Teaching English Abroad

Your expert guide to teaching English around the world

Susan Griffith

trotman t

While every effort has been made to ensure that the information contained in this book was accurate at the time of going to press, some details are bound to change within the lifetime of this edition, especially those pertaining to visa requirements for teachers, exchange rates and the conditions offered by the schools listed in the country directories, details of which have been supplied by the schools. Readers are invited to contact Susan Griffith, c/o Crimson Publishing Ltd, 19–21c Charles Street, Bath BA1 1HX, or email her at info@crimsonpublishing.co.uk with any comments or corrections. The best contributions will be rewarded with a free copy of the next edition or any other Crimson title.

DISCLAIMER

The opinions expressed in the case studies set in this style of box are entirely those of the featured organisation. Those in an italic script have been submitted independently, usually by readers of earlier editions of this book.

European Union Referendum:
This edition was revised after the referendum result on 24 June, 2016 regarding the UK's continued membership of the European Union, but before negotiations had begun with other member states. At the time of going to press, the UK remains a constituent member of the Union, which allows the free movement of people, capital, goods and services across the 28 Member States. Formal proceedings for negotiating the terms of the UK's withdrawal from the Union can only commence when the UK government triggers Article 50 of the Lisbon Treaty which is scheduled to be in 2017. It is impossible to predict how long it will be after that before the free movement of labour will be curbed. Until that time, the information provided on the European Union remains valid. The publisher acknowledges that the information provided in the book on the European Union will be subject to change following the UK's decision to leave the European Union. At the time of going to press, the UK remains a Member State of the Union and will continue to be subject to its obligations under EU law until it has finalised the terms of its withdrawal with the other 27 Member States.

NOTE: Most wages and prices are given in local currencies. For conversion to sterling and US dollars, use www.oanda.com.

Teaching English Abroad

This edition first published in Great Britain 2017 by Trotman, an imprint of Crimson Publishing Ltd, 19–21c Charles Street, Bath BA1 1HX

First edition 1991
Sixteenth edition 2017

A catalogue record for this book is available from the British Library.

ISBN 978 1 84455 644 1

Printed and bound in Malta by Gutenberg Press Ltd

CONTENTS

PREFACE

Tomorrow, the daughter of an old friend is flying to Hong Kong in order to start teaching across the Chinese border in Shenzhen, a job she arranged in September while spending four busy weeks acquiring a Certificate in English Language Teaching to Adults (CELTA) teaching qualification. Not long ago, the son of a neighbour moved to Barcelona without anything fixed up, and has been happily living and teaching in that enthralling city ever since. And those are just two examples from my immediate neighbourhood.

An ability to teach the English language is the most globally mobile skill there is. Teaching English after university is a rite of passage for large numbers of Britons and North Americans, and is a great way to begin a career, even if they don't continue in the field of eduction. Countries that continue to demonstrate a voracious demand for English teachers include Spain, Italy, South Korea, China, Vietnam, Taiwan, Indonesia, Turkey, Saudi Arabia, Russia, Chile, Argentina and Colombia. Opportunities are opening in new corners of the world all the time, from Myanmar to Kurdistan, and in a thousand more familiar places from Berlin to Bangkok. Even in countries without the tiger economies of the Pacific Rim, demand for English teachers persists. Economic conditions may be strained and unemployment high in Mediterranean Europe, yet many private institutes continue to hire appropriately qualified native speakers.

The governments of Spain, Colombia, Costa Rica, Georgia and many other countries have been investing in programmes to bring native speakers into contact with young language learners. Amid all these encouraging trends, the future uncertainty for British readers in the wake of Brexit is bound to be a worry. In the words of one language school employer in Spain: 'We employ only teachers who have an automatic right to work in Spain and it remains to be seen if this will always be the case for UK citizens.'

Those of us who speak English as our mother tongue tend to take for granted how universally dominant it has become. Aspirational families almost everywhere perceive English to be a route to prosperity, and are willing to invest in language study even when times are tough. A surge in opportunities for 'VYL' teachers, i.e. those who can teach Very Young Learners, indicates a developing trend to start teaching the language almost from infancy. An advertisement spotted in the Moscow Metro for a major chain of English schools carries the incentive that by learning English you can 'Become Your Boss's Boss'. Russians who know English earn, on average, 40% more than those who don't.

The TEFL industry has spawned hundreds of specialist websites that cover teacher training forums and publicise current vacancies worldwide. Some might wonder what a book can add. Here, I have tried to create a hand-held tool that makes it easy for the reader to compare at a glance destinations for teachers, institute requirements, visa regulations, possible problems and rewards. This book aims for clarity – to help make sense of the overwhelming clutter of unsifted information online.

In addition to all the hard information and vacancy listings that it includes, this book tries to convey a flavour of life as a teacher abroad, by including first-hand descriptions of everything from the extracurricular rewards of teaching in Hungary (lots of food festivals) to tips on apartment rental agencies in Japan. My aim has always been to make the information as concrete and up-to-date as possible, and to cut the waffle. This book can be the stepping stone to a brilliant year or two of adventure abroad.

Susan Griffith
Cambridge
December 2016

ACKNOWLEDGEMENTS

This new revised edition of *Teaching English Abroad* would not have been possible without the help of scores of English teachers and the people who employ them. They have generously shared their wealth of information, insights and anecdotes. As well as all the people who helped with the 15 previous editions, the following should be thanked for their contributions, some of them substantial, to the research for this updated edition:

Zeeda Anderson – Hungary
Davinna Artibey – Ecuador
Frederick Ball – Austria
Charles Beach – Colombia
Alan Chadwick – Spain
Miranda Crowhurst – Bolivia
Jonathan Davies – France
Stephen Dorosewicz – Spain
Martin Filla – Czech Republic
Libby Goldsmith – Latin America
Emily Handler – Hungary
Bradwell Jackson – Russia
Leah Morawiec – Poland
Gillian Murphy – Hungary
Geoff Nunney – Slovakia
Jamie Pinder – Iraq
Ailsa Randall – Czech Republic
Kathryn Saville – Turkey
Christine Smith – France
Susie Smith – Spain
Ben Stefano – Germany
Samantha Thornley – Vietnam
Rufus Vaughan-Spruce – Russia
Inge Visser – Turkey
Tanvi Warty – Spain
Catherine Wills – France

PART 1

INTRODUCTION

INTRODUCTION

It is estimated that a staggering one and a half billion people are, at this moment, learning English worldwide. The statistics illustrate the extent to which English dominates our globalised world: three-quarters of the world's mail is written in English, 80% of the world's electronically stored information is in English and well over a third of users of the internet communicate in the language you are reading at this moment. English dominates the world's business, sports, entertainment, aviation, science, technology … and karaoke bars. Citizens of the world strive to learn English, not only to conduct business, but to enjoy culture and entertainment, which explains why there are an estimated quarter of a million native-speaker teachers of English working worldwide. Mind-boggling statistics aside, the demand for instruction at all levels given by people who happen to speak English as their mother tongue is insatiable.

Just as Latin was the lingua franca of Europe in the Middle Ages, now English is the language used to communicate between persons not sharing a mother tongue, and this will not change after the United Kingdom isolates itself from the European Union (EU). When the newly liberated nations of Eastern Europe sloughed off Russian, they turned in very large measure to English rather than to the other main European languages. In fact, countries as far-flung as Myanmar, Namibia and Turkmenistan are busy making English one of the keystones of their educational systems. In some German-speaking cantons in Switzerland, English is replacing French as the preferred second language at school. Advertisers around the world often choose English, to avoid expensive multilingual campaigns. Switzerland's national airline is Swissair, not Air Suisse or Luft Schweizer.

This is bad news for all those Germans, Swedes and French Canadians who would like to market their language skills to fund a short or long stay abroad. When you learn that the Alliance Française in Russia is recruiting English teachers, as it was in 2016 in the small city of Obninsk, the dominance of English can't be disputed. It is English speakers, mainly from Britain, Ireland, North America, Australia and New Zealand, who accidentally find themselves in possession of such a sought-after commodity.

SOME DEFINITIONS

The commonly used acronyms ELT, TEFL, TESL and TESOL can be confusing, especially since they are often used interchangeably. ELT, which stands for English Language Teaching, has come to be the mainstream expression in the UK (preferred by such august bodies as the University of Cambridge and by the publishers of the main journal in the field). But most people still refer to TEFL (pronounced 'teffle'), Teaching English as a Foreign Language. TESL stands for Teaching English as a Second Language, and TESOL means Teaching English to Speakers of Other Languages. People learn English as a second language when they need to use it in their day-to-day lives, for example emigrants to the UK and the USA or inhabitants of ex-colonies where English retains official status and may well be the medium of instruction in schools. (English is the official or joint-official language in more than 75 countries.)

As this book is for people who want to travel abroad to teach, the term TEFL is mainly used here, as well as ELT. Teachers of English as a Second Language (ESL) are usually involved with multicultural education in their own countries. In the USA, the vast majority of English language teaching is of ESL because of the huge demand for English among those people who have emigrated to the USA and whose first language is not English. Therefore the term ESL dominates in American contexts, even when (technically) EFL is meant.

The acronym TESOL covers both situations, yet it is not widely used apart from in institutions which favour the Trinity College London qualifications known as the Certificate and Licentiate Diploma in TESOL (see Training section later) and also in the context of the American organisation TESOL Inc., which is the largest English teachers' organisation in the world, with more than 11,000 members.

There is no shortage of other acronyms and sub-categories in the world of TEFL. One of the main ones is ESP, which means English for Specific Purposes. ESP aims to match language teaching with the needs of various professions such as business, banking, tourism, medicine, aviation, law, etc. Business English is probably the most important in this category (and 'English for Shopping' as sometimes offered in Japan is the least important). Because a great many learners are motivated by a desire to use English at work, they want their teachers to adopt a functional rather than a structural approach. In other words they want to have lessons in which they can pretend to be telephoning a client, recommending, applying, advising, agreeing, complaining and so on. They are certainly not interested in the subjunctive.

EAP stands for English for Academic Purposes, i.e. English at an advanced level usually taught to students who are planning to study at foreign universities or English-medium institutions in their own country.

The acronym TOEFL can cause confusion. The Test of English as a Foreign Language is a US-based standardised test administered to language learners. Passing a TOEFL exam is widely held to be a reliable indicator of how well an individual can communicate in English. The focus of many language schools abroad is to prepare candidates for the exam, and so many advertise for teachers with 'TOEFL' experience. The UK counterpart, sponsored by the British Council and Cambridge English is IELTS (International English Language Testing System), commonly used by candidates worldwide who want to enrol in English-speaking universities.

SCOPE OF OPPORTUNITIES

The range of locations and situations in which English is in demand covers an enormous spectrum. If TEFL is booming in Kazakhstan and Laos and Colombia, there can be few corners of the world to which English has not penetrated. English has been called a 'barometer of western influence' and only a handful of countries in the world (notably North Korea) have rejected western influence outright, although even there a specialist tour operator in the UK was recently looking to recruit a handful of volunteer teachers to train tour guides at Pyongyang Tourism College. Myanmar used to fall into this category but not any more, since it is fast opening up to western influences including to the English language. The economic tigers of the BRIC nations (Brazil, Russia, India, China) were flagging somewhat in 2016, but their markets for the English language continue to grow massively. Economists predict that the MINT countries will be the next emerging economic giants: Mexico, Indonesia, Nigeria and Turkey. Apart from Nigeria, where English is already the official language, these countries already have huge ELT industries, which continue to expand.

Many years have passed since the arrival of the single European market, which precipitated a greater expansion of the English language than ever before in Europe's history. There has been an enormous increase in demand, especially from companies and professionals eager to participate in an integrated Europe. At least one German-based multinational has gone so far as to decree that all operations will be conducted in English. The question is, will this change after Britain leaves the EU? Already anxiety has been expressed in boardrooms in East Asia: if their head office moves from London to Frankfurt, should they be learning German rather than English? Perhaps it is arrogant to assume that English is so globally entrenched that corporate moves away from London would not seriously dent the supremacy of the English language.

The attraction of European Union countries for British teachers is enhanced by the fact that (at least for now) they have the legal right to work there. Looking ahead to a future where Britons might be excluded from the free movement of labour within Europe, the rules might have to be rewritten to prevent the decimation of an essential industry. Irish teachers will probably be in higher demand than ever.

The kinds of people who want to learn English are as numerous as the places in which they live. The worldwide recession saw a certain amount of cutting back in spending from Moscow to Madrid, for example on corporate training budgets, but it is remarkable how resilient the market has remained, even in struggling Greece. In an even more competitive employment market, a command of English is considered so essential that individuals are prepared to fund themselves and their children. The area of the industry that seems to be booming almost everywhere is the teaching of children, known as Young Learners or YL in the trade. Kids as young as 18 months are being immersed in an English-speaking environment and older ones are being sent to private English classes as their parents keep a weather eye on their future career prospects.

People around the world can think of a dozen reasons why they need to sign up for private English lessons.

- A Taiwanese student dreams of studying at UCLA.
- A Bulgarian bus driver, proud to be from a member state of the EU, wants to work in Denmark where he will be able to communicate in English.
- The wife of the Peruvian ambassador in Islamabad wants to be able to speak English at official functions.
- A Greek secondary school student has to pass her English exams in order to proceed to the next year and, like most of her classmates, attends a private tutorial college for English lessons.
- A Turkish youth wants to be able to flirt with tourists from Northern Europe.
- A Mexican waiter wants to get a job in the Acapulco Hilton.
- A Saudi engineer has to be able to read reports and manuals in English for his job.

The list is open-ended, and prospects for hopeful teachers are therefore excellent. There are also hundreds of international schools throughout the world where English is the medium of instruction for all subjects and there may be specific EFL vacancies. These will be of most interest to certified teachers who wish to work abroad.

As the profile of the English language has risen, so has the profile of the profession that teaches it, and the number of qualified and experienced English teachers has increased along with the rise in demand. The difficult employment situation for new graduates in the UK and elsewhere has prompted some to look abroad, and to equip themselves with a TEFL certificate in order to get some work experience on their CV. The explosion in the availability of training courses means that a much higher proportion of job-seekers have a TEFL certificate than was the case a decade ago, and (quite rightly) foreign language schools are becoming more selective when hiring staff.

People who cruise into a country expecting to be hired as an EFL teacher simply on the basis of being a native speaker are in most cases (though not quite all) in for a nasty shock. Employers at all levels will ask for evidence of the ability to teach their language or at least a university degree as proof of a sound educational background. Certainly without a degree, a TEFL qualification or any relevant experience, the scope of opportunities shrinks drastically.

WHO IS ELIGIBLE TO TEACH?

Anyone who can speak English fluently and has a lively, positive personality has a fighting chance of finding an opening as a teacher somewhere. Geordies, Tasmanians and Alabamans are all hired as English teachers (not to mention Norwegians and North Africans), though most employers favour native speakers of English without a heavy regional accent. Depending on the economic and cultural orientation of a country, schools will prefer British English or North American English. For obvious geopolitical reasons Europe and Africa incline towards Britain while Latin America and the Far East incline towards the USA and Canada. Many other countries have no decided preference, for example Indonesia and Turkey. Clear diction is usually more important than accent. On the American English versus British English debate, **Sab Will**, one-time director of a TEFL training company in Paris, says:

> ***I'm not convinced it's a major concern. There are certainly French who find one flavour (or should that be 'flavor'?) easier to understand than the other, and some people want to be taught mainly in one 'accent' based on their intended future use of English. But overall I think it all evens out. Most students are happy with a friendly, competent and enthusiastic teacher who is able to adapt to their needs and supply them with materials and learning situations relevant to their situation. In relation to that, the origin of the teacher pales in comparison. Of course the teacher should be able to 'neutralise' their accent if necessary, whatever their origins, so that the student has a model which will be understood throughout the English-speaking world.***

English language teaching is an industry that is seldom regulated, giving rise to the host of cowboy schools sometimes dubbed the 'McDonald's of English teaching'. The other side of the coin is the proliferation of cowboy teachers, who have no feel for language, no interest in their students and no qualms about ripping them off. The issue of qualifications must be considered carefully. It is obviously unwise to assume that fluency in English is a sufficient qualification to turn someone into an EFL teacher. Many experienced teachers of English come to feel very strongly that untrained teachers do a disservice both to their students and to their language. Certainly anyone who is serious about going abroad to teach English should turn to the relevant chapter to consider the training options.

Among the army of teacher–travellers, there are undoubtedly some lazy, spiritless and ungrammatical native speakers of English who have bluffed their way into a teaching job. Most books and journals about language teaching are unanimous in their condemnation of such amateurs. Yet there are some excellent teachers who have learned how to teach by practising rather than by studying. For certain kinds of teaching jobs, a background in business and commerce might be more useful than any paper qualifications in teaching. Therefore we have not excluded the unqualified teacher-traveller from our account. To get a sense of the range of individuals who pursue this course, the site www.teachingtraveling.com carries illuminating interviews with teacher-travellers of all ages and backgrounds. As long as they take their responsibilities seriously and bear in mind that their pupils have entrusted them with significant quantities of time and money to help them learn, they need not bring the EFL profession into disrepute. Some untrained teachers we talked to during the research for this book found the responsibility so unnerving that they promptly enrolled in a TEFL course before again unleashing themselves on an unsuspecting language-learning public.

Non-native speakers should not assume that their services will not be in demand outside their home countries. **Richard Ridha Guellala** was born in Holland, raised in Tunisia and partly educated in England, and went on to earn one of the most highly respected qualifications in TEFL, the Cambridge Diploma. While teaching in Thailand, he wrote:

> ***Most non-native speakers think that a position as an EFL teacher is impossible for them. However, I came to the conclusion that even unqualified non-native speakers are often hired by Asian schools, as long as they project a professional image during the interview, speak clearly, are well-groomed, know the basics of English grammar and are fluent in the language. Scandinavians and Dutch are sometimes even more successful in finding teaching jobs at top schools than native speakers. True, we non-native speakers possess a rather 'heavy' or 'funny' accent but, believe it or not, some Asian employers favour our accents to the native speaker's because we speak more slowly and use very simple basic vocabulary.***

Within the industry, the lobby that argues in favour of equal rights for non-native-speaking teachers is becoming more powerful, especially in western Europe. They claim that to advertise for native speakers only is discriminatory. Understandably, people from other countries who have gained near-native fluency in English feel aggrieved when they are excluded in favour of a native speaker who may have a much lower level of linguistic awareness and educational attainment. TEFL Equity Advocates (www.teflequityadvocates.com) was set up in April 2014 to speak out for equal professional opportunities for 'native' and 'non-native' English-speaking teachers in ELT. To illustrate the inroads the campaign is making, TESOL-France, the professional association of English teachers in France, no longer supports adverts that ask for native speakers only.

At an extreme opposite from the casual teacher-traveller is the teacher who makes ELT a career. Only a minority of people teaching English abroad are professional teachers. Career prospects in ELT are in fact not very encouraging. After teachers have achieved a certain level of training and experience, they can aspire to work for International House and then for the British Council. From there, they might become a director of studies at a private language institute, although one is unlikely to become a director without a primary interest in business and administration.

THE OLDER TEACHER

An increasing number of early-retired and other mature people are becoming interested in teaching English abroad for a year or two. Although it may be true that, in certain contexts, language institutes are more inclined to employ a bright young graduate, if only for image and marketing reasons, there are plenty of others that will value maturity, especially the growing number of establishments specialising in teaching young children. **Peter Beech**, Director of Anglo-Hellenic in Corinth, Greece, which trains and places teachers in jobs, has noticed increasing interest from people who have already had a career in the UK, in teaching or in any field, who want to move abroad.

Whereas only a few companies openly impose an upper age limit, some age discrimination does regrettably take place, more noticeably in Asia and the Middle East than elsewhere. The teacher recruitment agency Teach to Travel Ltd insists that candidates be less than 40 to be placed in Turkey, Thailand, Hong Kong and South Korea. A government scheme in Brunei accepts teachers up to age 52 for primary schools, 55 for secondary. Saudi Arabia will not issue visas to teachers over 55 and China likewise imposes a maximum age of 55 or 60 for issuing the Z-visa. In Indonesia, the government wants foreign teachers to be aged 25–54. A chart published in the International Schools Review sets out the restrictions for many countries (www.internationalschoolsreview.com/nonmembers/age-article.htm).

For older job-seekers it will be a matter of spreading their net as widely as they can by contacting as many relevant organisations, including voluntary ones, as possible. Older applicants may have to work harder to demonstrate enthusiasm, energy and adaptability to prospective employers; but this should be no bar to someone committed to creating adventures later in life. The issue of age will matter less if you can present yourself face-to-face to possible employers (unless you really are a decrepit old geezer or crone). Some keen candidates have volunteered in the first instance which gives them the chance to show their mettle. Others have had success by heading away from the competition of the big cities to focus on quiet backwaters.

After coming to the end of a career in his native United States, **Stephen Dorosewicz** and his wife decided to embark on a teaching adventure, partly because their son is living and working in Madrid. First, Stephen obtained a Polish passport through ancestry which gave him access to Europe:

> ***Prior to looking for work overseas, I initially received ESL training through volunteer positions at the local Literacy Council then followed up with a TESOL certificate at my local community college in northern Virginia. Age discrimination was the biggest problem (I am 68, my wife 65). Earlier I had discovered that in most Asian and Middle East countries, being over 50 means no job. In Spain, most school administrators are male and seem to be looking for young females as teachers. They are not so pleased with mature instructors unless pressed for teachers just before term begins. I wish I'd started my ESL training and teaching much earlier by local volunteering to develop more realistic expectations and also to treat ESL teaching as a job not an adventure.***

Australian journalists **Alexandra Neuman** and **John Carey**, aged 49 and 50 respectively, decided that having worked for 30-odd years it was time to do something different. They didn't want to do the sensible thing and wait until retirement, so started saving and planning, and after a couple of years had saved enough to fund a year in Italy. At first Alex didn't work but when they decided to extend their stay, she needed to find work. The only work available was teaching English, which is what she is doing right now in the lovely town of Bergamo:

> ***It won't matter what you read, who you speak to or how much planning you do once you arrive, your experience will be completely different. I have yet to meet one person who had a similar experience to mine, so above all you must bring with you tolerance, flexibility and an upbeat attitude. The rewards are well worth it. I love living here, I have never met such kindness and I know bureaucracy is terrible and I get paid badly but as I sit looking out of my hilltop apartment to the snow-capped Alps and the grapes ripening on the vine just below my bedroom window I think life is pretty wonderful!***

JERRY MELINN

Jerry Melinn enjoyed teaching English at an institute in Athens through Anglo-Hellenic so much that he signed on for another year:

I suppose you could say I don't fit the profile of a TEFL teacher. Usually they are unattached, young and out to see the world after finishing their university studies. I worked in the telecommunications industry in Ireland for almost 40 years and took advantage of an early retirement scheme when I was 56 years old. I didn't want to stop working and, as my four children were grown up, I decided, with the agreement of my wife, to try my hand at teaching English in Greece. I was interested in Greece because we have friends here and had been coming to Greece on holidays for many years.

WHAT EMPLOYERS ARE LOOKING FOR

Between the dodgy operators and the British Council is a vast middle ground of respectable English teaching establishments. Many would prefer to hire only qualified staff, yet they are not always available. On the whole these schools are looking for teachers with a good educational background, clear correct speech, familiarity with the main issues and approaches to TEFL, and an outgoing personality.

A bachelor's degree and/or TEFL certificate is no guarantee of ability as **Marta Eleniak** observed in Spain, where she taught during her gap year (after doing a one-week introductory TEFL course):

> ***I've seen graduate teachers make such a mockery of the enterprise that it's almost criminal. TEFL is creative teaching. Forget about your educational experiences. In TEFL you have got to be able to do an impression of a chicken, you've got to be a performer. And you have to be flexible. If the pupils are falling asleep, conduct a short aerobics class and change tack to something more interesting. A good teacher builds a rapport with the class, and is enthusiastic, patient, imaginative and genuinely interested in the welfare of the pupils.***

A sophisticated knowledge of English grammar is not needed, since in most cases, native speakers are hired to encourage conversation and practise pronunciation, leaving the grammar lessons to local teachers. On the other hand, a basic grasp is necessary if only to keep up with your students.

MOTIVES FOR TEACHING ENGLISH

There are perhaps five main types of individual to be found teaching English from Tarragona to Taipei:

- the serious career teacher
- the student of the prevailing language and culture who teaches in order to fund a longer stay
- the long-term traveller who wants to prolong and fund his or her travels
- the philanthropic or religious person sponsored by an aid organisation, charity or mission society
- the misfit or oddball, perhaps fleeing unhappiness at home.

Experienced English teacher in Spain **Deryn Collins** identifies just three types of folk who teach abroad:

> ***There are people who want to learn about how others live and take part, those who want to put a year out on their CV and those who leave their homeland because they cannot live with their 'own'. Which means you will on occasion work with a weirdo or maybe you are that weirdo. But mostly the mix of personalities is a marvellous thing. You can find good friends in teachers' rooms – some might even find love!***

In many countries, English teaching is the most easily attainable employment, in fact the only available employment for foreigners. Anyone who wants to transcend the status of mere tourist in a country such as Thailand, Bolivia or Japan will probably be attracted to the idea of teaching English. The assumption behind some thinking at the snobbish end of the EFL spectrum is that people who do it for only a year or two as a means to an end (e.g. learning Chinese, studying Italian art, eating French food) are necessarily inadequate teachers.

There are small pockets of people (mainly in the Far East) whose sole ambition is to earn as much money as possible to pay off student debts or fund further world travels. Seldom are these good teachers, if only because they take on so many hours of teaching that they can't possibly prepare properly for their lessons. But for most teachers, making a lot of money is not a priority or, if it was at the outset, they are soon disillusioned.

Salaries in popular tourist destinations (such as Paris, Barcelona, Chiang Mai) may actually be lower than in less appealing neighbouring towns, even though the cost of living is higher. Pay scales are relatively meaningless out of context. For example, high rents and other expenses usually eat up the high salaries paid in Japan, at least in the first year. When converted into sterling a salary in Romania might sound pitiful but will be perfectly adequate there. In some countries such as Kenya or Argentina, a TEFL salary may not be enough to fund anything beyond a spartan lifestyle, and savings from home are essential to fund any travelling. Yet the majority of people who spend time abroad teaching English are able to afford to live comfortably and have an enjoyable time without feeling pinched, although they end up saving little.

A summary of **Barry O'Leary's** round-the-world history as a TEFL teacher might be inspiring to others considering a new direction:

> ***The last time I counted, I'd taught more than 2,300 students in my eight years as a TEFL teacher. That's a lot of lost-looking faces, funny English accents, and spur of the moment questions that I've had to answer. I'm not saying I'm the most intelligent TEFL teacher – only last week I really grasped the difference between subject and object questions – but I can offer some advice to those willing to learn. After doing a TEFL course in London with St Giles College, I bought a one-way ticket to Australia with a stop-off in South America. I left alone and without any job prospects but I was pumping with adrenaline; my new life living abroad was about to start.***
>
> ***My first job was in Quito, Ecuador, where I got paid $2 an hour for teaching feisty Ecuadorian teenagers. I wasn't interested in the money, teaching was fun and I got a buzz from helping them. It was so much better than the pressurised sales jobs I'd escaped from. After three months teaching in Quito I was hooked. I travelled overland to Salvador (getting robbed in Rio on the way) and was lucky enough to get more work just before the Carnival. I stayed for four months and really fell in love with teaching, and Brazil. My time in Sydney wasn't such an adventure, but I learnt a lot teaching vigorous Chinese students. I saved up enough (the pay was pretty good) for an amazing three-week trip up the east coast, and shot off to Bangkok where I'd lined up a job.***
>
> ***I was met by a strict Catholic nun, my new boss, who pummelled me into shape, and that's where I first learnt how to teach younger learners. My seven months teaching in Thailand was amazing. I loved teaching tiny, funny kids who were smiling all day. I saved up enough for a six-week overland trip through Laos, Cambodia, Vietnam, China, and then to Moscow on the Trans-Mongolian Railway. I returned to England a new man. I'd travelled the world and had become a teacher, but my thirst for adventure continued. After the summer teaching in London, I headed for Seville, Spain, where I've been ever since. This year I married my Spanish wife. In my six years here I've really learnt how to teach, thanks to some excellent training and a stiff hand from my boss. I get excellent results and my students like my classes, well, the majority of them who can be bothered to learn.***

Barry is a blogger at www.baztefl.com and has self-published a book, *Teaching English in a Foreign Land.*

RED TAPE

At least for now, the European Union consists of the UK, Ireland, the Netherlands, Belgium, Luxembourg, Denmark, Sweden, Finland, Austria, Estonia, Latvia, Lithuania, Poland, Czech Republic, Slovakia, Hungary, Slovenia, Croatia, Malta, Bulgaria, Romania, the Greek populated area of Cyprus, France, Germany, Italy, Greece, Spain and Portugal, the latter six of which have enormous EFL markets. Within the EU, the red tape should be minimal for all nationals of member states who wish to work in any capacity. Outside the EU, legislation varies from country to country. In theory there is also 'free reciprocity of labour' within the European Economic Area (EEA). The EEA takes in those Western European countries that have decided to stay outside the Union, viz. Iceland, Liechtenstein, Norway and Switzerland.

The United Kingdom referendum of June 2016 delivered a shock result that could have radical consequences for British EFL teachers in the future. What a post-Brexit EFL industry in Europe will look like is anybody's guess at this stage. Decisions about visas and employment rights will be crucial. If all TEFL teachers from Britain have to obtain work permits, as teachers from outside the EU currently do, it would complicate and delay matters for job-seekers and especially for language institutes. One thing is for sure, it will be an excellent time to be a teacher from Ireland. It may be that each member state negotiates a different arrangement with the UK and, possibly, special provisions will be made for Britons teaching their language. If it turns out to be a 'hard' or 'clean' Brexit, perhaps the free movement of labour will cease, which could mean that opportunities will increase for North American and Antipodean teachers who may find themselves competing with Britons on a level playing field, bureaucratically speaking.

At present all of this is idle speculation. The UK must first trigger Article 50 of the Lisbon Treaty, which will begin a two-year negotiation period, so little is likely to change during the lifetime of this edition. Experts have predicted that it could take five to ten years before Britain is actually out. The monthly *EL Gazette* (www.elgazette.com) is a source of news and developments in the ELT industry and it would be wise to keep an eye on relevant articles; much of its content is available free in the digital edition. For the time being, both British and Irish nationals have a significant advantage over Americans, Canadians, Australians, New Zealanders and South Africans when job-hunting in Europe. Although not impossible for other nationalities, it is difficult for them to find an employer willing to undertake the task of proving to the authorities that no EU citizen is available or able to do the job. **Brian Komyathy** from Long Island, New York, was disappointed when he made enquiries about moving to an EU country:

> ***European walls of regulations do not exactly bespeak, 'Americans welcome aboard'. I'm technically eligible to acquire Irish and hence EU citizenship through my grandparents, so as soon as various documentary records are located and processed I'll not have the problems I do now. A slew of phone calls convinced me of the necessity of taking this course.***

Within the landmass of continental Europe, the Schengen Agreement means that there are no border controls among the 26 participating countries. Non-EU citizens who enter Europe are permitted to stay in one or more countries of the Schengen zone for up to 90 days within a six-month period. In the past, long-stay residents of European countries would cross the border to leave the Schengen Area to renew their tourist visa. However, when the regulations changed to limit stays to 90 days in six months, many non-EU semi-residents had to depart. Nationals of the US, Canada, Australia, New Zealand and many others do not need to obtain a Schengen visa, whereas citizens of Turkey, China, etc. do (see list at www.schengenvisainfo.com). Applicants will be required to provide their biometric data (fingerprints and a digital photograph) and pay the fee of €60. Non-Europeans should be careful not to overstay the 90-day limit on their Schengen visa. If it is picked up on departure, they will be liable for a huge fine. Some potential employers like English language summer camp companies accept North Americans and Antipodeans because the job lasts less than 90 days. A small number of European language schools will accept non-Europeans on an intern basis (i.e. unpaid or low paid) for periods of less than 90 days.

Some lucky Americans may gain access to the EU if they are fortunate enough to be able to prove European ancestry and acquire dual nationality. Rules differ among countries, but in some cases it is sufficient to provide the documentation showing that you have a grandparent of that nationality. Ireland, Italy and Poland are well known for offering citizenship by descent to those with family trees from those countries. Greece is also a possibility, though if you are a male and become resident in Greece, i.e. live there for more than six months in one calendar year, you will be called upon to do the obligatory year of military service.

Other Americans find ingenious ways to stay legal. In some cases non-Europeans with a student visa are permitted to work up to a certain number of hours, in France, for example and in Germany, where international students on a student visa are permitted to work 240 part-time days a year. International and student exchange organisations may be able to assist. Some US-based organisations cooperate with partner agencies in various countries to place native speaker teachers as live-in tutors or in schools or institutes, often as volunteers. For particulars, see page 88 of the Finding a Job chapter.

The immigration authorities of many countries accord degree-educated English teachers special status, recognising that their own nationals cannot compete as they can for other jobs. Other countries may lack the mechanism for granting work visas to English teachers and so will often turn a blind eye to those who teach on tourist visas, since everyone knows that locals are not being deprived of jobs, rather they're being given an advantage by having the chance to learn English.

Some organisations have developed a study-and-teach solution. While you are learning Russian in Moscow or Spanish in Quito, you do some English tutoring on the side. Since your status is primarily as a student, it is unnecessary to obtain a full work authorisation. Teachers who find a job before leaving home can usually sort out their visas or at least set the wheels in motion before arrival, which greatly simplifies matters. You can only start the process after finding an employer willing to sponsor your application, preferably one that is familiar with the processes. There is no point applying to the embassy or consulate until you have found an employer. The majority of countries will process visas only when they are applied for from outside the country. So if you have to visit your chosen country on a tourist visa in order to find a job (which is the usual process), you will have to leave the country to apply for the work visa, though often this can be done from a neighbouring country rather than your country of residence. The restrictions and procedures for obtaining the appropriate documentation to teach legally are set out in Part 2 of this book, country by country. A website for lawyers has a handy table of country-by-country work permit/residency regulations at http://us.practicallaw.com/2-509-3111?q=work+permits.

STAYING ON THE RIGHT SIDE OF THE LAW

Prospective teachers should contact the relevant consulate for the official line. If you do get tangled up in red tape, always remain patient with consular officials. If things seem to be grinding to a halt, it may be helpful to pester them, provided this is done with unfailing politeness. Suppliants have sometimes noticed how discretionary decisions can be. An application refused on one day might be accepted by a different official the next, so try not to give up at the first hurdle.

British graduates with student debt will have to investigate whether or not they might be liable for making repayments while teaching abroad. If a graduate works abroad but does not tell the Student Loans Company what their income is, a fixed monthly amount is deducted depending on what country they are in, from £40 a month in Indonesia to £241 in Australia. The calculation is made according to the prevailing exchange rate, so when the value of the pound plunged after the Brexit vote, some teachers, for example in Japan, discovered that they were over the repayment threshold. For a country-by-country list of income thresholds, go to www.tinyurl.com/grads-pay.

REWARDS AND RISKS

The rewards of teaching abroad are mostly self-evident: the chance to become integrated in a foreign culture, the pleasure of making communication possible for your students, the interesting characters and lifestyles you will encounter, a feeling of increased self-reliance, a better perspective on your own culture and your own habits, a base for foreign travel, a good suntan ... and so on.

A longer lasting benefit is to your CV: in future job applications and interviews you can highlight how teaching abroad has enhanced your ability to think on your feet and explain things clearly, bolstered your confidence when presenting information to groups, improved your inventiveness and so on (which will all be true).

After spending more than three years teaching around South America, **Libby Goldsmith** identified the downsides and rewards of life as an EFL teacher:

> ***In terms of drawbacks, I often feel as if I'm living a student's life, but without the studies. For example, trying to make ends meet, living with other people, limiting luxuries, even basic things like going out for a drink. Whilst your students may have exciting job prospects, I feel that as an EFL teacher you have already reached the heights of the profession. Personally the rewards have been in terms of discovering oneself, such as discovering new aspects of your personality. For example, I never realised how much patience I had, yet when you're with a student who is struggling on some particular point, it is amazing how you are happy to repeat or to slow down to help that student understand. Other rewards include the great sense of pride you get from the accomplishments of a student whom you have helped.***

Good teachers often find their classes positively fun and place a high value on the relationships they form with their students. Teaching is a lot of fun when it's done right. One-to-one teaching can also be enjoyable since you have a better chance to get to know your students or clients. (By the same token, it can be a miserable experience if you don't get on, since there is no escape from the intimacy of the arrangement.) Off-site teaching provides glimpses into a variety of workplaces and private homes, perhaps even resulting in hospitality and friendship with your students.

As competition for jobs has increased, working conditions have not improved. There is a growing tendency for EFL teachers to be offered non-contract freelance work, with no guarantee of hours, making it necessary for them to work for more than one employer in order to make a living. Job security is a scarce commodity. Part-time freelancers of course miss out on all the benefits of full-time work such as bonuses, holiday pay, help with accommodation, and so on. In some cases, they are obliged to form their own companies, which can be a costly and time-consuming exercise.

Uninitiated teachers run the risk of finding themselves working for a shark or a cowboy who doesn't care a fig about the quality of teaching or the satisfaction of the teachers, as long as students keep signing up and paying their fees. 'Client satisfaction' is their only criterion of success; business takes complete precedence over education. Exploitation of teachers is not uncommon since the profession is hampered by a lack of both regulation and unionisation.

The job of teaching English is demanding; it demands energy, enthusiasm and imagination, which are not always easy to produce when you are confronted with a room full of stonily silent faces. Instead of the thrill of communication, the drudgery of language drills begins to dominate. Instead of the pleasure of exchanging views with people of a different culture, teachers become weighed down by sheaves of photocopies and visual aids. Like most jobs when done right, teaching English is no piece of cake and is at times discouraging, but invariably it has its golden moments. It offers opportunities for creativity, learning about other cultures and attitudes, making friends and of course travelling. Not a bad job in many ways.

Roberta Wedge writes amusingly on a possible spin-off from a teaching contract abroad:

TEFL is one of the most sex-balanced job fields I know (though the Director of Studies is usually a man) and, for those who are interested, the possibilities of finding your one true love appear to be high. 'Thrown together in an isolated Spanish village, eating tapas in the bar, hammering out lesson plans together – we found we have so much in common.' And a year later they were married. (A true story.)

On a more serious note, teachers should inform themselves about the political situation before offering their EFL services and take stock of their particular sensitivities concerning issues such as political freedom, democracy, human rights, religion and so on. To take a couple of examples, teachers in China have been shocked by the overt racism. For instance a Ghanaian teacher working in a small city not that far from Beijing had to get used to the local people coming up to him to rub his skin to see if the black would come off. In the Central Asian Republics, home to ethnically diverse populations, certain groups are treated shamefully. If you are concerned by these matters, check the Washington-funded Freedom House website at www.freedomhouse.org for updates. Additional insight can be gained from Reporters Sans Frontières (Reporters without Borders) at www.rsf.org. With regard to 'press freedom' their Worldwide Press Freedom Index rates countries according to the freedom of their press; in 2016 Finland and the Netherlands were at the top, Eritrea and North Korea at the bottom of the list. China and Vietnam are both near the bottom.

the field of ELT: University of Cambridge English Language Assessment and Trinity College London. The Certificate qualification is acquired after an intensive 120–130-hour course offered full-time over one month or part-time over several months. Since 2011 Cambridge, in association with International House London, has been offering a CELTA course online that combines online study with live teaching practice (described below).

Most centres expect applicants to have the equivalent of university entrance qualifications, i.e. three GCSEs and two A levels, and some require a degree. Admission to the course is at the discretion of the course organiser after a sometimes-lengthy selection process. Places on courses at the well-established centres may be difficult to get at short notice, especially in summer, though the proliferation of training centres means that most are not as oversubscribed as they once were.

Applicants should be able to demonstrate a suitable level of language awareness and convince the interviewer that they have potential to develop as a teacher. Some centres won't consider applicants under the age of 20. Past academic achievement is less important than aptitude; even a PhD does not guarantee acceptance. Most schools will send you a task sheet or grammar research activity as part of the application. Sample questions might be 'How would you convey the idea of regret to a language learner?' or 'Describe the difference in meaning between "I don't really like beetroot" and "I really don't like beetroot"'.

Courses are not cheap but should be viewed as an investment and a potential passport to a worthwhile profession in many different countries. In fact, prices have been coming down over the past couple of years, with many centres trying to survive amid keen competition. The range is about £1,000 to £1,400 for a full-time or part-time course with an average of £1,250. Most centres include the validation body's fee, variously called assessment, moderation or examination fee, which in 2016 was £137 (Trinity) or £140 (Cambridge).

Many colleges of further education offer the Trinity or Cambridge certificate part time and these are usually less expensive. Timetables for part-time courses vary, but the norm is to attend classes one or two evenings a week for one or two terms of the academic year plus occasional full days for teaching observation and practice. The further education sector has been hit hard by government cuts in the UK, and a number of FE colleges are no longer offering certificate courses in TEFL, particularly those that used to offer the Trinity CertTESOL course. As one former convenor of a part-time course in a Home Counties college of FE explained:

> ***It was getting increasingly expensive for learners, and more and more seemed to want an intensive programme or at least one with fewer hours of classroom learning. I think more demanding work lives and more free time options have also had an impact, as they have on most areas of adult education … Many FE colleges are not well set up for intensive TESOL programmes (no classroom space available wholly just for 5 weeks; few students available for micro-teaches from June–early October in many cases) … So unfortunately we no longer offer the course.***

Some institutes of higher education, such as Anglia Ruskin University in Cambridge and the University of Hull, no longer offer a certificate course to all comers but embed the course into university modules on for example a BA course in English Language Teaching.

Once accepted onto a certificate course, you will usually be given a pre-course task to familiarise yourself with some key concepts and issues before the course begins. Full-time courses are very intensive and 100% attendance is expected, so you need to be in a position to dedicate yourself completely to the task in hand for four weeks. The standard of teaching is high, the course rigorous and demanding and the emphasis is on the practice of any theory taught. One of the requirements is that participants teach a minimum of six hours of observed lessons to authentic English language students.

Trinity's CertTESOL and the Cambridge CELTA are accredited by the Office of Qualifications and Examinations Regulation (Ofqual), the national body for the regulation of vocational qualifications outside the higher education sector. On the Qualifications and Credit Framework for England, both certificate courses have been accredited as a Level 5 qualification, which is considered equivalent in difficulty to the second year of an undergraduate degree course. CELTA and Trinity CertTESOL graduates may receive credits towards degree programmes at the discretion of the institution. The British Council has adopted the terminology 'TEFL-1 qualified teachers', which means they have a CELTA/CertTESOL or equivalent, and TEFL-Q which means they have a BEd, PGCE with Qualified Teacher Status or a DELTA.

INTERNATIONAL HOUSE BARCELONA

'I studied English for many years and had finally achieved a very advanced level, so I decided to do something with my English: teaching was the obvious job for me. I was offered a job in a small school where I'm from in the north of Spain even though I had no training as a teacher, but the school was awful: the owner was unprofessional and seemed uninterested in the students and I had the impression she was just in it for the money.

'However, I did my best but after eight months I realised I needed training and support if I was ever going to be a professional teacher.

'An English friend told me about the Cambridge CELTA and told me that International House Barcelona was the best, most professional and prestigious place to take the course so I applied and was accepted.

'I am now halfway through the course and am extremely happy that I was accepted. The tutors are amazing; right from the first day we all felt we were members of a special, very supportive group. There is no competition, we all help each other and we all feel we are learning an incredible amount and getting really supportive, constructive feedback on our work in the teaching practice classes when we teach real students who are here to learn English. The way the tutors teach us was a real eye-opener right from the start when we had an Arabic lesson – no English was used in the class and by the end of the lesson we were acting out role plays in Arabic confidently. The tutors don't lecture, they practise what they preach and their input sessions are fun as well as being very informative. The tutors put us in the students' shoes and the focus is very much on learning outcomes and how the teacher can help the students achieve these.

'When I finish the course I want to take the Young Learners course at IH Barcelona so that I feel confident teaching children as well as adults and then I'm going back to my hometown to open a small English language school of my own. My school will be nothing like the school I mentioned above. I will put into practice all that I've learned at International House Barcelona and I hope my students will soon be speaking fluent English.' Karla

CAMBRIDGE CELTA

Cambridge CELTA (Certificate in English Language Teaching to Adults) has established itself as a key passport to teaching opportunities overseas. It has a solid reputation in the international teaching community and high levels of recognition among employers around the world. CELTA is administered and regulated by Cambridge English (1 Hills Road, Cambridge CB1 2EU; ✆ +44 1223 553997; www.cambridgeenglish.org) and is sometimes referred to simply as the Cambridge Certificate. Many believe that CELTA is the most reliable route to jobs with better rates of pay and with employers who are willing to give more support to novice teachers.

You don't have to stay in the UK to take CELTA. Administered and regulated by the assessment wing of the University of Cambridge, CELTA courses are offered at 362 centres in 75 countries. For example, the British Council runs courses in Milan, Naples, Kuwait, Kiev, Dhaka, Casablanca and many others; CELTA courses are offered by 29 centres in Australia and New Zealand and steadily climbing in North America so that there are now 24 CELTA course providers in the USA (including 14 branches of Teaching House) and eight in Canada. A full list is available at the Cambridge English website: www.cambridgeenglish.org/find-a-centre/find-a-teaching-centre. International House Worldwide is one of the key providers, accounting for more than half of all CELTA courses taken.

The CELTA Online blends self-study with teaching practice. The course has been produced in partnership with International House London and leads to the same internationally recognised certificate as the face-to-face CELTA course. Candidates still have to do at least six hours of observed teaching practice in person, and the course will be carried out over at least 10 weeks. Note that it is no cheaper than the original; in fact there is often an extra charge of about £80 for course materials. Currently, 85 CELTA centres offer the CELTA Online, including 27 in the UK, five in Italy, six in Spain and five in Australia.

Securing a place on a CELTA course isn't automatic. Course providers are selective in order to ensure standards are kept high – and as a result, the pass rate is usually at least 90%. Grades available are Pass, Pass 'B' and Pass 'A', giving candidates the chance to distinguish themselves. CELTA provides a foundation of theory but focuses on effective teaching skills and practical tools for teaching English to adult learners. You'll gain hands-on teaching practice and the experience and support to build confidence in the classroom.

Many teachers believe that a CELTA plus some teaching experience is the perfect recipe for securing a good teaching job, as **Doug Burgess** wrote while teaching in Chile:

> ***If you are interested in job security and acquiring a work visa, it is highly advisable that you complete the CELTA and try to get some experience as it will give you flexibility and options when you are here so that you can have the most comfortable and enjoyable time possible.***

Some people have voiced surprise that a course which qualifies people to teach only adults is still so dominant, when much of the demand for English comes from young learners. Cambridge English used to offer a two-week extension course to the CELTA course for people who wanted to teach young learners, called the YL extension; however this was discontinued in December 2016.

Why Saxoncourt?

Saxoncourt is a well-established CELTA centre with over 16 years' experience of delivering high-quality training in a variety of formats. We run four-week full-time intensive courses and part-time courses over 12 weeks enabling trainees to develop new skills and opportunities while still holding down their current jobs. We have a dedicated team of highly experienced and qualified tutors who work hard to ensure that trainees get the best possible introduction to the challenges and rewards of EFL teaching.

What's the course like?

In a word 'intense' – but also incredibly rewarding. The learning curve is steep and the demands it places on trainees in terms of time and energy are high, but the benefits usually come pretty quickly too: you learn about teaching – the course's main focus is methodology; you learn about the English language – there's no surer way to learn than to teach; you learn about other cultures – you'll be teaching students from all over the world; you learn about yourself – if you've never taught before, the course gives you plenty of real and practical experience, and most people find their confidence improves as they find they *can* do it.

What does it involve?

Trainees must complete six hours of assessed teaching, write four assignments and plan lessons. They also have at least 60 hours of input where they learn the key elements of effective and successful English teaching.

What do I get out of it?

Passing the course means you are CELTA qualified. This means, quite literally, that a world of opportunities opens up. You will be equipped to start a career enabling you to travel, meet new people and make a real contribution to their lives – what are you waiting for?

TRINITY COLLEGE LONDON

The other principal initial Certificate in TESOL is awarded by Trinity College London (89 Albert Embankment, London SE1 7TP; ✆ +44 20 7820 6100; tesol@trinitycollege.co.uk; www.trinitycollege.co.uk). The Trinity Certificate (CertTESOL) has international recognition, is highly regarded by employers in the UK and around the world and is considered to have equal academic standing to CELTA. Currently there are just under 100 centres worldwide offering CertTESOL training full or part-time. More than a third are outside the UK, with six centres in Spain, three in New Zealand and centres in other countries such as Canada, Hong Kong, Czech Republic, Ireland, Italy, Malta, Japan, Argentina and Uruguay.

Trinity stipulates a minimum of 130 hours offered intensively over a minimum of four and often five weeks or part time over a longer period. All intensive courses must have a pre-course learning component in addition to the minimum hours. The course content includes grammar and phonology, a range of teaching approaches and methodologies, classroom management and motivation, hands-on experience of teaching aids (from adapting printed materials to interactive whiteboards), and introduction to the learning of an unknown language (in which trainees receive four hours' instruction and lesson planning). In addition, they must complete a minimum of six hours of observed and assessed teaching practice and spend at least four further hours observing experienced teachers of English.

The CertTESOL is accepted by the British Council as an appropriate initial TESOL qualification in its accredited English language teaching organisations in the UK and its own teaching centres overseas. In fact, British Council offices in Recife and Sao Paulo in Brazil, Seoul in Korea and Valencia in Spain offer the course. All courses meet the core Trinity requirements but there are variations in course delivery across the different providers to reflect different in-house practices and philosophy. Trinity seeks to ensure that its qualifications are in line with those of other comparable awarding bodies – principally Cambridge English.

A graduate of the Trinity Certificate course remembers her experience:

I got good grades for my four A levels and wanted to take a year out abroad. I did some research on the net – found out a bit about teaching English ('TESOL') – but realised that a weekend course wouldn't be cheap, or actually give me the qualification for a decent job. I looked into online teacher training – but I really wanted the experience of meeting other would-be teachers and experienced trainers. I therefore chose a five-week intensive Trinity CertTESOL course – I could have done it part-time, but I was in a hurry! I was warned about how intensive it would be – how I should tell my friends that I'd be really busy for five weeks – and sure enough when I was accepted for the course I had to start reading straight away for some written tasks to complete beforehand.

The course itself was an extraordinary experience. I started (and finished!) by feeling very enthusiastic and energetic. There were written assignments ('journals') to prepare over the four weeks and I was corrected on my grammar, punctuation and spelling, which was a surprise at first. I had to plan my time carefully – what I would do in the evenings and at the weekend, how much I could read. The most demanding but exciting part was the teaching practice with real students from different nationalities. It had never occurred to me I would feel so nervous. The first time I stood up in front of them I realised they expected to learn something from me, and I kept forgetting that there was no point in explaining difficult words or ideas in English – I had to learn very specific techniques to teach my own language. Overall . . . my own communication skills improved enormously, my students were very kind and I learnt to respect their feelings, the other trainees were (all bar one) very supportive, I learnt to manage a heavy workload in and out of school, and finally I feel I developed as a teacher and as a person – all in five weeks!

A new Trinity College London course called TYLEC (Teaching Young Learners Extension Certificate) has been developed in association with the British Council for trained ELT teachers to hone their skills teaching children and adolescents. The course is offered in 25 British Council offices worldwide from Tunisia to Taiwan.

CHOOSING A COURSE

It is up to prospective trainees to weigh up the pros and cons of the courses available to them and to establish how rigorously each course under consideration is monitored. One reservation that a few employers abroad have expressed is that the proliferation of providers of certificate courses, whether on behalf of Cambridge, Trinity or independents, has made it more difficult to maintain a uniform standard, especially since so much of the assessment of candidates is subjective. The general decline in standards of literacy in Britain and North America has also prompted some to complain of a decline in quality of TEFL training.

When it comes to workload, trainees in both CELTA and Trinity TESOL courses complain of a punishing schedule. But most come away claiming that the course elements are superb. At the time, participants sometimes feel as though they are drowning in information, but realise that the course has to pack a great deal of material into four brief weeks. When trying to identify differences between them, one view is that the CELTA concentrates more on the structure of language and classroom management, and Trinity on the use of authentic materials and practical teaching techniques. The majority who go on to teach abroad are very grateful for the training it gave them, as in the case of **Andrew Sykes**, teaching in Bordeaux:

As for the certificate course that I did in Leeds it was certainly one of the most stimulating, challenging and interesting things I have ever studied for. Initially I felt a bit out of place – I had a background of science A levels, a maths degree and two years as a (failed) accountant. The course was professionally run and there were good teacher-student relations. Most people had never taught anybody anything before in their life, but we were gradually eased into teaching by the supportive teaching staff who were refreshingly (and diplomatically) critical when required to be. A criticism which some students had was that there wasn't enough feedback about what was expected to gain a pass, let alone achieve an A or B. The best recommendation for the course is perhaps that I would never have felt comfortable teaching without it.

So even if your social life disappears for a month and all you can talk about at weekends is phrasal verbs and English idioms, the consensus is that it is worthwhile.

Many certificate courses are offered by independent companies outside the Cambridge and Trinity folds and these are more difficult to assess. Some are accredited by respected national organisations, such as TESL Canada (www.tesl.ca) or ACELS in Ireland (www.acels.ie). For many, one of the key factors will be cost. Generic certificate courses are available in dozens of countries and the cheapest ones are offered in the cheapest countries. **James Clarke** and his girlfriend Sally were looking for a course for under $1,000 inclusive in South America and ended up at one in Peru, which has since gone out of business, though that did not prevent them from thinking it gave them a good grounding:

We took (and both passed) a TEFL training course in Trujillo, Peru that cost $900 for four weeks including a homestay and all food – much cheaper than anywhere in Buenos Aires where we had been before. It was a very good experience, with only one other student on the course, unlike a rival course we observed in Cusco, Peru, where there were maybe 14 students. Every day of the first week we observed four hours of classes (with participation) as well as four hours of theory from 9am to 1pm. In the second week, the observation turned into actual teaching of the classes with the same theory lessons. The third week involved observation of a higher standard of classes and then the fourth week was teaching, but four hours per day instead of two hours in the second week. We taught grammar, conversation and pronunciation, all using games, activities, dynamics and motivational techniques using music. There was one drawback that we suspect was down to the price of the course – we did not receive any original textbooks, just photocopied pages from textbooks.

Possible advantages of doing a TEFL training course abroad are that you may already be teaching or living in that country and want to upgrade your qualifications locally; the course and cost of living may be cheaper than in your home country; and successful course participants will almost certainly be put in touch with local employers, making it much easier to land a job in that place.

Jonathan Davies, who runs a well-regarded TEFL certificate training course in Toulouse, speaks of the difficulties of choosing the right course, especially when big commercial chains dominate Google rankings:

If you do some googling for TEFL courses, you will often find a course in an attractive French location offered. But when you click on it suddenly you are back to generic photos on a home page, a toll-free number and the offer of a discount on a course on the other side of the world. Or you find that the '120-hour TEFL course' is not externally accredited, is offered only online or over a weekend in a hotel . . . Many TEFL course websites show no local addresses or local telephone numbers. This is because they offer locations either to gauge interest in the location, or will run that location only if they get enough trainers on board. This can create a lot of frustration and last-minute cancellations. The worldwide TEFL training organisations often seem to be targeting Americans after an adventure gap year anywhere exotic, i.e. 'We are not running our Bordeaux course – how about Thailand?' Here in Toulouse we do what we can to get our ex-trainees set up locally after the course, if that is what they want.

Teaching practice is key. Busy colleges such as Ealing, Hammersmith and West London College offer an insight into the diversity of ELT work because they teach such a wide range of students, to whom their CELTA trainees are exposed during teaching practice sessions.

OTHER RECOGNISED QUALIFICATIONS

In 2005, Cambridge English introduced the Teaching Knowledge Test (TKT), a new accessible test about teaching English to speakers of other languages, delivered to international standards. The test, which can be taken by both practising and aspiring teachers, involves three modules that cover the background to language learning and teaching, planning lessons/using resources and managing the teaching and learning process. Hundreds of TEFL training centres worldwide are offering short courses to candidates who want to prepare for TKT, which is more accessible than CELTA and does not include teaching practice as part of the assessment. A specialist module of most interest to aspiring teachers of English is called TKT: Young Learners, which focuses on teaching children aged 6-12. This 30-hour course covers principles of teaching English to young learners, plus planning and preparing lessons, teaching and assessing young learners; see www.cambridgeenglish.org/teaching-english/teaching-qualifications/tkt.

Beyond CELTA is the Diploma. Whereas CELTA is considered an initial qualification, the Diploma (as distinct from any old diploma with a lower case) is an in-service modularised course for experienced English language teachers. The Cambridge Diploma in English Language Teaching to Adults (DELTA) and the Trinity Diploma (Dip TESOL) are high-level qualifications usually open to graduates who have at least two years of recent ELT classroom experience. The three modules of the Diploma course are available intensively over a minimum of eight weeks but more usually part-time over several months or a year. A Distance DELTA option supported by International House (IH) and the British Council is increasingly popular (www.thedistancedelta.com) because it can be combined with full-time teaching. The fees – currently £2,950 plus assessment fees – are sometimes subsidised by employers. Of the three modules, you can do the second one face-to-face at International House in London intensively over six weeks or less intensively over 16 weeks. This is known as the Blended DELTA, which currently costs £3,100.

TEACHING HOUSE NEW YORK

The Blended Delta Program by Erica Lederman

'After two years of teaching English as a second language to adults, both in my home country of the United States and in Russia, I became stuck in a rut. Lessons were overly predictable and my knowledge of language ceased to expand. In 2010 I began working for International House/Teaching House New York, which coincidentally was beginning to offer the Blended Delta programme that same year. It was the perfect opportunity for me to get out of that rut and learn more about language, methodology and curriculum design.

'The Blended Delta is composed of three separate components: a written exam, a face-to-face course and a written thesis. Although it is possible to do these components in any order, it's highly recommended that candidates complete the modules separately and in sequence so that they can get the full benefit and devote the time necessary to each task. The Blended Delta programme at Teaching House treats the first and third modules as distance courses and the second module as an on-site, intensive course. This allows a lot of flexibility for candidates, who can participate from all over the world.

'Although thoroughly challenging and, at times, extremely stressful, the Delta was an invaluable experience. After completing the programme I have a better understanding of the teacher's role in the classroom and the beliefs that underlie every word and action spoken during a class. I am more confident experimenting with different methodologies and techniques, as I am able to evaluate them critically and predict how they might work with my learners.

'Furthermore, the Delta has opened up other avenues in ELT besides classroom teaching, such as publishing materials and teacher training. For anyone who wants to pursue a long-term career in the ELT industry, the Delta is a worthwhile investment.'

A few universities (especially the former polytechnics) from Brighton to Belfast offer their own certificate or diploma in TEFL. Most are one-year or two-year courses offered post-graduation, full- or part-time, and tend to be more theoretical than Cambridge and Trinity courses. It is important to do some research before committing yourself to a course so that you are sure that the qualification you obtain will be recognised by employers both in the UK and overseas. Once again find out if there is some form of external assessment and whether the course includes a reasonable amount of teaching practice.

Stephen Curry felt let down by the course he chose:

> ***I called my local university to see what courses were available and was advised that they could provide a course consisting of two modules, one from the PGCE and one from the MEd programme, which would be equivalent in status to a one-month certificate and would be 'recognised'. The course of study took from May to February to complete. It was a lot of hard work, research based and absolutely no fun whatsoever. I did the course on the understanding that it would lead to a stand-alone TEFL certificate. I have since tried to get the university to confirm in writing that this module carries the recognition they claimed it would but they now say that they cannot do this. Unfortunately it was not until the latter stages of the course that I (and others) began to see that the eventual outcome would be a qualification that was unlikely to be recognised in the eyes of anyone outside the university, let alone as being equivalent to the Cambridge/Trinity certificate.***

A number of undergraduate institutions such as Central Lancashire, Nottingham Trent and Wolverhampton offer TESOL as part of an undergraduate course; the UCAS directory lists all university courses in the UK and can be consulted online at www.ucas.com, or in any careers or general library. MA courses in ELT and Applied Linguistics are offered at dozens of universities and colleges. Some offer a master's by distance learning aimed at practising ELT teachers worldwide. Arguably, there is a world oversupply of MAs; however, an MA is a prerequisite for many posts in some countries, especially in the Middle East.

Anyone who wishes to specialise in the highly marketable field of Business English should enquire about specialist courses such as the First Certificate for Teachers of Business English (FTBE) validated by the London Chamber of Commerce & Industry or LCCI (www.lcci.org.uk/teaching-qualifications.asp) or the 50-hour blended Cert IBET (International Business English Training) validated by English UK and Trinity College. Yet another possibility is to undertake the course online, for example with The Consultants-E (www.theconsultants-e.com) which charges £695 for 70 hours over 10 weeks, plus a moderation fee of £160.

TEFL ORG UK

Katrin Winter had always wanted to see the world, travel and experience different cultures and ways of life. Now in her mid-twenties she has decided to take the plunge and finally take a gap year. She enrolled on the 140-hour Premier TEFL Course in July.

'The instructor miraculously managed to make the English grammar sound like the most interesting thing in the world. He was an experienced teacher himself and shared a lot of his knowledge with us. When the course was over, I soon received my certificate in the post. I used TEFL Org UK's website to look for jobs as I was looking to go to China. I found a job within three days of finishing the course and I am now in Xi'an.'

Despite vast cultural differences, which she admits sometimes can be a struggle, she said:

'I meet wonderful people every day, in and outside of the school; there is so much culture and so many experiences to be had here. I won't even try and start describing the wonderful food I've had! I work at a language school, so my working day usually starts at 2pm and lasts until 8.30pm. My weekend is Wednesday and Thursday, which is actually quite nice as most people will be at work and the city less hectic. The students at school are very motivated to learn and respect their teachers a lot. Older students are also keen to find out about where I am from, and more about my culture and traditions. We often have discussions on local affairs.

'It's been a very rewarding experience so far. I have had some maddening days when people can't understand me due to the language barrier and I miss home comforts and familiar faces, but those days are offset by so many more wonderful days full of learning new things and experiencing a whole different way of living.'

INTRODUCTORY COURSES

Although the Cambridge and Trinity certificates are sometimes referred to as 'introductory courses', cheaper, shorter and less rigorous introductions to the subject are available. With the dramatic rise in the popularity of certificate courses there has been a decline in what might be considered as more amateurish courses, though these do have a role to play, for example for school leavers who would not be accepted onto a certificate course or for the curious who do not want to commit themselves to a month-long course or pay £1,000+ until they have had some preliminary exposure to the field.

Because there are some commercial enterprises and 'cowboy' operators cashing in on the EFL boom, standards vary and course literature should be studied carefully before choosing. Most people who have done a TEFL training course claim that the most worthwhile part is the actual teaching practice, preferably to living, breathing foreigners rather than 'peer-teaching' in mock lessons to fellow participants. The fact is that most short introductory courses do not allow for much chance to do teaching practice. On the other hand they can provide lesson ideas and some hand out useful manuals full of lesson plans.

The more upmarket introductory courses often present themselves as an opportunity to sample the field to see whether you want to go on to do a certificate course at a later stage. Others make their course sound as if it alone will be sufficient to open doors worldwide. Some in the industry consider weekend courses to be money-spinning machines and their claims to dispense 'internationally recognised' certificates to be highly contentious. It would be unreasonable to expect a weekend or five-day course to equip anyone to teach, but most participants do find them helpful. After seeing an advertisement in the New York subway advertising for English teachers, **Roger Blake** was prompted to seek out some training. Back in England, Roger, who admits to being a not particularly academic type, enjoyed the 'crash' weekend training he did with i-to-i so much that he enrolled in a home-study module of a further 20 hours. Later, when he was asking about local teaching possibilities in Addis Ababa, he felt more confident being able to show two course certificates.

The majority of residential courses last a weekend or four to five days and cost between £300 and £500, not counting accommodation. Almost all will issue some kind of certificate that can sometimes be used to impress prospective employers. Anyone who wants a job after doing a short course should aim to do it in the spring when the majority of jobs are advertised for the following academic year. Many people who complete an introductory or 'taster' course go on to do an intensive certificate, often at the same centre.

A number of private language centres offer their own short courses in TEFL, which may focus on their own method, developed specifically with the chain of schools in mind (for example Berlitz) or may offer a more general introduction. You may come across schools looking for teachers to teach the Callan Method. Many people in the industry are sceptical (to put it mildly) about its efficacy, including an American teacher who worked at a participating school in Poland, a country where the Callan Method is popular:

The Callan Method is little more than a fraud. The material is so pedagogically and linguistically outdated that no well-informed student would ever use it. Further, the book is excessively morbid. I couldn't, in good faith, teach the Callan Method again.

A number of accrediting bodies and monitoring organisations exists, but competition between them does not make the task much easier. It is strongly recommended that you ensure that a recognised independent body accredits the course for which you are applying.

The new College of Teaching (www.collegeofteaching.org) is becoming established and may become involved with TESOL training courses. The International Accreditation of TESOL Qualifying Organisations (IATQuO) is another monitoring organisation, which has been run by an individual in Bristol since 2005 and has validated a handful of TESOL certificate courses in Europe; details from IATQuO in Bristol (ADMoller@aol.com; www.iatquo.org). A new international organisation is CALTEP (www.caltep.org), the Council for the Accreditation of Language Teacher Education Programs, based in the US and certifying the quality of short-term teacher preparation certificate programmes.

ONLINE AND DISTANCE LEARNING

The rise of the internet and increased use of electronic communications has made online TEFL training courses far more popular than the old distance learning and correspondence courses. Providers of face-to-face courses are suffering from the competition from cheap online courses, and some are cancelling courses due to low take-up rates. Not only is an online course much cheaper but it can also be done in the candidate's own time and/or in any part of the world.

Typically, online courses at the professional end of the spectrum involve at least 150 hours of tutor-led home study, as required for Level 5 of the Qualifications and Credit Framework. Some 'hybrid' or 'blended' courses including the CELTA Online offer distance learning in combination with a residential element. A new entrant to the profession is faced with a bewildering array of distance courses to choose from but does not always possess the knowledge or experience to judge between them.

Among accrediting bodies, which mostly operate as commercial enterprises, some specialise in online courses, for example Accreditat in Edinburgh (www.accreditat.com), which accredits TEFL/TESOL providers for both face-to-face and distance/online courses.

ACTDEC, the Accreditation Council for TESOL Distance Education Courses, was established in 1993 to improve on standards of distance TESOL/TEFL programmes. A copy of the ACTDEC code of practice and other details, including a list of accredited members (just a handful), can be viewed online at www.ACTDEC.org.uk. With these organisations, it is not always easy to ascertain the levels of quality control. Newer accrediting bodies have yet to prove their rigour, such as OTTSA (Online TESOL and TEFL Standards Agency; www.ottsa.org) and ALAP (Awarding Language Acquisition for Professionals; www.alapuk.org).

A NOTE ABOUT ACCREDITATION

Distance training varies enormously in quality. Some companies are successful primarily because of their advertising campaigns and skill with social media but offer very mediocre courses. Others offer good quality courses and receive excellent feedback on course work. Careful research is needed before choosing where to spend your money on an online course. Obviously a 100-hour online certificate that can be bought through Groupon for $40 is going to be of limited value.

People considering the distance learning route to TEFL training should be cautious. Some of the promotional literature does not inspire confidence: over the years I have spotted some egregious errors, including a course that 'is designed to suit you're learning speed' and another offering a 'life-long career gaurantee'. The most obvious disadvantage is the lack of face-to-face teaching practice, though some courses are more interactive, providing opportunities for blocks of teaching practice plus plenty of tutor feedback. Be aware that some employers, including ones whose details are included later in this book, specify that they will not consider applications from people with online certificates. For example Dave Fox, Director of Lexis TESOL Training Centres in Queensland, Australia, explained the situation in a recent interview: 'These days I come across lots of people looking for work who have "qualifications" from weekend-long TEFL courses or online courses with no practical element and I can't offer them anything. It's really important that you make sure your TEFL/TESOL certificate meets the criteria for work in your country of choice.' **Annabelle Laker** got in touch from Vietnam to report that the 120-hour TEFL course she had done in England before leaving did not really count for much, but fortunately she had also undertaken a 20-hour practical weekend TEFL course and had also worked as a teaching assistant in a school in England, which was experience valued more highly by her prospective employers.

More recently, **Susie Smith** wrote from her teaching job in northern Spain:

> ***I studied for the 120-hour combined face-to-face and distance learning TEFL Certificate with The TEFL Academy. While I would have preferred to have taken the internationally recognised CELTA, I didn't have the time to take a four-week, full-time course. My experience to date (in getting a job straight away and now securing another good role starting in September 2016 in Huelva) would suggest that while a CELTA is highly desirable, alternative TEFL qualifications aren't a significant hindrance, at least in Spain.***

A new development for distance students of TESOL is that they may be able to get actual teaching practice online or via Skype. One way of ascertaining the worth of a distance learning course you may be considering is to ask to be put in touch with past students. If you are not satisfied with the course but have paid your money (typically £400+ for a certificate course), you have little recourse.

Details of introductory, online and distance training courses both in Britain and abroad are provided in the Directory of Training Courses that follows.

TRAINING IN THE USA

Until 20 years ago, there were virtually no short intensive courses in TEFL available in North America. That has now changed. In addition to the 24 Cambridge CELTA providers in the USA, a number of independent TEFL training organisations offer four-week intensive courses (see Directory of Training Courses below). The major providers like Transworld are well connected with language schools abroad, particularly in Latin America and the Far East. Competition is keen among the schools, and prices remain fairly consistent at about $2,300–$2,800 for a four-week course, with the odd course available for around $2,000.

The American Language Institute in San Diego has been praised by its graduates, such as **Bryson Patterson** writing from Costa Rica:

> ***The ALI TEFL course is a solid teacher training programme encompassing methodology, live classroom practice, grammar and job placement. A day would begin with four hours of methodology (the theory and practice of second language acquisition). Trainees are then instructed in the ins and outs of lesson planning, and annual planning. Mock classes are video taped, helping students to evaluate their own performance. Afternoons are spent working as assistants for mentor teachers in live EFL classrooms and rotating through all the levels of EFL classes at the ALI.***

If one of your main criteria is the after-course job advice, make sure you investigate properly. **Melanie Twinning** felt let down by the choice she made:

> ***Despite being at least $1,000 more expensive than the competition, the course I chose really didn't do everything it promised. It has really no job placement to speak of and the man in charge of job placement is actually rather mean. Luckily I had your book and a bit of confidence and was able to find positions on my own but if you're paying $3,000 for a TEFL course I think you should get what it promises. I have to say the course itself was incredibly well done and the director is phenomenal. They just won't help you at all unless you are going to Korea.***

It is easier to get practical experience of teaching English (without a qualification) by joining one of the many voluntary ESL programmes found in almost every American city, run by community colleges, civic organisations and literacy groups. For a first-hand account see the chapter on North America at the end of this book. The membership organisation ProLiteracy Worldwide (www.proliteracy.org) operates in most states and offers volunteer tutors training workshops and access to specialist ESL materials that it publishes.

Note that the Peace Corps has been developing an on-the-job TEFL Certification Programme which involves pre-service training, online learning communities, and class observations by Peace Corps TEFL staff leading to a professional TEFL credential at the end of their 27-month posting. Pilots have been run in Armenia, Madagascar and Nicaragua and soon the programme will also be available in Thailand, Ecuador, Costa Rica, Benin, and Rwanda (see http://files.peacecorps.gov/volunteer/learn/TEFL_Comms.pdf). Its goals are different from those of commercial language schools, in encouraging cooperation with local teachers and engagement with the community, and focusing less on classroom management, as the CELTA does, for example.

DIRECTORY OF TRAINING COURSES

CAMBRIDGE CERTIFICATE (CELTA) IN THE UK

The following is a reasonably comprehensive (though not exhaustive) list of CELTA courses offered in the UK. In addition, various universities including Bath, Bristol, Nottingham Trent and Sunderland, along with many colleges of further education and adult education centres in London and around the country, plus some English language institutes offer occasional full-time or part-time CELTA courses. All are linked from www.cambridgeenglish.org/find-a-centre/find-a-teaching-centre.

ACTION ENGLISH LANGUAGE TRAINING LTD: Leeds; ✆ +44 113 244 9403; www.aelt.co.uk; full-time and blended online (15 weeks); rough frequency 12 per year; £1,250.

ANGLO-CONTINENTAL TEACHER TRAINING CENTRE: Bournemouth; ✆ +44 1202 557414; www.anglo-continental.com; full and part-time; rough frequency 6 per year; £1,296.

BASIL PATERSON COLLEGE: Edinburgh; ✆ +44 131 225 3802; www.basilpaterson.co.uk; full-time; rough frequency 8 per year; £1,195.

BELFAST METROPOLITAN COLLEGE: Belfast; ✆ +44 28 9026 5142; www.belfastmet.ac.uk; part-time; rough frequency 2 per year; £1,450.

BELL LANGUAGE SCHOOL: Cambridge; ✆ +44 1223 275598; www.bellenglish.com/teacher-training; full-time (4 weeks); 4 per year; from £1,395.

BELL LONDON: London WCI; ✆ +44 207 440 6770; www.bellenglish.com/locations/bell; twice a year; from £1,395.

BLACKBURN COLLEGE: Blackburn; ✆ +44 1254 292500; www.blackburn.ac.uk; part-time; £1,100.

BOLTON COLLEGE: Bolton; ✆ +44 1204 907333; www.boltoncollege.ac.uk; part-time.

BRASSHOUSE CENTRE: Birmingham; ✆ +44 121 303 0114; www.brasshouse.birmingham.gov.uk; part and full-time; rough frequency 3 per year; £1,200.

BRITISH STUDY CENTRES: Oxford; ✆ +44 1865 263200; www.british-study.com/teacher-training/centres/oxford; full-time; rough frequency 12 per year; £1,245.

BROMLEY COLLEGE OF FURTHER & HIGHER EDUCATION: Bromley; ✆ +44 20 8295 7000, ext 7127; www.bromley.ac.uk; part-time.

BROOKLANDS COLLEGE: Weybridge, Surrey; ✆ +44 1932 797774; www.brooklands.ac.uk; part-time; rough frequency 4 per year; £1,175.

CANTERBURY CHRIST CHURCH UNIVERSITY: Canterbury; ✆ +44 1227 767700, ext 2129; www.canterbury.ac.uk; full and part-time January to May; rough frequency 1 per year; £1,280.

CARDIFF & VALE COLLEGE: Cardiff; ✆ +44 2920 250400; www.cavc.ac.uk/celta; 1 full-time in summer, 2 part-time per year; £1,500.

CITY OF BATH COLLEGE: Bath; ✆ +44 1225 312191; www.bathcollege.ac.uk; part-time; £1,496.

CITY OF BRISTOL COLLEGE: Bristol; ✆ +44 117 312 5886; www.cityofbristol.ac.uk; part-time over 8 or 10 weeks, or 18 weeks if online; £1,495.

CITY OF OXFORD COLLEGE: Oxford; ✆ +44 1865 550550; www.cityofoxford.ac.uk; full-time in July; £1,288.

CONCORDE INTERNATIONAL STUDY CENTRE: Canterbury; ✆ +44 1227 451035; www.concorde-int.com; full-time; 5 per year; £1,163.

EALING, HAMMERSMITH & WEST LONDON COLLEGE: London; ✆ +44 207 565 1283; www.wlc.ac.uk; full-time 7 times a year and part-time; £1,150.

EMBASSY CES NEWNHAM: Cambridge; ✆ +44 1223 345650; www.embassyenglish.com/global/teacher-trasining-courses/celta; full-time; roughly 3 per year; £1,450.

ENGLISH LANGUAGE HOUSE: Milton Keynes; ✆ +44 1908 694357; www.elhuk.com; full and part-time; rough frequency 4 per year; £1,350.

GLASGOW CLYDE COLLEGE: Glasgow; ✆ +44 141 272 3638; www. glasgowclyde.ac.uk; 1 full-time in June, 1 part-time October-February; £1,150.

GLOUCESTERSHIRE COLLEGE: Cheltenham; ✆ +44 1242 532144; www.gloscol.ac.uk; full and part-time; rough frequency 4 per year.

GREENWICH COMMUNITY COLLEGE: London; ✆ +44 20 8316 6610; www.gcc.ac.uk; part-time only with various start dates.;£1,250.

ILS ENGLISH: Nottingham; ✆ +44 115 969 2424; www.ilsenglish.com; full-time in June, August, September, and October; £1,200 including moderation fee.

INTERNATIONAL HOUSE BELFAST: ✆ +44 28 9033 0700; www.ihbelfast.com; £1,230.

INTERNATIONAL HOUSE BRISTOL: tt@ihbristol.com; www.ihbristol.com; 7 times a year; £1,350.

INTERNATIONAL HOUSE LONDON: ✆ +44 20 7611 2414; www.ihlondon.com; infott@ihlondon.com; full and part-time; rough frequency 11 per year. This is the largest CELTA and DELTA centre in the world; £1,495.

INTERNATIONAL HOUSE LONDON

'After CELTA, the world is your oyster! I am a German student but during my semester breaks I can work abroad now. Doing the CELTA at IH London was an eye-opener for me; I am absolutely sure that being a teacher is my dream job. The course was difficult and stressful but you have to stay focused on your goals and see the immediate outcome. I already worked for an international college in England during summer school and term time and will work at the same college this summer again. Many opportunities ahead and definitely plan to do the DELTA as well!' **Simone Griener, German**

'I frequently tell people that my CELTA qualification from IH is the most challenging – and most rewarding – achievement on my CV. It has allowed me to follow my dream of moving to Japan, teaching elementary school children and adults, and it continues to open doors for me. On day three of training for my current job as an Assistant Language Teacher in one of Japan's elementary schools, I planned my lesson on one of the empty lesson plans from my CELTA. It had the IH logo in the corner. The head trainer called me to the head of the class while marking them and said, "You trained with IH? Wow – everyone who is anyone in this industry has been through their training." No matter where my career takes me to next, I know that IH's extensive training in all areas of ESL teaching will ensure that I am completely prepared, and is recognised as among the finest in the world. Thank you, IH!' **Alex Page, British**

INTERNATIONAL HOUSE NEWCASTLE: ✆ +44 191 232 9551; www.ihnewcastle.com; 6 per year. £1,300. Also offers IH Cert in Teaching Younger Learners and Teenagers (TYLT); 1 week, £320.

ISE HOVE: Sussex; ✆ +44 1273 384800; www.isehove.com; full-time (7 times a year), part-time (twice a year); £925–£1,075.

ITTC: Bournemouth; ✆ +44 1202 516289; www.ittc.co.uk; full-time and part-time; rough frequency 12 per year; £1,371.

ITTC

Lisa D – a not so average CELTA candidate

I originally come from Canada, but came to England in 2002 and got work in an office. The monotony got to me and I searched around for a CELTA course and decided on ITTC. I'm glad I chose ITTC as the course was so practical and the tutors on the course were really good role models who tried to get the best out of everyone.

I was lucky to be offered work at BEET/ITTC straight after the course, and I worked the whole summer for them before I went to teach overseas. I've taught in private language schools, I've set up and organised English immersion camps for teenagers where I had to design the whole course as well as produce materials, I've worked in secondary schools overseas and also trained up to be an examiner for English language examinations. So far I've spent time in Switzerland, Italy and Colombia, and I come back to England regularly to work on summer programmes.

Having the CELTA has given me an opportunity to use my brain more than I ever did working in an office. I love working with people from different cultures, and it has also allowed me to learn other languages more easily. I still don't like being asked to teach areas I haven't been trained for and I'm not much of a disciplinarian – but this hasn't really been a problem, as my students always seem so motivated.

In 2013 I decided I'd like to complete the Cambridge Delta so I studied at ITTC and in Argentina and now I'm a Delta qualified teacher.

(Lisa wrote this while in Bournemouth, but she is currently working for the British Council in Colombia.)

LAL TORBAY: Torbay, Devon; www.lalschools.com; 5 full-time courses a year; £1,250.

LANGUAGE LINK TRAINING: Earl's Court, London; ✆ +44 20 7370 4755; www.languagelink.com; full-time offered monthly; part-time 2 times a year; £1,240 including Cambridge assessment fee.

LANGUAGE TEACHING CENTRE BRIGHTON: Hove, East Sussex; ✆ +44 1273 735975; www.ltc-english.com/ltc-brighton/our-school; full-time; rough frequency 4 per year; £995.

MANCHESTER ACADEMY OF ENGLISH: Manchester; www.experienceenglish.com/celta; full and part-time; rough frequency 11 per year; £1,350.

MANCHESTER CENTRAL SCHOOL OF ENGLISH; Manchester; ✆ +44 161 236 7575; www.manchestercse.co.uk; 9 intensive courses plus 2 part-times/online.

NEWCASTLE COLLEGE: Newcastle; ✆ +44 191 200 4538; www.ncl-coll.ac.uk; part-time; £1,250.

NILE TEFL: Norwich; ✆ +44 1603 664473; www.nile-elt.com; full-time; rough frequency 8 per year; £1,431.

NILE TEFL, NORWICH

Thom talks about his career in ELT, which all started with a CELTA:

Little did I know when I first enrolled for a CELTA that it would lead to a postgraduate degree and a leading role at one of the largest teacher training institutes in Europe.

In my case, CELTA led to two years' teaching in Portugal, where a friend had told me he 'played football on the beach in the days and taught English in the evenings'. I still had the travel bug, so I returned to Britain for a year, finding work in ESOL classes at higher education colleges, and saved money to travel to Australia. During a year there, I taught in Surfer's Paradise and Sydney, and started to understand how people were making an interesting and fulfilling career from TEFL, rather than doing it as a means to an end.

I moved to Thailand from Australia, and after a year or so working at a university, I started at the British Council, where I was encouraged to think more long-term about teaching, and did the Delta by distance. This modular qualification is now one of a selection of online courses offered by NILE, and is done by distance learning with online and local supervision. I did really well with this qualification, and started to become involved in more and more interesting projects, and to develop an interest in teacher training. It was time to leave Thailand, however, and life then took me to Santiago de Chile where my work led me to take a Master's Degree in Language Testing, and the opportunity to develop in the area of Educational Technology.

I've been working in language testing, teacher training, technology in and out of the classroom, and language teaching and learning for the last eight years.

These days I work closely with the professional development and postgraduate students at NILE in Norwich, and enjoy a working environment that offers networking possibilities for teachers at every stage of their ELT career. Somewhere along the way I stopped playing football on the beach, but I haven't missed it as much as I once would have thought!

As Director of NILE I have had the opportunity to meet many teachers from around the world, all with different perspectives on what makes a good training course, and my team and I are constantly striving to improve our courses, from CELTA to our Master's Degree, in order to be able to continue to deliver world-class professional development. With experienced tutors, extensive resources onsite and home-stay accommodation near the course centre, NILE makes the perfect place to follow the CELTA course.

NOTTINGHAM TRENT UNIVERSITY: Nottingham; ✆ +44 115 848 6156; www4.ntu.ac.uk/hum/language-centre; part-time; £1,380.

OXFORD HOUSE COLLEGE: London; ✆ +44 20 7580 9785; www.ohcenglish.com; part and full-time; rough frequency 12 per year; £1,325.

RANDOLPH SCHOOL OF ENGLISH: Edinburgh; ✆ +44 131 226 5004; www.randolph.org.uk; part and full-time; rough frequency 9 per year; £990.

READING COLLEGE: Reading; ✆ +44 1189 554319; www.reading-college.ac.uk; part-time October to February; £1,284.

READING OPEN CENTRE: English Language & Teacher Training Centre, Reading; ✆ +44 118 939 1833; www.telc-reading.co.uk; semi-intensive; rough frequency 3 per year; £1,300.

ST GILES BRIGHTON: Brighton; ✆ +44 1273 682747; www.stgiles-international.com; full-time; rough frequency 11 per year; £1,230.

ST GILES INTERNATIONAL LONDON HIGHGATE: London; ✆ +44 20 8340 0828; www.stgiles-international.com/english-language-schools/uk/london-highgate; full-time; rough frequency 18 per year; £1,230.

SAXONCOURT TEACHER TRAINING: London; ✆ +44 20 7499 8533; 20 7491 1911; www.saxoncourt.com; full and part-time; rough frequency 12 per year; £1,199.

SKOLA TEACHER TRAINING: London; ✆ +44 20 7287 3216; www.skolacelta.co.uk; part-time; 3 times a year part-time; £1,295.

SOLIHULL COLLEGE: Solihull; ✆ +44 121 6787295; www.solihull.ac.uk; part-time; £1,391.

SOUTH THAMES COLLEGE: London; ✆ +44 20 8918 7366; www.south-thames.ac.uk; 3 full-time and one part-time; £1,250.

STANTON TEACHER TRAINING: London; ✆ +44 20 7221 7259; www.lscstanton.co.uk; full-time; rough frequency 12 per year; £1,311.

STUDIO CAMBRIDGE: Cambridge; ✆ +44 1223 369701; www.studiocambridge.co.uk; full-time; rough frequency 2 per year; £1,400.

SUSSEX DOWNS COLLEGE: Eastbourne; ✆ +44 1323 637240; www.sussexdowns.ac.uk; intensive course offered over 4.5 weeks in the summer. £1,100. Also part-time over 11 weeks from February and September; £950.

TEACHING HOUSE LONDON: London; ✆ +1 800 756 2003; www.teachinghouse.com/london; full and part-time; 6 courses per year; £1,384.

UNIVERSITY OF GLASGOW, EFL Unit: Glasgow; ✆ +44 141 330 6521; www.gla.ac.uk/schools/mlc/eas; full-time and part-time; £1,200.

UNIVERSITY OF SHEFFIELD, ENGLISH LANGUAGE TEACHING CENTRE: Sheffield; ✆ +44 114 222 1780; www.sheffield.ac.uk/eltc; full-time in June/July and August/September plus part-time, blended and online; £1,450.

WESTMINSTER KINGSWAY COLLEGE: London; ✆ +44 20 7802 8813; www.westking.ac.uk; part-time; rough frequency 1 per year.

CAMBRIDGE CERTIFICATE (CELTA) ABROAD

The following centres, listed alphabetically by country, offer the Cambridge Certificate in English Language Teaching to Adults.

ARGENTINA

INTERNATIONAL HOUSE BUENOS AIRES: Buenos Aires; ✆ +54 11 4788 1788; www.ih-buenosaires.com; full-time offered monthly plus 2 part-time courses a year; $1,260 plus registration fee $190.

ARMENIA

ESOLARM: Yerevan; ✆ +374 60 509 709 or 99 166 599; www.esolarm.org; 1 full-time course in July; €1,150.

AUSTRALIA

AUSTRALIAN TESOL TRAINING CENTRE (ATTC): Sydney, Brisbane and Perth; ✆ +61 2 8252 2821/1300 730 466; info.ATTC@navitas.com; www.attc.edu.au; full and part-time; rough frequency 12 per year.

CURTIN UNIVERSITY: Perth; ✆ +61 8 9266 4224; www.english.curtin.edu.au; full-time; rough frequency 2 per year; starting June and November; AUS$2,850–$3,100.

HOLMESGLEN LANGUAGE CENTRE: Chadstone (Victoria); ✆ +61 3 9564 1779; www.holmesglen.vic.edu.au; full and part-time; rough frequency 4 per year.

HOLMES INSTITUTE TEACHER TRAINING: Melbourne; ✆ +61 3 9662 2055; www.holmes.edu.au; full-time; rough frequency 4 per year.

INSEARCH UNIVERSITY OF TECHNOLOGY, SYDNEY (UTS): Sydney; ✆ +61 2 9218 8646; www.insearch.edu.au/courses/teacher-training; full and part-time; rough frequency 3 of each per year; AUS$3,090.

INSTITUTE OF CONTINUING & TESOL EDUCATION (ICTE): Brisbane; ✆ +61 7 3346 6734; www.icte.uq.edu.au/celta; full and part-time; rough frequency 4 per year; AUS$2,995 plus moderation fee.

INTERNATIONAL HOUSE SYDNEY: Sydney; ✆ +61 2 9279 0733; www.ihsydney.com.au; full-time courses offered monthly, 5 part-time; AUS$3,150 plus $250 Cambridge assessment fee.

LEXIS TESOL TRAINING CENTRE (LTTC): Maroochydore, Queensland; ✆ +61 7 54792272 or 5447 4448; www.lexistesoltraining.com/sunshine-coast; full-time from February, May and July; 10 weeks part-time from September; AUS$2,750.

MELBOURNE TRAINING ASSOCIATES: Carlton, Melbourne; ✆ +61 3 9041 5341; www.melbtraining.com.au; 5 full-time courses, and part-time blended courses; AUS$3,100–$3,300.

MILNER INTERNATIONAL COLLEGE OF ENGLISH: Perth; ✆ +61 8 9325 5444; www.milner.wa.edu.au/teacher-training/CELTA; full and part-time; rough frequency 5 per year; AUS$2,890.

PHOENIX ENGLISH LANGUAGE ACADEMY: Perth; ✆ +61 8 9227 5538; www.phoenix.wa.edu.au/teachertraining; 5 full-time (130 hours), 3 part-time per year; AUS$2,945-$3,100.

RMIT ENGLISH WORLDWIDE: Melbourne; ✆ +61 3 9657 5876; www.rmitenglishworldwide.com; full and part-time; rough frequency 3 per year; AUS$3,100.

SOUTH AUSTRALIAN COLLEGE OF ENGLISH (SACE Adelaide): Adelaide; ✆ +61 8 8410 5222; www.saceadelaide.sa.edu.au; full-time; rough frequency 4 per year; AUS$3,100.

TASMANIAN COLLEGE OF ENGLISH (SACE Hobart and SACE Whitsunday): Hobart, Tasmania; ✆ +61 3 6231 9911; www.sacehobart.edu.au; full-time; 1 per year in October; AUS$3,100.

TEACHING HOUSE MELBOURNE: Melbourne; ✆ +1 800 756 2003; www.teachinghouse.com; full and part-time courses year round; AUS$2,800.

AUSTRIA

BFI VIENNA: Vienna; ✆ +43 1 811 78 10152; www.bfi.at; 1 full-time in winter and 2 part-time courses per year; €2,590.

BAHRAIN

BRITISH COUNCIL, BAHRAIN: Manama; ✆ +973 1726 1555 ext 229; www.britishcouncil.bh/en/teach; 1 full-time from mid-May; 850 dinars (£1,450).

BELARUS

INTERNATIONAL HOUSE: Private Educational Institution Study Centre, Minsk; ✆ +375 44 7784328; www.ih.by; 2 full-time in summer; £850.

BELGIUM

LANGUAGE TEACHER TRAINING IN BELGIUM: Brussels; ✆ +32 488 516 955; www.lttb.eu; 5 full-time, 4 part-time; €1,680.

BRAZIL

ALLIANCE, Manaus, Amazonia; ✆ +55 92 35843764; www.alliancegroup.com.br.

BRITANNIA INTERNATIONAL ENGLISH: Rio de Janeiro; ✆ +55 21 2143 7630; www.britannia.com.br; full-time and part-time; R$4,300 (£885).

CULTURA INGLESA: Sao Paulo, Belo Horizonte, Bahia, Natal, Belém and João Pessoa; www.culturainglesasp.com.br; occasional part-time courses mainly for Brazilian teachers; sample price R$3,540 + R$480 Cambridge fee.

SEVEN ENGLISH: Sao Paulo; ✆ +55 11 2392 0017; www.sevenidiomas.com.br; full and part-time both twice a year; R$3,440 plus US$211 Cambridge fee.

TARGET LANGUAGE SERVICES LTDA: São Paulo; ✆ +55 11 3207 5400; www.targetlanguage.com.br; 2 full-time, 2 part-time.

UP LANGUAGE CONSULTANTS: Terreo; ✆ +55 11 5105 0200; www.uplanguage.com.br; 1 part-time.

BULGARIA

AVO-BELL SCHOOL OF ENGLISH: Sofia; ✆ +359 2 943 3943; www.teflcertificates-avo.com; full-time; rough frequency 4 per year; £983–£1,028 for course alone, £1,244–£1,289 including self-catering accommodation.

CANADA

ENGLISH CANADA WORLD ORGANIZATION: Halifax; ✆ +1 902 429 3636.

GLOBAL VILLAGE: Calgary; ✆ +1 403 543 7300; www.celtacalgary.ca; full-time 3 times a year, part-time twice a year; C$2,500.

GLOBAL VILLAGE: Vancouver; ✆ +1 604 684 1010; www.gvcareer.com; full-time; rough frequency 5 per year; C$2,500.

GREYSTONE COLLEGE: Toronto; ✆ +1 416 323 1770; www.greystonecollege.com/celta-program-toronto; 3 part-time courses a year.

INTERNATIONAL HOUSE CAREER COLLEGE: Vancouver; ✆ +1-604-739-9836; www.tesl-vancouver.com; 8 full-time courses a year; C$2,345 plus $150 registration fee.

INTERNATIONAL LANGUAGE SCHOOLS OF CANADA – MONTREAL: Montreal; ✆ +1 514 876 4572; www.celta.ilsc.ca; full-time; about 7 per year; also part-time and online with practicum; C$2,500.

LSC INTERNATIONAL COLLEGE: Toronto; ✆ +1 416 488 2200; www.ecenglish.com/en/teacher-training/toronto-celta; full-time every month; C$2,500.

SOL SCHOOLS: Toronto; ✆ +1 416 322 3405; www.solteacher.com; 4 part-time courses; C$2,500.

TEACHING HOUSE TORONTO: Toronto; ✆ +1 800 756 2003; www.teachinghouse.com; part-time courses year round; C$2,500.

CHINA

EDUCATION FIRST: Beijing; ✆ +86 6586 5550.

INTERNATIONAL HOUSE BEIJING: Beijing; ✆ +86 188 106 039 01; www.ihbeijing.com; 2 full-time in the summer; RMB 11,500.

LANGUAGE LINK CHINA TRADE CENTER: Beijing and Shanghai; ✆ +86 10 5169 5583; www.celtachina.com.cn; full-time; rough frequency 10 per year; RMB 12,500.

SYDNEY INSTITUTE OF LANGUAGE AND COMMERCE (SILC): Shanghai; ✆ +86 21 6998 0003; www.insearch.edu.au/Teacher-Training/CELTA-SILC-details; course is run once a year in August by Insearch in Sydney (entry above); RMB 15,550.

COLOMBIA

BRITISH COUNCIL BOGOTÁ: Bogotá; ✆ +57 1 325 9090; www.britishcouncil.co; full-time and blended; 4,300,000 pesos.

INTERNATIONAL HOUSE BOGOTÁ: Bogotá and Medellin; ✆ +57 1 336 4747; www.ihbogota.com; full-time 7 times a year; $1,795–$1,895.

CYPRUS

SHERIDAN PRIVATE INSTITUTE: Nicosia; ✆ +357 22590 556; www.sheridan.com.cy; full-time in summer.

CZECH REPUBLIC

AKCENT – INTERNATIONAL HOUSE: Prague; ✆ +420 2 6110 9249; www.akcent.cz; full and part-time; rough frequency 10 per year; £969–£1,049; also offered in Brno.

EVROPSKE CENTRUM JAZYKOVYCH: Ceske Budejovice; ✆ +420 387 204 662; www.celta-training.eu; 5 full-time courses May to September; £828 if booked more than 3 months in advance.

HELLO LANGUAGE CENTRE OSTRAVA: Ostrava; ✆ +420 261 109 249; www.akcent.cz.

MASARYK UNIVERSITY: Brno; ✆ +420 54 949 7785; http://cic.muni.cz/en; part-time over 15 weeks in autumn and spring; 35,000 crowns.

ECUADOR

BSL (BRITISH SCHOOL OF LANGUAGE): Montañita and Cuenca; ✆ +593 9 9885 4399; www.celtainecuador.com; offered 8 times a year in Montañita at eco-lodge by Pacific Ocean and 3 times a year in Cuenca; $2,595 in Montañita includes accommodation and meals; $1,595 in Cuenca without accommodation.

KAMALA EDUCATION AND TRAINING GALAPAGOS: Santa Cruz, Galapagos; ✆ +593 99 27 90079; www.CELTAgalapagos.com; minimum 4 full-time courses a year; $2,350, with last minute reduction to $1,700 recently; packages available that include a month of volunteering after the course.

EGYPT

BRITISH COUNCIL: Cairo; ✆ +20 2 3300 1845; www.britishcouncil.org.eg/en; full-time; frequency 6 per year; 18,400 EGP (£1,570).

FUTURE UNIVERSITY IN EGYPT: Cairo; www.fue.edu.eg; 3 times a year; 15,000 EGP.

PHAROS UNIVERSITY: Alexandria; www.pua.edu.eg; 7 times a year; 14,000 EGP.

FRANCE

BRITISH COUNCIL PARIS: Paris and Lyon; ✆+33 1 49 55 73 07; teacher.training@britishcouncil.fr; www.britishcouncil.fr; €1,850.

CIEL BRETAGNE: Le Relecq Kerhuon, Brittany; www.esolbrittany.com; new 5-week course running 4 times between May and October 2016; €1,700.

ESOL STRASBOURG: Strasbourg; ✆ +33 7 62 99 17 22; www.esolstrasbourg.com; 5 per year full-time; €1,500 winter, €1,600 high season.

ILC FRANCE (INTERNATIONAL LANGUAGE CENTRE): Paris; ✆ +33 1 44 41 80 20; www.ilcfrance.com; full-time; rough frequency 9 per year; €1,800.

GEORGIA

EDUCATION & TRAINING INTERNATIONAL LTD: Tbilisi; ✆ +995 32 225 0945; www.eti.uk.com.

INTERNATIONAL HOUSE TBILISI: Tbilisi; ✆ +995 32 294 0515; www.ihtbilisi.ge/en/celta; full-time in the summer (provisional), part-time in the autumn and online CELTA; all £780.

GERMANY

BERLIN SCHOOL OF ENGLISH: Berlin; ✆ +49 30 229 0456; www.berlin.school-of-english.de; 8 full-time per year and two part-time; €1,595 (including exam fee).

HAMBURG SCHOOL OF ENGLISH: Hamburg; ✆ +49 40 480 2119; www.hamburg.school-of-english.de; 3 full-time per year; €1,595.

INTERNATIONAL HOUSE FRANKFURT: Kaiserstr. 12, 60311 Frankfurt; www.suarez.de/celta-frankfurt; 8 per year; €1,595.

MUNCHNER VOLKSHOCHSCHULE: Munich; ✆ +49 89 48006 6265; www.mvhs.de/celta; full and part-time; rough frequency 2 per year (August/September); €1,595.

GREECE

BRITISH COUNCIL ATHENS: Athens; ✆ +30 210 369 2339; www.britishcouncil.gr; 4 full-time courses a year; €1,425 plus €150 Cambridge fee.

CELT: Athens; ✆ +30 210 330 2406; www.celt.edu.gr; 4 full-time, 2 part-time; €1,450, plus €160 Cambridge assessment fee; also offers its own TEFL certificate course (€1,300).

STUDY SPACE: Thessaloniki; ✆ +30 231 026 9697; www.studyspace.gr; part-time October to January or February to May; full-time in June; €1,800 including accommodation.

HUNGARY

INTERNATIONAL HOUSE: Budapest; ✆ +36 1 345 7046; www.teacher-training.hu; monthly full-time; 1 part-time per year; £899 for early booking, £999 otherwise.

INDIA

THE BRITISH COUNCIL ENGLISH LANGUAGE TEACHING CENTRE: New Delhi; ✆ +91 1800 102 4353; www.britishcouncil.in; full-time offered in Mumbai, Kolkata and Chennai as well as Delhi; Rs130,000 (£1,300).

PLANET EDU: Gurgaon, Haryana; ✆ +91 124 4684 800; www.theplanetedu.com; full-time in summer; Rs130,000.

INDONESIA

THE BRITISH INSTITUTE (TBI): Jakarta; ✆ +62 81 3204 33339 / 21 300 27988; www.tbi.co.id; 3 full-time in Jakarta, 1 in Bali; $1,800.

IRELAND

INTERNATIONAL HOUSE: Dublin; ✆ +353 1 635 5850; www.ihdublin.com; monthly and 1 part-time course; €1,750 inclusive.

KAPLAN INTERNATIONAL COLLEGE: Dublin; ✆ +353 1 672 7122; Dublin@Kaplan.com; 5 part-time; €1,700.

THE ENGLISH ACADEMY: Dublin; ✆ +353 1 872 6600; www.theenglishacademy.ie; 9 full-time courses a year; €1,600.

UNIVERSITY COLLEGE CORK, Language Centre: Cork; ✆ +353 21 490 3883; www.ucc.ie/esol; part-time twice a year, semi-intensive (7 weeks) in spring and one intensive course in June; €1,750.

ITALY

ANGLO-AMERICAN CENTRE: Cagliari, Sardinia; ✆ +39 070 654 955; www.angloamericancentre.it; 2 full-time over summer; €1,600 including exam fee and course materials.

BRITISH COUNCIL: Naples; ✆ +39 081 578 8247; www.britishcouncil.it; full-time in June/July; €1,850.

GIGA INTERNATIONAL HOUSE: Catania, Sicily; ✆ +39 095 715 2243; www.gigact.com; 4 full-time; €1,600–€1,750.

INTERNATIONAL HOUSE: San Donato Milan; ✆ +39 02 527 9124; www.ihmilano.it; full-time; rough frequency 3 per year; €1,880.

INTERNATIONAL HOUSE PALERMO: Palermo; ✆ +39 091 584954; www.ihpalermo.it; full-time; rough frequency 1 per year; €1,550.

INTERNATIONAL HOUSE ROME/ACCADEMIA BRITANNICA: Rome; ✆ +39 06 7047 6894; www.ihromamz.it; full-time and semi-intensive, 5 per year; €1,800; also run YL extension and DELTA modules.

INTERNATIONAL HOUSE ROME

'As a CELTA graduate, I can tell you that the course is the best professional decision that you could make. It will fundamentally change your approach to the classroom forever. You encounter supportive tutors and experienced mentors that help you unlock all your teaching potential. Together with other eager trainees you will learn how to manage the classroom successfully, engage with students effectively and to take with you all that you need.' **Maria A.**

'If you are reading this, it means you're thinking of doing a CELTA course. When you have your interview, they'll probably tell you that it's going to be hard, stressful and time-consuming – and they are absolutely right! What they don't tell you is that it's also a rewarding and life-changing experience. Tutors will help you through every stage, giving you advice, feedback and great tips. Likewise, you'll also learn a lot from your fellow trainees. My recommendation before starting the course would be to get as familiar as possible with the CELTA wikispaces and the suggested reading list, because once the course starts you won't have a lot of time for extra reading or research. I'm finishing my course this week and I can say for sure that I haven't regretted a single minute of it – or a single euro!' **Annachiara S.**

'Very intensive! Very stressful! But worth it! There will be little sleep, no social life, 100% commitment. But you will not do this alone – you'll have your fellow trainees and tutors' support to accompany you during this short but intensive journey.' **Dennis P.**

'The lack of sleep and demanding workload might be overwhelming in the beginning, BUT the eagerness of your students, the guidance of the tutors and the support of your fellow trainees make it all worthwhile in the end! Although challenging, you will leave with a new knowledge which you can confidently take with you anywhere you teach. Excellent! I liked it a lot!' **Sofia M.**

THE CAMBRIDGE SCHOOL: Verona; ✆ +39 45 800 3154; www.cambridgeschool.it; full and part-time; rough frequency 2 per year.

JAPAN

LANGUAGE RESOURCES: Kobe; ✆ +81 78 382 0394; www.language-resources.co.jp/teachers; part-time; 290,000 yen plus Cambridge fee.

JORDAN

BRITISH COUNCIL AMMAN: www.britishcouncil.org/jo; full-time twice a year (January and August); 1,750 dinars.

KAZAKHSTAN

INTERPRESS INTERNATIONAL HOUSE: Almaty; ✆ +7 727 272 2744; www.ihkazakhstan.com; www.celta.kz; full-time in summer; 600,000 tenge.

KOREA

INTERNATIONAL GRADUATE SCHOOL OF ENGLISH IGSE: Seoul; ✆ +82 2 6477 5151; http://sce.igse.ac.kr/community/TheCambridgeCELTA; summer intensive; 2,350,000 won.

KUWAIT

BRITISH COUNCIL KUWAIT: Kuwait City; ✆ +965 2251 5512; www.britishcouncil.com.kw/en/teach/celta; intensive course in August; 850 Kuwaiti dinars.

LATVIA

INTERNATIONAL HOUSE RIGA-SATVA: Riga; ✆+371 6722 6641; www.ihriga.lv; full-time in July and August; €1,050.

LEBANON

ALLC INTERNATIONAL HOUSE BEIRUT: Beirut; ✆ +961 1 500978; www.allcs.edu.lb; full-time; rough frequency 2 per year in the summer; one in Beirut, the other in Saida (Sidon); $1,800.

MACEDONIA

SOUTH EAST EUROPEAN UNIVERSITY LANGUAGE CENTRE: Skopje; ✆ +389 70 321 985; www.seeu.edu.mk/sites/celta; 1 intensive in June; €975.

MALAYSIA

THE BRITISH COUNCIL LANGUAGE CENTRE: Kuala Lumpur; ✆ +60 3 2723 7900; www.britishcouncil.my; part-time over 10 or 20 weeks or full time in August; 9,275 ringgits (£1,660).

MALTA

IELS MALTA: Sliema; ✆ +356 2132 0381; www.iels.com.mt; 3 full-time a year; €1,400.
NSTS ENGLISH LANGUAGE INSTITUTE: Valletta; ✆ +356 2558 8500; www.nsts.org; full-time; rough frequency 3 per year.

MEXICO

INTERNATIONAL HOUSE: Mexico City, Guadalajara and Quintana Roo; www.ihmexico.com; mostly full-time; $1,795.

MOROCCO

BRITISH COUNCIL CASABLANCA: Casablanca, Rabat and Tangier; ✆ +212 802 001045; www.britishcouncil.ma/en/teach; full-time and part-time; 25,000 dirhams (£1,650).

MYANMAR

BRITISH COUNCIL BURMA: Yangon; ✆ +95 1 246789/256290; www.britishcouncil.org.mm; full-time in May; 2,000,000 Kyat (£1,150).

NEPAL

BRITISH COUNCIL TEACHING CENTRE NEPAL: Kathmandu; ✆ +977 1 441 0798; www.britishcouncil.org.np/teach/courses-qualifications/celta; full-time September; £1,400.

NETHERLANDS

BRITISH LANGUAGE TRAINING CENTRE: Amsterdam; ✆ +31 20 622 3634; www.bltc.nl; 2 full-time and 2 part-time courses offered annually; €1,925 inclusive.

BRITISH SCHOOL NETHERLANDS: Den Haag; ✆ +31 70 315 4080; www.britishschool.nl; part-time on 18 Fridays from September; €2,250.

NEW ZEALAND

ARA INSTITUTE OF CANTERBURY: Christchurch; ✆ +64 3 940 8296; www.ara.ac.nz; 4 part-time per year.

AUT INTERNATIONAL HOUSE, Auckland; ✆ +64 9 921 9630; www.aut.ac.nz; 2 part-time; NZ$2,150.

CAMPBELL INSTITUTE: Wellington; ✆ +64 4 803 3434; www.campbell.ac.nz; full-time in June; NZ$3,195.

CHRISTCHURCH COLLEGE OF ENGLISH: Christchurch; ✆ +64 3 343 3790; www.ccel.co.nz; full-time; rough frequency 3–5 per year; NZ$3,050.

LANGUAGES INTERNATIONAL: Auckland; ✆ +64 9 309 0615; www.languages.ac.nz; full-time; rough frequency 6 per year; NZ$3,200.

NEW ZEALAND LANGUAGE CENTRES: Auckland; ✆ +64 9 303 1962; www.nzlc.ac.nz; 5-week courses run 5 times a year; NZ$3,200.

UNIVERSITY OF AUCKLAND: English Language Academy, Auckland; ✆ +64 9 919 7666; www.ela.auckland.ac.nz; 4 full-time, 2 part-time; NZ$3,300.

UNIVERSITY OF WAIKATO PATHWAYS COLLEGE: Hamilton; ✆ +64 7 858 5600; www.waikato.ac.nz; full-time; rough frequency 4 per year; NZ$3,300.

OMAN

BRITISH COUNCIL OMAN: Muscat; ✆ +968 2468 1000; www.britishcouncil.om/en; part-time; 1,000 Omani rials (£1,660).

INTERNATIONAL HOUSE MUSCAT: Ruwi, Muscat; enquiry@polyglot.org; www.pi.om; full-time in August; 1,050 Omani rials (£1,750).

POLAND

BRITISH COUNCIL KRAKOW: Krakow; ✆ +48 12 428 5930; www.britishcouncil.pl/en/celta; 6 full-time courses per year; 5230 zloty.

BRITISH COUNCIL WARSAW: Warsaw; ✆ +48 22 695 5900; www.britishcouncil.pl/en/English/schools/warsaw; 3 full-time courses in summer, 1 part-time throughout the year; 5,400 zloty (early booking discount available).

GAMA COLLEGE OF ENGLISH: Krakow; ✆ +48 12 6341259; www.gamacollege.pl/teacher-training-celta.

INTERNATIONAL HOUSE-INTEGRA KATOWICE: Katowice; ✆ +48 32 259 9997; www.ih.com.pl; 2 full-time in summer.

INTERNATIONAL HOUSE WROCLAW: Wroclaw; ✆ +48 71 781 7290; www.ih.com.pl; full-time; rough frequency 9 per year; from £805 if booked early.

LANG LTC: Warsaw; www.lang.com.pl/celta; twice full-time in summer and part-time in spring and autumn; 5,200 zloty (£900).

PORTUGAL

INTERNATIONAL HOUSE LISBON: Lisbon; ✆ +351 21 315 1493/1494/1496; www.ihlisbon.com; full and part-time; rough frequency 10 per year; €1,500.

INTERNATIONAL HOUSE LISBON

'Taking the CELTA course at IH Lisbon has been a life-changing experience. It is, without a doubt, an incredibly intense course, but ultimately, very rewarding. No sooner have you observed a veteran teacher in the classroom, than you are teaching your first class. The tutors, however, provide you with all the advice, support and encouragement you need to get through those first few nerve-racking lessons. Feedback is constant, fair and endlessly helpful. In addition, all the reference materials you could possibly need are either located in the school library, or accessible from the computer room. IH Lisbon provided me with the solid foundations on which to start my teaching career, and I would highly recommend the school to anyone wishing to undertake the CELTA certificate.' **Louise Marques**

QATAR

INTERNATIONAL HOUSE DOHA: www.ihdoha.com; 2 full-time in summer; 11,500 Qatari rials (£2,000+).

ROMANIA

SHAKESPEARE TRAINING SRL: Bucharest; ✆ +40 744 314 437 or +40 21 230 2006; www.celtatraining.ro; 2 full-time, 1 part-time; £1,100.

RUSSIA

BKC-EDUCATION WITHOUT LIMITS: Moscow; www.bkcih-moscow.com; full-time; rough frequency 7 per year; from £850.

LANGUAGE LINK ROSTOV-ON-DON: Taganrod, Rostov; ✆ +7 863 200 1444; www.languagelink.ru; full-time in July/August; £900.

LANGUAGE TESTING PROFI (LT-PRO): St Petersburg; ✆ +7812 2445488; www.lt-pro.ru; 2 full-time in summer; 85,000 roubles (+ £135 Cambridge fee).

URAL FEDERAL UNIVERSITY CENTRE OF LANGUAGE EXCELLENCE (UCLEX): Ekaterinburg; ✆ +7 902 267 0986; www.uclex.urfu.ru; intensive course in July; £1,200.

SERBIA

INTERNATIONAL HOUSE BELGRADE: Belgrade; ✆ +381 11 3612 218; www.ihbelgrade.co.rs; 4 full-time per year; £900.

SINGAPORE

THE BRITISH COUNCIL SINGAPORE: Napier Road; ✆+64 6473 1111; www.britishcouncil.sg; 2 full-time, part-time; S$5,900.

CA INTERNATIONAL COLLEGE: Singapore; ✆ +65 6536 2193; www.tesol.edu.sg; full-time (4 weeks) and part-time (8 weeks); S$5,100.

SLOVENIA

MINT INTERNATIONAL HOUSE: Ljubljana; ✆ +386 1 300 4300; www.mint.si; 2 full-time in summer; €1,250 plus €250/€350 for a month's accommodation.

SOUTH AFRICA

DURBAN LANGUAGE CENTRE: Durban; ✆ +27 31 201 3448; www.durbanlanguage.com.

GOOD HOPE STUDIES: Cape Town; ✆ +27 21 683 1399; www.ghs.co.za; full-time; rough frequency 6 per year; $1,690.

INTERNATIONAL HOUSE CAPE TOWN: Seapoint, Cape Town; ✆ +27 21 433 0546; www.ihcapetown.com; 6 full-time, 1 part-time; 14,250 Rand.

INTERNATIONAL HOUSE JOHANNESBURG: Johannesburg; ✆+27 11 339 1051; www.ihjohannesburg.co.za; full-time; rough frequency 6 per year.

SPAIN

CAMBRIDGE ENGLISH: London School of Languages, San Sebastian; www.languagetestingservices.com; 3 full-time courses; €1,550.

CAMBRIDGE SCHOOL: Granollers, Barcelona; ✆ +34 93 870 2001; www.celta-delta.com; 5 weeks full-time; rough frequency 4 per year; €1,535.

CAMPBELL COLLEGE: Valencia; ✆ +34 96 362 8983; www.cambridgeceltavalencia.com; 5 per year; €1,450.

CHESTER SCHOOL OF ENGLISH: Madrid; ✆ +34 91 401 9729; www.chester.es; full-time offered July, August, September, November, February and May; €1,450 including the Cambridge fee.

CLIC INTERNATIONAL HOUSE: Seville; ✆ +34 95 450 01316; training@clic.es; www.clic.es/tefl; full-time; rough frequency 12 per year; €1,575. Also available 4 times a year in Malaga; Spanish courses; ✆ +34 95 450 2131; www.clic.es.

CLIC INTERNATIONAL HOUSE SEVILLE

Emily Turner's testimonial

When I arrived at CLIC IH on the first day of the CELTA course, I was painfully aware of the weight of the decision that I had made: I had willingly given up a secure job in the middle of a recession to pursue a career in EFL teaching. My former colleagues thought that I was mad!

Now my only regret is that I didn't take the leap earlier! I have a job that I love which is both challenging and rewarding and gives you the opportunity to travel all around the world … although why anyone would ever want to leave Seville is beyond me!

I will always remember the first day of the CELTA course as the day that my new life began. All my nerves evaporated after the warm welcome that I received from the staff at CLIC IH and I soon felt at home. The most memorable part of that day was watching our tutors teach a lesson; observing them filled me with the determination to study hard and to one day teach as inspirationally as them.

And study hard I did! The CELTA course is demanding; after all, you only have a few weeks to be moulded into the teachers of tomorrow. It is testament to the quality of the course that after a month I felt filled with the confidence to teach an engaging, informative lesson to students of any age and ability.

This intensive nature of the CELTA means that it is a bond for life! My classmates and I became a family; we were all there to offer encouragement as each of us took our turn to stand in front of a class and teach for the first time. Although now we are scattered all over the world we all stay in touch and are planning a reunion. Equally, my tutors have remained important in my life and two months after the course has ended, they are regularly in contact, tracking my progress and continuing to offer support and advice.

Now to my great delight, I work for CLIC IH and I couldn't be happier. CLIC IH isn't just a language school, it's a community of people that have made a commitment to learning and development. It is a lively place to study and work and is bursting with interesting people and ideas. Just ask anyone in Seville and they will tell you themselves.

EL CENTRO BRITÁNICO: Santiago de Compostela; ✆ +34 981 597490; http://www.elcentrobritanico.es/celta; 3 full-time a year; €1,590.

EXAMS CATALUNYA: Barcelona; ✆ +34 93 411 1333; www.exams-catalunya.com; full-time in August; €1,625.

HYLAND LANGUAGE CENTRE: Madrid; ✆ +34 91 431 9757; www.hylandmadrid.com; 4 full-time (June, July, August and September) and part-time; €1,570.

INSTITUTE OF MODERN LANGUAGES: Granada; ✆ +34 958 225536; www.celtagranada.com; 6 per year; €1,350.

INTERNATIONAL HOUSE BARCELONA: Barcelona; ✆ +34 93 268 3304; www.ihes.com/bcn; full-time, part-time and online; rough frequency 19 per year; €1,650.

Finding work

IH Barcelona is well known in the EFL world. According to an independent survey on IH Barcelona, 20% of trainees who take the CELTA course here are offered work before they have completed the course, while 70% are working as teachers within four weeks of finishing.

Why Barcelona?

Barcelona has the largest Gothic quarter in Europe, modernist buildings designed by Gaudi, miles of beaches and offers art museums, opera halls, music festivals, and one of the best football clubs in the world! This combined with shops, fabulous tapas and wine bars, makes Barcelona one of the greatest cities to visit! Why not combine all this with an EFL course?

International House Barcelona Teacher & Translation Training Department C/ Trafalgar, 14. 08010 Barcelona; Tel +34 93 268 3304.
training@bcn.ihes.com; translation@bcn.ihes.com; www.ihes.com/bcn.

INTERNATIONAL HOUSE MADRID: Madrid; ✆ +34 91 319 7224 or 91 310 1314; www.ihmadrid.com; full and part-time; rough frequency 3 per year; €1,610.

INTERNATIONAL HOUSE PALMA: Palma; ✆ +34 971 726408; www.ihes.com/pal; full-time; rough frequency 4 per year; €1,545.

INTERNATIONAL HOUSE SANTANDER: Santander; ✆ +34 942 233 664; www.ihsantander.com/cursos/cursos-profesores.

IRISH ACADEMY: Palmas de Gran Canaria; www.theirishacademy.com; 5 per year; €1,530.

LENGUAS VIVA: Valencia; www.celtavalencia.com; €1,470–€1,520.

SRI LANKA

BRITISH COUNCIL: Colombo; www.britishcouncil.lk; intensive course every August; 375,000 rupees.

SWITZERLAND

ACADEMIA SCHWEIZ: Basel; ✆ +41 61 260 2020; www.academia-basel.ch; 1 full-time in July, 1 part-time October–January.

BELL LANGUAGE SCHOOL, SWITZERLAND: Geneva; ✆ +41 22 749 1616; www.bell-school.ch; full-time in July and 3 part-time courses per year; SFr3,950.

CAMBRIDGE ENGLISH: St. Gallen; ✆ +41 71 278 0040; www.celta.ch; 1 part-time; SFr3,500.

FLYING TEACHERS: Zurich; ✆ +41 44 350 3344; www.flyingteachers.ch.

SL&C CELTA CENTRE: Lausanne; ✆ +41 21 310 0300; www.supercomm.ch; full-time in July; online from September; SFr3,800.

TLC, THE LANGUAGE COMPANY: Baden; ✆ +41 56 205 51 78; www.tlcsprachschule.ch; part-time over 10 weeks, starting September; also offers one full-time course in July; SFr4,200 in both cases.

THAILAND

ECC (THAILAND): Chiang Mai; ✆ +66 2 655 3333; www.eccthai.com; full-time; rough frequency 2 per year; $1,600; also offered with an extra week of teaching young learners.

INTERNATIONAL HOUSE BANGKOK: Bangkok; ✆ +66 2 6326 790; www.ihbangkok.com; also offered in Chiang Mai and Phuket; $2,100 in Bangkok, $2,495 in Chiang Mai and $2,595 in Phuket, including accommodation.

TUNISIA

THE BRITISH COUNCIL, TUNISIA: Tunis; ✆ +216 71 145 300; www.britishcouncil.tn/en/teach3; full-time in summer; 4,040 Tunisian dinars.

TURKEY

BRITISH SIDE: Istanbul; ✆ +90 212 327 2701; www.britishside.com; 2 full-time in summer, several part-time; £1,200.

INSTITUTE OF LANGUAGE STUDIES - INTERNATIONAL HOUSE: Izmir; ✆ +90 232 484 2490; http://english.ilsizmir.com/index.php/teacher-training/celta; 4- and 6-week formats 5 times a year; £1,080.

INTERNATIONAL MEDITERRANEAN ACADEMY (IM ACADEMY): Fethiye; ✆ +90 252 616 64 06; www.im-academy.org; full-time in summer; £1,100.

INTERNATIONAL TRAINING INSTITUTE: Levent, Istanbul; ✆ +90 212 283 6466/6426; www.iti-istanbul.com; full and part-time offered frequently; £1,200; also offering the CELTA in Bursa in the summer in partnership with Uludag University.

IZMIR UNIVERSITY OF ECONOMICS: Izmir; ✆ +90 232 279 2525; www.ieu.edu.tr; 1 full-time, 9 part-time; £1,026 full-time, £899 part-time.

UKRAINE

GRADE EDUCATION CENTRE: Kiev; www.grade.ua; 2 full-time in summer; $1,299/$1,399.

ILC KYIV: Kiev; ✆ +380 44 238 9870; www.ilcentre.com.ua/en; 3 full-time (June–August) and 1 part-time); earlybird £899.

LONDON SCHOOL OF ENGLISH: Odessa; ✆ +380 48 777 50 15; www.lse.ua; 1 full-time in July; £700.

UNITED ARAB EMIRATES

THE BRITISH COUNCIL, ABU DHABI: Abu Dhabi; ✆ +971 2 691 0600; www.britishcouncil.ae; full and part-time; also in Sharjah and Dubai; 10,000 dirhams.

HIGHER COLLEGES OF TECHNOLOGY: Many locations; ✆ +971 2 681 2070; www.hct.ac.ae.

USA

DENVER BRIDGE TEFL: Denver; ✆ +1 303 785 8864 ext 862; www.bridgetefl.com; full-time; rough frequency 7 per year; $2,495.

ELS LANGUAGE CENTERS: Tacoma, Washington; ✆ +1 253 680 7296; celta@els.edu; www.els.edu; 9 full-time per year; $2,550.

INTERNATIONAL HOUSE SAN DIEGO: San Diego; ✆ +1 619 260 1113; www.ihsandiego.com; full-time; 5 courses per year; $2,695.

ST GILES INTERNATIONAL: San Francisco; ✆ +1 415 788 3552; www.stgiles-international.com/san-francisco; full-time; rough frequency 8 per year; $2,495.

MISSOURI STATE UNIVERSITY CELTA CENTER: Springfield; ✆ +1 417 836 6540; www.international.missouristate.edu; 5-week courses 4 times a year; $2,450.

ST GILES NEW YORK CITY: New York; www.stgiles-international.com/New-York; 6 full-time courses a year; $2,495.

SOL SCHOOLS MIAMI BEACH: Miami; ✆ +1 305 763 8520; www.solschools.com/destinations/miami/beach_profile.php; 5 full-time courses per year; $2,500.

TEACHING HOUSE NEW YORK

Opening Doors to Opportunities – Teaching House CELTA

Index finger outstretched, breath held, continents and bodies of water flashing before my eyes, fast at first then slower, as the outlines of countries became clearer, the oceans became visible. Slower still, as the spinning sphere began to reveal the names of places I'd learned long ago. Losing its momentum, the globe breathed one final breath, jerking to a stop, leaving the tip of my index finger trembling above the spot where I would spend the next year and a half of my life: Vietnam. I closed my eyes, submitted my résumé, completed a phone interview, accepted their offer, bought a one-way ticket, packed up my life into two small suitcases, hugged my family goodbye, held back tears, and fell asleep on the 24-hour flight to the other side of the world. I opened my eyes to find myself struck by two very intense feelings: fear and heat. There I was, alone, scared, and sweating outside international arrivals at Tan Son Nhat airport in Ho Chi Minh City. That was all it took to change my life: the blink of an eye ... and my CELTA.

I was very grateful for everything that I learned during my CELTA course. The foundation it gave me allowed me not to feel like a total fraud as I stepped into my first real class. Whether I was teaching three-year-olds the ABC song, listening to the latest Taylor Swift single with my teenage students, or delving into the depths of American culture with adults, my CELTA course at Teaching House prepared me to be creative and retrospective. It helped me to develop into the teacher I am proud to have become.

Like most people who uproot their lives to take on new and challenging adventures, I found myself in a state of constant self-discovery. I realised that I loved teaching English, and that I wisely (or unwisely) invested so much of myself into my classes that my students had the power to affect me long after I went home for the night. I realised that I had the ability to bridge cultural barriers, developing relationships with those I had very little in common with except the desire to grow. I realised that every choice I had made in my life had led me to that point, that time, that place, and I was happy.

My departure came in late spring, just as the dark clouds of rainy season were descending upon Vung Tau. The heavy rains seemed to wipe my slate clean, leaving my future open to just about anything. I could once again take out my globe, give it a spin, and hold my breath as my future lies just under the tip of my index finger.

TEACHING HOUSE ATLANTA: Atlanta; ✆ +1 800 756 2003; www.teachinghouse.com; full-time; 4 courses per year.

TEACHING HOUSE BOSTON: Boston; ✆ +1 800 756 2003; www.teachinghouse.com; full and part-time; rough frequency 8 full-time courses per year and 2 part-time courses per year.

TEACHING HOUSE BROOKLYN: Brooklyn; ✆ +1 800 756 2003; www.teachinghouse.com; full-time; 2 courses per year.

TEACHING HOUSE CHICAGO: Chicago; ✆ +1 800 756 2003; www.teachinghouse.com; 11 full-time and 3 part-time courses per year.

TEACHING HOUSE DETROIT: Detroit; ✆ +1 800 756 2003; www.teachinghouse.com; full-time; 2 courses per year.

TEACHING HOUSE HOUSTON: Houston; ✆ +1 800 756 2003; www.teachinghouse.com; full-time; 2 courses per year.

TEACHING HOUSE LOS ANGELES: Los Angeles; ✆ +1 800 756 2003; www.teachinghouse.com; full-time; 10 courses per year.

TEACHING HOUSE MIAMI: Miami; ✆ +1 800 756 2003; www.teachinghouse.com; full-time; 6 courses per year.

TEACHING HOUSE MINNEAPOLIS: Minneapolis; ✆ +1 800 756 2003; www.teachinghouse.com; full-time; 2 courses per year.

TEACHING HOUSE NEW YORK: New York; ✆ +1 800 756 2003; www.teachinghouse.com; full and part-time; rough frequency 28 per year.

TEACHING HOUSE PHILADELPHIA: Philadelphia; ✆ +1 800 756 2003; www.teachinghouse.com; 4 full-time courses per year.

TEACHING HOUSE PHOENIX: Phoenix; ✆ +1 800 756 2003; www.teachinghouse.com; 2 full-time courses per year.

TEACHING HOUSE PORTLAND: Portland; ✆ +1 800 756 2003; www.teachinghouse.com; 2 full-time courses per year.

TEACHING HOUSE SALT LAKE CITY: Salt Lake City; ✆ +1 800 756 2003; www.teachinghouse.com; 2 full-time courses per year.

TEACHING HOUSE SAN DIEGO: San Diego; ✆ +1 800 756 2003; www.teachinghouse.com; 3 full-time courses per year.

TEACHING HOUSE SAN FRANCISCO: San Francisco; ✆ +1 800 756 2003; www.teachinghouse.com; 5 full-time courses per year.

TEACHING HOUSE WASHINGTON DC: Washington DC; ✆ +1 800 756 2003; www.teachinghouse.com; 11 full-time, 2 part-time courses per year.

UNIVERSITY OF TEXAS AT AUSTIN CELTA CENTER: Austin; ✆ +1 512 471 2480; www.world.utexas.edu/celta; 6 full-time courses a year; $2,595.

VENEZUELA

BRITISH COUNCIL VENEZUELA: Caracas; ✆ +58 212 952 9965 Ext: 248; celta@britishcouncil.org.ve; www.britishcouncil.org.ve; full-time in January; 25,000 Bolivars (£2,500).

VIETNAM

APOLLO EDUCATION: Hanoi and Ho Chi Minh City; ✆ +84 4 3943 2053; www.teachatapollo.com; 4 full-time courses in both Hanoi and Ho Chi Minh City; 3,440,000 dong (£1,000).

INTERNATIONAL LANGUAGE ACADEMY (ILA): Ho Chi Minh City; ✆ +84 1207 267 159; www.teachenglishilavietnam.com; full-time; rough frequency 9 per year; $1,750.

LANGUAGE LINK VIETNAM: Hanoi; ✆ +84 4 3974 4999; www.llv.edu.vn; full-time; rough frequency 4 per year; $1,600.

TRAINING

DIRECTORY OF TRAINING COURSES

TRINITY COLLEGE CertTESOL IN THE UK

A+ ENGLISH LANGUAGE SCHOOL: Sheffield; ✆ +44 114 209 6292; www.aplusenglish.co.uk; 9 full-time courses, 1 part-time course; £1,050 plus £195 admin and moderation fee; 15% early booking discount.

ATHENA TEACHER TRAINING: Bournemouth; ✆ +44 1202 544166; www.tefl-training.co.uk; 4 full time courses a year; £1,074 plus moderation fee.

BOLTON COLLEGE: Bolton; ✆ +44 1204 482460; Suzannah.Redmond@boltoncc.ac.uk; www.boltoncollege.ac.uk; part-time courses from September and February; £1,350.

CITY COLLEGE PETERBOROUGH: Peterborough; ✆ +44 1733 761361 Ext. 241; www.citycollegepeterborough.ac.uk; part-time from January (6 hours a week for 6 months); £1,395.

COLCHESTER INSTITUTE: Colchester; ✆ +44 1206 712487; www.colchester.ac.uk; part-time 20 weeks from September; £1,500.

ENGLISH IN MARGATE: Margate, Kent; ✆ +44 1843 227700; Jake.Castaldi@leolanguages.com; www.traintoteachenglish.com; part of International Language Homestays; 130-hour course delivered 4 times a year; £1000 plus £50 registration fee; accommodation £600.

ENGLISH NATURALLY: Winchester; ✆ +44 1962 859700; www.english-naturally.com; 2 full-time in summer (£990); 2 part-time (£1200) plus moderation fee of £125; host family accommodation for £102 per week.

EUROSPEAK: Reading; ✆ +44 118 958 9599; trinity@eurospeak.org.uk; ww.tefl-certification.net; full-time monthly; £1,195.

GLASGOW CLYDE COLLEGE: Glasgow; ✆+44 141 272 3664; www.glasgowclyde.ac.uk; part-time for 36 weeks from end of August followed by 10 half days of teaching practice at Langside Campus; £1,100 plus £155 moderation fee and £80 for textbooks.

GOLDERS GREEN COLLEGE TEACHER TRAINING CENTRE: London; ✆ +44 20 8905 5467; www.teachertraininglondon.com; full-time; 2 times per year; £969.

INLINGUA: Cheltenham; ✆ +44 1242 250493; www.inlingua-cheltenham.co.uk; full-time; 6 times a year; £1,155 + £135 moderation fee.

KEELE UNIVERSITY: Keele; ✆ +44 1782 733013; elu@keele.ac.uk; www.keele.ac.uk; 1 intensive course in summer.

LANGUAGES TRAINING & DEVELOPMENT: Witney, Oxfordshire; ✆ +44 1993 708637; www.ltd-oxford.com; full-time; rough frequency 6–12 per year. LT&D has Erasmus partnership with school in Hungary and part of the course is delivered in Szekszard. Erasmus funding available; £950 to non-EU participants.

LEEDS ENGLISH: Leeds; ✆ +44 113 275 1964; www.leedsenglish.com; 20 weeks part-time from January; £950 plus £49 admin fee.

LEWIS SCHOOL OF ENGLISH: Southampton; ✆ +44 2380 228203; www.lewis-school.co.uk; 5 times a year full-time, £995; 1 time part-time £1,200; plus moderation fee of £130.

LIVERPOOL SCHOOL OF ENGLISH: Liverpool; ✆ +44 151 706 0730; www.lse.uk.net; 4 intensive courses per year.

THE MANCHESTER COLLEGE: Manchester; ✆ +44 161 203 2100; www.TMC.ac.uk.

NORTHAMPTON COLLEGE: Northampton; ✆ +44 1604 1232344; www.northamptoncollege.ac.uk; part-time, 1 per year; £700 for trainees under 24, £1,400 otherwise.

NORTHBROOK COLLEGE: Northbrook, Sussex; ✆ +44 845 155 60 60; www.northbrook.ac.uk; part-time 3 times a year (1 evening a week for 13 weeks); £1,575.

OPEN DOORS INTERNATIONAL LANGUAGE SCHOOL: Plymouth; ✆ +44 1752 258770; www.odils.com; 1 full-time, 1 part-time a year; £995 plus moderation fee.

OXFORD INTERNATIONAL EDUCATION GROUP: Greenwich, London; ✆ +44 20 8239 1444; www.uicteachertraining.com; full-time; rough frequency 9 per year; part-time courses offered at other Oxford International (formerly ISIS Education) locations in Oxford, Brighton and Central London; £995–£1,095 with possible discounts.

DOMINIC HARRIS

It was in September 2009 that I found myself at Bergamo train station in North Italy bound for Lecco, a small town near Lake Como. And as I stood alone on that platform in the early evening sunshine, with barely a word of the mother tongue and not entirely sure whether I definitely had somewhere to stay when I arrived there, I reflected on how I had got myself into this situation.

It all started in November 2008 when I was sitting with my fellow fresh TEFL-ites awaiting the beginning of our five-week TESOL guidance into the world of international EFL teaching. The course was as challenging and fulfilling as anything I had ever done. Along the way, I taught students from no fewer than 20 different countries, learnt rudimentary Japanese, taught, reflected, analysed, learnt about different languages and cultures, taught, made new friends, played the most international games of football ever, taught again and had a marvellous time whilst doing it all.

Now at the end of my eight months in Italy I have had a chance to reflect once again on how it has developed me as a teacher. Teaching abroad swept me out of my comfort zone and gave me a deeper connection with the plight of the language learner. Professionally, it has stretched and challenged me, with my having to integrate and, perhaps more essentially, assimilate into a new professional set up and "way of doing things". It has been tough at times indeed, and a zeal for the job at hand, i.e. teaching, is essential. But, in short, by making the jump into the unknown of international EFL teaching, I have come out a more fulfilled and better teacher than when I stood alone on the platform of Bergamo train station.

OXFORDTEFL LONDON: London; tesol@oxfordtefl.com; www.oxfordtefl.com; 6 full-time and 1 part-time course per year; £1,225; course also offered in Spain, Czech Republic and India.

ST BRELADE'S COLLEGE: St Aubin, Jersey; ✆ +44 1534 741305; www.stbreladescollege.co.uk; full-time; rough frequency 2 per year; £1,250 including exam fee.

ST GEORGE INTERNATIONAL: London; ✆ +44 20 7299 1700; www.tesoltraining.co.uk; 11 full-time and 3 part-time per year; £895 full-time, £995 part-time.

ST GILES EASTBOURNE: Eastbourne; ✆ +44 1323 729167; www.stgiles-international.com; full-time; rough frequency 3 per year; £995 plus £130 moderation fee.

ST GILES LONDON CENTRAL: London; ✆ +44 20 7837 0404; www.stgiles-international.com; full-time; rough frequency 7 per year plus one part-time; £1,095 + £130.

SIDMOUTH INTERNATIONAL SCHOOL: Sidmouth, Devon; ✆ +44 1395 516754; efl@sidmouth-int.co.uk; www.sidmouth-int.co.uk; full-time; 3 per year; £1,250 including moderation fee; accommodation arranged on request.

SUSSEX CENTRE FOR LANGUAGE STUDIES: University of Sussex, Brighton; ✆ +44 1273 877485; www.sussex.ac.uk; full-time in summer; £1,270.

SUSSEX COAST COLLEGE HASTINGS: Hastings; ✆ +44 1424 458342; www.sussexcoast.ac.uk; 6 months part-time starting January and September; £1,290.

SUTTON COLLEGE: Sutton, Surrey; ✆ +44 20 8770 6901; www.suttoncollege.ac.uk; part-time 1 per year; £950.

TAMESIDE COLLEGE: Greater Manchester; ✆ +44 161 908 6789; www.tameside.ac.uk; part-time; £1,300.

THE ENGLISH STUDIO: Bloomsbury, London; ✆ +44 20 7637 3813; https://englishstudio.com/courses; full-time monthly; £840 plus £110 moderation fee.

THE LANGUAGE INSTITUTE/TLI ENGLISH LANGUAGE TRAINING: Edinburgh; ✆ +44 131 226 6975; www.tlieurope.com; full-time; rough frequency 3 per year; £990.

TRAINING 4 TEFL: Rose of York Language School, London; ✆ +44 20 7637 2212; www.training4tefl.com; frequent full-time courses throughout the year; £830–£945.

UNIVERSAL LANGUAGE TRAINING (ULT): Woking, Surrey; ✆ +44 1983 853808; www.universal-language.co.uk; 2 full-time courses in summer, one in Woking, one at Royal Holloway University in Egham, Surrey; £845 plus £130 moderation fee.

UNIVERSITY OF CENTRAL LANCASHIRE: School of Languages and International Studies, Preston; ✆ +44 1772 894241; cenquiries@uclan.ac.uk; www.uclan.ac.uk; full-time in August; £1,295; also offers university-level courses in TESOL.

UNIVERSITY OF MANCHESTER LANGUAGE CENTRE: Manchester; ✆ +44 161 306 3397; www.languagecentre.manchester.ac.uk/teach-english/our-courses/cert-tesol; twice a year; £1,480.

WE BRIDGE INTERNATIONAL LTD: Cardiff; ✆ +44 2920 225656; www.we-bridge.co.uk; 4 times a year; £1,250.

TRINITY COLLEGE CertTESOL ABROAD

ARGENTINA

CASA DE INGLÉS: Resistencia-Chaco; ✆+54 362 432 2953; lauraalvarez@arnet.com.ar or casadeingles@ymail.com; part-time course between April and October.

AUSTRIA

ENGLISH TEACHER TRAINING COLLEGE/ABCi: Vorchdorf, Upper Austria; ; ✆+43 7614 514 00 17; admissions@abci-english.at; www.english-teacher-college.at; on-the-job training towards Trinity CertTESOL (see entry for ABCi in Austria chapter); also offers training for teaching Young Learners.

BRAZIL

THE BRITISH COUNCIL: Recife; trinitycert@britishcouncil.org.br; www.britishcouncil.org.br; course takes place at Cultura Inglesa Boa Viagem, Recife.

CULTURA INGLESA: Rio de Janeiro; ✆ +55 21 2528 8734; www.culturainglesa.net/wps/portal/inicio; courses also available in Goiânia and Sao Paulo.

CANADA

COVENTRY HOUSE INTERNATIONAL: Toronto; ✆ +1 416 929 0227; https://tesolcertificationcourse.com; full-time; rough frequency 2 per year; C$999 (with discount).

CHINA

EF EDUCATION FIRST: Beijing, Shanghai and Guangzhou; jake.whiddon@ef.com; www.ef-teachers.com.

CZECH REPUBLIC

OXFORD TEFL: Prague; www.oxfordtefl.com; full-time; rough frequency 10 per year; €1,300 if booked early.

GREECE

AMERICAN COLLEGE OF GREECE: Athens; www.acg.edu; 2 part-time over 8 weeks, 1 full-time in July blended with online; €2,000.

HONG KONG

THE EDGE LEARNING CENTER LTD: Causeway Bay; ✆ +852 92791395; www.theedge.com.hk.

ENGLISH FOR ASIA: Sheung Wan, Hong Kong; ✆ +852 2392 2746; www.englishforasia.com or www.teflhongkong.com; full and part-time; rough frequency 10–12 per year; HK$25,000 (£2,570).

INDIA

ILSC NEW DELHI (in association with Greystone College): Delhi; ✆ +91 84 70 866 266; www.ilsc.in; training courses including teaching business English.

OXFORDTEFL: Kerala; www.oxfordtefl.com; full-time 8 times a year; from €1,400.

INDONESIA

IALF BALI (INDONESIA AUSTRALIA LANGUAGE FOUNDATION): Bali; ✆ +62 361 225243; www.tesolbali.com; full-time; rough frequency 4 per year; $1,900.

IRELAND

ATLANTIC SCHOOL OF ENGLISH AND ACTIVE LEISURE: Schull, County Cork; ✆ +353 28 28943; www.atlantic-english.com; full-time; rough frequency 3 per year; €1,450 plus accommodation can be arranged for €80–€150 per week.

ITALY

BRITISH SCHOOL VICENZA: Vicenza; ✆ +39 0444 542190; www.britishschoolvicenza.net/tefl-teacher-training; full-time in summer; course exported from St George International of London; €1,450.

TEFL IN ITALY Rome; ✆ +39 06 92919464; www.tefl-in-italy.com; 4+ full-time courses a year; €1,749 (or €1,549 with discount).

JAPAN

SHANE ENGLISH SCHOOL: Tokyo; ✆ +81 3 5275 6756; sophia.mcmillan@shane.co.jp; www.tefljobsinjapan.com; full-time in summer.

MALTA

EC MALTA: St Julian's; ✆ +35 621 388500; www.ecenglish.com.

EUROPEAN SCHOOL OF ENGLISH: St Julian's; ✆ +35 621 373789; www.ese-edu.com.

MEXICO

ICLS (INTERNATIONAL CHRISTIAN LANGUAGE SCHOOL): Guadalajara; ✆ +52 33 38 25 97 65; course exported from ODILS, Plymouth, UK.

NEW ZEALAND

EDENZ COLLEGES: Auckland; ✆ +64 9 309 5208; www.edenz.ac.nz; intensive (5 weeks) and semi-intensive (10 weeks) with monthly start dates.

INTERNATIONAL PACIFIC COLLEGE: Palmerston North; ✆ +64 6 354 0922; www.ipc.ac.nz/tesol-courses.html; full-time 2 per year.

PARAGUAY

STAEL RUFFINELLI DE ORTIZ – ENGLISH: Asuncion; ✆ +595 21 226062/207017; www.stael.edu.py; part-time February to November.

SPAIN

ACTIVE LANGUAGE: Cadiz; ✆ +34 95 6 221426; training@activelanguage.net; www.activelanguage.net; 2 full-time in the summer, 1 part-time through the academic year; €1500 (€150 discount for early booking).

APP ACADEMIA DE IDIOMAS: Gandia, Valencia; ✆ +34 96 286 7281; www.appformacion.com/pa-teacher-training-525-400.html.

BRITISH COUNCIL VALENCIA: Valencia; ✆ +34 963392981; www.britishcouncil.es; full-time in July; €1,595.

FUNDACIÓ INSTITUT D'ESTUDIS NORD-AMERICANS: Barcelona; ✆ +34 93 240 5110; teachertraining@ien.es; www.ien.es.

LANGUAGE CAMPUS: Laguna, Tenerife; ✆ +34 922 630 302; www.lcidiomas.com; part-time from January; €1,400.

OXFORDTEFL: Barcelona, Malaga and Cadiz (summer only); ✆ +34 93 1740062; www.oxfordtefl.com; full-time; rough frequency 12 per year; €1,400 early bird, otherwise €1,500.

TEFL-IN-SPAIN: Malaga; ✆ +34 951 956 784; www.tefl-in-spain.com; full-time most months; €1,399 if booked 3 months in advance, otherwise €1,529; also 8-week part-time course in September/October; accommodation for €440 in single rooms, €360 in shared rooms.

TESOLSpain: Granada; ✆ +34 664 60 2846; www.tesolcourse.com/tesol/spain-granada; new course coming soon.

THAILAND

ST STEPHEN'S INTERNATIONAL SCHOOL: Nakhon Ratchasima 30130; ✆ +66 86 4688040; www.trinitytesolthailand.com; 4-week residential course includes private accommodation and meals in the national park area of Khao Yai, Thailand; 6 times a year; £1,499.

TURKEY

INKAŞ AŞ: Istanbul; ✆ +90 212 496 1010; efikri@superonline.com.

URUGUAY

DICKENS INSTITUTE: Montevideo; ✆ +598 2 710 7555 ext 105; www.dickens.edu.uy; part-time.

SHORT INTRODUCTORY COURSES

BERLITZ WORLDWIDE: www.berlitz.com/careers/33; all newly hired teachers (who must be university graduates) must join free 2-week training in-house in the Berlitz Method.

EF ENGLISH FIRST TEACHER TRAINING: 1- or 2-week course offered in Boston, Paris, Munich or Malaga; ✆ +44 20 7341 8500; www.ef.co.uk/tz; approx. $920–$1,100 for 1 week, and just under double for 2 weeks; cost varies depending on location.

FLYING CLASSROOMS: Norwich Study Centre, Norwich; ✆ +44 1603 619091; www.flyingclassrooms.co.uk; 2-week, 45-hour Introduction to TEFL; £350 per week; also specialist 1-week course in teaching Young Learners, Business English, Drama Techniques for Creative Language Teaching (12 hours in 3 days, £300).

GLOBAL LANGUAGE TRAINING LTD: London N1; ✆ +44 203 435 6821; www.globaltefl.uk.com. 2-day weekend courses in London, Birmingham, Manchester and Sheffield throughout the year; £150/£180.

i-to-i: Leeds, UK; ✆ +44 800 093 3148; www.i-to-i.com or www.onlinetefl.com; 20-hour weekend courses in London, Birmingham and Sydney; can be combined with online options; £149.

ITTC: Bournemouth; ✆ +44 1202 516289; www.ittc.co.uk; TEFL taster day £70 including lunch; frequency 10 per year; fee can be credited to CELTA if booked.

KRISTAL INTERNATIONAL: Carmarthen, Wales; ✆ +44 1994 231145; www.tefl-course.net; modularised 30-hour courses which combine on-site and home study; weekend courses offered in various UK locations; prices from £199 for Module 1.

SAXONCOURT TEACHER TRAINING: London; ✆ +44 20 7499 8533; www.saxoncourt.com; mainly a CELTA provider but run taster days with a grammar booster workshop for £59.

TEFL ORG UK: ✆ +44 1349 800600; info@tefl.org.uk; www.tefl.org.uk; classroom, online and combined TEFL courses throughout the UK, from 20 to 150 hours.

TEFL ORG UK

Rebecca is 18 years old and originally from Cambridgeshire. She took a 50-hour TEFL Course in April, and saw it as a great option for travel and work upon leaving school.

'My first TEFL job has been in Sant Sadurni D'Anoia, a small town in Catalunya (Spain) which is the birthplace of Cava. I'm working as a conversation assistant (alongside the English teacher) and living with local families. I teach children aged 7 to 16. It is very challenging, but so rewarding; we have a lot of fun too! I work 20 hours a week, but I am in school 9–5 most days. My main job is organising speaking activities, but I'm also involved in lots of other things and do private English classes; I currently do four hours a week but I am considering doing more. It's so wonderful to live in another culture: the food, the parties (they love their parties here) and it's the best way to learn another language and where I live there are two languages which is even better. Taking a TEFL Org UK course was one of my best decisions. I left school in June with average grades and started work in September. Being given such an opportunity in this economic climate is rare. I could not be happier. I intend doing a degree in a few years but for now, I am going to work and get the life experience that university cannot teach you. I'm currently planning where I want to go next – I am hoping France!'

Rebecca has just enhanced her qualification by completing a 100-hour Advanced TEFL Course, allowing her to specialise in teaching young learners, teaching business English and teaching English online.

UK-TEFL: Lytham, Lancashire; ✆ +44 871 222 1231; www.uk-tefl.com; intensive standard and advanced 2- or 3-day courses throughout the UK but mainly in the London area, Birmingham and Manchester; held on weekends and weekdays; £200–£250.

ONLINE TEFL TRAINING

AMERICAN CULTURE UK/TESOL TURKEY: Antalya, Turkey; www.onlinetesol.com; £1,416.

AMERICAN TESOL INSTITUTE: Tampa, FL, USA; ✆ +1 813 975 7404 and 877 748 7900; www.americantesol.com; from $295.

ANGLO CENTRES: Calle Unió, 41, bajo, Tarragona, Spain 43001; ✆ +34 977 251 437; www.tefl.anglocentres.com; 150-hour online course (£315) or combined with teaching practice (£750); endorsements for Business English or Young Learner teaching can be added; also offer 4-week intensive course in Tarragona.

CIEE (COUNCIL ON INTERNATIONAL EDUCATIONAL EXCHANGE): Portland, Maine, USA; tefl@ciee.org; www.ciee.org/tefl; online TEFL course.

ENJOY TEFL: Harrogate; www.enjoytefl.com; 120-hour course and access to two mindfulness courses for £90/$135.

ESL CERTIFIED: ✆ +1 888 661 8005; www.eslcertified.com; 100-hour ($350) and 120-hour ($425) instructor-led online courses; free demo lesson available online.

GLOBAL ENGLISH: Exeter, Devon, UK; ✆ +44 1392 411999; www.global-english.com; from £210 for 70 hours to £475 for 250-hour course; offers additional specialist components in Young Learners and Business English plus flexible teaching practice local to the trainee.

GLOBAL LANGUAGE TRAINING: London and New York; ✆ +44 203 435 6821 (UK), +1 646 688 2927 (US); www.globaltefl.uk.com; 150-, 120-, 60- and a variety of short 40-hour courses available for £189, £139, £79 and £59.

ICAL: London, UK; ✆ +44 845 310 4104; www.icaltefl.com £155; offers practical teaching placement; £245.

INTENSIVE TEFL COURSES (ITC): Darlington, UK; ✆ 0845 644 5464; www.tefl.co.uk; distance course for £135, nominated as Part 2; Part 1 should be a face-to-face weekend course but not being offered at present.

INTERNATIONAL TEFL ACADEMY: Chicago headquarters; www.internationalteflacademy.com; 170-hour online certificate course offered over 11 weeks including 20 hours of classroom observation and teaching to be arranged locally; $1,395.

INTERNATIONAL TEFL TRAINING INSTITUTE: New York, Sao Paulo, London; ✆ +1 646 762 6361; www.becomeenglishteachers.com; 120 hours, US$350 with tutor support, US$235 without tutor; can be combined with onsite tuition in many cities worldwide from Budapest to Tampa ($2,000).

INTERNATIONAL TEFL INSTITUTE: London W1; ✆ +44 20 7129 1063; admin@itefli.com; www.itefli.com; 120-hour Certificate (£115), 180-hour Diploma (£135) and 250-hour Master Diploma (£169) plus short specialised TEFL/TESOL courses.

INTESOL WORLDWIDE LTD: Northwich, Cheshire, UK; ✆ +44 1606 871001; www.intesoltesoltraining.com; online certificate and diploma courses (since 1993) from 120 to 390 hours, costing from £175 to £995; 120-hour Cert TEFL with TEYL (Young Learners) allows you to take up Intesol-arranged jobs; on-site courses available in Bolivia, Cyprus, Nicaragua, Thailand and Vietnam.

i-to-i: Leeds, UK; ✆ +44 800 093 3148; www.i-to-i.com; 140-hour course combines 20 hour face-to-face weekend course with 120 hours follow-up online, £349 with occasional internet reductions; range of online courses from £149 for a foundation course; also Level 5 EDI CertTEFL accredited by Ofqual that includes 6 hours of assessed teaching practice, £1,195.

ITTT (INTERNATIONAL TEFL & TESOL TRAINING): www.teflcourse.net or www.teflcorp.com; range of online courses from $190 to $1500 when combined with teaching practice; now affiliated to TEFL International, which offers 4-week in-class courses worldwide.

LearnTEFL: London SW19; ✆ +44 208 123 1585; and Chicago, +1 888 234 9318; www.learntefl.com; 60-hour foundation course (£125), 120-hour course (£225), 150 hours (£275).

LINGUAEDGE: Beverly Hills, CA, USA; ✆ +1 888 944 3343; www.linguaedge.com; 50-hour, 100-hour or 150-hour online courses; $149, $249, and $349.

LONDON TEACHER TRAINING COLLEGE: London, UK; ✆+44 20 8133 2027; lttc@teachenglish.co.uk; www.teachenglish.co.uk; 60 and 120-hour certificate courses (£175/£285 by download, £310 by post); 180 hour Diploma (£325).

LOVETEFL: Leeds, UK; ✆+44 113 829 3300; info@lovetefl.com; www.i-to-i.com; 120, 180 and 300 hours: £129, £169 and £239 (2015). Job and intern placement in Thailand, China, etc.

MIDWEST EDUCATION GROUP: Chicago, IL, USA; ✆ +1 773 382 1567; contact@midwested.us; www.midwested.us; 120-hour online TESOL training programme certified by Illinois Board of Higher Education with optional 30-hour practicum; shorter option 60 hours with tutor support.

MYTEFLWORLD: www.myteflworld.com; 100-hour TEFL course accredited by ACCREDITAT; £195.

NORWOOD ENGLISH: Laois, Eire; ✆+353 087 94 10148; www.norwoodenglish.com; from €160 for 120-hour distance course; does not offer practical teaching placement; other specialist courses on Grammar for EFL (€100), teaching Business English (€175), etc.; new joint online course and teaching practice in Vietnam.

ONTESOL: Toronto, Canada; ✆ +1 416 929 0227; toll-free in Canada +1 877 778 3749; toll-free UK +44 808 101 3459; info@ontesol.com; www.ontesol.com; online courses developed via Coventry House lasting 100, 120 or 250 hours; C$349 for 120-hour course.

PREMIER TEFL: St Mary's College, Co. Cork, Ireland; ✆ +44 1273 782869 / +1 415 800 3961; www.premiertefl.com; 120, 150, 180 or 220 hours.

TEACHING ENGLISH IN ITALY: Florence, Italy; sheila@teachingenglishinitaly.com; www.teachingenglishinitaly.com; Basic Online TEFL/TESOL English Teaching Certificate course (120 hours), $265/€200; Grammar course (20 hours) with guided tutor support, $110; Teaching Business English and Teaching English to Young Learners, both 30 hours, both cost $220.

TEFL 247: London and Co. Cork, Ireland; ✆ +44 8444 905078; tefl247.com; very cheap self-guided on-line courses starting at £30; organise 'TEFL bursts' i.e. short tasters of teaching in China, Thailand or Poland.

TEFL CAMBRIDGE: ✆ +44 208 816 8212; www.teflcambridge.com; 5 TEFL training courses ranging from 20 to 140 hours; accredited by ACCREDITAT.

TEFLEN TRAINING COLLEGE: Offices in Australia, India, UK and USA; www.teflen.com; 40, 60, 120 and 150 hours from $190 to $490.

TEFL EXPRESS: ✆ +44 20 3287 7796; www.teflexpress.co.uk; 150-hour online courses costing £349–£469; affiliated to Language Link and course provides passport to jobs and internships in their network of 100+ schools worldwide.

TEFL FULL CIRCLE: London WC1; www.teflfullcircle.com; 40, 120 and 160 hours costing £50, £150 and £200.

TEFL GRADUATE: ✆ +44 203 287 6161 (UK); +1 312 212 3416 (US); www.teflgraduate.com; 40, 60, 120 and 150-hour courses; £75–£245.

TEFLINK: ✆ +44 208 144 6901; www.teflink.com; range of 8 online TEFL courses; accredited by ACCREDITAT.

TEFLSTOP: www.teflstop.com; part of Intesol Worldwide (above); online course aimed at backpackers; £295 for 100-hour course; guaranteed jobs or internships in China.

TEFL TRAINING COLLEGE: London W1; ✆ +44 20 7129 1063; admin@go-tefl.com; www.go-tefl.com; Certificates/Diplomas of Educational Studies in TEFL from 100 to 300 hours, costing £115–£219; sister company to International TEFL Institute (see above).

TEFL UK: www.tefluk.com; 120-hour Advanced Interactive TEFL Course; normal price £349 with reductions to £99; also 150-hour course for £399.

TESOL-DIRECT: Birmingham; ✆ +44 121 449 2221; www.tesol-direct.com; 110-hour certificate course (from £295) and 150-hour course (from £345) plus specialist extension courses on teaching Business English (£295) and English for Young Learners (£195).

THE CONSULTANTS-E LTD: Weymouth; ✆ +44 1305 788523; www.theconsultants-e.com; specialise in online courses in International Business English Training; also some in-person courses, e.g. 10 week Cert IBET (Certificate in International Business English Training), £695 plus moderation fee of £160.

TRAIN-TO-TEFL: Bolton; www.train-to-tefl.com; 120-hour online certificate course; online interactive modules (17 units) written by experienced teacher and trainer Suzannah Redmond with regular assessment so that trainees can gauge their progress; £99; can be blended with 2-day face-to-face TEFL introduction course in Manchester.

TRINES: London; www.trines.co.uk/tefl; 120-hour basic course, £75; 160-hour Masters course combining online and classroom study, £995; guaranteed job.

TUTORGROUP ONLINE TESOL TRAINING INSTITUTE: Taipei, Taiwan; www.TGOTTI.com; 70-hour course.

UNIVERSITY OF TORONTO: Toronto, Canada; ✆+1 416 628 1386; http://teflonline.teachaway.com; online TEFL course offered in association with respected teacher recruitment agency Teachaway; 100-hour, 120-hour or 150-hour options ($995, $1,295 and $1,495).

WORDS LANGUAGE SERVICES: Dublin, Ireland; ✆ +353 1 6392984; www.wls.ie; 100-hour course for €225; grammar course for €50; does not offer practical teaching placement.

ACADEMIC COURSES

This represents a small selection of university courses in TEFL/TESL in the UK. On the www.ucas.com site, you can search by subject and find courses in TEFL/TESOL usually offered in combination with another subject such as a modern language or tourism.

ANGLIA RUSKIN UNIVERSITY: East Road, Cambridge CB1 1PT; ✆ +44 1245 493131; efl@anglia.ac.uk; www.anglia.ac.uk; offers BA in English Language teaching and an MA in Applied Linguistics and TESOL.

ASTON UNIVERSITY: Languages and Social Sciences Unit, Aston Triangle, Birmingham B4 7ET; ✆ +44 121 204 3762; lss_pgadmissions@aston.ac.uk; www.aston.ac.uk; MSc in Teaching English to Speakers of Other Languages (TESOL), MSc in Teaching English for Specific Purposes (TESP), MSc in Teaching English to Young Learners (TEYL), MSc in Educational Management in TESOL (EMT), part-time, 2–5 years, £8,000; MA in TESOL studies, MA in TESOL and Translation, MA in Applied Linguistics, all £5,250.

CANTERBURY CHRIST CHURCH UNIVERSITY: North Holmes Road, Canterbury CT1 1QU; ✆ +44 1227 767700 (Department of English and Language Studies); languagestudies@canterbury.ac.uk; www.canterbury.ac.uk; offers Diploma/MA in TESOL; full (12 months) or part-time; also offers the CELTA (see entry).

LONDON METROPOLITAN UNIVERSITY: 166–220 Holloway Road, London N7 8DB; ✆ +44 20 7133 4202; humanities@londonmet.ac.uk/admissions@londonmet.ac.uk; www.londonmet.ac.uk; MA TESOL and Applied Linguistics (for experienced teachers); full-time one-year course; £7,650 for EU students or £11,400 for non-EU students.

SHEFFIELD HALLAM UNIVERSITY TESOL CENTRE: Sheffield; ✆ +44 114 225 5515; www.shu.ac.uk/about-us/academic-departments/the-tesol-centre; MA in TESOL (full-time); M.Ed. in TESOL by distance learning; Postgraduate Certificate in Teaching English for Academic Purposes.

UNIVERSITY COLLEGE PLYMOUTH ST MARK & ST JOHN: Plymouth; www.marjon.ac.uk; MSc TESOL offered full-time for 12 months; £5,000 for UK/EU students and £10,000 for overseas; good honours degree or equivalent required for admission.

UNIVERSITY OF BEDFORDSHIRE: Park Square, Luton, Bedfordshire LU1 3JU; ✆ +44 1234 400400; www.beds.ac.uk; BA (Hons) in English Language Studies with Teaching English as a Foreign Language (TEFL), BA (Hons) in English Language for Business, BA (Hons)/Diploma in English for International Communication, MA in Applied Linguistics (TEFL), TEFL Certificate (summer school, £1200), TEFL Certificate (part-time evening).

UNIVERSITY OF BIRMINGHAM: Centre for English Language Studies, Westmere, Edgbaston Park Road, Edgbaston, Birmingham B15 2TT; ✆ +44 121 414 3239/5696; www.birmingham.ac.uk; MA in TESOL, on-site or distance learning or in Applied Linguistics.

UNIVERSITY OF BRIGHTON: School of Languages, Falmer, Brighton, East Sussex BN1 9PH; a.pickering@brighton.ac.uk; http://.arts.brighton.ac.uk; offers Diploma and MA in TESOL; 1 year full-time or part-time; these are both post-graduate courses; applicants must have some English teaching experience for the MA and 2 years for the Diploma; also offers a MA in English Language Teaching, 1 year full-time or part-time, for teachers with a limited amount of experience. The one-year Diploma course costs £1,750 (full-time) while the MA fees are £5,580.

UNIVERSITY OF CENTRAL LANCASHIRE: School of Languages and International Studies, Preston, PR1 2HE; ✆ +44 1772 892400; cenquiries@uclan.ac.uk; www.uclan.ac.uk; BA (Hons) in Teaching English to Speakers of Other Languages, BA (Hons) in TESOL and Modern Languages, MA in TESOL and Applied Linguistics.

UNIVERSITY OF EDINBURGH: 21 Hill Place, Edinburgh EH8 9DP; ✆ +44 131 650 6200; www.ed.ac.uk; MSc or Post-Graduate Diploma or Certificate in TESOL.

UNIVERSITY OF EXETER: School of Education and Lifelong Learning, St Luke's Campus, Heavitree Road, Exeter EX1 2LU; ✆ +44 1392 264837; ed-student@exeter.ac.uk; http://socialscience.exeter.ac.uk/education/tesol; EdD/PhD/MPhil/MEd/TESOL; full-time, part-time and intensive summer study.

UNIVERSITY OF LEEDS: Leeds; www.education.leeds.ac.uk; MA in TESOL with choice of specialities, e.g. Young Learners and ICT.

UNIVERSITY OF MANCHESTER: Postgraduate Admissions Office, School of Education, Faculty of Humanities, Oxford Road, Manchester M13 9PL; ✆ +44 161 275 3463; education-enquiries@manchester.ac.uk; www.manchester.ac.uk; offers MA TESOL or MA Educational Technology and TESOL in 3 modes of study: 1 year full-time or part-time, UK/EU £6,500 and overseas £14,500; and 3 years distance, £2,667 a year; entry requirements include 3 years' teaching experience; the university also offers an introduction to TESOL as part of an undergraduate degree (one term).

UNIVERSITY OF READING: Department of English Language & Applied Linguistics, Whiteknights, PO Box 218, Reading RG6 6AA; ✆ +44 118 378 8512; a.j.horn@reading.ac.uk; www.reading.ac.uk/English-language-and-applied-linguistics; MA ELT in both campus-based and distance-study modes, with an additional study track for novice teachers; also, MA in Applied Linguistics.

UNIVERSITY OF STIRLING: Institute of Education (CELT), Stirling FK9 4LA; www.stir.ac.uk; MSc in TESOL (Teaching English to Speakers of Other Languages); MSc in TESOL and CALL (Computer Assisted Language Learning) and PhD and EdD in TESOL Education available; General English, IELTS Preparation, English for University Study, Short Courses for Teachers, and a Summer School in August are also offered.

UNIVERSITY OF SUSSEX: Sussex Centre for Language Studies, Falmer, Brighton, East Sussex BN1 9RH; ✆ +44 1273 678416; UG.Admissions@sussex.ac.uk (for bachelor's degree programme) or PG.Admissions@sussex.ac.uk (for master's programmes); www.sussex.ac.uk; BA in English Language Teaching; 3 or 4-year joint major in ELT with English, English Language, Language(s) or Linguistics; includes opportunity to take Trinity TESOL Certificate as part of degree; MA in English Language Teaching; MA in International English Language Teaching and a Postgraduate Diploma in ELT (full-time 1 year, part-time 2 years).

UNIVERSITY OF WARWICK: Centre for Applied Linguistics, Coventry CV4 7AL; ✆ +44 24 7652 3200; appling@warwick.ac.uk; www2.warwick.ac.uk/fac/soc/al/; MA in ELT/ESP/English for Young Learners (all post-experience), English Language Teaching (Studies and Methods) (less than 2 years' experience), ELT (Multimedia) (either pre- or post-experience); one-term Postgraduate Certificate in any of the MA specialisms (January to March), 2 terms for a Postgraduate Diploma.

UNIVERSITY OF WOLVERHAMPTON: Wolverhampton; www.wlv.ac.uk; International Academy offers BA (Hons) in Linguistics and TESOL.

TRAINING COURSES IN NORTH AMERICA

USA

AMERICAN LANGUAGE INSTITUTE: San Diego State University, 5250 Campanile Drive, San Diego, CA 92182 1914; ✆ +1 619 594 5907; ali@mail.sdsu.edu or rhillier@mail.sdsu.edu; www.ali.sdsu.edu; TESL/TEFL Certificate validated by SDSU Dept of Education (3 graduate credits); 4 weeks, 130 hours, offered in January and June, and part-time in autumn and spring; $2,725; dormitory/homestay/apartment accommodation can be arranged through the ALI housing office; job placement assistant programme.

BOSTON ACADEMY OF ENGLISH: 59 Temple Place, 2nd Floor, Boston, MA 02111; ✆ +1 617 338 6243; info@bostonacademyofenglish.com; www.teflboston.com; 4-week intensive 120-hour CTE-FL course, $2,550; part-time over 12 weeks, $2,400.

BOSTON LANGUAGE INSTITUTE: 648 Beacon St, Boston, MA 02215; ✆ +1 617 262 3500; www.bostonlanguage.com; intensive 4-week TEFL Certificate course (120 hours) offered monthly; 12-week Saturday programmes also offered 3 times a year; special TEFL Certificate Programme for Non-Native Speakers of English also offered: course includes additional training on pronunciation, American culture and other relevant topics; tuition of $2,465 includes fees, all study materials and lifetime job assistance.

ETON INSTITUTE: New York; www.americas.etoninstitute.com; TESOL/TFL programme leads to City and Guilds Access Certificate in English Language Teaching (ACE), a TESOL qualification in communicative and modern language methods; 120 hours over 6 weeks; £2,480.

HAMLINE UNIVERSITY: TEFL Certificate Program, School of Education, 1536 Hewitt Avenue, St Paul, MN 55104; ✆ +1 651 523 2429; education@hamline.edu; www.hamline.edu; intensive 1-month courses in July and January and part-time extensive courses autumn and spring; current tuition $3,230; focus is on developing communicative language teaching strategies; ongoing career counselling provided. Graduate credit granted; course can be used towards Hamline's MA in ESL; advanced TEFL option offered.

HUNTER COLLEGE CONTINUING EDUCATION: New York; ✆ +1 212 772 4000; www.hunter.cuny.edu/ce/certificates/tesol. Intensive course with 20 hours of practice teaching in ESOL classrooms; $3,800.

INTERNATIONAL TEFL ACADEMY: Boston, Chicago, Honolulu, New York, San Diego and Seattle; 4-week course given at various intervals, e.g. 9 times a year in Chicago; from $1,995 in Chicago to $2,550 in Hawaii (at the Intercultural Communications College Honolulu).

LADO TEFL CERTIFICATE: 401 9th Street, NW, Suite C 100, Washington, DC 20004; ✆ +1 202 223 0023; tefl@lado.edu; www.lado.edu; 135-instructional-hour professional teacher training programme; intensive courses offered monthly; semi-intensive courses in spring, summer and autumn; $1,950.

NEW SCHOOL: New York; www.newschool.edu/matesol14; Masters in TESOL offered on-campus or online.

OXFORD SEMINARS: Santa Monica and New York; ✆ +1 800 779 1779; www.oxfordseminars.com; TESOL/TESL courses held in cities around the USA, usually on university/college campuses; 60 hours over 3 consecutive weekends; $1,095.

SCHOOL OF TEACHING ENGLISH AS A SECOND LANGUAGE (in cooperation with Seattle Pacific University): 9620 Stone Avenue. N., Suite 101, Seattle, WA 98103; ✆ +1 206 781 8607; STESLinfo@spu.edu; www.schooloftesl.com; offers both a TESOL/TEFL certificate and a Washington State ELL Endorsement programme; the certificate consists of four classes which may be taken in a 4-week intensive format or via evening and/or online classes; tuition for all formats is $245 per credit (2015); credits can be transferred into master's degree programmes in either the Seattle Pacific University School of Education or College of Arts and Sciences (MA-TESOL); Bachelor's degree required for admission; local housing list available on request; personal advising; employment seminars, graduates' networking services and an onsite ESOL class.

SIT GRADUATE INSTITUTE: Brattleboro, Vermont 05302-0676; ✆ +1 802 258 3310; tesolcert@sit.edu; www.graduate.sit.edu/sit-graduate-institute; 130-hour TESOL Certificate course taught intensively at various times throughout the year in New York, Houston and locations in Latin America including Costa Rica, Guatemala and Ecuador; affiliated to nonprofit World Learning and the Experiment in International Living; costs from $1,400 in Caserta, Italy to $2,595 in New York.

TRANSWORLD SCHOOLS: TESOL Certificate training courses at Transworld Schools, 551 Sutter Street, 6th Floor, San Francisco, CA 94102; ✆ +1 415 928 2835; transwd@aol.com; www.transworldschools.com; Comprehensive TESOL Certificate (4 weeks full-time, 10 weeks part-time, $2,100); TESOL Certificate (3 weeks full-time, 10 weeks part-time, $1,900); Intensive TESOL Certificate (for experienced ESOL teachers: 2 weeks full-time; 7 weeks part-time, $1,700); Advanced TESOL Certificate (for experienced ESOL teachers: 1 week full-time; 4 weeks part-time, $900); Distance Learning TESOL Certificate with 1 week on-site residency $1,000; all courses internationally recognised; approved by State of California, BPPE (Bureau for Private Postsecondary Education) and accredited by ACCET, Continuing Education Credits awarded; high-quality training, low tuition fees, and lifetime job placement worldwide; accommodation ($650–$1580 for 4 weeks); courses include evaluated Teaching Practice, teaching children and adults, grammar, Business English, TOEFL and syllabus design; facilities include multi-media lab, video and internet.

WASHINGTON ACADEMY OF LANGUAGES: TESL Graduate Certificate/Endorsement Program, 521 Wall St, Seattle, WA 98121; info@wal.org; www.wal.org; Graduate TEFL Certificate offered in conjunction with University of Seattle; 8 courses for total of 24 quarter credits; offered intensively as 8-week summer course, or online; tuition for each course is $400 or $600.

WESLI: 19 N. Pinckney Street, Madison, WI 53703; ✆ +1 800 765 8577 or +1 608 257 8476; info@mttp.com; www.wesli.com; practical, hands-on 5-week TEFL Certificate Course (130 hours including 10 hours of teaching practice) in a progressive university city; 4 times a year; tuition and course materials $2,595; housing arranged if needed; integrated with an ESL school providing an international environment; job placement assistance including resource library, job search workshop and personal résumé editing; graduates have found jobs in 40 countries.

WESTERN WASHINGTON UNIVERSITY TESOL PROGRAM: Bellingham, WA 98225; ✆ +1 360 650 4949; www.wce.wwu.edu/TESOL/teaching-english-speakers-other-languages; full-time and part-time university courses starting in September, with a summer intensive option; interdisciplinary course work and practical experience lead to a certificate of achievement and a supporting endorsement in teaching ESL; distance education and overseas practicum experiences in Mexico available; $6,750.

CANADA

Note that the website of TESL Canada (www.tesl.ca) has links to a large number of approved teacher training programmes across Canada.

CCLCS (Canadian Centre for Language and Cultural Studies): Toronto; ✆ +1 416 588 3900; www.cclcs.ca; full-time or part-time from September; TESL Diploma: C$140 registration fee plus C$1,495 for Part I and C$2,075 for Part II.

GLOBAL TESOL: Edmonton, Canada; ✆ +1 888 270 2941; info@globaltesol.com; www.globaltesol.com; office/training centres across Canada, and in many countries worldwide; world's largest TESOL Certificate and Diploma granting programme as described in a free Travel-and-Teach information package; 40,000 graduates teaching English in 85 countries; range of Canada Government certified TESOL Certificate and Diploma courses held regularly in cities throughout Canada and other countries; 5-day intensive format, or online and correspondence study options available worldwide; overseas job guaranteed; prices range from C$695 to C$3,495; 16 specialisation course options; 120-hour to 600-hour programme available; other courses offered online or by correspondence include Teaching Business English, Teaching TOEFL Preparation, Teaching Grammar, Teaching Children, Teaching Adults, Tourism English, Teaching CALL Computer English and more; accommodation can be arranged; franchises available; email for details.

GREYSTONE COLLEGE: 560 Granville St, 3rd Floor, Vancouver, BC V6C 1W6; www.greystonecollege.com; TESOL130 Certificate programme; 1 month full-time, offered monthly or 12 weeks part-time; practicum arranged after the course; C$1,620.

INTERNATIONAL HOUSE CAREER COLLEGE: 200–215 West Broadway, Vancouver, BC V6H 167; ✆ +1 604 739 9836; www.tesl-vancouver.com; IH Career College offers IH Certificate (130 hours and online) starting 4 times a year; C$1,650 (C$1,000 online).

INTERNATIONAL LANGUAGE ACADEMY OF CANADA (ILAC): 920 Yonge St, 4th floor, Toronto M4W 3C7; ✆ +1 416 961 5151 and 688 West Hastings, 3rd floor, Vancouver, BC V6B 1P1; ✆ +1 604 484 6660; www.ilacinternationalcollege.com; 4-week, 100-hour certificate courses offered 7 times a year in both cities; C$990.

LONDON LANGUAGE INSTITUTE: London, Ontario; ✆ +1 519 439 3350; www.llinstitute.com

OHC TORONTO: Toronto; www.ohcenglish.com/school/Toronto; 4-week TESL diploma offered monthly; C$1,450.

OXFORD SEMINARS: 131 Bloor St West, Suite 200–390, Toronto, ON M5S 1R8 and 10405 Jasper Ave, Suite 16–21, Edmonton, AB T5J 3S2; www.oxfordseminars.ca; 60-hour course held over 3 consecutive weekends; C$995 (plus GST).

PEAK TESOL: College of the Rockies, Cranbrook, BC; www.cotr.bc.ca/TESOL; online course or blended, with optional 20-hour practicum; C$1,995.

STUDY AT COVENTRY: Toronto; www.tesolcertificationcourse.com; 5-week TESOL Certificate, recognised by TESL Canada; 8 times a year; C$999.

TRAINING COURSES WORLDWIDE

WORLDWIDE

BRIDGE: Head office: 915 South Colorado Blvd, Denver, CO 80246; ✆ +1 303 785 8864; toll-free (USA and Canada): ✆ +1 888 827 4757 or +44 808 120 7163 (UK); www.bridgetefl.com; intensive 140-hour TEFL courses offered in centres in Argentina, Brazil, Chile, Peru, Colombia, Costa Rica, Guatemala, Mexico, Czech Republic, UK (Northern Ireland and London), Greece, Italy, Spain, Hungary, Russia, Thailand, Turkey, Vietnam, Cambodia, UAE, South Africa and USA; on-site TEFL course tuition starts at $1,695; online and blended-learning courses also available worldwide starting at $184.

EBC INTERNATIONAL: Headquarters, Madrid; ✆ +34 91 555 3975 plus toll-free numbers in UK, US and Canada; www.ebcteflcourse.com; 4-week certificate course offered at frequent intervals in Madrid, Buenos Aires, Boracay (Philippines), Chania, Prague and Phuket; course alone costs from €1000 but can also book accommodation.

GLOBAL TESOL COLLEGE: main website www.globaltesol.com and headquarters in Canada: 7712, 104 St, Edmonton, AB T6E 4C5; in North America: ✆ +1 888 270 2941/+1 780 438 5704, tesol@globaltesol.com; US-East in North America: ✆ +1 866 837 6565, tesol@tesol world.com; US-West in North America: ✆ +1 888 837 6587, info@globaltesolusa.com; Australia: ✆ +61 7 3221 5100, teachenglish@sarinarusso.com.au; China: ✆ +86 134 0508 0034, info@teflcoursechina.com; Greece: ✆ +30 274 302 9012, Georgia@globaltesol.gr; for accommodation: info@linguisticlab.com; India: ✆ +91 172 269 2682, info@tesolindia.com; Malaysia: ✆ +60 85 413778, joanne@globaltesol.com.my; Mexico: ✆ +52 818 368 2410, linda@engcanada.com; New Zealand: nz@globaltesol.co.nz; Philippines: ✆ +632 910 1438, global@edulynxcorp.com; Singapore: ✆ +65 6221 3957, info@globalelt.org; Taiwan: ✆ +886 2 2369 1181 (24 hrs), anne@globaltesol.com.

INTERNATIONAL TEFL TRAINING INSTITUTE: New York, Sao Paulo, London; ✆ +1 212 913 0591; www.becomeenglishteachers.com; 120-hour on-site tuition in many cities worldwide from Budapest to Tampa; prices from $1,200 but usually $2,000.

LANGUAGE CORPS: Stow, MA; ✆ +1 978 562 2100; toll-free (North America): +1 877 216 3267; www.languagecorps.com; 4-week TESOL training course offered in many places worldwide from Crete to St Petersburg, Rio to Phnom Penh, followed by job-placement assistance; courses accept school leavers; cost varies according to location but typically $1,750–$2,000 with varying options for paying more for extra services, e.g. guaranteed job placement.

PARADISE TEFL: http://paradisetefl.com; based in Cambodia with intensive courses offered in multiple locations in Cambodia, Vietnam, Laos, Malaysia, Thailand and Mexico; frequent start dates.

SIT (SCHOOL FOR INTERNATIONAL TRAINING) GRADUATE INSTITUTE: Kipling Road, PO Box 676, Brattleboro, VT 05302; ✆ +1 800 257 7751; tesolcert@sit.edu; www.sit.edu/tesolcert; full-time; 130-hour SIT TESOL Certificate course offered in various locations in the US and worldwide including Chicago, IL and Rohnert Park, CA, Quito (Ecuador), Oaxaca (Mexico), Bangkok and Chiang Mai (Thailand), Guatemala City and Quetzeltanango (Guatemala), Kharviv (Ukraine) and others; fees vary from $1,400 in Thailand to $2,295 in the US.

TEFL INTERNATIONAL: admin@teflinternational.org.uk; www.teflinternational.org.uk; USA Head office: 1200 Belle Passi Rd. Woodburn, OR 97071; TEFL International TESOL Certificate, 120-hour including observed Teaching Practice; available worldwide: full-time, part-time and distance learning; Special Projects with guaranteed work or internship (including volunteer projects); TEFL International World Wide Locations: Buenos Aires, Beijing, Hong Kong, Shanghai, Zhuhai, Manuel Antonio, Prague, Alexandria, Brittany, Corinth, Calcutta, Florence, Rome, Tokyo, Kathmandu, Cebu (Philippines), Lubin, Seoul, Barcelona, Seville, Ban Phe, Chiang Mai and Phuket, London, New York, Woodburn, Ho Chi Minh City; most centres offer the course every month; prices vary slightly from $1,390 to $1,790, but with regular specials and discount programmes.

VIA LINGUA: info@vialingua.org; www.vialingua.org; Proprietary 120-hour Certificate course (Via Lingua CTEFL) accredited by the College of Teachers and franchised to language institutes worldwide; moderated by ELT Institute, Hunter College, City University of New York; course available in Arequipa (Peru), Budapest, Buenos Aires, Guzmán (Mexico), Crete, Florence, Ho Chi Minh City, Istanbul, New York, Panama, Pattaya (Thailand), Phnom Penh (Cambodia), Porto (Portugal), Rio de Janeiro, St Petersburg, Santiago (Chile) and Sardinia; prices vary according to location from €1,175 course fee in Florence to $2,100 in New York.

ARGENTINA

ÍBERO TEFL SCHOOL: 113 Piedras Street, Buenos Aires; ✆ +54 11 6023 8375; info@iberotefl.com.ar; www.iberotefl.com; intensive 4-week TEFL certificate courses offered monthly; $990; can be combined with 3 weeks' Spanish tuition for $1,365; claim 99% of graduates find paid jobs after gaining certificate.

MENTE ARGENTINA: Av. Santa Fe 3192 piso 4'b', C1425, Buenos Aires; ✆ +54 11 3968 7861 (Argentina); +1 858 926 5510 (USA); +44 20 3286 3438 (UK); info@menteargentina.com; www.menteargentina.com; 4-week TEFL certificate course offered monthly; 150 hours including 24 hours of teaching practice; all-in prices including accommodation from $2,690 for student residence to $3,250 for private apartment, all in the best areas of Buenos Aires such as Palermo, Belgrano, Barrio Norte and Recoleta; Spanish course can also be arranged.

ROAD2ARGENTINA: Buenos Aires; ✆ +54 11 4826 0820; www.road2argentina.com/tefl-argentina; partner of EBC above with follow-on volunteer teacher placement programme (for a fee).

AUSTRALIA

AUSTRALIAN TESOL TRAINING CENTRE (ATTC): Sydney: Level 1, 31 Market Street, Sydney, NSW 2000; ✆ +61 2 9389 0249; Brisbane: Level 1, 295 Ann Street, Brisbane, QLD 4001; ✆ +61 7 3229 0350; train@attc.edu.au; www.attc.edu.au; CELTA centres that offer Foundation in TESOL course (4 weeks) full and part-time courses throughout the year; accommodation service available; internet enrolment AUS$1,500.

ENGLISH LANGUAGE SERVICES: Adelaide Institute of Technical and Further Education (part of the Government Department of Education, Training and Employment), 5th Floor, Renaissance Centre, 127 Rundle Mall, Adelaide, South Australia 5000; ✆ +61 8 8207 8805; els.tesol@tafesa.edu.au; http://els.sa.edu.au; Certificate IV in TESOL; 315-curriculum hour course AUS$3,300; TESOL for overseas teachers and TESOL online.

GLOBAL TESOL AUSTRALIA: Sarina Russo Centre, 82 Ann Street, Brisbane, Queensland 4000; ✆ +61 7 3221 5100; teachenglish@sarinarusso.com.au; www.globaltesol.com; 120-hour to 600-hour programmes available; tuition fees AUS$995–$2,300; all courses can be completed in-class, online or by correspondence; job overseas guaranteed.

LANGUAGE TRAINING INSTITUTE (LTi): PO Box 1061, Nambour, Queensland 4560; ✆ +61 7 5442 3511; admin@LTi.edu.au; www.LTi.edu.au; Certificate IV in TESOL; 5 weeks full-time or up to 12 months part-time. Course can be completed on-site at several centres in Victoria, NSW and Queensland (and also Singapore and Tehran) or by distance education (either online or traditional using printed textbooks and workbooks); AUS$2,000–$3,000.

LEXIS TESOL TRAINING CENTRE (LTTC): Maroochydore, Queensland; ✆ +61 7 54792272 or 5447 4448; www.lexistesoltraining.com/sunshine-coast; introduction to TESOL; 1 or 2 weeks in Maroochydore, Brisbane, Byrons Bay, Noosa and Perth; $499 or $999; Maroochydore centre also offers the CELTA.

TEACH INTERNATIONAL: Head Office, Level 2, 370 George Street, Brisbane, Queensland 4000; ✆ +61 7 3211 4633 ext 4; www.teachinternational.com; Foundation in TESOL, 100 hours, AUS$1,695; Certificate III in TESOL, 110 hours, AUS$2,295; Certificate IV in TESOL, 220 hours, AUS$2,995; accredited by Australian government; offered throughout the year.

BOLIVIA

INTESOL TESOL TRAINING: La Paz; www.intesolbolivia.com; 1-month intensive or mixed mode; monthly; $1,495 full-time, $1,195 combined modes.

BRAZIL

INTERNATIONAL TEFL ACADEMY: Rio de Janeiro; www.internationalteflacademy.com; monthly; $1,995.

TEFL INTERNATIONAL: Natal; www.teflinternational.org.uk; 2 full-time courses a year in January and July; $2000 excluding accommodation.

CAMBODIA

LANGUAGECORPS: ✆ +1 877 216 3267 toll-free (US); www.languagecorps.com; 4-week TESOL courses available monthly in Cambodia; $1,750.

TEACHERS IN CAMBODIA: Phnom Penh; http://teachersincambodia.com/tefl-course; in partnership with Learning Jungle International School 4-week TEFL training course programme that includes 20 hours of classroom observation, 20 hours of monitored classroom teaching experience and employment.

CHILE

INTERNATIONAL TEFL ACADEMY: Av. Las Urbinas 68, Providencia, Santiago; ✆ +56 9 9766 84301; info@tefl-academy.com; www.internationaltefl/academy.com/tefl-tesol-certification-courses/south-america/chile/santiago; 120-hour certificate course, 9 times a year; $1,995; life-long job assistance.

CHINA

APPLIED CAREER TESOL (ACT): Guangzhou; www.appliedtesol.com; on-the-job training with Canadian company; 160-hour TESOL Cert and 300 hours' teaching practice; $200 to start and then work is paid while learning.

TEFL IN CHINA: Room 50307, Friendship Hotel, Beijing 100873; ✆ +86 10 828 50464; tefl@safea.gov.cn or service@chinajob.com; http://tefl.chinajob.com; 7-day intensive course offered dozens of times a year usually in Beijing but also in Guangzhou, Shanghai and Chengdu, which leads to a TEFL in China Certificate and is considered a suitable alternative to two years' teaching experience when applying for a Z visa; RMB3,000.

TEFL INTERNATIONAL: At Gateway Language Village, Xiangzhou Culture Plaza, Ningxi Road, Zhuhai; ✆ +86 756 229 8967; admin@teflinternational.org.uk; www.teflinternational.org.uk; 120-hour accredited TESOL certificate course in Zhuhai and Beijing; good job and internship prospects all over China with the job placement assistance programme; course runs monthly and costs $1,690 (excluding accommodation) which costs $250–$300 in a shared dorm.

COLOMBIA

FUNDACION EDUCATIVA PERSONAL GROWTH: Bogota; www.pgrowth.com; training course in communicative teaching available in San Andres Island, Bogota and Cartagena (all in Colombia).

ISSO – INTERNATIONAL STUDENT SERVICES ORG: Cali; www.estudiosexterior.com; training centres in Bogotá, Cali, Medellin and Barranquilla; 120-hour course, semi-intensive and intensive; $950.

COSTA RICA

CENTRO ESPIRAL MANA: Invu de Peñas Blancas village, San Isidro de Peñas Blancas, near Chachagua, between San Ramon and La Fortuna; admin@espiralmana.org; www.espiralmana.org; School for International Training's TESOL Certificate Course; 1-month intensive offered monthly; contact Mary Scholl.

COSTA RICA TEFL: Heredia and Playa Samara; info@costaricatefl.com; www.costaricatefl.com; offers 10 TEFL Certification courses per year, 160 hours' contact time; costs $1,485, including job placement assistance, course materials, course portfolio and text and access to local cultural events as well as a 10% discount on Spanish classes at Intercultura; the core instructors all have masters degrees and/or higher in education and in teaching English as a second or foreign language with more than 22 years of professional teaching experience; Heredia courses affiliated to Intercultura Costa Rica; www.interculturacostarica.com; see entry in Central America chapter.

INTERNATIONAL TEFL ACADEMY: Heredia; www.internationalteflacademy.com; 4-week course given 5 times a year between July and December; $1799 including online discount; board and lodging with family cost $550.

MÁXIMO NIVEL EXECUTIVE LANGUAGE CENTER: de la Farmacia la Bomba 75m sur, San Pedro, San Jose (HQ in Cusco, Peru); ✆ +1 800 866 6358; info@maximonivel.com; www.maximonivel.com; 150-hour TEFL/TESOL Certificate (over 4 weeks) for $1,400–$1,700 offered monthly except December; 50-hour TEIB (Teaching English for International Business) Certificate and TIEEP (Teaching International English Exam Preparation) Certificate (over 3 days), $400 each; rough frequency 4 times a year; housing arranged with families, in shared apartments, hostels, etc. from $225 for 4 weeks; lifetime job-finding assistance; an average of 5 graduates are employed by Máximo Nivel each month.

TEFL INTERNATIONAL: TEFL International, S.A. Apartado #161 Quepos, Manuel Antonio 6350 Costa Rica; admin@teflinternational.org.uk; www.teflinternational.org.uk; 120-hour TESOL; optional Spanish as a Second Language Course; monthly start dates; course fee $1,790, homestays for $400.

CYPRUS

INTESOL: c/o Plato Institute, 8 Souliou Street, Limassol 3016: ✆ +357 25 564260; plato@cytanet.com.cy; www.teflcyprus.com; 4-week TESOL course with teaching practice; lifetime job guidance; €1,260.

CZECH REPUBLIC

HELLO ACADEMIES: Tyrsova 1832/7, Prague 12000; ✆ +420 607 733334; s.madl@smallerearth.com; www.helloacademies.com; 4-week course offered monthly; $1,480; IATQuO-accredited. Operated by Smaller Earth.

INTERNATIONAL TEFL ACADEMY: Prague; www.internationalteflacademy.com; 6 times a year; $1,465.

LIVE TEFL: Prague; www.liveteflprague.com; 4-week course offered monthly; €1200; accredited by the College of Teachers; graduates of the course are given a 6-month full-time contract with salary guarantee with its parent company, the large language school Spěváček.

TEFL IN PRAGUE: Edua Languages, U Pujcovny 2, 110 00 Prague 1; ✆ +420 739 540930; info@teflinprague.com; www.teflinprague.com; 4-week TEFL courses with job guarantee for Pass-1 graduates and visa support in the Czech Republic; €1,550 including 39 days of accommodation; under the umbrella of EDUA Group, the biggest private educational institution in the Czech Republic.

TEFL INTERNATIONAL: Prague; admin@teflinternational.org.uk; www.teflinternational.org.uk; 120-hour TESOL; optional free Czech language lessons; offered monthly; from €999 if booked early, otherwise €1,150 plus accommodation from €300.

TEFL WORLDWIDE PRAGUE: Freyova ul. 12/1, 190 00 Prague; ✆ +420 603 486 830; info@teflworldwideprague.com; www.teflworldwideprague.com; British and American-owned school offering 4-week TEFL course in Prague; courses offered monthly; job assistance worldwide; €1,300 plus accommodation.

TEFL WORLDWIDE

Haley Moore, January 2016 Graduate, Prague

'Hey there! My name is Haley Moore, I was born and raised in Columbus, Ohio, my hometown which I absolutely cherish and love. Three years after graduating from college I found myself in a stuffy corporate job thinking there has to be more to life. So, I quit, served at a restaurant for two months and followed my dream to move to Europe.

'I wasn't quite sure how I was going to do it, but after talking with a few friends and doing a little research I found TEFL Worldwide Prague. And wow, I am so happy that I did. I took the course in January 2016, and found my community (family) here in Prague. Not only did I make the best friends who understood all my struggles (it takes a certain type of person to do this course), I also learned an incredible amount and now feel completely prepared to teach English as a foreign language. And that's exactly what I'm doing. The first Monday after the course ended, I was hired by a language school. The next day I was hired by another school, and the interview requests have just kept on coming. Not long after I took on a public course with another school and began picking up many private lessons which I teach at my leisure.

'This experience has been nothing short of amazing. I won't say it's not without its hardships. At a few points since my time here I've considered moving to Asia to make more money, where I've seen a few of my friends go. But that's what's so cool – thanks to my TEFL certification (which NEVER expires) I have the option to do so and thus the keys to the world. I feel completely blessed to be able to have a skill that will never leave me. With this certification I can teach all over the world.

'As I write this I'm on a bus to Cesky Krumlov, a cute little town that all of my Czech students claim is the most beautiful in their country. My friends and I are going rafting there. And this is just one of the cool mini trips I've taken. So I will leave you with my favorite quote in hopes of inspiring you: "Twenty years from now you will be more disappointed by the things you didn't do than by the ones you did do. So throw off the bowlines. Sail away from the safe harbor. Catch the trade winds in your sails. Explore. Dream. Discover." – Mark Twain.'

THE LANGUAGE HOUSE: Education Center SPUSA, Na poříří 1038/6, 110 00 Prague 1; ✆ +420 224 210 813; info@thelanguagehouse.net; www.thelanguagehouse.net; 4-week course offered 10 times a year; €1,300 or €1,550 with housing included (€100 discount February–May and November); IATQuO-accredited.

WATTSENGLISH: Rohacova 77, Prague 3; www.wattsenglish.com; UK-registered company with franchised summer camps teaching young children throughout the Czech Republic and Slovakia; offer their own International TEFL Certificate (WITC) specialising in teaching English to young learners; 10,000 Czech crowns but free if candidate teaches a complete season with Wattsenglish.

ECUADOR

CEC-EPN (CONTINUING EDUCATION CENTER): National Polytechnic School, Quito; www.cec-epn.edu.ec/cursos/curso/tefl-tesl-cca; 150 hours in September including cross-cultural awareness module; $1,395. Job placement assistance.

CENTRO DE ESTUDIOS INTERAMERICANOS/CEDEI: Casilla 597, Cuenca; ✆ +593 7 283 9003; info@cedei.org; www.cedei.org; summer TEFL programme, $3,225 including accommodation.

EGYPT

AMERICAN UNIVERSITY IN CAIRO: PO Box 74 New Cairo 11835; ✆ +20 2 2797 4978; teflinfo@aucegypt.edu; www.aucegypt.edu; US enquiries to 420 Fifth Avenue, 3rd Floor, New York, NY 10018 2729; ✆ +1 212 730 8800; offers MA in Teaching English as a Foreign Language (MA/TEFL); American-style education in an overseas setting.

TEFL INTERNATIONAL: 4, Shohdy Basha Street, Stanly, Alexandria; admin@teflinternational.org.uk; www.teflinternational.org.uk; 120-hour TESOL; monthly start dates; course fee $1,690; optional teaching Internship programme with Arabic language and cultural programme, $1,990; steady supply of jobs in Cairo.

FRANCE

TEFL INTERNATIONAL: 275 rue Saint-Jacques, 75006 Paris; admin@teflinternational.org.uk; www.teflinternational.org.uk; 120-hour TESOL; monthly start dates; course fee $600+€950; accommodation from €250.

TEFL TOULOUSE: 9 Allees Frederic Mistral, 31400 Toulouse; ✆ +33 5 61 54 76 67; www.tefltoulouse.com; 4-week TEFL Certificate (validated by IATQuO); 9 per year; €1,600; accommodation costs €350–€600 with host family, in studio flat, etc.; specialist sessions on Business English, teaching Young Learners and how to set up as a freelance teacher in France; lifetime job guidance and discounted French language courses for trainees.

THE LANGUAGE HOUSE: Montpellier Espace Langues, 5 ter avenue Saint Lazare, 34000 Montpellier; ✆ +33 6 8483 8559; info@teflanguagehouse.com; www.teflanguagehouse.com; affiliated schools in Nice (English American Center, 22 rue d'Alsace Lorraine, 06000 Nice), as well as in Marrakesh (Morocco) and Antalya (Turkey); 4-week TEFL Certificate Program and 1-week Teaching Business English Program (also offered online); French programmes validated by IATQuO; offered monthly; Certificate course, €1,290; Business course, €690 on-site, €390 online; homestays, single studios and shared apartments can be arranged; job assistance focuses on Mediterranean countries; contact Gyl Golden.

GREECE

ANGLO-HELLENIC TEACHER TRAINING: 13 Vasilou St, Corinth 20006; ✆ +30 27410 53511; info@teflcorinth.com; www.teflcorinth.com; delivers training course for TEFL International; accommodation in Vrahati, 20 minutes from training centre.

CELT: 77 Akademias St, 106 78 Athens; ✆ +30 210 330 2406; www.celt.edu.gr; €1,300; 100+ hour Certificate course offered intensively in the summer months and part-time starting October, January, March and April; also offer CELTA course, €1,450.

TEFL INTERNATIONAL: Corinth; www.teflinternational.org.uk; 120-hour TESOL course over 4 weeks; 5 times between May and September; course fee $600+€920; accommodation for €250–€350; 10 hours' teaching practice with Greek children and adults; teacher placement service via Anglo-Hellenic Teacher Recruitment (www.anglo-hellenic.com).

VIA LINGUA CRETE: Chrysanthou Episkopou 48, 73 132 Chania, Crete; ✆ +30 28210 57438; maria@vialingua.org; www.teflgreece.com or www.vialingua.org; 5 offered per year between May and October; €1590 including shared accommodation.

GUATEMALA

MÁXIMO NIVEL EXECUTIVE LANGUAGE CENTER: 6a Avenida Norte #16 y 16A, La Antigua (HQ in Cusco, Peru); ✆ +1 800 866 6358; info@maximonivel.com; www.maximonivel.com; 150-hour TEFL/TESOL Certificate (over 4 weeks) for $1,400–$1,700 offered monthly except December; 50-hour TEIB (Teaching English for International Business) Certificate and TIEEP (Teaching International English Exam Preparation) Certificate (over 3 days), $400 each; rough frequency 4 times a year; housing arranged with families, in shared apartments, hostels, etc. from $225 for 4 weeks; lifetime job-finding assistance; an average of 5 graduates are employed by Máximo Nivel each month.

HONG KONG

CHINESE UNIVERSITY OF HONG KONG: 23/F, Tower, B, School of Continuing and Professional Studies, The Chinese University of Hong Kong, Mongkok Town Centre, 90 Shantung Street, Mongkok, Kowloon; ✆ +852 2209 0235; www.cuhk.edu.hk/English/index.html; two courses on offer: Diploma Programme in Teaching English as a Second Language, 10 months, tuition fee HK$13,500 plus HK$100 enrolment fee; Master of Arts Programme in Teaching English to Speakers of Other Languages (jointly organised by School of Continuing and Professional Studies, The Chinese University of Hong Kong and Lancaster University); 2 years; tuition fee HK$89,800, plus HK$200 enrolment fee; contact Carol To, Programme Coordinator.

HEADSTART GROUP LTD: Hong Kong & Macao; ✆ +852 2155 9602; www.headstartgroup.co; face-to-face TEFL course after candidates complete a 120-hour course with BridgeTEFL (www.teflonline.com); 40 hours of assessed teaching practice with Headstart partner schools (at a cost of approx. HK$11,800).

HUNGARY

VIA LINGUA BUDAPEST: Tavasz u. 3, 1033 Budapest; ✆ +36 1 368 1156; budapest@vialingua.org; www.via-lingua.hu; 4-week intensive Certificate in TEFL course offered 3 or 4 times a year; course run by Tudomany Nyelviskola (see entry in Hungary chapter); €830, cost can be paid in instalments after the course if graduates who have earned a distinction degree teach for the company for a specified period.

INDONESIA

TEFL INTERNATIONAL: Surabaya; www.teflinternational.org.uk; monthly; $1600 plus $150–$250 for accommodation.

IRELAND

ALPHA COLLEGE OF ENGLISH: 4 North Great George's Street, Dublin 1; ✆+353 1 874 7024; admin@alphacollege.com; http://alphacollege.com.

CENTRE OF ENGLISH STUDIES: 31 Dame Street, Dublin 2; ✆+353 1 671 4233; info@ces-schools.com; www.ces-schools.com.

CLARE LANGUAGE CENTRE: Erasmus Smith Building, College Road, Ennis, Co Clare; ✆ +353 65 684 1681; clarelc@iol.ie; www.clarelc.ie.

CORK LANGUAGE CENTRE INTERNATIONAL: Wellington House, 16 St Patrick's Place, Wellington Road, Cork; ✆ +353 21 455 1661; info@corklanguagecentre.ie; www.acetireland.ie.

DORSET COLLEGE: 66 Lower Dorset St, Dublin 1; ✆ +353 1 830 9677; info@dorset-college.ie; www.dorset-college.ie.

GALWAY LANGUAGE CENTRE: The Bridge Mills, Galway; ✆ +353 91 566468; info@galwaylanguage.com; www.galwaylanguage.com.

INTERNATIONAL HOUSE DUBLIN: 66 Lower Camden Street, Dublin 2; ✆ +353 1 475 9011/3; info@ihdublin.com; www.ihdublin.com.

MEI (MARKETING ENGLISH IN IRELAND): 1 Lower Pembroke Street, Dublin 2; ✆+353 1 618 0910; www.mei.ie; is an association of recognised schools and a representative body (similar to English UK); many MEI schools provide teacher training courses (CELT) and ACELS-accredited courses.

U-LEARN: 97 St Stephens Green, Dublin 1; ✆ +353 1 878 7339; www.ulearnschool.com.

ITALY

ACLE (ASSOCIAZIONE CULTURALE LINGUISTICA EDUCATIONAL): Via Roma, 54, 18038 Sanremo; ✆ +39 184 506070; info@acle.org; www.acle.org; 5–6 day intensive TEFL-TP (Through Theatre and Play) introductory course with full board and lodging included; €150 course fee; successful students work as paid tutors, teaching English at camps throughout Italy (see Italy chapter); this project offers a combination of theory plus invaluable practical experience with emphasis on drama and child-centred learning activities; tutors receive an introductory TEFL Certificate at the end of the working period.

CENTRO TOSCAN DI LINGUE: Piazzale Porta al Prato 14, 50144 Florence; www.centrotoscano.com; venue for TEFL International's 4-week certificate course given monthly; $500 + €1190.

INTERLINGUE LANGUAGE SYSTEM/ROME TEFL COLLEGE: Via Lucrezio Caro 67, 00193 Rome; info@interlingue-it.com; www.interlingue-it.com/tefl; TEFL International Certificate courses run 9 times a year; €400 deposit plus €1000 without accommodation, accommodation from €400.

TEACHING ENGLISH IN ITALY: Florence; www.teachingenglishinitaly.com; 3-day weekend TEFL courses (20 hours, Friday to Sunday) offered every other month at Europass, Florence; €195; 1-week TEFL Teacher Refresher (€500) and 2-week Creative Classroom courses also in collaboration with the Europass teacher training Centre, Florence (€820).

VIA LINGUA FLORENCE: Via Brunelleschi 1, 50123 Florence; ✆ +39 055 283161; florence@vialingua.org; www.cteflflorence.com; 1-month intensive; approximately 9 a year; course fee €1,195 plus from €650 for accommodation.

JAPAN

TEFL INTERNATIONAL: 4-25-16 Minamimizumoto, Katsushika-ku, Tokyo 125-0035; admin@teflinternational.org.uk; www.teflinternational.org.uk; 120-hour TESOL; monthly start dates; course fee $2,390; paid teaching work arranged.

VOLTA ASSOCIATES: Chiyoda-ku, Tokyo 101–0054; www.volta-associates.com/tesol-course.html; 30-hour in-class TESOL training (affiliated to American TESOL) for 60,000 yen including handbook.

MALTA

ETI MALTA: Teacher Training & Development, St Julian's, Malta; www.etimalta.com; range of short Continuing Professional Development courses offered.

INLINGUA MALTA: Sliema; www.inlinguamalta.com; 45-hour TEFL Certificate offered in-house. TEFL Course Coordinator, Donovan Gatt.

MEXICO

DUNHAM INSTITUTE: Avenida Zaragoza 23, Chiapa de Corzo, Chiapas; ✆ +52 961 616 1498; academic-coordinator@dunhaminstitute.com; www.dunhaminstitute.com; 4-week TEFL course in conjunction with Spanish courses and language exchange and tutoring of local students; minimum commitment 8 weeks if tutoring local students or 5 months if teaching in schools; $1,600 includes free homestay with local family.

HESLINGTON LANGUAGE PROGRAM / HELP ENGLISH MEXICO: Tehuacán; www.helpenglishmexico.org/tesol-certification-program; 4-month American TESOL course combined with intership, starting August, January and May; $2,500.

INTERNATIONAL TEACHER TRAINING ORGANIZATION: Madero No. 469, Guadalajara, Jalisco 44100; ✆ +52 33 3658 5858; toll-free from UK: ✆ +44 800 404 9800; toll-free from USA: ✆ +1 866 514 7479; www.tefl.com.mx; 4 weeks offered monthly; $1,490; guaranteed job placement.

INTERNATIONAL TEFL ACADEMY: www.internationalteflacademy.com; Ciudad Guzman (3 times a year), Puerto Vallerta (6 times) and Guadalajara (8 times).

TEACHERS LATIN AMERICA: Plaza Galerías, Circuito Interior (Calz. Melchor Ocampo) 193 Local J-11, Miguel Hidalgo, 11300 Ciudad de México; ✆ +52 155 1496 0227; www.teachers-latin-america.com; 80-hour plus TEFL Certificate Programme offered monthly; 40 hours' in-class study, 10–20 hours of instructor-assessed student teaching and at least 25 additional hours of self-study on grammar, lesson planning, etc.; $1,190 including accommodation; job assistance throughout Latin America.

TEFL INTERNATIONAL: Chiapa de Corzo; www.teflinternational.org.uk/mexico.html; monthly; $1,690; volunteer teachers programme $1,950.

TEFL TRAINING MEXICO: Jalisco; ✆ +52 341 412 8090; www.tefl-trainingmexico.com; 130 hours, including 16 hours of private Spanish tuition; total $1,500; $400 for homestay accommodation; affiliated to Via Lingua.

NETHERLANDS

BRITISH SCHOOL NETHERLANDS: Vrouw Avenweg 640, 2493 WZ Den Haag; ✆ +31 070 315 4080; www.britishschool.nl; 5-day intro to TEFL offered in mid-July; €502; also offer CELTA course.

NICARAGUA

INTERNATIONAL TEFL ACADEMY: Leon; ✆ +1 505 2311 7411; www.nicaraguatefl.com; face-to-face as well as online and blended; $1899 (discounts for early booking).

PERU

INTERNATIONAL TEFL ACADEMY: Arequipa; www.internationalteflacademy.com; offered in July and October; $1,550.

MÁXIMO NIVEL EXECUTIVE LANGUAGE CENTER: Avenida El Sol 612, Cusco; ✆ +51 84 581800; info@maximonivel.com; www.maximonivel.com (see also Costa Rica and Guatemala); 150-hour TEFL/TESOL Certificate (over 4 weeks) for $1,400–$1,700 offered monthly except December; 50-hour TEIB (Teaching English for International Business) Certificate and TIEEP (Teaching International English Exam Preparation) Certificate (over 3 days), $400 each; rough frequency 4 times a year; housing arranged with families, in shared apartments, hostels, etc from $225 for 4 weeks; lifetime job-finding assistance; an average of 5 graduates are employed by Máximo Nivel each month.

RUSSIA

BENEDICT SCHOOL: 4 Admiraltejskaya Embankment, St Petersburg 190000; ✆ +7 812 325 7574; www.eng.benedict.ru; 4-week Via Lingua course offered 4 times a year; €1300 plus 18,000 roubles for accommodation. 13-week Work-Study programme in autumn and spring, which combines 2-week introductory TEFL training with Russian language course and job guidance; £690.

SLOVAKIA

CANADIAN LANGUAGE SCHOOL: Nitra; ✆ +421 904 371 050; info@canadian.sk; www.canadian schoolnitra.sk; 2-week 'Teach the Teacher' summer course for new ESL teachers who are not confident about grammar and teaching techniques; 2 weeks of intensive lessons (8 hours per day, 80 hours) with various start dates in July and August; £320 including materials but not accommodation.

SPAIN

ANGLO CENTRES: Calle Unió, 41, bajo, Tarragona 43001; ✆ +34 977 546309; www.tefl.anglocen tres.com; 4-week residential Certificate course, accredited by College of Teachers; offered 6 times a year; £1,040; also offer online and blended courses; contact Vince Ferrer or Rob Bianchi.

CANTERBURY TEFL: Calle Covarrubias 22, 2° Derecha, 28010 Madrid; ✆ +34 91 838 0082; www.canterburytefl.com; 40 hours of teaching theory supplemented by 40 hours of lesson planning, 20 hours class observation and 20 hours paid internship; €1,275 reduced by €280 for paid teaching.

EBC INTERNATIONAL: Orense 16, 2E, 28020 Madrid; ✆ +34 91 555 3975; www.ebcteflcourse.com; offered monthly; approx €1,275; 1-year visa option for non-EU participants is a possibility.

EUROPE TEFL TEACHER TRAINING: Salvador Espriu 91, 08005 Barcelona; ✆ +34 932 215515 info@europetefl.com; www.europetefl.com; 4-week intensive full-time; TEFL courses run throughout the year in Barcelona, Seville and many other locations in Europe and Latin America; €1,300, including all course materials, expert job guidance, alumni network and more; accommodation in the city centre and close to the schools can be arranged, €400–€500 a month; contact Kevin Cline.

INTERNATIONAL HOUSE BARCELONA: Calle Trafalgar 14, 08010 Barcelona; ✆ +34 93 268 3304; training@bcn.ihes.com; www.ihes.com/bcn; Business English Teachers course, 36 hours over 2 weeks, July only, €450; also, Director of Studies Training Course and Trainer Training Course, both 1 week in July, €555; and the International Diploma in Language Teaching Management (IDLTM), 2-week on-site course in July followed by 8 months of online assignments, €3,150; help given with finding accommodation.

OXBRIDGE BARCELONA: Numancia 47 entl 2, 08029 Barcelona; ✆ +34 93 532 7565; UK: +44 20 8133 0043; tefl@oxbridge.es; www.oxbridgetefl.com; Oxbridge International TEFL Certificate with employment opportunities; 120 hours including 20 hours of real teaching practice; subsidised course price after a successful interview in Barcelona, with reduction of €400 from full price of €1,250.

OXBRIDGE MADRID: Corredera Baja de San Pablo 39, 28003 Madrid; ✆ +34 91 523 4243. As above.

TEFL IBERIA: Barcelona; www.tefl-iberia.com; 4 week course throughout the year, but more in summer. €1350 (€1200 with early booking discount).

TEFL INTERNATIONAL: in Seville and Barcelona; admin@teflinternational.org.uk; www.teflinternational.org.uk; 120-hour TESOL; monthly start dates; course fee from €1,390.

TTMADRID: C/ Montesa, 35 (esc dcha) 2° dcha, 28006 Madrid; ✆ +34 91 572 1999; info@ttmadrid.com; www.ttmadrid.com; 4-week intensive courses accredited by the College of Teachers; courses run 9 times a year; course fee €1,375; interviews with teaching agencies arranged on graduation; course emphasis on teaching Business English; real teaching experience with adults and elective inputs on how to teach children; non-EU nationals may obtain student visa while combining this course with Spanish; €2,750.

SRI LANKA

LANKA TEFL TRAINING INSTITUTE: Colombo; www.teflsrilanka.com. 120-hour TEFL certificate course offered intensively or over 10 weeks, partnered with LTTC in London; $1,100 for non Sri Lankan trainees.

THAILAND

AYC INTERCULTURAL PROGRAMS: 9/197, 7th Floor, GOT Building Soi Ratchadaphisek 29, Ratchadaphisek Road, Chatuchak, Bangkok, 10900; ✆ +66 2556 1533; h_r@aycthailand.com; www.aycthailand.com; 120 hour TESOL course validated by INTESOL; course runs in Bangkok, Koh Samui and Phuket and costs $799 ($999 with accommodation); job guarantee for native English speakers under 52 years of age, holding a bachelor's degree.

CHICHESTER COLLEGE, THAILAND: 1st Fl., Muangthai Phatra Complex, 252/193 Ratchadaphisek Rd., Bangkok 10320; ✆ +66 2 693 2901; www.chichester.ac.th; TESOL certificate and distance diploma courses in cooperation with Chichester College UK; 4-week certificate course runs monthly; $1,595; accommodation offered at a private lodge near the Chichester Training Centre in Bangkok, and provided at a special subsidised rate of $150 for the entire duration of the full-time course only; graduates are provided teaching placements through Spencer International, which has links with schools in Thailand, Cambodia, Vietnam, Myanmar, Indonesia and China.

FEECHERS TEACHER TRAINING: Thailand; http://feechers.weebly.com; teacher recruitment company that arranges free 6-day teacher training in cooperation with various training centres, and job placement programme in the coastal provinces of Suratthani, Chumphon and Prachuap Khiri Khan in southern Thailand and various locations in the north and northeast of Thailand.

GREEN TEFL: Chiang Mai; ✆ +66 53 226718; www.greentefl.com; 120 hours, offered 5 times a year, including considerable on-the-job training experience teaching in local NAVA school; 38,500 baht if booked early, 45,000 baht otherwise.

ISLAND TEFL: Phuket, also in Koh Samui, Surin and Bangkok; monthly; 120 hours over 3 weeks ($999), 150 hours in 4 weeks ($1,490); job placement programme $795.

PARADISE TEFL THAILAND: ✆ +66 840 513655; www.paradisetefl.com or http://tefltesolthailand.com; franchise in Koh Phangan of international network of training courses; 9 per year; 32,000 baht.

PENNIES FOR PAPA FOUNDATION: Chiang Rai 57240; ✆ + 66 84 756 3900; www.penniesforpapa.org; 120-hour online TESOL course combined with 4 or 12 week internships teaching Akha people in a Northern Thai village; 4 weeks for $999; 12 weeks for $1,997.

SEE TEFL (Siam Educational Experience): Chiang Mai; ✆ +66 53 266295/6; info@seetefl.com; www.seetefl.com; 4-week training course; 10–15 times a year; $1,495 (or $1,295 if booked early); accommodation can be provided for extra $350–$400; job guarantee and also internship programme.

TEFL CAMPUS: Phuket or Chiang Mai; ✆ +66 81 968 9334; www.teflcampus.com; 4 weeks; $1,690 or $1,790 with accommodation in Chiang Mai.

TEFL EAST/GLOBAL TRAINING ACADEMY: tefleast@gmail.com; www.englishjobsthailand.com; affiliated to American TESOL Institute; 7-day teaching orientation in Bangkok ($500) followed by placement throughout Thailand for 4-5 months, for degree-holders only; monthly salary 30,000 baht per month.

TEFL INTERNATIONAL: 32/185 Phunphon Road, Talad Neua Ampur Muang, Phuket 83000; admin@teflinternational.org.uk; www.teflinternational.org.uk; 120-hour TESOL certificate course at Chiang Mai and Phuket; $1,690 excludes accommodation.

TESOL COURSE THAILAND: Bangkok and Phuket; www.tesolcoursethailand.com; 120 hours (3 weeks) in-class course followed by 4–5 months of teaching in Thailand with free accommodation; course fee $1,590; affiliated to American TESOL Institute.

TEXT AND TALK ACADEMY: 1961 Phaholyothin Road (opposite Mayo Hospital), Lardyao, Chatuchak, Bangkok 10900; ✆ +66 2 561 3443; info@teflteachthai.com; www.teflteachthai.com; 6-week certificate courses (about $1,495), upgrade and refresher course, 16-week diploma course, 8-week TEYL course, 8-week advanced skills course and home study course; acts as hiring agent at end of course.

UNITED EDUCATIONAL CONSULTANTS CO. LTD: 4th Floor, Silom Plaza, Silom Road corner Narathiwat Road, Bangkok 10500; ✆ +66 2 233 2388; info@teflthai.com; www.teflthai.com; 120 hours over 5 weeks with 10 start dates throughout the year; 44,500 baht; course earns eligible graduates 9 US graduate credits in education; US master's degree can be completed in 1 year while teaching in Thailand; also offers graduate diploma in teaching; 3 and a half-year part-time bachelor's degree in education, and weekend study for 1 and a half-year dual US and Thai accredited master's degree (www.uecthai.com), including required Thai teaching licence.

UNITEFL THAILAND: T.Suthep, A.Muang, Chiang Mai 50200; ✆ +66 88-402-8217; www.unitefl.com; 120-hour course offered monthly in Chiang Mai and 7 times per year in Phuket; 45,000 baht (£820/$1,4950); affiliated to TEFL International.

WECI TEFL: 70/145 Soi; 112, Nongkae, Hua Hin, Prachuap Khiri Khan 77110; ✆ +66 32 900464; www.wecitefl.com; 120-hour course in seaside town 2 and a half hours south of Bangkok; starting from 36,000 baht with other options to include placement or preparation for ED (educational) visa.

TURKEY

ONLINETESOL TURKEY: Antalya; http://onlinetesol.com; American Culture U.K. TESOL 150-hour course including a teaching practicum in Turkey; TL1300 (including tax).

VIA LINGUA ISTANBUL: Kent English, Bahariye Cad. 15/2, Kadiköy, 34710 Istanbul; ✆ +90 216 347 2791/2; istanbul@vialingua.org; www.tefl-turkey.com; 4-week CTEFL course offered 6 times a year; €1,275 plus €300 for accommodation.

VIETNAM

MIDWEST EDUCATION GROUP: 4633 N. Western Ave., Suite 207, Chicago, IL 60625; ✆ +1 847 496 7919; contact@midwested.us; www.midwested.us; 4-week classroom-based TESOL programme in Vietnam; MEG has satellite offices in the two major cities plus Can Tho south of Ho Chi Minh City; $1,100.

AVSE-TESOL: Go Vap District, Ho Chi Minh City; ✆ +84 85427 3436; peter@avse-edu.vn; www.avse.edu.vn; Australian government accredited TEFL-TESOL programme offered monthly; 150 hours over 4 weeks with minimum 20 hours of practice teaching of 'real' language learners; US$1,599, includes free accommodation near the school and guaranteed paid employment.

INTERNATIONAL HOUSE

Teacher Training with International House

Choosing the right training course or applying for your first teaching job abroad can be a daunting prospect. There are so many courses available and potential job opportunities to consider that it is hard to know where to start – and you want to make the right choice as this is your future!

If you choose International House, you don't need to worry.

The International House (IH) network is committed to continually driving excellence in both language teaching and teacher training. International House led the way in creating the first training course specifically for English as a Foreign Language for teachers in 1962, which formed the basis for the current CELTA qualification, so we really are the experts.

As a network of 155 affiliated schools in 52 countries globally, International House is a fantastic option for both teacher training and a career in teaching English. We offer training courses for every stage of a teacher's career, delivered both face to face and online.

Why should you train with International House?

- IH has over 50 years of experience in developing and training teachers
- IH courses are moderated by the IH Assessment Unit and recognised globally
- The IH name is widely respected in the field of language teaching, and teachers that have trained with IH are widely sought after by employers
- Course participants who train with an IH school in any location within our network will receive the same high standard of training and assessment
- Training with IH means you are guaranteed to train with dedicated professional trainers

Why should you work for an International House school?

When starting a new career it is essential you begin with the right foundations and IH schools have the systems and support in place to help you.

You can progress with International House and work with other teachers that feel as passionately about teaching as you do. Our schools only employ professional teachers with recognised teaching qualifications and our quality charters ensure that all teachers receive regular training and support from academic managers.

We are a network of schools committed to the same values and quality standards, not a franchise, so each school has its own unique character and local flavour. Many of our teachers started their career with one IH school and have moved around the network. So International House really can be a career choice for life.

For more information please visit www.ihworld.com/teachers or email info@ihworld.com.

FINDING A JOB

You have only two choices: to search for a job from afar or go to the country of your choice and look around. Having a job arranged before departure obviously removes much of the uncertainty and anxiety of leaving home for an extended period. It also allows the possibility of preparing in appropriate ways: sorting out the right visa, researching the course books in use, etc. However, veteran teachers as well as confident newly qualified teachers prefer to travel to the city of their choice in the hiring season (e.g. April in Thailand, September in Spain ...) and set up interviews locally. It is always advantageous to meet an employer face-to-face, inspect a school and make contact with other teachers to get the real lowdown before signing a contract, rather than accepting a job in complete ignorance of the prevailing conditions.

While some employers choose their staff months before they are needed, many start to recruit and interview not long before the beginning of term when they have a rough idea of how many clients have signed up. Online advertisements for northern hemisphere positions starting in September generally appear between April and July though plenty of adverts can be found through the summer, too. If you want to look for a job in person, you will either have to go on a reconnaissance mission well in advance of your proposed starting date or take your chances of finding a last-minute vacancy.

FINDING A JOB IN ADVANCE

There are three ways of finding a teaching job in advance:

- ***by answering an online advertisement***
- ***using a recruitment agency or a large international English teaching organisations such as International House***
- ***conducting a speculative job search, i.e. making contact by email or telephone with all the schools whose addresses you can find in this book or from any other source, including social networks like LinkedIn.***

TEFL WEBSITES

For schools, an online advert offers an easy and instantaneous means of publicising a vacancy to an international audience. Teachers looking for employment can use search engines to look for pages with references to EFL, English language schools and recruitment. CVs can be emailed quickly and cheaply to advertising schools, who can then use email themselves to chase up references.

Arguably it has become a little too easy to advertise and answer job adverts online. At the press of a button, your CV can be clogging up dozens, nay, hundreds of computers. While opening up an enormous range of possibilities, the internet can be a bewildering and discouraging place to job-hunt. A host of websites promise to provide free online recruitment services for English teachers. Because many sites are struggling on the margins, they often seem to offer more than they can deliver and you may find that some offer little more than general waffle or that the number and range of jobs posted are disappointing, either undated (and therefore meaningless) or with dud links. Some inspire little confidence, such as www.esljobslounge.com whose tagline is 'Welcome to your one stop solution to search and find ESL teching [sic] jobs around the world'. That being said, everywhere you look on the internet, potentially useful links can be found. For many years Dave Sperling's 'Dave's ESL Cafe' (www.eslcafe.com) dominated the field and it is still the first port of call for many, especially North Americans, to check job vacancies and investigate further. Often the job discussion forums are useful, though always check the dates because many are very out-of-date. In any case 'Dave' provides a mind-boggling amount of material and many links to specific institutes and chains in each country.

Another key international site is www.tefl.com, which has gained in authority and popularity over recent years. When subscribing (for free), you can specify whether you want to be notified of vacancies by email on a daily or weekly basis. The site claims to have more than 23,500 registered employers. At the time of writing the countries with the most vacancies listed were China (91), Spain (89) and Italy (64). After **Susie Smith** got her TEFL certificate, she started looking for suitable jobs online:

> ***TEFL.com was one of a number of websites that was recommended while I was studying for my TEFL certificate through the TEFL Academy. The website is well-designed and easy to navigate. After creating a free online profile (a lengthy and somewhat frustrating process), searching and applying for jobs was incredibly easy. While I did check out a number of other resources, TEFL.com quickly became my favourite. At the end of August 2015, I applied for eight paid full-time teaching posts in different parts of Spain, all advertised on TEFL.com. My first interview took place on the telephone just a few days later. I was offered and accepted the post a few hours later. Although I subsequently received a further six invitations to interview I don't regret having made a quick decision to accept my first offer.***

When registering your details as a job-seeker try to be as targeted as possible. **Fergus Cooney** learnt the hard way not to be too general on ESL Cafe:

> ***I posted a message simply stating 'Qualified teacher seeking job'. Within two days I was inundated with many dozens of replies requesting my CV and, more surprisingly with job offers everywhere, although the majority were from Korea, Taiwan and China. 'Jackpot,' I thought (I have since realised that many schools/agents must have an automatic reply system which emails those who advertise in the way I did). I quickly began sifting through them, but not as quickly as they kept arriving in my inbox. Before a few more days had passed, I had become utterly confused and had forgotten which school was which, so I deleted them all, got a new email address and posted a second, more specific message on Dave's.***

In almost all cases, employers will contact an applicant only if they wish to proceed with their application, so do not expect any politely worded refusals.

While these two giants of the TESL world (www.eslcafe.com and www.tefl.com) have pushed some other sites out of business, many rivals survive and flourish.

Here is a brief survey of some of the key recruitment sites.

- www.englishjobsabroad.com: clear layout with range of dated and archived job postings with email addresses revealed.
- http://teflen.com/tefl-tesol-jobs-board-employment-job-portal.html: mainly recruitment agencies with live vacancies.
- www.tefl-jobs.co.uk: recruitment website from the 247recruit stable, with only a few undated postings.
- www.tefljobs.net: dated vacancies with possibility of clicking through to contact details; free to register but must upload a CV in order to apply.
- www.TEFLworld.com: calls itself a vertical search portal with a search engine that crawls major job boards across the Internet and finds posted positions matching the criteria of the job seeker. Part of the Icon Group (Thailand) and overlaps with www.tesall.com and www.totalesl.com. Strongest in vacancies in Asia.
- www.gooverseas.com/teach-abroad: searchable online directory of opportunities to teach, study, volunteer and intern abroad, based in Berkeley, California. Includes some first-hand reviews of employers and programmes.
- www.glassdoor.co.uk/index.htm: includes some relevant job vacancies and employer reviews posted by employees. Covers all kinds of work as well as English teaching so not always easy to filter relevant postings.

- http://tesljobs.com: vacancies mostly in China but a handful of others.
- BestTEFL.com: uses Facebook to list job contacts as they come in – www.facebook.com/teflcelta.teachersjobs.
- TEFLnow.com: Online TEFL training provider. Worldwide vacancies posted on Facebook (www.facebook.com/TEFLnow) as they arise.
- www.esl101.com: database of recent job postings with web addresses but no contact details.
- www.job.ihworld.com/jobs: International House maintains a clear website with links to its 155 affiliated schools in 52 countries displaying email addresses of directors and directors of studies. The recruitment and training sections of the website are accessible to all; enquiries to worldrecruit@ihworld.com.
- www.eslbase.com/schools: links to language schools, country by country but not always reliable (e.g. of a sample tested at the time of writing for the country of Georgia, six of the 13 links were dead); www.eslbase.com/jobs has current vacancies precisely dated and particularly strong in China and Spain, plus a useful TEFL forum.
- www.teflsearch.com: has an alphabetical employer directory as well as a good choice of vacancies in a range of countries with contact details revealed.
- www.teachinghouse.com/english-teaching-jobs: CELTA training provider in the US that maintains a huge TEFL jobs database with dates (often long in the past) and email addresses.
- www.teachoverseas.ca: EFL teaching jobs and resources with a bias towards Canadians. Partner site of the TESall Group.
- www.onlinetefl.com/tefl-jobs-abroad/tefl-jobs-board: maintained by the giant TEFL training and travel company i-to-i and Love TEFL. Most listings are for the obvious recruiters.
- www.tefllogue.com: discursive site with links to blogs and other sites that might be useful (but no current vacancies). Part of the BootsnAll travel network.
- www.tefljobsworld.com: another recruitment portal for English language school jobs worldwide with minimal listings.
- http://esljobs.biz: set up in 2002 by experienced teachers to match teacher CVs with vacancies.
- www.eslteachersboard.com: vast site and free community for EL teachers with current job postings (dated and with email addresses revealed) and teachers' CVs.
- www.eslemployment.com: decent selection of dated vacancies.
- www.tefl.org.uk/tefl-jobs-centre: job vacancies accessible to Scottish-based Tefl.org.uk's students but with links for anyone to application forms for major employers.
- www.onestopenglish.com: teachers' resource site (not a job site) maintained by the educational publisher Macmillan. An annual subscription costs £42/€53/$68; one-month free trial available.
- TEFLwork.com: launched in 2015 as a jobs portal designed to connect schools with English language teachers who hold a CELTA or DELTA (or equivalent). Part of the Frameworks Education Group that also includes teacher training-focused agency StudyCELTA and its sister brand ELTcampus.
- www.jobsabroadbulletin.co.uk: jobs board has a 'Teaching & TEFL' section, which remains archived and is easy to access.
- TeflGraduate.com: jobs board of an online TEFL training company listing different vacancies from the usual.
- www.teflcourse.net/tefl-jobs: good, easy to navigate with historic dated vacancies (part of online and in-class training company ITTT).
- http://worldoftefl.com: Quinn's World of TEFL tries to match qualified teachers who register with the site with vacancies, after conducting a brief chat by Skype.

Other websites that are country specific, e.g. www.ohayosensei.com (jobs in Japan), www.ajarn.com (teaching in Thailand) and www.lingobongo.com for Madrid/Barcelona, are listed in the relevant country chapters. One ESL blog site that is especially insightful is James Soller's jimmyesl.com.

For small-scale, out-of-the-way teaching opportunities, most of them voluntary, check out these excellent online directories: www.helpx.net and www.workaway.info. After subscribing for €20/$29 respectively, which covers a year's access to registered hosts' contact details, you will find inviting prospects to teach children at a summer camp in Moldova, live in the centre of Rome in exchange for teaching English to a family with two children at university or teach for an NGO in a beach town in Peru.

RECRUITMENT FAIRS

In an ideal world, prospective teachers could meet a range of employers all at once. Certified classroom teachers looking for vacancies in international schools have access to this kind of event (see section on Certified Teachers below). But it is not very common in TEFL. The energetic **Aidan O'Toole**, long-time resident of Andalucía, describes the advantages of the annual job fair he has spearheaded in Córdoba and recently extended to Bilbao, where language schools can meet job-seekers in May:

> ***The first Spainwise recruitment fair in 2009 was a success with many teachers and language schools attending. Each side invests a small amount of money into getting a job, which is far more efficient than teachers flying out from England for just one or two interviews. The chance to meet face-to-face is tremendously useful for both sides. Of course tefl.com (and similar) have transformed the recruitment process and the typed CV and letterbox seem to belong to another era. But it is just too easy for newly qualified teachers to lean on the wrong button on their computer and send out hundreds of CVs, sometimes in answer to adverts they haven't even read.***

Aidan thinks that meeting a range of job-seekers makes it much easier for language school owners to spot the best candidates than rifling through a pile of CVs from new CELTA graduates. Meeting face-to-face also allows candidates who do not fit the perfect profile a chance to shine.

Professional English language teachers often try to attend a regional conference sponsored by TESOL Inc. (tesol.org) or IATEFL (International Association of TEFL; iatefl.org), where a jobs market is hosted and interviews arranged. **Sandeha Lynch** describes the TESOL Arabia Conference he attended in Al-Ain in Abu Dhabi:

> ***These are serious ELT conferences not only as marketing fairs for publishers, booksellers and software companies, but also as an open job shop for the local employers. Teachers from all over the Gulf try to get there to socialise, look for a new job or just absorb enough academic wisdom to last them another year. If teachers are looking for a job then most of the time they'll be making appointments, checking off their interview scorecards and watching the clock. All of the local colleges and recruiting agencies have stands there, and they are busy from morning to night giving interviews to anyone who knows the local scene and has the right qualifications.***

RECRUITMENT ORGANISATIONS

Major providers of ELT and teacher placement organisations of various kinds may be able to assist prospective teachers in English-speaking countries to find teaching jobs. Some are international educational foundations; some are voluntary organisations such as the Peace Corps or charities; some are major chains of commercial language schools; and others are small agencies that serve as intermediaries between independent language schools abroad and prospective teachers. The companies and organisations listed in this chapter have been assigned to the following categories (though there is some blurring of distinctions):

- international ELT organisations (including the major language school chains)
- commercial recruitment agencies
- voluntary, gap year and religious organisations
- North American organisations, which cater primarily (though not exclusively) to citizens of the USA and Canada
- placement services for British and American state-qualified teachers.

Note that agencies and organisations that operate only in one country or one region are described in the country chapters in the second part of this book.

It is hardly worthwhile for a family-run language school in Northern Greece or Southern Brazil to pay the high costs which most agencies charge schools just to obtain one or two native-speaker teachers. Vacancies that are filled with the help of agencies and recruitment consultants tend to be either at the mass-market end where there are large numbers of unfilled entry-level positions or at the elite end of the ELT market for specialised or high-level positions.

HOW AGENCIES WORK

Agencies make their money by charging client employers; the service to teachers is usually free of charge. By law in the UK, no fee can be charged to job-seekers either before or after placement, except if a package of services is sold alongside (e.g. insurance, visas, travel, etc.). Note that different rules apply in other countries, so that placement fees are the norm in the USA. Some of the best recruitment organisations to deal with are ones that specialise in a single country and are located in situ, such as Anglo-Hellenic Recruitment in Corinth or MySayar in Myanmar (see Greece and Myanmar chapters). They tend to have more first-hand knowledge of their client schools. Beware of scam recruiters. If a job offer is made without a proper interview and sounds too good to be true, it is probably a fake. In no circumstances should you send bank details or money in advance (e.g. if requested for visas).

Bear in mind that the use of an intermediary by foreign language institutes is no guarantee of a smooth and supported ride. Small independent recruiters, especially in the context of Korea or the Middle East, are sometimes interested primarily in gaining their commission and then disappear. In some cases employers turn to the expensive option of using a recruiter because they have so many vacancies, they need help. In other cases, they do not have a good enough reputation as employers to attract applicants without help. Sometimes recruitment agencies abroad are trying to fill vacancies that no one in the country who is familiar with the employer would deign to fill. As the American **Rusty Holmes** said of his employer in Taiwan: '*The school was so bad it had to recruit from America.*' If you are in any doubt about the reliability of an agency or the client he/she represents, it is a sensible precaution to search online and ask for the name of one or more current or recent teachers whom you can ask for a first-hand account. It is a bad sign if the agency is unable or reluctant to oblige.

The hiring of teachers for chain schools abroad is done either at a local level, especially when they are franchises (so direct applications are always worthwhile), or centrally, if the school has trouble filling vacancies.

One way in which recruitment agencies work is to create a database of teachers' CVs and to try to match these with suitable vacancies as they occur. In order to be registered with such an agency it is almost always essential to have a relevant qualification, often at least the Cambridge or Trinity Certificate, since agencies tend to deal with high-level, difficult-to-fill vacancies. Smaller agencies may have fewer vacancies on their books but they can often offer a more personal service. A good agency will provide a full briefing and information pack on the school in particular and the country in general, and will make sure that the contract offered is written in English and offers reasonable terms.

Volunteer English teachers are in demand by dozens of commercial sending agencies which routinely charge volunteers £800–£2,000+ for placement and related services. Before her final year at university, **Susannah Kerr** took up one of these placements in Thailand, which she found to be less structured than the agency literature had promised, which seems to be typical. She felt that the school to which she was assigned did not really need English-speaking volunteers and she suspected that they invited foreigners merely as status symbols. With hindsight she felt that she had been naïve to assume that the school would be grateful for her efforts. She was allowed to teach whatever she liked, so naturally she concentrated on spoken English and taught no grammar and only occasional writing exercises. She was given no lesson plans and was not required to prepare the students for exams. When the teachers saw that the volunteers were coping, they took a holiday.

THE BRITISH COUNCIL

The British Council (www.britishcouncil.org) is the largest ELT (English language teaching) employer in the world. The Council represents the elite end of the ELT industry. At its own 80 or so teaching centres in more than 50 countries, it offers high-quality, face-to-face language teaching and employs the best qualified teachers. The standard minimum requirement is a CELTA (or equivalent), plus two years of full-time teaching experience. The British Council is a professional organisation whose jobs tend to come with attractive terms and conditions. However in a few locations, the Council has been recruiting 'apprentice' teachers or teaching assistants with a qualification but without experience.

The Council's offices abroad are usually well informed about opportunities for English language teaching locally. You should be able to access online a list of language schools that are Cambridge exam centres, which can be a useful starting point for a job search. In some countries the British Council has a School Finder, for example http://hr.bcschoolfinder.org/schoolfinder/easy123.php for Croatia and www.britishcouncil.gr/sites/default/files/school-finder-thessaloniki-10-2016.pdf for northern Greece.

Contact details for the offices worldwide are listed online at www.britishcouncil.org/organisation/our-global-network. The charter of the British Council defines its aims as to promote and develop a wider knowledge of the United Kingdom and the English language. It is non-profit-making and works non-politically. It employs over 7,000 staff overseas, a good 2,000 of whom are involved with the teaching of the English language in some capacity. Other work that the Council carries out includes the running of libraries, the organisation of cultural tours and exchanges, etc. But language teaching and teacher recruitment remain among its central concerns.

A useful starting place for qualified EL teachers is the Council's jobs portal where current vacancies are listed: https://jobs.britishcouncil.org. British Council teaching centres recruit both through London and locally. They especially welcome applications from teachers with experience or an interest in specialist areas such as Young Learners, Business English, skills through English, IELTS exam preparation, etc.

Most of the contracts offered through the website above are for two years and come with an attractive salary and relocation package (airfares, allowance for shipping belongings, etc.). Once you have secured one job with the Council, it is possible to move to other jobs in other offices. Internal vacancies are described separately at the jobs portal.

A completely separate programme run by the British Council is the placement of language assistants in schools for an academic year. The Language Assistants team administers exchange programmes with 14 countries worldwide. Applicants for assistant posts must be native speakers of English who have completed their secondary education and at least two years of degree-level study in the UK, often but not necessarily in the language of the destination country. In some countries (especially China and countries in Latin America) posts are of particular interest to graduates interested in a career in TEFL. The website is open for applications from 1 November to 28 February. For more information see the Languages Assistants website (www.britishcouncil.org/language-assistants/become/where-can-I-go) or contact the team by emailing language.assistants@britishcouncil.org or phoning the British Council ✆ +44 161 957 7755.

In conjunction with the BBC, the British Council also maintains a website called Teaching English (www.teachingenglish.org.uk) which is a free resource for teachers and includes lesson plans, worksheets, teaching tips, webinars, apps, etc.

The British Council is a large and complex institution with two headquarters: one at 10 Spring Gardens, London SW1A 2BN (✆ +44 20 7930 8466) and the other at Bridgewater House, 58 Whitworth Street, Manchester M1 6BB (✆ +44 161 957 7755). Some feel that it has lost some of its patrician credentials and has been rebranding itself along business lines in order to compete in an international market.

INTERNATIONAL ELT ORGANISATIONS

Bell English, Hillscross, Red Cross Lane, Cambridge CB2 0QU (✆ +44 1223 278800; www.bellenglish.com/jobs). Bell recruits teachers for senior ELT posts in its associated schools in Thailand, Macao, China, Jordan, Kazakhstan and Switzerland.

Bénédict Network International (www.benedict-international.com). Franchised business and language schools in Europe (15 in Germany, 8 in both Switzerland and Italy), plus 3 in Russia and 2 in Ecuador. Recruitment is not centralised.

Berlitz (www.berlitz.com/Careers/33; links to Berlitz sites for countries worldwide some of which indicate current job vacancies). Berlitz is one of the largest language training organisations in the world with about 550 franchised locations in 70 countries. It is also one of the oldest, founded in 1878. The company's core business is language and cultural training, and teacher vacancies occur most often in Germany, Turkey and Korea. All Berlitz teachers are native, fluent speakers and university graduates; all must undergo training in the 'Berlitz Method', a direct 'see-hear-speak' teaching approach that does not rely on translation. Berlitz is known for supervising its teachers' techniques very closely, and deviation from the method is not permitted. Berlitz schools abroad employ teachers directly, usually on a part-time basis initially, after they have completed a training course in the Berlitz Method. Berlitz has been expanding its summer programmes for young learners in Germany, Spain, etc.

Cactus TEFL (www.cactustefl.com). An advisory service that allows you to compare TEFL training courses but does not assist in job finding.

Education Development Trust, Highbridge House, 16-18 Duke St, Reading RG1 4RY (✆ +44 118 902 1000; www.educationdevelopmenttrust.com). Formerly CfBT (Centre for British Teachers) that manages EFL/EAP/ESP/Primary/Secondary teachers and instructors for various projects and contracts, mainly in Brunei, also in Singapore and Oman.

EF English First Teacher Recruitment and Training (www.englishfirst.com/esl-jobs). Online recruitment centre for 200 EF schools in China, Russia and Indonesia.

ELS Language Centers, Princeton, NJ (www.els.edu/en/careers). ELS, now owned by Berlitz, is a network of campus-based English language instruction and university preparation centres in the USA, Canada and Australia, with links to English teaching centres at universities in China, Malaysia, Turkey, Saudi Arabia, Panama, etc., but does not recruit teachers apart from in the US.

IH World Organisation, Unity Wharf, 13 Mill Street, London SE1 2BH (✆ +44 20 7394 6580; worldrecruit@ihworld.com; www.job.ihworld.com). International House (IH) is one of the largest and oldest groups of language schools, teaching English as a foreign language (and 25 modern languages) in 155 affiliated schools in 52 countries worldwide. IHWO Recruitment Services is based in London at the International House World Office, which is the co-ordinating body for all International House affiliated schools. It is responsible for managing the recruitment of teachers, trainers and senior staff for IH schools and annually expects to assist in the recruitment of between 350 and 400 teachers for International House schools worldwide. The minimum qualification requirement for teaching posts is the Cambridge CELTA or Trinity TESOL Certificate. All IH schools adhere to internal quality standards that provide strict guidelines on terms and conditions, working hours and working environment. (Note: IH London, a language school and teacher training centre, is a separate company; see training directory.)

Inlingua (www.inlingua.com). International chain of 309 language centres that operate autonomously in 35 countries across Europe, Africa, Asia, North and South America. Link to jobs on website especially in Germany, Italy and the Middle East.

Language Link, 6 Duke's Road, London WC1H 9AD (✆ +44 20 3214 8250; info@languagelink.co.uk; www.languagelink.com). International language training organisation with a network of affiliated schools in Russia, China, Vietnam and Uzbekistan which carry out teacher recruitment independently of London. Usually minimum qualifications are TEFL Certificate or PGCE or experience but visit the website of the country in which you wish to work. (See Training chapter for details of Language Link's CELTA courses.)

Marcus Evans Linguarama, 7 Elm Court, 1 Arden Street, Stratford-upon-Avon CV37 6PA (✆ +44 1789 203910; personnel@linguarama.com or dannycoughlan@linguarama.com; www.linguarama.com/employment). Linguarama specialises in providing language training for professionals. Applicants for trainer positions in centres abroad must have at least a degree and a Cambridge/Trinity Certificate (or equivalent). Linguarama finds placements for 50–100 teachers at 21 centres in six European countries; in the spring and early summer they usually advertise vacancies in Germany and Italy and sometimes France, Netherlands and Spain.

Richard Lewis Communications, Riversdown House, Warnford, Southampton, Hampshire SO32 3LH (✆ +44 1962 771111; www.riversdown.com/careers). RLC has partners worldwide and offices in Finland, Sweden and Germany, specialising in cross-cultural training and language teaching.

Saxoncourt, 59 South Molton Street, London W1K 5SN (✆ +44 20 7491 1911; recruit@saxoncourt.com; www.saxoncourt.com). One of the largest UK-based recruiters of EFL teachers, Saxoncourt places several hundred teachers per year with Shane English Schools and other clients worldwide, mainly in Japan, Taiwan, China, Singapore, Vietnam and Italy. Applications are welcome, particularly from candidates with a Cambridge CELTA, Trinity TESOL or equivalent qualifications. Interviews are held in London, where possible. Interested candidates should register online at www.saxoncourt.com. The website features a regularly updated current vacancies page, online registration and country-specific sections with downloadable information packs.

SAXONCOURT RECRUITMENT

A case study from one of our teachers

Why Taiwan?

'Taiwan is a unique and beautiful country. You can be in the centre of Taipei and then within 30 minutes you can be in the mountains. It has everything from beaches to mountains to bustling cities. Life goes on all night as there are many 24-hour shops and the retail stores are open till late into the night. Whether you want a nice relaxed coffee, a beer in a pub or a wee dance in a club the Taiwanese cities have it all.

'The food is cheap, tasty and there is something for everybody. You can go to the night markets where there is a lot of variety or you can go to one of the many restaurants that have food from all over the world.'

How did your recruitment company help you?

'Saxoncourt was very useful. It took the majority of the stress away and left me to concentrate on my teaching. Once I was recruited I was in regular contact with the recruiter who was constantly asking what I needed and giving me close support. Everything from my visa documents to my arrival pickup was organised for me and this left me feeling very supported as going to Asia for the first time was quite a scary prospect.'

How is the teaching?

'Teaching in Taiwan is a very rewarding experience. The majority of classes are Young Learners; however, there are other classes such as adults, teenagers and full-time kindergarten. The Taiwanese students are a lot of fun once they get to know you, and they work very hard at their schools all day, so appreciate the more active and fun classes here at Shane English School Taiwan (SEST).'

What are you doing now?

'Currently I'm working as the Human Resources Assistant Director of Studies (HRADoS) of SEST. The promotion opportunities are there at SEST for those who work hard and show a good attitude. I am now in charge of recruitment for the whole country and also play an integral role in scheduling for the teachers.'

Wall Street English International (teach@wallstreetenglish.com; www.wallstreetenglish.com). Now owned by Pearson, Wall Street operates both company-owned and franchised centres, and employs more than 2,000 teachers in nearly 450 centres in 28 countries and territories in Asia (China, Indonesia, Hong Kong, South Korea, Malaysia, Thailand and Vietnam), Europe (France, Germany, Italy, Portugal, Spain, Switzerland, Czech Republic, Russia, Turkey), Latin America (Argentina, Brazil, Chile, Colombia, Ecuador, Mexico, Nicaragua, Peru, Venezuela), the Middle East (Israel, Saudi Arabia) and Africa (Morocco and Angola). The most recent location to open is in Myanmar. The countries with almost continuous vacancies are China, Russia, Italy, Saudi Arabia, Turkey and Thailand. Applicants should have at least a bachelor's degree and the appropriate professional qualifications of a CELTA or equivalent TEFL certificate. One year's teaching experience is an advantage. Due to restrictions and visa legislation in many countries within the network, Wall Street hires teachers from the UK, Ireland, USA, Canada, Australia, New Zealand and South Africa. The interview process is as follows: a first-round interview is a 'get to know you' interview that will probably last around 45 minutes. Some countries will consider doing this on the phone with offshore applicants. A second-round interview will involve discussing a lesson plan created by the applicant and giving a brief teaching presentation of approximately 15 minutes. This interview will also last approximately 45 minutes. Qualified applicants can apply online.

COMMERCIAL AGENCIES

If you have a TEFL background, you can send a CV with covering letter via email or post to the relevant agencies. Agencies that specialise in a single country are not included in this chapter, but are mentioned in the relevant country chapters.

Arun Language Training & Recruitment Ltd, Littlehampton, UK (✆ +44 7495 368 499; barry.shorten@arunlanguagetraining.com; www.arunlanguagetraining.com/recruitment). Mainly for qualified status teachers but some ESL vacancies especially in China.

Astute Education, Nottingham (✆ +44 115 905 0148; colin@astuteeducation.co.uk; www.astuteeducation.co.uk). Specialise in recruiting contracted and permanent staff for nurseries, primary, secondary and tertiary education establishments around the world, with occasional TEFL/TESOL vacancies, especially in Malaysia and the Middle East.

BBD Education, Dubai (✆ +971 56 724 2373; recruitment@bbd.ae). Recruits teachers mainly for international schools but occasional TEFL posts in Turkey, the Middle East, Asia and Africa.

Brightspark Teachers Ltd, Gateshead (www.brightsparkteachers.co.uk). 20-30 positions worldwide but mainly Southeast Asia.

Carfax Education Recruitment, 48 Langham Street, London W1W 7AY (✆ +44 20 7927 6200; www.carfax-tutors.com). Offices in Dubai, Moscow, Baku, Monaco and London. EFL-qualified freelance tutors recruited from the UK to tutor children in Russia, Azerbaijan, Dubai, etc. Tutoring mainly in English but also in other core subjects needed for studying abroad.

English in Action, 2 Hawks Lane, Canterbury CT1 2NU (✆ +44 1227 818250 or +44 7876 865132; recruitment@englishinaction.com; www.englishinaction.com/jobs.php). Native-speaking teachers based in UK with British/EU passport and at least a CELTA/Trinity recruited to travel to Europe for short periods of 1–8 weeks to deliver specialised active programmes to children. Recent destination countries included Austria, Croatia, Germany, Italy, Slovenia, Spain and Turkey.

English Language Company, Sydney, Australia (✆ + 61 2 9267 5688; www.elc.edu.au/en/elc-worldwide/elc-teaching). ELC Sydney runs a range of teaching programmes in Malaysia (where they have a sister school) plus Vietnam, Thailand, China, Colombia and Peru.

ESL Certified Recruiting Services, Colorado (✆ +1 888 661 8005; teach@eslrecruitme.com; www.eslrecruitme.com). Recruitment of native speaker teachers for China, Korea, Vietnam, Ecuador, Georgia and Uzbekistan.

ESLstarter Ltd, Northwich, Cheshire (✆ +44 161 818 2191; USA: +1 209 348 9814; www.eslstarter.com). Family-run agency by Phil and Claire Negus, recruiting teachers, interns and volunteers for clients in Cambodia, China, Hong Kong, Japan, Korea, Myanmar, Thailand, Vietnam, UAE, Colombia, Peru and Uruguay normally after they complete 120-hour Intesol online or blended TEFL course (www.in-tesoltesoltraining.com). Training followed by placement incurs fees, e.g. £495 for Cambodia.

Evocation EFL, Bon Marché Centre, 241–251 Ferndale Road, Brixton, London SW9 8BJ (✆ +44 20 7274 8441; efl@evocationefl.net; www.evocationefl.net). Agency based in London and Dublin. Annually recruits about 200 teachers from English-speaking countries, after a face-to-face interview in the UK. Candidates must have CELTA/Trinity TESOL, first degree and at least some relevant experience. The majority of job vacancies are in Italy.

Flying Cows, Nottingham (✆ +44 115 824 0824; www.flying-cows.com). Jobs in Korea, China, Vietnam, Colombia and Spain.

Footprints Recruiting (www.footprintsrecruiting.com). A proactive and principled teacher recruitment agency based in Vancouver, Canada with vacancies mostly in Korea and China but also in Abu Dhabi, and other countries.

Global Recruitment Solutions (UK) Ltd, Wales (✆ +44 77 9047 9238; recruitment@globalrecruitsolutions.co.uk or alison.recruitment@gmail.com; www.globalrecruitsolutions.co.uk). Sole proprietor,

Alison Morgan, interviews and places teachers in Saudia Arabia, UAE, Europe and Asia. University degree required plus a teaching qualification such as PGCE + QTS or CELTA/TEFL for ESL positions.

Global Teacher Recruitment, Johannesburg (✆ +27 11 052 2865; www.globalteacherrecruitment.com). Part of the Monkey Tree Group of schools in Hong Kong and China.

Gold Star TEFL Recruitment, Taiwan (teach@goldstarteachers.com or jim.althans@goldstarteachers.com; www.GoldStarTeachers.com). Independent English-owned TEFL recruitment agency filling vacancies for a variety of English schools across China and less often for Indonesia and Saudi Arabia.

Hunt ESL, part of the international training organisation Intesol (see next entry).

Intesol Worldwide Ltd, (✆ +44 208 144 1233; www.intesolteachabroad.com). Teaching practice follows Intesol training courses in franchise schools in Nicaragua and Vietnam. TEFL jobs arranged in China, Thailand, Korea and Indonesia, and internships in Thailand, China and India.

Language Solutions International, 11 Coldbath Square, London EC1R 5HL (✆ +44 20 7689 1900; jobsoverseas@langsols.com; www.langsolsint.com). Global network of privately owned schools that specialise in teaching working adults in industry (especially the energy industry); welcomes applications from highly qualified and experienced EFL teachers for Budapest, Baku (Azerbaijan), Algeria, Dubai, Madrid and Basra. Minimum requirement is a CELTA certificate.

My ESL Recruitment (+44 20 3582 3363; www.myeslrecruitment.com). Most vacancies are in Saudi Arabia but also elsewhere in the Middle and Far East.

Norwood English, Laois, Eire (✆ +353 57 875 6325; info@norwoodenglish.com; www.norwoodenglish.com/jobs). TEFL training centre in Ireland that places teachers in, for example, China, Vietnam, Thailand, Korea and Georgia, plus internships in India.

Prime Teachers International, York Science Park, Heslington, York YO10 5NP (✆ +44 1904 567673; info@primeteachers.com; www.primeteachers.com). UK-based recruitment consultancy for the education sector with vacancies in Turkey, the Middle East, China, nurseries in Moscow, etc. Recruitment manager is Georgina Tognola.

Reach To Teach, head office in Iowa, USA (✆ +1 201 467 4612; UK ✆ +44 20 3286 9794, Australia ✆ +61 2 8011 4516; www.ReachToTeachRecruiting.com). One of the largest human resource companies for teachers in Asia, primarily Korea, China, Taiwan and Vietnam. All services are free to teachers.

Red Chair, Co. Kerry, Ireland (Adrien@redchair.ie; www.redchairrecruitment.ie). Positions advertised in Saudi Arabia, Oman, Bahrain, Kuwait, Malaysia, China, Korea, Japan and Bangladesh.

Tamaki TEFL Recruitment (✆ +44 7534 121468; tomoka.teflrecruitment@outlook.com; www.tamakiteflrecruitment.co.uk). Jobs in Taiwan, China and Saudi Arabia.

Teachaway, Toronto and Vancouver, Houston and Edinburgh (www.teachaway.com). Recruits for employers in Korea, China, Japan, Taiwan, Saudi Arabia, Mexico, Kazakhstan and others. Appointed recruiters for state-qualified teachers to work in the public school system of Abu Dhabi among others.

Teaching Nomad, www.teachingnomad.com. Shanghai-based company recruits qualified ESL teachers for Asia (China, Taiwan, Singapore) and the Middle East (Saudi Arabia, Qatar, Oman and UAE).

Teach to Travel Ltd, Room 4, Third Floor, Duru House, 101 Commercial Road, London E1 1RD (✆ +44 20 096 1214/7193 2546; hr@teachtotravel.co.uk; www.teachtotravel.com). English teachers placed in Turkey, China, Saudi Arabia and Thailand. TEFL/CELTA and university degree required. General Manager is Fiona Mendoza, and director is Geoffrey Thomas.

TEFL Express, London WC1 (✆ +44 20 3287 7796; US: ✆ +1 347 497 6124; jobs@teflexpress.co.uk; www.teflexpress.co.uk). TEFL training course provider partnered with Language Link, EF, Wall Street English and other major employers. Recruitment and internships in Russia, China, Thailand, Hong Kong, Indonesia, etc. Candidates must be TEFL/CELTA trained; two years of experience is required for some positions.

TEFL Heaven, Experience Teaching Abroad Ltd., Weston super Mare (✆ +44 20 8133 3885; teachabroad@teflheaven.com; www.teflheaven.com). Hundreds of internships and paid jobs in Thailand, Vietnam, China, Costa Rica, Peru, Argentina, Mexico, Guatemala, Spain and Czech Republic normally after doing a 2-week or 4-week in-country TEFL training course.

TEFLOne (www.teflone.com). Since 2006, Taipei-based TEFLOne has been recruiting TEFL-certified teachers for Shane schools among others in Taiwan, Japan, China, Vietnam and Indonesia. Positions start every month in all countries, and teachers can be placed well in advance. Positions can be teaching young learners, adults or a combination. All positions offer a competitive salary with training, academic and welfare support and opportunities for career progression. TEFLOne carries out the whole recruitment process from pre-screening for visa/work permit eligibility, interviewing, reference checking, visa and flight liaison and arranging arrival time. Due to the requirements of the schools, TEFLOne can proceed only with teachers who are native English speakers from the UK, USA, Canada, South Africa, Ireland, Australia or New Zealand and holders of a recognised degree and a TEFL qualification. Most successful candidates will have completed an intensive 120-hour classroom-based TEFL course that includes at least six hours' observed teaching practice. Contact David Coles (david.coles@teflone.com) for more information.

TEFL UK, www.tefluk.com. Online TEFL training company owned and run by former TEFL teachers. Also recruits teachers for Taiwan, Thailand, China, Japan, Korea, Vietnam and Georgia (free placement) and for Colombia (£299 placement fee).

Trines, London (www.trines.co.uk). Energetic recruiter principally for China, Taiwan and Vietnam plus Kenya (see entry at beginning of Asia chapter).

VOLUNTARY, GAP YEAR AND RELIGIOUS ORGANISATIONS

Christians Abroad (✆ +44 300 012 1201; recruit@cabroad.org.uk; www.cabroad.org.uk). Ecumenical charity providing information and advice to people of any faith or none who are thinking of working overseas, whatever their circumstances, whether short or long-term, voluntary or paid. Occasional openings for TEFL teachers in India, Sri Lanka, Tanzania, Kenya and Cameroon.

VSO (Voluntary Service Overseas), 100 London Road, Kingston upon Thames KT2 6QJ (✆ +44 20 8780 7500; enquiry@vsoint.org; www.vsointernational.org). VSO is a professional organisation that works in 23 countries in Africa, Asia and the Pacific. It receives requests, including a very few in English language teacher training. Volunteer requirements vary but the usual commitment is two years. Most placements are for skilled and qualified professionals aged 18–75 from a variety of backgrounds. VSO recognises the Trinity TESOL and Cambridge CELTA qualifications. The VSO package for its volunteers includes airfares, medical cover, National Insurance contributions, rent-free accommodation and a modest salary in line with local pay rates. VSO also provides full in-country support including pre-departure training and briefing, basic language and cultural orientation on arrival prior to starting placement.

A number of companies charge school-leavers and others to arrange volunteer placements abroad, known as voluntourism, many of which are in schools where volunteers teach English. Several of those listed here are founder members of the Year Out Group (www.yearoutgroup.org), formed to promote well-structured gap year programmes.

BUNAC (✆ +44 33 3999 7516; www.bunac.org). Teaching internships in China, Thailand and Vietnam; volunteer teaching in Nepal and Thailand. Prices from £795 include 120-hour online TEFL course.

Global Crossroad, Irving, TX (✆ +1 866 205 6515; www.globalcrossroad.com). Volunteer teaching and internships in 18 countries, from Uganda to Peru. For volunteer programmes in many countries, application fee of $299 plus varying weekly fee.

Global Nomadic, London (✆ +44 20 7193 2652; www.globalnomadic.com). Tries to minimise costs in its placements worldwide, including paid teaching in Thailand, China, Czech Republic and Costa

Rica in conjunction with 4-week in-country training courses. Prices from £1,050 in Thailand (excluding accommodation) to £2,500 for 8-week training in Costa Rica. Volunteer teaching placements in Brazil, Nicaragua, Madagascar, Myanmar, Cambodia and other countries.

Greenheart Travel, Chicago (www.greenhearttravel.org). Cultural exchange organisation that arranges teaching jobs in South Korea, China, Myanmar, Thailand, Vietnam, Colombia and Italy. (Greenheart won top prize at the Global Youth Travel Awards 2016 as Outstanding Volunteer Project.)

Inspire Volunteer Abroad, Newbury (✆ +44 1635 285666; www.inspirevolunteer.co.uk). Volunteer teaching placements from two weeks to six months in India, Nepal, Cambodia, Romania, Peru and Thailand. Prefers older candidates with teaching experience. Costs are steep, starting from £1,225 for 2 weeks. All accommodation and some meals are included.

International Volunteer HQ, New Plymouth, New Zealand (✆ +64 6 758 7949; info@volunteerhq.org; www.volunteerhq.org). Short-term volunteer teaching in many countries for varying fees.

IST Plus, Crest House, 102–104 Church Road, Teddington, Middlesex TW11 8PY, UK (+44 20 7788 7877; www.istplus.com). IST Plus administers Teach in China and Teach in Thailand programmes (see respective chapters).

i-to-i Love TEFL, Suite 2, Chantry House, Victoria Road, Leeds, LS5 3JB (✆ +44 113 205 4610; www.i-to-i.com/tefl-jobs-abroad). TEFL/TESOL training provider that arranges paid TEFL internships in Vietnam and China and short voluntourism TEFL experiences in Thailand, Cambodia, Colombia and South Africa. Fees include TEFL training course combining 120-hour online study with 20-hour intensive weekend in a classroom (worth £249).

Lattitude Global Volunteering, 42 Queen's Road, Reading, Berkshire RG1 4BB (✆ +44 118 959 4914; volunteer@lattitude.org.uk; www.lattitude.org.uk). Overseas volunteering opportunities for 17–25 year olds, including teaching in Argentina, China, Ecuador and Vietnam. Posts are for between three and five months and cost the volunteer from £2,300 to £2,500 plus airfare, insurance and medical costs. Board, lodging and (sometimes) a living allowance are provided.

Love Volunteers, New Zealand (✆ +44 1865 522688; US: ✆ +1 416 800 4993; www.lovevolunteers.org). Voluntourism teaching in many countries worldwide including Albania, Brazil (new), Cambodia, Cameroon, Ethiopia and Honduras. Many countries, from Bangladesh to Malawi, let volunteers assist in schools.

Plan My Gap Year, Unit 2, Orchard Business Park, Furnace Lane, Horsmonden, Kent, TN12 8LX (✆ +44 1892 722720; www.planmygapyear.co.uk/english-teaching-programmes). Choice of volunteer teaching projects lasting 1–24 weeks in 11 countries including Morocco, Tanzania and Nepal. Prices for a fortnight are mainly £200–£400 plus registration fee of £149.

Projects Abroad, Aldsworth Parade, Goring, Sussex BN12 4TX (✆ +44 1903 708300; info@projects-abroad.co.uk; www.projects-abroad.co.uk). Sends up to 4,000 people abroad annually on a variety of projects in developing countries, with English teaching projects in Ethiopia, Peru, Sri Lanka and Madagascar, among many others. Projects start from two weeks in length, with an average volunteer spending three months. Three-month placements start at about £2,700, excluding travel costs but including accommodation, food, insurance and in-country support.

The Project Trust, Hebridean Centre, Ballyhough, Isle of Coll, Argyll PA78 6TE (✆ +44 1879 230444; info@projecttrust.org.uk; www.projecttrust.org.uk). Sends school leavers (aged 17–19) on TESOL gap years to Senegal, China, Japan, India, Nepal, Thailand and Honduras. Participants must fundraise to cover part of the cost of their 12-month placement, at present £6,200. Teaching in primary and secondary schools in many other countries from Malawi to the Dominican Republic.

Travellers Worldwide, 2A Caravelle House, 17/19 Goring Road, Worthing, West Sussex BN12 4AP (✆ +44 1903 502595; info@travellersworldwide.com; www.travellersworldwide.com). Provides teaching as well as many other work experience and volunteer placements worldwide, including some unusual countries such as Zambia and Borneo. Prices start from £795 for a short 2-week stint.

Travel to Teach (T2T), Thailand (www.travel-to-teach.org). Thai-based organisation that provides volunteer teaching opportunities (among others) in Thailand, Cambodia, Laos, Vietnam, China, Bali, Sri Lanka, Maldives, India, Costa Rica, Guatemala, El Salvador, Nicaragua and Mexico. Fees start at £436 for a month in Thailand.

Usit, 19/21 Aston Quay, Dublin 2, Ireland (✆ +353 1 602 1906; www.usit.ie). Programmes for paying volunteers that may involve teaching in India, Nepal, Ghana, Vietnam and Sri Lanka. Prices are from €669 for a fortnight. Also assists Irish nationals to obtain working holiday visas for Taiwan, Hong Kong and Argentina (workandtravel@usit.ie).

Volunteering Solutions (✆ +44 800 014 8160; info@volunteeringsolutions.com; www.volunteeringsolutions.com/teaching-volunteer-projects). Short teaching placements in dozens of countries in Africa, Asia and South America, from teaching monks in Chiang Mai (Thailand) to children in Kampala (Uganda). One week costs about £400. Agency is based near Delhi.

OPPORTUNITIES FOR NORTH AMERICANS

Although the companies, agencies and charities listed here are based in the USA and cater primarily to North Americans, Skype makes it commonplace for a US organisation to have clients in Europe (and vice versa). Recruitment agencies in the USA have stronger links with Latin America and the Far East than with Europe. As in Britain, some organisations are involved primarily with English-medium international schools following an American curriculum, and are looking to recruit state-certified teachers; these are listed separately at the end of this section.

A Broader View, Pennsylvania (✆ +1 215 780 1845; www.abroaderview.org). A non-profit active in 24 countries with teaching placements in most locations including Cameroon and the Galapagos. The price for eight weeks starts at US$1,640 (in Nicaragua).

Center for Intercultural Education and Development (CIED), Georgetown University, Washington, DC (✆ +1 800 308 7649; fellow@elprograms.org; www.elprograms.org). Administers the English Language Fellow Program on behalf of the US Department of State (see below). The 65 or so destinations include unusual countries such as Algeria, Mauritania and Turkmenistan.

CIEE (Council on International Educational Exchange), 300 Fore Street, Portland, ME 04101 (www.ciee.org/teach). Administers teaching in Chile, Peru, China, Spain, Czech Republic, Dominican Republic, Morocco, Senegal, South Korea, Vietnam and Thailand. Participants are placed in local schools where they teach English as volunteers or are compensated with a local salary and temporary or permanent housing. Sample programme fee for 5 months teaching in Senegal is $1,600 which includes 150-hour CIEE TEFL Certification course (valued at $1,000).

Fulbright English Teaching Assistant (ETA) Program, Institute of International Education, New York (✆ +1 212 984 5525; http://us.fulbrightonline.org/eta-program-charts or http://exchanges.state.gov/us/program/fulbright-english-teaching-assistant-program). Recent college graduates and young professionals are placed as English teaching assistants for 6–12 months in primary and secondary schools or universities overseas to improve foreign students' English language abilities and knowledge of the United States. Candidates must be American citizens, have a BA and knowledge of the host country's language.

Geovisions, Guilford, Connecticut (✆ +1 203 453 5838; www.geovisions.org). Volunteer teaching in Malta, Costa Rica, etc.; English tutoring in Brazil, Chile, France, Italy; and paid teaching in China, Korea, Thailand and Vietnam.

InterExchange, 161 Sixth Avenue, New York, NY 10013 (✆ +1 800 597 3675; workabroad@interexchange.org; www.interexchange.org/teach-english). Arranges homestays with 15 hours a week of

English tutoring of the family in France, Spain, Italy, Austria and Germany (for 1–3 months) or as a part-time language assistant in schools. Also paid EFL teaching posts in China, Thailand and Vietnam. Programme fees from $795 for live-in positions in Europe and varying fees for further afield.

LanguageCorps, Sudbury, MA (✆ +1 978 562 2100; toll-free (North America): +1 877 216 3267; www.languagecorps.com). Company offers 4-week TESOL training course in many places worldwide, and then job placement in South-East Asia, Latin America, etc.

Peace Corps, Washington, DC (✆ +1 855 855 1961; www.peacecorps.gov). TEFL has historically been one of the major programme areas of the Peace Corps, which currently has programmes in 64 countries. Just less than 40% of the 6,818 volunteers work in the education sector, with many involved in ELT. Volunteers, who must be US citizens, over age 18 and in good health, are sent on 27-month assignments. All expenses, including airfare and health insurance, are covered. Peace Corps volunteers teach at both secondary and university level, and some become involved with teacher training and curriculum development. It can take 9–12 months between application and departure. Education volunteers must have a college degree (not necessarily in education) and varying levels of experience of ESL tutoring one-to-one or classroom teaching.

Scotia Personnel, 6045 Cherry St, Halifax, NS B3H 2K4, Canada (✆ +1 902 422 1455; info@scotia-personnel-ltd.com; www.scotia-personnel-ltd.com). Teaching placements in Korea and China; live-in tutoring in France, Italy and Spain. Substantial service fee.

TESOL International Association, Alexandria, VA (✆ +1 703 836 0774; info@tesol.org; www.tesol.org). A key organisation for professional ESL/EFL teachers worldwide, TESOL is an association offering various publications and services to 12,000 members in 120 countries. Full individual membership costs $98 per year, or $60 for those who have been in the field for less than three years. Members can receive assistance from TESOL's Careers Service and attend the Job MarketPlace, an ESL/EFL job fair held during TESOL's annual convention. Teaching vacancies are published at careers.tesol. org/jobs.

TravelnStudy, Amherst, USA (www.travelnstudy.com/programs/europe). Opportunities for 18–22 year olds to travel, volunteer and tutor in Germany, Austria, Switzerland, Czech Republic and Poland. For example live-in-tutoring positions in Switzerland last 2-12 weeks and cost $500–$2,000.

US Department of State English Language Fellow Program, Washington DC (http://elprograms.org). The Department of State English Language Fellow Program sends US citizens abroad to enhance English language teaching capacity and foster mutual understanding between the US and other countries. Fellowship projects are 10-month assignments for US TESOL professionals who possess a graduate level degree (preferably MA TESOL) and a minimum two years of TESOL classroom experience. Through a unique cultural exchange experience, Fellows work directly with local teachers, students, and educational professionals at universities in more than 80 countries around the world. Participants receive a $30,000 stipend, allowances to cover housing, food and other costs while in country, plus round-trip international travel, among other benefits. In addition, the programme provides participants with a platform to experience different cultures and build skills that can enhance their TESOL careers. The US Department of State also maintains a website for teachers and learners of American English abroad at http://americanenglish.state.gov. The site carries links to their offices worldwide, including Regional English Language Offices (RELOs).

WorldTeach, Cambridge, MA (✆ +1 857 259 6646; www.worldteach.org). Non-profit organisation that provides college graduates with one-year contracts (EFL or ESL) in American Samoa, Colombia, Ecuador, Guyana, Namibia, the Marshall Islands, China, Bangladesh, Chile, Pohnpei (Micronesia) and Thailand. Summer programmes are available in Ecuador, Poland, Namibia, Morocco, Nepal, Micronesia and South Africa. Participants pay a volunteer contribution ranging from zero to $3,990; several programmes are fully funded by the host country including Samoa, the Marshall Islands and Micronesia.

As mentioned earlier in the introductory section about Red Tape, Americans are permitted to travel in continental Europe, known as the Schengen Area, for up to 90 days at a time in a six-month period. Some summer jobs as English teachers on language camps are shorter than 90 days, and tutors and counsellors do not require a work visa. In some countries like Germany, employers are able to help some nationalities with visas. For example when **Brandon Howard** was 22 and finishing up his last semester at Montana State University in global and multicultural studies, he came across vacancies with the German summer camp company LEOlingo on a work abroad website:

> ***My application process for LEOlingo was straightforward and dynamic. I was asked anything from how many children's songs do you know, to are you good at riding a horse? I had no previous English teaching experience per se, but had multiple years of backcountry guiding for youth. Work permits were not as difficult to obtain as I had originally thought. After working closely with my German boss we found that the proper steps could be taken once I had landed in Germany. At the foreigners' registration office I had to present all required documents such as my work contract and the €50 transaction fee.***

CERTIFIED TEACHERS

International schools around the world that follow a British/American curriculum or teach the International Baccalaureate (IB) diploma programme employ mainly QTS (Qualified Teacher Status) teachers. Some have ESL teachers with lesser qualifications to act as teaching assistants. *The Economist* magazine recently dug up some fascinating statistics about the boom in international schools which teach in English in non-Anglophone countries: 22 countries have more than 100 international schools, headed by the United Arab Emirates with 478, and China with 445. Jobs with these schools can come with high salaries and attractive perks.

Certified primary and secondary teachers who want to work in mainstream international schools abroad should be aware of the following agencies and organisations, which match qualified candidates with vacancies. Most of the hiring for primary and secondary schools abroad (often referred to in the American context as K–12: kindergarten to grade 12) is done at recruitment fairs included in the list below. The files of job-seekers are added to a database that can be consulted by recruiters, who then choose whom they want to interview. Candidates who successfully land a job abroad with the help of a US agency may have to pay a placement fee of $300–$600, though in some cases the employer underwrites this expense.

Council of International Schools, Leiden, Netherlands (EducatorRecruitment@cois.org; www.cois.org). Educator Recruitment Service for certified teachers (BEd or PGCE) with at least two years' teaching experience. The agency hosts at least one recruitment fair in London in January, and has a searchable database online of more than 700 accredited international schools.

Gabbitas Education, London SW1 (www.gabbitas.co.uk). Established for 144 years, Gabbitas maintains a register of qualified and experienced teachers available for teaching posts in South America, Europe, Asia, etc. Gabbitas generally recruits subject-specialist teachers for English-medium schools. It has offices in China, Japan, South Korea and Russia.

Global Education Logistics, Brentford, UK (www.globaleducationlogistics.com). Recruits QTS teachers for international schools worldwide.

International Schools Services, Princeton, NJ (www.iss.edu). Offers teaching opportunities for educators in private American and international schools around the world. ISS hosts three international recruitment centres (IRCs) annually, where interviews are conducted by international school administrators. Applicants must have a bachelor's degree and relevant K–12 experience. IRC registration materials are provided on approval of application.

Queen's University, Kingston, ON (ed.careers@queensu.ca; http://info.educ.queensu.ca/torf/index.php). Organises the Teachers' Overseas Recruiting Fair. Fair takes place in late January. Teacher certification required plus at least two years' K–12 teaching experience. Registration opens in September.

Search Associates (www.searchassociates.com). 11 job fairs worldwide for fully qualified primary and secondary teachers with relevant experience. Search Associates is not usually appropriate for TEFL teachers who have no school experience but offers information and placement assistance for teachers with at least some mainstream school experience (with pupils aged 3–18). Long-term positions only (one to three-year contracts, renewable).

Seek Teachers (www.seekteachers.com). Educational consultancy for international teaching jobs, mainly in primary and secondary schools, but also advertise some ESL teaching jobs mainly in the Far and Middle East.

Teach Anywhere (www.teachanywhere.com). Online recruiter of licensed teachers for positions worldwide, mostly in international schools.

Teacher Horizons (www.teacherhorizons.com). Online recruiter for international schools.

Teacher Recruitment International (Australia), Perth, Australia (www.triaust.com). Places teachers in primary and secondary school posts in international schools in Europe, Asia, the Middle East and, to a lesser extent, South America. Initial registration fee of A$77 but no placement fee.

University of Northern Iowa, Overseas Placement Service for Educators, Cedar Falls, IA (overseas.placement@uni.edu; www.uni.edu/placement/overseas). UNI is a non-profit organisation and it does not charge any placement fees to schools or teaching candidates. All-in registration fee for teachers is $50. Recruiting fair is held in early February. Educators must hold current certification in elementary or secondary education.

SPECULATIVE JOB HUNT

The vast majority of language schools do not publicise their vacancies internationally and instead depend on local adverts, word of mouth, personal contacts and direct approaches. Because there is quite a high turnover of staff in TEFL positions, a speculative job search has a better chance of success than in many other fields of employment, especially if you get the timing right. For a successful campaign, only two things are needed: a reasonable CV and a list of addresses of potential employers. But always bear in mind that the majority of language schools won't offer you work until they have interviewed you, normally via Skype if you are not in the country.

APPLYING IN ADVANCE

Most job-seekers set up an alert with their favourite TEFL job sites so they hear of new vacancies in their preferred destinations as soon as they are posted. Language school websites very often have a recruitment or 'work for us' icon, sometimes the only web page that is in English, and increasingly applications are invited online. As in all facets of modern life, social networks play a key role, and some prospective employers constantly update and post the newest positions available on Facebook or other social networks profiles. Customs differ. In France, for example, many companies ask for a 'motivation letter'. Many request a photo (which some consider a dubious practice).

The other essential ingredient is the names and contact details of language institutes. Each of the country chapters in this book provides such a list and recommends ways of obtaining other addresses, for example by contacting a federation of language schools (if there is one) or specialist recruiters in your destination country. Note that the embassy or British Council is unlikely to be able to help. For example in some countries the US embassy website states categorically that 'the US Embassy does not maintain a database, either formal or anecdotal, of English schools or recruitment agencies'. The most comprehensive source of addresses of language schools is usually the *Yellow Pages*, which in many cases can be consulted online. Just type 'Yellow Pages' and your destination country into a search engine and then search for 'Scuole di Lingue' in Italy, 'Jazykova Skola' in the Czech Republic and so on. Some countries are much better than others, for example, the online Portuguese *Yellow Pages* are very helpful whereas the Russian are not.

Of course it has to be stressed that accepting a job offer without meeting the employer face-to-face carries risks. In some cases, a language school has to be fairly desperate to hire a teacher it has never met for a vacancy that has never been advertised. On the other hand, job-hunting in situ is not a realistic possibility for everybody. If applying from home, it is a good idea to follow up any hint of interest with a request for a Skype chat.

Usually the online application form is very basic and has to be accompanied by your curriculum vitae (CV). Entire books and consultancy companies are devoted to showing people how to draw up an impressive CV (or résumé as it is called in the USA). But it is really just a matter of common sense. Obviously employers will be more inclined to take seriously a well-presented document than something scribbled on the back of a dog-eared envelope. Any relevant training or experience should be highlighted rather than submerged in the trivia about your schooling and hobbies. If you lack any TEFL experience, try to bring out anything in your past that demonstrates your 'people skills', such as voluntary work, group counselling, working with children, one-to-one remedial tutoring, etc., and your interest in (and ability to adapt to) foreign countries. If you are targeting one country, it would be worth drawing up a CV in the local language; **Judith Twycross** was convinced that her CV in Spanish was a great asset when looking for teaching work in Colombia. If you get the job, however, be prepared for your new employer to expect you to be able to speak the vernacular.

Personality and adaptability can be as important as educational achievements in TEFL, so anything that proves an aptitude for teaching and an extrovert personality will be relevant, especially if you are going after a job teaching children. This is easier to convey over Skype than in an online application form.

If your credentials are not the kind to wow school directors, it might still be worth sending off a batch of warm-up letters, stating your intention to present yourself in person a couple of weeks or months hence. Even if you don't receive a reply, such a strategy may stick in the mind of employers, as an illustration of how organised and determined you are.

INTERVIEWS

As with the CV, so at interview: highlight anything that is remotely connected with teaching even if it has nothing to do with the English language, and do it energetically and enthusiastically. Yet keenness will seldom be sufficient in itself. You don't have to be an intellectual to teach English; in fact the quiet bookish type is probably at a disadvantage. An amusing illustration of this is provided by **Robert Mizzi**'s description of his interview for the JET Programme in the Japan chapter.

DON'T HAVE A TEFL BACKGROUND?

Do a certain amount of research, e.g. acquaint yourself with some of the jargon such as 'notional', 'communicative-based', etc. It is not uncommon for an interviewer to ask a few basic grammar questions. To help you deal with this eventuality, see the list of recommended reading in the chapter on Preparation. Visit the ELT section of a bookshop to begin familiarising yourself with the range of materials on offer. Always have some questions ready to ask the interviewer, such as 'Do you favour the Oxford or Cambridge course books?', 'What audio materials do you have?' 'Do you encourage the use of songs?' or 'Do you teach formal grammar structures?'

An interesting post was published on a Teaching English in Berlin blog recently that set out some of the questions that you should have ready to ask at an interview. Don't be shy to ask the obvious:

- How much freedom will I have to plan classes?
- How many hours can I realistically expect to get?
- How many teachers do you employ?
- Is there a teacher's room or preparation area?
- Is there a photocopier?
- What resources are available?
- What's your teaching methodology?
- Is there any training or career development available?
- How much administration or paperwork will I have to do?
- How much is the pay? Is travel pay included?

You will certainly be asked how long you intend to stay and (depending on the time of year) nothing less than nine months will be considered. They will also want to know whether you have had any experience. With luck you will be able to say truthfully that you have (at least) taught at a summer school in Britain or elsewhere (again, see chapter on Preparation). Some applicants who are convinced that they can do a good job make a similar claim, untruthfully, knowing that at the lower end of the TEFL spectrum this will never be checked. If you have done a TEFL course of any description, be sure to take along the certificate, however humble the qualification. Even schools in far-flung places are becoming increasingly familiar with the distinctions between various qualifications and are unlikely to confuse a Cambridge certificate with an anonymous distance learning 'certificate'. In Asia especially, nothing short of the original will do for the purposes of obtaining a visa, since there are so many counterfeit copies around.

If you have a university degree, be sure to take the certificate along. Even if the interviewer is prepared to take your word for it, the school administration may need the document at a later stage either to give you a salary increment or to obtain a work permit. If needed for a work permit, prepare to pay to have the document notarised or apostilled (legally authenticated). **Adam Hartley**, who taught English in China, hadn't realised that his MA would have earned him a higher salary; although he arranged for two separate copies to be sent from Britain, neither arrived and he had to be content with the basic salary. Americans should take along their university transcripts; any school accustomed to hiring Americans will be familiar with these. Also take along any references; something written on headed paper will always impress, even if your previous jobs were not in teaching.

While smart casual dress, neither flashy nor scruffy, may be appropriate for an interview in Britain, something more formal might be called for in certain cultures, such as France or Japan. Even if all your friends laugh when you pack a suit before going abroad, you may find it a genuine asset when trying to outdo the competition. As **Steven Hendry**, who has taught English both in Japan and Thailand with none of the usual advantages apart from traveller's canniness, says:

> ***You may not need a tailor-made suit but you definitely need to be able to present a conservative and respectable image.***

Increasingly, interviews for teaching posts are conducted over Skype, where you should take just as much care to dress smartly and be prepared with knowledge of the potential employer and pertinent questions to ask. Make sure you choose a quiet, well-lit place and look into your webcam throughout. If the interview touches on the terms of service, make notes as soon as you can. Often there are disappointing discrepancies between what is promised in the early stages and what is delivered; at least if these things have been discussed at interview, you will be in a stronger bargaining position if the conditions are not met.

Unrealistic expectations are a genuine hazard when contemplating an exciting stint of working abroad. A recruitment consultant in the field offers the following sensible advice:

> ***Teachers should be made aware that they are being employed to do a professional job and it is hard work and long hours. They should not underestimate the cultural differences even in countries they think they know. These often lead to misunderstandings and dissatisfied teachers. I am also constantly surprised by teachers who take jobs without knowing the first thing about the place, the job, the sort of classes they will have, etc. They should make a checklist of questions and if they are making applications on their own they should ask to speak to teachers who are there at the time or who have just left.***

Emily Handler realised that she had inflated notions of what her role would be in the classroom when she first arrived in Hungary:

> ***The idea of being a primary school 'conversational English teacher' was misleading for me, or maybe I was just too optimistic. I assumed I would be having conversations with the students. Imagine my reaction when I asked 'How are you today?' and a student answered, after a great amount of thought, 'It's Tuesday!' (plus, it was Wednesday). I think a job title like 'vocabulary builder and oral English practice teacher' would have been clearer to me.***

Research is the key. You wouldn't apply for a job in the UK without knowing quite a lot about it so why do so when you're going to another country? Online reviews are becoming an increasingly valuable tool for assessing potential employers. Ferret out feedback on forums such as www.eslcafe.com, www.eslwatch.info and www.gooverseas.com. The site www.reddit.com/r/TEFL carries employer reviews/complaints and a busy TEFL forum. In some cases, an old hand will have set up an online blacklist where this kind of inside information can be obtained. Be aware that notoriously bad employers can be slippery and pay certain sites to take down negative reviews or flood the internet with phony positive feedback. Occasionally, an embassy or consulate will assist, as in the case of the US Embassy in Seoul, which keeps a file of language schools about which it has received persistent complaints. But the best way is to ask around in the expat teaching community.

ON THE SPOT

It is almost impossible to fix up a job in advance in some countries, due to the way the TEFL business operates. For example, written applications to the majority of language schools in Ecuador or Peru or Vietnam would be mostly a waste of time since the pool of expat teachers and travellers on the spot is usually sufficient. Even in countries such as Spain and Germany, for which adverts appear in the UK, the bulk of hiring is done on the spot.

When you arrive in a likely place, your initial steps might include some of the following.

- Check online classified job ads on Craigslist, Gumtree, Kijiji or the local equivalent.
- Transcribe a list of schools from the *Yellow Pages*.
- Look for local English language papers and magazines, such as *FUSAC* in Paris.
- Check noticeboards in likely locations such as the British Council, US Embassy/Cultural Centres, universities, TEFL training centres, English language bookshops (where you should also check which EFL materials are stocked) or hostels which teacher-travellers frequent.
- Keep your ears open when you frequent favourite expat haunts, such as the Irish pubs in town.

Make sure that your CV is in a format that you can easily tweak to target specific employers. A reconnaissance trip is a good idea if possible, although **Andrew Whitmarsh** didn't even realise he was looking for a new job, when one found him in Indonesia:

> ***As often happens, I didn't find my job, my job found me. I was standing on top of a volcano in Indonesia when a gentleman in my hiking group asked me what I did for a living. Upon my reply of 'English Teacher', he declared that this was wonderful news to hear and he had just the job for me. The gentleman just happened to be the President Director of Wall Street Institute – and he needed teachers.***

With a little more purpose and a little less serendipity, **Fiona Paton** found a job teaching English in France. On her way back from a summer holiday in Spain, she broke her return journey in Vichy long enough to distribute her CV to several language schools, which resulted in a job for the academic year.

After compiling a list of potential employers, phone the schools and try to arrange a meeting with the director or director of studies (DOS). Even if an initial chat does not result in a job offer, you may learn something about the local TEFL scene, which will benefit you at the next interview, especially if you ask lots of questions. You might also be able to strike up a conversation with one of the foreign teachers, who could turn out to be a valuable source of information about that school in particular and the situation generally. It is very common to have to begin with just a few hours a week. Make it clear that you are prepared to stand in at short notice for an absent teacher. The longer you stay in one place, the more hours will come your way and the better your chances of securing a stable contract.

This gradual approach also gives you a chance to discover which are the fly-by-night schools, something that is difficult to do before you are on the scene. Disreputable profit-hungry schools flourish in Europe just as they do in other parts of the world. It is not always easy to distinguish them, though if a school sports a sign 'Purrfect Anglish' you are probably not going to need an MA in Applied Linguistics to get a job there. Working for a cowboy outfit may not be the end of the world, though it often spells trouble, as the 'Problems' chapter will reveal. But without many qualifications you may not have much choice.

FREELANCE TEACHING

Private English lessons are usually more lucrative than contract teaching simply because there is no middleman. Learners may prefer them as well, not only because of the more personal attention they receive in a private lesson but because it costs them less. As a private tutor working from your own home, your students' homes or a neutral space like a quiet café or park, you can undercut the big schools with their overheads. But at the same time you deprive yourself of the advantages of working for a decent school: access to resources and equipment, in-service training, social security schemes and holiday pay. The life of a freelance teacher can be quite a lonely one. Usually teachers working for a school take on a small amount of private teaching to supplement their income, provided this is allowed in their contract. Most employers do not mind unless your private teaching is interfering with your school schedule or (obviously) if you are pinching potential clients from your employer.

In order to round up private students, you will have to sell yourself as energetically as any salesperson. **Pete**, a blogger from Bratislava, shared some of his tips for making a good impression on new clients and keeping them coming at http://pete-teaches-in-bratislava.blogspot.co.uk. He recommends offering the first lesson at a discounted price, having credible references available on request, arranging meeting times and places to suit the convenience of students, and trying to be engaging and enthusiastic throughout. He also advises that you should gauge students' language level at the first meeting, which will give you the tools to tailor a personalised 'syllabus' for them.

You should be familiar enough with different course books to choose a suitable one for their level. No language learner wants to pay to listen to a native speaker just chat, so try to offer structured lessons and do far more listening than talking.

SELF-PROMOTION IS ESSENTIAL

Steven Hendry *plastered neatly printed bilingual notices all over town in Chiang Mai in Northern Thailand.*
Ian McArthur *made a large number of posters (in Arabic and English) and painstakingly coloured in the Union Jack by hand in order to attract attention in Cairo. (Unfortunately these were such a novelty that many posters were pinched.)*

Putting a notice on appropriate noticeboards (in schools, universities, public libraries, popular supermarkets) and running an advertisement on a local community website, such as www.expat.ru in Moscow or www.portaportese.it in Rome should put you in touch with a few hopeful language learners. You will also need a reliable mobile phone and frequent access to your email. Once you've made a good start, word will spread and more paying students will come your way, though it can be a slow process. Specialist language tutor search sites may be of help such as www.angoltanarok.com in Budapest or www.getstudents.net in Japan. Creating a profile on these sites is usually not expensive. A site that operates internationally is http://findmyfavouriteteacher.com, where you can post your bio and the prices you charge for a discounted trial lesson and for normal lessons.

Counterbalancing the advantages of higher pay and a more flexible schedule are many disadvantages. Everyone, from lazy Taiwanese teenagers to busy Barcelona businessmen, cancels or postpones one-to-one lessons with irritating frequency. People who have taught in Latin countries complain that the problem is chronic. Cancellations among school and university students especially escalate at exam time. It is important to agree on a procedure for cancellations that won't leave you out of pocket. Although it is virtually impossible to arrange to be paid in advance, you can request 24 hours' notice of a cancellation and mention politely that if they fail to give due warning you will insist on being paid for the missed lesson. But you can't take too tough a line, since your clients are paying above the odds for your flexibility. Another consideration is the unpaid time spent travelling between clients' homes and workplaces.

If you are more interested in integrating with a culture than in making money, exchanging conversation for board and lodging may be an appealing possibility. This can be set up by answering (or placing) small ads in appropriate places (the American Church in Paris noticeboard is famous for this). **Hannah Start**, a school-leaver from Merseyside, put up a notice at her local English language school indicating that she wanted to exchange English conversation for accommodation in Paris; a businesswoman on an intensive English course contacted her and invited her to stay with her.

ONLINE TEACHING

With more and more people having fast internet connections and not enough time (or money) to attend in-person lessons, online learning is a fast-growing market. New technologies make it straightforward to be beamed into a classroom on the other side of the world via Google Hangouts, which allow up to 10 people to join in a video call. The march to online teaching is relentless and the demand for tech-savvy online teachers rising exponentially. **Leah Morawiec** thinks it's simple:

> ***All you need is a good Internet connection and you're set. Most people want only conversations. It's a great option for people without cars, or those who want to fill in their schedule, or teach in their pjs. Looking for a school? Try mine: www.talkback.pl. Having your own company is great but it's a ton of work. You have to find the work yourself, advertise, have a website, make invoices, etc.***

Venerable companies such as Berlitz are expanding in that direction and now recruit for their Berlitz Virtual Classroom. Teaching by Skype, other online platforms or even via a chatting-app such as NiceTalk Tutor is now a common way to supplement a teaching income or even as a full-time job. A growing number of companies, such as Learnlight, SpeakPlus, FluentU and Learnship (for business English), have created marketplaces that connect language learners with tutors or coaches. Thirteen companies had adverts for online teachers on www.tefl.com at the time of writing, which is an attractive prospect if you can choose your own hours, rates of pay and teaching style. After being accepted as an online teacher, you normally start by creating a profile for yourself, then fix your price and think of ways to attract students by promoting yourself on the site.

A well-researched and valuable article on the subject by insider **Ruth Sheffer** was recently published on Jimmy's ESL blog (http://jimmyesl.com/teach-english-online/want-online-english-teacher), part of which is reproduced here, with permission:

> ***Every day more and more companies pop up promising lots of students and 'easy money'. Remember, most of the companies are actually more interested in taking a commission from you than providing an educational service, and many will offer you incentives if you sign up more teachers, which means more competition over available students. Some sites use their own platform and others allow you to use whichever communication method you choose. Some have a fixed pay rate, while others allow you to fix your own hourly rates. It is often really hard to find how much commission these companies take, as the rates are hidden on the websites in the terms and conditions, and not published in a clear way. Most seem to take 15%. Some companies are web-based only, while others also have an app, or are primarily smartphone-based. The latest fashion seems to be to offer immediate availability for chats with any native speakers online, and not really proper lessons with qualified teachers ... Your technological skills will come into play. How much do you know about Google Docs, RealtimeBoard and Zoom? There are many ways to share your screen and many online teaching tools you will need to master if you are going to stand out from the thousands of other online teachers already out there.***

The article goes on to compare the advantages and drawbacks of teaching for some of the main companies, including the big player iTalki (based in China, as many are), Verbling, VerbalPlanet and Cafetalk. The author also mentions a number of other sites that pay a fixed (low) hourly rate, such as Cambly ($10.20), Lingoda (€8.50), Skimatalk (from $14), Topica Native ($10) and TutorABC ($8) – rates of pay that might be acceptable to new teachers looking for experience.

PREPARATION

The preceding chapters on ELT training and job-hunting set out ways in which you can make yourself more attractive to potential employers. One of the best ways in which to prepare for a stint of teaching abroad is to teach English locally. Relevant experience can usually be gained by volunteering to tutor language learners in your home town; this is particularly feasible in the USA, where literacy programmes take place on a massive scale. It might also be a good idea to contact the director of a local commercial language school and ask to sit in on some lessons and to talk to teachers. A polite note expressing your interest in TEFL would probably meet with a positive response. EFL teachers are like everyone else; they are experts at what they do and don't mind sharing that knowledge with interested outsiders.

SUMMER CAMPS ABROAD

More prolonged exposure to TEFL can best be gained by working at a language summer school in the UK or a language summer camp abroad. **Rona Mackenzie**, who taught English in Southern Spain for a few years, started this way:

> *My first ESL teaching post was a fun, but gruelling, eight-week summer school in the south of England, where I cut my teeth. It was a baptism of fire, but something I would recommend. I didn't have to deal with a new country and a new language, as well as my first teaching job. Teaching classes of 14 unruly teenagers as a new teacher wasn't easy, but it was an invaluable experience. Next came the real deal. A move to Spain, a new job, a new life.*

You don't have to confine your hunt for a summer teaching post to the UK either. Summer camps that combine English tuition with sports and activities are held from the mountains of Romania to the Basque country. **Emma Lander** is another graduate who wanted to test the TEFL waters by accepting a summer position in the middle of a Finnish forest next to a lake:

> *I recommend working at a summer school if you're new to TEFL and you're not sure about it as a career. The informal approach to work and the freedom you are given in the classroom is an excellent way to ease in to teaching and see if it's right for you.*

Emma's employer was Nordic School (see entry in Scandinavia chapter).

This is the way **Ross O'Brien** from Ireland also started out, but at the opposite end of Europe, in Andalucía:

> *A word of advice: teaching English is a challenging, demanding job and I'd recommend working in a summer camp before you commit to a year round contract in an academy. My summer experience in TECS proved invaluable, and I really felt confident in my abilities starting in Blue Door, despite the fact they offer very different things.*

Both TECS and the Academia Blue Door have entries in the directory of employers following the Spain chapter.

UK SUMMER SCHOOLS

Language courses take place throughout the British Isles in the summer, especially in tourist areas. It is estimated that there are 600–800 English language schools in operation in Britain during July and

August, mainly catering for foreign students, especially from France, Spain, Italy and other EU countries, and increasingly from further afield, such as Russia and Turkey. Many of these schools advertise heavily in the spring, e.g. 'Teach English on the English Riviera'. Quality varies of course. The British Council has an accreditation scheme and a searchable database at www.educationuk.org/english, which allows you to search by region and type, e.g. junior vacation courses in Southern England. Schools are located throughout the UK including Wales and Scotland, but are concentrated in the South East, Oxford, Cambridge and coastal resorts such as Bournemouth and Hastings.

Newly qualified EFL teachers are often hired for these summer positions which not only provide a chance to find out whether you will enjoy English teaching for a longer period, but may put you in touch with people who are well informed on overseas possibilities. The pace is likely to be hectic with a full programme of extracurricular activities which might include anything from producing a magazine to chaperoning trips to the theatre in Stratford. Resources may be limited, though not many of the kind of employer **Marta Eleniak** found herself working for some time ago have survived:

> ***I have got nothing good to say about my employer. We were expected to do nearly everything including perform miracles, with no support and pathetic facilities. I can only liken it to being asked to entertain 200 people for four hours with a plastic bowl. The pupils got a raw deal too because of false promises made to them.***

She does admit though, that it was on the basis of this three-week job that she got a job in a Madrid language school.

Recruitment of summer teachers gets underway in the new year and is usually well advanced by Easter. The short-term nature of the teacher requirements means that schools sometimes have difficulties finding enough qualified staff. Wages are higher than for most seasonal summer jobs. The average starting salary for teachers with a TEFL certificate is about £300–£400 per week in addition to board and lodging at residential schools, and some salaries top £450 a week. Time off is normally non-existent in these intensive summer schools, and you may be asked to sign a waiver form regarding the 48-hour maximum working week. Since most schools are located in popular tourist destinations, private accommodation can be prohibitively expensive and the residential option attractive. Without a TEFL certificate or any TEFL background it is easier to get taken on as a non-teaching sports and activities supervisor, which at least would introduce you to the world of TEFL. EFL teachers must expect a number of extracurricular activities such as chaperoning a group of over-excited adolescents to a West End theatre or on an art gallery visit. In most cases, you will be required to obtain an enhanced DBS criminal records check.

Some of the major language course organisations that offer a large number of summer vacancies are listed below.

Anglo Continental Educational Group, 29–35 Wimborne Road, Bournemouth BH2 6NA (✆ +44 1202 557414; jhaine@anglo-continental.com; www.anglo-continental.com).

Anglophile Academics, 140–144 Freston Road, London W10 6TR (✆✪+44 20 7603 1466; tutors@anglophiles.com; www.anglophiles.com). Teachers needed for summer camps and schools in England plus Ireland and Europe.

Ardmore Language Schools, Hall Place, Berkshire College, Burchetts Green, Maidenhead, Berkshire SL6 6QR (✆ +44 1628 826699; jobs@theardmoregroup.com; www.theardmoregroup.com or www.ardmore-language-schools.com/working_for_ardmore.aspx). Successful applicants will be DBS-checked to work in one of about a dozen residential summer centres.

Bell Summer Schools, Red Cross Lane, Cambridge CB2 0QU (✆ +44 1223 275594; jobs.uk@bellenglish.com). Schools in Cambridge and St Albans, plus Oxfordshire and Berkshire. Pay rate for CELTA-holder from £375 per week plus statutory holiday pay.

Concorde International Summer Schools, Arnett House, Hawks Lane, Canterbury, Kent CT1 2NU (✆ +44 1227 453315; recruitment@concorde-int.com; www.concorde-int.com/recruitment).

Discovery Summer, 33 Kensington High St, London W8 5EA (✆ +44 20 7937 1199; www.discoverysummer.co.uk/employment.php). EFL teachers for various locations in England such as Radley (Oxfordshire) and Shrewsbury (Shropshire).

EC English Language Centres (www.ecenglish.com/en/work-for-ec). International company with UK summer schools in Brighton, London, Oxford, Cambridge, Bristol and Manchester. Teaching rate of about £16 per hour (including holiday pay).

EF Language Travel, 22 Chelsea Manor Street, London SW3 5RL (✆ +44 20 7341 8612; www. ef.co.uk/summer-jobs). Centres in Oxford, Torbay, Brighton, Hastings, London, etc.

EJO, Eagle House, Lynchborough Road, Passfield, Hampshire GU30 7SB (✆ +44 1428 751549; www.ejo.co.uk/work-with-us).

Embassy English (http://jobs.embassysummer.com). Teachers and other staff needed for 2–8 weeks at many summer schools. Also summer teaching jobs at three Embassy Academies.

Harrow House, Harrow Drive, Swanage, Dorset BH19 1PE (✆ +44 1929 424421; www.harrowhouse.com).

Kent School of English, 10 and 12 Granville Road, Broadstairs, Kent CT10 1QD (✆ +44 1843 874870; enquiries@kentschool.co.uk; www.kentschoolofenglish.com).

LAL UK Summer Schools, Conway Road, Paignton, Devon TQ4 5LH (✆ +44 1803 558555; jobs.england@lalgroup.com; careers.lalschools.com). Summer schools held in Tavistock, Taunton, Winchester, Brighton, Berkhamsted and Twickenham. Up to £350 per week.

OISE Youth Language Schools, OISE House, Binsey Lane, Oxford OX2 0EY (✆ +44 1865 258346; ylsrecruit@oise.com; www.oiserecruitment.com). 120 summer teaching jobs at 11 summer schools.

Oxford International, 259 Greenwich High Road, London SE10 8NB (www.oxfordinternational.com/recruitment). 800 teachers, activity leaders, etc.

Pilgrims Young Learners, 38 Binsey Lane, Oxford, OX2 0EY (✆ +44 1865 258336; recruitment@pilgrims.co.uk; www.pilgrims.co.uk).

Plus International, 8–10 Grosvenor Gardens, London SW1W 0DH (✆ +44 20 7730 2223; recruitment@plus-ed.com; www.plus-ed.com). 120 summer teaching positions in the UK plus Dublin. Non-residential pay of £13–£18 per hour.

Project International, 19 Catherine Place, London SWIE 6DX (✆ +44 20 7916 2522; recruitment@projectinternational.uk.com; www.projectinternational.uk.com/employment). Jobs at 10 centres from Dover to Brecon.

Stafford House Study Holidays, 19 New Dover Road, Canterbury, Kent CT1 3AS (✆ +44 1227 811506; recruitment@staffordhouse.com; www.staffordhouse.co.uk). Part of Cambridge Education Group, with 14 centres. Recruitment season opens in January.

SUL Language Schools, 31 Southpark Road, Tywardreath, Par, Cornwall PL24 2PU (✆ +44 1726 814227; claires@sul-schools.com; www.sul-schools.com/teachers). Base pay for starting teachers £258 per week, £278 with CELTA/TESOL.

Thames Valley Summer Schools, 13 Park Street, Windsor, Berkshire SL4 1LU (✆ +44 1753 852001; recruit@thamesvalleysummer.co.uk; www.thamesvalleysummer.co.uk/working-for-us.aspx). Salary from £365 per week for CELTA/TESOL certified teachers.

XUK, 48 Fitzalan Road, Finchley, London N3 3PE (✆ +44 20 8371 9686; www.xukcamps.com/jobs). Two residential summer camps in East Anglia (Ipswich and Attleborough, Norfolk). £325–£375.

Roberta Wedge found that working for a large summer school organisation was not only good preparation for a teaching contract in Italy, but was fun for its own sake:

> ***The big language mills in Britain are a good way to see the country. I signed up with OISE in Exeter because I wanted to tramp the moors. It's possible to spend the whole summer jumping around fortnightly from contract to contract, all arranged ahead of time through the same organisation.***

WHILE YOU'RE WAITING

After you have secured a job abroad, there may be a considerable gap which will give you a chance to organise the practicalities of moving overseas and to prepare yourself in other ways. If you are going to a country that requires immigration procedures your employer can start the visa procedures. You may have to do a lot of running around to embassies, getting your degree certificate legally endorsed, getting police clearance (ACPO or DBS disclosure, in the UK). In addition to deciding what to take and how to get to your destination, you should think about your tax position and health insurance, plus find out as much as you can about the situation in which you will find yourself.

If you are entering the world of TEFL as a beginner, you might want to get a little experience. While still in his home town of Portsmouth, and before taking up his gap year placement in China, **James Butcher** showed considerable enterprise:

> ***I volunteered at a local primary school so that I had an idea of how the classroom environment worked and it also gave me ideas on how to control and motivate the class. I also had the chance to work with a Moldovan lady living in England and I helped her develop her English.***

If finding local opportunities is difficult, go online to teaching sites such as Verbling, LRNGO or iTalki where you might be able to fix up some online teaching experience. You might be able to host a language learner in your house and get paid handsomely for it, provided you have a TEFL qualification. InTuition Languages (www.intuitionlang.com), partnered with International House, offers payment of £430–£1,000 a week for offering full board and lodging and 15–30 hours of tuition a week to a client.

ELT professionals should consider joining the International Association of Teachers of English as a Foreign Language (IATEFL, Kent; www.iatefl.org). Membership, which costs £57 to individuals, £37 to students or retirees and £176 to institutions, entitles teachers to various services including six magazines annually and access to special interest groups, job alerts, conferences, workshops and symposia.

The more information you can find out about your future employer the better. **Kathy Panton** thinks that she would have been a more effective teacher in her first year in the Czech Republic if she had asked more probing questions beforehand:

> ***Now that I have a better idea of what to teach I think I could handle it, but a first-year teacher should ask a lot of questions; such as, what books the students have used, teacher continuity, very detailed report of what the students can do (as opposed to what they have studied), and most of all what they will be expected to accomplish during the school year. If the report is vague, I don't think anyone should take the job unless they are really confident that they'll be able to develop the framework themselves. I would look for a school that said something like, 'You'll guide the students through Hotline 1 textbook, and also give them extra vocabulary and speaking exercises to supplement the text. You'll also work with a phonics text for a few weeks, because these students have poor pronunciation. You'll probably find it useful to bring some old magazines but the school has several ESL textbooks already.' This would show that the school takes both curriculum and organisation seriously.***

An invaluable source of information is someone who has taught at the school before; ask your employer for a couple of email addresses or (better) phone numbers. Obviously these contacts are best followed up at an early stage before you have committed yourself to the job. Once you know where you are going, you can try to cultivate an online acquaintance with your future colleagues who will be in a position to pass on priceless minutiae, not only recommending pubs, bakeries, etc., but (if the accommodation is tied to the job) to arrive early and avoid the back bedroom because of the noisy plumbing or to take your wellies since winter rains turn the streets to rivers.

CONTRACTS

This is the point at which a formal contract or at least an informal agreement should be drawn up. Any employer who is reluctant to provide something in writing is definitely suspect. Horror stories abound of the young unsuspecting teacher who goes out to teach overseas and discovers no pay, no accommodation and maybe even no school. For this reason you should not only sign a contract but also have a good idea about what you are committing to.

WHAT A CONTRACT SHOULD COVER

The following items should be covered in a contract or at least given some consideration.

- *Name and address of employer.*
- *Details of the duties and hours of the job. (A standard load might be 24 contact teaching hours a week, plus three hours on standby to fill in for an absent teacher, fill all the board markers in the staff room, etc.).*
- *The amount and currency of your pay. Is it adequate to live on? How often are you paid? Is any money held back? Can it be easily transferred into sterling or dollars? What arrangements are there if the exchange rate drops suddenly or the local currency is devalued?*
- *The length of the contract and whether it is renewable.*
- *Help with finding and paying for accommodation. If accommodation is not provided free, is your salary adequate to cover this? If it is, are utilities included? Does the organisation pay for a stay in a hotel while you look for somewhere to live? How easy is it to find accommodation in the area? If it is unfurnished what help do you get in providing furniture? Can you get a salary advance to pay for this and for any rent deposits?*
- *Your tax liability.*
- *Provisions for health care and sick pay.*
- *Payment of pension or national insurance contributions.*
- *Bonuses, gratuities or perks.*
- *Days off, statutory holidays and vacation times.*
- *Paid flights home if the contract is outside Europe, and mid-term flights if you are teaching for two years.*
- *Luggage and surplus luggage allowance at the beginning and end of the contract.*
- *Any probationary period and the length of notice which you and the employer must give.*
- *Penalties for breaking the contract and circumstances under which the penalties would be waived (e.g. extreme family illness, etc.).*

Obviously any contract should be studied carefully before signing. It is a wise precaution to make a photocopy of it before returning to avoid what happened to **Belinda Michaels**, whose employer in Greece refused to give her a copy when she started to dispute some points. In some cases the only contract offered will be in a foreign language (e.g. Arabic or Kazakh) and you will either have to trust your contact at the school for a translation or consider obtaining an independent English translation. **Amanda Moody** signed documents that were only in Japanese and later found out that she'd been diddled out of her end-of-year bonus.

HEALTH AND INSURANCE

Increasingly, the immigration authorities abroad will not grant a teacher a work permit until they have provided a medical certificate. Many countries such as Russia and Korea may insist on an HIV test and various other health checks, including for syphilis and tuberculosis. General practitioners (GPs) and clinics make a charge, often a hefty one, for carrying out these tests, whether you do it before you leave home or after arrival.

Reputable schools will make the necessary contributions into the national health insurance and social security scheme. Even if you are covered by a national scheme, however, you may find that there are exclusion clauses such as dental treatment, non-emergency treatment, prescription drugs, etc., or you may find that you are covered only while at work. Private travel insurance can be very expensive. Travel insurance companies offer a standard rate that covers medical emergencies and a premium rate that covers personal baggage, cancellation, etc. On a 12-month travel policy, expect to pay roughly £20–£25 per month for barebones cover and £35–£40 for more extensive cover. One of the cheapest policies is offered by Coe Connections International (www.coeconnections.co.uk), which offers 12 months of basic cover for just £166. Unusually, it can be purchased or extended after you have left home. Note that annual travel policies do not cover a single long stay, but will cover a number of trips with a maximum stay of 30 or 70 days or whatever the limit is.

Within Europe private insurance is not absolutely essential because European nationals are eligible for reciprocal emergency health care within the EEA. It is most unlikely that this will be withdrawn after the UK leaves the EU, although it is not known whether Britons will still be entitled to acquire the European Health Insurance Card (EHIC) which they are at present, and which simplifies the process for EU citizens to obtain emergency health care in any member state, but does not cover repatriation in the case of a serious problem. Specialist expatriate policies might be worth investigating, though these may exceed £400 for one year. Bespoke insurance policies can be drawn up by brokers such as Campbell Irvine (www.campbellirvine.com). Off-the-peg policies are of course cheaper – try Insure and Go (www.insureandgo.com) or Direct Travel Insurance (www.direct-travel.co.uk). MoneySupermarket.com allows you to compare lots of travel insurers.

The EHIC scheme entitles European citizens to free medical treatment in public hospitals within the 28 EU (eventually 27) member states, plus Iceland, Liechtenstein, Norway and Switzerland. You can apply online for it via the NHS or by phone (✆ +44 300 3301350) quoting your National Insurance number. The card is free, so be careful to use an official site such as www.nhs.uk/ehic, avoiding the tricksters who put up official-looking sites but charge a fee. Even if your employer will be paying into a health scheme, cover may not take effect immediately and it is as well to have the ordinary tourist cover for the first three months.

No matter what country you are heading for, you should check the travel advice available from the NHS. The Department of Health has discontinued its leaflet *Health Advice for Travellers* but go to www.nhs.uk/healthcareabroad for links to country-by-country information. Increasingly, people are carrying out their own health research on the internet; check, for example, www.fitfortravel.nhs.uk and www.travelhealth.co.uk. The website of the World Health Organization (www.who.int/ith) has lots of information, including a listing of the very few countries in which certain vaccinations are a requirement of entry, primarily a Yellow Fever certificate, if you are travelling from an affected country.

A company that has become one of the most authoritative sources of travellers' health information in Britain is MASTA (www.masta-travel-health.com). It maintains a database of the latest information on the disease situation for all countries and the latest recommendations on the prevention of tropical and other diseases. Customers can book a telephone consultation or visit one of MASTA's travel clinics that administer inoculations (see website for prices) and sell medical kits and other specialist equipment like water purifiers, mosquito nets and repellents. Note that arguably the advice errs on the side of caution (which means it also makes more profit). A worldwide searchable listing of specialist travel clinics is maintained by the International Society of Travel Medicine (www.istm.org) although many cities and some countries are not included.

NATIONAL INSURANCE CONTRIBUTIONS, SOCIAL SECURITY AND PENSIONS

Nationals of the European Economic Area (EEA) countries working in another member state are covered by European Social Security regulations. Information about national social security arrangements in Europe can be read online at http://ec.europa.eu/social/main.jsp. Similarly, contributions made in any EEA country count towards benefit entitlement when you return home. The UK also has social security agreements with other countries including Croatia, Israel, Jamaica, Turkey and the USA, so some commentators are confident that cooperation with EU countries will survive Brexit. The international section of the Department for Work and Pensions at Newcastle (helpline ✆ +44 191 218 7777; www.gov.uk/international-pension-centre) should be able to advise.

If you don't make national insurance contributions while you are out of the UK in a country with no reciprocal agreement, you will forfeit entitlement to benefits on your return. You can decide to pay voluntary contributions in the UK at regular intervals or in a lump sum in order to retain your rights to certain benefits. Unfortunately this entitles you only to a retirement/widow's pension, and not to sickness benefit or unemployment benefit.

The question of pensions may seem irrelevant if you are just taking off for a year or two to teach English abroad. However, anyone who remains in the job for more than a couple of years should give some thought to starting or maintaining a pension. Because most English language teachers move between countries, it makes sense to pay into a personal pension scheme in your home country and also to maintain your right to a state pension by keeping up voluntary contributions. The question becomes vexed in those countries where state pension contributions are compulsory, as in Germany. Regulations of course vary from country to country so that, for instance, you are entitled to receive a pension after paying into the German scheme for five or more years, but in Portugal you have to contribute for 17 years. If you pay into a scheme and leave before you are entitled to claim a pension, you will have to try to reclaim some of the money you paid in. In Germany you won't get back more than half. If you work in a number of countries you may find that you spend your retirement corresponding with national pension authorities, something that long-term expat teachers are understandably worried about. According to one who has lobbied the European parliament to consider the predicament of peripatetic English teachers:

> ***Social security regulations vary from country to country, so it is important to look into whether you will be entitled to a pension later if you intend spending any length of time in one place and have to pay pension contributions in a state scheme.***
>
> ***It's nice to hop around when you are young and full of energy and ideas. It's not so nice to find out that you have paid a lot of money into a scheme that won't pay you a pension later. English teachers are adventurers, but I'm afraid too many of us are forgetting a fundamental problem: how do we survive when we are old? We have managed to get the EU to realise that there is at least one group of professionals, i.e. TEFL teachers, who are living up to the European ideal of mobility of labour, but may well find they face a bureaucratic nightmare when they retire and apply for a state pension.***

TAX

Calculating your liability to tax when working outside your home country is notoriously complicated so, if possible, check your position with an accountant. Everything depends on whether you fall into the category of 'resident' or 'domiciled'. Most EFL teachers count as domiciled in the UK since it is assumed that they will ultimately return. Legislation has removed the 'foreign earnings deduction' for UK nationals unless they are out of the country for a complete tax year. Since most teaching contracts operate from September, this means that the vast majority of EFL teachers, including teachers on high salaries in the Middle East or on the Japan Exchange and Teaching scheme which were formerly tax-free, are liable to UK tax. If you are out of the country for a tax year, you will be entitled to the exemption, provided no more than 62 days (i.e. one-sixth of the year) have been spent in the UK. Anyone who is present in the UK for more than 182 days during a particular tax year will be treated as resident with no exceptions. HM Revenue & Customs has set out the requirements in the document RDR1 'Residence, Domicile and the Remittance Basis' updated June 2016 (accessible on www.hmrc.gov.uk).

If the country in which you have been teaching has a double taxation agreement with Britain, you can offset tax paid abroad against your tax bill at home. But not all countries have such an agreement and it is not inconceivable that you will be taxed twice. Keep all receipts and financial documents in case you need to plead your case at a later date. HMRC has a good website if you have the patience to look for the information you need (www.hmrc.gov.uk).

If US citizens can establish that they are resident abroad, full-time for 12 months less up to 35 days spent in the US, the first $100,800 of overseas earnings is tax-exempt in the USA, though it is compulsory for all US citizens to submit a tax return to the IRS (Internal Revenue Service).

TRAVEL

London is the cheap airfare capital of the world and the number of online and office-based agencies offering discount flights to all corners of the world is seemingly endless. General websites such as www.cheapflights.co.uk, www.travelsupermarket.com, www.skyscanner.net, www.expedia.com and www.opodo.com are good starting points, though comparison shopping this way can be time consuming and frustrating. Even after long hours of surfing, the lowest internet fares can often be undercut by a good agent, particularly if your proposed route is complicated, so don't hesitate to get on the phone. Online travel agencies such as www.netflights.com can come up with some good fares, but may not offer much assistance if something goes wrong at any stage. Some people are happy to pay the slight premium for talking to a human being rather than just clicking boxes.

The major student and youth (under 26) travel agency STA Travel is usually a good starting place. For bookings and enquiries call STA Travel or log on at www.statravel.co.uk to find fares and check availability. Other reliable agencies specialising in long-haul travel include Trailfinders with 29 branches in Britain and Ireland (www.trailfinders.com) and Travel Nation in Hove (www.travelnation.co.uk), which is staffed by real experts who specialise in finding the best deals on round-the-world flights, discounted long-haul flights and multi-stop tickets. Channel 4's *Dispatches* programme did an exposé in 2016 of sharp practice at the international travel company Flight Centre, showing that staff are encouraged to mark up the cost of flights for less savvy customers and that there is a culture of applying discretionary and excessive margins in particular cases. The company disputes these claims, but the moral is always to shop around as much as possible.

Within Europe, rail is often the preferred way of travelling, especially since the months of September and June when most teachers are travelling to and from their destinations are among the most enjoyable times to travel. Good discounts are available to travellers under 26. Websites to check include www.trainseurope.co.uk (✆ +44 871 700 7722) or the marvellous site for train travellers everywhere: www.seat61.com.

Thousands of travel websites in the US compete for custom. Discounted tickets are available, for example, from Air Treks in San Francisco (www.AirTreks.com). When **Cara McCain** was looking for a cheap flight from Texas to Korea to take up a teaching job, she booked on www.vayama.com.

HOSPITALITY EXCHANGES

If you are planning to travel and conduct a speculative job hunt, you might want to take advantage of one of the hospitality exchanges that flourish over the internet, the best known of which is the Couchsurfing Project (www.couchsurfing.com). Like so many internet-based projects, the system depends on users' feedback, which means that you can check on a potential host's profile in advance and be fairly sure that dodgy hosts will be outed straightaway. Airbnb.com started out as a website for individuals to rent out lodgings, usually a spare room in their house but is now more commercial, but always worth checking.

Roving English language teacher **Bradwell Jackson** had been mulling over the possibility of travelling the world for about a decade before he finally gave up his job as a drug abuse counsellor in Florida to take off. On his earlier travels he had discovered the benefits of paying to join Servas (www.usservas.org in the USA; www.servasbritain.net in the UK) and two other free hospitality exchange programmes Global Freeloaders (www.globalfreeloaders.com) and the Hospitality Club (www.hospitalityclub.org). His first destination was Mexico, where to his amazement he found English teaching work at the first place he happened to enquire in Mexico City:

> ***I really must say right away that Servas is not simply for freeloading in people's homes. However, once you take the plunge and commit to wandering the earth, things just start to fall into place. If you belong to clubs such as Global Freeloaders, Hospitality Club, or any of the other homestay organisations, don't be surprised if the family you stay with invites you for an extended stay. The first such family I stayed with in Mexico invited me to stay for six months. All they asked was that I help with the costs of the food they prepared for me and the hot water I used.***

Bradwell has continued his couchsurfing travels in some unlikely locations. His host in Bamako, Mali, let him stay for two months in exchange for two hours of English lessons a day. He was a wealthy man who gave Bradwell all his meals, internet access, laundry and so on. He commented that *'once one lands into a dream situation like this, you are apt to feel a bit guilty, and such hospitality takes time to get used to. Still, I am certainly not complaining'*. More recently, en route to his teaching job in China, he stayed with a host in Hong Kong; and while completing his CELTA training at International House in London, a Servas host took him to see the Saxon church at Bradwell-on-Sea (no relation to his name).

MAPS AND INFORMATION

Good maps and guides always enhance one's enjoyment of a trip, which no number of apps and GPS on your smartphone can replace. Most people you will meet on the road will probably be carrying a *Rough Guide* or a *Lonely Planet*. These are both excellent series, though try not to become enslaved by their advice and preferences. Even though so much advance information is available over the internet, nothing can compete with a proper guidebook to pore over and take away with you. If you are going to be based in a major city, buy a map ahead of time. Visit the famous travel bookshop Stanfords, with a branch in Bristol as well as the mother-store in Covent Garden, London; its searchable catalogue is available online at www.stanfords.co.uk. The Map Shop in Worcestershire (www.themapshop.co.uk) and Maps Worldwide in Wiltshire (www.mapsworldwide.com) both do an extensive mail order business in specialised maps and guidebooks.

The Foreign & Commonwealth Office (FCO) regularly updates its travel advice for every country in the world and includes risk assessments of current trouble spots; go to www.gov.uk/foreign-travel-advice. If you are living in a country with poor security, you will want to keep abreast of developments.

LEARNING THE LANGUAGE

GIVE AND TAKE

Even if you will not need any knowledge of the local language in the classroom, the ability to communicate will increase your enjoyment many times over. After a long hard week of trying to din some English into your students' heads, you probably won't relish the prospect of struggling to convey your requests to uncomprehending shopkeepers, neighbours, etc. A refusal to try to learn some of the local language reflects badly on the teacher and reinforces the suspicion that English teachers are afflicted with cultural arrogance.

If there is time before you leave home, you might consider making a start at learning the language of the place you are going to by enrolling in a part-time or short intensive course of conversation classes at a local college of further education or using a self-study programme with books and tapes or an online course. This will also have the salutary effect of reminding you how difficult it is to learn a language. Take a good dictionary and a language course at a suitable level, for example the *Oxford Take Off In* … series from Oxford University Press (global.oup.com) as MP3 downloads, the BBC (www.bbc.co.uk/languages), Linguaphone (www.linguaphone.co.uk) and Pimsleur, an audio-based learning system whose courses consist of half-hour sessions every day. The popular Duolingo is a free language-learning platform. Also, check out noticeboards in local cafés, etc., or on Facebook for info about language exchanges. A great resource is www.gumtree.com, which has a skills/language swap section. If you're lucky, your conversation partner might also be able to help you with advice/contacts for your trip or your job hunt.

Of course it is much easier to learn the language once you are there. Some employers may even offer you the chance to join language classes free of charge or swap English lessons for those in the local language; if you are particularly interested in this perk, ask about it in advance. Some cities, such as Barcelona and Istanbul, have regular informal 'English café' evenings (*intercambio*), although people you meet this way will be more interested in improving their English than your Spanish or Turkish. Check out the site www.lingobongo.com, which focuses on language exchanges in Berlin, Madrid and Barcelona as well as teaching jobs.

Minna Graber, who fell in love with the Romanian culture and language, tried to improve her Romanian while teaching English in Bucharest, but her colleagues and acquaintances did not make it easy for her:

> ***My main problem was that the English teaching staff were completely unable to understand that my main reason for being there was to improve my Romanian. They, in the main, refused to converse with me in anything other than English and on frequent occasions made fun of my efforts. This is despite the fact that I am at around level C1 in this language. They seemed to believe that if you know English you don't have to learn other languages. The other assumption was that English speakers can't learn other languages. This attitude was often replicated elsewhere in the town and I had to fight quite hard to persuade my Romanian friends that I was not a walking English conversation lesson.***

Signing up for language classes on location is a good way of finding out about local teaching openings, as **Till Bruckner** found:

> ***The first thing I do when I arrive somewhere new is to get myself language lessons. The teacher will have met many other foreigners, have local connections and speak some English. In other words he or she is the natural starting point in your job hunt. If you make clear that you can only continue paying for your lessons if you earn money too, you've found a highly motivated ally in your search for work.***

Surprisingly, it is not always an advantage to know the language, as **Jamie Masters** discovered in Crete:

> ***About speaking Greek. Well, no one told me. I assumed that they'd be quite pleased to have a Greek-speaking English teacher, best of both worlds. It's useful for discipline; the kids can't talk about you behind your back; you can tell when they're cheating on their vocab tests; and, I stupidly thought, you can explain things more clearly, really get them to understand … Well, I was wrong, and was laboriously reprimanded for it when they finally worked out what I was doing. But by that time it was too late: the kids knew I could understand Greek, and so knew they didn't have to make the effort to speak to me in English. No amount of my playing dumb worked.***

WHAT TO TAKE

The research you do on your destination will no doubt include its climate, which will help you choose an appropriate range of clothing to take. But there is probably no need to equip yourself for every eventuality. EFL teachers usually earn enough to afford to buy a warm coat or boots if required. Be sure to pack enough smart clothes to see you through the academic year; jeans are rarely acceptable in the classroom.

SAVE BEFOREHAND!
Even though you are expecting to earn a decent salary, you should not arrive short of money. It is usual to be paid only at the end of the first month. Plus you may need sizeable sums for rent deposits and other setting-up expenses.

A generous supply of passport photos and copies of your vital documents (birth certificate, education certificates, references) should be considered essential. Recreational reading in English may be limited, so you might consider taking an e-reader since a supply of novels will weigh you down. It could take time to establish a busy social life, so a laptop or iPad are *de rigueur*. BBC radio can be accessed online around the world but the fantastic BBC iPlayer sadly isn't available when you're abroad (though there are ways round it by using a secure proxy).

A wi-fi-enabled smartphone will probably do everything that you need, i.e. send emails and browse the web, not to mention take photos, play music and of course make Skype calls. To avoid floating off into a news vacuum, some people subscribe to the BBC daily email service, which sends out a selection of news stories according to the interests you register. Others relish the prospect of no longer having a clue who is who in the Cabinet or what scandal has befallen footballers and their wives. A further advantage of having access to the BBC is that you can record programmes for use in the classroom.

Find out from returned travellers what items are in short supply or very expensive. Some items that recur on teachers' lists of what they wish they had taken from home include their favourite cosmetics, vitamin tablets, a deck of cards, ear plugs and thermal underwear. If you are travelling directly to your workplace, there is little reason to travel light, as **Charles Beach** discovered when he went to teach in Colombia: '*I wish I had packed my bags as if I were moving to another country, instead of packing in my usual sparse, economical backpacker fashion.*'

TEACHING MATERIALS

Try to find out which course your school follows and then become familiar with it. Depending on the circumstances, there may be a shortage of materials, so again enquire in advance about the facilities. (For example, English texts being used in a few places in Cambodia dated from 1938 and contained such useful sentences as 'I got this suit in Savile Row'.) When **Rebecca Mallinson** went to Sudan to teach English through a London-based charity, SVP (see Africa chapter), she was none too impressed with the course books:

> ***English is taught in Sudan using the world's most boring textbook, entitled SPINE. It was seemingly produced to put the next generation off English and ensure that they will not have any speaking skills. Teachers are expected to rush through the chapters . . . regardless of whether the students have understood anything or not. When I queried this with one of the supervisors, he looked at me with total lack of comprehension, as though actually 'learning English' was not an aim at all.***

For new teachers the most useful thing to have is a really good course book to work from, with teachers' books and good supplementary materials such as Jill Hadfield's *Intermediate Communication Games* as invaluable support. Material from such sources can save a lot of preparation time when planning your own task-based lessons.

If you are going to have to be self-reliant, you may want to contact the major EFL publishers, primarily Oxford University Press, Cambridge University Press, Longman, Macmillan, and Heinemann to request details of their course books with a sample lesson if possible, and the address of their stockist in your destination country. For information, advice and free teaching resources, you can join the Oxford University Press Teachers Club at http://elt.oup.com. Online professional development is available from OUP's Oxford Teachers' Club.

Before leaving home, browse a specialist ELT catalogue either in the EFL department of a bookshop or online. KELTIC (www.keltic.co.uk) operates a specialist mail order service from Oxfordshire, offering an extensive range of ELT materials. You can use its user-friendly website anywhere in the world to get information and advice or to order materials or you can contact KELTIC by telephone (✆ +44 1869 363589) or email (keltic@btol-uk.com).

Another major stockist of ELT materials is BEBC, the Bournemouth English Book Centre in Dorset (www.bebc.co.uk). The company supplies books, CDs and ELT software by mail order to teachers worldwide. For a list of recommended titles, see the next section.

Here is a list of items to consider packing which most often crop up in the recommendations of teachers of conversation classes in which the main target is to get the students talking. Teachers expecting to teach at an under-resourced school might think about taking authentic materials including some of the following:

- good dual language dictionary, picture dictionary
- appropriate pop music downloaded on an iPod with speakers so that you can play songs with clear lyrics such as the Beatles or early Billy Bragg to your classes
- games and activities book
- illustrated magazines such as the *National Geographic* or unusual publications, for example old comic books, teen mags or the *Big Issue*
- maps (for example of London)
- tourist guides to your home country, travel brochures, blank application forms
- flash cards (which are expensive if bought commercially; homemade ones work just as well)
- grammar exercise book
- old Cambridge exam papers (if you are going to be teaching from its suite of exams).

Postcards, balloons, stick-on stars and photos of yourself as an infant have all been used to good effect. If you know that there will be a shortage of materials, it might even be worth taking general stationery such as notebooks, carbon paper, Blu-Tack, plastic files, large pieces of paper, coloured markers, etc.

Koober Grob spent an enjoyable time in Russia trying to hone the conversation skills of her highly motivated students. Her main regret was that she hadn't brought with her a 10-page list of possible discussion topics to help them practise their colloquial English, because she found that she was sometimes at a loss for topics (which may account for the conversation one day turning to chocolate-covered ants in Africa).

Richard McBrien, who taught English in China, recommends taking a collection of photos of anything in your home environment. A few rolls shot of local petrol stations, supermarkets, houses, parks, etc., can be of great interest to students in far-off lands. It may of course be difficult to anticipate what will excite your students' curiosity.

EFL teachers cannot escape so easily, so you should be prepared to be treated like a guru of contemporary British or American culture. If you know in advance that you will have to perform in this capacity, you might get hold of *Britain: For Learners of English* by James O'Driscoll (Oxford University Press, 2009; £42.50), which provides historical and cultural background of British society and institutions, as well as the private daily life of the British people.

ONLINE RESOURCES

More and more TEFL teachers are making use of the vast number of teaching resources available online. Also more schools are installing interactive whiteboards in classrooms, which can be a godsend for teachers. After getting used to using them at a well-equipped school in Kazakhstan, **Anthony Cook** concluded that *'they tend to inspire a lot of new ideas and approaches, especially in terms of incorporating video into lessons'*. He says that it's like having a cinema screen in the classroom, which makes it so much easier than getting 10 people to crowd around a laptop.

Teachers can access online a range of actual lesson plans and printable materials for immediate use with students as well as teacher forums and job sites.

Macmillan's onestopenglish.com is a good example of a useful website offering free teaching materials, although practically all the major ELT publishers now offer something similar. Here you will find masses of materials, either linked in to existing course books or stand-alone exercises, often with recordings, printable sheets, videos and teacher's notes. Along the same lines are websites which are not linked to publishers but which offer masses of exercises of all types. Again, there is usually a surprisingly rich free section, and a more comprehensive paying option, often aimed at organisations. The British Council's www.teachingenglish.org.uk is a good place to start, while www.eslprintables.com and www.enchantedlearning.com for children offer helpful printouts and worksheets. Try also EnglishZone for kids from LCF clubs (www.lcfclubs.com) which can be sampled in a free trial. Experienced TEFL teachers have generously shared masses of English teaching resources, like the non-profit site http://tomstefl.com geared for China and Hong Kong, or http://tefltastic.wordpress.com ('Publications and materials from TEFL lifer Alex Case, plus thousands of photocopiables and articles via the drop-down menus').

Then there are websites that are not specifically for English teachers or learners but that house much which teachers can make use of, such as the major newspaper and television sites, or cultural sites like www.visitbritain.com or www.royal.gov.uk. Some of these, such as the BBC and Voice of America even have special sections where they have created mini-websites full of exercises for English learners based on their own up-to-date content, which is great for keeping lessons fresh and stimulating. Bite-size news reports are sure to stimulate classroom discussion. Check out www.bbc.co.uk/learningenglish, and Voice of America's http://learningenglish.voanews.com. The US State Department's site http://americanenglish.state.gov brings together many resources and ideas for English language teachers around the world.

Hot on the heels of the resources above comes a whole raft of websites that are not explicitly for English teaching, have no derived exercises for use in class, are not always appropriate, and yet they offer incredible potential for the innovative and adventurous English language teacher. These belong to the online world of YouTube (free videos), Flickr (free photos), Wikipedia (free knowledge), Deezer (free music), the BBC (free news) and Google Earth (free maps). Once you have learnt how to adapt real English to your classroom and to your students you will find these sites to be an absolute goldmine which will help you inject some marvellously unexpected and highly appreciated moments into your classes.

An abundance of open source software makes it possible for tech-heads to experiment with creating their own interactive exercises. With Google's Blogger (www.blogger.com) or alternative user-friendly blogging tools such as WordPress (http://wordpress.org), Blogspot (www.blogspot.com) and Tumblr (www.tumblr.com), you and your students can create blogs and use them to extend their English learning to their outside class activities. The virtual world 'Second Life' (http://secondlife.com) is being used ever more creatively by teachers to hold 'in-world' English classes in a unique, fun environment. And sites such as Amazon and eBay can be used to assess buying opportunities, read product reviews, discover the auction process and why not spend a few pennies as a group to buy something for the class! The possibilities are endless.

Last, but not least, scores of teacher forums come and go for new and experienced teachers alike. These typically cover teaching techniques, difficult situations needing solutions, or simply mention useful new teaching resources which have come to light recently.

In reality, there is such an enormous amount of great stuff out there that the examples mentioned are a drop in the ocean. The best way to discover others is simply to type in 'English teacher training forum' or 'English teaching jobs Taiwan' or 'free English teaching resources' or whatever it is you're interested in and start surfing away. Googling for something specific will also provide useful leads, anything from ideas for teaching young learners to preparation for IELTS.

RECOMMENDED BIBLIOGRAPHY

There is such a plethora of books and materials that the choice can be daunting to the uninitiated. Every teacher should have a basic manual of grammar handy, such as:

Advanced Grammar in Use by Martin Hewings (Cambridge University Press, 2015; £23.59; with answers).

Collins Gem English Grammar (genuinely pocket-sized). Dubbed by at least one novice as 'the teacher's friend'. Out of print but available used.

English Grammar in Use by Raymond Murphy (Cambridge University Press, 4th edition, 2015; with answers and interactive eBook; £22.25).

Grammar for English Language Teachers by Martin Parrott (Cambridge University Press, 2010; £28.35).

Oxford English Grammar Course by Michael Swan and Catherine Walter (Oxford University Press, 2011; Basic: £22; Intermediate: £24; Advanced: £26). Short bite-sized grammar explanations with plenty of practice. The 'Pronunciation for grammar' CD-ROM helps students with the rhythm, stress and intonation of grammar structures.

Practical English Usage by Michael Swan (3rd edition, Oxford University Press, 2005; £32.50; intermediate to advanced). The world's most trusted reference grammar. Indispensable guide to problem points in the English language as encountered by learners and their teachers with clear, practical information and examples. Now also available Practical English Usage, an app for iPad, iPhone, Windows and Android, which is quick and easy to use. (See www.oup.com/elt/fingertips.)

Teaching English Grammar by Jim Scrivener (Macmillan, 2010; £25.50).

Here is a selected list of recommended books and teaching aids which you could consider.

Advanced Learner's English Dictionar (dictionaries published by both Collins and Cambridge).

Oxford Advanced Learner's Dictionary (8th edition, Oxford University Press, 2015; £38). The world's best selling advanced learner's dictionary. Helps develop all language skills with information on collocations, synonyms and writing. Available with DVD and premium online access code.

Children Learning English by Jayne Moon (Macmillan, 2005; £25.50). Introduces the theory behind good classroom practice with examples from around the world.

The English Language Teacher's Handbook by Joanna Baker and Heather Westrup (VSO, 2000; £15.99). How to teach large classes with few resources.

Grammar Games by M. Rinvolucri (Cambridge University Press, 1985; £27.50). Includes activities for all levels.

Grammar Practice Activities by Penny Ur (Cambridge University Press, 2009; £30.80). Paperback with CD-ROM. Teaching classic for all levels and ages. Includes photocopiable worksheets and visuals.

How Languages are Learned by Patsy M. Lightbrown and Nina Spader (4th edition, Oxford University Press, 2013; £29). A prize-winning, readable introduction to research in language acquisition and how it relates to the classroom.

Ladybird Key Words Reading Scheme (Ladybird's Books for English Learning). Inexpensive series for teaching young children.

Learning Teaching by Jim Scrivener (Macmillan, 2011; £37).

Lessons from Nothing by Bruce Marsland (Cambridge University Press, 1998; £21.70). From the Cambridge Handbooks for Language Teachers series.

Oxford Basics is a series of 11 short accessible books for teachers who are new to ELT or who are looking for new creative ways of teaching with limited resources. The series includes *Introduction to Teaching English* by Jill and Charles Hadfield (Oxford University Press, 2008; £21), a practical guide with lesson plans for new teachers of English, and *Simple Speaking Activities* by the same authors (Oxford University Press, 1999; £13).

Oxford Basics for Children is a series of five titles for teachers of young learners which provides adaptable teaching ideas in an easy-to-follow format. Series includes *Starting and Ending Lessons* by Naomi Moir (Oxford University Press, 2009; £13), *English Through Music* by Jane Willis and Anice Paterson (Oxford University Press, 2008; £15.50).

The Practice of English Language Teaching by Jeremy Harmer (4th edition, Pearson Longman, 2015; £40). A well-known core reference work for teachers from the author of *How to Teach English* (£38), a straightforward introduction to TEFL for new teachers.

PROBLEMS

Potential problems fall into two broad categories: personal and professional. You may quickly feel settled and find your new setting fascinating but may discover that the job itself is beset with difficulties. On the other hand the teaching might suit but otherwise you feel alienated and lonely. Those who choose to uproot themselves suddenly should be fairly confident that they have enough resources to rely on themselves, and must expect some adjustment problems. Only you can assess your chances of enjoying the whole experience and of not feeling traumatised. Women may encounter special problems in countries where women have low status. An informative site is www.journeywoman.com, among many others.

PROBLEMS AT WORK

Anyone who has done some language teaching will be familiar with at least some of the problems EFL teachers face. Problems encountered in a classroom of Turkish or Peruvian adolescents will be quite different from the ones experienced teaching French or Japanese business people. The country chapters attempt to identify some of the specific problems which groups of language learners present.

Although you are unlikely to be expected to entertain 200 people for four hours with a plastic bowl, there may be a lack of facilities and resources. The teacher who has packed some teaching materials will feel particularly grateful for his or her foresight in such circumstances. Some schools (especially cowboy ones) go to the extreme of providing very rigid lesson plans from which you are not allowed to deviate and which are likely to be uncongenial and uninspiring. Even when reasonable course texts are provided, supplementary materials for role play and games can considerably liven up classes (and teachers). You can obtain extra teaching aids after arrival from the nearest English language bookshop or make them yourself, for example record a dialogue between yourself and an English-speaking friend or cut up magazines or use postcards to make flashcards. If the missing facilities are more basic (e.g. tables, chairs, heating, paper, pens) you will have to improvise as best you can and (if appropriate) press the administration for some equipment.

PROBLEMS WITH STUDENTS

A very common problem is to find yourself in front of a class of mixed ability with incompatible aims. How do you plan a lesson that will satisfy a sophisticated business executive whose English is fairly advanced, a delinquent teenager and a housewife crippled by lack of confidence? A good school will of course stream its clients and make life easier for its teachers. But this may be left to you, in which case a set of commercially produced tests to assess level of language acquisition could come in very handy. Alternatively you can devise a simple questionnaire for the students to describe their hobbies, studies, family or whatever. This will not only display their use of English but also give you some clues about their various backgrounds. One way of coping with gross discrepancies is to divide the class into compatible groups or pairs and give tasks which work at different levels. Subdividing a class is in fact generally a good idea especially in large classes.

In some places you may even have to contend with racial or cultural friction among students, as **Bryn Thomas** encountered in Egypt:

> ***One of the problems I found in the class was the often quite shocking displays of racism by the Egyptians towards their dark-skinned neighbours from Somalia. Vast amounts of tact and diplomacy were required to ensure that enough attention was given to the Somalis (who tend to be shy, quiet and highly intelligent) without upsetting the sometimes rowdy and over-enthusiastic Egyptians.***

Your expectations of what teaching is supposed to achieve may be quite different from the expectations of your students. Foreign educational systems are often far more formal than their British or American counterparts and students may seem distressingly content to memorise and regurgitate, often with the sole motivation of passing an exam. But this doesn't always operate. Many teachers have had to face a class that doesn't seem to care at all about learning any English and merely wants to be entertained.

In many countries free discussion is quite alien, whether because of repressive governments or cultural taboos. It is essential to be sensitive to these cultural differences and not to expect too much of your students straightaway. The only way of overcoming this reluctance to express an opinion or indeed express anything at all is to involve them patiently and tactfully, again by splitting them into smaller units and asking them to come up with a joint reply.

Discipline is seldom a serious problem outside Europe; in fact liberal teachers are often taken aback by what they perceive as an excess of docility, an over-willingness to believe that 'teacher is always right'. In some cases, classes of bored and rebellious European teenagers might cause problems (especially on Fridays), or children who are being sent to English lessons after school simply as an alternative to babysitting for working mothers. Unfortunately, a couple of troublemakers can poison a class. You may even have to contend with one or two downright uncontrollable students as **Jamie Masters** did in Crete:

> ***At least two of my pupils were malevolent. There was one, Makis, who used to bring a 'prop' to every lesson, some new way of disrupting the class: an air pistol, a piece of string with a banknote tied to it, a whistle, white paint. He used to slap my cheeks, hug me and lift me off the floor, was quite open about not wanting to work . . . and then claimed I was picking on him when I retaliated. Well, call me a humourless unfeeling bastard, but . . .***

One teacher in Turkey found the majority of his students 'bouncy, bright, enthusiastic and sharp' but with one class he was always amazed that they walked upright when they got out of their chairs. It often turns out that each class develops a certain character.

Marta Eleniak, who taught in Spain, recommends taking a hard line:

> ***Be a tyrant at the start. The kids can be very wicked and take advantage of any good nature shown. Squash anyone who is late, shouts, gossips, etc. the first time or it'll never stop. The good classes make you love teaching. The bad make you feel as if you want to go back to filing.***

Each level and age group brings its own difficulties. Anyone who has no experience of dealing with young children may find it impossible to grab and hold their attention, let alone teach them any English. A lack of inhibition is very useful for teaching young children, who will enjoy sing-songs, nursery rhymes, simple puzzles and games, etc. A firm hand may also be necessary if **Aine Fligg**'s experience in Hong Kong is anything to go by. She was bitten on the ankle by one of her less receptive students. When the headmaster came in and remonstrated (with Aine!), the child bit him on the nose. The brat was then incarcerated in a cupboard, and emerged somewhat subdued.

Blogger and world traveller **Travis Ball** from California gradually learnt how to cope with young children at the rural language school at which he taught in Japan:

> ***I was brand new to teaching, so it was really rough getting started. With very little training, I was thrown in and expected to swim. I had 27 classes a week, 18 of them on different lesson plans. My youngest student was five while my oldest was 61. The sheer diversity of age and language experience threw me for a loop. In the first two weeks, I made two separate children cry, which I felt awful about. This was a cultural thing that I had to get used to. The first occasion involved my youngest student. We were doing a warm-up drawing activity and at the end I asked for the coloured pencils back so we could get onto the next game. The one word this child knew was 'no' which he kept repeating. I tried to take the pencil and move on with the class, which caused him to cry. I handed back the pencil and he basically coloured for the whole class.***
>
> ***The other instance involved this little boy's sister. I was attempting to teach the class the difference between the sound 'B' and 'V'. I started with one student and had her watch my lips as I said the word 'vanilla' and after***

a few attempts, succeeded in getting her to say the correct sound. Then I came to the next student and she tried twice and broke into tears on the third failed attempt. Not sure what to do, I kept going around the circle and the crying student calmed down after a few minutes, and was laughing with the next game minutes later. By the end of my nine months there, I was close to all my students, young and old. Leaving was especially rough with a few of the kids, and some of the adults as well.

Only 18 years old himself, **Sam James** had to teach a variety of age groups in Barcelona during his gap year and despite the problems, ended up enjoying it:

The children I taught were fairly unruly and noisy. The teenagers were, as ever, pretty uninterested in learning, though if one struck on something they enjoyed they would work much better. Activities based on the lyrics of songs seemed to be good. They had a tendency to select answers at random in multiple choice exercises. On the other hand they were only ever loud rather than very rude or disobedient. The young children (8–12) were harder work. They tended to understand selectively, acting confused if they didn't like an instruction. Part of the problem was that the class was far too long (three hours) for children of that age and their concentration and behaviour tended to tail off as the time passed.

Beginners of all ages progress much more rapidly than intermediate learners. Many teachers find adolescent intermediate learners the most difficult to teach. The original fun and novelty are past and they now face a long slog of consolidating vocabulary and structures. (The 'intermediate plateau' is a well-known phenomenon in language acquisition.) Adolescents may resent 'grammar games' (which are a standard part of EFL), thinking that games are suitable only for children.

Adult learners with a good grounding in the language often come to an initial class with wildly unrealistic expectations that need to be tactfully managed. No matter how fervently they wish for it, they are never going to speak unaccented English with native fluency after a handful of lessons.

The worst problem of all is to be confronted with a bored and unresponsive class. This may happen in a class of beginners who can't understand what is going on, especially a problem if you don't speak a word of their language. It can be extremely frustrating for all concerned when trying to teach some concept or new vocabulary without being able to provide the simple equivalent. If this is the case, you'll have to rely heavily on visual aids. Whole books have been written to show EFL teachers how to draw, for example *1,000+ Pictures for Teachers to Copy* by Andrew Wright (available second-hand). Some enjoy the challenge of teaching total beginners as **Hannah Bullock** did in the Czech Republic: 'because each lesson was like an invigorating game of charades'. Many new teachers make the mistake of doing all the talking. During his year of teaching in Slovenia, **Adam Cook**, like many others before him, came to the conclusion that silence is one of the teacher's most effective tools.

TIPS FOR DEALING WITH A LETHARGIC CLASS

The best way to inject a little life is to get them moving around, for example get them to do a relaxation exercise or have them carry out a little survey of their neighbours and then report their findings back to the class. If one or two eager beavers are answering all the questions while the rest of the class gently snoozes, you can use a ball to throw around the class – whoever has the ball speaks.

A blogger called **Emma** provides some useful ESL teaching tips on www.vesl.org. For the newly initiated teacher, she recommends having a few icebreakers prepared, as these can provide a simple and quick solution to help the teacher (and the class) feel more relaxed. She suggests that icebreakers can be used at any point in the lesson, for instance, to introduce yourself to the class, to put forward a new topic, or to help break up the lesson. For some of her practical suggestions of games and songs that work well, see www.vesl.org/2013/06/ice-breakers-progress.

In many countries foreign teachers come to feel like a dancing bear or performing monkey, someone who is expected to be a cultural token and an entertainer. If the students are expecting someone to dance a jig or swing from the chandelier (so to speak) they will be understandably disappointed to be presented with someone asking them to form sentences using the present perfect. At the other extreme, it is similarly disconcerting to be treated just as a model of pronunciation, and you may begin to wonder whether your employer might be better off employing a tape recorder.

PROBLEMS WITH YOURSELF

Lessons can fizz or fizzle. The latter may be the fault of the students but more often it is down to the teacher. One of the most common traps into which inexperienced teachers fall is to dominate the class too much. Conversational English can only be acquired by endless practice and so you must allow your students to do most of the talking. Even if there are long pauses between your questions and their attempts to answer, the temptation to fill the silences should be avoided. Pauses have a positive role to play, allowing students a chance to dwell on and absorb the point you have just been illustrating. Avoid asking 'Do you understand?' since the answer is meaningless; it is much more useful to test their comprehension indirectly.

A native speaker's function is seldom to teach grammar, though he or she should feel comfortable naming grammatical constructions. You are not there to help the students to analyse the language but to use it and communicate with it. It has been said that grammar is the highway code, the catalogue of rules and traffic signs, quite useless in isolation from driving, which gets you where you want to go. Grammar is only the cookery book while talking is cooking for other people to understand/eat. Persuading some students whose language education has been founded on grammar rather than communication that this is the priority may be difficult, but try not to be drawn into detailed explanations of grammatical structures.

Being utterly ignorant of grammar can result in embarrassing situations. You can only get away with bluffing for so long ('Stefan, I don't think it matters here whether or not it's a subjunctive') and irate students have been known to report to school directors that their teachers are grammar-illiterate. One useful trick suggested by **Roberta Wedge** is to reply with 'Very good question – we're going to deal with that in the next class.' Usually it will suffice to have studied a general grammar handbook such as *Practical English Grammar* or *Practical English Usage* (see the bibliography in the previous chapter). If you contradict yourself between one lesson and the next, and an eager student notices it, take **Richard Osborne**'s advice and say 'Ah yes, I'm sorry about that. You see, that's the way we do it at home. Bizness is often spelled with a Z in Canada.'

The worst fate that can befall a teacher is to run dry, to completely run out of ideas and steam before the appointed hour has arrived. This usually happens when you fail to arrive with a structured lesson plan. It is usually a recipe for disaster to announce at the beginning of the lesson 'Tonight let's talk about our travels/hobbies/animals' or whatever. Any course book will help you to avoid grinding to a halt. Supplementary materials such as songs and games can be lifesavers in (and out) of a crisis. If you are absolutely stuck for what to talk about next, try writing the lyrics of a popular song on the board and asking the class to analyse it or even act it out (avoiding titles such as 'I Want Your Body'). Apparently songs that have worked well for many teachers include George Michael's 'Careless Whispers', the Beatles' 'Here Comes the Sun' and 'When I'm 64' and 'Perfect Day' by Lou Reed. The site www.myenglishpages.com/site_php_files/lyrics_and_songs.php links to songs that have worked for learners. Another way of stepping outside the predictability of a course book might be to teach a short poem that you like, or even a short story (e.g. by Saki) if the class is sufficiently advanced.

LESSON STRUCTURE

A very popular way to structure a lesson is in 'notions'; you take a general situation like 'praising' or 'complaining', teach some relevant vocabulary and structures and then have the class put them into practice in role-play situations. Unfortunately repetition is the key to language learning, though you have to avoid boring drills, which will kill any interest in the language.

When a lesson goes well, it can be deeply satisfying. **Philip Tomkins** did his TEFL training in Greece in 2010 and identified the high point of his teaching experiences as sharing a joke in English with a class and all having a fit of the giggles. The low point was inadvertently using technical jargon in his first lesson, which temporarily killed it dead, and being faced with blank looks.

Culture shock is experienced by most people who live in a foreign country in whatever circumstances (see below), but can be especially problematic for teachers. Unthinkingly you might choose a topic which seems neutral to you but is controversial to the students. A little feature on the English pub, for example, would not be enjoyed in Saudi Arabia. A discussion about whaling might make a class of Norwegians uncomfortable. Asking questions about foreign travels would be tactless in many places where few will be able to afford international travel.

One of the more subtle problems is knowing how to approach teaching, as **J. W. Arble** discovered:

> ***I was caught up with trying to work out how to present myself to my students: whether to assume the role of friend, exotic or mentor; whether to be 'charismatic' or reserved, enthusiastic or dry, serious-minded or idiot savant. Given the limited time, I persuaded myself the aim was to make the subject interestingly different; with the hope a few might be triggered into curiosity. Less worthily, I just wanted to be liked.***

One of the hardest problems to contend with is teacher burn-out. If you invariably arrive just as the class is scheduled to begin, show no enthusiasm and glance at the clock every 90 seconds, you will not be a popular teacher. Getting hold of some new authentic materials might shore up your flagging enthusiasm for the enterprise. If not, perhaps it is time to consider going home (bearing in mind your contractual commitments).

PROBLEMS WITH EMPLOYERS

All sorts of schools break their promises about pay, perks and availability of resources. The worst disappointment of all, however, is to turn up and find that you don't have a job at all. Because schools which hire their teachers sight unseen often find themselves let down at the last moment, they may over-hire, just in the way that airlines overbook their flights in the expectation of a certain level of cancellation. Even more probable is that the school has not been able to predict the number of pupils who will enrol and decides to hire enough teachers to cover the projected maximum. Whatever the reason, it can be devastating to have the job carpet whipped from under your feet. Before you have got to this stage, you should have done an online search for feedback about your employer. Social media and sites like reddit, glassdoor and gooverseas.com can be very useful if your prospective employer has been reviewed. Sometimes an employer is bad enough for former teachers to set up their own Facebook page like one created by some disgruntled ex-employees of an institute in Kuwait, which did not beat around the bush: 'If you want to work for liars, work around violent types, work around drug users, work around colleagues who will spy on you and report your every move to your boss, and work around those teaching on false credentials, this is your place.'

Most employers are not this bad and merely fail to deliver some of the promised perks. Having a signed contract helps. If you feel that you are being shabbily treated, you could try losing your temper and threatening to tarnish the institution's good name. Nowadays, teachers who feel they have been exploited or abused have a ready outlet for their frustrations. They can use social media or write a negative review online on sites such as http://eslwatch.info. It is probably not advisable to take up a confrontational stance straightaway since this could mean a year of hostility and misery. Polite but persistent negotiations might prove successful. Find out if there is a relevant teachers' union, join it and ask it for advice (though EFL is notorious for being non-unionised). As the year wears on, your bargaining clout increases, especially if you are a half-decent teacher, since you will be more difficult to replace mid-term.

One recourse is to bring your employer's shortcomings to the attention of the British Council or, in extreme cases of exploitation, your embassy/consulate. If you are being genuinely maltreated and you are prepared to leave the job, delivering an ultimatum and threatening to leave might prompt improvements in your working conditions. Remember that if there are cowboy schools, there are also cowboy teachers. Many honest and responsible employers have fallen victim to unreliable and undisciplined individuals who break their promises, show up late and abuse the accommodation they are given. Try not to let your employer down unless the provocation is serious.

Language schools must function as businesses as well as educational establishments and in some case the profit motive overtakes everything else. In those cases, teachers soon realise that they matter less to the people in charge than the number and satisfaction of students. Some employers leave you entirely to your own devices and even look to you for teaching ideas. Others interfere to an annoying degree; we've heard of one school director in Spain who bugged the classrooms to make sure the staff were following his idiosyncratic home-produced course outlines. **Jayne Nash** worked for a chain of schools in France that use their own method; clients learnt basic phrases and words for everyday situations in parrot fashion:

> ***The courses were aimed at local business people, therefore students learnt mostly spoken English to introduce themselves, their company or product, language for meetings, telephone conversations, etc. The method seemed very effective, but can prove extremely tedious for the teacher. After you have repeated a word 10–20 times with 10 students, four times a day, five days a week . . .***

One of the most commonly heard complaints from teachers concerns the schedule. Eager only to satisfy clients, employers tend to mess around with teachers' timetables, offering awkward combinations of hours or changing the schedule at the last moment, which is extremely stressful. A certain amount of evening work is almost inevitable in private language schools, where pupils (whether of school or working age) must study English out of hours. Having to work early in the morning and then again through the evening can become exhausting after a while. It can also be annoying to have several long gruelling days a week and other days with scarcely any teaching at all (but still not days off).

H.P.W. = HOURS PER WEEK

One trick to beware of is to find that the 24 hours a week you were told you would be working actually means 32 45-minute lessons (which is much harder work than teaching 24 one-hour lessons). Even if the number of hours has not been exaggerated, you may have been deluded into thinking that a 24-hour week is quite cushy. But preparation time can easily add half as many hours again, plus if you are teaching in different locations, travel time (often unpaid) has to be taken into consideration.

In some situations teachers may be expected to participate in extra-curricular activities or marketing exercises such as dreary drinks parties for pupils or asked to make a public speech. Make an effort to accept such invitations (especially near the beginning of your contract) or, if you must decline, do so as graciously as possible. There might also be extra duties, translating letters and documents, updating teaching materials, etc., for which you are unlikely to be paid extra.

PROBLEMS OUTSIDE WORK

Your main initial worry outside your place of employment will probably be accommodation. Once this is sorted out, either with the help of your school or on your own, and you have mastered the essentials of getting around and shopping for food, there is nothing to do but enjoy yourself, exploring your new surroundings and making friends.

CULTURE SHOCK

Enjoying yourself won't be at all easy if you are suffering from culture shock. Shock implies something that happens suddenly, but cultural disorientation more often creeps up on you. Adrenaline usually sees you through the first few weeks as you find the novelty exhilarating and challenging. You will be amazed and charmed by the odd gestures the people use or the antiquated way that things work. As time goes on, practical irritations intrude and the constant misunderstanding caused by those charming gestures – such as a nod in Greece meaning 'no' or in Japan meaning 'yes, I understand, but don't agree' – and the inconvenience of not being able to do simple tasks without the help of a local will begin to get on your nerves. Unless you can find someone to listen sympathetically to your complaints, you may begin to think you have made a mistake in coming in the first place.

Emily Handler remembers when she went through a bad patch shortly after moving to Hungary to teach:

> ***My low point was the whole first six months. After the initial euphoria wore off, towards the start of October I got seriously depressed. Most days I pep-talked myself with things like 'C'mon, this is only a nine-month contract, you can do anything for nine months! People have jail sentences longer than that! Just finish the year and you can be gone! People survive the wilderness for longer than that! Just a few more months, you can do it!' Luckily for me, around February three things changed dramatically: spring showed up, I started to get over my first-year-teaching problems, and I made new friends in my town.***

Experts say that most people who have moved abroad hit the trough after three or four months, probably just before Christmas in the case of teachers who started work in September. A holiday over Christmas may serve to calm you down or, if you go home for Christmas, may make you feel terminally homesick and not want to go back. Teachers who survive this often find that things improve in the second term as they cease to perceive many aspects of life as 'foreign'.

Kathryn Saville has been teaching English as a foreign language abroad since 2004 in a variety of countries, and is currently teaching in Istanbul. She thinks she has become addicted to this perpetual rootlessness. In her case, it takes about three months to adjust to every new country she has worked in – to find the shops she needs, to learn the survival language, and navigate the city. She relishes recreating her life with each move and learning more about the world from all the places she has been and people she has met. She concludes, 'There is so much more to learn, not only of the world, but about myself!'

You're bound to suffer from low spirits occasionally, but remember not to broadcast your feelings randomly. Feeling contempt and hostility towards your host country is actually part of the process of adjusting to being abroad. If you feel you have to let off steam about the local bureaucracy or the dishonesty of taxi-drivers or the shockingly bad accent of the local English teachers, remember to do so in private, in emails or when there are no local people around. This is especially important if you have colleagues who are natives of the country. They may find some of the idiosyncrasies of their culture irritating too but, unlike you, they have to live with them forever.

The best way to avoid disappointment is to be well briefed beforehand, as emphasised in the chapter on Preparation. Gathering general information about the country and specific information about the school before arrival will obviate many of the negative feelings some EFL teachers feel. If you are the type to build up high hopes and expectations of new situations, it is wise to try to dismantle these before leaving home. English teaching is seldom glamorous.

TOP TIP

Don't go around saying 'In my country, we do this . . .' You're not in your country now, so let go of the things that frustrate you, and just enjoy the journey.

Some native-speaker teachers have found an unpleasant rift between local and foreign staff, which in some cases can be accounted for by the simple fact that you are being paid a lot more than they are. Sometimes new foreign teachers find their local colleagues cliquey and uncommunicative. No doubt they have seen a lot of foreigners come, and make a lot of noise, and go, and there is no particular reason why they should find the consignment you're in wildly exciting and worth getting to know.

LONELINESS

Creating a social life from scratch is difficult enough at any time, but becomes even more difficult in an alien tongue and culture. You will probably find that many of your fellow teachers are lots of fun and able to offer practical help in your first few weeks (especially any who are bilingual). If you find yourself in a one-foreigner village, surely there's another lonely teacher across the mountaintop. You could meet for a drink at the weekend to commiserate and to draw up a charter and call yourselves 'The Wonga Plateau EFL Teachers' Association' (and remember to put yourself down as founder the next time you are revising your CV). You may even want to take some positive steps to meet people and participate in activities outside the world of English language instruction. This may require uncharacteristically extrovert behaviour, but overcoming initial inhibitions almost always pays worthwhile dividends.

If you are tired of conversations about students' dullness or your director of studies' evident lunacy, you could try to meet other expatriates who are not EFL teachers. The local English language bookshop might prove a useful source of information about forthcoming events for English speakers, as will be any newspapers or magazines published in English. Seek out the overseas student club if there is a university nearby (though when it discovers what line of work you are in it may well have designs on you). Even the least devout teachers have found English-speaking churches to be useful for arranging social functions and offering practical advice. Bars that model themselves on British/Irish pubs are usually full of friendly expats.

The most obvious way to meet other foreigners is to enrol in a language course or perhaps classes in art and civilisation. Even if you are not particularly serious about pursuing language studies, language classes are the ideal place to form vital social contacts. You can also join other clubs or classes aimed at residents abroad, for example some German cities have English amateur dramatics groups.

Making friends with locals may prove more difficult, though circumstances vary enormously according to whether you live in a small town or a big city, with some gregarious colleagues or by yourself, etc. The obvious source of social contact is your students and their friends and families (bearing in mind that in certain cultures, a teacher who goes out to a bar or disco with students risks losing their respect). As long as you don't spend all your free time moping at home, you are bound to strike up conversations with the locals, whether in cafés, on buses or in shops. Admittedly these seldom go past a superficial acquaintance, but they still serve the purpose of making you feel a little more integrated in the community. Local university students will probably be more socially flexible than others and it is worth investigating the bars and cafés frequented by students. If you have a particular hobby, sport or interest, find out if there is a local club where you will meet like-minded people; join local ramblers, jazz buffs, etc. – the more obscure, the more welcome you are likely to be. You only have to become friendly with one other person to open up new social horizons if you are invited to meet their friends and family. Also make an effort to organise some breaks from work. Even a couple of days by the seaside or visiting a tourist attraction in the region can revitalise your interest in being abroad and provide a refreshing break from the tyranny of the teacher's routine.

COMING HOME

For some, teaching abroad can be addictive. The prospect of returning home to scour the local job adverts becomes distinctly unappealing as they drink Retsina, eat sushi or spend the weekend at a Brazilian beach. Once you have completed one teaching contract, it will be very much easier to land the next one, and it can be exhilarating to think that you can choose to work in almost any corner of the globe. By the same token, many people who go abroad to teach English get burned out after a year or two. The majority of English teachers do not think of TEFL as a long-term proposition. They talk about their colleagues who move on to other things as getting a 'proper job', i.e. one that does not require an early start followed by a long idle morning, where shoddy treatment by bosses is not the norm and where you do not have to correct anyone's phrasal verbs.

Homesickness catches up with most EFL teachers and they begin to pine for a pub or bar where repartee is quick and natural and for all the other accoutrements of the culture of their birth. The bad news is that there are few jobs in EFL in Britain except at summer schools. Even professional English language teachers can find it difficult to land a reasonable job in the UK. American teachers will probably fare better due to the growth industry of ESL in the US, though the majority of openings are part-time with few fringe benefits and opportunities for career development. The good news is that a stint of teaching English abroad is an asset on anyone's CV/résumé. Employers of all kinds look favourably on people who have had the get-up-and-go to work at a respectable job in a foreign land. On returning home from teaching in Chile, **Heidi Resetarits** began looking for jobs and found that having international work experience on her résumé was invaluable. Potential employers were intrigued by the fact that she'd lived in Chile. Such experience can always be presented as valuable for increasing self-assurance, maturity, a knowledge of the world, communication skills and any other positive feature which comes to mind. Very few teachers have regretted their decision to travel the world, even if the specific job they did was not without its drawbacks and difficulties.

PART 2

COUNTRY BY COUNTRY GUIDE

WESTERN EUROPE
CENTRAL AND EASTERN EUROPE
THE REST OF EUROPE
CENTRAL ASIAN AND OTHER REPUBLICS
MIDDLE EAST
AFRICA
ASIA
LATIN AMERICA
CENTRAL AMERICA AND THE CARIBBEAN
NORTH AMERICA
AUSTRALASIA

EUROPEAN UNION REFERENDUM

Following the European Union referendum result on 23 June, 2016, arrangements for UK citizens interested in living and working in another EU country are to be negotiated as part of wider discussions with the other Member States regarding Britain's exit from the EU. At the time of going to press, the UK remains a Member State of the Union and will continue to be subject to its obligations under EU law until it has finalised the terms of its withdrawal with the other 27 Member States. The information provided in this chapter will continue to be applicable to UK nationals while the UK remains a member of the EU.

AUSTRIA

The market for ELT in Austria is largely dominated by English for the business community, so teachers with any kind of experience of the business world have a sharp advantage over those with experience only of teaching general English.

As in Germany and Switzerland, most private language institutes depend on freelance part-time teachers drawn from the sizeable resident international community. An estimated 90% of EFL teachers in Austria are freelancers, which means that they do not have a contract with just one school and must pay tax as self-employed workers. Government cutbacks in the past year have resulted in the axing of subsidised language courses, for example for unemployed people, which means that there is an oversupply of native English teachers at present who are chasing fewer course contracts.

Teachers might consider joining the TEA (Teachers of English in Austria, www.tea4teachers.org/joomla), which costs €33 a year (€19 for students) although it doesn't specifically help job-seekers.

FINDING A JOB

The British Council in Austria has a short list of English language institutes and occasionally posts teacher vacancies on its noticeboard. Job ads and relevant employment information for English speakers appear on the site www.virtualvienna.net/jobs.

The online Yellow Pages for Austria are straightforward to use (www.herold.at). Search for *'Sprachschulen u-unterricht'* in the city or region in which you are looking for work.

Most of the 240 *Volkshochschulen* offer English courses in their programmes of general adult education. The co-ordinating office for the provinces in Austria is situated in Vienna. Browse www.vhs.or.at for more information. See the list of employers for details about salary/working conditions for Vienna's adult education centres.

More than 200 English language teaching assistants from the UK and USA are placed in Austrian secondary schools from 1 October to 31 May by the British Council and the Fulbright Commission. The British Council annually looks for about 100 assistants with a decent level of German to work 13 hours a week for a monthly salary of €1,440 gross or €1,162 after deductions for compulsory health insurance and tax are made (www.britishcouncil.org/language-assistants/become/austria). The Fulbright Commission is responsible for recruiting about 140 American graduates with a working knowledge of German and interest in teaching for the same scheme. Detailed information and an application form can be downloaded at www.usta-austria.at and submitted by 15 January.

The Austrian Bilingual Classroom Initiative (www.abcienglish.at) aims to reach every Austrian pupil with native speakers from English-speaking countries by 2020. In 2015 ABCi was absorbed by the newly formed English Teacher Training College in Vorchdorf in Upper Austria. The programme is now geared towards providing participants with a recognised TEFL certification (including the Trinity TESOL) and a chance to travel around Austria delivering free lessons in schools as a kind of apprenticeship or on-the-job training.

After obtaining his CELTA at the University of Sheffield, **Frederick Ball** happened upon ABCi on www.tefl.com and decided to add to his qualifications by enrolling in the CELT-P course in January 2016. This 120-hour Cambridge qualification for teaching primary-aged children is offered to groups of teachers as a combination of online study and practice teaching. Frederick describes the innovative programme:

The teaching centred around travelling to various schools in Austria and Germany to teach a week- or day-long programme of active, CLT-based student-centric English lessons. A day was usually spent with the same class for the majority of their usual lesson time . . . The programme that we worked from gave easily enough detail to follow minutely, but we were also offered the chance to be as flexible as we felt comfortable with in the content of our lessons. In addition, our course tutors were always close to hand in case we required additional assistance or guidance, and each day was followed by detailed feedback from both sides. The process of teaching in a different school each week, or even five different schools, meant that we had the chance to experience a wide variety of students from a variety of schools. Most of our work was in Neue Mittelschulen *(New Middle Schools) teaching children between 11 and 15 years of age, but at other times we taught students as young as six or seven or as old as 18, and with highly varying degrees of motivation and academic aspiration.*

Accommodation was always provided by the college, irrespective of the location of the schools we were attending, as was transport to and from work every weekday. Student teachers did not earn any monetary compensation for their work. Many found the experience costly as many other expenses, such as travel to and from the country, had to be paid out of pocket; but most found the Cambridge-accredited qualification which was to come at the end of it to be worth the investment. The job saw us travelling widely between rural Upper Austria and the capital Vienna, and thus much of our spare time was spent sightseeing, experiencing new places or simply relaxing in a variety of unfamiliar locations. I enjoyed it and found it beneficial to such an extent that I have now returned to the college as a paid Academic Intern, carrying out much of the same teaching work as I had been doing previously as a student teacher.

New arrivals in Austria's cities should visit a number of institutes and try to piece together a timetable. After working for three or four schools, it is better to cultivate just one or two since it is unrealistic to work for any more than this on a longer-term basis. A smart appearance and confident manner are always assets when looking for work teaching within the business community. Most Austrians will have an intermediate or higher level of English.

To give an idea of qualifications needed, MHC Business Language Training in Vienna asks for teachers who have some business background, ideally in a specialised area such as marketing, finance or law; it does not insist on a degree but welcomes a teaching certificate such as the CELTA.

The rate at reputable institutes starts at €18–€20 per lesson (normally 45 minutes) and more for 60-minute lessons (€20–€35). This is none-too-generous when the high cost of living in Vienna is taken into account, although taking seminars can pay fairly well (between €300 and €400 per 7+ hour day). Life in the provinces is less expensive of course. At the interview stage, always find out whether quoted rates are gross or net, if travelling time is covered, and when you will be paid. Some schools pay after the course has finished, which will leave you a pauper for an extended period.

TEACHING CHILDREN AND AT SUMMER CAMPS

The demand for teachers of children and young people is very strong in Austria as elsewhere in Europe. Summer camps provide scope for EFL teachers, as indicated in the entries for English for Children, English for Kids and LETA. Another major player is The Kids English Company (Kagraner Platz 8, 1220 Vienna; ✆ +43 1 263 8931; www.kidsco.at/working.htm) which mounts language courses for children aged 3–10. More than 30 native speaker teachers work at its language centre in Vienna plus teach lessons in kindergartens, private homes, etc. Recruitment takes place between May and September, and pay is generous, €28 per hour. Another company to try is educom, which runs immersion summer camps in the Austrian Alps (www.camps-for-friends.com/en/job) and takes on summer staff interested in sports and creative arts as well as language teaching. A Slovakian company, Sidas School (www.sidaschool.com), employs native English speakers for its Active English Weeks and Summer Day Camps which run in neighbouring countries including Austria (see entry in chapter on Slovakia).

REGULATIONS

Until the UK actually exits the European Union, British teachers are still entitled to the same freedom of movement as Irish teachers. Arrangements for British citizens looking to live and work in another EU country are to be negotiated as part of wider discussions with the other Member States concerning the UK's exit from the EU. Applications for work permits for non-EU citizens (*Beschäftigungsbewilligung*) are almost never granted. All schools claim that they will not hire a non-EU citizen unless they already have a work permit. One exception is the SWAP programme for Canadians under 30 (http://swap.ca/austria), who can get a six-month work visa. Otherwise, Austria is a hard nut to crack.

However, Austria has introduced a flexible new immigration scheme whereby highly qualified workers or skilled workers in shortage occupations may obtain a 'Red-White-Red Card' valid for an initial 12 months; more details of this can be found at www.migration.gv.at/en/types-of-immigration/permanent-immigration-red-white-red-card.html. A hefty percentage of earnings (typically 15%–17%) will be deducted at source (or should be) for health and social security contributions. Most employees and freelancers enrol in WGKK (www.wgkk.at) whereas the self-employed have to pay a minimum of €50 a month to SVA (http://svagw.at/portal27/svaportal/content?contentid=10007.713928&viewmode=content), which increases dramatically if your earnings rise.

Austria (like Germany) has many bureaucratic layers. New arrivals need to register with the police and obtain a *Meldezettel*, after presenting proof of accommodation and means of supporting yourself, either with savings or an employment contract. Wages will be paid directly into your bank account. You will also need to get a tax number from the local tax office.

GEOFF NUNNEY

Geoff Nunney, knowing that his job at a language school in Slovakia would end with the academic year, was anxious to sort out a summer job and had positive responses to his enquiries to summer employers in Austria, Italy and Spain, mostly sourced through this book. He accepted an invitation to Vienna, which is as accessible from where he was located in Nitra, as London is from his native Birmingham.

I walked away with the job on the day, which is a good feeling, and you couldn't wipe the smile off my face. I got six weeks' work with English for Kids, two in Vienna, and four in Linz. The programme is a mixture of English teaching, sports coaching and lots of things. It was quite a detailed application process: three lesson plans, two references, and then the director invited me to interview in Vienna. So I have more work than I did last summer, more time between camps and will be working in a beautiful country. Also, they pay travel expenses to Austria, and there are four days of training, before you start. It's not even the end of April, but I have my summer sorted. I can highly recommend them. The employer also responded positively to an admission of a chronic health problem I have, asked a couple of questions, not unreasonable, and checked if I have private health insurance, which I do (with Ace Travel Insurance).

LIST OF EMPLOYERS

ABCi
Austrian Bilingual English Classroom Initiative & English Teacher Training College, Bahnhofstrasse 13, 4655 Vorchdorf
+43 7614 5140017
office@abcienglish.at
www.abcienglish.at

An initiative of the English Teacher Training College.

NUMBER OF TEACHERS: 35 volunteer teachers.

PREFERENCE OF NATIONALITY: British. Also American, Canadian, Australian, New Zealand and Irish.

QUALIFICATIONS: Degree in education or similar teaching qualification.

CONDITIONS OF EMPLOYMENT: 3–5 months; 6–8 hours per day.

SALARY: Unpaid.

FACILITIES/SUPPORT: Accommodation is provided. No assistance with permits or travel expenses. Trainees can undertake a beginners or intermediate training course in combination with practical classroom experience, lasting 15 weeks in autumn, winter or spring.

RECRUITMENT: Adverts in the *Guardian*, tefl.com, etc. Interviews by Skype or phone.

CONTACT: Frank L. Carle, Managing Director.

BERLITZ AUSTRIA GmbH
Graben 13, 1010 Vienna
Also Mariahilferstrasse 27, 1060 Vienna; Schlosshoferstr. 13–15, 1210 Vienna; Getreidegasse 21, 5020 Salzburg, etc.
www.berlitz.at

NUMBER OF TEACHERS: No fixed number, teachers work on a freelance basis in Vienna, the Tirol, etc. Berlitz has 10 centres in Austria.

PREFERENCE OF NATIONALITY: None but it is very hard for non-EU citizens to obtain work permits.

QUALIFICATIONS: Perfect command of English and a talent for teaching. Academic background preferred; pedagogical experience is helpful but not vital. Any other background (business, engineering, IT, etc) is welcome.

CONDITIONS OF EMPLOYMENT: Freelance contract with no fixed hours. Schools are open Monday to Friday, 8am–8pm.

SALARY: Starting salary is €24 for a double unit (80 minutes).

RECRUITMENT: Interviews are essential.

BERLITZ AUSTRIA GMBH KIDS & TEENS
Schlosshofer Strasse 13-15, 1210 Vienna
erika.eckwolf@berlitz.at
www.berlitz.at/en/kids_teens

PREFERENCE OF NATIONALITY: Native speakers with EU nationality.

QUALIFICATIONS: Communicative personality and flexibility. TEFL training and childcare experience advantageous.

CONDITIONS OF EMPLOYMENT: Day camps in Vienna, and 5-day residential camps throughout Austria in July and August. Camp staff participate in sports and evening programme. Opportunities may arise to teach adults as well.

FACILITIES/SUPPORT: Initial training (4 days) in Berlitz Method given in late April, and specialised training for teaching children (3 days) in Vienna in early May.

RECRUITMENT: Application deadline mid-April.

CONTACT: Erika Eckwolf.

BIKU GmbH & Co KG
English Project Weeks and Summer Camps, Schneckgassse 14, 3100 St Pölten
+43 2742 77561
playandlearn@biku.at; project-weeks@biku.at
www.biku.at

NUMBER OF TEACHERS: 15–20.

PREFERENCE OF NATIONALITY: British, American, Australian, New Zealander, South African and Irish, but must have the legal right to work in Austria.

QUALIFICATIONS: Minimum TEFL certificate. Must be willing to travel.

CONDITIONS OF EMPLOYMENT: Freelance, so dates are flexible. Trainers travel around the country on project weeks on which they teach 6 lessons a day, during the school week.

SALARY: Negotiable.

FACILITIES/SUPPORT: No help with visas given.

RECRUITMENT: Interviews are essential and carried out in Austria.

CONTACT: Oliver Mayer (English Garden Manager) or Carina Donabauer (Project Weeks and Camps).

COLE INTERNATIONAL SCHOOLS
Weingartnerstrasse 108, 6020 Innsbruck, Tirol
+43 664 371 6063
admin@cole.at
www.cole.at/Employment-opportunities

NUMBER OF TEACHERS: 2 pre-school teachers or teaching assistants and 2 QTS (Qualified Teacher Status) primary school teachers. Also volunteer positions for part-time teacher in pre-school and in summer programme (www.cole.at/Summer-Programme-SUMEX).

PREFERENCE OF NATIONALITY: British.

QUALIFICATIONS: PGCE with English/German, or BA in English Language/Education. Well spoken British English.

CONDITIONS OF EMPLOYMENT: 1-year contract with either 10 or 20 hours per week.

RECRUITMENT: Usually via adverts on teaching and TEFL websites. Interviews are essential and can be conducted by phone; 1 month probationary period.

CONTACT: Rosie Ladner-Cole, Proprietor.

DELPHIN SPRACHSERVICE
Jeneweingasse 17, 1210 Vienna
+43 1 585 5347
delphin@dolphin.at
www.dolphin.at

NUMBER OF TEACHERS: 17 for one-to-one lessons, some of which are conducted in Viennese coffee houses.

PREFERENCE OF NATIONALITY: British, Irish, American.

QUALIFICATIONS: Charisma and competence, experience and appearance, resourcefulness and reliability, diligence and dynamics.

CONDITIONS OF EMPLOYMENT: Stage 1: freelance contracts from 1 to 6 months, starting at 1 hour/week; Stage 2: fixed contract (including health care and pension), open ended, starting at 10 hours/week.

SALARY: Stage 1, €15–€35 per unit (55 minutes); stage 2, €10–€25 per hour.

FACILITIES/SUPPORT: Centres provide preliminary accommodation for the first weeks and help teachers find a place on their own. Assistance with work permit only after a trial period.

RECRUITMENT: Interview essential: face-to-face, over the phone, review of references.

CONTACT: Mr Adrian Krois, Managing Director.

DIE WIENER VOLKSHOCHSCHULEN
Lustkandlgasse 50, 1090 Vienna
info@vhs.at
www.vhs.at

16 Vienna Adult Education Centres (VHS, life-long learning). English courses according to CEFR levels, 60 different languages offered, European language portfolio for adults, Cambridge Exams in collaboration with British Council Vienna, TELC Certificates.

NUMBER OF TEACHERS: Varies according to demand. All teachers are freelance.

PREFERENCE OF NATIONALITY: None, but normally hire teachers living locally.

QUALIFICATIONS: EUROLTA (ICC, The European Language Network, Die Wiener Volkshochschulen), EUROLTA-EUROVOLT Diploma (ICC, The European Language Network, Die Wiener Volkshochschulen), CELTA, DELTA and/or university training, or varied extensive experience of language teaching in upper secondary/adult/university education (at least 2 years' work experience).

CONDITIONS OF EMPLOYMENT: Self-employed freelancers. Minimum commitment 15 weeks (one term). Teaching hours Monday–Saturday between 6am and 9pm.

SALARY: €19–€22 per 50-minute lesson. Maximum: approx €560 per month.

FACILITIES/SUPPORT: Workshops and other in-service training courses available. Library and media facilities.

RECRUITMENT: Courses are planned 6 months in advance. European CV (google 'Europass' for information on the standard format), letter of intent and local interview essential.

ENGLISH FOR CHILDREN (EFC)/ENGLISH LANGUAGE DAY CAMP (ELDC)
Jägerstrasse 28, 2230 Gänserndorf
scott.matthews@englishforchildren.com; office@englishforchildren.com
www.englishforchildren.com

NUMBER OF TEACHERS: EFC: varies according to need. ELDC: about 25 counsellors.

PREFERENCE OF NATIONALITY: None, but must be a native English speaker.

QUALIFICATIONS: Minimum age 20. Experience of teaching children is required.

CONDITIONS OF EMPLOYMENT: EFC: freelance 10-month contract (September/October to June). Most of the work is part-time in kindergartens, primary schools and home groups. ELDC: the summer camp runs in Vienna during July for 4 weeks.

FACILITIES/SUPPORT: For the EFC programme teachers need to be living in Austria. Full training given, free of charge, before and during contract. All course materials provided. Housing not provided. ELDC: 4-week summer camp programme, lunch provided during camp days, 5 days a week, housing not provided; however, relevant contacts to student housing, hostels etc available.

RECRUITMENT: Direct applications by email and telephone interviews.

CONTACT: Scott Matthews, Director.

ENGLISH FOR KIDS
A. Baumgartnerstrasse 44/A7042, 1230 Vienna
+43 1 667 4579
magik@e4kids.co.at
www.e4kids.at.

NUMBER OF TEACHERS AND CAMP COUNSELLORS: 6–8 for full-immersion residential summer camp in Lachstatt near Linz in Upper Austria; 8–12 for day camps in Vienna.
PREFERENCE OF NATIONALITY: EU or others with work permit for Austria.
QUALIFICATIONS: CELTA or Trinity Certificate (minimum grade B) and some formal teaching preferred/required. Camp counsellors require no formal training/experience but must be outgoing, enjoy working with children and should like outdoor activities and sports.
CONDITIONS OF EMPLOYMENT: Duration: mid-July to end August. 2 weeks in Vienna and 3 weeks in Upper Austria. Pupil groups aged from kindergarten to age 10, and 10–15. Full-immersion courses with in-house methods following carefully planned syllabus and teachers' manual, supplemented with CD-ROMs etc. Pre-camp teacher training is mandatory.
SALARY: Varies depending on qualifications. Up to €1,650 per month gross, plus travel costs within Austria, full board and accommodation.
FACILITIES/SUPPORT: Good standard of accommodation and full board provided for teachers. Computer room, internet and video room available.
RECRUITMENT: www.e4kids.at/txt/jobs/apply/job_opportunity.html.
CONTACT: Irena Köstenbauer, Principal.

LETA e.U. (LEARN ENGLISH THROUGH ACTION)
Gyrowetzgasse 1/4, 1140 Vienna
+43 664 116 3140
pzt@leta.co.at
www.leta.co.at/en/careers

NUMBER OF TEACHERS: 4 full-time; up to 10 for summer camps in Salzburg and Vienna.
PREFERENCE OF NATIONALITY: Native speakers from UK, Canada, South Africa, Australia, USA and Ireland.
QUALIFICATIONS: TEFL, CELTA, TESOL or other qualification related to teaching English plus relevant experience working with adults.
CONDITIONS OF EMPLOYMENT: Working hours between 16 and 25 for full-time teachers. Hours are usually between 9am and 11.30am and between 2pm and 8pm. Open-ended contracts (unless teachers' visas expire).
SALARY: €18 per hour. Austrian labour law stipulates that an additional 13th and 14th month be paid. Bonuses may be paid to teachers who have excelled or brought in more clients.
FACILITIES/SUPPORT: Insurance provided. No assistance with accommodation. Help given with applying to AMS (Arbeitsmarktservice) for visa. Training workshops arranged. Owner personally trains teachers working with children aged 2–10 years.
RECRUITMENT: Direct application (up to 200 per year) without placing ads.
CONTACT: Precious Sandy Zeinzinger-Tuitz, Owner, Founder and Managing Director.

MHC BUSINESS LANGUAGE TRAINING GmbH
Wiedner Hauptstrasse 54/13A, 1040 Vienna
+43 1 603 0563
office@mhc-training.com
www.mhc-training.com/en/jobs

NUMBER OF TEACHERS: 50 for Vienna, Innsbruck, Linz, Salzburg, Graz and Klagenfurt. Also operate business language training in Bratislava (see entry in Slovakia chapter).
PREFERENCE OF NATIONALITY: Any.
QUALIFICATIONS: MHC trainers have a love of languages and an understanding of business experience, often specialising in areas such as marketing, finance, pharmaceutical or law. A degree is not necessary, although a teaching certificate such as CELTA would be of value.
CONDITIONS OF EMPLOYMENT: Freelance, teaching 15–25 hours per week.
SALARY: €26–€32 per 60 minutes, depending on experience and development with MHC. Seminars pay between €300 and €400 per day (7–9 hours). Trainers are responsible for paying their own taxes (about 21%) and social security (variable).
FACILITIES/SUPPORT: Resource library, photocopying, trainer development, course books for courses supplied for trainers. Trainers from non-EU countries require working papers.
RECRUITMENT: Interviews are essential and usually take place at premises. Possibility of Skype interviews if the applicant is based abroad.
CONTACT: Mark Heather, Managing Director (mark.heather@mhc-training.com).

MIND & MORE, MANAGEMENT AND EDUCATION SERVICES GmbH
Goldschmiedgasse 10, 3rd floor, 1010 Vienna
+43 1 535 9695
office@mindandmore.at
www.mindandmore.at/de/jobs

Management and Education Services is also the Representative Office of the British Open University and OU Business School in Austria, South Germany, Slovenia and Hungary.

NUMBER OF TEACHERS: About 70 language trainers in Vienna and more in many locations around the country and across the borders, plus management skills faculty trainers.

PREFERENCE OF NATIONALITY: None.

QUALIFICATIONS: Minimum university degree plus CELTA or TESOL and teaching experience; preferably also business experience.

CONDITIONS OF EMPLOYMENT: Freelance contracts. Hours vary.

SALARY: Language training: min €22 per 45-minute unit/€28 for 60-minute units; more for specialised language training and seminars; market rates for management skills training.

FACILITIES/SUPPORT: Support given.

RECRUITMENT: Via internet, personal recommendations, partner institutions including British Council, BFI and related institutions. Send cover letter, CV in EU-format and copies of certificates and references. Face-to-face interview essential.

CONTACT: Mag. Walter Grubanovitz (w.grubanovitz@mindandmore.at).

SPIDI SPRACHENINSTITUT

Franz-Josefs-Kai 27/10, 1010 Vienna

+43 1 2361 717

office@spidi.at

www.spidi.at

NUMBER OF TEACHERS: About 50 Business English/ESP trainers for Vienna, Tirol and Vorarlberg.

PREFERENCE OF NATIONALITY: EU citizens.

QUALIFICATIONS: Minimum CELTA or equivalent. Business English and ESP teaching experience preferred.

CONDITIONS OF EMPLOYMENT: Freelance. Flexible hours.

SALARY: €26–€28 per hour, depending on qualifications and experience.

FACILITIES/SUPPORT: No assistance with accommodation. Library with PCs for trainers. Monthly teacher development sessions.

RECRUITMENT: Local interview essential.

CONTACT: Martina Groh (martina.groh@spidi.at).

THE ENGLISH CAMP COMPANY LLC

Via Della Madonna Delle Grazie 6, Santa Maria Degli Angeli, Assisi (PG) 06081, Italy

+39 331 586 7751/320 3722 106

info@theenglishcampcompany.com

www.theenglishcampcompany.com

NUMBER OF TEACHERS: 15–25 for summer camps in Austria (and Italy) for children aged 7–14 years.

PREFERENCE OF NATIONALITY: None. Lots of North Americans join the summer camps.

QUALIFICATIONS: Previous teaching experience or experience working at summer camps with children.

CONDITIONS OF EMPLOYMENT: 2-month contract between June and early September. Working hours 9am–5pm. Compulsory 1-week orientation in Assisi must be attended in early June.

SALARY: €175 per week.

FACILITIES/SUPPORT: All teachers are housed with host families. Orientation week provided for all teachers in Assisi in early June (and sometimes late June as well). The programme gets good reviews on www.gooverseas.com.

RECRUITMENT: Closing date for applications beginning of April. Applications open in October.

CONTACT: Ashleigh McLean (ashleigh.mclean@theenglishcampcompany.com) and Nate Poerio (nate.poerio@theenglishcampcompany.com). Founders and Directors.

BENELUX

Belgium

As one of the capitals of the European Union, demand for all the principal European languages in Brussels is huge. Yet, despite the enormous amount of language teaching in Belgium, there are also a large number of well-qualified expatriates and spouses who take up teaching. This may meet some demand, but not all. To find contact details for language schools in Belgium, the online *Yellow Pages* is a useful tool. A search for 'language schools' in the Brussels Region on www.goldenpages.be will turn up about 80 institutes.

Newcomer is a bi-annual publication which remains in print, though its sister English language monthly magazine *The Bulletin* ceased publication a few years ago in order to go entirely digital (www.xpats.com). *Newcomer* contains information and contact addresses of interest to the newly arrived teacher, including a listing of major language schools (look for it in newsagents). The casual teacher will encounter a lot of competition from highly qualified candidates in Brussels and other cities, and will probably steer clear of schools that teach senior EU bureaucrats. Telephone/Skype teaching is popular in Belgium, especially among French learners of English; e.g. see Phone Languages (✆ +32 2 647 40 20; www.phonelanguages.com). Several language teaching organisations are represented in more than one Belgian city, especially Berlitz and CLL (see entries).

As throughout continental Europe, children attend summer camps which focus on language learning. Companies such as Kiddy & Junior Classes (part of Language Studies International) and Ski Ten International organise holiday English courses. Pro Linguis arranges week-long residential language courses in Thiaumont, a remote southern corner of Belgium near Luxembourg (✆ +32 63 220462; www.prolinguis.be) and employs some native English speaker teachers who must be willing to keep themselves amused. Courses are put on for all ages including children, so teachers may also be given pastoral duties patrolling dorms, etc. Another company to try for a summer job is Ceran Lingua International (www.ceran.com/en/ceran/jobs), whose children's centre is located in the town of Spa.

Social security payments are very high in Belgium. A full-time teacher should expect to be charged about €800 every three months. The first €7,130 can be earned free of tax; thereafter the rates are high.

FREELANCE TEACHING

It is feasible to put up notices in one of the large university towns (Brussels, Antwerp, Ghent, Leuven, Liège, etc) offering conversation practice. Almost all foreign teachers who begin to work for an institute do so on a freelance basis and will have to deal with their own tax and social security. Officially they should declare themselves *indépendants* (self-employed persons) and pay contributions that amount to up to one-third of their salary. In fact many English teachers take their gross salary without declaring it, and don't work long enough to risk being caught. Once a teacher has worked black (*en noir/in het zwart*), it is difficult to regularise his or her status, since they then have to declare all previous earnings. Therefore anyone who plans to spend more than a few months teaching in Belgium should consider this issue.

LIST OF EMPLOYERS

BERLITZ LANGUAGE CENTRES
Avenue Louise 306–310, 1050 Brussels
✆ +32 2 649 6175
joke.vandaele@berlitz.be
www.berlitz.be

NUMBER OF TEACHERS: About 225 (for Brussels, Waterloo, Namur, Charleroi, Liège, Antwerp, Bruges, Mouscron-Tournai, Ghent, Hasselt, Tienen, Mechelen and West Flanders).
PREFERENCE OF NATIONALITY: British or Irish.
QUALIFICATIONS: University degree.

CONDITIONS OF EMPLOYMENT: Freelance – flexible hours (mornings, evenings plus Saturday morning).

SALARY: €15 per 40-minute teaching unit.

FACILITIES/SUPPORT: No assistance with accommodation. In-house training lasts 8 days.

RECRUITMENT: Via adverts and direct applications.

CONTACT: Mrs Joke Van Daele, Country Manager of Instruction.

CALL INTERNATIONAL

Avenue Louise 65/11, 1050 Brussels

+32 2 644 9595

brussels@callinter.com

www.callinter.com/language-trainer

Centre for Accelerated Language Learning in Belgium (Brussels, Waterloo, Tournai and Liège).

NUMBER OF TEACHERS: 150.

PREFERENCE OF NATIONALITY: None.

QUALIFICATIONS: Degree necessary. Experience an advantage. Good communication skills needed.

CONDITIONS OF EMPLOYMENT: Freelance; car; flexible hours.

FACILITIES/SUPPORT: No assistance with accommodation.

RECRUITMENT: All year through.

CONTACT: Sylvie Laurent.

CLL CENTRE DE LANGUES

Place de l'Université 25, 1348 Louvain-la-Neuve

+32 10 470628/470629

jobs@cll.ucl.ac.be or eujobs@cll.ucl.ac.be

www.cll.be

NUMBER OF TEACHERS: 100 trainers for European institutions in Brussels, plus adult and business classes in Brussels and Wallonia. Also jobs teaching children and teens.

PREFERENCE OF NATIONALITY: From English-speaking countries.

QUALIFICATIONS: Experience in teaching English as a foreign language and, if possible, with a degree in languages.

CONDITIONS OF EMPLOYMENT: Freelance, variable hours (daytime, evenings, Saturdays, etc).

SALARY: €22.10–€27.50 per hour according to experience.

FACILITIES/SUPPORT: None.

RECRUITMENT: Advertisements on EURES, the European Job Mobility portal. Interviews in Belgium essential, followed by an integration session.

CONTACT: Mme Florence Baily (f.baily@cll.be).

LANGUAGE STUDIES INTERNATIONAL / KIDDY & JUNIOR CLASSES

Boulevard Clovis 83, 1000 Brussels

+32 2 217 2373

info@lsi-be.net

www.lsi-be.net

Children's school:

+32 2 218 3920

info@kiddyclasses.net

www.kiddyclasses.net

NUMBER OF TEACHERS: 30–60.

PREFERENCE OF NATIONALITY: None.

QUALIFICATIONS: Adult school: qualified university level teachers with TEFL experience; Children's school: qualified teachers or would-be teachers with experience in children's entertainment.

CONDITIONS OF EMPLOYMENT: Freelance, although 1–2 month contracts during the summer between late June and 1 September. Adult school hours: 9am–8pm; children's school: 9am–5pm.

SALARY: Varies.

FACILITIES/SUPPORT: None, although for the 2-month summer contract assistance is given finding accommodation.

RECRUITMENT: Via internet, newspaper, universities, company brochure. Interviews essential unless excellent references received. Interviews are carried out in Brussels.

CONTACT: Mme Caroline DeWitte for children's school; Mme Christelle Denay for adult school.

LC LANGUAGE CENTRE

Avenue de Broqueville, 113, 1200 Brussels

+32 2 771 7131

language.centre@skynet.be

www.lclanguagecentre.com

NUMBER OF TEACHERS: 20 (for English).

PREFERENCE OF NATIONALITY: UK and USA.

QUALIFICATIONS: TEFL or TESL and experience.

CONDITIONS OF EMPLOYMENT: Freelance/flexible contracts and work hours.

SALARY: Flexible.

FACILITIES/SUPPORT: None.

RECRUITMENT: Direct application. Interview essential.

LET'S SPEAK GOOD ENGLISH asbl

5, rue de Dinant, 1421 Ophain

+32 2 354 5786

letsspeakgoodenglish@gmail.com

www.letsspeakgoodenglish.com

NUMBER OF TEACHERS: 4 freelancers.
PREFERENCE OF NATIONALITY: English mother tongue.
QUALIFICATIONS: Teaching degree and TEFL experience needed. Experience with young learners / teens / adults and Business English sought.
CONDITIONS OF EMPLOYMENT: Full school year (September–June). Variable hours but usually 2pm–9pm.
SALARY: €1,200–€2,000 depending on hours worked and if accommodation is needed. Teachers are responsible for paying their own tax and social security contributions.
RECRUITMENT: Local advertising.
CONTACT: Helena Miziura, Director.

PRO LINGUIS
Rue de l'Eglise 228, 6717 Thiaumont
secretariat@prolinguis.be
www.prolinguis.be

NUMBER OF TEACHERS: 14 (freelancers) to work near Arlon close to the Luxembourg border.
PREFERENCE OF NATIONALITY: British.
QUALIFICATIONS: Kindergarten teacher or summer camp counsellor, primary school teacher, EFL training, BA in English or any other language, in business, law or social studies.1 year's teaching experience needed for summer positions.
CONDITIONS OF EMPLOYMENT: Minimum 1-year contract, or 2-month contract in summer; 7 hours per day, 4–5 days per week.
SALARY: €12.50–€14 per hour; free lodging on campus.
RECRUITMENT: Personal contacts and websites. Phone interviews. Summer recruitment carries on until mid-June.
CONTACT: Edward Young, Academic Director (edward.young@prolinguis.be).

SKITEN INTERNATIONAL
Chateau d'Emines, 45 rue de Rhisnes, 5080 Emines la Bruyere, Namur
✆ +32 81 213051
skiteninternational@gmail.com
www.skiten.com

NUMBER OF TEACHERS: 2 for English (plus 1 for tennis).
PREFERENCE OF NATIONALITY: None.
QUALIFICATIONS: Experience with children. Some knowledge of French useful. Mostly aged 18–25.
CONDITIONS OF EMPLOYMENT: Student contract for July or August. 6 hours of work per day including teaching and 'animation', i.e. supervising camp activities.
SALARY: €1,200 per month.
FACILITIES/SUPPORT: Board and lodging provided at camp.
RECRUITMENT: University exchanges, word of mouth.
CONTACT: Martine Goffinet, Director.

Luxembourg

With only a few private language schools, Luxembourg does not offer much scope for ELT teachers. **Fiona Hynd**, the *Responsable Pédagogique* for the English World Institute Luxembourg, described the typical situation:

> ***We do not recruit from outside the Grande Région of Luxembourg and the neighbouring regions in Germany, France and Belgium. When actively recruiting we do so locally and from CVs sent in on spec by people already living in the area. I think this is more or less true for most of the language schools here as Luxembourg is not a hot spot on people's lists of places to go. The cost of living is quite high and the work is mostly freelance and rarely full-time. I believe we are one of the few remaining schools to offer contracts.***

The national employment service (l'Administration de l'Emploi) at 10 rue Bender, L-1229 (Jobseekers' hotline ✆ +352 247 88888; www.adem.public.lu) has a EURES adviser who may have information about language teaching openings.

Informal live-in tutoring jobs are possible. Luxembourg Accueil Information (10 Bisserwee, L-1238 Luxembourg-Grund; ✆ +352 241717; www.luxembourgaccueil.com) is a centre for new arrivals and temporary residents. It provides a range of services from October to May, including workshops and language courses, and might be able to advise on teaching and tutoring possibilities. Annual membership costs €20.

Inlingua and Berlitz have centres in Luxembourg City (www.inlingua.lu/jobs and www.berlitz.lu), and the

Prolingua Language Centre hires professionally turned out teachers with a driving licence to teach in businesses (www.prolingua.lu/en/careers). Prolingua also runs language summer schools for school children.

Netherlands

Dutch people have a very high degree of competence in English after they finish their schooling. Educated Dutch people are so fluent in English that the Minister of Education once suggested that English might become the main language in Dutch universities, a suggestion which caused an understandable outcry. However, the schooling system has become increasingly international and university staff are being challenged to lecture and publish in English and to advance their English-language skills.

Yvonne Dalhuijsen, operational manager at UvA Talen (see list of employers), sees an increasing need for advanced levels of English within both companies and universities. She is always on the lookout for teachers who are native speakers of English. On the other hand, a few long-standing employers of freelance corporate trainers have ceased English teaching operations because of insufficient demand.

What private language schools there are tend to provide specific training in Business English and to be looking for language trainers with extensive commercial or government experience as well as a teaching qualification and – particularly outside the capital – some fluency in Dutch. Business English, Legal English and Academic English (writing papers, abstracts, etc.) are subjects in high demand. So many native English speaking citizens have settled in the Netherlands, attracted by its liberal institutions, that most companies depend on long-term freelancers. Candidates with just a CELTA and some teaching experience can try to pick up part-time work taking IELTS or other Cambridge preparation classes, for example, with CBE Languages in Rotterdam (www.cbelanguages.nl/jobs).

As of May 2016, the old Declaration of Independent Contractor (VAR-WUO) has been abolished and replaced with a system of model agreements between contractor and client, with the intention of cutting down abuse (from the tax office's point of view) of self-employed status. Information on the complicated procedure for freelance teachers and employers to implement the appropriate agreements is available from the tax office (www.belastingdienst.nl).

It might be possible to fix up some informal freelance lessons with university students from non-Dutch backgrounds, including Spanish, whose level of English is less advanced than their local counterparts'.

The *Yellow Pages* are easy to search online (www.detelefoongids.nl) under the rubric *Talenonderwijs* (Language Training). The site of NRTO (www.nrto.nl), the Dutch Council on Training and Education, links to a few English-training institutes. The British Language Training Centre in Amsterdam offers the CELTA course (see Training chapter) and may be able to give advice to qualified job-seekers and recommend other institutes or work. Linguarama Nederland has a sizeable operation in the business training field with centres in Amsterdam, the Hague and Soesterberg; send enquiries to personnel@nl.linguarama.com. Only applicants with a full TEFL/TESOL or CELTA qualification will receive a response (www.linguarama.com/nl/vacatures).

Outside the mainstream language institutes, it might be possible to arrange some telephone teaching. Try, for example, Dialogue Talen in the Hague (www.dialoguetalen.nl). Another possibility for those not interested in a corporate atmosphere is the network of *Volksuniversiteit*, adult education centres. Branches that teach English – 48 in all – can be found throughout the country, all listed at www.volksuniversiteit.nl.

LIST OF EMPLOYERS

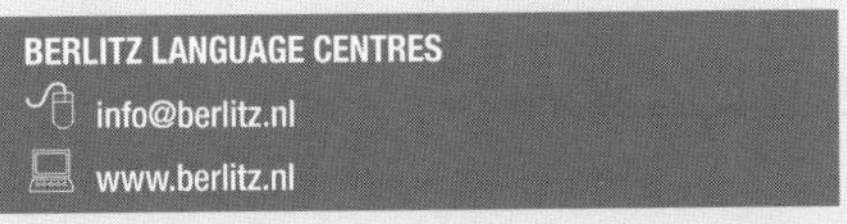
BERLITZ LANGUAGE CENTRES
info@berlitz.nl
www.berlitz.nl

Branches in Amsterdam, Maastricht, Rotterdam and 20 others.

NUMBER OF TEACHERS: 39.

PREFERENCE OF NATIONALITY: None.

QUALIFICATIONS: Minimum bachelor's degree and if possible TEFL and/or business-related work experience.

CONDITIONS OF EMPLOYMENT: 1-year contract. Working hours are between 7.30am and 9.45pm.

SALARY: €1,000–€2,500 per month depending on qualifications and hours worked.

RECRUITMENT: Via the website or on the spot. Interviews essential.

CONTACT: Mrs Joke Van Daele, Country Manager of Instruction (joke.vandaele@berlitz.be).

BOGAERS TALENINSTITUUT B.V.
Groenstraat 139–155, 5021 LL, Tilburg
+31 13 536 2101
administratie@bogaerstalen.nl
www.bogaerstalen.nl

NUMBER OF TEACHERS: 5 foreign out of total of 50.

PREFERENCE OF NATIONALITY: British.

QUALIFICATIONS: Degree and TEFL certificate. Experience in teaching conversational and Business English preferred. Candidates will be expected to register as ZZP-ers (freelancers). Teachers should have mastery of Dutch.

CONDITIONS OF EMPLOYMENT: From 1 week to 9 months.

SALARY: €22.50 per hour.

FACILITIES/SUPPORT: Will help with accommodation if needed.

RECRUITMENT: Speculative CVs and applications.

CONTACT: Jolanda Meijden, General Manager (jolanda.meijden@bogaerstalen.nl).

LANGUAGE PARTNERS
Sarphati Plaza, Rhijnspoorplein 24, 1018 TX, Amsterdam
+31 20 685 2991
afke.derijk@languagepartners.nl
www.languagepartners.nl

Offices also in The Hague, Rotterdam, Amersfoort, Zwolle, Breda and Nijmegen.

NUMBER OF TEACHERS: Approximately 200 (freelance/contract).

PREFERENCE OF NATIONALITY: None.

QUALIFICATIONS: Native speakers, CELTA or TEFL qualifications, and relevant experience in business-to-business training.

CONDITIONS OF EMPLOYMENT: 6–12 months. Variable hours.

FACILITIES/SUPPORT: No help with accommodation or visas.

RECRUITMENT: Online recruitment (e.g. on EURES job portal) and word of mouth. Interviews are essential.

CONTACT: Ms. Afke de Rijk, HR Manager.

PCI – PIMENTEL COMMUNICATIONS INTERNATIONAL
Bachlaan 43, 1817 GH Alkmaar
+31 72 512 1190/515 6518
hrdepartment@pcilanguages.com
www.pcilanguages.com

NUMBER OF TEACHERS: 50+.

PREFERENCE OF NATIONALITY: Mostly British; Irish, North American, Australians, New Zealanders and South Africans welcome.

QUALIFICATIONS: Experience in business and technical English. Cross-cultural communication skills and familiarity with modern teaching methods needed. Should have a VAR-WUO or be eligible to apply for one.

CONDITIONS OF EMPLOYMENT: Freelancers working mostly in-company nationwide.

SALARY: Starts at €27 per hour.

FACILITIES/SUPPORT: Most teachers already live locally.

RECRUITMENT: Adverts, word of mouth and recommendations.

CONTACT: Ms Iona de Pimentel, Director/Owner.

UvA TALEN
Roetersstraat 25, 1018 WB Amsterdam
+31 20 525 4637
trainers@uvatalen.nl
www.uvatalen.nl

Independent language institute, affiliated to the Universiteit van Amsterdam; consists of a translation agency and a training centre.

NUMBER OF TEACHERS: Varies, only freelance.

PREFERENCE OF NATIONALITY: None, provided native English speaker (with widely understood dialect).

QUALIFICATIONS: Experience in teaching adults and registered as a freelancer. Working knowledge of Dutch and/or the level system of the Common European Framework of Reference (A-B-C) is required.

CONDITIONS OF EMPLOYMENT: Freelance assignments only.

SALARY: From €25 per hour, plus compensation for preparation work or marking.

FACILITIES/SUPPORT: No assistance with accommodation or work permits. Project manager monitors content of the courses and is happy to advise teachers on content and materials.

RECRUITMENT: Teachers submit CVs and cover letter; face-to-face interviews required on arrival.

CONTACT: Yvonne Dalhuijsen, Operational Manager (YDalhuijsen@uvatalen.nl).

FRANCE

The French used to rival the English for their reluctance to learn other languages. A Frenchman abroad spoke French as stubbornly as Britons spoke English. But things have changed, especially in the business and technical community. Nearly every Parisian now has friends living and working in London whom they visit. French telephone directories contain pages of English language training organisations and the law continues to put pressure on companies to provide ongoing training for staff. Employees have the right to vocational training, and English language and computing training are the most popular objects of investment. Therefore many private language institutes cater purely to the business market. In fact a quick browse through the entries in the List of Employers at the end of this chapter will lead you to the conclusion that the majority of adult language training in France is business oriented, with most of it taking place on-site and the rest taking place in business and vocational schools. In this setting the term *formateurs* or 'trainers' is often used instead of English teachers. Private training companies involved with *formation* often produce very glossy brochures which look more like the annual report of a multinational corporation than an invitation to take an evening course. Most offer one-to-one tuition.

Many of the thousands of non-profit Chambres de Commerce et d'Industrie (CCI) around France have their own Centres d'Etude des Langues. In addition, a considerable number of town councils (*mairies*) offer simple English courses to locals for a reduced rate, or allow associations to offer courses using their premises, so you might be able to pick up a few hours of teaching this way.

Teaching children has traditionally been left mostly to French teachers of English, helped sometimes by foreign language assistants placed in schools (see later). According to the director of TEFL Toulouse, the teaching of Young Learners is on the up in France, with a current trend for teaching toddlers. Jonathan Davies speculates that teaching groups of children and teenagers after school will continue to take off, as it did in Spain in the 1990s. Children do not go to school on Wednesday afternoons, so this is a great time to offer to teach. Teaching by Skype or other online system is now a common supplement or even full-time teaching possibility in a growing market.

More and more language schools want to employ teachers on a freelance part-time basis to make their bureaucracy easier and more flexible. This means that teachers are becoming more savvy about drumming up their own freelance work, even if they have a contract with an employer elsewhere.

PROSPECTS FOR TEACHERS

Advanced ELT qualifications have been less in demand in the past than solid teaching experience, particularly in a business context. Nowadays the first question you are likely to be asked when approaching an employer is '*Vous avez le TEFL?*' Few schools accept candidates on the basis of being a native speaker and candidates may be asked to provide official certificates to show the educational level they have reached. However, anyone who has a university degree in any subject and who can look at home in a business situation (and possesses a suit/smart clothes) still has a chance of finding teaching work, particularly if they have a working knowledge of French.

All respectable language schools in France now want to see solid evidence of experience and competence, or at least a strong drive to work in the teaching field. A good CV showing past experience and a TEFL certificate from a reputable training organisation are almost guaranteed tickets at least to the interview stage.

Ironically, more 'serious' qualifications such as a BEd, PGCE or even the DELTA are not always a help. The fact is that language schools fight for contracts on price, and ordinary clients tend not to differentiate and believe language lessons are the same from whichever school. Therefore a teacher's experience and qualifications have little to do with schools winning training contracts. Most French students are happy with a friendly, competent and enthusiastic teacher, whatever their background, who is able to adapt to their needs and supply them with materials and learning situations relevant to their situation.

How much language schools have to pay teachers is a major issue. In other words, an enthusiastic new teacher clutching a shiny new TEFL Certificate may actually be more attractive than someone with a weight of experience and qualifications who expects to be paid accordingly. Salary scales are relatively fixed in France, and experience and advanced qualifications don't really give you much bargaining power. The situation is made worse by the rapidity with which language teachers move on, and language schools know that there are plenty of other good candidates hungry for work and experience, and more or less ready to work for the basic rate.

In some circles it is fashionable to learn American English, which means that, despite the visa difficulties for non-EU citizens, it is possible for Americans to find work as well. Most are already in France on a student visa, often studying the French language at a local Alliance Française.

FINDING A JOB

IN ADVANCE

France is such a popular and obvious destination for British and Irish people and also for North Americans that a job hunt from abroad can be disappointing. Most institutes in France consider primarily applicants who are already living locally. Major language-teaching organisations receive speculative CVs every day and can't promise anything until they meet the applicant.

Googling for 'Écoles de Langues' and your destination city is usually the best way to come up with contact details for language schools. The *Pages Jaunes* (Yellow Pages; www.pagesjaunes.fr) are a useful search engine; search under the heading *Cours Langues Étrangères* or *Formation Langues.*

The British Council offices in Paris, Lyon and Marseilles (www.britishcouncil.fr) teach English to adults, and to children and teenagers during the school holidays, and may have vacancies for well-qualified teachers, mainly to work part-time at their partner schools in Paris suburbs such as Vaucresson (teacherrecruitment@britishcouncil.fr). **Sab Will**, long-term English resident of Paris, worked at the British Council in Paris for several years and says to get in you will have to convince them you are good, with relevant experience and qualifications. It also has a useful online teaching resource centre (www.britishcouncil.fr/en/teach/online-resources) which offers a weekly collection of links to free materials from British Council websites.

TESOL-France (www.tesol-france.org) circulates weekly lists of job vacancies, mostly high-level posts e.g. in university language departments, which are accessible to members. Membership costs €49 a year (€27 if a student or unemployed) and brings other networking advantages.

Assistant programme

The Centre International d'Etudes Pédagogiques (CIEP) in France offers thousands of assistantships in France for students from many different countries (✆ +33 1 45 07 60 00; www.ciep.fr). Enrolled undergraduates and graduate students aged 20 to 35 can spend a (short) academic year working as English language assistants in primary or secondary schools throughout France and its DOM-TOMs (*départements et territoires d'outremer*), which refer to all overseas territories such as French Guiana and Réunion Island.

In return for giving conversation classes, providing classroom support and teaching pupils about their country for a mere 12 hours a week altogether, assistants receive a gross allowance of approximately €965 a month (€794 net) for seven months, beginning 1 October. Those who want to carry on teaching through the summer may apply to teach lycée students (aged 15–18) on intensive language summer courses fully funded by the French government. Similar posts for the academic year are also available in other francophone countries such as Belgium, Canada (Québec) and Switzerland.

Assistants must have a working knowledge of French, so modern languages students are encouraged to apply. Applications are considered from students who have at least A level, Higher Grade or equivalent in French. Some posts in primary schools require degree-level French because any help offered by colleagues and all discussion of pupil progress, curriculum, lesson planning, etc. is likely to be in French. British applicants should contact the Language Assistants Team, British Council (10 Spring Gardens, London SW1A 2BN; language.assistants@britishcouncil.org; www.britishcouncil.org/language-assistants).

North American students can participate in the scheme by applying through the Assistantship Program at the French embassies in Washington and Ottawa; for further information in the US contact assistant.washington-amba@diplomatie.gouv.fr or browse http://highereducation.frenchculture.org/teach-in-france; in Canada details are available from assistants-langue@ambafrance-ca.org. Applications for the Teaching Assistant Program in France can be found at www.tapif.org.

In some cases the description language 'assistant' is a misnomer in schools where there isn't much support from the rest of the staff. Whereas some might relish the responsibility, others might find the job quite isolating. Enthusiastic yet instructive feedback about the programme can be found at www.gooverseas.com/teach-abroad/france. The contrast in the experiences that participants describe highlights how much depends on unique circumstances in each placement, from Paris to the middle of nowhere, from being hamstrung by a creativity-destroying set curriculum to having carte blanche in planning lessons, from being assigned a spacious rent-free flat to struggling for accommodation on the open market. Much depends on how responsive your *professeur référent* is, since he/she will be your primary contact throughout. However, overall ratings of the assistants' programme are very high.

EMILY SLOANE

Emily Sloane from America was posted as an assistant to a small town in Lorraine (where the quiche comes from), unknown to any English language guidebook that she could find.

I taught English to about 170 students in three different primary schools, two 45-minute sessions per class per week, for a total of 12 hours of work each week. In general, the teaching and lesson planning were thoroughly enjoyable, although I wasn't given much guidance and received no feedback throughout the year, so I'm sure the fact that I was already comfortable and experienced with teaching and working with children made a big difference in my enjoyment. The kids, although adoring and very enthusiastic, were a lot rowdier than I had expected, and I was obliged to spend a lot more time on behaviour management than I'd anticipated. The kids were never mean, just excitable and chatty, especially so because my class offered a break from their usual blackboard-and-worksheet style routine. The fact that I was the only assistant in my town meant that my French improved noticeably, especially my slang and listening comprehension, although it made for some lonely weekends, because I was forced to get by in French all the time.

Teaching children & summer camps

The state Éducation Nationale system is highly regimented and difficult to get into without passing a very challenging test called the CAPES, and later on the Aggrégation. Native-speaker teachers might be able to find an opening in a specialised school such as a Montessori school, often run by expats. The British Council has a large and successful English teaching operation in Paris. Individual tutoring is most likely to take place on Wednesdays (when state schools are closed) and Saturdays.

It will be much easier to arrange part-time work tutoring children in a family context. An innovative company called the Speaking Agency (see entry) recruits up to 1,000 native speakers over 18 to work for a few hours a week either babysitting children aged 3–12 focusing on teaching English through play, or teaching older children. These are all live-out positions so the company is interested in hearing from people already living in France. As well as in Paris, it places tutors in Lyon, Lille, Bordeaux, Nantes and Toulouse. The hourly rate is €10–€13 for the childcare positions, €13–€20 for the tutoring, depending on number of children and travel distance. Details of the online application procedure are at www.facebook.com/jobinfrance. Other companies with similar programmes are Babylangues (see entry) and Eveil Bilingue (www.eveilbilingue.com/we-are-recruiting) who arrange for native English speakers in Paris to fill part-time babysitting and teaching positions.

Anyone who is interested in obtaining a childcare qualification and learning French while at the same time earning up to €1,100 (net) a month by tutoring children in English from September to June should investigate a programme run by the Paris Institute of Childcare Training (www.parisict.com/jobs.html).

The American model of the summer camp thrives in France and dozens of camps have a strong ESL component. Anglophone counsellors and tutors are employed, many of them from the US staying for less than 90 days on a Schengen visa. One of the biggest networks of camps is American Village (see entry) and another is Telligo (www.telligo.fr). For this edition, I received two enthusiastic accounts of working for American Village, one from an American with experience of working with children but no teaching background, and one from a qualified teacher from Australia. **Christine Smith** from the US reports that her days at camp started around 8.30am and finished any time up to midnight and describes the informality of the teaching:

> ***It is a long day and you need energy, but a lot of the work is fun. If you enjoy playing games and doing crafts and being silly, etc. it is enjoyable. It's not like teaching in a classroom. Even teaching the English classes in the morning is not the same as a regular classroom. We did lots of games and songs and not a lot of worksheets. One nice thing about this job is that if you are new to teaching, you get to have a new group of kids every week or two weeks. If you really don't like one group of kids, or if you really mess up and don't bond with the kids, you get to change kids! The attitudes of the pupils range from extremely enthusiastic to 'I'm only here because my parents made me come and I hate them for it.' It is a crash course in teaching.***

Christine goes on to describe the rewards of spending the summer in France (or six summers in her case): '*Camp is a place that you can form very deep bonds with other people. There are times sitting at a fire cooking marshmallows when you can be completely free and open about life. Also, you share with the other counsellors many first time experiences – first time eating some strange food, first time hitchhiking, etc.*'

Similarly, **Catherine Wills** from Melbourne was thoroughly satisfied with this chance to live and work in rural France while getting paid a reasonable wage on top of free bed and food.

ON THE SPOT

Prospective teachers should not automatically head for Paris but bear in mind that provincial cities have many language schools too. Due to the many French companies that have decided it is more cost effective to relocate in the provinces, many regional centres such as Orléans, Lyon, Marseilles, Toulouse, Lille and Rouen are crawling with medium and large international companies, all needing English-speaking staff, as confirmed by **Jonathan**

Davies, Director of the TEFL training company TEFL Toulouse (www.tefltoulouse.com): *'The good news is that outside Paris and some touristy and Mediterranean areas, most of France is still FAR from being saturated with qualified TEFL teachers, just at a time when the whole of France finally seems to want to learn English!'*

When applying to a training organisation, try to demonstrate your commercial flair with a polished presentation including a business-like CV (omitting your hobbies) preferably accompanied by a hand-written letter in impeccable French.

Although English teachers can still get away with more relaxed dress codes and a certain '*originalité*' is tolerated, you will still give yourself the best chance of employment if you follow typical French conventions: dress very smartly for interviews, be positive and enthusiastic, ask questions as well as answer them, and don't sell yourself too cheaply if you have a qualification or experience relevant to what they are looking for. Watch out for language schools trying to make you believe that working evenings or Saturdays is absolutely normal. You may not be able to get paid more for agreeing to do this, but you might be able to negotiate other concessions, such as more time off during the week.

The technique of making a personal approach to schools in the months preceding the one in which you would like to teach is often successful. On the strength of her Cambridge Certificate from International House, **Fiona Paton** had been hoping to find teaching work in the south of France in the summer but quickly discovered that there are very few opportunities outside the academic year. On her way back to England, she disembarked from the train in the picturesque town of Vichy in the Auvergne just long enough to distribute a few self-promotional leaflets to three language schools. She was very surprised to receive a favourable reply from one of them once she was home, and so returned a few weeks later for a happy year of teaching. Make it really easy for language schools to contact you by acquiring a French mobile phone (www.mobile.free.fr charges from €16 a month). Feature the number prominently on all your CVs and motivational letter (often requested by employers and recruiters).

Teaching English in exchange for room and board is not uncommon though it is normally combined with looking after the family's children or doing some domestic chores in order to pay for studies. The strings attached to a free room should be made very clear from the outset, or the candidate (quite often a young woman) might be in for an unpleasant surprise once installed if the family starts heaping on some decidedly non-linguistic tasks (ironing, washing, taking the kids to school).

While looking for something to do in her gap year, **Hannah Start** was put in touch with a French bank executive who had done an English language course in Hannah's home town and who wanted to keep up her English at home in Paris by having someone to provide live-in conversation lessons. So, in exchange for three hours of speaking English in the evening (usually over an excellent dinner), Hannah was given free accommodation in the 17th arrondissement.

SARA BREESE

Sara Breese described her job-hunt in Paris and the style of life teaching can pay for.

Finding work in France is a rather arduous process; however, with determination and zeal one can easily find work. I moved to Paris in September as a jeune fille au pair and doing side work teaching children English. The next year I decided to get my ESL teaching certificate at TEFL Paris which was one of the best decisions I ever made.

Not only did I love the process of getting my certificate, but I also discovered a love for teaching. ESL is probably the number one industry for Anglophones and is your best investment in terms of success in the job search. In order to find a teaching job I looked in the FUSAC [mentioned below] and applied to every English teaching organisation in the magazine. After about two weeks, I received some calls asking for interviews. I interviewed with three different places, accepting a job where I still work. I am paid €20 per hour gross, €16 after taxes. I immediately signed a CDII which is the ideal type of contract for a Business English teacher in Paris. It translates to basically a long-term intermittent contract meaning that you will receive work when it is available but you will not stop being considered an employee.

Sara was not able to save money because Paris is so expensive. She earned between €1,000 and €1,600 a month but spent half of it on rent. The cheapest accommodation takes the form of a *chambre de bonne* (maid's quarters) – small studios at the top of old buildings that are rented for no more than €600 per month.

If you do decide to give it a go in Paris, watch for adverts in the *métro* for English language courses, since these are usually the biggest schools and therefore have the greatest number of vacancies for teachers. Certain streets in the 8th arrondissement around the Gare St Lazare abound in language schools including some cowboy outfits whose standards are not always what they should be. Again, schools which insist on a TEFL certificate and use a rigorous recruitment process are probably the safest bet. If you are desperate, you might want to go for less reputable or well-known schools but be ready to be disappointed.

FREELANCE TEACHING

Well-off parents often pay for private lessons for their school-aged children. Business people with a pressing need for English, which they are reluctant to reveal to their employer, and worried exam students are other big markets for freelance English tutors. Private lessons are a very good supplement to an official contract and it is worth spending a bit of time putting notices up and spreading the word that you are available for this sort of work. **Sab Will** has charged €30 an hour for a minimum of two hours at a time and people seem to accept this if you can convince them you are well-qualified, experienced and pleasant to be with. In general €20 is considered a decent fee for an hour's private tuition, and should be the minimum charged in Paris by anyone with qualifications or experience. Outside Paris, you may do better charging €15, especially in places like Nice where there are so many English tutors. Many people advertise and then have to find a suitable public place to meet clients. Rather than choose a café where you might end up spending a couple of euros on a drink, the Luxembourg Gardens or other parks make a good meeting place in the summer.

It is not difficult to set yourself up as a freelancer ('*auto-entrepreneur*') in France provided you are officially based in France (i.e. with a French bank account and French social security number). The school that employs you as a freelancer should pay 20%–25% above the rate for employees since you will have to pay your own contributions and taxes.

Long-time teacher in France **Jonathan Davies** of TEFL Toulouse describes the trend:

Many teachers are now setting themselves up as freelancers or auto-entrepreneurs, which has added flexibility. You can bill language schools for hours you do for them, and also bill individual clients that you find yourself. You can even be both a freelancer and have contracts – you don't have to choose one or the other. Of course

if you are a freelancer you can choose your own rates and conditions too. It's a fun time to set up business in France, and really not that complicated. One of our TEFL Toulouse ex-trainees with a background in marketing refused to charge under €90 an hour – and got plenty of work!

Self-employed workers (*travailleurs indépendants*) are obliged to register at the social security office (www.urssaf.fr). The hourly fees (*honoraires*) paid to freelance teachers should be significantly higher than to contract workers (*salariés*), since they are free of deductions. There are many *panneaux* or noticeboards (see below) that might prove useful to someone looking for private tutoring. This is especially appealing to Americans who do this without worrying too much about visas.

As part of a well-organised teaching job hunt in Marseilles, American **Bradwell Jackson** tried to arrange to teach some private lessons:

Besides searching for jobs in schools, I also tried my hand at the tutoring market. I put up **petites annonces** *in the local* **boulangeries** *and bars, and I also put an ad in a free local paper called* **13** (**treize**)*, also called* **Top Annonces** *(www.topannonces.fr). The cost of placing the ad was not free, but it wasn't expensive (maybe €10). This did turn out to be fruitful, as I did get responses. My big disadvantage was that I didn't have a cell phone, and I was told that the French are not inclined to respond to someone only by email. I decided to counteract this by putting in a very low asking price, only €10 per hour. With that price, I got several responses, even with only an email address advertised. The problem was that there was a time lag of two weeks between my placing the order and its appearance, by which time I had booked a plane ticket back to Mexico. I also advertised on a free website service called Kelprof (www.kelprof.com). It was indeed free, but to contact referrals you have to use a password and 08 numbers which, I learned the hard way, are very expensive.*

According to an American blogger and school *assistant* called **Kelsey**, using sites like this takes patience, since so many native speakers are advertising their availability this way.

There are expatriate grapevines all over Paris, very helpful for finding teaching work and accommodation. The noticeboard in the foyer of the Centre d'Information et de Documentation Jeunesse (CIDJ) at 101 Quai Branly; ✆ +33 1 44 49 12 00; www.cidj.com (métro Bir-Hakeim) is good for occasional student-type jobs, but sometimes there are adverts for a *soutien scolaire en anglais* (English tutor). Access hours to the CIDJ without an appointment have been reduced to 1pm–6pm Tuesdays to Saturdays.

The other mecca for job and flat-hunters is the American Church at 65 Quai d'Orsay (métro Invalides), which has very active noticeboards upstairs, downstairs and outside. There is a charge for posting a notice and they are kept up to date. In the basement, the free corkboard is much more chaotic; it can take about half an hour to rummage through all the notices.

The American Cathedral in Paris (23 Avenue George V; www.americancathedral.org), near the métro stations Alma Marceau and George V, has a noticeboard featuring employment opportunities and housing listings. The free bilingual online newsletter *France-USA Contacts* or *FUSAC* (www.fusac.fr) carries dozens of teaching adverts. An advert under the heading 'Work Wanted in France' starts at €36 for 20 words. **Sab Will** placed a small ad in FUSAC when he first arrived in Paris and got responses from prospective students. It also provides effective ways to get into the English-speaking expat community in Paris. An online resource for openings in Paris is the expatriates magazine www.jobs-in-paris.fr, to which you can send your resumé.

It may be worth including a reminder here that anyone who advertises their services should exercise a degree of caution when arranging to meet prospective clients.

Outside the bigger cities, your chance of picking up freelance work is greatly improved. Working as a language assistant in a small town in Lorraine, **Emily Sloane** had no problem finding freelance work:

Through word of mouth and no active self-promotion, numerous townspeople contacted me about private English tutoring. By the middle of the school year I had five private students, whom I taught once a week each for a modest fee, with sometimes a meal on top. It was nice to be able to work through more complicated material with older students and really nice to have an inside look into various French households. Plus, the tutoring sessions kept me busy. I also earned some extra cash by doing freelance writing work for the mother of one of my students, which helped to supplement my fairly meagre salary and allowed me to take long and stress-free vacations during the numerous school breaks.

Despite not really needing French to teach – good teaching technique rarely involves having to translate or explain in French – many schools still prefer you to be able to speak some. Also you will get more private students if you can explain your prices and conditions over the phone. Some TEFL courses can offer a French course at a discount rate.

REGULATIONS

EU CITIZENS

While Brexit negotiations between the UK and the EU are ongoing, there is great uncertainty about the future status of British citizens. However during the transition phase, it seems to be business as usual.

Once you take up paid employment in France, your employer must complete all the necessary formalities for registering you with social security (*sécu*) and you will be issued with a registration card and then pay a percentage of your wages as contributions. French red tape is a pain in the neck, but once you've got it over and done with you are into a favourable system of benefits and help on anything from unemployment and housing aid to child benefit and income supplements if you don't earn much one year.

NON-EU CITIZENS

In France, it is much more difficult for Americans, Canadians, Australians and all other non-EU citizens to get a work permit. However, people with initiative are able to get some legal work, at least for a limited period. The easiest way (apart from marrying a French national) is to enrol in a French course at an official provider, such as the Alliance Française, and acquire a student visa, which allows the holder to engage in up to 20 hours of paid work a week, which is a typical teaching contract anyway, for up to one year. Possibilities exist for Americans who want to act as language counsellors and activity leaders at English immersion summer camps described above.

One American who did a TEFL training course in Paris describes the outcome of a well-organised job hunt:

I went to Paris on the big TEFL job hunt, and thought I might share my advice on how to get a job. They say it's 'almost impossible' for Americans to get a work visa or a good job in France, and I'd like to prove that theory wrong. Come prepared. Get a TEFL certificate. Bring your birth certificate and CV in both French and English, handwritten cover letters in both languages, passport photos and college transcripts. On the third day of my search, I got an interview. A few days later, I showed up and got the job. Overall I'd say it was not nearly as bad as I was warned it would be. Of course, I had to go back to the US for three months to get my work visa, but there's no other way to do it, besides working illegally (something I wasn't willing to do).

Another American, aged 22, took the student route, but doesn't mention what fees were payable for enrolling in a university. This advice is of use mainly to Americans who genuinely want to study for an MA:

Initially I decided to pursue a master's degree in a French university. Luckily, I had a professor who had studied at Paris III, so I emailed him and asked how I could apply, but if you contact the head of the department at any Parisian university and send a proposal (CV plus motivation letter), you can ask for an application. I started this process around March/April of last year for the fall semester. Getting accepted into a French university should not be too hard if you have a bachelor's degree. It helps to speak French, but if you don't, there may be some universities with French classes or you can consider an Anglophone university such as the American University in Paris. If and when you are accepted, you will receive a letter of enrolment with which you can apply for a visa in the States. Since you can only get a student visa before going to France, this letter is very important. I received this in about June/July. A law requires you to go through CampusFrance (www.campusfrance.org) for which you will probably need a translation of your diploma, etc. Applying for a student visa requires a lot of patience and setting up an appointment at the consulate weeks in advance. The important thing is never to get discouraged, have a lot of patience and remember – where there's a will, there's a way.

The Speaking Agency mentioned above employs a large number of non-EU people on student visas. Part-time work is available while you are in the process of obtaining or renewing your visa provided you can show a letter of acceptance from a French school.

More questions on long-stay (D) visas for studies will be answered on the French consulate website, for example at www.consulfrance-losangeles.org. One possibility open to some Americans with Irish or Greek ancestry is to obtain a passport from an EU member state. An easier route is to teach on a voluntary or occasional basis.

A long-time Nice-based expat offers an advisory service to prospective incomers on immigration and administrative questions and charges transparent fees (www.monamiandy.com).

CONDITIONS OF WORK

Teaching businessmen is not everyone's cup of tea, but it can be less strenuous than other kinds of teaching. Provided you do not feel intimidated by your students' polished manners and impeccable dress, and can keep them entertained, you will probably be a success. As mentioned above, one-to-one teaching is increasingly common – with some schools in Paris it constitutes 70% of their business – for which ELT training (including the CELTA or Trinity Certificate) does not prepare you. However, if you develop a rapport with your client, this kind of teaching can be most enjoyable as **Sara Breese** describes:

I have enjoyed teaching as most of my students are adults who have chosen to take English classes, either for pleasure or to advance their career. The majority of them are nice and very motivated, thus making my job a pleasure. The teaching is mostly one-on-one and you are allowed to teach in whichever style you please. I appreciate this freedom to be creative with my students. However, this freedom is becoming more and more rare as schools are imposing their personalised TEFL methods. I have friends who work for other companies and it makes them feel like robots repeating the same lesson over and over again. The only problems I have encountered in my time as a teacher have been in the planning. I am travelling constantly all over Paris which means your day is never dull, but also can make it rather stressful. As a mobile teacher I have to carry all of my teaching materials with me. I am often seen running through the métro with a backpack full of books, CDs and a stereo.

Language schools which offer this facility to clients, especially those in small towns rather than big cities, may well expect you to drive, perhaps even own, a car so that you can give lessons in offices and other workplaces. Most schools pay between €18 and €25 (gross) per lesson.

Salaried teachers should be covered by a nationally agreed and widely enforced *Convention Collective*, which makes stable contracts, sick pay, holiday pay, etc. compulsory as well as guaranteeing a monthly salary. The CDII (*contrat de travail à durée indéterminée intermittent*) is the norm, guaranteeing a low minimum such as 10 hours a week and paying an hourly rate for hours worked above that. A good language school should be able to allocate 20–25 hours a week to those who want them, but they are protected against paying for hours not taught when times are tough.

The annual holiday allowance for full-time teachers is five weeks plus an extra five days off. An unusual feature in France is that some schools calculate the salary according to a certain number of teaching hours per 9 or 12 months, and will pay overtime for hours worked in excess of this. Obviously the total can't be calculated until the end of the contract, which is a drawback for anyone considering leaving early.

Another legislated benefit is that workers in France are given a grant to spend on the training of their choice. The CPF (*Compte Personnel de Formation* or Personal Training Account) must be spent on training that leads to an official qualification such as FCE (First Certificate in English) or TOEFL. This also means that freelance teachers should be prepared to offer exam training and not just General English. **Sab Will** put the right to training to good use:

> ***My TEFL Diploma was paid for this way. But once I got it my employer didn't give me an extra centime more for my efforts. The three of us who had done the diploma stayed the obligatory year after the qualification and then left. So the language school lost its three most qualified teachers. Language schools that pay significantly more for experience or advanced qualifications are rare beasts.***

Telephone and internet teaching are popular for their convenience and anonymity, and a growing number of companies such as Phonalangue (www.phonalangue.fr/recrutement.php) and World Speaking affiliated to Berlitz (www.telelangue.com) specialise in this and employ native-speaker trainers. For many people, making mistakes over the phone is less embarrassing than face-to-face, though the lack of personal contact is felt by some to be detrimental to the learning experience. Many have been surprised by the good results. It is not necessary to be able to speak French and possibly even an advantage to be monolingual, so you won't be tempted to break into French in frustration. The basic requirements for phone trainers are normally an address in France, education to university level and experience in business. The standard rate of pay for telephone teaching is about €17–€19 an hour and schedules can be erratic.

Partly because of France's proximity to a seemingly inexhaustible supply of willing English teachers, working conditions in France are seldom brilliant. You can survive in France, and even Paris, on a typical 20-hour-a-week contract, but to live more than a basic existence you will need to supplement this with extra hours from somewhere else.

Although **Andrew Boyle** enjoyed his year teaching English in Lyon and the chance to become integrated into an otherwise impenetrable community, he concluded that even respectable schools treated teachers as their most expendable commodity.

EMILY SLOANE

Emily Sloane discovered that although the French do not often come across as the most approachable of people, having a slightly firmer sense of privacy than is common in some countries, they can be great company:

I joined the French Alpine Club, which had a thriving and spirited branch in my village. In addition to weekly indoor rock climbing sessions, I accompanied club members on various weekend hikes and climbing trips in the Jura and Vosges Mountains in France and Switzerland and even attended a 10-day climbing clinic in Northern Provence. Learning French climbing vocabulary while suspended 100 feet above the ground, when misunderstandings could have pretty serious consequences, was an experience I won't soon forget. The club members were fantastic people who generously shared the tight space of their homemade 'camping cars' and handcrafted liqueurs. I even convinced them to dress as Americans and speak English one night at the climbing wall. In return for their effort, I provided American snacks and music and a cheat sheet of useful American slang and insults that they enthusiastically tried out on each other. Through the club I even found my very own French lover, which proved to be the most efficient way to improve my language skills.

LIST OF EMPLOYERS

AMERICAN VILLAGE CAMPS IN FRANCE
SAS NACEL / American Village, BP 83329, 12033 Rodez CEDEX 9
+33 565 765 503
american.village@nacel.fr
www.job-americanvillage.fr

NUMBER OF TEACHERS: 200 native English language counsellors per year for English-immersion residential camps in 6 locations in France, attended by children aged 6–17.

PREFERENCE OF NATIONALITY: Programme is based not only on language, but on the culture, history, etc. of specific Anglophone countries, so American Village camps (the majority) are staffed by Americans and Canadians, while for British Village camps, English, Scottish and Welsh people are hired.

QUALIFICATIONS: Must be at least 20 years old (typically 20–35) with previous camp counselling or childcare experience, clear criminal history and high school diploma from a secondary school in an Anglophone country. Must be capable of organising ESL games for young learners with little knowledge of the language, plus other activities such as sports, arts and crafts and dance. Should be willing to get excited about performing in skits, telling stories, and leading songs and cheers. American Village counsellors should know enough about US history and culture to create lesson plans and games. Need to be team players, be organised, and be able to disconnect from technology during working hours (smartphones are not allowed while with the children).

CONDITIONS OF EMPLOYMENT: 4–10 weeks between March and October. Counsellors work from breakfast to bedtime, rotating through responsibilities with other counsellors. 2 hrs of ESL classes per day, so counsellors must create lesson plans.

SALARY: €770 per month (2016). Deductions in France amount to about 11%.

FACILITIES/SUPPORT: Housing and meals are paid for throughout the contract. Advice given to non-Europeans on obtaining a Schengen visa (maximum 90 days). Partial defrayal of train travel within France may be requested.

RECRUITMENT: Online application followed by telephone interview; recent professional reference required. Correct grammar and spelling required on application.

CONTACT: Amanda Pardue, Assistant Programme Director.

ANGLESEY LANGUAGE SERVICES (ALS)
1 bis, 3 Avenue du Maréchal Foch, 78400 Chatou
+33 1 3480 6515
als@alschatou.com
www.als-formationlangues.com

Company established 1978, located just outside Paris.

NUMBER OF TEACHERS: 50.

PREFERENCE OF NATIONALITY: Native speakers.

QUALIFICATIONS: CELTA plus 2 years of experience preferred but possibilities for trainees. Intermediate level or above in French an advantage. Ideally, teachers have a specialist area, such as finance or engineering. Car owner/driver an advantage.

CONDITIONS OF EMPLOYMENT: 10-month renewable contract. 15–25 hours per week. Pupils are adults and many are taught in their workplaces. Recent expansion, so group lessons at all levels offered in evenings and during the day. Some evening and Saturday work available.

SALARY: €18.50 per hour plus 12% on top for holiday pay. Travel expenses.

FACILITIES/SUPPORT: Some help with finding accommodation is available. No initial training but help with preparation provided plus ongoing professional development provided for teachers.

RECRUITMENT: Initial contact by email then one-to-one interviews held in school or in Anglesey (Wales).

CONTACT: Mike Webster, Manager and Pedagogical Director.

APPLILANGUE
16 E rue du Cap Vert, 21800 Quetigny
+33 3 8052 9898
contact@appli-langue.com
www.appli-langue.com

NUMBER OF TEACHERS: 12+.

PREFERENCE OF NATIONALITY: None.

QUALIFICATIONS: TEFL diploma and/or business experience.

CONDITIONS OF EMPLOYMENT: Open-ended contracts. Hours of teaching between 8.30am and 7.30pm.

SALARY: €1,449 per month starting, less about 20% for contributions.

FACILITIES/SUPPORT: School has contact who rents rooms while teachers are looking for an apartment. Help given with work permit applications including recommending a registered translator.

RECRUITMENT: Spontaneous CVs, word of mouth from former teachers.

CONTACT: John Diksa, Director.

ATRIBORD
62 bis rue des Peupliers, 92100 Boulogne Billancourt
+33 1 46 10 94 40/3
atribord@atribord.com
www.atribord.com/emplois

Operates in Madrid as well.

NUMBER OF TEACHERS: 33 business language teachers (all languages).

PREFERENCE OF NATIONALITY: None.

QUALIFICATIONS: Degree and TEFL needed plus good experience or real initiative (ideally both). Teachers should be able to go into companies and talk to their students as equals, sensitive to the demands of professional life.

CONDITIONS OF EMPLOYMENT: Open-ended contract. 15–25 hours of work a week depending on availability.

SALARY: €20–€30 an hour depending on experience.

FACILITIES/SUPPORT: No accommodation or visa help.

RECRUITMENT: Local ads e.g. FUSAC and interviews.

CONTACT: Niall Bickersteth, Partner.

BABYLANGUES
68 boulevard de Sébastopol, 75003 Paris
+33 1-44 61 44 72 / 73 74 92 00
recruitment@babylangues.com
www.job-in-france.babylangues.com

Operates in Bordeaux, Lyon, Lille, Nantes and many other cities as well as Paris.

NUMBER OF TEACHERS: 450 per year.

PREFERENCE OF NATIONALITY: None.

QUALIFICATIONS: Instructors must be native English speakers and must have had some professional experience working with children. No minimum level of French and no teaching experience are required, as instructors receive free training in Babylangues' innovative methodology.

CONDITIONS OF EMPLOYMENT: Normally 1 academic year (September–June) teaching children aged 3–12. Teachers work on open-ended contracts (CDI). Minimum stay is 4 months covering one semester. Flexible hours from 5 to 25 a week, based around instructors' availabilities. Usual slots are weekdays 4pm–8pm and Wednesday/Saturday 9am–5pm.

SALARY: €10.45–€16.50 net per hour.

FACILITIES/SUPPORT: Free medical check-up and possibility of full free coverage by French Social Security. Instructors receive a list of recommended rental agencies and websites for searching for accommodation. Babylangues does not sponsor visas for non-EU applicants. Free French classes. Free membership in shared bike scheme (Vélib in Paris).

RECRUITMENT: Adverts on FUSAC. Ongoing recruitment via video-conferences. If successful at this stage, candidates must also attend a meeting with the agency in France, to finalise paperwork, confirm availability and receive their teaching schedules.

CONTACT: Mathias Benoit-Levy, Director.

LE BUS BILINGUE
202 rue de Tolbiac, 75013 Paris
+33 782 75 41 67 and +33 601 73 31 74
jobs@busbilingue.com
www.lebusbilingue.com

NUMBER OF TEACHERS: 25.

PREFERENCE OF NATIONALITY: None, though so far all teachers have had the legal right to work in France.

QUALIFICATIONS: Experience teaching children aged between 3 and 12 years at a school, as a private tutor, etc. Teacher training would be ideal: TEFL, PGCE, etc.

CONDITIONS OF EMPLOYMENT: Rolling contracts with no fixed end point. 5-8 hours per week.

SALARY: €25 (gross) per hour. Deduction for tax and social security is 21% (which means net wage is less than €20).

FACILITIES/SUPPORT: Advice given on accommodation.

RECRUITMENT: Mainly via FUSAC, personal recommendations and word of mouth. 2-stage interview process whereby the candidate is interviewed by two members of the Bus Bilingue team and later observed in a classroom/lesson setting.

CONTACT: Ruth Skitt, Assistant Director (rskitt@busbilingue.com).

BUSINESS & TECHNICAL LANGUAGES
82 blvd Haussmann, 75008 Paris
+33 1 4293 4545
recrute@btl.fr
www.webbtl.com/fr

NUMBER OF TEACHERS: 70.

PREFERENCE OF NATIONALITY: British citizens for seconded contracts. EU citizen or candidate with working authorisation secured.

QUALIFICATIONS: TEFL training and experience, excellent communication and organisational skills, good IT skills, English mother tongue or equivalent are all needed. Business experience and French a definite plus.

CONDITIONS OF EMPLOYMENT: One-year extendable contracts from end of August/early September. Full-time posts are available as well as part-time, and may include extensive travelling around greater Paris to meet up with clients.

SALARY: On application.

FACILITIES/SUPPORT: Homestay accommodation is arranged for the first 2 weeks, while teacher looks for accommodation. No help with work permits.

CONTACT: Mme Shelli Chavet, Head of Pedagogical Coordination.

CITYLANGUES
Bât. C, Le Triangle de l'Arche, 11, cours du Triangle, Le Faubourg de l'Arche, Secteur Arche Nord, 92937 Paris La Défense Cedex; also 8 rue Louis Blériot, 92500 Rueil Malmaison
+33 1 5591 9670 (La Défense) and +33 1 4749 7946 (Rueil Malmaison)
ms@citylangues.com
www.citylangues.com

NUMBER OF TEACHERS: 25 for business clientele.

PREFERENCE OF NATIONALITY: None, but employ only teachers resident in Paris with French working papers.

QUALIFICATIONS: Degree and TEFL certificate.

CONDITIONS OF EMPLOYMENT: Teaching represents 72% of total paid hours as per French law.

SALARY: According to profile, graded accorded to experience.

FACILITIES/SUPPORT: No assistance with accommodation. Training available in how the French system works, emphasis on team work in school.

RECRUITMENT: Local interviews essential. Adverts on FUSAC.

CONTACT: Margaret Stewart, or Stefan Wheaton, Owner.

ENGLISH POINT
Head Office: 14E rue Pierre de Coubertin, Parc de Mirande, Dijon 21000
+33 820 626064
t.holland@englishpoint.fr
www.englishpoint.fr

NUMBER OF TEACHERS: 14.

PREFERENCE OF NATIONALITY: British, New Zealander, American, Canadian, South African.

QUALIFICATIONS: Preferably a CELTA or equivalent and/or significant teaching experience plus business work experience. The majority of courses are business-based so knowledge of how a business works is essential. Also, being an objectives-based school you should be able to think from the client's perspective and adapt your teaching accordingly.

CONDITIONS OF EMPLOYMENT: Contracts are from 3 months – permanent. Teaching hours 8am–9pm, Monday–Friday (possible Saturday mornings).

SALARY: €20–24 per hour depending on age/experience/ flexibility, etc.

FACILITIES/SUPPORT: School can help find accommodation for teachers, from organising viewings to full accommodation management.

RECRUITMENT: Through websites, training schools, word of mouth, etc. Telephone interviews essential followed by face-to-face meeting.

CONTACT: Tony Holland, Director.

FONTAINEBLEAU LANGUES & COMMUNICATION
47 Boulevard Marechal Foch, 77300 Fontainebleau
+33 1 6422 4896
recruitment@flc-int.com; dianne.riboh@flc-int.com
www.flc-int.com

NUMBER OF TEACHERS: 12 English teachers, 35 in total.

PREFERENCE OF NATIONALITY: British/Irish. Australians,

Canadians and Americans or other native English speakers with EU citizenship or French working papers.

QUALIFICATIONS: TEFL training (e.g. CELTA). Must be dynamic, creative, versatile and able to work in a team. Previous business experience a plus.

CONDITIONS OF EMPLOYMENT: 1 year minimum. Majority of teaching takes place in company premises so owning a car is necessary (transport costs reimbursed at €0.45 approx. per km). Variety of teaching situations including groups, one-to-one lessons and Business English. Hours are grouped as much as possible between 9am and 7pm, Monday to Friday.

SALARY: Starting at €19 per hour which includes 12% holiday pay. Social security deductions are about 22%.

FACILITIES/SUPPORT: Training workshops held regularly. Large teachers' library.

RECRUITMENT: Interview essential – usually by phone.

ICB EUROPE

45 rue d'Aboukir, 75002 Paris

+33 1 4455 3831

declankehoe@icbeurope.com

www.icbeurope.com/en/recruitment.php

NUMBER OF TEACHERS: 50 full-time and part-time.

PREFERENCE OF NATIONALITY: None but native English speaker.

QUALIFICATIONS: Prefer candidates who are TEFL/TESOL/CELTA qualified with a couple of years of business experience, ideally within the financial/insurance sectors. Working use of French needed. Excellent presentation and communication skills.

CONDITIONS OF EMPLOYMENT: Open-ended contracts. Trainers who can stay for at least 1 year are preferred. To teach during normal office hours Monday to Friday.

SALARY: Trainers who are available at all times can be guaranteed 800 teaching hours a year with an average remuneration of about €1,600 per month plus a monthly bonus programme based on student satisfaction and lesson observations. 21% deductions for tax and social security.

FACILITIES/SUPPORT: No assistance given with visas or accommodation.

RECRUITMENT: Adverts in FUSAC. Group interview involves candidates introducing themselves, a grammar test and some group discussion about different teaching techniques. If successful at this stage the candidate then goes on to have a one-to-one interview with the owner of ICB Europe, Eric Wrobley.

CONTACT: Declan Kehoe, Recruitment Manager/Résponsable Pédagogique.

ILC FRANCE (INTERNATIONAL LANGUAGE CENTRE)

13 Passage Dauphine, 75006 Paris

+33 1 4441 8020

info@ilcfrance.com

www.ilcfrance.com/recrutement

NUMBER OF TEACHERS: 34.

QUALIFICATIONS: CELTA or approved equivalent. Experience of business world essential.

CONDITIONS OF EMPLOYMENT: Teaching hours between 8.30am and 7pm. Contracts according to French labour laws. 80% of teaching is in-company.

SALARY: Variable according to contract.

FACILITIES/SUPPORT: Assistance with finding accommodation, teacher development and training. ILC offers full-time and part-time CELTA courses (see Training chapter).

RECRUITMENT: Spontaneous CVs and local adverts, although priority given to IH network. Interviews in Paris essential.

CONTACT: Marlene Regaya, Director (marlene.regaya@ilcfrance.com).

INLINGUA PARIS

109 rue de l'Université, 75007 Paris

+33 1 4551 4660/4946 1501

inlinguaparis@inlinguaparis.com

www.inlinguaparis.com

NUMBER OF TEACHERS: Many teachers for corporate students required for seven branches in Paris area (others at Bastille, La Défense, Roissy, Etoile, Vélizy and Saint-Denis).

PREFERENCE OF NATIONALITY: None.

QUALIFICATIONS: TEFL plus minimum 2 years' experience preferably with professional adults. Preferred minimum age 25. Candidates must be creative, independent, flexible, of excellent appearance and with a good cultural background.

CONDITIONS OF EMPLOYMENT: Minimum 12 months; open-ended contracts. Flexible hours, with guaranteed minimum, mostly 20–30 hours per week.

FACILITIES/SUPPORT: Assistance with accommodation, work permits and training possible.

RECRUITMENT: Adverts in FUSAC. Online application form. Interviews essential in France.

CONTACT: Philippe Fouque, General Manager.

LINGUARAMA
Tour Eve, 7è étage, 1 Place du Sud, La Défense 9, 92806 Puteaux Cedex
+33 1 4773 0095
paris@linguarama.com
www.linguarama.com

NUMBER OF TEACHERS: 30.
PREFERENCE OF NATIONALITY: Native speakers with working papers for the EU.
QUALIFICATIONS: Recognised TEFL qualification (CELTA or Trinity Cert) plus 1 or sometimes 2 years' teaching experience required. Must already be based in Paris. Driving licence useful.
CONDITIONS OF EMPLOYMENT: Full-time teachers work 25 hours per week September to June. Part-time teachers work flexible hours. Teaching is Business English, taught in-company and at school.
SALARY: Approx. €1,725– €1,875 per month.
FACILITIES/SUPPORT: Advice on finding accommodation. Regular training available. Opportunities for structured career development.
RECRUITMENT: Via marcus evans Linguarama, 101 Finsbury Pavement, London EC2A 1RS, and also locally.
CONTACT: Jo Dennison, Pedagogical Manager (JoDennison@linguarama.com).

PARIS CORPORATE LANGUAGE CENTER
59 rue Meslay, 75003 Paris
+33 1 5301 8150
otilghman@parisclc.com; contact@parisclc.com
www.parisclc.com

NUMBER OF TEACHERS: 15 (10 in Paris).
PREFERENCE OF NATIONALITY: Native speaker, with working papers for France.
QUALIFICATIONS: TEFL/CELTA/TESOL certificate and observed teaching experience.
CONDITIONS OF EMPLOYMENT: Minimum 1 year. CDI (open-ended contract). Approximately 25 teaching hours a week.
SALARY: To be discussed at interview.
FACILITIES/SUPPORT: No assistance with accommodation or work permits.
RECRUITMENT: Adverts in FUSAC and other sites. Face-to-face interviews in Paris are essential. For positions outside Paris, telephone interviews are held.
CONTACT: Olivia Tilghman-Osborne, Director of Methodology.

SPEAKING AGENCY / BABY-SPEAKING
33 Boulevard Saint-Martin, 75003 Paris
+33 1 8395 4176
developpement@speaking-agency.com; paris.recruitment@speaking-agency.com; paris.recruitment@baby-speaking.fr
www.speaking-agency.com; www.baby-speaking.fr

Babysitting and teaching positions with French families in Paris, Lyon, Lille, Bordeaux, Nantes and Toulouse.
NUMBER OF TEACHERS: More than 500 live-out part-time tutoring positions from September, 200 from January; up to 1,000 altogether. To work either with young children aged 3–12 or older children 12–18.
PREFERENCE OF NATIONALITY: Applicants must be native speakers and EU citizens or hold a student/working holiday/working visa for France.
QUALIFICATIONS: No specific diploma is required but applicants need to have experience in working with children (babysitting and/or tutoring). No minimum level of French language is required. Minimum age 18.
CONDITIONS OF EMPLOYMENT: Minimum stay 4 months. Starting September/October or January. All part-time positions. Flexible work schedules: 'Baby-speakers' choose the number of hours they want to work according to their availability, normally between 5 and 20 per week. Tutors for older children work 2–8 hours per week.
SALARY: Mostly €10–€13 per hour. For tutoring positions of adolescents, the range is €13–€20 per hour, depending on the number of children, location and the number of hours worked.
FACILITIES/SUPPORT: No accommodation provided, although agency has partnership with residences which offers a discount. Selected applicants are trained in an innovative early language acquisition method developed by specialists in child bilingualism. This counts as a declared job in France so tutors are entitled to French health insurance.
RECRUITMENT: Online application to HR Team. Skype interviews.

SYNDICAT MIXTE MONTAIGU-ROCHESERVIERE
35 Avenue Villebois, Mareuil, 85607 Montaigu
+33 2 5146 4545
anglais@sm-montaigu-rocheserviere.fr
www.gapyear-france.com

NUMBER OF TEACHERS: 5.
PREFERENCE OF NATIONALITY: British.

QUALIFICATIONS: Ages 18–25. Experience of and interest in teaching and a love of France are advantages. Must have GCSE and A level French.

CONDITIONS OF EMPLOYMENT: Standard contract length 9 months from early September, to teach 20 hours per week.

SALARY: €207 per month.

FACILITIES/SUPPORT: Accommodation provided with local host families/resident project coordinator. 10-day induction with Project Coordinator on arrival.

RECRUITMENT: Interview essential, possibly in UK or in France (Vendée April–June).

CONTACT: Julie Legrée, Project Coordinator.

TELAB LANGUAGE COURSES BY TELEPHONE

3 Place de la Poste, 71520 Tramayes

+33 3 8550 5858

s.evans@telab.com

www.telab.com

Specialises in teaching English by phone.

NUMBER OF TEACHERS: 60.

PREFERENCE OF NATIONALITY: None but must be native English speaker, resident in France and with necessary working papers.

QUALIFICATIONS: Language teaching qualifications (TEFL or equivalent), at least 2 years' experience in teaching languages to company employees, work experience in or knowledge of a specific field (e.g. marketing, finance, medical, technical, etc.), excellent communication abilities, independent, organised and rigorous at work. Must have a computer and know how to use the internet.

CONDITIONS OF EMPLOYMENT: Teachers work from home, flexible hours between 7am and 9pm. There is a trend for more teachers to work full-time rather than part-time.

FACILITIES/SUPPORT: Assistance given with social security registration (about 20% of gross salary is taken at source as contributions). No help with work permits or accommodation.

RECRUITMENT: Referrals, internet, press. CVs can be faxed to +33 1 3080 4458.

CONTACT: Stephanie Evans or Emmanuel Fays, Owner.

TLC – THE TURNER LEARNING CENTER

33&62 rue des Renaudes, 75017 Paris

+33 1 8364 5400

job@tlc-fr.com

www.tlc-fr.com/job

NUMBER OF TEACHERS: 40.

PREFERENCE OF NATIONALITY: Native English speakers, mainly to tutor children aged 6–18.

QUALIFICATIONS: University qualification, TEFL or CELTA trained, appreciation for corporate English, experience of ESOL exams preferred and for some courses fluent French is needed. Non-EU citizens must have a French work permit valid until the end of the academic year.

CONDITIONS OF EMPLOYMENT: 10-month contract September to early July. 10–20 hours a week of classes, depending on their specialism, experience and availability, though most teach 12–15 hours. TLC offers almost all lessons in clients' homes, between 5pm and 7.30pm, with all day Wednesday and Saturday possibilities. Timetabling is compatible with teachers already working in the French school system as well as the corporate English sector.

SALARY: Teachers working for TLC hold either a CDI work contract or, if they wish, are registered as independent. The CDI contract includes French national health insurance with an attractive hourly wage bringing the net salary up to €20 an hour, depending on experience, qualifications, quality and promptness of class reporting, completion of contract and training attendance if deemed necessary. Independent teachers have the same wage conditions but can see their hourly rate reach €30 because they pay their own contributions. They must provide TLC with an *attestation de vigilance* every trimester ensuring that they have settled their social taxes, which provides them with social insurance coverage.

FACILITIES/SUPPORT: No assistance with accommodation or work permits. Programme training provided.

RECRUITMENT: Monthly hiring drives. Adverts online and in magazines. Timetable of application and interview dates is posted at www.tlc-Fr.com/job. Skype interview in first instance then face-to-face interview in Paris.

CONTACT: Mala Moktar, Head Teacher.

TRANSFER

15 rue de Berri, 75008 Paris

+33 1 5669 2230

info@transfer.fr

www.transfer.fr

Also: 40–48 rue Cambon, 75001 Paris.

NUMBER OF TEACHERS: 90.

PREFERENCE OF NATIONALITY: None.

QUALIFICATIONS: Either professional or technical experience (law, finance, etc.) or solid teaching experience, Cambridge CELTA or similar qualification and degree.

CONDITIONS OF EMPLOYMENT: Short-term, long-term or permanent. Teaching takes place generally from 9am to 6pm and some evenings.

SALARY: On application. About 20% deducted for tax and social security.

FACILITIES/SUPPORT: Americans must have their own work papers as no assistance is given with arranging these.

RECRUITMENT: Application and CV. Interview.

CONTACT: Marian Casey (mcasey@transfer.fr)

WALL STREET ENGLISH

+33 1 7997 5650

recrutement@wseparis.com

www.wallstreetenglish.fr/recrutement

NUMBER OF TEACHERS: Varies; 58 franchised branches (addresses can be found on website). Largest ones are in Paris (with 6 branches), Amiens, Reims, Lyons, Orleans and French Riviera.

PREFERENCE OF NATIONALITY: EU or with valid working papers.

QUALIFICATIONS: CELTA or TESOL certificate. BA or 2+ years' teaching experience.

CONDITIONS OF EMPLOYMENT: Permanent contracts offered. To work part-time hours or full-time if necessary up to 136 hours per month.

SALARY: €1,470 per month plus bonuses; €16 per hour.

FACILITIES/SUPPORT: 5 weeks paid vacation, health insurance arranged.

RECRUITMENT: Via tefl.com and local advertising, e.g. FUSAC. Centralised recruitment with online application procedure.

CONTACT: Laetitia Bonnot, HR Manager, 1 Place de la Pyramide, Paris La Défense 92911.

GERMANY

The excellent state education system in Germany ensures that a majority of Germans have such a good grounding in English that very little teaching is done at the beginner level. If German students want exposure to a native speaker they are far more likely to enrol in a language summer course in Britain than sign up for extra tuition at a local institute. Furthermore, many secondary schools in Germany employ native speakers of English to assist in classrooms (programme details below). English is also offered at *Volkshochschulen* or adult education centres where various subsidised courses are run.

Cities in the former East Germany such as Leipzig, Dresden and Erfurt are less popular destinations for job-seeking teachers than Munich, Berlin and Freiburg, and may therefore afford more opportunities, especially since provision of English in the schools lags slightly behind that of Western Germany.

The greatest demand for English in Germany continues to come from the business and professional community, and with the continuing strength of the German economy, demand for English has held up well. Throughout the country the language teaching scene is remarkably stable. That does not mean that it is easy to walk into a job. Most firms that send English trainers into companies work with a stable list of expat freelancers resident in Hanover or Munich or wherever it is. However, highly paid in-company positions for EFL and ESP teachers can still be found, and the agencies and consultancies that supply teachers to business clients have increased the number of native-speaker freelance teachers they recruit. Demand is greatest outside cities such as Munich, where teachers complain about a lack of work.

PROSPECTS FOR TEACHERS

Many of the companies that market in-company English courses are desperate for professional teachers and trainers, though there is no shortage of inexperienced teachers looking for teaching opportunities. Any graduate with a background in economics or business who can speak German has a good chance of finding work in a German city. A TEFL certificate and a university degree have less clout than relevant experience, as **Kevin Boyd** found when he arrived with his brand new Cambridge certificate at the beginning of the academic year:

> ***I was persuaded by a teaching friend to go to Munich with him to try to get highly paid jobs together. As he spoke some German and had about a year's teaching experience, he got a job straightaway. Every school I went to in Munich just didn't want to know as I couldn't speak German and only had four weeks' teaching experience. After two days of this I decided to try my luck in Italy.***

Experience in commerce or a technical background is often a more desirable qualification than an ELT qualification. The question is not so much whether you know what a past participle is but whether you know what an 'irrevocable letter of credit' or a 'bank giro' is. Many schools offer *Oberstufe*, advanced or specialist courses in, for example, Banking English, Business English, or for bilingual secretaries, etc. Full-time, vocationally oriented courses in languages for business and commerce are offered by *Berufsfachschulen* (vocational schools). The regional English Language Teachers' Associations (ELTAs) have been moving to professionalise the industry and to offer and require more training in ELT skills.

Very few schools are willing to consider candidates who can't speak any German. Although the 'direct method' (i.e. total immersion in English) is in use everywhere, the pupils may expect you to be able to explain things in German. **Penny**, who worked in Berlin, was not put off so easily:

At the beginning they all expected me to talk to them in German. True to my CELTA training I insisted on English except in emergencies and they got used to it!

If the school prepares its students for the London Chamber of Commerce and Industry exams (LCCI), the teacher will be expected not only to understand the syllabus but to interpret and teach it with confidence. There is still a preference for British English, but the increasing number of course participants working for global or American companies prefer Canadian/American English.

Rates of pay vary. Some employers pay inexperienced teachers in the range of €12–€16 for a 45-minute lesson, whereas more senior positions are paid €18–€30+ an hour. Fees charged to companies by the most established and specialist teachers and trainers can be very high, which means few openings occur in this sought-after sector. These teachers also have high overheads and a staggeringly large percentage of their incomes will disappear in compulsory contributions (described below) and expenses. One further requirement of many employers is a driving licence and vehicle, so that teachers can travel easily from one off-site assignment to another.

FINDING A JOB

About 1,000 posts as English-language classroom assistants are available at secondary schools throughout Germany. Applications are encouraged from candidates under 30 years who have studied at least two years of German, preferably at university level. UK applicants should contact the Language Assistants Team at the British Council (assistants@britishcouncil.org; www.britishcouncil.org/language-assistants/become/germany). The salary is €800 a month (net) for 12 hours of work a week, unchanged for many years. Language assistants such as **Sarah Davies** (who was sent to a small town in the east) advise against agreeing to teach in a small village where conditions may be basic and the sense of isolation strong.

Other nationalities can also participate through Pädagogischer Austauschdienst (PAD; www.kmk-pad.org). About 140 American students and graduates are accepted as English Teaching Assistants through the Fulbright Program (administered by the Institute of International Education, 809 UN Plaza, New York, NY 10017-3580). Candidates planning to go on to become teachers of German are strongly preferred; contractual arrangements are as above plus help with travel and insurance.

Like so many embassies, the German Embassy in London is not noted for its helpful attitude to aspiring teachers or other job-seekers. Apart from directing students to enquire about the exchange programme run by the British Council and providing addresses of the state ministries of education, it recommends applying to the Zentrale Auslands-und Fachvermittlung (International Placement Services), ZAV, part of the German Federal Employment Agency (Villemombler Strasse 76, 53123 Bonn; ✆ +49 228 713 1313; zav@arbeitsagentur.de). All applications from abroad are handled by this office. Although people of any nationality can apply through the ZAV, only citizens of old EU countries (who have German language skills) are entitled to expect the same treatment as a German. As usual, it is next to impossible to arrange a teaching job without presenting yourself in person to language school directors and training companies, CV in hand. Determination, qualifications, experience and being on the spot are often deciding factors when an employer has to choose between large numbers of similarly qualified applicants.

The best source of language school addresses is the *Yellow Pages* (*Gelbe Seiten*), which can be consulted online (www.gelbeseiten.de), or try www.goyellow.de and search for *Sprachschulen.* Another way of accessing potential employers is via the local English Language Teachers Association, a branch of which can be found in most major cities. The Munich branch (MELTA) is especially vigorous and carries a few job vacancies and a page of employers (www.melta.de/jobs-listing). Look for English-language magazines aimed at expats and you may come across some relevant adverts.

Most of the major language school chains have a significant presence in Germany including Berlitz, whose many schools are always advertising vacancies, as are Inlingua and Linguarama. To the surprise of many, Wall Street English decided to close its 23 schools in Germany after more than two decades of operating there. According to the explanatory statement on their website: '*With a higher level of English being spoken by a larger amount of people in Germany, we feel it will, in the future, be increasingly difficult to deliver the full, high quality, WSE student experience.*'

Throughout Germany, more than 2,000 adult education centres or *Volkshochschulen* teach the English language (among many other courses) to adults. Native speakers with teaching experience might find a role within the Deutscher Volkshochschul-Verband e.V (www.vhs.de).

One of the easiest entrées to the TEFL world is as a tutor on a language summer camp. These have mushroomed in Germany, and take on lots of native speakers to help kids improve their English through interactive play, sports, music, etc. during the school holidays. Try for example:

Berlitz Kids: www.berlitz.de. See entry in List of Employers.

Camp Adventure: www.campadventure.de. English camps in various locations. Instructors must be over 19 year old and have training.

KCA (Kids Camp America): www.kidscampamerica.com/en/jobs. English immersion camps in Frankfurt, Wiesbaden, etc. €600 per week.

LEOlingo Sprachcamps: www.leo-lingo.de. See entry in List of Employers.

Oskar Lernt Englisch: www.oskar-lernt-englisch.de. Native-speaker teachers and counsellors should have a working knowledge of German and an *Erweitertes polizeiliches Führungszeugnis* (enhanced police clearance less than six months old).

Penguin Camp: www.penguincamp.de. See entry in List of Employers.

Sphairos: ✆ +49 89 187 03156; www.sphairos.de. They claim on their Facebook page that their 'melting pot' of teachers have 'charm and vigour'.

Sprachcamp Allgäu: www.sprachcamp-allgaeu.de/jobs. Looking for native English speakers also interested in outdoor education.

Sarah Paschke has spent many summers working for LEOlingo in Bavaria. She first applied after finishing her degree in the US when she knew she wanted to live in Europe and had to find something to justify this decision to her father. So she googled 'summer camps', knowing that she wanted to work for a small personal outfit rather than one of the giant language camp companies. To further overcome her parents' possible objections, she wanted to find a summer job that paid a wage and would assist with the visa issue:

> ***LEOlingo was delightful and timely in the application process. A couple of the 'megas' sent automated rejection replies to my email account or I never received any word back at all. After sending my résumé and questionnaire, a Skype interview was scheduled within a matter of two weeks. I had a background of teaching and tutoring youth; however, nothing with the intensive responsibilities of directing children 24/7. When I was applying around Europe, I was disappointed that so few employers offered a wage in addition to accommodation and food. LEOlingo pays well and gives you accommodation and food, which allowed me to save money to travel after camp.***
>
> ***The LEOlingo programme is a balance of language games, sports and crafts to keep the campers engaged, excited and interested in the topics. From writing and acting mini-dramas, to playing a camp-wide game of Capture the Flag, there is little time for campers to be bored! I knew it was going to be demanding, a high-energy and 'on-top-of-your-game' sort of job, and I was up for that challenge. LEOlingo really pushed me to interact with the German culture from the start since from the start we were staying with German host families in town. I don't speak German so I was lucky to have a family that knew English and was equally interested in me as I was in them. I still keep in contact with my host family and go to visit them a couple times a year when I can. Encounters with my pupils were always unpredictable, and they never failed to amaze me. Germans in***

general have a higher knowledge and capacity to learn English. Schools teach it well and the students at the summer camps are highly motivated and intrigued by the LEOlingo staff. Last summer my fellow teachers and counsellors represented all but two English-speaking countries. The highlight of camp is the correspondence between cultures, whether it is between counsellor and camper, or counsellor and counsellor. I learned so much about my own culture.

After her first summer as a LEOlingo teacher, **Sarah** decided to get her TEFL certification and then went on to teach in the Czech Republic, for which the training and experience in Germany were invaluable. Several other LEOlingo staff, Brandon Howard from the US and Laura Nichol from Bristol, also wrote to say how much they had enjoyed their summer employment in Bavaria.

INTERVIEWS

Most schools and institutes in Germany cannot, under normal operating circumstances, hire someone unseen merely on the basis of his/her CV and photo. Applicants should arrange for a face-to-face interview and be prepared to make themselves available at a moment's notice. Professional presentation is even more important for securing work in the German business world than elsewhere. Vacancies occur throughout the year since businessmen and women are just as likely to start a course in April as in September. Germans tend to be formal, so dress appropriately and be aware of your manners at an interview. Also, good references (*Zeugnisse*) are essential.

A good starting place is Frankfurt am Main, sometimes nicknamed 'Bankfurt' or 'Mainhattan'. Frankfurt has the highest concentration of major banks and financial institutions in the country and a correspondingly high number of private language schools. It is helpful, though not essential, to have some basic knowledge of German and business experience. In a job interview with a language school director, demonstrating a detailed knowledge of a handful of commonly used textbooks may be more important than business experience.

You can also impress a potential employer by showing some familiarity with current major German business news (bank mergers, etc.); follow the financial news on Bloomberg or download the BBC's *World Business Report*. Language schools are looking for teachers who can pose intelligent questions to business students about their jobs. There is a considerable demand from the business community for guidance on conducting 'small talk' in English, which is crucial in building rapport with clients and colleagues.

NINO HUNTER

Nino Hunter decided to go to Berlin, a city which is both exquisitely trendy and reassuringly relaxed, and one that appeals most to people in search of European culture at its finest. Despite his degree in modern languages from the University of Bath, he found it a struggle.

I did find it extremely difficult to find teaching posts in Berlin. I think the main reason would be the sheer number of English speakers in Berlin, many of whom wish to stay in this amazing city. Given the lack of industry, they have little alternative but to fall back on teaching English, with or without a CELTA/TEFL certificate. The English community is huge in Berlin (check Toytown Berlin at www.toytowngermany.com/berlin which has new postings every day). There are of course a huge number of schools in Berlin but given the number of teachers and the decreasing demand over the last two years due to the global economic crisis many of them have become exceptionally picky about who they choose to take on, often asking for at least two years' experience, etc. There was a particular demand for English teachers able to teach advanced students (Cambridge levels 1 and 2) and a few schools simply wouldn't take people on who didn't have experience teaching higher level students.

All of which means that the market in Berlin is extremely saturated and sending a CV off to each and every school usually doesn't help. The best way of finding teaching positions in the city is putting on a suit and going to the schools with a CV, introducing yourself and trying your hardest not to get fobbed off by a secretary, but rather to get an actual interview where they offer you a course. This obviously requires a little courage and a fair amount of energy but is the only way of being sure your CV isn't deleted immediately and is in fact the only way I or any of my colleagues got jobs at private language schools.

The teachers at the Berlin School of English where I did my CELTA course assured me that no one would pay less than €15 for 45 minutes to a teacher with a CELTA. My first school paid me just €12 and it took me 10 weeks to get up to €14, which was not at all uncommon.

Two pieces of advice I could give would be firstly to try to get on the lists for the Volkshochschulen (I think there are about seven in Berlin), as these pay more (if you have a university degree, even more) and the classes are large and quite fun. I also recommend joining ELTABB (English Language Teacher's Association (www.eltabb.com/main/index.php) which costs €40 a year but is undoubtedly the best place to network and sometimes perfect positions come up. Basically one needs to be as proactive as possible and not be too fussy. If Berlitz or similar offers you a course, take it.

A British teacher in Berlin maintains a blog www.teachingenglishinberlin.com with tips on job-hunting and settling into the city plus ideas for lesson-planning.

FREELANCE TEACHING

The majority of native speakers teaching for commercial institutes are not on contracts, but are employed on a freelance basis (*Honorarvertrag*) to work for between two and 20 hours per week. Schools employing freelance teachers are not in a position to make deductions, because they cannot know a teacher's full expenses. Teachers may also work for several different schools. Freelance teachers are responsible for paying their own tax, pension insurance contributions and (crucially) health insurance.

Upon successful completion of a Trinity TESOL certificate course in England, **Ann Barkett** from Atlanta went to Munich to look for freelance work, but found it tough going:

> ***During the period from December to March, I was putting up flyers for private and group lessons but received no response. I finally answered an advert for a private student whom I taught for a few weeks, but there just wasn't enough work or money coming in and I grew tired of trying at that point.***

Many freelance teachers find themselves for the first time required to design an ESP course (English for Specific Purposes), individually tailored to the needs of their business students. **Nathan Edwards** found that he got better at this:

> ***Experience has shown me that such a syllabus must be flexible, open to change and short-term adjustment so as to accommodate the complex and evolving needs of students who are also full-time working professionals. Students and their employers must be given the assurance of a clearly structured course outline, but this must be partly generated by an ongoing negotiated process with all the participants. Finally don't forget that the students themselves can be a valuable source of ESP course material such as authentic English email messages, business letters and company brochures from their offices.***

REGULATIONS

EU citizens are free to travel to Germany to look for and take up work, but like all German nationals must register their address with the relevant district authority (*Einwohnermeldeamt*) or local *Bürgeramt* within a week of finding permanent accommodation. For this they will need proof that they are living locally, e.g. a copy of a contract with a landlord, and possibly proof of employment or funding.

Useful guidance for the red tape affecting freelance teachers is available on the internet, for example on the relevant forums of ELTABB, MELTA, etc. Also try www.expatica.com/de/main.html and the Legal Guide to Germany at www.lg2g.info, which cover topics such as taxation, pensions and insurance.

NON-EU CITIZENS

Any non-EU citizen who wants to stay in Germany for more than the 90-day validity of a Schengen visa must obtain a residence permit (*Aufenthaltstitel*) before arrival in Germany. (Until a few years ago, citizens of the USA, Australia, Canada and a few others could apply after arrival, but that is no longer possible.) Applications must be lodged prior to entry at a German embassy or consulate in your country of residence. Canadians, Australians and New Zealanders should allow about two months, whereas Americans should apply four to five months in advance. You will need a valid passport, a letter from your employer stating what the position you have been offered is, what your projected income will be and the completed application form for a work permit.

According to the Residence Act, which governs residence permits for non-EU citizens, applicants must prove that they have a secure and regular income, which is next to impossible for freelance teachers. The only exceptions are if you can show that you can invest at least one million euros and/or create at least 10 new jobs and/or prove that the business will benefit the region economically.

TAX, HEALTH INSURANCE AND SOCIAL SECURITY CONTRIBUTIONS

About 95% of all the EFL teaching work in language schools and companies in Germany is offered on a freelance or self-employed basis. The hourly rates you are offered might sound good, but freelancers and self-employed teachers lose roughly 40% after paying tax and contributions. A trainer-recruiter in a small town near Frankfurt succinctly described the trade-off: '*Germany is comparable to Scandinavia in that you can expect to lose 40% … However, for this you get great health cover, a pension and some of the best social support in the world.*' Half of stoppages are payments into the German pension scheme. This is a compulsory contribution for all freelance teachers regardless of whether they already have a private pension scheme. These 'expenses', plus tax and rent, mean that most hard-working teachers are left with very little disposable income. **Sylvia Weismiller**, Director of Euro-Lingua, based in Freiburg, writes:

> ***Yes, it's very complicated, and lots of grey areas, unenforced requirements, etc. One of my American teachers is having problems getting his permits renewed. They said if he paid his pension contributions, they would renew it. What those two have to do with each other is a mystery! However, I don't know any foreigners who pay it, even though it is an official policy. At the moment the responsible government offices are swamped with applications from Eastern Europe so it's a huge plus if the applicant has an EU passport.***

Sylvia also mentions solidarity tax (about 5.5% of your income tax) and church tax (8%–9% of income tax), which you can avoid by registering as an atheist. However, medical insurance can be painful, particularly if you're a woman:

> ***Official health insurance depends on age, sex, etc. Also complicated. Women pay about double (for instance as a female in my 40s I was paying more than €400 per month). It doesn't depend on your income. If you are a registered student, however, you can get a much lower rate, I think €80 per month. As a student you can only work a limited number of hours, but as there aren't any tuition fees it's not a bad idea. There are also expat programmes which charge, I believe, €90 per month. They are limited to five years. You have to have health insurance to get your residence permit extended.***

If you are a non-EU citizen you can ask the Deutsche Rentenversicherung (German pension authority) to repay the contributions you have made if you have paid into the state scheme for less than five years, i.e. have paid less than 60 pension contributions.

Foreigners working in Germany must register with ELStAM (electronic PAYE).

CONDITIONS OF WORK

You can almost guarantee that you will be teaching adults except at summer camps, since school children receive such a high standard of English tuition at school. Contracts for full-time work are usually at least a year long, often with a three-month probation period. But it is rare to be *Angestellt*, i.e. fully employed by a school with guaranteed minimum hours, sick pay, holiday pay, etc. Wall Street English was one of the few that offered these contracts but, as of 2017, it has closed all its branches.

Hourly rates can be high: typically €17–€25 per lesson and double that and more for established teachers of Business English. Off-site teaching hours often incur a premium of €2–€5 to compensate for travel time, or sometimes employers pay 'three hours for two'. Freelancers who earn high incomes have normally been in Germany a long time, speak excellent German and have invested in acquiring relevant specialisations, resources, materials, etc. They have built up their clientele and reputation over years and defend their patch with understandable vigour. The majority of newcomers gain their initial experience at franchise language schools where the pay is much lower, sometimes on a par with cleaners, and where poor working conditions and no job security prevail. A 30-hour working week could consist of 40 45-minute lessons, which would be a very heavy workload.

However, after walking into a tiny English school on her street in Berlin and asking the owner if she needed any help, **Penny**, a British widow in her 50s, built up an enviable client base. She describes her experiences in Berlin:

> ***I do two classes a week, one in the morning and one in the evenings. The morning class is made up of retired ladies who come for fun and I have difficulty keeping them speaking English. I keep reminding them that I am being paid to teach them English and not to learn German from them. We have a good relationship and go out to the cinema occasionally. The members of the evening class are slightly more serious about learning English. Some of them sometimes join in the cinema outings.***
>
> ***The classroom has a table with eight chairs, which limits the size of the class. There is a blackboard – I would dearly love a whiteboard – and a CD/tape player. Most of my work, however, is one-to-one teaching, which I originally obtained through the school. I charge €14 and pupils come to me. Now, many pupils are recommended by a former or current pupil, so I have several German-Russians and several art historians together with some business ladies – there is a big demand for Business English.***

However, if Penny had to live solely on her teaching earnings, her standard of living would be much lower than it is. Monthly salaries for full-time *Angestellter* (employees) can be from €1,200 to €2,000 gross, with the possibility of paid overtime.

ACCOMMODATION

Considering that a one-bedroom flat in one of the big cities can easily cost €475–€675 per month, excluding bills, salaries need to be high. Most newcomers find rooms in shared houses or flats to rent from online communities. **Ben Stefano**, who lived in Berlin for part of 2016, describes the best sources of accommodation in Germany:

> ***As far as accommodation in any German city goes, www.wg-gesucht.de is definitely the first website that most people recommend. You can rent a whole apartment or a single room in a shared flat (*'Wohngemeinschaft',*** ***abbreviated to WG), which is what I did. I was paying €300 a month for my room in a three-bedroom WG in the well-connected suburb of Wedding, although in Berlin it's common to pay €350 or even up to €480 for a room in a hip area like Kreuzberg, Friedrichshain or gentrified Prenzlauer Berg. Another similar website www.immobilienscout24.de is also popular. These sites are free to use, but searching them can be difficult and time-consuming. Also you have to be wary of scammers, especially for apartments that are too good to be true in the big cities. Lots of young people also use Facebook groups where you can advertise your free room or write a post telling people you're on the hunt for a room. People often write profiles for themselves so others can get an idea of what kind of person they are.***

Cities may have their own portals of use to German speakers, such as http://schwarzesbrett.bremen.de for Bremen (which means notice board). An alternative to classified ads websites is the local *mitwohnzentralen*, which charges commission (usually one month's rent) for finding flats, or less for a sub-let. It is customary to pay your rent directly out of a bank account, so open a basic current account (*girokonto*) as early as you can. Often you pay the rent to the person whose name is on the lease (*Hauptmieter* or main renter).

LIST OF EMPLOYERS

ACADEMY OF EUROPEAN LANGUAGES
Kölnstrasse 19, 53113 Bonn
+49 228 242 5840
karriere@sprachakademie-bonn.de;
info@sprachakademie-bonn.de
www.sprachakademie-bonn.de

NUMBER OF TEACHERS: 200 in most German cities.
PREFERENCE OF NATIONALITY: None.
QUALIFICATIONS: University degree, education qualifications and experience in the private sector needed, preferably in finance, technology, medicine, and so on.
CONDITIONS OF EMPLOYMENT: Negotiable hours; open freelance contracts.
SALARY: €20+ for a 45-minute lesson.
FACILITIES/SUPPORT: Help can be given with accommodation and work permits if necessary.
RECRUITMENT: Personal recommendations and speculative applications. Letters of application and CVs can be submitted by email.
CONTACT: Tony Westwood, Director (t.westwood@sprachakademie-bonn.de).

BERLIN SCHOOL OF ENGLISH
Checkpoint Arkaden, Charlottenstrasse 81, 10969 Berlin
+49 30 229 0455
info@berlin.school-of-english.de
www.berlin.school-of-english.de

NUMBER OF TEACHERS: 30–40.
PREFERENCE OF NATIONALITY: None, but must be a native English speaker.
QUALIFICATIONS: University degree plus TEFL/CELTA Certificate and minimum 1 year's experience.
CONDITIONS OF EMPLOYMENT: Minimum 1 year on freelance basis. Between 16 and 30 hours per week. Focus on Business English and ESP in a diverse range of professions and industries.
SALARY: Details given at interview stage.
FACILITIES/SUPPORT: In-house training provided: accredited Cambridge CELTA Centre, regular teaching workshops and seminars, internet access for teachers, school library.
CONTACT: John Wills, School Manager (john.wills@berlin.school-of-english.de).

BERLITZ DEUTSCHLAND GmbH
Hahnstraße 68–70, 60528 Frankfurt
+49 69 666 089 258
jobs@berlitz.de
www.berlitz.de

Hiring is done locally by the 68 schools in Germany. All contact information is linked from www.berlitz.de. At the time of writing, nearly 50 Berlitz schools were looking for English instructors, but most vacancies were open to people already residing in the vicinity or having the required documents to work in Germany (visa and work permit).
NUMBER OF TEACHERS: Varies depending on the size of the language centre. Over 1,000 instructors employed in Germany.
PREFERENCE OF NATIONALITY: Native English speakers preferred.
QUALIFICATIONS: Teaching abilities, a professional attitude, good communication skills, willing to work a flexible schedule, and preferably have a business background.
CONDITIONS OF EMPLOYMENT: Open-ended, freelance contracts. Flexible hours between 8am and 9.30pm.
FACILITIES/SUPPORT: Training in the Berlitz Method given before start. Assistance with accommodation and work permits occasionally given.
RECRUITMENT: Adverts and personal referral.
CONTACT: Judith Schminke, Teamleader HR (judith.schminke@berlitz.de).

BERLITZ KIDS & TEENS – BERLITZ DEUTSCHLAND GmbH
Königin-Elisabeth Strasse 52, 14059 Berlin
+49 30 3030 8479
laurie.camargo@berlitz.de
www.berlitz.de

NUMBER OF TEACHERS: 250.
PREFERENCE OF NATIONALITY: Native English speakers. EU citizens preferred.
QUALIFICATIONS: Experience working with children aged 7–17 and also experience of teaching English preferred. Should be student or recent graduate.
CONDITIONS OF EMPLOYMENT: Freelance work in English holiday camps during German school holidays (Easter 1–2 weeks, summer 4–8 weeks, autumn 2–4 weeks). Camp programmes run all day from 8am to 11pm.
SALARY: €450 per week. Freelancers have to deal with tax and health insurance independently.

FACILITIES/SUPPORT: No help with accommodation. Support will be given in dealing with the German authorities. Free one-week counsellor training in Berlin in mid-July.

RECRUITMENT: Advertising in local magazines and word of mouth. Interviews are desirable and can be carried out over the telephone.

CONTACT: Laurie Castro Camargo, Kids Director (Quality and Training).

CAMBRIDGE INSTITUT
Residenzstrasse 22, 80333 Munich
+49 89 221115
info@cambridgeinstitut.de
www.cambridgeinstitut.de

NUMBER OF TEACHERS: Approximately 30.

PREFERENCE OF NATIONALITY: British.

QUALIFICATIONS: Formal teaching qualification essential, e.g. TEFL or PGCE (preferably in modern languages).

CONDITIONS OF EMPLOYMENT: 11-month contracts, renewable for a further 11 months. 26 hours per week. Lessons 9am–11.45am and 5.30pm–9.10pm.

SALARY: €2,600 per month less social security and income tax payments. Hourly rate is €23 for 45 minutes.

FACILITIES/SUPPORT: Assistance with accommodation. Induction course and ongoing workshops.

RECRUITMENT: Interview in UK or Munich essential.

CONTACT: Philip Moore, Principal.

CONTEXTINC
Elisenstr 4–10, 50667 Cologne
+49 221 925 4560
teaching@contextinc.com or office@contextinc.com
www.contextinc.de

NUMBER OF TEACHERS: 15–20 to teach and coach professionals.

PREFERENCE OF NATIONALITY: None.

QUALIFICATIONS: Must be native English speakers with academic education and experience.

CONDITIONS OF EMPLOYMENT: Freelance basis. Hours vary between 8am and 8pm, Monday to Friday.

SALARY: Varies according to qualifications/experience and degree of difficulty of class taught.

FACILITIES/SUPPORT: Accommodation and visas are responsibility of teachers. Some training given.

RECRUITMENT: Newspaper adverts, followed by local interviews.

DAVID BERRY LANGUAGES
Florastasse 2, 13187 Berlin-Pankow
+49 30449 9025
ped@dbl-berlin.de
www.dbl-berlin.de

NUMBER OF TEACHERS: 10–15.

PREFERENCE OF NATIONALITY: None.

QUALIFICATIONS: Minimum CELTA with preferably 2 years' experience.

CONDITIONS OF EMPLOYMENT: Freelance contract with flexible working hours.

SALARY: Negotiable depending on travel/course requirements.

FACILITIES/SUPPORT: Will refer teacher to the local ELTA for help with accommodation.

RECRUITMENT: Interviews are essential.

CONTACT: David Berry-Lichtenberg, Director of Studies.

DESK
Blumenstr. 1, 80331 Munich
+49 89 263334
info@desk-sprachkurse.de
www.desk-sprachkurse.de

NUMBER OF TEACHERS: 30 native speakers (70 teachers in total). For central Munich or Herrsching on Ammersee.

PREFERENCE OF NATIONALITY: None.

QUALIFICATIONS: Degree with TEFL experience of adult education (in-class or online).

CONDITIONS OF EMPLOYMENT: Duration of contract to suit. One of the few schools in Munich offering a full contract, as well as freelance openings. Flexible teaching hours mainly early mornings and evenings.

SALARY: €22 per 45-minute lesson.

FACILITIES/SUPPORT: No help with accommodation.

RECRUITMENT: CV and interview.

CONTACT: Erwin Schmidt-Achert, Owner (e.schmidtachert@desk-sprachkurse.de).

DIE NEUE SCHULE
Gieselerstrasse 30a, 10713 Berlin
+49 30 873 0373
bewerbung@neueschule.de
www.neueschule.de/jobs.htm

NUMBER OF TEACHERS: 80.

PREFERENCE OF NATIONALITY: British, American, Irish, Canadian.

QUALIFICATIONS: Cambridge or TEFL certificate and teaching experience needed. Mostly adults (ages 25–40) in small groups of no more than 8.

CONDITIONS OF EMPLOYMENT: Open-ended freelance contracts and some employed teachers. Variable hours in the daytime (9am–3pm) and evenings (6pm–9.15pm).

SALARY: Approx. €19 per hour.

FACILITIES/SUPPORT: Help with accommodation.

RECRUITMENT: Online application form. Personal interview necessary.

CONTACT: Martina Grebe, Director of Studies (Grebe@neueschule.de).

EURO INGOLSTADT

Esplanade 36, 85049 Ingolstadt

+49 841 17001

sw@euro-ingolstadt.de

www.euro-ingolstadt.de

State-recognised vocational language college.

NUMBER OF TEACHERS: 25.

PREFERENCE OF NATIONALITY: British, American, Canadian.

QUALIFICATIONS: At least a bachelor's degree (main focus must be German). PGCE preferred. At least 3 years' experience.

CONDITIONS OF EMPLOYMENT: Permanent contracts. Part-time work possible. 30 hours per week.

SALARY: Based on German state salary scale.

FACILITIES/SUPPORT: Assistance given with accommodation and work permits.

RECRUITMENT: Interview in Ingolstadt necessary.

CONTACT: Stuart Wheeler, Headmaster.

EURO-LINGUA

Beuggenerstr. 12, 79618 Rheinfelden-Nöllingen

+49 179 693 1898

info@euro-lingua.de

www.euro-lingua.de

Also has branch in Riehen, Switzerland near Basel.

NUMBER OF TEACHERS: 5.

PREFERENCE OF NATIONALITY: None, but native English speakers preferred.

QUALIFICATIONS: University degree, teaching experience, foreign language ability, preferably TOEFL or teacher training.

CONDITIONS OF EMPLOYMENT: Freelance.

SALARY: €15 per 45-minute lesson starting salary.

FACILITIES/SUPPORT: Advice given on local accommodation agencies. Non-EU teachers applying for a work permit outside Germany can be supplied with statement of projected income, etc. Support available as needed for lesson planning, books and other materials.

RECRUITMENT: Word of mouth, local ads, contact with schools abroad.

CONTACT: Sylvia Weismiller, Director.

FINER ENGLISH

Friedrich-Naumann-Strasse 19, 34131 Kassel

+49 561 766 9236

Joe.Finer@Finerenglish.com

www.Finerenglish.com

NUMBER OF TEACHERS: 25 for two branches in Kassel.

PREFERENCE OF NATIONALITY: British, Canadian, American.

QUALIFICATIONS: University degree plus a teaching qualification, if possible, plus at least 2 years' relevant teaching experience. However, personality is more important than a stream of qualifications.

CONDITIONS OF EMPLOYMENT: Teachers work as freelancers who teach only on clients' premises. School is looking for teachers able to commit for at least 1 year. Most teachers have a weekly timetable of about 17 90-minute classes.

SALARY: Teachers invoice Finer English for hours worked. Typical monthly earnings are €2,200–€3,000. Freelancers are paid in full but must organise the payment of income tax and health insurance.

FACILITIES/SUPPORT: Full teacher support provided including finding accommodation and dealing with red tape. Teachers need to arrange a medical examination with a German doctor in order to obtain medical insurance which is a pre-condition of receiving a work permit.

RECRUITMENT: Via internet. Intensive telephone interviews conducted from Kassel, Germany.

CONTACT: Joe Finer, Director or Oliver Grund, Director of Studies (Oliver.Grund@Finerenglish.com).

GERMAN AMERICAN INSTITUTE TUEBINGEN

Karlstrasse 3, 72072 Tübingen

+49 7071 795260

mail@dai-tuebingen.de

www.dai-tuebingen.de

NUMBER OF TEACHERS: 20–30.

PREFERENCE OF NATIONALITY: North American.

QUALIFICATIONS: College degree (minimum requirement BA or BSc). Applications from candidates holding a certificate in TESOL, TESL or TEFL are especially welcome. Candidates with a driver's licence valid in Germany are needed.

CONDITIONS OF EMPLOYMENT: Freelance positions only. Average workload 3–9 hours per week, teaching adults and high school students. Also summer camps for 10–14 year olds.

SALARY: Hourly wage.

RECRUITMENT: Local interview required.

CONTACT: Stephanie Krenze, Language Program Co-ordinator (07071 795 2614; stephanie.krenze@dai-tuebingen.de).

HAMBURG SCHOOL OF ENGLISH

Eppendorfer Landstr. 93, 20249 Hamburg

+49 40 480 2119

info@hamburg.school-of-english.de

www.hamburg.school-of-english.de

NUMBER OF TEACHERS: 60–70.

PREFERENCE OF NATIONALITY: British, North American.

QUALIFICATIONS: University degree plus ELT certificate. Preferred minimum 1 year's experience.

CONDITIONS OF EMPLOYMENT: Minimum 1 year on freelance basis. Between 16 and 30 hours per week.

SALARY: Approx. €29–€45 for 90-minute teaching session.

FACILITIES/SUPPORT: Assistance given with finding accommodation and obtaining work permits. Cambridge CELTA course provider.

RECRUITMENT: Via local or telephone interviews.

CONTACT: Bill Cope, Director of Studies (bill.cope@hamburg.school-of-english.com).

ICC SPRACHINSTITUT

Am Nordplatz 9, 04105 Leipzig

+49 341 5502 2460

info@icc-sprachinstitut.de

www.icc-sprachinstitut.de

NUMBER OF TEACHERS: 50.

PREFERENCE OF NATIONALITY: None.

QUALIFICATIONS: University degree, CELTA and preferably TEFL experience with corporate clients.

CONDITIONS OF EMPLOYMENT: Fixed term or freelance. Teaching in-company business courses, intensive and evening courses. Internships also available.

SALARY: €15–€20 per 45-minute lesson.

FACILITIES/SUPPORT: Assistance with accommodation and work permits (if necessary). Induction and regular training included. Good career prospects throughout the ASSET group.

RECRUITMENT: Walk-ins mainly though email applications welcome. Local interview essential.

CONTACT: James Parsons, Director (james.parsons@icc-sprachinstitut.de) or Mrs Teresa Lang, Director of Studies (teresa.lang@icc-sprachinstitut.de).

INLINGUA SPRACHCENTER KIEL

Alter Markt 7, 24103 Kiel

+49 431 981380

info@inlingua-kiel.de

www.inlingua-kiel.de

NUMBER OF TEACHERS: Approximately 10 trainers.

PREFERENCE OF NATIONALITY: None.

QUALIFICATIONS: Degree, CELTA certificate and some teaching experience preferred. Driving licence preferred.

CONDITIONS OF EMPLOYMENT: 6-month probationary period. Teaching hours Monday to Friday between 8am and 9pm and extra Saturday hours possible 8am–5pm. Full-time contract guarantees 100 teaching hours per month.

SALARY: From €12 per teaching hour.

FACILITIES/SUPPORT: Information is provided about the best way to find accommodation in Kiel. Necessary paperwork is provided for non-EU employee to take to foreigners' office to obtain a work permit.

RECRUITMENT: Through online advertisements and by receiving speculative CVs.

CONTACT: Armando Lizarzaburu (a.lizarzaburu@inlingua-kiel.de).

INLINGUA SPRACHSCHULE HANNOVER

Andreaestrasse 3, Ecke Schillerstrasse, 30159 Hannover

+49 511 324580

info@inlingua-hannover.de

www.inlingua-hannover.de

NUMBER OF TEACHERS: 15.

PREFERENCE OF NATIONALITY: English, American, Canadian; other native English speakers.

QUALIFICATIONS: Degree in any subject and minimum 1 years' TEFL experience.

CONDITIONS OF EMPLOYMENT: Minimum 12 months. Average at least 25 school lessons (45 minutes each) per week.

SALARY: Approx. €15 per lesson.

FACILITIES/SUPPORT: Assistance finding accommodation.

RECRUITMENT: Newspaper adverts and internet.

CONTACT: Ms Heiki Gleichmann.

INTERACT! LANGUAGE CONNECTS
Osdorfer Landstrasse 11, 22607 Hamburg
+49 40 2199 0400
info@interact-experts.com
www.interact-experts.com

NUMBER OF TEACHERS: 42.
PREFERENCE OF NATIONALITY: None.
QUALIFICATIONS: CELTA plus experience, business background and very good references.
CONDITIONS OF EMPLOYMENT: Various hours, Monday to Saturday, mornings and evenings.
SALARY: Approx. €18–23 per hour.
FACILITIES/SUPPORT: Assistance given with accommodation. Training. Access to internet/materials.
RECRUITMENT: Adverts, agencies, internet and word of mouth..
CONTACT: Kerstin Hansen, Manager (kerstinhansen@interact-experts.com).

LEOlingo SPRACHCAMPS FÜR KINDER
Seitzermühle 1, 92369 Sengenthal, Bavaria
Werderstrasse 35, 19055 Schwerin, North Germany
+49 385 581 5430 (North Germany)
baer@leo-lingo.de (Bavaria); goerner@leo-lingo.de (North Germany)
www.leo-lingo.de

Summer language camps for children in North-Eastern Germany (Hamburg, Baltic Sea, Mecklenburg-Vorpommern) and Bavaria.
NUMBER OF TEACHERS: 20–25 in Bavaria; 10–15 in North Germany.
PREFERENCE OF NATIONALITY: English-speaking countries (USA, UK, Canada, Australia, etc).
QUALIFICATIONS: College/university students preferred. Applicants should have previous experience of working with children aged 7–15, preferably as a camp counsellor or in similar fields such as teaching, au pairing, sports coaching, etc. Musicians welcome to apply.
CONDITIONS OF EMPLOYMENT: 7 weeks from mid-July in Bavaria; start date is a little earlier in North Germany. Day counsellors work 9am–5pm Mon-Fri. Night counsellors work 5pm–9am Sun/Mon–Fri, although the actual programme time is only 7–9.30pm.
SALARY: €200 per week for day counsellors plus either free bed and breakfast or full bed and board. The salary for a night counsellor is €100 per week, plus full bed and board.
FACILITIES/SUPPORT: Counsellors are provided with free accommodation during their working weeks (including the weekends), either with a German host family or at places such as youth hostels. If counsellors have a week off, they must arrange their own accommodation. For non-Europeans who are hired, LEOlingo sends the necessary information about work permits and they are responsible for the application process themselves, which usually involves arranging an appointment at their nearest German consulate and handing over the required documents, for example, completed visa application form, passport photo, copy of the working contract, proof of residence, proof of health insurance/funds. 8-day compulsory training is unpaid.
RECRUITMENT: Via job websites and university careers services. Application form followed by possibility of video interview.
CONTACT: Andrea Bär (Bavaria); Sabine Görner (North Germany).

LINGUA FRANCA
Mauerstrasse 77, 10117 Berlin
+49 30 8639 8080
info@lingua-franca.de
www.lingua-franca.de

NUMBER OF TEACHERS: 50.
PREFERENCE OF NATIONALITY: None.
QUALIFICATIONS: University degree plus TEFL experience and/or certificate. Experience in ESP preferred.
CONDITIONS OF EMPLOYMENT: Freelance only. Can generally give good teachers as many lesson hours as they want.
FACILITIES/SUPPORT: No help with accommodation. Will write the necessary letter to the employment office to support work permit application. In-house training available.
RECRUITMENT: Local interviews.
CONTACT: Douglas Werner, Director of Studies.

MARCUS EVANS – LINGUARAMA SPRACHENINSTITUT DEUTSCHLAND
personnel@linguarama.com
www.linguarama.com

NUMBER OF TEACHERS: From 25 Business English trainers in the smaller Linguarama schools to 70 in the larger ones; Linguarama schools located in Berlin, Cologne, Dusseldorf, Frankfurt, Marburg, Mannheim and many smaller towns. Vacancies at the time of writing in Cologne, Hannover and Dusseldorf, and often vacancies in Munich at Sendlinger-Tor-Platz 7, 80336 Munich; +49 89 2000 0930; munich@linguarama.com.
PREFERENCE OF NATIONALITY: Native English speakers only who must have valid working papers for the EU.
QUALIFICATIONS: Minimum university degree or equivalent and a recognised TEFL qualification (e.g. CELTA). 1–2 years' experience

of teaching Business English is preferred with a keen interest in business as a minimum.

CONDITIONS OF EMPLOYMENT: Mixture of contract and freelance teachers. Freelance teachers work variable hours, usually early mornings and evenings. Contract teachers usually contracted for 1 year, extendable to 2 years, but occasionally shorter contracts available. 23 days paid holiday per 12-month contract.

SALARY: €1,915–€2,020 per month depending on experience.

FACILITIES/SUPPORT: Contract teachers are given an initial 2-week accommodation entitlement and assistance with finding permanent accommodation. Travel expenses to the city are paid from the UK if recruitment is through head office. Help is given with obtaining a residence permit, etc. All teachers are given an induction course and ongoing training.

RECRUITMENT: Usually interviews locally for freelance teachers. Contract staff are sometimes recruited locally or via Linguarama Personnel Department, 101 Finsbury Pavement, London EC24 1RS.

CONTACT: Danny Coughlan, Personnel Manager.

PENGUIN CAMP

Tempelhof 3, 74594 Kressberg

+49 7957 9239 122

info@penguincamp.de

www.penguincamp.de/Jobs

NUMBER OF TEACHERS: 5-10 freelance language counsellors for day camps around Munich and some overnight camps in several locations in Bavaria.

PREFERENCE OF NATIONALITY: None.

QUALIFICATIONS: Native English or bilingual students, teachers, performing artists, etc. with creativity, independence, stamina, humour and organisational skills. Experience with children and some knowledge of German helpful.

CONDITIONS OF EMPLOYMENT: 4-day camp at Easter and Monday-to-Friday day and residential camps during the summer. Counsellors work 9-16 hour days.

SALARY: €240–€450 per week depending on hours and experience with Penguin.

FACILITIES/SUPPORT: Advice can be given on accommodation (hostels, etc.) in or near Munich and on permits (if non-EU). Counsellors are independent contractors so are responsible for their own tax and social security.

RECRUITMENT: Via websites and word of mouth. Skype interviews.

CONTACT: Alice & Holger Breit, Organisers.

PET-SPRACHEN

Baaderstr. 3, 80469 Munich

+49 89 2006 2090

team@pet-sprachen.de; info@pet-sprachen.de

www.pet-sprachen.de

NUMBER OF TEACHERS: 100 freelancers for 14 branches throughout Germany and occasionally in Austria and Switzerland.

PREFERENCE OF NATIONALITY: None.

QUALIFICATIONS: TEFL qualification and/or degree preferable, as are business experience and friendly, outgoing disposition.

CONDITIONS OF EMPLOYMENT: Travelling to companies to hold in-company courses on a freelance basis.

SALARY: Minimum €21 per teaching unit (45 minutes) plus travel.

FACILITIES/SUPPORT: No assistance with accommodation. Materials support given. Teachers' workshops held.

RECRUITMENT: Direct applications. Local interviews necessary.

CONTACT: Paul Bacon, Owner/Manager (paul.bacon@pet-sprachen.de).

SPRACHZENTRUM SUD

Bahnhofplatz 2, 83607 Holzkirchen

+49 8024 1733

info@sprachzentrum-sued.de

www.sprachzentrum-sued.de

NUMBER OF TEACHERS: 15 general and business trainers.

PREFERENCE OF NATIONALITY: British, Irish, American, Australian.

QUALIFICATIONS: Teaching certificate (e.g. CELTA, DELTA) or university degree. Teaching experience needed, especially in Business English.

CONDITIONS OF EMPLOYMENT: Freelance; employment possible after 1 year of successful freelancing. Also freelance teachers needed for summer camps in Munich, Jofestal and Spitzingsee.

SALARY: Between €15 and €25 per hour, depending on the qualification and contract.

RECRUITMENT: Telephone interviews possible. Candidates in Europe will be invited to interview and to teach a practice lesson with volunteer students.

CONTACT: Dr Karin Wiebalck-Zahn, Managing Director. Summer camp applications to Anissa Nasser (anissa.nasser@sprachzentrum-sued.de).

STEVENS ENGLISH TRAINING

Essen: Rüttenscheiderstr. 68, 45130 Essen

Cologne: Hohenstaufenring 29–37, 50674 Cologne

Dortmund: Westenhellweg 112, 44137 Dortmund

Münster: Olferstrasse 6, 48153 Münster
+49 201 877 0770
office@stevens-english.de
www.stevens-english.de

NUMBER OF TEACHERS: Approx. 80 full and part-time corporate language trainers.

PREFERENCE OF NATIONALITY: None but should be native English speakers.

QUALIFICATIONS: TEFL certificate or experience of the business world. Should be EU national with basic German and a driving licence, as well as a degree and CELTA if possible.

CONDITIONS OF EMPLOYMENT: 2-year contracts. Hours between 7.30am and 8.45pm Monday to Friday. Full-time contract with minimum 80 hours per month guaranteed. 80% of teaching is in-company with high element of ESP.

SALARY: Paid on points system per 45-minute session. Guaranteed minimum.

FACILITIES/SUPPORT: Furnished flats available at certain locations (e.g. Essen) for trainers recruited from the UK. Full induction programme. Extensive workshop training programme for trainers. Free training for the LCCI exam 'First Certificate for Teachers of Business English' (FTBE). Extensive library of teaching materials. Use of company car may be available.

RECRUITMENT: Recruit from UK and locally. Interviews essential and can be by Skype. Candidates receive €100 towards travel expenses and one night's accommodation provided.

CONTACTS: Michael Stevens, Managing Director.

NUMBER OF TEACHERS: 40 corporate trainers for Stuttgart, Bamberg and Mülheim.

PREFERENCE OF NATIONALITY: Ideally EU passport holders.

QUALIFICATIONS: Look for trainers with a university degree, CELTA (or equivalent) and 5 years' EFL experience (including corporate/business EFL training or technical/commercial background). Knowledge of German not obligatory.

CONDITIONS OF EMPLOYMENT: Initial contract is 2 years. 40 hours per week, during normal office hours.

SALARY: €2,600 per month (after completing a 6-month probation period on pay of €2,400). DELTA trainers receive a higher rate. Deductions amount to about 40% (depending on personal circumstances). €1,000 end-of-contract bonus.

FACILITIES/SUPPORT: Assistance with finding accommodation. 30 days paid holiday.

RECRUITMENT: Via www.tefl.com, social media (such as Xing and LinkedIn) and through website. Two telephone interviews followed by a task-based interview conducted face-to-face in Germany.

CONTACT: Helen Sinclair, Trainer Recruiter.

XCHANGE SERVICES

Hornschuchpromenade 20, 90762 Fürth

+49 911 950 990 10

jobs@xchange-services.de

www.xchange-services.de

Translation agency with language and intercultural training. Affiliated to English Camps for Kids (www.englishsummercamp.de).

NUMBER OF TEACHERS: 15–20.

PREFERENCE OF NATIONALITY: Native English speakers. Work permit required.

QUALIFICATIONS: Minimum teaching/training qualification, e.g. PGCE, CELTA/Trinity, TEFL/TESOL certificate. Business experience and commercial/industrial training experience also considered.

CONDITIONS OF EMPLOYMENT: Open-ended contract for freelancers; 24 contact hours per week; teaching hours between 7.30am and 8pm.

SALARY: Hourly rates to be negotiated.

FACILITIES/SUPPORT: May be able to advise on accommodation.

RECRUITMENT: Word of mouth. Interviews essential.

CONTACT: Thomas Hintze (thomas.hintze@xchange-services.de).

GREECE

For the past few years, Greece has been inching towards the cliff-edge of eviction from the Eurozone and then retreating after accepting serial bail-outs. The situation has been dire for a long time and is not improving. The unemployment rate remains stubbornly high at 24%, 250% higher than the EU average. Swingeing austerity has had a deeply detrimental effect on the Greek economy and yet has not reduced the debt mountain. The economy has shrunk by a quarter since 2008, with the private sector having been eviscerated. Every business has suffered, especially private language schools, because when money is tight, language learning is one of the first things to get the chop. Taxes are so high that school owners are finding it difficult to make a profit and don't see the point of staying open, especially as they generally have a problem collecting the fees from parents. This has led to a situation in which there is a serious over-supply of teachers compared to positions available.

English teacher **Jerry Melinn** has been able to observe the changes over the past decade that he has been living in Athens, and his assessment makes for depressing reading:

> ***There is no doubt that the financial crisis has had a very negative effect on the Greek people. Businesses – including foreign language schools – are closing daily and unemployment is at record levels. The number of students in language schools is falling and where students still attend, some parents don't pay the fees or are late paying. Competition among schools and from private teachers has increased. Private teachers have dropped their prices significantly and some parents are now finding it as cheap, if not cheaper, to hire a private teacher than to send their children to a private language school. There is also huge pressure on school owners to enter the students for the exams as fast as possible so the parents can save money. This is a big problem because if the students are not ready and fail the test the reputation of the school will suffer, which will result in a reduction in the number of new students.***
>
> ***Taking a medium to long-term view, I believe the ESL industry in Greece will continue to decline further from its peak. There will probably be little or no recruitment into the public service for a long time and employment in this area was one of the drivers for ESL. Tourism plays an important role in the economy and this will continue to stimulate demand but conversational English would be the main requirement here perhaps and not Lower or Proficiency certificates.***

The number of candidates sitting the Michigan Lower and Proficiency exams is declining. On the other hand there has been a spike in interest in the IELTS test, probably because Greeks see this as a route to finding work or study opportunities abroad. As for leisure pursuits, Jerry Melinn has noticed that cheap 'recession pastimes' like cycling and running have become popular.

The fact remains, teachers like Jerry Melinn continue to enjoy teaching in Greece. Schools continue to operate and the teacher recruitment agencies (see directory) remain in business. Thousands of private language schools – the term *kentra xenon glosson* has been replacing the term *frontisteria* – continue to supplement the language education of most children aged 6–16. A few years ago the state school system lowered the age when students begin to learn English, so parents want very young children to get ahead of the game and have a good grounding in English before they start their state school lessons. Secondary school students are all in pursuit of higher scores in the Panhellenic exams that determine university entrance.

Greek language schools are often run by local entrepreneurs and because they are limited to three or four classrooms are often housed in buildings which were not purpose-built as schools. Secondary school pupils in Greece are obliged to study 15 subjects, all of which they must pass before being allowed to proceed to the next year. In most areas the teaching of English in state schools is considered inadequate so that the vast majority of pupils also attend *frontisteria*, and it is not uncommon for a 15-year-old to have two or three hours of lessons a day (in other subjects as well as English) in one or more private establishments to supplement the state schooling. Despite this gruelling timetable, the students are usually motivated and generally participate enthusiastically in their lessons, reaching a good level of proficiency by age 16.

English language teaching in Greece has been described as an exam industry, and there is fierce competition among the international exam bodies. At one time Cambridge First Certificate and Cambridge Proficiency examinations dominated though they have been given a run for their money by the University of Michigan exams and more recently by the Pearson Test of English and the English Speaking Board (ESB) which won a tender for ESOL work from the beginning of 2014. The different exams are administered by two rival associations of language schools mentioned below, PALSO and EUROPALSO. More recently, City & Guilds English (www.cityandguilds.gr) has come onto the Greek scene, aggressively marketing its certification exams. Indigenous exams like Kratiko are preferred by some schools. In fact, there are now 15 exams to choose from, all administered by different examining boards, and the terminology can be confusing. A certificate in one of these exams earns points to help the applicant get on the waiting list for a job in the civil service or in a state school. Some teachers and students still refer to the exams by exam board names such as First Certificate and Proficiency (Cambridge), Michigan and Michigan Proficiency, Edexcel, etc. A structure for language learning and assessment has been laid down by the European Union (called the Common European Framework of Reference for Languages) which has gained widespread acceptance in Greece. B2 denotes someone who can function in English as an 'Independent User' and C2 denotes the highest level 'Mastery' of English.

PROSPECTS FOR TEACHERS

The employment situation for teachers is undeniably more difficult than it was in the boom years when schools were opening left, right and centre. **Jain Cook**, long-time Director of Studies at a successful language school in Patras paints a depressing picture:

> ***Things have changed a lot here, and it's much more difficult to find work. A lot of schools have shut down, so there are some very experienced teachers out there looking for work. The Koutsantonis school has been lucky because our student numbers haven't really dropped. The problem is parents not paying the fees, and this applies to all private schools. I finished at the school two weeks ago, and have already had 17 phone calls from ex-teachers or someone who is a friend of someone I know, asking me for work in September. I've had teachers asking for a job who are willing to work for two or three euros an hour! People are desperate for work. This also applies to private lessons, which are practically non-existent now and if you do get a student, you cannot charge much more than €5 an hour – and that's if you are a native speaker.***
>
> ***In some ways it's depressing here. Every time you go out another shop has shut down and people look miserable. It's really not the best place to come at the moment to work, especially when just under half of 18–25 year olds are unemployed and there is a lot of bad feeling towards foreigners, although more towards illegal immigrants.***

Yet prospects for EU citizens with a university degree and a TEFL qualification are not hopeless, particularly outside Athens. A fairly recent development is that ESP classes are becoming more popular in Greece and institutions organising company classes are sometimes on the lookout for professional, highly trained teachers.

A qualification is becoming essential, though not necessarily experience. The government stipulates that in order to obtain a teacher's licence, English teachers must have at least a BA in English Language and Literature or Education, so virtually all schools expect to see a degree certificate. Note that the government enforces a quota on all employers: for every foreigner they hire, they must employ 10 Greeks.

Having a TEFL qualification, as always, will make the job hunt easier. Given the size of the ELT market in Greece, it is surprising that so few training centres offer the CELTA or the Trinity TESOL certificate in Greece. The main teacher training organisations in Greece tend to concentrate on training Greek speakers to become English teachers, though Anglo-Hellenic in Corinth and Via Lingua in Crete run courses mainly attended by native English speakers. The main ELT training organisations in Greece are listed below:

American College of Greece/DEREE, 6 Gravias St, Aghia Paraskevi, 15342 Athens (✆ +30 210 600 2208; www.acg.edu). From 2016, offering an MA in TESOL, mixture of face-to-face with online studies.

Anglo-Hellenic, 13 Vasilou St, Vrahati, 20006 Corinth (✆ +30 27410 53511; www.anglo-hellenic.com; www.tefl.gr). TEFL International Certificate course (www.teflcorinth.com) held monthly between Easter and November; also offered part-time. Fee is €1,295. Accommodation is located in Vrahati on the seaside near Corinth. Shared accommodation €250; private room €350.

CELT, Georgiou Gennadiou 3, 10678 Athens (✆ +30 210 330 2406/1455; info@celt.edu.gr; www.celt.edu.gr). Offers CELTA (€1,450 plus Cambridge assessment fee of €160) and range of other courses including intensive DELTA taught over 8 weeks (€3,000 plus €400 Cambridge assessment fee). Also available part-time.

Study Space, D Gounari 21, 54622 Thessaloniki (✆ +30 231 026 9697; www.studyspace.gr). Teacher development centre whose CELTA package includes assistance with employment in its partner schools in Thessaloniki and throughout Northern Greece. Fee for full-time course (held in June) is €1,800 and includes accommodation. Also offered part-time October to January and February to May.

Via Lingua Crete, Chrysanthou Episkopou 48, Chania, 73132 Crete (✆ +30 28210 57438; www.teflgreece.com or www.vialingua.org). 5 times a year between May and November. €1,650 including shared accommodation (€100 supplement for single room).

Americans and other non-EU citizens will find it difficult to find a school willing to hire them, purely because of immigration difficulties. The government can impose stiff penalties on employers who break the rules and few, at least in the major cities, will risk it, as **Tim Leffel** found out some years ago: '*We had planned on teaching in Greece, but as Americans, we were not exactly welcomed with open arms in Athens; they told us to try the countryside.*' Tim moved on to Turkey instead.

A further complicating factor is the high number of Greek emigrés to North America and Australia who have returned (or whose children have returned) to Greece. In many cases, they are virtually native speakers of English but are favoured because of their ancestry. Of course there will always be schools prepared to hire Americans and others if well qualified, such as the Hellenic American Union, which has one of the largest programmes in adult EFL in Athens. The Betsis School in Piraeus (see Directory) has been known to accept one or two American TEFL graduates as interns who stay no more than the 90-day validity of their Schengen visas.

One reason why EU citizens with basic qualifications can expect to land a job in Greece is that wages are not high enough to attract many highly qualified EFL teachers. Greece tends to be a country where people get their first English teaching job for the experience and then move to more lucrative countries. Also, few schools place any emphasis on staff development or provide in-house training, so serious teachers tend to move on quickly. The majority of advertised jobs are in towns and cities in mainland Greece. Athens has such a large expatriate community that most of the large central schools at the elite end of the market are able to hire well-qualified staff locally. But the competition may not be so keen in Edessa, Larissa, Preveza or any of the numerous towns of which the tourist to Greece is unlikely to have heard.

FINDING A JOB

IN ADVANCE

Unless you elect to register with one of the recruitment agencies (that deal primarily with Certificate-qualified teachers), it may not be worthwhile trying to find a job in advance, since so much in Greece is accomplished by word of mouth. Getting a list of language schools from outside Greece is not easy. A considerable proportion of *frontisteria* belong to the Pan-Hellenic Federation of Language School Owners (PALSO Headquarters, 2 Lykavitou St, 106 71 Kolonaki, Athens). There are local branches of PALSO all over Greece though they are unlikely to offer much help to job-seeking teachers until they are looking on the spot. Note that the Athens association of language school owners is separate from PALSO and calls itself EUROPALSO (Akademias 98–100, Athens 106 77; ✆ +30 210 383 0752; www.europalso.gr). EUROPALSO consists of hundreds of schools in the Athens area and keeps a file of applications submitted by teachers (europalso@europalso.gr) or you can visit in person to see if any school owners have registered an interest in hiring teaching staff. PALSO-Chania has a separate web presence (only in Greek) at www.palso-chania.gr (Partheniou Kelaidi 72, Chania 73136; ✆ +30 28210 92622), while the Heraklion branch is at www.palsoher.gr.

An alternative association of language schools is QLS (Quality in Language Services), which aspires to be a Panhellenic Association of Accredited Language Schools. Overseeing its 24 member schools, the main office is in Athens; links to schools can be found on www.qls.gr.

The internet is not as useful for the job-seeker in Greece unless you can easily read the Greek alphabet. The *Yellow Pages* can be accessed in English at www.vrisko.gr/en/dir/foreign-language-schools or www.xo.gr/dir-az/F/Foreign-Language-Schools/?lang=en. Occasional classified job ads appear (mostly in Greek) on the site of the ELT News (www.eltnews.gr/news). For example in May 2016, the Omiros Association of Foreign Language Schools was inviting experienced English teachers (preferably native) to submit their CVs to s-omiros@otenet.gr for the academic year.

Most schools do their hiring for the following academic year between May and July. Obviously the major chains of schools offer the most opportunities, and it is worth sending your CV in the spring to organisations such as the Strategakis Group, which has about a hundred schools in Northern Greece (www.strategakis.gr). Other major organisations include Axon Hellas (www.axon.gr) and the Scholars Group (www.the-scholars.gr).

Fortunately there are several active recruitment agencies that specialise in Greece with offices in Greece and/or Britain. The number of teachers they recruit every year has been falling but is still substantial. These recruitment agencies are looking for people with at least a bachelor's degree and normally a TEFL qualification and/or experience (depending on the client school's requirements). All client employers provide accommodation. Long-established agencies Anglo-Hellenic Teacher Recruitment and Cambridge Teachers Recruitment both have entries in the Directory below.

When discussing your future post with an agency, don't be lulled into a false sense of security. It is wise to check contractual details for yourself and verify verbal promises. Check to see whether you are entitled to any compensation if the employer breaks the contract and similarly whether you will have to compensate the school if you leave early. Find out if there will be any other native English-speaking teachers in the area, and ask about the possibility of contacting your predecessor in the job.

After graduating from the TEFL Corinth certificate course, **Jerry Melinn** (aged 56) began working for the Katsianos School of Foreign Languages in Athens, where he remained teaching for four great years. As he developed as a teacher, he moved on to a different school where he is left mostly to his own devices and is allowed to cover the whole course including grammar:

> ***I read some horror stories on the internet about teaching in Greece but my experience has been great. The TEFL course in Corinth prepared me well for teaching. I have learned so much, made many new friends and grown very attached to the students. I have nothing but admiration for them as they come to lessons twice a week after Greek school and the vast majority are well behaved and good humoured.***
>
> ***I am still happy teaching here though things are more difficult as a result of the financial crisis. I now rent my own apartment and work on a contract for 15 hours a week at a school about 15 minutes by bus from my apartment. I occasionally work some extra hours especially coming up to exam time. I have much more autonomy as a teacher now and I like the responsibility of teaching exam classes on my own. The financial crisis has taken its toll and my pay has been reduced but I was able to negotiate a rent reduction, which offset my pay cut.***
>
> ***I still enjoy teaching and in my free time I go cycling, swimming and to the gym. As usual, my wife and I have holidays at Easter, June and September and I go home to Ireland for the summer and for Christmas.***

Phil Tomkins graduated from the Corinth TEFL course mentioned above and took up his first TEFL post on the small island of Kea in the Cyclades. His 'interview' with the director of the Kea school simply involved catching a bus to Athens and meeting her for an informal chat over coffee at a street café.

Given how many children study English outside school, it is surprising there are very few summer language camps or English programmes in Greece. The Russian-based Nordic School that operates English language camps in Finland has expanded operations to Crete (contact details may be found in its entry in the Scandinavia chapter).

The British Council is involved in supplying short-term ELT teachers to Skaramaga Refugee Camp in a port town just west of Athens. Positions last for nine months in an attempt to provide some stability and allow the children of secondary school age to continue their education. English lessons are offered every day; details from maria.nomikou@britishcouncil.gr.

IAN PARR

Ian Parr is yet another mature candidate who trained in Corinth and found work straight afterwards, in his case at a chain of three language schools in a suburb of Athens called Vyronas.

This has been my first job as an EFL teacher, having previously worked as a laboratory scientist in England for 10 years. I decided I wanted a new challenge and to travel so I completed the TEFL International course at Corinth. I first heard about this school in Athens through a contact I made on a Living in Greece website. I rang the school and spoke to the owner who asked me to come to Athens for an interview the same week. I met the school owner who was friendly and who checked my degree and teaching certificates, asked me a few questions about myself and told me that she expects her teachers to act professionally at all times whilst at the school. She then told me she would have work for me from January until the end of the school year in June, around 20 hours a week and that she would pay me €10 an hour. On returning to Greece after the Christmas holidays I soon found a small apartment to rent in the centre of Athens.

As is usual, the Greek teachers teach the younger children and also teach grammar to the older students. Native-speaker-teachers teach everything except grammar. This is common in Greece apparently and is a little frustrating as teaching grammar was a challenge I was looking forward to. Altogether my hours only added up to 12 hours a week which was disappointing considering I'd been promised 20. Over the months I have worked extra hours covering classes, doing mock speaking tests and giving extra classes close to the exams. The biggest difficulty has been surviving financially in what is an expensive city. Eventually it has gotten easier as I now have a private lesson and do some editing work for a local English man who owns a publishing company. I have been offered a full-time contract to work at the same school for next year and will take it as I have enjoyed my time here and want to learn more of the culture and language here in Greece.

ON THE SPOT

So many *frontisteria* rely on agents or personal contacts to find teachers for them that it can be difficult to walk into a job. The majority of schools have filled all their vacancies by July, so September is usually too late for prospective teachers to be looking for work. One of the best times to look is January. Greece is far less attractive in mid-winter than in summer, and many foreign teachers do not return to their posts after Christmas. Finding work in the summer is virtually impossible; most English language summer courses in resorts or on the islands are staffed by people who have taught for an academic year. **Will Brady** is one of the co-founders of Atlantis Books on the island of Santorini (www.atlantisbooks.org). He picked up a teaching job on the island:

> *It was just an opportunistic thing. I knew that I needed to earn some money so having recently got a TEFL qualification I thought I'd try my hand at a bit of TEFL teaching. I wandered around Fira and asked if there were any language schools, discovered that I was facing one, and walked in. I met a very strange man, who was the manager (the owner didn't speak English). This guy had studied psychology in England. I think he took a liking to me because I was English. I asked if I could do some work for them and he more or less told me straight away that I could, but kept things on very vague terms. Whilst I was back in England to arrange a few things, I negotiated with him over the phone. Then when I got back to the island I just went in and started. There was no interview whatsoever.*

Work was part-time, teaching (or assisting in the classroom) about 2–3 hours a day, 3–4 times a week. The language school had never hired a native English speaker before and all the Greek teachers would defer to Will on grammatical points, something he found 'quite strange', because he was considerably younger.

Although **Jamie Masters** knew that October was not prime time for job-hunting, that is when he arrived in Heraklion to look for work, some years ago now:

> *I advertised (in Greek) in the Cretan newspapers, no joy. I lowered my sights and started knocking on doors of frontisteria. I was put onto some guy who ran an English-language bookshop and went to see him. Turned out he was a linch-pin in the frontisterion business and in fact I got my first job through him. Simultaneously, I went to the PALSO office and was given a list of schools which were looking for people. The list, it turned out, was pretty much out of date. But I had insisted on leaving my name with them (they certainly didn't offer) and that's how I found my second job.*

Once you arrange an interview, be sure to dress well and to amass as many educational diplomas as you can. This will create the right aura of respectability in which to impress the potential employer with your conscientiousness and amiability. Decisions are often taken more according to whether you hit it off with the interviewer than on your qualifications and experience. **Jamie Masters** found that no one cared a fig about his PhD in classics.

When you elicit interest from a language school owner or a family, take your time over agreeing terms. Greece is not a country in which it pays to rush, and negotiations can be carried out in a leisurely and civilised fashion. On the other hand, do not come to an agreement with an employer without clarifying wages and schedules precisely. Make sure you read your contract very carefully so that you are familiar with what you should be entitled to. Anglo-Hellenic provides a detailed four-page contract in Greek and English, a sample of which is available on its website (http://anglo-hellenic.com/schools/contract.htm).

FREELANCE TEACHING

Private lessons are not as easy to find as they used to be. Established EFL teachers might now have three or four private pupils when before they had as many as 15. This is partly because of the falling birth rate in

Greece and also because the middle classes have less disposable income and prefer to send their children to the local *kentro xenon glosson* or to someone they know locally who has passed the B2 level examination and who charges much less than a native English speaker, sometimes as little as €4–€5. This is a huge contrast with the going rate for qualified private tutors of €25 per hour for B2 tuition, and €30 per hour for C2, probably more in Athens. Lesson prices are quoted on sites where tutors advertise their availability, such as www.findmyfavouriteteacher.com. Typically, a native speaker with basic TEFL qualifications will offer a trial lesson for €10 and charge €13–€15 for further individual lessons or stick with €10 per head in group classes.

Otherwise, private tutoring can materialise from the language schools (whose directors seldom seem to mind their teachers earning on the side) or from conversations in a café-bar.

Trading English lessons for board and lodging is a common form of freelance teaching in Athens and elsewhere. Sometimes contracted teachers are offered free accommodation in exchange for tutoring their boss's children. In Athens, the rich suburbs of Kifissia and Kolonaki are full of families who can afford to provide private English lessons for their offspring. The suburbs of Pangrati and Filothei are also well-heeled. It is also possible to start up private classes for children, provided you have decent accommodation in a prosperous residential area, though this will usually be too expensive if your only source of income is private teaching.

REGULATIONS

Long-term English teachers are meant to obtain a teacher's licence, though this is enforced more rigorously for Greek nationals. The bureaucratic procedures involved can be stressful, even with a supportive employer. The Ministry of Education considers a BA or higher degree in English Literature or a degree in Education a sufficient qualification, though a TEFL certificate strengthens an application of course. Your degree certificate must be officially translated and notarised/apostilled.

If and when the teacher's licence arrives from Athens, the teacher must take it along with his or her passport, photos and a lot of patience to the police station to apply for a residence permit, which should come through in about a month. The health certificate and residence permit must be renewed annually, though if you protest loudly enough you can usually get away with just having a chest X-ray. Keep photocopies of all forms.

Frontisteria usually tend to leave all the bureaucratic legwork to the teachers. If teachers work illegally, they will not be paying insurance contributions so will not be eligible for unemployment benefits, bonuses, pension, etc. Officially, applicants with non-EU passports must obtain a letter of hire from a language school which must be sent to an address outside Greece. The teacher takes the letter to the nearest Greek consulate and applies for a work permit; the procedures take at least two months. In practice, this rarely works.

It is mandatory for Greek employers to register full-time employees with the Greek national health insurance scheme, now known as EOPYY, which covers less than it used to. For example everyone has to pay more for medicines and contribute 15% to the cost of medical tests, treatments, etc. School owners have always been reluctant to pay contributions for their staff, especially when the rate of contribution rose to 30% of salary in the wake of Greece's financial catastrophe, while the employee's contribution of 16%–20% should be deducted at source. Many Greeks no longer see the point of paying, since it is much more expensive for them than it used to be and covers less. It is necessary to qualify for a pension but many are wondering if there will be any pensions in the future. Freelance teachers who teach privately will not be covered by social security unless they choose to pay TEBE contributions to the OAEE (insurance for the self-employed), which will be a minimum of €250 a month regardless of earnings.

CONDITIONS OF WORK

Standards vary among employers. Legislation that used to protect teachers is being watered down so that the government can cut its expenditure. Again **Jain Cook** provided a bleak account of recent changes and their impact on teachers:

> ***There is no longer a legal minimum wage. Our teachers took a 15% pay cut and another 20%–22% a year later. Married teachers used to get an extra 10% per hour, but this has been abolished. That means that the income of a married woman will have been reduced by 45% over two years. Things are not easy! As salaries have dropped, so have rents. Some rents in Patras have dropped from €350 per month to €150, and there are hundreds of empty flats. Everything else though, has gone up.***

The standard recommended hourly wage is €8.13 (gross), €6.84 (net), which can be multiplied by 100 to give a monthly wage based on 25 hours of teaching a week: €813 gross / €684 net.

In general the large chains are better, probably for no other reason than that they have a longer history of employing native English speakers. You also have some back-up if you have been hired through a mediating agency. Some of the small one-man or one-woman schools are run by barely qualified entrepreneurs who have had little contact with the English language; their teaching techniques involve shouting (usually in Greek) at their students and getting them to recite English irregular verbs parrot fashion. In fact this kind of school is on the decline, and standards have been rising.

The average number of hours assigned to teachers has been shrinking, to 18 per week or even as low as 12, which means reduced earnings and the possibility that the school will not be obliged to pay contributions. Teachers with superior training or experience may be able to ask for more hours and a higher rate. Schools that recruit from abroad tend to pay €700–€1,000 a month in addition to free accommodation. The custom in Greece has been to supplement low basic wages with a range of statutory benefits, e.g. holiday pay and Christmas and Easter bonuses, and these seem to have survived in the private sector at least, despite the imposition of so many austerity measures.

Teachers must find their rewards elsewhere, as qualified TEFL teacher **Phil Tomkins** did while teaching on the small island of Kea:

> ***Regarding finances, I long ago reconciled myself to the fact that I would never be a millionaire (certainly not from teaching!) and for some time have been re-adjusting what I want out of life. Peace and contentment, for me, far outweigh the benefits of the rat race and I am happy to live in comfortable 'poverty' on a sunny Greek island doing a job I enjoy, rather than working my fingers to the bone chasing the almighty dollar, and giving whoever is the current architect of our doom a big, fat slice of it. To measure one's successes solely in pounds, shillings and pence is a sure way to depression, disappointment and stress. Friends and family have all been very enthusiastic and supportive of me 'doing a Shirley Valentine' – and not a little jealous that even now, at the end of November, I'm still to be found at the beach most days. So far I have been thoroughly enjoying it, though I am missing my two main dietary requirements: curry and beer.***

The teaching year has been shrinking, so that an increasing number of schools now start their courses at the beginning of October and finish at the end of May. So some schools offer eight-month contracts rather than the nine months that used to be standard. Teachers should always check beforehand the date up to which they will be paid. Native English speakers are often employed to teach exam classes that finish before the end of May. Schools have been known to break the contract by paying off teachers as soon as their classes have taken the exams.

Employers who have suffered from staff desertions in the past may hold back some of your monthly pay as a bond (*kratisi*) against an early departure. Teachers with insufficient hours are forced either to work at more than one school or to take on private students. Split shifts are now very uncommon except in technical colleges or universities. Almost all teaching at *frontisteria* takes place between 5pm and 10pm.

It is not unusual to be expected to teach in two or more 'satellite' sites of the main school in villages up to 10 miles away. Local bus services are generally good and cheap but you could find yourself spending an inordinate amount of (unpaid) time in transit and standing around at bus stops.

PUPILS

Most native English speakers are employed to teach advanced classes, usually the two years leading to Cambridge or other exams. Because of the Greek style of education, pupils may not show much initiative and will expect to be tested frequently on what they have been taught. **Andrew Boyle** found the prevailing methodology of 'sit 'em down, shut 'em up and give 'em lots of homework' was moderately successful.

Another problem is that there is a great deal of pressure to assign pass marks just to retain the students' custom. Some school owners are so profit motivated, they have euros for eyeballs. Students expect to be told the answers and bosses want their teachers to be lenient with the marking so that the students all pass and parents will re-enrol them.

Will Brady, teaching on the island of Santorini, found the pupils quite challenging, particularly the girls:

> ***The job was littered with problems because the kids, for a start, were pretty uninterested. They were the offspring of hotel owners on the island, for the most part, whose only reason for having their kids learn English was so that they could be of use in the family business when the tourists came in summer. They had a level of MTV English but that was about it. They weren't motivated to learn and it was quite difficult to get them interested in the subject. I had a particular problem with a class of 15- to16-year-old girls who were quite difficult to discipline. For some lessons I was alone and they took advantage of the fact that I didn't speak Greek. They were not even bothering to whisper, but talking openly to each other, and playing footsie with me under the table, and it was very difficult to know how to handle that. The manager took me aside and told me in no uncertain terms that I should not respond to any of the advances. Thankfully, I hadn't entertained the idea.***

ACCOMMODATION

Since many schools provide a flat or at least help in finding a flat, teachers are often not too concerned about their living arrangements. Placements arranged by the recruitment agencies offer free accommodation in addition to the full salary. It is definitely worth checking in advance about furnishings. Flats are sometimes quite spartan but some of the better ones are comfortably furnished and may have a washing machine and television in addition to the essentials. However, some flats, especially in Athens, are unfurnished, which is a serious nuisance for someone on an eight-month contract.

Utility bills come every two months, and winters in Greece can be surprisingly cold. Even in a small flat, the electricity bill will run to hundreds of euros. Water bills are very cheap, however. Before taking over accommodation, try to find out if the bills have been paid. Changing the name is such a major hassle (involving tax returns, etc.) and unfortunately it is not uncommon for tenants to move on without paying their bills and the new tenant becomes liable. Non-payment of electricity and phone bills (but not water bills) will result in disconnection, and no final reminders are sent out.

LEISURE TIME

Teachers in Athens should have no trouble constructing a social life. Outside Athens, the social order is still fairly conservative. A further problem is the enormous language barrier in a country where it will take some time to learn how to read the alphabet. Watching Greek television is a good way to learn the language plus Greek lessons are run free of charge in many locations. **Cassandra**, based in the north of Greece, found that '*teaching was a bit more difficult and isolating than I expected, but once I was used to the lifestyle I enjoyed it … with hindsight I would have enrolled in Greek lessons sooner and tried to get out and meet more people.*'

Most teachers find the vast majority of Greek people to be honest, friendly and helpful and are seldom disappointed with the hospitality they receive. As anyone who has visited Greece knows, the country has countless other attractions, not least the very convivial tavernas. Eating out and drinking is no longer the bargain it once was, partly due to new government duties on pretty well everything. With the increase in VAT, many goods and services have risen in price, and even wine, which used to be exempt, is now taxed. Travel, particularly ferry travel, is affordable and a pure delight out of season. Despite all the hassles, most people enjoy a year in Greece.

LIST OF EMPLOYERS

ANGLO-HELLENIC TEACHER RECRUITMENT
13 Vasilou St, Vrahati 20006 Corinth
+30 27410 53511
applications@anglo-hellenic.com
www.anglo-hellenic.com or www.tefl.gr

NUMBER OF TEACHERS: About 50 vacancies every year in a wide choice of locations.

PREFERENCE OF NATIONALITY: British.

QUALIFICATIONS: University graduates with a TEFL certificate. Graduates of TEFL Corinth course are given priority. No experience needed.

CONDITIONS OF EMPLOYMENT: Most vacancies are in September, several in January and a few throughout the year. Teaching 25 hours a week, mainly to Young Learners.

SALARY: 9-month contracts pay the going rate of €700–€1,000 per month plus bonuses and 4 weeks' paid holiday. Starting salary is €813 gross (€684 net).

FACILITIES/SUPPORT: Free accommodation in a furnished flat. A four-page contract will be provided by agency (specimen copy available beforehand). Anglo-Hellenic also takes care of the bureaucratic essentials, and encourages meetings and exchange visits of its teachers and provides interactive web-based facilities for information, opinion and social chat. Several TEFL certificate courses (120 hours) are run every summer, with shorter professional development courses also being offered throughout the year.

RECRUITMENT: Interviews are conducted in London, Athens or Corinth, throughout the summer.

CONTACT: Peter Beech, Recruitment Director.

BETSIS LANGUAGE SCHOOLS
Thivon 109, 18542 Piraeus
+30 210 490 8926
Second site: Pyrgou 31, Karavas, 18542 Piraeus
abetsis@otenet.gr; abetsis@hol.gr

NUMBER OF TEACHERS: 15–20, also for two branches in small town of Drosia, north-west of Piraeus.

PREFERENCE OF NATIONALITY: British and Irish. As of April 2013, offering short internships to US nationals who have completed Anglo-Hellenic certificate course mentioned above.

QUALIFICATIONS: Bachelor's degree and Cambridge exams.

CONDITIONS OF EMPLOYMENT: 8-month contracts. 18–24 hours per week. Also opportunities for teachers to work at the publishing company, Andrew Betsis ELT, specialising in ELT exam books. Positions are available in the editorial and marketing departments.

SALARY: €9,000–€10,000 per year.

FACILITIES/SUPPORT: School helps teachers find rental accommodation and with the bureaucracy involved in applying for a work permit.

CAMBRIDGE TEACHERS RECRUITMENT
8 Daskalou-Kitsou, Maroussi, 15124 Athens
+30 210 258 5155; +30 694 655 8217
UK contact address of main interviewer (August only):
53 Green Acres, Parkhill, Croydon CRO 5UX, UK
+44 20 8686 3733
macleod_smith_andrew@hotmail.com

NUMBER OF TEACHERS: 10+ per year.

PREFERENCE OF NATIONALITY: British or EU.

QUALIFICATIONS: Degree and TEFL certificate, a friendly personality and conscientious attitude. Experience not needed.

CONDITIONS OF EMPLOYMENT: Contracts usually between September and May, although some summer work. Usual hours are Monday to Friday between 4pm and 10pm (25 hours per week). Teaching children and adults, elementary to advanced, in preparation for Cambridge exams.

SALARY: Roughly €650–€800 net per month plus flat, bonuses, 4-weeks' holiday pay and pension contributions.

FACILITIES/SUPPORT: Accommodation is provided (not necessarily free) plus health insurance and pension. Holiday pay and bonuses given at Christmas and Easter. Applicants can expect to receive plenty of information about working in Greece.

RECRUITMENT: Comprehensive interviews are conducted between mid-June and the end of August. Interviews are held in hotels in Central London.

CONTACT: Andrew Macleod-Smith, Director.

KOUTSANTONIS SCHOOL OF LANGUAGES

35 Gounari Ave, 26221 Patras

+30 2610 273925

info@koutsantoni.gr

www.koutsantoni.gr (Greek only)

NUMBER OF TEACHERS: Out of 35 staff in 9 schools, only 1 is British.

PREFERENCE OF NATIONALITY: Native English speakers with Greek ancestry.

QUALIFICATIONS: University degree. Preferably a teaching qualification and some experience.

CONDITIONS OF EMPLOYMENT: 8-month contracts. 10–12 teaching hours per week, evenings only, Monday–Friday.

SALARY: The legal minimum of €9 gross has been abolished so it is up to school owner and teacher to agree a rate.

FACILITIES/SUPPORT: School owner will help with search for an apartment and might be able to lend furniture.

RECRUITMENT: Generally teachers leave their CVs in person and are called back for interview when a vacancy occurs.

CONTACT: Cindy or Connie Koutsantoni (kapaflc@otenet.gr).

LAMBRAKI FOREIGN LANGUAGES CENTRES

Ionias Av 168, 71306 Heraklion; also Kamarioti 4, 71414 Gazi, Heraklion, Crete

+30 2810 323059; +30 2810 822292

info@lambraki.gr

www.lambraki.gr

NUMBER OF TEACHERS: 10 for several branches in Heraklion.

PREFERENCE OF NATIONALITY: Britain.

QUALIFICATIONS: University degree and TEFL qualification.

CONDITIONS OF EMPLOYMENT: Most teachers stay 2–3 years. 18–25 hours per week. Teaching children from the age of 7, adolescents and adults.

SALARY: From €700 per month (negotiable), less 16% deductions.

FACILITIES/SUPPORT: Assistance given in finding accommodation. School assists with residence permit after teacher provides a verified copy of his/her degree; official translation can be done in Heraklion.

RECRUITMENT: Via newspaper adverts, personal contact and PALSO Association. Telephone interviews.

CONTACT: Irene Lambraki Fasoulaki, School Director.

LORD BYRON SCHOOL

104, Tsimiski St, Diagonbios, 54622 Thessaloniki

+30 2310 278804

school@lordbyron.gr

www.lordbyron.gr

Member of QLS.

TEACHERS: 3–5 native English speakers.

PREFERENCE OF NATIONALITY: EU citizens.

QUALIFICATIONS: University degree, TEFLA, CELTA and EFL teaching experience.

CONDITIONS OF EMPLOYMENT: Standard contract 8 months. 24–26 hours per week. 40% of clients are adults or university students.

SALARY: €800 to €1,000 according to qualifications. 17% deductions for tax and social security.

FACILITIES/SUPPORT: Assistance finding accommodation and obtaining a legal status/teaching permit.

RECRUITMENT: Via detailed CV, interview, model lesson (with lesson plan). Interviews are carried out in Thessaloniki every May and June.

CONTACT: Harry J. Nikolaides, School Director (harry@lordbyron.gr).

PAPAELIOU SCHOOLS OF FOREIGN LANGUAGES

111 Karaiskou St, 18532 Piraeus-Athens

+30 210 417 3892

karaiskou@papaeliou.edu.gr

www.papaeliou.edu.gr

Branches in Piraeus and Nikea.

NUMBER OF TEACHERS: 45.

PREFERENCE OF NATIONALITY: British. Majority are

Greek-Americans or Greek. Must possess a valid visa.

QUALIFICATIONS: Minimum age 21. Bachelor's or master's degree from accredited institution and teacher training.

CONDITIONS OF EMPLOYMENT: 1–3 year contracts to teach at least 4 hours a day. Hours extend late into the evening.

SALARY: Approx. €850 net; €382 deductions.

FACILITIES/SUPPORT: No help with accommodation.

RECRUITMENT: Online application form. Interviewees usually teach a demo lesson. Successful candidates must then complete the in-service training programme and sign a probationary 3-month contract.

CONTACT: Ms Ino Panayotou, Director of Studies.

THE LINGUISTIC LAB

Adamapolou 10. 20400 Xylokastro (PO Box 12, Xylokastro), Corinthia

✆ +30 27430 22135/4 / 6945 580359

labisfilis@hotmail.com or info@linguisticlab.com

www.linguisticlab.gr (in Greek); www.linguisticlab.com

NUMBER OF TEACHERS: 6 for 3 branches.

PREFERENCE OF NATIONALITY: Native speakers, preferably with EU passport.

QUALIFICATIONS: Minimum BA plus TESOL certificate and experience. TESOL courses offered at Linguistic Lab.

CONDITIONS OF EMPLOYMENT: Standard contract period 1 year. To work 18–25 hours per week. Classes begin early September and finish in May/June. Summer classes may run in June and July.

SALARY: €700 a month; no deductions made.

FACILITIES/SUPPORT: Free accommodation is provided: furnished 2-bedroom apartments, to be shared between 2 teachers. Utilities are the responsibility of teachers. Option to have a private apartment, with a lower salary.

RECRUITMENT: To apply send a CV, copies of diplomas and passport, reference letters and a recent photo to the above address.

CONTACT: Bob Filis, Owner.

ITALY

Despite the Italian economy having stagnated for years, and rumours that the banking system is overwhelmed by bad debts, the English language teaching market seems to be flourishing in Italy. Companies that specialise in corporate training have no lack of clients, and neither do institutes catering to children and adolescents. English teaching in Italian state schools is generally acknowledged to be inadequate and many turn to the private sector to help them improve. Many children are being entered for externally moderated exams such as the Cambridge suite, for which private tutoring companies are on hand to prepare them.

Chances for teachers are always better in towns and cities that cannot boast leaning towers, gondolas or coliseums. Recently, it seems that the market has begun to boom in Sicily, Calabria and Puglia; of the 55 employers in Italy advertising for teaching staff on www.tefl.com in August 2016, a surprisingly high percentage were located in these southern provinces. Small towns in southern Italy and Sardinia, in the Dolomites and along the Adriatic coast have more than their fair share of private language schools and institutes.

PROSPECTS FOR TEACHERS

A complete range of language schools can be found in Italy, as the *Yellow Pages* will confirm. At the elite end of the market, there are the 40 schools that belong to AISLi, the Associazione Italiana Scuole di Lingue (www.aisli.it) which is involved with teacher employment (www.aisli.it/recruiting.html). Prospective teachers can submit their CVs to AISLi (aisli@aisli.com) who will circulate them round all member schools. Only ultra-respectable schools can become AISLi members so there are thousands of good schools outside the association. AISLi schools expect their teachers to have the right to work in Europe, which currently includes teachers from the UK, recognised TEFL qualifications and documented teaching experience. In return they offer attractive renumeration packages and conditions of employment.

At the other end of the spectrum, there is a host of schools which some might describe as cowboy operations, though these are decreasing in number. The CELTA is widely recognised and respected in Italy, as are other certificates. The days of finding work without a qualification are all but over. US qualifications are less well known for the simple reason that work permits are very difficult for non-EU citizens to obtain. There are so many job-seekers with TEFL training that qualifications are necessary in order to compete with all those native English speakers so keen to live, work and teach in Italy.

Strict employment regulations and red tape in Italy make small companies reluctant to offer full-time 'Italian' contracts or help with legal paperwork. Increasingly, schools are hiring teachers only on a freelance basis, whom they pay by the hour and offer no benefits. For example, Caledonian Communications in Milan commented: '*Unfortunately due to the economic situation in Europe we have had to change our staffing policy. We therefore no longer offer contracts, teachers are hired on a freelance basis.*' This means that most English teachers work for more than one private language school and also teach freelance lessons to make ends meet. However, these are exceptions. Another training company in Milan, The Language Grid (see entry) offers Italian contracts to long-term staff.

A few schools offer a British contract (i.e. one that is not subject to Italian legislation) in which the wages are lower than on an Italian contract but the benefits may be good and the red tape much less. For example, the UK agency Euroteach Ltd in Stratford-upon-Avon (✆ +44 7557 004515) recruits experienced British teachers to work for a chain of language schools in southern Italy; in this case tax and National Insurance contributions are paid in the UK.

The British and Irish recruitment agency, Evocation EFL, has a specialist section that places certified TEFL teachers with employers throughout Italy (www.evo.jobs). They are employed on a British contract and the agency maintains that the net earnings of about €1,200 are equivalent to their Italian counterparts, but much cheaper for the employer. Another UK-based agency to try is English Language Abroad, which was advertising multiple vacancies in Italy for a September start (✆ +44 7538 474 575; ally@englishlanguage abroad.co.uk).

Compulsory contributions for social security and expensive perks make hiring a permanent member of staff very costly so most of the jobs available are eight or nine-month contracts, October to May. The majority of English teachers in Italy work with no long-term job security, which is acceptable for those who want to spend only one or two years in the country. A lot of teaching work in Italy is paid under the table. Contracts shouldn't be expected at the start though they are more likely to be given by private language schools in smaller out of the way places.

Some private schools are contracted to provide teaching staff to state schools, but are trying to get away with paying teachers the same low wage from €12. If you are offered off-site work in the state sector (normally available only if you know Italian), do plenty of research and try to negotiate an hourly wage of at least €25 and read any contract carefully before signing.

A useful starting place for resources and information on training and teaching English in Italy is www.teachingenglishinitaly.com, a site maintained by **Sheila Corwin,** an American resident in Florence who has been working and living as an English language teacher and teacher trainer in Italy (on and off) since 2002. The company offers affordable online options in basic TEFL certification (from €200/$265), a 20-hour weekend TEFL course in Florence (€195) about 10 times a year and other teacher refresher courses; details from sheila@teachingenglishinitaly.com. Another repository of tips for teaching in Italy is www.tjtaylor.net with up-to-date resources in the Careers section covering qualifications, visas, tax and so on.

FINDING A JOB

IN ADVANCE

There is no single compendium of the hundreds of language school addresses in Italy. The relevant Yellow Pages, *Pagine Gialle*, are user friendly: go to www.paginegialle.it and choose the handy English version of the site. Typing in 'language schools' will produce more than 2,000 entries. The search engine allows you to search by city or more generally by region.

International language school groups such as Benedict Schools, Linguarama, Berlitz and Inlingua are major providers of English language teaching in Italy. International House has a dozen affiliated schools throughout the country. Wall Street English now has 70 centres in Italy and actively recruits native English speakers. Occasional vacancies are posted at www.wallstreet.it/lavoro-con-noi; in most cases applications should be sent directly to the school, whereas other recruitment is done by head office in Milan (staff@wallstreet.it). Applications to Berlitz should be sent to the individual schools hiring, e.g. workinrome@berlitz.com and workinmilan@berlitz.com.

A considerable number of Italian schools advertise vacancies on www.tefl.com. Several Italian-based chains of language schools account for a large number of teaching jobs. Many operate as independent franchises. For example you can get contact details for all 150 British Institutes on the website www.britishinstitutes.it (click on '*Sedi*'). Smaller chains to investigate include My English Schools (www.myenglishschool.it) which hire teachers for Bari, Bologna, Florence, Milan, Monza, Naples, Padua, Palermo, Turin, and a few others; Morgan Schools (www.morganschool.it) with a network of 25 schools around Italy; and Shenker Schools with 16 (www.shenker.com/work-with-us).

Other chains include the British Schools Group (www.britishschool.com/teaching-opportunities.html) with 70 member schools; the branches in Taranto, Brindisi, Ravenna, Casale Monferrato, etc. were all advertising for teachers at the time of updating. The Oxford Group (www.oxford.it) also has a centralised recruitment department (see entry). Most language schools in Italy seem to incorporate the word British, English, Oxford or Cambridge randomly combined with Centre, School or Institute, which can result in confusion, especially when it comes to the British School Group (www.britishschool.it/index.php/job-opportunities) which is quite separate from the – spot the difference – British Schools Group.

American citizens have a lot of problems finding work in Italy, largely because it is so difficult to obtain a work permit. However, a solution suggested by **Carla Valentine**, an English teacher in Venice, is to try working for one of the Department of Defense US army schools on the military bases in Italy. Under these circumstances, work permits are processed in the USA.

ON THE SPOT

The online *Yellow Pages* is probably still the best source of possible employers. Italians like face-to-face contact and, according to **Sheila Corwin**, director of www.teachingenglishinitaly.com, stopping by a school to meet the director often works better than blindly sending out résumés through snail or electronic mail. She urges job-seeking teachers to leave their CVs with directors even if the school is not hiring at the time because schools sometimes call back one or even three months later when they need a teacher. It is also a good ploy to offer to teach a few free lessons to their students to help get a foot in the door.

Often a few hours' teaching can gradually be built up into a full-time job by those willing to say yes. If you're there when they need you, you can usually get something. Most find that the longer they stay, the more hours they get, though there is still no job security working this way.

ALEX NEUMAN

Alex Neuman, a globetrotting journalist, describes how she set about finding teaching work in the town of Bergamo, where she and her partner had decided to spend a year or two.

The first step these days is to go online. I quickly found three or four English schools in Bergamo: Shenker, Wall Street, Inlingua and two small local firms run by individuals. I decided I should also look in Milan since it is only 45 minutes by train from Bergamo.

This is where you quickly realise this is not like job hunting in your own country and in your own language. Few Italians answer emails from strangers. You have to pick up the phone – a challenge when your language is rusty but as these were English schools most had an English speaking receptionist. Then I discovered the vagaries of the private teaching system, which basically is out to make as much money as possible while paying as little as possible to teachers and expecting infinite flexibility on the teacher's part and no flexibility on the school's part!

You will need patience and a sense of humour at this stage. I quickly got an interview with Wall Street and Shenker and was accepted at Shenker. Being accepted is not a problem it's actually getting onto the payroll and teaching that takes time. It was three months before I got on a two-week training course where I was promised €150 a week. In fact I received this money in December – two months after I'd done the course and five months after the initial interview. So it is best to have plenty of spare cash to see you through the first six months of finding work.

Shenker was good for me because I had no formal teaching qualification and it is based around a system so all your lesson plans are provided, you simply turn up and teach the system. For this you will be paid about €13.50 an hour before tax. I get about 15 hours of work a week, although they promised 20. But as I started working for them during the financial crisis their student numbers were considerably down.

Melanie Drake had much better luck in Bari:

> ***Italy has been a very positive experience for the most part, though living in the south without knowing the language can be quite problematic! It is really pretty easy to get work in Italy once TEFL-qualified, as the English level here is low (in the south especially). Money isn't fantastic but it balances out as life is fairly cheap, particularly if, like me, you can walk to work. Often accommodation is included with the contracts offered too. Ironically I am earning half of what I got in London, though here I can save fairly easily as my outgoings are halved. It works out pretty well.***

Scouring adverts in English language newspapers has worked for some. The fortnightly publications *Wanted in Rome* (www.wantedinrome.com) and *Wanted in Milan* (www.wantedinmilan.com) are very useful (particularly in the spring) as is the Italian-language classified ads paper *Porta Portese* (Rome and Lazio region). If you happen to see a request for 'mothers only', this means that they are looking for a teacher whose mother tongue is English (*insegnanti madrelingua*), not a female with small children. The majority of employers seek EMT (English Mother Tongue) teachers. Other publications with useful classifieds include *The Florentine* and *Easy Milano.*

FREELANCE TEACHING

Another possibility is to set up as a freelance tutor, though a knowledge of Italian is even more of an asset here than it is for jobs in schools. A participant on a *Guardian* web forum on ELT careers wrote in an encouraging vein for older job-seekers:

> ***I'm a career changer in my mid-50s and have had no problems here in Italy. I don't teach in language schools but contract direct with local state schools, libraries and private students, but that is based on having had means of support until I developed the requisite contacts.***

Alex Neuman is another teacher in middle life who has found Italy, and Bergamo in particular, a welcoming place. She supplemented her hours at local academies with private students:

> ***Italians are desperate to speak English so getting private students isn't that hard. The best students I have got are through word of mouth. A very friendly neighbour is always recommending me to friends and colleagues and I have managed to find myself three or four that keep me busy. I got my very first student by putting up a notice on the university noticeboard in Bergamo but have never had to do more than that. When writing an ad for private students you must always use the words 'mother-tongue speaker' – even though 'native English speaker' is more correct English!***

University students looking for private tuition might consult university noticeboards such as the one at the Città Universitaria in Rome, main campus of La Sapienza University of Rome. Qualified freelancers can broadcast their times of availability and rates on a specialist website such as www.insegnanti-inglese.it, which was set up in 2015 by native speaker teachers disgruntled at the low wages offered by the big institutes.

Porta Portese is another forum in which to advertise your availability to offer English lessons in Rome; women placing adverts should be careful when arranging meetings with prospective clients. As long as you have access to some premises, you can try to arrange both individual and group lessons. Whatever way you decide to look for work, remember that life grinds to a halt in August, just as it does in France. Competition is keenest in Florence and Venice, which are both saturated, so new arrivals should head elsewhere.

Freelance teaching can be very lucrative and you can expect to make from €25 to €45 an hour, which is still undercutting most of the language agencies who charge clients a lot, keep half and pay teachers half. New entrants to the market may have to offer lessons for €20 until they become established. If you can organise a group lesson for children or adults, you can charge as little as €10 per person.

SUMMER WORK

Paid work is available at a number of summer camps offering English instruction, a good opportunity for young people to spend a summer in Italy and learn more about teaching English to young learners. A number teach through the medium of theatre, so anyone interested in drama will be attracted by this idea. This opportunity is open to non-European nationalities, since the work period is less than three months and therefore within the duration of a Schengen visa. Some teacher training is often provided by the schools and companies that run these camp programmes. Most of these companies pay about €200 a week (less for city day camps). Successful summer teachers are often offered contracts for the academic year.

See entries at the end of this chapter for ACLE, Canadian Island, The English Camp Company, Kid's World, Lingue Senza Frontiere and International House in Campobasso. Other summer employers include:

Alice in Città Milan, (www.aliceincitta.org). Summer camps are based in Italian primary and secondary schools during summer holidays. Italian children learn English through games, art, sports, songs and acting.

Bell – Beyond English Language Learning, Liguria (recruitment@bellbeyond.com; www.bellbeyond.com/en/tutorsleaders). Minimum stay 2 weeks; €470 (gross) per fortnight.

Berlitz Italy (louise.thorne@berlitz.it or summercamps@berlitz.it; www.berlitz.it). Candidates must be native English speakers and experienced with children to work at two camps in Tuscany. Two-week minimum stay in June/July.

The English Experience, (www.englishexp.co.uk). Advertises 2-week summer contracts, including flights from UK, full board and accommodation, and a wage. Applications and interviews handled in Norwich office.

English is Fun, Bologna (direzionedidattica@englishisfun.it; www.englishisfun.it). Proprietary teaching method for young children taught in compulsory 3-day training course costing €610.

M B Scambi, Padua (www.mbscambi.com). Summer camp for month of July held on the beach at Lignano Sabbiadoro in the Venice area. Experienced teachers are paid €380 (gross) per week plus free room and board in shared en suite rooms.

Newbeetle Viaggi Studio, Jesi (www.newbeetleviaggistudio.it or www.ingleseinitalia.it). Language camp at Montecopiolo in the Marches. €300 net per week plus hotel accommodation and all meals.

Smile Modena (www.smilemodena.com). Employs summer tutors to mount English language theatre productions with groups of children. Summer staff are chosen after auditioning, including in London in October.

Scotia Personnel, Halifax, Canada (✆ +1 902 422 1455; info@scotia-personnel-ltd.com; www.scotia-personnel-ltd.com). This North American agency runs an organised scheme whereby young North Americans are recruited to tutor English in families for 3–12 months. Wage of €100–€200 per week.

REGULATIONS

The bureaucracy for citizens of EU member states has been simplified in recent years. EU citizens intending to stay in Italy longer than 90 days are required to register at the *anagrafe* office of the local town hall. Those who intend long stays of five years should apply for a *carta di soggiorno* or *certificato di residenza* (residence certificate). To obtain this, they must take proof of income (employment contract, financial backing from

PHILIP LEE

Philip Lee from New Zealand wanted to spend his summers working in Europe. After a successful camp job in Switzerland, his attention turned to Italy. Although he didn't have direct experience of teaching English as a foreign language, he had worked with children and given tuition and revision classes. Here he describes the highs and lows of the job.

I searched online for work over the summer in Italy. There were a lot of random jobs that didn't really lead to anything and a lot of misleading job adverts. However, I found some English teaching websites that were credible and I applied. After completing a written application on my background and experience in teaching, working with children and art/drama/games/sport and providing references, I was hired by Lingua Senza Frontiere. I taught English through various indoor and outdoor activities. About 90% of my time was spent playing a game/sport or completing an activity that was explained and conducted in English and there was very limited traditional 'classroom' teaching. The focus was to do as much as possible in English, including the instructions for each activity. Depending on the children's age and their familiarity with English, it was possible by using simpler words, shorter sentences and demonstrating my instructions at the same time. Teaching was very physical: I spent most of my day – about five hours of teaching and two of supervision – standing. Because a lot of the children were not very familiar/comfortable with English I had to be very energetic, positive and supportive throughout the day to keep them encouraged.

Lunch was up to two hours long and we were always treated to a good and big Italian lunch. Most schools were happy to cater to special diets as long as they were given prior notice. I stayed with the most hospitable and generous families, most of whom lived by the seaside. While living with the host families, who often had children in the camp as well, I was given my own room and sometimes my own bathroom. The families were very accommodating and understood that non-Italians did do some things differently, such as eating more than one biscuit for breakfast. They also understood that I wanted to experience as much of Italy as possible and took me out on numerous occasions. We went to vineyards, restaurants, farms, relatives' houses, shops, the beach, holiday homes, bars and clubs with the older host brothers and sisters, the pool, concerts and neighbouring towns and cities. They were also quite happy when I went out to socialise at night.

The wages are not high, however, I considered the English camp as a working holiday and was not aiming to leave with many savings. The biggest problem was the language difficulties with the children and at the schools. This was because it was uncommon for any of the tutors to speak much Italian. Any tutor who spoke Italian was instructed not to make this known so that the children would not take advantage of it. The difficulty in communication made our job harder, but arguably it gave the children a better learning experience. The training sessions that the camp organisation provides are really vital and it would have been a great benefit if I had written down all the ideas for games and activities for future reference.

There were a few behavioural problems with some children but we were not expected to deal with these. Each camp had a local Italian teacher in charge of the camp and we would tell her of any problems. If she did not handle it, we could inform our employer, who would communicate directly with the school.

Altogether it was a great opportunity to meet people from all over the world as well as Italians, to spend time in Italy not as a tourist, and incredible fun working with children, as all day is spent playing games or doing activities.

home) and must pass an Italian language test.

As mentioned earlier, non-EU citizens have very little chance of getting their papers in order for a longer-term job unless they are dual nationals or receive a firm offer of a permanent job while they are still in their home country. In the words of the recruitment agency, Evocation EFL: 'Please, don't waste your time (and ours) by applying if you are from outside the EU (we cannot get visas if you are from the US, Canada, etc).' Detailed information can be found at www.portaleimmigrazione.it According to the Italian Embassy in Washington, language teachers from the USA need a visa for *lavoro subordinato*. To qualify they must first obtain from their employer in Italy an authorisation to work issued by the Ministry of Labour or a Provincial Office of Labour (*Servizio politiche del lavoro*) plus an authorisation from the local *questura*. The originals of these plus a passport and one photo must be sent to the applicant's nearest embassy or consulate.

These procedures can take up to a year to complete and it is for this reason that so many Americans and other non-EU citizens work in Italy without work visas. However, there are two legal alternatives for US citizens. The first is to go to Italy on a student visa, which allows you to work for up to 20 hours a week (enough to live on). Interested Americans and other nationalities can contact private language schools that offer Italian classes to find out whether they can sponsor candidates signing up for a course of long duration. This is the route that Carla took some years ago:

> ***Getting a student visa is very easy. I enrolled for a year at Istituto Venezia to learn Italian. With a letter of enrolment from the school I was able to get a student visa from the Italian Consulate in Boston for one year (whether or not I attend classes is irrelevant, although obviously I do).***

Long-term language courses are expensive, but prices differ radically. **Sheila Corwin** provided a snapshot of the options in Florence, where she lives and trains TEFL teachers:

> ***A standard 20-hour Italian course runs €220 per week at Europass, the private Italian language school in Florence where I hold my weekend TEFL courses, but I am sure a cheaper quote would be offered for a longer stay (www.europass.it). The Istituto Europeo where I've studied Italian offers a year-long Italian course for €5,180 which covers 960 lessons for a duration of 48 weeks (www.istitutoeuropeo.it/indexENG.html). The Centro di Cultura per Stranieri, which offers Italian language courses through the University of Florence, is a lower-cost option. They offer 10-week courses in each of the four seasons costing €650–€800 (www.ccs.unifi.it/changelang-eng.html). Finally, the Centro di Internazionale Studenti Georgio La Pira offers the Italian-in-Florence programme, which is almost certainly the cheapest available. They offer semi-intensive month-long courses (40 hours) for €160 (www.centrointernazionalelapira.it).***

The second option is to become an independent contractor. This involves getting an expensive tax code number (*partita IVA*) from the local town government, which you have to do once you are earning more than €5,000, and work for more than one private language school. To get this number, you need a *codice fiscale* (similar to a social security number), which is available from the local town hall upon presentation of a passport or may also be obtainable online from the Agenzia delle Entrate (Revenue Agency).

With this number it is possible to obtain the *partita IVA* from the municipal authorities, though it will be necessary to use the services of an accountant. With these numbers you can find work and get paid. Australian and New Zealand citizens aged 18–30 plus Canadians aged 18–35 are eligible for a 12-month working holiday visa in Italy (6 months for Canadians). Holders are not meant to work for more than 90 days for one employer. They are obliged to obtain a *permesso di soggiorno* within eight days of arrival from the local *Questura* (police headquarters).

Tax is a further headache for long-stay teachers. As soon as you sort out the work documents, you should obtain a tax number (*codice fiscale*). The rate of income tax (*ritenuta d'acconto*) is usually about 23% in addition to social security deductions of 8%–9%. You'll be better off if you can work out an arrangement whereby the private language school deducts an amount from your wages in order to cover the taxes that you'd pay if you had a *partita IVA*.

CONDITIONS OF WORK

A typical salary for a full-time timetable would be about €1,300 net per month, though novice teachers sometimes earn not much more than €1,000. Staff on a *contratto di collaborazione* are paid by the hour, normally ranging from €12 to €19 net. Always find out if pay scales are quoted net or gross, since the two figures are so different. Take-home pay is not as high as might have been expected because of the high cost of compulsory national insurance, social security and pension contributions. Salaries tend to be substantially higher in Northern Italy than in the south to compensate for the higher cost of living. Business English, as always, can be very lucrative. Intensive Business English, based in Milan (see List of Employers) offers a gross salary of between €1,800 and €3,250. However, some teachers in Rome, Milan, Bologna, etc. have had to reconcile themselves to spending up to half their salaries on rent. Even for Italians, salaries are low when compared with the cost of living.

Only professional teachers will benefit from the industry-wide agreement or *Contratto Collettivo Nazionale del Lavoro* (CCNL), which sets a high salary for a regulation 100-hour working month. Because of the high costs of legal employment, there is a lot of dubious practice in Italy and prospective teachers should try to talk to an ex-teacher before committing themselves, especially if offered a job before arrival.

Few teachers complain about their students. Even when pupils attend English classes for social reasons (as many do in small towns with little nightlife) or are generally unmotivated, they are usually good natured, hospitable and talkative in class. In contrast to Greece, many language school directors are British rather than local.

LEISURE TIME

Italian culture and lifestyle do not need to have their praises sung here. A large number of teachers who have gone out on short-term contracts never come back – probably a higher proportion than in any other country. While rents are high, eating out is fairly cheap and public transport is quite affordable. Women teachers should be prepared to cope with some Mediterranean machismo, particularly in the south, and may have to contend with unwanted male attention.

Compared with many languages, Italian is easy to learn, though courses are expensive. It may be possible to swap English lessons for Italian ones, which might lead to further freelance teaching.

LIST OF EMPLOYERS

A.C.L.E. (ASSOCIAZIONE CULTURALE LINGUISTICA EDUCATIONAL)
Via Roma 54, 18038 San Remo
+39 0184 506070
info@acle.org
www.acle.org

NUMBER OF TEACHERS: 400 for city day camps and residential camps all over Italy from Sicily to the Alps.
PREFERENCE OF NATIONALITY: Native English speakers between 19 and 30 years of age.
QUALIFICATIONS: Minimum age 19. Must have experience working with children and the ability to teach English through the use of theatre and outdoor activities. A fun-loving personality and genuine interest in children, high moral standards and a flexible attitude to work required, preferably with some experience of living and travelling abroad.
CONDITIONS OF EMPLOYMENT: Camps start in June and run until September. Minimum of 3-weeks commitment required. The average tutor works for 4 weeks or more. Tutors change location every week or fortnight.
SALARY: From €520 for first 3 weeks, plus full board and homestay accommodation. Transport between camps provided plus insurance.
FACILITIES/SUPPORT: Intensive 5/6-day introductory TEFL-TP (Teaching English to Foreign Learners through Theatre and Play) course is compulsory and provided for fee of €150 usually deducted from wages.
RECRUITMENT: Application online at www.acle.org. Recruitment season for following summer opens 1 October. Deadline for applications is the middle of March, though recruitment can continue into July if vacancies remain.

ALPHA BETA PICCADILLY
via Talvera/Talfergasse 1a, 39100 Bolzano/Bozen
+39 0471 978600
info@alphabeta.it
www.alphabeta.it

NUMBER OF TEACHERS: 10–15 also for branch in Merano/ Meran, also in South Tyrol.

PREFERENCE OF NATIONALITY: Must have a passport from an EU member state.

QUALIFICATIONS: Minimum CELTA or equivalent. DELTA plus at least 2–3 years' TEFL experience preferred.

CONDITIONS OF EMPLOYMENT: 9-month contract with 18–22 contact hours per week.

SALARY: Around £1,530–£1,650 per month gross based on a British contract, depending on qualifications and experience. Standard UK income tax and social security deductions are made.

FACILITIES/SUPPORT: School has 2 flats available for teachers to share. Assistance given with work permits; however, these are relatively straightforward.

RECRUITMENT: Usually via www.tefl.com. Interviews are essential and are occasionally held in the UK.

CONTACT: Peter Marsh-Hunn, Director of Studies, English (marsh-hunn@alphabeta.it).

ANDERSON HOUSE
Via Bergamo 25, 24035 Curno, Bergamo
+39 035 463074
p.anderson@andersonhouse.it
www.andersonhouse.it

AH is a language school specialising in corporate language training and management training for companies (TIP, DPI, ICE and intercultural communication). It also offers courses to children and adults in preparation for Cambridge exams, and is a centre for language testing and certifications (Cambridge, BULATS, TOEIC and TOEFL). Anderson House is a founder member of SIETAR Italia (www.sietar-italia.org).

NUMBER OF TEACHERS: 4 full-time; 6 part-time for English; 10 part-time for other languages.

PREFERENCE OF NATIONALITY: British and Irish. European passport essential.

QUALIFICATIONS: Degree plus CELTA (minimum grade B), TESOL, DELTA or CertIBET (Trinity's Certificate in International Business English Training) and minimum 3 years' experience.

CONDITIONS OF EMPLOYMENT: Couples with car a bonus. Contracts from October to June (8/9 months) or from January for 5 months. All contracts renewable. To work 25 hours per week, 8am–10pm (one period of the day free). Some Saturday morning work; some summer work (June, July, September).

SALARY: €1,300 net for qualified teachers with 3 years' experience. Salary negotiable for those with more experience.

FACILITIES/SUPPORT: Italian lessons at cost. 70% is company work (general and business) both on and offsite. School has 3 small company cars and helps teachers with accommodation. Excellent facilities, staff resource centre, free internet access.

RECRUITMENT: Via www.tefl.com and direct application.

CONTACT: Peter Anderson, Director and Owner (p.anderson@andersonhouse.it).

ANGLO-AMERICAN CENTRE
Via Mameli 46, Cagliari 09124, Sardinia
+39 070 654955
info@angloamericancentre.it; angloamericancagliari@gmail.com
www.angloamericancentre.it

Member of AISLi. Offers the CELTA.

NUMBER OF TEACHERS: 20.

PREFERENCE OF NATIONALITY: Must be native speakers of English and have legal status to work in the EU.

QUALIFICATIONS: CELTA or Cert TESOL, 2 years' post-CELTA, reasonable Italian language competence, experience especially with younger learners, knowledge of Cambridge ESOL exams. Valid driving licence preferred.

CONDITIONS OF EMPLOYMENT: 1 October to 30 June for new teachers. 25 hours' contact time per week. Also summer school in July and possiblilty of contract renewal.

SALARY: €1,150–€1,300 per month (net of contributions).

FACILITIES/SUPPORT: School helps teachers to make contact with landlords and may accompany new arrivals to viewings. References can be provided to landlords and loans to cover initial deposit if necessary. Flight contribution.

RECRUITMENT: Direct applications, via www.tefl.com or the AISLi website. Interviews are held face-to-face in Cagliari or via Skype.

ASSOCIAZIONE ITALO BRITANNICA
Piazza della Vittoria 14/22, 16121 Genoa
+39 010 591605
mzacco@italobritannica.it
www.italobritannica.it/en

NUMBER OF TEACHERS: Approximately 15.

PREFERENCE OF NATIONALITY: None.

QUALIFICATIONS: Degree and CELTA or equivalent.

CONDITIONS OF EMPLOYMENT: Teachers are freelancers with approximately 12–15 hours' work per week.

SALARY: €14 per hour net, VAT is paid by the school.

FACILITIES/SUPPORT: Help may be given to find accommodation.

RECRUITMENT: Interviews may be held in London but preferably in Genoa.

CONTACT: Marina Zacco, Director.

BENEDICT SCHOOL
Via Industria 87, 41012 Carpi (MO)
+39 059 695921
info@benedict-carpi.it
www.benedict-carpi.it

NUMBER OF TEACHERS: 14.

PREFERENCE OF NATIONALITY: British, American, Irish. Minimum of 2 years' TEFL experience.

QUALIFICATIONS: Minimum TEFL (CELTA or equivalent certification).

CONDITIONS OF EMPLOYMENT: Mid-September until mid-July. Minimum 90 hours per month guaranteed (average 120 hours). 60% of work is with companies; 40% with private students.

SALARY: To be discussed at interview.

FACILITIES/SUPPORT: Accommodation provided by school.

RECRUITMENT: Internet and recruitment agency.

CONTACT: Ing. Philippe Bernet, General Manager and Owner.

BRITISH INSTITUTES – NEW SCHOOL
Via de Ambrosis 21, 15067 Novi Ligure
+39 0143 2987
noviligure@britishinstitutes.it
www.britishinstitutes.it/novi-ligure

NUMBER OF TEACHERS: 8.

PREFERENCE OF NATIONALITY: British, American.

QUALIFICATIONS: TEFL Diploma/degree plus 1 year's experience.

CONDITIONS OF EMPLOYMENT: 9 months, renewable. Average of 25 hours per week.

SALARY: From €11 per hour net.

BRITISH LANGUAGE SERVICES/LINGUAVIVA
Via C. De Cristoforis 15, 20124 Milan
+39 02 659 6401
segreteria@linguaviva.net
www.linguaviva.net

NUMBER OF TEACHERS: Approximately 20.

PREFERENCE OF NATIONALITY: British and Irish.

QUALIFICATIONS: Minimum CELTA or equivalent, degree plus some experience. Must be dynamic. Preference given to teachers with accommodation in the Milan area.

CONDITIONS OF EMPLOYMENT: October to June/July. 15–25 hours per week.

SALARY: Freelance rates.

RECRUITMENT: Adverts followed by personal interviews in Milan. Send full CV with photo and email addresses of 2 referees.

BRITISH s.r.l.
Via XX Settembre 12, 16121 Genoa
+39 010 593591
britishsrl@libero.it
www.britishgenova.it

NUMBER OF TEACHERS: 12.

PREFERENCE OF NATIONALITY: EU, American, Australian and Canadian.

QUALIFICATIONS: Bachelor's degree plus CELTA and some experience.

CONDITIONS OF EMPLOYMENT: 25+ hours per week between mid-September and mid-June.

SALARY: Variable according to hours worked.

FACILITIES/SUPPORT: Assistance given with accommodation, teaching materials and course programming.

RECRUITMENT: Interviews essential, usually take place in Italy or by phone.

CALEDONIAN COMMUNICATIONS
Viale Vigliani 55, 20148 Milan
+39 02 4802 0486/1086
info@caledonian.it
www.caledonian.it

NUMBER OF TEACHERS: 15–20, depending on time of year.

PREFERENCE OF NATIONALITY: EU citizens or others with permits already. British nationals can be hired on UK contract and given help to find accommodation. First 2 weeks are provided free and in some cases up to 1 month.

QUALIFICATIONS: Degree (preferably in a business subject) and TESOL, CELTA or DELTA. Prefer candidates who have worked in business for 5 years, have 2 years EFL experience and a driving licence. Good knowledge of EFL materials needed for positions that involve level-testing.

CONDITIONS OF EMPLOYMENT: All teachers are freelancers, and paid on an hourly basis.

SALARY: Varies according to age and experience.

RECRUITMENT: Word of mouth, newspapers, magazines, internet and CVs sent on spec.

CONTACT: Maria McCarthy, Managing Director (maria@caledonian.it).

THE CAMBRIDGE SCHOOL

Via Rosmini 6, 37123 Verona

+39 045 8003154

info@cambridgeschool.it

www.cambridgeschool.it

NUMBER OF TEACHERS: 12-15.

PREFERENCE OF NATIONALITY: None, provided they are native speakers with a valid EU passport/visa.

QUALIFICATIONS: Cambridge CELTA or Trinity CertTesol is essential. Minimum 2 years' experience as a teacher and experience with Cambridge English exam preparation is an advantage.

CONDITIONS OF EMPLOYMENT: 9 months, October-June, renewable with opportunities to work in the summer. 25 hours a week between Monday and Saturday lunchtime.

SALARY: Approximately €1,300 a month, net.

FACILITIES/SUPPORT: Medical insurance is provided. School usually knows of 2-3 flats as potential teacher accommodation or will accompany teacher to estate agents to ease the language barrier.

RECRUITMENT: Preliminary Skype interview and final face-to-face interview at the Cambridge School.

CONTACT: Director of Studies & Teachers' Coordinator.

CANADIAN ISLAND

Via Gioberti 15, 50121 Florence

+39 05 567 7567

info@canadianisland.com

www.canadianisland.it

NUMBER OF TEACHERS: 12 for summer camps.

PREFERENCE OF NATIONALITY: None.

QUALIFICATIONS: Overnight camp experience and an overall love and enthusiasm of working with children.

CONDITIONS OF EMPLOYMENT: 4 weeks. Working round the clock.

SALARY: €200 a week plus room and board.

FACILITIES/SUPPORT: Accommodation provided.

RECRUITMENT: Adverts on university career website. All interviews by Skype.

CONTACT: Maria Rocco, Director.

CLM BELL

Via Pozzo 30, 38122 Trento

+39 0461 981733

clm-bell@clm-bell.it

www.clm-bell.com

NUMBER OF TEACHERS: 25 approximately, also for Riva del Garda.

PREFERENCE OF NATIONALITY: Native English speakers.

QUALIFICATIONS: Minimum 2 years' experience with CELTA/DELTA qualification.

CONDITIONS OF EMPLOYMENT: 9-month contracts. To work 23 hours per week, can be extended. Positions also available at summer camp.

SALARY: €1,350–€1,550 per month.

FACILITIES/SUPPORT: Single subsidised accommodation on a limited basis. Help provided with work permits. Workshops given by teacher trainers.

RECRUITMENT: Via www.tefl.com or direct applications. Interview required.

CONTACT: Ivana Ferrari, Centre Manager, or Jane Nolan, Academic Coordinator for English.

DARBY SCHOOL OF LANGUAGES – ROME – MILAN

Via Mosca 51, Villino 14, 00142 Rome

+39 06 5196 2205

darby@darbyschool.it

www.darbyschool.it

NUMBER OF TEACHERS: 40–50, also for Milan.

PREFERENCE OF NATIONALITY: None, but must be native English speaker.

QUALIFICATIONS: TEFL certificate CELTA.

CONDITIONS OF EMPLOYMENT: Freelance. Teachers for both Rome and Milan can choose their hours which usually are an average of 20–25 hours per week. More hours available if wanted.

SALARY: The average salary of about €1,400 is sufficient and more than enough to live on in Italy.

FACILITIES/SUPPORT: New teachers are helped to find accommodation.

RECRUITMENT: Relevant CVs and interviews.

CONTACT: Gilda Darby.

ENGLISH CONVERSATION CLUB

Via Giuosè Carducci 5/1, 16121 Genoa

+39 010 540964

enquiry@thetrainingcompany.org; smurrell@thetrainingcompany.org

www.thetrainingcompany.org

NUMBER OF TEACHERS: 12.

PREFERENCE OF NATIONALITY: None.

QUALIFICATIONS: CELTA/DELTA or equivalent. Online certificates are not acceptable.

CONDITIONS OF EMPLOYMENT: 10-month contract. 100 working hours per month.

SALARY: €1,100–€1,300 per month net.

FACILITIES/SUPPORT: Assistance given to find accommodation prior to arrival.

RECRUITMENT: Usually via the internet. Interviews are essential and can be carried out over the phone or occasionally in the UK.

CONTACT: Stephen Murrell, Director.

EUROPLACEMENTS ITALY SRL – RECRUITMENT AGENCY

Piazzale Biancamano 8, 20121 Milan

+39 02 6203 3060

info@europlacements.it; g.taccone@europlacements.it

www.europlacements.it

NUMBER OF TEACHERS: 50–70.

PREFERENCE OF NATIONALITY: English-speaking countries; EU citizens preferred for visa purposes.

QUALIFICATIONS: BA in Education with specialisation in subjects for upper school.

CONDITIONS OF EMPLOYMENT: 12 or 24-month contracts. Hours are 9am–4pm Monday–Friday. Also part-time jobs available, and tutoring jobs in family settings.

SALARY: €1,400 per month (net) on average.

FACILITIES/SUPPORT: Some schools assist with accommodation.

RECRUITMENT: Advertisements on targeted websites plus many spontaneous applications. Preliminary interviews by Skype. Face-to-face interviews held in London three times a year or when necessary.

CONTACT: Gianna Taccone, Director of Educational Division and Family Division for English Mother Tongue Recruitment.

IIK ANCONA SCUOLA DI LINGUE

Scalo Vittorio Emanuele II, 1, 60121 Ancona

+39 071 206610

info@iik.it

www.iik.it

NUMBER OF TEACHERS: 5–6.

PREFERENCE OF NATIONALITY: British preferred; EU citizens.

QUALIFICATIONS: Minimum 3 years' teaching experience and TEFL/TESOL certificate. (Taster weekend courses and distance learning courses without observed and assessed teaching practice will not be considered.)

CONDITIONS OF EMPLOYMENT: Generally from September until end of June. Guaranteed minimum 25 hours per week. Teaching takes place between 8.45am and 9pm.

SALARY: €10 net per hour.

FACILITIES/SUPPORT: Assistance given with finding accommodation but teacher responsible for paying rent. School advises EU teachers on getting residence permit, fiscal code and enrolling in health services.

RECRUITMENT: Direct contact and www.tefl.com.

INTENSIVE BUSINESS ENGLISH

Corso Buenos Aires 7, 20124 Milan

+39 02 6900 2017

info@ibeschool.com

www.ibeschool.com

NUMBER OF TEACHERS: 45, for Milan, Bologna, Turin, Rome Venice and online.

PREFERENCE OF NATIONALITY: British, Irish, Australian, and New Zealander, already living in Italy.

QUALIFICATIONS: Minimum age 30. Minimum 3 years' experience and CELTA/TESOL qualified. A university degree and experience of the business world would be beneficial.

CONDITIONS OF EMPLOYMENT: 12-month contract. 25 contact hours between 9am and 7pm, Monday to Friday. Teaching corporate clients in-company and online.

SALARY: Between €1,800 and €3,250 gross depending on type of contract and experience. 20%–30% deductions for taxes.

FACILITIES/SUPPORT: Accommodation in flats owned by the school at very low rates. Cost of training with www.TeacherTraining.it may be reimbursed after 2 years' employment.

RECRUITMENT: Application form on website, advertising in local magazines and through the teacher network in Milan. Interviews essential.

CONTACT: Gordon Doyle, Director of Studies.

INTERLINGUE LANGUAGE SYSTEM COLLEGE – TEFL INTERNATIONAL

Via Lucrezio Caro 67, 00193 Rome

+39 06 321 5740

tefl@interlingue-it.com

www.interlingue-it.com

NUMBER OF TEACHERS: Approx. 20.

PREFERENCE OF NATIONALITY: None.

QUALIFICATIONS: Minimum TEFL certificate, university degree, some teaching experience.

CONDITIONS OF EMPLOYMENT: 9-month contracts, working between 20 and 30 hours per week.

SALARY: €12.50–€19 per hour, depending on contract.

FACILITIES/SUPPORT: Support in searching for accommodation. Also runs intensive TEFL training courses.

RECRUITMENT: Via students on their TEFL course, online application form and other methods. Interviews required, final interview must be carried out in Rome.

CONTACT: Angela Giordano, General School Manager.

INTERNATIONAL CLUB
P.le A. Moro, 6, 20034 Giussano
+39 0362 354057
info@internationalclub.it
www.internationalclub.it

NUMBER OF TEACHERS: 25.

PREFERENCE OF NATIONALITY: British, Irish, or any other native English speaker in possession of EU citizenship or *Permesso di Soggiorno* (work visa).

QUALIFICATIONS: For adult classes: CELTA/TESOL or any other TEFL qualification plus at least 1 year's experience with teaching groups at all levels. For children's classes: any qualification for teaching children (not necessarily as an EFL teacher) and experience with teaching children. Must have a driving licence. Other skills advantageous such as sports, music, arts or drama.

CONDITIONS OF EMPLOYMENT: Standard contract is 9 months or longer. Permanent teachers welcome. Sometimes teachers are employed shorter term and summer contracts from June to July are offered. Teachers work 25–35 hours per week.

SALARY: €12.50 net per hour.

FACILITIES/SUPPORT: Accommodation in flats owned by the school at very low rates. Free seminars for teachers.

RECRUITMENT: By direct contact or recruitment agencies. Interviews can be carried out on the phone or by internet. Occasionally interviews arranged in the UK or USA during the summer.

CONTACT: Mary Sposari, Director of Studies.

INTERNATIONAL HOUSE (CAMPOBASSO) ITALY
Via Zurlo 5, 86100 Campobasso
+39 0874 481321
risoreumane@ihcampobasso.it;
info@ihcampobasso.it
www.accademiabritannica.it

NUMBER OF TEACHERS: 20 for summer camp in Italy.

PREFERENCE OF NATIONALITY: British/American.

QUALIFICATIONS: Minimum age 21. CELTA qualification and experience teaching children and teenagers essential.

CONDITIONS OF EMPLOYMENT: Contract 2/4 or 6 weeks from end of June to August. 6 hours' teaching per day. Pupils aged 8–16.

SALARY: Approximately €65 per shift.

FACILITIES/SUPPORT: Accommodation and all meals provided.

RECRUITMENT: Direct application.

CONTACT: Linda Graziano, Director of Studies; Mary Ricciardi, Director.

INTERNATIONAL HOUSE (PALERMO)
Via Quintino Sella 70, 90139 Palermo
+39 091 584954
ihpalermo@ihpalermo.it; dos@ihpalermo.it
www.ihpalermo.it

NUMBER OF TEACHERS: 9 plus 1 Director of Studies and 1 Children's Coordinator. Most of the teaching is of Young Learners.

PREFERENCE OF NATIONALITY: Must have right to work in EU.

QUALIFICATIONS: Degree, CELTA (minimum grade 'B'), DELTA preferred. School interested in career teachers only.

CONDITIONS OF EMPLOYMENT: 8-month contracts from beginning of October. 25 hours per week, between 1.30pm and 9pm, Monday to Friday. Lessons last 75–80 minutes.

SALARY: From €1,250 plus increments.

FACILITIES/SUPPORT: Assistance with finding accommodation (rent €300–€400 per month). Weekly seminars and workshops. International House Certificate in Teaching Young Learners and Teenagers (IHCYLT) offered free of charge in September. CELTA courses offered in summer every year. School will subsidise in-service diploma course by distance learning for committed employees. Italian survival lessons. Flight refund up to €120.

RECRUITMENT: Via IH World Organisation or directly. Interviews essential.

CONTACT: Nick Kiley, Director of Studies.

KEEP TALKING
Via Roma 60, 33100 Udine, Friuli-Venezia Giulia
+39 0432 501525
info@keeptalking.it
www.keeptalking.it

NUMBER OF TEACHERS: 6.

PREFERENCE OF NATIONALITY: None, but must be native speakers.

QUALIFICATIONS: University degree and CELTA or equivalent required plus minimum 1 year of experience. Driving licence essential to carry out work in local companies.

CONDITIONS OF EMPLOYMENT: 9-month contracts (*contratto di lavoro a progetto*, which means an hourly paid contract with a guaranteed minimum number of hours). Minimum 750 contact hours over 9 months. 25 hours per week. Lessons mostly at lunchtimes and evenings and Saturday mornings.

SALARY: Starting hourly wage of €14.50–€16.50 (net); monthly €1,200–€1,330 depending on qualifications and experience.

FACILITIES/SUPPORT: Training seminars once a month. Excellent facilities. Income tax, pension, medical/accident insurance paid by employer. Accommodation provided. 30 hours of survival Italian.

RECRUITMENT: Face-to-face interview normally essential in Udine or in London in July. Candidates who are successful at interview will be told within about 2 weeks if they have been successful. Adverts via internet (www.tefl.com).

CONTACT: Kip Kelland, Director (kip@keeptalking.it).

KID'S WORLD

Via Lucrino 22a, 00199 Rome

+39 06 8621 2471

info@kidsworld.it

www.kidsworldenglish.com

NUMBER OF TEACHERS: 40 to teach children aged 7–13 at summer camps.

PREFERENCE OF NATIONALITY: None.

QUALIFICATIONS: Teachers should be dynamic and sporty.

CONDITIONS OF EMPLOYMENT: Summer camp period lasts 4–6 weeks between mid-June and the end of July. Teachers work around 8 hours a day.

SALARY: Approx. €900 per fortnight, less deductions of 25%.

FACILITIES/SUPPORT: Accommodation and meals are provided.

RECRUITMENT: Via local adverts for English teachers. Candidates applying from abroad can be interviewed by telephone or Skype.

CONTACT: Simon Charlesworth, Director (s.charlesworth@kidsworld.it).

LANGUAGES INTERNATIONAL SRL

Via Ippolito D'Aste 1/12, 16121 Genoa

+39 010 595 8889

robertson@languagesinternational.it

www.languagesinternational.it

NUMBER OF TEACHERS: 35–70 (depending on the time of year) in schools in Genoa and Rome.

PREFERENCE OF NATIONALITY: Native English speakers with passport from EU country.

QUALIFICATIONS: Prior teaching experience, university degree and recognised TEFL/TESOL certificate.

CONDITIONS OF EMPLOYMENT: Between 24 and 34 working hours per week, depending on which city the teacher is based in and their flexibility.

FACILITIES/SUPPORT: Assistance is given with accommodation, i.e. appointments to visit rooms are set up.

RECRUITMENT: Usually via the internet or word of mouth. Interviews are carried out over the phone if the candidate is not in Rome, Milan or Genoa.

CONTACT: Millica Robertson, Director of Studies.

LINGUE SENZA FRONTIERE

Corso Inglesi 172, 18038 – San Remo

+39 0184 533661

info@linguesenzafrontiere.org; raffaella.lsf.application@gmail.com

www.linguesenzafrontiere.com/work-with-us.html

NUMBER OF TEACHERS: Approximately 200 per summer for English immersion camps for children 7–14.

PREFERENCE OF NATIONALITY: Native English speaker.

QUALIFICATIONS: TEFL certificate or equivalent useful and/or relevant experience. Must be a native speaker with a bubbly personality and have a genuine interest in working with children. Italian is not required but is useful.

CONDITIONS OF EMPLOYMENT: 2-week contract plus a free 4–5 day training course, which is compulsory. Working hours are 8.45am–4.15pm, Monday to Friday. Some English-speaking actors are employed for the academic year as well.

SALARY: €450 net per 2-week camp all-in.

FACILITIES/SUPPORT: Accommodation is provided from beginning to end of contract. Online pre-training then 4-day on-site training course, when accommodation is in shared rooms. During camp, tutors stay with an Italian host family.

CONTACT: Raffaella, Tutor Coordinator.

LIVING LANGUAGES SCHOOL

Via Magna Grecia 2, 89128 Reggio Calabria

+39 096 533 0926

info@livinglanguages.it

www.livinglanguages.it

Also: via Madonna, 21 Gallico, 89135 Reggio Calabria

NUMBER OF TEACHERS: 8.

PREFERENCE OF NATIONALITY: Native English speakers.

QUALIFICATIONS: TEFL, CELTA.

CONDITIONS OF EMPLOYMENT: 9-month renewable contracts. British contract. Teaching hours 3pm–9pm, Monday to Friday.

SALARY: Approx. €826 (net) per month for an inexperienced teacher.

FACILITIES/SUPPORT: Help given with accommodation.

RECRUITMENT: Via adverts. Some interviews carried out in UK.

LONDON SCHOOL
Corso Rosmini, 66, 38068 Rovereto
+39 046 442 1285
info@londonschoolrovereto.it
www.londonschoolrovereto.it

NUMBER OF TEACHERS: 4–5.

PREFERENCE OF NATIONALITY: British.

QUALIFICATIONS: Degree, and excellent command of English language. Pronunciation and grammar must be perfect. Teachers who also speak Italian are preferred. For summer work, training or experience in teaching young learners is preferred, e.g. online TESOL plus TEYL course (via www.teachingenglishinitaly.com).

CONDITIONS OF EMPLOYMENT: 1-year contract which may be renewed. 20–25 working hours per week. Summer vacancies are also available at children's courses held between mid-June and mid-August at the BluHotel in Folgaria in the mountains of Northern Italy. Summer teachers work between 2 and 9 weeks.

SALARY: €12–€15 per hour. Summer teachers earn €300 (net) a week in addition to homestay accommodation; wages are paid at the end of the contract.

FACILITIES/SUPPORT: Help is given to find accommodation. Work permits are taken care of by the school's accountant.

RECRUITMENT: References, detailed CV and interviews essential.

CONTACT: Gordana Marjanovic, Owner.

LORD BYRON COLLEGE
Via Sparano 102, 70121 Bari
+39 080 523 2686
johncredico@lordbyroncollege.com
www.lordbyroncollege.com/teaching-opportunities

One of the largest independent language schools in Italy, with 40 years' experience and an annual attendance of nearly 2,000 students of all levels and ages. Authorised by the Italian Ministry of Education and member of EAQUALS (European Association for Quality Language Services).

NUMBER OF TEACHERS: 30 full-time, 30 part-time. Summer position: July 1st – August 8th.

PREFERENCE OF NATIONALITY: UK nationals. Canadian, American, Australian and South African applicants can be considered only if they have dual European citizenship.

QUALIFICATIONS: Degree, TEFL qualification, at least 1 year's teaching experience and knowledge of Italian or another foreign language.

CONDITIONS OF EMPLOYMENT: UK contracts for 8 months from October to June or 5 months from January, renewable. National insurance and pension coverage. Maximum 29.5 hours per week including paid training and on-call hours. Students of all ages and levels.

SALARY: Starting at €1,000 net per month in school year, €1,300 total for summer school. Paid orientation week. 5 weeks' paid holiday.

FACILITIES/SUPPORT: Free in-house DELTA course for teachers with minimum 1,200 hours' teaching experience. Teacher training and development programme for all teaching staff. Large self-access centre with video club, cinema, large TEFL resource centre and library and staff internet access. Participation in school's film dubbing and voiceover programme. Free Italian course. City centre accommodation found for teachers in shared flats; rent is €250 per month plus bills.

RECRUITMENT: Online application form in the Teaching Opportunities section of the website can be submitted by email or post with full CV, recent photograph, names and email addresses of 2 teaching-related references, copies of degree, TEFL qualification and passport from an EU member state. Interviews and hiring in June for October start and in December for January.

CONTACT: John Credico, Director of Studies (johncredico@lordbyroncollege.com).

MAC LANGUAGE SCHOOL
Formazione OK, Via Alessandro Cruto 8, 00146 Rome
+39 06 8366 4460
info@maclanguage.it
www.formazioneok.com

NUMBER OF TEACHERS: 57 for positions nationwide, including e-learning tutors.

PREFERENCE OF NATIONALITY: None if native English speaker.

QUALIFICATIONS: 3 years' experience or certified teachers.

CONDITIONS OF EMPLOYMENT: 4–8 hours per day.

FACILITIES/SUPPORT: None.

RECRUITMENT: Internet, newspapers, other. Interviews essential. Sometimes phone interviews can be arranged.

CONTACT: Mauro Bonello, Director.

MADRELINGUA SCHOOL OF ENGLISH
Via San Giorgio, 6–40121 Bologna
+39 051 267822
info@madrelinguaenglish.com
www.madrelinguaenglish.com

NUMBER OF TEACHERS: Around 10.

PREFERENCE OF NATIONALITY: None, but must be eligible to work legally in Italy.

QUALIFICATIONS: Degree plus CELTA (or equivalent) essential, YL qualification and/or DELTA preferred. The school contributes to course fees for staff wishing to extend their qualifications.

CONDITIONS OF EMPLOYMENT: Academic year is October to June. Teachers work evenings and Saturday mornings. Some permanent positions available.

SALARY: Depending on experience but above average for the local market. Minimum €20 per hour gross. Taxes are around 20%.

FACILITIES/SUPPORT: The school can arrange a 'homestay' on a temporary basis. English teachers may take subsidised Italian language courses.

RECRUITMENT: Speculative CVs.

MY ENGLISH SCHOOL

Via della Libertà 191, 90143 Palermo

+39 091 306962

palermo@myes.it

www.myenglishschool.it/palermo

Formerly Lucky Lion School. Second branch in Palermo at Viale Regione Siciliana Sud Est, 708/710.

NUMBER OF TEACHERS: 4.

PREFERENCE OF NATIONALITY: None.

QUALIFICATIONS: Native English speakers with CELTA or equivalent.

CONDITIONS OF EMPLOYMENT: Contracts are generally less than 1 year, but are renewable. Approx. 25 hours per week depending on the time of year.

FACILITIES/SUPPORT: Help provided to find private accommodation.

RECRUITMENT: Face-to-face interview and demonstration lesson essential.

CONTACT: Jacqueline Louise Scott, Director of Studies.

OXFORD GROUP

International Campus Baranzate, Via I Maggio 20, 20021 Baranzate (MI)

+39 02 872581

info@oxford.it

www.oxford.it/lavora-con-noi

A group of schools affiliated to the International School of Europe (www.internationalschoolofeurope.it) that offers an English-medium education to children aged 3–18.

NUMBER OF TEACHERS: 200+ ESL teachers for Milan, Rho, Florence, Bergamo, Asti, Seregno, Rome, Varese, Lecco, Merano, Brescia, Castiglione delle Stiviere (MN) and Reggio Emilia.

PREFERENCE OF NATIONALITY: EU passport required.

QUALIFICATIONS: Degree + TEFL certificate (or equivalent, including a teaching certificate). Experience and/or willingness to teach the younger age ranges needed.

CONDITIONS OF EMPLOYMENT: Normal term is mid-September until the end of July. Working hours vary, but average at 25 contact hours per week.

SALARY: To be discussed.

FACILITIES/SUPPORT: Schools may help teachers find accommodation but teachers pay their own rent.

RECRUITMENT: Via recruitment agencies, websites and newspapers. Interviews can be arranged by video conferencing or occasionally in the UK.

CONTACT: Ian George Bolton, Head of Language Department (igbolton@oxford.it).

OXFORD SCHOOL OF ENGLISH s.r.l.

Administrative Office, Via S. Pertini 14, 30035 Mirano, Venice

+39 041 570 2355

oxford@oxfordschool.com; rados@oxfordschool.com

www.oxfordschool.com; www.oxforditalia.it

NUMBER OF TEACHERS: 20–30 for 15 schools in North-East Italy; most are independent franchises (60–70 teachers employed altogether). Oxford School Busnago (MB) was advertising for EL teachers August 2016.

PREFERENCE OF NATIONALITY: British.

QUALIFICATIONS: Degree, TEFL and knowledge of Italian needed. Candidates must be holders of an EU member state passport.

CONDITIONS OF EMPLOYMENT: 9-month contracts or longer, 22 hours per week.

SALARY: Varies according to hours and length of contract but generally €1,000–€1,300. Tax deductions of about 23% give minimum health and welfare cover.

FACILITIES/SUPPORT: Accommodation at teacher's own expense, but school will help to find it.

RECRUITMENT: Interviews in London from mid-May or in Italy.

CONTACT: Philip Panter, Administrator.

QUAGI LANGUAGE CENTRE

Via Manzoni, 100/C, Erice C. Santa, 91100 Trapani, Sicily

+39 0923 557748

quagi@quagi.com

www.quagi.org

NUMBER OF TEACHERS: 7.

PREFERENCE OF NATIONALITY: Native English speakers with an EU member state passport.

QUALIFICATIONS: Preferably 2 years' experience, a degree and CELTA or TESOL certificate are required.

CONDITIONS OF EMPLOYMENT: Usually 8 months, October to the end of May. 4-month contracts also offered (January to May).

SALARY: €1,350 per month for 25 hours a week. Full-time Italian contract guarantees base salary per month.

FACILITIES/SUPPORT: Modern school offering training to become an official Cambridge ESOL oral examiner and/or invigilator. In-house training is provided before courses start. Perks include internet, a large range of resources and holidays are fully paid. The school will also help teachers find fully furnished accommodation, arrange tax file numbers and medical visits.

RECRUITMENT: Direct. Telephone interviews possible.

CONTACT: Teresa Matteucci, Director of Studies.

THE BRITISH LANGUAGE CENTRE

Largo Pedrini 2, 23100 Sondrio

+39 0342 216130

info@thebritish.it

www.thebritish.it

NUMBER OF TEACHERS: 6–7.

PREFERENCE OF NATIONALITY: British.

QUALIFICATIONS: CELTA (good grade) and minimum of 3 years' experience. DELTA preferred. Full, clean driving licence is essential. Some knowledge of Italian would be an advantage.

CONDITIONS OF EMPLOYMENT: UK-based contract is for 10 months from September 1st. 25 hours teaching per week plus meetings, admin, etc.

SALARY: £1,100 (gross) per month; deductions are about €300.

FACILITIES/SUPPORT: Assistance given with finding accommodation, e.g. helping to sort through ads and accompanying teacher to see possible places. Paid holidays. Outbound flight and setting in allowance given.

RECRUITMENT: Applicants should send CV, photo and a cover letter. Interviews can be face-to-face or by Skype.

CONTACT: Annika Paniga, Administrative Assistant; Steve Marsland, Director.

THE ENGLISH CAMP COMPANY LLC

Via Della Madonna Delle Grazie 6, Santa Maria Degli Angeli, Assisi (PG) 06081

+39 075 804 1402

info@theenglishcampcompany.com

www.theenglishcampcompany.com

NUMBER OF TEACHERS: 15–25 for summer camps throughout Italy, for children aged 7–14.

PREFERENCE OF NATIONALITY: None. Lots of North Americans spend the summer in Italy through this programme.

QUALIFICATIONS: Previous teaching experience or experience working at summer camps with children.

CONDITIONS OF EMPLOYMENT: 2-month contract. Working hours 9am–5pm. Compulsory 1-week orientation must be attended in early June.

SALARY: €175 per week.

FACILITIES/SUPPORT: All teachers are housed with host families. Orientation week provided for all teachers in Assisi in early June (and sometimes late June as well). The programme gets good reviews on www.gooverseas.com.

RECRUITMENT: Closing date for applications first week of April.

CONTACT: Ashleigh McLean (ashleigh.mclean@theenglishcampcompany.com) and Nate Poerio (nate.poerio@theenglishcampcompany.com), founders and directors.

THE LANGUAGE GRID srl

Via Carducci 35, 20123 Milan

+39 0349 7633507/034 016 7235

info@thelanguagegrid.com

www.thelanguagegrid.com

NUMBER OF TEACHERS: 14 business English trainers for this company which specialises in the banking and finance sector.

PREFERENCE OF NATIONALITY: Must be native English speakers, i.e. born and raised in an English-speaking country, with legal permission to stay in Italy.

QUALIFICATIONS: University degree (preferably in business or finance) and TEFL qualification (or be willing to acquire one).

CONDITIONS OF EMPLOYMENT: Long-term full-time Italian contract. 38 hours per week.

SALARY: National Contract with legislated benefits (no freelancers). Approximately €25,000–€30,000 (gross) per year, plus bonus. Deductions can amount to 46% in total for social security, taxes, etc.

FACILITIES/SUPPORT: Holiday and sick pay entitlements, etc. included in salary package. No assistance given with accommodation or visas.

RECRUITMENT: Internet, head hunter, word of mouth. Applications in writing with cover letter, CV and recent photo. Interviews take place face-to-face in Milan only.

CONTACT: Zoe Veronica Avlonitis, Managing Director.

TJ TAYLOR LANGUAGE TRAINING

Viale Bianca Maria 24, 20129 Milan

+39 02 4300 19075

work@tjtaylor.net; info@tjtaylor.net

www.tjtaylor.eu

NUMBER OF TEACHERS: 12 mainly for Milan and Padua.

PREFERENCE OF NATIONALITY: Native speakers of English with right to work in Italy.

QUALIFICATIONS: Minimum is a recognised TEFL qualification (CELTA or Trinity plus a few other recognised qualifications) and minimum 1–3 years' experience (5–10 preferred), with a strong preference for corporate training experience and an ability to design their own courses. Most new recruits comfortably exceed this minimum.

CONDITIONS OF EMPLOYMENT: 1 year if starting in January or September. 25 contact hours a week, Monday to Friday.

SALARY: From €1,300, after all taxes deducted. Freelancers have to invoice.

FACILITIES/SUPPORT: New teachers are assigned a local 'buddy' from the teaching staff, though the majority of teachers are already in Milan or the surrounding area.

RECRUITMENT: Ads on website, Twitter, Facebook and LinkedIn profiles, and normally also on www.tefl.com. Interviews essential and always held in Milan as positions tend to be long term.

CONTACT: Alex Taylor, Managing Director.

UNITED COLLEGE

Ronco a Via Von Platen 16/18, 96100 Siracusa

+39 0931 22000

info@unitedcollege.it; carolyn.davies@unitedcollege.it

www.unitedcollege.eu

NUMBER OF TEACHERS: 10.

PREFERENCE OF NATIONALITY: British (work contracts for non-EU nationals much more difficult to arrange).

QUALIFICATIONS: Degree plus Trinity or Cambridge certificate, plus 1 year's experience, especially useful if with Young Learners. Basic knowledge of Italian preferable.

CONDITIONS OF EMPLOYMENT: Mid-September to mid-June. Possibility of summer work. Up to 25 teaching hours a week between 3pm and 9pm, Monday to Friday.

SALARY: €1,100–€1,200 net per month (depending on qualifications and experience). Italian contract with contributions paid.

FACILITIES/SUPPORT: Assistance given with finding accommodation. Car available.

RECRUITMENT: Through www.tefl.com.

CONTACT: Carolyn Davies, Owner/Director of Studies.

WINDSOR INTEGRATED LANGUAGE & BUSINESS SOLUTIONS

Via Molino delle Lime 4/F, 10064 Pinerolo

+39 0121 795555

windsor@vds.it; info@windsorpinerolo.it

www.windsorpinerolo.it

NUMBER OF TEACHERS: 6–9.

PREFERENCE OF NATIONALITY: British or EU applicants only. Mother tongue speakers only.

QUALIFICATIONS: Education to degree level, TEFL Certificate, and minimum 1 year's teaching experience.

CONDITIONS OF EMPLOYMENT: 9–10 months (October to June). Courses offered in Military English.

SALARY: About €1,000 net per month.

CONTACT: Sandro Vazon Colla, Director.

PORTUGAL

After suffering badly from the European debt crisis, Portugal seems to be on the upturn with a higher minimum wage, a lower rate of unemployment (which dropped from 17% to 12% between 2013 and 2016) and moderate economic growth predicted for 2017. Outside the Lisbon area, the northern region around Porto has traditionally been the country's economic powerhouse and it especially looks set on a road to recovery, which means that there should be more disposable income around for English courses.

Teaching opportunities persist, especially in the teaching of young learners. Relations between Portugal and Britain have always been warm and historically there has been a preference for British teachers, though this may alter once Britain exits the EU. Most language institutes cater for anyone over the age of seven, so you should be prepared to teach children. As of 2016, the Ministry of Education has stipulated that primary school children will learn English for seven consecutive years. From 2016, a government initiative assists preschools and primary schools to join the new Bilingual Schools Programme in cooperation with the British Council. As a result parents are eager to start their children very young in private English classes. The enrolment for children's courses continues strong and a number of language institutes serve a student body that is 90% under the age of 17. Language schools often find it hard to recruit teachers who have experience of teaching children and a basic knowledge of Portuguese, which is useful when teaching young children. A recent trend is for established institutes to offer intensive summer courses. A job teaching on one of these is easier to secure and can provide a useful route into longer-term teaching.

In fact, some schools organise courses in nursery/primary schools for children from the age of three, sometimes as part of the Ministry of Education's 'Teaching and Understanding of the first level of basic English' programme. For example the Windsor School in Ovar, south of Porto, offers courses to 'toddlers' (www.windsorschool.ws/carrer.html).

The vast majority of British tourists flock to the Algarve, along the southern coast of Portugal, which means that many Portuguese in the south who aspire to work in the tourist industry want to learn English. Schools such as Wall Street English in Faro (www.wsenglish.pt) and the Centro de Línguas in Lagos cater for just that market. But the demand for English teachers is greatest in North and Central Portugal. Jobs crop up in historic centres such as Coimbra, Braga and Viseu and in small seaside towns like Aveiro and Póvoa do Varzim. These can be a very welcome destination for teachers burnt out from teaching in big cities, first-time teachers who want to avoid the rat race, or teachers who simply want to secure a steady wage and accommodation. The British Council (www.britishcouncil.pt) has seven English language centres in Coimbra, Greater Lisbon, Porto, etc. and recruits teachers, usually on a part-time basis initially. Candidates must have a degree, TEFL certificate and two years' post-TEFL qualification EFL teaching experience. CVs are kept on file for six months.

FINDING A JOB

Most teachers in Portugal have either answered adverts or are working for one of the large chains. International House (www.ihportugal.com) has 10 affiliated schools in Portugal. About three-quarters of all IH students in Portugal are children, so expertise with young learners is a definite asset. Wall Street English (www.wsenglish.pt) is well represented with 34 centres, some of which are always looking for dynamic teachers; CVs can be emailed to hr-recruitment@wsenglish.pt.

Outside the cities where there have traditionally been large expatriate communities, schools cannot depend on English speakers just showing up and so must recruit well in advance of the academic year (late September to the end of June). The Bristol School Group (see entry) offers the only possibility of which we have heard for working in the Azores, so if you want to work in the most isolated islands in the Atlantic

Ocean – more than 1,000km west of Portugal – this is your chance. Small groups of schools, say six schools in a single region, is the norm in Portugal. A number of the schools listed in the directory at the end of this chapter belong to such mini-chains. One of the most well established is the Cambridge Schools group that every year imports dozens of teachers.

A company that specialises in teaching children aged 3–13 is Fun Languages/Kids Club (www.kidsclub.pt), with dozens of clubs throughout the country. It is possible to submit an online application form, which is circulated round all the clubs and any with vacancies will make contact.

Many schools are small family-run establishments with fewer than 10 teachers, so sending off a lot of speculative applications is unlikely to succeed. As is true anywhere, you might be lucky and find something on the spot. The Cambridge CELTA is widely requested by schools and can be obtained at IH in Lisbon.

REGULATIONS

The standard requirement for EU residents is to register locally and obtain a registration certificate (*Certificado de Registo*) after an initial three-month stay. The documents needed to obtain this are proof of accommodation, health insurance and means of support. If you are employed, you must show that you have been registered in the social security system and are not being paid less than the Portuguese minimum wage (€618 per month from 2016). These must be presented to an immigration office – Serviço de Estrangeiros e Fronteiras (SEF; www.sef.pt) – or at your local Town Hall (*Câmara Municipal*). Forms can be downloaded from the SEF site, and the fee is €15.

Non-EU residents will have a much more difficult time trying to work in Portugal. Obtaining a work permit is next to impossible and therefore getting a contract job is out of the question for most. Self-employed teachers can try to make their tax status legal by using electronic invoice receipts called *faturas-recibo*. In order to qualify for these, you need an NIF (*Numero Identificação Fiscal*), for which you will need to be a legal resident. Without a contract, the only way to qualify is to have a Portuguese citizen sponsor you. For a detailed account of the bureaucratic battles fought by English teacher **Andrea Smith** from Washington DC, see http://americaninportugal.blogspot.it/2012/02/so-you-want-to-move-to-portugal-heres.html. She could achieve legal status only with the ongoing help of her Portuguese boyfriend. An alternative is to seek employment with schools that prefer American speakers, though even a school with 'American' in the title, such as the American School of Languages (see entry) or CAA (Centro Anglo-Americano) in Chaves and Vila Real (www.caaenglish.com), hire almost exclusively teachers who already have the right to reside in the EU.

Since most teachers working for nine months are working on a freelance basis, they are responsible for paying their own taxes and contributions. There are seven income tax brackets ranging from 10.5% to 42% and an array of tax deductions, credits and special benefits. Tax laws and regulations are frequently subject to change. The tax retention rate for the self-employed is 25% of earnings. The first 12 months of self-employment are exempt from social security payments.

CONDITIONS OF WORK

The consensus seems to be that wages are low, but the cost of living, at least outside the major cities, is reasonable. Imported consumer goods are taxed and expensive and the cost of domestic fuel and tolls on roads and bridges are high, but local produce such as olive oil, fruit, vegetables and wine is still relatively inexpensive. Public transport is quite cheap, as well as eating out. Working conditions are generally relaxed and students are generally helpful, as **Rachel Beebe** discovered:

Most students had a good attitude and tried very hard to speak the language. I spoke virtually no Portuguese in encounters or classes, and the students made every effort to use what they were learning to communicate with me.

The normal salary range is from €1,000 net per month. As in Spain, full-time contract workers are entitled to an extra month's pay after 12 months. Some schools pay lower rates but subsidise or pay for flights and accommodation. Several provide free Portuguese lessons. Teachers being paid on an hourly basis should expect to earn €12–€18, but they will of course not be eligible for the 13th-month bonus or paid holidays. If you are living in an urban centre, then you'll also need to factor in any unpaid travel time to find out how much you are 'really' getting paid.

LIST OF EMPLOYERS

AMERICAN SCHOOL OF LANGUAGES

22 – 1° Avenida Duque de Loulé, 1050 090 Lisbon

+351 21 314 6000; +351 967 907035

admin.asl@mail.telepac.pt

www.americanschooloflanguages.com

NUMBER OF TEACHERS: 5–10.

PREFERENCE OF NATIONALITY: EU citizenship is a plus but not essential.

QUALIFICATIONS: University degree, TEFL training course (preferably CELTA), EFL experience with adults preferable but not essential.

CONDITIONS OF EMPLOYMENT: Contract runs from October to June with some summer work an option. Contract is renewable for the next academic year, 21–24 working hours per week.

SALARY: €1,200–€1,600 per month with adjustments for inflation and opportunities for advancement.

FACILITIES/SUPPORT: Some assistance given to find accommodation, i.e. help making phone calls to prospective landlords, etc.

RECRUITMENT: Interviews in Lisbon are essential.

BRISTOL SCHOOL GROUP PORTUGAL

Bristol School – Instituto de Línguas da Maia,

Trav. Dr. Carlos Pires Felgueiras, 12–3°, 4470 158 Maia

+351 22 948 8803

bsmaia@bristolschool.pt

www.bristolschool.pt

Comprises a group of 9 language schools in Portugal: 4 in Oporto area, 2 in the Azores and 3 inland (Castelo Branco, Fundão and Colvilha). Addresses and email contacts all at www.bristolschool.pt.

NUMBER OF TEACHERS: 25.

PREFERENCE OF NATIONALITY: British and Irish (couples preferred).

QUALIFICATIONS: Bachelor's degree and TEFL qualification. EFL experience essential.

CONDITIONS OF EMPLOYMENT: Minimum period of work 15 September to 30 June. Full-time contract of 25 hours per week. Students aged from 8.

SALARY: Basic salary plus Christmas bonus and end-of-contract bonuses plus tax rebate. Legal contract of work.

FACILITIES/SUPPORT: Assistance with accommodation given.

RECRUITMENT: Direct application preferred.

CAMBRIDGE SCHOOL

Avenida da Liberdade 173, 1250 141 Lisbon

+351 21 312 4600

info@cambridge.pt; av.liberdade@cambridge.pt

www.cambridge.pt

Portugal's largest private language school with 9 centres, 5 in Lisbon and one each in Porto, Coimbra, Almada and Funchal (Madeira).

NUMBER OF TEACHERS: 90–110.

PREFERENCE OF NATIONALITY: EU citizens or in possession of a Portuguese *Autorizacao de Residencia.*

QUALIFICATIONS: Bachelor's degree plus CELTA, Trinity CertTESOL or an equivalent EFL qualification. Online qualifications are not acceptable. EFL experience preferred, however, newly qualified applicants may be successful.

CONDITIONS OF EMPLOYMENT: All contracts are Permanent Employment Contracts for full-time work, with a minimum commitment of 9 months, from 1 October to 30 June. 22 50-minute lessons a week. Also summer course teaching available.

SALARY: In a typical month, most starting teachers will average between €1,200 and €1,300 after deductions and extras. All staff receive a monthly meal subsidy of €141 and are included in the Portuguese National Health scheme. The school employs its own medical officers. One month paid summer holiday. Christmas and summer bonuses are paid.

FACILITIES/SUPPORT: All schools have 2–3 senior staff.

RECRUITMENT: Adverts on tefl.com. Applicants should send CV, recent photograph, contact telephone number and copies of degree and EFL certificate. Interviews are usually held in London in May and possibly mid-summer depending on requirements. Visitors to Portugal can be interviewed in Lisbon by prior arrangement.

CONTACT: Jeffrey Kapke, Adrian Mather, Robert Hart or Tony Hilzbrich, Pedagogical Administration.

CENTRO DE INGLES DE FAMALICAO

Edificio dos Correios, n° 116–4° Dto, Rua S. Joao de Deus, 4760 162 V.N. de Famalicao

+351 252 374233

centroinglesfam@gmail.com

www.fameli.pt

NUMBER OF TEACHERS: 3.

PREFERENCE OF NATIONALITY: Native speakers from UK or Ireland.

QUALIFICATIONS: Degree and CELTA (or equivalent) essential; experience an advantage but not essential. Online qualifications are not accepted.

CONDITIONS OF EMPLOYMENT: 9-month renewable contracts from late September to end of June. 24 contact hours per week, Monday to Friday only.

SALARY: At least €948 per month (net). Paid holidays at Christmas, Easter and Carnival. Travel expenses of €150 paid at beginning and end of contract.

FACILITIES/SUPPORT: Fully furnished flat near school provided rent free, sharing with other teacher(s). Help given with work permit procedures. Lessons are regularly observed and feedback given.

RECRUITMENT: Via adverts on the internet (www.tefl.com). Interviews essential, normally in London in July.

CIAL – CENTRO DE LINGUAS

Avenida Republica 14–2, 1050 191 Lisbon

+351 213 533733

linguas.estrangeiras@cial.pt

www.cial.pt

Also branch in Faro.

NUMBER OF TEACHERS: 15–17.

PREFERENCE OF NATIONALITY: EU citizens.

QUALIFICATIONS: University degree, CELTA, EFL teaching experience to adults (minimum 2 years); Business English teaching experience.

CONDITIONS OF EMPLOYMENT: Contracts October to June. Early morning, lunchtime and evening teaching hours.

SALARY: Depends on work agreement. Possibility of full-time, part-time or hourly basis. Monthly performance evaluation bonus paid as well as free Portuguese lessons and free health insurance as fringe benefits.

FACILITIES/SUPPORT: Family accommodation can be arranged for first 4 weeks if requested.

RECRUITMENT: Pre-selection through detailed CV; personal interviews compulsory.

CONTACT: Isabel Coimbra, Director (isabelcoimbra@cial.pt).

ENGLISH LANGUAGE CENTRE CASCAIS

Rua da Palmeira 5, 1A/B, 2750 459 Cascais

+351 21 483 0716/916 060170

caroline.darling@elc-cascais.com

www.elc-cascais.com

NUMBER OF TEACHERS: 12 including freelancers.

PREFERENCE OF NATIONALITY: Native speakers only, preferably from the UK.

QUALIFICATIONS: University degree and CELTA or equivalent.

CONDITIONS OF EMPLOYMENT: 10-month renewable contract from 1 September. 15–18 hours per week. Also part-time work teaching Young Learners from age 5.

SALARY: From €850 per month (for teaching a basic 15 hours per week). Extra private classes pay €14 per hour. End-of-year bonus and paid holidays.

FACILITIES/SUPPORT: Recruitment locally; pedagogical support – regular training workshops.

RECRUITMENT: Through www.tefl.com/local adverts. Face-to-face interviews essential normally held between April and June.

CONTACT: Caroline Darling, Director (caroline.darling@elc-cascais.com).

ESE – ENGLISH SCHOOL ÉVORA

Praça da Muralha, 12–1° esq. 7005 248 Évora

+351 266 743231/938 512574

jobs@ese.com.pt

www.englishschoolevora.com

NUMBER OF TEACHERS: 3.

PREFERENCE OF NATIONALITY: EU citizens, native English speakers.

QUALIFICATIONS: Degree, CELTA or equivalent, minimum 2 years' experience. Knowledge of Portuguese or a Latin language an advantage.

CONDITIONS OF EMPLOYMENT: 9-month renewable contract on freelance basis, 1 October to 30 June. 24 hours plus possible overtime. Most teaching in evenings till 10pm plus Saturday mornings.

SALARY: €1,664 (gross) per month. €16 per hour.

FACILITIES/SUPPORT: Some assistance with finding accommodation. 10 days' holiday at Easter/Christmas.

RECRUITMENT: Through the internet. Interviews are often on Skype.

CONTACT: Michael W. Lewis, Director.

FUN LANGUAGES – KIDS CLUB VISEU

rua Estevão Lopes Morago, Lote 326, 3510 085 Viseu

+351 232 426978

sandy@funlanguagesviseu.net; kidsclub@funlanguagesviseu.net

www.funlanguagesviseu.pt

One of 20 franchised branches throughout the country. HQ in Lisbon (geral@kidsclub.pt).

NUMBER OF TEACHERS: 9.

PREFERENCE OF NATIONALITY: Native speakers from Britain or North America.

QUALIFICATIONS: University education, teaching experience and teaching qualification preferred, although if a candidate shows potential, the employer is willing to train.

CONDITIONS OF EMPLOYMENT: Period of work September to July. 30 teaching hours per week.

SALARY: Variable from €700, depending on rent, bills, qualifications and circumstances. Arrangement will be discussed during the interview process. Teachers work freelance which means deductions are not made at source.

FACILITIES/SUPPORT: Accommodation is always provided for teachers moving to Portugal. Rent and bills are included in salary. Paid flights and transfers. The school registers teachers and takes care of permits, bank account and other issues involved in relocation.

RECRUITMENT: Advertising and headhunting at EFL summer camps in Britain. Online application form. Interviews are essential, and sometimes take place in the UK as well as Portugal.

CONTACT: Mrs Sandy Albuquerque, Director of Studies.

ILC INTERLEARNING CENTER

Rua Mouzihno de Albuqerque 56 1° esq., 2400 193 Leiria

+351 244 830950

leiria@ilc-escolalinguas.pt

www.ilc-escolalinguas.pt

Also has centres in Batalha and Fátima, in the same region.

NUMBER OF TEACHERS: 12.

PREFERENCE OF NATIONALITY: None.

QUALIFICATIONS: Degree.

CONDITIONS OF EMPLOYMENT: Standard contract is 10 months with 25 working hours per week.

SALARY: €12 per hour.

RECRUITMENT: Interviews carried out in Portugal.

INSTITUTO DE LINGUAS DE S. JOAO DA MADEIRA

Rua Durbalino Laranjeira S/N, 3700 108 S. João da Madeira

+351 256 833906

institutodelinguas@gmail.com

www.institutodelinguas.net

NUMBER OF TEACHERS: 14 working in schools/companies outside the Institute; 5 working at the Institute.

PREFERENCE OF NATIONALITY: British.

QUALIFICATIONS: DELTA/COTE plus 2 years' experience.

CONDITIONS OF EMPLOYMENT: 9-month contracts from mid-September.

SALARY: Dependent on qualifications.

FACILITIES/SUPPORT: No help given with accommodation, work permits; training sessions, workshops, seminars at the British Council Oporto.

RECRUITMENT: Interview essential.

CONTACT: Dr Helena Nicolau, Director.

INTERNATIONAL HOUSE (LISBON)

Rua Marquès Sá da Bandeira 16, 1050 148 Lisbon

+351 21 315 1493/4/6

info@ihlisbon.com

www.ihlisbon.com

NUMBER OF TEACHERS: 18.

PREFERENCE OF NATIONALITY: Native English speakers.

QUALIFICATIONS: CELTA minimum.

CONDITIONS OF EMPLOYMENT: Standard length of stay is 9 months. Flexible working hours to include evening and Saturday work. Pupils range in age from 8 to 80. Standard working week is 18 hours.

SALARY: From €1,355 per month for first year teachers, based on 18 hours per week teaching.

FACILITIES/SUPPORT: Assistance with finding accommodation. CELTA and IHCYLT courses offered regularly (see Training chapter).

RECRUITMENT: Local advertisements and by IH, London.

CONTACT: Colin McMillan, Director (colinmcmillan@ihlisbon.com).

INTERNATIONAL HOUSE (PORTO)

Porto: Rua Marechal Saldanha 145–1° Foz do Douro, 4150 655 Porto

+351 22 617 7641

info@ihporto.org; info@ihleca.com

www.ihporto.org; www.ihleca.com

Matosinhos: Leça da Palmeira, Rua Oliveira Lessa 350, 4450 751 Matosinhos

+351 22 995 9087

business@ihporto.org

NUMBER OF TEACHERS: 10.

PREFERENCE OF NATIONALITY: British, Canadian, Australian, New Zealander and American.

QUALIFICATIONS: CELTA/Trinity.

CONDITIONS OF EMPLOYMENT: 1-year contracts, 22 hours per week, pupils aged from 7.

SALARY: Depending on qualifications and experience.

FACILITIES/SUPPORT: Assistance with accommodation. Portuguese lessons available. Training provided.

RECRUITMENT: Direct application.

CONTACT: Shawn Severson, Educational Projects Manager (shawnseverson@ihporto.org).

INTERNATIONAL LANGUAGE SCHOOL

Av. Republica Guiné-Bissau, 26 A, 2900 588 Setubal

+351 26 522 7934

ilssetubal@gmail.com

http://ils.pt

NUMBER OF TEACHERS: 6.

PREFERENCE OF NATIONALITY: Native English speakers.

QUALIFICATIONS: CELTA or equivalent, 1 year's experience or more.

CONDITIONS OF EMPLOYMENT: October–July, 25 teaching hours per week.

SALARY: Approximately €1,300 per month (gross).

FACILITIES/SUPPORT: Accommodation provided.

RECRUITMENT: Via www.tefl.com. Direct applications by email with CV and photo are welcome. Phone interviews possible.

CONTACT: Tanya Garcia, Director.

LANGUAGE PROJECT – INSTITUTO DE LINGUAS

Rua de Camões 4, Quinta Nova de Sao Roque, 2670 513 Loures

+351 219 823084

info@language-project.com

www.language-project.com

NUMBER OF TEACHERS: 3.

PREFERENCE OF NATIONALITY: None.

QUALIFICATIONS: CELTA or equivalent, relevant degree and 2 years' experience including with young learners.

CONDITIONS OF EMPLOYMENT: Contract is 9 months (1 academic year) with 22–24 contact hours per week.

SALARY: €1,200 gross per month.

FACILITIES/SUPPORT: Assistance given with finding accommodation if necessary.

RECRUITMENT: Usually via adverts in schools, word of mouth or local websites. Interviews are essential either face-to-face or via Skype.

CONTACT: Christine Fonseca. Director (lproject@sapo.pt).

NEW INSTITUTE OF LANGUAGES

Avenida das Tulipas, N° 20B, 1495 159, Miraflores, Lisbon

+351 21 412 0929; 21 943 5238

admin@nil.edu.pt

www.nil.pt

NUMBER OF TEACHERS: 8 or 9 English teachers for 3 schools in and around Lisbon; branches in Miraflores, Portela and Massamá.

PREFERENCE OF NATIONALITY: British.

QUALIFICATIONS: Experienced and inexperienced graduates who have successfully completed a recognised minimum 4-week TEFL course (online courses are not considered).

CONDITIONS OF EMPLOYMENT: 9-month (1 October to 30 June) contract that is renewable, 24 contract hours per week (Monday–Friday). No Saturday hours.

SALARY: Depends on experience.

FACILITIES/SUPPORT: Secretarial and administrative help in finding permanent accommodation. Week-long orientation course end of September to aid teachers in the classroom.

RECRUITMENT: Website advertising (e.g. www.tefl.com) followed by face-to-face interviews in London in July and possibly September. No Skype interviews.

CONTACT: Nicholas Rudall, Director of Studies.

OXFORD SCHOOL

Lisbon: Rua D. Estefania, 165–1°, 1000 154 Lisbon

+351 21 354 6586; 796 6660

info1@oxford-school.pt

Cacém: Av. Bons Amigos, 37–1°Dto, 2735 077 Cacém

+351 21 914 6343

www.oxford-school.pt

Member of AEPLE .

NUMBER OF TEACHERS: About 40 employed at two branches in Lisbon and one in Cacém; 6 new hires per year. All teachers are native speakers.

PREFERENCE OF NATIONALITY: British.

QUALIFICATIONS: Minimum TEFL course (e.g. CELTA), qualifications and some experience.

CONDITIONS OF EMPLOYMENT: October–June. Hours mainly 1pm–3pm and 5pm–9pm.

SALARY: Minimum €17 per 1 teaching hour or €1,400 per month for 20 teaching hours per week. Deductions for taxes and social security approx. 15%.

FACILITIES/SUPPORT: Help given with finding a shared flat.

RECRUITMENT: Direct application. Interviews essential in Lisbon or London.

CONTACT: Zilda Amaro, Manager (Zildamaro@oxford-school.pt).

ROYAL SCHOOL OF LANGUAGES – ESCOLAS DE LINGUAS, LDA

Rua José Rabumba 2, 3810 125 Aveiro

+351 234 429156; 234 425104

rsl@royalschooloflanguages.pt

www.royalschool.pt

Schools also in Porto, Agueda, Guarda, Ovar, Viseu, Ilhavo, Sever do Vouga and Paredes. Languages taught: English, French, German, Italian, Spanish and Portuguese.

NUMBER OF TEACHERS: 30–35 in the whole group.

PREFERENCE OF NATIONALITY: British, Australian, Canadian and American.

QUALIFICATIONS: University degree plus TEFL/TESOL certificate.

CONDITIONS OF EMPLOYMENT: 9-month contracts. 25–27 teaching hours per week.

FACILITIES/SUPPORT: Assistance with accommodation and working papers. 5-day training course with Global TESOL College.

RECRUITMENT: Via CVs or interviews, which sometimes take place in UK.

SCHOOLSTOP

Travessa de Santa Quitéria 34B, 1250 212 Lisbon

+351 918 615364

want-to-teach@schoolstop.pt

www.schoolstop.pt

NUMBER OF TEACHERS: 6.

PREFERENCE OF NATIONALITY: British.

QUALIFICATIONS: CELTA.

CONDITIONS OF EMPLOYMENT: Standard contract is 1 year with 6 working hours per day.

SALARY: Variable.

RECRUITMENT: Interviews are not essential.

CONTACT: Mico Canavarro, Founder & Managing Director.

SELF ESCOLA DE LINGUAS

Rua Bela de São Tiago n° 20, 9060 400 Funchal, Madeira

+351 291 222894; 962 192323

info@e-self.net

www.selfunchal.pt

Schools also in Fogueteiro (Seixal) in Greater Lisbon.

NUMBER OF TEACHERS: 2 full-time and 3 freelancers (working on *faturas-recibo*).

PREFERENCE OF NATIONALITY: Native speakers of English with permission to work.

QUALIFICATIONS: Teachers with teaching or other degree, TEFL or formal teacher training or experience.

CONDITIONS OF EMPLOYMENT: Full-time teachers for 9-month contracts sometimes needed from beginning of academic year. Most vacancies are for part-time teachers to give short-term intensive courses.

SALARY: Variable.

FACILITIES/SUPPORT: School can assist teachers in finding accommodation and has been known to assist financially.

RECRUITMENT: CVs can be submitted by email in Microsoft Word or posted.

CONTACT: Rebecca Jardim, Director of Studies in Fogueteiro.

SPEAKWELL ESCOLA DE LINGUAS

Head office: Praça Mário Azevedo Gomes, N.421, 2775 240 Parede

+351 21 456 1771

speakwell@speakwell.pt

www.speakwell.pt

NUMBER OF TEACHERS: 12 full-time and 40 part-time freelancers for Oeiras, Cascais, Sintra and Lisbon.

PREFERENCE OF NATIONALITY: None, but must be native English speakers.

QUALIFICATIONS: TEFL certificate, preferably plus some business experience, or experience teaching children. Car owners preferred.

CONDITIONS OF EMPLOYMENT: Freelance, with the possibility of full-time hours. School opening times are weekdays and Saturdays. Business trainers and qualified school teachers also required.

SALARY: Above the average hourly rate for Portugal.

FACILITIES/SUPPORT: Good pedagogic and administrative support. Can help new teachers find accommodation through contacts, etc.

RECRUITMENT: Internet, local advertising, word of mouth.

CONTACT: Sue Munnion, Director.

SCANDINAVIA

Certain similarities exist in ELT throughout Scandinavia. The standard of English teaching in state schools is uniformly high, as anyone who has met a Dane or a Swede travelling abroad will know. Yet many ordinary Scandinavians aspire to fluency, so keep up their English by attending evening classes, if only for social reasons. Sweden, Denmark and Norway have excellent facilities for such people, which are variations on the theme of 'folk university', a state-subsidised system of adult education. Classes at such institutions are the ideal setting for enthusiastic amateur teachers.

But, as elsewhere in Europe, the greatest demand for the English language comes from the business community, particularly in Finland, thus enthusiastic amateurs tend to be less in demand than mature professionals. However, as Scandinavia is not a very popular destination for such teachers, despite its unspoilt countryside, efficient public transport and liberal society, there is scope for most kinds of teacher here.

Since Finland and Sweden are EU members, red tape is straightforward for EU teachers. But even in Norway, whose people voted by a referendum not to join, the formalities are straightforward for EU citizens and language institutes employ foreign teachers.

Denmark

There is little recruitment of English teachers outside Denmark, apart from the Cambridge Institute Foundation, which is Denmark's largest EFL institution with a number of branches that specialise in Business English. The Danish government has tightened up the immigration laws, making it virtually impossible for non-EU nationals to get working permits. Many schools expect their teachers to speak Danish, and there seem to be almost enough fully bilingual candidates resident in Denmark to satisfy this requirement. It is worthwhile for any native English speaker with an appropriate background who is staying in Denmark to enquire about part-time openings.

Like Scandinavians generally, Danes are enthusiastic self-improvers, which means that evening classes in English (and hundreds of other things) are very popular. These are purely recreational and are meant to be fun and informal (*hygge* in Danish). *Folkehøjskoler* (folk high schools) offer residential courses of varying lengths where working conditions are generally so favourable that there is very little turnover of teaching staff. The tradition of voluntary organisations, including trade unions, running courses is still strong in Denmark. It might be worth tracking down one of the voluntary organisations that run evening classes countrywide such as the Danish equivalent of Workers' Education, Arbejdernes Oplysnings Forbund or AOF (www.aof.dk). Addresses of the Danish Folkeuniversitet can be found on its website at www.folkeuniversitetet.dk.

Wages in Denmark are set by law and teaching English is no exception. The minimum is DKK170 an hour, and that is what most new arrivals earn. However, once you're established you can expect to earn about DKK220 an hour teaching in the state sector (which is much better funded and resourced than its UK counterpart). Denmark has among the highest taxes in the world, i.e. over 50% until you acquire a tax card (*frikort*), whereupon the rate drops and only earnings over a certain limit are taxed.

If you want to meet English language learners informally in Copenhagen, you could attend one of the Wednesday evening meet-ups organised by Mundo Lingo at Cafe Klaptræet on Kultorvet (www.meetup.com/Mundo-Lingo-Copenhagen-Free-Language-Exchange).

Finland

Although Finland's second language is Swedish, English runs a close second (or third). Finns are admirably energetic and industrious in learning foreign languages, possibly because their own language is so impenetrable (belonging to the Finno-Ugric group of languages along with Hungarian and Estonian). English is taught in every kind of educational institution from trade and technology colleges to universities, in commercial colleges (*kauppaloulu*) and in Civic and Workers' Institutes. Private language schools flourish too and traditionally have not been too fussy about the paper qualifications of their native English-speaker teachers. They seldom teach straight English courses but tailor-make courses for clients, e.g. 'English for presentation skills', so they are not looking for young first-timers to teach their wealthy corporate clients. Still, some private schools (such as Berlitz) may take on native English speakers without a teaching qualification.

Children start their primary education at age seven, and many children between the ages of three and seven are sent to private kindergartens, many of which are English (as well as German, American, etc.). These sometimes welcome a native English speaker with experience of teaching children. (The only skill that concerned one of these nurseries-cum-kindergartens looking to hire a young British graduate was singing.) Local teachers all have an MA degree since this is the minimum requirement. Provision of English is so good in state schools that there is little scope for picking up slack from disgruntled school leavers who feel they can't speak enough English. Neither is there much demand from an immigrant population since there are few foreigners or refugees in Finland compared with Norway or Sweden.

FINDING A JOB

Branches of the long-established Federation of Finnish-British Societies promote local language courses and publicise the availability of freelance tutors; its website www.finnish-britishsocieties.com carries links to English clubs and societies around Finland.

Another big player in the provision of English language teaching is Richard Lewis Communications (RLC), with offices in Finland and Sweden as well as England (see entry). RLC draws most of its students from senior management in both the public and private sectors, and also provides cross-cultural training. Of course not all the teaching takes place in the capital. There is a significant demand for freelance teachers for business in Turku, Oulu and other cities.

Teachers without EU nationality will encounter serious problems. American university students and recent graduates (within two years) over 21 can apply to the American-Scandinavian Foundation (58 Park Avenue, New York, NY 10016; ✆ +1 212 779 3587; www.amscan.org) for assistance in obtaining temporary work permits to cover a self-arranged internship (in Sweden as well as Finland). At one time there was a well-developed programme of teaching placements in Finland but that has expired. It is still worth asking ASF about TEFOL traineeships in Finland for the academic year, from the end of August until the end of May.

The Nordic School based in St Petersburg (see entry) mounts an ambitious series of children's summer schools at 11 different colleges in Finland (several of them Christian establishments) plus one in Sweden, for Russian children aged 7–18 learning English (age range varies among camps). Up to 50 native English speakers are recruited to implement an intensive programme of conversation lessons, at 24 fortnight-long camps. Teachers are given free accommodation and meals plus a wage at the end of each camp, and also offered transport to another location for those working at consecutive camps. The programme has expanded into the other seasons as well as summer. **Anthony Cook** has enjoyed three summers with Nordic School and hopes to do more in the future, which is a positive endorsement:

> ***I heard about the job from a colleague in Moscow who had previously worked for Nordic School. Although I am an experienced EFL teacher, it took me a couple of attempts before a vacancy came up. Since then, however, the school has sent me a list of available camps every year. Although I'm Australian and don't have an EU passport, there were no red tape problems; I suspect it's because staff are technically employed in Russia, which nicely avoids the Eureaucracy.***
>
> ***There are opportunities to use different spaces – including the Finnish outdoors – as your classroom. The lack of a set syllabus makes it essential to bring your own 'bag of tricks'. After my first year I arrived with a large folder full of stuff that I thought might be useful for various ages and levels, which made the experience much easier and more enjoyable.***

The biggest challenge is that you're dealing with four groups: the students of course, the Nordic School management (who are very approachable and helpful – though some of the managers on-site have limited English), the camp instructors and the Finnish staff at the rural colleges where most camps take place. Some camps are very remote, and isolation can be an issue. Ruokolahti camp, for example, is situated far from any town, at the end of a long promontory miles from the mainland, surrounded by a lake. The location is gorgeous – you've never taught anywhere prettier than this! – but the conveniences of city life are quite inaccessible.

I like the fact that Nordic School employs other professionals to look after the students outside of teaching hours. You'll never find yourself staying with a homesick child at night, dealing with minor injuries or removing a teenage girl from a teenage boy's sleeping quarters at 2am – that's someone else's job. If one of the camp instructors is a newbie, the school usually pairs them with a more experienced colleague, so there's generally someone there who knows how to deal with the tricky situations that can arise in camp.

Another fan of Nordic School is freelance writer, blogger and sometime English teacher **Emma Lander,** who spent one summer after university in Finland:

My school sat next to one of Finland's many lakes so in our free time we were able to swim, row boats and explore the forest area around the camp on bikes. As there was nothing around the area (and the bikes and boats were free for teachers) there was nothing really to spend money on, which made it a great place to save the €500 we were paid at the end of each two-week camp. The atmosphere at the school was great; everyone was always excited, active and happy to be there and the students were fun to teach. Because it was a summer school we were free to teach what and how we wanted and we often joined classes together to create big treasure hunts and other fun games.

CONDITIONS OF WORK

Back in the corporate world of Finnish cities, freelance arrangements have largely replaced contracts. A teaching unit of 45 minutes is the norm, with less evening work than elsewhere. Wages are high, but so is the cost of living. Some schools compress the teaching into four days a week, leaving plenty of time for weekend exploration of the country.

Taxes are high and are usually the responsibility of the teacher, whereas contributions should be paid by the employer; social security and unemployment insurance deductions will amount to at least 6% of the salary. Note that there is virtually no possibility of accepting payment 'under the table'. The system is highly controlled and everybody pays his or her taxes.

The Finnish Embassy in London's website (www.finemb.org.uk) has limited information about living and working in Finland. Helsinki has about 35 museums and art galleries plus a high density of sports facilities, ice rinks, etc. The long dark winters are relieved by a wide choice of cheerful restaurants, cafés, bars and clubs in the cities, and saunas almost everywhere.

Norway

The trend in Norwegian EFL is similar to that in Denmark, and most schools rely on a pool of native English speakers already resident in Norway. The instructional supervisor for Berlitz Norway says that he finds it next to impossible to recruit teachers from abroad because: '*They don't have a place to stay, a bank account, a work permit, can't attend interviews or training "next week". On top of this I have so many applicants who have all of these things in place and are in the Oslo area.*' Most jobs are for part-time work and of course do not offer accommodation. At least things are easier from an immigration point of view than they used to be. Although Norway is not a member of the EU, it does allow the free reciprocity of labour so that EU citizens are allowed to work in Norway without a work permit. Immigration restrictions on non-EU teachers remain stringent.

As throughout Scandinavia, the Folkuniversity plays an important role in language tuition in Norway and hires native English speakers, mostly on an occasional basis for *Engelskkurs* (evening classes) (www.folkeuniversitetet.no). There are branches in several hundred Norwegian municipalities, with fairly major teaching operations in Stavanger, Skien, Kristiansand and Hamar. Berlitz (see entry) hires native English speakers with no TEFL background provided they are graduates and successfully complete the Berlitz Instructor Training.

The basic hourly wage is about NOK160, though this can double for high-level business teaching. Expect to lose about a third in deductions.

Casual opportunities may crop up in unpredictable places. **David Moor** was simply intending to spend a month on holiday skiing in Norway, but then he saw an advert in a local supermarket for a native English teacher and jumped at the chance:

> ***A teacher put me up and fed me. I'd intended to stay in the hostel or a cheap hotel, but was finding Norway expensive. I was just working for keep, teaching three days a week, so I had lots of spare time. I had a fantastic time, much better than a normal holiday.***

Sweden

For many years the private EFL market has been in a slow, inexorable decline, as standards of English among school leavers have improved. The Folkuniversity of Sweden has a long-established scheme (since 1955) by which British and other native English speakers may be placed for nine months (one academic year) in a network of adult education centres throughout the country, but it no longer has a policy of actively recruiting applicants from abroad. It takes on new staff who are already resident in Sweden and even then, the work is part-time, at least initially (www.folkuniversitetet.se; look under '*Lediga Jobb*' meaning job openings).

Originally the teaching at the Folkuniversity (FU) consisted of evening classes called a 'study circle', an informal conversation session. Circumstances have changed, however, and the range of pupils can be very varied, from unemployed people to business executives, as well as people who want to prepare for Cambridge examinations or IELTS. People who need English at work are in the majority these days.

FINDING A JOB

Advertisements almost never appear on EFL job sites. Teachers with a solid ELT background might try the main state universities that put on English courses or the language schools listed in the *Yellow Pages* of Stockholm, Malmö, Gothenburg, Orebro and Uppsala. **Charlotte Rosen** decided to do a TEFL course in London before going to Sweden to be with her Swedish fiancé:

> ***I had visited Sweden several times before going to Gothenburg to work. I looked through the* Yellow Pages *for language schools and sent off my CV in English, which wasn't a problem because everyone speaks English really well. I was offered several interviews, including by the British Institute. Many of them said they were interested, but the terms only start in September and January so you have to time your applications quite carefully.***

Another possibility is to try some of the private schools in Sweden (not fee paying, as in Britain), particularly if you are interested in staying in Sweden longer term. The Swedish school system has changed dramatically over recent years and private schools (*friskolor* – free schools) are now plentiful. There are a few English schools within the state system but most of them are independent. Internationella Engelska Skolan (www.engelska.se) is one of Sweden's leading independent English-medium schools, founded by an American, and branches have opened all over the country. The website has detailed information about teacher recruitment which applies primarily to certified subject teachers. The schools follow the Swedish curriculum, are authorised by Skolverket and are free for the students.

Cathryn Lock, who had a Swedish fiancé and a degree from an English university, started working at a secondary school some time ago. She found the job through the national employment service, Arbetsförmedlingen (www.ams.se), sent in a letter of application and was interviewed by the headmaster. Cathryn has since gone on to pass a teacher exam in Sweden.

Although a business background will stand you in good stead, some of the private language schools accept certification, or even just a degree. The British Institute sometimes has vacancies for teachers with the CELTA. Making a breakthrough as a freelancer is difficult without a knowledge of the language, or the Swedish labour market and a functioning network of contacts.

CONDITIONS OF WORK

Teachers must pay tax in Sweden on a scale that varies according to the municipality. Swedish income tax is notoriously high, and the FU estimates that teachers lose about 30% in deductions. However, the upside of paying lots of tax is that Sweden is famous for the quality of its public services, its generous childcare and sick-day policies and its efficient and moderately priced public transport system. Although Swedes groan about tax, they do not often express frustration that their money is 'wasted'. Constructing a lively social life can be a challenge. **Ann Hunter** points out that it can be difficult to make Swedish friends:

> ***The only Swedes you meet regularly are your pupils and the professional relationship can make it awkward to socialise, though after your first term you can get to know ex-pupils quite well. Learning Swedish, if it is possible, is a good way to meet people, though your fellow students are foreigners of course.***

Andrew Boyle had mixed feelings about Sweden and Swedish people:

> ***Sweden is a pleasant place to live, if a little dull at times. It is a generally liberal place, although the increasingly multicultural nature of society is causing Swedes to have to face up to their own prejudices. The students are generally of a high level and although initially quiet not unfriendly and even chatty after they know you a little better.***

Still, once you meet one outgoing Swede you'll find yourself quickly drawn into a group, which manages to avoid the horrific cost of dining out/drinks by sticking to meals and parties in people's homes, trips to free galleries and museums and various meetings of social clubs/interest groups. There are also of course cheaper places to eat out, which you'll discover once you're able to find your way around. Stockholm has a great vibe, although the stylishness of its inhabitants can sometimes be intimidating. Gothenburg has a younger feel, and is the city of choice for hip young Scandinavians (and other nationalities, since the Swedish government is remarkably supportive of promising artists).

Outside the major cities, especially further north, you have to be independent and comfortable with your own company for long periods to enjoy Sweden. During the seven months of the winter the locals either hibernate or devote all their leisure to skiing. Anyone who enjoys outdoor activities will probably enjoy a stint in Sweden, especially ramblers and hill-walkers, who take advantage of the *Allemannsrätt*, the law that guarantees free access to the countryside for everyone. Island hopping around the (car-free) Stockholm archipelago with a tent is an excellent and cheap way to enjoy nature, eat far too many cinnamon buns and lie around in the sun. Summers are usually very warm, certainly more so than in Britain, which is why so many Swedes have an enviable golden tan.

LIST OF EMPLOYERS

DENMARK

BERLITZ LANGUAGE SERVICES SCANDINAVIA
Borgergade 28, 1300 Copenhagen
+45 70 215010
teaching@berlitz.dk
www.berlitz.dk

NUMBER OF TEACHERS: Varies for openings in Norway, Finland, Sweden and Denmark, usually Greater Copenhagen and Southern Sweden.
PREFERENCE OF NATIONALITY: None.
QUALIFICATIONS: Minimum bachelor's degree and/or business-related work experience.
CONDITIONS OF EMPLOYMENT: Freelance basis and mostly part-time. All new trainers must attend compulsory one-week Berlitz training course. Timetable changes from week to week; most teaching takes place in mornings and evenings.
FACILITIES/SUPPORT: No assistance with accommodation given.

CAMBRIDGE INSTITUTE
Vimmelskaftet 48, 1161 Copenhagen K
+45 33 133302
info@cambridgeinstitute.dk
www.cambridgeinstitute.dk

NUMBER OF TEACHERS: 26.
PREFERENCE OF NATIONALITY: British, Irish.
QUALIFICATIONS: Bachelor's degree, TEFL qualification and at least 1 year's TEFL experience abroad.
CONDITIONS OF EMPLOYMENT: 7-month renewable contracts (October to May). Minimum 20 hours per week, students aged 18–70.
SALARY: DKK270 (approx. £30) per teaching hour.
FACILITIES/SUPPORT: Furnished accommodation available in central Copenhagen. Training given.
RECRUITMENT: Direct application from teachers to email address above.
CONTACT: Richard Philp, Principal.

SANWES SPROGINSTITUT APS
Kokholm 1, 6000 Kolding
+45 75 517410
sanwes@sanwes.dk
www.sanwes.dk

Also branch at Andkaervej 19, 7100 Vejle (+45 75 724610).
NUMBER OF TEACHERS: 20–22.
PREFERENCE OF NATIONALITY: British, American, Australian.
QUALIFICATIONS: Should have some business background, be open-minded, cheerful and have lots of initiative. Must have appropriate training and experience.
CONDITIONS OF EMPLOYMENT: Freelance; preferred minimum period 6 months; daytime hours; total number depends on clients.
SALARY: Approximately DKK172 (about £20) per hour.
FACILITIES/SUPPORT: No assistance with accommodation. Pre-service training from other teacher. Help given with work permits.
RECRUITMENT: Local interviews.
CONTACT: Tina McCaffrey, Partner (tina@sanwes.dk).

FINLAND

AAC GLOBAL
Porkkalankatu 20, 00180 Helsinki
+358 9 4766 7800
recruitment@aacglobal.com
www2.aacglobal.com

Offices also in Tampere and Jyväskylä.
NUMBER OF TEACHERS: With growing operations in Sweden and Denmark, the company has over 300 trainers (80 native English speakers) and a total of 7 offices in Finland, i.e. Helsinki, Tampere, Turku, Jyväskylä, Kouvola, Vaasa and Oulu. It trains over 10,000 professionals yearly.
PREFERENCE OF NATIONALITY: British, American and Canadian.
QUALIFICATIONS: University degree plus CELTA/TEFL or equivalent or degree plus business background; teaching experience preferred. Driving licence is an asset.
CONDITIONS OF EMPLOYMENT: Trainers expected to deliver an interesting range of challenging language courses with a multicultural perspective.
FACILITIES/SUPPORT: Possibility of one-way airfare being paid. Induction training provided and a system of head trainers to support the trainers in each language.
RECRUITMENT: Direct application (see careers page of website), newspaper ads and recruitment websites.

MARK RICHARD'S BUSINESS ENGLISH OY
Kaisaniemenkatu 4 A, 00100 Helsinki
+358 9 6124 0362
office@mrbe.net
www.mrbe.net/fi

Sometimes openings outside Helsinki, e.g. Rovaniemi in Lapland.

NUMBER OF TEACHERS: 7 professional trainers.

PREFERENCE OF NATIONALITY: British, Australian or American.

QUALIFICATIONS: Degree plus CELTA or equivalent or PGCE.

CONDITIONS OF EMPLOYMENT: Teachers are freelance.

SALARY: €22–€28 per 45 minutes. Tax rate starts at 20% plus pension contribution of 4.5%.

RECRUITMENT: Interview is essential.

CONTACT: Mark Burton, Managing Director (mark.burton@mrbe.net).

NORDIC SCHOOL

15 Komissara Smirnova Street, Office 301, Saint Petersburg, Russia 194044

+7 812 303 8696; mobile +7 911 295 3187

lena1909@mail.ru

www.nordicschool.ru

Russian language school that has been hiring teachers to teach English to Russian children aged 7–18 in camps in Finland since 2000 (and also in Bulgaria, Greece and Russia).

NUMBER OF TEACHERS: 30–50.

PREFERENCE OF NATIONALITY: UK, Canada, USA, Australia, New Zealand.

QUALIFICATIONS: Teachers should ideally have experience of working with teenagers and should be familiar with conversational teaching/TEFL methods.

CONDITIONS OF EMPLOYMENT: 2–8 weeks for summer camps from mid-June. 1–2 weeks for winter camps; 1 week in spring and autumn camps. Teaching 5–6 hours a day from 9am to 2.15pm or 3.15pm with few breaks. 5 days per week.

SALARY: €400–€500 per fortnight (net) depending on season and number of teaching hours. No transport costs are covered.

FACILITIES/SUPPORT: Full-board accommodation provided in twin rooms and 3–5 meals per day provided.

RECRUITMENT: Mostly through TESL websites, job boards and TESL schools. Applicants should submit CV, application letter, scan of passport and recent photo. Skype or phone interviews acceptable.

CONTACT: Ms Lena Kostenyuk, Director.

RICHARD LEWIS COMMUNICATIONS / RIVERSDOWN LANGUAGES INTERNATIONAL

Westendintie 1, 02160 Espoo, Helsinki

+358 40 0380 439

info.finland@rlcglobal.com

www.riversdown.com/careers

Offices also in Turku, Tampere, Oulu, Jyaskyla and Kuopio and in the UK: Riversdown House, Warnford, Southampton, Hampshire SO32 3LH. RLC has a network of offices worldwide, especially Scandinavia, specialising in cross-cultural and communication skills training and language teaching.

PREFERENCE OF NATIONALITY: British, American, Australian, New Zealander or any native English speaker.

QUALIFICATIONS: University degree and TEFL preferred.

CONDITIONS OF EMPLOYMENT: Freelance work only.

FACILITIES/SUPPORT: Assistance with finding accommodation. New teachers are given thorough training in RLC's methods and cross-cultural tools/courses.

RECRUITMENT: Apply online.

CONTACT: Helen Teppo, Office Co-ordinator (helen.teppo@rlcglobal.com).

NORWAY

BERLITZ A/S

Akersgata 16, 0158 Oslo

+47 22 331030 / 23 003360

info@berlitz.no

www.berlitz.no

NUMBER OF TEACHERS: Varying number of freelancers only. Also has branch in Stavanger.

PREFERENCE OF NATIONALITY: None. Non-Europeans must obtain a contract after the compulsory one-week Berlitz training course and take it to the Ligningskontoret to have 3-month tourist visa extended.

QUALIFICATIONS: Minimum bachelor's degree and/or business-related work experience. Candidates who have business, financial, technical or legal backgrounds are preferred. Must be energetic, outgoing, creative and open to web-based instruction.

CONDITIONS OF EMPLOYMENT: Freelance basis with no guarantee of hours. Timetable changes from week to week; most teaching takes place in mornings and evenings. Offer crash courses in summer.

FACILITIES/SUPPORT: No assistance with accommodation given.

CONTACT: Thea Melberg, Instructor Coach (thea.melberg@berlitz.no).

FOLKEUNIVERSITETET/FRIUNDERVISNINGEN OSLO

Rolf Wickstrom vei 15, 0484 Oslo; PO Box 4293, Nydalen, 0402 Oslo

+47 22 476000

info.ost@folkeuniversitetet.no

www.folkeuniversitetet.no

NUMBER OF TEACHERS: 2 full-time, 8–12 part-time.

PREFERENCE OF NATIONALITY: None, but must be native English speaker.

QUALIFICATIONS: TEFL experience and/or qualification(s) (min. CELTA or equivalent).

CONDITIONS OF EMPLOYMENT: No contracts. Non-EEA residents will need a work permit. Students aged 18–65.

SALARY: Varies according to course (NOK270–300 per 45-minute lesson).

FACILITIES/SUPPORT: No assistance with accommodation, monthly teacher development workshops. Possibility of working at other centres around Norway.

RECRUITMENT: Local interviews only.

CONTACT: Wayne Kelly, Supervisor of English courses (Wayne.Kelly@fuost.no).

LINGU SPRÅKSENTER
Madlaveien 10, 4008 Stavanger
+47 40 300040
stavanger@lingu.no; post@lingu.no
www.lingu.no

NUMBER OF TEACHERS: 6 for clients in Oslo and Stavanger.

PREFERENCE OF NATIONALITY: British, American, Australian, etc.

QUALIFICATIONS: TEFL certification, if not a degree in teaching/English language. Experience with adults as private students and in groups is valuable.

CONDITIONS OF EMPLOYMENT: Freelance. Hours vary according to availability. Some teachers work full-time (28 teaching hours per week) while others work part-time.

SALARY: Hourly pay according to teacher's education and experience.

FACILITIES/SUPPORT: Advice given on finding accommodation but it is not provided.

RECRUITMENT: Vacancies are posted online. Good candidates are called in for an interview and teach a mini-lesson as part of the recruitment process. Skype interviews also possible.

SWEDEN

RICHARD LEWIS COMMUNICATIONS
Riversdown House, Warnford, Hampshire S032 3LH, UK
maria@rlcglobal.com
www.rlc.se

NUMBER OF TEACHERS: 40 in Stockholm, Göteborg, Malmö and Helsingborg.

PREFERENCE OF NATIONALITY: Must be native English speakers.

QUALIFICATIONS: Degree and recognised TEFL qualification essential. Teaching experience in Business English and some personal business experience would be an advantage.

CONDITIONS OF EMPLOYMENT: Various locations in Europe, mainly UK, Finland, Sweden and Germany. Full-time and freelance positions available.

SALARY: Depends on location and experience.

FACILITIES/SUPPORT: Varies depending on location.

RECRUITMENT: Online application process.

CONTACT: Maria Johnsson, Director; Annica Hallberg, General Manager.

SPAIN

Despite having been hit hard by the global recession, or maybe even because of it, Spain continues to offer masses of opportunities for native English teachers. Language schools of every description continue to cater to the enormous demand from young adults just out of school or at university who are now required to prove English proficiency before they can graduate. Demand for preparatory courses for the FCE (First Certificate in English) has skyrocketed. Unemployment is estimated to be a heart-sinking 44% among those under 26, which means that many are keen to fill their time productively and desperate to improve their CVs. Parents continue to push their young children and teenagers into English classes and summer camps, to help them pass school exams and eventually cope with a job market that demands fluency in English more than ever.

The national push to introduce English early continues; it is compulsory in state schools from the first year of primary school. This trend has filtered through to private language providers, many of whom offer courses to very young children. Spanish government-funded schemes to deploy native-speaking conversation assistants throughout the education system have been gathering pace. For example the Madrid Commune employs 1,880 native English speakers as assistants (*auxiliaries*) in both private and public institutions with bilingual programmes.

A fast growing sector of the market is in teaching young children. In fact there is a special category of teacher being sought by CALAC (www.calacschools.es), an association of four language schools in Andalucía, which is for Very Young Children (VYC), as young as three.

Another development that has benefited the English teaching industry is the increasing popularity of applying for European funds to put on English classes in the workplace, as administered by the Fundación Tripartita.

Thousands of foreigners teach English in language schools (*academias*), from the Basque north (where there is a surprisingly strong concentration) to Andalucía in the south and Galicia in the west as well as Madrid and Barcelona. The entries for language schools occupy many pages of the Madrid *Yellow Pages* and in the whole country total about 800 listings in the online *Yellow Pages*. Almost every main street in every Spanish town has an *Academia de Inglés*. *Academias* are privately run and are not regulated by the Ministerio de Educación.

Spain has always been a popular destination for EFL teachers. Who can fail to be attracted to the climate, scenery, history and culture? Economic expansion and increased prosperity in some quarters have brought about a dynamic, fast-paced society, while traditional stereotypes of flamenco and bull-fighting are completely outmoded. New arrivals discover that the various regions, from Asturias to Catalonia, have their own culture and do not consider themselves primarily Spanish at all.

With so many new schools opening to meet rising demand, in some places the ELT business has become very competitive, with academy owners competing for both teachers and students. Some do their best to squeeze out every last euro of profit, which can lead to poor working conditions. In some of the bigger cities a teacher's salary does not go all that far, although it is still possible to have a three-course meal (*menu del día*) with wine for less than €10 outside the big cities. In many parts of Andalucía, if you ask for a *caña* (a small glass of beer) or a glass of *tinto* you're given a decent tapa for free.

While teaching wages probably won't allow you to save much, they are usually enough to support a tolerably comfortable lifestyle. These are points to bear in mind when visions of paella and beaches dance before your eyes.

PROSPECTS FOR TEACHERS

While there are still schools desperate enough to hire any native speaker of English without a TEFL background, respectable schools these days require a solid TEFL certificate. Short/distance learning courses are often frowned upon. Many schools in some major cities echo the discouraging comments made by the director of a well-established school in Barcelona who said that he has found that there is a large supply of well-qualified native English speakers on hand so that his school cannot possibly reply to all the CVs from abroad that it receives as well. Schools report that the number of applications from candidates with a recognised TEFL certificate has increased simply because so many more centres in the UK and worldwide are churning them out.

Many Britons and Irish people still set off for Spain to look for teaching work on spec, preferably before the summer begins or in September, visiting, calling in and emailing their CVs once they get there. Many employers carry out much of their recruitment locally at the last minute, relying on word of mouth and local walk-ins. Less often, schools try to source teachers online. While speaking Spanish is not a must for most jobs, some knowledge of the language is a plus, both for job prospects and quality of life. The usual process in the big cities is to put together a timetable from several sources, and teachers in this situation should be reconciled to the fact that some or all of their employers in their first year will exploit them to some degree. Having said that, those who choose smaller cities or towns, or who stay on for a second or further years, can be choosier.

The situation for non-EU citizens has become almost impossible if they want to work legally in the private sector (see section on Regulations below). An important exception is the NALCA programme operating throughout Spain where a 'bilingual schools' campaign has been implemented. Native English speakers from North America work as assistants in state and private schools, at both the primary and secondary levels. The NALCA programme (North American Language and Culture Assistants in Spain) is administered by the Spanish Ministry of Education (details at www.mecd.gob.es/eeuu/convocatorias-programas/convocatorias-eeuu/auxiliares-conversacion-eeuu.html) and places about 2,500 Americans and Canadians in schools for the academic year October to May. Applicants must have a degree and at least an intermediate knowledge of Spanish; applications open in early January and are due by early April. Assistants receive a monthly allowance (*ayuda mensual*) of €700 (more in Madrid where the academic year finishes at the end of June); see http://comunidadbilingue.educa2.madrid.org/aux.conversacion for details of the Madrid language assistants programme. Note that mediating agencies such as CIEE (www.ciee.org/teach/spain) ease the application process for a fee of $1,100–$2,000. Various companies and organisations are involved with recruitment of native-speaker assistants, such as Multilingual Education Development & Support in Navarra (www.meddeas.com/recruiting-language-assistants-spain), UP International Education (www.upteachinspain.com), which places graduates as assistants in private schools throughout Spain and rewards them with grants of up to €845 per month, the BEDA programme which works with Catholic schools in the Madrid region (www.ecmadrid.org/en/language-assistant), and CAPS (has a directory entry).

The Meddeas programme recruits English speakers at three levels: Advanced are those with a BA in English and education, or a BA plus TEFL Certificate, who receive €912 a month; Graduate level are candidates with any degree, whose grant is €862; and the Speakers Program is for school leavers. Graduates may choose to receive half the grant in addition to accommodation with a host family. Participants on the Speakers Program earn €312 in addition to homestay accommodation and have a lighter load of conversation practice.

Summer language camps (*campamentos de inmersión*) are popular, in which sport and language learning are interwoven for children aged 5–18. For these, native English speakers are recruited in large numbers in March and April to teach the language and to coach sports and/or supervise swimming. Companies to try include ModLang in Zaragoza (www.modlang.es), Red Leaf with camps in Galicia (www.redleaf.es), English YA in Basque country (www.englishya.es), Eurobridge International in Cazoria and Alicante (www.eurobridge.net), McGrogans Summer School (www.mcgroganschool.com) and TECS (see entry).

FINDING A JOB

Because schools run the whole gamut from prestigious to rough-and-ready, every method of job-hunting works at some level. Many independent language schools are run by expatriate Britons and Irish people, and quite a few of these will offer guidance and support for newer teachers, as well as opportunities for further professional development.

IN ADVANCE

Candidates who know that they want to teach in Spain should consider doing their TEFL training with an organisation with strong Spanish links or, better still, do their training in Spain, for example with OxfordTEFL which offers the Trinity CertTESOL training in Barcelona, Malaga and Cadiz (see the Training chapter). This will allow candidates to get to know the country and the specific needs of the students, to take advantage of the job guidance of trainers that know the local job market well, as well as being on the spot for job vacancies. This option is often even cheaper than staying in the UK, given the lower cost of living and the fact that many centres offer a package that includes low-priced accommodation. International House has 15 centres, including in Barcelona, Madrid, and Santander, offering the CELTA course, as do the Chester School and Hyland Language Centre in Madrid, Campbell College in Valencia, and many others around Spain.

A great number of vacancies are advertised online, especially in May/June for an autumn start. For example the key site www.tefl.com carries scores of advertised jobs in Spain. The websites of Spanish language institutes tend to be reasonably transparent (unlike for Portuguese schools) and the majority display an icon 'Work with us' or '*Trabaja con nosotros*'.

At first, **Susie Smith** was anxious that her combined face-to-face and distance learning TEFL Certificate from the TEFL Academy wouldn't cut the mustard on a job hunt in Spain, but concluded that '*while a CELTA is highly desirable, alternative TEFL qualifications aren't a significant hindrance in Spain*'. She accepted the first job she was offered, which was with Sound English (see entry) in beautiful Cantabria, and really enjoyed the calibre of the students and the experience generally.

> ***I loved the buzz I got from my students, especially those who had previously struggled and then had a breakthrough in understanding and ability to communicate. They were excited, and I loved that I was able to facilitate their learning. I also really enjoyed indulging my creativity with my youngest students and then later each evening having much more academic discussions with my C1 and C2 adult classes. Halloween, Christmas and Easter were especially fun as my fellow teachers and I organised special craft lessons for the youngest children, decorated the Academy and wore costumes – something the children delighted in. The youngest students in Spain are generally enthusiastic, fast learners. They typically enjoy classroom activities and progress quickly. Older school-aged students often have to juggle a lot of extracurricular activities and this means that they can be tired by the time they arrive at a language academy.***
>
> ***In addition, the Spanish educational system appears to favour a more directed style of teaching and learning than most British teachers are used to. I found that I needed to modify my own expectations. My adult students were generally studying for educational or professional reasons and were therefore highly motivated. However, as with most adults, they were busy and sometimes struggled to prioritise study outside the classroom. I would highlight the need for perseverance and a hidden store of energy, especially towards Semana Santa before Easter when both students and teachers are a little tired but the term has a way to go.***

Susie is about to embark on a second year of teaching, this time with Kedaro in Huelva (see entry) in southern Spain. She is enjoying the life of a teacher so much that she has decided to apply to train as a certified teacher and is applying to do the PGCE in England in 2017.

For a listing of English language schools in Spain, one source is the *Yellow Pages*, which can be accessed on the internet (www.paginasamarillas.es) – you simply type in 'Academias de Idiomas' and the city or town of interest. You can find a list of members of FECEI, the national federation of private language schools, on the Spainwise website (www.spainwise.net). Some regional branches of FECEI invite CVs and cover letters which they will distribute to member schools with teacher vacancies; one of these in northwestern Spain is ACLID (Asociación Castellano Leonesa de Idiomas; www.aclid.es/trabaja-con-nosotros). On the Spainwise site you'll find current job offers in FECEI schools and details of the annual Spanish TEFL Jobs Fair. Held in mid-May in Córdoba and another a week later in Bilbao, the fairs are a showcase for FECEI schools. Schools from different parts of Spain have stands where teachers can meet employers face-to-face and find out about job opportunities for the following academic year. The fairs are good opportunities to meet lots of employers under one roof, compare what different locations have to offer and conditions offered by different schools, as well as attend talks on such issues as legalities and paperwork, adapting to life in Spain, etc. It's free so, if you're the type who likes to look before you leap, these fairs could provide the answers to many of the questions on your mind. For further details, contact Aidan O'Toole (info@spainwise.net).

ANDY HEATH

Andy Heath tells how he made good use of the Spanish TEFL Jobs Fair.

Fresh out of my CELTA course and with very little idea of what to do next, I was lucky enough to hear about the Spainwise Recruitment Fair in Córdoba, a kind of one-stop shop for TEFL jobs across the country. The only problem was I had already booked a return ticket home. Attending the fair would involve travelling to and from Spain twice in a month, difficult on a teacher's salary, almost out of reach of an unemployed one. I was serious about teaching, though, and equally serious about finding a good place to do it. I'd heard all the scare stories about exploitation, fly-by-night schools and shady operators. The chance to meet dozens of potential employers face-to-face and size them up while they did the same to me seemed too good to pass up.

A month later, as I mulled over three job offers, each in a different province of Spain and each from someone I was sure I would enjoy working with, I knew I'd made the right decision. The school I chose, Academia Blue Door in Córdoba, eased me through all the red tape and helped me with accommodation, as all the schools involved in Spainwise had offered to do. The job itself involved longer hours than you would ever teach without a break in England, but I appreciated the way that teaching in the evenings left mornings and afternoons free to sleep or enjoy life in a new city. A 10 o'clock finish coincides with when most Spaniards finish their dinner and start thinking about which bar to visit afterwards, so you don't miss much nightlife.

The recruitment agency EES Madrid run by Richard Harrison re-opened in September 2016 in Aranjuez, Madrid (✆ +34 602 462 079; richardinmadrid@gmail.com). His Teacher Presentation Service focuses on matching teaching assistants with state day schools in Madrid and other regions of Spain but also deals with standard EFL teaching positions. Applicants must be native speakers from Britain or Ireland with an EU passport and a university degree. The service is free of charge to qualified candidates.

Successful candidates from TtMadrid (see entry in Directory of Training Courses Worldwide; www.ttmadrid.com) are directed to several Madrid agencies such as Pembroke Educational Consultants (www.peceducacion.com). Another corporate language training agency to try is Training Express (see entry), which also offers teaching by telephone and has its principal offices in Madrid, Bilbao and Barcelona.

Although the teaching work in Valencia arranged by My TEFL Experience (see entry) is unpaid, it seems to have provided a very satisfying experience for **Tanvi Warty** who was a surgeon in Mumbai but in 2016 decided to test the waters of changing her profession. In preparation for a break from medicine, she did a 60-hour TESOL course at the TEFL Lab in London and then found this teaching opportunity on the site www.indeed.com.

> ***A simple questionnaire was to be filled out explaining why I wanted to work at the Academia Solidaria, which was followed by an interview. The application process was remarkably easy, and soon I was in Valencia teaching classes of between 5 and 15 students with levels ranging from absolute beginners to an intermediate level. I found myself lacking in terms of time management and lesson planning, but Paul Clare, owner of the Academy, helped me to stop being a teacher who nervously checks the time over and over during a class and become someone who goes through each stage with confidence. This is an ideal environment for new teachers, especially once the Academy implements a short observed training course for new teachers. I found myself confident of taking a decision to change my career and switch from Medicine to Linguistics and a large part of this decision was made during my stint with the Academia Solidaria. It allowed me to realise how much I enjoyed being in a language classroom in spite of all its challenges and demands.***

ON THE SPOT

Most teaching jobs in Spain are still found on the spot. While trying to flee recession in his native Ireland, **Ross O'Brien** was persuaded to give up on his plan to fix up a teaching job in Spain before leaving home:

> ***Mistakenly, I'd decided that I didn't want to leave Ireland until I had secured a job abroad, so every time I opened the advert for the May job fair in Córdoba (sponsored by Spainwise), I would close it again almost instantly, not even considering it. Then my dad talked some sense into me: 'You have to speculate to accumulate!' He was right and I knew it. Cheap Ryanair flights booked, CV uploaded to the Spainwise website and three weeks later I found myself in Córdoba attending the fair.***

Many language schools stipulate that they interview all candidates in person before hiring. The best time to look is between the end of the summer holidays and the start of term, which falls in the first two weeks of October, although you can find jobs in late October too. Since some teachers do not return to their jobs after the Christmas break and schools can find themselves left in the lurch, early January is also possible. Try outlying towns and suburbs if work is scarce in the city centres. In Madrid there are usually at least part-time jobs going most months of the academic year, though after Easter demand dies down. Many schools shut over the summer, but some work can be had in those that remain open, since most of their teachers disappear over the summer too, or teach kids in a number of English summer camps dotted around the country.

Alan Chadwick is convinced that it is better to look for a job after arrival than apply in advance. He has just completed two years of employment at BCN Languages in Barcelona (www.bcnlanguages.com) and is on the whole satisfied with the experience. He teaches with a good crew of about 20 teachers at his branch. Working conditions are reasonably good, with small classes, plenty of freedom in lesson planning and few admin or training requirements, so he finds that he has an easy and comfortable life. He can choose how many hours he teaches (usually 19–22) and the level of students (he prefers advanced adult classes taught on the school premises). His girlfriend Sophie works even fewer hours at her school, leaving time for her freelance graphic design work and for well-paid but occasional work appearing in online advertisements.

Once in Spain, the local press can be useful for tracking down the schools that are permanently recruiting, for example newspapers such as the twice-weekly *Cambalache* in Seville, *La Vanguardia* on Sunday and the daily *Segundamano*. In *El Pais* look in the classified section of the salmon-coloured supplement '*Negocios*', under '*Idiomas*', and in *Segundamano* under '*Ofertas de Empleo – Profesores*'. The classified advert papers *Cambalache* and *Segundamano* are also good for flat hunting.

The website www.madridteacher.com is a comprehensive source of information about teaching opportunities in Madrid (specifically), and also in the rest of Spain. It is run by a group of freelance teachers who teach in small and mid-sized companies, academies, schools and with private students in Madrid. The website www.lingobongo.com is also recommended for both Madrid and Barcelona for teaching jobs and language exchanges.

Local magazines may advertise the possibility of *intercambio*, which means an exchange of English for Spanish or Catalan conversation practice – a great way to meet locals. Some Irish pubs not only offer the opportunity to meet other expats but often organise weekly *intercambio* nights, which will be listed in the English-speaking press. Recommended expat teacher hang-outs in Madrid include J&J Books & Coffee on Wednesdays, Thursdays and Saturdays from 8pm, the Beer Station in Plaza Santo Domingo (Thursdays and Sundays), the Irish Rover in cooperation with Milingual (www.milingual.com) and the Triskel Tavern. For networking purposes you could join the Barcelona TEFL Teachers Association (see their Facebook page). They meet monthly at a bar in Gràcia where you could pick up informal advice about finding a job, living in Barcelona, etc.

Conventional wisdom says that summer is the worst time to travel out to Spain to look for work since schools will be closed and their owners unobtainable. With the recent boom in language learning (especially English) more and more schools are head-hunting for the following academic year before the summer break. With so many no-frills cheap flights on the market, a reconnaissance trip might be worth a gamble.

When knocking on doors, bear in mind that most language academies will be closed between 2pm and 4pm, when directors are invariably away from their desks. Leave a smartly produced CV with a local mobile telephone number. It is a very good idea to buy a mobile or at least an inexpensive local SIM card with a local number for your own phone. A serious director will probe into claims of experience and will soon weed out any bogus stories. Other directors are just checking to see that you are a reasonable proposition or at least not a complete dud.

For qualified teachers, opportunities abound. For the untrained, a more probable scenario is that they will elicit some mild interest from one or two schools and will be told that they may be contacted right at the beginning of term and offered a few hours of teaching as course start dates loom. It can become a war of nerves; anyone who is willing and can afford to stay on has an increasingly good chance of becoming established.

The great cities of Madrid and Barcelona act as magnets to thousands of hopeful teachers. Barcelona is full of teachers who have arrived after a less-than-happy year elsewhere in the world, spent in jobs to which they committed themselves sight unseen. There are language academies all over the country and a door-to-door job hunt in the area of your choice usually pays off for those willing to play a waiting game.

FREELANCE TEACHING

As usual, private tutoring can pay better than contract teaching because there is no middle man. Rates start at €20 an hour in the main cities and go up to €50. **Alan Chadwick** based in Barcelona is toying with the idea of going freelance to free up time for other pursuits. He would like to offer an evening class to about six learners, but of course would need premises. Teaching in the spare room of his flat would not be professional enough. Lots of people give private lessons in quiet cafés and parks, but that is trickier with a group. He could rent an office space for €150 per month and buy a whiteboard, but hasn't yet taken the plunge when he enjoys the reliability of the income he earns from teaching at an institute.

Freelance teachers must register as an *Autonomo* for tax purposes, i.e. an independent professional. *Autonomos* must pay a flat rate of €265 per month to cover compulsory social security contributions, no matter how little they earn.

It can be difficult starting up without contacts and a good knowledge of the language; and when you do get started it is difficult to earn a stable income due to the frequency with which pupils cancel. The problem is particularly acute in May when undergraduates and school pupils concentrate on preparing for exams and other activities fall by the wayside. Spaniards are fond of taking off extra days to link a mid-week fiesta with the weekend, known as *puente*, meaning bridge.

Getting private lessons is a marketing exercise and you will have to explore all the avenues that seem appropriate to your circumstances. Obviously you can advertise on noticeboards at universities, EOIs (*Escuelas Oficial de Idiomas*), community centres (*centros cívicos*), public libraries, corner shops and wherever you think there is a market. Major stores are a good bet, for example Alcampo supermarkets. A neat notice in Spanish along the lines of '*Profesora nativa de inglés da clases particulares a domicilio*' might elicit a favourable response. Introduce yourself at local state schools and ask them to pin up a notice broadcasting your willingness to ensure the children's linguistic future. Compile a list of addresses of professionals (e.g. lawyers, architects, etc.) as they may need English for their work and have the wherewithal to pay for it. Try export businesses, distribution companies, perhaps even travel agencies. Make the acquaintance of language teachers who will know of openings and advertise your availability on free ads websites, Craigslist, etc.

Because private classes can be better paid than institute teaching, they are in much demand, including by contract teachers, some of whom are engaged in some private tutoring. You could arrange a school contract with no more than 15 or 20 hours and supplement this with private classes, which are lucrative though unstable.

LIVE-IN POSITIONS

Some excellent programmes exist to place young people in families to do some tutoring in exchange for board and lodging. People from outside the EU who want to experience Spanish culture might like to consider a live-in position with a family who wants an English tutor for the children or a voluntary position as an English assistant on summer language/sports camps. Further details may be sought from Relaciones Culturales, the youth exchange organisation at Calle Ferraz 82, 28008 Madrid (✆ +34 91 541 7103; www.worktravelstudy inspain.com), which places native English speakers aged 18–40 with Spanish families who want to practise their English in exchange for providing room and board; the placement fee is €300.

Several American organisations, including InterExchange in New York (www.interexchange.org), arrange Teach in Spain programmes whereby fee-paying young Americans (mainly women) live with a family in exchange for speaking English and providing 15 hours of tutoring a week for 1–3 months; fees start at $795.

CHRISTOPHER WEEKS

One New Year's Day Chris Weeks noticed an advertisement on the useful job site www.jobsabroadbulletin.co.uk and decided 'New year: new start'.

I thought the volunteer programme would suit someone like me with no prior TEFL experience (though I had done a 140-hour online TEFL course with i-to-i).

In exchange for a room and food (all freshly home-cooked by the father of the family, José), I was expected to undertake English-speaking activities with the children for 15 hours each week. These ranged from homework help to English language games. The only problem I faced was tantrums and tears on occasion from the three-year-old, but she was cute so all could be forgiven.

My teaching was in the evenings so I was able to explore Madrid by day and undertake Spanish lessons at a great academy. I got to meet the extended family including Grandma, and went on holiday with the family to Andalucía, which was a great experience. I was made to feel very welcome despite my lack of Spanish. The low point was the weather. Unfortunately that year saw the coldest winter on record – it even snowed in Madrid in March, which was unheard of.

The contact through which Christopher organised the family stay is now called Culture Go Go and leaves subscribers to arrange their stays directly with host families (see entry). After his volunteer placement, Chris investigated finding paid work in Madrid and had plenty of offers of interviews. But he had a ticket to Glastonbury that he didn't want to sacrifice and this made it hard to land a longer-term job. He concludes: *'Madrid is a vibrant and exciting city which I may well return to in the future to live and work.'*

REGULATIONS

Until the UK actually exits the European Union, British teachers are subject to EU regulations. All EU teachers working on contract should possess a resident permit (*Certificado de registro de ciudadano de la Union*) and a foreigner ID number (NIE), which can be obtained from the Foreigners' Office (Oficina de Extranjeros) in the province of residence or at a designated police station (http://extranjeros.empleo.gob.es/es). A contract will not be issued until you have applied for an NIE (*Número de Identidad de Extranjero*). The application charge is €15. Since 2012, it has been necessary to demonstrate that you have medical insurance while in Spain and that you have an income of at least €400 a month, either from your employer, as a registered self-employed worker or from independent means (a credit card might be sufficient accompanied by a letter from your bank that you are well under the credit limit). If you are working legally, you will automatically be registered with the Social Security system for medical treatment; otherwise you will have to show a private policy that satisfies their requirements.

At present, the procedure for applying for a first-time Residency Certificate and NIE is as follows: go to the Oficina de Extranjería (which in Madrid can be found at Calle Manuel Luna, 29, 28020 Madrid near metro station Tetuán; ✆ +34 912 72 95 00) preferably after booking an appointment, though this is not always necessary. Beforehand you should download, fill out and print the form EX-15, the *Solicitud de Número de Identidad de Extranjero (NIE) y Certificados*. Otherwise pick up and complete the form on arrival. At the office you will be given a form to fill out, again with your personal information, which you must take to the nearest bank and pay the required fee. Return to the office to wait to collect your NIE, initially valid for three months but which can be extended to five years. With your NIE and passport, you can then go to the Social Security Office (Seguridad Social) to apply for a Social Security Number, with completed form *Modelo TA1* (www.seg-social.es). Your employer should be able to advise you on all the steps. The NIE is an important form of identification for filing taxes, establishing a business, opening a bank account and so on. All people with an address in Spain, including foreigners, are obliged to register at the *padrón* office in their local town hall (*ayuntamiento*), which is free of charge.

Some long-stay foreigners engage a specialist lawyer called a *Gestoria Administrativa* to assist in navigating the bureaucracy. Spain Expat (www.spainexpat.com) has pages of useful information about living and working in Spain, while the online community www.eyeonspain.com has some busy forums. Alternatively, teacher recruitment agencies like Spainwise can advise.

The immigration situation for people from outside the European Union is not at all easy. Most of the institutes that once hired North Americans now refuse to tackle the lengthy procedures involved in obtaining work permits. If inspectors discover illegal workers, the penalty for the company can be as much as €20,000. Berlitz cautions: '*Unfortunately, the European Union (EU), of which Spain is a part, seldom issues work permits to non-EU citizens unless they are married to an EU citizen.*' Americans with Irish or Italian ancestry often prefer to chase the papers that will get them a passport from an EU member state.

As mentioned above, the main exceptions for North Americans are the NALCA programme for Canadians and Americans, and also summer schools where the period of work is shorter than the 90-day validity of a Schengen tourist visa. Non-EU citizens may also live with Spanish families free of charge in exchange for tutoring the children in English. The Youth Mobility visa allows Canadians (18–35) and Australians (18–30) to work for up to a year; the Canadian quota for the year is 1,000.

The TEFL training company TtMadrid mentioned above has designed a combination of TEFL training course with Spanish language tuition which makes non-EU nationals eligible for a student visa and therefore able to live and work in Spain for up to 12 months. This Teaching and Cultural Immersion programme costs a cool €3,600; see further details at www.ttmadrid.com/course/spanish-teaching-and-cultural-immersion-program. Non-EU citizens who have studied for at least three years in Spain on a student visa can convert their visa into a work visa.

None of this means that there aren't any Americans or other nationalities teaching in Spain without permits. Many post-Hemingway Americans go to Spain for a year to learn the language and discover the romance of Spain. The teacher-training schools in major cities are full of American as well as British trainees, and Americans, Australians and New Zealanders also find work, not just teaching private classes but through numerous intrepid academies that hire them off-contract and send them off to teach in companies rather than on school premises. Any non-EU nationals who work on a tourist visa will have to renew it every three months by leaving the Schengen zone for 90 days. A new independent company called COMO Consulting run by two young American expats can advise on moving to Spain to live and work (www.comoconsulting-spain.com) for varying consultation fees.

The standard contribution to social security (*seguridad social*) is 6.35% of earnings. Together with taxes, which vary from month to month but will be less than 10%, the total deductions from a gross wage average 14%. People who are deemed resident for tax purposes are generally defined as those who live in Spain for more than 183 days in each calendar year. However, www.spainexpat.com suggests that in many cases you only need to file a tax return in Spain when you make more than €22,000 per year; unlikely if you are a language teacher. You do need to pay social security contributions if you earn more than €9,080 (equivalent to the national minimum wage). Currently, Spain and Britain have a double taxation treaty so Britons can't be taxed twice. Under EU legislation, language schools must give contracts and make contributions for all staff, whether full-time or part-time. In practice, this does not always happen. The majority of contracts are for nine months (October to June) but teachers receive an extra month's salary as holiday pay.

After 12 months of paying contributions you are eligible to claim *el paro* (unemployment benefit). Teachers on nine-month contracts have to work for two years before they can claim. Many claim when their second contract ends in June to sustain them over the summer, though this can be done only if you remain in Spain and don't (for example) leave to teach summer courses in your home country. Applications must be filed within 15 days of the end of your contract at the office of SEPE (*Servicio Público de Empleo Estatal*). For every year worked, you can claim four months of *el paro* usually at a rate of 75% of your wage.

CONDITIONS OF WORK

Most schools offer €1,100–€1,300 gross for 25 hours of teaching a week. Perks at the better schools include 2–3 weeks of paid holiday. A standard hourly wage for starter teachers would be €14, although some pay more than €20. Better hourly wages are paid to registered freelancers sent out to firms.

Spanish TEFL is no different from TEFL in other countries in that there are always some employers who offer low pay, long hours and poor conditions. For example, teachers have discovered that pay has been deducted when they have been unavoidably absent or that their bonuses have been withheld with no explanation. Your contract should guarantee a minimum number of hours.

BARRY O'LEARY

Barry O'Leary wrote from Seville in his third year of teaching there. In his first year he worked for a slightly disorganised and crafty academy where there was no mention of a contract, classes started at 8am and staggered throughout the day until 10pm and it was difficult to predict how much he would earn from month to month because he wasn't paid for local holidays. Luckily, in his second year, after mingling with the other expat teachers, he was able to land himself a job with a more professional establishment where he worked fixed hours in blocks from 4pm until 10pm, Monday to Thursday, leaving the mornings free, and with excellent ongoing training sessions on Friday mornings. The language school is one of the most successful in Seville with 12 academies scattered throughout the city and it takes care of its teachers, offering fixed contracts with long-term prospects.

The students, who are often passionate and keen to learn English, range in age from six to sixty so there is never a dull moment. Classes have a maximum of 12, all material is provided and there is scope to move away from the syllabus now and then. A lot of extra work is necessary in February and June when the exams take place but it's worth the agony.

Life in Seville is fun and varied, with an abundance of festivals including the religious Semana Santa and the livelier Feria. The city is a great place to live and a base for exploring Andalucía. Evenings can be spent in the many bars enjoying tapas, watching flamenco or Sevillanas (a local dance) or just mingling with the locals. Seville is generally safe and with the year round blue skies, it's a great place to brush up on your Spanish and experience a different way of life.

As always, you can gain an idea of an employer's integrity by talking to other teachers as well as by using your intuition at the interview. Asking lots of questions is a good idea since then you can find out your pay and minimum/maximum hours so that you will be in a stronger position to argue, should your employer try to mess you around. But realistically, many new arrivals feel exploited at least in some respects in their first year. **Laura Phibbs** was spared the possibility of being exploited, since her promised job evaporated overnight:

> ***The Madrid school director rang me to inform me that I had got the job and I was to start nine days later. When, as instructed, I rang to confirm the arrival time of my plane, I was told that there was no job for me after all since the school had gone bankrupt. I think what really made me angry was that I had rung him rather than the other way round. He did not even say sorry or sound in the least remorseful.***

It is possible that the bankruptcy was just an excuse in the face of insufficient pupils. There's far less demand for English during the summer months (apart from at summer camps), hence the near-universality of nine-month contracts. Most people find it impossible to save enough in nine months to fund themselves abroad for the rest of the year. Most pay agreements also already include the bonuses (*pagas extraordinarias*) that have already been adjusted pro-rata, of which there are two or three a year. Legal schools will pay *finiquito* (holiday pay) at the end of a contract, which should be equivalent to the pay for two and a half days of every month worked, based on your base (not full) salary.

The experience of teaching at a summer camp can be enjoyable and lucrative. The pay is generally fair (say, €800–€1,000 for a four-week stint plus free board and accommodation, rising to €1,200, including accommodation, if you're particularly fortunate) though some organisations offer little more than accommodation, meals and pocket money. **Glen Williams** describes his summer job at a summer language camp in Izarra in the Basque Country:

> ***The children learned English for three hours in the morning with one half-hour break (but not for the teacher on morning snack duty trying to fight off the hordes from ripping apart the bocadillos). Then we had another three or four hours of duties ranging from sports and/or arts to shop/bank duty. For many of us, inexperienced with dealing with groups of kids, there were a few problems of discipline. It was the kids' holiday and they quickly cottoned on that we English teachers in general were a bunch of hippie types.***

PUPILS

For a long time, Spaniards had the reputation for being somewhat challenged at learning languages. But now in the main cities, so many people speak decent English that foreign teachers find it hard to practise their Spanish. Often adult learners are more motivated than children. This was one of **David Bourne**'s biggest problems and one that he thinks is underestimated, especially as a high proportion of English teaching in some academies is with children and teenagers:

> ***I have found that a lot of the younger students only come here because their parents have sent them in order to improve their exam results. The children themselves would much rather be outside playing football. There are days when you spend most of the lesson trying (unsuccessfully in my case) to keep them quiet. This is especially true on Fridays. I have found it very hard work trying to inject life into a class of bored 10-year-olds, particularly when the course books provided are equally uninspiring.***

In such cases it might be a good idea to change your aim from teaching them English to entertaining them (and paying your rent). If students don't want to learn, you will only break your heart trying to achieve the impossible.

Adults are usually an easier proposition, willing to listen and think and with a good sense of humour. In general the Spanish will welcome opportunities to speak animatedly in class and express their opinions. A good knowledge of Spanish is helpful if not essential when teaching junior classes, as **Peter Saliba**, director of a language school in Malaga, explains:

We need teachers with a fluent command of Spanish, not the typical grasp of elementary phrases which may get them by in a social context. On a limited two or three hours per week teaching timetable, there simply is not time for cumbersome English explanations of English grammar and vocabulary. It is worse still with young learners and teens, who will 'run riot' or at the very least run circles round non-Castilian speaking teachers.

Needless to say, Spaniards are a nation of talkers. If things seem to be going awry in your classes, for example students turning up late or being inattentive, don't hesitate to make your feelings known, just as Spaniards do.

ACCOMMODATION

Rents usually swallow up at least a quarter of a teacher's income, more in the big cities and much more if you don't share. In small towns, it is not uncommon for schools to arrange accommodation for their teachers at least for an initial period. The director at a language school in the small Galician town of Marin estimates a modest starting rent of €150 per person in a shared flat, plus bills. **Alan Chadwick** reported recently that the standard price for a room in a shared house in Barcelona is €300 a month, which is often inclusive of all bills and internet. Spanish students sometimes want to share with English speakers, so check language school, EOI and university noticeboards for flat shares. Some teachers even arrange to share a flat rent-free in exchange for English lessons.

When renting a flat expect to pay a month's rent in advance, plus one or two months' rent as deposit. Since your first pay cheque may not arrive until November, you should arrive with £1,000+ to tide you over. Try to avoid using an *inmobiliaria* (letting agency), which will charge a further month's rent (at least). Be aware of the agencies or associations with seedy premises that charge you a fee before showing you anything. You will quickly distinguish their ads from private ones in the classifieds. In Madrid and Barcelona many people use the free ads paper *Segundamano*; if you do decide to compete for a flat listed in a paper or on a community noticeboard, get up early, since most decent flats are snapped up quickly. It is easier flat hunting in July/August than in September/October or February.

LEISURE TIME

Once you acquire some Spanish, it is very easy to meet people, since Spaniards are so friendly, relaxed and willing to invite newcomers out with them. Of course there is also a strong fraternity of EFL teachers almost everywhere, and some teachers find it tedious socialising almost exclusively with English teachers. As your Spanish improves, you will probably end up socialising with both groups in bars, at parties, *romerías* (pilgrimages), fiestas, etc.

If you're looking for traditional Spanish culture, don't go to Madrid, and certainly don't look for it in Barcelona, which is not Spanish at all but Catalan. Seville, Granada and Valencia are lovely Spanish cities. While teaching in Andalucía, **Joanna Mudie** appreciated the chance to learn about the traditional dances of Spain, e.g. Sevillanas, Malagueras and Pasadoble.

Rona Mackenzie was clearly enjoying a good quality of life while teaching at the Academia Blue Door in Córdoba:

So here I am, a few years down the line, loving my life in Spain. I still get driven to distraction by certain things. I will never get used to the lack of queuing, and the haphazard way in which certain things are dealt with can be very frustrating. But the climate, the wonderful people, the laid-back lifestyle, the food and the fiestas more than make up for that. Everything they say about Spain is pretty much true and I love this country. If you want to teach in Spain, go for it. Come with an open mind, a relaxed attitude, a willingness to learn the language and a serious commitment to hard work and you will doubtless love it. ESL teaching can be for anyone, at any age, as long as your attitude is right. I still miss a Sunday roast sometimes, but the food here's amazing. And I've found a shop where they stock Tetley's tea!

Glen Williams describes his spare-time activities in Madrid, a city with an enormous variety of nightlife where he was clearly enjoying himself to the full:

Madrid is a crazy place. We usually stay out all night at the weekend drinking and boogying. During the gaps in my timetable (10am–2pm and 4pm–7pm) I pretend to study Spanish (I'm no natural) and just wander the back streets. I suppose I should try to be more cultural and learn to play an instrument, write poetry or look at paintings, but I never get myself in gear. I think most people teach English in Spain as a means to live in Spain and learn the Spanish language and culture. But there is a real problem that you end up living in an English enclave, teaching English all day and socialising with English teachers. You have to make a big effort to get out of this rut. I am lucky to live with Spanish people (who do not want to practise their English!).

Of course Barcelona continues to lure many thousands of young expats. One of the best ways to get around the city is to join the shared bicycle scheme (BICING, pronounced 'bee-sing') for €47 a year. The city has a great nightlife, a beach and interesting markets. **Alan Chadwick** and **Sophie Wainwright** recommend going to the trendy flea market in the Raval area on the first Sunday of the month. While visiting, they were approached by a woman recruiting people to be in corporate promotional films. Sophie has been doing occasional filming work since. For example, she was paid €800 to be in a classy ad for Voll-Damm beer. An English friend of theirs appeared in an advert for a US cough syrup and was paid €2,000 for a fleeting appearance.

If the idea of teaching in Spain appeals at all, it is almost always a rewarding and memorable way for people with limited work experience to finance themselves as they travel and live abroad for a spell.

'The reason I wanted to do a CELTA course was because it is literally a passport to the world. No matter which country you want to stay in, you are very employable after completing the CELTA course.' **Kim – Hong Kong**

'Armed with the information we were given on job hunting (they didn't just kick us out the door), I ploughed on, vowing to give it one more week. On a CELTA course there is no time for procrastination. I would have previously considered myself a procrastinator, a perfectionist. I taught my first private class the very next day. I lined up three interviews with schools that same week.' **Muirne – Ireland**

'The CELTA course at Clic taught me how to be a good teacher in four gruelling but hugely rewarding weeks, and it is amazing to see these new skills put into practice in the classroom.' **Rebecca – Ireland**

LIST OF EMPLOYERS

ACADEMIA ANJO

Rua Rosalía de Castro 32, 27880 Burela, Lugo
+34 982 585593
angela.clare.ball@hotmail.com; director@academiaanjo.es

NUMBER OF TEACHERS: 4.

PREFERENCE OF NATIONALITY: None, but must have EU passport.

QUALIFICATIONS: Ideally candidates will have a view to a career in teaching and have teaching experience, a degree in languages and/or a reputable TEFL qualification.

CONDITIONS OF EMPLOYMENT: 9-month contract; working hours normally 3.30–9/9.30pm.

SALARY: €900-€1,300 (net) depending on experience, with accommodation provided.

FACILITIES/SUPPORT: Accommodation is provided; teachers pay for utilities. School helps teachers obtain a NIE and register for social security. Contributions are made amounting to €300–€400 a month.

RECRUITMENT: Via ads on www.tefl.com. Skype or telephone interviews.

CONTACT: Angela Clare Ball, Director.

ACADEMIA BLUE DOOR

C/Alhaken II, 6, 14008 Córdoba
+34 957 491535
recruitment@bluedoorspain.com; info@spainwise.net
www.bluedoorspain.com

NUMBER OF TEACHERS: 12.

QUALIFICATIONS: Native speakers of English with university degree and TEFL qualifications.

CONDITIONS OF EMPLOYMENT: Student groups no larger than 6. Contracts are from the end of September to the end of June.

SALARY: School offers a competitive package with salary above national pay agreements plus full national health and social security cover.

RECRUITMENT: Blue Door is a member of ACEIA and FECEI, and recruits at the Spainwise annual recruitment fair in May (www.spainwise.net).

CONTACT: Aidan O'Toole, Director (+34 692 613687).

ACADEMIA BRITANICA (INTERNATIONAL HOUSE CÓRDOBA)

C/Rodriguez Sanchez, 15,14003 Córdoba
+34 957 470350
info-cordoba@acabri.com
www.cordoba.acabri.com

NUMBER OF TEACHERS: 20, also for branch in Huelva.

PREFERENCE OF NATIONALITY: EU member state passport holders who can get residence permits easily.

QUALIFICATIONS: A or B in CELTA plus minimum 1 year's experience, especially in teaching younger learners.

CONDITIONS OF EMPLOYMENT: 9-month contracts, mid-September to mid-June, 22–25 hours per week. Majority of students are aged 4–17.

SALARY: Monthly average around €1,600 gross. Average 12% tax; 6.5% social security deductions.

FACILITIES/SUPPORT: Help with finding accommodation. Residence permits are applied for by the school and the teacher is accompanied to the permits office soon after arrival.

RECRUITMENT: Through IH recruitment system, or locally. Interviews in the UK for teachers recruited through IH World.

CONTACT: Simon Armour, Director of Studies (simon@acabri.com).

AMERICAN LANGUAGE ACADEMY

Plaza Conde del Valle de Suchil 15–17, 28015 Madrid

+34 91 445 5511

efl@americanlanguage.es

www.americanlanguage.es

NUMBER OF TEACHERS: 30 for summer and academic year positions.

PREFERENCE OF NATIONALITY: EU or non-EU with permission to work or with student visa. Canadians and Australians on Youth Mobility Visas are welcome to apply.

QUALIFICATIONS: Native speaker with BA degree or currently enrolled as an undergraduate, and language teaching qualifications (CELTA or TEFL). Prefer minimum 1 year's experience, though entry level positions open to candidates willing to take academy's own intensive training course.

CONDITIONS OF EMPLOYMENT: 1-year contract in first instance. Mostly block hours in mornings or evenings for a maximum of 28.5 teaching hours per week. To start July or September/October. Mostly teaching adults.

SALARY: Minimum €1,200–€1,350 per month (net) for average 26.5 hours per week.

FACILITIES/SUPPORT: No help with accommodation. Visa advice given to North American teachers. Lots of teacher resources and support.

RECRUITMENT: CV (no later than April), application form and personal or skype interview in Madrid including brief demo class. Interviews are held up to the end of May for positions beginning in October.

CONTACT: Jeffrey Locey, Director of Studies, Sergio Domene, Academic Coordinator and Language Consultant.

ASTEX SERVICIOS LINGUISTICOS

C/Hermanos Bécquer 7–6°, 28006 Madrid

+34 91 590 4921 / 3474

aslpedagogico@astex.es

www.astex.es

NUMBER OF TEACHERS: ASTEX employs around 350 ESL teachers at any one time, and usually hires 30 new teachers each September/October, with vacancies needing to be filled throughout the year. More than 50% of its classes are phone lessons which can be given from anywhere in the world.

PREFERENCE OF NATIONALITY: Native English speakers with EU citizenship or permission to work.

QUALIFICATIONS: Require CELTA or equivalent and minimum 2 years' EFL teaching experience. For telephone classes a specific training course (2 sessions of 3 hours) must be completed.

CONDITIONS OF EMPLOYMENT: 9-months contract/20–25 hours per week.

SALARY: Contracted teachers earn €17–€17.50 gross; freelancers earn €23–€24 gross.

FACILITIES/SUPPORT: Teachers' room: library, computers (free internet) and printer. Free workshops for teachers.

RECRUITMENT: Ads on www.madridteacher.com. Interview required.

CONTACT: David Warner (dwarner@astex.es); Kerry Rose (krose@astex.es).

AVILA CENTRE OF ENGLISH

Bajada de Don Alonso 1, 05003 Avila

info@avilacentreofenglish.com

www.avilacentreofenglish.com

NUMBER OF TEACHERS: 8.

PREFERENCE OF NATIONALITY: Any country where English is spoken as a standard language. Applicants must have automatic right to work in Spain.

QUALIFICATIONS: Minimum 2 years in mainstream TEFL, preferably in Spain, plus relevant degree and proper EFL training course.

CONDITIONS OF EMPLOYMENT: 9 months minimum. Usual hours are Monday to Thursday.

SALARY: Minimum salary (Scale II) is €1,300 gross.

FACILITIES/SUPPORT: Assistance given with accommodation search and temporary stay in hotel paid for while searching. Teachers are offered a variety of ongoing training opportunities every year, and costs are covered, along with transport where applicable. Some teachers have the chance to develop their own trainer talents and take part as presenters at relevant events.

RECRUITMENT: Via www.tefl.com, Spainwise Job Fair and website, and www.aclid.es. Speculative applications are not welcome, only applications in response to advertisements for specific vacancies.

CONTACT: Noni Gilbert Riley, Director.

BERLITZ (ESCUELAS DE IDIOMAS BERLITZ DE ESPAÑA)
HQ, Enrique Granados 6, Complejo Empresarial IMCE, 28223 Pozuelo de Alarcón. Recruitment office: Calle Jose Ortega y Gasset 11, 1° Izq, Barrio de Salamanca, 28006 Madrid
+34 91 577 7259
teach@berlitz.es
www.berlitz.es

Many centres in Spain, including Madrid (with few vacancies), Barcelona, La Coruña, Santander, Huesca and Seville.

NUMBER OF TEACHERS: Berlitz Spain employs approx. 100 native speakers.

PREFERENCE OF NATIONALITY: EU (for paperwork reasons).

QUALIFICATIONS: Degree level of education; TEFL qualification preferred though Berlitz provides 1-week compulsory training.

CONDITIONS OF EMPLOYMENT: 9-month contracts. Depending on contract type, hours range from an average of 9 (smallest part-time) to 28 hours (full-time) per week, but can vary. Schedules are also quite varied.

SALARY: Depends on which of 6 contract types. Sample contract pays €1,400 (gross) for one-to-one classes, €1,650–€1,800 for group courses. For first-year teachers, total deductions are around 9%.

FACILITIES/SUPPORT: Compulsory training usually in early October. No assistance with accommodation.

RECRUITMENT: Via adverts on various Spanish websites. Face-to-face interviews essential.

CONTACT: Simon Williamson, Country Manager of Instruction.

BRITISH SCHOOL
Plaza Ponent, 5–2nd floor, 43001 Tarragona
+34 977 211605
british@bstarragona.com
www.bstarragona.com

NUMBER OF TEACHERS: 5.

PREFERENCE OF NATIONALITY: Native English speakers with EU member state passport.

QUALIFICATIONS: University degree, CELTA or Trinity EFL qualification and minimum 1 year's experience teaching English abroad. Intermediate Spanish or Catalan would be an advantage.

CONDITIONS OF EMPLOYMENT: October to June, 21 class hours per week.

SALARY: Gross salary €1,190 per month for 21 class hours a week; end-of-contract bonus €234.

FACILITIES/SUPPORT: First week's accommodation paid in hotel; school video and book libraries.

RECRUITMENT: Internet with telephone interview.

CONTACT: Joe Hayes, Director.

BVRNS ACADEMY
Kalebarria 44–46 bajo, Durango, 48200 Vizcaya
+34 946 203668
info@bvrnsacademy.com
www.bvrnsacademy.com

NUMBER OF TEACHERS: 5.

PREFERENCE OF NATIONALITY: British, native English speakers; also bilingual French-English.

QUALIFICATIONS: Degree, TEFL qualification and experience. Teachers should be cheerful, lively, genuinely interested in teaching and enjoy working with both children and adults. Some knowledge of Spanish preferable.

CONDITIONS OF EMPLOYMENT: Standard 9-month contract. Students vary from young children to mature adults. Courses are grouped according to their level and age and take place mainly in the afternoon and evening (some in the morning). Maximum 8 in a class. 23 teaching hours per week.

SALARY: €1,325 per month for academic year. Bonus at the end of the course €500 on successful completion of contract.

FACILITIES/SUPPORT: Shared furnished room in a flat available for rent of about €270 monthly plus bills.

RECRUITMENT: Initial enquirers should send CV and recent photograph. Telephone interview required.

CONTACT: Ana Lopez, Director.

CAMBRIDGE ENGLISH STUDIES
Avenida de Arteixo 8–1°, 15004 A Coruña
+34 981 160216
www.cambridgeenglishstudies.com

NUMBER OF TEACHERS: 12 teachers, 8 in Coruña and 4 in Ferrol.

QUALIFICATIONS: EU citizens with a recognised TESOL qualification (e.g. CELTA/Trinity College London/RELSA).

CONDITIONS OF EMPLOYMENT: Contracts run from mid-September to end June, teaching 25 hours per week.

SALARY: Basic net salary is €1,000 per month plus increments for experience and qualifications. Taxes and social security paid by the school.

RECRUITMENT: Interviews required, but telephone interview is acceptable.

CAMBRIDGE HOUSE
C/Lopez de Hoyos, 95 1°A, 28002 Madrid
+34 91 519 4603/681 346677
teachers@cambridge-house.com
www.cambridge-house.com

NUMBER OF TEACHERS: 35 for 6 schools in central Madrid.

PREFERENCE OF NATIONALITY: British or Irish teachers. Non-EU teachers must already have their working papers.

QUALIFICATIONS: University degree, CELTA certificate and a minimum of 6 or 12 months' teaching experience.

CONDITIONS OF EMPLOYMENT: The average length of contract is 9 months (October to June) but summer work is available to teachers who want to stay on. Contact hours are between 22 and 26 with 3 hours' paid preparation. Most teaching is in block timetables until 10pm with 7.30pm finish on Fridays and no Saturdays.

FACILITIES/SUPPORT: Advice offered on accommodation and help in all matters of social security and residency application. Full social security payments and a work contract guaranteed. Workshops and staff meetings are held regularly to inform teachers of any extra courses available.

RECRUITMENT: Applications are received by email and acknowledged immediately. CVs are kept on file for future vacancies that crop up.

CONTACT: Penny Rollinson, Director of Studies.

CAMBRIDGE SCHOOL
Placa Manel Montanya 4, 08400 Granollers, Barcelona
+34 93 870 2001
alistair@cambridgeschool.com
www.cambridgeschool.com

NUMBER OF TEACHERS: 65 for 8 schools in the Vallès Oriental region near Barcelona.

PREFERENCE OF NATIONALITY: Native English speakers who can legally work in Spain, i.e. EU members or non-EU members with a work permit.

QUALIFICATIONS: At least CELTA (minimum Grade B) or equivalent. Clean driving licence, experience of teaching children or adolescents and/or experience of the business world would all be assets. Should already be living locally.

CONDITIONS OF EMPLOYMENT: Contract length mid-September to 22 June or possibly July. 20 contact teaching hours per week on average.

SALARY: Guaranteed minimum is €1,298 (gross) per month for 20 contact hours per week.

FACILITIES/SUPPORT: Assistance with accommodation, weekly seminars and workshops are part of the job, school library, teachers' room and extensive teachers' materials available. Offer the CELTA course 5 times a year.

RECRUITMENT: CVs should be sent to admin@cambridgeschool.com; interview will be either face-to-face or by phone.

CONTACT: Alistair Jones, Director.

CANADIAN LANGUAGE INSTITUTE
c/ París N° 25, Montequinto, 41089 Seville
+34 95 412 9016
rrhh@canadianli.es
www.canadianli.es

NUMBER OF TEACHERS: 10 for 3 branches in Seville.

PREFERENCE OF NATIONALITY: Any English-speaking country. EU member state passport essential.

QUALIFICATIONS: University degree and at least one year's experience of teaching Young Learners.

CONDITIONS OF EMPLOYMENT: Full-time contract from mid-September to end June. 1 or more years. 20–24 hours a week, teaching Monday–Thursday only.

SALARY: €1,300 per month.

FACILITIES/SUPPORT: Advice on accommodation given. 4 days paid training in early September, paid holidays at Christmas and Easter and end-of-contract bonus.

RECRUITMENT: Via posts on EFL boards. Local interview essential.

CONTACT: Victoria Mantecon, Director of EFL Department.

CAPITAL ENGLISH SCHOOL
La Janda Language Services S.L., Plaza Carretita s/n, Medina Sidonia, 11170 Cadiz
+34 670 734 145
becky@capitalenglishschool.com
www.capitalenglishschool.com

NUMBER OF TEACHERS: 5.

PREFERENCE OF NATIONALITY: Native speakers.

QUALIFICATIONS: Preferably a degree, and a Diploma/CELTA/Trinity qualification in TEFL with at least 2 years' experience.

CONDITIONS OF EMPLOYMENT: .9-month contracts. Usual tecahing hours are 4–9pm, Monday–Thursday. 20 hours a week, with extra hours in the mornings and on Fridays.

SALARY: €1,000–€1,080 per month. School pays social security; tax deduction of 9%.

FACILITIES/SUPPORT: Assistance given in finding accommodation. Ongoing staff development.

RECRUITMENT: Via www.tefl.com and word of mouth.

CONTACT: Becky Moon, Director.

CAPS (CONVERSATION ASSISTANT PROGRAMME FOR SCHOOLS)

Home to Home, Riereta 2, 08184 Palau-Solità i Plegamans, Barcelona

+34 93 864 8886

caps@hometohome.es

www.capsassistants.com

NUMBER OF TEACHERS: 150 for Catalonia and Valencia.

PREFERENCE OF NATIONALITY: Native English speaking countries, e.g. UK, USA, Australia and Canada.

QUALIFICATIONS: Minimum of A level or equivalent, and a native level of English. Most are aged 18–25. CAPS Plus programme open to graduates only. Must also have a desire to work with children. Desirable extras would include TEFL certificate or similar, some teaching experience and a desire to pursue teaching as a career.

CONDITIONS OF EMPLOYMENT: 9-month contract, though some come for shorter periods, e.g. 2 months. 25 hours per week.

SALARY: €315 per month for CAPS, €465 for CAPS Plus, which is considered a study grant. All deductions covered.

FACILITIES/SUPPORT: Participants live with families who are part of the programme. If a student visa is required, information is given.

RECRUITMENT: Marketing/advertising on various websites. CAPS representatives actively recruit in the UK, USA and Canada for example the Almondbury Agency in Devon recruits assistants for up to 250 schools (www.aupair-agency.com/Teaching-English-in-Spain.htm). All interviews are carried out via video conferencing.

CENTRO EDIMBURGO IDIOMAS

Edificio Edimburgo, Plaza Niña, 21003 Huelva

+34 959 263821 / 263862

info@centroedimburgo.com

www.centroedimburgo.com

NUMBER OF TEACHERS: 20.

PREFERENCE OF NATIONALITY: Must be EU citizen or hold work permit for Spain.

QUALIFICATIONS: Degree, CELTA plus 1 year's experience. Must speak conversational Spanish.

FACILITIES/SUPPORT: School helps find flats.

RECRUITMENT: Recent photograph and 2 references must be sent with application. Interviews essential.

CHALMORE LANGUAGE SOLUTIONS

Calle de Orense, 32 esc. izq. Oficina 1, 28020 Madrid

+34 91 555 1510

cv@chalmore.com

www.chalmore.com

NUMBER OF TEACHERS: 15.

PREFERENCE OF NATIONALITY: Must be native speakers of English, and be EU citizen.

QUALIFICATIONS: CELTA or TEFL (no online courses) and a minimum of 1 year's teaching experience.

CONDITIONS OF EMPLOYMENT: September–June. About 25 hours per week.

SALARY: On application. Taxes and social security paid by school.

FACILITIES/SUPPORT: No assistance with accommodation or work permits.

RECRUITMENT: Adverts in specialist media. Interviews are essential and are carried out in Madrid.

CONTACT: Frank Moerman, Director/CEO.

CIC

Via Augusta 205, 08021 Barcelona

+34 93 200 1133

iccic@iccic.edu

www.iccic.edu

NUMBER OF TEACHERS: 80 for 4 centres in Barcelona.

PREFERENCE OF NATIONALITY: Mix of native English speaking and teachers with 'native competence' from all around the world.

QUALIFICATIONS: Cambridge/Trinity certificate and 1 year's experience.

CONDITIONS OF EMPLOYMENT: Most new teachers are given a temporary 9-month contract running from October to June.

SALARY: Discussed during interview.

FACILITIES/SUPPORT: In-house training and professional development if funded by school.

RECRUITMENT: CVs via internet, all suitable candidates are interviewed.

CULTURE GO GO

hello@culturegogo.com

www.culturegogo.com

Formerly www.myfamilyabroad.com, based in Madrid.

PREFERENCE OF NATIONALITY: English native speakers from UK, Ireland, USA and Canada.

QUALIFICATIONS: No qualifications or experience necessary but candidates require enthusiasm to work with children.

CONDITIONS OF EMPLOYMENT: Flexible length of stay from a weekend to a year, according to agreement between host family and live-in tutor. Usually stays last 4–10 weeks. Recommended number of hours of language assistance is 15 per week.

SALARY: No wages are paid, only an exchange of food and accommodation for tutoring help.

RECRUITMENT: Interested candidates become members for 1, 3 or 12 months ($20, $30 or $48), which allows access to host contact details throughout Spain.

CONTACT: Tim Arnaudy, Co-founder.

DIVERBO
Calle de Orense 4, 7th Floor, 28020 Madrid
+34 91 391 3400
jobs@diverbo.com
www.diverbo.com

NUMBER OF TEACHERS: 80 for Madrid and Seville, and suburbs.

PREFERENCE OF NATIONALITY: Native speakers who already have NIE (residence card) and are registered as *autónomos* (freelancers who pay their own tax and social security).

QUALIFICATIONS: CELTA or equivalent plus 2 years' experience.

CONDITIONS OF EMPLOYMENT: Teaching mainly for companies face-to-face in small classes or online.

SALARY: From €19 per hour gross.

FACILITIES/SUPPORT: Compulsory training at beginning.

RECRUITMENT: Adverts on www.madridteacher.com. Interviews can be by phone.

CONTACT: Iñaki Cornago. HR Coordinator.

DIVERBO VOLUNTEERS
Calle de Orense 4, 7th Floor, 28020 Madrid
+34 91 391 3400
volunteers@diverbo.com
www.diverbo.com./en/volunteer-abroad/adults

Incorporates Pueblo Ingles programme of language holidays, in which an informal exchange of English conversation takes place over 8 days in various holiday resorts in Spain, where native English volunteers interact and converse with Spanish clients who want to improve their English. Native-speaking participants receive free room and board, and transport from Madrid.

EIDE SCHOOL OF ENGLISH
Genaro Oraa 6, 48980 Santurce (Greater Bilbao)
+34 94 493 7005
eide@eide.es
www.eide.es

NUMBER OF TEACHERS: 2.

QUALIFICATIONS: Bachelor's degree in English or languages and some teaching experience with children desirable. Driving licence.

CONDITIONS OF EMPLOYMENT: 9-month contract; 12 hours per week mostly in the evenings.

SALARY: €12 per hour plus bonus for holidays at the end of contract; 8% tax and social security deduction.

FACILITIES/SUPPORT: Room in school apartment offered for €250 per month plus bills.

RECRUITMENT: Interview essential.

CONTACT: Ruth Farpón Largo, Director.

ELA: ENGLISH LANGUAGE ACADEMY
Redonda de Santiago, 9, 1-D, 23400 Ubeda, Jaén
+34 953 756019
info@ela.org.es
www.ela.org.es

NUMBER OF TEACHERS: 9.

PREFERENCE OF NATIONALITY: EU citizens.

QUALIFICATIONS: Applicants must have the CELTA or TrinityTESOL certificate, a university degree and a minimum of 1 year's experience.

CONDITIONS OF EMPLOYMENT: 9 months. A full-time contract is 34 hours per week comprising 23 contact teaching hours and 11 hours on-site preparation, marking and meeting time.

SALARY: Minimum starting salary is €1250 per month (net). Settling-in allowance of €200 paid in second term.

FACILITIES/SUPPORT: New teachers are provided with up to 1 week's free accommodation organised by the academy and are assisted by the school to find more long-term accommodation. A representative of the school will arrange and accompany new employees when applying for all necessary permits, which usually include: application for residency and a national identity number (in the provincial capital Foreign Affairs Department), application for a social security number (local Social Security office) and also assistance with opening a local bank account.

RECRUITMENT: Via www.spainwise.net and www.tefl.com. Skype interviews are acceptable.

CONTACT: Paul Hillman, Director.

EL CENTRO DE INGLES
C/Caldereros 7, 23740 Andújar, Jaén
+34 953 506821
direccion@elcentrodeingles.es
www.elcentrodeingles.es

Sister school in nearby Bailen.

NUMBER OF TEACHERS: 2–4 new teachers required every year for September start.

QUALIFICATIONS: Degree required. CELTA/Trinity and 1 year's experience, especially valued if with young learners.

CONDITIONS OF EMPLOYMENT: 9.5-month contract. 21–24 contact hours per week (full-time 34-hour contract to cover class preparation, meetings and teacher training, etc.). Holiday bonus on completion of contract.

SALARY: Basic starting salary (21 teaching hours) is €1,330 gross, about €1,200 net. Bonus for DELTA-qualified teachers.

FACILITIES/SUPPORT: Help with accommodation, paperwork, settling in, induction. Full medical cover. In-service training.

RECRUITMENT: Interviews in Spain or England (as notified on website). Also recruit via www.spainwise.net.

CONTACT: Julie Hetherington, Director.

ENG-AGE LANGUAGE CENTRE

Calle Estrada 2, Baja Callejón, 36900 Marin, Pontevedra (Galicia)

+34 619 267765 / 986 883184

contacto@eng-age.es

www.eng-age.es

NUMBER OF TEACHERS: 4.

PREFERENCE OF NATIONALITY: UK, Ireland and native speakers from other English speaking countries if they hold an EU passport.

QUALIFICATIONS: University degree and English teaching qualification are essential. One year's experience, especially of very young learners, and a knowledge of Spanish would be advantageous.

CONDITIONS OF EMPLOYMENT: 9-month contract from 1 October with possibility to extend till end of July. 20–25 teaching hours per week.

SALARY: €1,085–€1,300 per month gross for 25 contact hours per week, less 6.4% social security and 2% tax.

FACILITIES/SUPPORT: Manager accompanies teacher on flat-viewing trip and to government offices to translate and help with obtaining a NIE and registering for social security.

RECRUITMENT: Via www.tefl.com and other sites. Skype interviews essential.

CONTACT: Mercedes Vivero Enjamio, Manager.

ENGLISH 1

Marqués del Nervión 116, 41005 Seville

+34 95 464 2098

info@english1sevilla.com

www.english1sevilla.com

NUMBER OF TEACHERS: 6.

QUALIFICATIONS: Degree and TEFL certificate (or diploma) and experience, especially with young learners preferred.

CONDITIONS OF EMPLOYMENT: 23 contact hours per week, Monday to Thursday only, teaching children, teenagers and adults. 9-month contract from October to June.

SALARY: Starting salary €1,100 gross plus extra payments for Cambridge exam preparation classes.

FACILITIES/SUPPORT: In-house training and great support in a very friendly and harmonious working atmosphere. Lots of assistance in finding accommodation.

CONTACT: Jennifer Fricker, Owner.

ENGLISH TEACHERS COLLECTIVE (ETC)

C/ Joaquín Costa 15, 28002 Madrid

+34 902 090166

info@etcspain.com

www.etcspain.com

NUMBER OF TEACHERS: 35. Most vacancies in Madrid, Barcelona and Seville, in company and private classes.

PREFERENCE OF NATIONALITY: British or American.

QUALIFICATIONS: CELTA/TrinityTESOL qualification plus 1 year's experience.

CONDITIONS OF EMPLOYMENT: 9-month contracts. 15 hours per week.

SALARY: €1,000 per month net.

FACILITIES/SUPPORT: No help with accommodation. Help given with residency permit and obtaining social security number. Monthly internal teacher training seminars.

RECRUITMENT: New post alerts via Facebook and Twitter. Local interviews essential.

CONTACT: Paul Hevicon, Director General.

ENGLISHYA

Baztan Berri Plaza 1 bajo, Elizondo, 31700 Navarra

+34 948 580322 / 680 624507

EnglishYA.es@gmail.com

www.EnglishYA.es

NUMBER OF TEACHERS: 6.

PREFERENCE OF NATIONALITY: None.

QUALIFICATIONS: Experience working with children.

CONDITIONS OF EMPLOYMENT: 6-month contract. 20 hours per week, follows school year so plenty of holidays and long weekends.

SALARY: €1,000 per month.

FACILITIES/SUPPORT: Assistance with finding accommodation.

CONTACT: David Rivas Iparrea, Managing Director.

ESIC IDIOMAS

Sancho el Fuerte 38, Bajo, 31011 Pamplona

 +34 948 173011

 idiomas.pam@esic.es

 www.esic.edu/idiomas

NUMBER OF TEACHERS: 28 (some part-time). Centres in Seville, Malaga, Zaragoza, etc. as well as Pamplona.

PREFERENCE OF NATIONALITY: Native English speakers.

QUALIFICATIONS: Recognised TEFL qualification and relevant experience.

CONDITIONS OF EMPLOYMENT: 9-month contract; 24 hours per week.

SALARY: €1,240–€1,320 depending on experience; €18 per hour self-employed.

FACILITIES/SUPPORT: Help is given to find accommodation and paperwork necessary to work in Pamplona. An initial induction course, with accompanying handouts, is given and various training and information sessions are given throughout the academic year.

RECRUITMENT: Sometimes interviewed by phone.

CONTACT: Fay Williams, Coordinator (fay.williams@esic.es).

EUROLANGUAGE CONSULTANTS (ELC)

Calle Alfredo Marquerie, 5 (bajo), 28034 Madrid

+34 91 740 5911

 recruitment@eurolanguage.org

www.eurolanguage.org

NUMBER OF TEACHERS: 20 natives, 18 non-natives.

PREFERENCE OF NATIONALITY: No preference, but EU working papers are necessary.

QUALIFICATIONS: TEFL, CELTA or TESOL certificates preferred, but also value other experience and interest in teaching.

CONDITIONS OF EMPLOYMENT: 9-month academic year. Part-time or full-time positions available.

FACILITIES/SUPPORT: Normally no help given with accommodation, but if a teacher does not speak Spanish employer can help with phone calls and general orientation.

RECRUITMENT: Web contacts, e.g. MadridTeacher, Lingobongo and Bolsa de Trabajo. Face-to-face interviews in Madrid.

CONTACT: Kerry Davis, Director of Studies (kerry.davis@eurolanguage.org).

EUROSCHOOLS

Plaza de la Independencia, Regueiro 2, 36211 Vigo

+34 986 291748 / 986 378600

info@euroschools.eu

www.euroschools.eu

NUMBER OF TEACHERS: 15.

PREFERENCE OF NATIONALITY: Must be EU.

QUALIFICATIONS: Good degree preferably in English, Spanish or modern languages, TEFL qualification, some experience preferred. Must have knowledge of Spanish and outgoing, friendly personality.

CONDITIONS OF EMPLOYMENT: 9 months from 1 October. 25 class hours per week.

SALARY: Competitive plus allowances are paid for university degree and TEFL teaching qualifications in proportion to qualifications.

FACILITIES/SUPPORT: Assistance given with finding accommodation. Holiday entitlement is 2+ weeks at Christmas, 1 week at Easter, 2 days at Carnaval. Access to internet and school computer network available to teachers.

RECRUITMENT: Good references, CV, photo and Skype interview.

CONTACT: Mr John Moriarty, Managing Director.

HOT ENGLISH LANGUAGE SERVICES

Paseo del Rey 22, 1 Planta, Oficina 1, 28008 Madrid

+34 91 543 3573

classes@learnhotenglish.com

www.learnhotenglish.com

NUMBER OF TEACHERS: 40–50 per year. Unpaid internships available.

PREFERENCE OF NATIONALITY: Native speakers, must be legally authorised to work in Spain because employer does not at present sponsor candidates for a work permit.

QUALIFICATIONS: TEFL/TESOL/CELTA or equivalent is a must. Teachers without formal qualifications, but possessing substantial verifiable experience, will also be considered. Candidates must be resident in Spain and have already applied for and received a Spanish NIE and social security number. Exceptions could be made in the future for teachers hired to teach telephone/Skype classes.

CONDITIONS OF EMPLOYMENT: September/October to 30 June. Minimum 8–10 hours up to as many hours as the teacher's schedule allows.

SALARY: €14–€18 per hour (gross), with adjustments based on class length and location. Deductions average 8.5%.

FACILITIES/SUPPORT: Hot English has a flat available for rent; otherwise, it can advise new arrivals on where to look for a flat.

RECRUITMENT: Adverts on local websites such as www.madridteacher.com and www.lingobongo.com. For Madrid positions, interviews must be held in person. For positions in other Spanish cities, interviews are held over the phone, as long as the candidate is already residing in the relevant city.

CONTACT: Mely Armstrong, Teacher Coordinator; Thorley Russell, Managing Director.

IDIOMAS TOP / LA ACADEMIA DE INGLES
Avda. de Moratalaz 139 (Lonja), 28030 Madrid
+34 91 430 5545
info@idiomastop.com
www.idiomastop.com

NUMBER OF TEACHERS: Approx. 40 per course.

PREFERENCE OF NATIONALITY: EU citizens or people with legal status.

QUALIFICATIONS: University degree and TEFL, plus competence in the Spanish language.

CONDITIONS OF EMPLOYMENT: 9–10 months. Any hours between 8am and 10pm, but mainly 4pm–9pm. Also run residential immersion camps in Asturias in July. Volunteers receive living expenses and transport from Madrid.

FACILITIES/SUPPORT: No help with accommodation.

RECRUITMENT: Interviews in Madrid are essential.

CONTACT: Ana Aparicio, Director.

IDIOMASTER LANGUAGE CENTRES
C/Juan Rico 8, 14900 Lucena, Córdoba
+34 957 591678
recruitment@idiomaster.es
www.idiomaster.es

NUMBER OF TEACHERS: 9 for a group of schools.

QUALIFICATIONS: Must be friendly and enthusiastic. University degree, CELTA or Trinity and at least 1 year's experience, preferably with children. Less experience acceptable if candidate achieved A/B on certificate course.

SALARY: Minimum monthly gross salary €1,250 plus end of contract bonus of 2.5 days' salary per month worked. Full social security and national health insurance cover.

FACILITIES/SUPPORT: Ongoing internal teacher training and support plus external teaching conferences and courses. Digital classrooms with interactive whiteboards. Help with finding accommodation. Preparation centre for the Cambridge suite of exams. A registered Trinity College, London examination centre and member of ACEIA, FECEI and CALAC (Central Andalusian Language Academies; www.calacschools.es).

INLINGUA SANTANDER
Avenida de Pontejos 5, 39005 Santander
+34 942 278465
inlingua.santander@inlingua.com
www.inlinguasantander.com

NUMBER OF TEACHERS: 12.

PREFERENCE OF NATIONALITY: EU native English speakers or having a work permit for Spain.

QUALIFICATIONS: TEFL certificate and/or teaching experience, university degree.

CONDITIONS OF EMPLOYMENT: Contract for academic year or summer, full-time contract: up to 26 teaching hours a week.

SALARY: Minimum net €1,057.

FACILITIES/SUPPORT: Assistance with finding accommodation, inlingua Method course, workshops, school library. Free Spanish lessons.

RECRUITMENT: Via www.tefl.com, etc. Interview by phone.

CONTACT: Mrs Ingrid Antons, Director.

INSTITUTE OF MODERN LANGUAGES
Puerta Real 1, 18009 Granada
+34 958 225536
info@imlgranada.com
www.imlgranada.com

NUMBER OF TEACHERS: 20.

PREFERENCE OF NATIONALITY: British, other native English speakers.

QUALIFICATIONS: University degree, TEFL qualification and relevant experience.

CONDITIONS OF EMPLOYMENT: Contract for the academic year, contract for part-time work, national insurance, social security.

FACILITIES/SUPPORT: Good resources, Examination Centre for University of Cambridge ESOL Examinations in Granada, Almería and Málaga. Offer CELTA course.

RECRUITMENT: EFL teachers are recruited from among the best qualified in Granada at the time. Initial short-list drawn up by director of studies from available CVs, then school owner carries out second interviews of short-listed candidates.

CONTACT: Monika Czernek, Director of Studies (monika.czernek@imlgranada.com).

INTERLANG
C/Antonia Mercé, 8 – 1°, 28009 Madrid
+34 91 515 8422
empleo@interlang.es
www.interlang.es

NUMBER OF TEACHERS: 90.

PREFERENCE OF NATIONALITY: None but must be native speaker and have EU working papers if non-EU citizen.

QUALIFICATIONS: Prefer TEFL qualification plus 2 years'

TEFL experience and sound knowledge of business English. Must be able to give engaging, high quality classes.

CONDITIONS OF EMPLOYMENT: Registered freelancers, or school offers standard 9-month contracts. Typical teaching hours 8.30am–10am/1pm–6pm. Teaching in-company one-to-ones, in small groups as well as telephone and online teaching.

SALARY: €18.50 per hour gross on contract, €24 per hour gross for registered freelancers. Tax deductions vary, but for freelancers there's a 7% deduction for the first two years and then 15%.

RECRUITMENT: Via the company website or via permanent advert at www.madridteacher.com. Candidates are asked to send recent CV and colour photo to empleo@interlang.es. A face-to-face interview in Madrid or Skype interview.

CONTACT: Sean O'Malley, Director of Studies.

INTERNATIONAL HOUSE MADRID

Calle Covarrubias 1, 28010 Madrid

+34 91 319 7224 / 902 141517

selection@ihmadrid.com

www.ihmadrid.com

NUMBER OF TEACHERS: 190 for 4 centres in Madrid.

PREFERENCE OF NATIONALITY: No preference, but applicants must have permission to work permanently in the EU.

QUALIFICATIONS: Candidates must have the Cambridge CELTA or Trinity CertTESOL. Applicants without one of these qualifications will not be accepted.

CONDITIONS OF EMPLOYMENT: Initially posts are for the academic year from October to June. 19–22 hours of teaching per week.

SALARY: Competitive salary for the market in Madrid. More details on application. As a rough guide, teachers on 25 hours a week can expect to receive more than €1,400 gross (€1,081 net) for 19 hours, €1,252 net for 22 hours depending on experience and qualifications. Deductions of 6% for social security and 10%–11% for income tax. Hourly rate of €20–€22 for freelancers

FACILITIES/SUPPORT: No assistance with accommodation; there is a plentiful supply in Madrid. No assistance with work permits. Paid holidays.

RECRUITMENT: Advertising through IH World organisation, other recruitment sites such as www.tefl.com, IH Madrid website, word of mouth and email applications to the above address. Face-to-face interviews in Madrid essential.

CONTACT: Mr Alex Bishop, Human Resources (abishop@ihmadrid.com).

ISE TENERIFE (ISE LANGUAGE LTD)

Calle Obispo Rey Redondo 52, 38201 San Cristobal de la Laguna, S/C de Tenerife

+34 922 194744; info@isetenerife.com

sindi@ise.uk.com; info@isetenerife.com

www.isetenerife.com

NUMBER OF TEACHERS: 3.

PREFERENCE OF NATIONALITY: UK, US.

QUALIFICATIONS: Any teaching certificate. Must be able to speak a little Spanish.

CONDITIONS OF EMPLOYMENT: Long-term work. From 12 hours per week.

SALARY: €12 per hour (net).

FACILITIES/SUPPORT: Advice given on finding accommodation and on applying for residence permits.

RECRUITMENT: Partner school of ISE Hove (www.ise.uk.com) that offers CELTA courses. Skype interviews are fine.

CONTACT: Sindi Ferrera Martínez, Director and Owner.

KEDARO INTERNATIONAL

Calle Murillo 8, 21001 Huelva

+34 959 87 37 12

info@kedaro.com

http://kedaro.com

NUMBER OF TEACHERS: 15-20.

PREFERENCE OF NATIONALITY: EU passport holders or valid work permit holders.

QUALIFICATIONS: CELTA or TESOL and 1 year's experience; less experienced candidates are considered with pass A or B.

CONDITIONS OF EMPLOYMENT: 9–10 months with optional summer work for 5 weeks. 24 hours a week.

SALARY: €1,000 net with 3 hours of Spanish lessons included.

FACILITIES/SUPPORT: Assistance given with flat-hunting.

RECRUITMENT: Via www.tefl.com, Dave's ESL Cafe and www.spainwise.net. Always 2–3 Skype interviews.

CONTACT: Richard McCulloch, Director of Studies (rich@kedaro.com).

KIDZ IN ACTION

Calle Cuesta 13, Majadahonda, 28220 Madrid

+34 912 540 554

info@kidzinaction.es

www.kidzinaction.es

NUMBER OF TEACHERS: 3.

PREFERENCE OF NATIONALITY: None.

QUALIFICATIONS: Ability to communicate at the level of young learners.

CONDITIONS OF EMPLOYMENT: 1–2 years. Usual hours are 12pm–8.30pm.

SALARY: €1,200 per month after tax.

FACILITIES/SUPPORT: Advice and contacts given for accommodation. No help given with visas.

RECRUITMENT: Interviews in Spain.

CONTACT: Jonathan Lipschitz, Owner.

KLEINSON: LA CONSULTORA DE IDIOMAS

C/Apodaca 7, bajo izquierda, 28004 Madrid

+34 91 140 0570

info@kleinson.es; formacion@kleinson.es

www.kleinson.es

NUMBER OF TEACHERS: 22 native English speakers out of 50 for companies throughout Spain.

PREFERENCE OF NATIONALITY: None whatsoever, although Kleinson does not provide work visas.

QUALIFICATIONS: Teachers become 'consultants' after working with Kleinson. Ideally, candidates come with at least 2 years' experience and/or a CELTA. Candidates who hold the company's values and are hard workers but with very little teaching experience can still be considered. It is important that staff share Kleinson's professional values and embrace diversity.

CONDITIONS OF EMPLOYMENT: Average contract is from September/October to June/July. All consultants start with morning, lunchtime or evening hours. After at least a year and receiving solid feedback they are moved up to block hours.

SALARY: All consultants, regardless of experience, start at €20 per hour gross (which is €15 net) for classes in the city centre. For classes outside the centre contract teachers can receive up to €25 per hour net. Teachers officially signed up as freelancers are paid €17 per hour (€22 if registered *autonomo*) and can go up to €30; NB: in Spain, 9% of wages are retained for tax from freelancers (*autonomos*) in addition to social security contributions. After 3 years of being taxed at 9%, the rate doubles. Rewards paid to teachers who bring in new clients.

FACILITIES/SUPPORT: All consultants are required to attend a training session. Informal advice given on finding accommodation. No assistance with work permits.

RECRUITMENT: Word of mouth, online ads or collaborations with TEFL academies throughout Spain and the USA. Online application procedure, 3-step interviews take place only in Madrid: telephone interview first followed by a group interview and finally an individual one.

CONTACT: Shiva Roofeh, Head of Training.

LINC, ENGLISH FOR LIVING

Calle Genaro Parladé, 4. Bajo B, 41013 Seville; also Calle Los Balbos S/N, 11009 Cadiz

+34 954 500459

sevilla@linc.es

www.linc.es/tefl-jobs-seville-cadiz

NUMBER OF TEACHERS: 15–20.

PREFERENCE OF NATIONALITY: Must be an EU member state passport holder and native English speaker.

QUALIFICATIONS: Degree, plus EFL qualification (CELTA or Trinity) and 1–2 year's teaching experience. Some knowledge of Spanish helpful.

CONDITIONS OF EMPLOYMENT: Standard contract is 9/10 months from September/October to June. Full and part-time contracts available. Full-time is 24 contact hours per week. Some summer work available.

SALARY: €1,200 (gross) per month for full-time contracts.

FACILITIES/SUPPORT: Help is given with finding accommodation. Regular in-service training programme. Free Spanish classes.

RECRUITMENT: Interviews held via Skype or phone.

MCGINTY SCHOOL OF ENGLISH

Avda, Cabo de Gata, 54, 04007 Almeria

+34 950 259745

dos@mcgintyschool.com

www.mcgintyschool.com

NUMBER OF TEACHERS: 26.

PREFERENCE OF NATIONALITY: None. Must be national of EU member state or have valid work permit.

QUALIFICATIONS: Minimum CELTA or PGCE, preferably language graduate with 3 years' relevant teaching experience.

CONDITIONS OF EMPLOYMENT: 1-year contract from early September with the possibility of summer work and contract renewal. Maximum 25 teaching hours per week, mainly between 4pm and 9.30pm, Monday–Friday.

SALARY: Starting full-time salary is €1,175 net per month but may increase depending on experience and qualifications. Bonus paid on completion of contract.

FACILITIES/SUPPORT: Assistance provided with finding accommodation and registering for social security, etc. Regular training and development sessions in school; support to attend training and conferences. Free Spanish lessons.

RECRUITMENT: Via Spainwise, etc. Applicants should send CV and photo in first instance. Interviews are essential and can be conducted in Spain or over the phone.

CONTACT: Tim Swillens, Director of Studies.

MAUCAL SL

Pol. Argualas Nave 35, 50012 Zaragoza
+34 976 350 205
maucal@maucal.com
www.maucal.com

Language consultancy with branches in Huesca and Granada as well.

NUMBER OF TEACHERS: Approximately 4.

QUALIFICATIONS: EFL qualification and bachelor's degree (with honours) preferable.

CONDITIONS OF EMPLOYMENT: Contracts of 9–10 months; from 12 to 34 hours a week.

SALARY: Depends on hours a week.

MERIT SCHOOL

Campo Florido 54–56, 2a, 08027 Barcelona
+34 93 243 1524
dos@meritschool.com
www.meritschool.com

NUMBER OF TEACHERS: 40–50 for 8 branches.

PREFERENCE OF NATIONALITY: Native English speakers. Must have EU member state passport or current work permit for Spain.

QUALIFICATIONS: University degree, TEFL certificate (preferably grade B or higher), 1 year's experience. Classroom experience with young learners or teenagers an advantage.

CONDITIONS OF EMPLOYMENT: Most contracts run from October to June with the possibility of extension into July for summer courses. Number of teaching hours varies – part-time and full-time teachers are sought.

SALARY: €15–€18 per hour. Travelling fee for off-site classes.

FACILITIES/SUPPORT: 3 centres plus in-company department: Campo Florido and Sant Cugat campuses (Young Learners, Teenagers, Adults), UPC campus (University students and staff) and in-company department (Business and General English for adults off-site in companies). Regular in-house workshops, financial assistance to attend external training events, good library of teaching resources, peer observation scheme, regular observations and feedback by senior staff. Spanish classes.

RECRUITMENT: Mostly local internet sites but sometimes on international sites like www.tefl.com. Applications from interested teachers are always welcome. Face-to-face interview required. Best time to apply is late May to July or in September.

CONTACT: David Corp, Director of Studies.

MY TEFL EXPERIENCE

Carretera Malilla, 11 bajo derecha, 46006 Valencia
+34 662 247 990
info@myteflexperience.com
www.myteflexperience.com

NUMBER OF TEACHERS: Up to 8 fee-paying volunteers per week to teach free English classes to Spanish people affected by the economic crisis.

PREFERENCE OF NATIONALITY: All volunteers must be fluent or have bilingual level of English. Non-EU participants will need a Schengen visa (maximum 90 days); My TEFL Experience can provide a letter of invitation.

QUALIFICATIONS: None required, but TEFL qualification and some teaching experience and/or transferable skills are preferred.

CONDITIONS OF EMPLOYMENT: 2–12 weeks. Teaching 2–3 classes per day; 12–16 hours per week, Monday to Thursday (approx. 2–3 classes per day).

SALARY: No salary. Volunteers pay a placement fee of €175 per week which covers accommodation in a private room in apartments shared with up to 3 other teachers.

FACILITIES/SUPPORT: Lesson plans and class materials are provided. Extra training offered where necessary and help given to new TEFL teachers to develop their skills through observation and feedback. Advice given on living and working in Spain to participants who want to stay on.

RECRUITMENT: Applicants fill out a short application form via the website, followed by a Skype interview.

CONTACT: Alyx Tzamantanis, Programme Coordinator.

PREMIER SCHOOL OF ENGLISH

C/ Perafán de Rivera 1 – Local, 41710 Utrera, Sevilla
+34 955 861951
info@premierenglish.es
www.premierenglish.es

Member of ACEIA, FECEI and CALAC.

NUMBER OF TEACHERS: 7.

PREFERENCE OF NATIONALITY: No real preference as long as they are native speakers and have EU residency permit.

QUALIFICATIONS: Must have a CELTA or Trinity TESOL plus 1 year's experience. Experience of teaching very young children would be useful.

CONDITIONS OF EMPLOYMENT: 9-month contracts from mid-September. Maximum 24 hours of teaching mostly in the afternoons and evenings: 4pm–9.45pm Monday to Thursday, 4pm–6.15pm Friday.

SALARY: Starting salary €1,300 (gross) for a maximum of 24 hours per week, which could increase depending on experience and qualifications. Deductions total about €100 a month. 2 weeks paid holiday at Christmas and 1 week at Easter.

FACILITIES/SUPPORT: School actively helps teachers find flats and negotiate with landlords, etc. Help given with red tape (the procedures vary from year to year). Paid one-week induction. Weekly in-house teacher training sessions. Free Spanish classes.

RECRUITMENT: Through recommendations, www.spainwise.net, www.tefl.com and elsewhere online. Interviews essential.

CONTACT: Francis Rodriguez, Director of Studies.

Q ENGLISH LANGUAGE TRAINING

Avd País Valencià, 129–131, 03820 Cocentaina (Alicante)

+34 96 559 2204

info@qeltcocentaina.com

www.qeltcocentaina.com

NUMBER OF TEACHERS: 3.

PREFERENCE OF NATIONALITY: British.

QUALIFICATIONS: CELTA or TESOL qualification (not short online introductory courses) and a minimum of 1 year's teaching experience.

CONDITIONS OF EMPLOYMENT: 9 months October to June. 25 hours a week.

SALARY: €950–€1,000 (net) according to experience.

FACILITIES/SUPPORT: Assistance offered with finding accommodation. Assistance given with obtaining identification documents for Spain.

RECRUITMENT: Via online advertising. Interviews are usually carried out over the phone or on Skype, but if the candidate is in the area a face-to-face interview is preferable.

SOUND ENGLISH

Jesús Cancio 2, Torrelavega, 39300 Cantabria

+34 942 086971

soundenglish@hotmail.com

www.soundenglishacademy.com

NUMBER OF TEACHERS: 2.

PREFERENCE OF NATIONALITY: British.

QUALIFICATIONS: Minimum degree and TEFL Certificate.

CONDITIONS OF EMPLOYMENT: 24 contact hours per week, normally 4–9pm.

SALARY: €1,100 (net).

FACILITIES/SUPPORT: Help given with accommodation. Full social security paid. Teacher training.

RECRUITMENT: Via www.tefl.com.

CONTACT: Jonathan Kinson, Owner.

SPEAK ENGLISH SCHOOL

Cimadevilla 17 Ent F, 33003 Oviedo, Asturias

+34 985 226136

speakschool@hotmail.com

www.speakschool.com

PREFERENCE OF NATIONALITY: British.

QUALIFICATIONS: TEFL certificate and a minimum of 2 years' experience.

CONDITIONS OF EMPLOYMENT: 9-month contracts, to work 25 hours per week.

SALARY: €1,200 per month (net) plus end-of-contract bonus.

FACILITIES/SUPPORT: The school can help with finding accommodation.

RECRUITMENT: Interviews essential, but can be carried out in the UK. Sometimes, telephone/Skype interviews can be arranged.

CONTACT: Mick Gordon, Director of Studies.

TECS (THE EDUCATIONAL CONSORTIUM OF SPAIN)

The English Centre, Apdo. Correos 85, 11500 El Puerto de Santa María, Cadiz

+34 956 853000

tecscamp@tecs.es

www.tecsemployment.com

NUMBER OF TEACHERS: 15–20 teachers required throughout the year for 5 language centres on the Costa de la Luz in southwest Spain. Up to 200 staff employed in summer (teachers, monitors, management and support staff) at 8 residential locations in Cádiz, Salamanca, Andalucía and one in Madrid region.

QUALIFICATIONS: Employees must be team players who are young at heart and full of energy, with a mature and responsible personality. EFL teachers require a 100-hour TEFL qualification or normal school teaching qualification (if candidate has experience working with foreign-language children). Police check required.

CONDITIONS OF EMPLOYMENT: Minimum 4 weeks (2 fortnight-long camps); academic year runs from 15 September or 1 October to 12 June.

FACILITIES/SUPPORT: 5 days' pre-start training.

SALARY: €550 per fortnight. Free board and lodging. Salary during year is €889–€1,410 (gross), based on 19–31 contact hours.

RECRUITMENT: Online and via www.spainwise.net jobs fair in May. Recommended dates to apply are February/March.

CONTACT: Douglas Haines, Summer Camp Recruitment; Gillian Thompson, Director of Language Centres.

THE FARM SUMMERCAMPS
Barrio Elizalde 11, 01193 Erentxun, Alava
✆ +34 945 063234
info@campamentosthefarm.com
www.campamentosthefarm.com

NUMBER OF TEACHERS: One for each 6–7 children on various camps in Basque country, i.e. in Gorozika, Lurkoi, plus one in Asturias.
PREFERENCE OF NATIONALITY: All, including fluent speakers of English from Scandinavia and Holland as well as Britons and Irish, Canadians and Americans.
QUALIFICATIONS: Experience desirable; must have good communication skills. Counsellors should find living communally a positive and inspiring experience, show flexibility and creativity when it comes to teaching workshops and classes and have maturity and sensitivity in helping to prevent and resolve conflicts.
CONDITIONS OF EMPLOYMENT: Camp takes place in July.
CONTACT: Mascha Snoijink (mascha.thefarm@gmail.com).

TICK IT ENGLISH
Calle Doctor Marañón, 1, Entr, 24402 Ponferrada, León
✆ +34 987 088256
info@tickitenglish.com
www.tickitenglish.com

NUMBER OF TEACHERS: 4.
PREFERENCE OF NATIONALITY: British.
QUALIFICATIONS: CELTA and 2 years' teaching experience, especially with young learners (ages 4–16).
CONDITIONS OF EMPLOYMENT: 9-month contract. 25 hours per week.
SALARY: €1,350 per calendar month, less approximately €100 in contributions.
FACILITIES/SUPPORT: Help given to teachers to find suitable accommodation. One flat is available to rent through the school. Help given to EU citizens to register with the local authorities and obtain the necessary paperwork.
RECRUITMENT: Via Spainwise and adverts on www.tefl.com. Some interviews held in the UK.
CONTACT: Derek Holloway, Director of Studies (derek@tickitenglish.com).

TRAINING EXPRESS
Madrid: Glorieta de Quevedo, 9, 6ª planta, 28015 Madrid; Barcelona: Rambla de Catalunya, 33, 08007 Barcelona; Bilbao: Torre Iberdrola, Plaza de Euskadi, 5, 48009 Bilbao
✆ +34 91 521 1554 (Madrid); +34 93 467 3603 (Barcelona); +34 94 439 7393 (Bilbao)
jobs@trainingexpress.es
www.trainingexpress.es; http://www3.trainingexpress.es/recruitment/recruitment-home

NUMBER OF TEACHERS: 300+ freelance trainers.
PREFERENCE OF NATIONALITY: None but must have native-level English. Agency likes to offer clients a range of accents.
QUALIFICATIONS: Must already have permission to work in Spain plus university degree, TEFL Certificate/CELTA and 2 years of ESL experience.
CONDITIONS OF EMPLOYMENT: Permanent contract with possibility of summer work. 40–80 hours per month (10–20 hours per week), depending on teacher's availability. Peak class times are normally early morning, midday and late afternoon.
SALARY: The rate per class depends on location, schedule and content (general English, Business, etc.).
FACILITIES/SUPPORT: No assistance with accommodation. HR Department gives information about how to obtain the papers necessary to work in Spain. Trainers are assigned a coordinator who offers them classes and helps with any issues related to their working life at Training Express. They are also assigned a senior teacher who is available to give pedagogical advice, material for their classes, etc. Free Spanish classes offered to trainers who have a minimum number of contracted hours.
RECRUITMENT: CVs sent in response to adverts and via company's website. Recruitment team (based in Serbia) filters CVs and carries out preliminary phone interviews. Successful candidates are invited to a face-to-face interview where they have to prepare a lesson plan or give a demonstration of their teaching methodology.
CONTACT: Ms Nikolina Tepic, Recruitment Resourcer; Ivana Raicevic, Head of Recruitment.

UCETAM (Union de Cooperativas de Enseñanza de Trabajo Asociado de Madrid)
Programa Bilingüe Ucetam (PBU), C/ Guzmán el Bueno 133, 1° I, 28003 Madrid
✆ +34 91 448 0622
bicucetam@ucetam.es; applications@ucetam.es
www.ucetampbu.es (English version)

NUMBER OF TEACHERS: About 136 native speakers who assist classroom teachers as 'native auxiliaries' in the Madrid region.
PREFERENCE OF NATIONALITY: Mainly American and British.
QUALIFICATIONS: University degree, not necessarily in education.

CONDITIONS OF EMPLOYMENT: One academic year (5 September until 22 June) with the possibility of extension for a further year. 18 or 26 hours per week (in the classroom) plus staff meetings.

SALARY: €981 for 18 hours a week; €1,441 for 26 hours a week. Free lunch at the schools. Schools cover social security costs and repatriation insurance but EU teachers must pay contributions of 2%; US teachers have no deductions.

FACILITIES/SUPPORT: No assistance with accommodation. Assistance given with red tape. The scholarship scheme is run in conjunction with Madrid local educational authority and assistant teachers work on a student visa. UCETAM presents documents to the immigration authorities, then non-EU participants are called for fingerprints.

RECRUITMENT: Via website. Interviews via Skype or in Madrid. Deadline for applications: 24 February. Decisions will be communicated in March or April.

CONTACT: Sarah Mackin, Program Coordinator.

VAUGHAN SYSTEMS

Edificio Eurobuilding 2, Calle Orense 69 – 1° planta, 28020 Madrid. Also offices in Barcelona, Valladolid, Vigo, Valencia, Seville and Santander

+34 91 748 5960, ext. 4370

http://grupovaughan.com/teaching-english-spain/vaughan-systems-job-center

NUMBER OF TEACHERS: 96, mostly for Madrid but also Barcelona, Bilbao, Santander, Valencia, Valladolid and Vigo.

PREFERENCE OF NATIONALITY: None but EU or work permit required.

QUALIFICATIONS: No experience needed; training given during free 2-week training course in the company's methods, in one of the cities where they have an office.

CONDITIONS OF EMPLOYMENT: Freelance and a few contract positions for an academic year. Mostly teaching in-company with a lot of travelling between workplaces.

SALARY: Teachers are all self-employed and bill Vaughan at the end of the month for the hours they have taught.

FACILITIES/SUPPORT: Teachers look after their own social security contributions. No accommodation.

RECRUITMENT: Online application system.

CONTACT: Natasha Pascua and Marta Martínez, Teacher Recruitment & Training Coordinators.

VAUGHAN TOWN

Edificio Eurobuilding 2, Calle Orense 69 – 1° planta, 28020 Madrid

+34 91 748 5950

anglos@vaughantown.com

http://volunteers.grupovaughan.com

Intensive 6-day cultural exchange programme or 'talk-a-thon', from a Sunday to a Friday, held almost every week year round. 15 Spaniards and 17 English speakers are put together in a relaxed environment, accommodation in 4 picturesque locations within 2 hours of Madrid, to re-create an English-speaking village. The programme is based on both one-to-one sessions and group activities, as well as excursions, parties and walks in the countryside.

PREFERENCE OF NATIONALITY: All native speakers welcome.

SALARY: None for 1-week language exchange, but free food, accommodation, and transport from Madrid to hotel are provided.

CONTACT: Vaughan Volunteers Recruitment Manager.

WAYMAN ENGLISH INTERNATIONAL, S.L.

Calle Narcisos 62-A, 28016 Madrid (Registered office)

wdarcy@waymanenglish.com; jobs@waymanenglish.com

www.waymanenglish.com

NUMBER OF TEACHERS: 20 freelancers teach English in businesses throughout the greater Madrid area.

PREFERENCE OF NATIONALITY: Mainly native speakers only. No assistance given with work, residency or student visas.

QUALIFICATIONS: CELTA, TEFL or other recognised qualification and a university/college degree are needed. Qualifications, teaching expertise (technique and classroom management skills) etc. are all desirable, but Wayman English also assesses personality, character, professionalism and a love for teaching. Candidates should provide an updated CV – preferably with a current photo – and confirm they already reside in Spain and have the ability to legally work in Spain. Ideally the candidate has a minimum of 5 years' teaching experience, especially with business English, though company sometimes takes on teachers with less experience (e.g. 2–3 years) in whom employer sees potential and is willing to mentor. Intermediate level of Spanish will be valued.

CONDITIONS OF EMPLOYMENT: Normally, teachers work throughout the academic year (September to June) but sometimes on a case-by-case basis depending on the client's demands or needs. Most work is part-time. Hours normally from 8am and/or from 1pm to 5pm Monday to Friday. Number of hours varies from 25 to 90+ a month. Timetables normally fill up once the teacher has demonstrated his or her ability. Some vacancies can be filled only by teachers with their own transport.

SALARY: Gross hourly rates for freelance teacher are €18–€21 for phone teaching; €21–€30 for one-to-one and group classes. Rates depend on the client, duration of assignment, volume of hours and whether they are block hours or not.

FACILITIES/SUPPORT: No help with accommodation, though advice will be given on most convenient areas of Madrid to live, to take advantage of teaching opportunities in the city centre and in the numerous companies in the northern part of the city.

RECRUITMENT: Mostly word of mouth and personal recommendation. Specific jobs are advertised on teaching websites and local newspapers in Spain. All plausible candidates are given a personal interview. The candidate needs to be in Madrid as business needs may mean the candidate needs to start immediately.

CONTACT: Wayne D'Arcy, Director and Co-owner.

SWITZERLAND

The status of English is unassailed in multilingual Switzerland, where English is the preferred language of communication between people from different regions. The tourist industry and the presence of many international organisations and businesses make a knowledge of English an absolute priority. English has been compulsory throughout the curriculum in all Swiss schools since 2010, which involved retraining Swiss teachers on a massive scale and somewhat more demand for foreign teachers of English. Many cantons start English lessons early in primary school, whereas others start later, such as Italian-speaking Ticino, where English is not taught until age 14, after French and German.

Yet prospects are gloomy for people who fancy the idea of teaching the gnomes of Zurich or their counterparts in other parts of Switzerland, unless they are ultra-qualified. Although immigration regulations are not as restrictive as they once were, Switzerland will not suddenly be welcoming an army of foreign language teachers. Teachers may also like to consider whether they wish to face the barrage of regulations that are part and parcel of living in Switzerland, from attempting to open a bank account without possessing a small fortune, to falling foul of strict rubbish disposal regulations.

The Swiss economy remains solid, but is not as invincible as it was once considered to be, as the director of a *Sprachschule* in Basel explained:

> ***As a small language school in a country and region which has been experiencing severe withdrawal symptoms (from full employment, job and financial security), it is unlikely that we will be recruiting staff from outside Switzerland, especially as there is a large reservoir of potential candidates here in the Basel region and work permits for staff from outside Switzerland are now a rarity.***

This was corroborated by **Estelle Bieri**, formerly of the chain of Migros Club Schools (www.ecole-club.ch):

> ***In order to teach English, we require teachers to be either native speakers or to have a C2 level of English, preferably with a good Cambridge Proficiency pass. Teachers must have a B residence permit. In addition, they require a qualification in teaching English as a foreign language to adults, for example a CELTA or equivalent, or higher. This is valid for any Swiss school which is Eduqua validated (Eduqua is an independent body for quality control). Many of our teachers have university qualifications. Teaching experience is welcome, particularly with regard to teaching certain levels and types of classes (ESP, etc.).***

There are eight branches each of Wall Street English and Bénédict Schools in Switzerland; a list of addresses is available at www.wallstreetinstitute.ch and www.benedict-international.com. At the time of writing the Geneva and Lausanne branches of Wall Street (see entry) were advertising vacancies for 'talented and motivated new teachers' with a valid Swiss work permit. If you are hired by a Swiss language school, wages are high: ranging from SFr30 to SFr60 for a 50-minute lesson.

Private tutoring is a possibility for those who lack a permit, as the American world traveller and free spirit **Danny Jacobson** discovered when some years ago he was living with his Swiss girlfriend in Bern:

> ***A Swiss friend advised me to apply at one of the English schools but I didn't think it would work without a permit. So I just made my own flyer and put it up around town and the next thing I knew I had a bunch of people calling me up to help with proofreading seminar papers/assignments and to give private lessons. I figured I'd go for quantity and low-ball the market, charging only SFr20 per hour. But I found a few adverts for people looking for teachers and with those, I went with their offered price, which was much more.***

A qualified teacher can charge about SFr80 an hour in the cities, so even SFr40 might be considered a bargain.

The English Teachers' Association in Switzerland (www.e-tas.ch) operates a jobs board with a few vacancies, mainly for part-time trainers for business or for summer programmes. For example, at the time of writing the English Club in Villeneuve (www.theenglishclub.ch) was advertising for locally resident native speakers with experience of teaching children while Sight + Sound in Geneva (www.sight-sound.ch) was looking for part-time tutors to teach general classes and one-to-one.

REGULATIONS

No permit is needed for EU citizens who stay for less than three months though there is an obligation to register online. If they want to stay beyond that, e.g. to continue job-hunting or to do a seasonal job, they must obtain an L-permit (labour permit) for jobs lasting less than a year. If they are able to submit an employment contract from a Swiss employer, the Migration Office can complete residence formalities and no additional work permit is required.

If the contract of employment is going to extend beyond one year, it is necessary to apply for a B-permit, valid for between one and five years. There are strict quotas which have been reduced in recent years due to anti-immigrant feelings within Switzerland. So they are available only to highly qualified people for senior positions.

Detailed information about the regulations is published by the State Secretariat for Migration (www.sem.admin.ch) and is sometimes available from the cantonal authorities, for example downloadable brochures about living and working in Zurich are available at www.awa.zh.ch. The canton of Zurich also allows foreigners to apply for a work permit online (in German language only), which shortens the application time. The searchable forum www.englishforum.ch can also be helpful on technical matters.

As a result of Switzerland moving towards integration with Europe, non-EU citizens are finding it harder to gain legal access to Switzerland's English-teaching market unless they apply in special categories like spouse or trainee. If a non-European does find an employer willing to sponsor their application, the applicant will have to collect the documents from the Swiss embassy in his or her home country. Even summer employers are reluctant to hire from outside Europe, as the long-established summer camp organisation Le Rosey makes clear: '*To our great regret, Swiss law makes it impossible for international schools like Le Rosey to obtain work permits for non-EU citizens.*'

VACATION WORK

More possibilities for teaching English exist at summer camps than in city language institutes, as can be seen from the programmes listed in the directory below. There are a number of international schools in Switzerland, some of which run English language and sports summer schools. The Swiss Federation of Private Schools produces a list of summer schools in Switzerland held at its member schools, indicating which ones teach English, available at www.swiss-schools.ch. Watch for occasional job adverts on this site or, if you are in Switzerland, make local enquiries.

In addition to the organisations with entries below, the following organisations offer summer language courses between June and September and may need teachers or monitors (or some combination of the two):

Aiglon College Summer School, 1885 Chesières-Villars (✆ +41 24 496 6161; www.aiglon.ch). Summer school runs from 1 July to 1 August.

Collège Alpin International, Beau Soleil Holiday Language Camp, 1884 Villars-sur-Ollon (www.beausoleil.ch).

PHILIP LEE

Philip Lee from New Zealand spent his summers during university working at English language summer camps on the Continent, including one summer with Village Camps (see entry). The application for the position of counsellor involved a formal application and phone interview, plus he had to complete a basic first aid/CPR course (CPR etc) at his own expense. This opportunity is open to non-European nationals, as Philip reported recently.

There wasn't much of a visa problem as most tutors from outside the EU (US/Canada/Australia/NZ) had a three-month tourist visa I believe. I never encountered any problems in relation to my visa and working and even when I was working in Switzerland, where I expected more regulation and controls, there wasn't a problem at all. I worked in Switzerland for a two-week camp. But there were people who stayed there for up to 12 weeks working without problems.

I was paid cash in hand for the Swiss camps. I think payment was always a bit of concern for people working in this line of work for the first time, in the sense that there were no 'employment rights', but at the organisations I worked with, payment was always managed very professionally.

Alpadia Summer Camps, 1820 Montreux (www.alpadia.com/en/about-us/jobs.htm). Holiday language courses in Leysin, Ascona and Zug, for which it hires tutors and activity leaders.

Institut Le Rosey, Camp d'Eté, 1180 Rolle (✆ +41 21 822 5500; summercamp@rosey.ch; www.roseysummercamps.ch/jobs). Qualified or experienced EFL teachers over 20 for co-educational summer camps with sports coaching in Gstad and Rolle on Lake Geneva. Teachers must be capable of carrying out boarding school duties.

Institut Monte Rosa, 57 Avenue de Chillon, 1820 Montreux-Territet (✆ +41 21 965 4545; info@monterosa.ch; www.monterosa.ch).

International Camp Suisse is a British-based language camp with an office in West Yorkshire and the camp held in Torgon (www.campsuisse.com/job-description/language-teachers). Activity leaders and language teachers are needed to fill many summer positions.

Les Elfes in Verbier (www.leselfes.com/about-us/jobs). Another camp operator looking for seasonal summer or winter staff, most of whom will be over 20, though younger candidates are eligible to do work experience.

Leysin American School in Switzerland, 1854 Leysin (www.las.ch/summer/staff). Contact the director of Summer Programs.

St George's School in Switzerland, 1815 Clarens/Montreux (www.st-georgescamp.ch).

Surval Mont-Fleuri, Route de Glion 56, 1820 Montreux 1 (www.surval.ch). For teenage girls.

TASIS (The American School in Switzerland), Summer Language Programs, Via Collina d'Oro, 6926 Montagnola-Lugano (✆ +41 91 960 5151; http://summer.tasis.com/page.cfm?p=303). Hiring takes place between January and March. Net salaries are SFr2,600 for counsellors and SFr4,000 for teachers. American staff may be eligible for a SFr1,400-1,500 contribution to their transatlantic airfares and Europeans up to SFr500.

LIST OF EMPLOYERS

BERLITZ SCHOOL OF LANGUAGES AG
Gerbergasse 4, 4051 Basel
+41 61 226 9040
basel@berlitz.ch
www.berlitz.ch/en/vacancies

NUMBER OF TEACHERS: 15.

PREFERENCE OF NATIONALITY: Must be living in Basel and have residence permit.

QUALIFICATIONS: Bachelor's degree or professional experience, e.g. business, banking. Berlitz is looking for motivated and enthusiastic employees who can openly engage with others, have a love of language and culture, and a positive disposition. Must have teaching experience with adults and be a communicative person.

CONDITIONS OF EMPLOYMENT: No limit on contract length. Candidates must be available for at least 20 hours per week. Flexible hours of work. Pupils are adults whose average age is between 30 and 40.

SALARY: SFr22.50 per 40-minute lesson plus 10%–20% supplements for some programmes.

FACILITIES/SUPPORT: No assistance with accommodation. Training provided.

RECRUITMENT: Through adverts. Local interviews essential.

CONTACT: Martijn Morren (martijn.morren@berlitz.ch).

THE CAMBRIDGE INSTITUTE
Seidengasse 6, 8001 Zurich
+41 44 221 1212
zuerich@cambridge.ch
www.cambridge.ch

Schools also in Luzern, Basel and Bern.

PREFERENCE OF NATIONALITY: Native English speaker who is already resident in Zurich.

QUALIFICATIONS: English teaching certificate or diploma (e.g. CELTA or equivalent). The candidate must have already obtained the required permits to live and work in Switzerland.

CONTACT: Roger Bourne, Director of Studies.

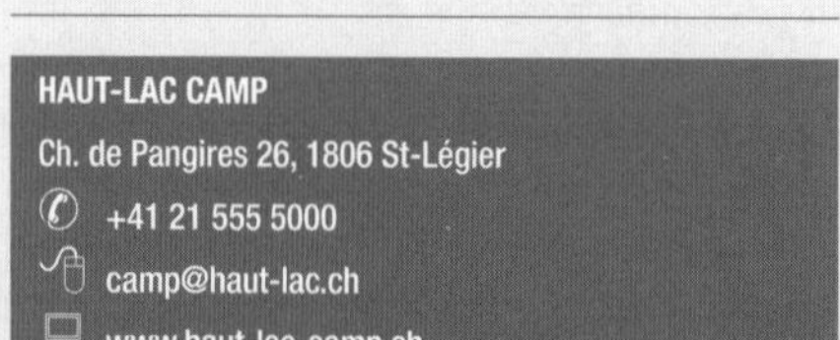

HAUT-LAC CAMP
Ch. de Pangires 26, 1806 St-Légier
+41 21 555 5000
camp@haut-lac.ch
www.haut-lac-camp.ch

NUMBER OF TEACHERS: Teachers/monitors needed for summer, spring and winter language camps for adolescents.

PREFERENCE OF NATIONALITY: Native English speakers, preferably with a passport from an EU member state.

QUALIFICATIONS: TEFL, CELTA or equivalent plus it is useful to have experience in sports, drama, art or games organisation.

CONDITIONS OF EMPLOYMENT: Language and sports summer camp (late June to end of August); winter ski camp (end of December to early April); spring camp (early April to early May).

FACILITIES/SUPPORT: Full board and lodging provided in single, twin or three-bedded rooms. Help given with travel expenses. Free laundry facilities and use of sports equipment.

RECRUITMENT: Send for an application form to jobs@haut-lac.com.

CONTACT: Steve McShane, Director.

INLINGUA – BASEL
Dufourstrasse 50, 4052 Basel
+41 61 278 9933
sprachkurse.basel@inlingua.com
www.inlingua-basel.ch

NUMBER OF TEACHERS: 50–55.

PREFERENCE OF NATIONALITY: Must be a Swiss or EU citizen and be in possession of a Swiss residence permit.

QUALIFICATIONS: University degree is essential. If the degree is not a teaching degree then CELTA or equivalent is required in addition (online courses are not accepted).

CONDITIONS OF EMPLOYMENT: Generally open-ended contracts but a two-year minimum commitment is expected. Lessons are held from 7am to 9.30pm and the teachers' workload depends on their availability.

SALARY: Starting full-time salary is approximately SFr5,500. Salary is directly dependent on number of lessons taught. It could take a few months before a full-time workload is built up.

FACILITIES/SUPPORT: The school handles all paperwork for work permits. No help with accommodation.

RECRUITMENT: Usually via ETAS (English Teachers' Association of Switzerland), advertising online or unsolicited applications. Interviews are essential. First round is conducted via telephone followed by one or two rounds of personal interviews held at the school.

CONTACT: Ms Anja Georg, Personnel Assistant (anja.georg @inlingua.com).

THE LANGUAGE FACTORY
Bionstrasse 4, 9015 St Gallen
+41 71 383 4185
info@thelanguagefactory.ch
www.thelanguagefactory.ch

NUMBER OF TEACHERS: 3.
PREFERENCE OF NATIONALITY: None.
QUALIFICATIONS: CELTA.
CONDITIONS OF EMPLOYMENT: Open-ended period of employment.
SALARY: Depends on qualifications and experience.
FACILITIES/SUPPORT: No help with accommodation. Most teachers are already resident.
RECRUITMENT: Job ads, mainly on www.e-tas.ch (English Teachers' Association in Switzerland). Interviews carried out via Skype or face-fo-face.
CONTACT: Judith Vogt, Teacher Trainer.

LANGUAGES FOR FUN
Place des Perrières 1, 1296 Coppet
+41 86 931 530
alex@languagesforfun.ch
www.languagesforfun.ch

NUMBER OF TEACHERS: 3.
PREFERENCE OF NATIONALITY: British.
QUALIFICATIONS: Minimum CELTA and a few years' experience.
CONDITIONS OF EMPLOYMENT: 1-year renewable contract. Usual hours are 2.30–6.30pm.
SALARY: Hourly pay.
FACILITIES/SUPPORT: No assistance with accommodation. The school takes care of work permit procedures.
RECRUITMENT: Based on CV and individual interview.
CONTACT: Alessandra Ginsberg.

TLC–INTERNATIONAL HOUSE
Bahnhofstrasse 44, 5400 Baden
+41 56 205 9796
hr@ihbaden.ch
www.ihbaden.ch

NUMBER OF TEACHERS: 25, mainly for in-company courses in Zurich and Baden areas.
PREFERENCE OF NATIONALITY: Native English speakers.
QUALIFICATIONS: Minimum CELTA plus experience teaching English to adults. DELTA preferred. Some business experience is preferable plus experience of teaching exam courses. Must be willing to travel.
CONDITIONS OF EMPLOYMENT: Open-ended contract. Classes start at 8am and finish at 9.30pm and include Saturdays. If the teacher is flexible in terms of location and time they can work up to 26 hours per week.
SALARY: SFr60–SFr72 depending on qualifications, experience and range of teaching.
FACILITIES/SUPPORT: Training opportunities and free language training.
RECRUITMENT: Usually through ETAS (English Teachers' Association of Switzerland), adverts on websites such as www.jobs.ch or through word of mouth. Interviews are essential. Preliminary interview can be done by phone and successful candidate will need to take a trial lesson in Switzerland.
CONTACT: Tanja Bechtiger, HR Manager.

VERBIER LANGUAGE SCHOOL
Centre de l'étoile, Rue de Médran 6, CP 475, 1936 Verbier
+41 79 653 2227
info@verbierlanguageschool.com
www.verbierlanguageschool.com

NUMBER OF TEACHERS: 2 full-time and varying numbers of part-time staff depending on the season.
PREFERENCE OF NATIONALITY: None.
QUALIFICATIONS: Teachers must be bi or tri-lingual. Obviously it's better if potential employees have experience, but language skills and personality are highly important. Classes do not always focus on grammar but should make learning fun and relaxed. Conversational skills are paramount.
CONDITIONS OF EMPLOYMENT: Seasonal contracts are June to August and December to April. Usual teaching hours are 9am–12pm and 4pm–7pm.
SALARY: SFr25 per hour. Less deductions required by Swiss law (pension, second pension, accident insurance, taxes).
FACILITIES/SUPPORT: Teachers must find their own accommodation but employer provides list of agencies and people who may be able to offer help. Assistance given with work permits.
RECRUITMENT: Selection made from CVs received and interviews arranged, by Skype if necessary.
CONTACT: Rosi Pickard, Director.

VILLAGE CAMPS
14 Rue de la Morache, Nyon, 1260 Vaud
+41 24 493 3064
personnel@villagecamps.com
www.villagecamps.com

Language summer camp at Leysin near Lake Geneva in French-speaking Switzerland (also in York, England and Cyprus).

PREFERENCE OF NATIONALITY: European, North American, Australian and New Zealand passport holders may apply.

QUALIFICATIONS: Applicants must be at least 21 years of age, possess a recognised qualification in language teaching (minimum 4 weeks) and be a native English speaker. Must have proven teaching experience of at least a year. A second language is desirable and experience in sports, creative and/or outdoor activities is essential. A valid first aid and cardiopulmonary resuscitation (CPR) certificate is required while at camp.

CONDITIONS OF EMPLOYMENT: Employment periods vary from 3 to 8 weeks between June and August. Unpaid orientation (last week of June) must be attended.

SALARY: Room and board, accident and liability insurance and a weekly allowance of SFr425 provided.

RECRUITMENT: Starts in January. There is no deadline to submit applications, but positions are limited. Interviews are by telephone. For information on dates, locations, and positions available and to apply directly online, visit www.villagecamps.com.

CONTACT: Personnel Director.

WALL STREET ENGLISH

Rue du Simplon, 34, 1006 Lausanne

+41 21 614 66 14

brad.elliott@wallstreetenglish.ch

www.wallstreetenglish.ch/en/jobs

Head office of WSE Switzerland which comprises 8 schools.

NUMBER OF TEACHERS: 12 in Lausanne, 60 in Switzerland.

PREFERENCE OF NATIONALITY: None. Due to restrictions on work permits, candidates who are already established in Switzerland are preferred.

QUALIFICATIONS: CELTA or equivalent is a minimum.

CONDITIONS OF EMPLOYMENT: Open-ended contract. Variable hours but usually evenings 5pm–8pm.

SALARY: SFr37–60 per hour, depending on type of lesson given. Tax deducted at source for non-long-term residents plus various insurance deductions.

FACILITIES/SUPPORT: Assistance given with obtaining insurance card and sorting out tax but only after candidate has arranged his or her own work permit.

RECRUITMENT: Teachers for other WSI branches in Switzerland and the Czech Republic are generally recruited by a team leader in each school individually, and therefore candidates are encouraged to apply directly to their chosen school/area. Interviews are essential and occasionally conducted via Skype.

CONTACT: Brad Elliott, National Academic and HR Director.

CENTRAL AND EASTERN EUROPE

The transition to a market economy throughout Eastern and Central Europe initially resulted in a huge demand for professional assistance, especially in improving the skills of communication in English. In the 1990s and early 21st century this was matched by an enthusiastic demand from young westerners to live and work in Eastern Europe. But now the standard of state language education has improved to the extent that there are now many more competent homegrown teachers in Hungary, Poland and so on, and far less call for native speaker teachers. And with the improvements in state provision of language teaching, fewer Eastern Europeans feel compelled to invest in private instruction. Hundreds of thousands have been learning English on the spot in Britain and Ireland while living and working there. Post-Brexit, it is simply not known what form the arrangements for Eastern Europeans living and working in the UK will take.

Yet despite having moved past making 'Western' synonymous with 'desirable', the majority of Central European people are still remarkably welcoming to Britons and Americans. Thousands of temporary and longer-term visitors continue to fall under the spell of famous destinations such as Prague, Budapest, Kraków, as well as many other beautiful towns in Slovakia and Bulgaria. Even those who find themselves in the less prepossessing industrial cities usually come away beguiled by Central European charm. The English language teaching industry in these countries has grown up, and hires native speaker teachers with proven experience or an appropriate qualification. For qualified English teachers the market is now more stable, realistic and developed.

The explosion in the number of training centres for TEFL/TESL teachers in all English-speaking countries means that the pool of certified available teachers is fairly large. Teachers who can claim to specialise either in teaching Young Learners or in teaching Business English are especially attractive since both these areas of ELT are buoyant. Tourism training colleges in Hungary, the Czech and Slovak Republics and the Baltics are especially keen on encouraging conversational English. The easiest way to become more employable is to acquire a TEFL qualification, which could prove especially useful (and incidentally cheaper) if obtained in Eastern Europe. For example International House in Prague, Budapest, Katowice and Wroclaw all offer the CELTA course, while others offers proprietary TESOL certificates (see the Directory of Training Courses).

North Americans have found that the accession of most of the former Eastern bloc countries to the EU has resulted in immigration regulations favouring English teachers from Britain and Ireland. Whether the playing field will be more even after the United Kingdom negotiates an exit from the EU remains to be seen. Language institutes understandably do not want to become involved with the delays and expense of supporting non-EU candidates to obtain a residence permit, though some are willing. One of the first language-teaching organisations to break into Eastern Europe has continued to be one of the most active and energetic in the region, International House. IH-affiliated schools are flourishing in the main cities of Belarus, Lithuania, Latvia, Estonia, Ukraine (where there are six), Poland, Romania, Bulgaria, Hungary, Russia and Slovakia, among others. The affiliation agreement with all IH schools states that the schools can employ only teachers who have passed the CELTA course. Similarly the British Council is often in need of suitable candidates to fill vacancies in its teaching centres in Bulgaria, Romania, Ukraine, etc.

Local salaries can seem absurdly low when translated into a hard currency. Some schools pay what is usually a generous salary by local standards but which can leave little after paying for food and accommodation. It is difficult to generalise, but a typical package would include a monthly net salary of £500–£600 in addition to free or subsidised accommodation and possibly some other perks such as a travel stipend. The best-paid jobs are for firms that teach in-company courses, especially in Poland, though they are unlikely to offer accommodation.

A host of private language schools that are either independent or part of larger language-teaching organisations are represented in Eastern and Central Europe. Most of the Central European schools listed in the directory are well established and offer above-average working conditions. In the more volatile climate of Russia and former Soviet republics (which are several years behind the stable democracies of Central Europe), locally managed schools come and go, and tend to choose their teachers from the pool of native English speakers on the spot, who also come and go. Intrepid travellers visiting the Central Asian Republics with no intention to work are still sometimes invited to stay a while and do some English teaching, as was happening in off-the-beaten-track towns in Poland and the former Czechoslovakia in the 1990s.

One interesting option for those who do not wish to commit themselves for a full academic year is to work at one of the many language summer camps which are offered to young people, usually in scenic locations from Lake Balaton in Hungary to Lake Baikal in Siberia to the Black Sea resorts of Bulgaria.

CONDITIONS OF WORK

The financial rewards of working in the old Russian Empire are usually so negligible that trained/experienced teachers cannot be enticed to teach there unless they have an independent interest in living in that part of the world or are supported by a voluntary organisation. Even the large language chains which offer reasonable working conditions (e.g. flat provided, plenty of support) do not pay high enough wages to allow ordinary EL teachers to save any money. Russia itself can offer reasonable wages, but the cost of living can be very high in Moscow and St Petersburg and inflation continues to be a problem.

Most of the Central European cities and larger towns have sprouted western-style supermarkets – Tesco stores have proliferated in Hungary, Poland, etc. – and other consumer outlets, often to the disgruntlement of the older generations who have a fondness for their local shops. Living in these cities begins to feel not so very different from living in France or Italy, particularly with the influx of international companies. The nightlife of Budapest rivals that of Berlin. Smaller towns and rural areas can still be a very different proposition (until you come across expats who have bought property on the cheap in Bulgaria, etc.).

FINDING A JOB

Far fewer vacancies in Central and Eastern Europe are being advertised in the educational press and on the internet, especially in Poland, but it is still worth checking the main EFL job sites such as www.tefl.com, which at the time of writing carried job ads for 57 different employers in the region, with the majority of 25 being in Russia. The possibility of creating your own job in the more obscure corners of this region still exists. Much of what takes place happens by chance, and protocol is often given a back seat to friendly encounters. Obtaining work often comes down to the right (or wrong) hairstyle or whether you've got any Polish/Lithuanian/Slovak/Azerbaijani ancestry. Looking professional, being persistent and asking as many questions as you answer, rather than sitting back on your heels, usually pays off. EU teachers will have an advantage in EU member countries, although other nationalities do succeed in finding employers willing to take on the expense and hassle of applying for the documentation.

Michael Todd from the US describes a typical trajectory for the TEFL teacher taking his or her first tentative steps into Eastern Europe to becoming established. When he arrived, he had done one undergraduate course in teaching English and a tutoring seminar for volunteer teachers, both back in Michigan. Initially he spent nine months near Katowice in Poland teaching the Callan Method, then two years at the Technical University of Liberec in the Czech Republic, and after five years in Bratislava he became a Senior Teacher. Along the way he acquired a CELTA from International House Budapest (which he wishes he had done earlier), and a Business English Teaching certificate (BET) from International House Bratislava:

I found my first job in Slovakia online. I don't remember which site. They turned out to be bloodsuckers, so after a year I moved to International House Bratislava. Another teacher and I walked into IH and asked for an interview. The DOS promptly interviewed us. Because I didn't have a CELTA, the DOS had me do a teaching demonstration a few days later. Having impressed her in the teaching demo, we discussed the contractual terms. I decided, stupidly, to return to my first employer, but IH was still willing to hire me for the following fall.

According to Michael, teaching one-to-one at international businesses around Bratislava gave him lots of autonomy and variety. Some of his students just wanted to chat but most were looking for competently delivered lessons and they expected to be corrected often. Students over the age of 45 tend to be more difficult to teach, and they complain about how hard the language is. It would be easier to save money if it wasn't so tempting to visit nearby Vienna, Budapest and Prague. Fortunately there is a healthy market for private lessons, so it is not difficult to supplement your income.

In addition to International House, the major chains have some franchise schools in the region, chief among them EF English First, which sends many teachers to Russia, and Language Link with affiliated schools in Russia, Uzbekistan and one school in Kazakhstan (www.languagelink.co.uk). The Peace Corps (toll-free ✆ +1 855 855 1961; www.peacecorps.gov) provides volunteer teachers on 27-month contracts to a few countries in Central Asia plus Ukraine where it runs a TEFL Project. The only other destination countries for Peace Corps teachers in the region are Albania, Armenia, Georgia, Kosovo, Kyrgyz Republic, Macedonia and Moldova. Candidates must be US citizens, have a degree and be in good health. All expenses, including airfare and health insurance, are covered. Volunteers teach at both secondary and university level and become involved with teacher training and curriculum development.

Angloville (www.angloville.com/teach-english) is the biggest provider of language immersion programmes in Central & Eastern Europe, with operations year round at country hotels in Poland (where the programme started), Hungary, Romania and the Czech Republic. Volunteers stay for three to ten days helping local clients to improve their conversational English by practising. In return they receive free accommodation and full board, transport from their gateway city after having a tour of it; with a choice of Warsaw, Wroclaw, Poznan, Krakow, Budapest, Bucharest, Prague or Dublin. Angloville is offering a new Anglo-TEFL Scholarship programme (www.anglo-tefl.com) aimed at students, which involves subsidised online training with Premier TEFL, followed by at least two weeks of providing speaking practice to Polish, Hungarian, Romanian or Czech clients at Angloville holiday destinations.

The rest of this chapter is organised by country: Bulgaria, Czech Republic, Hungary, Poland, Romania, Russia Slovakia, followed by Russia's former satellite states (the Baltic States, Ukraine and Moldova). The former Yugoslav republics of Slovenia, Croatia, Bosnia-Herzogovina, Serbia and Montenegro are included in the chapter 'The Rest of Europe' along with Albania, Cyprus and Malta. Finally the Central Asian Republics are covered.

BULGARIA

Since Bulgaria joined the EU in 2007 it has attracted more EU tourists as well as property speculators and foreign businesses. The demand for English teachers is substantial, although opportunities in the private sector are still relatively scarce. Almost all schools ask for at least a degree and teaching certificate. The cost of living is among the cheapest in Europe and indeed the world.

FINDING A JOB

A Bulgarian agency of long standing appoints 60–80 native speakers to teach in specialist English-language secondary schools for one academic year starting mid-September, for which the deadline is 31 May, though admissions are also accepted on a rolling basis. Details are available from Teachers for Central and Eastern Europe (21 V 5 Rakovski Boulevard, Dimitrovgrad 6400; ✆ +359 391 24787; tfcee@usa.net; www.tfcee.8m.com). Graduates, preferably with a TEFL background, are accepted from the USA, UK, Canada and Australia to spend an academic year teaching. The weekly teaching load is 19 40-minute classes per four-day week. The monthly salary in Bulgarian leva is equivalent to $100. Benefits include free furnished accommodation, 60 days of paid holiday, paid sick leave and work permit. A summer programme is also available at Black Sea resorts for which the application deadline is 20 June and the monthly wage is $200. TfCEE charges an application fee of $60.

A number of other companies offer English-language summer schools and camps at resorts near Varna. The Orange House English Language Centre in Varna (www.orangehousevarna.com) has been seen advertising pay rates of £1,000 for a nine-week summer stint.

The British Council in Sofia has a thriving English centre, which offers courses for young learners, adults and businessmen and women; to enquire about any forthcoming part-time teaching vacancies email learnenglish@britishcouncil.bg. Pharos is the biggest chain of foreign-language and computing schools in Bulgaria (www.pharos.bg), and affiliated to the Strategakis Schools network of Northern Greece; however, this book has never heard of any native speakers being hired by a Pharos school.

Outside the official education system a reasonable number of language institutes and educational establishments are on the look-out for well-presented, confident candidates. One of the first private schools to be established after the revolution of 1990 was the AVO School of English, with two schools in Sofia affiliated to Bell Worldwide. It runs CELTA courses that are at the cheaper end of the scale for Europe (see entry in the Directory of Training Courses) and often advertises for native English-speaking staff who must have a degree, preferably in English and at least a year of teaching experience, preferably with young learners (www.avo-bell.com/en/work_offers).

American teachers with at least a master's degree could try the AUBG, a private American-style liberal arts university located in Blagoevgrad (www.aubg.edu). All classes are in English and the university's English Language Institute prepares future AUBG applicants for the TOEFL and SAT exams, as well as teaching courses every semester to absolute beginners and intermediate students.

EFL vacancies hardly ever crop up on the internet, but this does not mean that they do not exist, as **Darren Quinn** reported:

> ***Before I came to Bulgaria I had no idea what the job market was really like. All the information and advice I found online was negative. However, when I arrived here, even though I didn't speak the language very well, I walked into every school I could find and asked them for work. I had obtained my CELTA and had worked in South Korea for one year before I moved here, though it would have been possible to work at some schools here without***

the CELTA. Within a few months I was working part-time at four different schools and also had some private students. Work was a difficult grind for a long time here. However, two years ago, my wife and I were able to open our own small school, which has since grown into one of the biggest in the city (see entry for ABC School).

I would have to say that overall my experience in Bulgaria has been a very good one. The students are excellent and the Bulgarian people are very friendly and relaxed. The culture is fascinating and varied. Many people are put off coming to Bulgaria, perhaps because they think there are few job opportunities and much of the information online concerning employment is quite negative. From my own experience, I can say that this is not true: if you put in the leg-work you can find work here and if you aren't worried about making a fortune, this is a very enjoyable place to teach English.

REGULATIONS

Bulgaria's accession into the EU has made it easier for teachers in terms of red tape. EU citizens only need a letter from their employer in order to get permission to stay for one year. It's a little time consuming, but basically unproblematic, and is done at the local police station. US citizens, on the other hand, need a visa obtained from one of the four Bulgarian consulates in the US. For this reason the Real English School (see entry), among others, employs only EU citizens or non-EU citizens who have a right to stay for some other reason (e.g. marriage to a Bulgarian). The English Academy, however, will consider employing US citizens, who are responsible for their own visas, although some assistance is given with paperwork.

LEISURE TIME

Vicky Williams, who was director of the Real English School in Veliko Turnovo and Pleven until it closed in 2016, reported that living in Bulgaria was never dull:

> *As for living and working in Bulgaria, it is a country that is changing rapidly. There are still some vestiges of communism around in terms of architecture, cars, bureaucracy and lack of choice in shops, etc., but on the other hand there is a huge amount of building going on and many people now do have a lot of money. It's a fascinating place to live at the moment – it is a country of contrasts.*

The current minimum wage in Bulgaria is 420 leva a month, about €215, among the lowest in Europe. Since a month's rent for a one-bedroom flat can cost more than that in central Sophia, the majority of Bulgarians live together in family units, often with several generations squashed together in one house.

Most big cities are well equipped and Bulgaria is striving to meet the guidelines put in place since joining the European Union. In towns, you'll find everything you would expect from a modern European city. In rural areas, on the other hand, wages are still much lower and living conditions can be more traditional, for example in the countryside you can still see peasants with donkeys and carts and stooped old ladies lugging branches of trees home to burn for firewood. In these areas indoor toilets may be something of a luxury. The Bulgarian countryside, especially mountain areas, is expansive and unspoilt, with plenty of affordable opportunities to hike or ski in the winter. The Black Sea coast is mostly built up as holiday resorts and is a popular place for a cheap seaside break.

LIST OF EMPLOYERS

ABC ENGLISH LANGUAGE CENTRE
23 Marno Pole Street, Veliko Tarnovo
+359 899 915 486
abc-bg@hotmail.com
www.abcenglish.eu

NUMBER OF TEACHERS: 4.
PREFERENCE OF NATIONALITY: EU passport holders only.
QUALIFICATIONS: CELTA.
CONDITIONS OF EMPLOYMENT: 1 year minimum. Variable hours between 9am and 9pm.
FACILITIES/SUPPORT: Assistance given with accommodation and work permits.
RECRUITMENT: Website advertising, followed by interview.
CONTACT: Darren Quinn, Director.

ENGLISH ACADEMY PLOVDIV
28 Gladston Street, Plovdiv 4000
+359 32 623457
plovdiv@englishacademybg.com
www.englishacademybg.com

NUMBER OF TEACHERS: 4.
PREFERENCE OF NATIONALITY: Only native English speakers.
QUALIFICATIONS: Recognised teaching certificate such as the Cambridge CELTA.
CONDITIONS OF EMPLOYMENT: 3, 6 and 12-month contracts. Full-time: Tuesday to Friday, 5.40pm–9.40pm and Saturday 9am–1pm and 2pm–6pm. Part-time: less than 24 hours per week within the same time frame.
SALARY: 15 Bulgarian leva per hour.
FACILITIES/SUPPORT: Arranges with local agents for accommodation viewings and assists with translation. Non-EU citizens are responsible for their own visas although the school gives assistance.
RECRUITMENT: Telephone and/or in-person interviews.
CONTACT: Mark A Faulkner, Director of Studies (markfaulkner@englishacademybg.com).

ENGLISH ACADEMY VARNA
48 Preslav Str, Nezavisimost Square, Varna 9000
+359 52 622351
varna@englishacademybg.com
www.englishacademybg.com/en/varna-jobs

NUMBER OF TEACHERS: 14 for academic year and summer school.
PREFERENCE OF NATIONALITY: Only native English speakers.
QUALIFICATIONS: Degree in any subject and teaching certificate are essential, 3 years' experience preferred. Must be friendly and outgoing.
CONDITIONS OF EMPLOYMENT: 12-month contracts preferred starting in July (over 4 terms), 20–24 teaching hours a week, 5 days a week (Monday to Friday at summer school or Tuesday to Saturday during academic year, although a lot of teaching takes place at weekends). Part-time positions 8–20 hours. July/August summer schools run in association with charitable foundation (www.arkutino-school.eu).
SALARY: 23 leva per hour, more for technical/non-standard teaching. 10% flat rate tax. Summer teaching rate is 20 leva per hour net with a guaranteed minimum of 18.
FACILITIES/SUPPORT: Free shared accommodation given for full-time summer work.
RECRUITMENT: Over the internet (mainly www.tefl.com). Interviews essential, either by telephone/Skype or face-to-face. Non-EU citizens are responsible for their own visas, but assistance given with the relevant paperwork.
CONTACT: Mark Mctaggart, Director of Studies (markmc@englishacademybg.com).

CZECH REPUBLIC

The proliferation of TEFL-qualified teachers has allowed language schools to become far more discerning, especially in Prague. Language institutes generally do not accept online TEFL certificates, and adhere to the international standard of looking for teachers who have had at least 106 class hours in a four-week on-site programme, with at least six hours of observed teaching practice. Smaller Czech towns, including some rather uninspiring places in the steel-producing heart of the country and the Moravian capital Brno, offer interested teachers more scope for employment than the tourist-clogged capital. Be prepared for living and working conditions to change significantly once you leave the capital, especially for EFL teachers. Prague offers low pay, split shifts and intense competition between language schools that leads to job insecurity for teachers. Teaching private lessons is the most lucrative but the most difficult to fix up for new arrivals. Private lessons can be charged at 350+ crowns an hour, but most teachers working for a run-of-the-mill institute start at a base rate of 200–250 crowns which has not risen in some years. A good way to attract students initially is to charge at the lower end of the scale but to teach in groups of three or four.

FINDING A JOB

Most schools prefer a mixture of accents though Irish people have a red tape advantage, as do Britons while the UK remains in the EU. But there are also plenty of Americans and Canadians, along with Australians who are generally well received partly because of the large number of Czechs who emigrated to Australia.

STATE SCHOOLS

Qualified teachers are seldom recruited to teach in Czech primary and secondary schools as they once were. However the centralised contact, the Academic Information Agency (AIA) in Prague (see entry), part of the Ministry of Education, continues to offer a placement service into one-year positions. Far fewer positions are registered with the AIA than used to be the case, and any that are will likely be in obscure towns rather than Prague. The school year runs for 10 months from 1 September to 30 June, though some vacancies occur in January between semesters. In some cases, TEFL qualifications are not required, though normally the minimum requirements accepted are BA/MA in English/Applied Linguistics, a teaching qualification and experience. Applications should be submitted before the end of April. The AIA simply acts as a go-between, circulating CVs and applications to state schools that have requested a teacher. Schools then contact applicants directly to discuss contractual details.

One British teacher with extensive teaching experience in Slovakia was delighted and relieved to be hired by the Technical University of Liberec. On application he was upfront about having failed the CELTA course the previous summer and also about having severe epilepsy, and was 'really encouraged by the Director's promotion of equal opportunities and non-discrimination'.

PRIVATE INSTITUTES

A wide range of well-established academies offer high standards of instruction. The main international chains of language schools, such as Berlitz, have large established operations in the country. Most teachers are recruited locally, often through a TEFL training centre, such as TEFL Worldwide Prague (www.teflworldwideprague.com), or via noticeboards, for example at the British Council and English-language bookshops.

It is not difficult to find contact details for English-language institutes in Prague and elsewhere. The most established schools that are externally vetted and their standards monitored belong to the professional association of language schools, AJS (Asociace jazykových škol; www.asociacejs.cz). Member schools could be worth approaching since many of them include teacher recruitment information in English on their websites. Also the *Yellow Pages* (Zlaté Stránky; www.zlatestranky.cz) are an excellent source of addresses under the heading *Jazykove skoly* as is the listing of schools at www.expats.cz/prague/directory/language-schools.

Of the institute websites that are available in English, a selection that provides teacher vacancy information, and in some cases online application forms, includes James Cook (www.icl.cz/en/teachers), Lexis (www.lexis.cz) and Tutor (see entry) plus:

English Link s.r.o., Prague: www.englishlink.cz
Glossa skola jazyku: www.glossa.cz
Tandem Jazykove, Prague: www.tandem.cz/work-for-tandem.

Even though most schools in Prague claim to receive plenty of CVs on spec from which to fill any vacancies that arise, their willingness to describe their recruitment procedures online (in contrast to the main language schools in Poland) indicates that the demand for teachers is still strong. Anyone who is well qualified or experienced should have few difficulties in finding a job on the spot, particularly if they are lucky with their timing. The market in Brno is booming too, with more than 120 language schools listed as operating in the country's second-largest city (many will be one-person outfits), catering to a population of less than 400,000. Most people wait until they arrive in Prague before trying to find teaching work, which is what **Linda Harrison** did:

> ***I arrived in September, which was too late, but if you persevere there are jobs around. A lot of teaching work here seems to be in companies. Schools employ you to go into offices, etc. to teach English. After a short job hunt, I was hired by a company called Languages at Work which paid well and provided food and travel vouchers as well as helping with accommodation.***

Languages at Work has since morphed several times and is now the Spevácek Education Centre (see entry). People end up teaching in Prague via the most circuitous routes, as **Anne Morris** from the USA describes:

> ***Although I'm near retirement age, I'm still a free spirit and am living in Prague now more or less by chance. I ran into an American couple at a jam-packed event in Old Town Square on a visit to Prague two years ago who said they were teaching English here. I've always loved this city so I asked how one would get a job like that and they scratched out a website on the back of an envelope (TEFL Worldwide). I lost them in the crowd but on return to the US came across the envelope in a coat pocket and decided to check it out – and now here I am teaching English. Just wish I'd made this discovery much earlier in my life!***

Outside of Prague, chances are reasonable of finding jobs in the private sector all year round, with the greatest selection available in late August through to November and in January/February. Those without qualifications or experience will find it very difficult because they will be competing with all those keen new graduates of TEFL training courses in the Czech Republic (see Directory of Training Courses). Private schools in Prague will give preference when hiring to anyone who is already resident.

If you are stuck for a job during the summer months, a good option is to work in a summer camp until the school year starts. There are a number of children's summer camp options available, as well as intensive one-week courses for adults at holiday resorts. Children's camps do not generally pay very well, but food and accommodation are included, and many teachers use the camps as an opportunity to get to know a bit more of the country before going back to their city jobs in September. One to try is a British company,

Wattsenglish, which runs city summer day camps as well in Prague, Liberec, Usti nad Labem, Teplice, Karlovy Vary, Mlada Boleslav, etc. and a residential camp in the Giant Mountains (www.wattsenglish.cz/for-teachers/employment-opportunities). Teachers are paid 6,000 crowns per week gross (4,000–5,000 crowns net).

There are some advertisements for teaching jobs in the local English language online press, primarily at www.expats.cz. Quite a few advertised positions seem to be in nurseries and pre-schools. It may be worth advertising your speciality as a freelance English tutor (e.g. marketing, law, etc.). **Kathy Panton** suggests enlisting the help of a Czech friend to translate 'Native speaker will tutor English to intermediate or advanced students', and send it to a free ads site such as *Annonce* (www.annonce.cz). Otherwise, you can post your bio and prices on www.findmyfavouriteteacher.com or similar. Trial lessons are offered for 125–200 crowns, with private lessons earning the teacher on average 300–400 crowns.

REGULATIONS

Since accession, EU citizens no longer have to apply for a visa or work permit. Those who intend to stay more than 90 days can obtain a certificate of temporary residence from the regional office of the Ministry of the Interior, though this is not a requirement; see the Immigration section at www.mvcr.cz for contact details or phone the information hotline on ✆ +420 974 832421.

Correspondingly it has become more problematic for non-EU citizens to obtain the necessary permission to live and work in the Czech Republic. The sought-after document is the blue card, which entitles foreign nationals with good qualifications (minimum university degree) to both live and work in the country. This requires gathering a raft of documents including employment contract, proof of accommodation, health insurance cover, etc. and presenting it at the Czech embassy in your country or, in some circumstances, to the Ministry of the Interior. Foreigners do sometimes pick up work on their Schengen tourist visa but, before it expires after 90 days, the holder must exit the country and is not allowed to return until a further 90 days have elapsed.

The Czech Republic has Youth Mobility agreements with New Zealand and Canada which allow young people aged 18–35 who meet the acceptance criteria to reside in the Czech Republic for up to 12 months; the administration fee is currently 2,500 crowns.

Working as a self-employed freelancer is becoming more common, partly because the earnings can be higher than employees. For example the Swallow School (see entry) says that teachers working with their own business licence can invoice the school for 20,000–30,000 crowns, whereas employees are paid in the region of 14,000 crowns plus benefits such as paid holidays. EU citizens who want to set up as self-employed freelancers must obtain a Czech trade licence (*živnostenský* list) as **Martin Filla** did:

> ***It took me about 6 months to get a business licence. Before then some people took me on just as a temporary teacher and without a contract. After I got my business licence, more schools were willing to give me work and also a (standard) contract with it. According to law, it took me about three years to get my permanent residence visa and this also shows schools I plan to live in the Czech Republic.***

CONDITIONS OF WORK

People teaching at private institutes in Prague, where there is a definite glut of foreign teachers, attracted by the cultural chic of the city, have been called the 'sweat shop labourers' of the TEFL world because of the low wages that employers can get away with paying. Salaries in the capital are sometimes lower than in smaller cities such as Brno, even though the cost of living is higher.

Working conditions in state schools are generally better than in private schools, though opportunities are far fewer than they used to be. The guaranteed salary at state schools, even if you're sick or there is a holiday, is a definite advantage. If you are lucky enough to be teaching mostly final-year students, your working hours in the exam month of June will be minimal, even though the teaching day at a state school might start at 8am. This counts as a lie-in compared with teaching in private companies, which is often underway by 7am or 7.30am. And of course in state schools there is no evening or weekend work.

The monthly wage range in state schools of 20,000–35,000 crowns gross is catching up with wages in the private sector. If you are renting on the open market, expect to spend between a fifth and a quarter of your earnings on simple accommodation. Hourly fees start at roughly 200 crowns net, though a more usual wage is 230–250 crowns. A full-time salary should be adequate to live on by local standards but will not allow you to save anything, unless you take on lots of private tutoring.

The scramble for getting teaching hours did not appeal to the 40-something Australian author **Rachael Weiss** whose long stay in Prague resulted in the amusing and revealing book *The Thing About Prague*, first published in 2014 (Allen & Unwin). Her spin on English teaching is more negative than most:

> ***I suppose I could have got a teaching certificate and joined the hordes of Brits and Americans working for horrible cowboy outfits for a pittance, but two things stopped me. First. I don't have what it takes to work for a horrible cowboy outfit. There are plenty of them in Prague. 'Schools' set up by glassy-eyed bandits, mainly from Russia and America – men who'd arrived in Prague like rats off a cargo ship that'd washed up on a tropical paradise, filled with vulnerable foreigners who had no other way of earning a living, and natives desperate to learn the language of the internet. Living was cheap, wages were low and labour was plentiful.***
>
> ***I heard tale after tale of teachers working for minimal rates a few hours a week, having to travel three hours for every one they worked and not getting paid for their travel time, being done out of their pay, being promised visas that never materialised. I kept hearing of jobs lost with no notice and of ghastly bosses.***
>
> ***Second, I didn't want to teach English because that was the job that all the expats did, and I didn't want to be in the expat crowd. I didn't want to work with a whole lot of Americans and Brits, where I'd have to talk endlessly about the food and television we'd left at home. I wanted a job, any job, one that was more like an ordinary job.***
>
> **Weiss, R., (2014). *The Thing About Prague ... How I gave it all up for a new life in Europe's most eccentric city.* Crows Nest, New South Wales: Allen & Unwin.**
>

In Brno, wages nearly match those of Prague, but you should expect less in smaller cities such as Olomouc, Xlin, Hradec Kralove, etc. However, outside the Czech Republic's major cities the cost of living drops and many teachers in smaller cities and towns find that they are able to save more despite actually earning a lower monthly salary.

Qualified teacher **Ailsa Randall** has been teaching in the Czech Republic for years and comments on the quality of her students:

> ***The students are wonderful – it is so exciting for them to have a British teacher and they are eager to learn. I have taught people of all ages, including children and almost all of them were fantastic students. I still enjoy teaching them 15 years later! Great sense of humour. They needed English for work but also for travelling or just for fun. The teaching was so much more fun than the teaching I had been doing before in a secondary school in England. If someone is thinking about coming to the Czech Republic and is put off by the low salaries I would say don't worry. So many people want private lessons and the language schools give you plenty of free time so you can make ends meet no problem. You will encounter enthusiastic and very sweet students and the level of English is a lot higher now than when I arrived.***

The majority of private language school clients are adults who are available for lessons after work, so most teaching takes place between 4pm and 8pm, Monday to Thursday. Long-time resident **Martin Filla** (originally from Australia but with a passport from an EU member state) reported that in the past he had struggled due to the financial crisis and a reduction in the number of students. He now teaches only 25 hours a week, with half his students from language schools, and 40% in private lessons. Martin encounters the problem familiar to all EFL teachers, trying to balance encouragement of students to speak with trying to get them to speak accurately, as he reported while working for David's Agency (see entry) in the Moravian spa town of Luhacovice:

> ***Most of the teaching was conversation based, to students who were intermediate or upper intermediate. One great challenge was to make it comfortable and interesting for everyone to speak, and help the students overcome their shyness. It was difficult to make every lesson interesting for everyone, and I was unsure about how much I should correct the students' bad grammar habits. Adult students especially have bad habits from earlier learning and these are very difficult to correct.***

Accommodation in Prague is more plentiful than it used to be and easier to find thanks to various Facebook groups. If you have a friend to translate for you, you can try the accommodation listings in *Annonce*, the Prague free ads paper, or Craigslist in English (http://prague.craigslist.cz). Most employers are prepared to help newcomers to find accommodation, usually a room in a small shared flat or university hostel. In the rest of the country there is less competition for affordable accommodation. However, those moving to Brno or Zlin will find that the real-estate agents rule the market, so those without local support may find themselves having to pay one month's rent to the agent as a finder's fee. On the other hand, agents do offer the advantage of providing a wide selection of furnished flats covering a range of budgets and in a variety of neighbourhoods. Many people place an advert in the local *Inzert Expres* or classifieds in other magazines, looking for accommodation. Many Czech students welcome the opportunity to share a flat with a native-English speaker in order to practise their English for free.

Students are reported to be 'a delight to teach, alert, intelligent, fun-loving, keen and interested'. Many English teachers avail themselves of the excellent resource centres run by the British Council in Prague and Brno. The British Council's teaching centre in the centre of Prague has very occasional openings for teachers who are TEFL certified with two years' relevant experience. One of the strongest motivations among secondary school (*gymnasium*) students to learn English is the prospect of the 'Maturita' (school-leaver's) exam. At the beginning of the year they are given 25 topics (e.g. the British Royal Family, the influence of the media) and at the end of the year they must talk in English about one topic (chosen at random) for 15 minutes. This is a very good incentive for class participation.

LEISURE TIME

The cost of living in Prague continues to creep up, though most things are still affordable in other towns. For example a decent midday meal at a Brno restaurant (soup, main course and beer) will cost about 120 crowns, whilst rents for one-bedroom flats outside the Brno city centre start at 8,000 crowns a month. It is possible to survive on 600+ crowns a day. Prague has a vibrant nightlife with clubs and cafés, cinema, opera, poetry and dance. There is so much expat culture that a new arrival serious about getting into Czech culture will encounter many distractions.

In Prague theft is a problem, though walking the streets is reasonably safe. In small towns, however, English teachers are more likely to be treated as honoured guests with occasional offers of hospitality and invitations, for example to join skiing trips (which are very cheap).

Ailsa Randall who now lives in Brno reminisces about how much she enjoyed living in a smaller place where friendly locals often invited her to their wine cellars. She went cycling in the local forests, travelled every weekend, visited beautiful castles and generally had a great time socially.

LIST OF EMPLOYERS

ACADEMIC INFORMATION AGENCY (AIA)
Centre for International Cooperation in Education (Dum zahranicníspolupraçe),
Na Poricí 1035/4, 110 00 Prague 1
+420 221 850504
aia@dzs.cz
www.dzs.cz/cz/akademicka-informacni–agentura/english-teachers-6

NUMBER OF TEACHERS: Teachers needed for state primary and secondary schools throughout the Czech Republic though numbers have been decreasing over the years.
PREFERENCE OF NATIONALITY: Native English speakers from UK, Canada, USA, Australia.
QUALIFICATIONS: Professional teachers are preferred for teaching at primary and secondary schools. All candidates are required to have a college or university-level degree, preferably in English or in a related field. Additional qualification in teaching English as a foreign language (e.g. CELTA) is necessary for applicants who are graduates of courses in non-related subjects. Previous experience in teaching English in a classroom setting is greatly welcomed. High motivation is expected.
CONDITIONS OF EMPLOYMENT: 10-month contracts, 1 September to 30 June, 24 hours per week.
SALARY: Same as local Czech teachers.
FACILITIES/SUPPORT: Accommodation provided by schools (free or subsidised). Non-EU citizens – work and residence permits organised before arrival.
RECRUITMENT: Interested applicants register their availability with AIA, which circulates details to schools looking for a teacher.
CONTACT: Karla Benesová.

AKAIA JAZYKOVÁ AGENTURA
Benátská 1078, 570 01 Litomyšl
+420 731 103727
akaia@akaia.cz
www.akaia.cz

NUMBER OF TEACHERS: 4.
PREFERENCE OF NATIONALITY: EU preferred but other nationalities are also welcome.
QUALIFICATIONS: CELTA or equivalent plus degree and at least 1 year's experience.
CONDITIONS OF EMPLOYMENT: 10 months, renewable. 30 hours per week.
SALARY: 27,000–30,000 crowns less 2,000 crowns for social security.
FACILITIES/SUPPORT: School has a flat and information about other flat rentals. Assistance given with red tape. All teachers need a criminal record check; EU citizens must register with the different authorities; non-EU teachers have to get a visa.
RECRUITMENT: Interviews generally by Skype.
CONTACT: Tomáš Fila, Director.

AKCENT INTERNATIONAL HOUSE PRAGUE
Bitovská 3, 140 00 Prague 4
+420 2 6110 9218
akcent@akcent.cz
www.akcent.cz

NUMBER OF TEACHERS: 100.
PREFERENCE OF NATIONALITY: None (need to comply with Czech immigration laws).
QUALIFICATIONS: Degree plus CELTA or equivalent (minimum).
CONDITIONS OF EMPLOYMENT: 10 or 12 months from September/October. Approximately 22 contact hours per week (i.e. 26 45-minute lessons). Mostly teaching General English to adults, though some YL teaching. Teaching both on-site and in-company.
SALARY: 10,000–14,000 crowns (before tax) per month plus shared accommodation, end-of-contract bonus and other benefits. Teachers can also choose to work as freelancers earning 210–252 crowns per 45 minute lesson.
FACILITIES/SUPPORT: Health insurance covered and 25 days paid holidays per calendar year. Contribution made to cost of travelling to Prague. Offers CELTA/DELTA courses plus courses in teaching Young Learners and Business English. Help given to freelancers who want to obtain the business licence.
RECRUITMENT: Helena Linková, Teacher Recruitment (helena.linkova@akcent.cz).

BRNO ENGLISH CENTRE
Starobrnenska 16/18, 602 00 Brno
+420 541 212262
martin@brnoenglishcentre.cz
www.brnoenglishcentre.cz

NUMBER OF TEACHERS: 16.
PREFERENCE OF NATIONALITY: Native English speakers with EU citizenship or valid visa.

QUALIFICATIONS: A university degree plus an internationally recognised TEFL/TESOL qualification (not online), together with a minimum of 1 year's teaching with a similar institution.

CONDITIONS OF EMPLOYMENT: Standard contract is from September to May (9 months). Up to 24 lessons (45 minutes) per week, plus preparation, training and meetings. Contracts may be renewed.

SALARY: Around 24,600 crowns per month (gross) for average of 24 teaching hours a week. The average teacher would take home about 18,000–19,000 crowns.

FACILITIES/SUPPORT: Centre finds affordable accommodation (e.g. monthly rent of 7,000 crowns), pays the fees associated with this and advances the first month's rent. Work permits are generally not a major problem. It is more problematic gaining the residence permit needed for non-EU citizens, although the centre provides assistance.

RECRUITMENT: Normally by direct application. The centre does not go through agencies or intermediaries. Interviews are essential and can, in theory, be carried out in the UK or else by phone.

CONTACT: Martin Kleinwächter, Director; Nigel Briggs, Director of Studies.

CALEDONIAN SCHOOL
U Půjčovny 2, Prague 1
+420 210 084221
jobs@caledonianschool.com
www.caledonianschool.com

NUMBER OF TEACHERS: 100 in various locations in Prague and in schools around the Czech Republic (also in Slovakia).

PREFERENCE OF NATIONALITY: Teachers with EU citizenship preferred due to visa requirements. Non-EU applicants should have or be in the process of obtaining a business visa and trade licence.

QUALIFICATIONS: Teachers must have TEFL/TESOL/CELTA qualification with or without teaching experience.

CONDITIONS OF EMPLOYMENT: One year contract, usually from September, with possibility of renewal. 22 to 26 45-minute lessons a week. Part-time schedules also offered. School teaches adults and young learners in-school and in-company.

SALARY: Approx. 18,000–20,000 crowns per month (after 15% deduction for tax) for qualified teachers, depending on number of hours worked. Pay rise after 6 months. Health insurance must be arranged independently.

FACILITIES/SUPPORT: No help given with accommodation. Free Czech lessons. Transport reimbursed to full-time teachers.

RECRUITMENT: Interviews carried out in person or via Skype. Applicants must complete a lesson plan task as part of the interview. School hires year round.

CONTACT: Dušan Laščiak, HR Consultant.

CLOVERLEAF LANGUAGE SCHOOL
Dolni 31, Ostrava - Zabreh 700 30
+420 777 2 89 841; +420 553 4 01 822
gabriela.martinaskova@cloverleaf.cz
www.cloverleaf.cz

NUMBER OF TEACHERS: 6.

PREFERENCE OF NATIONALITY: EU citizens preferably.

QUALIFICATIONS: Degree in (English) teaching and/or CELTA course or TEFL course (120hrs), 2–3 years' experience in teaching.

CONDITIONS OF EMPLOYMENT: 1-year contract, teaching 15–20 hours a week.

SALARY: Deductions from gross salary consist of 10% for taxes (which can normally be reclaimed at end of the calendar year) plus 2,000 crowns per month for social and medical insurance.

FACILITIES/SUPPORT: School offers cheap hostel accommodation while teacher is house-hunting, and can help translate when viewing flats with an estate agent. Course in Communicative Teaching (25 hours) offered, plus chance to attend Cambridge Conference in September and various workshops and seminars throughout the year. Work permit assistance given to American and Canadian teachers.

RECRUITMENT: For the interview, candidates write a brief lesson plan, justify parts of a lesson, elicit/explain a context of several grammatical issues and check understanding. Other professional and motivational questions will be asked.

CONTACT: Gabriela Martinásková, Senior Teacher and Methodologist.

DAVID'S AGENCY
Dr. Veseleho 1042, 763 26 Luhacovice
+420 603 346618
catto@davidsagency.cz

NUMBER OF TEACHERS: 2 in Zlin and 2 in Luhacovice spa town.

PREFERENCE OF NATIONALITY: British or other native English speakers.

QUALIFICATIONS: University degree and TEFL.

CONDITIONS OF EMPLOYMENT: 10-month contracts, 8am–noon and 1pm–4.30pm.

SALARY: 24,000 crowns (gross) less about 25% for tax, health insurance and social benefits.

FACILITIES/SUPPORT: Accommodation arranged for 5,000 crowns per month. Assistance with work visa process.

RECRUITMENT: Via email. Early application encouraged to allow visa-processing time. Interviews are held in Britain in the summer.

CONTACT: David Catto, Director.

EDCENTRE SCHOOL S.R.O.
1414 Jasenicka, 755 01 Vsetin
+420 775 115039
lance@edcentre.cz
www.centrumjazyku.cz/job-opportunity

NUMBER OF TEACHERS: 6 for schools in Vsetin and Valasske Mezirici.

PREFERENCE OF NATIONALITY: None, but EU member state passport or residence preferred.

QUALIFICATIONS: Bachelor's degree, EFL qualification (CELTA or equivalent) and 1–2 years' experience teaching abroad. Good knowledge of grammar needed.

CONDITIONS OF EMPLOYMENT: 10–12 months from September. 30–35 45-minute 'teaching hours' a week which fall between 7am and 8pm with a large gap in the middle of the day. Most teachers are on *Zivnostensky* list (sole trader's business licence).

SALARY: From 220 crowns per 45 minutes, depending on qualifications, experience and whether teacher is on *Zivnostensky* list. Deductions for registered self-employed teachers approximately 15% of earnings.

FACILITIES/SUPPORT: School accommodation is sub-let to teachers. Help given with red tape.

CONTACT: Lance Adam LaSalle, Co-director.

ENGLISH IN ZLIN
Kvitkova 248, 76001 Zlin
+420 731 085 073
englishinzlin@gmail.com
www.englisihinzlin.cz

NUMBER OF TEACHERS: 7 freelancers.

PREFERENCE OF NATIONALITY: USA, Canada, Australia, New Zealand, Great Britain.

QUALIFICATIONS: None specified.

CONDITIONS OF EMPLOYMENT: Open-ended vacancies. Hours worked according to demand.

SALARY: From 250 crowns per 60 minutes, depending on qualifications and experience. Tax of 15% deducted from contracted teachers, but none from freelancers' pay.

FACILITIES/SUPPORT: Local contacts in local property market assist teachers. Regular observations, appraisals and workshops. No assistance given with work permits.

RECRUITMENT: Head-hunting and local recommendations.

CONTACT: Karl Martin, CEO / Founder.

NUMBER OF TEACHERS: 15.

PREFERENCE OF NATIONALITY: EU citizens or those with legal right to work in the Czech Republic.

QUALIFICATIONS: Normally CELTA or Trinity CertTESOL plus experience and preferably a degree. Newly qualified TEFL graduates with positive reference from course tutor will be considered.

CONDITIONS OF EMPLOYMENT: 1-year contract. Teaching hours are between 7.30am and 8.30pm. School tries to avoid assigning split shifts.

SALARY: Varies according to experience. Deducted contributions usually amount to 10% of salary.

FACILITIES/SUPPORT: Office staff help teachers find the right flat or room. Assistance willingly given with obtaining visas, though it is a long process for non-EU teachers.

RECRUITMENT: Mostly local or direct approach from recently qualified TEFL teachers.

CONTACT: Ralph Davies, Director of Studies (ralph@skolapark.cz); for in-company training elsewhere in the country: Roman Koznar, Managing Director (roman@skolapark.cz).

POLYGLOT SPOL S.R.O.
Mecislavova 8, 140 00 Prague 4
+420 241 740566
skola.praha@polyglot.cz
www.polyglot.cz

NUMBER OF TEACHERS: Approximately 50 for branches in Prague, Brno, Ceske Budejovice, Plzen, Ostrava, Jihlava and Liberec and for summer programme.

PREFERENCE OF NATIONALITY: None.

QUALIFICATIONS: CELTA/TEFL or other certification of at least 120 hours of training plus experience.

CONDITIONS OF EMPLOYMENT: Between 7 and 20 hours' teaching per week depending on whether the employee teaches in the morning or afternoon.

SALARY: 200–300 crowns per hour.

RECRUITMENT: Interviews are not always essential.

CONTACT: Barbora Sedlarova (barbora.sedlarova@polyglot.cz).

SPEVACEK EDUCATION CENTRE

Namesti Miru 15, 120 00 Prague 2

+420 222 517869

centrum@spevacek.info

www.spevacek.info

NUMBER OF TEACHERS: 150.

PREFERENCE OF NATIONALITY: Must be a native English or Czech/Slovak speaker. EU citizens only unless non-EU candidate already holds a valid visa.

QUALIFICATIONS: Minimum requirements are university degree and a recognised TEFL certificate. Online TEFL training is not acceptable unless combined with extensive experience. Formal EFL teaching experience is valued and rewarded. Professionalism, reliability, enthusiasm and smart appearance expected.

CONDITIONS OF EMPLOYMENT: 10-month renewable contracts. 80–90 teaching units per month (more if requested). Minimum 17 scheduled hours a week teaching all sorts of courses: adults, mainly in-company General and Business English, public courses, pre-school courses, post-secondary courses, small groups and individuals. Teaching kindergarten children, teenagers or (optional) public courses in a sister school. More experienced teachers may get 25 hours of work. Hours normally 7.30am–10am, 9.30am–12.40pm, and 3pm–7pm. Lots of public transport involved. Summer work also available.

SALARY: Teaching is paid on an hourly basis. Approx. 23,000 crowns (gross) per month plus bonus.

FACILITIES/SUPPORT: Affiliated to sister school for TEFL training, Live TEFL Prague. Orientation training in September. Full academic support with teacher development workshops. Free Czech lessons.

RECRUITMENT: School recruits year round but main recruiting time is June–August. Résumés/CVs and cover letter welcomed via career web page. Interviews conducted in Prague or via Skype.

CONTACT: Ms Lucie Prisovska, DOS (lucie.prisovska@spevacek.info).

STATE LANGUAGE SCHOOL BRNO

Jazyková skola s právem státní jazykové zkousky, Kotlárská 9, 602 00 Brno

kucerova@sjs-brno.cz

www.sjs-brno.cz

NUMBER OF TEACHERS: 2.

PREFERENCE OF NATIONALITY: British.

QUALIFICATIONS: Must have TEFL qualification.

CONDITIONS OF EMPLOYMENT: 1 academic year (September to June). Approximately 20 hours per week.

SALARY: About 18,000 Czech crowns per month.

FACILITIES/SUPPORT: Assistance with finding accommodation, full help with work permits and training available at staff meetings.

RECRUITMENT: Liaise with other schools.

CONTACT: Iveta Kucerová, Deputy Director.

SWALLOW SCHOOL OF ENGLISH

Mrštíkova 399/2a, 460 07 Liberec III

+420 603 829171

info@swallow.cz

www.swallow.cz

NUMBER OF TEACHERS: 15, for young learners and in-company.

PREFERENCE OF NATIONALITY: EU citizens, or others with permission to work in EU.

QUALIFICATIONS: CELTA + 1 year's experience.

CONDITIONS OF EMPLOYMENT: 10 months. Teaching 26 45-minute lessons per week about half on-site and half off-site. Teachers choose whether to work as employees or freelance with their own business licence.

SALARY: Freelancers can invoice school and earn 20,000–30,000 crowns per month (gross) less about 3,000 crowns in contributions. Employees earn 14,000 crowns but get paid holidays.

FACILITIES/SUPPORT: Advice given on finding affordable accommodation in the range of 4,000–7,500 crowns per month. Assistance given with negotiating red tape and obtaining a business licence.

RECRUITMENT: Via www.tefl.com. Interviews mainly by Skype.

CONTACT: Richard Hunter, Director.

THE PHILADELPHIA ACADEMY s.r.o.

T.G.M. 916/111, 293 01 Mladá Boleslav

+420 326 733386

philadel@philadel.com

www.philadel.com

NUMBER OF TEACHERS: Approx. 40 in total.

PREFERENCE OF NATIONALITY: None (though visas for Canadian and Australian citizens are problematic).

QUALIFICATIONS: BA/MA in English plus TEFL/TESOL/CELTA.

CONDITIONS OF EMPLOYMENT: 1 school year at least. About 25 hours per week (20 guaranteed – more is possible).

SALARY: 200 crowns per hour. Deductions depend on agreement.

FACILITIES/SUPPORT: Fully furnished flat with satellite dish, DVD player, etc. located 15 minutes walking distance from the school building – paid for by school, except for utilities.

RECRUITMENT: Internet advertising. Interviews essential.

CONTACT: Dana Zbíralová, Director.

TUTOR SCHOOL

U Půjčovny 2, Prague 1

+420 210 084210

tutor@tutor.cz; zamestnani@eduagroup.cz

www.tutor.cz

Part of EDUA Group (www.eduagroup.cz) and associated with Caledonian School (see above entry) though a separate legal entity.

NUMBER OF TEACHERS: Most vacancies in Prague and Brno.

PREFERENCE OF NATIONALITY: Teachers with EU citizenship preferred due to visa requirements.

QUALIFICATIONS: Teachers must have TEFL/TESOL/CELTA qualification with or without teaching experience.

CONDITIONS OF EMPLOYMENT: 1-year contract, usually from September, with possibility of renewal. 22 to 26 45-minute lessons a week. Most teaching takes place in-company.

SALARY: Approx. 18,000–20,000 crowns per month (after 15% deduction for tax) for qualified teachers, depending on number of hours worked. Health insurance must be arranged independently.

FACILITIES/SUPPORT: Assistance in finding accommodation is not provided.

RECRUITMENT: Interviews carried out in person or via Skype. Applicants must complete a lesson plan task as part of the interview. School hires year round.

VISTA WELCOME

Volsinach 2300/75 (Atrium House), Strašnice,100 00 Prague 10

+420 284 862345

vista@iol.cz

www.vista-welcome.cz

NUMBER OF TEACHERS: 6 native speakers. 32 Czech teachers.

PREFERENCE OF NATIONALITY: British, Canadian and American.

QUALIFICATIONS: TEFL certificate and/or proven ELS teaching experience. Mature teachers preferred, though enthusiasm important. School does not want to hire people who are just looking for a way to see the world. Experience in teaching Business English a plus.

CONDITIONS OF EMPLOYMENT: 1-year contract minimum. Teaching hours vary. Full-time teachers guaranteed at least 20 lessons (45 minutes each) per week. Courses aimed at firms and organisations looking for in-house courses. Teachers often work for more than one school to get enough teaching hours.

SALARY: 230 crowns per hour plus medical and social insurance; or 320 crowns without insurance.

FACILITIES/SUPPORT: No accommodation provided though advice may be given to new arrivals.

RECRUITMENT: Adverts in the local English-language newspaper for expats, the internet and via other schools in Prague.

HUNGARY

English is compulsory for all Hungarian students who wish to apply for college or university entrance, and university students in both the arts and sciences must take courses in English. The Hungarian education system has much to be proud of, not least the efficacy with which it retrained its Russian teachers as English teachers after the return to democracy in 1989. The network of bilingual secondary schools (*gimnazia*) has produced a large number of graduates with a sophisticated knowledge of English. In cities and even some small towns, bilingual schools now operate at the elementary level as well. From first grade onwards, students study basic subjects in English and Hungarian. The vast majority of private language schools are owned and run by Hungarians rather than expats. Even though the calibre of Hungarian teachers is very high, some schools still seem keen to employ native English teachers.

The invasion of foreigners in Budapest was never as overwhelming as it was (and is) in Prague. Although there might be an abundance of native speakers offering to teach general English, people with the skill to teach business English are in high demand. It is different of course in the state education system, where opportunities that do exist will be in the provinces. Even in the more remote parts of the country, formal academic qualifications are important. It is a legal requirement that the bilingual schools employ a native English speaker as lector. Most *gimnazia* liaise with the Fulbright Commission or the Central European Teaching Program (described later) and take on Americans, though Britons are also eligible.

Teachers are poorly paid in Hungary, aside from in the top-notch private schools. Rents in Budapest are high and take a major proportion of a teacher's salary; some schools help by subsidising accommodation, or it may be possible to arrange accommodation in return for English lessons. Teachers through the Central European Teaching Program have housing and utilities provided. **Emily Handler** found the flats provided by CETP in the county town of Szolnok to be '*a bit old-fashioned with furniture and art from the 1970s*', but nice enough, and with everything provided. She says '*I can remember expecting my flat would be a cold, damp, dark concrete single room, and it turned out much better than that.*'

Low as the salaries may seem, native English speakers can console themselves with the thought that they are usually better paid than Hungarian teachers and even university lecturers.

FINDING A JOB

Very few jobs in Hungary are advertised in the international TEFL press and only a handful of teaching companies publish information for job-seekers on their sites, for example Cambridge Schools (www.cambridge.hu), though first you have to figure out that Magunkról is the tab meaning 'About Us', Angol Intezet (English Institute) with seven branches in Budapest (www.angolintezet.hu) catering for corporate clients, M-Prospect (www.m-prospect.hu/nyelvtanari-poziciok in Hungarian only) and Berlitz (recruiting@berlitz.hu).

Recruitment of conversational English teachers and sometimes of other academic subjects takes place via the Central European Teaching Program (CETP, see entry). The programme offers 'cultural immersion through teaching' and is open to native English speakers with a university degree, preferably some experience of TEFL and overseas teaching/study experience and a willingness to pay the programme fee. CETP liaises with the relevant government department in Hungary to place teachers in state schools and dual language grammar schools, as well as in some parochial schools throughout the country. In Budapest it cooperates with a non-profit company Szoloto (http://bilingual.hu/en), which provides an accredited bilingual education programme to three public primary/middle schools and two kindergartens. A co-teaching model is used whereby classes are taught by a native Hungarian and a native English speaker.

The website of the Professional Association of Language Schools (NYESZE) has a searchable listing of its 30+ member schools at www.nyelviskola.hu.

AFTER ARRIVAL

The British Council in Budapest (www.britishcouncil.hu) operates teaching centres on both the Buda and Pest sides of the capital. In 2016 it was looking to hire 'high performing hourly-paid teachers of English' particularly of young learners aged 6–17 (teaching@britishcouncil.hu).

As of 2016, the Regional English Language Office (RELO) for Central and Southeastern Europe, which was located at the US Embassy in Budapest, is closed and is relocating to Belgrade.

THE PRIVATE MARKET

While it has become increasingly difficult for foreigners to find teaching jobs in Hungarian state schools, private institutes provide more scope, primarily to meet the needs of the business community and also for children whose parents are keen for them to supplement the English teaching at state schools. It is estimated that there are over 100 private language schools in Budapest alone and 300 around the country, both very fluid numbers since schools open and close so quickly. Many private schools use native English speakers as live commercials for the schools, though nowadays they want to advertise the qualifications of their teachers too.

Anyone with a recognised TEFL Certificate and experience of the business world has a chance of finding at least some hourly teaching after arrival in Budapest or other cities. Institutes catering to the business market seem to have weathered a national policy change that stipulated that language training did not count as vocational training for the purposes of state subsidies. Companies that had received some funding to send employees to English courses have had to retrench.

To find the less well-established schools on the spot, keep your eyes open for the flyers posted in the main shopping streets or check out the English-language weeklies. Occasionally teaching jobs are advertised on English-language sites such as www.budapestjobs.net and www.xpatloop.com/classifieds. The majority of vacancies seem to be in Budapest nurseries or after-school clubs.

Gillian Murphy from Ireland was living and teaching in Budapest until summer 2016 and found plenty of work in the business community:

> ***In my experience of teaching business people in private institutes, there is a shortage of native English teachers at the moment. I think this is connected to the low pay and extremely complicated tax system here for teachers. My pay ranged from 2,700 forints for 45 minutes to 4,000 forints for one hour, depending on the arrangement between the school and the student.***

Private tutoring provides one way of supplementing a meagre salary. Freelance teachers may find a developing market for their linguistic expertise among company executives. The Department of Commerce, for example, employs teachers to train bankers, traders and top electrical engineers. A UK-based online service was launched in 2014 to match prospective native-speaker tutors with learners in Budapest: www.LearnEnglishBudapest.com vets aspiring teachers who, once approved, can post mini-biographies on their site for Hungarians to contact directly. They have fixed prices for lessons in the range of 3,500–6,750 forints an hour, according to qualifications and experience as well as location and time of lessons. A home grown tutor-search site is www.angoltanarok.com; advertising yourself on that site will cost a modest 1,990 forints for one month. Another company that connects freelance teachers with adults, children and companies seeking private tuition is PENNA Native English Teachers (www.AnyanyelviAngolTanarok.hu). Obviously these companies do not assist with teaching premises, so you will have to find a suitable place for your tutorials. Apparently upstairs at Burger King is a favourite. Note that Hungarian taxes quickly become a headache for freelance teachers, since the government by law takes 26% of earnings.

REGULATIONS

Since Hungary is a full member of the EU, EU citizens do not require a residence permit, and immigration procedures have been much simplified. However, before the 93rd day of their stay, they should report their presence to their nearest regional Office of Immigration and Nationality. The office will issue a registration certificate, which permits indefinite stays. EU citizens working full-time in Hungary are subject to the same social security and pension obligations as Hungarians. Employees must make payments into the National Health Insurance Fund and into a pension fund.

Non-EU citizens must arrange a visa before leaving their country of residence and then apply for a work/residence permit. A foreign employee cannot be legally paid until she or he has a work permit (which costs 5,000 forints). This fee is covered for those applying to teach through the Central European Teaching Program (CETP), and also income tax is waived for the first two years. When **Emily Handler** was applying to CETP from the US some years ago, '*it seemed like a never-ending collection of paperwork, certificates, notarised copies, everything in triplicate … Later when I arrived in Hungary and started the Hungarian paperwork it made the first bit seem like child's play. Working with the immigration office in Hungary was so confusing and frustrating; the first year I had to go four or five times, and each time they came up with some paper that was missing, some stamp that was misaligned, something not signed or dated properly, etc. etc.*'. Those nationals who require a work permit must find a Hungarian employer who is entitled to apply for a work permit from the relevant Regional Employment Office.

To obtain a one-year residence permit, non-EU nationals must jump through a series of hoops, and provide everything from a title deed for their accommodation to bank statements. An American teacher and blogger set out all the steps he took a couple of years ago; he rose to the challenge of what he describes as a 'highly ordered scavenger hunt' and helpfully describes the process at https://budabeats.wordpress.com (search for 'Residence').

CONDITIONS OF WORK

Salaries vary, but teachers at private institutes tend to earn from 2,500 forints (€8) an hour or 250,000 forints a month. It is essential to find out whether pay is net or gross since Hungarians lose more than a quarter of their already meagre wages in tax and contributions. It is also important to check whether your employer is taking out insurance on your behalf: an insurance mix-up turned **Ellen Parham**'s 'satisfactory' high-school salary into something worse than meagre.

American graduate and CETP participant **Genevieve Pierce** found that teaching teenagers in a state school could be challenging:

> ***They were totally uninterested in learning, didn't complete their homework, and lacked any opinion or view-point. This is a result of the political situation in Hungary and the low salaries. I am sure my students overhear their parents complain about money and politics constantly, which has to drain the students' hope for a future. I think they feel trapped in Hungary. One student even said, 'Why should I do my homework when I'm going to live in Hungary and be a shop clerk like my mother?'***

In general students in the rural areas of Eastern Hungary are better behaved than their counterparts in Budapest, though their level of English will be lower. This kind of problem won't arise if you are teaching in a bilingual school with high entrance requirements as Emily Handler now is.

Culture shock is inevitable. CETPer **Emily Handler** (who is now married to a local) remembers the problems she encountered in her first year:

> ***There was the confusion of working in a totally unfamiliar educational system. Although the other teachers at my state primary school (all Hungarian) did their best to help me, none of them had ever lived abroad and found it hard to understand some of the things that I didn't know. A great example would be the five or six times I went in to work and found the school completely closed. It was always because there was some local holiday or school event which everyone knew about because they had been doing it for years.***

LEISURE TIME

The Opera House in Budapest is one of the most beautiful in the world, the Széchenyi thermal baths are the perfect place to unwind graciously and the cutting-edge 'ruin bars' set up in derelict buildings make for a fantastic and arty nightlife. If high culture is your bag, you can attend symphony concerts and dances for 500 forints. For shopping, the Christmas and Easter markets are superb. It is easy to make a strong argument for living in Budapest, but there are downsides, as long-stay American teacher **Ellen Parham** explains:

> ***Everything is convenient for me here in Budapest, but some of the others in the CETP programme who are teaching in smaller towns are treated like celebrities and everyone knows them. Living in a big city is hindering my ability to speak Hungarian, too. Everyone speaks English and I am never forced to speak Hungarian.***

Zeeda Anderson is one of those CETP participants who came to see the advantages of living in the remote countryside and enjoyed herself so much that she returned to the same place in September 2016:

> ***I decided to teach in Hungary with my heart set on living in Budapest. When I was told that I would be placed in Ebes, a tiny town in the countryside, I had mixed feelings about whether I would enjoy the experience. I decided to come with an open mind, and now, after returning for a second year of teaching, I am extremely glad I did. I know teaching in Budapest would have been a great experience as well, but here in the countryside, in a town of almost no English speakers, I have been able to make friends with Hungarians, and experience first-hand their traditions. Last week I went to a bacon frying party (szalonnasütés), where I sat around a campfire with Hungarians and roasted pork fat over bread. It is this experience, and many others like it, that have allowed me to appreciate living in a quieter place. Here I am able to (creatively) attempt to cross language barriers to get to know families and friends living a very different way of life than they would in an international city. Of course, there are moments when things get difficult, but overall the key has been allowing myself time to develop relationships and become accustomed to the way of life.***

Emily Handler still goes off travelling most weekends, often to attend a festival: '*Festivals take place around Hungary year round: Szolnok Goulash Festival, Makó Onion Festival, Gyula Sausage Festival, etc. And yeah, most of them are food or drink related. Hungary is a good country to be a food lover in!*'

LIST OF EMPLOYERS

AMEROPA LANGUAGE SCHOOL
Október Huszonharmadika u. 5, 1117 Budapest
+36 1 209 3993
ameropa@ameropatraining.hu
www.ameropatraining.hu

NUMBER OF TEACHERS: 60.
PREFERENCE OF NATIONALITY: None.
QUALIFICATIONS: Minimum bachelor's degree and teacher training (TEFL, CELTA or equivalent).
CONDITIONS OF EMPLOYMENT: Ongoing contracts, usually between 6 and 24 months with 10–20 working hours per week.
SALARY: Competitive.
FACILITIES/SUPPORT: Assistance given with work permits.
RECRUITMENT: Interview and demonstration lesson are essential.

BUDAPEST AFTERSCHOOL
Kiraly utca 73, 1077 Budapest
+36 6 308 913901
budapestafterschool@gmail.com
www.budapestafterschool.com

NUMBER OF TEACHERS: 6–10, mainly freelancers.
PREFERENCE OF NATIONALITY: British, Australian.
QUALIFICATIONS: BA and teaching credentials preferred. Leaders of specialist activities for children are also appointed, e.g. for theatre arts and photography, where prior experience and expertise are important.
CONDITIONS OF EMPLOYMENT: Open-ended stays with variable hours.
FACILITIES/SUPPORT: Personal recommendations made on accommodation. Curriculum training given by school director.
CONTACT: Melanie Sefton, School Director.

CENTRAL EUROPEAN TEACHING PROGRAM
3800 NE, 72nd Avenue, Portland, OR 97213, USA
+1 503 287 4977
mary.cetp@gmail.com; hildie.cetp@gmail.com; hajni.cetp@gmail.com
www.cetp.info

NUMBER OF TEACHERS: 90–100 for 100 schools in cities and the countryside.
PREFERENCE OF NATIONALITY: Native English speakers: USA, Canada, the UK and native English-speaking Europeans.
QUALIFICATIONS: Minimum: bachelor's degree plus some TEFL training; an online TEFL certificate (minimum 40 hours) is adequate. Must have 20 hours of classroom teaching experience, voluntary or paid, before departure. Retired people welcome to apply.
CONDITIONS OF EMPLOYMENT: Standard contract 10 months (1 school year), although teachers can sometimes be placed for winter semester only, January to June. To teach 22–26 hours per week.
SALARY: $450–$1,000 per month (average $500) after taxes, paid in local currency, plus free housing and utilities. Salary fluctuates according to exchange rates and teacher's experience.
FACILITIES/SUPPORT: All teachers receive a furnished apartment with utilities paid. Apartments range from a small studio to a spacious 1 or 2-bedroom flat. All are equipped with TV and washing machine, among other amenities. CETP provides teachers with all necessary documents for residence and work permits and health insurance cover. A week-long orientation is provided in Budapest prior to the start of the school term. A Hungarian director and her assistant oversee CETP teachers throughout the year.
RECRUITMENT: Via word of mouth, the internet and university placement offices. CETP programme fee is $1,800/$1,900–$2,500 for an academic year, $1,500–$1,800 for one semester. The lower fees are for rural high schools and Budapest preschool/kindergartens.
CONTACT: Mary Rose, Director.

FUNSIDE ASSOCIATION
Villanyi ut 14, 1114 Budapest
+36 1 950 950 2
tabor@funside.hu
www.funside.eu

NUMBER OF TEACHERS: 5–6 per summer season for English language children's residential camps at Balatongyorok on Lake Balaton and at day camps in Budapest.
PREFERENCE OF NATIONALITY: None as long as they are native English speakers.
QUALIFICATIONS: Minimum age 20. Teaching English as a second language experience, as well as experience working with children. Camp experience preferred. University students and teachers staying in Budapest are welcome to apply. A criminal records check may be required.
CONDITIONS OF EMPLOYMENT: 2–5 weeks during the 5-week period that camps are run from beginning of July. Long hours,

since as well as delivering English lessons in the morning, staff act as camp counsellors in the afternoons and evenings.

SALARY: Agreed on an individual basis. Some expenses covered.

FACILITIES/SUPPORT: Accommodation and meals provided (at overnight camps only). 1-day orientation in Budapest held the day before the camping season begins.

RECRUITMENT: Only via online application form from beginning of February. Interviews are essential between February and May, preferably in person, alternatively on Skype.

CONTACT: András Kittka, Director (+36 30 9776 111).

INTERNATIONAL HOUSE BUDAPEST
Language School & Teacher Training Institute, Vermezo u. 4, 1012 Budapest
+36 1 212 4010
dos@ih.hu
www.ih.hu

NUMBER OF TEACHERS: 40.

QUALIFICATIONS: Minimum: Cambridge CELTA.

CONDITIONS OF EMPLOYMENT: Contracts are for 25 contact hours per week including in-company teaching, teaching young learners, groups, one-to-one and special projects.

SALARY: 198,000 forints per month (net).

FACILITIES/SUPPORT: Assistance given with finding accommodation. In-service teacher development.

RECRUITMENT: Through direct application. Interviews essential, conducted if necessary by telephone or Skype.

CONTACT: Zsofia Jakab, Director of Studies.

KARINTHY FRIGYES GIMNAZIUM
Thököly ucta 7, Pestlorinc, 1183 Budapest
+36 1 291 2072
info@karinthy.hu
www.karinthy.hu

NUMBER OF TEACHERS: About 70.

PREFERENCE OF NATIONALITY: Native English speakers.

QUALIFICATIONS: MA in English (preferred) or TEFL/TESL qualification.

CONDITIONS OF EMPLOYMENT: 1–2 year contracts, 22 lessons a week.

SALARY: National salary plus all costs of accommodation in a pleasant, fully furnished and equipped flat near the school. 10% taxes and social security deduction.

FACILITIES/SUPPORT: Assistance with work permits; authorised copies of degrees and/or certificates are needed by the end of June.

RECRUITMENT: Application directly through agencies and foundations. Interviews preferred and conducted via Skype, webcam or telephone.

CONTACT: Deputy Head: nemcsics@karinthy.hu.

KATEDRA LANGUAGE SCHOOL NETWORK
Anker köz 1–3, 1061 Budapest
+36 1 700 0137; +36 323 137 7000 (mob)
tanar@katedra.hu
www.katedra.hu/karrier

NUMBER OF TEACHERS: 15 for franchised schools in 30 towns and cities plus 5 locations in Budapest.

PREFERENCE OF NATIONALITY: Most teachers are Hungarian, but a few are native English speakers.

QUALIFICATIONS: CELTA, DELTA or equivalent.

CONDITIONS OF EMPLOYMENT: Standard contract is 6–12 months, 12 to 16 45-minute lessons per week.

SALARY: From 2,750 to 3,250 forints per lesson.

FACILITIES/SUPPORT: Assistance given with applying for work permits. Also offer teacher training certificate courses (see Training Directory).

RECRUITMENT: Teachers are recruited by individual schools (linked from main site above). Applications can be emailed with CV, diploma and photo to addresses in the format eger@katedra.hu, debrecen@katedra.hu, and so on. Face-to-face interview and the teaching of a mock lesson are normally required.

LIVING LANGUAGE SEMINAR
Eló Nyelvek Szemináriuma, Fejér György u. 8–10, 1053 Budapest
+36 1 317 9644
info@elonyelvek.hu or elonyelv@t-online.hu
www.elonyelvek.hu

NUMBER OF TEACHERS: 3–5 native English speakers.

PREFERENCE OF NATIONALITY: British, American, Canadian.

QUALIFICATIONS: A great deal of ESL teaching experience, registered City & Guilds, Local State Examinations centre. Preparation for City & Guilds, Cambridge and local ITK-Origó exams, TOEFL, IELTS, iBT, business English.

CONDITIONS OF EMPLOYMENT: Contracts from 3 months. Negotiable hours. Mainly teaching adults (aged 16–40).

SALARY: High by local standards.

FACILITIES/SUPPORT: No assistance with accommodation at present.

RECRUITMENT: Through adverts. Interviews required.

CONTACT: Paul Biró, Director.

MANHATTAN LANGUAGE SCHOOL
Örs vezér tér 25/C, 1106 Budapest
+36 1 431 8630
info@manhattannyelvstudio.hu
www.manhattannyelvstudio.hu

NUMBER OF TEACHERS: 8–10 depending on the term.

PREFERENCE OF NATIONALITY: None.

QUALIFICATIONS: Teaching qualification (preferably CELTA or equivalent) and some teaching experience, especially of corporate work.

CONDITIONS OF EMPLOYMENT: Teachers work on freelance basis. Working hours depend on the type of course that is taught, e.g. company courses can start as early as 7am or in-house courses can finish after 8pm.

SALARY: €7–€11 per hour depending on the level taught and location of the course.

RECRUITMENT: Face-to-face interview although on rare occasions a phone interview may suffice. Candidates must also conduct a mock lesson.

CONTACT: Anna Bradák, Manager.

OPEN MIND EDUCATION CENTER

Maros Street 12, 1122 Budapest

+36 1 793 2293

allasopenmind@gmail.com

www.openmindacademy.hu

NUMBER OF TEACHERS: 3 for English (and Mathematics) departments.

PREFERENCE OF NATIONALITY: None.

QUALIFICATIONS: University degree in any subject. Should have passion for teaching, and be a disciplined, goal-oriented team member.

CONDITIONS OF EMPLOYMENT: 1–2 years, extendable. 35 hours per week full-time. The institute is open 8am–8pm, 7 days a week.

SALARY: Above the Hungarian average.

FACILITIES/SUPPORT: No assistance with accommodation. Training in the Open Mind teaching method. Work permit provided.

CONTACT: Katalin Szilágyi, Manager.

TUDOMANY NYELVISKOLA
Tavasz u.3, 1033 Budapest
+36 1 368 1156
info@tudomanynyelviskola.hu
www.tudomanynyelviskola.hu;
www.cegesnyelvoktatasok.hu

NUMBER OF TEACHERS: 10–15.

PREFERENCE OF NATIONALITY: British and American.

QUALIFICATIONS: TEFL/TESL preferred.

CONDITIONS OF EMPLOYMENT: 10-month contracts, hours vary.

FACILITIES/SUPPORT: Assistance with accommodation not usually given. Training sometimes available. Affiliated with ELT training centre Via Lingua Budapest at the same address (see Training listings). Refund of course fee (starting at €875) to those who teach at Tudomany for 3+ months.

RECRUITMENT: Local interviews essential. Must teach demo lesson.

CONTACT: Ms Krisztina Tüll (dos@europainyelvek.hu).

POLAND

Prospects for English teachers in Poland, eastern Poland in particular, remain reasonable, even if the seemingly insatiable demand for English teachers that characterised the Polish teaching scene is now a thing of the past. Poles are still keen to learn English, but with the explosion of no-frills flights, millions of Poles simply get on a plane and come to Britain or Ireland, to acquire the language while they work.

This has, of course, had a knock-on effect on the quality of Polish English teachers working in their home country, although the reverence for 'native speakerhood' still runs high. A famous Polish poet described (in perfect English) how his teenage daughter and her friends largely communicate in English, or at least a form of English picked up from TV shows and pop songs, and that some of the older generation are worried that Poland is becoming swamped by the English language and western culture. Like the rest of Europe, Poland is also moving to introduce English to very young learners from the age of three, so experience of teaching children is highly prized.

For now, certain types of English classes, largely taught by native English speakers, are still popular; according to one director of studies: 'realistic' conversation classes teach Poles how to rent a flat or order a drink, while others teach students how to fill in forms (good luck to them).

Major cities such as Warsaw, Wroclaw, Krakow, Poznan and Gdansk are possible destinations, especially for people with experience of preparing for Cambridge exams or those looking for in-company work. The smaller towns in eastern Poland and in Silesia in southern Poland are more promising destinations, where the competition for jobs will be less intense and you may still receive preferential 'foreigner' treatment if you gain a dependable reputation as a teacher. A contributor to www.polishforums.com wrote to an enquirer:

> ***You should be looking at smaller places, less competition for jobs and less competition means more money for you. I live in Katowice and know that schools around here are always looking for teachers. However, . . . how to put this . . . it ain't no Paris. Kato has a bad image, but once you know the places to go it's fine. And it's only a 45–60 min drive from Krakow.***

An even more extreme view was posted on the same site: *'The market here in Poland is truly saturated. There are plenty of private language schools in Warsaw now and Krakow is stuffed with native speakers all chasing the same work. The best bet is to look at somewhere in the back woods.'*

Foreign teachers usually find their students friendly, open and keen to learn more about the world. Discussion classes are likely to be informed and lively, with students well up to date on developments and very well motivated to practise their English. In some companies, promotion depends on the level of English achieved, which spurs students from the business world to be especially committed. On the other hand, if the company is paying for an employee's lessons, there may be little incentive to attend regularly or with enthusiasm.

FINDING A JOB

Interested teachers should not expect to be snapped up unless they have at least a TEFL certificate and some sort of teaching experience. International House has a sizeable presence in Poland, with major schools in Bielsko-Biala, Bydgoszcz and Wroclaw among others; vacancies are posted at http://job.ihworld.com. BELT Schools (Business Education Language Training, formerly Bell Schools) can be found in Gdansk, Gdynia, Szczecin and Warsaw (www.belt.edu.pl). These high-profile ELT organisations are founding members of PASE, the Polish Association for Standards in English, which promotes ethical practices in the private sector. PASE (www.jezykowo.pase.pl) has 23 member schools. PASE members employ almost exclusively teachers with a recognised teaching qualification and the vast majority have graduated from philology programmes at universities in Poland. Schools approved by the Polish Ministry of Education insist that their teachers have a university degree and a teaching qualification.

In 2016 the British Council was advertising for part-time teaching assistants for Warsaw (teach@britishcouncil.pl). The Council also recruits teachers of children and adults for residential summer camps.

ON THE SPOT

Semesters begin in late September and on 15 February, and the best time to arrive is a month beforehand. After arrival, try to establish some contacts, possibly by visiting the English department at the university. Although some school directors state a preference for British or American accents, many are neutral provided you are a native English speaker.

Private language schools can be found everywhere, catering for all kinds of English. The Warsaw *Yellow Pages* carries several pages under the heading *Jezykowe Kursy, Szkolenia.* Check out www.nativespeaker.com.pl where individuals advertise private tuition and language schools post vacancies in the 'Native Speaker Job Center', searchable by region. **Leah Morawiec**, owner of the online teaching company TalkBack based in Gliwice, recommends two Polish language sites, www.olx.pl and www.e-korepetycje.net, for posting job announcements. While some institutes have high standards in those they hire, others are looking more for personality.

Freelancing is popular, and there is demand for tailor-made one-to-one courses, though the corporate market hasn't quite recovered from the economic crisis. When **Kathy Cooper** was based in the small town of Raciborz in Silesia she worked for three language schools over seven years and also freelanced on the side. She found that once her name was established around town, she had a waiting list of willing students. Banks are likely clients and often pay well by Polish standards. Kathy also taught corporate clients (signed through the school), including in the fields of '*food/chocolate, cement, power plants, furniture, steel, industrial cleaning and sanitation, automotive, banking, industrial equipment, manufacturing, legal profession, doctors, and hotel industry. Yes, I am in Poland, land of opportunity for teachers.*'

Competent freelancers ask for 50–90 zloty an hour, though corporate clients pay upwards of that. As usual, private students can be unreliable, so try to get them to pay for a block of lessons in advance. For this work, teachers should have enough ELT awareness to be able to devise their own syllabus. They will also have to put up with early or late hours (8am/9pm) and the inevitable cancelled lessons as business execs reschedule due to important meetings. Kathy Cooper got around this problem simply by calling another business client who wanted to make up lost hours.

With only a couple of months as a volunteer English teacher on her CV, American **Leah Morawiec** landed a two-year contract with a language school. A condition of her employment as a freelancer was that she had to set up her own company. This is much cheaper for the school, which is why they force you to do it:

> ***For me it was a bit of a drawback because you have to have an accountant, pay income tax, your own ZUS (health insurance and social security), which is all quite expensive. So, in the end, you don't earn what you thought you would, and you have to have someone help you with all the bureaucracy if you don't speak Polish. Thus, if possible, I'd recommend avoiding any employer who requires you to open a company. Of course, it does have its advantages if you're planning on staying in Poland for longer, because you can have your own private students and invoice them directly. In the long run, having a company gives you your freedom from the language schools.***

More of Leah's insights can be found on her blog page www.polonization.pl/why-poland-is-a-great-place-to-teach-english.

HOLIDAY LANGUAGE CAMPS

Some private language-teaching organisations run short-term holiday courses in summer and occasionally winter, requiring native English speakers.

To take one example, the Perfect English private language school (www.perfectenglish.pl) in southern Poland has been seen advertising vacancies for its summer courses held in the mountains or on the seaside, as well as for the academic year. American young people might be interested in volunteering to work at one of the several English-language immersion camps run by the Kosciuszko Foundation's Teaching English in Poland (TEIP) Program (www.thekf.org/programs/teaching_english_in_poland). The three to four-week programme takes place in July and early August. One American who applied through the Foundation's New York branch blogged about her successful summer on the programme in the town of Limanowa. She reported that, with the exception of flights, the programme covered the cost of everything, including accommodation, food and weekend trips to Polish towns and cities. Despite noting certain key cultural differences between her host country and the USA, she found it relatively easy to settle into Polish life. Although she had studied Polish for a semester in college before her departure, her spoken Polish improved markedly once she arrived in the country, and she made many friends, both among fellow expat teachers and local staff.

As mentioned in the introduction to the Central & Eastern Europe section of this book, short holidays in which paying language learners mingle and interact with native speakers who are given free room and board and transport from the nearest city are organised by Angloville (see entry).

REGULATIONS

Poland's requirements for EU teachers are broadly in line with the rest of Europe. Teachers wishing to stay for more than three months must register their address at the town hall to obtain a *Zameldowanie*, which can then be used to apply for a social insurance number (ZUS) and a tax number (NIP). The latter will be needed in order to be paid by an employer if on a real contract (*umowa o pracy*) or to issue invoices if a registered independent contractor (i.e. freelancer). Employers should assist with the documentation and the necessary translation of official documents into Polish. The minimum monthly ZUS contribution from teachers is under 350 zloty for the first two years, but after that it more than doubles, regardless of earnings.

Non-EU citizens who want to stay for more than 90 days and for less than a year will have to jump through the usual hoops prior to departure from their home country. The required documents must be presented in person to a Polish Consulate: a valid work permit certificate issued by the Office of Wojewoda in Poland or a promissory work permit from your Polish employer, your passport, two photos, a completed application form and the current fee for a work visa. To get a work permit your employer needs to submit copies of all the stamped pages of your passport, a copy of the company's CEIDG (confirmation of company registration) and proof of payment. Most schools will assist with the documentation but may not bear the financial cost. When the initial visa expires (after three months), it is possible to apply for a residency card from inside Poland, which will be valid for two years. Most employers who take on foreign teachers are well aware of the procedures which, according to one, could fill a book on their own. The Polish Embassy in Washington can provide further details (www.washington.mfa.gov.pl).

CONDITIONS OF WORK

Generally speaking, private language schools in Poland offer reasonable working conditions. Instead of hearing complaints from teachers about employers, it tends to be more often the other way round, as the Director of Studies of a private language school makes clear:

> ***My boss, who has been employing British native speakers for seven years and who has proved to be a very patient person, could provide you with some hair-raising stories of teachers signing their contracts and withdrawing at the very last minute (having probably found a more lucrative job in Asia), teachers returning a couple of days late after the Christmas break without presenting any adequate excuse (or not returning at all), not to mention the state of flats and equipment which, after being used for nine months, are often left in a wrecked condition.***

Wages are higher than they used to be, but the cost of living has risen too. The current average wage in the private sector is about 45–60 zloty an hour less about a fifth in tax. That means that a teacher working 20 hours a week is likely to clear $750–$1,000 a month. For a full-time timetable at a language school you can expect to earn between 2,500 and 3,500 zloty. If you have to rent on the open market, expect to pay the equivalent of at least $500 a month for a one-bedroom flat outside the centre of a big city, but that may or may not include utilities and internet access. Food bought in supermarkets is cheap but eating out has become more expensive, as have bars unless you stick to beer and Polish vodka.

Leah Morawiec finds that Polish students are generally shy to speak, especially in big groups. They are much more reluctant to share their opinions than westerners, and it takes time to get them to open up. Generally, students are very nice, fun, intelligent and they usually have a good base of English knowledge. They prefer speaking in class because that's what they're usually lacking.

Heidi Rothwell-Walker enjoyed company teaching, which was a contrast with the basic adult education she had been doing in Britain.

> ***I was expected to work any time from 7am to 6pm. Sometimes the early hours (especially in the long winter) can get you down, but you will be rewarded financially for starting at 7am. There was a lot of travelling and waiting at bus stops, but working conditions in the companies were excellent. Not every company gave you access to a whiteboard or overhead projector but they could be made available upon request.***

KATHY COOPER

Kathy Cooper is an American grandmother who suddenly decided to live in Europe. Immediately after obtaining a Trinity certificate in TESOL in the UK, she was offered a job in southern Poland and fell in love with her life there, the chemical-free foods, the teaching and the culture. She began her Polish teaching career in the town of Opole, where she was thrown in at the deep end. With time, she was able to refine her teaching schedule.

Teaching varies from school to school, and from classroom to classroom. Starting out, I was thrown immediately into a range of beginning children to executive business and British Council exam classes. It was either to be my death or destiny. I now specialise in only executive business and exam classes. Periodically, I embark on a student who wants to attend either high school or university in America, hence I teach TOEFL exams for both. SLEP (Secondary Level English Proficiency) testing is the new format for high school entrance in America, it is part of the TOEFL system. I can proudly relate that my last student attending a foremost university in the States has just been asked to return, and on scholarship, to obtain her MA in Graphic Design. She was their first Pole of several thousand foreign students. Teachers are a mix of English-speaking nationalities; I have worked with all, including other Americans. It is most common you will teach with Polish teachers. In my case, again, I have some executives and advanced students that require only native speakers because of their language level. Facilities vary; I've been lucky to have had beautifully renovated and comfortable buildings and classrooms. It's not always the norm. Your resource library can often depend on the age of the company. I am with a young school now, and we are stocking year by year.

Despite a considerable amount of disorganisation at many schools, no one complains of a lack of hospitality from the Poles. Poles even seem to have the ability to crack jokes in English when their English is very elementary, so lessons are not usually dull. On the whole they are also very well motivated and hard working, including adolescents. One teacher warns against working for a school that employs a regimented learning method like Callan or Avalon which takes a lot of the fun out of teaching.

LEISURE TIME

Poland offers no shortage of sights to see, pubs to visit, museums, theatres and parks to enjoy. Films are usually in English with Polish subtitles. Travelling is fairly cheap and easy. The transport system in Warsaw and some other cities looks complicated at first glance but is in fact straightforward. People in shops and so on can seem rude and abrupt, though this should not be taken personally.

Kathy Cooper has fallen for the food:

Poland yields the most amazing hams, kielbasas and bacon that have ever melted in my mouth. Add the dense and daily purchased homemade breads that taste like my grandmother's, the variety of local and international cheeses, harvests of the freshest chemical-free fruits and vegetables that can be found, plus ice creams, baked goods and phenomenal yoghurts abound. Need I say more? . . .

Kathy does go on to say that unfortunately the western plague of hypermarkets, including Tesco, has led to the closure of traditional small shops.

Heidi Rothwell-Walker is convinced that she made the right decision when she chose to work for a school in Poland rather than at one of the other schools around the world that offered her a job:

The language is difficult, comprising such wonderful names as 'Sczcyrk', a tiny ski village, but it can make for a good atmosphere in the classroom as you struggle with Polish pronunciation whilst your students try to get their tongues round English words.

Poland can seem a bit of a backwater, but it's a tremendous experience. It'll change your thinking completely and you'll either love it (like 98% of people) or hate it, but you must try it. I have just renewed my contract for another year because I have been very impressed by them and am very happy here.

LIST OF EMPLOYERS

ANGLOSCHOOL
ul. Ks. J. Popieluszki 7, 01–796Warsaw
+48 22 663 8883
agnieszka@angloschool.com.pl
www.angloschool.com.pl

NUMBER OF TEACHERS: 10–12 native English speakers in 4 centres in Warsaw and Lomianki.

QUALIFICATIONS: CELTA or equivalent and a BA or MA. Teaching experience preferred. Experience of teaching children is valued.

CONDITIONS OF EMPLOYMENT: 9-month contract from mid-September, up to 28 hours per week teaching 3pm–8.30pm Monday to Friday. Some morning classes 8.30am–10am. Combination of work in the primary academy and the language school.

SALARY: Competitive. School pays taxes and social security (45%).

FACILITIES/SUPPORT: Accommodation is provided by the school in the form of two- or three-roomed shared flats or single rooms in a house. Accommodation includes all necessary facilities, i.e. furniture, a phone, cable TV, a washing machine, kitchen with necessary equipment. Initial induction course in August or September and ongoing workshops.

RECRUITMENT: Cooperates with schools running CELTA, TEFL courses, which provide a job placement service. Advertising in newspapers, internet (www.tefl.com) and recruitment agencies. Direct application with CV and photo welcomed.

CONTACT: Ms. Agnieszka Heintze, Director of Studies (agnieszka@angloschool.com.pl).

ANGLOVILLE POLAND
Ul. Sw. Leonarda 1/8, 25-311 Kielce
+48 73 310 9133
info@angloville.com
www.angloville.com

NUMBER OF TEACHERS: 20–80 a month for short language exchanges in a variety of locations.

PREFERENCE OF NATIONALITY: None.

QUALIFICATIONS: No experience/qualifications. Native English speaker, over 18. Must be enthusiastic conversationalist willing to engage in English conversation for up to 12 hours a day with adults or teenagers. Participants of the Anglo-TEFL Scholarship programme (www.anglo-tefl.com) can be subsidised to obtain an online qualification with Premier TEFL, followed by a minimum of 2 weeks at one or more Angloville holiday destinations.

CONDITIONS OF EMPLOYMENT: 6-day language exchange programme operates year round at a number of hotels and resorts in scenic locations around Poland. 5 hours of structured conversation a day plus social activities and making conversation over all meals.

SALARY: None, but free board and hotel accommodation are given. Some venues have swimming pools, spa, tennis courts and other facilities. Volunteers get a free tour and lunch in their jumping-off city, mostly Warsaw but also Wroclaw, Poznan and Krakow.

RECRUITMENT: Application process is online. Occasionally interviews take place by telephone/Skype. Processing of applications takes up to three weeks.

CONTACT: Marlena Kedzior.

BELT GDANSK
ul. Targ Drzewny 3/7, 80–886 Gdansk
+48 58 308 4777
gdansk@belt.edu.pl
www.bellschools.pl

Formerly part of Bell Schools International.

NUMBER OF TEACHERS: 90 for centres in Gdansk, Gdynia, Szczecin and Warsaw.

PREFERENCE OF NATIONALITY: British and Irish. Non-EU considered with relevant experience.

QUALIFICATIONS: CELTA or Trinity TESOL plus university degree. Minimum 1 year's experience.

CONDITIONS OF EMPLOYMENT: September to June, 20–26 hours a week. Annual workload is 680 hours. Part-time contracts also available. Also runs summer camps for young learners (aged 9–17).

SALARY: 2,400–2,800 zloty net per month, plus end-of-contract bonus of 1,000 zloty. Warsaw wages are higher: 3,000–3,600 zloty.

FACILITIES/SUPPORT: Accommodation assistance. Costs of obtaining work permits and visas are reimbursed by school. Health insurance. In-house teacher development programme. Warsaw centre also runs CELTA and DELTA courses.

RECRUITMENT: Ads on internet. Interviews necessary, usually by phone.

BRITISH CENTRE S.C. – ENGLISH LANGUAGE COURSES
ul. Dabrowskiego 8/6, 42–202 Czestochowa
+48 34 361 5914
office@britishcentre.pl
www.britishcentre.pl

NUMBER OF TEACHERS: 2.

PREFERENCE OF NATIONALITY: British.

QUALIFICATIONS: CELTA and experience with preparing students for Cambridge ESOL exams.

CONDITIONS OF EMPLOYMENT: 1-year contract with between 15 and 20 lessons per week.

SALARY: 35 zloty per lesson (45 minutes). 25–26 zloty after tax and social security deductions.

FACILITIES/SUPPORT: Room provided in English teacher's house.

CONTACT: Ms Henryka Rabenda, Co-owner.

ENGLISH COLLEGE
ul. Zeromskiego 31, 26–600 Radom
+48 385 8033
biuro@englishcollege.pl
www.englishcollege.pl

Centres located in Radom and 6 nearby towns including Kozienice, Iłza, Pionki and Zwoleń.

PREFERENCE OF NATIONALITY: Native speakers of English with clear standard British, Irish or North American accent.

QUALIFICATIONS: Degree (preferably in education or TESOL), TEFL/TESOL Certificate and experience. Should be enthusiastic, energetic, open minded and enjoy contact with people and eager to learn new things. Could be teaching kindergarten or adults.

CONDITIONS OF EMPLOYMENT: 9-month contracts (30 teaching weeks) from end of September. 22–24 hours per week, teaching all ages: children, teenagers and adults. Hours mainly 3pm–8.30pm.

SALARY: 20,000–22,000 zloty per contract depending on the hours. Monthly advance of 2,000 zloty plus contract completion bonus (up to 10% of salary).

FACILITIES/SUPPORT: Single furnished studio flat provided free, but not utilities. Cost of work permit covered by school (including courier delivery) but not visa if required. Transport paid for to off-site schools (30–40 minutes away from Radom) by bus or company car. Half of the cost of health insurance will be reimbursed.

RECRUITMENT: Application form, photo and copies of teaching certificates to be submitted and 2 references received directly before Skype interview is arranged.

CONTACT: Anna Machlarz, Director of Studies.

ENGLISH LANGUAGE CENTRE 'RIGHT NOW'
Pszczynska 17, 44–240 Zory, Silesia
+48 32 434 2929
info@rightnow.com.pl
www.rightnow.pl/employment

NUMBER OF TEACHERS: 1–2.

PREFERENCE OF NATIONALITY: EU member state passport holder.

QUALIFICATIONS: Bachelor's degree and some teaching experience an asset, but prepared to give training.

CONDITIONS OF EMPLOYMENT: 10 months mid-September to mid-June. 12 90-minute lessons per week plus private tuition.

SALARY: About 2,500 zloty per month after deductions and taxes.

FACILITIES/SUPPORT: Subsidised accommodation at school's flat within walking distance of the school. Assistance with work permits.

RECRUITMENT: Internet ads followed by interviews in person or by telephone.

CONTACT: Rafal Zurkowski, Owner/Manager.

GLOBAL VILLAGE
Al. Legionów 42, 25–035 Kielce
+48 41 362 1393
office@gv.edu.pl
www.gv.edu.pl

NUMBER OF TEACHERS: 7. Also for branches in Kielce, Starachowice and Skarzysko.

PREFERENCE OF NATIONALITY: EU citizens preferred.

QUALIFICATIONS: Bachelor's or master's degree plus a CELTA, DELTA or TEFL certificate.

CONDITIONS OF EMPLOYMENT: Standard contract length 1 academic year, to work 3pm–8pm, Monday to Friday.

SALARY: Competitive.

FACILITIES/SUPPORT: The school organises accommodation.

CONTACT: Urszula Szczepanczyk, Director (+48 602 313 274, urszula@gv.edu.pl).

INTERNATIONAL HOUSE INTEGRA BIELSKO
ul. Zielona 32, 43-300 Bielsko-Biała
+ 48 33 822 33 30
bielsko@ih.com.pl
www.ih.com.pl/Bielsko; www.facebook.com/IHBielsko

School has bilingual Kindergarten and primary school.

NUMBER OF TEACHERS: 11.

PREFERENCE OF NATIONALITY: EU candidates preferred (as they do not require a visa to live and work in Poland). In view of extra costs and administration involved in employing non-EU citizens, only particularly strong applicants can be considered.

QUALIFICATIONS: CELTA or equivalent, degree and 1 year's teaching experience required, especially of young and very young learners.

CONDITIONS OF EMPLOYMENT: 9 months. 21 hours a week. In-school group teaching is mostly from 3.30pm to 8.30pm. One-to-one lessons and in-company classes are in the mornings, afternoons and evenings, but teachers are not required to teach outside a 12-hour band during the day.

SALARY: 2900–3700 zloty depending on qualifications and experience. Tax deductions differ between nationalities (eg 0% for Britons, 18% for Irish).

FACILITIES/SUPPORT: The school assists new teachers with finding accommodation. If a non-EU teacher is employed, the school covers the costs of obtaining the visa (excluding travel and hotel costs). 20 days paid holiday.

RECRUITMENT: International House World Organisation; www.tefl.com. Interviews are carried out via Skype (with a webcam) or in person.

CONTACT: Katarzyna Jakielaszek, Director of Studies (katarzyna.jakielaszek@ih.com.pl).

INTERNATIONAL HOUSE TORUN

ul. Legionów 15, 87–100 Torun

+48 56 622 5081

torun@inthouse.pl

www.inthouse.pl

NUMBER OF TEACHERS: 10.

PREFERENCE OF NATIONALITY: None.

QUALIFICATIONS: CELTA needed. Experience not essential.

CONDITIONS OF EMPLOYMENT: 9 months.

SALARY: 1,600–1,875 zloty (net) depending on experience.

FACILITIES/SUPPORT: Shared accommodation provided. Help given with registration of EU teachers who stay more than 3 months, and to non-EU teachers who need work permits.

RECRUITMENT: Through IH World and also direct contact to school. Interviews necessary and sometimes carried out at IH London.

CONTACT: Glenn Standish, Director of Studies.

INTERNATIONAL HOUSE – WROCLAW

ul. Ofiar Oswiecimskich 19a, 50–069 Wroclaw

+48 71 372 3698

biurowroc@ih.com.pl

www.ih.com.pl/wroclaw

NUMBER OF TEACHERS: 8. Also for Bielsko-Biala and Wroclaw.

PREFERENCE OF NATIONALITY: EU citizens, but non-EU citizens may also be considered.

QUALIFICATIONS: Minimum CELTA or Trinity certificate. 1 year's experience or CELTA Pass 'A' or 'B' preferred.

CONDITIONS OF EMPLOYMENT: 9-month standard contract, 21 contact hours per week.

SALARY: 2,600–3,400 zloty per month net (in first year) depending on qualifications and experience.

FACILITIES/SUPPORT: The school helps new teachers find suitable accommodation before and on arrival.

RECRUITMENT: Via IH Human Resources in London or direct at wrocdos@ih.com.pl. Interviews are carried out by IH Human Resources in London or else directly in Wroclaw in person or by phone.

CONTACT: Richard Mason, Director of Studies (richard.mason@ih.com.pl).

LEKTOR SZKOLA JEZYKOW OBCYCH

ul. Olawska 25, 50–123 Wroclaw

+48 71 372 5292

biuro@lektor.com.pl

www.lektor.com.pl

NUMBER OF TEACHERS: 70.

PREFERENCE OF NATIONALITY: British, Irish, American, Canadian and Australian.

QUALIFICATIONS: Certificate in TEFL required (CELTA, DELTA or equivalent).

CONDITIONS OF EMPLOYMENT: Contracts for 1 or more years, 20–25 lessons per week. Students are young adults. Company organises intensive summer courses and language camps as well.

SALARY: From 55 zloty per hour.

FACILITIES/SUPPORT: Assistance with finding accommodation and obtaining work permit if necessary.

RECRUITMENT: Adverts on www.tefl.com. Personal interviews essential.

MCGREGOR LANGUAGE SCHOOLS

ul. Jagietty 2, 32–400 Myslenice

+48 12 372 2895

jobs@mcgregor.home.pl

www.mcgregor.net.pl

NUMBER OF TEACHERS: 8–10. Also for other branches in Limanowa and Wadowice.

PREFERENCE OF NATIONALITY: None.

QUALIFICATIONS: A successful candidate must have completed an ESL/EFL training course. Experience is not necessary but is an advantage.

CONDITIONS OF EMPLOYMENT: Length of stay October to June. 24 teaching hours per week between 3pm and 9pm.

SALARY: 2,800 zloty gross per month, less 19% for income tax and social security contributions.

FACILITIES/SUPPORT: Free fully furnished accommodation provided, 5 minutes' walk from school. The school takes care of all paperwork and covers the cost of the work permit, as well as providing full support to non-EU citizens to obtain a residence visa (though teachers cover the cost, currently 1,800 zloty (£50).

RECRUITMENT: Applications should include CV, 2 referees and copies of degree and TEFL certificates. Skype or face-to-face interviews.

CONTACT: Maria Garczynska-Payne, Academic Manager.

MULTISCHOOL SZKOLA JEZYKOW OBCYCH

ul. Niedzwiedzia 46, 02–666 Warsaw

+48 22 638 2339

biuro@multischool.pl

www.multischool.pl

NUMBER OF TEACHERS: 45 in 3 branches in Warsaw for kindergarten, primary and middle school pupils.

QUALIFICATIONS: TEFL course, higher education; experience not necessary. Must have degree or master's in early childhood education.

CONDITIONS OF EMPLOYMENT: 12 months. Teaching hours 8am–3pm and 3pm–8pm.

SALARY: $1,000 a month average, varies according to timetable. Less 10% for deductions.

FACILITIES/SUPPORT: Help given in finding a flat to rent and in obtaining a work permit.

RECRUITMENT: Résumé to be sent online. Prefer to interview candidates but can rely on CVs, letters of motivation and telephone conversations.

SPEED SCHOOL OF ENGLISH

ul. Sobieskiego 10/2c, 31-136 Krakow

+48 60 359 9919

krakow@myspeed.pl

www.myspeed.pl

NUMBER OF TEACHERS: About 40 for 5 branches in Gliwice, Bielsko-Biala, Krakow, Tychy and Wroclaw.

PREFERENCE OF NATIONALITY: English-speaking countries.

QUALIFICATIONS: Ideally a BA degree plus CELTA, TESOL or equivalent. Experience is not essential but considered an asset.

CONDITIONS OF EMPLOYMENT: 10–12 months starting July or September. Afternoon and evening shifts plus mornings on a rotational basis.

SALARY: About 3,000–3,500 zloty per month (net). Airfare allowance paid on completion of contract.

FACILITIES/SUPPORT: Accommodation is ready for teachers' arrival. Full assistance given with work visa application including official translations and trips to the Labour Department on teachers' behalf. Free intensive teacher training and induction course.

RECRUITMENT: Internet, walk-in, cooperation with British organisations. Interviews take place face-to-face or by Skype.

CONTACT: Martyna Olszowska, Recruitment Coordinator.

STUDIUM JĘZYKÓW OBCYCH 'NEW ENGLAND'

ul. Pomorska 34, 66-400 Gorzów Wlkp.

+48 95 732 3087

newengland@pro.onet.pl

www.newengland.pl

NUMBER OF TEACHERS: 1.

PREFERENCE OF NATIONALITY: None, but prefer EU citizens.

QUALIFICATIONS: BA preferably in philology, linguistics or education, plus TEFL or equivalent. No experience needed.

CONDITIONS OF EMPLOYMENT: 10-month contract. Usual hours are 2pm–9pm.

SALARY: Decent local salary, depending on experience and qualifications.

FACILITIES/SUPPORT: School finds accommodation for teacher.

RECRUITMENT: Skype interview.

CONTACT: Beata Kulik, Owner.

TALKBACK

ul. Słowików 17, 42-677 Szałsza, Silesia

+48 789 087 387

leah@talkback.pl

www.talkback.pl

NUMBER OF TEACHERS: 6 to teach via Skype.

PREFERENCE OF NATIONALITY: Open to all native speakers, especially American and British.

QUALIFICATIONS: No experience or qualifications necessary other than speaking English as a native. Most students want conversation practice, though IT would be useful to be able to explain points of grammar. Should be familiar with using Skype and other basic computer programmes.

CONDITIONS OF EMPLOYMENT: Flexible hours to fit in with clients. No contracts.

SALARY: 35–45 zloty per hour.

FACILITIES/SUPPORT: Advice on finding accommodation can be given. One-to-one training possible with owner of the company. Access to materials created by other teachers in the school. School will apply and pay for a work permit, which takes about a month. Foreign teachers then apply for a residence permit; advice available from owner who is a US citizen.

RECRUITMENT: Via the Polish website www.olx.pl to scan for adverts placed by teachers offering lessons. Also via owner's blog www.polonization.pl.

CONTACT: Leah Morawiec, Owner.

THE BEST SZKOŁA JEZYKÓW OBCYCH
M Reja 50, 66-470 Kostrzyn nad Odra
+48 79 558 9871; +48 69 836 4523
k.naruszewicz@szkolathebest.pl
www.szkolathebest.pl

NUMBER OF TEACHERS: 1–2.

PREFERENCE OF NATIONALITY: None.

QUALIFICATIONS: BA or MA in Teaching English or TEFL/CELTA/ TKT/TESOL certificates (or an equivalent).

CONDITIONS OF EMPLOYMENT: Contracts last an academic year. 25 hours teaching a week, afternoons and evenings, with 15 office hours.

SALARY: $1,100 less $450 contributions (to cover unemployment insurance, paid sick leave and paid holidays).

FACILITIES/SUPPORT: Subsidised accommodation offered in the schoolhouse for $150. Financial support for teachers pursuing further qualifications. Help given with visa application, arranging necessary visits and travels, etc.

RECRUITMENT: Advertise online.

CONTACT: Kornel Naruszewicz, School Director.

WARSAW ENGLISH ACADEMY
Mokotowska 1, 00-640 Warsaw
+48 73 000 1053
we@WeAcademy.pl
www.WeAcademy.pl

NUMBER OF TEACHERS: 4.

PREFERENCE OF NATIONALITY: British, American.

QUALIFICATIONS: CELTA.

CONDITIONS OF EMPLOYMENT: 8-month contracts. Teaching hours between 7am and 9pm.

SALARY: 50–70 zloty per hour, less 18% for taxes and contributions.

FACILITIES/SUPPORT: No assistance with accommodation or work permits.

RECRUITMENT: Candidates teach a trial lesson.

CONTACT: : Izabela Wroblewska, Co-Founder.

WARSAW INTERNATIONAL TRILINGUAL SCHOOL
Karowa 14/16 lok 6; 00-324 Warsaw; also at ul. Cicha 5, 00-353 Warsaw
+48 503 072 119
amjup2000@yahoo.com
www.3languages.pl

NUMBER OF TEACHERS: 5.

PREFERENCE OF NATIONALITY: None.

QUALIFICATIONS: Early years education certified teachers.

CONDITIONS OF EMPLOYMENT: 3-year contract. Hours of work 7.30am–1pm or 1pm–6.30pm.

SALARY: US$1,000 per month (net).

FACILITIES/SUPPORT: Shared flats provided. Full assistance given with red tape.

CONTACT: Anna Maliszewska, Pre-school Founder and Owner.

YORK SCHOOL OF ENGLISH
ul. Bursztynowa 20–22, 31–214 Krakow
+48 12 415 1818
info@york.edu.pl
www.york.edu.pl.

PASE (www.pase.pl) and Quality English (www.quality-english.com) recognised school, City & Guilds and LCCI approved examination centre. Has branches in Bochnia and Brzesko as well.

NUMBER OF TEACHERS: 30, including approximately 10 full-time native English speakers.

PREFERENCE OF NATIONALITY: British and Irish, also American, Canadian or Australian (EU visa holders preferred).

QUALIFICATIONS: BA/MA (preferably in English or Linguistics). TEFL certificate (CELTA/Trinity or equivalents). Minimum 1 year ELT experience preferred, references.

CONDITIONS OF EMPLOYMENT: 9-month full-time renewable contract (September to June). Average 26 hours per week.

SALARY: Monthly average salary 3,000 zloty gross depending on qualifications and experience. Paid overtime.

FACILITIES/SUPPORT: Free accommodation for the first 3 days. Help given with accommodation. Bonuses. Professional development, regular workshops and conferences.

RECRUITMENT: www.tefl.com.

CONTACT: Ewa Krupska, Director of Studies (e.krupska@york.edu.pl).

ROMANIA

Since the collapse of communism, English has been taught in Romanian primary schools all the way through, so most people under 30 can communicate reasonably well. The vast majority of English teaching is carried out by Romanian teachers, who seem to do a splendid job, judging from the extremely high pass rate their students achieve in the Cambridge exams. Young Romanians possess an enthusiasm for the English language that dates from the arrival of the Cartoon Network in their country and which is driven, as throughout Europe, by the ubiquity of English-language films and music. Teenagers are also motivated to learn English if they harbour an ambition to live and work abroad. Since January 2014 restrictions have been lifted on the right of Romanians (and Bulgarians) to work in the UK, which spurred even more to master English. Even with Britain voting to leave the EU, Romanians continue to see English as a passport to success. A foreign language exam is compulsory for graduating from school and university, which has boosted demand for private tuition. Yet there are relatively few private language institutes in Romania, partly because of the small size of the corporate sector. The arrival of western investment and global companies and hotel chains has created more demand for commercial English though not necessarily the prosperity to pay for it.

The Ministry of Education in Bucharest does not recruit EFL teachers directly, though it cooperates with the British Council to improve standards of local teachers and place unpaid interns. The British Council (www.britishcouncil.ro) has been active in promoting English in Romania at all levels and runs its own Teaching Centre in Bucharest at Calea Dorobantilor 14 (✆ +40 21 307 9600) and also in Iasi. At the time of writing, it was recruiting both hourly paid teachers of corporate English and full-time teachers to join the team of 40 teachers, to start September 2016. As always with the British Council, applicants must have at least the Cambridge/Trinity Certificate and a minimum of two years' full-time post-qualification teaching experience.

QUEST Romania (www.quest.ro) is the Romanian Association for Quality Language Services, though its website is not maintained and it is of limited interest to foreign teachers.

Some language schools are listed under the heading *Limbi Straine – Cursuri* in the *Golden Pages* (www.paginiaurii.ro), but these are unlikely to employ a native English speaker. Romanian language schools find it next-to-impossible to attract native English-speaker teachers because they simply can't afford to pay them.

As the director of one QUEST member school wrote:

> ***While we would welcome having native English teachers on our staff (we do occasionally receive enquiries from interested people), it is true that given how small our school is (approximately 400 students a year altogether) we cannot afford spending too much on employing them. For the moment, we only employ highly qualified local teachers on part-time contracts. I do not want to mislead people before we reach a more secure position and financial situation, in a very unstable country, economically speaking.***

MINNA GRABER

Many years ago, Minna Graber arrived in Romania to celebrate the New Year and has been besotted with the country ever since.

We went straight into a Carpathian village at the top of a mountain complete with gypsy fiddlers and not an internal combustion engine for miles around. I fell for the place hook, line and sinker and haven't been able to kick the habit. I wanted to teach in the north-east of the country and so contacted the British Council in Iasi, who in turn referred me to SOL. I met the director, Grenville Yeo, at a café and we talked for a long time about the challenges, rewards and requirements. In the end the job offer was with one of the best schools in Bucharest where the students all go on to university (and a significant minority are these days applying for British university places). I work for 18 teaching periods a week. I am not supposed to teach grammar, which at least in my school is seen as the Romanian English-language teachers' prerogative partly, I fear, because they assume native speakers are not capable of this. This is despite the fact that I am fully trained to do so.

The wages sound terrible – 1,100 lei a month after deductions for tax and National Insurance. The other teachers have to pay for accommodation out of this so in comparison I have a big advantage (the school's parents' association provides and pays for my very simple small studio flat and for the running costs). I am very good at living frugally but find that I still have to take on a couple of private students to make ends meet. The rest of the staff work long hours, giving these private lessons.

According to Minna, native speakers of English can command a high fee for giving private tuition. She charges around 60 lei an hour (£11.50). If you work in a private kindergarten, as she did at one point, you can charge even more. Despite her modest earnings, she is far from discontent with her lifestyle:

I go to all the best concerts, have private lessons in Romanian, attend martial arts classes and choir every week and travel a lot. I am even able to put a little by at the end of the month. My students are all completely delightful. I love teaching them. They are respectful and talented. I do have to mother them a little over matters such as getting work in on time. Occasionally they, and their parents, try to exert pressure on me over marks. If a form tutor asks my help in rescuing a student who has problems or who might otherwise get expelled I always do so, otherwise I resist changing marks.

As for leisure time, many a Saturday has been spent haring up the mountains with Bucharest's enormous and enthusiastic mountain club. As a result of my wanderings over the mountains in the summer I made friends with some traditional shepherds and peasant farmers and am always welcome to visit. The times spent with these friends in the countryside are like a journey back into a far distant past. Of course, for all of this a command of the Romanian language is essential.

Nobody knows anything about Romania and the upside of this is that it is a very tourist-free area and you enjoy status as a visitor from the outside world. People are interested and welcoming largely because there are so few visitors. Catch it whilst it still lasts.

A few British exchange organisations and charities recruit volunteers for summer language camps. For example, BREDEX (British Romanian Educational Exchange) is a volunteer student-led organisation which sends about a dozen university students from the UK to five cities in Romania to teach conversational English (see entry), starting in early July. It is also possible to make contact directly with language camp organisations, such as InAction Camps (www.tabereengleza.ro) located in the Carpathian Mountains. DAD International UK-Romania in Iasi (✆ +40 772 201399; www.dad.ro) has been sending volunteer teachers to several camps in mountain or seaside locations around Romania since 2001, but seemed to be retrenching at the time of writing. The arrangement has been for flights and accommodation to be paid.

Americans might also investigate People to People's Language Ambassador programme (www.ptpe.org). Recently, PTPE chapters in the towns of Lugoj, Roman and Vaslui have expressed an interested in hosting a native speaker for two to four weeks so that the volunteers can immerse themselves in Romanian culture while teaching English conversation lessons.

Projects Abroad in Sussex (www.projects-abroad.co.uk) recruits paying volunteers to work as English language teaching assistants during the summer or academic year in Romania, the only teaching project in Europe. No TEFL background is required. Packages cost from £1,895 for one month to £3,295 for three months and include placement, accommodation, three meals a days, full medical and travel insurance and 24 hour staff support.

Since the accession of Romania to the EU in 2007, red tape for EU citizens has become simpler. Any teacher wishing to stay for longer than 120 days should apply for a temporary resident permit. So far there is no date for Romania to join the Schengen Area. If or when it does, non-EU citizens will be allowed a maximum stay of 90 days within 6 months unless they obtain a work/resident's permit.

Romania is not a particularly expensive place to stay, but not dirt cheap either. According to the director of the Bredex programme, a recent teacher estimated a total outlay of about £1,000 for the summer including flights, but goes on to qualify this: '*Considering her frenetic travel and impressive/spectacular beer and pizza consumption, we would confidently say that is an upper-end estimate.*'

LIST OF EMPLOYERS

BREDEX (BRITISH ROMANIAN EDUCATIONAL EXCHANGE)
41 Penge Road, London E13 0SL, UK
✆ +44 7956 946786
ridwanatbredex@gmail.com
www.facebook.com/BREDEX.info

Programme for British university students to teach conversational English in summer programmes, founded by Oxford students in 1991 but now open to all UK universities.

NUMBER OF TEACHERS: About 12 volunteers.

PREFERENCE OF NATIONALITY: Native speakers (or with native proficiency) at British universities.

QUALIFICATIONS: Must be students or recent graduates in any discipline from a British university. Candidates should be keen on fostering the educational development of others. Enthusiasm, intellectual curiosity and a willingness to get involved in something different are necessary.

CONDITIONS OF EMPLOYMENT: 7 weeks from early July. 3 weeks of teaching, 1 week to travel and explore Romania, 3 more weeks of teaching. Minimum of 3 hours of teaching on weekdays but usually 2 teaching sessions a day of 3 hours each.

SALARY: Unpaid. Teachers cover their own travel costs and pay an admin fee of around £40.

FACILITIES/SUPPORT: Free accommodation is provided at Romanian university dorms for the duration of the programme. Prior to the programme, participants receive a cheat sheet of resources from previous years to help plan their lessons but teachers have complete creative control of their classes. The weekend before teaching begins is spent in Bucharest, where participants are given a crash-course introduction to Romanian culture and nightlife, with discussions on teaching.

RECRUITMENT: Contact with universities during autumn and spring terms, via student volunteering bodies, posters and the Bredex Facebook page. A short personal statement, followed by a telephone interview or a meet-up, location permitting.

CONTACT: Ridwan Ibrahim, Director.

PROFESSIONAL LANGUAGE CENTRE

4/1 Semanatorilor St, Targu-Mures 4300

+40 265 251180; mobile +40 723 241042

acotoara@gmail.com

www.professionalcentre.ro

NUMBER OF TEACHERS: 1.

QUALIFICATIONS: Bachelor's degree or equivalent.

CONDITIONS OF EMPLOYMENT: 1-year contract. To work 4pm–8pm, 5 days a week.

SALARY: $7 per hour. Taxes and social security paid by the school.

FACILITIES/SUPPORT: Assistance with finding accommodation and acquiring work permits.

RECRUITMENT: Interview required.

CONTACT: Angela Cotoara, Director.

RUSSIA

The Russian economy is in dire straits. The rouble has been tumbling, mainly because of the fall in the world price of oil, and at the time of writing was trading at an all-time low of 65 roubles to the US dollar. Recession seems to be looming. National morale is low, not helped by the disgrace of the doping scandal that resulted in the ban of so many of its athletes from the Rio Olympics. The geopolitical situation is no rosier, with the EU agreeing to extend sanctions against Russia as punishment for its aggression towards Ukraine and annexation of Crimea. Inevitably these problems will mean some contraction of the English language market, especially in the corporate sector. Yet both old and new language training businesses are eagerly recruiting teachers via advertisements abroad. Hosting the 2018 FIFA World Cup may act as a spur just as the Winter Olympics of 2014 did.

With the economic squeeze, Russians are slowly discovering language learning via the internet, although courses at private language schools continue to be popular. Reflecting the views of their clientele, many schools feel obliged to hire a native speaker teacher, if only to burnish their image, despite the high cost. The large chains, such as Language Link, International House and EF English First, are constantly recruiting native speaker teachers for their schools, even though Russian English teachers are cheaper and do not require visa support and other costly add-on benefits such as accommodation, health care and travel allowances. Yet the collapse of the rouble has had a devastating effect on Russian schools' attempts to recruit teachers from abroad. **Julie Nagay**, Director of Studies at Pilot School in Rostov-on-Don (www.pilot-school.ru) lamented that two years ago they could offer a monthly salary equivalent to $1,000 net, but now the same salary is worth $500–$600 '*and not every foreigner is ready to work for such money*'. Almost all schools are looking for applicants who hold TEFL certificates obtained on credible 100+ hour training courses with teaching practice. If you do not hold a certificate but have gained valuable experience teaching General English, Business English and/or international examination courses (IELTS, FCE, CAE and their like), and you have taught both adults and children, you should have little difficulty finding a job teaching English in Russia.

Robert Jensky, Managing Director of Language Link Russia, is convinced that high standards are essential:

> ***I have personally seen many unqualified teachers fail because they did not fully realise the difference between speaking English and teaching English. Although Russians can vary in temperament and personality, they share a respect for education. Russians who under communism did not have to pay for education have come to accept the fact that it is now necessary to do so. There is little debate among Russians as to the significance of the English language both domestically and globally. Their only concern is that they get their full money's worth from each and every lesson. Russian students are demanding and place high expectations on their teachers, and so do the companies that employ them (including those that hire EFL teachers illegally). Given these circumstances, it is strongly recommended that any teacher coming to Russia has with them a good grammar book, a dictionary and a concise guide to TEFL methodology.***

Many young Russians are already fairly competent in the language and want to become more conversant with western culture, not just for its own sake but to enhance their career prospects. Jobs in international firms are often advertised only in English. Russians young and not-so-young who want to work in advertising, banking, computing and so on often need to speak English and therefore are drawn to the intensive English courses advertised all over the Moscow metro and on lamp posts.

There are also plenty of jobs tutoring and looking after young children, as affluent parents hope to give their children a head start by showing off at the same time. This sector is definitely expanding, with several companies and individuals posting adverts in newspapers and websites such as www.expat.ru; for example, an advert seen in 2016 invited native speakers, qualified teachers and tutors of English (and other languages) with a linguistic background or TEFL Certificate to join the teachers team of the Native Speakers Club, which arranges private lessons at the teacher's or student's place (hr@nsc24.org). Kindergartens and specialist companies that offer tutors, nannies and governesses for children have also realised that native English speakers '*create a good image for your company*', according to the director of Little Angels Kindergarten in Moscow (see List of Employers). Other specialist agencies include Gouverneur International (www.guvernior.ru), Home Story (ns.homestory@gmail.com), Duke & Duchess International (www.dukeandduchess-int.com) and Bonne International with offices in London and Moscow (www.bonne-int.com). ESL-qualified native candidates are needed to tutor children aged 3 to 12 years and can command high salaries when they have an appropriate background in early childhood education.

FINDING A JOB

Finding a vacancy in Russia shouldn't be too difficult. Russia is, after all, the largest country on earth, spanning 11 time zones. You only need to decide where in Russia you'd like to settle down to teach English. As a rule, salaries can drop the further you go from Moscow. A lower salary, however, is usually more than made up for by the lower costs of living found in many of the big cities away from Moscow; and a lower cost of living usually means a higher standard of living. Likewise, you're more likely to experience real Russia and real Russians.

Rob Jensky cautions against focusing your job hunt entirely around salary and perks:

> ***For newly qualified teachers, academic support can mean the difference between success and failure as a teacher. And speaking of success as a teacher, having tons of personality is imperative. Students want to like their teachers and the way to gain their affection is by truly liking them back. Teachers who like their students will spend the time needed to prepare for their lessons adequately and this is where the value of proper academic support cannot be overestimated. The availability of a good Director of Studies and other experienced teaching staff who can help you with lesson preparation is a benefit that cannot be counted in terms of dollars and cents or pounds and pence.***

Teachers who are capable of performing in a variety of EFL classroom settings (Young Learners, adults, General, Business English, examination preparation) are in the greatest demand. Likewise, teachers who are prepared to be flexible with regard to teaching schedules will find a far greater number of employment opportunities. This is especially true in the great metropolitan areas, where so many business and one-to-one clients want to be taught before or after the working day.

The two most popular international websites used by Russian employers looking to hire English teachers are www.tefl.com and www.eslcafe.com. A typical advert might read: '*British-owned and managed school based in the centre of Moscow is always looking to recruit teachers of English (and other European languages) to work with large Russian and multinational companies.*'

When considering potential employers in Russia make sure that the company has the right to invite and employ teachers in Russia (see visa section for details), check whether the salary is net or gross and ask if accommodation is free/included.

The main international language chains, such as Language Link and EF English First, recruit large numbers abroad; for example, EF has 35 language schools across Russia. Benefits packages standardly include accommodation, travel reimbursement, medical insurance and visa costs. Many foreign teachers prefer the security of working for a western-owned company. Even if the wages are not brilliant, the support and fringe benefits usually make up for it. Language Link (see entry) offers an array of different employment opportunities designed to fit the needs of most EFL applicants from qualified to unqualified willing to be interns or volunteers. International House has its main operation in Moscow (see entry for BKC) and affiliated schools in Novokuznetsk (Siberia), where the lower salary of 40,000 roubles goes much further than in Moscow. The IH branch in Stavropol (http://ihstavropol.com) in the deep south of Russia pays its teachers considerably more, especially if they have experience of teaching young learners and very young learners.

Another experienced TEFLer is **Bradwell Jackson**, who ended up accepting a contract in Shakhty, a city in Rostov oblast in southern Russia. The Language Link franchise here was the first to offer Brad a contract with limited hours, and he has since bargained them down to a 15-hour teaching week, plus a large apartment paid for by the school:

> ***The fact that Russia was the first to offer a favourable contract may say something about their need for native speakers. I only agreed to start the visa procedure after I saw that the contract specifically stated that I couldn't work over 22 hours a week. I believe that this particular town of Shakhty was willing to agree since they are such a small town it's not easy for them to inveigle a foreigner to come to live. This makes this a perfect symbiotic relationship, as I am happy to live in such a village-like atmosphere where I don't need to have a car and can walk to work. The teachers are quite friendly to me, and the manager almost never does anything to ruffle my feathers, since she probably doesn't want to see me take off (as some previous foreign teachers have done apparently). Upon arriving in-country, I didn't notice as much of the supposed 'Russian cold exterior' as I had been apprised of. It is true that I couldn't just smile at people on the street. My colleague told me that people will think that I'm crazy if I do that. I asked him, 'Even if I smile at the girls?', and he said, 'Yes.' I found out that he was right.***

The monthly salary of 35,000 roubles (less than $550) is at the low end, though more than three times what the local Russian teachers are paid. In Brad's case, the easy workload and comfortable free apartment are sufficient compensations. Small town pastimes seem to suit Brad too: '*For the most part, Russians seem just as sociable as any other people I've known. When I go out for dancing or karaoke, I'm often inundated by the local tipsy Russians who demand that I come over to their table for a drink, which they say is a Russian tradition.*'

The oilfield areas of Tyumen and Nizhnevartovsk are a popular and somewhat better paid region to work in than most: CET (cetschool.com) is an example of an independent British-owned and -run chain of schools which employ teachers on yearly contracts from September to May. Others are now popping up in more remote areas such as Irkutsk, Novosibirsk or Yakutsk, the coldest city in the world and the centre of Russia's gold and diamond-mining industry. In none of these places is a newly qualified teacher likely to get rich or pocket more than $600–$800 a month, but it's a fascinating cultural experience. Flights, visa expenses and accommodation will normally be provided and paid for, as well as Russian lessons and an opportunity to live in and experience a part of the world that can often be as far removed culturally from life in Moscow or St Petersburg as they themselves are from London or New York.

FREELANCING

The vast majority of English teachers in Moscow, especially those with a little more experience and knowledge of the local market, supplement what can often be a rather meagre income from an EFL school with much more lucrative private tuition, normally conducted at the homes of wealthy individual clients. It is generally accepted among Moscow employers that most, if not all, teachers supplement their income by freelancing, which causes no problems unless a teacher is trying to poach students.

Check the online message board community for English speakers living in Moscow (www.expat.ru, mentioned above), which always carries a selection of clearly set out adverts for native English-speaker teachers, preferably already resident in Moscow. Even newly qualified teachers can normally start building up private students fairly quickly, particularly if they offer a free trial lesson. Personality and likeability are as highly valued in Russia as purely academic skills, such as grammatical and linguistic knowledge.

RUFUS VAUGHAN-SPRUCE

In recent years, veteran EL teacher and CELTA trainer Rufus Vaughan-Spruce has spent time living and teaching in Moscow, the hub of the ELT market. He has generously supplied this illuminating account of working as a well-paid freelancer, on top of having a part-time contract with a school.

Well-off students are relatively easy to come by with some effort, time and patience, either through personal contacts, word of mouth, other teachers, friends of friends, or websites such as www.expat.ru. Most of the network of private clients I built up over three years living and working in Moscow originated from a single original student who passed my name onto friends and colleagues, and they then to theirs, etc. A typical rate for a 90-minute lesson would be between 3,000 and 4,000 roubles in cash, depending on the time of day (weekday evenings are always in higher demand), how far away the location of the client is (and how far from a metro station) and, of course, the level of experience and qualifications of the teacher. Demand is somewhat lower in St Petersburg, as are rates, i.e. 2,000-2,500 roubles for 90 minutes. Make a good impression in a first lesson (offer the first lesson for free if necessary) and a decent, personable teacher should quickly be able to build up a bank of private students which can double or even triple your income from working officially for a language school. IELTS tuition is particularly in demand, and teachers who are or have been IELTS examiners can command premium rates.

In an ideal world, a teacher could do such work full-time and enjoy a comfortable lifestyle for a schedule that involved no more than 20-24 hours of teaching time (plus the inevitable travel) each week. The travel itself, outside key rush hour times at the busiest stations on the Circle line, is generally reliable, cheap and not unpleasant. The entire Moscow Metro network is now blessed with free wifi, and trains run every 1-2 minutes from 5am until 1am. Clients are likely to be interesting and varied, and often have specific needs or requirements. Over the past two years, those I have taught have included a popular radio show host, the chairman of a major Russian bank, a senior FSB (security service) official, a well-known chef and a number of government or senior business figures.

However, one requires a sponsored visa to live and work legally in Russia, and herein lies the biggest hurdle to independent work. One solution to this quandary, especially for better qualified teachers with extensive experience (DELTA, etc.), is to approach one of the larger business-oriented schools, such as IPT or British Business Language Centre, and offer to work for them on a part-time basis in exchange for visa sponsorship. You may be on a relatively low rate for what you do for them: 750-900 roubles per academic hour is typical in Moscow, 550-700 roubles in St Petersburg. But if you agree to teach, say 10-16 academic hours per week for a school like this – likely to be concentrated in the busy early morning hours – in exchange for visa sponsorship and the understanding that the rest of your time is your own, this can often be a mutually beneficial arrangement. This is especially true since the collapse of the rouble in recent years, as many of the better or more experienced teachers have upped and left, and many such schools can be desperate for experienced teachers for their more important VIP clients. In general, the less experienced you are as a teacher, the greater the number of hours they will probably want you to agree to teach for them.

EXCHANGE PROGRAMMES

Since 1992, the Serendipity Russian-English Program has been sending Americans to work at the American Home in Vladimir Russia, a city 180km north-east of Moscow. In addition to teaching regular classes, the teachers give lectures on American society and participate in other activities. Contracts last nine to 11 months (renewable) starting in the second week of August. The annual deadline for applications is 1 March or until all the places are filled. Complete application information is at www.serendipity-russia.com.

Students of Russian should investigate the programme run by the Pro-Ba Centre in St Petersburg where four or eight weeks of intensive study of Russian is followed by a period of work in schools teaching evening classes, kindergartens or summer camps (www.russian-learning.com/course/study-and-work). Fees are €2,750 for two months and €3,750 for four months, accommodation included. A cultural exchange organisation GeoVisions arranges live-in tutoring jobs in Russia for volunteers willing to live with a Russian family for one, two or three months, speaking as much English as possible. Programme details, including the fee (currently $1,489) can be found at www.geovisions.org/program/teach-english-in-russia. Young people without a TEFL background might also investigate the intern teaching programme or the au pair-teacher combination programme operated by the Hudson Group in Moscow (www.encounterrussia.com).

The youth exchange company CCUSA (www.ccusa.com/programs/campcounselorsRussia.aspx or www.ccusa.co.uk) recruits volunteers for English-immersion summer camps in Russia whereby teacher/counsellors from the USA and UK are placed in youth camps in Russia lasting four or eight weeks between mid-June and mid-August. Participants must have experience of working with children and/or abroad, and have an interest in learning about the Russian language and culture. Camps are widely scattered, from Lake Baikal in Siberia to the shores of the Black Sea. The programme fee of $2,900 from the US and £999 from Britain includes return flights to Moscow and onwards to your assigned camp, insurance, orientation on arrival and room and board. Applicants of all ages are accepted: the CCUSA record so far was a 63-year-old American woman who worked at a Russian camp.

PAUL JONES

Australian Paul Jones spent the summer in Russia.

I worked as a counsellor in a summer camp near the city of Perm. When I first arrived, my heart sank because it looked like a gulag (for which the area around Perm is famous!). But you soon forget the physical conditions, mostly anyway. If I didn't like the food at the start, I definitely learnt to like it by the end and now reminisce about the worst of it! My job, as with American summer camps for kids, was to help lead a group of up to 30 children for their three-week stay at the camp. Because I did not speak the language, I was placed with two other leaders so my services weren't really necessary. However, this region of Russia doesn't exactly get many international visitors so the role I played at camp sometimes felt more like being a rock star! The types of activities the kids did ranged from football, basketball and swimming (the colour of the pool was scary) to singing, dancing and crafts. But while I tried as best I could to lead my group of kids in their daily activities, every single kid in the camp wants a piece of you because you're the foreigner! So a lot of the job is to just be there and share a different culture with the kids (and their parents sometimes), other Russian counsellors and the Camp Director. I found that a few words in Russian go a long way to bridging the culture gap. And if possible take some souvenirs for the kids. Even a pack of cards with the British flag on them provides 52 little gifts.

CONDITIONS OF WORK

The majority of language schools that recruit teachers from abroad offer a package that includes a salary, free accommodation, subsidised flights, and support for a multiple entry visa. The accommodation will usually be shared with other teachers. Wages are normally quoted in roubles rather than dollars to protect against currency fluctuations. The net wage range is normally 40,000–60,000 roubles. When you see salaries of up to 90,000 roubles advertised (as by the Orange Language Centre in St Petersburg in 2016), this will be for highly qualified candidates working long hours. Outside the cities, starting wages will be closer to the lower end.

For those who choose to (or have to) live out, the housing market has calmed down somewhat and it is no longer as difficult as it was for foreign teachers to find independent accommodation. According to **Rufus Vaughan-Spruce**, '*accommodation is still expensive in Moscow, but not (in dollar terms at least) anything like as pricey as it was. Paying around 30,000–40,000 roubles a month for a private one-room apartment somewhere two to six stops outside the Circle line is typical (currently £350–£450). You'll normally be expected to put down a month's rent, a month's deposit and (if you've used an agent) a month's commission payment on the day you move in.*'

Rufus Vaughan-Spruce was remarkably lucky on his first stint of working in the city. He was chatting to a private student about the problems of finding accommodation in Moscow. It turned out that this man had a rather beautiful and very spacious apartment he wasn't using and let Rufus stay there rent-free for a year. The only payment he ever agreed to accept was that he stopped paying for his weekly English lesson.

A cultural difference which many newcomers find difficult to accept is the apparent unfriendliness of the Russian people. However, the cold face of Russian officialdom could not be in starker contrast to the warmth that will greet you when you get to know Russians better. **Elizabeth Bearman**, a teacher in Moscow, goes some way to unravelling the mystery of the cold Russian exterior:

> ***The Russian man in the street does not smile unless he is happy, he does not engage complete strangers in meaningless conversation and he does not suffer fools gladly. There is a Russian proverb that perhaps sums it up: 'Only a fool smiles all the time'. However, while Russians can appear rude and unfriendly, when you get to know them they are considerate, helpful, generous and well . . . friendly. The Russian concept of friendship is much deeper and less superficial than elsewhere.***

The clichéd cold exterior of the Russian is nothing compared to the literal cold of the Russian winter, as described by **Travis Boyle** who worked in Moscow (and is from Texas!):

The hardest thing about my job is probably the weather. Because I work in-company, I have to trek to all of my students' offices, and because this is Moscow, that means that nine months of the year are cold, snowy, and icy. But the students almost always offer hot tea or coffee.

Moscow winters last a good four or five months, when temperatures regularly fall below minus 15°C.

At first American teacher **Bradwell Jackson** had trouble controlling his classes of children in the little town of Shakhty:

Whereas in China, I noticed a culture of respect for teachers, here there is no such respect and teachers are mistrusted. When I first started teaching here, the kids ran roughshod over me and had a heyday driving me to the brink. My experiences in China hadn't prepared me for handling such behaviour. The only country I've seen where children behave worse is my own. I was able to overcome this situation fairly quickly, because I genuinely like my students; otherwise I would have been toast in the bin. Russian adults are business-like and want to get their money's worth. Yet, at the same time, if they like you, they are happy to joke around when it's appropriate.

Katherine Hyvärinen was delighted with her adult students in Moscow, whom she described as '*enthusiastic, motivated and with a positive and at times humorous attitude*' towards her lessons. Her boss **Tim Newton,** MD at IPT (see entry), has no complaints about the intermediate and advanced students he has taught in Moscow, who are mostly sponsored by their companies and are committed and hard working. He compares his school favourably with some of the alternatives:

Don't be fooled into believing that just because you choose to work for a chain school, you are going to be working in either a large school or one staffed by native English-speaking teachers. Many major chains operate small teaching operations in far-flung locations. Proximity to good health care cannot be taken for granted, and could be an issue for people with medical conditions. If proximity to cultural and recreational outlets such as theatres, cinemas, museums, parks, circuses and other tourist attractions is important to you psychologically, then be sure to investigate locations prior to accepting a job.

REGULATIONS

A sponsored visa is necessary to live and work legally in Russia. There are exceptions: for instance, if you are married to a Russian you can get residency fairly quickly. Some old hands do live and work on business visas, but this involves either returning to your home country every three months for the complex and expensive process of getting a new one, or leaving the country for 90 days in each 180-day period. US passport holders are permitted an initial stay of up to 180 days. Employers must keep abreast of the Federal Migration Service's changing legislation. In order to qualify for a multiple entry work visa, teachers must provide certified copies of their passport, TESOL certificate, letter of invitation from the employer and university degree certificate, and must undergo an HIV test. The proof of being HIV-negative must be dated within three months of the visa application. You will have to collect your visa from the Russian Embassy in your home country. The visa application process is anything but streamlined and routinely takes three months as it did in **Bradwell Jackson**'s case, though at least he was able to submit simple copies of his degree and CELTA certificates, rather than originals or apostilled copies. If your employer is not being particularly helpful, specialist visa agencies may be able to advise such as Real Russia (www.realrussia.co.uk). In the UK, the Russian Consulate has outsourced its visa activities to VFS Global (http://ru.vfsglobal.co.uk), which has offices in London, Manchester and Edinburgh. Agencies such as Legal Stay (www.legalstay.ru) advertise in Russia their ability to provide working visas for teachers for a colossal fee (e.g. €1,450 initially).

The company that holds your visa has considerable leverage over you, so it is not a good idea to fall out with them. They can cancel your visa at a moment's notice for any (or no) cause, though it's worth noting that they do need physical possession of your passport in order to carry out this step.

Employers are supposed to deduct pension contributions from employees who have contracts of more than six months.

LIST OF EMPLOYERS

AAA/SGI ENGLISH
Bldg 6/7, No 8 Staromonetniy Pereulok, Moscow 119180
+7 495 951 7038
admin@aaaenglish.ru
www.aaaenglish.ru

School is a joint venture between AAA English and St George International in London; both are British owned and managed.
NUMBER OF TEACHERS: Up to 15 for 2 locations in Moscow (second location at Building 2, No 16 Prospect Mira, Moscow 129090).
PREFERENCE OF NATIONALITY: British.
QUALIFICATIONS: 1-year minimum teaching experience, first degree, CELTA/TESOL/TEFL.
CONDITIONS OF EMPLOYMENT: 1 year. 40 academic hours per week. Also liaise with Russian summer camp organisation to provide native-speaker teachers for the vacation.
SALARY: 60–75,000 roubles net per month for 160 academic hours (40 per week). However, salary does not depend on doing a minimum of 40 hours per week. The school policy is to find enough students to keep the teaching staff fully occupied. Hours taught above 40 are paid an overtime rate of 500 roubles.
FACILITIES/SUPPORT: Employer finds apartments for staff and pays the finder's fee and security deposit. First return flight from London to Moscow is also paid. Assistance with work permits given. AAA English is licensed by the Moscow City Government as an education establishment and authorised by the Russian Foreign Migration Service to invite and issue work permits and contracts direct to teachers. The school covers the cost of the issue of the work visa and permit.
RECRUITMENT: Via www.tefl.com. Interviews normally conducted by Webex video over the internet.
CONTACT: Michael Lang, General Director/Owner/Head Teacher (mlang@aaaenglish.ru).

BKC – INTERNATIONAL HOUSE Moscow
3–5 Gazetny Pereulok, Office No 8, Moscow 121019
+7 495 737 5225
recruit@bkc.ru
www.bkcih-moscow.com/jobs;
http://job.ihworld.com (when hiring)

NUMBER OF TEACHERS: Approximately 200 contract and hourly paid teachers in Moscow, 50 teachers in the Moscow region. 38 schools in total.
PREFERENCE OF NATIONALITY: None.
QUALIFICATIONS: CELTA, Trinity TESOL, SIT Tesol, TESL Canada or any 100–120 hour onsite course. Higher qualifications such as degree in business/economics needed for some posts along with 2 years' experience. Entry-level teachers with no experience needed for some positions. Job guaranteed in Moscow to successful graduates of the BKC CELTA course.
CONDITIONS OF EMPLOYMENT: 6 or 9 months.
SALARY: Up to 50,000 roubles (net) for 30 hours per week over 9-month contract; up to 40,000 roubles for 24 hours a week (9-month contract). End-of-contract bonus of up to 30,000 roubles.
FACILITIES/SUPPORT: The school provides visa support (pays for multiple-entry work visa), shared accommodation, airfare reimbursement, health care, metro pass, paid holidays and 50% discount for Russian classes. Opportunities for professional development – an active in-house training programme, consisting of regular monthly training seminars and different workshops.
RECRUITMENT: All year round, though main intake for end of August/beginning of September.
CONTACT: Ms Svetlana Ryzhenkova, Recruitment Manager.

BRITISH EDUCATIONAL CENTRE
Ul. Proletarskaya, d7, Zheleznodorozhny, Balashikha, Moscow Oblast
+7 495 514 2376
dos@bec-russia.com
www.bec-russia.com

NUMBER OF TEACHERS: 5.
PREFERENCE OF NATIONALITY: British, American, Canadian, Australian, New Zealand.
QUALIFICATIONS: CELTA/TESOL with at least a year's experience.
CONDITIONS OF EMPLOYMENT: 9-month contracts. 30 academic hours per week (45 minutes) / 22.5 real hours, with some groups in the mornings from 10am, but most of the activity takes place from mid-afternoon to evening (4pm–10pm).
SALARY: 50,000 roubles (net) per month for teachers with little

experience, increasing to 65,000 roubles for a senior teacher.

FACILITIES/SUPPORT: Free shared accommodation is provided in modern apartment with bills paid for. Return flight reimbursed, free gym membership, visa fees reimbursed, end-of-contract bonus of 30,000 roubles and paid holidays. Regular fortnightly professional development, including both methodology workshops and language analysis practice. Work invitation provided, enabling teachers to get a work visa, which can be extended if teacher renews contract.

RECRUITMENT: Competency-based interview of selected candidates to assess knowledge of English grammar, ability to analyse language and formulate CCQs (Concept Checking Questions), and lesson structuring skills. Candidates will also be asked about the nature of teaching vocabulary and about teaching teenagers. Those who wish to teach young learners will have a second interview with the Senior Teacher for YLs.

CONTACT: Daniel Clayton, Director of Studies.

CAPITAL & LETTERS ACADEMY

Tverskaya 16, Moscow 125009

+7 495 777 9757

feedback@c-n-l.ru

www.c-n-l.ru/en

Offices also in St Petersburg at Nevskiy Prospekt 55.

NUMBER OF TEACHERS: Up to 6.

PREFERENCE OF NATIONALITY: British, American, Canadian.

QUALIFICATIONS: CELTA/TEFL and at least 3 years of experience.

CONDITIONS OF EMPLOYMENT: 3-month trial period preceding open-ended stay. 40 working hours a week: Monday–Friday 9am–6pm with 1-hour lunch-break. Roughly 20 hours of teaching, 20 hours of lesson preparation and admin. Should be able to tailor courses to client needs.

SALARY: Minimum 60,000 roubles per month (net). Possibility of salary increase every 4 months depending on performance.

FACILITIES/SUPPORT: School offers teachers a choice of apartments. Assistance given with permits.

RECRUITMENT: Interviewing people in Moscow and seeking candidates abroad.

CONTACT: Nicole Nee, Managing Director.

CARFAX PRIVATE TUTORS

Meriten House, Nevskiy Prospekt 21, St Petersburg 191186

Moscow office: Blagoveshchenskiy Pereulok 1b, Office 306, Moscow 123001

Head office: 48 Langham Street, London W1W 7AY, UK

+7 812 325 5552 (St Petersburg); +7 495 775 4260 (Moscow); +44 20 7927 6200 (London)

russiarecruitment@carfax-education.com; petersburg@carfax-education.com; moscow@carfax-education.com

www.carfax-tutors.com/become-a-tutor; www.carfax-education.com

Offices also in Baku, Dubai, London and Monaco.

NUMBER OF TEACHERS: 25–30 freelance tutors for school-age children, plus nannies and governesses for pre-school children.

PREFERENCE OF NATIONALITY: British.

QUALIFICATIONS: Good standard of school and university education, plus CELTA or Trinity TESOL. Experience needed for some posts.

CONDITIONS OF EMPLOYMENT: Part-time positions are always available to candidates living for up to 6 months in St Petersburg. Flexible timetabling. Up to 20 hours per week with 2-day weekend.

SALARY: £20 an hour. From 45,000 roubles (net) for full-time work.

FACILITIES/SUPPORT: Depends on location. Temporary accommodation provided for initial period or assistance given. Visa invitation is generated after receiving copy of passport. All costs are reimbursed, including flights.

RECRUITMENT: Via TEFL websites such as www.tefl.com. Interviews can be held in London office or via Skype.

CONTACT: Hugh Willan, Director (St Petersburg).

EF ENGLISH FIRST

Citydel Business Center, Zemlyanoy Val 9, 3rd Floor, Moscow 105064

+86 21 6133 6133 (in Shanghai)

efrecruitment@ef.com

www.englishfirst.com/ESL-jobs/teaching-jobs-in-russia.html; www.ef-russiateachers.com (community site)

NUMBER OF TEACHERS: About 40 for 35 schools in 20 cities (including 20 in Moscow and others in St Petersburg, Stavropol, Rostov, Tyumen, Nizhny Novgorod, Novosibirsk, etc.).

PREFERENCE OF NATIONALITY: British, Irish, North American, Australian, New Zealander or South African.

QUALIFICATIONS: CELTA/TESOL/EF TEFL certificate plus a university degree (preferably in English, linguistics or arts), minimum 1-year ESL teaching experience. Minimum age 22.

CONDITIONS OF EMPLOYMENT: 9 months September–May or 12-month renewable contracts. Schools open 9am–9pm, Monday to Friday, and 9am–6pm, Saturday. 28 teaching hours per week within a 40-hour working week.

SALARY: 65,000 roubles (gross) a month.

FACILITIES/SUPPORT: Modern classrooms all fitted with computers and LCD screens with online supplementary materials. Support with finding accommodation. Visas and work permits arranged. Up to 28 days' paid holidays. Flight allowance of up to 3,500 roubles a month. Orientation upon arrival and ongoing training. Medical insurance provided.

RECRUITMENT: All online.

ENGLISH CENTRE ANGLETICA
54 Mira St, Krasnodar 350000
+7 952 832 5480; +44 7817 902134 (Bournemouth)
www.angletica.ru

School in Moscow as well as Krasnodar and Syktyvkar in Komi region west of the Urals.

NUMBER OF TEACHERS: 3–9 per year, depending on contract duration.

PREFERENCE OF NATIONALITY: British.

QUALIFICATIONS: Candidates should be well organised, enthusiastic, able to communicate with adults and children alike. Previous work experience is not necessary, as full training is provided on arrival.

CONDITIONS OF EMPLOYMENT: 3 weeks (for summer language camps) to 9 months. Minimum 22–24 hours per week over 6 days.

SALARY: From £5 per hour net.

FACILITIES/SUPPORT: Free accommodation provided. Candidate covers cost for Russian visa application process but visa support and letter of invitation are arranged. The school pays for the cost of registration upon arrival. Reimbursement for travel by public transport.

RECRUITMENT: Via direct search, e.g. online adverts on www.jobsabroadbulletin.co.uk. Recruitment between January and 1 June for early October start. Face-to-face interviews preferred but can be via Skype for global applicants.

CONTACT: Mr Stanislav Sukhanov, General Director.

FLC (FOREIGN LANGUAGE CENTRE) REWARD
Building 32, Kommunisticheskaya St, Volgograd 400131; Building 17, Naberezhnaya Reki Fontanki, St Petersburg 191023
+7 8442 33 31 46; +7 988 028 98 31 (Volgograd)
+7 812 570 59 17; +7 812 952 59 90 (St Petersburg)
resume.reward@gmail.com; flc.reward@gmail.com
www.flc-reward.ru; www.flc-reward.com; www.reward.spb.ru

NONGOVERNMENTAL EDUCATIONAL ESTABLISHMENT.

NUMBER OF TEACHERS: 15.

PREFERENCE OF NATIONALITY: British, American, Canadian and Australian.

QUALIFICATIONS: TEFL/TOEFL or CELTA and university degree. Teaching experience preferred but not necessary.

CONDITIONS OF EMPLOYMENT: 8–12-month contracts, possibility of extension on mutual agreement. 24–30 academic hours (45-minute lessons) a week. 103–129 academic hours a month.

SALARY: To be discussed at interview. Deductions of 20% for pension fund and 30% for personal income tax during first 183 days, dropping to 13% thereafter.

FACILITIES/SUPPORT: Free, furnished shared accommodation is provided. Free methodology seminars and group Russian lessons. Free visa invitation letter and visa registration during the contract; compensation of consular fees (half on arrival, half on successful completion of contract). Flight reimbursement on successful completion of contract. Free medical insurance. Free internet access, plus copying and printing equipment in all offices. Invitations extended to social events organised by FLC Reward.

RECRUITMENT: TVia database of tecahers' CVs o ww.eslcafe.com, www.tefl.com, www.esl101.com, etc.

CONTACT: Alexandra Melnikova, Recruitmnet Manager; Anna Mitina, Director.

GLOBUS INTERNATIONAL
Makarenko St 5, Building 1A, 3rd floor, Office 5, Moscow 105062
+7 495 645 2158
info@globus-int.ru
www.globus-int.ru (Russian only)

British-owned company with branches in Moscow, Pushkin (Moscow Region) and St Petersburg.

NUMBER OF TEACHERS: 26 corporate language trainers.

PREFERENCE OF NATIONALITY: British, Irish, Australian, New Zealander, Canadian, American.

QUALIFICATIONS: Minimum CELTA or equivalent, plus ideally 2 years' experience in corporate environment.

CONDITIONS OF EMPLOYMENT: 12-month standard contract, up to 26 academic hours per week. Lots of travelling within Moscow. Summer intensive courses offered.

SALARY: From US$1,600 (net) per month, depending on experience.

FACILITIES/SUPPORT: A housing manager helps to accommodate all teachers based on what they would like. Centre organises a work visa invitation, then when the teacher is in Russia, organises all the necessary documents to make sure the teacher is fully registered and has all correct documentation. Medical insurance, survival Russian and in-house teacher training.

RECRUITMENT: Through TEFL websites. Telephone interviews are essential. If possible the school tries to set up face-to-face interviews in London.

CONTACT: Crichton Brauer, Managing Director.

GLORY SCHOOL FOREIGN LANGUAGES
46 Gorokhovaya St, Off 5, St Petersburg 190005
+7 812 438 3083
edu@gloryschool.ru
www.gloryschool.ru/vacancy.html

NUMBER OF TEACHERS: 10.

PREFERENCE OF NATIONALITY: British, American or Canadian.

QUALIFICATIONS: Native speaker with higher education and some experience. Prefer candidates with 3 years or more EFL teaching experience or EFL certificate.

CONDITIONS OF EMPLOYMENT: 1-year contract. Part-time in-company classes available.

SALARY: $20 per hour.

FACILITIES/SUPPORT: Assistance is given with renting a flat and applying for work permits and visas. Russian-language lessons can be exchanged for English conversation practice.

RECRUITMENT: Usually via the internet.

IPT (INTERNATIONAL PROFESSIONAL TRAINING) LTD
Office 207, Petrovka Ulitsa 15/13, Moscow 107031
+7 495 228 3513
info@iptrussia.ru
www.iptrussia.ru

NUMBER OF TEACHERS: 40 native speaker corporate trainers out of total staff of 200 in Moscow. IPT also teaches in over 50 regional cities across Russia.

PREFERENCE OF NATIONALITY: Native speaker (or Russian national). Company is British-owned and managed.

QUALIFICATIONS: University degree and certified EFL teaching qualification, plus minimum 3–5 years' EFL experience. Business English and/or Corporate Language Teaching experience required. Teachers must have a creative teaching approach. Experience in Russia or Eastern Europe preferred, but not essential. Experience of financial or legal presentations would be valuable.

CONDITIONS OF EMPLOYMENT: 16–20 academic hours per week. Part-time contract according to Labour Code regulations. Stable schedule of minimum 80 academic hours per month. Students are all at intermediate level or above. Hours mainly 8am–9:30am and 6pm–7:30pm with some afternoon classes.

SALARY: Negotiable. All salaries are paid net of tax; employer pays all income taxes and social fees. Flight cost reimbursement.

FACILITIES/SUPPORT: Free accommodation and/or assistance given in search for accommodation, with agents and transport provided. Teachers receive a 12-month, multiple-entry, teaching visa for the duration of the contract. IPT provides native-speaker teachers with free Russian lessons (subject to availability) and teaching workshops on different themes. Free Moscow travel card.

RECRUITMENT: Telephone interviews (at least 3), references, qualifications check, receipt of sample lesson plans.

CONTACT: Tim Newton, Managing Director (tim.newton@iptrussia.ru).

ISTRA SCHOOL
Of. 337, 6 Revolution Square, Istra, Moscow Region 143500
+7 985 915 6319
info@istra-english.ru
www.istra-english.ru

NUMBER OF TEACHERS: 2 (Istra is an hour by train from Moscow).

PREFERENCE OF NATIONALITY: British, American, Australian.

QUALIFICATIONS: Minimum 1–2 years' teaching experience plus CELTA or TEFL certificate. Experience of exam preparation (FCE, TOEFL, IELTS) would be a big advantage.

CONDITIONS OF EMPLOYMENT: 9–10 month contracts. Normal load is 86 hours in a 4-week period which may include Saturdays and Sundays. This comprises 78 hours of teaching (equivalent to 104 academic 'hours' which last 45 minutes) plus 8 normal hours for other duties, e.g. stand-by, placement testing, paperwork, meetings, seminars, open days, English clubs and presentations.

SALARY: 65,000 roubles per month (net) plus annual bonus. Compulsory insurance contributions paid by school.

FACILITIES/SUPPORT: School arranges invitation and other documents to enable teacher to obtain a visa in their home country. Free accommodation is provided in a 2-room shared flat 20-minute walk from the school. Guidance is given on legal requirements, e.g. doctor's examination and HIV test; school covers expenses. Teachers are enrolled in free Russian state health care scheme (does not cover medications or dental services). Flight reimbursement of 17,000 roubles.

RECRUITMENT: Adverts on www.tefl.com. Interviews by Skype.

CONTACT: Tatiana Krouglova, Director.

LANGUAGE LINK RUSSIA

Moscow

job@languagelink.ru

www.jobs.languagelink.ru

NUMBER OF TEACHERS: 200 in various programmes for 60 schools throughout Russia (Moscow, Moscow Region, St Petersburg, St Petersburg Region, Volgograd, Samara, Togliatti, Ufa, Rostov na Donu, Stavropol, Shakhty, Orenburg, etc.).

PREFERENCE OF NATIONALITY: British, American, Canadian, Australian, New Zealander and South African.

QUALIFICATIONS: CELTA or Trinity Certificate/Diploma (or equivalents) required unless teachers apply with relevant EFL/ESL experience. Candidates without a 100-hour TEFL qualification may enter Language Link's Teacher Internship Programme. Openings also available to those without experience or qualifications as volunteers, work-study participants or summer camp staff. All applicants should be enthusiastic, cheerful and open-minded.

CONDITIONS OF EMPLOYMENT: 6-, 9- or 12-month contracts. Up to 30 teaching hours per week; experienced teachers have negotiated lighter timetables. Adult, children and in-company classes. Runs English-language summer camps near major cities starting in early June.

SALARY: 67,000–77,000 roubles per month (gross) for full-time teachers at Moscow branch. Salaries negotiable at different branches.

FACILITIES/SUPPORT: Teachers are generally provided with free accommodation in 2-room flat (for 2 teachers). Paid time off, paid medical services, full work visa support and academic support. Flight reimbursement up to 30,000 roubles.

RECRUITMENT: Application is online. Minimum 2 professional references. Telephone/Skype interviews are compulsory unless carried out by Language Link in London. Branch schools carry out recruitment independently of the Moscow HQ.

CONTACT: Robert Jensky, Managing Director; Liam Jennings, Director of Studies of 2 Moscow branches.

LITTLE ANGELS KINDERGARTEN

St Novocheremushkinskaya no 49, Office 12, Moscow

+7 8495 332 1603

litang@mail.ru

www.littleangels.ru

Bilingual kindergarten for children aged 2–6.

NUMBER OF TEACHERS: 5.

PREFERENCE OF NATIONALITY: British, Canadian or Australian.

QUALIFICATIONS: Experience or diploma in early childhood education needed and a TEFL qualification. Also he/she should have experience of teaching.

CONDITIONS OF EMPLOYMENT: Standard 1-year contract, usual hours are 9am–5pm or 6pm.

SALARY: Depends on qualification and experience but at least $1,500. If the employee has a work permit from Little Angels, 13% of the tax is deducted from their salary.

FACILITIES/SUPPORT: Visa, but not accommodation, support.

RECRUITMENT: Advertise on www.expat.ru. Interviews and sample class are essential.

CONTACT: Mrs Sveta or Mrs Zemfira.

Private kindergartens offering bilingual education to young children.

NUMBER OF TEACHERS: 2.

PREFERENCE OF NATIONALITY: UK, Canada, Australia, New Zealand, South Africa.

QUALIFICATIONS: Higher/college degree in Humanities/Psychology/Education/Social Studies; a certificate in TESL/TEFL would be a bonus. Minimum of 1 year's experience of teaching English to children of pre-school and primary school age, preferably abroad (e.g. South Korea). If candidate has only TEFL/TESL certificate, 1–2 years' experience of teaching English to young children is obligatory. Knowledge of early development of children and of teaching methodology needed. Supplementary skills and abilities welcome, e.g. in art, music, sports or acting. Want young, optimistic, hard-working teachers with experience.

CONDITIONS OF EMPLOYMENT: Minimum 1 year. 10-hour days starting at 8.30am, 9am or 11am with hour off for lunch. 2-day weekends off. Summer camp work may be available.

SALARY: Around 80,000–120,000 roubles per month.

FACILITIES/SUPPORT: Foreign teachers are provided with comfortable accommodation (separate or shared) close to the school. Full work visa sponsorship and reimbursement. Flight reimbursement up to 400 euros.

RECRUITMENT: Ads on ESL/EFL websites and Facebook's TEFL-CELTA Jobs page. Skype interviews obligatory.

CONTACT: Elena Panfilova, CEO (e.panfilova@milcentre.ru).

NUMBER OF TEACHERS: 3–5.

PREFERENCE OF NATIONALITY: None.

QUALIFICATIONS: Higher pedagogical education and work experience.

CONDITIONS OF EMPLOYMENT: 24 hours per week, 12 months.

SALARY: 45,000 roubles per month.

FACILITIES/SUPPORT: School pays for rented flat. Working visas arranged.

RECRUITMENT: Skype interview essential.

CONTACT: Olga Pokrovskaya, Headteacher.

PREMIUM ENGLISH
Chistopolskaya 20A, Kazan 420111, Republic of Tatarstan
+7 843 518 6060
info@premiumenglish.ru
www.premiumenglish.ru

British-owned and managed.

NUMBER OF TEACHERS: 12–15.

PREFERENCE OF NATIONALITY: None.

QUALIFICATIONS: CELTA or equivalent plus degree and 1 year's ELT experience. Young Learners' experience an advantage.

CONDITIONS OF EMPLOYMENT: September to July, or 12 months from September. 25 clock hours per week, 5 days a week (2 consecutive days off: Sat/Sun or Sun/Mon). To teach children and adults in the business and professional community both in-company and on school premises.

SALARY: Up to 60,000 roubles (net).

FACILITIES/SUPPORT: The school provides furnished single accommodation close to school. Employer provides teachers with a multiple-entry work visa. Teachers need to provide apostilled copies of passport and qualification. An HIV test is required for the visa. Survival Russian lessons given. Weekly teacher training. Contribution to travel expenses given on completion of contract.

RECRUITMENT: Via www.tefl.com.

CONTACT: Steven Mott, Owner/Director of Education.

WINDSOR ENGLISH LANGUAGE SCHOOL
7 Komsomolsky Prospect, Moscow 119146
+7 495 221 0832
job@windsor.ru
www.windsor.ru/eng/tefl

NUMBER OF TEACHERS: Vacancies almost all year round, especially for part-time teachers experienced with IELTS preparation, for chain of language schools in Moscow, St Petersburg and Vladimir.

PREFERENCE OF NATIONALITY: British, Canadian, Irish, American, Australian and New Zealander.

QUALIFICATIONS: Bachelor's degree or higher (preferred) and a TEFL certificate essential (CELTA, Trinity College TESOL, etc). Minimum 1-year's experience of teaching.

CONDITIONS OF EMPLOYMENT: Part-time teaching mainly, but also 9–12 month contracts from August/September. Most teaching takes place on mornings and weekends. Corporate trainers work 20–24 hours per week (in Moscow only). Summer openings in Siberia (Abakan in the Republic of Khakasia).

SALARY: Starting salary for contract work 40,000–50,000 roubles per month net, for 26–30 academic hours per week. 40-minute lessons. Paid overtime.

FACILITIES/SUPPORT: The school provides good-quality shared accommodation close to a metro station; sponsors, assists and pays for work visas. Employer pays for utilities, health insurance, monthly travel card and bonus. Full in-house academic support and professional development.

RECRUITMENT: Via adverts on www.expat.ru, www.tefl.com, etc. Interviews are essential, usually done by telephone or Skype.

CONTACT: Alina Zasorina, Human Resources Manager.

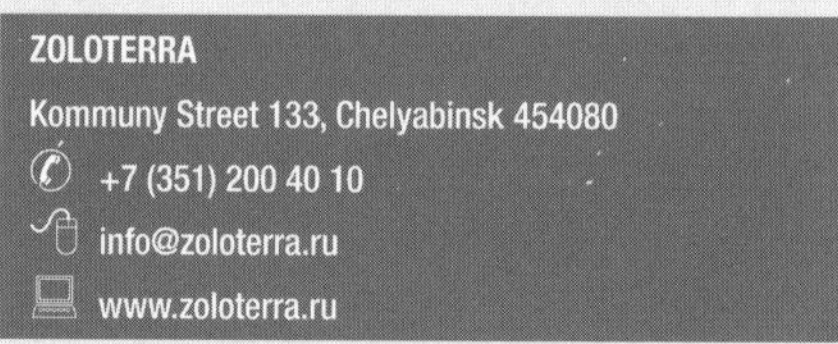

ZOLOTERRA
Kommuny Street 133, Chelyabinsk 454080
+7 (351) 200 40 10
info@zoloterra.ru
www.zoloterra.ru

NUMBER OF TEACHERS: 5 for 3 branches.

PREFERENCE OF NATIONALITY: British.

QUALIFICATIONS: CELTA or Trinity.

CONDITIONS OF EMPLOYMENT: One-year contract. Approx. 30 academic hours per week with the possibility of paid overtime.

SALARY: Average US$900–$1200 per month (net, after 13%–30% has been deducted for taxes and social security).

FACILITIES/SUPPORT: Accommodation is provided and all bills are paid by the company. Full working visas are provided and the cost reimbursed. A letter of invitation is provided so the applicant can apply (in person) in London or Edinburgh. An HIV certificate is required.

RECRUITMENT: Adverts on Tefl.com and Dave's ESL Cafe, followed by Skype interview.

CONTACT: Dr Sergey Zolotykh, Director.

SLOVAKIA

Slovakia has been somewhat neglected not only by tourists but by teachers as well. As one language school director put it a couple of years ago:

> ***Many teachers head for Prague, which is why Slovakia stands aside of the main flow of the teachers. That's a pity as Prague is crowded with British and Americans while there's a lack of the teachers here in Slovakia.***

Another wrote from a small Slovakian town: '*It would be wonderful if through your book more native speakers come to Slovakia.*' The density of private language schools in the capital, Bratislava, and in the other main cities such as Banska Bystrika makes an on-the-ground job hunt promising.

Once considered a backward part of Europe, huge resources have been poured into the country's development including into increasing access to English instruction. The European Social Fund has targeted groups who need English and provided subsidised or even free courses for people working in education or the civil service. As a result, a substantial demand exists for native English teachers, although the wages are fairly low, forcing many teachers to take on private students and/or economise. The salary range for teachers is €550–€800 net, €750–€1,100 gross. Many schools pay by the lesson, which should start at around €12, though entry level teachers can be offered as little as €8 as was being advertised in 2016 by SPEAK Jazykova Skola in Banská Bystrica. Schools that provide free accommodation of course offer a lower wage. The flat rate of tax in Slovakia is 19%.

EU citizens need only to confirm residency at the local police station. In order to obtain a trade licence, which is necessary for self-employed freelancers, you will have to supply a sworn declaration that you have not been convicted of any crimes for the previous 10 years, something that can be done at the British Embassy in Bratislava (for a fee). Many teachers go freelance after one or two years of working for a school, which is advantageous for both schools and teachers. Freelancers may have less security but earn more.

For candidates from outside the EU, the Slovak visa process is expensive and time consuming. The main costs are getting a criminal record check from the teacher's home country (cost varies) and the visa fee. The applicant will have to submit a medical certificate, evidence of accommodation (i.e. a document from your landlord) and so on. A blood test must be carried out at the Oddelenie cudzokrajnych chorob, Fakultna Hospital in Bratislava, Martin or Kosice, as a pre-requisite for a residence permit. All documents will have to be translated, notarised and/or apostilled. Most employers guide their teachers through the process but not many will cover the cost.

A programme open to both EU and non-EU candidates is run by Edulink Language School (see entry). This semi-volunteer programme recruits a couple of native speakers to teach English for an academic year.

The British Council at Panská 17 in Bratislava's old town (www.britishcouncil.sk) sometimes advertises vacancies for freelance teachers to start in September. The English-language weekly newspaper, the *Slovak Spectator* published on Mondays, doesn't have a classifieds section, but does publish its annual Career Guide for €5. The useful business directory, the *Green Pages* (see http://greenpages.spectator.sme.sk/en/c/language-schools.html) links to a list of language schools with full contact details.

Although wages can be low, prices for food and meals out are not expensive. Accommodation in Bratislava is about twice as expensive as in small towns in Central Slovakia.

Budapest, Vienna and Prague are all within easy reach. Slovakia also offers good conditions for mountain walking in the Tatras along thousands of miles of hiking routes up to an altitude of 2,500m and for mountain cycling.

Michael Todd, who was a senior teacher at IH Bratislava, enjoyed living in Slovakia, but had a few reservations:

Typically, teachers stay one or two years and move on to another country. Bratislava is more a place to get experience. It's nice enough, well located, but turnover is very high as Bratislava just doesn't have enough to hold teachers, unless of course, they start dating a local. I've met a lot of people from different countries, seen a lot of interesting places around Bratislava and have been introduced to literatures I hadn't known about. It's rewarding that I'm helping people and can believe in my work rather than working for some company that sells some product. But the pay is low and the hours can be long. Accommodation is ok but it's kind of like being in university again as we share apartments with other teachers and tend to have hand-me-down furniture. Landlords/ladies are often controlling and seem to view your renting from them not as a business arrangement but as if they are doing you some personal favour. On a further note, I wouldn't have stayed in Slovakia as long as I have except that I've been dating an Austrian woman and, as an American, moving to Austria just wasn't an option. Bratislava is ok, it's not hard to live here but it's not in the league of Prague or Budapest. Usually when I visit some nearby city, I feel a little depressed coming back to Bratislava.

GEOFF NUNNEY

Geoff Nunney has had various teaching contracts in Slovakia in recent years, and was pleased when one of the 30 schools in Nitra to which he had written in 2016 offered him an interview and then a job starting in March. In previous years he has worked at the Vages School (www.vages.sk) in Nitra, the Rain School in nearby Šala (www.rainschool.sk), and a bilingual *gymnázium* or grammar school in Cadca. Unfortunately, conditions were far from ideal at his recent job and he felt obliged to leave early. The boss was a control freak who tried to rule by fear, and who paid such low rates per unit that Geoff couldn't break even. He has now returned to the Lingua School, also in Nitra, where he will have part-time work but is confident he can gradually fill up his timetable.

It's thanks to your book that I found Slovakia. The people here are great and were incredibly supportive when I lost both parents in one year and also when I returned to England for treatment for a chronic health problem.

I teach kids, teenagers and adult conversation classes. The schools provide good teaching resources, internet, copying and up-to-date textbooks. The recruitment processes were very thorough, consisting of a face-to-face interview with the head teacher, who was very informative, approachable and asked relevant questions.

The best thing you need in Slovakia is a sense of humour. I have been in school plays, and they are a very friendly nation of people. Their standard of English is very good, and they are great fun to teach. For example, once, a student stopped me and said, 'Geoff, the walls have ears' to demonstrate his mastery of an English idiom. I have dated a Slovak teacher, who asked me out - very forward people the Slovaks - she stole my business card, rang my mobile, and we had a night out at the Irish Pub in Nitra. I still play cricket, go 10-pin bowling, and play pool with some students and colleagues.

Teaching wages in Slovakia allow you to cover the basic cost of living, but not much else. You can survive, pay the bills, but don't expect to save a lot. Although wages aren't great here, the locals and the scenery and the supportive staff make up for it. I speak a little Slovak, and if you immerse yourself, you will get the rewards. I love it out here, and it has stunning mountains and walking country. I would describe it all as a Slovak adventure!

LIST OF EMPLOYERS

ACADEMIA ISTROPOLITANA NOVA

Prostredna 47/A, 900 21 Svaty Jur

+421 2 4497 0452

ainova@ainova.sk; ruth@ainova.sk

www.ainova.sk

NUMBER OF TEACHERS: 6.

PREFERENCE OF NATIONALITY: UK citizens.

QUALIFICATIONS: University graduates preferably with pedagogical degree or holders of CELTA, TEFL or other internationally recognised certificate.

CONDITIONS OF EMPLOYMENT: 1-year contract, 80 teaching hours per month. Part-time teachers to work on trade licence (*živnosť*) or on an agreement basis (*dohoda*) in and around Bratislava.

SALARY: By agreement.

FACILITIES/SUPPORT: Assistance given in finding accommodation but teachers pay rent.

RECRUITMENT: Personal recommendation and ELT training centres. Phone interviews possible.

CONTACT: Ruth Zorvan, Director of Professional Communication and English Programmes.

AGENTÚRA VZDELÁVANIA s.r.o.

Pečnianska 6, 851 01 Bratislava

+421 2 6225 0765

info@agenturavzdelavania.sk

www.agenturavzdelavania.sk

NUMBER OF TEACHERS: 6 part-timers.

PREFERENCE OF NATIONALITY: None.

QUALIFICATIONS: Higher education, teaching experience. Having some expertise in a specific profession, such as law, medicine, accounting, finance or marketing is an advantage.

CONDITIONS OF EMPLOYMENT: Open-ended employment. 6–10 hours a week.

SALARY: €12–€25 per 60-minute lesson. All taxes and levies are paid by the teacher.

FACILITIES/SUPPORT: No help with accommodation or visas.

RECRUITMENT: Internet job boards, interviews.

CONTACT: Alžbeta Rigáňová, Managing Director.

AKADEMIA VZDELAVANIA – ACADEMY OF EDUCATION

Sekretariát, Jarná 13, 010 01 Žilina

+421 904 838 999 (Mobile)

www.akademiavzdelavania.sk

Non-profit adult education association.

NUMBER OF TEACHERS: Approximately 20 full-time posts in branches throughout Slovakia. Branches recruit individually and are linked from website.

PREFERENCE OF NATIONALITY: Native English speaker holding an EU member state passport.

QUALIFICATIONS: CELTA or TESOL qualification (or recognised equivalent) and degree. Energy, enthusiasm and an interest in people required. Must be willing to teach a range of classes, including teenagers or young learners.

CONDITIONS OF EMPLOYMENT: 1 academic year (mid-September to end of June). Teachers' contracts are for a maximum of 22.5 contact hours per week.

SALARY: Competitive salary plus accommodation allowance, local travel pass, health insurance, luncheon vouchers and contribution to airfares.

FACILITIES/SUPPORT: Work and residence permits arranged and paid for. Academic and pastoral support, regular seminars and workshops; orientation for new teachers.

RECRUITMENT: CVs and brief covering letter to be emailed to your chosen branch, e.g. for Zwolen, avzvolen@stonline.sk.

CONTACT: Director of Studies.

CANADIAN LANGUAGE SCHOOL NITRA
Kupecká 6, 94901 Nitra
+421 904 371 050 (Office)
info@canadian.sk; phil@canadian.sk
www.canadianschool.sk

Schools also in Trenčín and Trnava.

NUMBER OF TEACHERS: Currently 6, but intending to expand to 8.

PREFERENCE OF NATIONALITY: EU citizen (due to slow and expensive bureaucratic processes in Slovakia). Teachers must have clear English.

QUALIFICATIONS: TESOL/CELTA is generally the minimum; however, director is more interested in finding exciting and effective teachers with 'the right stuff' who will never be boring.

CONDITIONS OF EMPLOYMENT: Minimum 6 months with ongoing opportunities. 35 actual hours per week, spread across the spectrum of the day.

SALARY: Above the average local salary to attract and retain the best teachers.

FACILITIES/SUPPORT: All taxes, health and social insurance and flat are provided from the gross salary. Non-EU teachers have to pay their own visa-related expenses, including waiting up to 3 months to see if their visa will be approved, prior to being able to start work. School offers intensive 2-week 'Teach-the-Teacher' summer courses.

RECRUITMENT: Skype interviews are possible.

CONTACT: Philip Le Mottee, Director.

EDULINK LANGUAGE SCHOOL S.R.O.
Kollárova 17, 91701 Trnava
+421 910 428 281
trnava@edulink.sk
www.edulink.sk

NUMBER OF TEACHERS: 2 semi-volunteers to teach English for an academic year to adults and children in Trnava.

PREFERENCE OF NATIONALITY: Countries where English is spoken as a first language.

QUALIFICATIONS: TEFL certificate and a can-do attitude.

CONDITIONS OF EMPLOYMENT: 1 academic year. 38 'scholar hours' (each hour is 45 minutes).

SALARY: €500 a month.

FACILITIES/SUPPORT: Homestay or shared accommodation is arranged and paid for, plus medical insurance, visa support and holidays. Guidance given on how to apply for documentation in their home countries to apply for work permit; red tape within Slovakia is paid for by school.

RECRUITMENT: International TEFL websites or referrals. Skype interviews.

CONTACT: Pero Hattingh, Owner/Director.

EUROTREND 21
Namestie slobody 16, 811 06 Bratislava
+421 2 5249 4350
info@eurotrend21.sk; office@eurotrend21.sk
www.eurotrend21.sk

NUMBER OF TEACHERS: 4.

PREFERENCE OF NATIONALITY: None.

QUALIFICATIONS: Minimum university degree, TEFL certificate and experience.

CONDITIONS OF EMPLOYMENT: Minimum contract 6 months. Hours are available mornings, afternoons and evenings.

SALARY: Dependent on experience. Starts at €12 per 45-minute lesson.

RECRUITMENT: Interviews are essential and are carried out on-site.

CONTACT: Coordinator of Language Courses.

HARMONY SCHOOL
26 Kapitulska, 917 01 Trnava
+421 33 534 4982
info@harmony.sk
www.harmony.sk

NUMBER OF TEACHERS: 15 full-and part-time teachers.

PREFERENCE OF NATIONALITY: EU citizens.

QUALIFICATIONS: CELTA/DELTA or equivalent.

CONDITIONS OF EMPLOYMENT: 1-year contract with 25 teaching hours and 10 admin hours per week.

SALARY: €1,000–€1,200.

FACILITIES/SUPPORT: Assistance given with finding accommodation.

RECRUITMENT: Interviews are essential.

CONTACT: Jana Chynoradska, Director (jana@harmony.sk); Katarína Divileková.

INSTITÚT EURÓPSKYCH JAZYKOV
Nam. Osloboditelov 10, 071 01 Michalovce
+421 907 448 408
institut.ej@gmail.com
www.institut.sk

NUMBER OF TEACHERS: Rolling vacancies.

QUALIFICATIONS: Must be university graduate. School is looking for professionalism, strong educational background, experience, personality, and communication and people skills. Teachers should be patient, enthusiastic, good team players, with a sense of humour.

CONDITIONS OF EMPLOYMENT: Semesters start mid-September, early January and early April. 90-minute lessons. Many clients are graduates and civil servants, since the European Social Fund pays for free English courses for these categories.

FACILITIES/SUPPORT: Accommodation provided and help given with settling into local area.

CONTACT: Petra Gondkovicova, Owner/Manager.

INTERNATIONAL HOUSE BRATISLAVA
Namestie SNP 14, 811 06 Bratislava
+421 2 5296 2675
info@ihbratislava.sk
www.ihbratislava.sk

NUMBER OF TEACHERS: 20, especially Young Learner specialists.

PREFERENCE OF NATIONALITY: EU citizens.

QUALIFICATIONS: Minimum Cambridge CELTA/Trinity Cert and preferably 1 year's experience in YL teaching or Cambridge exam preparation. A degree is not essential.

CONDITIONS OF EMPLOYMENT: 10 months from early September. Average 25 teaching hours per week starting at 7:30am (no weekends). Mainly off-site teaching, plus children's classes, general and business English.

SALARY: Full-time contract teachers are paid €1,000–€1,200 per month gross unless they want to live in a shared school flat, in which case pay is reduced to €800–€1,000 gross. Freelancers must pay their own contributions, usually about 20%.

FACILITIES/SUPPORT: Full-time teachers are offered accommodation in shared flats. Assistance given with obtaining a Trade Licence. Workshops and training sessions. 20 days' paid holiday.

RECRUITMENT: Via http://job.ihworld.com or www.tefl.com. Interviews are essential and can be carried out by telephone/Skype.

CONTACT: Jon de la Fuente, Director of Studies (dos@ihbratislava.sk).

JAZYKOVÁ SKOLA START
Hlavná 37/68, 040 01 Kosice
+421 917 642230
recruitment@jazykova.sk
www.jazykova.sk/jobs.php

Also has a branch in Presov.

NUMBER OF TEACHERS: 10.

PREFERENCE OF NATIONALITY: Native English speakers from the EU. Willing to sponsor (but not pay for) work visa applications for native speakers from outside the EU, but this is rare.

QUALIFICATIONS: University education; TEFL or previous experience is an advantage.

CONDITIONS OF EMPLOYMENT: 1 academic year, extendable to a permanent contract. Usual hours are 3pm–8pm with some morning lessons.

SALARY: By negotiation.

FACILITIES/SUPPORT: School helps new arrivals find accommodation.

RECRUITMENT: Via the internet. Preliminary stage is to take a short online English test, which is easy for native speakers to pass. Interviews are carried out by phone or Skype. In the case of teachers already in Slovakia, they are carried out in person.

CONTACT: Richard Swales, Director.

MHC BUSINESS LANGUAGE TRAINING s.r.o.
Zamocká 30, 811 01 Bratislava
+43 1 603 0563 (HQ in Vienna)
office@mhc-training.com
www.mhc-training.com/en/jobs

Sister school of MHC in Austria.

NUMBER OF TEACHERS: 25.

PREFERENCE OF NATIONALITY: Any.

QUALIFICATIONS: MHC trainers have an understanding of business experience, often specialising in areas such as marketing, finance, pharmaceuticals or law. A degree is not necessary, although a teaching certificate such as CELTA would be of value.

CONDITIONS OF EMPLOYMENT: Freelance, teaching 15–25 hours per week.

SALARY: €16–€20 per 60 minutes, depending on experience and development with MHC. Seminars pay between €200 and €250 per day. Trainers are responsible for paying their own taxes (about 19%) and social security (variable).

FACILITIES/SUPPORT: Resource library in Vienna, photocopying at clients' premises, trainer development. Books required for courses. Trainers from non-EU countries require working papers.

RECRUITMENT: Interviews are essential and usually take place at premises. Possibility of Skype interview if the applicant is based abroad.

CONTACT: Brosnan Lockesley, Regional Director for Slovakia; Mark Heather, Managing Director (mark.heather@mhc-training.com).

NATIVE SPEAKER NETWORK INTERNATIONAL

Michalska 9, 81101 Bratislava

✆ +43 664 348 5292

office@nsn-int.com

www.nativespeakernetwork.com

NUMBER OF TEACHERS: Up to 40.

PREFERENCE OF NATIONALITY: None.

QUALIFICATIONS: Minimum college degree and TEFL/CELTA qualification.

CONDITIONS OF EMPLOYMENT: 6-month stays. 30 lessons per week.

SALARY: €400 (net) per month plus expenses.

FACILITIES/SUPPORT: Accommodation is organised for teachers. Reimbursement for travel is paid and food compensation. No assistance with work permits.

CONTACT: Margit Derler, Manager.

SIDAS LANGUAGE SCHOOL

P.C. Strojar, Juzna Trieda 93, 040 01 Kosice

✆ +421 905 853127 (mobile)

schofield@sidaschool.com

www.sidaschool.com

Also operate in the Czech Republic and Austria.

NUMBER OF TEACHERS: 15–20 for both set-location and peripatetic posts.

PREFERENCE OF NATIONALITY: British and Irish, but native speakers from other countries welcome.

QUALIFICATIONS: Ideally applicants will have a first degree and TEFL qualifications. Training and assistance are provided to people with no real experience.

CONDITIONS OF EMPLOYMENT: Three programmes: Natives in Schools in which teachers teach primary and secondary school children as part of the normal English-medium curriculum in all subjects; Active Language Weeks, which require teachers to travel town-to-town for a minimum of 4 weeks delivering week-long courses of active English to children of mixed abilities; and children's Summer Day Camps in varying towns which involve sport, drama and very little classroom teaching. Also after-school opportunities in nursery schools for teachers based in one town for the academic year. Hours for set-location teachers typically 8am–2pm Monday to Friday, but some work 1pm–7pm.

SALARY: Competitive local salary that can increase over time.

FACILITIES/SUPPORT: Free accommodation during the working week. Company finds a flat, usually shared with fellow Sidas teachers, for teachers in set locations. Help given with permits. Training provided before and during the working period.

RECRUITMENT: Via tefl.com, etc. Skype interviews.

CONTACT: Dave Schofield, Managing Director.

THE ENGLISH CLUB

Pri Suchom mlyne 36, 811 04 Bratislava

✆ +421 904 415490

oravecmartin@ba.telecom.sk

www.theenglishclub.sk

NUMBER OF TEACHERS: 2–4.

PREFERENCE OF NATIONALITY: British.

QUALIFICATIONS: University degree plus TEFL/TESL/CELTA and 1 year's experience.

CONDITIONS OF EMPLOYMENT: 10-month contract from September to June. Working hours between 7am and 9.45pm, 30 hours per week.

SALARY: From €7 per 45 minutes.

FACILITIES/SUPPORT: Shared flat with wi-fi is available. All necessary paperwork for work permits is completed by the school.

RECRUITMENT: Usually via the internet. Interviews are essential.

CONTACT: Martin Oravec, Director.

THE BALTICS

Arguably the most Westernised part of the old Russian Empire, the Baltic countries of Lithuania, Latvia and Estonia all became fully fledged members of the EU in 2004. This eased the bureaucracy for passport holders from EU member states, and it is to be hoped that Britons will retain this privilege after the Brexit negotiations are completed. If not, they may be in the same position as Americans and other non-EU citizens who need to apply for a work permit, which can take many months. For this reason and due to extra costs, most schools strongly prefer to employ EU citizens. A number of budget airlines as well as national carriers operate to the region (e.g. Ryanair to Kaunas, Vilnius and the Baltic seaside resort of Palange, plus Riga and Tallinn) plus Wizz Air to Riga, Kaunas and Vilnius. Despite new business and tourism links, the market for English-language teachers has not been expanding, and few vacancies are advertised abroad.

Latvia and Lithuania

Of the three Baltic States, Latvia has been slowest to embrace change, although its beautiful capital, Riga, has become a mecca for a certain type of British tourist (at the stag-party end of the spectrum). English is increasingly necessary for anyone working in the hospitality sector, although there are still relatively few commercial language schools and virtually no job postings on the TEFL sites.

Qualified ELT teachers could make contact with the Latvian Association of Teachers of English (LATE) in Riga (www.late.lv), or the Lithuanian Association of English Language Teachers (LAKMA), though they don't get involved with job assistance and are mainly for professional development of English teachers at gymnasiums and other state schools.

One Latvian language school that may be able to offer decent facilities is the Language Centre International House Riga-Satva (www.ihriga.lv), which can also help with visas, flat-finding and teaching support. It does its hiring in April–May for a September start.

The market in Lithuania seems to have shrunk in recent years, with EF English First scaling back and the ILS franchise having closed down. The only vacancies seen advertised recently were for English for Academic Purposes and summer courses at a private Christian university in Klaidepa (www.lcc.lt) affiliated to the heavy-duty proselytising City Church.

A number of schools offer intensive summer programmes, for example a private language school with three branches in Vilnius and one in Kaunas that sources summer teachers over the age of 23 through the members-only site Workaway (www.workaway.info/643191928465-en.html). Volunteer teachers stay for two to 12 weeks and are provided with shared accommodation in exchange for teaching 4–5 hours a day.

Estonia

Estonia is arguably the most progressive of the three Baltic countries. The demand for native English-speaker teachers is not very high, as illustrated by the language institute in Tallinn that communicated with this book to say that it already has plenty of native-speaking English teachers in its database, with few vacancies. However once in a while a private institute advertises on an international TEFL site: for example In Down-Town Language School in Tallinn (www.indowntown.ee) was looking to recruit well-qualified teachers for an August 2016 start and offering a decent monthly salary of €800–€1,000 net.

As throughout the Baltic region, summer language camps for children are popular, often depending on native speakers who come for the cultural experience rather than to earn money. One such is Bellnor's international summer camp held at the Baltic resort of Kloogaranna near Tallinn (see entry).

LIST OF EMPLOYERS

AMES LANGUAGE ACADEMY/AMERICAN ENGLISH SCHOOL
Naugarduko 4/12, 01309 Vilnius, Lithuania
+370 85 279 1011
vilnius@ames.lt
www.ames.lt

NUMBER OF TEACHERS: 40 for 8 branches throughout the country.
PREFERENCE OF NATIONALITY: None.
QUALIFICATIONS: TEFL certificate required in addition to background in pedagogy.
CONDITIONS OF EMPLOYMENT: 5 days per week (mornings and afternoons). Other conditions negotiable. Students are teenagers, adults and corporate clients, private and public sector.
SALARY: $9–$12 per contact hour.
FACILITIES/SUPPORT: Initial in-house training provided; continuous in-house training and teacher support provided.
RECRUITMENT: Demo class to be taught after the interview.
CONTACT: Ms Egle Kesyliene, Director.

BELLNOR INTERNATIONAL SUMMER CAMP
Office: Tuukri põik 10 – 16, Tallinn
+372 660 9606
info@bellnor.ee
www.bellnor.ee

Camp takes place in Kloogaranna on the Estonian coast, west of Tallinn. Parent cultural exchange organisation is NPO International Education.
NUMBER OF TEACHERS: 8–12.
PREFERENCE OF NATIONALITY: British, American or any English-speaking country.
QUALIFICATIONS: Basic teaching and volunteering experience.
CONDITIONS OF EMPLOYMENT: 2-week camps during July. 5 levels of English taught for 3 hours a day.
SALARY: None, this is a volunteer position. Pocket money given.
FACILITIES/SUPPORT: Accommodation and 4 meals a day provided. Pre-arrival training via Skype and one-day orientation on arrival.
RECRUITMENT: Mainly via partner universities and other institutions abroad.
CONTACT: Valeria Bondareva, Executive Assistant.

INTERNATIONAL LANGUAGE SERVICES
Roosikrantsi 8B, 10119 Tallinn, Estonia
+372 627 7170
info@ilstallinn.ee
www.ilstallinn.ee

NUMBER OF TEACHERS: 7 full-time and 3 part-time.
PREFERENCE OF NATIONALITY: Locally based freelancers preferred.
QUALIFICATIONS: Minimum CELTA or Trinity certificate plus 1 year's experience. Some business knowledge preferred.
CONDITIONS OF EMPLOYMENT: 9 months from 1 September with a good chance of staying on for summer work. 96–120 45-minute 'hours' per month with most lessons lasting 90 minutes.
SALARY: €600 per month net guaranteed for 80 hours a month. Hourly rate of €12.75 paid thereafter. Full-time teachers normally take home €1,000–€1,500.
FACILITIES/SUPPORT: Regular seminars and teacher-development programme leading to LCCI Further Certificate in Teaching Business English. Sponsorship for the Trinity DipTESOL by distance for teachers on longer contracts. No accommodation since plenty of rental accommodation is easily available; a 1-bedroom flat should cost €300–€350 a month, more if it is within walking distance of the school.
RECRUITMENT: Internet ads (www.tefl.com) usually between March and August. Initial application to be made via tefl.com's InstApply system. Three recent and relevant referees needed. Phone interviews.
CONTACT: Phil Marsdale, Director.

UKRAINE

After the February revolution of 2014, hopes ran high that a closer alliance to the west would gradually strengthen and reform democratic institutions and boost the economy. Then along came the humiliating annexation of Crimea by Putin's Russia, and pro-Russian separatist violence in the east of Ukraine. The economy suffered badly in 2015 and the Peace Corps pulled out all its volunteers. But that is changing. As of 2016, the EU and Ukraine have signed a Deep & Comprehensive Free Trade Agreement (DCFTA) which will open markets in goods and services and should lead to modernisation and reform. English teachers are in higher demand than they have ever been, including in a reviving corporate sector. The Peace Corps is in the process of implementing a TEFL Project, whereby volunteers will work in secondary schools and universities to enhance the English communication skills of students and teachers. A decent number of language schools advertise vacancies on the main job sites like www.tefl.com.

Native English-speaking teachers in Ukraine often remark on the enthusiastic reception they receive from students. Many of the younger pupils express an adoration for the teachers, which can at first be quite overwhelming, and prospective teachers in out of the way places can expect to receive occasional invitations to students' homes in order to meet their families. Although this can initially be a little unnerving, most teachers find that the generous hospitality is one of the things that makes teaching in Ukraine such a worthwhile experience.

After more than a decade in Kiev, **John Hall** is full of the rewards of teaching in Ukraine:

> ***You may ask, why teach in this part of the world and not sunnier climes? Well, I did a degree in English Lit and Russian at the University of Westminster. For part of the course I enjoyed nine months in St Petersburg and got hooked on the Slavic mentality, people, culture, literature and general way of life. I guess that feeling has never left me.***
>
> ***My situation in Ukraine is not typical, but not unusual either. I have worked for three private language schools since my arrival here, most recently the London School of English and now International House Kyiv, where I have been promoted to Assistant Director of Studies. I have also been married to a lovely Ukrainian woman for the last eight years. The reason for my long stay and subsequent happiness in Kyiv is mainly down to the friendly atmosphere within the city and the pleasing and professional work conditions I have encountered here. The social life is quite lively, though to master the language is a life-long goal!***
>
> ***Please don't get me wrong. Ukraine is not the easiest place to live. There are many schools out there that are not as foreigner friendly as my current school. Work permits and visas are a constant nightmare. But here at IH, everything is done legally, which is a major plus, which everyone admires and respects. The students are lovely, polite and hard working on the whole. There are some who fit the first two qualities, but not the latter, and that's to be expected everywhere in the world. They are generally inquisitive and have high expectations of their teachers, which comes out of the national character. They are paying – sometimes quite highly – for a service and expect the teachers to deliver top-notch lessons and answer all their questions confidently. This can be a bit daunting for some teachers, but a challenge and a happy one for most. Children aged 5–16 make up more than half of the overall student number and this has a huge bearing on planning, timetabling and recruitment, as all teachers are expected to be capable of teaching all these groups.***

For professional opportunities, well-qualified candidates can try the British Council in Kiev, which has a teaching centre and hires freelancers on an ongoing basis (job.applications@britishcouncil.org.ua). In addition to the Kiev branch where John Hall worked, International House has a strong presence in the country, with vacancies from time to time at its schools in Dnipropetrovsk, Kharviv, Odessa, Poltava and Lviv (the latter has an entry below). The IH school in Dnipropetrovsk (shortened to DNK), situated only 150 miles from rebel-held Donetsk in the unstable and potentially risky east of the country, has been trying to attract candidates straight out of their Certificate training courses. They offer contracts lasting five or ten months with many perks such as free accommodation and subsidised travel (check www.job.ihworld.com).

The British-owned Educational Solutions Group is Ukraine's largest privately owned chain of ELT schools, with a centralised Human Resources office. The group comprises three London Schools of English (see entry) and two Language Academies, in Kiev and Odessa. Teachers with a minimum of a degree, CELTA or equivalent and a little experience will not find it difficult to be hired on 12 or 18-month contracts. US nationals must obtain the long-stay visa, for which they will need a labour authorisation form (*dozvil na pratsevlashtuvannia*) from their employer.

As in Russia, the process for schools of getting permission to hire foreigners is both expensive and labyrinthine. Business visas for British teachers cost twice as much as for other nationalities. For years, many schools didn't bother and asked their teachers to leave the country every three months and re-enter as tourists. However, the same rule now applies as in the Schengen Area, which is that you are permitted to stay 90 days in 180, and cannot re-enter straightaway. The fine for overstaying is a modest 900 hryvnias (£27) which permits you to stay for a further 90 days.

As is noticeable throughout Europe and elsewhere where English is in high demand, English-language summer camps have arrived on the scene. This huge country has many beautiful landscapes for hosting such camps, from the Carpathian mountains to the Black Sea. One company seen advertising for summer staff is Dec Camp Ltd (www.dec-camp.com), which runs an English-immersion activity camp at a recreational centre 70km south of Lviv in Western Ukraine, affiliated to the Dec School in Kiev (www.dec-school.com/about/vacancies) which hires teachers for the academic year.

LIST OF EMPLOYERS

BUCKEYE ENGLISH
Dnipropetrovsk
+380 63 729 6608
andy.buckeye@gmail.com
www.buckeyeenglish.com

PREFERENCE OF NATIONALITY: USA and Canada. Conversation American English instructors for corporate classes and via Skype.

QUALIFICATIONS: 4-year degree from accredited college. CELTA or other TEFL certificate or equivalent experience preferred. Ability to build speaking confidence in students. Must be adaptable to foreign cultures, creative, energetic, professional and willing to learn.

CONDITIONS OF EMPLOYMENT: 3-, 7- or 9-month contracts.

SALARY: 15,000–20,000 hryvnia per month. Increments based on teaching load and performance.

FACILITIES/SUPPORT: Travel and visa-related expenses are the teacher's responsibility. School picks up arriving teachers from train station, arranges the loan of a mobile phone and offers Russian language tutoring.

RECRUITMENT: Via www.tefl.com. Skype interviews.

CONTACT: Marianna Ilyina, Director (marianna_ilyina@mail.ru).

INTERNATIONAL HOUSE – KYIV
Business centre 'Vector', section B, 10-G Starokyivska Street (near Politekhnichnyi Instytut metro)
+380 44 238 8870
info@ihkyiv.com
www.ihkyiv.com

PREFERENCE OF NATIONALITY: Native English speakers.

QUALIFICATIONS: Minimum TEFL/CELTA certificate.

CONDITIONS OF EMPLOYMENT: 1-year contracts. Teach up to 25 hours per week.

SALARY: $1,000–$1,500 a month based on experience, paid in Ukrainian hryvnia.

FACILITIES/SUPPORT: The school provides the teacher with a single room or shared apartment.

CONTACT: Tetyana Oratovska, Director.

INTERNATIONAL HOUSE LVIV
3 Petrushevych Square, Lviv 79005
+380 32 225 5190
ihlviv@gmail.com
www.ihlviv.com

NUMBER OF TEACHERS: 15.

PREFERENCE OF NATIONALITY: None, but should be native English speakers.

QUALIFICATIONS: CELTA/TESOL/IHC/Trinity certificate.

CONDITIONS OF EMPLOYMENT: 10 months plus 3 weeks' paid holidays. 24 teaching hours per week plus one meeting/seminar.

SALARY: From 6,800 hryvnias ($800 approx.) per month, depending on experience.

FACILITIES/SUPPORT: $400 of return ticket covered by the school. Furnished accommodation is provided for up to $200. Half the cost of the D-type visa and apostille is covered. The cost of the work permit, translation and registration is fully covered by school.

RECRUITMENT: Locally, via the internet and through IHWO recruitment services.

CONTACT: Marianna Ilyina, Director (marianna_ilyina@gmail.com).

LARISA SCHOOL OF LANGUAGE

Shevchenko 63, Second Floor, Mikolaiv

+380 512 7171 96; +380 94 944 0196

larisaschooloflanguage@gmail.com

www.larisaschooloflanguage.net

Main office and language school for the LSL Education Network.

NUMBER OF TEACHERS: 10.

PREFERENCE OF NATIONALITY: American, British or Canadian.

QUALIFICATIONS: TEFL/TESL/CELTA.

CONDITIONS OF EMPLOYMENT: Minimum 3-month contract depending on the time of year. Usual working hours are Monday to Saturday, late afternoons and evenings.

FACILITIES/SUPPORT: Assistance is given with finding accommodation and applying for work permits.

RECRUITMENT: Usually via the internet. Interviews are essential and can be carried out through Skype.

CONTACT: Larisa Nemchenko, Director, and Bill Green.

THE LONDON SCHOOL OF ENGLISH GROUP

Room 105, Building 19, 39 Politekhnichna Street, Kyiv 03056

Also: The Language Academy, 14 Lunacharskogo Street, Kyiv 02002

The London School of English Odessa. Office 20, 14 Ekaterininskaya Street, Odessa 65026

+380 44 277 8654 (LSE Kyiv); +380 44 541 0602 / +380 503 801 390 (Language Academy); +380 48 777 5015 (LSE Odessa)

admin@lse.kiev.ua (LSE Kiev); lacademy@lse.kiev.ua (Language Academy); educationalsolutions2015@yahoo.co.uk

www.lse.ua/vacancies

Part of British-owned Educational Solutions Group. Also affiliated to Pearson Group.

NUMBER OF TEACHERS: 25–35 at several schools around Ukraine to teach adults and children, on- and off-site.

PREFERENCE OF NATIONALITY: None.

QUALIFICATIONS: CELTA or Trinity TESOL certificate required (other certificates will not be considered). Degree needed. Minimum 1 year's teaching experience preferred but newly qualified teachers are welcome.

CONDITIONS OF EMPLOYMENT: 12 or 18 months starting September. 24 hours per week. Also summer contracts.

SALARY: 16,500–19,000 hryvnias per month for teachers with up to 2 years' teaching experience. Well-qualified employees with 5+ years' experience can earn 22,500 hryvnias.

FACILITIES/SUPPORT: Fully furnished, shared, rent-free apartment is provided. Sponsorship on the Cambridge CELTA or DELTA is available. Assistance given in obtaining work permit and long-term visa which are paid for by school. Free return flight from UK.

RECRUITMENT: Via www.tefl.com. Initial phone/Skype interview followed by a face-to-face interview, sometimes held in London in summer as well as Ukraine. Walk-in candidates will be given an interview whatever the time of year.

CONTACT: Nick Morris, Head of Recruitment.

MOLDOVA

Few people can find Moldova on the map (between Ukraine and Romania) and fewer know that it is famous for its wine. It languishes at the bottom of the table of the poorest countries in Europe which means that a few agencies recruit paying volunteers. For example Love Volunteers (www.lovevolunteers.org/programs/volunteer-moldova) cooperates with a Moldovan NGO to place volunteer teachers to help school children with conversation practice. Participants stay with families in Causeni. Programme fees start at $340 for one week.

And yet, a handful of commercial language schools is in business and occasionally one will seek to employ a native speaker or two. Sharp-eyed readers of the international TEFL websites will spot the occasional appeal for a teacher, for example at a language summer camp with My English Planet or with the well-respected International Language Training Center in the capital, Chisinau (see entry).

LIST OF EMPLOYERS

INTERNATIONAL LANGUAGE TRAINING CENTER (ILTC)
43 Petru Rares str., Chisinau 2005
+373 22 29 29 88
iltcmoldova@gmail.com; iltcmoldova.hr@gmail.com
www.iltc.md/teaching

NUMBER OF TEACHERS: 3–4 to teach General English to young learners, teenagers and adults, Business English and TOEFL preparation.

PREFERENCE OF NATIONALITY: UK and USA, and other English-speaking countries.

QUALIFICATIONS: CELTA/TESOL/TEFL Certificate and Bachelor's degree.

CONDITIONS OF EMPLOYMENT: 10-month contracts. 24 hours a week, mostly in afternoons and evenings.

SALARY: Fixed salary of US$650 a month (net).

FACILITIES/SUPPORT: Shared or single accommodation is provided by the school, or monthly accommodation allowance of US$300. Support given in obtaining a work and residence permit. Teachers must bring their degree certificate, CELTA or equivalent and criminal background check all apostilled in their home country. The process takes about two months. End-of-contract contribution of up to US$750 to travel expenses. ESL workshops and teacher mentoring.

RECRUITMENT: Web adverts and Skype interviews.

CONTACT: Oksana Malcenco, Academic Director.

THE REST OF EUROPE

Outside the mainstream European nations, demand for native speakers of English obviously exists though immigration problems often occur. As of 2015, Albania, Macedonia, Montenegro and Serbia are officially recognised as candidates for membership of the European Union, while Bosnia Herzegovina and Kosovo are still in the category of potential candidates. This chapter contains a miscellany of European opportunities. Of the countries included, Croatia, Slovenia, Malta and Cyprus are members of the EU.

ALBANIA

Information about teaching in this European country wedged between Greece, Macedonia, Serbia and Montenegro has not always been easy to find, but Albania is now fairly stable and offers some opportunities for teachers keen to escape the traditional EFL circuit. The number of paid teaching jobs is severely limited by the country's poverty, but Albania is signatory to a Stabilisation and Association Agreement with the EU that came into force in 2016, so there is hope that demand will increase if the country's economy slowly continues to grow.

English is certainly the favoured foreign language and is compulsory from the fifth grade through to university. Some language schools at least aspire to employ a native English-speaking teacher, although few can currently afford it. There is a need for volunteer teachers to come to Albania to expose children from deprived backgrounds to English spoken by a native. The Language Schools in Albania Foundation (LSIA) is the largest non-profit private language tuition provider in Albania, founded in April 1994 by a group of Albanian university teachers and students. It has been more active in the past than it is now, and it is not clear whether it can be of any assistance to aspiring teacher-volunteers, despite its having a 'Careers' tab on its website. It is affiliated to the long-established international cross-cultural charity People-to-People (www.ptpe.org), which sends short-term teaching volunteers to a few countries in Europe but not as yet to Albania.

Albania is still considered to be close enough to a developing country to have a sizeable contingent of Peace Corps volunteers in place, including a number who are teaching English at foreign-language high schools and other institutes. **Margaret Sheridan** was a Peace Corps volunteer, who said: '*I had a terrific experience, teaching English in high school and to adults, then opening a TOEFL test site, the first in Southern Albania, with a terrific Albanian colleague.*'

Other institutions that may be worth contacting are the Memorial International School of Tirana (Ish Shkolla e Partise, Rruga Dritan Hoxha Nr.1, Tirana; ✆ +355 4 223 7375; www.mist.edu.al), which currently employs a handful of Americans, Britons and Canadians who are qualified ESL teachers. The school's minimum requirement is that teachers have some years of experience in their own fields, although the majority have completed university courses with components in education. The Albanian International School in Tirana (www.ais-tirana.org) was recently advertising on Dave's eslcafe for ESL and kindergarten teachers. A language school in Vlora called the Smart Center (www.smartcenter.al) has been seen advertising a vacancy at a monthly salary of $500. Another commercial institute we have heard of hiring native speakers is the Lincoln Center of Albania (see entry). A number of US non-profits that were and in some cases still are active in the field of education, such as the American School of Peshkopi, which sponsors an English summer camp, have a religious agenda in spreading the gospel.

Visa guidelines can be checked at the Embassy of the Republic of Albania in the UK or USA. If a European's stay is going to be less than 90 days, they do not need to apply for a visa. It is not possible to cross out of Albania and straight back in again to renew your tourist visa. If you intend to stay longer than 90 days, you must apply for a residency permit. US nationals can stay for up to a year without a permit.

Living costs are very cheap by US and UK standards, though choice can be limited. One volunteer teacher complained that he had to travel five hours by bus to Tirana to buy ketchup. Albania has plenty of scenic attractions, including rugged mountains, ancient Greek ruins and a marvellous stretch of Adriatic coastline, blissfully free of package-holiday tourists.

LIST OF EMPLOYERS

LINCOLN CENTERS OF ALBANIA
Rruga Qemal Stafa Nr. 184, Tirana; also at Rr Ismail Qemali 31
+355 4 223 0880
info@lincoln.org.al
http://lincolnalbania.org

School has branches in Shkodër and Lezhë.
NUMBER OF TEACHERS: Few native English speakers.
PREFERENCE OF NATIONALITY: American and others.
QUALIFICATIONS: Degree or TEFL certificate required; MA preferred.
CONDITIONS OF EMPLOYMENT: Part-time teachers for courses offered at all levels and special English programmes for several professional institutions in Albania.
RECRUITMENT: Mainly via www.anegino.gen.al (recruitment site in Albanian).
CONTACT: Edita Nikolla (enikolli@lincoln.org.al).

ANDORRA

Andorra lies in the heart of the Pyrenees, between Spain and France, and can be seen as an extension of both countries, though it has its own elected government. It is too small to have many language schools, but the two listed here are possibilities (and you would be there over the skiing season). Technically, Andorra is not a member of the EU so it is necessary to obtain a work permit which involves completing forms in Catalan.

LIST OF EMPLOYERS

CENTRE ANDORRA DE LLENGUES (CALL)
Av del Fener 17, 1-F/G, 500 Andorra-la-Vella
+376 804030
idiomes@call.ad
www.call.eu.com

NUMBER OF TEACHERS: 2.
PREFERENCE OF NATIONALITY: British, Irish and American.
QUALIFICATIONS: BA in English or a foreign language plus TEFL qualification and 2–3 years' experience abroad most welcome. A good knowledge of Spanish and/or French can help. Non-smokers preferred.
CONDITIONS OF EMPLOYMENT: 9–10-month renewable contract that runs from October to June. 27 hours per week, 5 days a week. Teaching hours spread throughout the day. Teaching very young learners (6–7 years) and all other ages including professionals.
SALARY: €1,800 per month (plus overtime if any available).
FACILITIES/SUPPORT: Board and lodging available within walking distance costs from €550 per month. Work permit arranged and paid for by the school.
RECRUITMENT: Direct application with CV and photo by email.
CONTACT: Claude Benet, Director.

INLINGUA ANDORRA
Carrer Prat de la Creu 30, AD500 Andorra la Vella
+376 807060
inlingua@inlingua.ad
www.inlingua.ad

NUMBER OF TEACHERS: 10 for four branches.
PREFERENCE OF NATIONALITY: None.
QUALIFICATIONS: University degree and TEFL certificate needed

plus 2 years of experience.

CONDITIONS OF EMPLOYMENT: 9.5 month contracts. 25 teaching hours a week.

SALARY: €1,300 a month less 10% deductions.

FACILITIES/SUPPORT: Assistance given with red tape; teachers must provide criminal record check and university diploma and transcripts with the Hague apostille. No help given with accommodation.

RECRUITMENT: Spontaneous applications, inlingua HQ and other web portals. Skype interviews.

CONTACT: Ferran Costa, Director.

BOSNIA-HERZEGOVINA

There are still few private language schools in Bosnia, and most operate on a small scale. As usual, you could check the list of 27 schools provided at www.eslbase.com/schools/bosnia-and-herzegovina for leads.

LIST OF EMPLOYERS

NEW ACADEMY

Muharem Suljanovic Street, 79101 Prijedor

+387 65 586469

new_academy@yahoo.com

www.new-academy.com

PREFERENCE OF NATIONALITY: None.

QUALIFICATIONS: 2 years' TEFL experience.

CONDITIONS OF EMPLOYMENT: 1-year contract with working hours between 4pm and 10pm. Also offers summer courses.

RECRUITMENT: Interviews are essential.

CONTACT: Principal.

CROATIA

In July 2013 Croatia celebrated its acceptance into the European Union. This is unlikely to have much immediate impact on its struggling economy, but long-term integration will boost business and lead to more demand for a high standard of English.

Building on its strong indigenous English teaching infrastructure, Croatia's private language schools flourish in Zagreb, Varazdin and Karlovac, as well as in other towns. For many schools, the idea of employing a native English-speaker teacher is very attractive; particularly given Croatia's popularity as a British tourist destination, accessible by cheap flights. Teachers who go to work in Croatia are likely to find themselves being made welcome and treated well, certainly outside the usual tourist hot spots. Salaries are likely to be quoted in euros even though the national currency is still the kuna.

The market for private teaching is strong; however, native English teachers need to be well qualified to secure a job. A good source of language schools can be found by searching the British Council Croatia's School Finder, aimed at prospective English exam-takers (http://hr.bcschoolfinder.org/schoolfinder/easy123.php). Occasionally, teaching vacancies are posted on the Croatian jobs site www.moj-posao.net/EN. For example, at the time of writing the Lingoteka School in Zagreb (www.lingoteka.com) was looking to hire a native speaker able to teach both children and business people (but not at the same time).

Non-EU citizens wishing to work in Croatia must apply to the Embassy of the Republic of Croatia for a visa. An application form must be completed by your employer and returned together with a passport, two photographs and details of the job (e.g. a copy of your contract, length of employment, type of work, location and full address of employer).

The British Council in Zagreb can offer informal assistance to prospective teachers and should be able to put you in touch with the Association of Croatian Teachers of English (HUPE), which organises teacher-development activities but can't help foreign teachers to find jobs.

With its beautiful coastline and accessibility, Croatia has developed summer camps, some of which teach English. The exchange company CCUSA sends volunteer counsellors to Camp California in Pakostane near Zadar on the Adriatic; counsellors pay a programme fee of £245 (www.ccusa.co.uk/PROGRAMS/Camp-California) but get free room and board. A few years ago, **Geoff Nunney** wanted to find a summer job after the academic term finished at the language school in Slovakia where he had spent the year. He got a job at Euroclub on Solta, an island off the coast near Split (www.euroclub.hr), the largest international youth camp on the Adriatic:

> ***I have a return invitation for this year, kids of all nationalities from 10 to 20. There's a big mixture of teachers – I was known as the 'Crazy Teacher'. Lots of sports, lessons and a holiday atmosphere. I did four weeks there, and the pay is enough to live on.***

LIST OF EMPLOYERS

FOREIGN LANGUAGE SCHOOL – ZIGER
S. Vraza 37, 42000 Varazdin
+385 42 330385
info@skola-ziger.hr
www.skola-ziger.hr

NUMBER OF TEACHERS: 1–2.

PREFERENCE OF NATIONALITY: British, American and Canadian.

QUALIFICATIONS: At least 1 year's experience, CELTA/DELTA, university degree.

CONDITIONS OF EMPLOYMENT: Minimum 1-year contract, teaching hours are usually late afternoon and evenings.

FACILITIES/SUPPORT: Assistance with finding accommodation and work permit (school applies and translates documents).

RECRUITMENT: Via email contact. Interviews by phone.

CONTACT: Irena Ziger, Director.

MHC BUSINESS LANGUAGE TRAINING
Petrinjska 26, 10 000 Zagreb
+385 99 793 6363
zagreb@mhc-training.com
www.mhc-training.com

Company headquarters in Vienna (see entry).

NUMBER OF TEACHERS: 15.

PREFERENCE OF NATIONALITY: Any.

QUALIFICATIONS: MHC trainers have an understanding of business experience, often specialising in areas such as marketing, finance, pharmaceuticals or law. A degree is not necessary, although a teaching certificate such as CELTA would be of value.

CONDITIONS OF EMPLOYMENT: Freelance, teaching 15–25 hours per week.

SALARY: €10–€15 per 60 minutes, depending on experience and development with MHC. Seminars between €100 and €150 per day. Trainers are responsible for paying their own taxes (12%–25%) and social security (variable).

FACILITIES/SUPPORT: Trainer preparation room, resource library, photocopying, trainer development and social networking events. Trainers require working papers.

RECRUITMENT: Interviews are essential and usually take place at premises. Possibility of Skype interviews if the applicant is based abroad.

CONTACT: Bashkim Fazliu, Regional Director South East Europe (bashkim.fazliu@mhc-training.com).

CYPRUS

A visitor to the Republic of Cyprus will be struck by the similarities with Greece – cuisine, architecture, landscapes, culture, economy on the skids – but then be surprised at the relative prominence of English. Signs are printed in both Greek and English, many (if not most) local people even outside the cities speak some English, and the British influence can be noticed everywhere. Because of the long-standing relationship between Cyprus and Britain, the English language is given much prominence in the state educational system. As a result the density of *frontisteria* is not as high as it is in Greece, though there are still a fair number of private institutes preparing children for external examinations.

At least one organisation is trying to market Cyprus (to Germans, Russians, etc.) as a destination in which to learn English, as Malta has successfully done. In a joint venture between a British language school and the English Learning Centre in Limassol (www.englishlearningcentre.com.cy), the English in Cyprus summer programme (www.englishincyprus.com) was developed to put on holiday English courses for children, adults and families. Its sister school in Limassol, the English Learning Centre (www.englishlearningcentre.com.cy), employs a number of native English-speaking teachers. The long established language camp company Village Camps in Switzerland has inaugurated an English language camp in Droushia in the west of the country, for which it employs one counsellor for every six campers. The promised pay was €245 per week for the two weeks of the camp, plus €225 in travel expenses.

Cyprus has a small population of not much more than one million and therefore opportunities are not extensive. Also a large number of Cypriot students leave the island each year to study in the UK and USA, although there are still a number of afternoon language schools in the cities and towns.

To find an ELT job in Cyprus before you arrive is extremely difficult because very few of the ELT schools advertise except locally to a sizeable expat community from which native English-speaker teachers can be drawn. Some expats will also informally help Cypriot friends with their English over a glass of beer.

Sending speculative CVs is unlikely to succeed. It is more fruitful to visit schools in person and hand them round. One freelance opportunity might be to approach businessmen and women in the property sector, who have (or would like to have) English-speaking clients. You'd need a solid business background to succeed, and would be required to provide specialist vocabulary ('grouting', anyone?).

Since Cyprus joined the European Union, visas are no longer a major hurdle for EU members. Nationals of all the other 27 EU countries have the automatic right of residence in Cyprus. Those who intend to work and stay in the country are obliged to apply for a registration certificate within four months of arrival. In Nicosia this can be done at the Migration Department; elsewhere applicants must visit the Immigration Police. The fee for registration is a modest €20; however, the fine for failing to register is in excess of €2,500.

If you wish to advertise your services as a tutor on English-language sites, try www.angloinfo.com/cyprus or www.cy.bazaraki.com. Most schools offer a contract of 20–25 working hours a week for the academic year September to May/June. The hourly pay is above average for Southern Europe, usually in the range €12–€16 per hour. As in Greece, there are usually two paid holidays during the academic year: two weeks over Christmas and two weeks for the Greek Orthodox Easter.

Most Cypriot schools have very good facilities, although they may be lagging behind somewhat in technology. Teacher support is readily available, with regular free seminars organised by various publishers. In language classrooms, there is a wide range of levels for all ages. The majority of children enrol at language schools when they are about eight and finish around the age of 16, attending lessons twice a week. However, there is a growing demand for children as young as four to start learning English as a foreign language, so schools are introducing classes for younger children. A lesson can last from one to two hours for higher levels. Young students and adults are usually motivated and love interactive teaching. However, those teaching teenagers will need to be firm and to make lessons particularly interesting.

People move to Cyprus more for the lifestyle than for cheap living. The downside is that eating out, etc. is not cheap; however, the improved infrastructure (like the good motorways) makes life easier. Note there is no train service on the island. Government plans to take the country upmarket by building more marinas and golf courses have had to be set aside because of the economic problems. The global downturn saw a sharp decline in the number of tourists arriving in Cyprus and many small businesses were forced to close. If reunification with the Turkish north takes place on the island (a long way off but positive moves have been made), then the country could really flourish.

A decent studio apartment can be rented for €350–€450 per month. By opening the English-language newspapers, you will be able to find out what's on and where to meet new friends. If you want to find out more about life in Cyprus for expats, visit the forums at www.cyprusliving.org based in Paphos and www.easterncyprus.com.

TURKISH CYPRUS

There are six private universities, four private schools and at least two language schools in the Turkish Republic of Northern Cyprus (TRNC). The main industry in Northern Cyprus is tourism, largely catering for an English-speaking clientele, so there is local demand to master the languages for employment purposes. However, it should be pointed out that the expatriate community numbers more than 4,000, so there is already a substantial pool of native English speakers on hand to fill any teacher vacancies that occur.

MALTA

Malta is a very appealing destination for the peripatetic English teacher, and not just because of its climate. The capital Valletta, along with all the islands of Malta, have been chosen as European Capital of Culture for 2018. Although somewhat off the beaten track, the tiny island of Malta (where English is an official language) has a booming EFL market. A number of private language schools cater to groups coming from other Mediterranean countries on short courses in the spring, summer and at other times. The Malta Tourism Authority promotes language courses; you can check the list of language schools on www.visitmalta.com/en/language-learning. The EFL Monitoring Board of the Ministry for Education and Employment publishes online a list of 42 licensed language schools.

The interests of the mainstream English-language institutes are represented by FELTOM, the Federation of English Language Teaching Organisations Malta (✆ +356 2131 0927; www.feltom.com); the site has good links to the 19 member schools and basic information about teaching on the island. Many of the schools have teacher recruitment information on their websites, for example the Maltalingua School in St Julian's (www.maltalingua.com/jobs). Another school in that same resort, EC English Language Centre (http://jobs.ecenglish.com), offers summer jobs to entry-level teachers provided they are able to do an intensive induction course for the first half of June.

All EU citizens have the right to live and work in Malta, although it is necessary to obtain an ELT Permit from the ELT Council (https://eltcouncil.gov.mt/en/Pages/Requirements-for-an-ELT-Teaching-Permit.aspx). In order to be eligible for the permit, a candidate must have an A level in English (grade C or above) from a recognised institution and have completed a TEFL course such as a CELTA. A home-grown alternative qualification that satisfies the government requirement is TELT (Test for English Language Teachers); many schools offer preparatory courses in advance of the exam. All teachers also need a clean police conduct certificate. Note that self-employed freelancers do not need to obtain a work permit. Australians and New Zealanders under the age of 30 should be entitled to apply for a one-year working holiday visa to Malta, reciprocal with Maltese citizens being eligible for WHVs down under, although that could not be confirmed at the time of writing.

Wages are paid hourly and are in the €8–€12 bracket, with a steady average of €10. Many professional teachers join MATEFL, the Malta Association of TEFL (www.matefl.org), which lists occasional job vacancies/wanted on its site. Membership costs a modest €20. The NSTS English Language Institute in Gzira (HQ, 220 St Paul St, Valletta VLT1217; ✆ +356 2558 8000; http://nsts.org/vacancies) markets its English courses in conjunction with sports holidays for young tourists to Malta. NSTS runs weekly vacation courses from June to August, and it might be worth approaching it for a job, particularly if you are a water sports enthusiast. NSTS was keen to hire **Robert Mizzi** from Canada once it learned that he was half-Maltese:

> ***I was offered a job quite casually when NSTS found out I was volunteering conversational English in the main youth hostel in Valletta. Perhaps one reason they wanted to hire me was they knew the visa would not be a problem. However, I was surprised by how relaxed the offer was. It was just mentioned in passing rather than at an actual interview. I guess it is the Maltese way: once you are one of them, then everything is gravy.***

JESSICA STONE

Four years ago Jessica Stone decided to leave the States to embark on a Mediterranean adventure, even though she was older than most who entertain such dreams.

I feel extremely lucky: after carefully examining all the countries I was interested in visiting/teaching/travelling in, I selected Malta as my first choice. I sent out about 15 letters and résumés and received roughly six responses. Three of them asked me to touch base when I arrived, saying they could probably give me part-time work in the summer. One made a definite appointment to meet and one asked if I could do a Skype interview. The latter ended up offering me an excellent position as the Executive Director of Academic Programme Development and Marketing, a far cry from the teaching job I'd originally applied for. Just happened to have the skill set they were looking for at the time. I should say that I am 58 years old and hold a Masters and PhD in Communications, and have taught Business and Business Communications at US universities for over 20 years. In preparation I did a 100-hour TESOL course with LCC in Seattle.

So now I'm living in Malta, have a great flat with a view of the Med and a super job. The school is going to get the work permit for me, which will result in a one-year residency visa to follow on from the initial three months as a tourist. From my understanding, the issues with visas are the same everywhere - lots of paperwork and rubber stamps and moaning about not being able to get one, but anyone who really wants one gets one. And the schools hire people right and left even though you can't officially work without a work permit. The money you earn teaching English is not very good, especially for people my age. But the adventure and cultural experience are truly priceless.

LIST OF EMPLOYERS

AM LANGUAGE STUDIO
299 Manwel Dimech Street, Sliema SLM 1054
+356 21 324242
info@amlanguage.com
www.amlanguage.com

NUMBER OF TEACHERS: 3.
PREFERENCE OF NATIONALITY: British.
QUALIFICATIONS: CELTA or CertTESOL.
CONDITIONS OF EMPLOYMENT: Teachers are employed on a freelance basis and are required to work from July to August with 22.5–30 hours per week.
SALARY: €11 per hour.
FACILITIES/SUPPORT: As teachers are freelance they just have to register as self-employed with the local authorities and do not need to apply for a work permit.
RECRUITMENT: CV and telephone interview.
CONTACT: Edwina Caruana Galizia, Director of Studies.

ELANGUEST ENGLISH LANGUAGE SCHOOL
Keating House, Ross Street, St Julian's STJ 3243
+356 21 374777
dos@elanguest.com
www.elanguest.com

PREFERENCE OF NATIONALITY: British, Canadian and Australian.
QUALIFICATIONS: TEFL course plus A level in English. Applicants with CELTA or DELTA are given preference.
CONDITIONS OF EMPLOYMENT: No contract; however, applicants who can work all year round are given preference. Between 4.5 and 5.5 working hours per day.
FACILITIES/SUPPORT: Assistance given with work permits.
RECRUITMENT: CV, photo and telephone interview.

GV MALTA ENGLISH CENTRE
St George's Street, St Paul's Bay SPB 3476
+356 21 573417
info@gvmalta.com
www.gvmalta.com

Formerly Global Village Malta.
NUMBER OF TEACHERS: All staff are native speakers of English.
PREFERENCE OF NATIONALITY: None.
QUALIFICATIONS: Experience and TEFL qualification needed plus minimum 1-year's experience.
CONDITIONS OF EMPLOYMENT: Open-ended contracts. 15–20 hours per week in low season, 20+ hours per week in peak season.
SALARY: Varies according to experience and qualifications.
FACILITIES/SUPPORT: Advice given on rental accommodation.
RECRUITMENT: Mainly via teacher-training courses run on-site. Interviews are essential and are usually carried out face-to-face with the Director of Studies and include analysis of lesson planning.
CONTACT: Mrs Gaby Huhn, Director/Head of School.

IELS MALTA
Matthew Pulis Street, Sliema SLM 3052
+356 21 320381
hr.malta@iels.com.mt
www.lalschools.com; www.ielsmalta.com

NUMBER OF TEACHERS: 60.
PREFERENCE OF NATIONALITY: None.
QUALIFICATIONS: Minimum CELTA but no experience required.
CONDITIONS OF EMPLOYMENT: Open-ended contract with 15 or 22.5 hours per week, depending on preference and availability.
SALARY: €10.50 per hour.
FACILITIES/SUPPORT: Assistance given with work permits.
CONTACT: Angie Conti, Academic Manager (angie.conti@lalgroup.com).

INLINGUA SCHOOL OF LANGUAGES
9 Triq Guzi Fava, Off Bisazza St, Sliema SLM 1632
+356 20102000
dos@inlinguamalta.com
www.inlinguamalta.com

Cambridge accredited centre. Member of FELTOM.
NUMBER OF TEACHERS: 30–100+ depending on time of year.
PREFERENCE OF NATIONALITY: Native speakers if they are able to work in Malta. (inlingua does not apply for work permits.)
QUALIFICATIONS: Matriculation standard of education, A level English and TEFL qualification minimum. Holders of CELTA qualification or higher will be given preference.
CONDITIONS OF EMPLOYMENT: Casual and freelance employment only.
SALARY: Depends on qualifications.
RECRUITMENT: Local interviews essential.

INTERNATIONAL HOUSE MALTA-GOZO
Triq Is-sirk 128, Swieqi SWQ 3211
+356 21 384139
info@ihmalta.com
www.ihmalta.com

PREFERENCE OF NATIONALITY: None. Most staff are recruited locally. Teachers are required to be able to work in the EU and have a valid ELT Permit issued by the ELT Council of Malta.

QUALIFICATIONS: CELTA or equivalent is minimum requirement. Minimum C1 English, excellent written and spoken communication abilities, and must be flexible and able to work as part of a close-knit team.

CONDITIONS OF EMPLOYMENT: Teaching in Malta is often seasonal so hours may fluctuate during the year. A contract may be for a year, the summer period or on an indefinite basis. Teaching takes place in mornings and/or afternoons.

FACILITIES/SUPPORT: No assistance with accommodation. Monthly teacher development sessions based on the teachers' and institutional needs. IH staff can also participate in IH Online Conferences and other training opportunities offered within the network. Sick benefits and leave are paid on a pro rata basis.

RECRUITMENT: Local advertising on Facebook, *The Times of Malta*, MATEFL, etc. Staff may also be chosen for interview from CVs received.

CONTACT: Lisa Phillips, Director of Studies.

SKYLARK SCHOOL OF ENGLISH / EUROCENTRES MALTA
29, Victor Denaro Street, Msida MSD 1604
✆ +356 21 316604
info@skylarkmalta.com
www.skylarkmalta.com

NUMBER OF TEACHERS: 30 freelancers.

PREFERENCE OF NATIONALITY: EU citizenship preferred though willing to consider any CV as long as teachers are native English speakers.

QUALIFICATIONS: Minimum of a TEFL course and a high school-level qualification in English Language (A level or equivalent). However, a CELTA/DELTA/TESOL certificate is preferable.

CONDITIONS OF EMPLOYMENT: Freelance basis only. Flexible timetable according to teacher's availability. Normally 15–30 class hours a week.

SALARY: €8–€12 per hour.

FACILITIES/SUPPORT: Non-local teachers are given assistance in finding housing as close to the school as possible and at the best rate possible.

RECRUITMENT: Face-to-face interview and on occasion class observation. Occasionally telephone interviews are conducted.

CONTACT: Sigo Gatt, Director of Studies.

SERBIA, MONTENEGRO AND KOSOVO

After the short-lived union of Serbia and Montenegro (where Serbian is spoken) broke down, followed by Kosovo's declaration of independence from Serbia in 2008, the dissolution of the former Yugoslavia became final, with much underlying tension remaining.

The ELT industry has been developing but mainly supplied by local teachers. International House has a school in Belgrade, the Syllabus School, which offers the CELTA course at a reasonable price, and another affiliate, the Cambridge Centar in Podgorice, Montonegro. One possible lead is the Bejza Education Centre (Kosovska 39, 3rd Fl, 11000 Belgrade, Serbia; ✆ +381 11 334 3077; www.bejza.edu.rs). The US State Department's Regional English Language Office (RELO) for Central and Southeastern Europe has just moved from Budapest to Belgrade, so there may be some English language programmes in the pipeline.

In order to get a residence/work permit for Serbia, you must submit a contract of employment and a translated copy of your diploma. Further information on the regulations for entering and working in Serbia can be found at www.london.mfa.gov.rs.

The first group of approximately 20 Peace Corps Kosovo volunteers arrived in June 2014 in order to teach English at local secondary schools after three months of cross-cultural, language and technical training. Another interesting volunteering opportunity is offered by the Balkans Peace Park Project (www.balkanspeacepark.org), a proposed park that straddles the borders of Kosovo, Montenegro and Albania in rugged mountainous country. Foreign volunteers spend a week or two in the summer teaching English to young villagers, while local volunteers provide environmental awareness education.

IBCM (International Business College Mitrovica), not far from Pristina in Kosovo, has a few native English teachers, including for its High Schools English Programme (vacancies@ibcmitrovica.eu).

LIST OF EMPLOYERS

ANGLOLAND LANGUAGE SCHOOL
Starine Novaka 19/I, 11000 Belgrade, Serbia
+381 69 2787 251 (mobile)
angloland@sbb.rs; office@angloland.rs
www.angloland.rs

NUMBER OF TEACHERS: 1–2.
PREFERENCE OF NATIONALITY: None.
QUALIFICATIONS: Bachelor's degree plus CELTA minimum. DELTA or MA in TESOL/Applied Linguistics and/or long-standing experience preferred.
CONDITIONS OF EMPLOYMENT: Two 90-minute lessons per week in some cases.
FACILITIES/SUPPORT: Assistance may be available for accommodation, and work permits may be possible.
RECRUITMENT: Interviews arranged on basis of submitted CV.
CONTACT: Natasha Jovanovich.

OXFORD CENTAR
64 Rimiski trg, 81000 Podgorica, Montenegro
+382 20 234425
oxfordcentar@t-com.me; oxfordcentar@gmail.com
www.oxfordcentar.com

Language centres also in Bar, Budva, Bijelo Polje, Niksic and Cetinje.
NUMBER OF TEACHERS: 6.
PREFERENCE OF NATIONALITY: British, American, Australian, New Zealander and Canadian.
QUALIFICATIONS: 3–5 years' practical experience. Staff are graduate philologists, some with an MA or PhD.
CONDITIONS OF EMPLOYMENT: 4- or 9-month contract with 22 to 27 working hours per week.
SALARY: €750–€850 per month plus flat allowance of €200 per month.
FACILITIES/SUPPORT: School pays for 2 nights in a hotel as teacher looks for accommodation. Assistance also given with applying for work permits.
RECRUITMENT: Usually via adverts on www.eslbase.com or www.tefl.com. Interviews are essential and can be via phone or Skype.

SLOVENIA

As in Croatia, there are plenty of private schools and opportunities can be created by energetic native English speakers both as freelance teachers for institutes and as private tutors. Slovenia is a sophisticated little country with high standards of education and many well-qualified native teachers of English.

The British Council in Slovenia keeps an up-to-date list of schools that prepare candidates for Cambridge English exams (www.britishcouncil.si/en/exam/cambridge/prepare), which would be a starting point. The average hourly wage should start at €10.

As one of the countries that joined the EU in May 2004 and the Schengen Agreement in 2008, Slovenia now has fairly straightforward regulations for EU members. All EU citizens are able to work in Slovenia under the same conditions as Slovene citizens in their countries. However, teachers should obtain a temporary residence permit within three months of entering the country, and will need a valid passport whose expiry date exceeds by at least three months the intended period of stay, health insurance, sufficient means of subsistence and a legitimate purpose for their residence (like a job). Your school should report your post to the Employment Service of Slovenia (*Zavod za zaposlovanje*) in Ljubljana within eight days of starting the job. Canadians aged 18–35 can apply for a Youth Mobility visa that will allow them to work for a year, while New Zealand citizens up to the age of 30 can do likewise.

LIST OF EMPLOYERS

BERLITZ LANGUAGE CENTER
Gosposvetska 2, 1000 Ljubljana
+386 1 433 1325
ljubljana@berlitz.si; workinslovenia@berlitz.si
www.berlitz.si

Also centres in Maribor, Kranj, Novo Mesto and Celje. Also organise summer camps in the ski resort of Krvavec and at the seaside at Debeli Rtic.
NUMBER OF TEACHERS: 60.
PREFERENCE OF NATIONALITY: EU or candidates already with permission to work in Slovenia. Candidates should be already living in Slovenia.
QUALIFICATIONS: Tertiary educational background, good communication skills, professional attitude and appearance.
CONDITIONS OF EMPLOYMENT: Minimum 1 year. All work on freelance basis. Number of hours assigned on merit; no guaranteed minimum. Good teachers work 20–40 hours per week.
SALARY: From €10+ per unit (40 minutes).
FACILITIES/SUPPORT: No assistance with accommodation. Compulsory training in Berlitz Method offered twice a year. Regular support through observations and workshops.
RECRUITMENT: Adverts and personal recommendation. Applications welcome at any time and are kept on file for 6 months. Face-to-face interviews are compulsory.
CONTACT: Gregor Sergan, Director.

EVROPA BLED d.o.o.
Finzgarjeva 15, 4260 Bled
+386 45 741563/644988
cilka@evropa-bled.com
www.evropa-bled.com

NUMBER OF TEACHERS: 1–2.
PREFERENCE OF NATIONALITY: None.
QUALIFICATIONS: Experience essential. Teacher training course for TEFL required.
CONDITIONS OF EMPLOYMENT: School year from October to May. Minimum 30–40 lessons a month.
FACILITIES/SUPPORT: Help is given with finding accommodation but the rental charge is borne by the teacher.
RECRUITMENT: Contacts through the British Council.
CONTACT: Cilka Demsar, Director.

JEZIKOVNA AKADEMIJA
Akademija INT d.o.o. Valjhunova 11, 1000 Ljubljana
+386 7079 5792
info@jezikovna-akademija.si
www.jezikovna-akademija.si

NUMBER OF TEACHERS: 5–10, part-time.
PREFERENCE OF NATIONALITY: EU citizens.
QUALIFICATIONS: Teaching experience and suitable education are required.
CONDITIONS OF EMPLOYMENT: Upwards of 3 months per project. Hours begin in the mornings before 10am or in the afternoons after 3pm.
SALARY: Upwards of €12 (gross) per 45 minutes. Depending on type of contract, taxes required by the local authority are deducted.
FACILITIES/SUPPORT: No assistance given with accommodation. Internal training available with in-house personnel.
RECRUITMENT: Online.
CONTACT: Mr Matija Kovač, Managing Director.

NISTA LANGUAGE CENTER
Smarska C.5D, 6000 Koper
+386 5625 0400
info@nista.si; nista@siol.net
www.nista.si

Located on the Adriatic not far from Trieste, Italy.
NUMBER OF TEACHERS: 15.
PREFERENCE OF NATIONALITY: England, Scotland, New Zealand and Australia.
QUALIFICATIONS: Bachelor's degree (Hons) and TEFL certificate

plus a year's teaching experience. Business background useful. Some opportunities for final year students.

CONDITIONS OF EMPLOYMENT: Minimum 10 months September to June (preferably longer). Usual 24–26 hours' contact time per week. Also part-time openings.

SALARY: About €13 per lesson. No tax or social security deductions.

FACILITIES/SUPPORT: The school provides an apartment for teachers and provides necessary documents for them.

RECRUITMENT: Email, internet.

CONTACT: Mrs Alenka Rajčič, Director.

NUMBER OF TEACHERS: 5.

PREFERENCE OF NATIONALITY: British.

QUALIFICATIONS: English teacher with a variety of TEFL experience (TEFL or CELTA certificate).

CONDITIONS OF EMPLOYMENT: Standard length of contract 1 year. 20–30 hours per week including morning, afternoon and evening lessons.

SALARY: €10 per hour (45 minutes of teaching).

FACILITIES/SUPPORT: Help is given with finding accommodation and acquiring the necessary permits.

RECRUITMENT: CV must be submitted. Successful applicants will be invited to attend an interview.

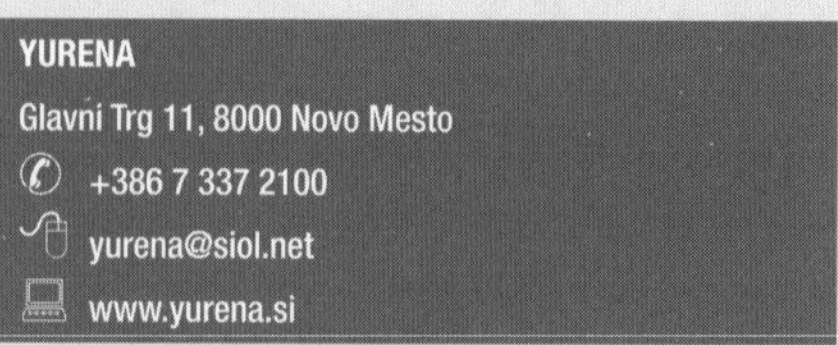

YURENA
Glavni Trg 11, 8000 Novo Mesto
+386 7 337 2100
yurena@siol.net
www.yurena.si

NUMBER OF TEACHERS: 2–3.

PREFERENCE OF NATIONALITY: English.

QUALIFICATIONS: TEFL qualification.

CONDITIONS OF EMPLOYMENT: 1-year contracts. 25–30 hours per week.

SALARY: Approximately €1,000 per month.

FACILITIES/SUPPORT: Accommodation and help with work permits provided.

RECRUITMENT: Interviews essential.

CONTACT: Marija Trunkelj.

CENTRAL ASIAN AND OTHER REPUBLICS

The former Soviet republics have gradually resumed their own national and regional identities. Whereas the Baltic States (Estonia, Lithuania and Latvia) desire few if any ties with Russia, other former Soviet republics, especially those in North Central Asia (Kazakhstan, Kyrgyzstan, Tajikistan, Turkmenistan and Uzbekistan), have joined with Russia (and China) to form a number of economic and security-related treaty organisations. In between these two extremes are the eastern European states such as Belarus and Moldova and the Caucasian States (Armenia, Azerbaijan and Georgia) that drift from one side to the other depending on the nature of the area of cooperation. Prospective EFL teachers seeking to find employment in this vast region would do well to study their atlases carefully and then investigate the prevailing influences affecting the particular country or area in which they are interested at the time of their job search.

Prospective incomers should give some thought as to whether they will be able to tolerate different attitudes to human rights, religious freedoms, etc. On the question of the religious flavour, not to say fervour, of the republic in question, as a general rule, the former western republics are mostly eastern Orthodox Christian and the Southern Central Asian Republics are Sunni Muslim, so there are noticeable differences (including among individuals) between levels of tolerance in matters of sexual freedom, alcohol, dietary habits and even smoking.

An internet job search should yield a few results, for example a post teaching corporate English in Northern Tajikistan or another teaching teenagers in Pavlodar region of Kazakhstan. Many established institutes operating in the various countries of the former Soviet republics are off the radar of search engines. It is not difficult to find contact details for institutes of higher education, technical colleges and pedagogical institutes, some of which may employ native English-speaking teachers at various times. It can also be worth trying international schools. English teaching is still largely delivered by the state. University faculties often have their own international relations office, which may have two or three vacancies for highly educated foreign specialists; try, for example, the Kazakh-British Technical University in Almaty where Louise Wheeler works (see her account below in the section on Kazakhstan). The US government deploys a number of Language Teaching Assistants to most of the countries of the region, from Armenia to Tajikistan, through the Fulbright Program (http://exchanges.state.gov/us/program/fulbright-english-teaching-assistant-program). Assistants are university graduates in their 20s who are normally placed in universities, but also in schools and other venues, to serve as a resource for conversation, vocabulary and reading and writing courses.

Another source of ELT employment can be the NGOs operating in a number of former Soviet republic countries. In response to the increase in demand for English, the Peace Corps sends a substantial number of volunteer English teachers to the Kyrgyz Republic, Georgia and Moldova.

Much of the demand has been spurred by the influx of businesses connected with the Caspian oil industry, which has particularly affected Kazakhstan, Uzbekistan, Turkmenistan and Azerbaijan. Opportunities with international companies exist for professional teachers where the salaries are approaching those of the oil-rich states of the Middle East. Net salaries of up to $2,000 per month on top of free accommodation and travel expenses are not too uncommon.

Chain schools such as Language Link, EF and International House can provide sources of TEFL employment. For example Language Link operates teaching centres in Atyrau, Kazakhstan (atyrau@languagelink.ru) and Tashkent, Uzbekistan (applications to jobs@languagelink.com.cn) and may in future open others, as long as the petrodollars flow.

International House has been active in opening up the region to English-language learners. IH's partner in Almaty, Kazakhstan is Interpress, which does some of its own teacher hiring (see entry).

Belarus is another republic with various language-teaching opportunities, for example at International House Minsk (www.ih.by) and SOL Minsk (www.sol.by). The International Language Training Center in Chisinau, Moldova (www.iltc.md) might be persuaded to hire a native speaker teacher. Another US-oriented school in Chisinau is the American Language Center (www.alc.md), though it tends to hire only local staff. Few foreigners would be able to survive on the low monthly stipends offered in Moldova.

A base in Central Asia allows you to explore this fascinating region, as **Anthony Cook** did when he was working in Almaty, Kazakhstan:

> ***I tended to try and save up a bit, then splurge on one or two longer trips each year. Travelling around Central Asia is quite the adventure. To mention just two of the 'stans': Kazakhstan itself has a unique multicultural history and awe-inspiring, dramatic landscapes, with wide regional variation (though you have to make a real effort to get to the good bits, because they're separated by vast stretches of nothingness and the transport infrastructure is not the best!). Uzbekistan has some of the world's most impressive Islamic architecture, plus the desert of Karakalpakstan in the west, dotted with ancient, deserted fortresses. The Uzbek people are an added bonus; they're every bit as warm and eccentric as the Kazakhs, and a lot chattier and more inclined to strike up a conversation with strangers. So you meet a lot of 'characters' when you visit their country. If I were to go back to the region, I'd definitely want to continue exploring – the list of intriguing destinations is quite long.***

In searching for a job, perhaps the best advice might be to limit your search to a couple of countries and thereafter do your research. A thorough understanding of the country, its culture and its regard for foreigners is absolutely essential. And be sure to check out the legality of any employment that you are thinking to engage in. As **William Kinsey** found out while working in Almaty, things are not always what they seem:

> ***Our school was raided by the police, who demanded our visas and claimed incorrect registration. Our boss/owner was useless and two of my fellow teachers were brought to the police station and had their apartment raided. Further, the boss asked us to lie on his behalf and say that we are not paid, rather we are only English consultants not accepting salary. I can only speculate, but I surmise it creates a tax escape for him.***

Given this, teachers are well advised to check with consulates rather than potential employers as to how legal working status is obtained. As laws change often, employers may not be lying to potential teachers, they may simply be out of date in their current thinking.

GEORGIA

Five years ago the Ministry of Education took the dramatic decision to fund a native English-speaker teaching programme called Teach and Learn with Georgia (TLG). Semester start dates fall in August/September and January/February. The programme offers foreigners the chance to teach in state schools throughout the country, as part of a cultural exchange programme. Airfares, homestay accommodation, medical insurance and a round-trip ticket for one vacation are all covered by the programme plus a modest stipend (see entry below). Full details are on the TLG website www.tlg.gov.ge.

Reviews of the programme on sites like www.gooverseas.com are generally favourable, like this one posted by a participant, while others focus on the disorganisation:

> ***Georgia has been a wonderful experience. The people are very friendly and welcoming. Most of the villages and schools are just excited that they have an English speaker and are very cooperative. Georgia has its share of discomforts: most volunteers are placed in smaller villages (mine has about 1,000 people); bathroom facilities are low tech, which means showers once a week and sometimes Turkish toilets; schools are limited in what materials they have, expect little to no technology used in classrooms. All of that said, the people more than make up for these minor discomforts! Everybody in my village talks to me when we meet. I've received three bouquets of flowers this week already and I got more apples and nuts than I could eat during the fall. The teachers in my school got some useful phrases translated and hung them in our coffee room. And it's always great to hear kids improve their reading and become more confident. The little boys I live with delight in using their***

English, like yelling from the bathroom 'I want toilet paper!' to saying 'Let's go!' as we leave the house. Even now they are hovering around, asking me what I'm doing. I would not trade my time in Georgia for anything.

The private sector is expanding quickly in the capital Tbilisi. A Georgia-specific business directory at www.city24.ge lists dozens of foreign language centres in the capital with optimistic names such as Future World and Classy Profile. Most of them are too small to be in a position to hire foreign teachers, but a few do, such as International House (www.ihtbilisi.ge/en/recruitment) and Lingua House One (see entry). A language camp organiser is Education & Training International (eti_sales@caucasus.net).

Georgia has now fallen into line with Europe by instigating a policy of allowing foreigners to stay for 90 days in 180 days. Those staying longer need to apply for a D1 (work) immigration visa from outside Georgia.

LIST OF EMPLOYERS

EDUCATION AND TRAINING INTERNATIONAL LTD
ETA Georgia, 4 Kuchishvili Street, Tbilisi
UK office: Burstow Road, London, SW20 8SX
+995 555 217 252 (Georgia); + 44 208 542 0646 (UK)
md@eti-georgia.ge
www.eti.uk.com

ETI is a Language and Business Skills Training Company with offices in Georgia, Azerbaijan and Kakhstan.

NUMBER OF TEACHERS: 5.

PREFERENCE OF NATIONALITY: None.

QUALIFICATIONS: Bachelor's degree or higher qualification essential for Azerbaijan and Kazakhstan, preferably in a teaching-related subject. CELTA qualifiation or equivalent essential. Minimum 3 years' teaching experience preferable; experience teaching exam courses, especially Cambridge, IELTS and TEFL desirable.

CONDITIONS OF EMPLOYMENT: 1-year contract. Approx. 100 class hours per rmonth any time between 8.30am and 9pm.

SALARY: $1,100–$1,800 gross depending on location. Some offices offer part-time hourly paid positions only. Less 20% for tax and contributions.

FACILITIES/SUPPORT: Teachers on full-time contracts are given a package of apartment plus utilities and internet, local medical insurance, visa and associated costs, retrun airline ticket to a hub airport, 15 days' paid holiday (plus public holidays) in addition to salary. Annual teacher training courses on a variety of topics, plus exam-specific training and the opportunity to be trained as a Cambridge speaking examiner.

RECRUITMENT: Via www.tefl.com, ETI website and local websites/contacts.

CONTACT: Pamela Kemsley-Dugladze, ManagingDirector.

LINGUA HOUSE ONE
68 I. Chubinaashvili St, Tbilisi
+995 595 502 957
linguahouse2005@gmail.com
www.linguahouse.ge

NUMBER OF TEACHERS: 5.

PREFERENCE OF NATIONALITY: British, American, Canadian, New Zealander.

QUALIFICATIONS: Diploma or Teachers' Training Certificate. School seeks to hire qualified, trained and experienced specialists.

CONDITIONS OF EMPLOYMENT: Minimum stay 6 months; can stay indefinitely. Flexible hours.

SALARY: Individual classes pay 15 lari an hour (net), group classes last an hour and a half and pay 20 lari.

FACILITIES/SUPPORT: No help with accommodation, but assistance given on submitting documents to obtain a work visa.

CONTACT: Nino Mgeladze, Director of Lingua House Tbilisi.

TEACH AND LEARN WITH GEORGIA (TLG)
1 Gmir Kursantta str, Tbilisi 0167
+995 322 200 220 ext. 4855
tlgadmin@tpdc.ge; tlbinbox@tpcd.ge; applications@tlg.gov.ge
www.tlg.gov.ge

NUMBER OF TEACHERS: 50+ for state schools, mostly in rural areas.

PREFERENCE OF NATIONALITY: British, American, Canadian, Australian, New Zealander, Irish and South African are preferred, but all native speakers will be considered. Since 2015, other languages, such as French and German, are also taught.

QUALIFICATIONS: Minimum 2 years of post-secondary education.

A TEFL qualification and teaching experience are not required. Must have criminal record check and medical test including HIV.

CONDITIONS OF EMPLOYMENT: All job placements are full-time positions. Most start in September. One or two semesters, renewable. Teaching schedules vary but are generally through daytime hours Monday–Friday.

SALARY: Volunteers are paid a monthly stipend of 750 lari per month. After taxes are withdrawn and the host family are paid 200 lari to cover food and utilities, only 400 lari are left for spending (about US$175). Free return airfare is paid upfront. Teachers who commit to a year-long contract receive an additional flight ticket equal in value to their tickets to and from Georgia.

FACILITIES/SUPPORT: Homestay accommodation provided. Visa guidance, airport collection, teacher orientation, etc. are provided.

RECRUITMENT: After initially registering on website, application enclosing photo and letter of motivation must be submitrted. Applicants are interviewed by videoconference.Deadline for September intake is 1 July.

AZERBAIJAN

Tucked away between Georgia, Iran and the Caspian Sea, the republic of Azerbaijan produces great oil wealth. Because of the capital, Baku's, key role in the production and distribution of oil and gas, language institutes have a lot of money to throw around in pursuit of the country's commitment to making English the second language, and have been offering more than comfortable salaries to teachers. Yet teacher retention is not very high, partly because of the hardships of living in Central Asia and because the employers have not provided enough pastoral support to new arrivals. Many teachers arrive in Baku with no idea how to do the job well or to adapt to the culture.

John Gahan had a head start since he had spent two years as a volunteer with the Peace Corps in Gumlag Village in the Oghuz Rayon of Azerbaijan before deciding to move to the big city:

While I was completing my last couple of months in my village for Peace Corps, a friend of mine and I decided to seek employment in Baku because we heard the salaries were good, and we felt the adjustment wouldn't be terribly difficult. I found out about English First, arranged an interview, taught a trial lesson to a large group of children and was offered a job. EF had me working immediately, since my visa from Peace Corps hadn't expired and EF arranged my work visa for me within that time. Having completed Peace Corps, I was expecting to roll into Baku and live a comfortable, lucrative life with all the cultural bases already covered. It didn't exactly happen that way because, as many people can attest, there's a big difference between volunteer and 'real' work. I had to make that adjustment rather quickly.

Thus far, the working conditions have been pleasant (well-equipped classrooms with whiteboards and computers and so on) and wages have been satisfactory for a single male on a modest budget. As long as my expenses haven't gotten out of hand, I've been able to save around a thousand dollars a month after student loan payments. I can count on one hand the number of times I've had to deal with behavioural problems, which were efficiently dealt with by the school. Nonetheless, the 'orientation period' at EF is essentially non-existent. Though I had two years of volunteer teaching in a village under my belt, I had no idea about the expectations in the classroom at EF, and I had not taught in a setting like this before. This made my first groups mediocre at best, and particularly scary towards the ends of the levels because I was in a panic that the paying students weren't prepared for their final tests. I was also unaware of what I needed to do to get tests effectively graded and student reports and certificates completed. At this point, however, those problems are water under the bridge, and I fully enjoy working here now. For my own work, help is always available if I ask for it.

When a group of students clicks, it's really wonderful, and the students are extremely grateful for what you do for them. The biggest issue with students here is getting them to think outside the box and discuss topics other than national meals and weddings. For most of them, they want English as a skill, so they can 'find a good job' or study abroad. Teaching here forces idealistic foreign teachers to face the reality of many places, namely that people wish to adopt a language ability from you, but that does not mean that they want to adopt ideas or culture from you. Any strong, independent-minded teacher who wants to save some money and be in a fascinating region can do well in Baku. It's not the liveliest city, but it is changing rapidly, with new buildings going up all the time.

Note that the Peace Corps no longer has a programme in Azerbaijan.

Several British and international companies recruit qualified teachers for Azerbaijan, such as Language Link Tashkent, which was advertising for native English-speaking teachers to begin September 2016, and stay for six, nine or 12 months. ETI Ltd (www.eti.uk.com) in London, Language Solutions (jobsoverseas@langsols.com; www.langsols.az), Teachaway, and Carfax Recruitment with an office in Baku all recruit teachers from time to time. One of Carfax's tutors working in Baku in 2014 blogged on their site:

After having graduated last summer, I began looking for a job which would offer me the opportunity to teach the subjects I love with a little adventure on the side! I chose to work in Baku, Azerbaijan, with Carfax Education because I knew little about the country, but had always been fascinated by the various cultures of the former Soviet empire, and I wanted to learn more about the former Soviet Republics. So far I have thoroughly enjoyed my time here and find the work very rewarding.

Carfax Baku has an office on the outskirts of the city, though I do most of my teaching at students' homes. This means using taxis to get between lessons – a daily battle with traffic and the frequent road closures caused by the president's convoy! Such time is not wasted, however, because they pepper my day with 15-minute Russian and Azeri lessons. Taxi drivers make great teachers and I now have a very colourful vocabulary.

For a capital city with 2 million people, Baku feels more like a large village. It really seems as if everyone knows each other. This has made making friends much easier than I expected. On top of this the city has a great selection of small coffee shops, bookshop cafés and old style tea houses in which to hang out. I'm truly glad of the opportunity to work in this part of the world. Between Russia and the Middle East lies a country defined by its proximity to both but with an intrinsic national identity and complex history. Luckily I have six more months here to explore it!

LIST OF EMPLOYERS

CARFAX PRIVATE TUTORS

25E Nobel Ave., White City, AZ1025 Baku; Head Office: 48 Langham Street, London W1W 7AY, UK

+995 12 488 1026

baku@carfax-education.com

http://carfax-baku.com/en

Offices also in Russia, Monaco and Dubai.

International private tutors to work in Baku, tutoring candidates for entrance to schools in the UK and Switzerland.

LINE-LEADER IN EDUCATION LANGUAGE CENTER

Shafayat Mehdiyev 83, 4th Floor, AZ 1141, Baku

+994 12 539 3396/97

info@bakuline.com

www.bakuline.com

NUMBER OF TEACHERS: 1.

PREFERENCE OF NATIONALITY: British, North American, Australian, and New Zealander.

QUALIFICATIONS: EFL/ESL certificate.

CONDITIONS OF EMPLOYMENT: 9-month contract from October. Schools open 9am–9pm, Monday to Saturday, 24 contact hours per week. Mainly adult students.

SALARY: $2,000 per month.

FACILITIES/SUPPORT: Modern facilities, teacher library, computer laboratory, guidance and support of academic coordinator, flights paid on completion of contract, paid holiday, orientation and ongoing seminars and development. Assistance given with finding flat (not shared). Medical insurance and visa provided.

RECRUITMENT: Applications through English First (EF) teacher recruitment in offices worldwide.

CONTACT: Lala Talishli, Director of Studies.

KAZAKHSTAN AND KYRGYZSTAN

Kazakhstan is another prospering Central Asian Republic where the demand for IELTS preparation continues to soar and the market among young learners is also expanding. Culturally, the country is changing away from the one that was referenced in the film *Borat* (full title: *Borat: Cultural Learnings of America for Make Benefit Glorious Nation of Kazakhstan*).Yet Kazakhstan has not enjoyed a very positive reputation amongst the ELT community, something which **Anthony Cook** thinks is undeserved.

Since obtaining his CELTA a few years ago, Anthony (originally from Australia) has had several contracts with Interpress-IH, which, on balance, he says is probably his favourite school, and Almaty is definitely one of his favourite places to live in.

I first went to KZ to work for Interpress IH the year after Borat *was released, with no specific expectations except that it probably wouldn't be quite what Sacha Baron Cohen had depicted. I know the school often has trouble enticing teachers to Kazakhstan, so I'd like to say why I think they're worth considering as employers. There's no such thing as a perfect language school in this world, of course, but I really enjoyed working there and hope I might have the chance to go back one of these days.*

Overall, the hours are pretty good, and it's a relief to discover that, unlike in some other countries, there are no Kazakhstani people mad enough to request lessons at 7.30 in the morning! It can be a bit scary for a teacher who has never taught exam prep before to be thrown in at the deep end, but the 'teachers' room culture' is generally very good, with people around who are willing to help you get your head around unfamiliar material.

The students in KZ are probably the best I've taught anywhere. They're lively and talkative, and noticeably more 'worldly' than students in other ex-Soviet republics I've worked in. That's probably because KZ was historically a dumping ground for the USSR's unwanted, from North Koreans to Azeris and everyone in between, so now it's a relatively multicultural place, and the people there like it that way. Kazakhstani students are also keen on the more technical sides of learning a language – they want to master the grammar of English, because they see a connection between speaking correctly and getting the respect of those they speak to. They're inclined to bond well with classmates and, if you're a capable teacher, they'll be grateful for your presence in the classroom and you'll feel their loyalty. Also, in contrast to some Asian countries, in KZ it's considered acceptable and even good to be outspoken, so you generally don't have to struggle to wring opinions out of your students (excluding the occasional surly teenager, of course!). They are also generally quite sociable, and the culture doesn't have the 'barriers' between teacher and student that limit out-of-classroom interaction elsewhere. So it's not difficult to hang out with the locals and make some friends if you want to.

LOUISE WHEELER

With a Masters in TEFL and eight years of teaching experience, Louise Wheeler is also happily working in Almaty, at the Kazakh-British Technical University with which she had had previous contact through her university:

Whilst it is not essential for foreign staff, it can help to bear in mind that personal connections are often important for employment in Kazakhstani society. Therefore, it can help for potential international applicants to at least make a good impression on a personal level, as well as professionally. My job at the university involves teaching English to students between the ages of 17 and 22 in General, Academic, Business and Professional English aimed at supporting them in their study of Business, Oil and Gas, Chemical Engineering or IT subjects in English. I really enjoy working with KBTU students. Like many Kazakhstani students they are enthusiastic, creative, active and willing to share their opinions in class. We are lucky here, in as far as the students are generally pre-intermediate level and above, but the level can be much lower in less prestigious institutions and as you move outside the main cities of Almaty and Astana. The only problem I have experienced with Kazakhstani learners is in motivating them to do independent work out of class. Many have no experience of being asked to work independently prior to university and unfortunately, it can be a challenge to combat certain practices such as plagiarism and cheating in written work.

The wages are definitely good in comparison with many local wages and even with many other organisations employing foreigners in Kazakhstan. I was able to save money and maintain a comfortable quality of life. The thing I love about teaching in Kazakhstan is the 'can do' attitude and enthusiasm to try new things. My colleagues and managers have always been open to new ideas and are generally supportive of teachers who want to implement new systems and projects. It's a fantastic and challenging environment in which to develop as a teacher.

In Almaty we are lucky to have the stunning Alatau mountain range just 15 minutes away by bus, so it is easy to get out to mountains for walking and picnicking in the summer and skiing and skating in the winter. In town there are lots of parks in the centre, which are especially good if you enjoy running. There is a good selection of restaurants and bars in the city too. I personally enjoy the chance to explore different parts of this varied and multicultural city, especially the bazaars. In addition, I have found it a very rewarding experience to learn some Kazakh and Russian. This really helps you to get under the skin of Kazakhstan's culture and society.

Winters in Almaty can seem very long, dark and cold at times. Moreover, Christmas is not celebrated and for our university the 25th is a normal working day. For this reason, my first Christmas period spent in Kazakhstan was a bit of a low point. However, the next year I organised to take a trip home at this time (as most of the expat community do). On the other hand, the Kazakh spring festival of Nawrus, in late March, is a wonderful time. Normally people have a week off and there are lots of cultural events happening around the city and beyond. It is a great chance to see traditional yurts, people in national costumes, try Kazakh speciality foods, watch traditional games and listen to folk music. Moreover, it's a time when you are most likely to experience the much celebrated 'Kazakh hospitality', with local colleagues and friends keen to invite you to their homes. Kazakhstan remains an exciting, multicultural, friendly and fascinating place to live and work.

Visas and work permits need to be sorted out before arriving in Kazakhstan but the school should handle all or most of the paperwork. One thing that may present an obstacle is the relative scarcity of Kazakh embassies and consulates around the world, and their possible lack of cooperativeness. The one in London has a dreadful reputation: it randomly refused to renew one returning teacher's visa, without offering any explanation, and the subsequent appeal process dragged on for weeks. Anthony Cook has had better luck applying in Seoul and Bangkok.

Louise Wheeler confirms that the process can cause difficulties:

> ***The visa must be applied for on your behalf through the organisation you work for. You will be asked to submit notarised, apostilled copies of degrees, masters degrees and teaching certificates (with transcripts), police record checks, a medical certificate and three years of references (stamped by HR departments or equivalent). This process can be very time consuming – up to two years in my experience – and be prepared for the Ministry to change its requirements or processes without warning.***
>
> ***After being issued with a work permit and visa you are also required to get a blood test for HIV/AIDS. However, whilst your application for a work visa is being processed, your employer may make arrangements for you to stay under the terms of a business visa. This kind of visa is valid for three months, provided you leave the country every 30 days.***

A large English language school in Reading, England with multiple links to Kazakhstan recently opened a school in Almaty for which it was hiring native speaker teachers to start September 2015. The offered salary was 260,000 tenge plus a housing allowance to cover a studio flat and other benefits (www.eurospeak.kz). Try also Study Innovations Language Schools (www.studyinn.kz) in Almaty, Astana, Karaganda, Shymkent and Kostanay.

More opportunities will develop in mountainous Kyrgyzstan over the coming years. The Government of the Kyrgyz Republic has determined that English will play an important role in education to support the transition to a market economy, and to that end has been deploying Peace Corps TEFL volunteers (among others) in secondary schools since 1993.

LIST OF EMPLOYERS

KAZAKHSTAN

INTERPRESS-INTERNATIONAL HOUSE – ALMATY

InterPress-International House, Keremet 7, Almaty 050040

+7 727 315 7986

recruit@ihkazakhstan.com

www.interpress.kz

Largest English language school in the country with 7 branches in Almaty, 2 each in Astana and Karaganda, and 1 in Shymkent.

NUMBER OF TEACHERS: About 60 foreign and local teachers employed, 35–40 new ones taken on each year.

PREFERENCE OF NATIONALITY: Native English speakers from UK, USA, Ireland, Canada, Australia.

QUALIFICATIONS: Cambridge CELTA, IHC, Trinity TESOL, MA in TESOL as a minimum and at least 1 year of post-qualification teaching experience preferred. Young Learners qualification and experience in teaching for exam preparation (IELTS and TOEFL) are preferable.

CONDITIONS OF EMPLOYMENT: 9 or 12-month contracts from September/October. Teaching load 120 hours (or 100 teaching hours) monthly plus 8 hours per month set aside for teachers' meetings, workshops and standby hours.

SALARY: 200,000–240,000 tenge net ($1,000–$1,250) in Almaty, and 220,000–260,000 tenge ($1,150–$1,400) in Astana, depending on qualifications and experience. Overtime hourly rates paid after 1,080 contracted hours. Bonus paid on completion of contract amounting to 150 tenge per hour taught (e.g. could be total of 216,000 tenge for 12-month contract). Paid holidays: 20 days in 12 months, 15 days in 9 months. Free survival Russian course.

FACILITIES/SUPPORT: Airfare allowance of 120,000 tenge if from Europe, 180,000 tenge if from North America or Australia.

Free shared accommodation, all bills paid by the school (excluding long-distance telephone calls, cable TV and internet) or accommodation reimbursement. Airfare allowance. The school assists and covers the costs of a multiple-entry 1-year work visa. Limited health care and 24-hour hotline emergency assistance. Opportunities for promotion and transfer in one of the world's leading educational organisations.

RECRUITMENT: Direct applications to the school and through IHWO Recruitment Services (www.ihworld.com) and online advertising. Phone/Skype interviews essential.

CONTACT: Yelena Olshanskaya, Recruitment Manager (yelena.ih@gmail.com).

LANGUAGE LINK KAZAKHSTAN
1a Kulmanova St, Atyrau 060002
+7 7122 272907
jobs@languagelink.ru
www.jobs.languagelink.ru

QUALIFICATIONS: Degree and CELTA or equivalent required.

CONDITIONS OF EMPLOYMENT: Similar to Language Link Russia (entry in Russia chapter).

SALARY: US$2,000 net per month.

CONTACT: Amangali Utaleyev (utaleyev@gmail.com).

KYRGYZSTAN

CALLAN SCHOOL
49a Suumbaeva Street, Bishkek 720000
+996 770 890405
callanschool@mail.ru
www.kallan.on.kg

NUMBER OF TEACHERS: 10 for work in English-language conversation clubs and workplace lessons.

PREFERENCE OF NATIONALITY: American or British.

QUALIFICATIONS: Native speakers of English only, though relevant background would be appreciated.

CONDITIONS OF EMPLOYMENT: 3 months to a year. Variable number of lessons that last 85 minutes.

SALARY: $6 per lesson. Out-of-office lessons pay $8. Total earned is $300-$700 per month depending on number of hours worked (which is more than enough to live in Kyrgyzstan). Tax is about $8 per month.

FACILITIES/SUPPORT: Free homestay accommodation; private room in family home. Assistance given in obtaining a work permit, which will cost the teacher $150 (if they are staying for a year). Opportunities to join excursions organised by Callan School, e.g. Saturday horse treks for picnics and barbecues.

RECRUITMENT: Interviews normally done through Skype.

CONTACT: Sabira Soorbekova, Senior Manager.

LONDON SCHOOL OF LANGUAGES AND CULTURES
Baitik Baatyr 39, Bishkek 720005
+996 312 544474/545430
info@londonschool.kg
www.londonschool.kg; http://thelondonschool.org/en/tefl-jobs.php

NUMBER OF TEACHERS: 8.

PREFERENCE OF NATIONALITY: American and British native English speakers.

QUALIFICATIONS: Degree, CELTA and at least 1 year's teaching experience. Teachers without experience also would be considered. Must be aged under 40.

CONDITIONS OF EMPLOYMENT: Minimum 6 months starting all year round. 22 hours per week, 5 hours per day, 4 days a week plus 1-hour interview with new students four times a month. Also has volunteering programme, teaching English to village children.

SALARY: From $650 to $800 a month with free accommodation and monthly cultural excursions within the country all year round.

FACILITIES/SUPPORT: Free room provided plus all accommodation expenses. Help given with work permits for which teachers must have CELTA certificate and 2 references from previous teaching jobs.

RECRUITMENT: Online application. Teachers hired on basis of CV and references.

MIDDLE EAST

Oil wealth has meant that many of the countries of the Middle East have long been able to afford to attract the best teachers with superior qualifications and extensive experience. Most employers can afford to hire experienced professionals and there are few opportunities for newcomers to the profession. MENA, the common acronym for the Middle East and North Africa, is a region with a lot of recruitment activity. However, the tangled web of explosive conflicts throughout the Middle East has caused many teachers to look elsewhere. Multiple wars have undoubtedly destabilised the area and fanned the flames of Islamic distrust of the West. In fact some radicalised groups are opposed to the teaching of English.

With the tragic destruction of Syria, ongoing civil war in Yemen and increasing numbers of suicide bombings orchestrated by so-called Islamic State, some countries have been rendered completely off-limits. Ongoing tensions between Israelis and Palestinians and an escalation of anti-western sentiment have resulted in many prospective teachers being in fear for their personal security.

Even once peaceful Turkey, where thousands of native English-speaking teachers find work, has been destabilised by the failed coup of 2016. All but a fraction of the population identifies itself as Muslim, yet Turkey does not fit comfortably into a chapter on the Middle East. What is more, despite Turkey's desire to join the EU, its membership of the community of Europe is far from imminent. But whatever its geographical classification, Turkey is a very important country for EFL teachers, whatever their background, and is treated at length later in this chapter.

The wealthy countries of Saudi Arabia, Qatar, Oman and the Gulf states generally employ teachers with advanced qualifications. Higher qualifications attract a premium on salaries; for example, a teacher with a BA might earn a package (salary, housing, transport) worth £2,400 a month, whereas someone with an MA will be rewarded with £3,000 a month. Other Middle Eastern countries without oil wealth, such as Jordan and Lebanon, may have more casual opportunities. Anyone interested in teaching English to the Palestinians scattered throughout the Arab world is likely to be working on a voluntary basis or for accommodation and a local stipend, rather than for expatriate salaries. Institutes of higher education throughout the region, especially those training engineers, pilots or other professionals, routinely incorporate intensive English language programmes into the courses at Vocational, BA and MA level. Many offer a Preparatory Year Programme (PYP) or foundation year that involves a lot of English study. These institutes employ a staggering number of native speaker teachers.

Teachers who sign contracts in a strict Islamic country should be aware of what they are letting themselves in for. People usually spend a year or two teaching in Saudi Arabia to make some money or are students of Arab culture, rather than because they enjoy the lifestyle. When the amount of money accumulating back home is the principal or only motivation, morale can degenerate. The situation can be especially discouraging for women. Yet not everyone is gasping to get home to freely available alcohol, etc. A certain percentage of teachers are recruited locally from a stable expatriate community. Demand for native English-speaker teachers continues strong in Saudi Arabia, mainly due to the opening of new colleges and universities, both in the public and private sector, some of which employ scores of ESL teachers and lecturers. Note that many of them accept candidates from appointed recruitment agencies or online applications. A list of institutes of higher education can be found at www.university-directory.eu.

Middle Eastern language departments are also more likely to recruit non-native English speakers, specifically well-heeled teachers with pristine qualifications. **Ahad Shahbaz**, CEO of Interlink Language Center, asks: '*If a non-native speaker is highly educated, has earned his credentials from the Harvards of ESL teacher training institutions, and has near-native and at times superior proficiency and eloquence in the language, should we not be hiring him or her?*'

FINDING A JOB

Unless you are more or less resident in the Middle East, it is essential in most cases to fix up a job in advance. Casual teaching is not a possibility in most countries for a number of reasons, including the difficulty of getting visas, the prohibitively high cost of staying without working and the whole tradition of hiring teachers. There are a few countries that can be entered on a tourist visa (e.g. Qatar and the United Arab Emirates) if you want to inspect potential employers, but this would be an expensive exercise. Visa difficulties vary from country to country. In Jordan, for example, schools that would like to hire foreign teachers are often put off by the cost of securing a work permit and paying the attendant lawyers' fees.

As always, it is worth checking with the British Council office in the country that interests you. The British Council has teaching centres in Bahrain (Manama), Jordan (Amman), Oman (Muscat), Occupied Palestinian Territories (Jerusalem and Ramallah), Qatar (Doha), Saudi Arabia (Riyadh, Jeddah and Al-Khobar), Kuwait and the United Arab Emirates (Abu Dhabi, Dubai, and Sharjah). The Council carries out teacher recruitment for MENA (Middle East and North Africa) centrally, with a deadline of 21 March and interviews about a month after that (see entry). As with major ELT organisations, the British Council has a sizeable presence at the Recruitment section of the annual TESOL Arabia conference held every March (www.tesolarabia.co).

American teachers should investigate the US-sponsored Regional English Language Offices, some of which are involved with delivering English-language courses. The RELO in Bahrain is also responsible for Kuwait, Yemen, Qatar, UAE and Oman; and Saudi Arabia comes into the orbit of the RELO in Cairo. The RELO in Amman delivers English-language courses through its American Language Center that employs some native English-speaking teachers (info@alc.edu.jo) and organises language exchange events every Wednesday afternoon.

America-Mideast Educational & Training Services or Amideast is a private, non-profit, non-government organisation with headquarters in Washington DC, which provides English-language test preparation and other professional training through its network of operations throughout the Middle East (and North Africa). Recruitment of teachers is done by the individual centres, linked from www.amideast.org.

The usual suspects are active in the region. International House has a big operation in Dhahran in Saudi Arabia, one in Iran, two in Lebanon, one in Qatar, one in Syria and one in Oman. Berlitz has schools in Bahrain, Beirut, Oman, Qatar, UAE and others.

In Saudi Arabia and other strict Islamic countries, jobs are advertised by gender. Males probably have the advantage because there are openings for them in military academies, aeronautical colleges, etc. But female-only institutions are on the increase and at the time of writing the Middle East recruiter m2r Global was advertising multiple positions for female ESL teachers with schools, vocational colleges and universities in Mecca, Al-Khobar and Unaizah. The remuneration promised to the most highly qualified was well over $50,000 plus free housing, flights, visas and so on. But in some respects, women continue to be treated as second-class citizens since some adverts firmly warn: '*A female CANNOT sponsor her family*'.

Job adverts regularly appear on websites such as www.tefl.com, www.eslcafe.com and www.esl101.com, with a preponderance of vacancies being in Saudi Arabia. The site www.seekteachers.com acts as an employment agency for Middle Eastern employers; enquiries about advertised posts in Saudi, Bahrain, etc. can be sent to zayd@SeekTeachers.com. The largest display ads in the British educational press (in print) are quite often for Middle East vacancies, many placed by recruitment agencies on behalf of high-spending Saudi clients. A requirement often mentioned in job details is experience of the Middle East, in acknowledgment of the culture shock that many foreigners encounter in adapting to life under Islam. It is also worth checking classified jobs in education in regional newspapers and websites such as the *Khaleej Times* (www.khaleejtimes.com) from the UAE.

RECRUITMENT AGENCIES

In theory, being hired by an established recruitment agency in your own country should offer some protection against problems. However, it can be the case that people working on commission may say anything to reach their recruitment targets, and will shamelessly exaggerate conditions, such as the distance from accommodation compound to workplace or the staff turnover rate. In an ideal world, you would be able to talk to your prospective employer directly or make contact with other staff members, but in practice, agencies are seldom able to put new teachers in touch with anyone on-site. Check the fine print of any contract, looking for a get-out clause for the employer, such as '*the parent company may amend or re-issue benefits, policies and procedures pertaining to the better conduct of its business*'. Such a contract means nothing because the employer reserves the right to change whatever they like.

A typical agency advert for corporate language instructors for the Middle East might read: '*Client seeks applications from male instructors for its corporate training programmes in the petrochemicals, utilities and heavy industries sectors. We can consider UK, Canadian, American, Irish, New Zealander, South African, Egyptian, Jordanian and Filipino nationals. Applied language practice is more important than descriptive language or grammar-bound approaches to language teaching. Applications from enthusiastic candidates who are interested in multimedia are especially welcome. We have projects available in several cities.*'

Reputable agencies to check out include Teachaway (www.teachaway.com), which at the time of writing was recruiting licensed teachers for many positions in Abu Dhabi, among others; the UK-based m2r Global (see entry); Footprints Recruiting (UAE and Kuwait); www.tefl.org.uk; English Today Recruitment (www.englishrecruitment.com); In Advance Recruitment (www.inadvance.uk.com); Red Chair Recruitment in Ireland (www.redchairrecuritment.ie) and many others.

CONDITIONS OF WORK

Many teachers complain about the low standards achieved by students due to lack of motivation, and say that it is difficult to be a serious teacher in many Middle Eastern classrooms. Others take a less dim view, including **Rufus Vaughan Spruce**:

> ***It's absolutely not a universal truth and presents a very unfair and overly negative view of teaching in the region. When recruiting in the Gulf I usually sought out teachers a couple of years off a CELTA who still had enthusiasm and understood they had things to learn (and wanted to learn!), rather than the jaded older types.***

LEISURE TIME

Most teachers live in foreigners' compounds provided by their employers; these are often well provided with sports facilities such as tennis courts and swimming pools. In some locations, such as Jubail in Saudi Arabia, water sports are a popular diversion. Some describe expat life in the Middle East as a false paradise.

The principal pastimes are barbecues, reading out-of-date copies of the *International New York Times*, playing on computers (which are cheaply available), home-brewing to get round the alcohol ban (Saudi Arabia and Kuwait are completely dry states), and complaining about the terrific heat. Others try to learn Arabic and make local friends, always taking care not to offend against local sensibilities. The constraints of living under Islam are well known. For example, in some countries anyone found eating, drinking or smoking in a public place during the month of Ramadan could face a jail sentence, large fine and/or deportation. Teachers may be expected to work very unsocial hours during Ramadan, i.e. starting class at sunset. Ramadan lasts 30 days and in 2017 will start on 27 May.

LIST OF EMPLOYERS

BRITISH COUNCIL – MENA

MENA-TeacherRecruitment@ae.britishcouncil.org

www.britishcouncil.org/jobs/careers/english

The British Council – Middle and Near East, and North Africa has teaching centres in Bahrain, Iraq, Kurdistan, Kuwait, Oman, Qatar, Saudi Arabia, United Arab Emirates, Occupied Palestinian Territories and Jordan (plus Morocco, Tunisia and Egypt in North Africa).

NUMBER OF TEACHERS: Fluctuating vacancies across the region, with a considerable number in Saudi Arabia (ksa.recruit@sa.britishcouncil.org).

PREFERENCE OF NATIONALITY: Most countries will accept applications from teachers across the globe providing they have the required qualifications and a high level of English, if English isn't their first language. Exceptions to this are stated in individual post information.

QUALIFICATIONS: Minimum CELTA or Trinity Cert plus 2 years' full-time (1,600 hours) ELT experience, for hourly teaching. DELTA or Trinity Diploma may be needed for more senior posts. Maximum age 60.

CONDITIONS OF EMPLOYMENT: Most contracts start 1 September and are for 2 years.

FACILITIES/SUPPORT: Accommodation arranged in some countries plus medical insurance.

RECRUITMENT: Batch recruitment via British Council Recruitment Unit in Dubai. Deadline is mid-March; interviews in April. Recruitment also takes place at TESOL Arabia conference in March and IATEFL Jobs Market in April each year.

CONTACT: Ms Jalpa Trivedi (MENA-TeacherRecruitment@ae.britishcouncil.org).

ENGLISH TODAY RECRUITMENT

Arabian Street, Riyadh, Saudi Arabia

+966 758 584 999

HR@englishrecruitment.com

www.englishrecruitment.com

NUMBER OF TEACHERS: About 60 teachers per year each for Saudi Arabia, UAE and Bahrain.

PREFERENCE OF NATIONALITY: Preference given to British and American teachers. Must be native speakers.

QUALIFICATIONS: Teaching, Linguistics is preferred. BA in TESOL, Language Education or English is acceptable, or BA in a related field plus teaching certification such as TESOL, TEFL, CELTA, DELTA or similar from an accredited university or institute.

CONDITIONS OF EMPLOYMENT: 1- or 2-year contracts. 24 hours per week.

SALARY: $3,000–$4,500 (full package) depending on qualifications and experience.

FACILITIES/SUPPORT: Agency sends visa papers and contract to the teacher's home country so they can submit them to the relevant embassy. Air tickets are provided free. Suggestions made on the best places to live.

RECRUITMENT: Interviews by Skype are recorded and passed to clients. Sometimes schedule walk-in interviews in UK and US.

CONTACT: Imran Mureed, Recruitment Director (imranmureed007@gmail.com).

---

m2r EDUCATION

24 Cheapside, Wakefield, West Yorkshire WF1 2TF

+44 1924 201973

info@m2rglobal.com; charlotte@m2rglobal.com

www.m2rglobal.com

Global recruitment consultancy.

NUMBER OF TEACHERS: 50 per year, sent to various organisations and employers in the Gulf Cooperation Council (GCC) region, i.e. Bahrain, Kuwait, Saudi and the UAE.

PREFERENCE OF NATIONALITY: Native speakers of English only.

QUALIFICATIONS: Minimum BA degree, ideally in English Language, recognised ESL qualification and 1-year's experience. Overseas experience is preferred also.

CONDITIONS OF EMPLOYMENT: Minimum 1-year contract, renewable. 40 hours per week, though number of contact hours varies.

SALARY: Minimum $30,000 plus benefits such as housing and flights. Saudi salaries up to $42,000 tax-free.

RECRUITMENT: Video or telephone interview can be arranged if face-to-face interview in Yorkshire is not possible.

CONTACT: Charlotte Watson, Recruitment Account Manager, or Mr Munir Mamujee, Managing Director (munir@m2rglobal.com).

MIDDLE EAST JOBS

28 Pipers House, Manor Row, Bradford BD1 4QU

+44 7446 814735 (mob); +44 1274 9250938

info@middleeastjobs.org.uk

http://meastjobs.com

NUMBER OF TEACHERS: 200+ for positions around the Middle East, especially Saudi Arabia.

PREFERENCE OF NATIONALITY: None.

QUALIFICATIONS: Degree plus CELTA or 120-hour TEFL qualification. Most schools accept teachers with 2 years' experience.

CONDITIONS OF EMPLOYMENT: 1-year renewable contract. 20 teaching hours a week plus 20 hours of preparation.

SALARY: Depends on teachers' experience and qualifications. Salaries (e.g. $28,000–$50,000 per year) are paid tax-free.

FACILITIES/SUPPORT: Housing is provided. Help given with visa application process. Employers often provide many perks, such as free airfare.

RECRUITMENT: CV, copies of credentials, transcripts/diploma, EFL certificate and passport, plus 2 references, to be sent to the recruiter at the email address above. Skype or face-to-face interview.

CONTACT: Ambereen Hayat, Director.

RED CHAIR RECRUITMENT

91 New Street, Killarney, County Kerry, Ireland

+353 64 66 22 007

Adrien.king@redchairrecruitment.ie

www.redchairrecruitment.ie

Described as a 'boutique recruitment agency' based in Ireland, Red Chair recruits for Saudi Arabia, Oman, Kuwait and Bahrain, as well as countries in Asia.

NUMBER OF TEACHERS: 50+ worldwide.

PREFERENCE OF NATIONALITY: USA, Canada, UK, Ireland, New Zealand, South Africa and Australia only. Some employers want extensive experience, e.g. 7 years for an engineering college in Muscat, Oman.

QUALIFICATIONS: Degree in discipline related to English or Education is highly sought after. MA or above often required.

CONDITIONS OF EMPLOYMENT: 1- or 2-year contracts. Usually 40 hour weeks with 20–25 classroom contact teaching hours.

SALARY: Varies according to qualifications, experience and clients' budgets.

RECRUITMENT: Interviews by Skype.

CONTACT: Adrien King, Director.

AFGHANISTAN

Afghanistan is unlikely to be a destination that any sane teacher would contemplate at present. Longstanding government advisories advising against all but essential travel remain in place. Security fears are higher than ever in Kabul, where just a few days before updating this chapter, the American University of Afghanistan was attacked by gunmen who killed 13 people (24 August, 2016). Not long before that, two lecturers, an American and an Australian, were kidnapped. The only private, non-profit, co-educational university in the country, The American University, has about 1,700 students, many of them studying English alongside their other courses. The university was advertising early in 2016 for native English instructors to work in its Professional Development Institute (jobs@auaf.edu.af). However, the fate of the university was not known at the time of writing. For interest, this account of working in Afghanistan several years ago, from American Tom Clark, is included.

TOM CLARK

While teaching in Kuwait, Tom Clark saw an advert on Dave's ESL Cafe that he followed up later. It turned out that the American University in Kabul was desperate to get teachers in place for a summer project funded by USAID. Since the US government controlled the programme, his visa was sorted out quickly. According to Tom, you could get a lot of stories about the funding and where it was going and how it got disbursed … It wasn't so much red tape as corruption, but that is everywhere in Afghanistan. The job was teaching at the university prep programme, plus he was doing extra work for the UN and a human rights organisation. Tom describes the job.

The contract with the university was the best I have had in the ESL world. It paid $5,000 a month with danger pay and other bonuses. It was better than Saudi. It offered holiday pay, housing, transportation, laptop, cell phone, we could fly on UN planes, etc. We stayed in a guesthouse with a beautiful garden, had security guards 24/7 and were fenced in, and we had electricity more than four hours a day. Our money went a long way, as the cost of living was so low there and the American dollar was welcome. Transferring money in and out was not easy, nor setting up bank accounts. Security was a problem, as we were not free to travel around or mix with the locals. If an aid worker was killed, we would be on lock-down/house arrest for weeks at a time. Sometimes we wore bulletproof vests, were always in the presence of security guards, had to be very careful associating with local people and would have to come up with colourful stories to get out and about into the 'field'.

The workplace was quite unorganised and a lot of people were disgruntled. We wanted to teach different subjects, but things were always censored there. My fellow teachers were of a higher calibre than I was used to. All had masters in specialised areas and

I had the feeling they all worked for organisations they did not mention on their CVs. They spoke multiple languages and seemed to have alternative agendas other than just teaching. Many of them had prior links to the State Department. It was an odd assortment at best.

The pupils were the cream of the crop. They were not from typical backgrounds, they were from high-ranking military, intelligence and diplomatic families. Occupying our spare time was difficult since we always had to get permission to go anywhere, unless we hid under the radar. There were a handful of 'safe' establishments for foreigners, but after a while you got bored with those and had to find a way to entertain yourself. If it were not for the money, it would be quite hard to stay and live there, unless you really liked reading books all the time. For a journalist, spy or a madman, Afghanistan was a great place at that time.

Employment information about the university can be found at www.auaf.edu.af, where current openings for native-speaking English instructors are listed. Several public universities in the Afghan capital are in the process of transitioning to teaching in English as part of an Afghan Ministry of Higher Education and British Council agreement concluded in October 2013. Most advertised positions are with government agencies and NGOs such as ACBAR in Herat (Agency Coordinating Body for Afghan Relief & Development) at www.acbar.org. For example, a Canadian charity was recently seeking fluent English speakers with teaching experience to take after-school classes of girls at a community school in Kabul (Recruitment-Kabul@CW4WAfghan.ca).

IRAQ

Iraq is probably not high on the list of must-see destinations for many TEFL teachers, but **Jamie Pinder** has no complaints about his ongoing teaching contracts in Iraq. He says he has been lucky enough to have had three jobs with oil and gas companies based on camps, two in Basra through a recruiter and one in Iraqi Kurdistan, which was a direct hire. Relaxation after work consists largely of eating, watching TV and going to the gym:

> ***After a quick chat and submitting an updated CV, I was offered the job. With many of these jobs it's about knowing people and, of course, experience in oil and gas and the Middle East helps a lot. I have already worked in Libya, Kuwait, Qatar, Jordan and KSA, so I had the experience. I also have a TEFL and CELTA. Overall, Iraq was relatively easy to get the paperwork done, but the immigration on arrival at Basra was another matter. Lots of patience was needed, as opposed to arriving in Erbil, Kurdistan, where UK passport holders get a visa on arrival which is converted into residency.***
>
> ***All three were rotational jobs, working 28 days on, 28 days off. When you're at work, you really DO work, and the highlight is you get to fly home for four weeks off. At all three gigs, accommodation and three meals a day were provided. Rooms varied from old rusty containers to modern, hotel-style rooms. Wages are well below those earned by the technical staff but still some of the best around for TEFL. No problem saving money as you spend nothing, though the temptation to spend when you go home is strong. Typical of the Gulf, some students had very low educational levels and struggled to read and write in their own language. Those who were on higher level courses were excellent and keen to learn as it was very important for their work and their future. Recently we've been doing some work in the local community in Kurdistan which has been very interesting, with young people aged 18–25 trying to learn a few words of English.***

ISRAEL

Because of the large number of English-speaking Jews who have settled in Israel from the USA, South Africa, etc., many native speakers of English are employed in the state education system and there is little active recruitment of foreign teachers. There are a number of private language schools, for example about 11 Wall Street English centres (applications to hrcv@wsi.co.il) and nine Berlitz schools. The Wall Street branch in Nazareth is the first to open in the Arab sector. The British Council (www.britishcouncil.org.il) maintains a presence in Israel but does not have a teaching centre. Some English teaching opportunities are available to Jewish candidates, for instance at the summer camp (Kefiyada) run in conjunction with Berlitz which is partnered with the Jewish Agency.

Employers normally stipulate that applicants must have a work permit for Israel before they can be considered. Sorting out the red tape for living in Israel is difficult unless you speak fluent Hebrew. Chances are improved if you are in a relationship with an Israeli or Jewish foreigner.

TOM BALFOUR

Tom Balfour discovered there were openings in Israel, shortly after reacquainting himself with a girl he knew in Tel Aviv.

I sent emails with my CV to various English schools, mostly branches of the two big companies Berlitz and Wall Street, explaining my situation – that I would be leaving Israel in a week to return to England for my summer job, but that I wanted to come back in September and teach English in Tel Aviv. Most of the schools simply sent me a reply saying 'get back to us when you return' but Wall Street in Tel Aviv invited me for an interview. In the interview I was asked various questions about teaching, and then the director pretended to be a low-level student and asked me to explain various words to her. When she asked me what a model was, I said 'Naomi Campbell, Kate Moss' and then got up and did a pretend catwalk round the room. Although I'm sure that my qualifications helped, I think that might be what got me the job: knowing how to keep explanations simple, and being prepared to look silly if it helped. She told me that if I came back I would be offered a contract.

I had heard (from this book in fact!) that with the high number of native English-speaking immigrants in Israel there wasn't really a market for English teachers. I think, however, that my Trinity qualification and my planned work at the summer school made me stand out from the native candidates, some of whom were hoping for a job simply on the strength of being English speakers.

Israel is an amazing country and Tel Aviv is a great, cosmopolitan city with a good beach and fantastic nightlife.

PALESTINE

Education, like all aspects of life, is very difficult for many Palestinians in the West Bank and Gaza. Although the demand is there, the circumstances do not allow the vast majority of Palestinians to achieve their ambition. The British Council in Palestinian Territories operates English language centres in Jerusalem and Ramallah, and occasionally runs adult and children's courses in other parts of the West Bank and Gaza (www.britishcouncil.ps). The Council runs an interesting Teacher Apprenticeship Scheme which sponsors candidates who want to teach for the Council in Palestine to do the CELTA course in Amman or Cairo by paying half the expenses upfront and lending the other half; intakes are in March/April or September/October.

The US non-profit organisation Amideast is also active in the same range of towns (www.amideast.org/west-bank-gaza). In 2015 it taught nearly 750 students from refugee camps in Ramallah at its annual Camp Discovery. Amideast partners with the UNRWA (United Nations Relief & Works Agency for Palestine) to host a 13-day camp in July at the Gaza Training Centre, where children can improve their English language skills by interacting with native-speaking interns. Amideast also employs qualified teachers for their Ramallah and Jerusalem offices. Advertised posts in 2016 came with a monthly salary of $1,100 for 96 teaching hours, but with no accommodation or travel perks.

The charity UNIPAL (Educational Exchange with Palestinians – see entry) operates an educational and cultural exchange with Palestinian communities. Another charity that arranges for English tutors to spend the summer in Nablus or nearby refugee camps for Palestinians is Project Hope (see entry). Palestinian schools struggle on and anyone who supports their cause might be prepared to become a volunteer teacher. Senior people who can set up programmes would be especially welcome.

LIST OF EMPLOYERS

PROJECT HOPE (Humanitarian Opportunities for Peace and Education)
00970 29 An-Najah, Al Qadim St, Nablus
+970 9233 7077
recruiter@projecthope.ps; nablus@projecthope.ps
www.projecthope.ps

Canadian-registered charity. Non-profit volunteer organisation that supports children denied access to basic services in the refugee camps and villages of the Nablus region of the Northern West Bank.

NUMBER OF VOLUNTEER TEACHERS: 15–30 for the largest provider of free English classes in the West Bank (1,000 students enrolled per month).

PREFERENCE OF NATIONALITY: None.

QUALIFICATIONS: Teachers must have a TEFL qualification or teaching experience along with experience of working with groups of children and young people. Minimum age 21.

CONDITIONS OF EMPLOYMENT: 5 weeks to 1 year, 20–25 hours of teaching a week, with 2 full days off.

SALARY: None. Volunteers must contribute 500 shekels ($150) per month to accommodation in a shared apartment.

RECRUITMENT: Teachers fill in an application form and are then interviewed over the telephone (the recruiter calls the teacher).

CONTACT: International Volunteer Recruiter.

UNIPAL
BCM Unipal, London WC1N 3XX, UK
info@unipal.org.uk
www.unipal.org.uk

NUMBER OF VOLUNTEER TEACHERS: 30 volunteers for summer camps in Jerusalem and the West Bank.

PREFERENCE OF NATIONALITY: Native English speakers and living in the UK.

QUALIFICATIONS: Experience with children or teaching. TEFL a bonus. Volunteers should have sensitivity, tolerance and political awareness. Must be at least 20 at time of application.

CONDITIONS OF EMPLOYMENT: 3–5 weeks between mid-July and end August. 5 hours a day.

SALARY: None. Volunteers must pay £300 plus flights, etc.

RECRUITMENT: Application forms are downloadable from website from November and are due mid-February for interviews in March and training days in mid-April and July. Candidates must be available to attend.

CONTACT: Brenda Hayward, Director.

KUWAIT

Although teaching salaries are no longer in the stratosphere, as some were in the past, many organisations still seek to lure expat teachers with favourable terms. Educational standards are variable, as encountered by **B. P. Rawlins** in Kuwait:

> ***There are simply too many schools in Kuwait acting like pigs at a trough, all of them out there for the money. They dare not criticise any anti-social behaviour by pupils, parents or adult students for fear of losing fees in a competitive market. Professionalism is viewed with hostile suspicion in some quarters.***

This negative view is not subscribed to by all who have spent time in the region. Many agree that English learners in Kuwait, as throughout the Arab world, can be a pleasure to teach because they are so eager to communicate, and so unhesitant to speak English in class.

As well as keeping an up-to-date list of the many international and English-medium schools in Kuwait, the British Council in Mansouriya (info@kw.britishcouncil.org) employs teachers year round and for July/August summer courses.

LIST OF EMPLOYERS

AMIDEAST
Mail: PO Box 44818, Hawalli 32063, Kuwait
Physical Address: Ahmed Al-Jabeer St, Opp. Al-Awadhi Mosque, Commercial Bank Building, 2nd Fl, Sharq
+965 2247 0091
kuwait@amideast.org
www.amideast.org/kuwait

PREFERENCE OF NATIONALITY: North American. AMIDEAST emphasises American-style English.

QUALIFICATIONS: BA/BEd and MA in TESL are essential. 5 years of teaching experience are required.

CONDITIONS OF EMPLOYMENT: Hired as part-time independent contractors. Contracts are usually 6 weeks long and renewable according to demand. Average 2 hours a day, 3 days a week; generally evenings.

SALARY: Depends on qualifications and experience.

RECRUITMENT: Newspaper ads and referrals.

CONTACT: Ms Samar Khleif, Country Director (skhleif@amideast.org); Janice Quinn, Director of Training (jquinn@amideast.org).

LEBANON

Lebanon has traditionally been an important commercial hub for the Middle East, a forward-thinking, artistic and entrepreneurial country. However, progress is being set back by heightened terror threats and sectarian tensions that have escalated with the deepening crisis in Syria. Hezbollah, the main Shi'ite party in Lebanon, has a close alliance with Syria's Bashar al Assad, while the vast majority of Lebanese Sunnis support the mainly Sunni-led uprising in Syria. Furthermore, fear of cross-border strikes from Israel is never far below the surface, and a permanent ceasefire seems further away than ever. There continues to be a heavy UN presence along the 'Blue Line' in the south and many foreign embassies advise against non-essential travel to the area as well as to many other areas of the country.

Most teaching jobs in Lebanon are found in Beirut. Locals are generally open minded and many speak three languages: English, French and Arabic. Male and female teachers will find it relatively easy to adjust (compared to the major culture shock experienced in other Middle East destinations), although the pace of life is slower and more conservative outside Beirut. In 2015, a new programme was implemented in Lebanon called 'Accessing Education: Language Integration for Syrian Refugee Children' funded by the EU and assisted by the British Council. This ambitious English language teaching programme for children aged 8–14 who arrive from Syria with almost no English is being carried out mostly by local teachers after receiving specialised training.

Finding an English teaching job in Lebanon can be difficult as there is a local pool of qualified teachers. Few schools advertise abroad and almost none recruit on teaching websites. A further impediment is mentioned by Amideast's Programme Manager, which is that work permits are expensive in Lebanon. Occasionally Amideast hires expatriates who are already in Lebanon taking classes at the American University of Beirut or living with friends or relatives.

If you cannot find a posting, find the contact information of any school online and start sending off your CV. Most full-curriculum schools are English or French, with the other language plus Arabic taught as second languages, although English continues to gain ground over French, to the chagrin of the French.

However, even schools that do not use English as the medium of instruction employ English teachers. The website www.lebweb.com is an online directory for everything from banks to schools in Lebanon; www.schoolnet.edu.lb/schools.htm has links to some private schools around Lebanon; and the classified section of www.dailystar.com.lb carries very occasional teaching vacancies (but is normally dormant). For info about teaching English to adults try the American Lebanese Language Center (see entry) or it could be worth trying the Lebanese American University (www.lau.edu.lb).

While the demand for teachers exists, the wages can be low unless you are lucky enough to be hired by a large, foreign-operated school or university. The minimum wage is about $500 per month and local teachers earn about $750 per month as a starting salary. Foreign teachers can expect to earn about $900–$1,500 a month, depending on credentials, experience and how the contract is negotiated. Contact hours are often high and teachers may be assigned additional tasks. Lebanon has 20 official holidays.

A few larger schools offer on-site housing and those that do not will help teachers find decent accommodation. Finding a flat from abroad is difficult, although some English websites and newspapers list private and shared accommodation.

LEISURE

Shelley Beyak-Tarabichi, a Canadian who used to work for International House in Beirut, came to appreciate life in Lebanon:

Lebanese hospitality is renowned, the food is fantastic (healthy and vegetarian friendly) and the weather is comfortable. You can swim at a beach resort in the summer, ski in the winter and hike all year round. There are gyms, malls, outdoor groups, concerts, art schools and mountain resorts along with traditional Arabic cafés, monasteries, mosques and historical sites dating back thousands, if not millions, of years. While the political situation in Lebanon is termed unstable, it is not evident on a day-to-day level as one would expect.

LIST OF EMPLOYERS

ALLC IH BEIRUT

American Lebanese Language Center – International House Beirut, Dimitri El Hayek St, Confidence Center, 7th Floor, Sin el Fil, Beirut

+961 1 500978; +961 70 944684

recruitment@allcs.edu.lb

www.allcs.edu.lb.

Teaching centre in Saida and affiliated centres in Hamra and Tyre.

NUMBER OF TEACHERS: Approx. 20.

PREFERENCE OF NATIONALITY: American, British.

QUALIFICATIONS: CELTA or approved equivalent, 2+ years' post-CELTA experience. Business English experience desirable.

CONDITIONS OF EMPLOYMENT: 12-month standard contract. 26 contact hours per week, split shift between 9am and 9.30pm.

SALARY: $1,000–$1,500, depending on experience and qualifications. No deductions.

FACILITIES/SUPPORT: The Centre finds suitable accommodation but does not pay for it. The Centre deals with all paperwork relating to work and residency permits. Health insurance provided.

RECRUITMENT: Normally through IHWO recruitment page, unsolicited applications and emails. Interviews are essential, usually carried out via Skype.

CONTACT: Elaine Kniveton, Academic Director (elainek@allcs.edu.lb).

OMAN

According to experienced American teacher **Tom Clark**, who has worked in Afghanistan, Egypt, Syria, Turkey, Kuwait and Saudi, Oman is '*the best in the Middle East for being friendly and open and laid back*'. Tom thinks Oman has been experiencing a boom in tourism and employment and is growing and developing very fast, which has had some negative outcomes, such as local residents moved from waterfront locations to make way for luxury hotels. Technical colleges such as the Salalah College of Technology, where Tom worked alongside 59 other ESL teachers, have periods of hiring on a big scale.

Since the 1970s Oman has had to import the majority of its skilled labour, including teachers. Teachers of English are employed from Sudan, Sri Lanka, India and North Africa, which means that there is a much broader mix of accents than usual. Positions for native English speakers from the UK etc. become available each year with the British Council and Amideast in Muscat, and the major employers of western teachers are the Ministry of Higher Education and Sultan Qaboos University (which hire primarily through TESOL conventions in Dubai and the US each spring).

Despite an expanding EFL market, there's no room at all for visiting job-seekers, since a tight hold is kept on tourist visas. It will make it much easier to land a job if you have an MA in TESOL or Applied Linguistics (or at least are enrolled in a distance learning ELT master's degree) with at least three years' experience, preferably at university level. IH Muscat (Polyglot Institute) in Oman asks for teachers with a degree plus CELTA or Trinity TESOL and three to five years' EFL experience post-CELTA. If the first degree is a BSc, the approving body requires five years' experience post-CELTA. The main recruiting season begins in March, just prior to the annual TESOL Arabia conference. Itinerant teacher **Bradwell Jackson** investigated possibilities at Polyglot and reported that it is both the oldest and largest school in Muscat. According to the school's marketing manager, the market for English is ever expanding, possibly as much as 13% year on year. The students prefer British English to American, partly for political reasons and also because they are more likely to go to Britain for further studies. Bradwell concludes: '*In the very short time I have been here, Oman strikes me as a very pleasant place to live. It seems a very well-kept secret. Everyone is talking about UAE, as Oman quietly and slowly gains more and more gravitas. The city is very clean and surprisingly modern. I would love to work here myself.*'

TATI, the Technical & Administrative Training Institute in Medinat Qaboos (✆ +968 246 05086 ext 25; esljobs@tatioman.com; www.tatioman.com) does some hiring of well-qualified native speaker lecturers for Salalah mentioned above as well as government colleges of technology around Oman. Positions are for September to June.

Exactly why an MA in TESOL should be necessary is not very clear. One wry description of students in higher education could apply equally to students throughout the Middle East:

> ***Unfortunately there is a widespread idea that experts in linguistics and the like have what it takes to teach English. It can come as a bit of a shock, therefore, for teachers who have studied phonics, syllabus design, methodology and socio-linguistics to discover that they are teaching 'Headway Elementary' units 1 to 5 to groups of up to 40 students per class. Not exactly what the MA prepares you for. One could say that the school-leavers who come to the colleges and higher institutes are ill prepared.***

On the other hand **Tom Clark** found his students to be polite and really engaged with their studies. This is not life in the fast lane of academic endeavour but something of an academic lay-by. If you choose to work in one of the colleges of higher education, you may find that the concept of rigorous academic standards is imperfectly understood, and therefore rarely applied.

Tom Clark found the quality of life congenial. Newly arrived teachers were presented with a choice of places to live, from villas in the mountains to plantations in the woods, luxury apartments in the suburbs to places on the beach. It is possible to acquire a drinking licence for the five bars in town. Other recreations include scuba diving, boating, desert camping Bedouin-style, picnicking in the mountain valleys, camel racing or just haring around in a 4WD. The countryside and coasts are stunning, and if you can handle the heat and at times the humidity, mountain walking is popular. Just try not to get bored with these activities. There are no others, unless you happen to live near Muscat, where you can indulge in wandering around glossy shopping malls, watching Hindi movies and eating sushi.

LIST OF EMPLOYERS

AMIDEAST OMAN
Al Jama'a Al Akhbar Street, Building 93, Airport Heights, Ghala (Muscat)
+968 2 2459 0309
oman@amideast.org
www.amideast.org/oman

NUMBER OF TEACHERS: 10 part-time EFL instructors for on and off-site assignments. Based on a memorandum of understanding with the Ministry of Education, AMIDEAST is one of the only institutes legally able to employ teachers on a part-time basis.
PREFERENCE OF NATIONALITY: Americans and other native English speakers.
QUALIFICATIONS: Bachelor's degree plus recognised international certificate in TEFL/TESL and a minimum of 2 years' successful experience teaching English to non-native speakers. Teachers are usually on family visa because their spouse or parent is working in Oman, or have full-time work with local colleges or universities.
CONDITIONS OF EMPLOYMENT: Mostly freelancers. General English classes for children, teenagers and adults held between 8am and 9pm. Business English and other ESP courses conducted for public and private sector organisations on a per contract basis.
SALARY: 10 rials per hour ($25).
FACILITIES/SUPPORT: AMIDEAST will offer assistance in locating affordable housing. All visa-related fees and procurement will be managed by AMIDEAST upon arrival.
RECRUITMENT: Via www.amideast.org plus regional and international TEFL conferences.
CONTACT: Paul Steele, Director of Training Programs (psteele@amideast.org).

CfBT EDUCATION SERVICES AND PARTNERS LLC
PO Box 2278, Ruwi, PC 112, Muscat, Sultanate of Oman
+968 24560239
gcowley@cfbtmena.com; gen@cfbtoman.com
www.cfbt.com

Affiliated to Education Development Trust in the UK (www.educationdevelopmenttrust.com), formerly CfBT Education Trust.
NUMBER OF TEACHERS: Up to 12 at the British Training Institute in Muscat; over 40 in projects with Ministries of Education and Higher Education.
PREFERENCE OF NATIONALITY: British, North American, Australian, New Zealander.
QUALIFICATIONS: Usually DELTA. Salary increments paid for MA and PhD.
CONDITIONS OF EMPLOYMENT: 1 year renewable, 1 September to 31 August. Up to 25 teaching hours a week. Short-term contracts for consultants.
SALARY: Market rate. Tax free.
FACILITIES/SUPPORT: Accommodation allowance; work permit; annual return flight.
RECRUITMENT: Normally through advertisements on internet (www.tefl.com, www.jobs.edufind.com) or agents abroad.
CONTACT: Gavin Cowley, Country Director and General Manager.

IH MUSCAT / POLYGLOT INSTITUTE OMAN LLC
PO Box 221, Ruwi, Post Code 112, Sultanate of Oman
+968 24 666 666
vacancy@polyglot.org
www.polyglot-institute.com

NUMBER OF TEACHERS: 15.
PREFERENCE OF NATIONALITY: UK, Australia, South Africa, USA.
QUALIFICATIONS: First degree in any subject, CELTA or equivalent (IHWO standard), minimum 3 years' EFL teaching experience post-qualification. Driving licence required for some positions.
CONDITIONS OF EMPLOYMENT: 1–2 years. Up to 26 contact teaching hours per week from a 40-hour working week. Teachers often work split shifts; classes run Sunday to Thursday.
SALARY: Dependent on qualifications and experience, e.g. 850–900 rials a month.
FACILITIES/SUPPORT: Shared, furnished accommodation may be

provided or 250 rials accommodation allowance. Flights paid. All documentation is arranged and organised by HR team, according to legal requirements; process takes place in 3 phases and normally takes 3-4 weeks.

RECRUITMENT: IH website (http://job.ihworld.com) and interviews normally carried out by IH Recruit Services.

CONTACT: Mrs Jean Scopes, Director of Studies (jean.scopes@polyglot.om).

MODERN COLLEGE OF BUSINESS & SCIENCE (MCBS)

PO Box 100, Al-Khuwair, 133 Sultanate of Oman

+968 24583583 / 24583538

jobs@mcbs.edu.om

www.mcbs.edu.om

NUMBER OF TEACHERS: Full-time teachers, faculty positions and interns for intensive ESL programme.

QUALIFICATIONS: Minimum of relevant bachelor's degree and 2 years' teaching for some positions, new graduates with CELTA qualification considered to teach in General Foundation Program.

CONDITIONS OF EMPLOYMENT: Starting in autumn or spring.

SALARY: According to qualifications and experience.

SUR UNIVERSITY COLLEGE

PO Box 440, Postal Code 411, Sur, Oman

job@suc.edu.om; suc@suc.edu.om

www.suc.edu.om

PREFERENCE OF NATIONALITY: Native English speakers.

QUALIFICATIONS: Bachelor's or master's degree in English or related areas, TEFL or CELTA certificate plus minimum 2 years' experience of teaching adults.

CONDITIONS OF EMPLOYMENT: 1 year renewable. 21 hours per week. To teach on foundation course for Omani students who want to study business, IT or engineering at university.

SALARY: $2,000–$2,500 per month basic salary, tax free. 40 days' paid summer holiday.

FACILITIES/SUPPORT: Free furnished accommodation and assistance with work permit. Transport provided, medical insurance, utilities allowance and annual round-trip air ticket.

QATAR

The tiny traditional emirate of Qatar is surrounded by Saudi Arabia, Bahrain, the United Arab Emirates and Iran, and has a stable ELT industry. Past reforms by the Emir of the state between 1995 and 2013, Sheikh Hamad bin Khalifa Al-Thani, promoted English over Arabic as the medium of instruction in the state school curriculum, while trying to balance respect for the heritage and conservative nature of Qatar's people.

As a country high in natural gas and oil reserves, Qatar has a per capita income that exceeds some of the leading industrial countries of Western Europe, and as such offers some enticing expatriate packages to teachers. Because of Qatar's booming economy, the cost of living is high, particularly for accommodation, and it is increasingly difficult to afford a decent place to live. A standard expat housing allowance for a single person might be 5,500 rials a month (as paid by the Ta'allum Group of Schools for the first two months of a contract) which is enough to rent a small studio flat only.

After completing a Master of Education in Canada, **Arshiya-Nageen Ahmed** went to Qatar to teach and to research education practice in the Middle East:

> ***I was actively looking for careers related to my field while volunteering to gain additional experience. After receiving three job offers I had to decide my best option. The interview procedures were long, however, I got the job in Qatar and have been working ever since. Students are hesitant to speak English at times since they do not want to make mistakes. Thus the best way is to build good student-teacher rapport so that the students become comfortable in an English-language environment. I was already aware that students would find some difficulty in adjusting to a foreign accent but from their feedback, they seem at ease in understanding a Canadian accent. Furthermore, it is important to encourage students to speak English with their peers so that they stay in practice.***

The main teaching opportunities are to be found in state schools and post-secondary education institutes. There are also opportunities for in-company development of Business English for those with the appropriate qualifications. The British Council has an English language centre in Doha (99 Al Sadd Street, PO Box 2992, Doha; general.enquiries@qa.britishcouncil.org) offering English courses to adults and children and possible advice on finding teaching work.

There are also possibilities within private language institutes. The expat site www.qatarliving.com carries job adverts, but mostly for in-country hires and part-time positions. International House Doha has a standing request on its website for hourly paid English teachers (www.ihdoha.com), while Inlingua Qatar is partnered with Score Plus Education to help candidates gain admission to foreign universities. Originating in Canada, Oxford Learning uses native speakers to help Qatari children progress in English (qatar@oxford learning.com).

LIST OF EMPLOYERS

EDUCATE LEARNING CENTER
Aamal Tower, 1st Floor, West Bay, Doha (PO Box 24635, Doha)
+974 4417 7103
info@educate.com.qa
www.educate.com.qa

NUMBER OF TEACHERS: 8–10.

PREFERENCE OF NATIONALITY: Canada, US, UK, New Zealand, Australia.

QUALIFICATIONS: Must be a native English speaker with a diploma or degree for post-secondary education. Some knowledge of Arabic is preferred. Junior trainers with 6 months' to 5 years'

experience are generally preferred for their fresh approach. Employer is looking for candidates who are extroverts, highly organised, professional and with a positive attitude. They should have the ability to teach upper management in corporate settings.
CONDITIONS OF EMPLOYMENT: Minimum 1 year. 40 hours per week: 20–24 hours' teaching time, the rest for lesson planning and preparation.
SALARY: 6,000–10,000 riyals per month, depending on experience and qualifications. No deductions because Qatar is a tax-free country.
FACILITIES/SUPPORT: Accommodation is provided or an allowance in lieu if teachers choose to find their own accommodation. Employer covers costs and takes responsibility for the processes involved in obtaining a work permit after teachers provide the necessary documentation (i.e. proof of higher education, valid passport etc.) and pass the Qatar medical examination.
RECRUITMENT: Referrals, online advertising, via AIESEC International. Interviews are completed over Skype or by telephone.

QATAR AERONAUTICAL COLLEGE
PO Box 4050, Doha
+974 4440 8813
careers@qac.edu.qa; doha.hr@gmail.com
www.qac.edu.qa

NUMBER OF TEACHERS: 35–40.
PREFERENCE OF NATIONALITY: Native English speakers.
QUALIFICATIONS: Bachelor's degree, CELTA, DELTA, TEFL certificate or master's plus minimum 3 years' experience.
CONDITIONS OF EMPLOYMENT: Length of contract is 6–12 months. Working hours are 7am–2pm.
SALARY: $3,600–$4,000 per month.
FACILITIES/SUPPORT: Furnished accommodation, government health card and assistance with work permits provided.
RECRUITMENT: Interviews required, usually carried out in the UK.
CONTACT: Hester Drewry, Training Manager of Foundation Programme (hdrewry@qac.edu.qa); HR department.

SAUDI ARABIA

Recruitment of English teachers is booming and the recruitment websites are full of advertised vacancies. Whereas at one time employers had very high standards and expected their teachers to have many years of experience, now there are some teachers in the kingdom who don't even have a university degree. Part of the problem is that the country is so wealthy that many from the elite classes know that they will never have to work for a living and do not particularly value education. The teaching is not always very serious and there is an expectation that everyone will 'pass', no matter what. The days of fabulously high salaries are also over, and rising persecution of foreigners has acted as a further disincentive. But expatriate packages are still attractive, with substantial salaries, free airfares and accommodation plus generous holidays and other perks.

Teaching in a naval academy or petrochemical company while living in a teetotal expatriate ghetto is not many people's idea of fun, especially after a request for an exit visa has been denied. Women who get jobs as teachers (at a women's college) may live to regret it when they find that Saudi women are prohibited by law from driving a car and must not appear in public without being covered from head to foot in an *abaya*.

Specialist ELT recruiters like Desert Recruiting Services (www.desertrecruiting.com) in Canada which specialises in the Middle East, Global Recruitment Solutions in Wales (www.globalrecruitsolutions.co.uk), GoldStar TEFL Recruitment (www.GoldStarTeachers.com) and D1 Resourcing in Ireland (www.d1resourcing.com) all advertise vacancies, often for certified teachers. Other recruiters active in Saudi include Tamaki TEFL Recruitment (www.tamakiteflrecruitment.co.uk), Teach to Travel (www.teachtotravel.com) and English Today Recruitment (http://englishrecruitment.com). Experienced recruiters warn that mobilisation to Saudi Arabia takes three to four months from the interview. There are also recruitment companies operating in Saudi Arabia like Quality Education Holding Company in Riyadh (www.qehc.edu.sa) and Pimento Connection (www.pimento-soe.co.uk), but they often operate mainly in Arabic, so dealing with them is not straightforward.

TOM CLARK

Tom Clark has also taught in Saudi Arabia. He describes the interview process in the UK with a large group of recruiters who rush the applicants through like cattle and then make them wait around all day to hear the outcome as an 'awful experience'.

Saudi is by far the oddest place to get paperwork done. The embassy people are not friendly and really try your patience. Every day they told me to come back, which meant I was paying for a hotel and paying for taxis and food, etc, waiting for nothing. Yet the company told me the visa was all ready and signed by the Ministry.

I have worked in Saudi on three separate occasions. The contract means nothing, as everything is done by favours and whom you know. Accommodation is normally in a compound, some of which have pretty high security with maybe three different checkpoints, jeeps with machine guns, barricades, etc. The job in Jeddah put us up in a hotel though, where there was no security at all.

I hate to be negative about any place, but Saudi is not an easy place. Depending on where you are, you could be in a very conservative place where shops close for two hours every prayer time. You need to keep covered and to be careful about what you say about most topics, but especially religion, politics and even history. There is no drinking and forget talking to the opposite sex. It is a very regimented lifestyle and you need some pretty tough skin to stay there. The religious police are everywhere, and as a foreigner in the kingdom you are always being watched by someone. I had an all-women's class that by law had to be in a separate building. The students could see me on a screen, but I couldn't see them. An official was present to censor my lesson and shut down the power if I got off topic, even talking about how some battles were fought and won.

Depending on where you are, it is pretty slim pickings to find things to do in your spare time. Even to go around the country is not easy without proof of being Muslim. To the best of my knowledge there is only one cinema in Riyadh, for mothers and children only. Jeddah offers some variety with the beaches and old town and more liberal culture. If you are going to be anywhere, try to be in Jeddah.

Teachers educated to MA level can expect to earn from $37,000, while teachers with superior qualifications and experience can command salaries of $70,000.

Professional teachers tempted by the money should bear in mind the drawbacks, as **Philip Dray** did:

I decided against Saudi Arabia. The money was appealing, but I couldn't think myself into a situation where there was no nightlife and limited contact with women. A year may seem short when you say it fast, but you could get depressed in a situation like that. Money is nearly everything but it can't buy peace of mind. So I opted for a job at a school for boys in the UAE that, from the description, sounded sociable, inviting and accessible.

Morris Jensen points to the good things about Saudi Arabia, including the hospitality, ease of finding lucrative private work, excellent sports facilities, shopping and accessibility of places of interest in the Middle East. He also acknowledges the problems, such as the religious and cultural clashes that arise in the classroom and the frustrating bureaucracy.

Among the documents required for a work permit are a medical certificate notarised by the Foreign & Commonwealth Office in London, an authorisation from the Saudi Ministry of Foreign Affairs, copies of diplomas, a contract of employment and accompanying letter from the sponsoring company. You must also provide a statement of religion; atheism is not an option. The maximum age is 60 for visa purposes. The fee payable before leaving your home country is only the beginning. Your passport is held by your sponsoring employer, while you carry around an official copy as identification, at least until you are issued with a *muqeem* (resident identity card that replaced the *iqama* in 2015) by the Ministry of the Interior. Every time you want to leave the country you must request an exit and re-entry visa, which is given at the discretion of your employer. Some foreign workers have reported having to pay a very substantial sum for an exit visa.

The US State Department publishes cautionary guidelines for English teachers at http://photos.state.gov/libraries/saudi-arabia/768382/yoderja/guide.pdf, advising all prospective employees to obtain an official Arabic translation of any contract before signing. Verbal assurances and covering letters are not binding under Saudi law. In the case of an employment dispute, an employee cannot just leave the country (because the employer holds the passport). 'Absconding' is a crime that can result in a heavy monetary fine, detention, deportation and a five-year ban.

LIST OF EMPLOYERS

BERLITZ LANGUAGE CENTRES AL-AHSA
Qatar Road, Hofuf and Mulhim Tower, Thurayat Road, Mubarraz 31982
+966 3 581 131
recruitment@berlitz-ksa.com
www.berlitz-ksa.com; www.berlitz.sa/en/careers

NUMBER OF TEACHERS: Variable for 10 language centres (half male, half female).
PREFERENCE OF NATIONALITY: British preferred. Must be native speaker of English.
QUALIFICATIONS: Minimum BA or MA in any subject plus 2 years' teaching experience; or BA + CELTA or equivalent + 3 years' experience; or PGCE + 1 year's teaching experience. Experience of TOEFL preparation would be useful. Married couples preferred.
CONDITIONS OF EMPLOYMENT: Summer-only or one-year renewable contracts. 8 hours per day, all but half an hour of timetabled teaching. At busy times, teachers will be required to work overtime (up to 11 hours per week), which will be paid at one and a half times normal salary.
SALARY: From 96,600 riyals to 123,000 riyals per year tax-free.
FACILITIES/SUPPORT: Furnished single person's or family accommodation provided rent free. Travel allowance covers air travel to and from Saudi Arabia. Full training in Berlitz Method is given. Compulsory training workshops are held.
RECRUITMENT: Online application, with photo.

EUROPEAN CENTRE
PO Box 60617, Riyadh 11555
+966 11 455 0505

NUMBER OF TEACHERS: 20–40 corporate instructors in various cities across Saudi Arabia.
PREFERENCE OF NATIONALITY: British and American.
QUALIFICATIONS: Most positions are for males only. Bachelor's degree in a language-related field as a minimum plus a CELTA/Trinity or equivalent teaching certificate with at least 1 year's experience. Occasionally there are positions for newly qualified teachers.
CONDITIONS OF EMPLOYMENT: Standard 12-month contract renewable, 7.45am–4.00pm, 5 days per week. Average load of 27 contact hours per week.
SALARY: Salary details on application. The range is from 8,600 riyals gross to 11,300 riyals gross with additional 3,600 riyals or 7,200 riyals per month overtime available in certain locations. Salary scales undergo periodic review.
FACILITIES/SUPPORT: Free, fully furnished accommodation and transport allowance provided. Company provides valid work visas and residence permits (*iqamas*) at company cost and medical cards (*Tawuniya*) for private medical cover with £80 approx. of the annual fee paid by the employee. The company also refers candidates at point of hire to a visa broker who does all the necessary paperwork for visa processing. The company covers the broker and visa medical charges, as well as the cost of the actual visa. Prepaid flights are provided. British management. Centre uses labs, tactile learning and simulator facilities, plus Adobe format materials for projectors and smart boards. On-the-job training provided.
RECRUITMENT: Adverts on www.tefl.com. Via recruitment agency Al Rajhi Co. for HRD (www.al-rajhi4hrd.com). CV with scanned copies of qualifications and a photo should be sent by email. A comprehensive PDF information pack is sent out to a candidate within 24 hours of receipt of a suitable application. Candidates may apply at any time of year.
CONTACT: Aidan Chalk, Managing Director.

GOLD STAR TEFL RECRUITMENT
Taipei, Taiwan
apply@GoldStarTeachers.com
www.GoldStarTeachers.com

Specialises in recruitment into Asia, but helps teachers into jobs with Wall Street English, Saudi Arabia, which has 22 branches in many cities: Riyadh, Jeddah, Al Khobar, Al Madina Al Munawara, Makkah, Al Taif, Abha, Khamees Mushait, Jazan, Najran, Qatif, Bureida, Tabuk and Al Kharj.
PREFERENCE OF NATIONALITY: Native English speakers from UK, Ireland, USA, Canada, Australia, New Zealand or South Africa to teach communicative English to adults.
QUALIFICATIONS: Bachelor's degree in English, TEFL, Linguistics or Literature. TEFL experience and/or certificate preferred but not required. Must be male teacher or a couple (government regulation for visa). Outgoing sociable personality.
CONDITIONS OF EMPLOYMENT: Minimum 2-year commitment. 30 days paid holiday after 12 months of work.
SALARY: $2,100 per month plus flight, housing allowance and other perks. Total package worth 12,375 riyals per month (salary of 8,000 riyals, flight paid upfront, housing contribution 2,000 riyals and transport allowance 800 riyals).
FACILITIES/SUPPORT: Legal work visa obtained (but fees paid by teacher). Ongoing training. Medical insurance provided.

INTERLINK LANGUAGE CENTERS
Al Yamamah University, PO Box 45180, Riyadh 11512
esl@interlink.edu
www.interlink.edu/careers-2; www.yu.edu.sa

NUMBER OF TEACHERS: About 50, 80%–85% of whom are native English speakers.
PREFERENCE OF NATIONALITY: Visa regulations stipulate that teachers must have a passport from Australia, New Zealand, Canada, US, UK, Ireland or South Africa.
QUALIFICATIONS: MA in TESL or MA in related field with CELTA/DELTA or another 120-hour residential TEFL training course. At least 2 years of EFL/ESL teaching experience with adult learners; at least 1 year of working or living in another culture.
CONDITIONS OF EMPLOYMENT: Minimum 2-year contract, longer preferred. 20–25 hours per week, plus participation in programme of activities.
SALARY: $38,000–$40,000, tax-free.
FACILITIES/SUPPORT: Free furnished housing, medical insurance and round-trip transport to Saudi Arabia.
RECRUITMENT: Résumés to be submitted via www.appview.interlink.edu. Interviews are essential; can be by conference call.
CONTACT: Dr Nebila Dhieb-Henia, General Director.

JUBAIL UNIVERSITY COLLEGE
English Prep Year Programme, PO Box 10074, Jubail Industrial City 31961
+966 3 342 9000 ext. 1008
ucjjobs@gmail.com; jobs@ucj.edu.sa
www.ucj.edu.sa

NUMBER OF TEACHERS: 25+.
PREFERENCE OF NATIONALITY: British, Irish, American, Canadian, South African, Australian, New Zealander.
QUALIFICATIONS: BA/MA/PhD in English, Linguistics or TESOL. CELTA/Trinity TESOL certificate desirable, plus 2 years' full-time ESL/EFL/EAP/ESP teaching experience at university/college level. American graduates should have a GPA of at least 3.0. Maximum age 50.
CONDITIONS OF EMPLOYMENT: Initially 2-year contracts, renewable annually thereafter. 40 hours per week (20 contact teaching hours, 10 prep hours, 10 office hours).
SALARY: Varies depending on qualifications and experience. Salary is tax-free.
FACILITIES/SUPPORT: Free furnished accommodation provided. Full details are supplied to teachers when salary offer accepted on how to get medical clearance and visa application.
RECRUITMENT: Web-based advertising. Interviews conducted by Skype or telephone.
CONTACT: Mike Creed, Academic Recruiting Co-ordinator.

KING FAHD UNIVERSITY OF PETROLEUM & MINERALS
Preparatory English Program, College of Applied and Supporting Studies, Box 5026, Dhahran 31261
+966 3 860 0000
recruite@kfupm.edu.sa; faculty@kfupm.edu.sa
www.kfupm.edu.sa

NUMBER OF TEACHERS: 90, including for affiliated colleges such as Dammam Community College (dccjobs@kfupm.edu.sa).
PREFERENCE OF NATIONALITY: American, Australian, British, Canadian, Irish, New Zealander.
QUALIFICATIONS: Master's degree or full-time postgraduate diploma in TESOL/Applied Linguistics, or Cambridge DELTA, plus minimum 4 years' overseas experience. Cambridge CELTA or equivalent may be acceptable with particularly relevant experience.
CONDITIONS OF EMPLOYMENT: Male teachers only for all-male university; native speakers of English. 2-year contracts starting September and February. 20-hours per week, Saturday–Wednesday.
SALARY: 124,000–180,000 riyals ($33,000–$48,000) per year.
FACILITIES/SUPPORT: On-campus furnished accommodation with all services available for married or single status. Annual airfares. Local education. Contract completion bonus.
RECRUITMENT: Send cover letter and CV by email to recruite@kfupm.edu.sa. Videoconference interviews are required.
CONTACT: Paul Brown, Director of the Preparatory English Program (pbrown@kfupm.edu.sa).

SKYLINE GLOBAL SOLUTIONS
1055 Westlakes Drive, Berwyn, PA 19312, USA
+1 610 230 0296
positions@skylinetechsolutions.com
www.skylinetechsolutions.com

NUMBER OF TEACHERS: 200+ for positions in Riyadh and Dammam universities, such as Princess Noura University.
PREFERENCE OF NATIONALITY: American, British, Canadian, South African, Australian, Irish and New Zealander.
QUALIFICATIONS: BA degree minimum. TEFL/TESL/CELTA qualification. Some positions are available only to females.
CONDITIONS OF EMPLOYMENT: 1-year contract, 20–25 contact teaching hours, total of 40 working hours per week.
SALARY: Tax-free salary package of $2,600–$4,200 per month.
FACILITIES/SUPPORT: Furnished shared accommodation provided or stipend for those who live independently. Recruiter manages the visa process.
RECRUITMENT: Print media and internet. Interviews are essential and are conducted in the US.

UAE (UNITED ARAB EMIRATES)

The oil-rich UAE consists of seven emirates or principalities, each governed by a hereditary emir (Muslim ruler). The most important are Abu Dhabi the capital, Dubai and Sharjah. The great draw for TEFL teachers is the money that can be made, as **Ben Naismith** admitted not long after moving to Dubai:

> *Having spent a number of years working in countries that English teachers typically flock to (Costa Rica, Thailand, etc.), my wife and I decided it was time to earn more than the usual ELT pittance. So after a brief look at the available options, we settled on the UAE and Dubai. As with many teaching professionals, this decision was made in the hopes of finding a balance between financial stability and quality of life. And, although we have been here only a relatively short time, our expectations have thus far been pleasantly exceeded.*
>
> *In terms of the schools, there are a number of the usual chains including Berlitz and the British Council. In addition, there are plenty of teachers working at high schools, colleges and universities. Although I personally work full-time for one school, it seems that the majority of the teachers I have met freelance at a number of different places. Getting a work visa is a bit tricky though, as you need to either be sponsored exclusively by one employer (or else be married to someone who is) or pay to get an office in a free zone.*
>
> *Regarding the make-up of classes, Dubai truly is a modern cosmopolitan city, and the learners come from all over the world, with the majority either from around the Middle East, South Asia, or South-East Asia. Due to the massive demand for English speakers, there are all types of classes ranging from Young Learners, to General English, to Business English, to ESP – truly something for everyone.*
>
> *One of our greatest fears moving here, a common one I'm sure, was how we would adapt to the local surroundings. Prepared for an extremely conservative society, we were amazed at how liberal it is here in terms of clothing, attitudes, etc. The people are also, by and large, extremely friendly, probably as they too are mostly immigrants in a foreign land! What did live up to the hype though was the heat, which is truly unlike anything I have experienced before, so be prepared.*

The huge diversity of nationalities that makes up the population of the Emirates means that English is the main lingua franca, and almost everyone is eager to improve his or her knowledge of the language. The respected organisation Amideast (www.amideast.org/uae), with offices in Abu Dhabi, Dubai and Sharjah delivers Intensive English and TOEFL programmes, for which it recruits experienced English-language teachers.

Many institutes hire only teachers who are already living locally with a residence visa, drawing from a pool of freelance teachers and never hiring from abroad except for occasional senior positions.

Most advertised jobs in the UAE, as throughout the Gulf, say that they require three to five years of EFL experience, and in some cases a master's degree as well. Check www.jobsindubai.com and www.khaleejtimes.com. You will be at an advantage if your teaching experience covers exam preparation, TOEFL-iBT, academic and Business English. Beware of small local recruitment agents and manpower supply companies advertising on local websites. One in Sharjah recently attracted a spate of terrible reviews along the lines of: '*They ask for money to get you a second interview, but actually they don't, and never return your money. They are cheaters and a waste of time.*'

STEPH FUCCIO

When Steph Fuccio and her husband (whom she met on the international EFL circuit) applied to universities and similar in Oman and the UAE, most places cited the lack of an MA as the reason their applications were not progressed. In the end they were hired by Abu Dhabi University.

This is the first place I've lived where the British Council does not pay the highest English teaching wage, although it has a nice location on the island and still offers its high standard of organisation and good professional development. The rule of thumb for getting on here, much like Italy and some other countries I've been in, is it depends on who you know, no matter what your experience and education are. 'Wasta' is key here: it's who you know, your connections, that get things done, including internet service, speeding tickets and teaching jobs.

The pace in the classroom, much like the pace of life here in general, is slower than most western institutes. Adult students expect a lot of personal attention (not to be confused with correction) but usually this dedication is not expected of them in return, i.e. they rarely will do any work outside of class, and sometimes will come up with amazing reasons not to do work even in class. Overall, they are good humoured. Although their sense of humour is different from mine, there is always an intersection of silliness that is available. They will always be late for class and want many breaks. They will usually have their 3-4 cell phones on the seat next to them, ready to take a call at the first ring. Emiratis are very well taken care of by their government. Although 80% of the population of the UAE is comprised of foreign nationals, it is the Emiratis who get the best jobs with the highest salaries and best benefits.

I wish I could make it sound more glamorous and inviting. The weather is great for the region, the low humidity is a relief after living in South-East Asia. The food is amazing. The money is spoiling and the lifestyle isn't as strict as in neighbouring Saudi and Bahrain. But this isn't for the faint of heart or first-timer.

Once again, the financial rewards are the principal attraction and make the red tape hassles bearable. Entry-level jobs pay about 8,000–10,000 dirhams (US$2,200–US$2,700) per month tax-free plus free housing. The cost of living is not as expensive as you might expect, so most people can save a lot of money. Abu Dhabi and Dubai look very western and familiar, though these similarities are only skin deep. After **Philip Dray**'s arrival at the Oasis Residence in Dubai, he was well pleased with his decision to move to the UAE, since living conditions in his luxury apartment complex, complete with pool, steam room, squash court and gym, were just as lavish as he would have been given in Saudi.

Certified primary and secondary school teachers might want to investigate the recruitment drive currently underway by the Abu Dhabi Education Council (ADEC), which is attempting to reform the UAE educational system and place expat teachers in public schools throughout the country. Footprints Recruiting is one of several recruitment agencies that act as intermediaries for this programme (http://adec.footprintsrecruiting.com); TeachAway is another.

LIST OF EMPLOYERS

BERLITZ LANGUAGE CENTER

PO Box 47120, Abu Dhabi

+971 2 667 2287

info@berlitz-uae.com

www.berlitz.ae/careers

Centres also in Dubai and Sharjah.

NUMBER OF TEACHERS: 45.

PREFERENCE OF NATIONALITY: None.

QUALIFICATIONS: University graduates with teaching diplomas. For candidates with non-education or teaching university degrees, a CELTA or TEFL certificate is essential. All instructors need to undergo and successfully complete training in the Berlitz Method of instruction.

CONDITIONS OF EMPLOYMENT: Minimum contract is 2 years. Usual hours are Sunday to Thursday, between 7.30am and 9pm, Saturdays between 9am and 1.30pm. A weekly schedule is provided by the Centre Director specifying working days and hours.

FACILITIES/SUPPORT: Accommodation is provided in a shared teachers' apartment. A work visa and labour card are issued to new candidates on full-time contracts. Original degrees/diplomas and a reference describing the candidate's experience is necessary, with attestation from the UAE Embassy or Ministry of Foreign Affairs in country of origin, plus copy of passport and passport photos.

RECRUITMENT: Through email applications, referrals and adverts in newspapers or websites. Applications should include letter of intent, updated CV and recent passport photo. Interviews are important; for international applicants phone interviews are carried out.

CONTACT: Ms Manal Mahshi Azar, Director, Abu Dhabi (manal.mahshi@berlitz-uae.com); Mrs Reem Shehab, Director, Dubai; Ms Sereen Masri, Director, Sharjah.

HIGHER COLLEGES OF TECHNOLOGY

+971 2 692 2635

recruit@hct.ac.ae

http://recruit.hct.ac.ae

NUMBER OF TEACHERS: Up to 450 English faculty teachers involved in teaching ESL for Foundation Programme at 17 colleges throughout the UAE.

PREFERENCE OF NATIONALITY: None. Should be native or near-native speaker for English faculty positions.

QUALIFICATIONS: English faculty minimum requirements are master's degree in TEFL (preferred), Applied Linguistics or similar; TEFL qualification e.g. DELTA desirable; 3 years' teaching experience (tertiary preferred).

CONDITIONS OF EMPLOYMENT: Teaching year is from September to June. To teach up to 24 50-minute lessons a week (Sunday to Thursday).

SALARY: Tax-free income. Salary based on experience and education. Annual rises are given upon receiving positive performance evaluations.

FACILITIES/SUPPORT: Visa arranged by HCT. Singles and families welcome. Unfurnished accommodation and a furniture allowance, excellent benefit package offered – details provided upon request or to short-listed candidates.

RECRUITMENT: Online HCT application required. Interviews can be conducted via video teleconference.

TURKEY

Turkey is a wonderful country to travel in, with a wealth of historic sites such as Troy and Ephesus, marvellous food and warm, friendly people. But its tourist industry has been decimated by recent terrorist attacks, namely the Ankara bombings that killed more than 100 people, the attack on Istanbul Airport in June 2016 and, of course, the coup attempt that came not long after. Deepening political unrest in the aftermath of the unsuccessful military coup and warnings of a 'high' terror threat have discouraged prospective tourists and teachers from choosing Turkey as a destination.

Immediately following the coup, President Erdogan declared a state of emergency and suspended more than 15,000 people working in education accused of having links with the Gülen Movement, which he blames for masterminding the coup. Many suspect that the purges were an excuse to strangle political opposition. The economy has suffered and the Turkish lira has dropped to a record low. Turkey is certainly not moving towards admission to the European Union.

Nevertheless, Turkey's ELT industry continues to absorb an enormous number of globe-trotting English teachers and the country is a good choice of destination for fledgling English teachers with a university degree and a TEFL certificate, both of which are required for visa reasons. Over the years, pay and perks have been cut back to some extent. However, every teacher who has complained about employers breaking their promises, run-down accommodation and so on has concluded by saying that Turkish people are amazingly hospitable and the country fascinating. By describing below the problems which some teachers have encountered on short teaching contracts in Turkey, it is to be hoped that readers can guard against them.

PROSPECTS FOR TEACHERS

Turkey's prosperous classes are more eager than ever to learn English and, furthermore, seem to have the money to pay for it. The boom in English is not confined to private language schools (*dershane*), which have proliferated in the three main cities of Istanbul, Ankara and Izmir. In order to prepare students for an English-language engineering, commerce, tourism or arts course, many secondary schools hire native-speaker teachers. Hundreds of private secondary schools (*lises*) consider as one of their main priorities the teaching of the English language. Similarly at the tertiary level, some universities, both private and public, use English as the medium of instruction and offer intensive English preparatory programmes.

A few institutes still offer a package which includes free accommodation and free airfares (London–Istanbul) on completion of a contract. All of these employers want to see a university degree and a TEFL Certificate of some kind, preferably the Cambridge CELTA or equivalent. Both a degree and a specialist qualification are required by the Turkish Ministry of Education before it will approve a work permit (see Regulations below).

The bias in favour of British English over American is not particularly strong. Many schools claim to have no preference and yet, because they advertise on UK-based sites and are more familiar with British qualifications, there is a preponderance of British teachers. Also, the requirement that work visas be applied for in the country of origin makes matters more difficult for teachers from the USA, Australia, etc.

A near-native-speaking English specialist who had been working for eight years in marketing communications decided it was time to change direction. Having learned that a TEFL qualification was a requirement for teaching in Turkey, she enrolled in a CELTA course and then moved to Istanbul:

Having travelled to Turkey as a tourist on a number of occasions, I decided to move there in the summer of 2015. Something drew me, even if I haven't found what it is. I had talked to an expat who was on leave in the Netherlands, and she advised me to become a teacher. She shared some of her experiences, not all of them rosy. I managed to arrange my first teaching hours within the first month of my stay and had already signed up with

one of the top language schools a few months later. There is a real need for language teachers in Turkey, and native and near-native speakers (as in my case) are embraced. A lot of teaching in Turkey goes without contract, work permit and a set amount of teaching hours, so that one may get by in one month to fall short in the next. Many schools offer minimum wages. Classes may be at nights or weekends and split between teachers. Colleagues may not all be master of the language they are teaching. Students who are used to a 'mug-and-jug' kind of teaching, may be very passive in their learning, unwilling to participate in activities and are sometimes in the wrong level, frustrating their learning process.

In the end, however, that doesn't take away from the genuine interest – and need – that Turkish pupils have to learn English. They bond to their teacher like little puppies and, once they have gotten past the threshold of their limitations, love to discuss and are quite happy to go along with all you are offering. This, the fruits of teaching itself, makes teaching in Turkey rewarding, if you do not mind a few bumps along an uncertain road.

FINDING A JOB

IN ADVANCE

While old hands claim that it is always preferable to arrive in Istanbul or other cities and knock on doors of language schools to find a decent job, newcomers to the profession may prefer going through an agency. International recruitment agencies sometimes seek both entry-level and more experienced teachers for private academies and public schools in Turkey. For example, Teach to Travel in London (www.teachtotravel.com) collaborates with the Turkey-based teacher placement agency Teachers in Turkey (see entry). Another agency is Marmaris Recruitment, also in the directory at the end of this chapter; they charge an administration fee of £40 to register. A former coordinator at Teachers in Turkey set up his own EL teacher matching agency in 2016 called Boz Academy Consulting Services (hr@bozacademy.com). You might also try www.teachingenglishinturkey.com, which has expanded from recruiting teachers for the Oxford as Academy in Bursa to placing teachers more widely.

English-medium universities employ considerable numbers of language instructors, such as Bilkent in Ankara and Istanbul Sehir University (see entries for both). Many of the major chains, such as Wall Street English, hire frequently; and English Time (see entry), Just English (www.justenglishtr.com) and Bank Street (www.bankstreet.org) advertise regularly; while one of the largest companies is Amerikan Kultur Dernegi, which with dozens of schools claims to have the biggest network in Turkey. Telephone and online teaching is a large part of its business. Teacher recruitment information is not easily accessible on the websites of these companies, which tend to be only in Turkish and have only a basic web form for applications.

When the British Council closed down its teaching operations in Turkey, some ex-Council teaching staff set up British Side (see entry), which hires highly qualified teachers on a full-time basis, as well as others hired on an hourly basis, who are well paid.

The CELTA training centre ITI Istanbul (www.iti-istanbul.com) administers a recruitment service for language schools in Turkey and can send notification of current vacancies to subscribers to their mailing list free of charge. Quite a few ads for Turkish schools appear on the main TEFL job sites, such as www.tefl.com and www.learn4good.com in the spring and through the summer. Also check out www.englishjobsturkey.com, www.employeebul.com (for jobs in Istanbul) and the Istanbul expat site www.yabangee.com/category/jobs.

Another avenue to explore is to teach in a large company: for example the Marriott Hotel in Ankara sometimes looks for teachers. A lucky few will find summer work in a coastal resort, for example with the International Mediterranean Academy in Fethiye (www.im-academy.org).

Some ads specify that they are looking to hire teachers already in Turkey, though some offer travel expenses. If you are considering accepting a job with an advertiser, ask for the name and telephone number of a previous teacher for an informal reference before accepting. An even better indication is if it has been able to keep its teachers for two or more years. If the school is reluctant to provide this kind of information, be suspicious. It may also be worth phoning the British Council office in the relevant city, since it keeps a file of complaints about language schools.

ON THE SPOT

Although not the capital, Istanbul is the commercial, financial and cultural centre of Turkey, so this is where most of the EFL teaching goes on. On the negative side, there may be more competition from other teachers here and also in Izmir than in Ankara or less obvious cities.

Given the huge demand for native-speaker teachers, Turkey is one country where scouting out possibilities on the ground can pay off, rather than signing a contract at a school you have never seen. After **Bruce Lawson** had a terrible experience with a private language-teaching organisation in Istanbul (*'their contract was a fiction that Tolstoy would have been proud of'*), he concluded that he could have earned half as much again if he had been employed by a school that interviewed and hired locally.

Tim Leffel and **Donna Marcus** from New Jersey were amazed by the ease with which they made their way as English teachers:

> ***There's a huge demand for teachers (any nationality really) in Istanbul. We lined up work on our second day of interviews. We interviewed at three schools and all of them offered us positions. We chose one in Bakirköy because there were two jobs available in the same place and we were allowed to wear anything within reason (no ties, no new clothes to buy). They were satisfied that we could only commit ourselves for four months. We did see a lot of applicants turned away, even when there was a need for new teachers, because they lacked TEFL credentials.***

FREELANCE TEACHING

The standard Ministry of Education contract prohibits private teaching outside the bounds of the signed contract. In fact, unless you are blatantly pinching students from the institution that employs you, most employers turn a blind eye. University English departments might be a place to look for private students. The top rate of pay goes over £20 an hour, though a more usual hourly rate would be less than half that, i.e. 35 lira.

REGULATIONS

Since 10 April 2014, it is no longer possible to process the residence/work permit after arrival in Turkey. You must now apply to the Turkish Consulate in your home country, with the originals of crucial documents, i.e. the job offer from a Turkish employer, your university degree diploma, teaching/TEFL certificate plus a police check, all of which will be forwarded to the Ministry of Labour. If approved, you must enter the country within 90 days and then apply for a residence permit from the Ministry of the Interior within 30 days of arrival, which can take months to be processed by the General Directorate of Migration Management. It may also be possible to apply for a resident's permit after arrival and later your employer can apply for your work permit. For information see www.turkishconsulate.org.uk/en/work_visa.asp. The current fee for a work permit is 191 lira (about £50) with an entry visa costing about twice that. Large fines can be levied on foreign employees without the necessary permits and much more on employers, though enforcement seems fairly lax. Naturally, employers prefer to hire a teacher who is already in Turkey with a residence permit, and only a tiny percentage of schools recruit from outside Turkey.

In line with the Schengen system, foreigners are allowed to stay 90 days within a period of 180 days. If you are planning to enter as a tourist to fix up a job, be aware that tourists must obtain an e-visa online. Prices differ among nationalities, so check www.evisa.gov.tr for information: the fee for Britons and Americans is $20, whereas Canadians pay $60. If you overstay, you become liable for a hefty exit fine.

All salaries in Turkey are quoted net of deductions, which amount to about 25% for contributions and tax. If the school makes social security contributions on your behalf, you will have medical cover from the first day your work visa becomes valid. The scheme pays all your doctor's bills and 80% of prescriptions. Once again it is prudent to confirm that your employer keeps any promises he or she makes. More than one teacher has realised at a critical moment that, despite assurances, insurance premiums have not been paid by the school.

A complication for people who intend to teach English in a *lise* (state secondary school) or *kolej* (private school) is that the Ministry of Education rules specify that teachers of English should have a university degree in English, Linguistics or related degree and preferably a PGCE or a BEd with English as a main subject. However, this is not strictly enforced.

CONDITIONS OF WORK

The normal deal is a one-year contract (which can usually be broken with one month's notice) and a monthly salary in Turkish lira starting at about £500, which may be supplemented by a relocation allowance, free or subsidised accommodation and insurance. Hourly employment used to be fairly unusual in Turkey, but increasingly employers are finding it more profitable to pay by the hour, especially during low seasons, when the number of teaching hours goes down.

Over the years many employers have come in for criticism, with words such as 'cowboy', 'unprofessional' and 'untrustworthy' being bandied about by disappointed teachers. Browsing the web will eventually bring you to sites which name and shame schools that sack their teachers to save money, slash wages or pay late, fail to honour contracts, assign inflated marks to students to keep or attract custom, withhold certificates to prevent staff from leaving prematurely, expect teachers to work on a tourist visa and so on. It is not always easy to establish how current some of this information is, plus some of it must be taken with a pinch of salt. One poster on the web forum www.turkeycentral.com holds out against the tide of negativity:

> ***I'm working at a language school in Taksim, Istanbul, and with no experience teaching and a freshly acquired CELTA. I have to admit I couldn't be happier. My school has walked me through the residence permit and now I have a work permit too. On top of that I've made a bunch of good friends, and the students are super enthusiastic. Our school hires on a rolling basis, but the salary is nothing to brag about. It's a beginner's salary, though it can be supplemented by giving your own private lessons, but it's a start. And if you consider it temporary, a really good start at that! I should note that my school, in particular, had terrible reviews all over the net. That said, I still came to check it out when I got an interview. And I can testify that life in a language school is what you make of it – don't believe everything you read online about them. Just visit and find out.***

Some people in the ELT business believe that the situation is gradually improving, and that with increased regulation, there are fewer dodgy operators and swashbuckling and unscrupulous employers. One of those optimists is the director of studies at a major Istanbul school:

> ***I have worked for approximately four years in Turkey, in Istanbul and in a small remote town in the south. Prospective teachers always hear many horror stories about working in Turkey and to an extent they are well founded. In the past, schools and employers openly abused teachers' rights. But this is definitely changing. There are many good, up-and-coming organisations which can be trusted. Teachers should ask around, be careful about contracts and conditions, and not agree to the first job they are offered without checking out the school, its size, reputation, etc.***

It is important to remember that some teachers have a marvellous time, as **Raza Griffiths** had at the first school he worked for, which was in the town of Ordu on the Black Sea coast:

> ***It would be no exaggeration to say that as a native English person in a region of Turkey unused to foreigners, I enjoyed celebrity status, with lots of inquiring eyes and lots of invitations to dinner. Although the town did not exactly have a thriving cultural life as we would understand it, this was more than compensated for by the sociableness of the people and their deep desire for communication. Because it was a private school, money was not in short supply and the facilities were excellent, with computers, etc. The free furnished flat I was given was large and very comfortable, and there was a free school minibus service that took teachers to the school. On either side of the school there were hazelnut gardens, behind there were mountains and in front the Black Sea, all quite idyllic, especially in summer. The other teachers (all Turkish) were very welcoming from day one, despite the fact that I was less experienced and was getting four times their salary. I could live very comfortably on my salary and still have a lot left over for spending on holidays and clothes.***

The standard paid holiday allowance for teachers is 15 days. At inferior schools, national holidays must be taken out of this annual leave, including Muslim holidays such as Seker Bayrami, usually celebrated at the end of Ramadan, and Kurban Bayrami. The former lasts three days, the latter four days, and it is customary to make the bridge to a full week. Christmas is not observed much and you may be offered very little time off, especially in smaller schools where the majority of the staff is Turkish. Big chains of schools, where native English speakers are in the majority in the staff-room, tend to close for a week.

Most things can usually be negotiated in Turkey, be it the price of a carpet or the terms of a contract, so it is wise to shop around carefully before accepting a job. One non-negotiable condition in some schools is a proscription on facial hair for men and revealing clothing for women.

THE STUDENTS

The major schools are well equipped with computers, language labs and course materials. But better than the back-up facilities is the enthusiasm of the students, who are usually motivated, conscientious and well behaved, and enjoy group discussions. Teachers should not, however, expect too much interaction between teacher and pupil, as **Tara Dermot**, a teacher in Istanbul, describes:

> ***Walk into a classroom in Turkey and you are likely to find every kind of student that you would find all over the world: the eager, the shy, the lazy, the clever one . . . What sets Turkish students significantly apart in my experience is their passivity. Turks grow up in an incredibly teacher-centred learning environment so that is what they are expecting. Having them participate in a far more student-centred, communicative course can therefore be frustrating, but given time and perseverance they will soon see the benefits and the fun to be had.***

'*Willing if unimaginative*' was one teacher's description of her students. One undesirable aspect of Turkish education is that many *lises* (high schools) are strongly oriented to exam preparation and university entrance. On the whole, however, the friendly openness of young Turks may cause a foreign teacher to forget that Turkey is still 98% Muslim, where only 29% of women are in the workforce and outside the cities dress is conservative. Teachers are regarded as important figures in society and, as such, are expected to dress fairly conservatively.

Student behaviour differs radically, depending on what kind of institution you teach in. Private secondary schools tend to be populated with spoiled and immature kids who do not always respect their teachers. **Joan Smith** found this hard to stomach at the private school in Kayseri where she taught:

Turkish parents indulge their children something rotten. Rich spoilt students abound in my classroom and discipline goes out the window. Foreign teachers are regarded as inferior and are given even less respect than the Turkish teachers.

Joan did not think that she should have to tolerate some of the innuendos her male students were getting away with, but had little hope of justice if they and their friends denied her allegations.

DICK BIRD

Dick Bird's (and others') experiences have been very different. Dick, a veteran EFL teacher, taught in Turkey a long time ago but his description of his pupils is still apt:

I have found women students defer to a far higher level of male chauvinism than would be acceptable anywhere in the West. Turkish women also seem to have exceptionally quiet voices and I can't help feeling that this irritating characteristic is somehow related to their role in society - a case of being seen but not heard until you are very very close perhaps? Sometimes my students know too much grammar to be able to express themselves freely. As their own language is radically different to Indo-European languages they have a lot of difficulty adapting to the sentence structure of English: they regard relative clauses as a perversion and are baffled, if not mildly outraged, by the cavalier way English seems to use any tense it fancies to refer to future actions but is puritanically strict about how one may describe present and past events. Another difficulty Turks have is that we EFL teachers like to use a lot of words in our metalanguage (i.e language about language, e.g. adjective, verb) which do not have cognates in Turkish as they do in other European languages, for example a teacher may inform their students that 'will' expresses probability, not intention; this will be readily understood by an elementary-level Spaniard but is total gibberish to a Turk (as I suspect it is to a great many native speakers of English).

Dick's analysis of Turkish EFL students ends with a light-hearted description of their irrepressible energy and enthusiasm. I have retained it for many editions of this book since it is so much fun:

Whenever the class is asked a question they would fain prostrate themselves at their teacher's feet were it not that years of instilled discipline keep them penned by invisible bonds within the confines of their desks until the ringing of the bell, whereat pandemonium breaks loose as a thousand berserk adolescents fling themselves across the (highly polished) corridor floors and down the (marble) steps headlong into the playground. (This phenomenon may help to explain why fire drills are not a regular feature of Turkish school life.)

A long-time TEFL teacher **Kathryn Saville** was offered a job by Neville Wells, founder and director of the Business English Academy in Istanbul (see entry), after a Skype interview.

> ***I had done this kind of teaching before, travelling around the city to students at their places of work, teaching in meeting rooms, offices and cafés, sometimes to large groups but usually one-to-ones. My contract is written in Turkish for the purposes of getting my visa, however I had a recommendation from a friend who had worked for BEA, one of the better paying companies in the city, assuring me that the employer was reliable and fair. I feel that he is my agent to link me with work. I enjoy this style of work as it leaves me plenty of free time to do my own thing (in my case creating art) and can rearrange my schedule to suit both me and my students. Travelling around the city can be gruelling though and sometime finding the address is a challenge. The most important and satisfying element of this job is getting to know the students who are mostly professionals or students and very motivated to learn.***

ACCOMMODATION

Accommodation is almost never offered to teachers hired in Turkey, but is sometimes made available for foreign hires. If accommodation is provided as part of your contract, it may be located close to the school in a modern flat which you will have to share with another teacher or it may be some way away, possibly in an undesirable neighbourhood. Fortunately not many teachers are assigned accommodation as gruesome as **Philip Dray**'s in Izmir:

> ***Cockroaches, centipedes, noisy neighbours, a filthy shower room and a fitted kitchen circa 1920 – I was slowly adjusting to it all. But one day, while I was having a shower, I saw a rat looking at me from the ventilation shaft and I knew that my patience had run out. I asked for a new flat but they said they couldn't get a new one before May. So, reluctantly (as there were some very nice people at the school) I had to leave.***

If the school doesn't provide a flat it should help you find one and act as go-between with the landlord. Most provide some kind of rent subsidy, since rents in Turkey are high relative to the cost of living. The situation in over-crowded Istanbul is especially tight. One agency estimates that shared accommodation will cost at least 500 lira a month per person in smaller towns, but 700–1,000 lira in Istanbul. It is not uncommon to bargain over the rent as if you were buying a second-hand car. Flats and rooms in shared apartments are advertised on Craigslist etc., or there are estate agencies called *emlak*, but these tend to charge a month's rent. Foreigners are usually considered an attractive proposition as they tend to be undemanding tenants.

In Istanbul, the nicest flats are along the Bosphorus, where the air is clean, the views stunning and a lot of the buildings are older properties with a lot of character; this is why they have been snapped up by well-heeled diplomats and multinationals. The Asian side of the city might have less charm but it also has less pollution and many people prefer it.

LEISURE TIME

Even if you are earning a salary at the lower end of the scale, you should be able to afford quite a good life, especially if you eat a lot of bread, drink local wines and use public transport. Basic meals and food, transport, hotels and cinemas (most films are subtitled rather than dubbed) are still very reasonable, especially away from the seaside and Istanbul. Depending on your smartphone can be problematic. Foreign visitors are prohibited by law from using their own mobile devices after the first 90 days without registering them. You will need to register the phone (for a fee) before applying for a residence permit. You can buy used mobiles for 70–100 lira and a SIM card starts at about 50 lira.

With the benefit of hindsight, **John Boylan** decided the hassles of life in Turkey weren't so bad after all:

> ***Recognise why you are in Turkey – for the experience – and try to enjoy that. You have a chance to live in a fascinating city for a year on the basis of a one-month certificate. You may live near Taksim and, let's be honest, could you afford to live a stone's throw from the equivalent in London or New York? Don't fall into the trap of mixing only with EFL teachers. Broaden your horizons and don't spend all your time in expat bars with a clique of English teachers. Socialising all the time with the same teachers can lead to a climate of moaning. Constructive criticism/advice is fine but too many teachers become bitter and vengeful. Most Turks are OK. If you want to make Turkish friends, get involved in sport or something where you'll see the same people regularly.***

Travel in Turkey is wonderfully affordable. The efficiency, comfort and low cost of Turkish bus travel put the coach services of most other countries to shame (though not their safety record).

Turkey generally is a great place to live and work. It's a fascinating country, full of contradictions, as befits a land that is the bridge between East and West.

LIST OF EMPLOYERS

BILKENT UNIVERSITY SCHOOL OF ENGLISH LANGUAGE
06800 Bilkent, Ankara
+90 312 290 5401

intrec@bilkent.edu.tr
www.busel.bilkent.edu.tr

Privately funded not-for-profit English-medium university, part of the national university system, within the Times Education Worldwide Top 50 New Universities.

NUMBER OF TEACHERS: 280 EFL/ESP teachers in preparatory and freshman programmes.

PREFERENCE OF NATIONALITY: Bilkent employs Turkish nationals and native English speakers from Australia, Canada, Britain, USA, South Africa and Ireland.

QUALIFICATIONS: Must be degree holder, preferably BEd or language degree; previous teaching experience not essential but a distinct advantage.

CONDITIONS OF EMPLOYMENT: Contracts from September to August. 20 contact hours per week.

SALARY: Salary quoted net in US dollars and Turkish lira, starting at approximately $900 plus 1,450 lira per month.

FACILITIES/SUPPORT: Free accommodation on campus, private health insurance, airfare and baggage allowance, residence permit, work visa, etc. Good facilities and opportunities for career advancement, e.g. to study for an ICELT, DELTA and/or MA on full scholarship.

RECRUITMENT: Directly via www.bilkent.edu.tr/~busel/interrec/index.html. Recruitment process for EFL/EAP instructors begins in February each year.

CONTACT: Head of Teacher Services.

BRITISH SIDE LANGUAGE SCHOOL
Barbaros Bulvarı No.91, Beşiktaş, Istanbul
+90 212 327 2700
frontoffice@britishside.com
www.britishside.com

British Side aspires to be the closest thing to a British Council teaching centre that exists in Turkey, since the British Council closed in Istanbul in 2006/7.

PREFERENCE OF NATIONALITY: None provided they are native speakers.

QUALIFICATIONS: CELTA or equivalent, i.e. an externally assessed course with a minimum of 120 hours of input and at least 6 hours of observed teaching practice with feedback. 2 years of full-time teaching experience (applicants with less experience will be considered based on feedback from their teaching course tutor).

CONDITIONS OF EMPLOYMENT: 2-year contracts. Full-time is considered to be 76+ hours per month. Most courses run in the evenings and at weekends. Usually those who work on Saturdays and Sundays have 3 days off in the week. Other work patterns are available.

SALARY: Net salaries are competitive, among the highest of language schools in Istanbul. Hourly pay range is 39.60–50.30 lira, depending on qualifications and experience.

FACILITIES/SUPPORT: No official help given but the large network of teachers usually assists newcomers in finding flats/rooms within a few weeks. Structured professional development programmes, with weekly training workshops (which teachers are paid to attend), bonus schemes and private health insurance provided free for full-time teachers (discounted price for hourly paid teachers). New teachers submit their details and passport photos to HR department, who make an appointment with the relevant authorities.

RECRUITMENT: Face-to-face interviews with candidates already residing or recently moved to Turkey is the preferred method, though occasionally Skype interviews are conducted.

CONTACT: Moudood Sayeed, Branch Manager & Corporate Courses (moudood.sayeed@britishside.com).

THE BUSINESS ENGLISH ACADEMY
Lati Lokum Sokak, Alp Han No.3, Kat 5, Mecidiyeköy, Istanbul
+90 212 356 0248/49/50
bea@bea-tr.com
www.bea-tr.com

NUMBER OF TEACHERS: 15.

PREFERENCE OF NATIONALITY: None.

QUALIFICATIONS: CELTA plus minimum 3 years' experience, and a background relevant to teaching professionals and business people.

CONDITIONS OF EMPLOYMENT: 1-year contract teaching 25 hours a week.

SALARY: 5,000 lira a month (net).

FACILITIES/SUPPORT: No assistance with accommodation. Help given with red tape.

RECRUITMENT: Recommendation, word of mouth and internet. Nearly all apply from in-country.

CONTACT: Neville Wells, Managing Director.

EARLY AMERICAN ENGLISH
Gaziosmanpasa Branch, Mevlana Mah 869/1, Sok No: 62/A, Gaziosmanpasa, Istanbul
+90 212 650 4650
gaziosmanpasa@erkeningilizce.com
www.erkeningilizce.com/gaziosmanpasa

NUMBER OF TEACHERS: Up to 3.

PREFERENCE OF NATIONALITY: Good clear accent for teaching young learners aged 7–14.

QUALIFICATIONS: Must be cheerful and communicative.

CONDITIONS OF EMPLOYMENT: 1-year contract. To work 6 days a week, 8.30am–4pm with some variation in weekday and weekend schedules.

SALARY: Depends on whether hired as a full or part-time teacher. School normally pays a retainer plus a fee per lesson taught.

FACILITIES/SUPPORT: No assistance with accommodation or visas.

CONTACT: Dincer Demir, Head Teacher of ELT Department.

ENGLISH LIFE LANGUAGE SCHOOLS
Kapani Ishani, Konak, Pier Karsisi, TEB ustu Kat 2, Daire 2, Konak, Izmir
+90 232 441 1111
info@dilokulum.com
www.englishlife.com.tr

Group of franchise schools in Izmir, Denizli, Kusadasi, Konya and Usak in Western Turkey, affiliated to Deren & Koray International Tourism and Education Center and the English West group (entry below).

NUMBER OF TEACHERS: 7.

PREFERENCE OF NATIONALITY: English, Scottish, American, Australian, Canadian and New Zealander.

QUALIFICATIONS: Schools licensed by the Ministry of Education require teachers to have at least a 2-year university/college degree, however, a 4-year bachelor's degree is preferred. Those with a 2-year degree or bachelor's degree in a non-relevant field require a TEFL/TESOL certificate. This can be obtained online (preferably TEFL/TESL certification module and a special grammar module). Outgoing personality needed, with the ability to work in a team. The Callan Method of teaching English requires a sense of urgency, the use of miming and gesticulation, and the presentation of a clear accent with excellent pronunciation skills.

CONDITIONS OF EMPLOYMENT: 1-year contract, renewable for a second year, 20–25 hours per week.

SALARY: Salary is calculated on either hourly or salary-package basis. This varies by school and location, and will be discussed with candidate. All teaching positions have a 6-month probationary period with an increase in pay provided after successfully completing the probationary period.

FACILITIES/SUPPORT: Free accommodation for at least a month. Once teacher finds own accommodation, accommodation allowance of 250 lira is paid. Help with work permits and expenses met. Intensive 1-week teachers' training programme via the Callan Method given at time of hire and before starting teaching.

RECRUITMENT: Via www.eslcafe.com and others.

CONTACT: Koray Altan, MSc (Manager) and Chuck Militello (Regional Director/Education Group Coordinator).

ENGLISH TIME LANGUAGE SCHOOLS
Time Education Group (TEG), Açelya Cd, Beylikdüzü OSB, 34520, Istanbul; Istiklal Caddesi, Örs Turistik s Merkezi No:151, Taksim/Beyoğlu, Istanbul 34300
+90 212 879 2926
www.englishtime.com

NUMBER OF TEACHERS: 200+ part-time and full-time for 40+ branches throughout Turkey, including Izmir, Izmit, Antalya, Bursa, Ankara and Eskisehir.

PREFERENCE OF NATIONALITY: US, Canada, UK, South Africa, Australia, New Zealand.

QUALIFICATIONS: Teachers must have a university degree and a TEFL, TESOL or CELTA certificate. Experience is preferred.

CONDITIONS OF EMPLOYMENT: Full-time teachers are offered a 6 or 10-month contract based upon experience. Classes run 7 days a week. Choice of 4 programmes: weekday morning course (10am–2pm for 6 weeks); weekday evenings (7–10pm for 8 weeks); weekend mornings (9am–1pm for 15 weeks) and weekend afternoons (3–7pm for 15 weeks). Rolling start dates according to when classes fill rather than according to semesters or terms. Part-time work also on offer.

SALARY: 3,000 lira per month for whole package. Housing or housing support, end-of-contract bonus and travel allowance. Hourly salary 18–20 lira (£4.50–£5) net.

FACILITIES/SUPPORT: Furnished housing provided on arrival and then help with accommodation search, with rent subsidy. Help with red tape given.

RECRUITMENT: Internet job searches, blogs, current teachers' recommendations, word of mouth. Interested applicants to complete online application form and send CV and photo. Interviews carried out by phone or Skype.

ENGLISH WEST/DEREN KORAY GROUP

Cumhuriyet Bulvari, No 36 Kapani Ishani Kat 2, Konak, Izmir (Pier Karsisi, Konak-Izmir)

+90 232 489 4747

info@englishwest.com; info@derenkoray.com.tr

NUMBER OF TEACHERS: 36.

PREFERENCE OF NATIONALITY: English, Scottish, American, Canadian, New Zealander and Australian.

QUALIFICATIONS: Schools licensed by the Ministry of Education require teachers to have at least a 2-year university/college degree, however, a 4-year bachelor's degree is preferred. Those with a 2-year degree or bachelor's degree in a non-relevant field require a TEFL/TESOL certificate. This can be obtained online (preferably TEFL/TESL certification module and a special grammar module). Outgoing personality needed, with the ability to work in a team. The Callan Method of teaching English requires a sense of urgency, the use of miming and gesticulation, and the presentation of a clear accent with excellent pronunciation skills.

CONDITIONS OF EMPLOYMENT: 1-year contract, renewable for a second year, 20–25 hours per week.

SALARY: Salary is calculated either on hourly or salary-package basis. This varies by school and location, and will be discussed with candidate. All teaching positions have a 6-month probationary period with an increase in pay provided after successfully completing the probationary period.

FACILITIES/SUPPORT: Free accommodation for at least a month. Once teacher finds own accommodation, accommodation allowance of 250 lira is paid. Help with work permits and expense met. Intensive 1-week teachers' training programme via the Callan Method given at time of hire and before starting teaching.

RECRUITMENT: Via www.eslcafe.com and others.

CONTACT: Koray Altan, MSc (Manager) and Chuck Militello (Education Group Coordinator).

GENCTUR

Istiklal Cad. No.108, Aznavur Pasaji, Kat: 5, 34430 Galatasaray, Istanbul

+90 212 244 6230

workcamps@genctur.com; workcamps.in@genctur.com

www.genctur.com.tr; http://dilkurslari.genctur.com.tr; www.upegem.com (all in Turkish)

NUMBER OF TEACHERS: 10 volunteers for summer camps in Izmir.

PREFERENCE OF NATIONALITY: Native (or good) English speakers.

QUALIFICATIONS: Experience with children, workcamp or teaching experience is preferred.

CONDITIONS OF EMPLOYMENT: Volunteering for teaching English to children aged 12–17 at summer camps for 2 weeks, through outdoor activities, games and songs.

SALARY: Free board and lodging. Volunteer registration via IVS £210.

RECRUITMENT: Only through partner voluntary organisations abroad (e.g. IVS GB, Thorn House, 5 Rose Street, Edinburgh EH2 2PR; +44 131 243 2745; info@ivsgb.org; www.ivsgb.org).

CONTACT: Zafer Yilmaz (zafer.yilmaz@genctur.com); Kevser Cimenli (kevser@upegem.com).

INTERNATIONAL HOUSE ISTANBUL

Aydin Sok. F Blok No. 12/1, Levent, Istanbul 34300

+90 212 282 9064

www.ihistanbul.com.tr

NUMBER OF TEACHERS: 30 full-time and part-time.

PREFERENCE OF NATIONALITY: Must be native speaker or Turk.

QUALIFICATIONS: Must be from a country where the primary official language is English. Minimum requirements: university degree and a CELTA/TESOL certificate. At least 1 year's post-

CELTA teaching experience desirable; Business English experience especially useful. Turkish teachers need degree as English teacher plus pedagogy certification.

CONDITIONS OF EMPLOYMENT: 9-, 10-, or 12-month contracts based on a 5-day working week with 2 consecutive days off and 30 contact hours teaching per week. Part-time contracts are also available. Paid holiday, number of days depending on the length of the contract, plus state and religious holidays.

SALARY: 2,300–4,000 lira monthly, depending on experience and qualifications, including accommodation allowance of 500 lira.

FACILITIES/SUPPORT: Relocation allowance of up to $750. Full private health and life insurance.

RECRUITMENT: IH Recruitment or via internet or direct application. Interviews essential but can be by telephone/Skype. Some recruitment via www.iti-istanbul.com (email olga@iti-istanbul.com).

CONTACT: Mrs Zeynep Gunduzyeli, Director of Studies (zgunduzyeli@ihistanbul.com); Mr Bora Gunduzyeli, Director.

INTERNATIONAL HOUSE IZMIR

Necatibey Bulvari No 19 K5, Cankaya, Izmir

+90 232 484 2490

info@ilsizmir.com

http://english.ilsizmir.com

NUMBER OF TEACHERS: 4.

PREFERENCE OF NATIONALITY: None.

QUALIFICATIONS: Degree and CELTA Certificate (or equivalent).

CONDITIONS OF EMPLOYMENT: 1 year. 24 hours per week.

SALARY: Varies according to experience.

FACILITIES/SUPPORT: Advice given on finding accommodation. Help given with obtaining work permit after original degree and CELTA certificates plus passport are provided; school covers all costs.

RECRUITMENT: Carried out locally because local interviews needed.

CONTACT: Billy Hasirci, Director of Studies (bhasirci@ilsizmir.com).

ISTANBUL SEHIR UNIVERSITY SCHOOL OF LANGUAGES ENGLISH PREPARATORY PROGRAM

Istanbul Sehir University, Dogu Kampusu, Kusbakisi Cad. No:27, Altunizade, Uskudar, 34662 Istanbul

+90 444 4034

sepp@sehir.edu.tr

www.sehir.edu.tr

NUMBER OF TEACHERS: 10–15 per year.

PREFERENCE OF NATIONALITY: None.

QUALIFICATIONS: BA + CELTA or TESOL certificate is minimum requirement. MA in ELT or Applied Linguistics is preferable.

CONDITIONS OF EMPLOYMENT: 1-year contracts. Hours of teaching 8.30am–5.30pm with an afternoon off in the week.

SALARY: 3,500–4,500 lira (£975–£1,250) per month.

FACILITIES/SUPPORT: No assistance with accommodation. The HR Department is in charge of work and residence permits.

RECRUITMENT: Via ads posted on International Training Institute (ITI) Istanbul Joblist (http://jobs.iti-istanbul.com) and British Council mailing lists. Face-to-face interviews are essential; Skype interviews are not possible.

CONTACT: Dr Ilke Buyukduman, Director (ilkebuyukduman@sehir.edu.tr).

KENT SCHOOL OF ENGLISH – ISTANBUL

Bahariye Caddesi No. 15/2, 34710 Kadiköy, Istanbul

+90 216 347 2791 / 347 2792

info@kentenglish.com

For job applications:

dos@kentenglish.com

www.kentenglish.com

NUMBER OF TEACHERS: 10+.

PREFERENCE OF NATIONALITY: Native speakers of English from the USA, UK, Canada and Australia.

QUALIFICATIONS: Bachelor's degree and TEFL certificate required. Priority given to candidates with teaching experience.

CONDITIONS OF EMPLOYMENT: 8, 10 or 12-month contracts. Weekend, weekday and evening classes in and away from school premises (in-company training programmes). Weekly teaching hours 25+. Also run English summer courses.

SALARY: Average $1,200 per month.

FACILITIES/SUPPORT: Work and residency permits arranged. Some training provided. Paid vacation. Health insurance. Intensive CTEFL course (Via Lingua) available for those without a teaching certificate.

RECRUITMENT: Local interviews.

MARMARIS RECRUITMENT LTD

info@marmarisrecruitment.com

www.marmarisrecruitment.com

Online agency that charges £39.99 to register.

NUMBER OF TEACHERS: 100+.

PREFERENCE OF NATIONALITY: The partner academies prefer native English speakers from UK, USA, Canada and Europe.

QUALIFICATIONS: University degree in any subject and/or a teaching certificate such as TEFL.

CONDITIONS OF EMPLOYMENT: Contracts September–June. Monday–Friday, 9am–5pm, with some academies assigning weekend hours as well.

SALARY: 2,000–5,000 lira per month depending on qualifications and experience.

FACILITIES/SUPPORT: If accommodation is not provided by the academy, the agency will try to advise. Academies are responsible for facilitating visas.

RECRUITMENT: Skype interviews.

CONTACT: Sarah Jones, HR.

OXFORD VISION EDUCATION & VISA CONSULTANCY

Inebolu Sokak Sozer Apt. No: 9/6 kat: 2, Kabatas-Istanbul

+90 212 293 8350

istanbul@oxfordvision.com

www.oxfordvision.com

NUMBER OF TEACHERS: 35.

PREFERENCE OF NATIONALITY: USA, UK, Canada, Australia, New Zealand.

QUALIFICATIONS: Minimum 3 years' experience in primary or secondary school with BA degree in any subject and TEFL, TESOL or CELTA certificate.

CONDITIONS OF EMPLOYMENT: 8–9 months. 25 hours a week.

SALARY: Approximately $1,600 per month net.

FACILITIES/SUPPORT: Assistance given in finding accommodation. Government requires employers to apply for work permits after submitting original degree and TEFL certificates.

RECRUITMENT: Via Skype or local interviews.

CONTACT: TEFL Recruitment Manager.

SDM LANGUAGE SCHOOL AND EDUCATION AGENCY

Halaskargazi Caddesi No: 336/1 Kat:3–4, Sisli 34456 Istanbul

+90 212 233 0999

sts@sdm.com.tr

www.sdm.com.tr

PREFERENCE OF NATIONALITY: Native English speakers.

QUALIFICATIONS: University graduate, ELT qualification and experience of teaching adults.

CONDITIONS OF EMPLOYMENT: 6-day working week (with Fridays off). Working hours between 10am and 10pm. To teach mainly professionals.

FACILITIES/SUPPORT: Assistance with work permit given.

TEACHERS IN TURKEY

Fulya Mah. Buyukdere Cad., Defne Apt. No: 56 9/19, 34394 Mecidiyekoy, Sisli-Istanbul

+90 212 347 0348

tt@teachersinturkey.com

www.teachersinturkey.com

NUMBER OF TEACHERS: 100–150 per year for private schools, kindergartens, primary schools, secondary schools and universities throughout Turkey. Also summer camps.

PREFERENCE OF NATIONALITY: UK, USA, Canada, Australia, New Zealand, Ireland, South Africa.

QUALIFICATIONS: Native English speaker, undergraduate degree, and teaching certificate (e.g. TEFL, TOESL, CELTA).

CONDITIONS OF EMPLOYMENT: September/October to June. 30 teacher hours per week normally Monday–Friday 8.30am–5pm. Pay day is 15th of month.

SALARY: Starting at 2,500 lira (£600) per month. Completion bonus of 2,000 lira.

FACILITIES/SUPPORT: Assistance given in locating suitable housing, connecting roommates and translation help with contracts/landlords. Visa fees of $300–$500 will be reimbursed. Museum card given for free or discounted museum entrance nationwide. Orientation and teacher training seminars organised where possible.

RECRUITMENT: Via internet and in association with Teach to Travel agency in London (www.teachtotravel.co.uk). Personal interviews in UK and Turkey or Skype interviews.

CONTACT: Mr Oguzhan Imamoglu, Co-Founder & Academic Coordinator (oguzhan@teachersinturkey.com); Aydin Kurnaz, Recruiter (aydink44@hotmail.com).

TURCO-BRITISH ASSOCIATION

Bestekar Sokak No. 32, Kavaklidere, 06680 Ankara

+90 312 419 1844

dos@tba.org.tr

www.tba.org.tr

NUMBER OF TEACHERS: 20–30.

PREFERENCE OF NATIONALITY: British.

QUALIFICATIONS: Degree plus EFL qualification. Experience desirable.

CONDITIONS OF EMPLOYMENT: 2 years, 27 contact hours per week (45 minutes each lesson).

FACILITIES/SUPPORT: Shared, fully furnished accommodation, paid utilities, close proximity to school (about a 5-minute walk). Assistance with travel costs at the beginning and end of a 2-year contract. Residence and work permit procedures undertaken and costs met. 4 weeks' paid annual leave, Christmas holiday, national Turkish holidays. Settling-in bonus, national social security covered. TBA is the only association in Turkey acting as an independent Cambridge English Language Assessment Authorised Centre.

RECRUITMENT: Via the *Guardian*, internet and locally.

CONTACT: Ms Özlem Fraser, Administrative Co-ordinator.

TURKISH-AMERICAN ASSOCIATION

Güvenevler, Cinnah Cd. No:20, 06690 Çankaya/Ankara

+90 312 426 26 44

coursesinfo@taa-ankara.org.tr

www.taa-ankara.org.tr

Long-established binational centres affiliated to US Embassy.

NUMBER OF TEACHERS: 7–8 per year. Full-time and part-time.

PREFERENCE OF NATIONALITY: American, British, Canadian, Australian.

QUALIFICATIONS: All candidates need to have a higher education degree in language teaching or a TEFL/TESOL certificate. Candidates must be comfortable with the Communicative Approach. Some work with pre-school children for Young Learner specialists.

CONDITIONS OF EMPLOYMENT: 1-year contracts from June can be extended upon mutual agreement. Flexible hours with courses running mornings and evenings during the week, and all day at weekends. 2 days off per week.

SALARY: 2,140 lira for a 120-hour month, 2,500 lira for working 150 hours, both paid net.

FACILITIES/SUPPORT: Social security, housing and lunches are provided plus airfare upon completion of the contract. Shared housing is provided free of charge (not including domestic expenses). TAA runs the necessary paperwork in Turkey for visas.

RECRUITMENT: Via websites such as www.tefl.com and professional recruitment companies. Interviews can take place online.

UKLA ACADEMY LANGUAGE SCHOOLS

Dikkaldirim MH. Zübeyde Hn Cd. 15/A Demir Apt 16090 Osmangazi – Bursa

+90 224 232 1440

english@ukla.com.tr

www.ukla.com.tr; http://tr-tr.facebook.com/UKLAACADEMY

NUMBER OF TEACHERS: 15–20 per year. Branches also in Eskisehir and Izmir.

PREFERENCE OF NATIONALITY: Must be native speakers as this is government policy for foreign English teacher employment.

QUALIFICATIONS: Bachelor's degree and CELTA or equivalent certification. Relevant experience, e.g. one year of teaching adults, is an advantage; minimum 2 years experience for certain posts.

CONDITIONS OF EMPLOYMENT: 1-year contract from August/September, with 28–30 classroom hours per week.

SALARY: Starting at 2,000 lira per month (after tax).

FACILITIES/SUPPORT: Fully furnished shared housing, work visa, residence permit, health insurance, professional development support (seminars and workshops), airfares reimbursed.

RECRUITMENT: Process involves an application essay, lesson plan and a final interview carried out over the phone or by Skype.

CONTACT: Ms Jennifer Dodds, Director of Studies (Bursa); Elif Egilmez Sevinc, Eskisehir Branch Manager.

AFRICA

Contradictions abound in a continent as complex as Africa, and one of them pertains to the attitude to the English language. On the one hand, the emergent nations of Africa want to distance themselves from their colonial past. On the other hand, they are eager to develop and participate in the world economy and so need to communicate in English. Yet, linguistic questions are often eclipsed by various humanitarian crises and ongoing conflicts. Chaos in Congo and Somalia, government collapse in Libya, the Ebola outbreak, communal violence in the world's newest state, South Sudan, emergence of terrorist groups like Boko Haram in North-Eastern Nigeria and al-Qaeda in the Maghreb in Mauritania … none of these adds to Africa's allure. Scrolling through the Foreign & Commonwealth Office's travel warnings with their repeated 'advice against all but essential travel' in many regions is enough to put off many. Tunisia was a good-news story until June 2015 when terrorists killed 38 tourists including 30 Britons on a beach in the resort of Sousse. The tourist industry collapsed overnight and is still in tatters.

What makes much of Africa different from Latin America and Asia (vis-à-vis English teaching) is that English is the medium of instruction in state schools in many ex-colonies of Britain, including Ghana, Nigeria, Kenya, Zambia, Zimbabwe and Malawi. Some countries would like to get rid of English because it is seen as a colonial relic, without knowing which African language to use in its stead. For example, the Gambian president announced in 2014 that English would be dropped in favour of Arabic but nothing has changed to date. As in the Indian subcontinent, the majority of English teachers in these countries are locals. But there is still some demand for native English speakers in the secondary schools of those countries. The only countries in which there is any significant scope for working in a private language institute are the Mediterranean countries of Morocco, Tunisia and Egypt.

The drive towards English extends to most parts of the continent. Across Southern Africa, the dominant language of business and commerce and the language of university textbooks is English. It is typical that when Namibia acquired independence, it decided to make English its official language to replace Afrikaans. Ethiopia at present is pursuing a policy of improving the levels of English across the country, although its remarkable rate of 10% economic growth suffered a reversal in 2016 because of the drought. A demand for hundreds of native English speakers, mainly at the advanced teacher-trainer level, is created from time to time, which organisations such as the Department for International Development, VSO and Skillshare Africa attempt to supply. For example, the British Council in Dar es Salaam was running a large-scale project called EQUPT-ELT (part funded by DFID) in 34 training colleges across Tanzania to improve the English-language proficiency and teaching skills in the country, to make it easier for the country's students to move from Swahili-speaking primary school to secondary school where English is the medium of instruction. As of March 2016 the project was handed over to the Tanzanian Ministry of Education.

To balance the picture, it must be said that in some countries (such as Zambia, Nigeria, Sudan) the demand for English teachers has fallen off in favour of science, maths, technology and other languages. Even in ex-colonies of France (Morocco, Tunisia, Senegal, Mali, etc.) and of Portugal (Mozambique), English is a sought-after commodity. World traveller **Bradwell Jackson** several years ago discovered paid on-the-spot teaching opportunities in Mali, Mauritania and Senegal.

PROSPECTS FOR TEACHERS

Few language schools exist in African countries and fewer can afford to employ expat teachers. The British Council maintains offices in most African countries and is discouraging of the prospects for teachers. The English language is taught from a very early stage in many countries and, as a result, there are no institutes which specifically teach it. However, you may want to enquire at universities and colleges that teach English at an advanced level.

Because a high proportion of teaching opportunities in Africa are in secondary schools rather than private language institutes, a state teaching certificate is often a prerequisite. Missionary societies have played a dominant role in Africa's modern history, so many teachers are recruited through religious organisations, asking for a Christian commitment even for secular jobs. Apart from work with aid or missionary agencies, there are quite a few opportunities for students and people in their gap year to teach in Africa. Students and other travellers have also stumbled upon chances to teach on an informal basis.

FINDING A JOB

Many organisations, including a range of gap-year agencies, send people to Africa to teach English. These postings are normally regarded as 'voluntary' since wages, if paid at all, will be on a local scale though positions often come with free housing. In some cases a substantial placement fee must be paid. For links to smaller local charities that charge no placement fee, search the listing of Volunteer Programs in Africa at www.truetravellers.org/free-volunteer-programs-in-africa for teaching opportunities. See the chapter 'Finding a job' in Part 1 of this book for further details of the general agencies that send students such as **Sarah Johnson** from Cardiff who went to Zanzibar to teach English and geography at a rural secondary school. Once she started work Sarah discovered that:

> ***The expectations which Zanzibari children have from school are worlds away from those of British school children. They expect to spend most of their lessons copying from the blackboard, so will at first be completely nonplussed if asked to think things through by themselves or to use their imagination. I found that the ongoing dilemma for me of teaching in Zanzibar was whether to teach at a low level which the majority of the class would be able to understand, or teach the syllabus to the top one or two students so that they would be able to attempt exam questions, but leaving the rest of the class behind. Teaching was a very interesting and eye-opening experience. I believe that both the Zanzibari teachers and I benefited from a cultural exchange of ideas and ways of life.***

Networks like Couchsurfing (www.couchsurfing.com) have hosts registered all over Africa, who might be interested in exchanging hospitality for English lessons. **Bradwell Jackson** stayed with a couchsurfing host in Bamako, Mali for two months:

> ***He is a wealthy man who lives in a nice house, and I get all my meals, internet, my laundry and a few other odds and ends done for free. I teach him two hours every day, which leaves me lots of time to explore Bamako and do whatever else I like.***

Just one word of caution about internet offers: if you see a job advertised that looks too good to be true, do not be tempted to investigate further. Although thankfully rare, scams aimed at 'greedy' foreigners can be sophisticated and seemingly plausible.

PLACEMENT ORGANISATIONS

Africa & Asia Venture (www.aventure.co.uk). Offers students and recent graduates the chance to spend three to five months teaching a wide variety of subjects, especially English in Africa (Uganda, Kenya, Tanzania, Malawi and South Africa). The 2016 participation fee ranges from £1,645 for a 5 week summer programme to £3,285 for 16 weeks plus airfares.

Link Ethiopia (www.linkethiopia.org/volunteering). London-based charity that places volunteers (including gap-year students) for one to six months in partner schools in Ethiopia. Fee for standard three-month placement is £495 plus an equal amount to be fundraised to help the schools.

Peace Corps, 1111 20th St NW, Washington DC 20526 (✆ +1 855 855 1961 toll-free; www.peacecorps.gov). Nearly half of Peace Corps volunteers are posted to Africa, many of whom teach on 27-month assignments in 27 African countries, ranging from Mali to Mozambique. Must be US citizen, over 18 and in good health. All expenses, including airfare and health insurance, are covered.

Projects Abroad (www.projects-abroad.co.uk). Work placements in schools in Ethiopia, Ghana, Kenya, Madagascar, Morocco, Senegal, South Africa, Tanzania, and Togo.

Project Trust (www.projecttrust.org.uk). Sends school leavers (aged 17–19) to teach (often other subjects as well as English) in schools in seven African countries including Malawi, Botswana, Senegal and Swaziland. Participants must fundraise to cover part of the cost of their 12-month placement, at present £6,200 (2016).

Sazani (www.sazani.org). 6-week voluntourism placements as teaching assistants in nurseries and state schools in Zanzibar; cost for individuals is £3,500.

Travellers (www.travellersworldwide.com). Placements to teach conversational English in Ghana, Morocco, South Africa and Zambia, plus other teaching in Zimbabwe.

Village-to-Village (http://v2vtanzania.org/volunteers). Volunteers are sent to the Kilimanjaro region of Tanzania to assist on various projects including teaching English in primary schools and orphanages, teacher training as well as construction and sustainable agriculture projects.

Village Africa, Hampshire (www.villageafrica.org.uk). Teaching volunteer programme in the West Usambara Mountains of Tanzania suspended in 2012 due to changes in the immigration rules, but visitors still welcome on 90-day tourist visa to help children practise their English.

WorldTeach, One Brattle Square, Suite 550, Cambridge, MA 02138, USA (✆ +1 857 259 6646; www.worldteach.org). Non-profit organisation that recruits volunteers to teach English in Namibia, Morocco and South Africa, among other countries around the world. A 12-month placement in Namibia costs $2,490, while a summer in Morocco costs $3,990.

ON THE SPOT

The best chances of picking up language-teaching work on the spot are in North Africa, in Egypt, Morocco or Tunisia (treated separately below). Language schools are thriving in South Africa, staffed in large measure by English-speaking South Africans but also by foreigners. Tourists can enter South Africa on a tourist visa for three months, renewable for a further three (for a fee) at an office of the Department of Home Affairs, provided the application is lodged at least 45 days before the original visa expires.

If teachers (British as well as American) are prepared to travel to an African capital for an interview with one of the US State Department-sponsored English teaching centres in Africa (often attached to American embassies), they may be given some freelance opportunities. Virtually all hiring of teachers in these government-run language programmes takes place locally, so speculative applications from overseas are seldom welcome. This is how one American got her foot in the door and went on to become the director:

> ***Work in an American Cultural Center is a great way to start off. I myself did it five years ago and am now running a programme. It allows a person to work in Africa but also provides up-to-date material which teachers in the national programmes are often forced to go without. Classes are small and the hours are not too heavy but can usually be increased, depending on the capabilities of the teacher. We also do outside programmes in specialised institutions and thus give teachers experience in ESP (hotels, oil companies, Ministries). People with degrees in EFL are very much in demand.***

The regional offices are located in Dakar for West Africa, Dar es Salaam for East Africa and Pretoria for Southern Africa.

At the opposite end of the spectrum, grassroots voluntary organisations may have teaching positions. For example The Volta Aid Foundation (www.voltaaidfoundation.org) places teaching volunteers in the eastern province of Ghana; the necessary qualifications are 'a big smile, warm heart and a good grasp of English'. Volunteers stay with local Ghanaian families and cover their living expenses by paying $500 for the first month and $350 for subsequent months.

Till Bruckner is a veteran world traveller who has a decided preference for fixing up teaching and voluntary placements independently:

> ***My advice to anyone who wants to volunteer in Africa (or anywhere else) is to go first and volunteer second. That way you can travel until you've found a place you genuinely like and where you think you might be able to make a difference. You can also check out the work and accommodation for yourself before you settle down. If you're willing to work for free, you don't need a nanny to tell you where to go. Just go.***

Opportunities crop up in very obscure corners of the continent. Travel blogger **Kim Reuter** spent several years exploring possibilities in Africa:

> ***There are a ridiculous number of job positions just waiting to be filled in Africa ... but you have to be THERE to find them. For example, while living in Madagascar, I visited the local university and was offered a teaching position on the spot because of my English speaking skills. This position, never advertised online, will only become available to you if you are in the right place at the right time. Obviously the 'right place' is not your faux leather couch in South-West Florida.***

Even further off the beaten track is the island of La Réunion, a département of France between Madagascar and Mauritius. Apparently there is a market for freelance teachers; consider advertising in the paper *Quotidien* (www.lequotidien.re).

PROBLEMS AND REWARDS

Rural Africa can, without doubt, lead to culture shock. Whether it is the hassle experienced by women teachers in Muslim North Africa or the loneliness of life in a rural West African village, problems proliferate. Anyone who has fixed up a contract should try to gather as much up-to-date information as possible before departure, online or by attending some kind of orientation programme or briefing. Otherwise local customs can come as a shock. On a more basic level, you will need advice on how to cope with climatic extremes. Even Cairo can be unbearably hot in the summer (and surprisingly rainy and chilly in January/February).

One unexpected problem is when locals are overawed by foreigners, as **Mary Hall** describes:

> ***A white person is considered to be the be-all and end-all of everyone's problems for whatever reason. It's quite difficult to live with this image. Stare and stare again, never a moment to yourself. I'd like to say the novelty wore off but it never did. Obviously adaptability has to be one of the main qualities. We had no running water, intermittent electricity and a lack of such niceties as cheese and chocolate.***

A certain amount of deprivation is almost inevitable; for example teachers, especially volunteers, can seldom afford to shop in the pricey expatriate stores and so will have to be content with the local diet, typically a staple cereal such as millet usually made into a kind of stodgy porridge, plus some cooked greens, tinned fish or meat and fruit. The cost of living in some African cities such as Freetown and Douala is in fact very high, and a teaching wage does not normally permit a luxurious lifestyle. **Peter Kent** taught in Tanzania and kept a journal throughout his stay:

> ***Bit worried about the food situation, only seems to be tomatoes, onions and potatoes at the market so a pretty boring diet. Sijaona is, if I understand her right, going to show us where you can buy more exotic veg . . . Taught standard one (ie year 1) today for the first time since they started this term. There are 105 kids, five or six to a bench which fits three normally. Quite a sight really, 105 bright-eyed kids staring expectantly at you. Mrs Msigwa, their teacher, seems really nice, keen and capable. We may get somewhere between us. You get the impression that if you stuck with them for years to come they'd be speaking English.***

But of course volunteer teachers can't stick around that long and after less than a year it was time for Peter Kent to bid farewell to his school amidst present giving, choir singing and emotional speeches.

Health is obviously a major concern to anyone headed for Africa. The fear of HIV-contaminated blood or needles in much of Central Africa prompts many teachers to outfit themselves with a complete expat medical kit before leaving home (see Introduction). Malaria is rife and there is an alarming amount of mosquito resistance to the most common prophylactics, so this too must be sorted out with a tropical diseases expert before departure.

The visa situation differs from country to country of course but is often a headache. Whereas in Cameroon it is not really necessary to obtain a work permit, in Ethiopia it is much more problematic. The rules in Tanzania are complicated too: whether on a three-month tourist visa or two-month visa (both $50 for Britons at the border) you are not permitted to work or volunteer without a valid work permit, which should be arranged with your sponsoring agency.

If all that Africa could offer was a contest with malaria and a diet of porridge, no one would consider teaching there. But anyone who has seen David Attenborough's 'Africa' series can imagine how the continent holds people in thrall. A chance to see the African bush, to climb the famous peaks of Kilimanjaro or Kenya, to frequent the colourful markets, these are the pleasures of Africa which so many people who have worked there find addictive.

TEFL training can lead to unexpected opportunities in Africa. After graduating from York University **Miranda Crowhurst** was pleased to be accepted for one of the 12 places on a CELTA course in her hometown of Cambridge with the Bell School, and really enjoyed the course. While searching for jobs abroad she came across an intriguing opening in Tanzania to teach the young children of two expat families, and secured the seven-month position. She sent back descriptions of her life and adventures, divided between a prospering avocado farm and the nearby town of Mbeya, in a picture postcard Africa:

> ***The farm is just in front of Rungwe volcano and right up against the jungle – you would not believe how beautiful it is looking out over the mountains from my cottage. At dawn when we set off for town, the sun rises spectacularly, lighting up trucks piled with farm labourers, forested mountains silhouetted against the pink sky, and sweeps of mist lying lazily over the villages. I also love walking round town – lots of people say hello in Swahili, and hi, and good afternoon. I'm the only white person I ever see and it makes me feel a little bit like a light bulb, but although people definitely notice me, no one hassles me, is pushy or unfriendly.***

EGYPT

The aftermath of the Arab Spring has decidedly failed to bring about the move to democracy that Egyptians who demonstrated hoped to achieve. The situation in 2015 and 2016 has been calmer, but the politics still polarised. High inflation and a shortage of foreign currency led to the Egyptian pound being devalued by 13% in 2016 and an increasing differential between the official rate (8.80 to the dollar) and black market rate (up to 12 to the dollar).

However, media reports can present an unduly negative image of everyday life in Egypt, and there is anything but hostility to the English language. The British Council's English teaching operations have expanded to take in new partners in suburban Cairo and a teaching centre in Alexandria. Of Egyptians who want to learn English, a large percentage is from the business community, though there is also a demand among university students and school children. Many young Egyptians who aspire to work in their country's computing or tourist industry want to learn English. Students at computer training schools or at tourism training centres like the one in Luxor might be looking for some private tuition from a native speaker.

Check the online *Yellow Pages* in English at www.yellowpages.com.eg; a search for 'Language schools and instruction' reveals more than 300. At one end of the spectrum there are the British Council's Teaching Centres in Alexandria and Cairo (Agouza, Heliopolis – a second is soon to open – and Sheikh Zayed City, 40km west of the city centre). At the other there are plenty of dubious establishments. Whereas you will need a professional profile for the former, back-street schools will be less fussy.

The British Council employs more than 100 teachers at five centres in Egypt. For many years Cairo has been one of the few large teaching centres in the British Council network where a recently qualified EL teacher has a good chance of being hired and quickly promoted. The minimum requirements are native English-speaker status, UK passport, CELTA or Trinity TESOL and two years' post-qualification teaching experience. If you are already in Egypt and there are suitable vacancies you will be invited for an interview and demonstration lesson (having sat in on another class beforehand). Summer is a good time to look, when the regular teachers tend to go away to escape the heat. During exam time there is also a need for one-to-one tutors and paid invigilators. The British Council (as always) has a great library and is a good place to teach. The main branch is located centrally in Agouza with another large centre in Heliopolis, which is quite a way from the centre of town and therefore has its own social world. The El-Alsson International School in Giza (www.alsson.com), out near the Pyramids, employs a number of expat teachers.

When **Dan Boothby** spent time in Cairo he found it almost alarmingly easy to find work:

> ***I taught one-to-one lessons to several people and got about five hours a week work and charged £10 an hour. Frankly this was much more than I was worth but if you charge less than the market rate then it is felt that you are an amateur. I taught an isolated and lonely five-year-old, son of the Georgian Consul, where I was more a babysitter than a tutor. I felt so guilty about the fee I was charging that I spent an hour trying to get him to learn something. I didn't feel so guilty charging to tutor the Georgian Ambassador, since he probably passed the bill on to his government.***
>
> ***I got a lot of students through friends that I made who were teaching at the international schools. The kids at these schools are often in need of extra tuition towards exam times when their parents realise that they've been mucking about all year and are close to failing. The problem is that the kids tend to be very uninterested and so it is difficult to make them concentrate. But I enjoyed one-to-ones. You could build up a large group of students and earn a decent wage but equally teach less hours and have more time – one of the reasons for getting out of England.***

Cairo seems to be a city where work seeks out the casual teacher rather than the other way round. Taxi drivers and hotel staff may ask you, unprompted, if you are available to teach. Most of these are genuine offers but it is best (especially for women) to be cautious. Most job-seekers find that potential bosses are not as interested in their educational background and experience as in how much confidence they can project. It is not unknown for an interview to take place over a game of chess and plenty of glasses of tea so that your general demeanour can be assessed. Jobs seem to be available year round, so there is no right or wrong time to arrive.

Language schools are not all located in Central Cairo but also in the leafy, prosperous residential areas such as Heliopolis, Maadi and Zamalek. Residential areas are also the best areas to look for private clients, as **Ian McArthur** found:

> ***In Cairo I sought to work as a private English tutor. I made a small poster, written in English and Arabic, with the help of my hotel owner. I drew the framework of a Union Jack at the top, got 100 photocopies and then meticulously coloured in the flags. The investment cost me £3. I put the posters up around Cairo, concentrating on affluent residential and business districts. I ended up teaching several Egyptian businessmen, who were difficult to teach since they hated being told what to do.***

More recently an American traveller about to start law school posted the following on Lonely Planet's Thorn Tree forum:

> ***Back in December I posted a message asking people if they thought it was possible to get short-term jobs abroad or if it was a good idea to possibly make tutoring flyers to put up around town. Both were ideas to supplement the money I already had saved and to have some new adventures/meet locals while travelling. I got a ton of negative responses telling me those ideas wouldn't work, etc, etc. Just wanted to post back on here six months later that it IS possible and my friend and I just did it. We got teaching jobs in Egypt that paid fairly well, without having work permits, without having TEFL, and the classes were for business professionals and thus were short term (five weeks). Also, we put up tutoring flyers all over Cairo and made a decent amount of money doing private tutoring.***

The American University, centrally located at the eastern end of the famous Tahrir Square, is a good place to find work contacts though teaching for the AUC itself is difficult; only five candidates a month are granted an interview so they can afford to be highly selective. Also try the noticeboards at the Community Services Association (CSA No. 4, Road 21, Maadi, Cairo; www.livinginegypt.org), where a range of services for expats is offered including a tutor referral list. In fact beginners' English and conversational English are taught on the premises.

The best places to meet other expats and find out about work opportunities are expat meeting places like El Horreya Café downtown, or the Ace Club in Maadi. Also try the café-bars near the American University.

STUDENTS

In an article in the *EL Gazette*, Jonathan Gayther of the British Council Cairo described their students as '*lively, welcoming, and always ready to venture an opinion*'. Another teacher describes his Egyptian students at a language institute in the north-west suburb of Sahafeyeen as '*rowdy and sometimes a little over-enthusiastic*'. Having just obtained a Cambridge Certificate in London, he went to visit some friends in Cairo and was immediately offered a three-month summer contract where they were desperate for a teacher. He had to adapt his lessons to please both the ebullient Egyptian youths and a group of shy and industrious Somalis and describes his predicament with such a mixed class:

> ***Different religions, different ways of thinking and (as I learnt in my first week at the school) different modes of dress must all be taken into consideration. One of the problems that English students in this area have difficulty with is hearing the difference between B and P. The exercise for this is to hold a piece of paper in front***

of the mouth and repeat the letters B and P. Since more air is exhaled during the sounding of the letter P than with B, the paper should fly up when P is said, and move only a little with B. The first time I made the students do this we went round the class, first Hamid the engineer from Alexandria, then Mona who was trying to get a job at the reception in the Hilton and then we came to Magda from Mogadishu (the capital of Somalia). All the Egyptians started to laugh – her whole face apart from her eyes was covered with a yashmak. I decided that this should not impede the exercise so if the yashmak moved it was a P, and not a B!

Living expenses are creeping up, as are taxes, though a teacher's salary still permits a comfortable lifestyle. The CELTA course offered by the British Council in Cairo used to be one of the cheapest in the world; however, the current fee of 18,400 Egyptian pounds works out at £1,570.

Most teachers enter Egypt on a tourist visa ($25 on arrival) and then ask their school to help them extend it. The multiple-entry tourist visa is valid for a maximum of six months and costs £32. However, a business visa can be issued if you have a letter of invitation from a company (£65 for single entry, £105 for multiple). This is valid for six months and schools will help to extend it. British citizens can find up-to-date visa information at www.egyptianconsulate.co.uk. Work permits must be applied for by your employer to the Ministry of the Interior in Egypt.

LIST OF EMPLOYERS

AMIDEAST EGYPT

Cairo Office: 38 Mohie El Din, Abou El Ezz Street, Dokki-Giza, Cairo

+20 2 19263

HR-egypt@amideast.org; egypt@amideast.org

www.amideast.org.egypt/careers

Alexandria Office: 28 Damitte St, Roushdy, Alexandria

alexandria@amideast.org

www.amideast.org/egypt/careers

NUMBER OF TEACHERS: 15–22. Possible openings with 13 partner Off-site Service Providers, such as Skills Castle Academy, linked from website.

PREFERENCE OF NATIONALITY: North American, but all native English speakers are welcome to apply.

QUALIFICATIONS: Minimum CELTA or TESOL certification, university degree and preferably 2–3 years of teaching adults.

CONDITIONS OF EMPLOYMENT: Local term-to-term hire agreements according to student numbers. 8–15 hours per week, 9 5-week sessions per year. Students are working adults and university students.

SALARY: $5.50–$8 an hour (paid in local currency). Contracted teachers earn $13, less 17.65% for tax and contributions.

FACILITIES/SUPPORT: Good teachers' resources, internet access, friendly working environment. Operates out of three historic mansions on the Mediterranean. No financial assistance with accommodation given, but temporary housing can be arranged with no cost. No assistance given with work permits.

RECRUITMENT: Pre-interview questions sent to applicants via email, and then a classroom demonstration.

BRITISH COUNCIL EGYPT

192 El Nil Street, Agouza, Cairo. Also in Heliopolis and Alexandria.

+20 2 33001666

MENA-TeacherRecruitment@ae.britishcouncil.org; information@britishcouncil.org.eg

https://jobs.britishcouncil.org/Login.aspx; www.britishcouncil.org.eg

NUMBER OF TEACHERS: 100+ employed in Alexandria and Cairo area to teach 4,000+ adults and 1,650 young learners at centres in Agouza and Heliopolis, with branches in Nasr City and Sheikh Zayed City. Also take on trainee teachers newly qualified.

PREFERENCE OF NATIONALITY: British (or Egyptian).

QUALIFICATIONS: UK passport, CELTA or Trinity TESOL and 2 years' post-qualification teaching experience. For visa reasons candidates must be less than 60. Enhanced DBS disclosure is mandatory.

CONDITIONS OF EMPLOYMENT: 2-year contracts from mid-August. Classes offered 7 days a week, though most teachers teach either over 5 days each week or 4 days with 1 (non-teaching) work day. 25 contact hours per week.

SALARY: Local annual salary from about 8,700–12,000 Egyptian pounds (net) paid monthly into an Egyptian bank account plus sterling supplement to teachers recruited outside Egypt paid into a UK bank account. Airfares, visa costs and medical insurance are also provided.

FACILITIES/SUPPORT: Compulsory in-service training offered. Assistance given with pursuing DELTA, IBET or YL extension. Help given with accommodation and visas.

RECRUITMENT: Ads are placed many months in advance of vacancies but recruitment is ongoing. Batch recruitment via the British Council MENA Recruitment Unit in Dubai. Deadline is mid-March; interviews in April.

CONTACT: Carol Ashen (Carol.Ashen@britishcouncil.org.eg).

SUDAN

According to the constitution of the Republic of Sudan, drawn up in 2005, the two official languages are Arabic and English. After many years of diplomacy, South Sudan achieved national autonomy in July 2011 and its official language is only English, though most people speak Arabic or dialects of Arabic. Unfortunately, conflict returned to South Sudan in 2016, and in July of that year most foreigners were evacuated, especially from the capital Juba, and many local people fled to refugee camps across the border in Uganda.

Most of Sudan is relatively peaceful at present, with the important exception of Darfur in the west. The long-established NGO the Sudan Volunteer Programme, based in London and Khartoum (see entry), sends volunteers to help young Sudanese improve their English through contact with British volunteers. The volunteer's responsibilities might include running discussion groups, providing support for teachers at universities, training for public servants, teacher-training course design and developing course materials for English for legal purposes. Other volunteers have run General English courses and helped with English clubs, especially for pre-sessional and inter-sessional groups of university students. Some volunteers have produced and participated in radio programmes for learners of English and done editorial work for an English-language newspaper, so there is plenty of scope for pursuing individual talents and interests. In collaboration with the Sudan Ministry of Education, SVP has been developing a programme for volunteers to teach in secondary schools where the emphasis is on teaching the teachers and setting up English Clubs.

This is all good news for a country in which the current government has shown little inclination to support the teaching of English as a second language and has instead promoted the Arabisation of the country's educational system. As a result, the general standard of English has sharply declined over the past generation. Some are worried about their personal security, based on media coverage and FCO travel warnings.

Undaunted by bad publicity, **Rebecca Mallinson**, a mature volunteer, described in her revealing blog her motivations and feelings on the eve of departure for Khartoum:

> ***I am now at a stage of life where my children have left home and have their own lives. This is the first time in my adult life that I have been footloose. I decided to re-train as a TEFL teacher and look at possible places to go. I got a wonderful book out of the library called* Teaching English Abroad *that contains details of many countries and mentioned Sudan and SVP. I did a bit of background reading about Sudan and was hooked. It is a country with a lot of archaeology and interesting and diverse cultures. It is a country with a lot of problems, both war and poverty. SVP sends volunteers to enhance understanding of the outside world in Sudan and at the same time increase understanding of Sudan elsewhere. As they are a very small charity, this is obviously a drop in the ocean, but at least it is a start.***
>
> ***I have spent the last nine months preparing to go. I have achieved my TEFL qualification, had some lessons in Sudanese Arabic, reverted to my maiden name, bought suitable clothes for an Islamic country and had a large number of vaccinations. I have also got rid of most of my possessions as I intend this to be a lifestyle change, hopefully doing alternate years of volunteering and paid work for the foreseeable future. As from Thursday I have rented out my home (a boat on the Thames). It is almost time to say 'Goodbye boat,* salaam alekum *(peace be with you) Sudan!'***

Since leaving Sudan, Rebecca has taken up a new volunteering challenge in South Sudan and as of summer 2016 is reporting about the experience in her fascinating blog http://living-in-nimule-blog.blogspot.co.uk. Holding out against the tide, she is struggling to keep a little school called Cece open.

MARK TANNER

Mark Tanner, a New Zealand adventurer, found out about the Sudan Volunteer Programme by searching the web and was accepted onto the scheme.

While some volunteers were required to use the syllabus as a guide, I had a free rein over what I taught and how. This prompted me to ask the students to suggest topics that were of interest to them and allowed me freedom to encourage discussion about parts of the Sudanese culture I was interested in. The main objective was to provide the students with a native English speaker and get them used to conversation. We were encouraged to do less-formal sessions called the English Club. For example we themed the cooking class, as our university was all female and cooking was something they considered important. Some classes stand out in my memory such as the one where we tried to teach the students to juggle. The classrooms could be quite hot and were equipped with blackboard and chalk, although we used teaching aids based on our own initiative.

The lodgings provided were basic, but by Sudanese standards good. The stipend was enough to subsist in Sudan, living like the Sudanese. As lovely as the Sudanese are, things are not as organised in the country as we would expect in the West. Yet it would be difficult to find more hospitable people than the Sudanese and there is never a shortage of offers for dinner or to visit a village, which provided a fantastic opportunity to experience the culture in a way many other NGO workers never saw.

There are many interesting things to see in Khartoum, such as Nuba Wrestling, fish markets, Dervish dancing and museums. SVP has a deal with the Blue Nile Sailing Club which allows students to try their luck at sailing on the Nile. Many of the volunteers did other voluntary work for NGOs. I helped an NGO with marketing and to develop a website. My principal motivation for being in the Sudan was to paddle through Sudan on the Nile, and I spent a lot of my spare time trying to source permits for this.

One of the highlights for me was seeing the English of the students improve and the relationships develop from that. Teachers are greatly respected in the Sudan so volunteers are revered and treated with respect.

Not everyone is so positive about being placed by an agency, especially if their motives are strictly philanthropic. The placement that was fixed up for **Till Bruckner** in Sudan didn't live up to his expectations:

> ***They'd told me at my interview in London that I'd be teaching international politics but when I arrived the local branch didn't know what I'd come for and wanted me to teach conversational English at a university in Khartoum. I figured that if I was going to teach English to kids from well-off families while living in a city of outstanding natural ugliness, I might as well go elsewhere and get paid for it. There'd be no problem finding***

work as an English teacher in Sudan. There's great demand and little supply as nobody (including most Sudanese) wants to live there. In a country with poverty on that scale, there's more useful things you can do with £500 than pay for a scheme to tutor English. If you want fun, go elsewhere; if you want to help, put the £500 in an Oxfam charity box.

However, that is just one point of view and many people have felt that their contribution as a volunteer teacher has not been futile, either from the point of view of broadening their own horizons or of helping others.

The SVP site carries illuminating first-hand accounts by recent volunteers, pointing out some of the highs ('the overwhelming friendliness and hospitality of the people') and lows ('the oppressive heat').

LIST OF EMPLOYERS

SUDAN VOLUNTEER PROGRAMME

34 Estelle Road, London NW3 2JY, UK

+44 7910 940819

david@svp-uk.com

www.svp-uk.com

UK registered charity which promotes English teaching among university students and other adults.

NUMBER OF TEACHERS: 10–20 at any time in and outside Khartoum.

PREFERENCE OF NATIONALITY: None but should be native speakers of English and if not, they should be qualified English-language teachers.

QUALIFICATIONS: TEFL certificate, experience of travelling in developing countries and some knowledge of Arabic are helpful but not obligatory. Volunteers must be over 22, in good health and have some university education.

CONDITIONS OF EMPLOYMENT: Preferred minimum 8 months to tie in with university semesters: October–January or January–May. Secondary school terms run June to February/March.

SALARY: SVP's partner schools pay a stipend which should be enough to live on (e.g. 800 Sudanese pounds/£100) and modest accommodation. Volunteers must raise the cost of the airfare to Sudan (currently £400) plus £80 (towards the cost of the group insurance policy). Wage can be supplemented by private teaching.

FACILITIES/SUPPORT: Accommodation with self-catering facilities is arranged.

RECRUITMENT: Applications accepted year round. Two referees are also required. Prior to departure, medical check-up required plus selection interviews, orientation and briefings take place. Volunteers are required to write a report of their experiences and to advise new volunteers.

CONTACT: David Wolton, Director.

KENYA

Kenya is another country with a chronic shortage of school teachers. Since 2003, when the government kept its promise to abolish school fees for primary schools, there has been a steady increase in student numbers. The worst teacher shortages are in Western Province. English is the language of instruction in many Kenyan primary schools, so not knowing Swahili need not be an insuperable barrier for foreign teachers. The Kenyan Ministry of Education restricts jobs in the state sector to those who have a university degree, teaching certification and at least one year of professional teaching experience. The few private language institutes that there are in Nairobi are not subject to this restriction. The British Council in Nairobi at Upperhill Road (information@britishcouncil.or.ke) may be able to offer advice. One institute which carries information about year round job openings on its website is the Language Center (see entry), which hires native speakers with a degree and a recognised TEFL qualification.

According to the Kenyan High Commission in London (45 Portland Place, London W1B 1AS; ✆ +44 20 7636 2371), all non-Kenyan citizens who wish to work must be in possession of a work permit issued by the Principal Immigration Officer, Department of Immigration, PO Box 30191, Nairobi before they can take up paid or unpaid work. Teachers who have been offered employment should apply for a Class A permit, aimed at those who are suitably qualified and 'whose engagement in that employment will be of benefit to Kenya'. The school should apply for work permits for the teachers even before they enter Kenya. Proof of professional qualifications is required. However, it is not certain that immigration regulations would be strictly enforced in the case of native English speakers looking for teaching work on the spot. Certainly in the past it was possible to fix up a teaching job by asking in the villages, preferably before terms begin in September, January and April. Be prepared to produce your CV and any diplomas and references on headed paper.

Also ascertain before accepting a post whether or not the school can afford to pay a salary, especially if it is a Harambee school, i.e. non-government, self-help schools in rural areas. A cement or mud hut with a thatched or tin roof will usually be provided for the teacher's accommodation plus a local salary, which would be just enough to live on provided you don't want to buy too much peanut butter or cornflakes in the city. Living conditions will be primitive, with no running water or electricity in the majority of cases. The Kenyan version of maize porridge is called *ugali*. In Daisy Waugh's book *A Small Town in Africa* (no longer in print) she describes how, when she arrived at the village of Isiolo (a few miles from Nairobi) where she had arranged to teach, she was told that they didn't need any teachers and there were no pupils. She patiently waited and, five weeks into term, her class arrived.

People who choose to teach in Kenya do it for love, not money. In the words of **Ermon O. Kamara**, PhD, former Director of the American Universities Preparation Institute in Nairobi:

> ***Candidates must view being in Kenya as a holiday with pay. The cost of living and corresponding local salaries sound quite low to foreigners. Consequently they must think of the opportunities to enjoy Kenya's beaches, mountains and game parks as well as experiencing a new and interesting culture. During weekends and holidays, one can travel the breadth of Kenya. Also the proximity to other countries in East and Southern Africa permits a traveller to see a good deal of our continent.***

LIST OF EMPLOYERS

THE LANGUAGE CENTER LTD

Ndemi Close/Ndemi Road off Ngong Road, PO Box 40661, 00100 Nairobi

+254 20 386 9531, 386 9532, 387 0610, 387 0612

tlc@language-cntr.com

www.language-cntr.com

NUMBER OF TEACHERS: Approximately 6.

PREFERENCE OF NATIONALITY: British, American.

QUALIFICATIONS: Minimum first degree plus CELTA, TEFL or any other recognised teaching qualification.

CONDITIONS OF EMPLOYMENT: Standard length of contract is 2 years. Normal working hours are 8.30am to 4pm.

SALARY: Around $8.50–$11 per hour for the first year plus medical insurance and gratuity. PAYE tax deductions of 20%–30% of salary.

FACILITIES/SUPPORT: Employer will handle the application process for work permits and pay half of the total expenses.

RECRUITMENT: Online application form or word of mouth. Interviews are essential and are conducted locally.

ROKO 20 ACADEMY

PO Box 10233, Murang'a, Central Highlands

+254 7298 50539

roko20academy@gmail.com

www.jaffa17.wordpress.com

Primary school set up in Kambira near Murang'a to provide free education to orphans and children from disadvantaged backgrounds.

NUMBER OF TEACHERS: 2–3 volunteers.

PREFERENCE OF NATIONALITY: All native-speaking countries.

QUALIFICATIONS: TEFL or TESL qualified with a minimum of 2 years' teaching experience. Minimum age 21, average age 30.

CONDITIONS OF EMPLOYMENT: Standard length of stay is 3 months, for one of the school terms January–April, May–August or September–November. School hours are 8am–3pm. Volunteers follow an ESL programme to improve the standard of English for pupils aged 3–12, complementing the class teacher using the Kenyan syllabus.

SALARY: None. Volunteers must be self-funding, though basic accommodation at the school can be provided.

FACILITIES/SUPPORT: Charity can secure a rented flat in the town or provide accommodation at the school. Initial orientation and teaching programme. Advice on visas: initial 3-month visa can be extended in Nairobi for further 3 months.

RECRUITMENT: Via volunteer websites such as Workaway (www.workaway.info) and Help Exchange (www.helpx.net) as well as ELT sites such as www.tefl.com.

CONTACT: Tracey Neale-Ferreira, Patron.

MADAGASCAR

KIM REUTER

Kim Reuter from Florida is primarily interested in conservation and development, but during her long stay in Madagascar she couldn't help but notice how many opportunities there are to teach English both formally through institutions and informally to individuals.

It is not difficult to find teaching work and to my knowledge there is not a significant administrative burden, especially if you are teaching privately or in certain English schools. Many work without an official contract. There may be more red tape if you plan to teach at the university level. Usually you do not need any sort of certification, apart from being a fluent speaker. Teaching materials are extremely hard to find, so be ready to create your own lessons or bring your tools into the country with you. It is also much easier to find these positions if you know some working French (very few people speak any English and it is helpful to know French, if just enough to set up appointments with students). Note that English-French dictionaries are hard to come by.

I was offered a contract job teaching English at the university level in Madagascar. Do not expect to get help in finding accommodation, though this is easily set up in-country either staying in the house of a local family, or in a cheap hotel/apartment. The wages paid for a good private instructor of English are enough to live on (food, accommodation and sightseeing). You should establish early on the teacher-student relationship, especially as a woman, since there are stigmas associated with being a foreigner in Madagascar. It could be that your students perceive your friendly and open attitude (which is normal in western countries) as an invitation for flirtation or a romantic relationship. However, being upfront about the student-teacher relationship can discourage these encounters.

In your spare time, there are so many things to do in Madagascar. It is one of the most amazing places in the world and there is no shortage of things to see. The people here are some of the friendliest I have ever met - expect to meet your students' families, be invited to their school graduations, etc. I highly recommend teaching in Madagascar, and you will find that there are a lot of unexpected perks ... like learning French or Malagasy, as you go through the process of teaching English.

MOROCCO

Although Morocco is a Francophone country, English is a requirement for entrance to university or high-ranking jobs, and there is strong demand from the business communities of the main cities. Like so many African countries, Morocco has sought to improve the standards of education for its nationals, so that almost all teaching jobs in schools and universities are now filled by Moroccans. But outside the state system there is a continuing demand for native English speakers.

The Moroccan Ministry of Employment stipulates that the maximum number of foreign staff in any organisation cannot exceed 50%. It also insists that all foreign teachers have at least a Bachelor's degree in TESOL or a degree plus TESOL/TEFL certificate before they can be eligible for a work permit. The maximum age is 60 years. Work permits are obtained after arrival by applying for authorisation from the Ministère de l'Emploi, Quartier des Ministères, Rabat. You will need copies of your diplomas, birth certificate and so on. Although a knowledge of French is not a formal requirement, it is a great asset for anyone planning to spend time in Morocco.

A number of commercial language schools employ native English speakers. The hourly rate of pay at most schools is less than £10 (equivalent in dirhams). The American Language Centers are located in the main cities of Morocco and most hire native speakers; see the website www.aca.org.ma/jobs for details. They are private institutes but are affiliated to and partially funded by the US State Department. Two are included in the list of employers, including the Casablanca branch, which recruits native English-speaker teachers from a number of courses including academic institutes in the USA such as the University of North Texas, which offers a graduate certificate in TESOL. Other branches to try are in the Atlantic port city of El Jadida (eljadida_dir@aca.org.ma) which was advertising for teachers at the time of writing, Marrakech (alcmarr@aca.org.ma) and in Mohammedia (director@alcmohammedia.com).

The workcamps movement is active in Morocco and some of these summer volunteer projects take place on English-language camps for Moroccan adolescents (see CSM entry below). A similar volunteer teaching programme in Casablanca is organised by El Jadida Voluntary Work Association (http://jvwork.webs.com). A participant from summer 2016 wrote of the challenges: '*We had no common language, meaning that my instruction was limited to examples, drawings and actions. In spite of this, my students kept returning to class. I was inspired by their determination and I worked hard to improve myself as a teacher.*' He went on to recommend bringing some simple English story books to make lessons more engaging, and lots of whiteboard markers since they run out quickly and are hard to find locally. He warns that the food served by host families is so delicious that you must be prepared to gain a few pounds.

LIST OF EMPLOYERS

AMERICAN LANGUAGE CENTER
1 Place de la Fraternité, Boulevard Moulay Youssef, Casablanca 20000
+212 522 277765
diretor.casa@aca.org.ma
http://casablanca.aca.org.ma/en/test-efl-jobs

NUMBER OF TEACHERS: 12–15 full-time teachers (mostly native speakers) plus about 40 part-time Moroccan teachers.

PREFERENCE OF NATIONALITY: North American, but British teachers are also welcome to apply.

QUALIFICATIONS: Bachelor's degree, TEFL Certification (CELTA preferred) and a minimum of 1 year's EFL overseas teaching experience.

CONDITIONS OF EMPLOYMENT: A standard contract is for 12 months from 1 October to 30 September. 18 contact hours a week are standard for the Adult Program, mostly evenings and weekends. However, some teachers have additional classes, including Young Learners.

SALARY: 188–208 dirhams per hour (£14.50–£16) according to qualifications and experience. There is also a tax-free housing allowance of up to 3,000 dirhams per month plus a 10,000 dirhams settling-in allowance (over $1,000), which is also tax free. Taxes on a monthly salary amount to about 15% of earnings. Complete medical insurance (80% reimbursable) is provided for all full-time teachers. A ticket to the teacher's residence in the USA (for North Americans) or UK (for British teachers) is provided if a teacher successfully completes 1 year at the centre. There is also an end-of-contract bonus equal to 1 month's pay.

RECRUITMENT: Send CV, letter of introduction, scanned copies of first page of passport and original diplomas and 2 letters of recommendation. All paperwork necessary for teachers to obtain work permits is done by administration staff. New teachers have to bring a copy of their birth certificate and their original university diplomas and certificates.

CONTACT: Richard Martin, Director.

AMERICAN LANGUAGE CENTER, RABAT

4 Zankat Tanja, Rabat 10000

+212 537 767103

dir@alcrabat.org

www.alcrabat.org/en/employment/

NUMBER OF TEACHERS: 20 full-time and 25 part-time teachers.

PREFERENCE OF NATIONALITY: Applicants should be from a country where English is the first language.

QUALIFICATIONS: BA preferably in Education, TESOL, or related field; knowledge of French or Arabic highly desirable. TEFL certification required (not online).

CONDITIONS OF EMPLOYMENT: 1-year renewable contracts. 18–22 contact hours per week full-time. Hours of work generally between 2pm and 9pm weekdays (Tuesday to Friday) and 9am and 5pm on weekends. Students aged from 7, mostly aged 14–35.

SALARY: Approximately $1,500 per month (gross) for October to July school year. Possibility of paid overtime. Paid sick leave and medical insurance provided as well as vacation allowance and round-trip airfare upon completing 2 years.

FACILITIES/SUPPORT: Free housing/homestay provided for 2 weeks while permanent accommodation is sought. Pre- and in-service training fully supported. Free access to high-speed internet, free language classes (French and Arabic) and other benefits.

RECRUITMENT: Through TESOL convention in early spring in the US and some local hiring. Video-conference interviews are also used.

CONTACT: Michael McMillan, Director.

AMIDEAST

35 Rue Oukaimeden, Agdal, Rabat

+212 537 67 50 75/81/82

Also: Zenith 1, Etage 3, Sidi Maarouf, Casablanca

+212 522 259393

anovelli@amideast.org

www.amideast.org/morocco

NUMBER OF TEACHERS: Approximately 35.

PREFERENCE OF NATIONALITY: Must be native English speakers.

QUALIFICATIONS: TEFL qualification.

CONDITIONS OF EMPLOYMENT: 1-year contracts, preferably with a view to extending. To work around 70–100 hours per month.

FACILITIES/SUPPORT: Settling-in allowance. Assistance with apartment search and work visas, which must be acquired within 3 months of arrival.

RECRUITMENT: CV and cover letter to knorris@amideast.org. Telephone interview required.

CONTACT: Alex Novelli, Director of Programs.

CHANTIERS SOCIAUX MAROCAINS (CSM – ICYE MOROCCO)

PO Box 456, Rabat or CSM IMM 13 APP 06 Rue Elmowahidine, 10000, Rabat

csm_morocco@yahoo.fr

www.csmorocco.org

NUMBER OF TEACHERS: Around 40 volunteers for 5 'Scholar Support' summer workcamps in Rabat, Salé, Kenitra, Casablanca, etc.

QUALIFICATIONS: Skills teaching children are required. French or Arabic an advantage. Independent attitude and the ability to work in difficult circumstances with little support.

CONDITIONS OF EMPLOYMENT: Voluntary work teaching English to Moroccan youths aged 15–18 from modest or poor families on summer workcamps in July or August. Volunteers teach 25–30 students for 4 hours a day, Monday to Friday.

SALARY: Voluntary work. Volunteers pay for their own flights, insurance, induction and administration fee of €80.

FACILITIES/SUPPORT: Local host families provide board and lodging. For summer projects, pre-camp orientation at the beginning of July.

RECRUITMENT: Online application through CSM.

TUNISIA

As with its neighbour in the Maghreb, Tunisia's young people have been turning away from the language of the country's former colonial master and embracing the dominant language of international music and business. Although the young generation speak fluent French because they have been taught it in school, many teenagers prefer English. Both Amideast (see entry) and the British Council Tunis Teaching Centre employ qualified native English-speaker teachers. The latter runs a summer school for children and teenagers in June and July with extra vacancies; teachers earn £1,800 for the whole period plus accommodation and flights.

ROGER MUSKER

Roger Musker found that people would be interested in paying you for lessons, even though you plan to be in the country for a relatively short time. He was in Tunisia for one winter.

I decided to take a month off work as a kind of sabbatical and, if well planned, at no cost. I found all young people in Tunisia keen to practise and speak English whenever possible. I had one good contact in Sousse, who worked for the Tunisian Tourist Agency. I wrote to him from England and he replied that he could line up students on my arrival, which included himself and his 10-year-old daughter (who turned out to be my best student). At their house I was plied with extremely sweet tea and sticky cakes, which you are obliged to eat. Altogether I had eight keen fee-paying students, including a blind telephone operator, a teacher of English on a revision course and students from the Bourguiba Institute at Sousse University, which claims to be the second-oldest university in the world. For the latter it was necessary to get permission from the Ministry of Education via the headmaster.

Every day I tutored 8-10am and 5-7pm. The hourly rate was about £8, allowing me to cover basic costs while having a working holiday. Even without the contact and knowing Arabic, work is there for the asking. It just takes initiative. Go to any official institute, the tourism or municipal offices, demonstrate your availability and enthusiasm, give them your contact number and await replies.

The Bourguiba Institute in Tunis (47 Av. de la Liberté, 1002 Tunis; www.iblv.rnu.tn) occasionally hires well-qualified teachers.

LIST OF EMPLOYERS

AMIDEAST TUNISIA
33 rue Ahmed, Ramy, 1002, Tunis
+216 71 145 700/707
elteachers@amideast.org
www.amideast.org/tunisia

NUMBER OF TEACHERS: 50 full or part-time independent contract TEFL/TESL teachers. Also for Sousse.
PREFERENCE OF NATIONALITY: Native or near-native speakers of English.
QUALIFICATIONS: Ideally a degree and accredited 100+-hour international certificate in TEFL/TESL. 1 year's successful experience of teaching English to non-native speakers would be a plus. Should have knowledge of US standardised tests like TOEFL and GMAT.
CONDITIONS OF EMPLOYMENT: Minimum 9 months. Classes for children, teenagers and adults held between 8.30am and 9pm. Courses also run for public and private sector organisations.
SALARY: 20.28–23.40 dinars per hour depending on qualifications and experience.
FACILITIES/SUPPORT: Hotel accommodation provided on arrival for up to 15 days until teacher finds accommodation (with help of school). During the 4 months that American and Canadian citizens are allowed to stay as tourists, the school handles arrangements for getting a work permit and visa. A 500-dinar travel grant is paid at the end of the 1-year contract.
RECRUITMENT: Via www.amideast.org plus regional and international TEFL conferences.
CONTACT: Mariem Salhi, EL Coordinator (msalhi@amideast.org).

BRITISH COUNCIL TUNISIA
87 Avenue Mohamed V, BP 96 Le Belvédère, 1002 Tunis
+216 71 145 302
ian.bowman@tn.britishcouncil.org; recruitment@tn.britishcouncil.org
www.britishcouncil.tn

QUALIFICATIONS: UK first degree (required for work visa). Minimum certificate in EFL (CELTA or Trinity) plus 2-years' post-certificate teaching experience in EFL. Demonstrable ability to teach across the range of courses offered, especially of Young Learners. Experience of IELTS and Cambridge Exams desirable. Maximum age 58 for visa reasons.
CONDITIONS OF EMPLOYMENT: 2-year full-time contracts from end of August. Also run summer school programme for which they need teachers for 8 weeks (June/July).
SALARY: Flights, baggage, medical insurance and pension contributions in addition to salary for full-time work. Salary for 2-month summer school is £2,000 plus flights, accommodation and medical insurance.
CONTACT: Ian Bowman, Deputy Teaching Centre Manager.

ENGLISH CULTURAL CENTRE
Av 14 Janvier Imm Itkan, 3000 Sfax
+216 74408949
contact@englishculturalcenter.com
www.englishculturalcenter.com

NUMBER OF TEACHERS: 4.
PREFERENCE OF NATIONALITY: British or American.
QUALIFICATIONS: 3 years' experience.
CONDITIONS OF EMPLOYMENT: 6 months or annual contract. Most classes are in the afternoon/evenings, 4pm–6pm and 6.30pm–8.30pm.
SALARY: 28 dinars (£9.50) per 2 hour lesson.
FACILITIES/SUPPORT: Assistance given with applying for work permits.
RECRUITMENT: Interview is essential and can be conducted on the phone or Skype.
CONTACT: Ahmed Zayani, Administrative and Financial Manager.

LIBYA

On 23 October 2011, the National Transitional Council (NTC) proclaimed the liberation of Libya after more than 40 years under Colonel Gaddafi, who had isolated himself and his country from the western world for so long. Many hoped that this potentially prosperous little country would cohere and flourish after the revolution. Unfortunately, the country is now a failed state and has descended into chaos. A black market flourishes in dollars and diesel, while corruption is endemic and the financial system has completely broken down. The country continues to be in the news for being the unpoliced jumping-off point for migrant boat people from Africa and the Middle East, so many of whom drown in the Mediterranean. The Foreign Office advises against all travel to the country and has closed the British Embassy. It warns of Islamic State-affiliated groups carrying out bombings and kidnappings in 2015. The brief flowering of institutes offering English instruction that came in the wake of the Libyan revolution was soon extinguished, and many fledgling schools and organisations like the English Teachers' Forum for Libya are now defunct.

If, at some point in the future, the country stabilises, demand for native-speaking teachers is bound to increase, in the oil, gas and engineering sectors as well as the population at large.

LIST OF EMPLOYERS

ALMAQAR IT & ENGLISH LANGUAGE TRAINING

Al-Fornaj, across from Tripoli Medical Centre, next to the General Mills Company, Tripoli

+218 92-6626114

info@almaqar.ly

www.learnenglishlibya.blogspot.co.uk; https://www.facebook.com/AlmaqarITC

Primarily an IT training centre. Native-speaking director (expat American) has moved back to Florida after 26 years in Libya. It is not known if the training centre still employs foreign teachers

MAURITANIA

After gaining some popularity among travellers overlanding from Morocco to Senegal, Mauritania has dropped off the radar again. The FCO advises against all travel to most of the country and all but essential travel to the south, including the capital, Nouakchott.

When **Bradwell Jackson** visited before the rise in terrorist attacks in the Western Sahara, he was surprised by how few westerners he saw: '*It seems as though this country is up and coming as one of those unexplored gems that travellers haven't yet discovered.*' With a terrorist threat rating of 'high', this gem will probably remain undiscovered by travellers for some time to come.

Bradwell, who supplied information several years ago, found a teaching job by a '*happy accident of fate*'. On striking up a conversation with a westerner walking on the other side of the street in Nouakchott, he asked her about English language schools, and was promptly taken to the front door of The English Language Centre (now called Sahara English – www.facebook.com/saharaenglish):

> ***I was lucky enough to speak with the owner right away. I was talking to her while she was busy doing some other things, so it was not a formal interview. I did not have to fill out an application, though she asked me to write a letter explaining why I wanted to work in Mauritania. She seemed very interested, and asked me to come back in a couple of days to do a mock class in front of her teachers. I was hired based on this.***

Bradwell's wages started at 50,000 ouguiyas (now worth $135) a month and increased to 68,000 ouguiyas ($185) a month. He was told that a person hired from within the country is paid much less than a person hired from outside. Getting a work permit was refreshingly simple. The school simply took his passport to the employment office and paid for a one-year work permit.

Bradwell found the students to be a joy to work with, because they were 'serious' and hungry to learn. British English is as popular as American English.

EQUATORIAL GUINEA

After 12 editions of this book came the first report of possibilities for teaching English in the former Spanish colony of Equatorial Guinea, now one of the smallest countries of Africa, surrounded by Cameroon and Gabon. Although **Kim Reuter** has no first-hand experience of teaching English here, she did run a non-profit organisation in the country, so is familiar with the small but growing market for English teachers:

> ***It is basically impossible to get a job before you land in country, but you can easily find one in the capital city of Malabo. There are several small English schools that will hire English speakers, and you can also set up English classes through the Spanish and French cultural centres in Malabo. You do not need formal training in teaching English, though you need to be a fluent English speaker and you should bring your teaching tools with you. It is very difficult to enter the country unless you are American because Americans do not need visas. You are technically required to get a resident permit if you plan to stay for more than three months but I do not know of many people who have gone through that long and costly process. I have heard it costs $1,000, but I am still unclear as to what the process is.***

The hours at the English schools are mostly part-time, and pay is approximately $25 per hour. The wages are more than enough to live on in Malabo, though the capital is very expensive (e.g. $10 to eat, and rent can be around $900 for a one-bedroom apartment). You may or may not have a contract, but you will be expected to teach English courses from start to finish. Finding accommodation can be hard in Equatorial Guinea, but there are a few non-profits that will house you at very low cost, and the English schools may help you find accommodation in the house of a local family (though you should not rely on this). The fellow teachers are usually Equatoguineans who have had English training, which is why native English fluency is so prized. Working in Equatorial Guinea can be very difficult, so be sure to do thorough research on the country before arriving. On the other hand it will pay dividends for years to come. Once you are there, people can be extremely kind and giving. You will be invited into their homes and most students (if you teach at a school) will respect the student–teacher relationship. The upside about Equatorial Guinea is that it is a place that almost no one goes to. Your English-language skills will be prized, you will find that you are one of only a handful of foreigners and you are guaranteed to have experiences that are unmatched in any other country.

SENEGAL

The British Council has a flourishing teaching centre in Dakar (Rue AAB–68, Amitie Zone A et B, BP 6232; ✆ +221 33 869 2700; information@britishcouncil.sn) that actively recruits teachers and interns. It will want to see your CV and certification and then (here's the rub) want you to attend an interview. Anyway, they accept applications year round, so those who are interested should submit a short motivation letter in English and CV to recruitment.senegal@britishcouncil.sn.

The British Senegalese Institute in Dakar (www.britishbsi.com) is the oldest English teaching centre in the country. It does not require teachers to have a specific certificate or experience, although these are certainly desirable. The average hours per week are 15, and the pay is around 3,500 CFA ($6) per hour. Another possibility is the Centre Africain d'Etudes Supérieures en Gestion (Boulevard du General De Gaulle, B.P. 3802, Dakar; courrier@cesag.sn). The school is located in a large, official complex and tends to cater for more affluent students.

The English Language Program run by the US Embassy (RELO-Dakar@state.gov) in Senegal continues to recruit. Although Dakar is an interesting city of contrasts, **Bradwell Jackson** was not tempted to stay. He found the city sprawling and unwieldy, as well as expensive.

OTHER AFRICAN COUNTRIES

LIST OF EMPLOYERS

MOZAMBIQUE

LYNDEN LANGUAGE SCHOOL
Av Zedequias Manganhela 267, JAT Building, 2nd Floor (PO Box 456), Maputo
+258 21 360494
info@lynden.co.mz
www.lynden.co.mz

NUMBER OF TEACHERS: 5.
PREFERENCE OF NATIONALITY: British, Australian, South African, etc.
QUALIFICATIONS: CELTA or Trinity plus 2 years' experience.
CONDITIONS OF EMPLOYMENT: 1 year, 25 hours per week.
SALARY: $1,000; half paid in the local currency (meticals).
FACILITIES/SUPPORT: School finds and pays for accommodation. School applies to Ministry of Labour for work permit once teachers gather necessary documents.
RECRUITMENT: EL Gazette, internet or via recruitment partners www.tefl.org.uk. References checked by phone.
CONTACT: Denise Lord or Lynne Longley, Co-Directors.

SOUTH AFRICA

INTERLINK SCHOOL OF LANGUAGES
1st Floor, 4 Regent Road, Sea Point, Cape Town 8005
+27 21 439 9834
info@interlink.co.za
www.interlink.co.za

Member of EduSA, the national association of quality English language centres in South Africa (www.edusouthafrica.com).
NUMBER OF TEACHERS: 10.
PREFERENCE OF NATIONALITY: South Africans preferred but will consider native English speakers with permission to work in South Africa.
QUALIFICATIONS: Recognised TEFL qualification, CELTA preferred.
CONDITIONS OF EMPLOYMENT: Full-time contracts last for 1 year. Part-time contracts reviewed weekly according to demand.
SALARY: Varies according to experience and qualifications. Part-time salary 70 rand per hour.
RECRUITMENT: Interview required.
CONTACT: Luanne McCallum, Manager.

TANZANIA

INDIGENOUS EDUCATION FOUNDATION OF TANZANIA
PO Box 54, Monduli, Arusha Region, Tanzania
US address: PO Box 300067, Jamaica Plain, MA 02130
+255 784 870097 in Tanzania;
+1 617 390 8752 in USA
volunteer@ieftz.org; info@ieftz.org
www.ieftz.org

Non-profit, community-collaborative organisation that provides affordable educational opportunities to an under-served population of youth in rural Tanzania.
NUMBER OF TEACHERS: 10 volunteers of whom 1–3 are English teachers for Orkeeswa School.
PREFERENCE OF NATIONALITY: All native speakers.
QUALIFICATIONS: Minimum BA and ESL qualification. Preferably with classroom ESL teaching experience, and an understanding of the challenges of teaching to an exam-driven curriculum while trying to broaden the students' skills. Ideally certified English teachers with experience teaching EFL. Average age is 27.
CONDITIONS OF EMPLOYMENT: Minimum 1-year commitment if teaching forms 1–6. 3–4 months for English Immersion Programme from the end of August to December. School hours are 7.30am–5.30pm with some Saturday classes.
SALARY: None for volunteers. A living stipend is available for volunteers who commit to a full year.
FACILITIES/SUPPORT: Shared housing with basic utilities/amenities is provided for all volunteers. Orientation provided on arrival. Volunteer covers other expenses, including return airfare to Tanzania, visa fees $200 for CTA (Conducting a Temporary

Assignment) visa that covers less than 2 months, $1,000 for a resident permit if staying more than 3 months. Basic living expenses (food, travel, etc.).

RECRUITMENT: Online. Interview and orientation with US Volunteer Coordinator via email/Skype/phone.

CONTACT: Lisa Heinert, US Volunteer Coordinator.

SERIAN UK

charley.nussey@gmail.com
www.serianuk.org.uk

Serian means 'peace' in Kimaasai.

NUMBER OF TEACHERS: 15–20 teaching assistants and qualified teachers in ESL and other subjects placed at Serian UK, Noonkodin Secondary School, in the rural Maasai village of Eluwai.

PREFERENCE OF NATIONALITY: All nationalities accepted. Non-native speakers of English should have IELTS 6.5 or above.

QUALIFICATIONS: Volunteers who want to be considered as independent class teachers of English should have the CELTA, TEFL or similar. Classroom assistants who work alongside a qualified Tanzanian teacher should ideally have completed a minimum of 1 year of undergraduate-level study in English, although school leavers with strong motivation and above-average qualifications will also be considered. Previous teaching experience in a school is strongly preferred, even if it is no more than a 2-week work experience placement. Maths and science teachers also needed.

CONDITIONS OF EMPLOYMENT: 2–3 months recommended for short-term volunteers though arrangements are flexible. Ideally 6–12 months from January or July for qualified teachers.

SALARY: Volunteers are asked to cover their living costs, $40–$50 per week, and are encouraged to carry out additional fundraising for the project.

FACILITIES/SUPPORT: Volunteers stay in a staff house at the school. Volunteers can also take up (at reduced rates) a range of additional activities such as walking tours, homestays in traditional Maasai boma or Swahili tuition.

RECRUITMENT: Applications can be made online. Pre-departure interview desirable.

CONTACT: Ms Charley Nussey, International Volunteer Co-ordinator (charley.nussey@gmail.com).

UGANDA

SOFT POWER EDUCATION (SPE)

UK: 55 Guildhall St, Bury St Edmunds, Suffolk IP33 1QF
Uganda: PO Box 1493, Jinja
+256 774 162541
volunteering@softpowereducation.com; info@softpowereducation.com
www.softpowereducation.com

British-registered non-religious charity improving quality of life through education. Among numerous other projects, SPE offers TEFL courses for men and women in the community.

NUMBER OF TEACHERS: 1 or 2 at a time based at the Amagezi Education Centre. Female teachers needed to work with women in Kyabirwa community near Bujagali Falls, Jinja.

QUALIFICATIONS: TEFL qualification and some experience preferable but not essential. Creativity and ability to work independently using one's own initiative essential.

CONDITIONS OF EMPLOYMENT: Minimum 3 months.

SALARY: None. Volunteers must cover their own living and travel expenses as well as a donation to the charity. Recommended amount is £75 a week.

FACILITIES/SUPPORT: Camping, dorms, private bandas or living within the local community. Guest houses in Jinja are also an option, but they are located some distance away from the Amagezi Education Centre, so travel costs would be higher.

CONTACT: Sharon Webb, Volunteer Manager and Country Manager (sharon@softpowereducation.com).

ASIA

Although the English language is not a universal passport to employment, it can certainly be put to good use in many Asian countries where the demand for English teachers is substantial, even extraordinary as is the case with China, Korea and Taiwan, which have been described as 'black holes' for EFL teachers.

Conditions and remuneration differ wildly between industrialised countries, such as Japan, Korea and Singapore, with their western-style economies, and developing countries, such as Nepal and Cambodia, where both wages and the standard of living are lower. Thailand and Vietnam are in between. China combines rapidly industrialised cities with vast stretches of rural backwaters. A concerted job hunt in Asia will almost always turn up possibilities, and sometimes the difficulty comes in choosing among them. **Ross McKay** from Glasgow writes of his job hunt:

> ***I was 50 and fed up for various reasons. So I wrote to about 500 institutions all over South-East Asia. Whilst waiting for replies I did a distance TESOL course and College of Further Education teaching certificate. I got three offers, one in Hanoi, one in Bangkok and I chose Jakarta as I knew nothing about Indonesia. My colleagues come from all over the English-speaking world and often become great pals. But there are some head-cases. I guess one has to be a little crazy to live this life, and a few people crack up. The great thing about life in Indonesia is that every morning you wake up and have no idea what the heck is going to happen next.***

The powerhouse economies of South-East Asia – Indonesia, Thailand, Malaysia, Singapore, Philippines and Vietnam – together with Brunei, Myanmar, Cambodia and Laos, formed the Asean Economic Community (AEC) at the end of 2015, having brought forward the implementation date from 2020. The appointed common language for the AEC single market is English, so the drive to raise linguistic competence in the region will only become more intense over the coming years.

In contrast to Thailand, Vietnam and Indonesia, with their strong demand for native English-speaker teachers, other countries between Pakistan and the Philippines (with a few exceptions) are not easy places in which to find paid work as an English teacher. The largest growth area has been in Cambodia, Myanmar and Laos, where a number of language schools employ native English-speaker teachers who can be paid a decent wage … or peanuts (or something in between).

International recruitment organisations such as Reach To Teach and Saxoncourt are active in the region. Saxoncourt recruits for the group of Shane English Schools (www.shaneschools.com) in Japan, China and Taiwan mainly, and also Vietnam, Indonesia, Thailand and Korea where the first Shane school opened in September 2016. The education broker Teach to Travel (see entry) fills vacancies in Thailand and China, while the newer agency Trines with an office in London has many client schools in China, Taiwan and Vietnam. TEFLOne offers a placement service to native English-speaking EFL teachers with a degree and a 120-hour certificate qualification in TEFL for reputable schools throughout China, as well as Taiwan, Japan, Vietnam and Indonesia. The package on offer normally consists of a monthly salary, end-of-contract bonus, paid return flight, free accommodation and welfare support (www.teflone.com). Many online recruiters are busy filling posts in China, Hong Kong, Korea, Taiwan, Japan and Thailand such as www.findworkabroad.com, based in Guangzhou, China, and www.asiateachingjobs.com with vacancies shown to account-holders. Another agency with its headquarters in Asia is Brightspark Teachers (see entry) run by an expat living in Kuala Lumpur. The Teachers in Cambodia agency, (see chapter), run by an American in Phnom Penh, has recently broadened its horizons to fill vacancies in other Asian countries (www.teachersinasia.com).

In North America dozens of recruiters and agencies mediate between language schools in Asia and job-seekers, for example Footprints (www.footprintsrecruiting.com) and Reach to Teach (see entry below).

For American citizens and residents, both Princeton and Stanford universities have affiliated programmes that operate in various Asian countries and include TEFL teaching. Stanford's VIA (formerly Volunteers in Asia) has been providing international exchange opportunities since 1963 and continues to send volunteer

English teachers to summer programmes in Indonesia and Myanmar. These placements (www.viaprograms.org) are open to college students or graduates and require a participation fee of about $2,500. Details of the Princeton programme can be found at http://piaweb.princeton.edu. It currently places about 130 full-year fellows in 20 Asian countries.

Exposure to the radically different cultures of Asia is fascinating. **Allison Williams** was writing from Korea about her exhilarating experiences and frustrations, but this could apply equally to much of Asia:

> ***Among the highlights have been meeting and getting to know such awesome little people, by which I mean the kids! Some things here are so alien but then with other things you really do see that we are all pretty much the same. I've had quite a few of those whoa-man-I-live-in-Asia moments. For example you will have an old woman squatting on the road selling garlic right next to a couple that look like they just stepped out of Vogue magazine. I love eating all sorts of weird and wonderful things. Among the lowlights have been clothes that don't fit and being told you are a big size, lol. You get tired of not being able to do anything for yourself, like banking or simple things like exchanging a product. Of course it gets better the longer you stay. Accepting the hierarchy and educational views has sometimes been tricky, and it has been frustrating not being allowed to do more teaching on my own. All in all I am really happy with the whole experience, but after two years I'll be ready to go home. I'm excited about clothes that fit, being able to understand everything and eating cheese!***

One issue that rears its ugly head from time to time is discrimination on the grounds of age and also race. For marketing reasons in Asia, employers prefer their employees to look younger than 30, and many applicants have complained that too much emphasis is placed on the photograph requested at the time of application. Racism is also a potential problem, as highlighted by a contributor to a *Guardian* TEFL forum:

> ***Myself and my girlfriend, both in our mid-20s and university graduates with good work experience, have been looking into TEFL in Asia for over a year now. We've gotten so far as getting interviews, but on several occasions we've been denied a job as my girlfriend is mixed race (Chinese/British). This hasn't been the explicit reason for not getting a job, of course, but it's been heavily implied. For instance, my girlfriend was asked whether she could dye her hair blonde in order to be considered for a job in a school in Hong Kong.***
>
> ***I think that racism in Asia is hushed over by many, especially recruiting companies and advisors. It's a serious issue and one that affects many people applying for work in China, Hong Kong, Korea and Japan especially. If you don't 'look' western, you'll struggle significantly compared to your Caucasian brethren.***

LIST OF EMPLOYERS

BRIGHTSPARK TEACHERS LTD
Diamond House, Kingsway North, Team Valley, Gateshead, Tyne and Wear NE11 0JH
info@brightsparkteachers.co.uk
www.brightsparkteachers.co.uk

NUMBER OF TEACHERS: 20–30 positions worldwide but mainly Southeast Asia.

PREFERENCE OF NATIONALITY: All native English speaking countries.

QUALIFICATIONS: Must hold recognised qualifications from their own countries.

CONDITIONS OF EMPLOYMENT: Most contracts are for 2 years.

SALARY: Depends on position and school.

FACILITIES/SUPPORT: Most schools assist teachers with accommodation.

RECRUITMENT: Websites, job sites. Interviews in UK are possible, but usually conducted by Skype.

CONTACT: Pam Sutton (Director); Terri Hounsom (Business Development Director).

ESLSTARTER LIMITED
Winnington Hall, Winnington, Northwich, Cheshire CW8 4DU, UK
✆ +44 161 818 2191
info@eslstarter.com
www.eslstarter.com

NUMBER OF TEACHERS: Up to 100 interns, volunteers and teachers per country for China, Taiwan, Hong Kong, Japan, Korea, Nepal, India, Thailand, Cambodia, Myanmar and Vietnam (among others outside Asia).

PREFERENCE OF NATIONALITY: All native English-speaking countries. Also, applicants with near native English fluency are welcome to apply.

QUALIFICATIONS: ESLstarter looks for applicants with a passion for teaching. Bachelor's degree is not always necessary.

CONDITIONS OF EMPLOYMENT: 4–12 months. Average 22 hours per week.

SALARY: Variable from volunteer positions to a salary of RMB8,000 in China and 252,800 yen in Japan. Programme fee is charged in some cases.

FACILITIES/SUPPORT: ESLstarter assists applicants with the visa process. Either the accommodation is provided or assistance can be arranged to help teachers find accommodation on arrival.

RECRUITMENT: Application documents and Skype interview.

CONTACT: Philip Negus, Recruitment Director (phil@eslstarter.com).

REACH TO TEACH
1606 80th Avenue, Algona, IA 50511, USA.
Also #319 Minsheng Road, Taipei, Taiwan
✆ +1 201 467 4612 (USA)/0203 286 9794 (UK & Ireland)/2 8011 4516 (Australia)
info@ReachToTeachRecruiting.com
www.ReachToTeachRecruiting.com

Reach To Teach is one of the largest human resource companies for teachers in Asia and all services are free to teachers. See separate entries in chapters on China, Korea and Taiwan.

NUMBER OF TEACHERS: 500+ per year to work in Taiwan, Korea, China, Hong Kong, Singapore and Vietnam.

PREFERENCE OF NATIONALITY: In order to qualify for permission to work in Asia, you must be from one of the following countries: USA, Canada, UK, Ireland, South Africa, Australia or New Zealand.

QUALIFICATIONS: A positive, enthusiastic, dedicated and flexible attitude is the most important qualification. Most positions in Asia require a 120-hour TEFL certification. Teaching experience is a plus.

CONDITIONS OF EMPLOYMENT: All job placements are full-time positions and for one full year. Teaching schedules vary but are generally either mornings and afternoons or afternoons and evenings.

SALARY: Competitive packages that reflect the local market rate. Ability to save depends on lifestyle. Some job placements (especially Korea and China) offer free flights, free accommodation and bonuses.

FACILITIES/SUPPORT: Recruiter offers personal attention to every job placement. Through a partnership with a TEFL course provider, Reach To Teach can assist teachers in getting course discounts. All placements come with guidance on visas, flights, accommodation, etc. and workplace teacher training. All teachers have the option of continued support throughout year-long placement.

RECRUITMENT: Applications submitted via Reach To Teach website. Interviews conducted over Skype, by phone or occasionally in person.

CONTACT: Carrie Kellenberger, Co-President (Carrie@ReachToTeachRecruiting.com).

TEACH TO TRAVEL LTD
Room 4, Third Floor, Duru House, 101 Commercial Road, London E1 1RD, UK
✆ +44 207 096 1214
hr@teachtotravel.co.uk
www.teachtotravel.co.uk

NUMBER OF TEACHERS: Scores of positions mainly in Thailand and China.

PREFERENCE OF NATIONALITY: Must be native English speaker.

QUALIFICATIONS: University degree and teaching qualification, such as TEFL/TESOL/CELTA/PGCE, required. Must be under the age of 40.

CONDITIONS OF EMPLOYMENT: Most jobs last 10 months, requiring 20–25 contact hours per week, 40 hours on site.

SALARY: £600–£1,300 per month (net).

FACILITIES/SUPPORT: Free accommodation in Hong Kong and Korea.

RECRUITMENT: Skype interview.

CONTACT: Geoffrey Thomas, Director (geoff.thomas@teachtotravel.co.uk).

TEFL HEAVEN LTD
Experience Teaching Abroad Ltd, Dr Fox's Building, Badger House, Oldmixon Cresent, Weston-super-Mare, North Somerset BS24 9AY, UK
✆ +44 208 133 3885
teachabroad@teflheaven.com
www.teflheaven.com

NUMBER OF TEACHERS: Around 250 English teachers to be placed in Thailand, Vietnam and China as interns (among other countries).

PREFERENCE OF NATIONALITY: Teachers need to be of a native English speaking origin.

QUALIFICATIONS: TEFLHeaven programmes normally include an in-country TEFL qualification followed by a guaranteed job. For all paid teaching positions a Bachelor's degree is a requirement.

CONDITIONS OF EMPLOYMENT: 6–12 months is standard. 25–32 hours a week (with exceptions).

SALARY: Varies dramatically between countries and according to experience/qualifications.

FACILITIES/SUPPORT: If accommodation is not supplied as part of the package, assistance will be given in finding accommodation.

RECRUITMENT: Via direct marketing with universities, advertising online and word of mouth. Skype interviews mainly.

CONTACT: Ben Hesketh, Recruiter/Marketer & Director.

TRINES

5 St John's Lane, London EC1M 4BH, UK

+44 207 549 2898

info@trines.co.uk; sue@trines.co.uk

www.www.trines.co.uk

NUMBER OF TEACHERS: About 120 each for China, Vietnam and Thailand.

PREFERENCE OF NATIONALITY: Must be a passport holder from the UK, Ireland, USA, Canada, Australia or New Zealand.

CONDITIONS OF EMPLOYMENT: 10–12 months. Around 20–25 teaching contact hours per week + preparation time.

SALARY: £1,000–£2,000 per month. Bonuses sometimes offered for signing a contract.

FACILITIES/SUPPORT: Agency advises on documents needed for work permit; schools deal with the application.

RECRUITMENT: Skype interview.

CONTACT: On receipt of a CV, agency assesses suitability and if approved, recommends to client school. If school is interested, further documents are requested from applicant (passport, certificates, etc.) and an interview is arranged by Skype or in person in the UK, sometimes followed by a further interview with the school.

CONTACT: Susan Jones-Miranda, Director.

CHINA

Recruitment of English teachers for the People's Republic of China is absolutely booming in the private sector. People inside and outside China keep wondering when this romance with the language will fade. Jobs are not as easy to pluck from the vine as they were a couple of years ago, because the authorities have begun to tighten up the visa regulations, making it more difficult to pick up a teaching job on the spot and to sort out the paperwork later. This means that it is preferable to arrange a job in advance that allows you the chance to obtain the appropriate working visa before arrival. Fortunately the internet is plastered with any number of adverts from recruiters and language institutes. Cyberspace is a-buzz with new companies and organisations recruiting thousands of native English speakers to teach at schools and academic institutions around the country, in companies and in private language institutes. It is still the case that more positions are notified than there are foreign applicants to fill them, so the demand is huge.

English is compulsory for school pupils from the age of nine. Although optional, English is now even taught from kindergarten. A foreign language is a compulsory component of the entrance exam (*gaokao*) to enter higher education; of the more than nine million candidates who take this exam, the vast majority choose English over Russian, French, Spanish or Japanese. Unfortunately the *gaokao* does not test real acquisition of language, but requires the memorisation of vocabulary lists and grammar structures. The majority of candidates are not taught communicative English by native speakers, though this is slowly changing. Just as in Taiwan, Korea and Japan, the emerging middle class of China aspires to send its children for private tuition in English and in some cases 'real English' instead of exam English. Many students and teachers are very keen to improve their English to Cambridge Proficiency standard, in the hope of being accepted to study overseas. Competition can be cut-throat although children from the wealthiest families may be less inspired, knowing that they'll be going abroad eventually, whether their English is fluent or not. But most are eager to learn, even if the style of rote learning to which they have become accustomed can be difficult for foreign teachers to adopt.

English is ubiquitous. Many street and shop signs in the capital and other major cities are written in English as well as Chinese, though most Beijing citizens, especially the older generation, can say little more than 'What is your name?' It is easy to forget that, amid the well-reported stories of sprawling urban metropolises rising almost in the night, nearly half of China's population still lives in the countryside. **Sam Meekings** was surprised to discover that although he headed off to Beijing every other weekend to stock up on western foods and see the sights, most of his students had never left the small city of Hengshui; only 15 years previously it had all been farmland.

Bill Lehane was pleasantly surprised by his encounter with China:

> ***I spent six months with my partner teaching teenagers at a school in Lishui City in Zhejiang province. As a journalist by trade with no prior interest in China or indeed teaching experience, I had perhaps an even steeper learning curve than most expat teachers in the Middle Kingdom. Undoubtedly switching the mild climes of Ireland for the hot and humid surrounds of provincial China is a big change, but I found the hours were good and the pay quite adequate as long as you stayed in-country. I would say the worst aspect for me was having to give a blood sample when I arrived, and the best was the ubiquitous, delicious street food. As a writer accustomed to hearing only bad things about communist China and its leaders in Beijing, I have to say I experienced a very different place on the ground. People are happy and friendly and have an interesting, varied and ancient culture.***

PROSPECTS FOR TEACHERS

'*With just a university degree and a little determination anyone can find an opportunity to challenge themselves somewhere in twenty-first century China,*' writes **Sam Meekings**, who taught in a state-run normal college (i.e. teacher training institute) before accepting an editing job with Oxford University Press in Shanghai (and is now a published novelist). However, the better schools have recently started to become more stringent in their recruiting methods and foreigners cannot simply walk into highly lucrative jobs in the same way that they did in the early days. Nevertheless, there are still schools in rural areas so desperate that they will employ anyone simply to have a 'token foreigner' and hence enhance their status.

Teachers are classified as Foreign Experts (FEs) who must have at the very least a university degree. In some popular places like Shanghai where jobs are competitive, a master's degree in a relevant area (English, Linguistics, TEFL/TESOL, etc.) and some teaching experience at the tertiary level may be a requirement. Teachers must have their dossier assessed by the State Administration of Foreign Experts Affairs (SAFEA) before a Foreign Expert Certificate will be granted. As of 2016, the demand for native speakers has escalated, since the passing of a new law that prohibits non-native speakers from being eligible for an FE Certificate unless they have a university degree from a native English speaking country. The percentage of non-native speaking teachers has been very high hitherto, more than 50% in the case of some big employers, but now those positions will have to be filled by native speakers. For the present, non-native teachers can renew their annual Certificate if they continue to work for the same employer who gives them a good recommendation. But unless prospective new teachers are from or have been educated in Britain, Ireland, North America or the Antipodes, they will not be eligible to become a Foreign Expert.

Most foreigners teach oral English rather than grammar, which means that younger candidates without qualifications may also find positions in Chinese schools but as interns on much less generous stipends. Gap year students can pay a fee from £795 to £6,200 to join China teaching programmes organised by (for example) Lattitude Global Volunteering, BUNAC (www.bunac.org/uk/intern-abroad/teaching/teaching-internship-china) and Project Trust, and be placed in primary schools, middle schools (public secondary schools, often boarding schools) or vocational schools. The more remote or deprived the area or the more hostile the climate, the easier it will be to find a job. But there are also plenty of vacancies in comfortable cities such as Kunming and Dalian, fewer in Shanghai and Beijing.

Even ordinary secondary schools employ native English speakers; applications can be made through provincial education bureaux. Writing direct to the Foreign Affairs Office (*waiban*) of institutes of higher learning may lead to a job offer. Chinese institutes seem to attach more weight to the letter of application than to the curriculum vitae, but the CV should still be sent and should emphasise any work or experience in education. Also enclose a photo, a photocopy of the first page of your passport, a copy of any education certificates and two references. **Jessie Levene** notes that schools seem to prefer female teachers, particularly for younger students, and as a result, she was given more and more classes, despite an already full timetable.

Some schools have also introduced a probationary period of between two and 10 weeks. Although this may sound a bit daunting if you have already paid for flight tickets, it can work in the applicant's favour, as it allows time to ensure that the school is suitable for you. It is always best, wherever possible, to visit a school before signing a contract and talk to other teachers, to make sure that the school is everything it says it is. After teaching in China and realising how great the demand for native speaker teachers is, **Caryn-Ann Langley** from Scotland set up a teacher placement agency, which she and her father ran for a few years. Her emphatic advice is:

> ***Speak to other foreigners working at the schools! We cannot express how important this part of the application process is; it will save so much trouble if you can just speak with a foreigner. If there are none, ask to see the school's licence to employ Foreign Experts. If they won't show this, stay away because they probably don't have one. If the school is checked and you are found working, you may be deported for working illegally.***

China is the biggest market in the world right now for IELTS tests, so it is a good place to get trained and start testing. Once you are an official IELTS examiner, you can examine anywhere in the world, but have to keep your certification up to date by examining at least once every three months.

FINDING A JOB

With the explosion in opportunities, the job hunt is more complex and varied than it was a few years ago, when most teacher applications were for state institutes and had to go through the Chinese Education Association for International Exchange (CEAIE) or one of its provincial offices. Nowadays, CEAIE leaves recruitment to online companies and private recruiters, foundations or China-linked companies eager to sign up native English speakers (with or without relevant experience) for an academic year.

Some of the tried and tested old schemes are still in place and still work. The British Council's Language Assistants Programme, in cooperation with the Chinese education authorities, places graduates in schools across China. TEFL training is provided on a two-week course in Beijing which is free to participants. Assistants receive free accommodation and utilities and a flight back to the UK. Teaching experience and/or qualifications are not necessary. Details of the application procedure can be seen at www.britishcouncil.org/language-assistants/become/china. The British Council accepts applications up until the end of January. Applications are screened and then candidates are invited to attend an assessment day in February/March for departures in mid-August. The minimum requirement is a university degree, though a TEFL certificate and/or teaching experience, preferably abroad, improve your chances of acceptance. Opportunities are available in a large variety of cities throughout mainland China, though initial training and orientation take place in Beijing before teaching starts on 1 September. Wages are not brilliant at the lower end, i.e. RMB4,000 per month, though those with relevant experience earn up to RMB13,000, and all teachers are provided with free accommodation. The required medical check in the UK – sometimes a full medical exam while other schools will be content with a letter from your GP – must be paid for by the candidate as well as an International Child Protection Certificate which costs £60.

Most jobs begin with the school year in August/September and are advertised in the months beforehand. Schools hire teachers for the whole year, though one-term contracts are sometimes available. Recruiters in the UK to try are Teaching English in China based in Newcastle and Cardiff (www.teic.co.uk), Flying Cows in Nottingham (www.flying-cows.com/teaching-china), TEFL Panda with offices in Twickenham and Fuzhou (www.teflpanda.com) and London-based Teach English in China (www.teach-english-in-china.co.uk). A couple of others are listed at the end of this chapter.

Any web search or a trawl of the major ELT job websites is bound to turn up plenty of contacts. The majority of vacancies are for candidates who have a degree and a TEFL certificate; without the latter many agencies make it a requirement that you take at least an online TEFL course. Long-lived online agencies include http://jobs.echinacities.com, http://teachingchina.net, www.newworldesl.com and www.cathayteacher.com, which have long lists of jobs, all dated and described in detail. Other places to look on the web include www.networkesl.com, www.clickchn.com for jobs in public schools and universities, www.en.xhgjedu.com (New Time International Teaching Agency), Good Teachers Union (see entry), and Gold Star TEFL Recruitment (www.GoldStarTeachers.com), which advertises salaries at the high end, i.e. RMB6,000–RMB16,000 per month. The classified sections of regional expat websites such as www.gochengdoo.com and www.thebeijinger.com/classifieds/english-teaching are also worth searching.

Tefl.chinajob.com regularly offers a seven-day training course in Beijing, Shanghai and Wuhan, and less often in Guangzhou, Suzhou and Chengdu. This TEFL training is approved by SAFEA which will grant FE status to graduates who pass it.

Demand for qualified teachers is so high that any who advertise their services online may get an instantaneous response, as happened to a teacher writing from Shanghai:

I put my CV on TEFL.com and the DoS of EF Academic Partnerships contacted me by email enquiring about my current location and availability. I replied that I was at home and currently seeking employment and asked for some more information. He promptly replied and we arranged an interview for the following Saturday morning.

PRIVATE LANGUAGE TRAINING

An ever-growing number of private companies operate in the fields of media and education, especially English-language kindergartens and tutorial centres. **Jane Pennington**, who taught for four years in China, carried out a little research and estimates that there were about 100 private language companies in Kunming, only about 15%–20% of which were officially licensed. The ratio is better nowadays but there are still plenty of cowboy outfits. Such institutes are not authorised to invite foreign teachers, yet some persuade native English-speaking teachers to work for them without admitting that it is illegal. Like private schools everywhere, a number are run by unscrupulous entrepreneurs interested only in profit. Similarly there are independent recruiters and agencies that advertise vast numbers of vacancies and try to slot people in as quickly as possible so that they can collect their commission. If considering working in the private sector, try to find out the degree of professionalism of the company that has expressed interest in hiring you, and talk to other foreigners working there, especially with regard to payment.

International ELT organisations such as EF English First or Longman Schools (see entries) have been expanding and usually offer a solid introduction to life as an English teacher in China. Shane English School has more than 40 schools across China which recruit directly (which many teachers recommend) via the Shanghai headquarters (recruitment@shane.com.cn) or via recruitment agencies such as Saxoncourt Recruitment in London. Placement of teachers by Language Link (see entry) is concentrated on the Beijing area. The Taiwanese company Kidcastle specialises in teaching very young children; already it has 200 schools in mainland China, with new schools opening all the time. Recruitment of teachers is done centrally at http://ft.kidcastle.cn.

The internet is a prolific source of possibilities and expanding all the time. According to the Wall Street Journal, more than half of the population of China is now online, i.e. 688 million people. Any web search or a trawl of the major ELT job sites can inundate you with job contacts. In the private sector, some large companies such as hotel chains have their own language-training facilities for staff, especially if they are joint ventures with western companies. Most recruitment of teachers by business and industry takes place locally, since they do not offer accommodation.

PLACEMENT AGENCIES AND ORGANISATIONS

Many companies recruit teachers from abroad for China. Whereas many merely make the initial match, others have an ongoing relationship with their teachers. Australian **Shane Johnson** taught all over China for seven years, and preferred to be hired through an agency, in his case Buckland International Education Group (see entry below), because they could sort out any problems that arose:

I have had a very smooth seven years and the only real problem was when I arrived at my current school to find that they wanted me to share an apartment and teach only Grades 1 and 2, even though they had assured me I would have my own apartment and my timetable would be Grades 3–6. It took only one phone call to my boss at Buckland before a second apartment was found and I had older classes added to my timetable. This is the reason I sign with a recruiter and not directly with a school. I have a contract with my boss/recruiter and they have a contract with each school.

A number of North American organisations involved in teacher placements in China have entries in the listings at the end of this chapter, including the Colorado China Council, Appalachians Abroad and the

US-China Educational Exchange. WorldTeach (www.worldteach.org/programmes/china) is a non-profit organisation that sends volunteers to teach in secondary schools in Hunan province for a full academic year (August to July). Volunteers pay $500 for the year. A Canadian-Chinese joint venture directly hires, trains, manages and assists their foreign teaching staff (www.panda-education.ca).

CONDITIONS OF WORK

With the rise of the free market many reward packages are now open to negotiation. Higher degrees or diplomas attract higher salaries, so if you have earned qualifications beyond a BA, take along the certificates to prove it. Employers generally offer to reimburse airfares after you have completed your one-year contract. The general monthly salary range for most ordinary native English-speaker teachers should start from RMB5,000 ($750/£550) but can rise in the private sector (especially in sophisticated Shanghai and Beijing) to well over RMB15,000. (Note that an alternative term for the Chinese currency is yuan, so salaries are sometimes quoted in CNY, which is exactly the same as RMB.)

With the explosion of the English teaching market, dodgy operators have entered the fray and the number of complaints from teachers who feel badly exploited has escalated alarmingly. A good source of information on how to avoid this may be found at www.chinaforeignteachersunion.org, where users can post complaints and warn of scams, to protect the interests of foreign teachers in China (which they claim number 29,642). The site publishes a blacklist of poor employers and more usefully, a list of '*12 clauses every foreign teacher should insert into their contract before signing it*'. These mainly protect teachers from having to pay for things such as the invitation letter, school supplies or excursions, travel to off-premises lessons, and so on. All the big chains like EF (see entry), Disney (http://disneyenglish.disneycareers.com) and Wall Street English (www.wsi.com.cn/career/en/index.aspx) have attracted complaints in the past, though problems are usually particular to a single branch rather than to the whole company so beware of attaching too much importance to negative feedback online.

The experience of teachers in the big cities is very different from that of native speakers who go to more obscure locations. Be aware that what are called cities in China are more like counties or small states, so even when you think you are going to a big city, you could in fact end up in a small town with few recreational outlets, as happened to **Dan Casaletto**:

> ***I was in a much smaller town than I had expected where there was no expat community. My fellow teachers were a bunch of Chinese men and women with whom I could not communicate. The few teachers who could speak English were friendly, but busy with their own lives. There was one other foreign teacher from the West and although we had little in common it was great to have a conversation in English and someone to commiserate with. The presence of a university nearby did give me a chance to make friends with English-speaking Chinese college students.***
>
> ***I was living in a small town, where some of the more repugnant features of Chinese culture are brought to the fore (spitting, including indoors, children defecating on the sidewalk, yelling in confined quarters and market sellers charging grossly inflated prices for inferior merchandise). The school curfew was terrible, school gates were locked from 11.30pm to 6am. If I could do it again I would have demanded to be placed in a larger city.***

Although higher wages can be earned in the big cities of Beijing, Guangzhou, Shanghai, the megalopolis of Chongqing and in the Special Economic Zones such as Hainan, life in Chinese cities has many drawbacks in terms of crowds and pollution. Kate Devlin, who taught at the China Agriculture University in Beijing, found the city 'polluted, very ugly and soulless'. For quality of life, South-Western China is probably better than much of the east. Yunnan province has a particularly congenial climate. This area is also reputed to be less money oriented than the east coast cities, which may have the drawback that it may be more difficult to find paying private students.

CARYN-ANN LANGLEY

Caryn-Ann Langley traded Scotland for China and wrote enthusiastically about her situation:

I was in a bit of a pickle about what I wanted to do next, so when a school friend posted on Facebook about teaching jobs in China, I decided to give this a go. In my first job, in a government school, I was living in a hotel with my friend and two other girls. It got a bit much – whenever you walked out of your bedroom in your Spongebob PJs you'd come face-to-face with a half naked old Chinese man in the corridor. You can't move to a flat without the permission of the company you work for. After a bit of a breakdown in communication with that employer, I went onto a website called echinacities.com and found my new job here in Hainan, a tropical island of China, where I hope to stay for a long time. When I came down to Hainan I was apartment shopping within two days, and moved into this little place on the third. Such a difference it makes.

While most small cities in China are full of people who have never travelled far from their homes, Hainan is mostly populated by mainland Chinese people who have come for a more relaxed lifestyle on a tropical island. There are many local Hainanese people as well from small villages dotting the island, which makes communication very fun.

I don't have any teaching qualifications and neither do my friends teaching in Guangzhou and Kuitun. Working conditions in my kindergarten are really good for me. It is a private school so parents pay a lot of money and everything is clean and modern. The kids are four years old and spoilt rotten but I love them all. As long as they learn their new words in English and have fun, their parents are happy, and so is the school.

Foreign teachers generally earn double the Chinese English teachers' wage, which is plenty to save for travelling unless you spend it on a lot of luxuries. I only work four hours a day, so I get to do what I want in the afternoons, like go to the beach. I get at least four weeks' summer holiday with lots of other holidays as well. I can say I am in love with China.

Outside the major eastern cities you can live on less than RMB2,000 a month if your accommodation is provided. Even teaching interns on low wages (normally people on a gap year or who don't have a university degree) can usually afford to eat out and travel a bit. However, in the major eastern cities, the cost of living will be much higher and those who aspire to a little glamour in their lifestyle will find themselves spending up to RMB5,000 per month. Inflation has been creeping up in China, especially for food, so hanging out in expat bars and taking taxis has become more expensive.

The three- or four-week holiday over Chinese New Year should be paid, as should vacation periods in state schools if you are contracted to continue teaching afterwards. Companies in the private sector may not offer payment during enforced breaks from teaching. **Paul Carey** identified the sudden six-week break from working and earning with little notice given by the employer as one of the low points of his experience with EF English First in Shanghai, which was otherwise '*a worthwhile experience both personally and professionally*'. Many employers offer free internet access and some offer free Chinese lessons. **Shane Johnson** appreciated the large number of holidays:

The Chinese are one of the most festive people I have ever known and they celebrate each festival with a lot of food, beer and a public holiday. In addition to all the school and statutory holidays, traditional festivals are celebrated such as Tomb Sweeping Festival and the Dragon Boat Festival. China is such a wonderful country to live in and life really is an amazing journey.

While teaching in a suburb of Shanghai, **Marybeth Hao** noticed many Chinese parents were more than willing to pay native English-speaker tutors high fees to tutor their children outside school hours.

Foreign teachers can be expected to teach anything from 15 to 30+ hours a week. Twenty hours is typical, though this sounds lighter than it actually is because there are bound to be extra duties. Often there is a heavy load of marking, not to mention marketing. Teachers in the private sector are routinely asked to attend student recruitment events, for example to hand out flyers or to appear at drop-in evenings whose main purpose is to rope in new clients. Some teachers are expected to staff an 'English corner' or English club, or deliver a weekly lecture on western culture. In out-of-the-way places, you might find yourself playing the part of 'token foreigner' at the many banquets you will be invited to when you first arrive. For **Dan Casaletto** one of the high points of his time in China was dancing at a nightclub on his birthday while a crowd chanted 'foreigner' and 'beautiful' in Chinese. He was humbled and amazed at the generosity of many whom he encountered and befriended.

In cases where teachers are given a huge number of classes, the administration's main ambition is to maximise your exposure, which may have the effect of minimising your usefulness. On the whole **Michelle** enjoyed her time in China, but she thinks that foreign teachers should be given more advice on what is required of them before they start teaching. It is not unusual for the school to leave it up to the teachers to find out if any national exams are looming for which you should be helping the students to prepare. Hours of teaching are unpredictable and the teaching days can be very long. Students get up at 6am and work at night in supervised sessions. Michelle was asked to take classes at weekends, which left little time for travel. If you want to keep your weekends free for travel and relaxation, firmly decline teaching hours on Saturday and Sunday, and be aware that it is all too easy to over-commit yourself in the first few weeks. It should always be your choice to take on extra hours and when you do, you should be paid accordingly.

Sam Meekings describes how attendance at several Chinese banquets can lead to a succession of nasty hangovers:

Every foreigner in China quickly becomes familiar with **baijiu**, *a sharp, clear liquor with a cloying aftertaste, which is measured out into shot glasses in front of you at the start of a meal. Though beer is increasingly popular, no large event is complete without* **baijiu**. *At any large banquet, especially with officials or high-ranking teachers at the school or college, you will be encouraged to drink with them. Your glass will be topped up throughout the meal, and often many people will wish to toast you, meaning you must once again down your drink as a sign of mutual respect. This is why, by eight or nine in the evening, restaurants begin to clear out – many diners are too wasted to do anything but go home and sleep. It should be noted, however, that women are usually exempted from this custom, and though I would have liked to have been spared the attention (and the subsequent hangovers), my female colleagues were not impressed that they were simply expected to sit and slowly sip beer or Coca-Cola while all the men went through the intricate tradition of getting each other as drunk as possible. Similarly, while almost all the male teachers in the college were heavy smokers (one of the best gifts to present to someone is a box of cigarettes), women smoking were frowned upon. Though these attitudes cannot be found in big cosmopolitan cities, I am certain that they persist throughout the smaller towns that make up the bulk of this vast country.*

On the other hand, you may find your colleagues and bosses bend over backwards to help and support you, as **Bradwell Jackson** reported:

I was offered a job with Aston in China on the basis of a telephone interview. Aston is good to me, and my co-workers scramble to help me whenever I have even a mild matter that needs attention. For example, when I told them I was looking for a kung-fu school, they took this as a very important issue and had many long discussions-cum-negotiations with each other in order to come up with the best option for me. I think it might be hard to convince a westerner to come and stay in an out-of-the-way city like Tangshan.

Really, I'm living the life of Reilly here. I've got nothing to complain about. The school has given me a free apartment complete with cable TV, washing machine, toaster oven, microwave and refrigerator. Whenever I'm hungry, I just mosey on down to the street vendors and get some proper Chinese food for a friendly budget price. Who can ask for more?

THE STUDENTS

There are not many corners of China these days into which foreigners, whether teachers or travellers, have not penetrated, although in Hengshui, three hours south of Beijing, **Sam Meekings** was amazed at the reaction he received from people in the town, who would stop and gape at him as though they had seen 'dinosaurs or dragons'. **Yasmin Peiris**, based in Shenzhen, one of China's newest cities, agrees that the attitude towards teachers is generally favourable, even though there is a language barrier. She chose to ask her students for advice on where to go at weekends and what to do (a foot massage, a little shopping and sampling tempting varieties of Chinese food were some of the suggestions). In Beijing, **Kate Devlin** reckoned that the students in her university classes came from very wealthy families and were spoiled rotten: '*Out of a class of 20–25 students, maybe five or six kids would listen to my lecture. Students would openly sleep, read, watch movies on their laptop or mostly talk. They were required to be in class so they were, but nothing more.*'

Perhaps the younger age groups are preferable. The students that **James Butcher** taught were not quite as he expected:

I think our general expectations are that Chinese students will be well behaved and silent in class, but this is far from the truth! They can be a rowdy bunch. But with the right methods they can be controlled. The younger grades are very enthusiastic and pick up things quite fast. I found the Chinese students to have a very positive, energetic attitude. They are also hilarious to watch and I guarantee they will put a smile on your face every day. The older grades are generally good too. They don't want to be treated like children, once they trust you they will enjoy your lessons and always run to give you a hug when they see you! I taught kindergarten for a few sessions at the start of my contract and discovered that age group wasn't for me so they assigned another teacher to that class. I found the children hard to control and much too young to learn English really. I had to teach kindergarten after a long day at school and I just didn't have the energy at that point!

Bradwell Jackson identified another interesting new trend in modern-day China from his experiences of teaching in a small city:

There is another interesting phenomenon in China, which is the syndrome of the 'Little Emperor'. Chinese children are well behaved, but they were even better behaved 10 or 20 years ago. With the advent of the one-child policy, some interesting changes took place. It seems that with just one child in the house, and especially if it's a boy, the child is much more likely to be spoiled and accommodated. Any English teacher here will probably get his/her small share of little brats who just can't understand why they can't do what they want.

I agree with the premise that a teacher has to be a bossy boots in order to establish the discipline straight off the bat. I certainly did this, maybe even a bit too much, so that now the (naughty) kids are just a tad bit resistant sometimes. The parents, on the other hand, are deliriously happy with me. They specifically love the fact that I'm strict with the kids.

Slowly, newer pedagogical methods are being accepted by students and administrators alike, although most teachers are warned not to stray into dangerous territory in their lessons, like politics and sex. **Bradwell Jackson** identified the three forbidden 'T' topics: Tiananmen, Taiwan and Tibet. One recent teacher struggled with the contradictions: '*We're invited here to teach Western Culture, then instructed not to behave like westerners.*' However, it is impossible to generalise, because in one place, techniques that smack of innovation will be greeted with blank stares, while in another, there can be lively class discussions.

Bill Lehane from Ireland blogged while he was teaching in China and gave an amusing account of a less than triumphant lesson:

> ***The assignment, on the face of it, should have been simple. Choose your favourite foreign country, write seven sentences about it and then read your work out to the class the following week. The results were, well, pretty bad. Many of them obviously hadn't bothered to do the homework at all, and were just bluffing their way through about two and a half sentences in the hope they would get away with it. And many couldn't even do that much: at least one stood up and said: 'USA. I like NBA. Thank you'. And promptly sat down. X is for fail, mister! The most popular country was Canada, but only because loads of students had found a stodgy piece about it in their English textbook. The result of this was that I must have heard the same spiel: 'My favourite country is Canada. It is north of the United States. It is the second largest country in the world. It has a population of only slightly over 30 million people' – about 40 or 50 times over the course of the week.***
>
> ***Out of the 350-odd students, a few, to be fair, were quite good. One girl gave a presentation on Switzerland that could have doubled as a Wikipedia entry. One boy said his favourite country was South Africa because it had lots of gold, and that when he found it he would be very rich. A few chose Ireland but seemed not to know what to say about it except to ply me with compliments. They all passed! Many more in the middle ground had perfectly acceptable mini-speeches. Even where they just regurgitated what I had said in my introduction, I felt that they had done their job for what was an Oral English assignment.***
>
> ***Culturally, the exercise was instructive, despite the flawed results. Boys liking basketball while girls liking romance (or clothes!) seemed to be the benchmark of Chinese teenagerdom. In the end, then, my first foray into assigning homework was a bit of a mixed bag. But addling, lazy assholes aside, it's mostly a pleasant job being a foreign teacher in China I reckon. You draw up a simple lesson on PowerPoint and just run with it for a week, improvising and fine-tuning as you go along. And once you're plugged in to it, the work goes by really quickly, leaving plenty of time for fun.***

Jessie Levene, reaching for some colourful similes, identifies the low point of her first teaching job was feeling like a 'robot' and a 'teaching monkey'. It seems that you may have to work fairly hard to introduce modern teaching techniques into the classroom, as from a very early age Chinese children are taught in a very traditional style, as **Nina Capek** found while teaching in a primary school:

> ***The teaching style does take a bit of getting used to. The children are used to learning by rote and the general ethos is: whatever the teacher says, we copy. Teaching 'my name is . . .' to 50 six-year-old children proved very entertaining as they all copied me and said 'my name is Nina'.***

A teacher who started work at Shanghai Lixin University of Commerce was delighted with the standard of students:

> ***Their attitude has been excellent on the whole. I have only a couple of disruptive students, but they all seem to be very motivated to learn English and realise how important it can be to their future careers. I know little of their real expectations other than most are concerned more with fluency than complexity or accuracy.***

At university, students expect to pass, as it has been difficult for them to get in, while some have paid to get in or used connections (*guanxi*), which means they expect to sail through. Don't be surprised if just before exam time your students ply you with gifts, expensive meals and even offer money. Teachers who accept these offers may find that their students expect high marks even if they do not turn up to the exam!

SAM MEEKINGS

Sam Meekings, like some other teachers, found that there is a demand for any English provided it is clearly enunciated. Imaginative interactive teaching methods can work, as Sam discovered when he had to teach a 60-strong class of university students, whose homework left something to be desired.

Each week I was supposed to go through the excerpts from Shakespeare or Dickens in the book, despite the fact that close to half of the class could barely communicate with me in English at all. Though the impulse was strong to follow the example of the Chinese teachers and teach only to the brighter students and hope the others kept quiet at the back, I soon found that it was much more enjoyable to try and work the material into games and activities that everyone could take part in. This took time, however, since some students were so used to either being ignored or simply learning by rote and repetition that they were too shy to speak up. This is a problem I have noticed even teaching in private school in bigger cities – students are often so heavily criticised for mistakes in their normal classes that they lack the confidence to risk answering a question or attempting to join a game or discussion in case they do something wrong.

It sometimes feels as if you are not only in a different country but also in a different century. None of the students I taught had any real concept of exploring or questioning an idea. When I set some homework essays for my literature class or set debate topics for my English speaking class to try to engage with, I was invariably met with 60 identical responses. Students are taught to pass exams in China, to memorise the single correct response and then repeat it when instructed – there is no concept of coming up with your own ideas. My students were all adamant that there was always one right answer and that everything else could therefore be discounted as wrong. This meant most essays and debates were very, very short. Coupled with the fact that we were not allowed to fail any students (even if they could not write more than their name on the biannual exam papers we had to set), it quickly became clear that we would have to set aside most of our preconceptions about education. Yet when students do finally open up or try something new, there is no better feeling.

REGULATIONS

As mentioned at the beginning of this chapter, the bureaucratic free-for-all of a decade ago is over. Enforcement of the new regulations is not universal especially in small obscure towns, but the state regulates foreign teachers much more tightly than it once did. If possible, try to jump through the hoops to regularise your status to avoid the possibility of punitive fines and being cheated by your employer. The most recent crackdown has been on non-native speakers who are no longer entitled to obtain a visa for teaching English.

Before leaving home or even buying a flight ticket, you should have in hand a signed contract and a Z-visa. For the letter of invitation to be approved by the authorities, you will need to supply your university degree,

TEFL certificate (which can be an online course), a medical report from your home country and a criminal records check. At the beginning of the process, scanned copies of these documents suffice, but hard copies will have to be posted before the work permit can be issued. The contract and letter of invitation from your employer must be taken to your nearest Chinese Consulate or Embassy to apply for a Z-visa (work visa).

People arriving with a Z-visa have 30 days to convert this to a Foreign Expert Certificate and Residence Permit from the Division of Exit-Entry Administration of the Beijing Public Security Bureau. SAFEA (State Administration of Foreign Experts Affairs) is trying to streamline and improve the process of recruitment and also to make foreign experts eligible to join the social security insurance system. Keep receipts of all the visa expenses you incur because your employer might reimburse them at a later stage.

Requirements are more stringent in the popular destinations of Shanghai, Beijing, etc. where Foreign Experts are expected to have two years' post-university working experience and/or an MA. In neglected regions like north-west China, the threshold will be much lower. Everything has to be officially stamped. If you are found without the appropriate documents you will be harshly fined. For example, a teacher whose papers were mostly in order but hadn't got the resident's permit was fined RMB3,000 (more than half a month's wages). State institutes of education usually do everything by the book but you shouldn't expect the same of private language schools or commercial recruiters.

A couple of summers ago **John Ramage** answered an ad on Dave's ESL Café and describes the application process and red tape requirements in detail:

> ***I sent the agent a statement of interest plus the picture page of my passport plus my CV plus a reference letter plus photos. The agent then set up an interview with the private university, Huanghe College of Science and Technology in Zhengzhou (Henan Province). They called me on my mobile during a lunch break in the office, in Scotland. This was amazingly quick and easy and I got the job fast. The agent then sent me a long contract in bits and pieces, which made it a bit awkward and finicky.***
>
> ***Before going to China, there were unexpected hiccups. Hiccup no. 1 was the medical. This is required for people teaching in China. A form is downloadable from the Chinese website which the doctor must complete. My GP flatly told me it was not NHS work. The MASTA Travel Clinic did help and promptly scheduled a comprehensive medical, exactly what the Chinese authorities were looking for, but it cost me £380.***
>
> ***The second hiccup was the elastic time taken over visa processes. The Chinese Consulate suggests one month, but it can take much longer. I gathered my documents and sent them to the Public Security Bureau in China for processing. The college sent me the invitation letter and work permit to take to the Consulate to apply for the visa. Getting the visa took one week after that. My documents spent far longer than expected in the PSB. The agent made it worse by promising it would be over in several weeks, so I left my UK job. As the weeks turned to months, I got really annoyed. The agency seemed to have a mañana, mañana attitude (although they were Australian). Surely he ought to have known! Fortunately I didn't book my flight until after I got my Z-Visa, otherwise I could have lost money.***

LEISURE TIME

Foreigners who teach in Beijing can lead a standard expatriate life if they want to, socialising at expat bars and clubs. Life in the provinces will be very different. You may still be one of the very few foreigners that the local people have ever seen and are bound to be the object of curious stares (which will be even more persistent if you happen to be a non-white person).

The main way of socialising in China is going to restaurants, because a large banquet shared by many people is only marginally more expensive than cooking for yourself. However, as most people go out to eat around 6pm–7pm, restaurants do not usually stay open later than 10pm. Students in state institutions can be restricted by a strict curfew, but when everything closes at 10pm, native English teachers start to realise why the students are not so bothered.

In smaller settlements, there may be no restaurants even to rival the Chinese take-away in your home town; but the locals will be far more interested in you and perhaps even teach you to cook your own Chinese food. If there are several foreigners, communal dining facilities (often segregated) will usually be provided. Glutinous rice, soy beans and cabbage are staples and fresh produce may be in short supply in winter. In Tangshan, **Bradwell Jackson** reports that he could have a 'killer meal' of dumplings, quick and right off the street, for only a couple of renminbi.

Learning Chinese is the ambition of many teachers and is a great asset, especially outside cosmopolitan areas. Take a good teach-yourself book and CD/tapes, since these are difficult to obtain outside Beijing and Shanghai. Mastering Chinese characters is a daunting business, though the grammar is straightforward. Others prefer to study Tai Chi, Wushu or other exotic martial arts.

Despite China's rapid 'westernisation' in economic terms, its cultural differences remain both a challenge and a delight. Be prepared for noise and air pollution even in small towns, though it is usually possible to escape into the countryside by bicycle or bus. **James Butcher** found that everyone heads for the park to relax. His local one in a quiet town in Guangdong province had amusement rides and boating lakes. When it got really hot, everyone headed to the mall, where the air conditioning was on full blast.

School and college vacations take place over Spring Festival (Chinese New Year) in or around February, when the trains are very crowded and the weather is cold. Chinese people are renowned for making last-minute arrangements, so be prepared for the frustration of finding out at the last minute when your holidays will be, by which time the trains may be booked up and flying is much more expensive.

Some cities such as Kunming have a good expat community to which the Chinese cater with western-style cafés and restaurants. There are plenty of films to watch (all pirated) and a couple of galleries to visit. Much of the time you will be responsible for your own amusement, so take plenty of reading matter, including *Wild Swans*, an astonishing account of life in the Cultural Revolution or perhaps *Under Fishbone Clouds* by Sam Meekings, quoted in this chapter, an interweaving of 20th-century Chinese history and folklore. **Jessie Levene** found lots to do in Chengdu: '*learn Chinese, take photos, enjoy the amazing Sichuan food, hang out with friends, go to bars …*'.

Bradwell Jackson would urge anybody to do TEFL in China:

> ***My first impressions were that of a fascinating country with a splendid culture, and I wasn't even in a well-known city. The people are organised and respectful, and the food, of course, is a revelation. If you have just a little bit of travel experience to a non-western country, you should be fine and have no worries at all. There is certainly no problem with safety. My school has been very good to me. You will find that most schools bend over backwards to get you here. All you need is a fair amount of teaching experience (and a college degree) and the whole new world of China awaits you.***

American **Ed Flok** was similarly enamoured of teaching in China and in his third year began teaching at the North China University of Technology in Beijing:

> ***Don't believe all the negative articles you read about China. Everywhere I taught the people were awesome, and very polite, reaching out to make me their friend. I ate at personal dinner tables, swam in the Yellow Sea with students, ate at restaurants, went bike riding and socialised. The best of this experience was actually teaching the students English, and seeing how fast they learn. To this day I keep in contact with some of my first students. They really get attached to you as a role model, and want you as their friend.***

LIST OF EMPLOYERS

AMITY FOUNDATION
71 Han Kou Road, Nanjing, Jiangsu 210008
+86 25 8326 0836
amitynj@amity.org.cn
www.amityfoundation.org

A Chinese Christian NGO.

NUMBER OF TEACHERS: 40–50 for Young Adult Teaching Programme and 1-month summer programme.

PREFERENCE OF NATIONALITY: None, but must be native English speaker or have a high level of proficiency in English and language teaching experience.

QUALIFICATIONS: Ages 18–28 for Young Volunteer Programme. Teaching experience, a knowledge of Chinese or of living in Asia are useful but not essential. A Christian faith commitment is generally required, however, the 'mission' expected is to serve rather than to proselytise.

CONDITIONS OF EMPLOYMENT: 1-year placement in underdeveloped parts of China. Also Summer English Programme (SEP) for volunteers to provide oral English training to Chinese middle and primary school teachers of English in rural and minority areas, for 4 weeks from early July.

SALARY: None. Volunteers pay participation fee to cover orientation, admin, etc. e.g. US$3,900 for 5 months, $4,500 for 11 months.

FACILITIES/SUPPORT: Accommodation is usually provided in the form of an apartment on the school campus.

RECRUITMENT: Teachers are recruited primarily through church sending agencies, i.e. mission agencies of various denominations in a range of countries including the UK, Canada and the USA. See above website for contact details of these organisations. Interviews in person are expected and generally take place in the applicant's own country.

CONTACT: Helen Zhao, Educational Exchange Programs (helenzhao@amity.org.cn).

APPALACHIANS ABROAD TEACH IN CHINA PROGRAM
Center for International Programs, Marshall University, One John Marshall Ave, Huntington, WV 25755, USA
+1 304 696 6265
gochina@marshall.edu
www.marshall.edu/gochina

NUMBER OF TEACHERS: 40–60 annually.

PREFERENCE OF NATIONALITY: American, Canadian and British.

QUALIFICATIONS: Bachelor's degree is essential; accepted ages range from new college graduates to early retirees.

CONDITIONS OF EMPLOYMENT: 10-month teaching contract from 1 September. Teaching 15–18 hours per week, at public and private primary and secondary schools and in institutes of higher education, mainly in Shanghai but other areas as well.

SALARY: RMB8,000–15,000 per month, up to RMB22,000. Maximum 1 month paid winter school break and full international airfare paid on completion of teaching contract.

FACILITIES/SUPPORT: Accommodation provided free by hosting school. Free orientation in Shanghai in late August before arriving at Chinese host school. Discount given on 11-week online TEFL training course with International TEFL Academy.

RECRUITMENT: Internet adverts and phone or Skype-video interviews. Application deadline 31 March/16 April. Application fee is $150; job placement and administrative fee is $1,050 which includes 4–5 day orientation in Shanghai and 1-year travel and medical insurance card.

CONTACT: Ms QingQing Zhao, Director of China Projects.

ASTON ENGLISH
435 MinZheng Street, ShaHeKou District, Dalian, Liaoning Province 116021
+86 411 8451 8248
www.astonrecruiting.com

NUMBER OF TEACHERS: 300+ annually for 120 schools mostly in Sha'anxi and Shandong but in provinces all over China.

PREFERENCE OF NATIONALITY: American, Canadian, British, Irish, Australian, New Zealander and South African.

QUALIFICATIONS: University degree (any subject) and a TEFL certificate and/or TEFL experience. Candidates without a TEFL background can take a 1-week course in China which meets this requirement, at a cost of $315, which is part refunded on renewal of contract.

CONDITIONS OF EMPLOYMENT: Contract lengths of 6–7 weeks in summer or winter. Term-time contracts are for 6 or 12 months starting September and March, 7.5 or 13.5 months starting mid-January and mid-July. Most contracts are for 20 teaching hours plus 3 office hours. Most teaching takes place at weekends. Teachers get 3 days off a week.

SALARY: Up to RMB12,000 a month, but most earn much less. Varying flight allowances of up to RMB7,000 (approximately $1,050) based on hours and length of contract. Small deductions made for income tax.

FACILITIES/SUPPORT: Contracts provide teachers with private bedrooms in a 2 or 3-bedroom Chinese-style apartment. Teachers must pay for utilities. Proper documents provided for work visas before arrival and residence permit after. Chinese lessons provided. Online and face-to-face training is ongoing.

RECRUITMENT: Via all methods such as internet (www.tefl.com, etc.), phone and drop-ins. Phone/Skype interviews.

CONTACT: Gavin Parker, Recruitment Manager.

BEIJING TEACH
38 St. Marks Place, Roslyn, NY 11577, USA
+1 516 535 9236
info@BeijingTeach.com
www.BeijingTeach.com

NUMBER OF TEACHERS: 200 per year for partner schools in Beijing and region.

PREFERENCE OF NATIONALITY: Native English-speaking teachers preferred.

QUALIFICATIONS: Teachers must be energetic and patient because most pupils are young children. Teaching experience preferred but not required.

CONDITIONS OF EMPLOYMENT: 10–12 months. 25 teaching hours, 40 total work hours per week.

SALARY: RMB7,000–14,000 per month.

FACILITIES/SUPPORT: Free shared accommodation. Round-trip airfare reimbursement, free Chinese lessons, a free TEFL certificate, visa sponsorship and free lunches at place of work.

BERLITZ CHINA
211 Shimen Yi Lu, Unit 701-3, Wang Wang Plaza, Shanghai, 200041
+86 21 5213 8393
teaching.cn@em.berlitz.com
www.berlitz.com.cn

NUMBER OF TEACHERS: 140.

PREFERENCE OF NATIONALITY: USA, Canada, UK, Australia, New Zealand preferred.

QUALIFICATIONS: Bachelor's degree or higher, certification in language teaching (TESOL, TEFL, CELTA or equivalent preferred) and teaching experience preferred. Must have interest in teaching adults as well as children, and have organisational and communication skills. Instructors should be dynamic, mature, professional and culturally sensitive. Business experience, knowledge or qualifications also desirable.

CONDITIONS OF EMPLOYMENT: Minimum 1 year, but standard contracts are 2 years. Operation hours are Monday–Friday 8.30am–9.30pm and Saturday and Sunday 8.30am–4.30pm. Full time instructors are required to work 40 hours a week in shifts during the operating hours with 2 days off (1 weekend day and 1 week day).

SALARY: RMB14,000 per month.

FACILITIES/SUPPORT: First week's hotel accommodation is paid for overseas hires during which the centre staff help the instructor to find a place to live. Help given with red tape. Requirements vary among cities but always include Bachelor's degree or higher, 2 years post-university working experience. Approximate processing time is 1–2 months.

RECRUITMENT: Internal company postings, employee referrals, job fairs, as well as some international, national and local websites. Skype interviews.

CONTACT: Angelica Arango, Country Manager of Instruction.

BOND LANGUAGE INSTITUTE
2nd Floor, Bai Hui Zhong Xin, Lang Qing Xuan, Bo Ai 5th Road, Zhongshan, Guangdong 528400
+86 760 8887 6667
bond_ Institute@hotmail.com
www.tefl-bond.com

NUMBER OF TEACHERS: 100+ including fee-paying interns.

PREFERENCE OF NATIONALITY: All major English-speaking countries.

QUALIFICATIONS: Preferably those with TEFL/TESOL certificates and college diploma and above. Ages 21–55.

CONDITIONS OF EMPLOYMENT: Usually a 6-month or 1-year contract. The maximum weekly workload is about 20 hours.

SALARY: Interns receive RMB2,900 (£300) a month; recruited teachers will be paid RMB6,200 or more.

FACILITIES/SUPPORT: Free accommodation; furnished apartment units equipped with major domestic and electric appliances. School is nationally accredited and authorised to employ western teachers and process work permits.

RECRUITMENT: By word of mouth and through partners throughout the world, e.g. the Teach and Travel China programme administered by ImmerQi in Beijing (www.immerqi.com). Interviews are essential and are often carried out in the UK and in North America.

BUCKLAND INTERNATIONAL EDUCATION GROUP
#78 Lane 1, Longyue Road, Yangshuo, Guilin 541900
+86 773 882 7555
bucklandping@gmail.com
www.bucklandgroup.org

Cultural Exchange Teaching Program in 65 franchised schools throughout China.

NUMBER OF TEACHERS: 120 teachers per year in 8 provinces.
PREFERENCE OF NATIONALITY: Native English speakers: British, American, Canadian, Australian, Irish or New Zealander.
QUALIFICATIONS: Bachelor's degree or TESOL certificate preferable.
CONDITIONS OF EMPLOYMENT: 5- or 10-month renewable contracts available, starting in August. 15 teaching hours per week from Monday to Friday.
SALARY: RMB4,000–RMB5,500 after tax per month. Taxes paid by the school. Bonus of RMB2,200 paid on completion of 1-year contract.
FACILITIES/SUPPORT: Free housing provided: furnished, private apartments with utilities (phone, TV, air-conditioning, western toilet, internet, etc.). Up to RMB200 per month utilities allowance. Paid public holidays and up to 15 consecutive days of paid sick leave. Free visa service: work visa invitation letters, work permit and resident permit sponsorship and visa updates. Airfare reimbursement and assistance. Teacher training, cultural orientation and post-training teacher assistance. Mandarin lessons provided.
RECRUITMENT: Usually via the internet, e.g. www.tefljobs.net. No application fee. The first step is to submit a résumé in Word, recent full body photo and application form. Interviews not essential.
CONTACT: Ping Wang (bucklandping@gmail.com); Owen Buckland (owenbuckland@gmail.com).

CLICK CHINA CULTURAL EXCHANGE CO LTD

Room 2308, Building#13 Wanda Plaza, Jiyuqiao, Wuchang District, Wuhan, Hubei Province
+86 27 8275 1218
emilyclickcn@qq.com; clickchina@qq.com
www.clickchn.com

NUMBER OF TEACHERS: Job agency that hires about 100 teachers for schools in Mainland China.
PREFERENCE OF NATIONALITY: North America, Oceania and European countries. Also jobs available for non-native speakers.
QUALIFICATIONS: Bachelor's degree essential, with TEFL/TESOL/CELTA or teaching experience from English-speaking countries preferred.
CONDITIONS OF EMPLOYMENT: 10-month contracts in public schools, with Monday-Friday hours 8am–12pm and 2pm–5pm. Language training institute contracts are for 12 months with most teaching taking place Wednesday to Sunday during the day and evening classes.
SALARY: In primary/middle schools: RMB6,000–RMB13,000 (subject teaching positions up to RMB16,000); universities: RMB4,500–RMB8,000; and language schools: RMB7,500–RMB15,000.
FACILITIES/SUPPORT: Local teachers from schools help with finding housing. Agency sends teachers a detailed list of documents required by China Foreign Experts Affairs Bureau for work permits application. When documents are ready, schools apply for work permits and invitation letters from the Bureau, which normally takes 3–7 weeks, and then post them to the teachers who can then apply for a Z-visa at their nearest Chinese embassy.
RECRUITMENT: Email applications with resumé, photo, passport page and copy of degree and certificate. Interviews can normally be arranged within 2 working days.
CONTACT: Emily Liu, Senior Account Manager.
EMAIL: emilyclickcn@qq.com

COLORADO CHINA COUNCIL

4556 Apple Way, Boulder, CO 80301, USA
+1 303 443 1108
alice@asiacouncil.org
www.asiacouncil.org

NUMBER OF PARTICIPANTS: 15–20 per year in the year-long programme. Participants are placed at universities throughout China.
PREFERENCE OF NATIONALITY: North American with no discernible regional accent.
QUALIFICATIONS: Minimum bachelor's or higher degree (all majors and professional backgrounds considered, though English, TEFL, linguistics, business, accounting, economics and engineering especially welcome). Universities prefer that applicants have some teaching/public speaking/tutoring/seminar presentation background. People with a master's degree or PhD are strongly encouraged to apply, as are couples. Must be 60 or under at time of application and in excellent mental and physical health.
CONDITIONS OF EMPLOYMENT: Full academic year programme runs from September to June/July. 16–20 hours per week; 2-week intensive TESL and Mandarin Training Institute in Sichuan in August.
SALARY: Monthly stipend of RMB5,000–RMB10,000 depending on university and academic or professional background. Free housing in FTs' complex, medical benefits, most or all of round-trip transportation costs reimbursed and 5–8 week paid vacation over Chinese New Year.
FACILITIES/SUPPORT: CCC provides full support if any problems or issues arise at any point. Most universities invite CCC's teachers to teach for a second year. Housing is adequate to excellent depending on city and university. CCC is the oldest non-religious China teaching, training and placement organisation in the USA which accepts people from all over the country. CCC has published *Yin Yang: American Perspectives on Living in China* (Rowman and Littlefield, 2012), which takes prospective applicants through the entire process of teaching in China, from attending the Summer Institute, through the joys and frustrations of the classroom, travel, making

friends and how families cope with this challenging transition.

RECRUITMENT: Initial application fee of $150. Rolling admissions with fees between $800 and $1,200. Details on website.

CONTACT: Alice Renouf, Director.

CUBEL CULTURE & EDUCATION LIAISON UK LTD

15th Floor, Brunel House, 2 Fitzalan Road, Cardiff CF24 0EB

+44 292 032 9143

j.song@cubel.co.uk; info@cubel.co.uk

www.cubel.co.uk

CUBEL works as a direct contractor for JESIE (Jiangsu Educational Services for International Exchanges) of the Department of Education for Jiangsu Province.

NUMBER OF TEACHERS: 2-6 appointments every year and about 10 short summer placements. Also recruit football coaches.

PREFERENCE OF NATIONALITY: Native speakers of English to teach CUBEL's partners and clients in Jiangsu, Beijing and Henan. Britons preferred for ease of interview and training.

QUALIFICATIONS: Anyone with a bachelor's degree from a British or North American university can be considered. TEFL or teaching qualification preferred.

CONDITIONS OF EMPLOYMENT: Short contracts of 2–5 weeks at summer camps across China and longer contracts 6–12+ months available in Jiangsu, Beijing and Henan. Average 20 hours per week. Summer teachers get one day off per week.

SALARY: For summer positions, the cost of visa, plane tickets, accommodation and meals is provided by CUBEL. Teachers are not paid for delivering lessons but will be given a £250 allowance for each week spent on the camp. For contracts of 6 months and longer: RMB8,000–RMB10,000 per month (£920–£1,150), depending on the status of the schools/organisations.

FACILITIES/SUPPORT: Accommodation provided.

RECRUITMENT: As soon as vacancies are notified by partners in China, they are advertised on website, TEFL forums, Gumtree, etc. Interviews are essential; for summer positions these take place before 1 May. Skype interviews are possible.

CONTACT: Jane Song, Head Liaison Officer (j.song@cubel.co.uk).

EF ENGLISH FIRST

Teacher Recruitment Office, 1F Jiu An Plaza, 258 Tongren Road, Shanghai 200040

+86 21 6039 5868; +86 21 6133 6422

efrecruitment@ef.com

www.englishfirst.com/esl-jobs

Many franchise schools recruit directly (for example, see the next entry and adverts on www.tefl.com).

NUMBER OF TEACHERS: 2,400 for more than 200 EFL schools in Beijing, Shanghai, Shenzhen, Guangzhou and 60 cities across China.

PREFERENCE OF NATIONALITY: Native English speakers.

QUALIFICATIONS: University degree, internationally recognised TEFL certification and teaching experience.

CONDITIONS OF EMPLOYMENT: 12-month contracts. Teaching 21 (real) hours between 9am and 9pm, 5 days a week.

SALARY: RMB12,500–RMB13,750 per month basic salary.

FACILITIES/SUPPORT: Shanghai, Beijing, Guangzhou and Shenzhen schools provide comprehensive benefits package including relocation assistance, flight allowance, health insurance, paid vacation, official working visa, Mandarin lessons and ongoing training and professional development.

RECRUITMENT: Via EF's Online Recruitment Centre at www.englishfirst.com/esl-jobs or send résumé and qualification details to efrecruitment@ef.com. Recruiters can put applicants in touch with current teachers.

EF ENGLISH FIRST CHANGCHUN

EF ChangChun Mega Center, Education First C30, Tiandi Shierfang, Linhe Street (130011) Changchun, Jilin Province 130000

+86 431 8468 0999

hotjobs.ef@gmail.com

www.efchangchun.com/job

EF Changchun has four branches in the city.

NUMBER OF TEACHERS: 50.

PREFERENCE OF NATIONALITY: USA, UK, South Africa, Canada, New Zealand and Australia.

QUALIFICATIONS: Bachelor's degree needed; TEFL or CELTA and 1 year of teaching experience are both desirable. Age 20–50.

CONDITIONS OF EMPLOYMENT: 12 or 18 months. Evenings Monday–Friday (3pm–7pm) and all day Saturday–Sunday (9am–6pm). 2 consecutive days off during the week.

SALARY: RMB6,5000–RMB7,500 (net) per month plus free accommodation, insurance, flight allowance (up to RMB10,000) and final bonus (up to $4,500).

FACILITIES/SUPPORT: Teachers are provided with their own furnished apartment (not shared) near the school. Hired teachers are sent the necessary paperwork to apply for a visa via courier. School then deals with all the necessary paperwork such as obtaining a foreign expert certificate, residency permit and so on. Costs are reimbursed after arrival. ERIKA insurance is provided by school, including medical and accident insurance, baggage and property insurance and liability insurance.

RECRUITMENT: Advertising on TEFL recruitment websites such as www.tefl.com and Dave's ESL Cafe, recruitment agencies and some local agents in different countries. Interviews by Skype.

CONTACT: Lynn, HR Specialist or Chris Marshall, Director of Studies.

ENGLON GLOBAL TEFL RESOURCING LTD

24 Hampshire Terrace, Portsmouth, Hampshire PO1 2QF, UK

+44 23 9229 7144

info@TEFL-in-China.com

www.TEFL-in-China.com

Affiliated with Helen Group Corporation in China (www.helengroup.com) with 5,000 client schools.

NUMBER OF TEACHERS: 50 for Shenzhen City in Guangdong Province, Hangzhou City, Zhejiang Province and Jiangsu Province.

PREFERENCE OF NATIONALITY: British, American, Canadian, New Zealander and Australian.

QUALIFICATIONS: Bachelor's or master's degree, TEFL certificate preferred. Internships available for those without degrees. Without TEFL qualification or experience, new arrivals will have to do a SAFEA-approved TEFL training course; the cost of RMB3,000 will be advanced and paid back out of your salary over 5 months.

CONDITIONS OF EMPLOYMENT: One academic year (10 months) from September or February in Chinese kindergartens, primary schools, secondary schools and colleges. Up to 22 contact hours a week.

SALARY: RMB5,000–RMB8,000. The first RMB4,800 are tax-free.

FACILITIES/SUPPORT: Free accommodation provided. Return air ticket reimbursed at end of contract up to RMB5,000.

RECRUITMENT: Via www.tefl.com, etc. Interviews held in the UK.

CONTACT: Polly Whitworth, Consultant; Ms Weidan Liu, Director (liuweidan@hotmail.com).

FIND WORK ABROAD

Office 1412, 6–8 Zhong Shan DaDao,Tian He, Guangzhou 510000

+86 20 3730 3381 (China); +1 312 273 1868 (USA)

apply@findworkabroad.com

www.china.findworkabroad.com

NUMBER OF TEACHERS: Recruitment agency deals with 1,000 applicants a year.

PREFERENCE OF NATIONALITY: UK, USA, Canada, NZ, Australia and South Africa.

QUALIFICATIONS: BA degree or higher. No experience is needed for most positions.

CONDITIONS OF EMPLOYMENT: 12-month contract. 20 hours per week Monday to Friday.

SALARY: RMB7,000–15,000 per month. Deductions of RMB300–600 unless school pays contributions.

FACILITIES/SUPPORT: Accommodation is usually offered, or a housing allowance given. Schools assist with work permits: after signing a contract, completing the medical exam and supplying copies of résumé, BA and certificates, the school will issue authorisation to get the working visa at the Chinese embassy.

RECRUITMENT: Adverts on ESL job websites. Interviews online if applicant is abroad, or in person.

CONTACT: Amy Wen, Office Manager (amywen@findworkabroad.com).

GOLDEN APPLE CHILD EDUCATION (GROUP)

Floor 4, Bldg 6, Tianfu Xingu, 399 Fucheng Avenue, Gaoxin District, Chengdu, Sichuan 610041

+86 28 8597 6013

eslapplication@163.com

NUMBER OF TEACHERS: 50+ for 33 kindergartens in Chengdu.

PREFERENCE OF NATIONALITY: American, British, Canadian, Australian, New Zealander, Irish and South African.

QUALIFICATIONS: Minimum bachelor's degree in any subject and 2 years' post-graduation work experience in any field, preferably teaching. Qualified teachers with PYP (Primary Years Program) experience needed for positions in two IB-accredited kindergartens.

CONDITIONS OF EMPLOYMENT: Standard 1-year contract. 20 teaching hours per week (ESL); 28 (PYP).

SALARY: RMB10,000–12,000 per month depending on experience.

FACILITIES/SUPPORT: School provides furnished accommodation or a stipend towards housing, and a FE's licence and working 'Z' visa. 7–8 weeks of paid holiday, one month's salary as contract completion bonus, RMB3,000 arrival bonus and a 'cultural helper'. The procedure requires teachers to sign a contract with the school, and get a medical in their own country on the official Chinese embassy paperwork. The school then applies for a government invitation letter using the paperwork, which takes about a month or so to receive. An invitation letter to the teacher is then posted and teachers apply for a Z visa from the Chinese embassy.

RECRUITMENT: Through internet adverts e.g. on gochengdoo.com, forums, ESL recruitment agencies and word of mouth.

CONTACT: Nigel Jones, Director of English Education.

GOLD STAR TEFL RECRUITMENT

12/F, 221, Zhong Xiao East Road, Da An District 106, Taipei City, Taiwan 106

www.GoldStarTeachers.com

English-owned and managed, independent TEFL recruitment agency filling vacancies for a variety of kindergartens, primary, middle and high schools plus universities across China including Inner Mongolia. Also recruit for private institutes including Wall Street English and Disney English.

NUMBER OF TEACHERS: 40 a month.

PREFERENCE OF NATIONALITY: Native English speaker from UK, USA, Canada, Australia, New Zealand or South Africa.

QUALIFICATIONS: Bachelor's degree, TEFL certificate preferred, teaching experience preferred, plenty of passion and energy.

CONDITIONS OF EMPLOYMENT: 1 year. 20 hours per week (maximum 40). Choice of age from Kindergarten to adult.

SALARY: RMB9,000–RMB17,000.

FACILITIES/SUPPORT: Schools provide accommodation, flight, allowance, health insurance and Z-visa.

CONTACT: Jessica, Recruitment Consultant.

GOOD TEACHERS UNION

Beijing Inn, Group 4 Unit C, Building 11 Room 301, DongShuiJing HuTong, 100011 Dongcheng, Beijing

+86 185 0006 5857; +86 138 3635 8190

goodteachersunion@gmail.com; esljobsinchina@outlook.com

www.goodteachersunion.org

NUMBER OF TEACHERS: 300–400 yearly in various locations around mainland China.

PREFERENCE OF NATIONALITY: Most partner schools prefer teachers from native English speaking countries such as the USA, Canada, Australia and the UK, though some positions are open to non-native speakers who have studied and graduated in one of these countries or have impeccable English language skills.

QUALIFICATIONS: Vary with position and school location. Bachelor's degree (or higher) needed for jobs apart from internship positions, available for candidates on a gap year from university, Associate degree holders or others. TEFL/TESOL/CELTA certificate (minimum 12 hours) is a plus; most schools strongly prefer evidence of TEFL training and some will be willing to reimburse candidates who study for one.

CONDITIONS OF EMPLOYMENT: 1-year contracts are standard, though internship options allow shorter contracts. 32–40 working hours per week, including office hours for lesson preparation. Public schools and kindergartens operate Monday-Friday, while most language centres operate Wednesday to Sunday. 2 days off per week.

SALARY: Salary dependent on educational background, experience and interview performance. Starting at RMB8,000 ($1,200) a month and going up to RMB25,000 ($3,750). Deductions are calculated according to the Chinese progressive taxation system. Some schools quote salaries net, so the situation should be clarified in advance.

FACILITIES/SUPPORT: GT Union covers cost of hotel during the first 2 weeks (1 week initial training and 1 week to look for an apartment). Housing allowance or free apartment. Advice given on finding accommodation in the desired district, and help with negotiations, signing the contract and any other issues that arise. Full assistance with work permits, available to teachers aged 24–60. Partner schools are obliged to provide Junior Employee training on the curriculum to all new arrivals, whether or not they are experienced. Training lasts 1–3 weeks and is paid. Possible benefits provided by schools include free flight to China (flight reimbursement upon completing the contract), relocation bonus of RMB8,000–RMB10,000, paid sick leave/personal leave; free Chinese classes, and medical and/or accident insurance.

RECRUITMENT: Via high profile recruiting websites, job fairs and events organised in China. New positions posted on social networks. At least one interview with HR required.

CONTACT: Daisy Mitova, Recruiter; Tine Zhao, Recruiter.

INTERLINGUA SCHOOL

Guiyang: 60 Jincang Road, Guiyang, Guizhou 550001

+86 85 1867 69226

jobs@interlinguaschool.com

www.interlinguaschool.com/eng

NUMBER OF TEACHERS: 20 for four branches in Guiyang and Zunyi.

PREFERENCE OF NATIONALITY: British, American, Canadian, Australian and New Zealander.

QUALIFICATIONS: Minimum bachelor's degree. ESL/EFL qualification or 1 year's teaching experience essential. Experience of working with young children would be useful.

CONDITIONS OF EMPLOYMENT: 1 year or longer. 30–36 hours per week.

SALARY: RMB11,000–RMB13,600, depending on qualifications and length of contract. International flight allowance up to $1,000, end-of-contract bonus up to $2,000, and other perks.

FACILITIES/SUPPORT: Accommodation offered free of charge or accommodation allowance of RMB2,200. Free Mandarin lessons.

CONTACT: Pamela Zhang, HR Officer; Maosi Yan, Programme Director; Manuel Gomez, Co-ordinator.

IST PLUS – TEACH IN CHINA PROGRAMME
Crest House, 102-104 Church Road, Teddington, Middlesex TW11 8PY, UK
+44 20 7788 7877
info@istplus.com
www.istplus.com/teachinchina

NUMBER OF TEACHERS: 10–15 each year.
PREFERENCE OF NATIONALITY: Native English speakers; non-native speakers must have near-native proficiency in English.
QUALIFICATIONS: University degree in any field essential. TEFL training or experience is not essential but preferred. Maximum age 65.
CONDITIONS OF EMPLOYMENT: 5- or 10-month renewable contracts starting in August or February, teaching 16–18 classes a week, which works out at a working week of 30–35 hours.
SALARY: RMB4,000–RMB10,000 net per month.
FACILITIES/SUPPORT: Free accommodation (usually on campus), all-inclusive 7-day orientation in Shanghai on arrival including basic TEFL training, accommodation, sight-seeing and airport transfer. IST Plus arranges school/college placement, visa and work permit, insurance and 24-hour emergency hotline.
RECRUITMENT: Deadlines are mid-December for February departure and mid-June for August departure. Teach in China fees are £1,100 for 5 months, £1,295 for 10 months. All teachers who complete their contracts will receive a TEFL certificate.
CONTACT: Ralph Allemano, Director (rallemano@istplus.com).

LANGUAGE LINK
InterChina Building, Room 708–722, 33 Denshikou Da Jie, Dong Cheng District, Beijing 100006
+86 10-5169 5591/92/93
darrenyihai@languagelink.com.cn

NUMBER OF TEACHERS: 12.
PREFERENCE OF NATIONALITY: Native speakers only due to visa restrictions (UK, USA, Ireland, Canada, Australia, New Zealand).
QUALIFICATIONS: TESL Certificate, BA/BS degree, experience preferred but not essential.
CONDITIONS OF EMPLOYMENT: 12-month contracts. 20 teaching hours per week maximum.
SALARY: Beijing: RMB16,000 (gross) + $1,000 contract completion bonus. Smaller cities: RMB12,000 (gross) + free apartment + $1,000 contract completion bonus. Tax deductions around RMB2,000
FACILITIES/SUPPORT: In Beijing company pays accommodation fees, deposit, upfront rent, and then teacher is responsible for monthly rent. In smaller cities accommodation is provided free. Full assistance with obtaining a Z-visa. Free ongoing training during employment; 30% discount offered on CELTA for teachers. Free Chinese classes.
RECRUITMENT: Online adverts on www.eslcafe.com, etc.
CONTACT: Darren Fox, Academic Coordinator.

LONGMAN SCHOOLS SHANGHAI
Rm 1901, Tower A, 388 West Jiangwan Rd, Hongkou Plaza, Shanghai 200083
+86 21 6031 7131
recruit@longmanschools.com.cn
www.longmancareers.com

15 campuses throughout Shanghai catering to young learners aged 3–12.
NUMBER OF TEACHERS: 80+.
PREFERENCE OF NATIONALITY: Native English speakers.
QUALIFICATIONS: Minimum bachelor's degree, TEFL and 2 years' teaching experience.
CONDITIONS OF EMPLOYMENT: 1-year contract. Standard contract is for 16 hours a week but usually lots of overtime. Most classes take place at weekends and evenings. 2 days off per week.
SALARY: RMB12,000–RMB15,000 base plus paid overtime and year-end bonus.
FACILITIES/SUPPORT: Assistance provided with finding accommodation and applying for work permit. All teachers are enrolled in New Teacher Training programme to become acquainted with structured curriculum.
RECRUITMENT: Usually via the internet and recruitment agencies. Candidates are asked to write a lesson plan prior to interview (carried out by phone if the candidate is not local) and submit a 3–5 minute video.

MIDDLE KINGDOM GROUP
Office in Xiamen, Fujian Province
apply@middlekingdomteachers.com
www.middlekingdomgroup.net

NUMBER OF TEACHERS: 50 each September.
PREFERENCE OF NATIONALITY: Native-speaking teachers of any origin.
QUALIFICATIONS: Bachelor's degree and good transferable skills.

CONDITIONS OF EMPLOYMENT: 10-month contracts. 12–20 teaching hours per week.

SALARY: RMB5,000–9,000 per month (depending on location and qualifications).

FACILITIES/SUPPORT: Each partner school provides a private apartment, a 1-year working visa and reimbursement of airfare. 7-day orientation offered in August in China which leads to TEFL certificate and meeting up with other teachers in the new intake; inclusive cost of orientation is RMB2,500.

RECRUITMENT: University presentations, word of mouth, advertising. Skype interviews and often an interview with a partner school.

CONTACT: Chris Thomas, Director (chris@middlekingdomteachers.com).

RAY ENGLISH TEFL RECRUITMENT

K.I. Business Building, North Street, Xi'an, Shaanxi Province 710075

+86 29 8931 2020

teachers@rayenglish.com

www.rayenglish.com

NUMBER OF TEACHERS: Agency that recruits more than 1,000 English teachers per year for jobs all over China including Mongolia.

PREFERENCE OF NATIONALITY: Native speakers of English from UK, Ireland, US, New Zealand, Australia, Canada and South Africa. Non-native speakers with exceptional English skills may also apply.

QUALIFICATIONS: University degree + TEFL certification. No experience needed. Applications from non-TEFL holders may be considered.

CONDITIONS OF EMPLOYMENT: 12-month contracts. Hours in the public system (middle schools, high schools, university) are Monday–Friday 8am–5pm, around 16–20 teaching hours per week. Hours are longer in private language centres (20–25 hours) and include weekends/evenings. 2 days off during the week.

SALARY: Depending on city and local living costs: RMB7,000–8,000 in smaller cities; RMB9,000–10,000 in larger cities; RMB13,000–16,000 for Beijing/Shanghai (since cost of living in those cities is wildly expensive). School deducts income tax of around 10%.

FACILITIES/SUPPORT: All public jobs and private language centres for younger learners come with free housing for teachers. Adult language centres in China give a housing allowance towards rent. Full support is given to find teachers modern places. School complies with Chinese law by sponsoring the work visas for teachers. Each school has a dedicated staff member whose assistance is free of charge.

RECRUITMENT: Skype interviews set up between teachers and schools.

CONTACT: Stuart Allen, Operations Director.

REACH TO TEACH

1606 80th Avenue, Algona, IA 50511, USA

+1 20 1467 4612

info@reachtoteachrecruiting.com

www.ReachToTeachRecruiting.com/teach-english-in-china.html

For contacts in other countries, see entry at beginning of Asia chapter.

NUMBER OF TEACHERS: 200+.

PREFERENCE OF NATIONALITY: British, American, Canadian, Australian and New Zealander, Irish and South African.

QUALIFICATIONS: A full university degree (any discipline) is enough for most schools in the smaller cities or towns. Teachers in the bigger cities face tougher requirements as the government will only issue work papers to those that have a TEFL qualification plus preferably 2 years' work experience after leaving university (with one of those years being in a teaching or training-related field). Through a partnership with a TEFL course provider, Reach To Teach can assist teachers in getting course discounts.

CONDITIONS OF EMPLOYMENT: All job placements are full-time positions and for 1 year (and usually extendable). Teaching schedules vary but are generally either daytime, or afternoons and evenings.

SALARY: Depends on school, but commonly: reimbursed flights to and from China, free furnished apartment, salaries from RMB8,000–RMB22,000 per month depending on qualifications and location.

FACILITIES/SUPPORT: China visa guidance, airport collection, teacher orientation, etc. are provided. Teachers have the option of continued support and contact with Reach To Teach throughout their year-long placement.

RECRUITMENT: Applications submitted via website. Interviews conducted over Skype, by phone and occasionally in person.

CONTACT: Dean Barnes, Director of Recruiting – China & Vietnam (Dean@ReachToTeachRecruiting.com).

ROCKIES ENGLISH EDUCATION

No 7 Bandaotingtao, 461Zhongshan Road, Shahekou District, Dalian City, Liaoning Province

+86 137 9515 3990

hr@rockiesenglish.com; rockiescc@163.com

www.rockiesenglish.com

Rockies English Education recruit outgoing and qualified ESL teachers to teach in kindergartens, public primary schools and language training schools in cities throughout China.

NUMBER OF TEACHERS: 30.

PREFERENCE OF NATIONALITY: Native English speakers from USA, UK, Canada, Australia, New Zealand, Ireland and South Africa.

QUALIFICATIONS: Minimum age 24. Bachelor's degree (or diploma/certificate), TESL/TESOL/TEFL/CELTA, criminal records check and in good health. Candidates should be responsible, motivated and have a positive attitude.

CONDITIONS OF EMPLOYMENT: Contracts are for 1 year. 25 hours per week.

SALARY: RMB10,000–RMB15,000 per month, less deductions of about RMB500.

FACILITIES/SUPPORT: Free single furnished non-shared apartment provided, or an allowance to rent an apartment independently. Work visa provided for all foreign teachers. Orientation training in Rockies' own teaching and materials development systems. Ongoing training given. Free Chinese language lessons. Medical and accident insurance provided. Airport pick-up on arrival.

RECRUITMENT: Interview, contract signing, collection of documents for work visa including medical examination, application by employer for work permit, invitation letter couriered to teacher, application for Z visa in teacher's home country or Hong Kong. Travel can be booked when work visa is issued.

CONTACT: Kevin Zhang, HR Manager.

SPEAKEASY
12 LingShiGuan Road, Wuhou District, Chengdu
+86 187 8029 8993; +86 186 2829 1690
jb.englishtutor@gmail.com

NUMBER OF TEACHERS: 8.

PREFERENCE OF NATIONALITY: USA, UK, Canada, New Zealand, Australia. Others can be considered provided candidates have native pronunciation and fluency.

QUALIFICATIONS: TEFL qualified (CELTA, TESOL, etc.). Minimum 2 years' relevant teaching experience (preferably both adults and children).

CONDITIONS OF EMPLOYMENT: One year contracts. Flexible hours, with teachers working on an hourly basis, as much or as little as they want. Teachers must provide a free demo class for prospective students, but no extra office hours are required.

SALARY: RMB160–RMB200 per class hour plus signing/ re-signing bonuses.

FACILITIES/SUPPORT: Teachers find their own accommodation. No help given with work permits.

RECRUITMENT: Word of mouth, online advertisements (e.g. on www.gochengdoo.com) and recruitment services. Interviews are essential, sometimes by Skype.

CONTACT: James Baxter, Headmaster.

TEACHING EXPERIENCE
Travel Agent G-L-E UG, Baumeisterstrasse 2, 20099 Hamburg
+49 393 1318 2487
apply@teaching-experience.com
www.teaching-experience.com

NUMBER OF TEACHERS: As many as possible.

PREFERENCE OF NATIONALITY: UK, USA, Canada, Australia and New Zealand.

QUALIFICATIONS: BA degree, TEFL/TESOL certificate is preferred.

CONDITIONS OF EMPLOYMENT: 1-year contract. 60–90 hours per month.

SALARY: RMB10,000–RMB20,000 net.

FACILITIES/SUPPORT: Private language schools, public schools, colleges and international schools will offer accommodation or help in finding it. Assistance given with work permits.

RECRUITMENT: Online marketing.

CONTACT: Melvin Hastedt, CEO.

TEACHING NOMAD
Kangding Rd No 1018, Yi Ge Bldg, 3rd Fl, Suite 306, Shanghai
+86 21 3319 9715
info@teachingnomad.com
www.teachingnomad.com

NUMBER OF TEACHERS: 20–25 per month.

PREFERENCE OF NATIONALITY: Americans and Britons preferred but applications from other 5 native-speaking countries also considered.

QUALIFICATIONS: ESL teachers must have BA, 120-hour TEFL qualification and 2 years' teaching experience. Teachers at International Schools need BA/MA, state teaching licence or QTS, plus 2+ years of relevant teaching experience.

CONDITIONS OF EMPLOYMENT: 15–25 teaching hours spread over the week including evenings, and weekends.

SALARY: RMB8,000–20,000 per month, plus benefits.

FACILITIES/SUPPORT: Some client schools offer housing, others assist in finding an apartment.

RECRUITMENT: Online marketing, direct marketing, word of mouth, hosting events, conventions, etc. All candidates are screened and interviewed over Skype or in person.

CONTACT: Ila Afshar, Personal Placement Consultant team.

TEIC (TEACH ENGLISH IN CHINA)

37 Haversham Close, Newcastle, NE7 7LR, UK

+44 753 178 9984

phil@teic.co.uk

www.teic.co.uk

PREFERENCE OF NATIONALITY: UK, US, EU.

QUALIFICATIONS: All applicants must be graduates prior to departure for China.

CONDITIONS OF EMPLOYMENT: 1 academic year. 18 contact hours a week.

SALARY: RMB5,000–RMB8,000 a month.

FACILITIES/SUPPORT: Self-contained furnished apartments are provided free. Full visa support given.

RECRUITMENT: Website, recommendations, presentations, Facebook. Interviews not essential but preferred, can be done by Skype or phone. Programme placement fee of £190.

CONTACT: Professor Phillip Thomas, Director.

TOPVIEW INTERNATIONAL EDUCATION GROUP LTD (TOPEDU)

509-510, Timeson Tower, B 12, Chaoyangmen North Ave., Chaoyang, Beijing 100020

+86 10 6551 9637

bd@top-intern.com

www.top-intern.com

NUMBER OF TEACHERS: Many for hundreds of partner schools throughout China.

PREFERENCE OF NATIONALITY: Native English speakers from US, UK, Canada, Ireland, Australia, New Zealand and South Africa (due to Chinese visa restrictions).

QUALIFICATIONS: Bachelor's degree or higher. Teaching experience or teaching certificates are not mandatory but highly preferred.

CONDITIONS OF EMPLOYMENT: Vacancies throughout the year. Contracts are for 12 or 24 months. Hours are 25–40 hours per week depending on position.

SALARY: US$1,200–$2,400 per month, depending on school location and teacher qualifications.

FACILITIES/SUPPORT: Schools provide all the teachers with free shared or private accommodation. Medical insurance and fees for Z visa are paid; airfare reimbursement given.

RECRUITMENT: Online paid advertisement channels.

CONTACT: Laura Rampazzo, Business Development Director.

US-CHINA EDUCATIONAL EXCHANGE

15 Locust St, Jersey City, New Jersey 07305, USA

+1 201 432 6861

edexchange@gmail.com

www.US-ChinaEdExchange.org

NUMBER OF TEACHERS: 200–300.

PREFERENCE OF NATIONALITY: Native English speakers: British, American, Canadian, Australian and New Zealander.

QUALIFICATIONS: Minimum bachelor's degree and commitment to teaching.

CONDITIONS OF EMPLOYMENT: 6 months or 1 year. 15 hours per week.

SALARY: Varies.

FACILITIES/SUPPORT: Schools provide free housing and send candidates visa approval documents. 7-day TEFL training course in Beijing or Shanghai in August or February.

RECRUITMENT: Internet and newspaper ads. Interviews always conducted by phone.

CONTACT: Dr Yong Ho.

VERBAL EDUCATION CHINA

Room 728, Tongyuan Plaza, Qinghe Third Street, Haidian District, Beijing

+86 10 6284 2160

verbaledu@outlook.com; verbaledu@126.com

www.sinoteacher.com

NUMBER OF TEACHERS: Recruitment agency for many candidates, to teach oral English mainly to middle school students throughout China and Mongolia, from remote villages to large urban centres.

PREFERENCE OF NATIONALITY: English-speaking countries only.

QUALIFICATIONS: Bachelor's degree and teaching experience are required. TEFL/TESL/TESOL preferred.

CONDITIONS OF EMPLOYMENT: Minimum 3 months (September–December or March–June) but 1 year preferred. 18 teaching hours per week Monday to Friday.

SALARY: RMB5,000–RMB8,000 depending on qualifications and experience.

FACILITIES/SUPPORT: Private accommodation provided and all meals at the school. Orientation given on arrival. Visa sponsorship and medical insurance provided.

RECRUITMENT: Via recruitment websites, e.g. www.cathayteacher.com. Interview required. Video of yourself needed.

XI'AN JIAOTONG-LIVERPOOL UNIVERSITY ENGLISH LANGUAGE CENTRE

No.111 Ren'ai Road, Suzhou Dushu Lake Higher Education Town, Suzhou Industrial Park, Suzhou, Jiangsu 215123

+86 512 8816 1300/1345

recruitment.hr@xjtlu.edu.cn; expats.hr@xjtlu.edu.cn

wwww.xjtlu.edu.cn/departments/centres/language-centre; http://job.xjtlu.edu.cn

NUMBER OF TEACHERS: Approx 135 for fast-growing university. EAP. Specialists needed.

PREFERENCE OF NATIONALITY: Local visa rules restrict employment to the following nationals: UK, Ireland, Australia, New Zealand, Canada and the US.

QUALIFICATIONS: Tutors need an MA in TESOL/Applied Linguistics or equivalent, plus a teaching qualification (e.g. CELTA/DELTA or BEd) and at least 2 years' experience.

CONDITIONS OF EMPLOYMENT: Renewable contracts for 1–3 years from August. Office hours are between 9am and 5pm with 20 hours of teaching per week (Monday–Friday only). Currently around 47 days of paid holiday per year.

SALARY: RMB14,898–RMB30,099 per month for a qualified and experienced tutor. Some lower-level tutor positions are available occasionally.

FACILITIES/SUPPORT: Housing allowance of up to RMB3,000 per month and HR will assist with finding local accommodation and applying for work permits. Travel allowance of up to RMB15,000 per year. BUPA health insurance (basic) paid.

RECRUITMENT: Usually via adverts on www.jobs.ac.uk and other websites. Applications are welcome all year round but main recruitment drives are in March and May each year. Interviews and some pre-interview tasks are essential and can be carried out over the phone or internet.

CONTACT: Dr Stuart Perrin, Director of Centre (stuart.perrin@xjtlu.edu.cn); Carly Ridyard, Deputy Director (carly.ridyard@xjtlu.edu.cn).

MONGOLIA

A romantic notion of nomadic horsemen living in yurts on the vast Mongolian steppes is seldom matched by the experience of expat teachers in the country. Most work in the far-from-beautiful capital city. Ulaanbaatar offers the same range of teaching possibilities as any major city, including private English language institutes (e.g. www.talktalkmongolia.com), business English academies (www.letumongolia.com), IELTS preparation for candidates who want to study at foreign universities (www.esp.mn), international schools (www.british-school.edu.mn) and voluntary organisations like the one in the entry below. A few other institutes seek native speaker teachers; for example try contacting englishworldmongolia@gmail.com.

LIST OF EMPLOYERS

NEW CHOICE MONGOLIAN VOLUNTEER ORGANIZATION
POB–159, Ulaanbaatar–210646 A
+976 9911 8767

info@volunteer.org.mn
www.volunteer.org.mn

NUMBER OF TEACHERS: 5 paying volunteers.

PREFERENCE OF NATIONALITY: Native speakers of English from UK, Ireland, USA or Australia.

QUALIFICATIONS: Minimum age 17. Should have teaching skills.

CONDITIONS OF EMPLOYMENT: 1–12 weeks. 5–6 hours per day, up to 30 hours per week, Monday to Friday.

SALARY: Volunteers pay a fee of $250 per week, $1,445 for 8 weeks. Volunteers must cover visa costs, airfares and insurance.

FACILITIES/SUPPORT: Accommodation and meals provided by host families.

CONTACT: Bayarjargal Damdindagva, Founder and Executive Director.

SANTIS EDUCATIONAL SERVICES
16 Student Street, 8th Khoroo, Sukhbaatar District, Ulaanbaatar
+976 1131 8319

marketing@santis.mn; santisbranch@santis.mn
www.Santis.mn; www.inlingua.mn

Joint US-Mongolia company and IELTS testing centre. Affiliated to inlingua.

NUMBER OF TEACHERS: 12–20.

PREFERENCE OF NATIONALITY: None.

QUALIFICATIONS: CELTA or equivalent as a minimum.

CONDITIONS OF EMPLOYMENT: Annual commitment, variable hours.

SALARY: To be discussed, paid net in US dollars.

FACILITIES/SUPPORT: Accommodation is provided. All aspects of work permits are dealt with before teacher's arrival.

RECRUITMENT: Web (e.g. www.gooverseas.com), agency, word of mouth and local. Skype interviews.

CONTACT: Andrew Orgill, Director of the International Office & President of inlingua Mongolia.

HONG KONG

Since the former British colony became the Hong Kong Special Administrative Region (HKSAR) of the People's Republic of China on 23 June 1997, '*everything has changed and nothing has changed*', or so the saying goes. Only international schools and specialist 'ESF' (English Schools Foundation) schools offer a curriculum using English as the medium of instruction (EMI) though other government schools have been given more freedom to choose to teach in English rather than (or alongside) Putonghua (simplified Mandarin Chinese). Many parents are willing to spend vast sums on extracurricular English courses for their children and there is a high demand for native English speakers willing to teach children from as young as six months. Many of these companies have proprietary learning systems and systematic phonics programmes. The lingering pro-British bias in some circles means that you still get language schools (English Focus is one example) boasting that all their teachers come from England and speak with clear British accents.

To meet the demand for English teaching, the Hong Kong government employs hundreds of English speakers to teach in the state education system and in non-government schools too as part of the NET (Native English Teacher) scheme described below.

It is illegal to enter Hong Kong as a tourist and take up work, so that those graduates who arrive on holiday and want to change their status are out of luck. However, it is possible to visit the city, find a teaching job and then apply for a work visa from a neighbouring country, which will take from six to eight weeks to process; Macao is the most convenient. The work visa is attached to the passport before entering Hong Kong. The authorities will expect to see a university degree, relevant work experience and/or a TEFL certificate and a corporate sponsor. Teachers who satisfy these requirements should have no difficulty obtaining a visa/entry permit.

FINDING A JOB

NET SCHEME

The NET scheme is administered by the Hong Kong Education Bureau (EDB) (NET Administration Team, Room 1110, 11th Floor Wu Chung House, 213 Queen's Road East, Wan Chai; ✆ +852 2892 6495; netrecruit@edb.gov.hk; www.edb.gov.hk (suffix '/pnet' for Primary and '/snet' for Secondary)).

The website carries full details of the scheme and an application form. Foreign Teachers, known as 'NETs', can interview for any school with a vacancy and have some control over where they're placed. The NET community maintains an online 'blacklist' of schools to avoid. The reason the scheme is so popular is that salaries and benefits are generous.

The competition has become much keener, partly because so many graduates and trainee teachers are looking for work outside their own countries. Acceptance is easier if you have a postgraduate diploma in education, though some categories of the programme are open to university graduates of language-related subjects with a TEFL certificate. The salary range for primary NETs is HK$26,700 (£2,775) to HK$54,230 (£5,650) per month and for secondary NETs even higher, HK$28,040 (£2,900) to HK$65,150 (£6,750). Superior qualifications are well rewarded in Hong Kong. Exact salaries are dependent on experience and qualifications. Every NET whose home is outside Hong Kong gets a monthly cash housing allowance of HK$20,989 (£2,175) which really bumps up the salary.

Also, there is a 15% gratuity on everything you earn, less contributions the employer has made into a pension fund, awarded at the end of the 24-month contract, provided your conduct and performance have met with approval. Flights, medical allowance and baggage allowance are all additional perks.

Applications are usually accepted until mid-February, and term begins in mid-August. It may be possible to be interviewed in London through a recruitment agency such as ESLstarter. After working in the private sector for the Chatteris Foundation (described below), **Tom Grundy** became a Netter and compares the two teaching schemes:

> ***The government NET programme is more highbrow and demanding but offers a better package and wage. However, you don't get the 'instant social circle' you would with an employer like Chatteris. NET is ideal should you decide to remain in HK and great if you already have a TEFL or PGCE qualification.***

He recommends the 'NET Teacher Survival Guide' at https://en.wikibooks.org/wiki/NET_Teacher_Survival_Guide to answer any questions about the programme.

OTHER EMPLOYERS

Almost any English institute you locate on the internet will have a Recruitment or Careers page. The British Council has a teaching operation which has an ongoing need for certificate-qualified teachers with at least two years' experience, preferably with children. Hiring takes place on a rolling basis; details are at https://jobs.britishcouncil.org or you can apply locally for hourly jobs (www.britishcouncil.hk). Those applying for part-time hourly work should already have a valid Hong Kong work visa. The wage goes up to HK$550 per contact hour for Certificate-holders and more for teachers with a DELTA or PGCE. In 2016, the UK-based teacher recruitment agency Prime Teachers (www.primeteachers.com) was looking to fill a number of EFL vacancies on behalf of a Hong Kong client running a large programme teaching children aged 2½ to 12. Applications were invited from Native English Speakers with a BA and a 100+ hour TEFL Certificate (online acceptable).

One of the largest employers is the Chatteris Educational Foundation (see entry), which offers recent university graduates from English-speaking countries the opportunity to teach in Hong Kong for one academic year. Like the government NET programme, this scheme has become more difficult to enter, although there are sometimes vacancies still being advertised in the summer for a mid-August start.

Tom Grundy completed the nine-month programme before he became a Netter:

> ***The wages were just enough to live on and save some for travel. I saved hard and was able to travel for three months around South-East Asia afterwards, and even afforded two laptops. Chatteris has its problems and its 'charitable' status is questionable, but they support and train you. You'll be placed with another British, Canadian or American in a primary or secondary school, there'll be several dozen others who you'll train with and so you'll immediately have a big social network. With Chatteris, your emphasis will be on oral English with a 'non-formal' approach, i.e. games, crafts and other 'fun' activities.***

The basic wage of HK$14,000 hasn't risen at all in the past few years and by about Christmas many CNETs (Chatteris Native-speaking English Tutors) conclude that their wages are exploitative. Furthermore you must pay a HK$2,000 deposit at the beginning against the completion of your contract, which will be returned to you at the end, minus bank charges. Participants often complain of an interfering management who require constant paperwork and attendance at workshops and meetings.

HK Education Provider Company Ltd (www.hkedu.com.hk) recruits ESL teachers from the seven English-speaking countries and places these university graduates in teaching positions in reputable public and private schools throughout Hong Kong. The agency provides training, shared accommodation with clubhouse facilities, teaching materials and online support. For a position as an Oral English Teacher, a Bachelor of Arts (BA) or Science (BS) degree is a prerequisite with a TEFL, TESOL or CELTA certificate. Further information is available from HKEDU (9A, Heng Shan Centre, 141–145 Queen's Road East, Wanchai, Hong Kong; ✆ +852 2156 2248).

Ready to Learn is now in its 21st year in Hong Kong of implementing its own system to teach English. It sponsors a few teachers from the UK and elsewhere (see entry), although it is not interested in '*travellers seeing the world with a TEFL qualification or similar*'. It is looking for teachers who will commit longer term and take an interest in the company and its methods.

The English Schools Foundation mentioned earlier hires 120 teachers during an annual recruitment drive for its five secondary schools, nine primary schools and five kindergartens. The campaign gets underway in November with interviews in January/February for an August start date (http://recruit.esf.edu.hk).

Dramatic English, also with an entry, employs drama graduates on 10- or 12-month contracts, who are able to use their arts degree and possible performance skills to help children learn English.

Demand is strong for native English speakers to work in English-speaking kindergartens, for which a degree and a TEFL qualification are generally sufficient. Typically, candidates who hold a degree in early childhood education, or a teaching related degree, do not require a TEFL qualification. Adverts abound for TEFL-trained graduates to work for companies with names like Cheerful Kids, Mini Minds, First Little Step, Blooming Buds, Little Beanies and Kidz-n-us. English for Asia (nisha@englishforasia.com) in Kowloon is another major recruiter, though it can usually employ graduates of its own Trinity CertTESOL course (see Directory of Training Courses).

Both internet adverts and more traditional print-based means of advertising jobs are still going strong. For example the bumper Saturday edition of the *South China Morning Post* might contain some useful leads; its classified section often carries teaching posts and can be consulted online at www.cpjobs.com/hk (search 'Native English Teacher'). The online community http://jobs.asiaxpat.com carries many ads for teachers, though most require that applicants already have a valid HKID/working visa. Another good searchable resource for jobs in HK is www.hk.jobsdb.com. The *Yellow Pages* are an alternative source of institute addresses or consult the list of English Learning Centres at www.englishtutor.hk. Landline calls within the city limits are free, by phoning around you can easily get an idea of the possibilities. Hiring is continuous, though the summer months bring even more openings, while the Chinese New Year in January/February is a bad time.

Some companies specialise in recruiting and outsourcing teachers, saving schools the administrative burden of employing a foreigner. Elton Educational Services (see entry) provides English courses and English teachers to Hong Kong kindergartens and primary schools.

Freelance teaching can prove lucrative although it's always a risk for non-permanent residents, as work visas forbid foreigners to work for anyone other than their named sponsor. An attractive advertisement strategically placed in the letterboxes of the ritzy apartment estates in Mid Levels, Jardine's Lookout and Causeway Bay suburbs or in busy supermarkets might winkle out some private students. It is also possible to pick up tutoring work where you visit a family's home and help their child with homework/English games. The standard payment is £20–£30 an hour. Summer schools, English drama organisations and language schools are also options in Hong Kong, but all foreign workers doing paid or voluntary work require a work visa, so make arrangements with an employer beforehand.

Although Hong Kong is famous for its big-city smog and vivacity, there are quieter places and it is worth researching the exact place where you will be living and working. **J. W. Arble** worked at a secondary school in the New Territories in a suburban town 30 miles to the north of Hong Kong Island. '*I lived alone in a 12 by 16ft flat, 17 floors above a colossal shopping centre of six hundred stores, 30 restaurants and a single bookshop that mainly stocked self-help guides and comics. Everything shut at 10pm.*'

REGULATIONS

British citizens may visit the HKSAR as tourists without a visa for up to 180 days provided they can satisfy the immigration officer on arrival that they are entering as bona fide visitors with enough funds to cover the duration of their stay without working and, unless in transit to the Mainland of China or the region of Macao, hold onward or return tickets. USA citizens are given 90 days. The visa requirements are posted at www.immd.gov.hk. As already mentioned, visitors are not allowed to change their status after arrival.

Once you have an employer willing to sponsor you, it is relatively straightforward obtaining a work visa by submitting form ID990A (Application for Entry for Employment as Professionals in Hong Kong). After both parties have signed a contract, the employer sends this and all necessary documents including police checks, a medical certificate, academic certificates and references to the Immigration Department. The employer must do a lot of paperwork so teachers should try to honour their commitments instead of flitting off to a better-paying school after a month or two. The HKSAR Immigration Department is located on the 2nd Floor of Immigration Tower, 7 Gloucester Road, Wan Chai (✆ +582 2824 6111; enquiry@immd.gov.hk). The work visa must be renewed annually.

The government rules stipulate that teachers recruited from overseas must be paid at least HK$20,000 a month. Salaries are taxed at roughly 3% at the end of the year, because there is no PAYE system in Hong Kong. Nor is there any social security. However, after their first year, employees must pay 5% into the Mandatory Provident Fund (MPF), which is matched by the employer. Medical care is not free in Hong Kong, but as soon as the teacher is given an HKID card, he or she can use the Government hospitals for a nominal fee. A visit to a private GP will cost about HK$400.

CONDITIONS OF WORK

If you do not have an official contract and are picking up some teaching at a private institute, you are likely to be paid on an hourly basis and not very well.

Hong Kong children are usually well behaved, eager and well mannered, even though so many are under huge pressure from exams, extra tuition, band practice, kung fu, lion dancing and extra sports. It can be just as important for teachers to help their pupils enjoy English and gain confidence as to instil the finer points of English grammar. Hong Kong's British past can also lead to some interesting situations, as **J. W. Arble** discovered:

> ***It is traditional for Hong Kong students to adopt an English name alongside their Chinese ones. These too have, in fact, become family names, passed down with little variation and as a result I found myself surrounded by ghosts from the Edwardian era, Sibyls and Mabels and Ethels and Normans and even an Algernon. Other students chose their own English names: King Kong was the moniker of one five-foot 14-year-old, School Bully was that of another, there was a Ferrari Vespa, an Ω – the student formerly known as Wong – and a Beckham, a 15-year-old covered in tattoos who literally slept through all my lessons undisturbed, who was rumoured to drive a minibus for the Triads. My favourite student name was Frozen Chicken Drumstick, belonging to a girl who had plucked it from a packet in the supermarket deep-freeze.***

ACCOMMODATION

Hong Kong has overtaken Singapore (just) and Tokyo as the most expensive city in Asia, and rents keep climbing. Flat shares are obviously the cheapest option; check out http://hongkong.craigslist.hk/roo for listings. The outlying islands such as Lamma and Lantau and the New Territories are cheaper than the central areas; the same money can buy double the floor space. Even with HK's superb public transport system, the commute can be time consuming, so living in Kowloon just north of Hong Kong island might be a happy medium. **Tom Grundy** suggests that the best deals are in old walk-up buildings without lifts, where your money will buy comparatively more floor space. He goes on to recommend looking up flat shares on Asia Expat (the main expat community online: http://asiaxpat.com) or Geo Expat (http://geoexpat.com) in addition to the online communities mentioned above.

Areas in Kowloon that are considered to be quite poor are becoming popular with foreigners, such as Sham Shui Po or Tai Kok Tsui, as they are cheaper and still on the MTR red line, which goes direct to Central on HK Island.

LEISURE TIME

Not surprisingly, culture shock is kept to a minimum in Hong Kong by the western affluence and the lingering traces of Britishness. Hong Kong is famed as a shoppers' paradise in which the cheap food, clothing and travel help to alleviate the problem of expensive accommodation. **Tom Grundy** concludes that Hong Kong is an ideal place to live:

> *In Hong Kong, tax is low to non-existent, it's super clean, has a huge expat community with lots of English clubs, activities, sports, events and the public transport is the world's best. It's very compact and all of Asia is on the doorstep (cheap flights and trains to China, Indonesia, Philippines, Thailand, Cambodia, Vietnam, Laos, etc.). The territory has dozens of tropical beaches, temples, a mind-blowing metropolis at its heart, fantastic hiking and outdoor activities, 248 idyllic outlying islands, huge country parks (70% of HK's area is actually green) and everything's a good deal cheaper than home, what with China next door. It's an ideal balance of East and West, English is widely spoken and western food and luxuries are available everywhere. Though Hong Kong is an aggressively consumerist, capitalist society, it is 'tempered' with Chinese tradition and Buddhist beliefs.*

LIST OF EMPLOYERS

BERLITZ LANGUAGES LIMITED
2/F, Lee Garden Six, 111 Leighton Rd, Causeway Bay
+852 2157 2222
info@berlitz.com.hk
www.berlitz.com.hk

NUMBER OF TEACHERS: 7, increasing to 10.
PREFERENCE OF NATIONALITY: UK, US, NZ, Australia.
QUALIFICATIONS: TESOL/TEFL, Bachelor's degree, business experience. Teaching experience good but not essential.
CONDITIONS OF EMPLOYMENT: 1 year with option to renew. Depending on agreement, business hours are 7.30am–9pm Monday–Friday, and 9am–6pm on Saturdays and Sundays.
SALARY: Starting salary HK$100 per unit (40 minutes teaching time). Contribution to pension scheme is 5%, to a monthly maximum of HK$1,250. Low tax rates, paid annually to HK Inland Revenue Department.
FACILITIES/SUPPORT: No help with accommodation. Sponsorship for work visa is provided for full-time teachers only. Successful applications usually take 4–6 weeks.
RECRUITMENT: Ads posted online or in local newspapers. Interviews conducted locally or via Skype.
CONTACT: Richard Li, Manager of Instruction.

CHATTERIS EDUCATIONAL FOUNDATION
Flat A, 13F, Block 2, Camel Paint Building, 62 Hoi Yuen Road, Kwun Tong, Kowloon
+852 2520 5736
hr@chatteris.org.hk; info@chatteris.org.hk
www.chatteris.org.hk

NUMBER OF TEACHERS: 65–70 CNETs (Chatteris Native-speaking English Teachers) per year for schools all over Hong Kong.
PREFERENCE OF NATIONALITY: Primarily British, American and Canadian.
QUALIFICATIONS: Bachelor's degree from the past 4 years or higher qualification in any subject, no teaching experience necessary as training is given. Undergraduates in their final year may also apply. Must have clean police record.
CONDITIONS OF EMPLOYMENT: 9-month contracts, 1 September–31 May (mandatory 3-week orientation in August). 8 hours per day with 1 hour lunch break, weekends free.
SALARY: HK$14,000. Must have enough funds on arrival to cover start-up costs and pay a refundable deposit of HK$2,000. Total recommended to have up front is about £3,750.
FACILITIES/SUPPORT: Accommodation is provided free of charge

by Chatteris during the 3-week orientation period. During this time, flat-hunting workshops are provided to familiarise employees with the property system of Hong Kong. Chatteris office staff are also available for assistance with negotiation of rental agreements and any issues that may arise during this time. After acceptance into the programme support is provided to applicants regarding the organisation and processing of work visa. Chatteris will request a number of documents such as original degree certificates, police clearance checks, doctor's letter and employment visa form ID990A in order for the visa to be processed.

RECRUITMENT: Through online job postings and websites, word-of-mouth and seminars. Applications accepted from November; closing dates are 31 May and 1 July. Interviews are conducted via Skype or in person, and carried out in the UK during a recruitment trip in February/March, in Sydney in May and sometimes in the USA.

DEBORAH ENGLISH KINDERGARTEN & INTERNATIONAL PRE-SCHOOL

Kindergarten Tower, Beverly Garden, Tseung Kwan, Kowloon

+852 2217 7933

dktko06@yahoo.com.hk

www.deborah-intl.edu.hk

NUMBER OF TEACHERS: More than 60 for all schools; eight kindergartens in HK and two in Shenzhen, China.

PREFERENCE OF NATIONALITY: Canadian, Australian, British or American. Must be native English speakers.

QUALIFICATIONS: Any university degree or an early childhood certificate plus minimum 6-months' teaching experience.

CONDITIONS OF EMPLOYMENT: 2-year contract. School hours from 8.30am to 5pm Monday to Friday plus occasional Saturdays for special events. Must love children, since teaching children aged 2–6.

SALARY: From HK$16,000, depending on experience. Airfare, medical cover and 8–9 weeks' approx paid holiday provided.

FACILITIES/SUPPORT: Free shared accommodation per 2–3 teachers or HK$2,000 accommodation allowance. Visa sponsorship may be available.

RECRUITMENT: Via the internet, please send résumé/CV by email. Recruiting goes on year round. Interviews not essential.

CONTACT: Mr Anderson.

DRAMATIC ENGLISH

Unit 802, New Kowloon Plaza, Olympic, Kowloon

+852 2880 5080

apply@dramaticenglish.com

www.dramaticenglish.org

NUMBER OF TEACHERS: Around 40 full-time native-speaking teachers for Hong Kong (plus for Shanghai, Shenzhen and Dongguan).

PREFERENCE OF NATIONALITY: None but must be native English speakers.

QUALIFICATIONS: Company largely deals with recent drama and English graduates, as well as specialists in Early Childhood Development. Candidates should have a degree in theatre/drama, English or related field. ESL qualification/experience is preferred, but not essential. Non-degree tertiary qualifications adequate for Early Childhood specialists.

CONDITIONS OF EMPLOYMENT: Contracts run for 10–12 months. Teachers may continue for another contract term. Working hours fall between 7.30am and 9.30pm with 9-hour working days, 5 days per week, depending on school programmes and timetabling.

SALARY: HK$20,000 per month starting salary plus end-of-contract bonus. Employees are required to pay their own taxes at the end of each financial year. There are tax-free thresholds, and due to the timing of contracts, first year employees end up paying little, if any tax.

FACILITIES/SUPPORT: Temporary accommodation for new teachers can be organised. Local staff are happy to support teachers who experience communication problems with local real estate agents and/or property owners.

RECRUITMENT: Via direct contact with universities, referrals and some websites. Dramatic English Recruitment has its own Facebook page. Phone interviews are essential. In 2016, the company interviewed teachers in Europe, visiting Birmingham, Bristol and Barcelona in September/October to recruit for the following year.

CONTACT: Luke Yick, CEO (yick.luke@gmail.com).

ELTON EDUCATIONAL SERVICES LTD

10th Floor, Wai Hing Building, 146 Prince Edward Road West, Kowloon

+852 2850 6967

info@eltoneducation.com

www.eltoneducation.com

Recruitment agency that provides Native English teachers (NETs) to Hong Kong kindergartens, primary and secondary schools.

PREFERENCE OF NATIONALITY: UK, Australia, USA, South Africa, Europe.

QUALIFICATIONS: Good English pronunciation, experience and qualifications, i.e. degree, TESOL/TEFL, BA (Ed) or other teaching qualifications like PGCE/PGDE.

CONDITIONS OF EMPLOYMENT: 1 year, often extended. Hours are 8.30–4.30 Monday–Friday plus one Saturday morning per month.

SALARY: HK$18,000–HK$23,000 per month depending on experience, qualifications and duties.

FACILITIES/SUPPORT: Teachers are responsible for their own accommodation.

RECRUITMENT: Via Global English (online TESOL Provider), local media (e.g. www.cpjobs.com), word of mouth and internet. Face-to-face interviews in Hong Kong with agency and client schools.

CONTACT: Toby White, Director.

ENGLISH EXCEL SCHOOL OF ENGLISH

3/F Wealthy Plaza, 138 Shau Kei Wan Rd, Sai Wan Ho, 01

+852 2893 3559

careers@english-excel.com

www.english-excel.com/career.php

British-owned and operated network of 12 schools around Hong Kong Island and Kowloon for children aged 3–16. The largest extra-curricular English school in Hong Kong.

PREFERENCE OF NATIONALITY: Native level speakers.

QUALIFICATIONS: Degree and teaching certificate, e.g. TEFL, CELTA. Applications from those without a teaching cert will be considered if they have demonstrated experience of working with children in other capacities. Classes are limited to four students per class and are highly interactive, so potential teachers need to be energetic and friendly.

CONDITIONS OF EMPLOYMENT: To teach students aged 3–16. Minimum contract duration is 12–16 months. Generous completion gratuities reflect the importance of the contract. Saturday is a working day so working week covers Monday to Saturday with two long mornings off till 3.30 pm.

SALARY: Revealed to short-listed candidates. Monthly bonus paid.

FACILITIES/SUPPORT: Affordable accommodation made available in Quarry Bay area. School applies for visas on behalf of the candidates before arrival in HK.

RECRUITMENT: Applications must include a cover letter and CV with photo. Recruitment is done via telephone interviews throughout the year.

HEADSTART GROUP LTD

Unit 2508, Nanyang Plaza, 57 Hung To Road, Kwun Tong, Kowloon, Hong Kong

+852 21559602; Macao: +853 6268 6001

juliechu@headstartgroup.co

www.headstartgroup.co; http://hkmacau.headstartgroup.co

NUMBER OF TEACHERS: Nearly 200 Native English Teachers (full-time and part-time).

PREFERENCE OF NATIONALITY: None as long as they are native speakers. Company has links with universities in the UK, US, South Africa, Ireland, Australia and New Zealand.

QUALIFICATIONS: Minimum requirement is a bachelor degree (preferably in education or English-related subjects) and TEFL/TESOL/CELTA, etc. 1–2 years' teaching experience an advantage.

CONDITIONS OF EMPLOYMENT: 12 months starting in September. Monday to Friday 8am–5pm.

SALARY: HK$18,000+ net.

FACILITIES/SUPPORT: Package available whereby accommodation is provided and a lower salary paid. Full assistance given with work permits. After the necessary documents have been received, Headstart lodges the visa application which normally takes 4–6 weeks to be processed. Cantonese classes and cultural orientation provided.

RECRUITMENT: University recruitment fairs, paid job posting websites, referrals from teachers and social media. Skype interviews.

CONTACT: Julie Chu, General Manager.

HK INSTITUTE OF LANGUAGES

6/f Wellington Plaza, 56–58 Wellington Street, Central

+852 2877 6160

recruit@hklanguages.com

www.hklanguages.com

NUMBER OF TEACHERS: 5.

PREFERENCE OF NATIONALITY: British or American.

QUALIFICATIONS: University degree, CELTA or equivalent ESL teaching certificate or state teaching certification, e.g. PGCE. Should have 2 years' teaching experience.

CONDITIONS OF EMPLOYMENT: 1-year renewable contract with 20–25 contact teaching hours per week.

SALARY: HK$20,000 per month.

FACILITIES/SUPPORT: Accommodation provided for the first week then assistance is given to find suitable permanent accommodation. Sponsorship offered for work permits and all paperwork is taken care of.

RECRUITMENT: Usually via advertisements on corporate and professional websites. Interviews are essential.

LITTLE COSMOS LANGUAGE & ART CENTRE
Shop 208, Level II, Park Central, 9 Tong Tak Street, Tseung Kwan O
+852 3162 3168
recruitment@littlecosmos.hk; info@littlecosmos.hk
www.littlecosmos.hk

NUMBER OF TEACHERS: 3–4.
PREFERENCE OF NATIONALITY: British, Canadian, American, Australian, South African.
QUALIFICATIONS: Preferably degree holder in Education or English, Linguistics or Literature discipline with TESOL, TEFL or CELTA certificate (120+ hours) and at least one year of teaching experience with children. Degree holder of other discipline will also be considered.
CONDITIONS OF EMPLOYMENT: 1 year contract, rolling renewals thereafter. 40 hours a week; maximum 30 hours of teaching.
SALARY: Between HK$23,000 and HK$26,000 per month depending on experience. Deduction of 5% as contribution to the Mandatory Provident Fund after working for 13 months. Tax rate is 12% for income of HK$80,000–120,000, going up to 17% above that threshold.
FACILITIES/SUPPORT: Assistance given with accommodation search including accompanying teacher to targeted locations and offering guidance with leasing agency. 1 week paid training to familiarise new teachers with the curriculum, lesson plans and teaching materials while shadowing and observing classes. Work visa sponsorship provided.
CONTACT: Ms. Angela Cheung, Manager.

MONKEY TREE ENGLISH LEARNING CENTER
1002, 101 Kings Road, Fortress Hill, Hong Kong Island
+852 3563 6771
careers@monkeytree.com.hk
www.monkeytree.com.hk

NUMBER OF TEACHERS: 208 for 44 centres altogether throughout Hong Kong plus one in Macau.
PREFERENCE OF NATIONALITY: In order of preference: England, America, Canada, South Africa, Ireland, Australia, Wales, Scotland, New Zealand.
QUALIFICATIONS: Degree + TEFL/TESOL/CELTA/PGCE.
CONDITIONS OF EMPLOYMENT: 12-month contracts. Teaching hours between 9.30am and 7.30pm.
SALARY: Average HK$23,000 per month. Teachers pay taxes of 5% of cumulative salary at end of contract.
FACILITIES/SUPPORT: Subsidised shared housing provided; teachers pay HK$5,500–7,000 per month rent. Arrangement is flexible so teachers can move out easily. Fully paid 2-week training programme covering theory and practice. Full sponsorship available for teachers to obtain a visa.
RECRUITMENT: Online advertisements, referrals from current teachers and agencies such as Global Teacher Recruitment.
CONTACT: Kirstin Aitken, HR Manager.

READY TO LEARN HONG KONG LTD
1G/F, 1/F, 2/F Wing Sing Commercial Building, 2–4 Wing Sing Lane, Yau Ma Tei, Kowloon
+852 2512 9338
help@rtlenglish.com
www.rtl.edu.hk

NUMBER OF TEACHERS: 15–25 part-time and full-time for Educational Centres in Fortress Hill (North Point), Yau Ma Tei (Mong Kok) and Hung Hom (Whampoa) teaching children 3–18.
PREFERENCE OF NATIONALITY: Majority are permanent residents who have been in HK for some time. Teachers can be sponsored from English-speaking countries especially UK.
QUALIFICATIONS: University degree necessary for getting a working visa. 120-hour TEFL Certificate required; any ESL courses that emphasise grammar are useful. A willingness to teach a structured curriculum in the form of prepared and printed lesson books.
CONDITIONS OF EMPLOYMENT: Minimum 1 year, renewable. Full-time in Hong Kong is 19 hours, but overseas sponsored teachers usually work 30 hours. Teaching hours between 9am and 7 pm, including weekends. Very structured material used for teaching, including a lot of grammar.
SALARY: Basic HK$20,000 per month, as stipulated by the HK government as minimum payment for overseas teachers. The teacher pays tax annually (on average about HK$5,500).
FACILITIES/SUPPORT: Return airfare paid (up to HK$6,000) if returning to home country. Up to HK$6,000 contribution to expenses during the first month. Help with finding accommodation initially can be given. New teachers will be met at the airport.
RECRUITMENT: Locally to find candidates who already have a working visa or permanent residence, internet advertising and word of mouth. Interviews necessary and can be by Skype.
CONTACT: Elaine Shannon, Principal and Founder (elaine.shannon@rtlenglish.com); Claire Askham (claireaskham@rtlenglish.com).

MACAO

The lesser-known of China's two special administrative regions is Macao, a former Portuguese colony that lies west of Hong Kong across the delta of the Pearl River. The territory's economy is booming from its successful gambling and tourist industries. With a doctorate in Linguistics, **Joanna Radwanska-Williams** is an ELT professional at the Macao Polytechnic Institute and with MPI Bell (see entry) who makes Macao her home:

> *Macao is a very international city with a high standard of living. It's definitely a pleasant living environment, and the historic city centre is on the UNESCO World Heritage list. Macao feels like a 'happy place' and is welcoming to families and newcomers. Many people speak English as the international and regional lingua franca and there is a high demand for English. There is a lot of English-language local press. The health care is good. There are many churches, especially Catholic ones, and freedom of worship. It is basically a western-type setting, though with lots of Chinese tourists from the mainland.*
>
> *The unusual factor – not necessarily a low – is the presence of the casino industry. This comes with incredibly luxurious shopping, good restaurants, etc. For the most part, we reap lots of benefits from this: good salaries, great public facilities funded by the government, such as parks, swimming pools, museums, cultural activities and tourist attractions. Macao has far surpassed Las Vegas in terms of revenue from the casino industry. To the extent that there is crime (much less so than in the US, I would think), it does not impact ordinary citizens. Macao is perfectly safe to walk in, day or night. The public transportation is great.*

LIST OF EMPLOYERS

ENGLISH FOR ASIA LTD (MACAO BRANCH)
10E, Edificio Comercial Rodrigues, No. 599 Av. Praia Grande, Macao
+853 2870 5784
nathan@englishforasia.com; macao@englishforasia.com
www.englishforasia.com

NUMBER OF TEACHERS: 10–15 (at present).

PREFERENCE OF NATIONALITY: Native English speakers of any nationality.

QUALIFICATIONS: Minimum bachelor's degree and TESOL certificate (or other equivalent teaching certificate). Minimum of 2-years' experience essential.

CONDITIONS OF EMPLOYMENT: 1-year rolling contracts (due to local labour laws). 27 teaching hours a week, plus an allocated 13 hours for preparation and admin work (40-hour working week). Hours usually stretch over 5 days, with 2 full days off per week. Operational hours are 8am–9pm; teaching schedule can accommodate teacher's outside commitments. Working during the weekends and summer months essential. Around 40 days of paid holiday per academic year (includes 2-week break at Christmas/New Year, 1 week at Chinese New Year, 5 days for Easter and a 5-day pre-summer holiday in June).

SALARY: HK$21,000 (depending on qualifications and experience). At current exchange rates, this is equivalent to £1,700, about double the average wage in Macao. Tax deductions are made quarterly and are very low (approximately £50 per quarter).

FACILITIES/SUPPORT: Teacher trainer on hand to give on-the-job coaching and guidance. Reasonably priced temporary accommodation will be provided upon arrival until an employee finds a home in the territory. No housing allowance is given. Visa sponsorship is given; teachers provide a copy of their CV/résumé and original certificates for inspection. UK syllabus is followed. The process can take up to 3 months and teachers will be required to pay a fee of around £10 upon collection.

RECRUITMENT: Usually direct application for teachers already in the region. Interviews essential.

CONTACT: Nathan Fox, Centre Manager.

HEADSTART GROUP LTD

Unit 2508, Nanyang Plaza, 57 Hung To Road, Kwun Tong, Kowloon, Hong Kong

+852 21559602; Macao: +853 6268 6001

juliechu@headstartgroup.co

www.headstartgroup.co; http://hkmacau.headstartgroup.co

See entry above in Hong Kong chapter.

MPI-BELL CENTRE OF ENGLISH (BELL PARTNER SCHOOL)

Macao Polytechnic Institute, 3rd floor, Meng Tak Building, Rua de Luis Gonzaga Gomes, Macao

+853 8599 3162

mpibell@ipm.edu.mo; davidq@ipm.edu.mo

http://bellcentre.ipm.edu.mo

NUMBER OF TEACHERS: 11 in Macao plus three in Xinjiang, China.

PREFERENCE OF NATIONALITY: None, but must be native speaker of English.

QUALIFICATIONS: Minimum bachelor's degree, CELTA and 5 years' experience, preferably in China.

CONDITIONS OF EMPLOYMENT: 2-year renewable contracts. Normally 20 contact hours per week over 5 days.

SALARY: Varies but approximately RMB400,000 gross per year. Approximately 8% deductions.

FACILITIES/SUPPORT: Accommodation or accommodation allowance provided. Work permit and visas arranged. End-of-contract payment. 22 days' paid holiday per year plus public holidays. Local medical insurance cover provided.

RECRUITMENT: Direct application.

CONTACT: David Quartermain, Deputy Director (davidq@ipm.edu.mo).

INDONESIA

Indonesia is the fourth most populous nation on earth. The economist Jim O'Neill, who coined the term BRIC to represent the economic powerhouse nations of the early 21st century, has now identified the next wave. Indonesia conveniently provides the vowel in MINT (Mexico, Indonesia, Nigeria and Turkey). This nation embedded in Southeast Asia and with longstanding ties to China seems at ease with Western ways of doing business, and some predict that the present rate of growth (above 5%) will continue.

For years schools have been attracting professional ELT teachers from abroad with benefits packages and reasonable salaries of more than 16 million rupiah (£900). The best jobs continue to crop up in the oil company cities. Although oil production has been declining, the industry is still crucial to the country's economy. The so-called 'native English speaker schools' with multiple branches in Jakarta and the other cities continue to deliver English courses to the millions of Indonesians who want to learn the language. These organisations can still afford to hire trained foreign teachers and pay them about 10 times the local wage. EF English First is the biggest and most well known chain of the franchised language schools, with schools in Jakarta as well as on Sumatra, Java, Sulawesi and Bali. Wall Street English (www.wallstreetenglish.co.id) has several branches in Jakarta – including a plush branch on Jalan Jend. Sudirman, the capital's most prestigious thoroughfare. In their ads on tefl.com etc., they explain 'why teaching at Wall Street English is your dream job'. It has captured market share by targeting office workers using a highly flexible schedule, which means teaching schedules can be awkward.

Over the past few years, the Association of National & Private Schools (ANPS) has become established. These accredited schools for the children of the Indonesian middle class tend to follow an international curriculum, often with some local content, and the medium of instruction is English, or a mix of Bahasa Indonesian and English.

FINDING A JOB

The CELTA is highly regarded in Indonesia and anyone who has acquired the certificate has a good chance of pre-arranging a job in Jakarta, Surabaya, Bandung or Yogyakarta (one of the most interesting cities in Indonesia), provided they satisfy the other visa requirements. The government stipulates that teachers must be native English speakers from the UK, USA, Canada, Australia or New Zealand in order to be awarded a work permit. (Oddly, neither Irish nor South African nationality is listed, though it is assumed that if a school made a case to hire a native English speaker from these countries, their application would be viewed favourably.) Teachers are required to hold a bachelor's degree preferably in Linguistics, English Language, English Literature or Education, to satisfy government visa requirements. In certain cases the specification of degree subject is enforced, whereas some major employers of English teachers do not. For example the English Division of LPIA (Indonesian American Educational Institution) with 70 branches hires American, British, or Australian teachers who have a BA or BSc (all majors OK) and asks only for applicants to be able to speak and write English well, be aged 18–35, in good health with no criminal convictions and to love working with Indonesians, especially children; see www.lpia.co/p/lpia-job-vacancies.html.

Among the main schools in Indonesia it is standard to reimburse airfares and visa costs at the end of a successful contract. A number offer medical insurance and many offer free housing.

EF English First advertises extensively and constantly for teachers in Indonesia. They are split into separate franchises, even within Jakarta, which are responsible for recruiting teachers for their own groups of schools, including the Swara Group, the Depok Group and the Harmoni Group which advertise independently of each other, though there is also a central recruitment system via www.englishfirst.com/ESL-jobs/teaching-english-in-indonesia. Employment conditions are fairly standard across the groups.

ON THE SPOT

More and more teachers are being hired on the spot, which suits the major schools, which then don't have to pay for airfares. Local recruits can negotiate shorter contracts, for example six months, unlike teachers recruited abroad, who usually have to commit for 12 months. Most teaching jobs start in July or September/October. With a Cambridge/Trinity or equivalent certificate and university degree in an approved field your chances of being offered a job are high. Under-qualified applicants would have to be extremely well presented (since dress is very important in Jakarta), able to sell themselves in terms of experience and qualifications and prepared to commit themselves for a longish spell or to start with some part-time work in the hope of building it up. Caution is advised at the interview stage, because promises are not always kept or the full extent of deductions mentioned.

Local schools staffed by Indonesians abound, many willing to hire a native English speaker at local wages, though they may not be in a position to arrange a work permit. There is no 'easy answer' for how prospective teachers should try to sell themselves, as **Ross McKay**, a long-term expatriate in Jakarta, is keen to point out:

> ***Each school has it own ethos. One place likes lots of chat but others are sober-sides who keep students' noses to the grindstone. I went to one interview and kept the class happy for an hour, only to be told that 'we're educators, not entertainers'. But another school didn't call me for interview because I'd stated that I took the job seriously and didn't go easy on students who habitually arrived late. Jam Karet, rubber-time, is a bad habit here, and you either adjust to it or get driven nuts.***

Opportunities exist not only in the large cities but in small towns too. Travellers have stumbled across friendly little schools up rickety staircases throughout the islands of Indonesia.

Tim Leffel from New Jersey, USA noticed a large number of English schools in the Javanese city of Solo, and others have recommended Denpasar (Bali). Volunteer Programs Bali was set up in 2013 to recruit international volunteers to provide free English classes to underprivileged children in Ubud; a full table of fees in rupiah (e.g. £750 for eight weeks) can be found at www.volunteerprogramsbali.org.

At local schools and institutes unused to employing native English-speaker teachers, teaching materials may be in short supply. One of the problems faced by those who undertake casual work of this kind is that there is little chance of obtaining a work permit. It is difficult for freelance teachers to become legal unless they have a contact who knows people in power. The problem of visas doesn't arise if you teach English on a completely informal basis, as **Stuart Tappin** did:

> ***In Asia I managed to spend a lot of time living with people in return for teaching English. The more remote the towns are from tourist routes the better, for example Bali is no good. I spent a week in Palembang, Sumatra, living with an English teacher and his family. You teach and they give their (very good) hospitality.***

If you get stuck job-hunting in Jakarta, go to Jalan Jaksa, a small but lively street where many teachers hang out.

REGULATIONS

The work permit regulations are rigidly adhered to in Indonesia and all of the established language schools and chains will apply for a visa permit on your behalf. Some even employ a dedicated visa coordinator and employ an agent in the Indonesian Embassy in Singapore where most people collect the visa. The Consular section of the Indonesian Embassy in London issues 'General Information for Foreigners Wishing to Work in Indonesia', which starts with the warning: '*Please be informed that it is not easy for foreigners to work and stay in Indonesia since Indonesia has very strict and complicated immigration/visa requirements and regulations, and the process can be very long*' (www.indonesianembassy.org.uk). As mentioned, the Indonesian government limits work permits to teachers holding passports from English-speaking countries (UK, US, Canada, Australia and New Zealand) and with degrees in an approved field as listed above, which one school director called 'nonsensical', but that is the situation. Candidates are also expected to have three to five years of post-qualification experience and be aged 25–57, though these rules are more flexible.

If the job is arranged in plenty of time before you leave home, you may be sent a letter of sponsorship from your employer to take to the Indonesian Embassy in your country and, subject to current visa requirements, it will issue you with a Temporary Stay visa (VITAS), which gives permission to apply for a Temporary Resident Card (KITAS) within a week of arrival in Indonesia. The total processing time will be at least 12 weeks. Most legitimate employers will pay the considerable cost of the visa and will therefore expect their teachers to stay for the duration of their contract.

It is possible to enter Indonesia on a tourist visa and, after being hired, have the school arrange the work permit, but for this you will have to leave the country after supplying your CV, originals of your TEFL course and university degree certificates, photocopies of your passport and application forms. You must also obtain a health certificate proving that you are free of HIV and of drugs. According to one school, the photos submitted must be in three different sizes and on a red background! The application is sent to the Indonesian Ministry of Education, the Cabinet Secretariat and the Immigration office. If and when the application is approved, the work permit will be valid for one employer only and will be revoked and the offending teacher deported if work is undertaken outside the terms of the contract.

After your work permit and temporary stay permit have been granted (with a maximum validity of one year), the documentation will then be sent to the nearest Indonesian Embassy (normally Singapore), where the teacher can have it stamped in his or her passport. These visa runs only take a day or two and should be paid for by your employer, although some, such as Berlitz, consequently withhold 10% of your salary for the first six months, then reimburse the 10% monthly, starting in the seventh month, to ensure that teachers fulfil the year's visa.

CONDITIONS OF WORK

Salaries paid by the 'native English speaker' schools can provide for a comfortable lifestyle, including travel within Indonesia during the vacations. Most schools pay at least 11 million rupiah per month, after Indonesian tax of 7%–10% (on earnings of up to 25 million rupiah) has been subtracted. Teachers with at least a year's experience were being recruited by TEFL One (wwww.teflone.com) not long ago on a salary starting at 15–20 million rupiah. As mentioned, reimbursement for airfares is commonplace, as described by **Bruce Clarke**, who worked for EF English First:

> ***In addition to a decent starting salary, my school also agreed to reimburse me at the end of my contract for both the price of my plane ticket and my work visa. Basic living is relatively cheap. I spend about half my salary on western luxuries like beer, CDs, movies, etc. I bank the rest so at the end of my year I expect to head home with a few thousand dollars saved. Most of the teachers I meet are in their early 20s, and are generally still at the 'let's party every night' stage of their lives. They complain about constantly being broke because they tend to go clubbing two or three nights a week and waste a lot of money.***

Many schools offer generous help with accommodation, ranging from an interest-free loan to cover initial rent payments or deposits, to free housing complete with free telephone, electricity and maid service. This perk may be at the expense of free choice though, and it is worth considering if you mind where you live/who you live with. It is customary in the Jakarta housing market to be asked to pay the annual rent in a lump sum at the beginning of your tenancy, and so access to a loan from your employer is often essential. **Ross McKay** warns that housing contracts should not be undertaken lightly, since one of his ex-colleagues who refused to pay a year's rent on a house he had occupied for two months ended up behind bars and subject to a huge fine.

If you happen to work for a school which takes on outside contracts, you may have the occasional chance to work outside the school premises, possibly in a remote oil drilling location in Sumatra, for up to double pay. The majority of teachers, however, conduct lessons at their school through the usual peak hours of 3.30pm–8.30pm, with some early morning starts as well. Many supplement their incomes with private students (provided their employer permits it). For example, Ross McKay was paid by a doctor to teach him while they drove into Jakarta in the morning, which boiled down to him being paid to be given a lift to work. Freelancers will have to get used to *jam karat*, which means 'rubber time', or the Indonesian habit of time (non)keeping.

THE STUDENTS

Outside the big cities, the standard of English is normally quite low, with students having picked up a smattering from bad American television. Classes also tend to be large, with as many as 40 students, all expecting to learn grammar by the traditional rote methods. According to a VSO volunteer teaching in Western Java (as quoted in the *Times Educational Supplement*): '*If I want to do something interesting, the students complain that it isn't in the exam.*' As is the case elsewhere in the world, the average age of English learners is getting younger, so anyone with experience of teaching children or teenagers will be appreciated. When **Andrew Whitmarsh** was a teacher for Wall Street in Jakarta, he enjoyed being able to entice his students into university-style discussions:

> ***As I look back over my experience, I would say that the best times have come during the classes when I almost forgot I was a teacher and they were my students, and instead felt like I was leading a discussion group back at university. At the other end of the scale there were certainly days that some classes felt repetitive, but I got through these by being sure to make creative and engaging social clubs to balance it all out.***

LEISURE TIME

Although Jakarta is a hot, dusty, overcrowded and polluted city, there is a great deal to see and do, and most teachers end up more than tolerating it. After quitting his job in information technology at age 37, **Bruce Clarke** obtained a TEFL certificate in Vancouver and immediately landed a one-year teaching contract with EF English First in Indonesia and concluded that Indonesia is 'okay', though not quite as glamorous as he had hoped. He liked his school and staff, but found Jakarta just another big, crowded city. On a happier note, a past Director of Studies at Executive English Programs (EEP) writes:

> ***Jakarta has moved on in leaps and bounds in many ways since I first arrived. The traffic may be viler than ever, but while it still certainly isn't Hong Kong or Singapore food-wise, the variety of good quality, reasonably priced restaurants is very impressive these days. Once you know your way around!***

Indonesia is a fascinating country and most visitors, whether short-term or long, agree that the Indonesian people are fantastic. Travel is cheap and unrestricted, and excursions are very rewarding in terms of scenery and culture. Travel by public transport can be time consuming and limiting for weekend trips, so you might consider getting a motorcycle, especially if you don't have to contend with Jakarta's traffic. A recent teacher for the respected IELC in Solo (see entry) recommends acquiring a motorbike in order to visit and explore local waterfalls, temples and the big city delights of Jogja.

The draw for **Dan Quinn** was gamelan music, which he studied in his spare time from teaching in Jakarta, as well as climbing hills like Papandayan, Guntur and Cikuray, which are all within reach of Jakarta by Primajasa bus. He has returned to the UK to live in the Outer Hebrides and manages the website Quinn's World of TEFL http://worldoftefl.com.

Predictably, the community of expatriate teachers participates in lots of joint activities such as football and tennis matches, chess tournaments, beach excursions, diving trips and parties. Most teachers have DVDs but occasionally go out to see an undubbed American film. The pleasant city of Bandung might prove an attractive alternative to Jakarta and offers a good-quality lifestyle to teachers, with a good mixture of rural and city life. Since the opening of the toll road from Jakarta to Bandung, a journey time of two hours is possible. It's choked at the weekends, but fine during the week.

Speaking of weekends, **Andrew Whitmarsh** had no problem finding something to do, often with the help of his students:

> ***This is one of the wildest and most wonderful countries I've worked in, so a lot of my time is spent getting out and seeing the city or jumping a train to check out the surrounding countryside. The traffic in Jakarta is tough to deal with and the air quality isn't great, but the opportunity for adventure and excitement is always just around the corner. Many of my students-turned-friends are great guides to the sights and always know the best nightclubs to visit, when the concerts are and where the best food is.***

Bahasa Indonesian, almost identical to Malay, was imposed on the people of Indonesia after independence in 1949 and is one of the simplest languages to learn both in structure and pronunciation.

LIST OF EMPLOYERS

AIM FOR ENGLISH
Jalan Padang 5C, Manggarai, Jakarta Selatan 12580
+62 21 8378 5238
ian@aimjakarta.com; info@aimjakarta.com
www.aimjakarta.com/english

NUMBER OF TEACHERS: 11.

PREFERENCE OF NATIONALITY: British, American, Canadian, Australian, New Zealander and Indonesian.

QUALIFICATIONS: Must have a bachelor's degree in English Language, English Literature, Linguistics or Education. At least CELTA, and 3–5-years' experience (teaching adults, test preparation, Business English and Academic English).

CONDITIONS OF EMPLOYMENT: 12-month contracts. 24 hours' contact. 7 hours in the office 5 days a week. Some evening work. Teachers will also visit clients in their workplaces around Jakarta.

SALARY: 17 million rupiah (after tax), equivalent to around $1,275 per month.

FACILITIES/SUPPORT: Return ticket home, end-of-contract bonus and full health insurance. Ongoing career development. Visas and work permits taken care of: outsourced to a reliable agent.

RECRUITMENT: Through online advertising and word of mouth. Interviews essential, and can be via web-meeting (via Skype/ Yahoo messenger with webcam). Face-to-face interviews preferred, as teaching a demonstration class is often necessary.

CONTACT: Ian Bishop, Managing Director.

BERLITZ LANGUAGE CENTRES
PT Berlitz, Hotel InterContinental MidPlaza Jakarta, Shopping Gallery R-26, Jl. Jendral Sudirman Kav. 10–11, Jakarta 10220
+62 21 251 4589
berlitz1@berlitz.co.id
www.berlitz.co.id

NUMBER OF TEACHERS: 10.

PREFERENCE OF NATIONALITY: British, American, Canadian, Australian and New Zealander (essential for visa).

QUALIFICATIONS: Degree with a major in English (required). TEFL certificate (CELTA, Trinity or equivalent). 3 years' teaching experience. Minimum age 25.

CONDITIONS OF EMPLOYMENT: 12-month contracts. School hours: 7.30am–9pm, Monday to Friday; 7.30am to 3pm Saturday. Lessons scheduled as available between these hours.

SALARY: Approximately $1,000–$1,200 (net) depending on qualifications and experience.

FACILITIES/SUPPORT: Housing allowance paid and first month's housing arranged. Berlitz Instructor Training free of charge. Visa agent assists with permits and school bears the cost.

RECRUITMENT: Word of mouth, newspapers and via internet. Interviews by phone or held at nearby language centre.

CONTACT: Manager of Instruction.

EF ENGLISH FIRST
Indonesian Head Office, Wisma Tamara Lt. 4, Suite 402, Jl. Jend. Sudirman Kav. 24, Jakarta 12920
+62 21 520 6477
efrecruitment@ef.com
www.englishfirst.com/ESL-Jobs/teaching-english-in-Indonesia

NUMBER OF TEACHERS: More than 700 for 77 schools throughout Indonesia. New vacancies every week.
PREFERENCE OF NATIONALITY: British, Canadian, Australian, American or New Zealander (due to work visa restrictions).
QUALIFICATIONS: Degree needed plusTEFL/TESL certificate, indicating 120 hours of class work, observations and evaluated practice teaching. Possibility of sponsorship available for EF's TEFL qualification.
CONDITIONS OF EMPLOYMENT: 12-month renewable contracts. Usual hours are early afternoon until evening (1pm–9pm).
SALARY: Varies significantly between cities: 11–14.million rupiah per month (net) depending on experience.
FACILITIES/SUPPORT: Cost of airfares reimbursed. Most schools provide shared housing free or a monthly housing allowance. Teachers preferring to live alone are given advice and help but bear the contractual responsibilities themselves. Schools provide and pay for Kitas (work-residency permit). Standardised induction programme on arrival, ongoing training and development, medical insurance and 10 days' paid holidays provided.
RECRUITMENT: Advertises heavily on main ELT sites like www.tefl.com. Via EF's Online Recruitment Centre or via individual Ef groups of schools, e.g. EF Harmoni Group in Jakarta (www.englishfirstjakarta.com), EF Depok/HS Group with 7 schools on the outskirts of Jakarta and EF Swara Group with 10 schools.
CONTACT: Simon Staniland or Rob Morgan, Academic Recruitment Team.

EXECUTIVE ENGLISH PROGRAMS (EEP)
Jalan Diponegoro 7, Bandung 40115
+62 22 426 3020
dos@eepbdg.com
www.eepbdg.com

PREFERENCE OF NATIONALITY: British, American, Canadian, Australian and New Zealander.
QUALIFICATIONS: CELTA/Trinity certificate plus university degree in English, English Literature or Linguistics (as laid out in the Department of Education regulations) and at least a year's experience preferred.
CONDITIONS OF EMPLOYMENT: 1-year contracts to work a maximum of 28 hours per week.
SALARY: Minimum 11 million rupiah per month for in-centre training. Increments for higher duties, in-company work and specialised training projects. Contract renewal bonus. Salary includes 25 days' paid holiday per year and limited medical coverage.
FACILITIES/SUPPORT: Will provide documentation and assist in finding accommodation.
RECRUITMENT: Through local newspapers (*The Jakarta Post*). Local interviews almost always necessary. Local interviews preferred, although online interviews are also acceptable.
CONTACT: Ian Mulyana, S.Pd., MM, Director of Studies & Operational Manager.

IELC (INTERACTIVE ENGLISH LANGUAGE CENTER)
Jl Moh Yamin 83, Solo, Central Java
+62 271 634 746
contact.ielc@gmail.com
www.ielc-indonesia.com

NUMBER OF TEACHERS: 5–6.
PREFERENCE OF NATIONALITY: Anglophone countries as per government regulations.
QUALIFICATIONS: Entry-level qualification, such as CELTA or equivalent; varing levels of experience required.
CONDITIONS OF EMPLOYMENT: 12-month contracts. Teaching hours from noon to 8pm.
SALARY: Total package which includes flight allowance and accommodation, approximately US$1,000 per month (net).
FACILITIES/SUPPORT: Clean, comfortable, modern rent-free accommodation is provided, shared with 1–2 other teachers. Internet, satellite TV and maid service are included. Comprehensive professional development programme which includes DoS and peer observation, weekly workshops, seminars and opportunities for funded qualifications and action research. All permits, as required by law, are handled by the school including permits and licences from the Ministry of Education, Department of Labour and immigration authorities.
RECRUITMENT: Online through job boards, e.g. www.tefl.com.
CONTACT: Nina Wexler, Director of Studies/Owner.

KELT SURABAYA (formerly International Language Programs)
Jalan Jawa 34, Surabaya 60281
+62 31 502 3333
jawa@k-elt.com
www.k-elt.com

NUMBER OF TEACHERS: 25 in 3 schools, mostly teaching general English to adults and children.

PREFERENCE OF NATIONALITY: Must be classified native English speaker (to satisfy work permit requirements) i.e. British, American, Canadian, Australian and New Zealander. Most teachers are British

QUALIFICATIONS: Degree and recognised EFL qualification required, e.g. CELTA or Trinity; short intro courses and online courses not acceptable. No experience needed.

CONDITIONS OF EMPLOYMENT: 1-year contracts, e.g. from July, October, etc. 20 hours per week, teaching 5 days a week, afternoons and evenings. Pupils from age 4.

SALARY: Starting salary is 13.5 million rupiah (net) per month with increments for experience.

FACILITIES/SUPPORT: Accommodation provided, including electricity, local phone calls and maid service. Regular workshops held. 8 weeks' paid holiday.

RECRUITMENT: Adverts on the internet (www.tefl.com). Recruitment 4 times a year.

CONTACT: Ian Ramsdale (ian@k-elt.com), Academic Coordinator of Studies.

PRIME ONE SCHOOL
Jl. Jenderal Besar A. H Nasution No.88 A, Medan 20147
✆ +62 61 785 3630/785 3672
info@pos.sch.id
www.pos.sch.id

NUMBER OF TEACHERS: 4.

PREFERENCE OF NATIONALITY: American, British and Australian.

QUALIFICATIONS: Must have a degree preferably in Education, Linguistics or English, and 1 to 5 years' teaching experience.

CONDITIONS OF EMPLOYMENT: Standard 2-year contract. Minimum 30 sessions per week.

SALARY: Up to 18 million rupiah before tax.

FACILITIES/SUPPORT: Shared accommodation in staff house provided. Assistance with work permits given. Airfare reimbursement.

RECRUITMENT: Writing test, interview and psychology test. Interviews via webcam.

CONTACT: Ms Fauzia Lubis, Academic Director.

SANG TIMUR
Karmel St No 2 Kebon Jeruk, Jakarta 11530
✆ +62 21 5302256
antorejekipurba@yahoo.co.id;
sangtimur_smak@yahoo.co.id
www.smaksangtimur-jkt.sch.id

Catholic high school of East Jakarta.

NUMBER OF TEACHERS: 8 native teachers for Jakarta and also Medan, Pematang Siantar, Pekanbaru and Makasar.

PREFERENCE OF NATIONALITY: All native speakers, aged 22–40.

QUALIFICATIONS: Bachelor degree in any field. TESOL qualification preferred but school's British academic director will train fresh graduates in Jakarta.

CONDITIONS OF EMPLOYMENT: 1 year from mid-July, renewable to 3 years. 30 teaching hours per week is usual out of a 40-hour week, 5 days a week. 40 days of holiday per year comprising 15 Indonesian public holidays, 13 days at Christmas, and 12 days in summer.

SALARY: From $700 per month, up to $2,000, according to experience and qualifications. Tax deductions total 8%. Overtime paid in excess of 40 hours.

FACILITIES/SUPPORT: Free housing and transport to school, plus free lunches at school. Employer will assist successful candidates to obtain visa before arrival and then apply for and cover costs of a work permit, which takes 1–2 months. Agent in Singapore can assist with one-day pick-up of permit. Possibility of reimbursement for flights. Free insurance paid by affiliated foundation (Enormous Wishing Foundation).

RECRUITMENT: CV to be sent by email and then chat and interview by Skype (anto_rejeki).

CONTACT: Anto Rejeki Purba, Managing Director.

THE BRITISH INSTITUTE (TBI)
Head Office, Sequis Center lantai 4, Jl Jendral Sudirman Kav. 17, Jakarta 12190
✆ +62 21 527 7860
recruit@tbi.co.id
www.tbi.co.id

TBI has 16 schools across Indonesia (8 in Greater Jakarta, 3 in Bandung, one each in Medan, Surabaya, Bali and Malang) and is the only CELTA centre in the country.

NUMBER OF TEACHERS: Approximately 150 expatriate and local teachers.

QUALIFICATIONS: CELTA or equivalent plus university degree in English-related subject minimum. TBI teachers must meet Indonesian education department criteria, e.g. be aged 25–57. One year's experience. Aspiring teachers with degrees in English disciplines approved by the Indonesian Department of Education may be considered for contracts that include CELTA sponsorship.

PREFERENCE OF NATIONALITY: British, American, Canadian, Australian and New Zealander only (for visa reasons).

SALARY: Base salaries vary and are based on relative cost of living and number of teaching hours per week (22–24). Monthly salary after tax ranges from 10 million to 15 million rupiahs. End-of-contract bonuses and airfare contributions are also paid.

FACILITIES/SUPPORT: Free health insurance coverage, settling-in loan, work permits and documentation paid. 6 weeks' paid leave per annum. Professional development programme of workshops and observed teaching with feedback. Good career development prospects, including supervisory positions.

RECRUITMENT: Local hire or distance. Local applicants must teach a demonstration lesson. Distance applicants must complete tasks and have a Skype/telephone interview.

JAPAN

Despite the Prime Minister's repeated attempts to stimulate the Japanese economy, which has stagnated for decades, growth remains elusive. Wages never rise and deflation remains stubbornly in place. However, in the run-up to the Tokyo Olympics in 2020, and ever increasing numbers of international tourists choosing Japan, a desire to master English is still in the ascendancy. The marketplace in which English-language academies are now competing may have shrunk since the glory days but it is still a flourishing industry. Groups of *eikaiwa* (conversation schools) remain in business, alongside thousands of independent English schools in Tokyo, Osaka and many other Japanese cities which hire *gaijins* (foreigners) to teach. Many are still eager to hire native speakers of English with no teaching qualification as long as they have a university degree and preferably some relevant experience.

The demand among Japanese people to learn English from native speakers will survive, no matter what. One of the booming areas of the market is the teaching of English to pre-school and primary-aged children. English has become compulsory for fifth and sixth grade pupils (from age 10) throughout Japan, and many parents are sending their children to cram schools in order to prepare them. Some lessons in Japanese secondary schools are taught using the medium of English. Japanese families devote a colossal percentage of their household income to promoting education, and English language schools are among the main beneficiaries.

The basic monthly salary of 250,000 yen for full-time entry-level EFL teachers has not risen for a dozen years, which is less at the current exchange rate than it was a few years ago. Wages are of course meaningless without balancing them against the local cost of living, which is notoriously high. The availability of part-time work has risen at the expense of full-time jobs. People used to say that you can't expect to break even and begin to save before you've been in Japan for at least a year, but the cost of living has stabilised and many teachers who live frugally do manage to save. Developments such as the increase in the number of '100 yen shops' (the equivalent of 'pound shops' or 'dollar stores') have made it easier to outfit an apartment or buy teaching materials at reasonable prices.

A university degree is a prerequisite for getting a teaching job, simply because it is a requirement for a work visa. However, despite the increase in competition for teaching jobs, there is still surprisingly little emphasis on TEFL qualifications. Image and personality are of paramount importance to the Japanese and many employers are more concerned to find people who are lively and a touch glamorous than they are to find people with a background in teaching.

As long as your expectations are realistic, Japan should turn out to be a rewarding choice of destination. Native English speakers are hired in a surprising range of corporate and other contexts: in-house language programmes in steel or electronics companies, state secondary schools, hot-house crammers, 'conversation lounges' where young people get together for an hour's guided conversation, vocational schools where English is a compulsory subject, 'ladies' classes' (quaintly so-called) where courses called 'English for Shopping' are actually offered, and also classes of children from as young as two, since it has become a status symbol in Japan to send children of all ages to English classes. In fact, studying English for many Japanese is still more a social than an educational activity.

Culture shock grips most new arrivals to Japan. Incoming teachers are often so distracted by the mechanics of life in Japan and the cultural adjustments they have to make to survive that they devote too little energy to the business of teaching. On the other hand, anyone who has a genuine interest in Japan and who arrives reasonably well prepared may find that a year or two in Japan provides a wonderful experience.

PROSPECTS FOR TEACHERS

Jobs teaching English in Japan can be looked for in a variety of establishments from kindergartens (increasingly popular) to universities (difficult to crack until you have been living in Japan for years). Most private language schools in Japan are looking for native English speakers with a bachelor's degree and possibly some TEFL experience. Although only a minority are looking for professional qualifications in their teachers, there has been a noticeable increase in the number of qualified EFL teachers (especially from Australia) looking for work, and naturally schools prefer to take them over complete novices.

Old Japan-hand **Joseph Tame** reported on his blog that he was interviewed by an agency recruiting teachers: '*CELTA was once again highlighted by the interviewers as one of the main reasons they'd contacted me in the first place – it's good to know that it has an impact in the real world recruitment*.' Many schools have no set intake dates and serious applications are welcome at any time of the year, though most contracts begin in April and finish the following March (i.e. one year), which corresponds to the academic year. Try to avoid starting your job hunt during Golden Week at the end of April or Obon in mid-August when no one is in work mode.

The demand for Business English and TOEIC (Test of English for International Communication) preparatory courses is considerable. Japanese workers who have paid employment insurance for over three years are eligible to take courses with accredited learning institutions and claim a portion of the cost back from the government. The growth in the demand for Business English is also due to companies expecting new recruits to be able to communicate in English in an increasingly global marketplace. In fact one maverick boss of a giant e-commerce company, Rakuten, decreed a few years ago that all meetings and correspondence would be conducted in English.

The favoured accent is certainly American and to a lesser extent Canadian. In fact, not many Japanese can distinguish a Scot from a Queenslander, or an Eastender from an Eastsider. What can be detected and is highly prized is clear speech. Slow, precise diction together with a smart appearance and professional bearing are necessary to impress some potential employers. One way round this is that Skype and telephone teaching have penetrated the language-teaching market.

FINDING A JOB

University graduates shouldn't find it too difficult landing a job before arrival, which means the employer can sort out visas and help with initial orientation and housing. The disadvantage is that the salary and working conditions will probably compare unfavourably with those of teachers who have negotiated their job after arrival; but most new recruits (*nama gaijin*, or raw foreigners) conclude that the trade-off is a fair one. Of course the pool of foreign job-seekers already in Japan is large enough that the jobs offering good conditions tend to be snapped up quickly. Some organisations do not welcome speculative applications from outside Japan, and quite a few advertisements specify that they will consider only candidates who already have the right visa. By contrast, the giant companies like Gaba, Interac and Aeon (see entries) mount ambitious recruitment drives in North America, the UK and Australia. One of these mass-market *eikaiwa* hired **John Ramage** a few years ago:

> ***After several frustrating trips to London, I did manage to get a job, which seemed like falling through an open door. Interac interviewed me in Edinburgh, rather close to home, and it was a positive experience. I arrived in Japan just in time for the cherry blossom, and I met many memorable people. I started learning to write Japanese. My experiences were so vivid that my life back home and in the West generally seemed less real.***

One of the best ways of arranging a job in advance is to join the Japan Exchange and Teaching (JET) Programme, which is a prestigious government-sponsored programme that offers what many consider to be a 'dream job' for new graduates (described in detail below). Whereas at one time the majority of ALTs (Assistant Language Teachers) in the public school system entered Japan as JET participants, many are now hired by private language-teaching companies known as 'dispatch companies', which do not always enjoy a favourable reputation. In fact **Del Ford**, with many years' teaching experience in East Asian countries, takes a decidedly dim view of this shift:

> ***Now, many of the public school ALT jobs are filled by the poor saps who accept dispatch company contracts. These companies represent pure evil: low salaries, no benefits, no support system, no paid airfare, health insurance, etc. I really think a section in your next edition should include a blurb on the pitfalls of working for these gangsters. Some smaller eikaiwa outfits have this type of nonsense for ads: '200,000 yen per month, prefer experience, basic Japanese language ability, TEFL Cert., International Driving Licence, etc.' Simply put, it's gotten grimmer over the last decade.***

A third route is to be hired directly as an ALT by a local education authority, as **Will Mercer** describes:

> ***In practice, your roles and responsibilities are identical to that of the other ALTs but, generally speaking, the salary and benefits are more in line with that offered by the JET programme. As you are hired by your local education authority you tend to have a closer relationship with your bosses. In my case, I dislocated my knee at my school's judo club and had to have an operation. I stayed in hospital for over two weeks and missed several weeks of work but was given a very high level of support and help from both my fellow teachers and employers at city hall and was later able to return to my post. I'm sure that wouldn't have been the case if I had been employed by a private ALT dispatch company.***
>
> ***These direct-hire positions also have the potential for real longevity. Some of my colleagues had held their job for a number of years, certainly more than the maximum of five offered by the JET programme.***

It seems that the proportion of direct hires is increasing over the number of dispatch-company hires, a trend that is likely to continue as education authorities realise they don't need a middle man. Direct-hire positions are not always well advertised. The first one **Will Mercer** got was after he made a speculative application, and the second position was posted on www.jobsinjapan.com.These ALT positions tend to go to strong candidates who have already been in Japan for a couple of years.

THE JET PROGRAMME

JET is an official Japanese government scheme aimed at improving foreign language teaching in schools and fostering good relations between the people of Japan and the 47 participating countries (www.jetprogramme.org). The programme has been in existence since 1987 and is now responsible for placing about 4,300 native English speakers for a minimum contract of one year in state junior and senior high schools within Japan, an increasing number in rural areas. Many consider the emphasis to be more on cultural exchange than on English teaching. The programme's number have been increasing, after a long period of decline. The long-term plan is to provide native English-speaker teachers to all primary, junior and high schools. The government is also moving towards making a Test of English as a Foreign Language compulsory for entry to and graduation from college, which would galvanise the demand for tuition.

The majority of JET participants are from the USA (contact details below). Britain annually recruits graduates to the programme and JET is among the largest employers of new graduates after the UK government. Acceptance has become more competitive and the prospects for people who become ALTs in English on the JET Programme are excellent. Any UK national who is under 40 with a bachelor's degree and an interest in Japan is eligible to apply.

In the UK the scheme is administered by the JET Desk at the Embassy of Japan, 101–104 Piccadilly, London, W1J 7JT (✆ +44 20 7465 6668; ukjet@ld.mofa.go.jp; www.jet-uk.org). Non-British applicants should contact the Japanese Embassy in their country of origin for information and application forms. US applicants can obtain details from any of the 16 consulates in the USA or from the JET Office: Japanese Embassy, 2520 Massachusetts Avenue NW, Washington, DC 20008 (✆ +1 202 238 6772/3; jetprograms@ws.mofa.go.jp; www.jetprogramusa.org).

The timetable for applicants from the UK is as follows: application forms are available online from early October; the deadline for applications is the last Friday in November; interviews are held in January and February; an intensive two-day orientation for successful candidates is held in London at the start of July and departures for Japan take place in late July/August.

Robert Mizzi from Canada worked hard on his application, which paid off since he was called to an interview:

> ***The interview was probably the most difficult interview I have ever had. It was only 20 minutes, but a painful 20 minutes. Besides the usual 'why' and 'tell us about yourself' questions, I was asked to teach a lesson on the spot using dramatic techniques I would use in class. Stunned, I managed to get out of my seat and draw some pictures of the stars and moon on the board, taught them the meaning of those words and then proceeded to ask the interview team to stand up and learn a little dance to the song 'Twinkle Twinkle Little Star'. All I wanted to do was to create an impression and to stand out of the 300 people being interviewed. People remember you best when you are acting like a complete fool. When it is teaching English as a foreign language, the ability to act like a fool is one of the main requirements of the job. Getting Japanese men in suits up and dancing during a job interview with the prestigious JET programme was a half-crazed risk, but a successful one at that.***

Often government-run exchanges of this kind do not offer generous remuneration packages; however, pay and conditions on the JET scheme are excellent. In addition to a free return flight, JET participants receive 3,360,000 yen a year (£23,900/$29,750). This is the salary before income and inhabitant taxes have been paid (though some participants are exempt) and there are further social and medical insurance fees of 40,000 yen a month. The salary is standard for all JET participants. Contracts are with individual contracting organisations in Japan, so there can be discrepancies in working conditions. It is the luck of the draw that determines who goes where, although stated preferences will be taken into consideration. Any income tax and pension contributions can be refunded after you leave Japan, though it is a big palaver.

ALTs are theoretically expected to work a seven-hour day and quite often teachers are assigned an average of three classes a day; however, hours spent in the classroom will vary between placements. **Mark Elliot** feels that the JET programme is 'probably the best job in the world' and described his situation:

> ***I lived on a wonderful island, three hours' ferry ride from Nagasaki, nearer Shanghai than Tokyo. There was a lot more to the job than teaching. After all, the programme was just as much about meeting people and participating in cultural exchange as it was about teaching.***

All JET participants teach in partnership with a native Japanese teacher so those without significant teaching experience are not thrown in at the deep end. The degree of responsibility varies depending on the relationship built with the Japanese teacher, with some ALTs effectively teaching the class in large part by themselves. Unfortunately this was not the case for **Charlotte Steggall** from Suffolk, who majored in Japanese and TESOL at university and was serious about pursuing TESOL at a master's level and as a career. She felt the ALT role to be of little actual value, but rather felt they were treated as 'singing, dancing white people to wheel out and show off in events in the town'. This was not what she signed up for, yet she loved the students and so agreed to stay on for a second year:

> ***What I do depends on which teacher I'm working with. Some ask me to do a 10-minute game in a lesson, some ask me to be a living tape recorder, some ask me to do full classes. Training Japanese teachers to work with ALTs is very hit and miss, and most have no idea what to do with us. What we do has little meaning to the kids, who***

see us and say 'Yay! She's here today so we get to play games!' They would never ask us to do a lesson to prepare for a test, or anything else with responsibility. I love teaching. But we are here mainly to allow country kids to interact with us and to overcome racism for when they are older. When I try to help or do something more because I have passion, I am batted down again.

I have a lot of spare time at work. I study Japanese, read books, use the internet. After school, I earn more money and brush up my teaching skills by doing private lessons, which allows me to break free and try different teaching styles.

Other teachers are delighted with the easy timetable. As **Rabindra Roy** wrote from Shizuoka prefecture, '*I can think of very few jobs where a freshly qualified graduate with an irrelevant degree and no experience can walk straight into such a big salary for this little work.*' He also describes the programme as '*desperately well organised*'. But partly because of the variety in locations and schools and partly because Japan is such a weird and wonderful place, it is impossible to predict what life will be like, no matter how many orientations you attend. About two-thirds of JET participants renew their contract, which indicates its success. A third of the second-years stay for a third year, with five years being the maximum a candidate can stay. The programme offers a tremendous amount of support and even those who are placed in remote or rural areas are usually within striking distance of other JET participants. In retrospect, **Susannah Kerr** who taught for a private company in Tokyo was not too sorry to have been turned down by JET because its teachers have little control over where they are sent and end up in small towns (however, she wouldn't have minded a JET salary).

IN ADVANCE

There are many other ways to fix up a job in Japan ahead of time, though these will usually require more initiative than embarking on the JET selection process. Some Japanese language schools have formed links with university careers departments, particularly in the USA and Canada, so anyone with a university connection should exploit it.

One or two language training organisations operate on a huge scale, with many branches and large numbers of staff. For instance AEON (see entry) has recruiting offices in New York and Los Angeles as well as Tokyo, and Interac interviews in cities throughout English-speaking countries. They want to interview anyone with a university degree and a perfect command of English. AEON's sister company, Amity Teachers, recruits many teachers of children for its 85 schools throughout Japan (www.amityteachers.com/teaching).

Some chains have been described as factory English schools, where teachers are handed a course book and told not to deviate from the formula. They depend on a steady supply of fresh graduates who want the chance to spend a year or two in Japan. Often new recruits do not have much say in where they are sent and in their first year may be sent to the least desirable locations, as **John Ramage** discovered after a successful interview with Interac in the UK:

I was so keen to go to Japan that I accepted a job in a very rural location. I knew this could be problematic and I was right, it was. Coming with limited funds meant I could not afford to buy a laptop and have internet, which might have made things bearable. I tried to be frugal but found the isolation hard to take. Later I moved to Tokyo, with Shane English School and stayed for much longer. After suffocating small towns I found Tokyo positively exciting.

For its recruitment in the UK, Shane English Schools relies on its partner agencies like Saxoncourt Recruitment and TEFL in Japan (London W1; www.tefl-in-japan.com). An energetic agency operating mainly online is TEFLOne Recruitment (www.teflone.com), which also recruits for Shane in Japan as well as for other countries in the Far East. A major employer is iTTTi Japan, which trades as Peppy Kids Club. The head office is in Nagoya but it has recruiting representatives in the UK, USA, Canada and Australia (see www.ittti.com/pkc) as well as an online application system. The company hires 400 native English speakers from overseas to work in its network of 1,300 children's conversation classrooms all over Japan, with the exception of Central Tokyo and the islands of Okinawa. With 70 schools, the US-centric IB Group based in Funabashi City hires on a smaller scale but still needs scores of teachers mainly for Chiba prefecture (www.ib-group.jp/american/english/job.html). The giant Gaba Corporation (http://teaching-in-japan.gaba.co.jp) operates 42 Learning Studios around Tokyo, Osaka and in Nagoya where clients are taught individually, and in off-site corporate settings. Gaba vigorously recruits year round.

Quite often schools and groups of schools will appoint a foreign recruiter. Many schools have no need to advertise abroad as they receive so many speculative résumés (the American term for CV is used in Japan).

Of course the internet is a valuable job-search tool. The site www.teflsearch.com carries a large number of vacancies in Japan. Using any of the popular household search engines, type 'English teaching in Japan' and dozens of job-related websites will appear. *O-Hayo-Sensei* (which means 'good morning teacher') has pages of teaching positions across Japan at www.ohayosensei.com. Many ads specify that 'candidates must currently reside in Japan'. The site www.Jobsinjapan.com is also excellent. *ELT News* (www.eltnews.com/jobs) lists ELT jobs around Japan, again mostly for candidates already in Japan, and the site carries news, classroom ideas, etc. for ELT teachers in Japan. It is a good idea to send your CV to the big employers before arrival, make some follow-up calls and hope to arrange some interviews in your first week.

Once you have some international experience of teaching, particularly of IELTS testing, you can aim to fix up short lucrative contracts as **Steph Fuccio** and her husband **Evan** did for a three-month period:

> *Nagoya is a very 'livable' city, a million times more so than Tokyo was. My love for bicycling was rekindled along with a craving for sushi. We worked for a company called Westgate Corporation both in Nagoya and Tokyo. It's a very reputable, trustworthy organisation. I would do this programme again in a heartbeat, it's that easy and lucrative.*

The Westgate Corporation has been providing English-language instruction programmes for corporations, residents, public schools and universities since 1983 and operates an online application programme (www.westgate.co.jp). Rates of pay are higher than at some of the other big companies and they offer flight reimbursement.

ON THE SPOT

As has been mentioned, native English speakers with a bachelor's degree have a chance of landing a job as an English teacher on arrival in Japan. The crucial question is how long will it take. The murderous cost of living means that job-hunters spend hundreds of dollars or pounds very quickly while engaged in the time-consuming business of answering ads, sending round CVs and going for interviews.

Travis Ball from Los Angeles set off on what he intended to be five years of world travels and chose Japan as his first destination because he had come to the conclusion that it would be one of the easier countries to find work teaching English without any experience or certificates:

> *I was basically sitting in my travellers' hotel room in Osaka sending out as many résumés as I could while attempting not to spend any money. I started by sending emails to every address listed in the chapter on Japan in your book and kept looking using the web and other resources. After filling out an online application and sending my résumé to a big chain, I was asked if I could attend an interview in Tokyo, which took place over two days and included a couple of tests and a mock 20-minute lesson we all had to prepare the evening before the second day. I was told that I had a job in a very small rural school (one other teacher who was Japanese and a manager). With hindsight I would probably have voiced my preference for a bigger city with more going on. That being said, I think it was my flexibility that helped me get the job in the first place.*

Joseph Tame from Herefordshire arrived in Tokyo with two big advantages, a working holiday visa and a Japanese girlfriend (now wife) with whom he could stay:

Having spent virtually all of my travel funds in my first 21 days in the city, I eventually decided to face the fact that I'd have to find a job, for a couple of months at least. What with all this talk of a global recession, I really didn't feel too positive. Furthermore I have virtually no experience teaching, have no teaching qualifications and indeed no university degree, which all employers insist on. My first stop was the Japan Association for Working Holiday Makers. I was fortunate in that as I was being registered, a phone call came through from a private English school who were desperate for a teacher. Thirty minutes later I had a job paying £17 an hour. The catch was that it was only four hours per week, but that was my pocket money taken care of. I actually spent time surfing the web in an attempt to remember what pronouns and adjectives are; I only ever remember that a verb is a 'doing' word.

Later Joseph Tame made good use of www.gaijinpot.com, which remains a superb resource for jobs, accommodation and news for foreign residents in Japan. He also recommends www.getstudents.net for those wanting to teach English (or other languages). Other teacher–student matching services are at www.senseibank.com, www.findstudents.net, www.hello-sensei.com/en/sensei and www.watashino-sensei.biz/teacher_site.html. You simply enter the relevant information about what you teach, what area of Japan you teach in, how much you charge, etc. and the students will come to you.

GaijinPot (www.gaijinpot.com) is the largest job site for foreigners and has a near monopoly on the English teaching jobs in Japan among the English conversation schools, dispatch schools (for teaching in the public schools) and everything in between. The site stores more than 150,000 résumés, most of which are searchable by potential employers. GaijinPot is also a useful general portal for foreigners in Japan, with popular forums for sharing information, experiences and questions.

One potentially useful site is *Tokyo Notice Board* (www.tokyonoticeboard.co.jp). A typical advertisement randomly selected might read: *'We are seeking an energetic, gregarious and reliable job applicant who wishes to share their experience with Japanese Community. Part-time job (1,000–1,500 yen per hour free talk; 2,160 yen per hour for teaching a lesson; 3,000 yen for a dispatch lesson).'* A 'dispatch lesson' is a private lesson given at company premises.

Few things could be more intimidating for the EFL teacher than to arrive at Narita International Airport with no job and limited resources. The longer the job-hunt takes, the faster the finances dwindle and the more nerve-racking and discouraging the situation becomes. One way to lessen the monumentality of the initial struggle would be to get out of Tokyo straightaway. Although there are more jobs in the capital, there is also more competition from other foreigners, to the point of saturation. Enterprising teachers who are willing to step off the conveyor belt, which takes job-seekers from the airport to one of Tokyo's many '*gaijin* houses' (hostels for foreigners) may well encounter fewer setbacks. Osaka seems a good bet since it is within commuting distance of the whole Kansai area, including Kobe, which is 20 minutes away by train. In Osaka the cost of living is as much as a quarter less than it is in Tokyo. Another promising destination is Sapporo in the north, the fifth largest city in the country. **Ken Foye**, a reader of this book, chose to teach on Hokkaido, the northern island on which Sapporo is located:

I have been teaching here for a year and a half now and I would recommend Hokkaido to anyone, especially those who don't find living in a large urban metropolis very appealing. Here the people seem much friendlier than in Tokyo, the cost of living isn't as high, there's fresh air and the scenery is magnificent. And I probably would not have ended up here if not for your book.

A company called Atlas (www.atlasp.net) provides one-to-one English language lessons both online and face-to-face in Sapporo, Yokohama, Nagoya and Osaka.

After the large company that employed her collapsed, **Susannah Kerr** swiftly began 'on the spot' job-hunting courtesy of websites such as www.gaijinpot.com. She considered a large employer, Gaba (mentioned above), which specialises in one-to-one teaching and offers the advantage of being able to choose your hours. The disadvantage is that earnings are dependent on your popularity as a teacher, since students vote with their feet. Susannah was interviewed by a company called Balloon Kids (www.bkje.co.jp) which employs up to 20 teachers and pays 200,000–250,000 yen per month. Instead of working from its own institute, the company hires rooms in (for example) suburban shopping malls, where 12–15 kids show up. The teacher would be expected to go to an office to pick up teaching materials and a key, and then let him/herself into the room, so there would be no contact with other teachers.

The six-month contract that Susannah eventually accepted was with MLS (see entry for Model Language Studio), a school that uses a proprietary Drama Method to teach English. With 30 branches in Tokyo and Yokohama, it is a small company by Japanese standards. Susannah was impressed with the efficacy of the method, and because the teachers were '*interesting, creative, often musical types, the children were often engaged and excited, and their spoken English really did improve. The teachers were always trying to use attention-grabbing games like charades.*'

TOKYO

One of the most often recommended places to start a job hunt in Tokyo is the Kimi Information Center (Oscar Building, 8th Floor, 2 42 3 Ikebukuro, Toshima-ku, Tokyo 171 0014; ✆ +81 3 3986 1604; kiminfo@kimiwillbe.com). Its website (www.kimiwillbe.com) carries teaching job adverts. Like so many postal addresses in Japan, it is difficult to find without a map (print one off from its website or follow these detailed directions: from Ikebukuro station take the West Exit, walk straight past the McDonald's for one block and turn right when you see Marui Department Store. Go three blocks past SMBC Bank. Kimi is on the right).

The Kimi Center offers extensive services for foreigners such as a translation service, free guided tours with Japanese students as well as advising on cheap short and long-term accommodation, where tenants are not liable for key money. If you register with it online, you can receive information about new jobs daily. With this free service, Kimi can assist with searching for a suitable job and even setting up interviews.

Another useful source of guidance for new arrivals on a working holiday programme (described in the next section) is the Japan Association for Working Holiday Makers (www.jawhm.or.jp/eng), whose services are available to those with the appropriate visa (see section on Regulations below). They post vacancies on their own searchable job board (www.job-board.info). **Joseph Tame** was a satisfied customer when he was on the programme:

> ***My first stop was the JAWHM, whose office was 20 minutes by bicycle from where I was staying. They were very helpful. After registering I had access to their lists of jobs. Essentially it's a job centre for foreigners. They also have the latest copies of all the relevant magazines and newspapers with sits vacant columns. They will advise on housing, etc.***

Even tourist offices such as the one at Hibuya station (exit A-3) have free noticeboards where private lessons may be sought or offered, as well as accommodation. **Amanda Searle** describes what she found when she was job-hunting:

> ***Most companies give little idea in their adverts of the hours and salary, let alone the age and number of students or the textbooks used. They are not very willing to give that information over the phone, explaining that you will get the opportunity to ask questions if you are called for interview. I sent cover letters out with my résumé, explaining that I was looking only for full-time positions which offered visa sponsorship. I sent out about 20 applications and about 10 companies contacted me and I went to eight interviews. I ended up being offered two full-time positions and three part-time ones.***

The initial phone call is very important and should be considered as a preliminary interview. Since you may be competing with as many as 100 people answering the same ad, you have to try to stand out over the phone. Speak slowly, clearly, and be very *genki*, which means bubbly and fun. You may be asked to send your CV to them electronically; the cover letter should be short and intelligent, and the CV should be brief and interesting, emphasising any teaching experience. Always carry a supply of professional-looking business cards (*meishi*).

Demonstration lessons form an integral part of most job interviews in Japan, regardless of one's qualifications. Try to prepare yourself as much as possible, if only because travelling to an interview in Tokyo is a major undertaking which can take up to three hours and cost a lot of money; it would be a shame to blow your chances because of a simple oversight. Dress as impeccably and conservatively as possible, and carry a respectable briefcase, since books are often judged by their covers in Japan. Inside you should have any education certificates you have earned, preferably the originals, since schools have long since realised that a lot of forgeries are in circulation. Your résumé should not err on the side of modesty.

REGULATIONS

Britons, Irish, Canadians, Australians and New Zealanders (among a few other, non-English speaking, countries) are eligible to apply for a working holiday visa for Japan; details can be found at www.uk.emb-japan.go.jp/en/visa/working-holiday.html.

Applicants must be aged 18–30. Applicants must show that they have sufficient financial backing, i.e. savings of £2,500, or £1,500 and a return flight. Visa holders may accept paid work in Japan for up to 12 months, provided it is incidental to their travels. The quota of working holiday visas for Britons is 1,000. Note that applications are accepted from April and once the allocation has been filled, no more visas will be granted until April of the following year.

Some schools rely on a stream of Canadians, Australians and New Zealanders on working holiday visas, which they must obtain in their home countries through the SWAP Japan Programme. SWAP allows Canadians aged 18–30 to work for six months in the first instance but is extendable to 12 months. To qualify you must prove that you have $2,500 at your disposal.

For those ineligible for a working holiday visa, the key to obtaining a work visa for Japan is to have a Japanese sponsor. Documents which will help you to find a sponsoring employer are the original or notarised copy of your bachelor's or other degree and résumé. Most teachers are sponsored by their employers, although on rare occasions it is possible for the sponsor to be a private citizen. Not all schools by any means are willing to sponsor their teachers, unless they are persuaded that they are an ongoing proposition. If your visa is to be processed before arrival, you must have a definite job appointment in Japan. Your employer must apply to the Ministry of Justice in Tokyo for a Certificate of Eligibility which he or she then forwards to you. You must take this along with a photocopy of it, your passport, photograph and application form to any Consulate General of Japan. The regulations stipulate that anyone who works in Higher Education must have an MA in Education or TEFL. Sponsoring schools warn that the visa application process takes between three and five months.

The UK and US have a visa exemption arrangement with Japan whereby they can stay for up to 90 days with a possibility of extending for a further 90 days. It is possible to enter Japan, look for work and then apply for a work visa. Those found to be overstaying as tourists can be deported. Furthermore, employers who are caught employing illegal aliens, as well as the foreign workers themselves, are subject to huge fines, and both parties risk imprisonment.

Finding an employer to sponsor you for a work visa is very important. A number of schools advertising for teachers state in their ads that they are willing to consider only those who are in Japan and already have a work visa. Whereas previously it was necessary for the teacher to leave the country, at great personal expense, to change their visa status (the Korean Visa Tour), these days the teacher need only take their Certificate of Eligibility into the local immigration office, where the visa will be processed. However, those on a student visa still need to leave the country to complete the visa process. According to **Alan Suter** the cheapest way is to take a ferry from Kobe to Busan, Korea. The work visa may be valid for 6 months, 12 months or 3 years. After you have worked for one year on a work visa, you can renew it for a further three years. When renewing, one of the most important requirements is a tax statement showing your previous year's earnings. It is difficult to obtain a new visa unless you can show that you have earned at least 250,000 yen per month. Cash-in-hand and part-time jobs may be lucrative but they do nothing to help your visa application. If you break your contract with your employer, you will have to find another sponsor willing to act as sponsor the following year.

You are permitted to work up to 20 hours a week on a cultural or student visa. Cultural visas are granted to foreigners interested in studying some aspect of traditional Japanese culture on a full-time basis. In this case you must find a teacher willing to sponsor you. Cultural visas are often granted for *shodo* (calligraphy), *taiko* (drumming), karate, aikido, *ikebana* (flower arranging) and *ochakai* (tea ceremony). At one time these study visas were liberally handed out but nowadays you must produce concrete evidence that you actually are studying.

Teachers usually have the basic rate of national income tax in Japan (6%–7%) withdrawn at source. Deductions for tax and social security as of 2016 normally total 7,000–8,000 yen per month.

CONDITIONS OF WORK

Despite the high cost of living, most teachers seem to be able to save money without having to lead too frugal an existence. Some even save half their salary in their first year by avoiding eating out and going to the cinema. **Antoinette Sarpong** spent one year teaching in Osaka and preferred to enjoy herself to saving:

> ***I enjoyed Osaka's nightlife thoroughly. I also opted to save for travel, so I only put a small dent in my student loans. Having said that, I lived very comfortably and had a lot of friends who did save quite a bit of money because they stuck to a budget. Japan is an expensive country but it is possible to save heaps of money if you stick to a budget. I would also suggest living rurally, if you can – less temptation than the big cities.***

The longer you work in Japan the higher the salary and better the working conditions you can command. Rank beginners outside Tokyo and Osaka can earn as little as 200,000 yen a month, but the steady average of 252,000 yen persists almost everywhere. Perks such as increments for higher qualifications, end-of-contract bonuses, free Japanese lessons and travel tickets, etc. are in fairly wide evidence. Teaching schedules can be exhausting. Teachers are increasingly asked to work 'outside their job description', helping out with advertising, student retention and the sale of study materials. Some companies organise informal conversation sessions with native speakers. The companies look for outgoing, reliable people to work as chat hosts who can lead lively conversations with a diverse clientele in exchange for a low hourly wage of 1,000–1,500 yen. One company called Leafcup English Café and School (www.leafcup.com/job.php) facilitates chat sessions between native speakers and learners, and has become stricter about the visa status of the people it hires.

Timetables may be announced at the last minute, though it is more difficult to opt out in Japan than in other countries because of the dedication Japanese workers show to their firms. Some schools remain open all weekend and on public holidays too.

One of the advantages of working in state schools (as JET teachers and other ALTs do) is that they close for holidays, usually three weeks at Christmas and two weeks in August between semesters. Most schools offer one-week holidays (paid or unpaid or a combination of the two) at the start of May (the 'Golden Week') and in the middle of August ('Obon vacation'). Holidays for those lucky enough to work in institutes of higher education are much more generous.

Private tutoring is still lucrative, paying from 3,000 yen an hour. **Susannah Kerr** managed to hold on to six hours of private teaching a week (teaching three children in one family), which netted her 18,000 yen, enough to eat. Occasionally you will meet someone who has been paid $100 just to have dinner with a language learner and converse in English, but these plums are few and far between.

THE STUDENTS

The stereotype of the diligent Japanese pupil has become somewhat outmoded. The younger generation of Japanese is not always willing to play by the rules that their elders lay down, and there is increasing tension in schools which may manifest itself in (mildly) unruly behaviour. But mostly teachers find their students eager, attentive and willing to confer great respect on their teachers, and in some out-of-the-way places even celebrity status. All teachers are expected to look the part and most schools will insist on proper dress (e.g. suits and dresses). But they do not want a formal approach to teaching.

Adults will have studied English at school for at least six years, and their knowledge of grammar is usually sound. They go to conversation schools in the expectation of meeting native English-speaker teachers able to deliver creative and entertaining lessons. Yet some are crippled by diffidence or excessive anxiety about grammatical correctness. **Michael Frost** is one teacher who experienced a clash of cultures when trying to encourage discussion in his classroom:

> ***It is very difficult for Japanese students to come out and express an individual opinion. The best tactic is to get them in pairs, so that together they can work something out. They are more productive and open in pairs, and it takes the pressure off them. Then get the pairs into fours, to express a mini-group opinion, then work for a total group agreement. The thing to avoid at all costs is to stroll into class, saying, 'OK, today we are going to discuss environmental issues. Tetsuya, you set the ball rolling: What do you think of pollution?' It will not work.***

It is a popular myth that Japanese students have good reading abilities in English and require only conversation practice. This was not the experience of **Nathan Edwards**, a diploma-qualified teacher from Canada:

> ***I am currently teaching at the Tokyo YMCA College of English, a pioneer in English teaching in Japan, established in 1880. The fact is that both reading and speaking in English present major challenges even to students with years of English instruction in the Japanese school system. It is highly advisable for teachers to bring a good supply of realia with them (various English brochures, used tickets, maps, coins, etc.) and old lesson plans.***

Problems can arise in team-teaching situations if your Japanese colleague has not attained a high enough level of English. While teaching in the JET programme, **Robert Mizzi** came to admire Japanese culture, but he did find some aspects of his job frustrating:

> ***A lot of times I cannot introduce a game idea because, literally, it will take 20 minutes for the teacher to understand (never mind the students).***

Amanda Moody worked in a small school in Nagoya, where she taught pre-school children using a mixture of the 'Gentle Revolution' and Rosetta Stone software:

> ***My pupils were very smart and the children of successful Japanese. Some were the products of brain surgeons or music producers. Others were businessmen's kids. But most of them were reading and writing around the age of three. Their parents expected the world of both us and their children.***

Amanda loved her students, but thought poorly of her employer, who fined teachers for 'infringements' such as 'smelled strange and suspicious acting: 500 yen fine'. Among the many strange aspects of Japanese culture is one which most foreigners find particularly disturbing. A native English speaker who happens to have non-Caucasian features will almost certainly be discriminated against.

ACCOMMODATION

It is not uncommon for teachers who are hired overseas to be given help with accommodation, which is a tremendously useful perk, even if the flat provided is small and over-priced, with poor insulation and a badly equipped kitchen, and located an hour away from work. Westgate for example arranges accommodation for all its teachers and then deducts the rent of 80,000 yen from wages. If you are on your own, you may be forced to use a foreigners' rental agency. Rental costs are likely to range from 50,000 yen to 75,000 yen per person per month (more in Tokyo, less in more distant prefectures). When you find a place through an agency, you will have to pay a commission of one month's rent.

When looking for accommodation on arrival in Tokyo, pick up a list of *gaijin* houses from an information or tourist office and look for ones which charge a monthly rather than a nightly rent, since these are the ones which attract long-term residents. Apple House (www.applehouse.ne.jp/english/applehouse.html) is recommended for being affordable, friendly and in a good location. A good place to look is Fontana Co (✆ +81 3 3382 0289; www.tokyocityapartments.net), which provides an excellent service. Because it is so difficult to rent flats, some teachers continue living in *gaijin* houses after they find work. Many foreigners live and work in the Roppongi district of Tokyo.

A couple of years ago, **Susannah Kerr** rented a two-bedroom flat in a nice traditional Tokyo neighbourhood of Kagurazaka for 160,000 yen a month, but when her flatmates moved on and she had to pay the rent by herself, she decided to move. Even when accompanied by a local, using a local rental agency proved impossible so she used an English-speaking rental agency to find a one-bedroom apartment for 80,000 yen in Okubo, a bustling 24-hour-a-day area known as Koreatown, with a mildly sleazy reputation but gradually improving. Foreign letting agencies offer the advantage of not insisting that you provide a local guarantor. The Sakura House agency, which caters for non-Japanese accommodation-seekers (www.sakura-house.com), has become a prominent feature of the accommodation landscape in Tokyo, but there are many others. Expect to pay 65,000–75,000 yen for a '1LDK' which refers to a small apartment consisting of one main room with kitchenette and bathroom.

A sizeable deposit called 'key money' is payable on signing a tenancy agreement, which can cause problems, as it did to **John Ramage**:

> ***A word of warning. I came to Japan with relatively little money. Interac will help you set up in a new place but they will offer you a loan because no one gets paid until they have been working for two months. It takes time for the loan to come through, and meanwhile there was a landlord on day one with his hand stretched out asking for £1,000 of key money. So, I used my credit card in an ATM. Bad move. My debt soared and this happened to other people too. Fortunately when I moved on to Tokyo, Interac returned part of the key money, and paid me the end-of-contract bonus, which was a great help.***

According to John, housing is more likely to be subsidised in Korea, Taiwan and China.

A further problem is the near total absence of furnished apartments because Japanese people do not like to use belongings that have been used by other people, which means you may have to go shopping for curtains and cookers on top of all your other expenses. Again, schools which normally hire foreign teachers may keep a stock of basic furnishings which they can lend to teachers. They may also have a member of staff willing to translate unpaid bills notices (a common affliction). If all this sounds too much hassle, perhaps staying in a *gaijin* house long term is not such a bad idea.

An alternative recommended by **Will Mercer** is a rental agency called Leopalace (http://en.leopalace21.com):

> ***I stayed in several different places during my time in Japan, and on three occasions I stayed in an apartment owned by Leopalace, a huge company that owns flats all over the country. Their website can be accessed in several languages and you can arrange to move in from outside Japan (I think). Their flats are relatively expensive and although they don't have key money they nonetheless charge a large amount in other move-on costs and administration fees. They have something of a mixed reputation amongst the foreigner community. Personally, I think they're a good place to start. They go out of their way to rent to foreigners and provide services and support in English. Their flats come in a handful of styles and are virtually identikit. Their flats tend to be new, very clean and to come with furnishings such as a washing machine, fridge, microwave, TV, internet, etc. On the other hand they're generally pretty small and the walls are quite thin. I had to move from Gunma prefecture to Osaka at short notice and so chose Leopalace because it was the most convenient option. I saw the flat I wanted on their website and arranged a viewing over the phone. As I had lived in one of these flats previously I knew exactly what I was getting, in fact the flats were identical down to the tiniest detail, despite being located several hundred kilometres apart. As I didn't have time to visit the local estate agents it was the perfect solution for me, at least in that situation.***

John Ramage paid an inflated rent for the convenience of staying in an apartment provided by Shane in Tokyo and suggests ways to keep the cost of living down:

> ***In Tokyo internet cafés are expensive if you use them a lot, but an internet connection to your house is cheap. It took me a while to find the cheap shops. The 100-yen shops sell cheap stuff for the house and the recycle shop is where you get second-hand electric goods, which is helpful because Japanese flats tend to be unfurnished.***

Obviously it is to your advantage to live as close to your place of work as possible but, as noted above, many teachers are forced to spend a sizeable chunk of their earnings and a lot of time commuting. Ask your employer to pay for your travel, preferably in the form of a monthly travel pass, which can be used for your leisure travel as well. If you're in Tokyo, bear in mind that city buses charge a flat fare of 210 yen.

LEISURE TIME

According to some veteran teachers, leisure time and how to spend it will be the least of your worries. Depending on your circumstances, you may be expected to participate in extra-curricular activities and social events which it would cause offence to decline and will eat up lots of your leisure time. Although **Bryn Thomas** enjoyed the sushi which his school provided for teachers still at work at 9pm, he was less keen on the '*office parties when teachers were required to dress up in silly costumes and be nice to the students*'. Most teachers are happy to accept occasional invitations to socialise with their Japanese colleagues or students, even if it does mean an evening of speaking very, very slowly and drinking heavily. Many teachers find the socialising with students fun if expensive. Knowing a *gaijin* is a considerable status symbol for many Japanese, many of whom are willing to pay good money just for you to go to their houses once a week and eat their food.

But it is not like that everywhere. A glut of westerners in Tokyo means that your welcome may be less than enthusiastic. In fact non-Japanese are refused entrance to some Tokyo bars and restaurants. Many people head straight out of Tokyo for the more appealing city of Osaka. **Julie Fast** describes the contrast:

> ***I am still enamoured of Osaka; it is like a village after Tokyo. I am constantly amazed at the trees we see everywhere. I never realised in Tokyo how much I hated being constantly surrounded by people. I never had personal space in Tokyo. No one does – which explains the distant, sour looks on most people's faces. What a difference in Osaka. Osaka people have the roughest reputation in all of Japan. From a western point of view, they are the friendliest. I have been invited to houses for lunch, children say hello and people in shops actually talk to you. Which proves you can't judge a country by its largest city.***

All cities are expensive. Any entertainment which smacks of the West, such as going out to a fashionable coffee house or a nightclub, will be absurdly expensive. However, if you are content with more modest indigenous food and pastimes, you will be able to save money. A filling bowl of soba noodles from a corner shop costs £3, though you may never take to the standard breakfast of boiled rice and a raw egg. Convenience stores sell tasty rice balls (*onigri*) which cost about 150 yen. Kappazushi is a reasonably priced chain of conveyor-belt sushi restaurants (*kaiten-zushi*) where all the plates are charged at a fixed 100 yen. Also look for all-you-can-drink *nomihoudai* pubs for a good night out.

Staying home to listen to Japanese-language tapes or to read a good book (e.g. *Pictures from the Water Trade*, a personal account of life in Japan) costs nothing. Obviously the more settled you become, the more familiar you will be with the bargains and affordable amusements. For example, while some Tokyo superclubs impose a cover charge equal to $40, **Susannah Kerr** found much cheaper ones and in fact one where she got to know the DJs was free.

Learning to live cheaply is easier in small towns, but there will be fewer entertainments. **Travis Ball** had to depend on his own resources to fill his leisure time:

> ***Unfortunately, due to the rural nature of where I was living, there wasn't really a whole lot to do with my spare time. In addition to a lack of activities, the weather was much colder than what I was used to at home in California and this limited my getting around via bike and on foot. I tried to use the time to work on personal projects such as teaching myself how to cook and working on my photography. I was occasionally able to organise day trips with my co-worker and some students, but found myself on my own more often than not. I took the time to develop a personal travel blog for flashpackers (www.flashpackerhq.com) that I'm still working on to this day.***

Finding your way around is nothing if not a challenge in a country where almost all road and public transport signs are incomprehensible. On the other hand things are easier than they were 10 years ago, when finding a menu in English or anyone who could communicate in English was all but impossible. Even though there is more English signage around, many feel that it is worth making an effort to master at least something of the written language. There are three alphabets in Japanese: *kanji* (ancient pictograms, impossible), *hiragana* and *katakana* (the characters used to spell loan words from English). It is possible to master the two latter alphabets which will make it possible to read station names and menus. Learning some of the script not only impresses students and shows that you are making an effort to absorb some of the culture, it also helps you to survive. **Joseph Tame** signed up for Japanese lessons so he could get beyond 'large beer please' and 'I don't understand' to a variety of expressions to exclaim 'how much?' in disbelief.

Japanese addresses are mind-bogglingly complicated too: the numbers refer to land subdivisions: prefecture, district, ward, then building. When in doubt (inevitable) ask a friendly informant for a *chizu* (map). It is also a good idea to get a Japanese person to write your destination in both *kanji* and transliterated into *roma-ji* (our alphabet). Japanese people will sometimes go to embarrassing lengths to help foreigners. This desire to help is wedded to a reluctance to lose face which means that they may offer advice and instructions based on very little information, so keep checking. Young people in jeans are the best bets. Outside the big cities the people are even more cordial. Wherever you go, you don't have to worry about crime. Not long after **Will Mercer** arrived in Gunma prefecture, he went for a hike in nearby hills, as so many local people seemed to do at weekends. Unfortunately he had no map, and he was also unaware of how early it got dark, so it was no joke when he found himself completely lost. Using his mobile phone to illuminate his way, he finally stumbled out onto a road. A car stopped for him and insisted not only on driving him to the railway station (which turned out to be a very short distance up the road) but on giving Will a torch, later returned by post.

Travel is expensive. For example the 320-mile journey by bullet train from Tokyo to Kyoto costs over £100 one way. Yet the pace of a teacher's life in Tokyo or another big city can become so stressful that it is essential to get on a local train and see some of the countryside. Tour operators do sometimes have special deals on train fares. For example in 2015, JREast (which operates in Kanto in Northern Japan) was offering a five-day pass to foreigners for 11,850 yen, excluding all bullet trains (Shinkansen). Shopping around for package tours is another good way to get to see Japan at the lowest possible price.

The alienness of Japanese culture is one of the main fascinations of the place. It is foolish to become bogged down worrying about transgressing against mysterious customs. But new arrivals soon discover that the Japanese allow foreigners a great deal of latitude. **Antoinette Sarpong** got better at her encounters with the local people after she realised that Japanese people do not like to say 'No' or directly express disagreement, so she gradually learned to read between the lines and to interpret their subtle communication style.

The expat scene is also not to everyone's taste, as **Antoinette Sarpong** from Canada described:

> ***One aspect of being here in Japan that was a little difficult was dating and body image. A conversation with a female mate from England the other day reminded me that it can be difficult for women first arriving in Japan, which is so patriarchal, and experience the highs and lows of the dating scene. However, for foreign men, it is often thought of as being much easier to meet women for relationships.***
>
> ***Japan is a fascinating country, but don't expect to blend in or go incognito; it is very difficult to be 'accepted' by the Japanese.***

Will Mercer is of the opinion that it would be misguided to aim for total acceptance:

> ***By sheer demographics you will, unless you have Asian features, stand out constantly. On more than one occasion a stranger opened a conversation with me by saying (in Japanese) 'wow, blue eyes!' This does not mean that foreigners will find themselves shunned or treated poorly. Rather, I think it is possible to be accepted within Japanese society, but always as a foreigner. You'll find it much easier to live comfortably if you accept just how exotic you appear to most Japanese. I didn't find it at all difficult to make Japanese friends and I found people, on the whole, to be very friendly, considerate and welcoming.***

LIST OF EMPLOYERS

ACC ENGLISH SCHOOL

252 Genjishinmei-Cho, Hekinan-Shi, Aichi-Ken 447 0872

+81 566 422 332

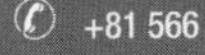

info@acc-english.co.jp

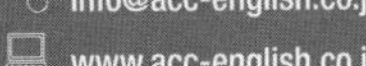

www.acc-english.co.jp

PREFERENCE OF NATIONALITY: Native English speakers for chain of schools in Aichi Prefecture (Nagoya, Anjo, Kariya, Handa, Hekinan, Nishio and Toyoake).

QUALIFICATIONS: University graduates. Teaching experience, basic Japanese language ability or TESOL training an advantage. Applicants must be prepared to teach all levels, from very young children to adults.

CONDITIONS OF EMPLOYMENT: 1-year full-time positions available to teach approximately 25 hours per week. Approximately 4 weeks of paid vacation. Part-time positions sometimes available.

FACILITIES/SUPPORT: 1-week pre-service training provided. Subsidised furnished accommodation arranged (monthly rent is around 40,000 yen).

RECRUITMENT: Speculative applications should be emailed/posted to the above address with a photo of yourself in business attire.

AEON CORPORATION
222 Sepulveda Blvd., Suite # 2000, El Segundo, CA 90245, USA
+1 310 662 4706
aeonla@aeonet.com
Also: 535 Fifth Avenue, Rm 413, New York, NY 10017
+1 646 277 7333
aeonnyc@aeonet.com
www.aeonet.com

One of the largest chains of English conversation schools in Japan with over 320 branches.

NUMBER OF TEACHERS: 800.

QUALIFICATIONS: Bachelor's degree in any subject and a perfect command of the English language. Teaching experience beneficial but not necessary.

CONDITIONS OF EMPLOYMENT: 1 calendar year renewable contract starting every month. 5 days a week. 40 hours/week work schedule. Maximum 25 teaching hours a week.

SALARY: 270,000 yen per month.

FACILITIES/SUPPORT: Single occupancy apartment furnished to Japanese standards. Subsidised monthly rent of 55,000 yen. Flight allowance of 70,000 yen for qualifying teachers. Pension and sickness insurance provided under Japan's Socialised Health Insurance plan. 3 weeks of paid vacation and 1 week paid training.

RECRUITMENT: 2 full-time recruiting offices in the US (as above). Group and personal interviews held on a regular basis in the USA, and 3 times a year in London, Toronto, Vancouver and Sydney. Positions start every month. Rolling deadlines. Initial applicants should send résumé and 500-word essay entitled 'Why I want to live and work in Japan'. For up-to-date information regarding recruiting trips and application instructions see www.aeonet.com.

CONTACT: Paul Hunt, Personnel Recruiter, New York office.

ARK FOREIGN LANGUAGE ACADEMY
4519–4 Innoshima Takuma, Onomichi, Hiroshima 722–2324
+81 845 228511
contact@arkgaigo.com
www.arkgaigo.com/jobs

NUMBER OF TEACHERS: 3. Also part-time positions.

PREFERENCE OF NATIONALITY: None.

QUALIFICATIONS: Degree.

CONDITIONS OF EMPLOYMENT: 1-year contract with 6–8 working hours per day.

SALARY: From 205,000 yen per month. 1,600 yen per 40-minute lesson. Trainees are paid 1,000 yen.

FACILITIES/SUPPORT: Accommodation provided free and sponsorship given for work visas.

RECRUITMENT: Interviews are essential.

CONTACT: Matt Winfield, Owner-Manager (matt@arkgaigo.com).

AUSTRALIAN CLUB
2F Manju Bldg, 8-banchi, San-ei-cho, Shinjuku-ku, Tokyo 160-0008
+81 3 6380 6024
edu@australianclub.net
www.100dreams.co.jp/au

Online school so teachers do not need to be resident in Japan.

NUMBER OF TEACHERS: 2–6.

PREFERENCE OF NATIONALITY: Australian teachers preferred.

QUALIFICATIONS: Applicants must be native English speakers with Australian citizenship. Must have TEFL/TESOL certificate, IELTS experience and experience with Japanese learners.

CONDITIONS OF EMPLOYMENT: No contracts; online teaching is on casual basis. Teachers nominate a 3-lesson shift (each lesson is 30 minutes in length). Shifts are on weekday nights or weekends (Japan time).

SALARY: 1,500 yen per 30-minute lesson (net).

FACILITIES/SUPPORT: No accommodation or work permits.

RECRUITMENT: Via TEFL/TESOL job boards. Skype interviews.

CONTACT: Rocco Nigro, Director of Studies.

BERLITZ JAPAN
Shin Aoyama Bldg., East 16F, 1–1 Minami Aoyama 1-chome, Minato-ku, Tokyo 107–0062
http://teach.berlitz.co.jp

NUMBER OF TEACHERS: Over 1,200 for 63 locations, about half of which are in Greater Tokyo.

PREFERENCE OF NATIONALITY: None, must be native English speaker. For many vacancies, only candidates already in Japan will be considered.

QUALIFICATIONS: Minimum university degree, business experience and/or teaching experience needed for some posts.

CONDITIONS OF EMPLOYMENT: Choice of 3 contracts: semi full-time is open to all applicants; part-time and hourly contracts available only to people already in Japan with current visa. Working hours vary.

SALARY: Starting salary of 250,000 yen, plus possibility of a contract completion bonus of 17,000 yen. Hourly paid teachers earn 1,990 yen per 45-minute lesson.

FACILITIES/SUPPORT: Visa sponsorship may be available for qualified applicants who are successful at a face-to-face interview.

RECRUITMENT: Via the above website. Interviews are essential and are conducted in Japan. Applicants must be available to attend an unpaid 5-day Instructor Qualification Program (IQP) at head office (dates on website).

BERNARD ENGLISH SCHOOL OF JAPAN
Shamotto Tsukuba 2F, 4–2-7 Matsushiro, Tsukuba City, Ibaraki-ken 305–0035
+81 298 565093
recruitment@bernard.co.jp
www.bernard.co.jp

NUMBER OF TEACHERS: 15+ for multiple schools in the Tsukuba area.

PREFERENCE OF NATIONALITY: American, Australian, British and Canadian.

QUALIFICATIONS: Must have a 4-year university degree (any field), TESOL-type qualifications are a plus, must have a valid driver's licence (either a Japanese or an international licence).

CONDITIONS OF EMPLOYMENT: 1 year contracts from August, renewable on mutual agreement. Contracts are a salary/hourly hybrid. Full-time teachers work 23–28 hours per week, with 8 weeks of school holidays spread throughout the year.

SALARY: Base salary of 185,000 yen plus 2,300 yen per hour for hours worked over 80 per month. Contract completion bonus of 60,000 yen.

FACILITIES/SUPPORT: Modern, fully equipped apartments are available for lease through the company. Staff are free to choose other lodgings, if desired. Visa sponsorship can be provided. Company cars are available for lease. A vehicle is necessary for travel between schools. Weekly Japanese language classes available for all teachers free of charge.

RECRUITMENT: Usually takes about 2 months from initial contact. Telephone interviews will be conducted. References are also required.

CONTACT: Frank Pridgen, Foreign Staff Manager.

THE BRITISH ENGLISH AND NEW DANCE ACADEMY
9–23 Hinodemachi, 3 chome, Sanyoonoda-shi, Yamaguchi-ken 756-0091
+81 836 842390
englishbenda@yahoo.co.uk; ennutton@gmail.com
http://bendaacademy.jimdo.com/esl-jobs

NUMBER OF TEACHERS: 6.

PREFERENCE OF NATIONALITY: Native English-speaking countries.

QUALIFICATIONS: At least a BA degree or 2-year college diploma. Experience is a plus.

CONDITIONS OF EMPLOYMENT: 12 months with option to renew. Teachers work a maximum of 24.5 teaching hours per week, with little or no office time.

SALARY: 245,000–260,000 yen per 98-hour month. Part-timers earn 2,350 yen per hour. National tax is paid from the first year and city tax from the second year. End-of-contract bonus after 12 months is 25,000 yen.

FACILITIES/SUPPORT: Academy covers key money expenses for teachers' apartments. Teachers pay for their own rent, usually 40,000–55,000 yen. Employer provides work visa sponsorship which is mainly carried out in Japan, but requires the teacher to complete the process in his/her home country. Company car provided.

RECRUITMENT: After receiving applicant's documents by email and airmail, school will arrange telephone interview.

CONTACT: Ted Nutton, Principal (ennutton@gmail.com).

ECC FOREIGN LANGUAGE INSTITUTE
General Headquarters: 3rd Floor, ECC Honsha Building, 1 10 20 Higashi-temma, Kita-ku, Osaka 530–0044
Regional offices in Tokyo, Nagoya and Osaka
+81 3 3365 4155
jobs@eccjapan.com; globalhr@ecc.co.jp
www.eccteachinjapan.com

NUMBER OF TEACHERS: 650+ at 180 schools in Japan.

PREFERENCE OF NATIONALITY: Applicants for whom English is their native language.

QUALIFICATIONS: Minimum bachelor's degree.

CONDITIONS OF EMPLOYMENT: 1-year contracts, ending yearly on 31 March; 35 total working hours per week, mostly evenings. To work 5 days a week with variable days off. 7 weeks' paid holiday per annum. Teachers work some Saturday or Sunday shifts. Opportunities for paid overtime are plentiful.

SALARY: 270,000 yen per month. Annual performance stipend of up to 100,000 yen for first 3 years.

FACILITIES/SUPPORT: Assistance with accommodation. Compulsory 50–70 hour pre-service training course over 2 weeks. 7 weeks' paid vacation. Social, health and pension benefits. ECC has been more sympathetic to teachers' unions than its rivals.

RECRUITMENT: Visit the website www.eccteachinjapan.com for recruitment schedules. No Skype interviews. Main hiring period is September/October/November. UK recruitment manager

Justin Dowding; recruitment events in London and Manchester. Permanent recruiting office in Toronto. Australian recruitment via AMAC Recruitment, www.amacrecruitment.com.au (+61 404 951271; ECC@amacrecruitment.com.au). Visa processing takes 2–3 months.

ENGLISH ACADEMY & HARVARD-KIDS ACADEMY
2–9-6 Ichibancho, Matsuyama 790–0001
+81 89 931 8686
marinbu@post.harvard.edu; e8686@dokidoki.ne.jp
www.eigo-academy.com

NUMBER OF TEACHERS: 7–9 including Harvard-Kids Academy in Yokohama.
PREFERENCE OF NATIONALITY: None.
QUALIFICATIONS: Teachers with at least a 4-year degree. Some experience in teaching is also helpful although training is given. Native English speakers preferred. Experience with young children is preferred for Harvard-Kids Academy, which is an immersion kindergarten/pre-school.
CONDITIONS OF EMPLOYMENT: 18-month contracts. Hours 12pm–9pm, Tuesday to Friday, 10am–6pm on Saturday.
SALARY: Starting at 250,000 yen per month. Income tax is withheld and different arrangements are made for social security or health insurance depending on the circumstances of the teacher.
FACILITIES/SUPPORT: Help in finding accommodation and loan in making initial deposit. Academy has two apartments which require only minimal deposits. Help to apply for Certificate of Prior Permission for a work visa and in visa renewal when the time comes.
RECRUITMENT: Advertise in publications in Japan and sometimes at Ohayo-Sensei. Telephone and Skype interviews.
CONTACT: K Marin Burch Tanaka.

THE ENGLISH VILLAGE
4-2-1-113 Taihei, Sumida-ku, Tokyo 130 0013
+81 3 3624 3300
englishvillage@msg.biglobe.ne.jp
www.englishvillage.gr.jp

NUMBER OF TEACHERS: 7 for branches in Kinshicho (area of Tokyo) and Funabashi in Chiba.
PREFERENCE OF NATIONALITY: British.
QUALIFICATIONS: Degree (any discipline) and CELTA qualification or equivalent. Valid visa essential.
CONDITIONS OF EMPLOYMENT: 1-year renewable. 30–50-minute lessons per week and sessions supervising free conversation room. School specialises in teaching British English to adults learners.
SALARY: 250,000 yen per month plus 200,000 yen completion bonus.
FACILITIES/SUPPORT: Subsidised accommodation is arranged. New teachers are given a period of thorough training before they start teaching, followed by in-service training.
RECRUITMENT: British press adverts. Interviews in the UK.
CONTACT: Neil Pearson, Principal.

GABA CORPORATION
23F Shinjuku Front Tower, 2-21-1 Kita Shinjuku, Shinjuku-ku, Tokyo, 169-0074
+81 3 5338 5715
recruiting@gaba.co.jp
http://teaching-in-japan.gaba.co.jp

NUMBER OF TEACHERS: 1000 positions for teaching one-to-one at 42 learning studios in Kanto, Kansai and Chubu.
PREFERENCE OF NATIONALITY: None.
QUALIFICATIONS: TEFL/TESOL experience and certification is preferred but not essential. An outgoing, adaptable personality with an interest in dealing with adult students one-to-one is a must. Must be proficient with computers.
CONDITIONS OF EMPLOYMENT: 6-month contracts, though instructors who require visa sponsorship are expected to stay 12 months. Busy times are weekday evenings and early mornings plus weekends. Instructors can choose their schedules on a monthly basis.
SALARY: Pay is on a per-lesson basis. Currently the rate is 1,500–2,200 yen per 40-minute lesson. Deductions are very low due to the contract type.
FACILITIES/SUPPORT: Accommodation is not provided but instructors can benefit from company links with established housing providers in Japan who may offer a discount. Help given with work visas, provided candidates have an accredited Bachelor's degree taught in English (any discipline) or else 3 years' full-time English language teaching experience.
RECRUITMENT: Face-to-face/Skype interviews. Company holds recruiting events especially in autumn in the UK, USA and elsewhere; applicants can meet a recruiter and attend interviews.
CONTACT: Jim Green, instructor Recruiting Manager.

HEART ENGLISH SCHOOL
310–0805 Ibaraki-ken, Mito-shi, 2–6–10 Chuo
+81 29 226 8010
yoshinaga@heart-school.jp; info@heart-school.jp
www.heart-school.jp/en/index.html

ALT provider company, placing teachers in public schools to assist Japanese teachers of English in Kanagawa Prefecture (including Yokohama and Kawasaki).

NUMBER OF TEACHERS: 300 Assistant Language Teachers (ALTs) per year, but varies by season.

PREFERENCE OF NATIONALITY: Native or near-native English speakers. Visa sponsorship possible only for passport holders of the US, Canada, UK, Ireland, Australia and New Zealand.

QUALIFICATIONS: Should already have working visa and live in the area. Key qualities are flexibility and a good personality with children. Experience is a plus but not essential if candidates have the right personality and are able to cooperate effectively with their Japanese co-teacher.

CONDITIONS OF EMPLOYMENT: Contracts are usually from the start date – normally April or September – through March, which is the end of Japan's public school year. If both parties agree, contract can be renewed in 1-year increments. Rarely, contract lengths are non-standard due to a specific school board request. In most cases the number of contracted hours is 4–5 per day, over 4 days a week.

SALARY: Pay depends on the municipality, and on number of working hours and days. Range from 160,000 yen per month to 240,000 yen. After rent, taxes, utilities and other compulsory expenses, an ALT earns the equivalent of $1,200–$2,400 in take-home pay, with an average of about $1,850. No payment when school is closed (as in August). Some companies provide a 100,000 yen stipend in these fallow periods, which is enough to cover rent, taxes, utilities and have enough left over for food, but not much else. Employees are expected to prepare for lulls.

FACILITIES/SUPPORT: Housing can be arranged and subsidised in a private apartment, usually furnished. School cooperates with legalities, and does most of the leg-work in obtaining and renewing Instructor visa.

RECRUITMENT: Via Japan-specific recruitment websites or via university career fairs in North America, UK and Australia. Interviews are required in person or via phone or video connection online.

INTERAC CO. LTD.

Iidabashi Grand Bloom, 5F, Fujimi 2-10-2, Chiyoda-ku, Tokyo 102 0071

+81 3 3234 7840

www.interacnetwork.com

Non-governmental provider of Assistant Language Teachers (ALTs) in Japan.

NUMBER OF TEACHERS: Over 2,000 full-time employees throughout Japan.

PREFERENCE OF NATIONALITY: None, though majority are Australian, New Zealander, Canadian, American, British, Irish and Jamaican.

QUALIFICATIONS: Minimum university degree, 12 years' education in the medium of English (all subjects taught in English at school for at least 12 years) plus a passion for teaching and a strong desire to live in Japan and work in Japanese public schools. Japanese language skills and teaching qualifications preferred but not a necessity. Driver's licence and willingness to drive are an advantage.

CONDITIONS OF EMPLOYMENT: 12-month contracts from early April to late March. Up to 29.5 teaching hours per week, Monday to Friday 8am–5pm; 7 months' contract available from late August to following year late March.

SALARY: Average 230,000–250,000 yen per month; 10% deducted in tax.

FACILITIES/SUPPORT: Comprehensive orientation programme on arrival with follow-up training sessions. Single occupied apartments arranged before arrival. Company acts as guarantor for apartment contracts and visa sponsor. Private health insurance cover available. Free Japanese lessons available in some locations. Company car available to lease.

RECRUITMENT: Heavy online advertising. All recruitment is done through global online system. Phone screening or interviews may be conducted by reps in Oxford, several US cities and elsewhere. Face-to-face interviews strongly preferred. Intakes in late August and late March.

INTERNATIONAL EDUCATION CONSULTANTS/KULZ ACADEMY

Shin Yokohama, IK Bldg. 604, 2 12 12 Shin Yokohama, Kohoku ku, Yokohama shi, 222–0033

+81 45 308 6280

info@ieconsultants.co.jp

www.ieconsultants.co.jp

Language institute and cram school for young learners.

NUMBER OF TEACHERS: 4.

PREFERENCE OF NATIONALITY: Native English speakers.

QUALIFICATIONS: University graduate. Must be in the country and have work visa already.

CONDITIONS OF EMPLOYMENT: Approximately 100 hours per month. Lessons take place between 6am and 9pm but are mostly in afternoons and evenings, including Saturdays.

SALARY: Hourly rate. 2,000–3,000 yen. Local taxes deducted.

FACILITIES/SUPPORT: No assistance with accommodation or visas. Transport is paid.

RECRUITMENT: Word of mouth. Face-to-face interview required.

CONTACT: Ulrich Kulz, CEO (ulikulz@ieconsultants.co.jp).

INTERNATIONAL EDUCATION SERVICES

Rose Hikawa Building, 22-14, Higashi 2-Chome, Shibuya-Ku, Tokyo 150–0011

+81 3 3498 7101

jobs@iesnet.co.jp

www.iesnet.co.jp/english

NUMBER OF TEACHERS: 15–20 ALTs, Business English trainers and language teachers for specialised fields like engineering.

PREFERENCE OF NATIONALITY: Mostly from North America, UK, Australia and New Zealand.

QUALIFICATIONS: University degree required. An assessment of any candidate's English Language proficiency may be required as part of the hiring process. English communication courses offered in management, engineering, pharmaceuticals, etc. so ESP background useful.

CONDITIONS OF EMPLOYMENT: Initial annual contract with option for renewal. Majority of positions start in March/April and August/September. Total teaching hours vary per month but average 25–35 per week and associated travel time.

SALARY: Varies between the yen equivalent of £19,000 and £21,000 less deductions of 5%–7%. End-of-contract bonus.

FACILITIES/SUPPORT: Administrative coordinator assists teachers in finding accommodation. Work visa sponsorship. In-house learning materials provided.

RECRUITMENT: Interviews are an essential part of the recruitment process and are sometimes carried out in the UK and the USA, but increasingly online. Applicants should apply 5 months before intended start date.

CONTACT: Rob Strachan, Director of Studies.

JAMES ENGLISH SCHOOLS

4-16-6 Teraoka Izumi, Sendai, Miyagi 981 3204

+81 22 772 0161

www.james.co.jp/english

NUMBER OF TEACHERS: 50–100 for 15 branches in the Tohoku region of Northern Japan.

PREFERENCE OF NATIONALITY: None.

QUALIFICATIONS: Bachelor's degree and TESOL certificate.

CONDITIONS OF EMPLOYMENT: 1-year contract. Expect teachers to stay at least 2 years. 30 teaching hours per week (average).

SALARY: 250,000–280,000 yen per month.

FACILITIES/SUPPORT: Loan provided for initial settling-in costs. Visa sponsorship. Training and regular professional development offered.

RECRUITMENT: Adverts on www.GaijinPot.com etc. Application process completed through website. Skype interviews.

CONTACT: Mr Yoshi Kigawa, Owner and President.

JET PROGRAMME UK

JET Desk, Embassy of Japan, 101–104 Piccadilly, London W1J 7JT, UK

+44 20 7465 6668

info@jet-uk.org; ukjet@ld.mofa.go.jp

www.jet-uk.org

NUMBER OF TEACHERS: Approximately 150 from the UK going to educational institutions all over Japan.

PREFERENCE OF NATIONALITY: UK passport holders only.

QUALIFICATIONS: Must hold a bachelor's degree by the time of departure and be under 40 years of age. TEFL training or experience preferred but not essential. Tattoos and body piercings are not well tolerated in Japan.

CONDITIONS OF EMPLOYMENT: 12-month renewable contracts starting in August up to maximum of 5 years. Normal working hours are 35 hours per week, although teaching hours are between 15 and 20. Conditions of service vary according to the policies of different contracting organisations.

SALARY: Annual remuneration is about 3.36 million yen per year.

FACILITIES/SUPPORT: JET finds placement, organises visa and insurance, hosts 2-day pre-departure orientation day in London, beginners' TEFL training and basic Japanese language course, 2-day orientation in Tokyo, language books; return flights provided upon completion of contract.

RECRUITMENT: Application process begins in October. Deadline for application is the last week in November. Interviews in following January/February with decisions given in April. All application info is online or contact JET Desk with any queries.

KENT SCHOOL OF ENGLISH

Shoppers' Plaza 706, 1–4-1 Irfune, Urayasu-shi, Chiba Ken 279–0012

+81 47 353 8708

kyagawa@tryon.co.jp

www.kent-english.jp/recruit

NUMBER OF TEACHERS: 8.

PREFERENCE OF NATIONALITY: None.

QUALIFICATIONS: Minimum university degree plus TEFL certificate or PGCE plus 2 years' TEFL experience. Must like children.

CONDITIONS OF EMPLOYMENT: 1-year contract. 23 contact

hours per week. School is open Tuesday-Friday 1–10 pm and Saturday 10am–6pm. 5–6 weeks' paid holiday.

SALARY: From 260,000 yen per month (gross) plus outward flight provided. Tax and insurance deductions are less than 8%.

FACILITIES/SUPPORT: Subsidised furnished flats available, some shared, some single. All deposits/key money/gratuities paid, so teachers pay only the rent and utilities charges. Visa sponsorship and initial training.

RECRUITMENT: Interview held in London in July. Adverts on the internet (e.g. www.tefl.com). Interviews held in the UK in the summer. Once contract is signed, permits are arranged and issued in mid-September.

CONTACT: Kaoru Yagawa, Principal.

KEVIN'S ENGLISH SCHOOLS

Iizawa 242–23, Minamiashigara Shi, Kanagawa Pref. 250-0122

+81 465 744458

kevinsenglishschools@hotmail.com

www.eikaiwamachida.wordpress.com; www.how-to-teach-english-in-japan.com

NUMBER OF TEACHERS: 3.

PREFERENCE OF NATIONALITY: None.

QUALIFICATIONS: College or university degree and some extra training in how to teach English. A TEFL certificate and experience are pluses.

CONDITIONS OF EMPLOYMENT: 1-year contract. Most teaching hours fall in the afternoon and evening up till 9pm.

SALARY: 250,000 yen per month.

FACILITIES/SUPPORT: Apartment is provided for a rent of about 60,000 yen per month. Assistance given with all official paperwork.

RECRUITMENT: Via www.how-to-teach-english-in-japan.com. Interviews by phone or in person are essential; many candidates are interviewed by phone.

CONTACT: Kevin R Burns, Owner.

MODEL LANGUAGE STUDIO (MLS)

2–31–8 Yoyogi, Shibuya-ku, Tokyo-to 151–0053

+81 3 3320 1555

careers21@mls-etd.co.jp

www.mls-etd.co.jp/recruiting_e/index.html

NUMBER OF TEACHERS: 55 across 30 studio locations in metropolitan Tokyo, Osaka, Chiba and one in Saitama.

PREFERENCE OF NATIONALITY: All native speakers.

QUALIFICATIONS: Experience working with students aged 1–12. Valid Working Visa or minimum BA Certification in which case sponsorship is possible.

CONDITIONS OF EMPLOYMENT: 1-year contracts mainly from February-November, though other openings year round. Up to 30 hours per 5-day week (of which 25–27 are teaching hours).

SALARY: Starting from 250,000 yen (gross) per calendar month. Up to 80,000 yen end-of-contract bonus.

FACILITIES/SUPPORT: 2-week basic training course in Drama Method. Company can temporarily house new arrivals. It has links to large number of apartments and can help staff source a suitable one (key money not required). Transport to and from work is paid. Various other monetary incentives. Long paid vacations and all national holidays paid. Company can help sponsor appropriate candidates for a visa before arrival in Japan.

RECRUITMENT: Via company website, wwwgaijinpot.com and various Japanese recruitment agencies. Face-to-face interview essential. Non-Japan-based applications must include an mpeg/DVD of the candidate in action.

PEACE BOAT / GET UNIVERSAL

1-32-13-4F Takadanobaba, Shinjuku-ku, Tokyo, 169–0075

+81 3 5287 3192

getprogramme@peaceboat.gr.jp; pbglobal@peaceboat.gr.jp

www.peaceboat.org/english/?menu=114

Peace Boat is a Japan-based international non-governmental and non-profit organisation that travels the world on peace voyages.

NUMBER OF TEACHERS: 8–12 volunteer language teachers onboard each cruise, to teach as part of the onboard language programme known as GET (Global English/español Training).

PREFERENCE OF NATIONALITY: Aim to recruit a linguistically and culturally diverse team. Non-native highly advanced speakers of English and applicants with multiple language teaching ability are welcome to apply.

QUALIFICATIONS: At least 18 months of relevant full-time language teaching experience. Flexible, good communication skills and an interest in peace building and global education. A degree, qualification in language teaching and conversational Japanese ability are highly regarded. Average age is 27.

CONDITIONS OF EMPLOYMENT: Voyages depart three times a year, e.g. 12 April, 2017 from Yokohama and last approximately 100 days to circumnavigate the globe. Teachers can expect to teach 2–3 intensive classes and some private lessons as well as organising language-related events onboard. While in port, teachers normally have free time.

SALARY: None. Participation fee for the voyage, which covers meals, accommodation onboard and port taxes is covered by GET Universal Co. Ltd. Teachers must cover transport to and from Tokyo, and compulsory travel insurance.

FACILITIES/SUPPORT: Structured online preparatory study period of 4–6 hours a week over 2 months before departure. Intensive orientation lasting 3–4 days in Tokyo. Professional development workshops conducted onboard. Documents for the necessary visas are provided.

RECRUITMENT: Recruiting websites and the Peace Boat website as above. Deadline for applications is mid-August; interviews in Tokyo (or by Skype) in early September.

CONTACT: Nicholas Sutton, International Coordinator.

RED ROOF ENGLISH SCHOOL

Okinawa Prefecture, Ginowan City, Samashita 175–1-102 (Kasa G2)

+81 98 890 1228

info@redroof.jp

www.redroof.jp

NUMBER OF TEACHERS: 3.

PREFERENCE OF NATIONALITY: None.

QUALIFICATIONS: University degree is essential for visa sponsorship. Experience working with children is preferred.

CONDITIONS OF EMPLOYMENT: 1-year contract. Usual teaching hours between 1pm and 9pm Monday to Friday or Tuesday to Saturday.

SALARY: Starting from 185,000 yen to 225,000 yen per month depending on expertise; 40,000 to 50,000 yen deducted per month for rent and utilities.

FACILITIES/SUPPORT: Apartment with modest furnishings is provided. Assistance is also given with setting up telephones and banking, etc.

RECRUITMENT: Usually through the internet or word of mouth. Interviews are essential and can be held via webcam or occasionally in Canada.

SHANE ENGLISH SCHOOL JAPAN (SESJ)

Kenkyusha Fujimi Building 4F, 2-11-3 Fujimi, Chiyoda-ku, Tokyo 102-0071

+81 3 5275 6756

drp@shane.co.jp; teflrecruitment@shane.co.jp

www.tefljobsinjapan.com; www.saxoncourt.com/jobs-abroad/japan

Chain of language schools in the Greater Tokyo region that has been part of Japanese cram school company Eikoh Inc since 2010.

NUMBER OF TEACHERS: 400+ in 180 schools, especially Tokyo, Kanto areas, Nagoya and Osaka.

PREFERENCE OF NATIONALITY: Native speakers of British English, i.e. from Commonwealth countries.

QUALIFICATIONS: University degree required plus CELTA or Trinity CertTESOL.

CONDITIONS OF EMPLOYMENT: 12-month renewable contracts. Maximum 30 contact hours per week. Students from age 2. 5–6 weeks' paid holiday.

SALARY: Starting salary 252,800 yen per month plus possible bonuses. Deductions for income tax work out at about 6.5% of gross income.

FACILITIES/SUPPORT: Accommodation sub-lets provided for teachers who require it or information on guesthouses that accept long-stay foreigners. All documentation for work visas is provided. 1 week Young Learner teacher training given.

RECRUITMENT: Via face-to-face interviews in Japan or via recruitment agencies in the UK, i.e. Saxoncourt International (www.saxoncourt.com), TEFLOne or TEFL-in-Japan.com.

CONTACT: Director of Recruitment and Personnel (teflrecruitment @shane.co.jp).

TEFL IN JAPAN

76 Mortimer Street, London W1W 7SA, UK

+44 207 079 3330

tim@tefl-in-japan.com

www.tefl-in-japan.com

NUMBER OF TEACHERS: 40 per year (for Shane English Schools).

PREFERENCE OF NATIONALITY: None.

QUALIFICATIONS: University degree, CELTA/Trinity CertTESOL or 120-hour online TEFL training and two years' experience.

CONDITIONS OF EMPLOYMENT: 12 month contracts. 29.5 hours per week, to include approx. 25 contact hours.

SALARY: 252,800 yen per month. 247,800 yen for teachers who don't have the CELTA or equivalent.

FACILITIES/SUPPORT: Accommodation is found for teachers, and rent is deducted from salary. After sending documents to Tokyo that are processed, the teacher visits a Japanese Embassy to have the visa stamped into their passport; no need for notarised copies or medical reports!

RECRUITMENT: Web advertising and contacts at TEFL teacher training centres, leading to a face to face or Skype interview.

CONTACT: Tim Langley, Director.

VOLTA ASSOCIATES
Chiyoda Platform Square 1005, 3–21 Kanda Hishikicho, Chiyoda-ku, Tokyo 101–0054
+81 3 3427 4227
info@volta-associates.com
www.volta-associates.com/recruitment.html

NUMBER OF TEACHERS: 5 corporate trainers to teach one-to-one.
PREFERENCE OF NATIONALITY: None.
QUALIFICATIONS: Bachelor degree with TESOL.
CONDITIONS OF EMPLOYMENT: 1-year contract. 4–6 lessons a day, 5 days a week.
SALARY: Approximately 230,000 yen.
FACILITIES/SUPPORT: Assistance given with finding accommodation (translating paperwork, finding estate agents, etc.). TESOL course is provided (affiliated with American TESOL, www.americantesol.com).
RECRUITMENT: Online application to Human Resources department. Interviews are essential.
CONTACT: Benard Oppong-Kusi, President and CEO.

WESTGATE CORPORATION
Human Resources Department, Yushima Daido Bldg 2F, 3-17-1 Yushima, Bunkyo-Ku, Tokyo 113–0034
+81 3 3836 0362
westgate_recruiter@westgate.co.jp
www.westgate.co.jp

NUMBER OF TEACHERS: 400.
PREFERENCE OF NATIONALITY: USA, UK, Canada, Australia, Ireland, New Zealand.
QUALIFICATIONS: Bachelor's or higher degree plus EFL/ESL teaching experience. 500+ hours of classroom teaching experience (including non-EFL/ESL) needed by applicants with EFL/ESL teaching certificate/degree and/or elementary/primary/secondary teaching credentials/qualifications; or 1,000+ hours of classroom teaching experience (including non-EFL/ESL) for those without any of the above credentials.
CONDITIONS OF EMPLOYMENT: 3–5 months. 9 working hours a day including 4–6 teaching hours. Work available in universities.
SALARY: From 260,000/275,000 yen per month. Deductions made for income tax, employment tax, National Health Insurance premium, rent (if teacher lives in a Westgate-arranged apartment), and Nursing Care Insurance premium (for teachers over 40).
FACILITIES/SUPPORT: Westgate arranges a fully-furnished single apartment (teacher pays rent of 81,000 yen including utilities) and sponsors all instructors to obtain the visa necessary to work in Japan. Flight reimbursement up to $1,200.
RECRUITMENT: Online application form. Skype or phone interview.
CONTACT: Miho Akiyama, HR Coordinator.

WISHBORN ENGLISH ACADEMY
Blooming Chateau #101, Kimiidera 811-43, Wakayama-shi 641-0012
+81 7 3445 8639
teach_at_wishborn@yahoo.com
http://wb-arida.wixsite.com/wishborn-ea

NUMBER OF TEACHERS: 8, teaching babies to seniors at a chain of schools, local kindergartens, public and private schools, businesses and community centres.
PREFERENCE OF NATIONALITY: No preference as long as applicant is from a country that uses English as its primary and official language.
QUALIFICATIONS: Bachelor's university degree and International Driving Permit (or Japanese driver's licence) essential. Past experience teaching or working with children is a plus. Teachers must be hard-working, flexible, focused, passionate about EFL teaching, creative and energetic.
CONDITIONS OF EMPLOYMENT: 1-year renewable contract preferably starting in March. Stays of 2–3 years preferred. Up to 30 scheduled hours per week (up to 25 teaching hours). Classes may be scheduled between 10am and 9pm. Most shifts begin early afternoon, and finish before 9pm.
SALARY: Base salary is 250,000 yen per full working month before taxes or other deductions. Monthly bonuses of up to 50,000 yen per month based on sales. Performance-based raises every year.
FACILITIES/SUPPORT: School sets up apartments for teachers before they arrive. Monthly costs must be paid by the teachers but school covers the initial key money and deposits. 2 weeks initial training with the manager and observing other teachers' classes. Additional training days (between 5 and 8 per year) and formal training 2 or 3 times per year conducted by the company that designed the children's curriculum used by the school. Reimbursement for work-related travel. 10 days paid vacation. Full assistance given with work visas.
RECRUITMENT: Internet ads including sites such as GaijinPot.
CONTACT: Greg Hodson, Manager.

KOREA

Anyone who has witnessed the early-morning scramble by students and businessmen to get to their English lessons before the working day begins in Seoul might be surprised to learn that the motto for South Korea is 'Land of the Morning Calm'. Because Korea's economy is increasingly globalised, English is seen as essential for success in business. The level of affluence in Seoul and the other major cities is striking, and many of these ambitious young Koreans are not only keen but also able to afford English lessons (or their parents can). An English proficiency test must be passed by all aspiring university students, which is why so many students of secondary school age study the language so feverishly. With the 2018 Winter Olympics taking place in PyeongChang, a mountainous region 100 miles east of Seoul, English is being prioritised among any Koreans involved. All these groups have probably studied English for many years at school but need to practise conversation with native English speakers.

It is estimated that eight out of every ten students from primary school upwards study English after school, though a percentage of these are doing it online. The Korean government spends more per capita on English language education than any other country in the world. So the demand is insatiable. School and university vacations (July and January) often see a surge in student enrolment at private language institutes and at seasonal camps. The teaching of children is booming more than ever. This must be the only country in the world where it is possible to have your international airfare covered in return for teaching for a couple of weeks at a camp (see description below). Major language teaching organisations rely heavily on recruitment agencies abroad to fill their recurring vacancies for native English speaker staff. The market in Korea is ever changing. There are still lots of jobs around but it is becoming harder to find good positions, especially for male teachers and couples.

The bias is strongly in favour of North Americans, Canadians in particular, and there are still relatively few British TEFLers in Korea, despite the activities of UK-based recruiters such as Flying Cows in Nottingham (see entry), which recruits for positions in both the private and public sectors. Note that in the case of Korea, 'schools' normally refers to the state sector whereas 'institutes' means private language academies run as businesses. The number of small to medium-sized *hagwons* (private language institutes) in all Korean cities interested in hiring a few native English speakers is massive. One agency in Korea's third city, Daegu, estimates that there are 800 native speakers of English teaching in that one city. When dealing with either *hagwon* owners or recruiters, ask for the email address of a current English-speaking teachers and use them to ask about the school, students, the town/city and accommodation. (For an account of what can happen if you don't do this, see Emma Lander's story later in this chapter.) Fortunately the language industry's reputation for shamelessly exploiting foreign teachers seems to be slowly improving.

Of broader concern than the possible shark-like practices of some potential employers is the looming proximity of North Korea. Kim Jong-un has no intention of giving up Pyongyang's nuclear arsenal, as he demonstrated in 2016 when five nuclear tests were carried out, perceived internationally as a dangerous escalation. **William Naquin**, a well-qualified American who taught in Kyunggi-Do, sums up the politics as he saw them when he was there:

> ***Korea is a divided country. We were quite nervous that war might break out here between the two Koreas. The situation in the north is universally reported to be extremely bad, with summary executions and food riots. The North Koreans have nuclear missiles, nerve gas and chemical weapons, and are led by the most isolated, despotic lunatic and paranoid military strongmen in the world. Prospective teachers need to know that this is one of the most likely flashpoints for war on earth, and that coming here necessarily involves some degree of risk.***

For the curious, it is possible to visit the Demilitarised Zone (DMZ) between South and North Korea on a day trip (from about $50 from Seoul). However, it is not possible to enter the reclusive Democratic Republic from the south.

PROSPECTS FOR TEACHERS

According to long-term American expat teacher **Dwight Gauer**, globalisation and Tiger Mothers (so-called because of their vaulting ambition on behalf of their children) are the key drivers of Korea's fanatical pursuit of the English language. He has written a comprehensive and valuable book, *Teaching English in South Korea: A Guide And Critique*, available on amazon.

> ***As I used to watch new high-rise apartments being constructed around me, I was quick to notice that hagwons were fast to follow. In many cases, they are the first businesses to be constructed in the neighbourhood of new apartments. Some here, me included, call this the 'hagwonisation' of Korea. This is a billion dollar business.***

According to **Amanda Middlecote**, director of the Nottingham-based recruitment agency Flying Cows, the market in Korea is so static that it is difficult for people to progress beyond the entry level salary of 2.1 million won. Hundreds of *hagwons* in Seoul, Busan (Korea's second city, less than four hours south of Seoul) and in smaller cities are run as businesses, where profit is the primary or even sole raison d'être. ELT training is not a priority in the majority of cases. Native-speaker status and a bachelor's degree are usually sufficient to persuade the owner of an institute to hire an English speaker. Education is greatly respected in Korea and degrees generally matter far more to potential employers than specialist qualifications. For now, a bachelor's is sufficient and a master's (no matter in what field) counts heavily in one's favour. Having a TEFL certificate and/or teaching experience usually attracts more job offers, although some schools are suspicious of candidates with experience because they view them as potentially picky, plus they don't want to pay more than a basic entry-level salary.

If you wait until you get to Korea, it is easy to fix up a job, but the visa is more difficult to arrange (see section on regulations below). If you want to find a good job make sure you present yourself well. **Peter Burnside** offers three brief tips to people considering going to teach in Korea: '*follow your heart, trust your instincts and take insane risks*'.

FINDING A JOB

IN ADVANCE

The Korean government administers an official teacher placement programme, not unlike JET in Japan, which means that it is competitive to be accepted. EPIK (English Program in Korea) is run by the Ministry of Education which places about 3,000 foreign graduates in state schools (mostly primary) and education offices throughout the country. Private recruiters are also involved and are chosen as official representatives by EPIK every spring. For 2017, the appointed agencies remained Korvia Consulting in Seoul (www.korvia.com), Korean Horizons (www.koreanhorizons.com) Vancouver, Reach to Teach in the US (www.reachtoteachrecruiting.com), www.Gone2Korea.com and Canadian Connection (see entry). Many subscribe to the view that it is easier and faster to apply directly to EPIK (www.epik.go.kr), though its deadline for applications falls earlier than recruiters' deadlines, for instance 1 February instead of 1 April for an autumn intake (though deadlines are extended until places are filled). Applications and documents can be submitted all year round in case of openings.

The salary offered on the EPIK programme is 2–2.7 million won per month (depending on qualifications and experience) plus free furnished accommodation, visa sponsorship, a settlement allowance of 300,000 won on arrival in Korea, 50% contribution to medical insurance and an end-of-contract extra month's salary called severance pay. The requirements were made stiffer a couple of years ago. Unless candidates are certified teachers or have a BA/MA in Education, they must also hold a 120-hour TEFL/TESOL/CELTA certificate. Training courses that include at least 20 hours of face-to-face teaching practice are favoured over purely online courses. Details of the programme are available from the EPIK website (www.epik.go.kr). Applicants cannot specify the location in which they would like to live/work and couples cannot apply together. You can select a preference of metropolitan, provincial or Seoul, but with no guarantee that your request will be honoured.

A subsidiary government programme is called TaLK or Teach and Learn in Korea (talkkorea@korea.com; www.talk.go.kr), which has been threatened with closure in recent times but seems to be continuing. TaLK is open to people with at least two years of university education. The teaching here takes place in after-school clubs in rural primary schools, the commitment can be shorter (6 months is possible if starting in August though 10 months from April is preferred) and the pay is lower (1.5 million won a month).

RECRUITMENT AGENCIES

Identifying the good recruitment agencies interested in more than collecting their commission from the hagwons is tricky. The fact that recruiters come and go indicates that some are just out to make a fast buck. Most private recruiters offer one-year contracts to English speakers with a university or college diploma. Candidates with additional EFL/ESL qualifications and teaching experience should be able to negotiate higher monthly salaries than the standard 2–2.1 million won. Recruited teachers are asked to commit themselves to teach 120 hours a month, which is a heavy load. Return airfares, free accommodation, paid holidays, contribution to medical insurance and completion bonus are all routinely promised. Applicants who cannot be interviewed locally can do so by telephone or Skype. Note that recruiters should not charge teachers any fee since they earn their commission from the schools and institutes. An agency in the UK called Flying Cows, formed in 2004, aims to be as honest as possible about the rewards and drawbacks of teaching in South Korea (see entry). The London-based recruitment agency Saxoncourt announced in 2016 that Shane English Schools has acquired a master franchise in the southern city of Ulsan.

Here is a list of Korea-based recruiters active at the time of writing, followed by a list for North American readers, all of which are located in Canada.

Daegu TEFL Job, Daegu (✆ +82 10 4254 4656; www.daegutefljob.com/tefljobs). Daegu Foreign Language Education Association consists of over 300 reputable private English language institutes in Daegu which employ foreign English teachers every year.

English Work, Seoul (✆ +82 2 532 4273; www.englishwork.com). Alternative name for TeachAbroad-Korea below.

Korea Global Connections, Seoul (see entry).

Morgan Recruiting, Seoul (✆ +82 070 8880 8855; www.morganrecruiting.com).

Park English Recruitment Agency, Seoul (✆ +82 2 749 1011; www.parkenglish.wixsite.com/parkenglish).

People Recruit, Busan (www.peoplerecruit.com). Calls itself a 'Competent Persons Database'.

Say Kimchi Recruiting, (anne@saykimchirecruiting.com; www.saykimchirecruiting.com) operates solely online.

SeoulESL Recruiting, Seoul (✆ +82 2 585 7871; esl@seoulesl.com; www.seoulesl.com).
TeachAbroadKorea.com, Top Placement Inc, Seoul (teachabroad22@gmail.com, www.teachabroad-korea.com). Cooperates with recruiter in Salt Lake City in the US.

The following Canadian agencies are willing to place more than just Canadians provided they meet the requirements.

Adventure Teaching, Vancouver (www.adventureteaching.com).
Canadian Connection Educational Services, (see entry).
Education Adventure, Vancouver (www.educationadventure.org).
Gone2Korea Recruiting, 2 Bloor Street W, Suite 700, Toronto M4W 3R1 (www.gone2korea.com).
Korea Connections (see entry).
KorJob Canada Recruiting, Vancouver (✆ +1 604 733 2850; www.korjobcanada.com).
Scotia Personnel, Halifax (✆ +1 902 422 1455; www.scotia-personnel-ltd.com). Refers Canadians with university degree to teaching English in schools in South Korea.
Teach Koreans, Cheongju (✆ +82 10 4582 0247; www.teachkoreans.com).

Cara McCain found a good way of dipping her toe in the water of teaching in Korea without committing herself for a whole year. The camp she worked for paid round-trip airfares from the US and provided accommodation, food and a wage of 800,000 won for a commitment of three to four weeks. In order to apply, you need to have a university degree, no criminal record and be willing to jump through all the bureaucratic hoops to prove it in order to qualify for a C4 (short-term business) visa:

> ***I was looking for a way to finance my trip to Korea, and a winter camp seemed like a perfect opportunity. Don't bother to apply unless you already have the documents, which include a notarised background check and an apostilled degree certificate. I contacted a couple of camps while I was waiting for my paperwork in the mail, but they turned me down flat because I didn't have the documents in hand. I was hired to teach a three-week intensive camp, seven hours a day with Sundays off. The camp that hired me was iHUFS [see entry] through a recruiter in Australia who worked with me over Skype and email.***
>
> ***The next step was buying my plane ticket. It was the winter holiday season, so airfares came out at about $1600. I told the recruiter that I didn't have the money to pay for my own ticket. He suggested that I just buy the ticket on a credit card, and the camp would transfer the money into my American bank account once I got to Korea. I took a leap of faith and it worked out fine. The camp went great. The staff was professional and took good care of all the teachers at the camp. We were picked up at the airport, and were given food and adequate accommodation. The students were great and enjoyed learning English. Couldn't ask for more. Overall the experience was a great way to jumpstart my ESL career. I gained relevant teaching experience, got to try the food, learned about the culture, and met people that I still keep in touch with to this day.***

Another camp company to try is Camp Korea (hr@ck.co.kr), which pays 2 million won (US$1,750) for 14 days work from mid-July, but no travel. Vacancies crop up at the last minute so they are interested in hearing from native speakers already in Korea on a working visa (see their facebook page). The internet is well equipped to keep track of the volatile English-language market and many Korean employers rely exclusively on sites like http://koreajobfinder.com, http://koreabridge.net/jobs and www.hiteacher.com. More than one web page (e.g. http://blacklist.tokyojon.com) lists good and bad employers along with quite a few horror stories.

Another possibility for anyone with an MA or advanced TEFL/TESL qualifications is to work for the language department of a Korean university (of which there are several hundred). Universities probably offer the best-paid and most stable employment.

EMMA LANDER

Emma J. Lander's story is typical and may be instructive. In most respects the *hagwon* job she was assigned through an agency was satisfactory and certainly lucrative, but there was one defect she couldn't overlook.

Like most people who move to Asia with a teaching contract I had signed on the dotted line to stay there for 12 months, but it didn't work out and I was home in England again within four months. I have written this account of my experience in the hope that if you decide to teach abroad (which you really should, by the way) you will learn from my mistakes and avoid making them yourself.

I found the job through an online recruitment agency. I read the testimonials, all of which were great, and proceeded to send my CV. They found me a job within a couple of weeks and before I knew it a telephone interview had been arranged on my behalf. I had secured my TEFL qualification a year earlier and I had already had two short-term teaching contracts so I felt confident that this was the job for me.

I was offered the job the day after the interview and I asked if I could speak to the other foreign teachers at the academy. The principal refused, saying that she was confident that I would be happy in my new role. I had done a lot of research regarding working abroad and all the advice I had come across was the same: 'Never go to a school if they don't let you speak to the foreign teachers beforehand because it probably means they've got something to hide.' This should have been a red flag for me. I should have kindly refused the offer and looked elsewhere. I should have ... but I didn't. I was so excited that I had secured a job that I ignored everything I had researched and I accepted the position without a moment's hesitation.

When I arrived in Korea I was met at the airport by my agency and taken to my apartment. It was very small but comfortable and I soon settled in. I was due to start the next day and I spent two days observing classes and learning the ropes before being given my own students. My working hours were Monday-Friday 2pm-9.30pm, although we often worked much later. The school provided textbooks for me to work through but I was free to teach them how I wanted. For the most part my students were polite and appeared to genuinely enjoy learning English. I taught ages 7-16 and found that each age range presented its own enjoyments and challenges.

The wages I received were excellent; I was earning around £1,000 per month and my outgoings were small. The school paid for my apartment and my monthly bills came to approximately £20. I was in a position to save around £800 a month if I so desired and still have an active social life. I was lucky as my weekends were always free so I spent my spare time either exploring the city of Seoul, or going further afield to see temples and climb mountains.

My job was great fun for about two months; however, I started to encounter problems when it came to testing time. I had already advised the head teacher that some of my students should be moved down a class because they did not understand the lessons. My requests were ignored. When I graded their papers, the students I was worried about were only receiving 30%, but, instead of them being moved down, I was forced to mark them at 70% (the pass rate at the academy) and then watch as some of them were moved up a level! 'We have to do that to keep the parents happy', I was told; that was when I decided to leave. The lowlight for me was watching my wonderful students struggle unnecessarily, simply because they were in the wrong classes. Seeing the academy put so much effort into making money and minimal effort into teaching was very sad.

You must be aware that if you break your contract the penalties can be harsh. I had to pay back my flight ticket and I lost 60% of my wages during the last two months. Even with the experience, I would (and will) do it again in a heartbeat. The highlight of my time in Korea was having the opportunity to explore a new culture and experiencing something entirely different to my life back home.

ON THE SPOT

Looking for a job on arrival is not recommended. The immigration laws stipulate that any foreigners who arrive in Korea to teach English must get their final visa processing completed in their own home country. There are all kinds of interesting conversations happening in Korea as to whether this regulation is really necessary, but the rules are mostly obeyed because the penalties for being caught are harsh. It is said that the government offers a reward to citizens who inform on offenders.

REGULATIONS

To reiterate, teachers must get their final visa processing completed in their home country if they are going to a *hagwon* job or even a short-term camp job, although some exemptions exist for visa processing in a third country if you are going to a public (state) school job. Anyone working without a visa risks fines and possible deportation. Similarly, the schools which hire freelance foreigners without permits can be closed down by the government. So, if at all possible, obtain a teaching visa (E2), which is available only to people with a 3 or 4-year bachelor's degree. The alternative C4 (short-term business) visa valid for single entry and maximum 90 days is also available only to degree holders. All must be native speakers of English and nationals of the UK, Ireland, USA, Canada, Australia, New Zealand or South Africa. Unfortunately some schools (such as Berlitz) want to hire only those with an F2 or F4 residency visa (for spouses of Koreans or people of Korean heritage) and will not accept E2 visas.

The procedures are ludicrously complicated. In the words of **Del Ford**, who has taught throughout the Far East for nine years: '*The application and immigration documentation requirements, especially for jobs in public schools, have entered the realm of Kafkaesque absurdity.*' Recruiters and employers accustomed to the procedures will set them out as clearly as they can. Here is a summary: you must gather together the contract of employment from your prospective employer, your passport, your original degree officially notarised/ apostilled, which must be from an approved institution in an English-speaking country, a notarised criminal record/DBS check, medical certificate, ID and forms. After mailing these and other documents to the employer in Korea, they are used to obtain a visa issuance number. With a visa issuance number, you can proceed to apply for the E2 visa at the Korean consulate in your home country. The consular officer may schedule a short interview that can be by phone and then stamp your passport with an E2 visa stamp. Within 90 days of arrival in Korea you'll have to subject yourself to a full medical at an approved centre, including blood and urine tests to check for HIV and any trace of illegal drugs, in order to qualify for an Aliens Registration Card. The medical exam will be at your expense and costs at least 100,000 won. Finally, your visa becomes valid and you may commence work immediately. **Emma Lander** summarises the ordeal:

> ***Securing the working visa for South Korea was a long and arduous process. I had to have my degree certificate verified, copied and signed by a solicitor and I had to acquire a background check and have that signed off too, none of which came cheap. I also had to get passport photos, copies of my CV and the contract, and complete a self-assessment medical check. It took roughly six weeks before my visa arrived. If you're going to work in Asia you must be committed because it takes a lot of effort on your part to get there.***

Since September 2010, Korean Embassies and Consulates General are accepting only notarised degree certificates and criminal record checks that have been affixed with the relevant 'apostille' (French for 'certification'). This can be done by specialist companies, for example in the UK see www.apostille.org.uk, where each stamp will cost £54 or £66. US nationals must obtain a criminal record check issued by the FBI rather than a state-level check, and these can take up to three months to process. Note that the Korean authorities do not return your submitted documents.

The E2 visa is valid for employment with the sponsoring employer, meaning if you change employers, you must have your E2 visa officially endorsed, which is much easier than applying from scratch. If you have obtained an E2 and completed your contract, you can transfer the visa to a new employer with minimal fuss. Freelance teaching is not permitted under the terms of your work permit and leads to fines and deportation.

Teachers are liable to income tax from their first day of work. The rate of income tax for most teachers should be 4%–7%, so beware employers who try to hold back much more from earnings. Most teachers participate in the Korean National Medical Insurance Union; most employers pay half of the total, leaving teachers to pay about 2% of earnings.

CONDITIONS OF WORK

Discontentment seems to be chronic among English teachers in Korea, and many foreign teachers have entered into contract disputes, partly due to cultural differences. They slowly discover that contracts in Korea are not set in stone, and are instead viewed as a starting point or a rough working agreement, subject to change and further negotiation depending on the circumstances. Culturally, the unwritten or oral agreement between employer and employee is generally considered just as valid. On the other hand, employers may consider a contract violation by a foreign worker to be a serious matter.

Whereas the internet reveals that a great many teachers end up disillusioned with *hagwon* owners who are variously branded crooks and rascals, a more considered view comes from a Scottish blogger called Lauren (http://livelauren.wordpress.com/tag/flying-cows) who taught in Korea through the Flying Cows agency after having been turned down for the EPIK programme. She points out that for every disreputable *hagwon*, there are a dozen decent ones, and advises prospective teachers to get an insider's view if at all possible from a foreign employee currently teaching at the institute.

The issue of severance pay (*taechikum*) is a sore point for many teachers. By law, anyone who completes a 52-week contract is entitled to one month's salary as severance pay. Employers have been known to make life quite unpleasant for their teachers near the end of their contracts, so that they're tempted to leave and forgo the bonus. According to the blogger Alex Stevenson (www.ninjateacher.com) eleventh month firings are less common than they once were because the immigration department is aware of the problem.

Bear in mind the quality of *hagwons* varies enormously. While some are excellent, others are run by sharks who may make promises at interview that they can't fulfil and overfill classes to maximise profits. Many schools do not use recognised course books but rely on home-made materials of dubious usefulness. On the other hand, standards are rising in some schools and the experience of teachers in the private sector is not all bad.

ALLISON WILLIAMS

Allison Williams was accepted onto the government's EPIK programme, which she thinks is vastly preferable to teaching for a commercial institute.

I applied through the agency Gone2Korea, who accepted me onto the EPIK programme and gave me the opportunity to apply for whichever city or province I wanted. We arrived on 18 February for a week-long orientation which covered tips on teaching and advice. I really found it very useful. I also was able to make contacts with other people teaching in Daegu. Since then I have taken a 100-hour TEFL course while in Korea, which has resulted in a $100 a month pay rise.

I co-teach, which in Korea can be one of three options: you do everything, you do nothing or you do about 50%. Many of the Korean teachers' English ability is very low so their own lack of confidence inhibits them from interacting or working with the native teachers. When co-teaching, the experience is very dependent on the teacher you work with. Last year I did the 50% option. I prepared worksheets and games for the lessons, I taught about half of the class, monitoring or assisting for the other half. Because this year our school has to improve on its national English test scores, I'm pretty much doing very little to nothing. I don't prepare games for lessons any more as they have cut down on the games in place of tests. This is not the norm but it can happen. It is a bit frustrating going from being so involved to doing so little, but I'm looking forward to being more involved next semester again. We follow the national curriculum and the teachers don't deviate from it, even if the grammar and/or phrases are incorrect or inappropriate, though they do add supplementary materials.

Working conditions are great! Since my accommodation is provided and paid for by the government, I have very few living costs and can save $1,000–$1,300 per month, without having to eat beans on toast, or should I say instant noodles. The teachers and students are all fantastic, very welcoming and kind. From day one I felt like a celebrity and still do after 15 months at the same school. I have my own desk and computer and have been helped with everything from my personal bills to getting a cell phone. In terms of pay, hours, vacation and working conditions public schools are the way to go. If you are looking for autonomous teaching and complete control over what you teach then public schools are not always the best option. I think the biggest problem is that the government has come up with this idea to have native English speakers in every school, but at the level of the school they have little or no idea what to do with them.

The majority of Korean language learners are serious (some attend two-hour classes three or four times a week) and want to be taught systematically and energetically, though even those who have been studying for years often show precious little confidence in conversing. They also expect their teachers to direct the action and are not happy with a laid-back 'let's have a chit-chat' approach.

ACCOMMODATION

Most schools that recruit teachers from abroad will sort out accommodation for their teachers. If you are looking for accommodation independently, be prepared (as in Japan) to be required to pay a large deposit or a year's rent in advance ('key money'). This should be returned to you at the end of your tenancy, though, as in Japan, disagreements can arise. If you don't hear about available flats from your school or other foreigners, check English-language community noticeboards online or find an English-speaking rental agent.

LEISURE TIME

Visitors are often surprised to discover the richness and complexity of Korean history and culture, partly because Japanese culture is far better known. Despite being a bustling metropolis of more than 10 million, Seoul has preserved some of its cultural treasures. Assuming your teaching schedule permits, you should be able to explore the country and, if interested, study some aspect of Korean culture such as the martial art Tae Kwon Do. The country's area is small, the public transport good, though traffic congestion at weekends is a problem.

Teachers often find that their students are friendly. Anyone homesick for the West will gravitate to the area of Seoul called Itaewon, where international restaurants and clubs are concentrated, not to mention a jazz club, a decent bookstore and other expatriate forms of entertainment. Teachers in the provinces will have to become accustomed to a very quiet life.

A contributor to a *Guardian* web forum on TEFL reported the following:

> ***Last year I worked in South Korea and it was the best year of my life. I have made friends all across the globe and loved every minute of my adventure in Busan, Korea's second largest city. It is a wonderful place and you can get to Seoul for a fun-filled weekend quite easily. The exchange rate is great and the free flights and accommodation allow for a high spending and saving lifestyle even though when the wage is measured against the pound it sounds fairly average. There are of course risks. But with Korea being a country unburdened by any large amount of crime and [with] a love for westerners, especially Brits, you are in good hands. Kids run around till midnight in the summer with no trouble. Old men drink*** **soju** ***all day and pass out on the benches at night;*** **ajumas** ***(old women) make you feel at home while joking about men and making harsh but delicious Korean treats. It's also wired up to the hilt with an extremely fast internet and a love for online gaming. Teaching can be challenging but it can also be a slacker's heaven, but I urge you to give it your all and you will feel better about yourself. Oh – and the beer is crap but you'll learn to love it.***

LIST OF EMPLOYERS

BERLITZ KOREA CO. LTD
3F, Apple Tree Tower, 144-25, Samseong-dong, Gangnam-gu, Seoul 135-090
+82 2 3453 4266
recruit@berlitz.co.kr or admin@berlitz.co.kr
www.berlitz.co.kr/etc/JobOpportunities.asp

NUMBER OF TEACHERS: 60 for 3 language centres in Seoul: Samseong, City Hall and Yeouida.
PREFERENCE OF NATIONALITY: Instructors must hold a passport from a country where English is a native language.
QUALIFICATIONS: Candidates with teaching and/or business backgrounds preferred, as majority of clients are professional people. Instructors must be professional, customer service-minded and able to teach using the Berlitz teaching principles.
CONDITIONS OF EMPLOYMENT: 1-year contracts. 3 schedules: morning block (6.45am–4.30pm); evening block (11.15am–9pm); split shift (6.45am–11.15am and 4.30pm–9pm). Instructors must be available to teach during their schedules, but if no classes are booked, attendance at the office is not required.
SALARY: Starting salary is 13,000 won per 40-minute lesson. Minimum guaranteed salary per month is 1,716,000 won (excluding housing). Monthly salary fluctuates, but is expected to average 2,500,000 won per month over the year. Tax deductions of 3–4% of earnings plus compulsory deductions for national pension and health insurance amount to 200,000 won per month.
FACILITIES/SUPPORT: Monthly housing stipend of 400,000 won per month. Loan for deposit for accommodation available (up to 5,000,000 won). Staff member assigned to help find housing and organise moving. All instructors must be in possession of a valid Korean working visa (F2 or F4) or be eligible for a new or transferred E-2 teaching visa.
RECRUITMENT: Berlitz Korea recruiting web page, current employee referrals, and recruiting websites such as www.worknplay.co.kr and www.eslcafe.com. Interviews are essential, preferably face-to-face in Seoul, but can be via Skype for overseas recruitment.
CONTACT: Vicky Hill, Country Manager of Instruction (vicky@berlitz.co.kr).

CANADIAN CONNECTION EDUCATIONAL SERVICES INC
2017 Danforth Ave, Suite 301, Toronto, ON M4C 1J7, Canada
+1 416 203 2679
esl@canconx.com
www.canconx.com

NUMBER OF TEACHERS: 300 per year.
PREFERENCE OF NATIONALITY: Canadian, American, British, Irish, Australian, New Zealander, and South African.
QUALIFICATIONS: Bachelor's degree in an English-related field, EFL qualification and teaching experience minimum.
CONDITIONS OF EMPLOYMENT: 1-year contract. To teach 22–30 hours per week.
SALARY: 1.8–2.5 million won per month.
FACILITIES/SUPPORT: Accommodation is supplied and paid for (teachers pay utilities). Agency handles all visa applications, teachers must supply documentation including notarised copy of their degree, criminal record check, 2 reference letters, passport photos, university transcripts and valid passport.
RECRUITMENT: Interview required.
CONTACT: Shane Finnie, Director.

CHUNGDAHM LEARNING INC
Chungdahm Faculty Recruiting Center, Baeksong Bldg, 5th Floor, Gangnam-gu, Cheongdam-dong 68–16 Seoul
+82 2 6257 0256
job@chungdahm.com; esljobs@aclipse.net
www.teachinkorea.com; www.aclipse.net

One of the largest private language institutes in South Korea, with 180 campuses teaching English to children. Aclipse Recruiting has offices in Boston and Seoul.
NUMBER OF TEACHERS: 1,000.
PREFERENCE OF NATIONALITY: Canadian, American, British, Australian, New Zealander, Irish and South African.
QUALIFICATIONS: College graduates, with clean criminal records (apostilled), from English-speaking countries. Candidates ideally have previous experience working with children, although previous teaching experience is not a requirement. Employer is looking for a professional, patient, flexible and outgoing demeanour. A strong desire to teach children overseas is required.
CONDITIONS OF EMPLOYMENT: 12 months. 4–5 days a week. Usual hours are 4pm–10pm for learners aged 10–16, or 1pm–7pm for younger learners aged 5–10. Hourly teachers work 120 hours per month, with a guarantee of 96 hours per month.
SALARY: Varies according to previous teaching experience, level of education and other factors, including performance on the Aclipse interview and evaluation. Standard range of salary is 2–2.8 million won for working 120 hours in a month. Hourly teachers are paid 25,000–35,000 won per hour. Teachers on a monthly salary are taxed at a rate of 7%–8% on their monthly income by the Korean government. Teachers on an hourly salary are taxed at rate of 3%.

FACILITIES/SUPPORT: Teachers on a monthly salary are given rent-free single furnished studio accommodation. Flight reimbursement. Training on arrival in ChungDahm curriculum. Company pays half of compulsory health insurance and pension payments. On the hourly salary, ChungDahm Learning helps its teachers find housing either before they arrive or upon arrival, assists with the key money (security deposit), and the teachers then pay rent directly to their landlord each month. Aclipse in the US assists candidates with obtaining the E2 visa. Teachers are responsible for obtaining the necessary visa documents, such as a state-wide criminal background check and original diploma, which the Aclipse office in Boston checks and forwards to ChungDahm in Korea. The visa code is then emailed to the candidate, who takes it to their nearest Korean consulate and gets visa stamped in passport.

RECRUITMENT: Online advertisements, social media, career fairs and campus events/information sessions. Interviews are essential: initial interviews are typically done over the phone, with recruiters from the Boston office or by US recruiter Aclipse (www.aclipse.net) with offices in Boston and Seoul.

CONTACT: Brendan Bryce, Social Media Manager.

FLYING COWS
The Hive, Nottingham Trent University, Nottingham, NG1 4BU UK
+44 115 824 0824
placement@flying-cows.com
www.flying-cows.com

Agency so-named because it aims to provide a service 'without the bull'.

NUMBER OF TEACHERS: Up to 30 teachers placed per month in schools throughout South Korea (as well as China and Colombia).

PREFERENCE OF NATIONALITY: Mostly British although can be Canadian, American, Irish, Australian, New Zealander and South African.

QUALIFICATIONS: Minimum degree in any discipline. Experience of teaching or working with kids is a bonus. TEFL not essential but can help attract job offers (but not any financial advantage).

CONDITIONS OF EMPLOYMENT: 12-month contracts. 6 hours per day, with varying hours, usually 30 per week. Positions available in after-school academies and public schools.

SALARY: From 2.1 million won per month. Deductions made for health insurance and income tax.

FACILITIES/SUPPORT: School arranges and pays for accommodation and flights. E2 visa assistance given. Support in all aspects of placement – contract negotiation, location advice, etc.

RECRUITMENT: Via ESL internet sites, university careers centres, media advertising and careers fairs. Applicants are usually interviewed by an FC representative over the phone, then by the school also by phone. FC staff have personal experience of teaching in Korea. Recruitment for private schools takes place year round 1–2 months before arrival, but for public school intakes in spring and autumn, deadlines fall 5–6 months in advance of the start dates.

CONTACT: Amanda Middlecote, Director/Senior Consultant.

---

i-HUFS ENGLISH CAMP
Recruited by English Beyond Borders, Toronto, ON Canada
Camps@englishbeyondborders.org
www.englishbeyondborders.org

HUFS stands for Hankuk University of Foreign Students. English Beyond Borders also recruits for year-long positions in Korea.

NUMBER OF TEACHERS: 40 teachers in summer, 20 in winter.

PREFERENCE OF NATIONALITY: Canadians only.

QUALIFICATIONS: Minimum Bachelor's of Education, and candidates must hold a Canadian passport.

CONDITIONS OF EMPLOYMENT: 2–4 weeks in January and July. Teachers work 46–48 hours per week, and get one day off each week depending on contract conditions.

SALARY: Airfare, accommodation in university residence and 1,000,000 won at end of a 4-week contract.

FACILITIES/SUPPORT: Teachers are provided with contracts and supporting documents necessary for the work permit.

RECRUITMENT: All online. Summer recruitment completed in June. Telephone interviews are conducted.

CONTACT: Linda Lee, Recruitment & Global Mobility Specialist.

KOREACONNECTIONS EMPLOYMENT LTD
#71, 583–6 Tap-Rib-dong, Yoosung-gu Daejon 305–510
+82 2 2058 2888
North American office: 211–3030 Lincoln Ave, Coquitlam, BC V3B 6B4, Canada
admin@koreaconnections.net; jaymlee@koreaconnections.net
www.koreaconnections.net

NUMBER OF TEACHERS: Approximately 150 annually for private and public schools.

PREFERENCE OF NATIONALITY: None; however, the Korean government only issues E2 visas to English teachers from UK, USA, Canada, Ireland, New Zealand, South Africa and Australia.

QUALIFICATIONS: Minimum bachelor's degree. BA in English, Education, Linguistics, TESOL or qualified teacher status is a plus though not mandatory. Clear spoken English and experience with working with young children.

CONDITIONS OF EMPLOYMENT: 1-year contract. Usual hours are 9am to 5pm Monday to Friday for public schools. Hours may be longer at private language institutes.
SALARY: Average basic salary is between 2.1 million and 2.3 million won at franchised private schools and can be between 1.8 and 2.7 million won at public schools, depending on experience and qualifications.
FACILITIES/SUPPORT: Accommodation is provided – usually single accommodation within walking distance of work. Sponsorship and assistance provided when applying for E2 visas; help with flight booking arrangements and airport pick-up.
RECRUITMENT: Usually via word of mouth, university career centre and online advertising. Interviews are essential and can be held over the phone or Skype. Face-to-face interviews can be arranged internationally depending on where the consultants are located at that time. Interviews have also been arranged while visiting TESOL conventions and job fairs in USA, UK, Canada and Ireland.
CONTACT: Jay Lee, HR Director/ Owner.

KOREA GLOBAL CONNECTIONS
Ga-301 Daenong B/D, 35-50 Guui 2-Dong, Gwangjin-Gu, Seoul
+82 2 452 9857
kgcabc@gmail.com
www.kgcesl.com

NUMBER OF TEACHERS: 200 per year.
PREFERENCE OF NATIONALITY: The Korean government allows only people from native English speaking countries: UK, USA, Canada, Ireland, Australia, New Zealand and South Africa.
QUALIFICATIONS: Bachelor's degree in any subject.
CONDITIONS OF EMPLOYMENT: 12 months. Contracted hours are 25–30 per week.
SALARY: 2.1–2.2 million won per month (£1,200–£1,250).
FACILITIES/SUPPORT: Benefits include free one-way flight, free semi-furnished housing and an extra month's wages as bonus upon finishing 12-month contract. Full visa assistance given. Airport pick-up.
RECRUITMENT: Skype interviews.
CONTACT: Anna Jeon, Director/Owner.

PLANET ESL RECRUITING
#201 Bogwang-dong 3-154, Yongsan-gu, Seoul 140–822
+82 10 9012 0579
Jobs@PlanetESL.com
www.PlanetESL.com; www.teach-english-korea.com

Recruiter for many schools in Korea.
PREFERENCE OF NATIONALITY: Teachers must be citizens of one of the seven designated English-speaking countries (Australia, Canada, Ireland, New Zealand, UK, US and South Africa).
QUALIFICATIONS: Bachelor's degree from an accredited university in one of the seven designated English-speaking countries.
CONDITIONS OF EMPLOYMENT: 1-year contracts are standard. Teaching hours range from 20 to 40 per week depending on whether it is a public or private institute. Private institutes normally operate an afternoon/evening schedule, while public schools have a 9.30am–4.30pm schedule.
SALARY: Average salary range 2–2.3 million won depending on experience and qualifications.
FACILITIES/SUPPORT: Accommodation is provided.
RECRUITMENT: Via online job postings and through recommendations. Interviews can be carried out by Skype or telephone.
CONTACT: Ms Jiyeon Kim, CEO and President.

REACH TO TEACH (SOUTH KOREA)
1606 80th Avenue, Algona, IA 50511, USA
+1 201 467 4612
applications@reachtoteachrecruiting.com
www.ReachToTeachRecruiting.com/Teach-English-in-Korea.html

Also has contacts in UK, Australia and New Zealand (see entry at beginning of Asia chapter).
NUMBER OF TEACHERS: 200+.
PREFERENCE OF NATIONALITY: Canadian, American, British, Australian, New Zealander, Irish and South African.
QUALIFICATIONS: Teaching experience is a plus, but not a requirement. A 120-hour TEFL certificate is a requirement for most positions, unless candidates have more than a year of teaching experience, an MA, or a BA in English or Education. Limited number of placements for non-TEFL qualified applicants.
CONDITIONS OF EMPLOYMENT: Public (EPIK, etc.) and private school positions. All job placements are full-time positions and for 1 year (and usually extendable). Schedules are generally either morning/afternoon (pre-school or public elementary, middle or high school) or afternoon/evening (elementary school).
SALARY: 2.1–3 million won per month (from $1,850–$2,650) plus reimbursed flights to and from Korea.
FACILITIES/SUPPORT: Free housing always given in a furnished one-bedroom apartment or studio. Teachers pay a deposit that is reimbursed. Teachers are also helped with work permits from beginning to end. All teachers are welcome at various teacher social events and gatherings (often held in Seoul).
RECRUITMENT: Detailed Skype or telephone interviews are essential. The company also carries out in-person interviews periodically in the USA and UK. Public school positions start twice

a year (March and September) and the application process ideally needs to start 6 months in advance. Private school positions can be applied for year round and the time between application and arriving in Korea is often much quicker.

CONTACT: John Kellenberger, Co-President (John@ReachToTeachRecruiting.com).

TEFA (THE ENGLISH FRIENDS ACADEMY)

733, Banghak-3 Dong. DoBong-gu, Seoul 132–855

+82 2 3493 6567

tefaenglish@yahoo.co.kr

NUMBER OF TEACHERS: Approximately 50 western teachers in 16 franchises of a private academy.

PREFERENCE OF NATIONALITY: Must be a native English speaker of a nationality eligible for an E2 visa.

QUALIFICATIONS: Minimum 3 or 4-year bachelor's degree. Love of kids and mature, interactive outlook.

CONDITIONS OF EMPLOYMENT: 12-month contract. Less than 30 hours' teaching. School covers medical insurance and 10 days' vacation. End-of-contract bonus (1 month's salary).

SALARY: 2.2–2.3 million won per month. Overtime hours paid at 20,000 won.

FACILITIES/SUPPORT: Close to all amenities and the schools, free, fully furnished, single or shared accommodation. Well-resourced schools, supportive work environment, job security.

RECRUITMENT: Via email and phone. No recruitment agents used.

YBM EDUCATION ECC

YBM ECC Head Office, 28-2 Inui-dong, Jongno Gu, 8th Floor, Seoul 110–410

+82 2 590 7818

eccmain@ybmsisa.co.kr

www.ybmecc.co.kr

NUMBER OF TEACHERS: 200 at 31 company-owned ECC branches and about 450 at 74 franchise ECC schools that are not placed by YBM Head Office. YBM Language Institutes (see next entry) are for adults and offer slightly less advantageous terms of employment.

PREFERENCE OF NATIONALITY: Canadian, American, British, Australian, New Zealander, Irish and South African.

QUALIFICATIONS: Minimum bachelor's degree, criminal background check, academic transcripts. No teaching experience required but candidates must enjoy teaching young children using curriculum provided (training given).

CONDITIONS OF EMPLOYMENT: 12-month contracts. 26 hours per week. Schedule 1: 9.30am–6pm. Schedule 2: 1pm–8pm.

SALARY: 2 million to 2.4 million won per month.

FACILITIES/SUPPORT: YBM provides rent-free, furnished accommodation near the school plus prepaid airfare, medical, severance pay and pension compliance, guaranteed contracts backed by the YBM Head Office, and assistance with E2 visa.

RECRUITMENT: Job postings via internet, word of mouth referrals from previous teachers. Every applicant undergoes either a phone interview or a face-to-face interview if they are in Korea.

CONTACT: Danny J. Kim, HR Manager, YBM Education ECC Head Office.

YBM LANGUAGE INSTITUTES

YBM Building, 13th Floor, 820-8 Yeoksam-dong, Gangnam-gu, Seoul 135–080

+82 2 3466 3519

gregstapleton@ybmsisa.com; ybmrecruiter@ybmsisa.com

www.ybmhr.co.kr

Various divisions cater to different markets; e.g. YBM Pine schools serve children aged 18 months to 16 years.

NUMBER OF TEACHERS: Between 250 and 300.

PREFERENCE OF NATIONALITY: Canadian, American, British, Australian, New Zealander Irish, South African.

QUALIFICATIONS: Minimum bachelor's degree plus 1-year formal teaching experience with adult learners. Candidates with graduate degrees in applied linguistics or CELTA/TESOL certification are preferred.

CONDITIONS OF EMPLOYMENT: 1-year renewable contract, six 50-minute classes per day (30 hours per week).

SALARY: Depending upon academic qualifications and teaching experience, salaries range from 2.1 million won to 2.5 million won per month, plus 200,000 won housing allowance. YBM Pine tends to pay more than YBM ECC (see above).

FACILITIES/SUPPORT: During the initial paid 5-day training period, teachers are provided with accommodation in a motel near the training centre in Seoul. Training takes place in the third week of the month preceding start date. Upon completion of training, instructors return to their school and are shown several apartments from which the teacher can choose. The school then provides up to 10 million won in key money (leasing) to secure the apartment plus a monthly housing stipend of 200,000 won. Visa processing costs are reimbursed. Instructor development and support is overseen by native-speaker English academic supervisors.

RECRUITMENT: Primarily through web-based job postings e.g. www.eslteachingonline.com and www.teflsearch.com, followed by telephone/Skype interviews when candidates are outside South Korea. Candidates applying from within Korea must attend a face-to-face interview.

CONTACT: Greg Stapleton, National Academic Director.

INDIAN SUBCONTINENT

Although India's phenomenal economic growth has slowed, business and industry are charging ahead. One of the most notable by-products of globalisation has been the outsourcing of services to countries with cheaper labour costs, which has been accelerated in India by the widespread knowledge of English, a legacy of the Raj in the educational system. After a long period in which nationalistic sentiment tended to view British colonial rule and therefore the English language as a tool of enslavement, there has been a softening of attitudes, partly in acknowledgment that India's technology boom owes a huge debt to the country's English-medium education. The bias against English is weakening, and it is now taught in state schools from the age of six. Interestingly, it is especially popular among the marginalised castes (once called 'untouchables' and now called Dalit), who see English as a job skill that will help them achieve social and financial emancipation.

This does not mean that there is a huge demand for native-speaker teachers. Very few ordinary citizens in much of South Asia can dream of affording the luxury of English conversation classes. This is particularly true in Nepal after the horrendous earthquake that struck in April 2015, killing and injuring 32,000 people and devastating the country's infrastructure. Few westerners could manage on the wages earned by ordinary teachers in India, Nepal, Sri Lanka, Pakistan, etc. However, those foreigners prepared to finance themselves and volunteer their time can find eager students by asking around locally.

Mainstream commercial voluntourism companies are of course active in the region, placing unskilled paying volunteers in various settings in India, Nepal and Sri Lanka. Examples include Travellers Worldwide in the UK and Global Crossroad in the US (www.globalcrossroad.com). A cheaper option for gap-year students and anybody else is available from the recruiter www.ESLstarter.com which sets up four-month teaching internships in Kerala for £590 (including free accommodation and meals provided by the school). For an extra £100, a 120-hour online TEFL training course with Global English can be added.

Grassroots organisations are also active, especially those concerned with improving literacy among women and children, such as Rajasthan-based Sankalp Volunteer (info@volunteersindia.org) which runs volunteer teaching programmes lasting from one to 16 weeks or longer in rural primary schools in Jaipur, Dharamsala, Delhi and Bangalore. After paying the initial application fee of $210, volunteers pay (for example) $1,745 for a 4-month placement in Jaipur. Other opportunities can be tracked down on www.omprakash.org (free to join) which connects volunteers with grassroots organisations around the world. The site clearly sets out the estimated daily cost of living, usually $8–$20 a day. Plenty of paid language teaching also goes on, for example in business colleges, though usually with local teaching staff.

India

The emerging economy of India has some commentators predicting that, together with China, its capacity and markets will before long overtake those of the West. High standards of education in the dominant class and an entrepreneurial spirit have helped India to flourish. English has been the medium of instruction in the elite schools and universities since India was a colony, and now is spreading to many ordinary middle-class Indians who want to participate in the booming global economy. Much of the demand for teaching is met by English-speaking Indians rather than foreigners. Whereas at one time elite institutes such as the British Council looked to employ British English teachers they now prefer Indian nationals if possible. However, with tens of thousands of students registering at British Council teaching centres, hourly teaching is also available to expat teachers (see entry).The most exciting development at the British Council in India is its programme to place teaching assistants in schools around the country; see entry for the Generation UK-India Programme.

Travelling English speakers have arranged to teach in the state sector simply by entering a school and asking permission to sit in on an English class. Provided they do not expect a wage, some teaching role could probably be found for them. A volunteer from Derbyshire teaching in several village schools in Andhra Pradesh wrote that she and her teaching partner were in such demand that a busload of volunteers would find work. But it can be very challenging and discouraging. Facilities can be brutal, with no teaching materials and no space. The majority of local English teachers, who have not really mastered the language, are very badly paid and can be transferred without appeal at any time; it is not too surprising to find that most are demoralised.

Jenna Bonistalli from New York City found an inexpensive volunteer option. She decided to use a windfall to fund six months off work to volunteer in India as a teacher:

> ***Colleagues, friends and family were surprised upon hearing my decision to take off for half a year, especially when they learned my destination. The first three months were spent in the Himalayan hill town of Kalimpong in West Bengal. My boyfriend and I volunteered through HELP, the Himalayan Education Lifeline Programme, an organisation that places teachers in primary schools throughout Indian and Nepali Himalayan regions. We chose to go through them for a number of reasons, mainly location (we were both interested in going to this region mainly due to religious and cultural interest) and cost (their fees and donation requirements were very reasonable compared to some other outrageously high prices). This was after months of searching online, in books, on www.idealist.org and through recommendations. We had some choice in where we wanted to be placed and were able to read descriptions and see photos of the school and family, so this was helpful. There were no real requirements for being accepted, aside from an application form and references. Both of us had experience as educators in different capacities, so this made us more confident. Our experience in the Himalayas was unsurpassed – the setting, our students, the people we met; everything (aside from a bout of dysentery) was utterly amazing.***

The current combined admin fee and donation to HELP (see entry) is £480, plus volunteers contribute about £100 a month to cover accommodation with host family or in school hostel accommodation.

Another voluntary agency that works in rural Himalayan communities is iSPiiCE which stands for Integrated Social Program in Indian Child Education (www.volunteerindiaispiice.com) whose projects take place around Dharamsala, home in exile of the Dalai Lama. Participation prices start at £410 for a fortnight, rising to £1,075 for eight weeks in addition to a £150 application deposit. The programme offered by Sagreen International (see entry) is not nearly as expensive. They also help volunteers to obtain an Employment Visa initially granted for one year.

Jon Walker was surprised by how contented he felt living in rural India as a volunteer teacher, where the atmosphere struck him as entirely calm, peaceful and beautiful. He spent the month of January volunteering through Dakshinayan (www.dakshinayan.blogspot.co.uk), a grassroots development charity that works with tribal peoples in the hills of Rajmahal and nearby plains:

> ***The children are of course what makes Dakshinayan so special. We were teaching Maths and English for three hours a day, and I really enjoyed the teaching. Although I had difficulties trying to translate to them what I wanted them to do, particularly to Class 2 whose English isn't so good, this was all part of the challenge. It was quite different from any teaching I had done before and meant that I really had to learn how to adapt lessons and make them the most beneficial. But we had some good fun along the way singing songs and playing games – educational of course! Their enthusiasm to learn is what motivates you every day and I miss their smiles and laughter that radiated around the school when they were there.***
>
> ***Life at Dakshinayan is very simple and a way of life that I adapted to very quickly. Waking up at 5.30am and being in bed by 9.30pm seemed very natural. Initially I was apprehensive that I would get bored when we weren't teaching. But after planning our lessons and helping with the chores around the school, it was very easy to fill our time and the days flew by. We also learnt some Hindi on the way and it was good fun having conversation exchanges with Bansi and Shanku.***

A number of mainstream gap year companies in the UK send volunteers to teach English in India and charge high fees. Interestingly, Projects Abroad closed its India programme in 2016. Just before

Raymond George (age 62) started his official retirement from his job as a university physics lecturer, he noticed an advertisement on a college noticeboard for volunteer teachers with Travellers Worldwide (www.travellersworldwide.com). They were offering teaching placements in Southern India, a region he was keen to see, so he enrolled for a two-month placement teaching spoken English in a primary school. This proved to be hugely rewarding, giving him a wonderful opportunity to experience life in a family and local community with enough spare time to travel to see the amazing temples of South India.

LIST OF EMPLOYERS

BRITISH COUNCIL – NEW DELHI

17 Kasturba Gandhi Marg, New Delhi 110001

+91 11 2371 1401

recruitment.corporatetraining@in.britishcouncil.org; careers.bcdelhi@in.britishcouncil.org

www.britishcouncil.in/about/jobs

NUMBER OF TEACHERS: The British Council has Teaching Centres across India (Bangalore, Hyderabad, Chennai, Coimbatore, Mumbai, Pune) offering increased partnership and corporate training. A large number of posts for freelancers to support examination events and to work in-company.

PREFERENCE OF NATIONALITY: Indian nationals preferred.

QUALIFICATIONS: Minimum CELTA qualification and varying levels of experience.

CONDITIONS OF EMPLOYMENT: 1 year hourly paid contracts are available for freelance trainers.

SALARY: Starts at approximately 1,000 rupees per hour for CELTA-qualified; more for DELTA qualified.

FACILITIES/SUPPORT: No help can be given with visas or accommodation.

RECRUITMENT: Interview required. May be conducted over the telephone. Deadline falls in September, though applications accepted year round.

BRITISH LINGUA

1/48, Lalita Park, Laxmi Nagar, Vikas Marg, Delhi 110092

+91 11 4302 6787

britishlingua@gmail.com

www.britishlingua.com

NUMBER OF TEACHERS: 1–2 to implement Spoken English training to Mahadalit (the poorest of the poor) in Bihar state.

PREFERENCE OF NATIONALITY: None.

QUALIFICATIONS: University graduate.

CONDITIONS OF EMPLOYMENT: 1 year. 8 hours per day.

SALARY: Negotiable.

FACILITIES/SUPPORT: Assistance given with accommodation. No help with visas.

RECRUITMENT: Local interview necessary.

CONTACT: Dr Birbal Jha, Managing Director.

GENERATION UK-INDIA PROGRAMME

British Council, Bridgewater House, 58 Whitworth Street, Manchester M1 6BB

+44 161 957 7755

www.britishcouncil.org/study-work-create/opportunity/work-volunteer/teach-india; www.britishcouncil.in/generationuk

NUMBER OF TEACHERS: 500 teaching assistantships across India including the states of Delhi, Gujarat, Madhya Pradesh, Maharashtra, Tamil Nadu, Uttar Pradesh and West Bengal with most schools based in large or medium cities.

PREFERENCE OF NATIONALITY: British only.

QUALIFICATIONS: Minimum age 18 and have completed at least one year of higher eduction. Must have British passport and permanent address in the UK. Positions available for all levels of teaching experience. Formal or informal experience of working with children, and ability to provide an overview of life in the UK are needed.

CONDITIONS OF EMPLOYMENT: 2–5 months from the beginning of July or August. Participants support English across the school both in lessons and in extracurricular activities. 20 classroom hours a week. Most schools are private or boarding schools. Must undergo a child protection check (£60), pay a £200 placement fee and obtain an Indian visa costing up to £300.

SALARY: Schools pay a monthly contribution of £150–£400 to living costs.

FACILITIES/SUPPORT: Pre-departure briefing held in early June. 3-day induction provided on arrival. Accommodation and meals provided free by host schools. Teachers are all assigned a mentor teacher.

RECRUITMENT: Recruitment begins in autumn. Applicants who pass initial screening will be invited to assessment days in March, held in Belfast, Edinburgh, Manchester, Cardiff and London.

HELP (HIMALAYAN EDUCATION LIFELINE PROGRAMME)
30 Kingsdown Park, Whitstable, Kent CT5 2DF, UK
+44 1227 263055
jim.coleman@help-education.org
www.help-education.org/volunteer.html

HELP recruits volunteer teachers to teach in primary and secondary schools in poor communities in the Indian Himalayas (Sikkim, West Bengal, Ladakh and Uttarakhand) as well as Nepal. See entry below in Nepal section. Volunteers pay an admin fee of £180, a donation of £300/£150 for students plus 9,300 rupees a month (£105) for board and lodging (13,000 rupees in Ladakh).

CONTACT: Barbara Porter (barbara.porter@help-education.org).

LHA CHARITABLE TRUST
Temple Road, McLeod Ganj-176219, Dharamsala, Dist. Kangra, Himachal Pradesh 176219
+91 189 222 0992
office@lhasocialwork.org
www.lhasocialwork.org

NUMBER OF VOLUNTEER TEACHERS: 5 at any one time to work with Tibetan refugees in Dharamsala, India.

PREFERENCE OF NATIONALITY: No preference, but fluency in English is required.

QUALIFICATIONS: Native speakers with prior teaching experience preferred, but non-native speakers with a high level of English language skill and/or documented proof of completion of a TEFL course are accepted.

CONDITIONS OF EMPLOYMENT: Minimum 2 months, maximum 6 months. One or two hours of class time per day, Monday through Friday, plus any time needed for preparation and grading. Additional hours may be needed if teachers are also participating in Lha's one-on-one tutoring programme.

SALARY: None; these are voluntary positions. Average daily cost of living is $20.

FACILITIES/SUPPORT: Lha is unable to provide room and board for volunteer teachers, though advice and orientation are given. Dorm rooms cost from 500 rupees per night or units with cooking facilities cost 9,000–15,000 rupees a month.

RECRUITMENT: Volunteer applications through Lha website and via partner websites like www.omprakash.org. In-person interviews are not essential. All communication prior to volunteers' arrival is carried out via email or telephone.

CONTACT: Ngawang Rabgyal, Executive Director of Lha Charitable Trust.

MANJOORANS GROUP
Corporate Office: Municipal Building, Kanjikuzhy, Kottayam, 686004 Kerala
+91 484 2396816
hr@manjooransacademy.com
www.manjooransacademy.com/careers

The group also has offices in Cochin, Trivandrum, Thrissur and Kollam, and runs 10 academies mainly preparing students for standardised exams like IELTS but also delivering an English-language programme called 'Speak Perfect'.

NUMBER OF TEACHERS: 50+ in ELT centres throughout the state of Kerala.

PREFERENCE OF NATIONALITY: British, American, Canadian, Australian, etc.

QUALIFICATIONS: TEFL, TESOL, etc. with a passion for teaching. Anyone with a good command of spoken English and knowledge of computers is eligible even without professional qualifications. IELTS trainers need 1–5 years' experience. For positions as English teachers, B.Ed or MA in English preferred.

CONDITIONS OF EMPLOYMENT: 6-month visas only are available. Hours of work are 9.30am–1pm and 2pm–4pm. To teach IELTS, TOEFL, conversational English.

FACILITIES/SUPPORT: Accommodation provided. Assistance given with sorting out visas.

RECRUITMENT: ESL websites. References needed. Interviews not essential.

CONTACT: Babu Manjooran, CEO.

SAGREEN INTERNATIONAL EDUCATIONAL TRUST (SIET)
TC 66/655(7), Poonkulam,Vellayani-PO, Thiruvananthapuram, 695522 Kerala
+93 4942 2304
info@sagreenintl.com; sagreenintl@gmail.com
www.sagreenintl.com

NUMBER OF TEACHERS: 500–800 paid volunteer English teachers all over India.

PREFERENCE OF NATIONALITY: UK, Australia, New Zealand, USA.

QUALIFICATIONS: Native speakers who are graduates and preferably have a TEFL background.

CONDITIONS OF EMPLOYMENT: Academic year June-March. Stays of 4–12 months. Minimum of 2 sessions per day out of 5. 45-minute lessons between 9am and 3.30pm. Teaching classes independently or alongside a local teacher.

SALARY: Volunteer teachers receive a monthly stipend of 8,000-20,000 rupees (£90-£225).

FACILITIES/SUPPORT: Free accommodation with food, wifi,

laundry and transport to work. 2 weeks' training on arrival. Unrestricted access to library and other teaching resources. Free 20-day beach holiday in Kerala upon arrival. Free horse riding, swimming and/or cricket lessons. All Employment Visa documents will be processed and forwarded to the participant.

CONTACT: Adv.B.Sathiq (International Coordinator); Sabira (Director).

VALUEPOINT ACADEMY
2nd floor, Shankar House, 1 RMV, Extension, Mekhri Circle, Bangalore, 560080
+91 80 40793777
hr@valuepointacademy.com
www.valuepointacademy.com

Four centres in Bangalore and one in Pune. Most students are from outside India especially the Middle East.

PREFERENCE OF NATIONALITY: None.

QUALIFICATIONS: Degree, preferably MA or PhD, in English plus preferably 5 years of teaching experience. English-language trainers must be passionate about the job.

CONDITIONS OF EMPLOYMENT: 1-year contract with a minimum of 6 and a maximum of 8 working hours per day.

FACILITIES/SUPPORT: Assistance can be given with finding accommodation and applying for work permits.

RECRUITMENT: Interview and demonstration lesson.

CONTACT: Ms Meenu Sood, Director.

Nepal

Just as Nepal was becoming more stable after emerging from civil war between pro- and anti-Maoists and then abolishing its backward-looking monarchical system, the country was plunged into chaos in 2015 by a destructive earthquake and its aftershocks. It seems that once again most areas of Nepal are safe to visit and most schools are operating. In September 2015 a new constitution was agreed so Nepalis are hopeful that street protests and strikes will become less frequent. The price of basic food and travel has increased substantially over the past couple of years. Nepal Immigration operates an online visa application system, though tourist visas can still be purchased on arrival for $100 cash and are valid for 90 days (shorter stays for less money are also available) and can be extended for $2 a day thereafter, up to a maximum of 150 days. Return is prohibited until the next calendar year. Note that a hefty fine or even prison sentence can be imposed on foreigners found overstaying their visas.

A range of organisations makes it possible for self-funding volunteers to teach. Of course living expenses are very low by western standards, though the fees charged by mediating or gap-year organisations as well as by Nepali agencies (some listed below) can increase the cost significantly. If you want to avoid a voluntourism agency fee, you can make direct contact with schools on arrival.

Relevant organisations in addition to the ones in the directory are listed below.

Alliance Nepal (www.volunteerworkinnepal.org). Opportunities to teach English, help in an orphanage, etc. in the Pokhara Valley for two weeks to three months. Prices from €200 for two weeks to €600 for 12 weeks.

Education & Health Nepal (www.ehn-nepal.org). NGO based in Kathmandu offering low-cost volunteering including teaching in rural schools and orphanage work. £80 admin fee plus £12 a day.

KEEP (Kathmandu Environmental Education Project), Thamel, Kathmandu (www.keepnepal.org). KEEP is eager to recruit volunteers to help deliver English-language training to guides and porters in July/August and December/January. KEEP also places volunteer teachers in government schools. Volunteers stay with a host family and must be self-funding.

RCDP Nepal Volunteer, GPO Box 8957, Tasindole Marg 95/48, Kalaniki 14, Kathmandu, Nepal (www.rcdpnepal.org). Paying volunteers work on various programmes lasting 1–12 weeks, starting every other Monday, including teaching English. Volunteers stay with families in villages including with Sherpa families. Registration fee of $269 plus a weekly charge which goes down the longer you stay, up to $850 for 12 weeks in Kathmandu and Chitwan, $1,915 in Pokhara.

After **Melissa Evans'** placement in Kenya was cancelled at the last moment, her gap year agency, Adventure Alternative (www.adventurealternative.com), had to live up to its name and quickly find her an alternative adventure. It arranged for Melissa to fly a month later to Nepal, where she taught in a school:

> *It was very, very rewarding, as the children really thrived off the teaching from a foreign teacher. I found the teaching a challenge as the children struggled with English, and also pronunciation. Sometimes, I found myself unable to understand the children and vice versa. However, familiarity over the three months allowed the language barrier to break down, and conversing with the children was easier by the end of my placement, as I had learned a little Nepali and they had grown used to my pronunciation. Before my gap year I had the ambition of being a teacher. However, after travelling for the first time my ambition changed, and now I aim to found an orphanage.*

Rachel Sedley spent six months between school and university as a volunteer teacher at the Siddartha School in Kathmandu, arranged through a UK gap organisation, and conveys some of the flavour of the experience:

> *The sun is shining and the kids are running riot. New Baneshwar is a suburb of Kathmandu, very busy and polluted, but of course so friendly. I do get tired of being a novelty, especially when I'm swathed in my five metres of bright turquoise silk (we wear saris for teaching) but I'm really loving it here. Already after one month, the thought of leaving the kids and my simple lifestyle is terrible. I find it funny that as a westerner I'm seen to represent infinite stores of knowledge and yet the servant girl is having to patiently teach me to wash my own clothes. And the general knowledge people have of the fundamentals of life makes me feel helpless and incapable. The children are so gorgeous (most of the time) and the Principal's family with whom I am living are lovely. It seems to me unnecessary to come to Nepal through an organisation. Everyone here is so keen to help.*

Rachel's main complaint about her situation was that she was teaching in a private school for privileged children, when she had been led to believe that she would be contributing her time, labour and money to more needy children.

LIST OF EMPLOYERS

HELP (HIMALAYAN EDUCATION LIFELINE PROGRAMME)
30 Kingsdown Park, Whitstable, Kent CT5 2DF, UK

+44 1227 263055
jim.coleman@help-education.org
www.help-education.org/nepalschools.html

HELP enables young people from poor communities in Nepal (Kathmandu Valley, Pokhara and Manang in the Western District) to improve their employment opportunities through education by providing financial and volunteer resources to their schools.

NUMBER OF PLACEMENTS: HELP supports some 25 schools in Nepal and the Indian Himalayas.

QUALIFICATIONS: Ages 19/20–60+. Appropriate teaching experience and/or a basic TEFL qualification is essential. Volunteers should be mature and resourceful. Qualities needed include resilience and adaptability, an open mind and an interest in other cultures, good mental and physical health, plus tact and diplomacy. A love of and experience with children is vital.

CONDITIONS OF WORK: Minimum 8 weeks. Volunteers can stay for a maximum of 6 months (for visa reasons).

SALARY: None. Admin fee £180, donation to project £300 (£150 for student volunteers) plus contribution to board and accommodation of 15,000 rupees (£105) per month. Accommodation is provided with host families or in school hostel. Everyday expenses should be about £1 a day.

FACILITIES/SUPPORT: Volunteers receive a briefing pack. Once in post, a local HELP representative is on hand to help with any problems.

RECRUITMENT: Applications accepted year round. Telephone interviews conducted after receipt of the online application form.

CONTACT: Barbara Porter, Volunteer Coordinator (barbara.porter@help-education.org).

HOPE AND HOME TRAVEL

PO Box 119, Lazimpat, Kathmandu

+977 1 443 9097

info@hopenhome.org; North America: volunteerhimalaya@gmail.com

www.hopenhome.org

Community-oriented volunteer opportunities for international volunteers with homestay and cultural exchange.

NUMBER OF PLACEMENTS PER YEAR: 55–60 in the Kathmandu Valley, Pokhara, and Chitwan areas of Nepal.

QUALIFICATIONS: Ages 18–35. A desire to help people.

CONDITIONS OF WORK: Volunteer opportunities lasting 2 weeks to 3 months are in the fields of teaching English, as well as community, health and environmental programme.

SALARY: None. Volunteer fees entirely fund programme and include homestay accommodation and food. From $400 for 2 weeks to $1,000 for 12 weeks plus registration fee of $200.

FACILITIES/SUPPORT: Language class, cultural information and project information provided.

RECRUITMENT: Online applications accepted year round.

CONTACT: Rabyn Aryal, Director.

INSIGHT NEPAL

PO Box 489, Pokhara, Kaski

+977 98560 22368

info@insightnepal.org

www.insightnepal.org

NUMBER OF TEACHERS: 60 volunteers accepted each year for development projects mainly in the Pokhara Valley.

PREFERENCE OF NATIONALITY: All.

QUALIFICATIONS: Minimum A levels for UK volunteers, high school diploma for Americans. Age limits 18–65. Teaching or volunteering experience desirable but not necessary.

CONDITIONS OF EMPLOYMENT: Placements last 7 weeks or 3 months starting year round.

SALARY: None. Programme participation fee is $1,260 for 3 months, $850 for 7 weeks.

FACILITIES/SUPPORT: Accommodation and two meals a day provided, usually as homestay. Programmes include pre-orientation training, placement in a primary or secondary school in Nepal to teach mainly English or in community development projects, and a 1-week village or trekking excursion. The 3-month programme also includes 3 days of jungle safari in Chitwan National Park.

RECRUITMENT: Application forms, 3 photos and introductory letter should be sent 3 months in advance of proposed starting date.

CONTACT: Naresh Shrestha, Programme Coordinator.

TREK TO TEACH

5129 Via Cinta, San Diego, CA 92122, USA

+1 619 405 8818

namaste@trektoteach.org

www.trektoteach.org

NGO status since March 2012.

NUMBER OF PLACEMENTS PER YEAR: 3–7 (because programme is new).

QUALIFICATIONS: Minimum age 22. Schools want teachers who can teach English, Maths and Computers. The Nepali students want teachers who can teach them new hobbies and new ways of looking at the world. Candidates should be academically able with a degree or heading towards one and be passionate about life.

CONDITIONS OF WORK: Programme combines teaching in Himalayan Nepal with a family stay and trekking. Minimum of 3 months, maximum of 8.

RECRUITMENT: No deadline. Applications must be in at least 1 month prior to expected teaching date. Nepali school year is March–December. Telephone interviews necessary.

SALARY: None because this is a volunteer programme. Programme costs: 10 weeks cost $3,600; extra weeks $200.

CONTACT: Brad Hurvitz, Founder (Brad.hurvitz@gmail.com).

Pakistan and Bangladesh

The need for English in Pakistan and Bangladesh is frequently replaced by the desperate need for more basic aid, following floods and earthquakes. The desire of teachers to work in these countries has been greatly dented by the fear of terrorism. The Foreign & Commonwealth Office advises against travel in many regions of Pakistan, including Peshawar and the Karakoram Highway north of the capital, Islamabad, warning that Al Qaeda in the Indian Sub-continent (AQIS) are active and have been responsible for some recent terrorist atrocities. In the wake of the terrorist attack in Dhaka in July 2016 which resulted in 29 deaths, 18 of them foreigners, the British Council decided to close its offices in order to review security, but reopened them a few months later.

Prospects are further curtailed by the lack of remuneration and difficulty with visas. Most opportunities are available only to teachers willing to finance themselves and to work on a three-month tourist visa. Security clearance and visa processing can take months, and is very difficult unless you have someone to push for you. A new concern is the spread of polio which is endemic in only two countries, Pakistan and Afghanistan, and a new requirement is that anyone who has spent more than a month in Pakistan is required to show evidence of recent vaccination before they can depart.

The British Council in London recruits qualified teachers for its six teaching centres in Dhaka and Chittagong and also employs hourly paid teachers who are recruited locally. People who are established in Dhaka, such as spouses of expat managers, etc., sometimes manage to earn reasonable part-time wages teaching private classes.

Almost no gap year or volunteer placement agencies or educational charities send volunteers to Pakistan and Bangladesh, unlike India and Nepal. One notable exception is the year-long placement of female volunteers by Worldteach (www.worldteach.org) at the Asian University for Women in Chittagong, which provides housing, visa and a stipend. Few private language schools exist in Pakistan. The British Council organises exams, but does not run teaching courses. The US counterpart is the Pakistan American Cultural Center (PACC; www.pacc.edu.pk) with two branches in Karachi and one in Hyderabad.

While loitering in a second-hand bookshop in Scotland, **Hannah Adcock** fell into conversation with a Pakistani university professor who promptly offered food and board in exchange for working at his wife's private school for children near Karachi. Having a native English speaker is apparently a real status symbol for a school. Many international schools hire certified teachers but positions for native-speaking EFL teachers may crop up, as well as opportunities to tutor businessmen, university students and children, if teachers are respectful and resourceful.

Tibet

Tibet (known as Xizang province in Mandarin), in the far west of China, has fascinated people in the West for centuries and until 1986 was inaccessible to the outside world. On the highest plateau in the world and encompassing a large section of the Himalayan mountains, Tibet offers something quite different from the rest of China. While there is a certain appetite to communicate with the outside world and learn English, there is also anxiety about incursions into Tibetan culture. The opening of a rail link from Lhasa to Beijing has hastened and increased the influx of Han Chinese visitors and settlers, whereas the number of international tourists has been sadly decreased by the intermittent closure of Tibet's borders.

Free travel is not permitted in Tibet and all visitors must have an authorised guide who holds the permit. Almost all NGOs that were active in the Tibetan Autonomous (so-called) Region have been expelled. The Chinese authorities have been made very nervous by the tragic spate of self-immolations by Tibetans (144 since March 2011) as a final despairing act of protest against the occupation of their country and suppression of their culture. The security crackdown has been ferocious, particularly in Lhasa. So for the present time, there is very little chance of entering Tibet as a teacher. A brave charity based in Scotland called ROKPA UK (www.rokpauk.org) sends the occasional solo volunteer teacher for a year to teach in schools that it supports on the Tibetan Plateau, most recently to the country town of Jiantsar in the north of Huangnan Tibetan Autonomous Prefecture, Qinghai Province, where 70% of the population is Tibetan.

Despite a decision taken some time ago to change the medium of instruction used in Tibetan schools-in-exile from English to Tibetan, there are plenty of volunteering opportunities in places such as Dharamsala in the Indian Himalayas. Try for example the Lha Charitable Trust (see entry above in India section). Other NGOs looking for volunteer English teachers (who pay no fees) include Education Support Tibet (lugyal.gerster@gmx.ch; www.estibet.org) registered in Switzerland, which runs Kunpan Cultural School in a village near Dharamsala. Also consider the Tibet Charity (http://tibetcharity.in) which was recently advertising on Dave's eslcafe for a volunteer to teach adults in Macleod Ganj; applications to tceducation@gmail.com.The Buddhist nunnery Jamyang Choeling Institute in the same area looks for female volunteers (jamchoe@yahoo.com).

LIZZI MIDDLETON

Lizzi Middleton's gap year was spent teaching English in a completely unexpected setting.

Not quite believing that I was embarking on what was to be the biggest adventure of my life so far, I arrived in Delhi and a few days later caught a 15-hour overnight bus to McLeodganj in North-West India, seat of the Tibetan government in exile and home of His Holiness the Dalai Lama. It was a further hour's hair-raising bus journey down into the valley to my placement at the Jamyang Choeling Himalayan Institute for Buddhist women. The nunnery is in a very secluded area of the countryside, set in front of the stunning backdrop of the snow-capped foothills of the Himalayas. It was unbelievably picturesque and was a welcome relief after the madness of Delhi!

Finding out what we were meant to be doing, and where we were meant to be, was our first major challenge. Tibetans are notoriously vague - we had been warned about this but it was vague on a level that I've never experienced vague before! This was one of the real cultural differences that I had to adapt to. Having just completed my A levels and the careful structuring of time that they had required, and coming from a family where we always let each other know where we are, life at Jamyang Choeling was quite a change. I had to learn to be very easy going, to not mind when a class just didn't turn up or when there was only half a class there.

My classes were loosely organised according to ability but to be honest that didn't mean much. Lessons were fun - I realised soon after I arrived that these women needed their hour with me to be educational but light-hearted. They get up at 5am every day and apart from an hour for lunch and an hour for dinner they don't stop until 10 or 11pm - they're studying Buddhism all day. My first few lessons were pretty diabolical as I tried to find my feet in a completely alien situation. I had no idea of how I was going to learn the names of 90 women, none of whom had any hair and who all wore exactly the same clothes!

So the teaching was the reason that I was there but there were lots of other things to be done at the nunnery too. Cooking for more than 90 people three times a day is no mean feat and so every day from 10am to noon I cut up vegetables with a small team of nuns. I found that it was a great time for the nuns to practise the English that they were sometimes too shy to use in front of each other in the classroom, and it was also an opportunity for me to learn some Tibetan and to listen to their stories - often of escape over the Himalayas from Tibet. I made some amazing friends. Together we had a huge amount of fun - riding on the roofs of local buses, swimming in the river, shopping for food for our leaving party, teaching each other national dances (I'm afraid we ended up opting to teach the Macarena), blowing up balloons, and a lot of the time just sitting and chatting about the similarities and most of all the differences between our lives, religions and cultures.

Specialist tour operators may be able to advise. For example, Tibetan Wild Yak Adventures publishes a little information about volunteering on a page of its website (www.tibetanwildyakadventures.com/teach_english.htm), including in orphanages in Tibet, although it is likely the information is not up to date.

Sri Lanka

The opening up of the country including Jaffna peninsula after the 26-year-old civil war has fuelled a demand for English-language education. English is sometimes seen as a neutral choice between rival Tamil and Sinhalese and, as in India, is used in some elite private schools.

The British Council at 49 Alfred House Gardens in Colombo (www.britishcouncil.lk) has offices with libraries and teaching centres in Colombo, Kandy and Jaffna, with partner schools in Galle and Matara. The teaching centres offer classes to adults and young learners. Teachers need a minimum of two years' post-certificate experience to be considered. The Council runs a part-time CELTA course from September to December costing more than £1,900.

The Senahasa Trust based in London (www.senahasa.org) has been working in rural state schools in Southern Sri Lanka since 2005 and recruits volunteer English teachers for the four schools rebuilt after the tsunami. Most of these are provided by the Project Trust (www.projecttrust.org.uk). A charitable foundation runs the SVS school for English in Colombo (www.svsenglish.org) which gives teachers who stay for the preferred six months free accommodation. Bond International Schools in Colombo, Trincomalee and Jaffna take on experienced teachers to prepare candidates for Cambridge ESOL exams (www.bond.lk/career.php).

LIST OF EMPLOYERS

BRITISH TEACHERS ABROAD
Mulberry Studios, Mulberry Road, Canvey Island, Essex SS8 0PR, UK
01268 695714
info@britishteachersabroad.com
www.britishteachersabroad.com

NUMBER OF TEACHERS: Unspecified number of nursery, Montessori and primary teaching assistants for several centres in Sri Lanka.
PREFERENCE OF NATIONALITY: British or Irish.
QUALIFICATIONS: Graduates in English with relevant experience of preparing candidates for the suite of Cambridge exams such as FCE and CAE. Montessori-trained teachers also needed.
CONDITIONS OF EMPLOYMENT: 9–12 month commitment. Up to 25 hours a week.
SALARY: Competitive salary and package.
FACILITIES/SUPPORT: Accommodation provided with utilities and internet. Visa is arranged. Teacher pays for the flights.
CONTACT: Vincent Cox, Project Coordinator.

SCHOOLHOUSE ABROAD
Schoolhouse, Anderson Road, Ballater, Aberdeenshire, AB35 5QW, UK
+44 1339 756333
info@school-house.org
www.school-house.org

Schoolhouse Abroad offers well-researched and supported English teaching volunteering opportunities in both formal and informal situations in Sri Lanka and India. Student groups such as trainee nurses or Buddhist monks are generally from poor backgrounds.
PREFERENCE OF NATIONALITY: Native or fluent English speaker.
QUALIFICATIONS: English teaching qualifications are not always essential as there is a range of placements to match a range of skills and experience. However, student teachers, newly qualified teachers seeking experience, teachers seeking a refreshing sabbatical or holiday and retired teachers may be particularly interested. Volunteers must be good communicators, be enthusiastic and open to contributing to and learning from new and challenging experiences, in and out of the classroom.

CONDITIONS OF EMPLOYMENT: Placements last 2 weeks to 6 months, according to volunteer's choice.

FACILITIES/SUPPORT: Individualised pre-departure support by phone, Skype and email. Volunteers stay in campus accommodation, with selected host families or in a shared house with other volunteers. Local specialised training or via Skype.

RECRUITMENT: Applications welcome all year. After submitting the online application form (via Schoolhouse site), Schoolhouse will develop a rapport with applicants to ensure an effective matching and good preparation.

COST: £900 for first month (covers placement admin, pre-departure support, airport pick-up, accommodation, most meals and support during placement). Subsequent months will cost less.

CONTACT: Cathy Low, Founding Director (cathylow@mac.com).

Maldives

A country that is normally associated with celebrities' luxury holidays, the island nation of the Maldives in the Indian Ocean promotes the use of English and encourages native speakers to spend time working in schools. The government used to administer an International Volunteer Programme whereby volunteers spent an academic year volunteering in the Maldives. Since the violent removal of the democratically elected government a few years ago, the volunteer programme has been suspended. As the founder of the UK organisation Friends of the Maldives confirmed: *'Sadly, since the coup in the Maldives, the programme has been dissolved. The new regime would prefer less outside influences.'*

A privately run scheme affiliated to a travel agency is called Volunteer Maldives (www.volunteermaldives.com). The two company founders offer a structured volunteering programme in various locations in the Maldive Islands, mainly involved with teaching and community programmes. Participants stay for a minimum of four weeks, up to three months. Possible extra activities include snorkelling trips, visits to uninhabited islands for swimming and sunbathing, and night fishing with the locals. Costs start at $1,600 for four weeks and rise to $3,400 for 12 weeks.

A similar programme is open to paying volunteers from Atoll Volunteers based on Naifaru Island (www.atollvolunteers.com); volunteers who enjoy working with children are assigned to one of the six primary and secondary schools on the various islands of Lhivayani Atoll, but mainly at Madhurasathul Ifthithaah institute. The fees here are a little more expensive: $1,750 for four weeks and $4,450 for 12 weeks.

When **Louise Sim** from Singapore was researching scuba diving in the Maldives, she chanced upon Volunteer Maldives and decided to apply as a pre-school teaching assistant. With minimal fuss she was assigned to Roashanee Pre-school and was billeted with a host who happened to be the principal and his family. Louise quickly picked up a few essential words of Dhivehi, especially when the little ones urgently needed the loo.

> ***Like most children, they took time to warm up, but once they get to know you, they are very sweet, which will make you want to take up professional teaching for pre-schoolers. They were very creative in art and crafts, and some of them would want to bring me to the reading corner to select an English book to read together. A few of them were a little hyperactive and had tantrums, which required more attention. In my spare time, I hung out with the local children and families, attended barbecues, birthday parties and picnics, and swam in the sea. I learned about simple happiness and that you don't have to earn a lot to be happy. The heat was a trial – it is quite hot on the atoll of Naifaru as there aren't many trees.***

Only a handful of English language institutes are active in the Maldives and they rarely advertise abroad. You could give Bond international Language Learning Centre a try (www.bondinternationalllc.com) in the unpronouncable Kulhudhuffushi in northern Maldives. Occasionally, the Language Learning Centre in the capital Male (newteacher@llcmaldives.com) advertises for teachers of young children. According to the advert on www.englishjobsabroad.com, the job was offering a monthly salary in Maldivian Rufiyaa equivalent to $950–$1,075, reimbursement of airfare, accommodation and health insurance.

MALAYSIA

For the many Malaysian students who aspire to go to university in the UK, USA or Australia, intensive English-language tuition is an essential part of their training. The government has increased the profile of English as a medium of instruction in the state education system and is now going it alone without much international input. For example a government-backed mentoring programme for native-speakers to work in schools with local primary school teachers came to an end in 2015 because the funding was not renewed, removing one of the best prospects for working in Malaysia. Malaysia is not at all like Taiwan or Thailand with thousands of private language institutes. Most of the teacher vacancies in Malaysia are for certified teachers to work in international schools. You can keep an eye on vacancies posted by the agency Bright Spark Teachers (www.brightsparkteachers.co.uk).

Job-finding search engines such as www.jenjobs.com and www.malaysia.recruit.net may be helpful, with occasional postings of ELT vacancies by companies like Windsor Learning Centre (www.windsor.my) and IMEC (www.imec.edu.my/career-opportunity), plus quite a few jobs in kindergartens and day care centres. One major player in the early education field is Lorna Whiston Schools (www.lornawhiston.com) which accepts applications year round for the position of Graduate English Speaking Teacher to work with young learners either in English enrichment programmes or in speech and drama training. Candidates must have a bachelor's degree plus CELTA/DELTA (or PGCE).

The British Council (www.britishcouncil.my) has teaching centres in Kuala Lumpur, Penang and Mutiara Damansara (near KL) that recruit CELTA-qualified and experienced teachers on an hourly or rolling basis. Recruitment takes place through the East Asia office in Singapore (EAteacher.Recruitment@britishcouncil.org.sg). The council in the Malaysian capital offers the CELTA course part-time for 9,275 ringgits (£1,700). As an employer the British Council is highly regarded, as long-time TEFLer **Steph Fuccio** from the USA reported after a stint of teaching in Kuala Lumpur at a different institute:

> ***My husband and I moved to Malaysia right after we got married and worked for different branches of the same language school. After a lot of pondering and trying to make it work, we left after six months. While we were there the government switched from using English as the primary language in the schools back to Bahasa Malay. This switch apparently happens often, and with an unfortunate effect on the kids in the school system. Thus, there weren't as many jobs open to us as initially thought.***
>
> ***The British Council was by far the best-paying language school in town, pretty much doubling standard language school salaries, with more benefits to boot. We interviewed at many places and finally decided on another school because it offered set daytime hours, good pay (5,000 ringgits before tax), and they had locations near our apartment. Unfortunately, what we didn't bargain on was the materials that we were supposed to use, their own cut and paste versions of difficult grammar books, the method they wanted us to teach with (lecture, not communicative method) and just how penny pinching they were. My husband's school gave them a ream of paper each month for photocopies, my school had a copy tally. We were all 'talked to' monthly on lowering our copy numbers.***

Other occasional employers of overseas teachers include the Cempaka Group of Schools (www.cempaka.edu.my), a small network of private and international schools in Kuala Lumpur, Selangor and Negeri Sembilan. The English Language Company in Sydney has a sister campus in Kuala Lumpur which accepts a steady stream of Teaching Assistants to work on Malaysian university campuses for a semester (http://englishlanguagecompany.com.my/recruitment.php); the salary is about 3,500 ringgit ($850) a month, and a placement fee is charged. To investigate a volunteer teaching opportunity, go to www.sols247.org/volunteer-teacher. Sols247 is a humanitarian organisation in Kuala Lumpur that runs educational and social empowerment programmes among poor communities. Volunteers teach English, computer and life skills at a network of community centres.

The government issues work permits only to highly qualified applicants. It is a stipulation that candidates must have worked for at least three years in their field, and must be under 60. Also enquire about a minimum age stipulation, since the government has been known to limit the issuing of work permits to people over 27. People caught working on tourist visas can expect to be fined and deported. Work permits can take a long time since the immigration department is slow to act; however, it is permitted to start work with an application pending. You will need to produce your degree and TEFL qualification certificates, university transcripts, reference letter from previous employer, medical report and passport photos. Employment Passes are divided between EP1 which covers work assignments lasting between two and five years, and EP2 for shorter term jobs of three months' to two years' duration. Once you are earning, be sure to register at the tax office as soon as you start employment, and ensure your employer is taking taxes regularly from your pay. Otherwise you can be hit by a colossal bill when you leave, as happened to one of Steph's fellow teachers. Suddenly huge amounts were missing from his pay cheque with no itemisation, and they heard that this was not uncommon. The Erican Language Centre (see entry) offers teachers willing to relocate to various parts of Malaysia to teach children or adults an attractive package. Australians and New Zealanders are eligible for working holiday visas for Malaysia.

One aspect of life in Malaysia which can be difficult to accept is that racial Malays are accorded special privileges over other citizens of Chinese, Indian or tribal origins. For example, places at the universities are available exclusively to *bumiputeras* or '*bumis*', which means literally 'sons of the soil', i.e. ethnic Malays. Otherwise Malaysia offers a pleasant multicultural environment and teachers usually experience less culture shock than they do in some neighbouring countries. Kuala Lumpur is a model of modernity and efficiency when compared with the neighbouring capitals of Jakarta and Bangkok.

LIST OF EMPLOYERS

ENHANCE EDUCATION SDN BHD
Unit 3H-2-1 Straits Quay, Jalan Seri Tanjung Pinang, Tanjung Tokong 10470, Pulau Pinang
+60 4 890 3390
careers@enhance-education.com
www.enhance-education.com

NUMBER OF TEACHERS: 22 for 4 schools in Penang State, two on the island, one each in Butterworth and Bukit Mertajam. Usually about 5 vacancies a year.

PREFERENCE OF NATIONALITY: None, provided they are native speakers.

QUALIFICATIONS: University graduate (any subject); CELTA or Trinity TEFL Cert (no on-line TEFL certs); minimum of 2 years' full-time teaching experience.

CONDITIONS OF EMPLOYMENT: Minimum 2-year contracts. 40 hours per week of which up to 24 may be teaching hours. Working week is from Wednesday to Sunday with Monday and Tuesday off.

SALARY: Starting pay of 7,250–7,600 ringgits per calendar month + 12% pension addition + 500 ringgit monthly location allowance for mainland centres. Income tax banded from 11% to 25% for residents, 25% for non-residents. Teachers become residents once their work visa has been issued. No compulsory social security. Optional local pension scheme (EPF) at 11% but not compulsory for foreigners.

FACILITIES/SUPPORT: School assists and pays for teachers to obtain a valid work permit and to register as foreign teachers with the Malaysian Ministry of Education. Procedures take up to 3 months. Assistance with relocation and settlement costs is available including 14 nights in a hotel on first arrival and an interest-free car purchase loan. 36 days paid annual leave plus 12 local public holidays.

RECRUITMENT: Via Dave's ESL Cafe. Interviews by Skype after candidate sends a recent lesson plan they have taught.

CONTACT: Dr Tom Craig-Cameron, Principal (tom@enhance-education.com).

ERICAN LANGUAGE CENTRE
C-19-4 Megan Avenue II, Jalan Yap Kwan Seng, 50450 Kuala Lumpur
+60 3 2164 9999
career@erican.edu.my
www.erican.edu.my/LanguageCentre/career.php

Language education and training company with 20+ centres across the peninsula.

NUMBER OF TEACHERS: 5 full-time.

PREFERENCE OF NATIONALITY: British, American, Canadian, Australian or New Zealander.

QUALIFICATIONS: Minimum TEFL/TESOL or CELTA qualification and one year's teaching experience.

CONDITIONS OF EMPLOYMENT: 12–24-month contracts to teach children and adults. Usual working hours (25–30 per week) between 9am and 5pm Monday to Friday. Lots of IELTS preparation.

SALARY: Approximately $1,200 per month plus monthly performance incentive, less 10% deductions for tax and social security.

FACILITIES/SUPPORT: Free shared room in teachers' hostel is normally available or the teacher will be subsidised by the centre (typically 500 ringgits per month) for private accommodation. The centre applies for work permits and covers all required visa charges. The visa application process may take 2–3 months.

RECRUITMENT: Usually via online advertisements. Interviews are essential and are normally via online video conferencing.

CONTACT: Ki Chong, Human Resource Manager (Erican Education Group).

SINGAPORE

Malaysia's tiny neighbour clinging to the tip of the Malay peninsula is a wealthy and westernised city-state in which there is a considerable demand for qualified English teachers on minimum one-year contracts. Once a teacher gets established in a school, freelance teaching is widely available paying from S$32 an hour (US$24).

The Foreign Recruitment Unit of the Ministry of Education in Singapore (www.moe.gov.sg/careers/teach) recruits foreign teachers in English language/English literature, as well as humanities, sciences etc. on one to three-year contracts in secondary schools and junior colleges (Grades 7 to 12). The scheme is very competitive, so only suitably qualified applicants should consider this option, though there are options to train for a Diploma in Education (even people with only A levels) while doing contract teaching.

The British Council at 30 Napier Road oversees teaching operations in five centres that constantly hire qualified Singapore-based teachers especially for teaching young learners (and can also provide a list of approved language schools). The recruitment office for all of East Asia is located in Singapore; enquiries may be sent to EAteacher.Recruitment@britishcouncil.org.sg. Many private institutes are located in the ubiquitous shopping centres, especially along Orchard Road, for example Berlitz (391b), Geos Language Centre (Singapore Shopping Centre, near Orchard Road), Ikoma Language School (350), Native Hills (321) and Goro (268). The majority of commercial language centres are Chinese-owned with a high proportion of teachers from Australia.

Not strictly for ESL teachers, a number of companies offer after-school or pre-school English enrichment programmes to local children. Sometimes all that is necessary to be hired is experience of working with children. Try, for example, My English (www.myenglish.com.sg/about-us/job-opportunities) and LCentral English Enrichment Centres (HumanResources@LCentral.net) offering a tasty salary of S$4,800 a month at its 11 centres. Similarly native English speakers are recruited to teach literacy skills to children with a company called I Can Read. Candidates must have either a university teaching qualification or a degree in a humanities subject such as English literature, linguistics or education, in order to qualify for the Employment Pass. Two-year contracts start in July/August (www.career.icanread.asia).

Singapore is not a recommended destination for the so-called 'teacher-traveller' who, without qualifications but with a smart pair of trousers, hopes to be able to impress a language school owner. Even people who have qualifications cannot count on landing a job without effort. However, persistent enquiries have resulted in the offer of hourly work. Once a job is found, a variety of Work and Employment Passes of varying grades may be applied for from the Ministry of Manpower; see www.mom.gov.sg for clarification. Students and graduates aged 17–30 from universities in the UK, US, Australia, New Zealand and other countries can easily qualify for the Work Holiday programme which permits participants to do any job for up to six months; the processing fee is S$150 and the total quota is 2,000.

Once you have a sponsoring employer, the prospective employer must contact the Singapore Immigration and Checkpoints Authority (10 Kallang Road, ICA Building, Singapore 208718; www.ica.gov.sg) for an application form and approval letter, or simply apply online. The process usually takes between six and eight weeks, and it is necessary to wait for the approval letter before travelling as you will be required to present it at Immigration Control in Changi Airport.

Some teachers have reported that they have quickly tired of Singapore, coming to see it as one giant shopping mall. So if shopping malls and a repressive regime (for example there are signs threatening to fine you up to S$1,000 if you drop litter, jaywalk, feed the pigeons or fail to flush the loo) leave you cold, Singapore is perhaps best avoided.

LIST OF EMPLOYERS

INLINGUA SCHOOL OF LANGUAGES
51 Cuppage Rd, #10–12, Singapore 229469
+65 6737 6666
info@inlingua.edu.sg
www.inlingua.edu.sg

NUMBER OF TEACHERS: 8 full-time English teachers (62 teachers in total in 13 language sections). Also positions as interns for students on working holiday visas.
PREFERENCE OF NATIONALITY: Multinational team from the UK, USA, Canada and Australia. Teachers from the UK preferred.
QUALIFICATIONS: University degree and post-graduate teaching qualification required (CELTA, TESOL or TEFL). Experience is not necessary but candidates must be effective teachers who can work well in a team.
CONDITIONS OF EMPLOYMENT: Standard 18-month contract. 40 hours per week (8 hours per day maximum) on school premises. This includes up to 25 hours of teaching (30 lessons lasting 50 minutes each). Group lessons are usually Monday to Friday 9am–1pm but trainers may also have to teach until 9pm Monday to Friday and 8am–3pm on Saturdays.
SALARY: Starts at S$3,100 per month. After a 6-month probationary period and satisfactory performance, salary increases to S$3,300. 18-month contracts are taxed at around 3%. Teachers do not need to pay Central Provident Fund contributions.
FACILITIES/SUPPORT: Temporary homestay accommodation can be arranged for at least 1 month at a cost of S$900. Teachers are given help by school's admin when looking for more permanent accommodation.
RECRUITMENT: Please apply by email by sending detailed CV. Interview and demonstration lesson in Singapore preferred but not essential.
CONTACT: Graham Sage, Managing Director.

MORRIS ALLEN STUDY CENTRES
#03–02, Block 51 Bishan Street 13, Singapore 579799
+65 6258 3229
administration@morris-allen.com
www.morris-allen.com

NUMBER OF TEACHERS: 40+ for six branches (also in Malaysia).
PREFERENCE OF NATIONALITY: British, Australian, New Zealander, Canadian, American and South African.
QUALIFICATIONS: Minimum 3 years' experience plus degree in education; or bachelor's degree plus teacher training specialising in English, primary or early childhood education. Most teachers have classroom experience with children whose mother tongue is English.
CONDITIONS OF EMPLOYMENT: 2-year contract strongly preferred. 28 teaching hours per week out of total working week of 35 hours between Wednesday and Sunday. Teaching Singaporean children aged 3 to 16 years, in an English-medium education system.
SALARY: S$3,500 per month, tax free plus bonus of S$3,000 at the end of 2-year contract.
FACILITIES/SUPPORT: S$700 per month per person provided for accommodation expenses in first year, S$900 second year, plus S$500 freight allowance. Medical insurance provided. 2 weeks' initial hotel accommodation and assistance given in finding an apartment. Employer will submit visa applications.
RECRUITMENT: Adverts in foreign teachers' journals and online, e.g. at www.englishjobsabroad.com. Face-to-face interview preferred; telephone interview possible.
CONTACT: Renee Stone, Principal.

NYU LANGUAGE CENTRE
The Adelphi 04–35, 1 Coleman St, Singapore 179803
+65 6338 3533
admin@nyu-online.com
www.nyu-online.com

NUMBER OF TEACHERS: 5.
PREFERENCE OF NATIONALITY: American, British.
QUALIFICATIONS: Degree with teaching experience in English.
CONDITIONS OF EMPLOYMENT: 1-year contracts. Hours are 9.30am–5.30pm, Monday to Friday.
SALARY: S$2,500–S$3,000.
FACILITIES/SUPPORT: Help given with work permits.
RECRUITMENT: Via advertisements or recommendation.
CONTACT: Nance Teo, Principal.

BRUNEI

Few people can locate Negara Brunei Darussalam (Brunei, the Abode of Peace) on a map of the world, let alone anticipate that there is a steady demand for qualified English teachers there. This wealthy oil state on the north shore of Borneo can afford universal education for its population of 415,000. For many years the Ministry of Education has been implementing a bilingual educational system which '*ensures the sovereignty of the Malay language while at the same time recognising the importance of the English language*'.

Brunei, mostly covered in luxuriant tropical rainforest, has a pollution-free, healthy environment, few traffic jams and one of the lowest crime rates in the world. It provides a very pleasant place to live and work for those who like the outdoor lifestyle and don't crave a wide variety of nightlife. For water sports enthusiasts, the warm, calm waters of the South China Sea provide an ideal environment for diving, sailing and power boating. Most expatriates join one of the many sports and social clubs which provide excellent facilities.

Brunei has a rich cultural heritage and still boasts the largest water village in the world, Kampong Ayer, where 10% of the country's population live in stilt houses. There are many opportunities to participate in colourful cultural extravaganzas to mark national events such as the Sultan's birthday on 15 July and National Day on 23 February. In the rural areas there is an opportunity to see how the other indigenous groups celebrate their traditional harvest festivals. Although Brunei is a Malay Islamic monarchy, other religions are allowed to practise freely and Chinese New Year and Christmas Day are also national holidays, in addition to the numerous Islamic public holidays.

There are currently over 200 expatriate primary and secondary EFL teachers working in Brunei in state sector schools. CfBT Education Services (Block D, Units 5 & 6, Kiarong Complex, Lebuhraya Sultan Hassanal Bolkiah, Bandar Seri Begawan BE1318, Brunei; http://careers.educationdevelopmenttrust.com or www.cfbt.org/bn) recruits suitably qualified and experienced individuals along guidelines set by the Brunei Ministry of Education. All teachers must have Qualified Teacher Status, e.g. PGCE or equivalent, plus a degree, a minimum three years' experience including EFL/ESL and be under 52 (primary) or 55 (secondary). The package currently includes a tax-free salary package worth B$49,000–B$72,000 a year (£26,700–£39,000). Contracts are usually for two years initially. A car driving licence is strongly preferred though some teachers can arrange to be driven to work by a spouse or a maid.

VIETNAM

The market in English-language training is still fizzing. Vietnam's economy is charging ahead and is now on target to achieve more than 6% growth this year. Student numbers are ever on the increase, and the established language schools are offering teachers a full timetable. Many urban Vietnamese want to learn English with a view to joining a profession such as banking or tourism or to have a chance of acceptance at institutes of higher learning overseas. From Ho Chi Minh City (HCMC) in the south to Hanoi in the north, opportunities abound for both trained professionals and freshly certified CELTA/TESOL graduates.

Although Vietnam is still a one-party socialist republic (which has been accused of blocking websites and blogs that are critical of the government), it bears all the trappings (complete with garish advertising hoardings and American pop music) of a capitalist society with an expanding young middle class who invest in electronic goods, luxury items and English lessons. The British Council offers many types of English course, from those aimed at primary school children to 'English for international business'. It employs 50 teachers and is always looking for hourly paid teachers, for its four centres in HCMC and Hanoi.

FINDING A JOB

Prospective teachers in Vietnam should be aware that the country is becoming increasingly savvy about qualifications. A degree is often no longer seen as sufficient and EFL teaching qualifications are very desirable. Many employers are not impressed with online courses or those without a classroom component. However, it is still possible to get work in a local institute, gain experience and move up the ladder. The principal teaching organisations included in the list of employers are the most prestigious employers with relatively high standards and high pay. Both Hanoi and HCMC have scores of other language schools which often employ staff within two weeks of arrival. Ask around before accepting a job to make sure they reliably pay the promised wages.

On the whole teachers are highly respected in Vietnamese culture, and it is not unusual for students to present their foreign teachers with flowers, presents and dinner invitations. However, caution should be exercised if you are advertising 'private English tuition', which can sometimes be misconstrued for other services. **Annabelle Laker** reported from Ho Chi Minh City that she got in a tangle when she went to meet a prospective student and he thought he could buy sex.

Vietnam is a good place to acquire the CELTA, since there are four course providers – Language Link, Apollo English in two cities and ILA Vietnam – all with entries at the end of this chapter. **Steph Fuccio** had no trouble getting work in Hanoi with Language Link after doing the CELTA course:

> ***Language Link is a great place to do a CELTA and start working. They have all the usual trappings of an EFL job such as unpredictable schedules, weekend work and so on. But, they do have a huge amount of resources, keen students and there is real opportunity to build up your teaching skills quickly. In my second year I taught English for Academic Purposes and TOEFL-iBT along with my regular Business and General English classes.***

Often the best way to find work is simply to arrive in one of the major cities and look around. Check out Craigslist (http://vietnam.craigslist.org), which has scores of job ads and is useful for accommodation listings as well, and www.expat.com/en/jobs/asia/vietnam, which is also good for posting private tuition ads. The site www.vietnamteachingjobs.com enables you to target your search for Academic English, Business English, General English or young children. Other community sites for expats such as http://tnhvietnam.xemzi.com can be equally productive for jobs, accommodation, etc. especially in Hanoi.

The demand for Young Learners' English is rocketing. On arrival at her job with Language Link Hanoi, **Amalia Pesci** was taken aback to be told that she would be mainly teaching young learners, because all of her extensive experience had been in teaching Adult English. She coped with teaching children for her first year but found the parental pressure hard to deal with: 'The parents wanted their children to learn English in about six months.'

Originally, **Annabelle Laker** from Exeter had signed up and paid to do an internship programme in Vietnam through the i-to-i TEFL website (www.i-to-i.com/teach-and-travel-abroad/teaching-internships/vietnam.html). However, at just four days' notice, the internship fell through and, after a concerted effort, she got all her money back:

> ***I was suddenly faced with no job, no apartment and no safety net for my first adventure overseas! I decided to travel to Vietnam anyway and see if I could make it work by myself. For my first two months in the country I travelled around and found voluntary positions by ringing up and visiting orphanages. Then I decided to settle in Ho Chi Minh City and printed out about 20 copies of my CV. I spent a few days running around the city dropping off CVs and copies of my TEFL certificates and degree at the head offices of language schools: I found this face-to-face approach worked better than sending emails or applying online for jobs. I was called for an interview a week later at a large language school called SuperYouth. Once they had seen that I could dress smartly and was a native speaker, I had the job so long as I worked the hours they wanted, i.e. 15 hours a week, almost all evenings and weekends. Friends of mine had clued me up to say I was currently being paid $20 an hour by private students and to use this to push up the original offer from the language school. In the end I was able to negotiate $17 an hour, but I did have to be quite firm to get this.***
>
> ***I work three jobs at the moment, which is very manageable and gives me variety which I love. The other two jobs I created really – I put up adverts on Craigslist and expat-blog as a private English-language tutor and from responses to these ads I now have a job with an agency as a conversation tutor for a group of four teenagers and as a Business English tutor for the reception staff at a western dental clinic based in the city.***

By asking around you will soon discover which schools might be hiring. Some of the best-established companies in HCMC are ACET, which specialises in academic English (see entry), RMIT (affiliated to an Australian university), VUS and many others like Compass Education (www.compass.edu.vn/en/job-opportunities), American Academy (www.ama.edu.vn/en) and Washington Language School.

In her late 20s, **Dawn Wilkinson** decided to use some money she had inherited to take a year off from her publishing job in the UK. After five months of travelling around South-East Asia with friends, she felt she wasn't ready to go home, so decided to find out how far her BA and MA in English would get her in landing a teaching job. After meeting up with a uni friend in Saigon – the old name for HCMC is still in wide use – and making friends with a few expats and locals, she decided to base herself there. After trawling through numerous ads placed by tutors looking for work, she finally stumbled across an ad placed by a wealthy French-Vietnamese woman looking for an English tutor for her seven-year-old daughter and Dawn got the job:

> ***The family were lovely and, as the sessions were at their house, they always invited me to eat dinner with them afterwards. This family were middle class, I guess, so working for the two families gave me a great insight into Vietnamese life and I spent a lot of time chatting with the parents about their lives and to the girls about their hopes for the future (they were all keen to improve their English as a means to travel and work in Europe or America).***
>
> ***Exams are taking off in Vietnam and many students strive to obtain a good TOEFL score in the hope of going to America, while the Cambridge suite of exams and IELTS are popular with those wanting to take up scholarships to Australia and the UK.***

SAMANTHA THORNLEY

Samantha Thornley shied away from joining the corporate world after graduation from Northeastern University in Boston, and was delighted to be accepted by Teachers for Vietnam in the USA (see entry), which has a well-run programme; unusually, funding is available for qualifying volunteers.

I lived and taught English in Vietnam for a full academic year, and I can honestly say that these were the hardest, scariest, best and most rewarding months of my life. Through challenges and adjustments, I was continually amazed at the generosity and hospitality of the Vietnamese people, especially my students.

Upon arrival I was continuously challenged by my surroundings. The first obvious problem I encountered was the language barrier. Simple things like ordering and paying for food, saying thank you or I'm sorry, can get lost in translation. I took a crash course in Vietnamese – numbers, food, all the necessities for my daily needs. It turns out that I was capable of learning how to get by in a strange land. The more I explored Can Tho, the more I realised how fast English is becoming a second language for the locals, and how valuable my time there was for both their education and mine.

My placement was as a volunteer English teacher at Can Tho University. I worked about 20 hours a week in class, although lesson preparation added at least another 10 hours a week. I also taught at a private English school at nights; although not required by the programme, it was a great way to meet more students and make some extra travelling cash. In most places in Vietnam (especially Saigon and Hanoi) you can find private schools easily, and as long as you are certified or have prior teaching experience you can work there. Most of the smaller cities, such as Can Tho, love to have foreign teachers and are more than willing to find a way to accommodate you.

Other organised schemes charge substantial fees such as Teach and Travel in Vietnam (www.teachandtravelvietnam.com) run by the English Language Company in Sydney. Smaller Earth with its headquarters in Connecticut also has a Teach and Travel Programme in Vietnam (www.smallerearth.com/us/asia/tefl-in-vietnam) which costs $999 for a 5-month placement.

CONDITIONS OF WORK

Base pay at the high-end schools and universities starts at $20 per teaching hour and rises to about $25, but a more usual hourly rate at language schools is $15–$18, with private tuition paying a little more and lessons delivered by Skype a little less. This should allow a comfortable lifestyle since the cost of living remains low (for example, HCMC is much cheaper to live in than Bangkok), so Vietnam is a good country for those trying to save some money. ESL teachers are exempt from tax, so earnings are net of deductions.

Teachers often complain of the unsuitability of some of the teaching materials in use. Course books are often designed for European learners so materials have to be constantly adapted, as the cultural references mean nothing to Asian learners.

Annabelle Laker noted that lesson structuring tends to be very book focused in language schools, as opposed to in universities and international schools:

> ***Language institutes want you to stick to the book and get through it. You have zero preparation time. You turn up to be given a printed schedule of room numbers and book pages to teach and review and away you go. Ad-libbing and thinking on your feet become your strengths. For one particular lesson I opened the book and it appeared to be some sort of song . . . I had no idea what the tune was meant to be and neither did the teaching assistant. Trying to think of a song tune on the spot felt a bit too much for me on this day . . . I wasn't feeling in jolly big purple dinosaur mode. Thankfully I had a light bulb moment and decided to turn the song into a clapping game! Turns out this is not something the Vietnamese kids are used to, so the whole concept was quite novel and exciting for them. It worked a treat. They learnt the song and we all had fun too. One successful lesson.***

She goes on to explain why the best thing about the job for her is the students:

> ***Although they are sometimes very naughty and hard to control or engage, for the most part they are a lot of fun and very cute. Some of the children have clearly never interacted with a 'real life' westerner before, which can initially mean they are very frightened. But it's not long before they are bouncing up to you saying 'Teacher, teacher, what's your name? Play game!' and stroking your arms.***

REGULATIONS

New work permit requirements came into force at the end of 2013, making the process more difficult. You will need to submit the originals of your university degree, TEFL certification and recent police clearance certificate and copies which have been notarised as being 'true and correct' and any differences in the names written must be notarised as belonging to the same person. The original or notarised documents are submitted to the immigration office with a medical report, and the work permit should be issued within about six weeks. It remains valid for two years.

Dawn Wilkinson commented that the laws are not always strictly observed though. Her employers assured her that it was fine to work on a tourist visa, as they were in the process of securing her a full work permit. In order to get this she would have to complete some kind of TEFL course, and was told that even a basic 60-hour/$200 online course would be enough to fulfil the criteria for a work permit. It is so costly for schools to obtain full work permits for their teachers that a lot of skulduggery takes place to avoid the hassle and expense, and rumours abound of schools paying off the authorities to turn a blind eye.

LEISURE TIME

According to **Annabelle Laker**, a shared western-style apartment in HCMC costs about $200 per person per month. Teaching afforded her an 'amazing expat lifestyle' while still being able to save a third of her wages. The cost of living is higher in Hanoi than Saigon, with rents and wages following suit. There is a two-tier system for utilities and travel in Vietnam, which means foreigners pay substantially more than locals for almost everything. You will soon learn that the first 'western price' quoted will always be two if not three times more than the price westerners should actually pay. Bear in mind that what you see is not always what you get. Behind that charming Vietnamese smile is more often than not the intent to extract money. Of particular note are the numerous women in search of a foreign husband, a foreign passport and an airline ticket. Single men should beware.

Hanoi is smaller and more beautiful yet bustling and noisy, whereas HCMC is a Bangkok in the making. This sophisticated, sprawling commercial centre boasts a skyline already dotted with fledgling skyscrapers. The main complaints thus are traffic, noise, pollution and street hassle. Vietnam is a developing country and although the wealth of the nouveau riche classes in the cities is very visible, the countryside is still desperately poor. Countryside and cities alike experience frequent power cuts and things in general don't always work as they are supposed to. Internet access is widely available and improving although it is still unreliable, slow and government firewalls prohibit prying eyes from seeing things they don't want you to see.

As usual, the drawbacks of living in a large Asian city may begin to intrude, as happened to **Dawn Wilkinson**:

> ***On the whole, I didn't find Saigon a particularly pleasant city to live in (apart from the fantastic food): it was either stiflingly hot or pouring down with rain, heavily crowded and polluted and had no green spaces at all. I tended to sleep through the day (directly in front of my fan!) or watch TV, then go out with friends late in the evenings after I'd finished working – Saigon does have a great, tight-knit expat social scene.***

The cities are wonderfully packed with cheap restaurants (*com binh dan*) and fantastic street food. Soon you will be addicted to *bun cha* (pork patty), *pho* (noodle soup), banana flower salad and *bia hoi* (draft beer). International restaurants and cafés are more expensive but still affordable for the average teacher. **Annabelle Laker** loves the chaos of street life in HCMC and the buzzing and vibrant nightlife, with many places offering free drinks for women on set nights.

Travelling round the region is very affordable, and has become more so with the rise of low-cost airlines such as Jetstar Pacific based at HCMC airport and Viet Jet Air, which flies from north to south for an astonishingly cheap $30. Regular tourist night buses are a great way to explore the country and cost just a few dollars for an eight-hour trip.

The *Reunification Express* is a train that runs the full length of the country (over 1,300km). The cheapest fare for the Hanoi–Saigon trip is about $50, though you will have to pay nearly 50% more for an air-conditioned soft sleeper.

Annabelle Laker feels that she wasn't really prepared for the assault on all her senses, but in an amazing way.

ZACHARY KEESTER

Zachary Keester reflects on his experiences as an English Teacher with ILA Vietnam:

I decided to teach English as a foreign language after I graduated from University. The economic climate in the United States was extremely volatile at the time, especially for an undergrad with very limited work experience. I looked around at my peers and myself and realised that there weren't any doors opening for us anytime soon. I wanted to live my life and see the world. Deciding to go into EFL teaching was the best and easiest decision I had ever made.

Originally, the plan was to go to South Korea and work in their public school system through the EPIK programme. I had a successful interview with the EPIK coordinator and was all set to go. However, I was told the position would not be available until

February; it was August and I didn't want to wait. Meanwhile, my friend who had taught in Korea, Vietnam and had just come back after teaching in Turkey, told me about the CELTA training course offered at ILA in Vietnam. I looked online and discovered that the next available course started in early November. I enrolled and booked my round-trip ticket to Vietnam immediately.

Two weeks into the CELTA at ILA, I cancelled my return flight and notified the school in Korea that I would not be teaching there in February. I would stay and teach in Vietnam.

Directly after completing the CELTA course, I was hired by ILA on a full-time contract. It was great. I couldn't think of a better place to start my teaching career. ILA offers its teachers so much support and really encourages professional development. I knew immediately that it was the right school for me. It wasn't your run-of-the-mill EFL school that hired under-qualified backpackers off the street. It was highly respected by both teachers and locals alike.

The best part about working for ILA in Vietnam is the hours and the location. As a full-time teacher you generally work on Saturday and Sunday, leaving you with five days off to relax or travel. As for location, Vietnam is centrally located, making travel to Thailand, Burma, Cambodia, Indonesia, Laos and Malaysia incredibly easy.

I have recently completed a Young Learner course at ILA that was offered to me completely free of charge. I am currently planning on earning my MA in Education online, while I continue to develop my teaching skills and methodology by working for ILA. ILA hasn't just opened doors for me; it has opened the world to me.

LIST OF EMPLOYERS

ACET (AUSTRALIAN CENTRE FOR EDUCATION AND TRAINING)

187 Vo Thi Sau, District 3, Ho Chi Minh City

+84 8 3932 6202

recruitment@acet.edu.vn

www.acet.edu.vn/recruitment.html

ACET is a NEAS-accredited partnership between IDP Education and the University of Technology Sydney's language centre.

NUMBER OF TEACHERS: Approximately 50 for 3 branches in Ho Chi Minh City and 40 for 2 branches in Hanoi.

PREFERENCE OF NATIONALITY: No preference but they need to be able to obtain a work permit in Vietnam and have native English speaking ability.

QUALIFICATIONS: University degree and CELTA or equivalent teaching qualification (minimum 6 hours observed lessons) required. Preferred qualifications and experience: 2 years' teaching experience to adults with reputable organisations, demonstrated experience in teaching Academic English and/or IELTS preparation. Experience of teaching in Asia is a plus. A clean police clearance certificate is required.

CONDITIONS OF EMPLOYMENT: Teachers will be on term contracts (5 weeks) until they obtain a work permit. Then ACET has contract signings twice a year but most teachers stay for at least 1 year. Reliable and stable teaching schedules with minimal travel. Typical hours are Monday–Friday: 4-hour classes in the mornings and afternoons, and 2-hour classes in the evenings. Classes for teenagers are taught on weekend afternoons.

SALARY: Ranges from $23.50 to $32.50 per teaching hour, depending on qualifications and experience. Teachers are taxed according to Vietnamese laws; personal income tax is between 12% and 20%.

FACILITIES/SUPPORT: No help given with accommodation, though finding affordable accommodation is not a problem, from shared housing to villas. Opportunities for professional development, and academic support given. Full assistance given with visa application provided teacher has brought necessary documents (degree, teaching certificate and police check). Local costs are met by school.

RECRUITMENT: Advertisements posted on www.tefl.com, Dave's ESL Cafe, and the ACET website. Most teachers are hired locally but also some are hired overseas. Email applications should include CV with referees, covering letter, preferred start date and location (Hanoi or HCMC) and scanned copies of teaching certificate and university degree. All teachers will have an initial interview with the Director of Studies either face-to-face or over the phone.

APOLLO EDUCATION & TRAINING

20 branches in Hanoi, Ho Chi Minh City, Danang, Haiphong, etc.

✆ +84 4730 02999

recruitment@apollo.edu.vn

www.teachatapollo.com; www.apollo.edu.vn

Established in 1995, Apollo is affiliated to International House and offers training in English, professional development and overseas study consultancy as well as teacher training (Cambridge CELTA). Apollo also has an increasing number of younger learners and corporate classes in addition to partnership contracts with local schools.

NUMBER OF TEACHERS: More than 100 nationwide, more in the summer months.

PREFERENCE OF NATIONALITY: None, but must be native English speaker or have IELTS band 8–9 or equivalent.

QUALIFICATIONS: Teachers must have a CELTA or equivalent (i.e. 120 hours minimum with at least 6–8 hours of observed classroom teaching practice). Vietnamese work permit regulations stipulate that teachers must also have a degree.

CONDITIONS OF EMPLOYMENT: 1-year contract (some 3-month short-term contracts are available, particularly for the summer programme, and part-time positions). 18–25 teaching hours a week between 7.30am and 10pm, Monday to Friday; 7.45am–8.15pm Saturday and Sunday.

SALARY: From $1,200 per month depending on qualifications and a competitive package including 15 paid annual leave days, 11 paid public holidays, contract completion bonus and re-signing bonus.

FACILITIES/SUPPORT: $500 contribution to medical insurance, sponsorship plus visa and internal work permit costs. For 1-year contracts teachers are given agents' names and/or a Vietnamese member of staff can visit accommodation with the teacher to assist with translation and negotiation.

RECRUITMENT: Through http://ihworld.com, local adverts and internationally using posters, websites, etc. Interviews are essential and are occasionally carried out over Skype.

CONTACT: Ms Ngan Nguyen, Nationwide Recruitment Coordinator.

ASIAN INSTITUTE OF TECHNOLOGY IN VIETNAM

Education Management Section, Building B3, University of Transport and Communications, Lang Thuong Dong Da, Hanoi

✆ +84 4 3766 9493 ext. 143

linh@aitcv.ac.vn

www.aitcv.ac.vn

NUMBER OF TEACHERS: 2.

PREFERENCE OF NATIONALITY: None.

QUALIFICATIONS: At least 5 years' experience and preferably a master's degree. TEFL cert also needed.

CONDITIONS OF EMPLOYMENT: Hours vary according to course availability. Classes last 2.5 hours. Mostly part-time.

SALARY: $22 per hour (diploma in TEFL/TESOL or TESOL certificate), $25 per hour (master's in TEFL or TESOL).

FACILITIES/SUPPORT: Some assistance with finding accommodation. No assistance with work permit.

RECRUITMENT: Word of mouth and interviews.

CONTACT: Ms Pham Ngoc Linh, HR Administrator.

ASTON EDUCATIONAL GROUP VIETNAM

231 Nguyen Thi Minh Khai St, District 1, Ho Chi Minh City; Alternative: 614-618 3/2 Street, Ward 14, Dist 10, Ho Chi Minh City

✆ +84 8 3863 3654

nguyentrucminh@gmail.com

www.aston.edu.vn

NUMBER OF TEACHERS: Full-time and part-time positions at several branches in HCMC with plans to expand the brand that specialises in teaching children.

PREFERENCE OF NATIONALITY: Americans and Britons preferred.

CONTACT: Mr Minh.

AUSTRALIA-VIETNAM SKILLS & EDUCATION (AVSE-TESOL)
1300 Quang Trung Street, Go Vap District, Ward 14, Ho Chi Minh City
+84 933883731
peter@avse.edu.vn
www.avse.edu.vn

NUMBER OF TEACHERS: 10–15.
PREFERENCE OF NATIONALITY: None.
QUALIFICATIONS: University degree and prepared to undertake an Australian government accredited TESOL programme in HCMC.
CONDITIONS OF EMPLOYMENT: 3, 6, 9 or 12 months. 20–25 hours per week.
SALARY: US$15–US$25 per hour (net).
FACILITIES/SUPPORT: Assistance given to teachers to find accommodation in the local area. Help given with work permits.
RECRUITMENT: Interviews are essential.
CONTACT: Peter Goudge, Managing Director.

FISHER'S SUPERKIDS ENGLISH CENTER
74 Nguyen Thi Minh Khai Street, Hai Chau Dict, Danang City
+84 511 625 1881
apply@fishersuperkids.com
www.fishersuperkids.com

NUMBER OF TEACHERS: 25+ for young learners and teenagers.
PREFERENCE OF NATIONALITY: All native speakers.
QUALIFICATIONS: University degree, and TEFL certificate. Candidates with at least 1 year's teaching experience preferred.
CONDITIONS OF EMPLOYMENT: 1-year stay. 18 teaching hours per week plus 17 office hours.
SALARY: $1,300 per month gross; less about 10% for taxes. 3 different bonus systems: completion bonus, quarterly performance review bonus, and parent satisfaction bonus.
FACILITIES/SUPPORT: School has contacts with local real estate companies, will advise on accommodation and assist in translation of documents if needed. Initial 1–2 weeks of training and orientation, and on-going training by the Academic Management team, which includes quarterly observations and monthly professional development workshops. Assistance given with work permits once teachers provide original degree certificate, TEFL certificate and a recent clean criminal background check from their home country. The school takes the documents which must all be notarised and pays government fees.
CONTACT: Luke Ferch, Academic and Recruitment Manager (lferch@fishersuperkids.com).

ILA VIETNAM
146 Nguyen Dinh Chieu St, Dist 3, Ho Chi Minh City
+84 8 3521 8788
recruitment@ilavietnam.com
www.teachenglishilavietnam.com

NUMBER OF TEACHERS: 450+ for 29 centres in Ho Chi Minh City, Danang, Vung Tau, Binh Duong, Haiphong, Hanoi and Bien Hoa.
PREFERENCE OF NATIONALITY: Native English speakers.
QUALIFICATIONS: Minimum requirements are university degree (any discipline), plus a recognised ELT qualification (CELTA, Trinity or equivalent preferred). Preference is given to applicants who have experience with young learners. Also positions for untrained volunteers.
CONDITIONS OF EMPLOYMENT: Standard 12-month contract. Approx. 25 hours per week.
FACILITIES/SUPPORT: School provides an airport pickup and pays for initial accommodation at a guesthouse. Information and contact details for estate agents are provided. Other teachers are always on the lookout for flatmates and there is an accommodation board in each school. School provides a relocation bonus for overseas applicants as well as paying for and obtaining visas and work permits. Free health insurance and Vietnamese lessons plus quarterly social events are paid for by the school. Bonus paid on successful completion of contract.
RECRUITMENT: Via the internet (www.tefl.com; www.eslcafe.com) and recruiters. Telephone interviews for overseas hires; face-to-face interviews for applicants in Vietnam. Applicants must send CV with cover letter, supporting documents, passport details and realistic start date. Must bring recent police clearance certificate and certified copy. Local applicants must also provide visa details.
CONTACT: David Thompson, Teacher Recruitment Executive/ Expatriate Human Resources.

LANGUAGE LINK VIETNAM (LLV)
62 Yen Phu St, Ba Dinh, Hanoi
+84 4 3927 3399 ext 453
recruit@languagelink.vn
www.llv.edu.vn/en/recruitment

NUMBER OF TEACHERS: 100+ for 40 schools.
PREFERENCE OF NATIONALITY: Native English speakers.
QUALIFICATIONS: Bachelor's degree in any discipline plus 120-hour intensive teaching certificate with practicum (online certificates are not eligible).
CONDITIONS OF EMPLOYMENT: Minimum 1 year if hired from

overseas; 6 months if already local. 70–100 contact hours per month. Teachers placed in primary and secondary schools for the academic year September to May.

SALARY: Hourly rate from $19 to $24; 70 hours minimum guaranteed after probationary period. Tax deductions 5%–30% on progressive scale, average 13%.

FACILITIES/SUPPORT: Advice given on finding accommodation and assistance with obtaining work permit. CELTA course offered on premises. Partial costs reimbursed for candidates who work for 1 or more months after the course.

RECRUITMENT: Internet advertising and local press. Local interviews necessary.

CONTACT: Greg Robertson, Teacher Recruitment and Welfare Manager.

SHELTON DEVELOPMENT GROUP

No. 40, Lane 2 Vuong Thua Vu, Thanh Xuan District, Hanoi

+84 4 7306 2688

recruitment@shelton.edu.vn

www.shelton.edu.vn

NUMBER OF TEACHERS: 25–30 for ESL centres in 5 provinces in northern Hanoi region. Shelton also provides teachers to the state school system.

PREFERENCE OF NATIONALITY: UK, Canada.

QUALIFICATIONS: Professionally qualified teachers as they tend to be substantially better trained than ESL teachers.

CONDITIONS OF EMPLOYMENT: 9.5 month contracts. Minimum 18 hours a week.

SALARY: $20–$25 an hour (net).

FACILITIES/SUPPORT: School advises on reliable landlords, helps negotiate issues and deals with local registration with the police. School covers two-thirds of the cost of obtaining the permits, but expects teachers to refund the difference if they leave after 1 year. No sick or holiday pay, and limited remuneration for cancelled lessons.

RECRUITMENT: Interesting cover letter, CV, scanned copies of qualifications, security and health checks to be sent. Interviews essential. Main hiring deadline for applications is mid-August.

TEACHERS FOR VIETNAM

PO Box 362, Salisbury, CT 06068, USA

+1 860 480 5041

info@teachersforvietnam.org

www.teachersforvietnam.org

NUMBER OF TEACHERS: About 5 teachers of ESL for university posts in Vietnam to further Vietnam's educational development by increasing fluency of spoken English and to build bridges between people in Vietnam and the West, particularly the USA.

QUALIFICATIONS: Must be university graduate so most volunteers are over 21. Some experience and/or training in TESL needed, plus eagerness to live and work in Vietnam.

CONDITIONS OF EMPLOYMENT: Academic year (August to May).

SALARY: Programme application fee $50. Programme pays for airfare, health insurance and travel during Tet holiday. Host universities pay a cost-of-living salary (e.g. $115–$200 per month) and in most cases provide free housing, usually a room or suite in a campus guesthouse.

FACILITIES/SUPPORT: In-country orientation session provided, which covers cultural issues as well as practical matters for foreigners newly arrived in Vietnam.

RECRUITMENT: Deadline for applications is 1 April. Face-to-face interviews in New York area in early May required.

CONTACT: John Dippel, Executive Director.

UNIVERSAL EDUCATION CENTER

R4-55-56-57 Hung Gia 5, Phu My Hung, Tan Phong Ward, District 7, Ho Chi Minh City 700000

+84 8 5410 4649; +84 162 811 9483 (mob)

harlyn@uec.edu.vn; info@uec.edu.vn

www.uec.edu.vn

NUMBER OF TEACHERS: Currently have 46 native English teachers and 21 Filipino teachers. UEC hires teachers almost every week.

PREFERENCE OF NATIONALITY: Countries in which English is the official language, e.g. USA, UK, Australia, Canada and New Zealand. Also teachers accepted from Ireland, Philippines and South Africa.

QUALIFICATIONS: Must be a native English speaker, be certified after formal training in TESOL (CELTA or equivalent is a plus but not required; online training is acceptable). Teachers with a 4-year degree are strongly preferred.

CONDITIONS OF EMPLOYMENT: Minimum 6 months. Teaching hours are weekday afternoons (between 4pm and 7pm) and weekend mornings (9am–11.30am).

SALARY: $17.55–$19.55 per hour net (for part-time teachers) and $20 per hour (for full-time teachers).

FACILITIES/SUPPORT: No assistance with accommodation, though full-time teachers receive housing allowance, vacation pay, sick leave and year-end bonus. Training workshops are held quarterly. Assistance with work permit for teachers who arrive with their university diploma and transcript and police certificate authenticated by the embassy/consulate in their own country. The compulsory health check will be arranged in an accredited hospital in HCMC.

RECRUITMENT: Email applications and some walk-ins.

CONTACT: Harlyn D. Dimabuyu, Academic and Hiring Manager.

VUS (VIETNAM USA SOCIETY) ENGLISH CENTERS

Head Office, 189 Nguyen Thi Minh Khai, District 1, Ho Chi Minh City

+84 8 3925 9899 ext 165

stephenthomas@vus-etsc.edu.vn; tutran@vus-etsc.edu.vn

www.vus.edu.vn

NUMBER OF TEACHERS: Approximately 160 part-time and full-time.

PREFERENCE OF NATIONALITY: None.

QUALIFICATIONS: Minimum BA degree in any discipline and teaching certification (CELTA, TESOL, TEFL or equivalent). Teachers with prior classroom experience have priority but inexperienced teachers are encouraged to apply.

CONDITIONS OF EMPLOYMENT: 1-year contract. Full-time teachers can expect 80–100 hours per month of student contact. Weekend classes are scheduled between 8am and 9.30pm (with Sunday finish at 5pm). Weekday classes are from 5pm to 9.30pm and a small number in the mornings. Most classes are in 2-hour blocks.

SALARY: $17–$24 per hour (net) based on qualifications, experience and outcome of demonstration lesson.

FACILITIES/SUPPORT: VUS provides guidance in completing the work permit application process and reimburses the cost ($300). Additional benefits for full-time teachers include free Vietnamese lessons and vacation allowance. VUS works closely with an accommodation agency run by Americans and Canadians which has proven itself to be pro-active and supportive.

RECRUITMENT: Local recruiting and posting on sites such as Dave's ESL Cafe. Interviews are essential. Local interviewees conduct a demonstration lesson as part of the interview process. Overseas candidates must submit a lesson plan as part of the interview process. Interviews with candidates located abroad are conducted via Skype.

CONTACT: Stephen Thomas, HR Manager (Foreign Teachers).

CAMBODIA

Cambodia is now a stable and welcoming country, having emerged from the shadow of its tragic past. The ELT market has been wide open to private enterprise in Cambodia for a number of years and is now well established. Yet the British Council does not have a presence in the country.

It is one of the last bastions for the so-called 'backpacker teacher' where a knowledge of the English language is in many cases sufficient to land a job. Things have not changed all that much from the early days when it was possible to rent a moto for the day, take a spin around Phnom Penh and ask for teaching hours at one of the language schools to be found on most street corners. The standards are more professional in the reputable schools like ACE, but there are many others who are not very fussy and do not expect to see a qualification.

Cambodia operates on a dollar economy, so few wages are quoted in riels. People normally use the local currency only for items that cost less than a dollar, i.e. 4,000 riels. Wages at the upmarket schools start at $15 an hour, whereas most others pay about $10–$12 regardless of credentials. Regulation of schools is non-existent. Prospective teachers should arrive with extra passport photos and buy a Business E visa on arrival for $50, valid for one month. This can be extended at the Ministry of Foreign Affairs for up to a year at a time for $278. According to some long-stayers, this bureaucratic laxity attracts a high proportion of misfits and dubious types. Girlfriend-hunting often seems to be a stronger motivator than education, rather like Thailand used to be. One commentator on www.asiapundits.com taught in Cambodia for more than a year and went further by saying that '*the country is a true degenerate's playground*'.

Of course there are plenty of serious teachers in the country too. A teacher placement agency in Phnom Penh (www.teachersincambodia.com) recruits for positions in primary and secondary schools starting in August/September. One of the longest established schools is the Australian Centre for Education or ACE (see entry), which is flourishing. Other commercial institutes in Phnom Penh include American-biased ELT (www.eess.edu.kh) and Home of English International (www.homeofenglish.edu.kh/job-openings), while others have gone bankrupt. When experienced teacher **Bradwell Jackson** from the US visited, he ascertained that the American Intercon Institute at 217 ABCD Mao Tse Tong Blvd (www.aii.edu.kh) is happy to hire foreign teachers who are in Phnom Penh.

Willing volunteers will find plenty of options, for example in one of the several rural schools run by the charity CESHEO (www.ceshe.org/volunteering.html) near Siem Reap and also Savong's School (www.savong.com) for children who can't afford tuition fees. The upfront volunteering fee is $250. On her gap year **Pascale Hunter** from Cambridge noticed a flyer for Savong's School up in her hostel in Siem Reap and spent a short time teaching teenagers and younger children there. Although she found the experience interesting, she felt it was '*fairly commercial, with the kids clamouring for western souvenirs*'. However, plenty of other volunteers have enjoyed their visit and are impressed by the dedication of the students. Volunteers should be prepared to provide a copy of their passport and police check.

Another organisation to try is Volunteer in Cambodia (www.volunteerincambodia.org), which recruits volunteers to teach at Conversations With Foreigners (CWF), a local conversational English school in Phnom Penh (No 247C, Street 271, Toul Pumbung II). Money raised by the programme goes towards the Cambodian Rural Development Team, a local organisation working to improve livelihoods in rural communities. Volunteers stay three months (there are specific group starting dates) and do not pay to volunteer, though they do pay for their accommodation and meals, which currently costs $725 in the shared volunteer house for three months. Teaching qualifications/experience are an advantage, but not required. Also in the capital is AHHA Education (www.ahhaeducation.org) which claims to cover living expenses of volunteers who stay for more than three months.

LIST OF EMPLOYERS

AMERICAN EDUCATION CENTER
7E Mao Tse Tung Blvd, Sangkat Boeung Keng Kang I, Khan Chamkarmorn, Phnom Penh
+855 11 092666345 (mob)
recruit@aec-cambodia.com
www.aec.edu.kh

NUMBER OF TEACHERS: 6 part-time and full-time.
PREFERENCE OF NATIONALITY: None.
QUALIFICATIONS: BA in English or similar, or BEd, ESL experience. Teacher Assistants just need to be good communicators and patient with toddlers and children.
CONDITIONS OF EMPLOYMENT: 1 year. 5 hours a day.
SALARY: Negotiable depending on experience.
FACILITIES/SUPPORT: No assistance with accommodation. AEC arranges for processing business visas.
RECRUITMENT: Via local advertisements in newspapers and on websites. Skype interviews are possible.
CONTACT: Janet English, Director.

AUSTRALIAN CENTRE FOR EDUCATION
Samdech Pan Campus: 46, Street 214, Sangkat Boeung Raing, Khan Daun Penh, Phnom Penh; Tuol Tom Poung Campus: No. 167, St 163 corner 480, Sangkat Phsar Deumthkov, Khan Chamkarmon, Phnom Penh
+855 23 724204; +855 23 881026; +855 232 22325
recruitment.cambodia@idp.com
www.idp.com/cambodia

NUMBER OF TEACHERS: 200 teachers at three campuses in Phnom Penh and one in Siem Reap.
PREFERENCE OF NATIONALITY: Any native English speaker is acceptable, though Australians preferred.
QUALIFICATIONS: Undergraduate degree plus CELTA or 120-hour equivalent. 1 year's teaching experience, with proven ability to work autonomously. IELTS experience valued. Police clearance may be required.
CONDITIONS OF EMPLOYMENT: 22 hours of classes a week, but teachers are expected to attend at the school 40 hours per week. Minimum commitment 6 months for terms starting in January, April, July and September. Hours vary: the school is open 6am–8pm and on Saturday mornings. Teachers needed for general courses, business English, young learners and English for Academic Purposes.
SALARY: $18–$25 hourly freelance; $1,700–$2,100 per month.
FACILITIES/SUPPORT: Advice given on affordable accommodation which is not hard to find in Phnom Penh (rents from $150 a month plus utilities). Assistance given before arrival on obtaining visas and school contributes to costs. The school is well equipped and resourced and a variety of professional development sessions are held each term. School pays half of contributions to medical insurance. Free Khmer lessons.
RECRUITMENT: Web advertisements, word of mouth. Interviews are required, but can be over the phone and are carried out in Australia from time to time. Professional references are checked.
CONTACT: Theara Chea, HR Co-ordinator (theara.chea@idp.com) or Kety Dy, Senior HR Officer.

CONVERSATIONS WITH FOREIGNERS (CWF)
#247c, Street 271, Sangkat Toul Tom Poung II, Khan Chamcarmon, Phnom Penh
+855 23 636 3040
info@volunteerincambodia.org
www.volunteerincambodia.org

Free 3-month voluntary programme to teach conversational English in Phnom Penh.
NUMBER OF VOLUNTEERS: 17–30.
PREFERENCE OF NATIONALITY: None. Must have a native level command of the language.
QUALIFICATIONS: TEFL or teaching experience not essential, though many come with some. Volunteers should have a real commitment to education and development and be capable of teaching English in a way that is sensitive to the development context and of encouraging the students to express pride in Cambodia. All ages from 18, with average in mid-20s.
CONDITIONS OF EMPLOYMENT: 3 months beginning in December, March, June and September each year. Volunteers teach up to 5 hours a day on week days. Classes can be any time 6–8am, 11am–1pm or 4–8pm.
SALARY: None. Volunteers fund their own living and travel expenses. Any profits go to fund the rural development work of partner agency, the Cambodian Rural Development Team.
FACILITIES/SUPPORT: Accommodation provided in volunteer house which costs $725 for 3 months including meals Monday to Friday, excluding public holidays. If volunteers prefer to live independently CWF can help with finding a place to stay. 2-week orientation programme includes lessons in Khmer language and culture, child safety training, teacher training and an optional trip to the province where volunteers learn more about rural development work and participate in a homestay. Assistance

given in renewing Type E business visa which volunteers can buy on arrival.

RECRUITMENT: Direct application through website or through partner agencies: such as www.WorkingAbroad.com and Volunteer Forever.

CONTACT: Volunteer Recruitment & Marketing Manager.

TEACHERS IN CAMBODIA

House: #6B, Street 270, Sangkat Boeung Salang, Khan Toul Kok, Phnom Penh

+855 77574427

cheryl@teachersincambodia.com

www.teachersincambodia.com

Teacher recruitment agency in Phnom Penh.

NUMBER OF TEACHERS: About 100 per year.

PREFERENCE OF NATIONALITY: Native English-speaking countries.

QUALIFICATIONS: Bachelor's degree or higher, TEFL or TESOL certified.

CONDITIONS OF EMPLOYMENT: 1-year contract. 20–30 hours per week.

SALARY: Negotiable.

FACILITIES/SUPPORT: Schools provide accommodation and work permits.

RECRUITMENT: Online ads, via universities. Skype interviews.

CONTACT: Cheryl Glorch, Director.

WESTERN INTERNATIONAL SCHOOL

#46, St. 566, 337, 335 Boeung Kok II, Khan Toul Kork, Phnom Penh

+855 23 990699

jobs@western.edu.kh

www.western.edu.kh/wis

NUMBER OF TEACHERS: 40 for main campus and Sihanoukville campus.

PREFERENCE OF NATIONALITY: None.

QUALIFICATIONS: Degree holders are preferred, but positions for non-degree holders are also available. In-house training is offered, and professional development is encouraged under guidance of the team leaders.

CONDITIONS OF EMPLOYMENT: 12-month contract. Students study in 3 shifts: morning session 7.30am–11.30am, afternoon session 1pm–5pm, and evening session 5.30pm–8pm. Teachers are offered a choice of classes within these time frames.

SALARY: Up to $10 per classroom hour. Teachers submit a 5% tax return.

FACILITIES/SUPPORT: School has a library, computer laboratory and large play area which teachers may use during class time. All classrooms are air-conditioned.

RECRUITMENT: Via email to HR Dept.

LAOS AND MYANMAR

Laos was the last country but one in the region to open its doors to foreigners, while Myanmar (formerly Burma) is the last. Over the past few years a number of English schools have opened in the Laotian capital of Vientiane, ranging from well-established institutions to small, shop-front enterprises staffed with locals or expats passing through on tourist visas. When English institutes first started opening in Vientiane, most were fly-by-night operations. But there are now several international English-medium schools such as the Lao-American College and the Vientiane International School (www.vislao.com), and also better-organised private language schools like ARDA Language Centres (www.ardalaos.com) which rely on volunteer teachers.

The visa procedures have settled down in Laos. If possible, a letter of invitation should be obtained from your employer before arrival which entitles the holder to enter Laos on a B2 visa (non-immigrant, business visa) instead of a tourist visa. With the B2 visa you can apply for a work permit which will cost around US$240 for a year while the resident card costs $90. Only the most elite schools will cover the cost of the visa, although most will assist you in obtaining it. In order to obtain the invitation, your sponsor needs a copy of your passport and probably copies of any educational credentials. Otherwise it is possible to buy a one-month tourist visa at the border for US$35. After arrival, the employer will have to make the invitation for a B2 visa. Then the teacher will be required to leave the country (usually across the border to Thailand) and re-enter on the B2 visa for a further fee.

Salaries and conditions of work can vary as much as the schools themselves. Vientiane College (see entry below) provides the best working conditions, staff development programme and benefit package. The majority of language schools pay by the hour, from as little as $5 up to $15 at the higher end of the range.

Demand for native English speakers also occasionally comes from bilingual schools such as the Oscar School and pre-schools or nurseries. Teaching opportunities also exist in the larger provincial centres such as Luang Prabang and Svannakhet and, in Vientiane, in larger companies and ministries for in-house teachers. Again, conditions vary greatly and there are often delays with payments and payments may be made in the local currency (kip).

Some volunteer opportunities exist in Laos, for example with the Thai organisation Openmind Projects (www.openmindprojects.org) and with the Sunshine School (see entry). The former programme costs $295 admin fee plus $395 for the first fortnight, which covers homestay accommodation, local meals and a three-day orientation in Nong Khai on the Thai-Laotian border. Stays can be extended for $95 a week.

Until a few years ago, there was almost no scope for teaching English in reclusive, repressive Myanmar. But the pace of change was highlighted when Aung San Suu Kyi, on her first visit to the US in September 2016, announced that it is time to remove all sanctions 'because our country is in a position to open up to those who are interested in taking part in our economic enterprises'. (Because her late husband and children are British nationals, she can't be head of state, even though she won a landslide election, so bears the title 'State Counsellor'.) With the move to democracy, a more open and pro-western system will certainly support English language schools. The scene is expanding to such an extent that there is now a TEFL recruitment agency MySayar (www.mysayar.com) in Yangon, the capital (formerly Rangoon). Schools are recruiting teachers who have a BA, CELTA or equivalent and preferably some experience, and offering reimbursement of travel costs and visas in addition to a monthly salary of $1,200–$2,200.

Business visas can be obtained ahead of time (for $36) or purchased on arrival at the airport for $50 provided you have a letter of invitation and sponsor letter. These single entry visas, which are valid for 70 days and can be renewed by crossing the border to Thailand, can be turned into a Multiple Journey Entry Visa for Business (MJEV) costing $180 and lasting for six months. Some schools will reimburse the costs at the end of the academic year.

The number of language schools that employ native speakers is still small, but rising. It is worth checking Asian teaching sites and also investigating possibilities at international and private schools such as Yangon Academy, which follows an American curriculum (www.yangon-academy.org), and Horizon International School, which has several branches and kindergartens around the capital.

Several voluntourism organisations like Greenheart Travel in Chicago (www.greenhearttravel.org/program/adult/teach/teach-in-myanmar) operate a Teach English in Myanmar programme with four start dates a year. Participants pay a programme fee of $1,520 for three months or $2,095 for a year-long placement; a 120-hour TESOL training course in Yangon can be added for an extra $730/$405 respectively. Teachers earn a monthly salary of $800–$1,200. Other agencies offer the same programme such as Geovisions (www.geovisions.org). Note that some agencies such as Thailand-based XploreAsia (www.xploreasia.org/teach-in-myanmar) promise only to facilitate interviews after the TEFL training course rather than guarantee placement.

NGOs are becoming more active in the country. The British Council has an expanding teaching centre in Yangon, and was advertising for teachers with a TEFL certificate and at least two years of experience in summer 2015.

The lack of basic infrastructure in Yangon, such as faltering electricity, very slow internet and pot-holed roads makes everyday life difficult. The stock of rental housing has not kept pace with the influx of people, and what you can find is either very expensive or very grotty. This situation should improve as investment starts to flow into the country. Teachers in international schools earn decent salaries (e.g. $2,000+ a month) with few outgoings. Eating and drinking is very cheap (e.g. about $3 a day) and basic apartments can be found starting at $200 a month plus next to nothing for utilities.

For information about teaching programmes for Burmese refugees in Northern Thailand, see the chapter on Thailand.

LIST OF EMPLOYERS

21ST CENTURY SCHOOL OF ENGLISH

74/6 Sisangvone Rd. That Luang Tai, Vientiane, Lao PDR

+856 21 452500

info@21centuryeducation.com

www.21centuryeducation.com

NUMBER OF TEACHERS: 13.

PREFERENCE OF NATIONALITY: American, British, Australian, New Zealander.

QUALIFICATIONS: CELTA/TESOL/TEFL.

CONDITIONS OF EMPLOYMENT: 1-year or 6-month contract with 13.5+ teaching hours per week.

SALARY: $13–$17 per hour.

FACILITIES/SUPPORT: School will arrange 6- or 12-month work visas; payment terms vary.

RECRUITMENT: Usually via the internet or word of mouth. Interviews are essential and can be carried out from the UK or USA.

ARDA LANGUAGE CENTRE VIENTIANE

Vientiane, Lao PDR

+856 21 217162

vientianelc@ardalaos.com

www.ardalaos.com

ARDA stands for Anglican Relief and Development Agency and is a foreign-owned private company. Centres also in Pakse (see entry) and Luang Phabang.

NUMBER OF TEACHERS: 2–6.

PREFERENCE OF NATIONALITY: None.

QUALIFICATIONS: Initial TESOL certificate or equivalent.

CONDITIONS OF EMPLOYMENT: Minimum stays 5–16 weeks; 1 year preferred. 6-week terms, standard 14 hours per week contact time.

SALARY: None because teachers are volunteers.

FACILITIES/SUPPORT: Accommodation not provided but appointments arranged with housing agents and assistance given with translation and transport. School pays for up to 2 tourist visas. Those who stay more than 16 weeks can obtain a multiple entry business visa.

RECRUITMENT: Via word of mouth.

CONTACT: Daniel Whetham, Centre Manager.

ARDA LANGUAGE CENTRE PAKSE

13 South Road, Pakse, Champasak Province, Lao PDR

+856 312 14674 / +856 205 4090773

pakselc@ardalaos.com

www.ardalaos.com

NUMBER OF TEACHERS: 2–3 every two years.

PREFERENCE OF NATIONALITY: None.

QUALIFICATIONS: TEFL/TESOL/CELTA is mandatory.

CONDITIONS OF EMPLOYMENT: 1 year contract. 48 teaching hours a month.

SALARY: Volunteer role, though if the teacher does not have sponsorship, the school can support teachers up to $5,400 a year.

FACILITIES/SUPPORT: Assistance given with inspecting housing options and with negotiations with the landlord. One room apartments with bathroom cost $100–$120 per month. School admin staff assist with visa applications and school pays for the visa and work permits.

RECRUITMENT: Letter of interest, submission of CV and educational documents, references and interviews in Laos.

CONTACT: Biju Abraham, Centre Director (ardapakse@gmail.com).

BRAINWORKS SCHOOL – TOTAL GROUP OF SCHOOLS

1 Thumingalar St, 16/4 Quarter, Thingangyun, Yangon; 280 U Wisara Road, Kamayut Township, Yangon, Myanmar

+ 951 8551360 – 3; +95 1501976

hr@brainworksschool.com

www.brainworks-total.com

The Total Learning Academy has 9 K-12 schools.

NUMBER OF TEACHERS: Lots.

PREFERENCE OF NATIONALITY: USA, Canada, UK, Australia or New Zealand.

QUALIFICATIONS: TEFL/CELTA plus preference given to those with BA or MA. Must have one year's classroom experience and experience of living in a developing country.

CONDITIONS OF EMPLOYMENT: 12 months. 43-hour week, 24 contact hours.

SALARY: $1,200–$2,000 (net) depending on experience.

FACILITIES/SUPPORT: Shared air-conditioned accommodation provided. Employer takes care of all government taxes and registration requirements including paying for flights every 70 days to complete visa renewal process.

RECRUITMENT: Online advertising, e.g. www.tefl.com and www.asiateachingjobs.com. Applications by email then Skype inteviews.

CONTACT: Bob Allwright, Owner

MOTE OO EDUCATION

182/194, Hnin Si Condo A/B, 7th floor, Botahtaung Pagoda Road, Pazundaung Township, Yangon

+95 931 115 669

info@moteoo.org; moteooeducation@gmail.com

www.moteoo.org

Mote Oo Education works with civil society organisations and post-secondary schools in Myanmar and on the Thai-Myanmar border.

NUMBER OF TEACHERS: Varies according to number of requests for Learning Support Volunteers from partner organisations.

PREFERENCE OF NATIONALITY: Must have native/advanced level English language proficiency.

QUALIFICATIONS: Minimum 2 years' teaching background. Enthusiastic, experienced volunteers needed, mainly over 24. Must be self-reliant, adaptable people who can fit into challenging environments and provide guidance and assistance to future community leaders, teachers and activists. As well as teaching English, suitable volunteers will assist with teaching social science and civic education courses, training teachers and helping with curriculum development.

CONDITIONS OF EMPLOYMENT: Minimum 3 month stay. 6–12 teaching hours per week.

SALARY: None. Where possible, host organisation provides a small stipend. Volunteer teacher must cover cost of travel, business visa, food, health insurance and accommodation (unless host organisation is able to provide).

FACILITIES/SUPPORT: Basic orientation package on Myanmar and its culture is provided. Advice given to volunteers on logistics, cheap accommodation and travel. Host organisation can usually issue visa invitation letter for business visa; tourist visa is fine for urban regions.

RECRUITMENT: Online advertising, websites, social media.

MYSAYAR: TEACHER RECRUITMENT FOR MYANMAR

209 Anawyahtar Road, Pabedan Township, Yangon, Myanmar

+95 0945 715 4892

Recruiter@MySayar.org

www.MySayar.org

Only teacher placement agency that operates exclusively in Myanmar.

PREFERENCE OF NATIONALITY: Native-English speakers who are currently teaching in countries adjacent to Myanmar are preferred. Approximately 30% of teachers are from UK, 30% from Australia, 20% American, 10% South African and 10% from other countries.

QUALIFICATIONS: Ideally teachers have an undergraduate degree, a CELTA or equivalent and at least one year of teaching experience.

CONDITIONS OF EMPLOYMENT: 12 months. 43-hour week, 24 contact hours.

SALARY: $1,200–$2,200 a month.

FACILITIES/SUPPORT: Schools typically provide housing, a stipend, or a no-interest loan for their teachers. Agency also provides accommodation tips and local insight not found on the internet. Visa sponsorship is primarily the responsibility of the school which provides all required documents. When these documents are shown at the immigration desk, the teacher's passport is stamped on entry.

RECRUITMENT: Online adverts. Teachers are interviewed by MySayar staff and usually also by the school that wants to employ a native speaker teacher.

CONTACT: Alexander Dorudian, Senior Recruiter.

SUNSHINE SCHOOL
Ban Si Meung, Vientiane, Laos
+856 21 214522
sunshinelaos@gmail.com

NUMBER OF TEACHERS: 2 volunteers at a time.

PREFERENCE OF NATIONALITY: English-speaking countries.

QUALIFICATIONS: Creative approach to working with the kids is important; experience in teaching or experience with young kids are both good assets.

CONDITIONS OF EMPLOYMENT: 1–10 months between September and July. School hours include 7 teaching periods from 8am to 4pm on weekdays. Volunteers usually have 4–5 teaching periods a day (maybe less depending on the volunteer's needs), in kindergarten, primary or junior secondary classes. Volunteers may also be involved in creative activities with the children or teachers' classes or teaching village children and youth on the weekends

SALARY: Voluntary basis only. Long-term volunteers staying 6–12 months may get a small living allowance (max $100 a month) or help with housing, depending on the financial condition of the school at the time.

FACILITIES/SUPPORT: Long-term volunteers will be supported with working visas (which cost $250–$450). All volunteers get a vegetarian lunch provided on school days. No accommodation provided, but local guesthouses charge only $60–$90 per month.

RECRUITMENT: Direct application to school.

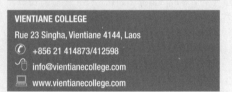

VIENTIANE COLLEGE
Rue 23 Singha, Vientiane 4144, Laos
+856 21 414873/412598
info@vientianecollege.com
www.vientianecollege.com

NUMBER OF TEACHERS: 40.

PREFERENCE OF NATIONALITY: Native English speakers from any region.

QUALIFICATIONS: Minimum bachelor's degree and CELTA. ESP/EAP experience preferred.

CONDITIONS OF EMPLOYMENT: Sessional and contract.

SALARY: From $1,500–$2,800 per month less 10% income tax.

FACILITIES/SUPPORT: Assistance with finding accommodation. School arranges and pays for work permit and residence visa. In-house training programme.

RECRUITMENT: Personal interview necessary.

CONTACT: Denley Pike, Director.

TAIWAN

The ELT industry is more than thriving in Taiwan, a country that remains a magnet for English teachers of all backgrounds. Part of the appeal of teaching in Taiwan is that the wages compare favourably with countries such as Japan, yet the cost of living is significantly lower. Equally important is that finding a job here is fairly easy. It used to be the case that schools were looking for only three things: a passport from an English-speaking country, a bachelor's degree and a pulse. These days, however, the better schools are becoming choosier, it is a little more difficult to get a working visa and many schools and local education departments are looking for an ELT qualification and prior experience. Nevertheless, the opportunities for teaching English in Taiwan are endless. Despite the fact that the birth rate is falling, there are hundreds of kiddies' schools and private cramming institutes or *buxibans* preparing high school students for university entrance examinations.

However, there is more regulation than there used to be. Only the reputable language schools, those that are fully licensed as foreign language schools, are permitted to employ English-speaking foreigners and sponsor them for visas, provided the teachers are willing to sign a one-year contract. Native English-speaker teachers with a university degree (in any subject) are eligible.

The market for teaching children from age two seems boundless at the moment, so anyone who enjoys working with young children, i.e. likes to sing songs, play games and comfort little ones who miss their mums, may be able to find a job. However, government regulations require that teachers working in kindergartens be fully qualified kindergarten specialists. This means that CELTA-trained teachers can no longer legally work in kindergartens. Some do, and a few have been deported. Language organisations that specialise in teaching early primary school-aged children generally provide detailed lesson plans, which means that little time needs to be spent on lesson preparation.

FINDING A JOB

Taiwanese consumers of English have a clear preference for the North American accent because of strong trading and cultural links between Taiwan and the USA. However, many schools will hire presentable native English speakers, whatever their accent. Few want their staff to be able to speak Chinese; in fact one teacher reported seeing a sign in a *buxiban* window boasting 'Teachers Not Speak Chinese'. Language teachers and tutors working in Taipei are predominantly American; native English speakers of other nationalities tend to gravitate to Southern Taiwan. **Amanda Searle** from the UK felt only slightly discriminated against:

> ***My employer claimed that they did not discriminate between people of different nationalities, but this is not what I have found. North Americans are the first choice when hours are allocated. I have had students complain that they wanted an American teacher because they wanted to learn 'real' English, though I have never had a student complain to the secretaries or me that my accent was difficult to understand.***

On the subject of discrimination, it seems that the ideal age for teachers is late 20s, and that both schools and agents are often accused of passing over older candidates, even those in their late 30s.

A few of the major organisations hire from overseas such as the giant Hess Educational Organization (see entry below). Interviews are conducted either in Taiwan or by telephone/Skype from Taiwan. The agency TEFLOne Recruitment (www.teflone.com) is one of many that recruit qualified teachers for posts in Taiwan as well as other countries in the Far East. The company Kid Castle (www.kidcastle.com.tw/en/jobs/teaching.html) has more than 200 franchise schools in Taiwan whose managers recruit individually, only after a face-to-face interview.

JAMES ROBINSON

James Robinson is one satisfied client of www.teflone.com and wrote from the small town of Taoyuan in Kaohsiung County in Taiwan's interior. After being made redundant as a welder/fabricator, he did a TESOL course, which he describes as 'the best move I ever made'. Soon afterwards he met the chief recruiter for TEFLOne, David Coles, to hear about opportunities with the Shane School.

My interview was a very positive experience. I knew that Shane would offer peace of mind, a highly efficient service and above all a friendly interview. It is for these reasons that Shane stood out from amongst the rest. Many other interviewers from other organisations sounded a bit officious and none of them offered as realistic and honest information about life in Taiwan as Shane did. It also sorted out all the administrative requirements such as work permits and bank accounts and patiently answered questions it had probably been asked a hundred times before!

My hours are currently about 25 a week, a lot more if you include the preparation, but a million times more interesting than welding! Most of the children are so eager to learn and I was astonished how the really young children retained new information.

Entertainment is the key. Yes, it was a learning curve and, yes, I made mistakes. But after a few weeks the preparation became far easier and it was a far more rewarding and positive experience. I think it's important to make things happen for yourself, e.g. to go climbing and cycling and participate in activities you like. This can be hugely rewarding for your inspiration as a teacher, to meet local people and get to know your new environment. As a result, my spare time is incredible. I still find it amazing that I can be out of the city and in the national park in 45 minutes, with its new aromas, wildlife and breathtaking scenery.

Many websites contain a wealth of detail about Taiwan and what it's like to teach there. Jobs and lots of information about teaching in Taiwan can be found at www.tealit.com (one of the best), www.orseek.com and www.englishintaiwan.com. The US-based recruiter for Asia Reach to Teach (www.reachtoteachrecruiting.com) is very active in Taiwan, where its main centre is located. Another possibility is ESL Dewey (www.esldewey.com.tw) that posts ads.

Reports sometimes surface of teachers accepting jobs via an agent or directly before arriving in Taiwan, only to find that they have been placed not in Taipei as they agreed, but in some three-goat mountain village. Discrepancies also sometimes occur between the contracts given to teachers in English and those given to employers in Chinese. The Chinese part is the legal part of the contract, so it would be a sensible precaution to have this translated before signing.

Many people arrive on spec to look for work. This is straightforward for Britons, Americans, Canadians and a few other nationalities who can stay for 60 or 90 days (renewable once) without a visa. Finding a *buxiban* willing to hire you is not as difficult as finding a good one willing to hire you. If possible, try to sit in on one or two classes or talk to another teacher before signing a contract. If a school is unwilling to permit this, it doesn't bode well. Read the fine print of the contract to find out what the penalties are for breaking a contract.

On the strength of the TEFL course she had completed at the American Language Institute in San Diego and a year spent teaching in Poland, freelance photographer **Alicia Wszelaki** wanted a taste of teaching in the Far East. She joined a short summer teaching project in Taiwan for adolescent girls, run by the American Language Village (www.kidscamp.com.tw) that she had noticed on Dave's ESL Cafe. Teachers were housed in a hotel not far from the camp and she found working conditions to be very good although the hours were long over 10 straight days:

> ***I realised a few days into the camp that this was indeed a summer camp and the kids were there not only to learn English but also to have fun. We played games, had lessons on pizza and hamburgers and other subjects that were more real world. The students really enjoyed these. There were lots of songs and dancing. If you choose to do a camp of this nature, bring lots of energy, smiles, optimism, an open mind and water. It was a wonderful and rewarding experience. The students were great and the teachers were some of the most incredible people I have met – a truly great blend of personalities and experiences.***

The best time to arrive is at the beginning of summer (the end of the school year), when Chinese parents enrol their offspring in English-language summer schools. August is another peak time for hiring, just before the new term begins, though there are openings year round. Word of mouth is even more important in Taiwan than elsewhere because there is no association of recognised language schools.

As always, travellers' hostels will be helpful, as reported by **Bradwell Jackson** from a trip to investigate the teaching scene:

> ***I couldn't believe all the English schools in Taipei. I presumed that the market must be saturated by now and that it would be too difficult to find a job, but after talking to the people in the know at the Taipei Hostel (www.taipeihostel.com/teach.html), I found out that this was not the case. The hostel is English-teaching central for foreigners and the common room is where all the newcomers meet to get the latest on the English teaching situation. Once you get the low down from the old hands there, just pick a direction and start walking. After passing about three corners, you'll definitely see an English school, probably two. Have your introduction ready, march on in there and sell yourself.***

Apparently some hostels feature blackboards on which job vacancies are chalked up as the hostel manager is notified. A good noticeboard is located in the student lounge on the sixth floor of the Mandarin Training Center of National Taiwan Normal University at 129 Hoping East Road.

Once you have decided to approach some schools for work, make contact by email or telephone in the first place. Next you must present yourself in person to the schools. Many schools in Taiwan are used to and expect cold-callers. Take along your university certificate and any other qualifications, and take the trouble to look presentable. **Peter McGuire** was told point blank that your appearance and how you conduct yourself at interview count for everything, and concluded that '*all your experience in life or teaching in other countries really doesn't mean a thing here*'. **David Hughes** specifically recommends paying attention to your feet:

> ***Bring plenty of socks/tights. You have to leave your shoes at the door of Chinese homes, and it's difficult to appear serious and composed with a toe poking through.***

Anyone with a high level of education (i.e. a master's degree or PhD) might find work attached to one of the scores of universities and colleges, where working conditions are very good. Foreigners are also allowed to work in public high schools, though it is difficult to function without knowledge of the language.

FREELANCE TEACHING

Work visas are valid only for employment with the sponsoring employer. However, many teachers teach private students, which pays handsomely from NT$700–$1,000 per hour. In a country where foreigners are sometimes approached in bars or on trains and asked to give English lessons, it is not hard to set up independently as an English tutor. **Peter McGuire** found the dream job of tutoring a travel agent three to six hours a day, seven days a week and was invited to accompany his client on a trip to Hawaii: *'Some of my lessons are given at private clubs, saunas, in taxicabs and fine restaurants. Actually, it's kind of unbelievable.'*

Although it would be possible to make a good living by teaching privately, you will need to work for a school in order to obtain the visa. A helpful hint is to have business cards printed up, calling yourself 'English consultant'. It is even more lucrative if you can muster a small group of students and charge them, say, NT$300 ($10) per person. Women usually find this easier to set up than men. The main problem is finding appropriate premises.

Cancelled hours are a perennial problem. Freelancers will find it prudent to explain to students gently but forcefully that they will be liable to pay if they cancel without giving sufficient notice; most will not object. You can even request one month's fees in advance. Once you are established, other jobs in the English field may come your way such as correcting business communications, transcribing lyrics from pop tapes or writing CVs and letters of application for Taiwanese students hoping to study overseas.

REGULATIONS

To stay legally in the country, teachers need to obtain an Alien Resident Certificate (ARC) from one of the many national immigration offices. Once you are accepted by a recruiter or find a school offering a one-year contract, the employer applies to the local education authority for a working permit, for which they will need a copy and translation of your degree diploma, contract and passport. A compulsory health check at an approved hospital can be carried out after arrival and will cost NT$1,000–$1,700. Some companies (like Hess) insist on a criminal record check from your home country. The good employers will make a contribution towards permit costs, especially if you renew for a second year. Canadian, American, British, Australian and New Zealand passport holders are permitted to stay visa-free for 90 days (apart from Australians who can stay for only 30 days). If in that time you secure a job, your future employer can then apply for a work permit, which should take 3–4 weeks if the application is in order. After that the teacher will have to obtain a formal visitor visa before applying for the ARC (Alien Resident Certificate).

Information on visas should be requested from the Taiwan Economic & Cultural Office in your country of origin, all linked from www.taiwanembassy.org.

After the work visa has been issued, tax will be withheld from your pay. The tax rate for foreigners who stay in Taiwan for less than 183 days in one calendar year (category A) is 18%. After six months, the rate of tax drops to between 6% and 13% (normally 6%) on income beyond the standard exemption of NT$85,000.

CONDITIONS OF WORK

Most jobs are paid by the hour, and for the past five years the minimum hourly rate a teacher should expect is NT$550–600 (approximately US$18). For a monthly salary you should expect to receive between NT$50,000 and NT$65,000 (average US$1,800) for 25 hours per week. Occasionally the rate for cushy morning classes drops below, and unsociable hours are rewarded (if you're lucky) with a premium rate of NT$600–$700. Rates outside Taipei (where the cost of living is lower) tend to be slightly higher due to the relative scarcity of teachers.

As usual some schools are shambolic when it comes to timetabling their teachers' hours. In a profit-driven atmosphere, classes start and finish on demand and can be cancelled at short notice if the owner decides that there are too few students to make it economic. When you are starting a new job, ask your employer to be specific about the actual number of hours you will be given and how scattered they might be throughout the day and evening. It is not uncommon for teachers who have been promised a full timetable at the point of hiring to find themselves with fewer hours than promised and a considerably lower pay packet.

Although exploitation of teachers (and students) is not as rife as in Korea, you should be prepared for anything, as **Rusty Holmes** had to be:

> ***The real reason there was such a high turnover rate of staff at one school was because of the supervisor's habit of barging into class at unpredictable moments and accusing the teacher (especially my Scottish colleague) of mispronouncing words, when she herself could barely speak English. The worst incidents occurred when she beat her own children in the face for getting poor grades, when she engaged a parent in a fistfight over a tuition dispute and when she physically ran her husband out of the school, all right in front of our students.***

However, unacceptable behaviour can be found in the teaching population too, as Sesame Street's one-time HR Manager **Adrian Maskery** explained:

> ***Foreign teachers in Taiwan don't have a good reputation amongst the local population here. Too many unskilled teachers take advantage of the situation. We have a word for being drunk and taking advantage of the local girls. This is what we are trying to change here, we would like to promote our image and turn things around.***

The usual problems which bedevil TEFL teachers occur in Taiwan, such as split shifts, often ending at 10pm, and compulsory weekend work, especially if you are teaching children. Few schools provide much creative training or incentives to do a good job. Like the educational system of China and so many other countries, Taiwanese state schools rely heavily on rote learning, making it difficult to introduce a more communicative approach, especially at the beginner level. Whereas some schools offer no guidance whatsoever, others leave almost nothing to the teacher. What is termed a 'training programme' often consists of a paint-by-numbers teaching manual. This certainly makes the inexperienced teacher's job easier but possibly also very boring. Not everyone will be comfortable with such a regimented curriculum.

LEISURE TIME

Flats are predictably expensive in Central Taipei so many teachers choose to commute from the suburbs by MRT where living conditions are more pleasant in any case. Rents tend to be in the region of NT$8,500–$20,000 per month per person. There are so many foreigners coming and going, and the locals are so friendly and helpful, that it is not too difficult to learn of flats becoming vacant. You will have to pay a month's rent in advance plus a further month's rent as a deposit or bond. Several schools will appoint a Chinese member of staff to chaperone new arrivals and translate on house-hunting trips.

Taipei has a rapid transit system that is far more enjoyable (and cheaper) than running a motorbike. Some teachers stay in hostels near the central station and commute to work in a satellite city where wages are higher than in Taipei (e.g. Tao Yuan and Chung Li). Without doubt, the biggest inconvenience and danger in Taiwan is on the roads. Taiwanese drivers often commit driving manoeuvres that would result in lynching in other countries. Red lights and traffic laws are more often than not ignored and foreigners compound the problem by riding too fast on scooters, with little experience, and often under the influence.

Not a single visitor to Taipei, which is one of the most densely populated cities in the world, fails to complain of the pollution, second only to that of Mexico City. Not only is the air choked with the fumes and noise of a million motorised vehicles, but there are also occasional scares that chemicals have infiltrated the water table, contaminating locally grown vegetables. One blogger maintains that you have to carry an umbrella to protect your skin and clothes from falling acid rain (www.roadjunky.com/article/654/teaching-english-in-taiwan). The weather is another serious drawback. The typhoon season lasts from July to October, bringing stormy wet weather and mouldy clothes. The heat and humidity at this time also verge on the unbearable.

Taipei is not the only city to suffer from pollution; Taichung and Kaohsiung are also bad. Even Tainan, the most historic city in Taiwan, with many old temples, has some pollution and far too many cars. Kaohsiung, on the south-west coast, is a large industrial city with a high crime rate by Taiwan's standards but has the advantage of being near the popular resort of Kenting Beach and within reach of mountain campsites such as Maolin. The geographical advantage of Taichung, further north, is proximity to the mountains as well as a good climate and cultural activities. The east coast is more tranquil, though some find it dull.

Wherever you decide to teach, one of the highlights of living in Taiwan is the hospitality of the locals. In fact some people report being smothered by kindness, since the Taiwanese will not accept a refusal of any food or drink offered, and even paying for meals or drinks can be a struggle. In general, apart from some petty crime, corrupt politicians and fairly well-hidden gang activity, Taiwan is virtually crime free, so you are free to follow your leisure pursuits without worry. Taipei has a 24-hour social scene that can seriously cut into savings. Heavy drinking is commonplace. Films are usually shown in English with Chinese subtitles. For the truly homesick there are some English-style pubs with pool tables and darts boards. For **Rusty Holmes**, the food was a highlight:

> ***Eating out is just as much a pastime in Taiwan as it is in Hong Kong. There are countless little mom-and-pop restaurants that offer delicious and inexpensive food. My favourite is the black pepper steak. Considering the high price of food in supermarkets, it would be cheaper to eat out than to cook at home. Taiwan is also a fruit-lover's paradise, though most are expensive by American standards. My favourite is the outstanding sugarcane Taiwan produces.***

LIST OF EMPLOYERS

GLORIA ENGLISH SCHOOL
22 Alley, 17–14, Lane 66, Huan-Nan Road, Ping-Jen City, Taoyuan
+886 3 495 1751/2
ges.job.tw@gmail.com; gloria@glo.com.tw
www.glo.com.tw

NUMBER OF TEACHERS: 100 for 18 cram schools in Taoyuan County (near Taipei).

PREFERENCE OF NATIONALITY: American or Canadian.

QUALIFICATIONS: Bachelor's degree, or 2-year college diploma and TESOL/TEFL certificate.

CONDITIONS OF EMPLOYMENT: 12-month contracts. Most classes are between 4pm and 9pm on weekdays and all day Saturday. Average minimum 20 hours per week; most teach 24–30.

SALARY: NT$660 per hour for teachers without previous teaching experience (approximately US$20). About NT$55,000 per month after tax. Deductions vary from nothing to 10% depending on length of employment. End-of-contract bonus of NT$30,000 plus other bonuses given throughout the year, including NT$25,000–NT$30,000 bonus for contract renewal.

FACILITIES/SUPPORT: Rent-free accommodation at one of the school's dormitories provided for 15 months. School will provide assistance with all related visa paperwork, but teachers are responsible for paying for their work permits. Training given including one-to-one workshops.

RECRUITMENT: Online job postings, e.g. on www.mytefljobs.com, newspaper job postings, referrals by current or previous employees. Phone interviews are mandatory. If the applicant is already in Taiwan, in-person interviews are preferable.

CONTACT: Celia Chou, HR Manager.

HESS INTERNATIONAL EDUCATIONAL GROUP
No 107, Section 2, Minquan E Road, Zhongshan District, Taipei City 104
+886 2 2592 6998
hess.info@hesseducation.com
www.hess.education.com

NUMBER OF TEACHERS: 600 native English-speaking teachers in more than 180 branches throughout Taiwan plus Singapore, China and Korea. About 250 new teachers hired each year.

PREFERENCE OF NATIONALITY: American, Australian, British, Canadian, Irish, New Zealander and South African.

QUALIFICATIONS: Bachelor's degree (in any subject) plus desire to work with varied age groups and to experience Chinese culture. Those holding an associate degree are welcome to apply provided they hold a TEFL/TESOL certificate as well. Applicants must provide a criminal background check from their home country.

CONDITIONS OF EMPLOYMENT: 1-year renewable contract. Three contract options are available to suit each teacher's preference. 1) 20-hour Contract: 20–25 hours a week guaranteed; teaching hours are generally between 1.30pm and 9pm, Monday to Friday and between 8.30am and 6.30pm on Saturdays; students aged 5–16; classes are 100 minutes. 2) 20M Contract: 20 hours a week guaranteed minimum; teaching hours are generally between 8.30am and 9pm, Monday to Friday and between 8.30am and 6.30pm on Saturdays; students are aged 2–16. 3) 25-hour Contract: same as 20M Contract except guaranteed minimum number of hours is 25 per week.

SALARY: NT$580 per hour (gross) starting salary. Tax rate is 18% for first six months then drops to 5%. A raise and bonus system is also part of the pay structure.

FACILITIES/SUPPORT: Airport pick-up and free hotel accommodation during initial 9-day training period. Free TEFL certification training programme and curriculum training provided with 4 follow-up training sessions after 1, 3, 6 and 9 months. Assistance given to obtain work permits and accommodation. Application process should be started 3 months in advance to allow time to collect visa and work permit documents.

RECRUITMENT: Apply online through Hess website; 4 major new teacher intakes per year. Applications accepted year round.

CONTACT: Amy Simpson, North American, British and Irish Applications and Interviews Consultant, English Human Resources Department (amy.simpson@hess.com.tw).

JUMP START

9F, No. 214, Heping East Rd., Sec 1, Taipei 106

+886 2 2369 4128

eric@jumpstart.com.tw

www.jumpstart.com.tw

English immersion schools for children aged 2–12.

QUALIFICATIONS: Native English speakers. Early childhood education/elementary teachers needed, e.g. with degree, preferably BEd (especially early childhood or elementary specialists). Must be enthusiastic and enjoy teaching children.

CONDITIONS OF EMPLOYMENT: To start mainly from 1 July or 1 September but other dates are possible. Guaranteed hours with extra hours available. Planned curriculum with complete teaching materials. Teachers should arrive a week in advance in order to receive a 2–3 day induction.

SALARY: Depends on qualifications and experience.

FACILITIES/SUPPORT: Work visa and health insurance provided. Airport pick-up. Accommodation provided on arrival.

CONTACT: Eric Ma, Human Resource Manager.

KANG NING ENGLISH SCHOOL

No. 39 Park Road, Jhudong 310, Hsinchu County

+886 3 594 3322

tammy.lin@kangning.com.tw

www.kangning.com.tw

NUMBER OF TEACHERS: 13 native English-speaking teachers for Language Department and Kindergarten Department in 7 branches in Jhudong Township and Jhudei City.

PREFERENCE OF NATIONALITY: British, American, Canadian, Australian, South African and New Zealander.

QUALIFICATIONS: Minimum bachelor's degree or 2-year associate degree (e.g. from US community colleges) and a TESOL certificate.

CONDITIONS OF EMPLOYMENT: Minimum 15 month commitment from July/August or January. Working hours in the Language Department 12.30pm–9.30pm. Working hours in the Kindergarten Department 9am–6pm.

SALARY: NT$58,000–$68,000 per month, depending on professional and academic qualifications, with end-of-contract bonus, partial airfare compensation, performance bonus and additional overtime pay and bonus. Average tax rate 6%.

FACILITIES/SUPPORT: Free Chinese lessons, staff trips, free meals, health insurance and paid national holidays/vacation. Fully formed curriculum cuts down on preparation time. Free accommodation for the first month during compulsory training and assistance to find suitable housing thereafter. KNES will also help teachers to obtain an Alien Residence Card (ARC) and open a bank account.

RECRUITMENT: Via website. Interview and reference check required. Occasional possibility of interviews in the US.

CONTACT: Tammy Lin.

KNS LANGUAGE INSTITUTE

313 Wunxin Road, Gushan District, Kaohsiung

+886 7 550 5611

knsleon@yahoo.ca

www.kns.com.tw

NUMBER OF TEACHERS: 45 teachers over 6 branches, mainly to teach children.

PREFERENCE OF NATIONALITY: North American, though all native English speakers accepted (American, Canadian, British, Irish, Australian, New Zealander and South African).

QUALIFICATIONS: At least a bachelor's degree. Teaching experience, TESOL certification or BEd preferred. Applicants must pass a medical examination.

CONDITIONS OF EMPLOYMENT: 1-year contracts. Full-time hours 2pm–9.10pm, Monday to Friday, in one location. Regimented teaching system. 30 teaching hours a week.

SALARY: NT$580 per hour plus end-of-contract bonus of NT$40 for every hour worked, so maximum NT$56,000 for the year.

FACILITIES/SUPPORT: Assistance with accommodation, and acquiring scooter and phone. No-interest loans available, 2-week paid training, paid work permit fees, health insurance, and a 3-week summer vacation.

RECRUITMENT: Via internet, university placement offices, etc. Online application form. Interviews in Taiwan or via Skype. Deadlines are 15 January for spring intake, 15 July for autumn start and 15 April for summer. Teachers must arrive at least 2 weeks early for training and set-up.

CONTACT: Leon Ranger, Human Resource Consultant (knsleon@yahoo.ca).

KOJEN ELS

6F, #9, Lane 90, Sung Chiang Road, Taipei

+886 2 2581 8511

kojenjobs@kojen-els.com.tw

www.kojenels.com

NUMBER OF TEACHERS: Around 300 for 35 centres teaching pre-schoolers, children and adults in Taipei, Kaohsiung and Taichung.

PREFERENCE OF NATIONALITY: American, Canadian, British, Irish, Australian, New Zealander and South African.

QUALIFICATIONS: Minimum bachelor's degree. ESL experience and/or TESOL/TEFL certificate will increase chance of employment.

CONDITIONS OF EMPLOYMENT: 1-year contracts. Afternoon, evening and Saturday work. Pupils range in age from 4 to 13 in the children's department.

SALARY: Starting wage NT$580–$590 per hour. Bonuses paid at end of contract, calculated according to number of hours taught for hourly teachers.

FACILITIES/SUPPORT: 1 week's free accommodation in shared apartments. Training provided. National health and labour insurance provided. Library has 6,000+ handouts.

RECRUITMENT: Direct application/walk-ins and online adverts, e.g. on www.teachergig.com, placed by independent recruiter Luisa Sia (luisarecruit@hibox.hinet.net). Local interviews compulsory. Applicants may be asked to teach a sample lesson. The original university degree certificate must be brought to Taiwan.

MICHAEL'S EFL SCHOOL

261 Tong-Nan Street, Hsin-Chu City

michaelseflschool@gmail.com

A small privately owned school managed by a Brit and his Taiwanese wife since 1985.

NUMBER OF TEACHERS: 3 native English speakers to teach children and teenagers (not kindergarten).

QUALIFICATIONS: Native English speakers with recognised university degree. Teaching/coaching experience/EFL qualifications are an advantage. References required. A genuine interest in teaching is essential. (Ideal for candidates considering teaching as a career.)

CONDITIONS OF EMPLOYMENT: Minimum 1-year contract. Afternoon and evening work only. Student-centred classes for 7 to 17-year-olds with average class size 7–10 pupils. School aims to offer parents a family-focused approach to education in contrast to the franchise schools.

SALARY: NT$600 per teaching hour.

FACILITIES/SUPPORT: 1-month (paid) induction course. 10 days' paid holidays, 10 days' unpaid. Gratuity fund. Free airport pick-up. Assistance finding accommodation. Work visa, national health care, ARC, all available through school.

RECRUITMENT: Via UK education newspapers and the internet. In first instance send dates of availability and photo plus CV. Interview with Michael Weatherley (School Owner) by Skype or in person.

PHOENIX GROUP ASIA

987-2 Chur Ri Road 3rd Floor, Taoyuan 33050

+886 3 3586567

phoenixgroupasia@gmail.com

www.phoenixgroup.asia

NUMBER OF TEACHERS: 50.

PREFERENCE OF NATIONALITY: USA and Canada.

QUALIFICATIONS: College degree and overseas English teaching experience.

CONDITIONS OF EMPLOYMENT: One year. Usual teaching hours in afternoons and evenings.

SALARY: US$1,700 per month less 5% tax (if entry to Taiwan is before July 1st,) or 18% (if after July 1st).

FACILITIES/SUPPORT: Assistance given with finding suitable housing but teachers pay their own deposit and rent. Initial one-week training given before teaching starts. Assistance with 5 steps in managing the bureaucracy: get medical check, send out work permit application, transfer landing or other visa into work visa, get resident visa and Alien Resident Card, and finally arrange health insurance card and labour insurance.

RECRUITMENT: Online job banks and social media.

CONTACT: Sandra King, CEO.

REACH TO TEACH

1606 80th Avenue, Algona, Iowa 50511, USA. Also #319 Minsheng Road, Taipei, Taiwan.

+1 201 467 4612

info@reachtoteachrecruiting.com

www.ReachToTeachRecruiting.com

For contacts in other countries, see entry at beginning of Asia chapter.

NUMBER OF TEACHERS: 150+.

PREFERENCE OF NATIONALITY: American, Canadian, British, Irish, Australian, New Zealander and South African.

QUALIFICATIONS: Positive, enthusiastic, dedicated and flexible attitude are the most important qualifications. Must have full BA for visa reasons and a TEFL qualification. Teaching experience and/or a 120-hour in-class TEFL qualification will often lead to a higher salary or more job placement options.

CONDITIONS OF EMPLOYMENT: 1 year full-time. Schedules are generally either morning/afternoon (pre-school) or afternoon/evening (elementary school). Pre-school positions start twice a year (February and August) and applications are needed 3 months in advance. Elementary school positions can be applied for year round.

SALARY: Salaries are competitive with most elementary and pre-schools in Taiwan. Salaries vary depending on teaching experience, qualifications, location and benefits. Salaries usually range between NT$50,000 and NT$65,000 per month.

FACILITIES/SUPPORT: Taiwan visa guidance and airport collection are provided plus teacher orientation/training (when available). Teachers have the option of continued support and contact with Reach To Teach throughout their year-long placement. Agency hosts teacher social events and gatherings (mostly in Taipei).

RECRUITMENT: Applications submitted via website. In-depth interviews conducted over Skype, by phone or occasionally in person.

CONTACT: Carrie Kellenberger, Co-President (Carrie@ReachToTeachRecruiting.com) or Dean Barnes, Recruiting Coordinator.

SESAME STREET ENGLISH

No. 6, Alley 32, Chang Rung Rd, Tainan City

+886 6 511 8086 ext 13

service@sesamevillage.tw; admin@sesamevillage.tw

www.sesamevillage.tw (Chinese only)

NUMBER OF TEACHERS: 25–28.

PREFERENCE OF NATIONALITY: UK, South Africa, Australia, Canada, USA and New Zealand.

QUALIFICATIONS: Minimum of a BA degree and TEFL/TESOL.

CONDITIONS OF EMPLOYMENT: 1 year renewable. Hours 2pm–8pm.

SALARY: NT$50,000 per month.

FACILITIES/SUPPORT: Handbook for new teachers written by recent teachers with advice on documentation, mobile phones, transport, food shopping, etc. Assistance given with finding but not paying for accommodation. Help given with applying for ARC, etc. at local immigration department.

RECRUITMENT: Via websites or word of mouth. Interviews in Tainan required.

CONTACT: Kristian Chen (HR Manager).

SHANE ENGLISH SCHOOL

6F-1, 41 Roosevelt Road, Section 2, Taipei

+886 2 2351 7755 ext 116

john.yates@shane.com.tw

www.shane.com.tw/sest

NUMBER OF TEACHERS: 180 in 61 franchise schools and 3 English-immersion kindergartens. Majority of lessons for children.

PREFERENCE OF NATIONALITY: Must be citizen of native English-speaking country.

QUALIFICATIONS: 120-hour TEFL/CELTA/Trinity certificate and Bachelor's degree. No experience required.

CONDITIONS OF EMPLOYMENT: 1-year renewable contracts. Guaranteed salaries for 80 hours per month for first 6 months. 5 days per week schedule.

SALARY: NT$44,800–$60,000 per month depending on hours taught.

FACILITIES/SUPPORT: Up-to-date facilities and teaching resources. Work permits, assistance with accommodation and comprehensive initial and Teacher Development Scheme.

RECRUITMENT: Applicants can apply directly to arrange face-to-face or Skype interview. Saxoncourt in the UK (www.saxoncourt.com) also recruits for Shane Taiwan.

CONTACT: Steve Lambert, Principal; Chris Redpath, Director of Studies; or Rachel Nickson, Recruitment Manager at Saxoncourt.

THAILAND

The English teaching scene is flourishing, especially in schools that teach English to children. For several years the government has been making efforts to extend the instruction of English in state schools as well as private ones, by introducing 'EP' (English Program), a bilingual stream within Thai schools which involves the teaching of English and other subjects, preferably by native English-speaker teachers willing to accept a modest wage.

Knowledge of English is eagerly sought by most urban young people and, in the context of Thailand, 'urban' is almost synonymous with 'Bangkok', which is more than 20 times larger than its nearest rival, Nonthaburi. The *Bangkok Post* is a less fruitful source of vacancies than Thai-specific websites such as www.teachingthailand.com, www.teachteflthailand.com and www.ajarn.com described below. The latter is a treasure trove of teaching information, contact details and job advertisements.

In its aim to improve the quality of English teaching in Thailand and to ensure that 'fake' teachers cannot be so easily accepted into the expat community, the government has tightened up the visa regulations and issuance of teachers' licences, which might provide an incentive for people who do not qualify to consider joining one of the many volunteer teaching schemes that operate throughout the country.

PROSPECTS FOR TEACHERS

The word on the street is that it takes no more than a nanosecond to find a job in Thailand provided you arrive in the main hiring season (April is best) with the right passport and a degree. Only a small percentage of recruitment takes place outside Thailand. The major schools use foreign recruitment agencies and the internet to make contact with potential teachers, but most organisations depend on finding native-speaker teachers locally, including Thai universities and teachers' colleges, as well as private business colleges, which all have EFL departments. Hundreds of foreigners graduate from one of the many TEFL training courses offered in Thailand (see Directory of Training Courses) and many of them have links with local schools. One of the most active is See TEFL (Siam Educational Experience) (www.seetefl.com), which guarantees employment if graduating job-seekers follow nine steps.

Thailand also appeals to English speakers who would like a career break and find that teaching is the best job going. **Ed Reinert** worked as a salesman for 25 years before becoming a teacher in Thailand, while **Carlos Vega** was a computer technician who realised that teaching was the only job he would be able to find in Thailand. Whereas few language companies openly impose an upper age limit, some age discrimination does take place, especially with companies that specialise in the teenage market (a key sector in summers).

Thais are exuberant and fun-loving people and their ideas about education reflect this. They seem to value fun and games (*sanuk*) above grammar, and an outgoing personality above a teaching certificate, although this attitude may be changing. Of course, there is already a nucleus of professional EFL teachers working at the most prestigious institutes in Bangkok. Many international and Thai bilingual schools look for individuals who can teach art, maths and science through the medium of English. Originally set up as teacher-training colleges, there are about 40 Rajabhat Universities around Thailand which are autonomous and hire their own English teachers. Some schools and language institutes may be keener to hire women on the assumption that they are less likely to become distracted by the seamier side of Thailand's nightlife.

One thing to consider is that Thai salaries have not really increased in recent years, even though the government wants to attract more professional teachers. This is something of a sticking point, and teachers who want to make a good living in Asia would be better off looking at Korea or Taiwan. However, living costs are still fairly low in Thailand (Bangkok and tourist resorts excepted) and many teachers have such an exciting time that they don't give a thought to saving, or indeed to returning home.

FINDING A JOB

IN ADVANCE

Among the many teacher-placement agencies attempting to place suitably qualified candidates in schools throughout Thailand, try the following:

AYC Intercultural Programs Thailand, Bangkok (✆ +66 2 556 1533; h_r@aycthailand.com; www.aycteachthailand.com). 200 native English speakers with a bachelor's degree are recruited for EP schools in Thailand, and also for summer language camps. New teachers may take 4-week Intesol-accredited training course for $799 ($999 with accommodation) that guarantees a job afterwards.

BFITS (Bright Future International Training & Services) – see entry.

Echo English Ltd – see entry.

Global Education Solutions, Nonthaburi; www.gesthailand.co.th. Teaching internships May-October or October-May for certificate-holders.

Global Training Academy, alex@globaltraining.co.th; www.englishjobsthailand.com. 4-week TEFL course in Koh Samui followed by placement throughout Thailand for 4–5 months, for degree-holders only.

Teach Thailand, Songkhla (roadexperience10@gmail.com; www.teachthailand.org). Recruits teachers for all regions: Northern, Isan (Northeastern), Central and Southern; salaries are lower in Southern and Northern provinces. Guaranteed job placement and visa assistance.

Teach to Travel Ltd, London, UK (www.teachtotravel.co.uk). 70 teachers under the age of 45 are placed in government primary and secondary schools in South and Central Thailand. Wage of 25,000–30,000 baht per month with jobs starting May and November.

London-based exchange travel companies such as IST Plus (see entry) and Global Nomadic (www.globalnomadic.com) arrange paid teaching jobs in Thailand but charge an administrative fee for their services. Global Nomadic's programme involves a four-week TEFL training course in Koh Samui and job-placement package costing $1,375.

The British Council in Thailand (www.britishcouncil.or.th) runs the Thailand English Teaching (TET) Programme (www.britishcouncil.org/study-work-create/opportunity/work-volunteer/thailand-english-teaching-programme) whereby a large number of undergraduates and recent graduates from participating UK universities spend nine weeks over the summer or four months in the winter working as English Language Assistants in Thai education institutions across the country. For longer-term teaching positions in the six British Council teaching centres, candidates will need a degree and at least 2 years' post-CELTA experience. Applications should be submitted to the East Asia Recruitment Team located in Singapore (EAteacher.Recruitment@britishcouncil.org.sg).

One of the best all-round sources of information about teaching in Thailand, with an emphasis on Bangkok and inside information about the main hiring companies, is the website www.ajarn.com – *ajarn* is the Thai word for teacher – with stories and tips and current job vacancies posted on www.AjarnJobspace.com. The site is run and constantly updated by a teacher, Phil Williams, who has been in Thailand for many years. Various online recruitment sites such as www.teachteflthailand.com and www.totalesl.com carry current vacancies in Bangkok and beyond. The Icon Education Group based in Thailand is a cluster of TESOL websites for teacher recruitment.

DAWN WILKINSON

Dawn Wilkinson taught from July to December at St Joseph Convent School in Silom, Bangkok, which she found through the BFITS agency advertising on www.ajarn.com.

Although it wasn't my favourite part of Thailand, I had made a few friends in Bangkok, so thought this would be the best place to live and look for work. I was surprised to discover how low teaching wages were in comparison to Vietnam; Thailand is so much more developed as a country (and living costs are much higher), but teaching wages far from reflect this, something that is complained about regularly on internet forums. There seemed to be hundreds of teaching jobs available in Bangkok. I only really looked at www.ajarn.com and, although I didn't struggle to find a job, I knew I could have got a better and higher-paid position if I had a TEFL qualification. After a successful Skype interview while in Vietnam, I accepted a full-time position as a Prathom (primary) grade 4 teacher in a prestigious Catholic girls' school in Silom. The agency arranged all my paperwork and visa, changing my tourist visa into a non-immigrant B visa which allows you to work while applying for your teaching licence (I wouldn't advise attempting to work in Thailand without the right visa – the authorities regularly catch and fine many people).

Teaching in Thailand seemed much more formal and serious than Vietnam. The Convent School was particularly strict in its enforcement of the 'proper' conduct and dress code of the teachers (no trousers or skirts above the knee for females, no sleeveless tops, no tattoos on show, etc). I taught more than 250 eight-nine-year-old girls, across eight classes, who were very sweet and affectionate, but who were also very hard to tell apart in their identical uniforms and French plaits (their self-styled nicknames, like Coffee, Ice and Bogey, also made me laugh somewhat!). I earned 35,000 baht a month, which, after 7,000 baht rent for a studio apartment (I lived in a cheaper 'Thai' rather than expat area), plus bills (3,000 baht), as well as the cost of travelling to work on public transport and food, didn't leave as much as I had had in Saigon. However, on the plus side, during just five months at the school I had about seven weeks of paid holiday – which I thoroughly enjoyed on the Thai beaches and islands!

Melanie Drake is another young teacher who landed a job in Thailand with ease, this one with ECC (see entry), after gaining a TEFL qualification at TEFL International Corinth in Greece:

My soon-to-be boss contacted me after he had spotted my CV on www.tefl.com. After several emails and a simple visa application process I was in Thailand. Culture shock all round. My job required me to teach in businesses, poor government schools with cramped, sometimes a bit unsanitary conditions and also in a local private language school. My tiny, basic but clean apartment was free and came with the job. My wages were more than satisfactory to save some as life was incredibly cheap. I was pretty lonely before I got to meet the other members of staff. I was living alone quite far out from the school and was unable to communicate with anyone due to language difficulties. I was terrified of dogs and it turns out that my city, Ayutthaya, had some of the highest numbers of stray dogs in the country, and dealing with this was easily my biggest hurdle. Classes were also over-populated in the schools, sometimes 60 to a class; with no air-conditioning. Students were for the most part quite lazy and more interested in the novelty of a foreigner than learning English. But, in hindsight, they showed more respect than the average British/American kid probably would.

The placement agency Teach Thailand (listed above) maintains that preparing to teach at a school in Thailand is more about adapting to the culture than honing your skills as a teacher.

VOLUNTEERING

For those who do not qualify for a salaried teaching position, the option of volunteering is attractive. Many worthy agencies operating internationally or at a grassroots level supply volunteer teachers to local schools who would otherwise not be exposed to native English speakers. Schools particularly want help from volunteers in spoken English. They usually have local teachers who are reasonably competent in grammar, vocabulary, spelling, teaching reading, etc., but value help from first-language speakers of English.

The visa regulations governing volunteers changed recently. The Non-Immigrant Category 'O' visa was previously issued to volunteers for 12 months, however the maximum on that visa is now 90 days, shorter than the standard semester which lasts four or five months.

A charity founded by an American, Volunthai (www.volunthai.com), runs a teaching programme in rural North-Eastern Thailand. Teachers' accommodation is provided as homestays, and the fee is $375 for the first month and $200 thereafter. Small-scale charities such as this can respond flexibly to individual requirements. For example, Volunthai once incorporated an American family with four children aged 3–13, all of whom participated in school activities. Looking back on their experiences of travelling around the world, the **Battye** family concluded that becoming part of a rural Thai village through Volunthai was the highlight of the year for them.

In rural parts of Thailand, schools cannot afford to pay salaries to foreign teachers, and local children have little or no exposure to fluent English. Yet the children who dream of going to university and into the professions need to achieve a certain standard of English. To meet this need various organisations enlist the help of volunteer teachers including the following:

Gift School of English, see entry.

International Volunteer HQ, New Zealand (www.volunteerhq.org/volunteer-in-thailand). 250 volunteers placed in Thailand every year including English teachers for young children, especially among hill tribes around Chiang Rai. Sample price $1,320 for 12 weeks (plus $279 registration fee).

Mundo Exchange Organization, Portland, Oregon, USA (✆ +1 503 227 8442; www.mundoexchange.org). Volunteers teach English and computer skills to disadvantaged children and/or adults mainly in Isan province in North-Eastern Thailand. Volunteers can be placed at short notice but 2–3 months' advance warning is preferred. The placement costs are $400 for the first week (which includes 2–3 day orientation), $685 for 2 weeks, to $1,075 for 8 weeks, then $105 per additional week. Fees include pre-arranged accommodation, travel within the project and support before and during the stay.

Openmind Projects, 43000 Nong Khai (www.openmindprojects.org). The fee for this volunteer teacher programme in different regions in Thailand starts at $295 for the first fortnight, and is $95 per week thereafter. Three-day orientation included. Teaching is taught by role play.

Starfish Volunteers (www.starfish-adventure.com). UK voluntourism company that places volunteer teachers in government schools in Surin. The 2017 fee is £800 for 8 weeks.

Travel to Teach, T2T, 77/4 Chaitalay Road, Prachuap Khiri Khan 77000 (✆ +66 9 2818 5929; www.travel-to-teach.org). Thai-based organisation that provides volunteer teaching opportunities (among others) around Chiang Mai and mainly in the north. Sample fees £436 for a month, £1,213 for six months.

Volunteer Teacher Thailand, 4/91 Soi Bang La-On, Moo 7, Khao Lak, Phang Nga 82190 (✆ +66 845290616; volunteer.teachers@yahoo.com; www.volunteerteacherthailand.org). This charity continues the work of the now disbanded Tsunami Volunteer Centre set up by British teacher Ken Hyde. Registration fee of 4,000 baht for any length of stay (minimum 2 weeks).

The Karen Hill Tribes Trust, York, UK (✆ +44 1904 612829; www.karenhilltribes.org.uk). Sends self-funding volunteers, including gap-year students, to North-West Thailand to work in upland and hill communities of Karen tribespeople, some as language teachers, for 10 or 20 weeks, costing £1,000 and £1,600.

Barbara Darragh also saw for herself how extremely popular English teachers are:

> ***My first volunteer trip to Thailand was with an organisation set up after the tsunami. I then went to Chiang Mai for six months and after completing a month's TEFL course with SeeTEFL I offered my services to a local school. I loved working there and made many Thai friends who are always emailing me and asking me when I plan to return, which I hope to do again in September. It is very easy to find good, cheap accommodation and the Thai people are so friendly. The children are a delight to teach and are so excited when you go into the school. The poorer schools where I volunteer would never normally be able to afford an 'English' English teacher. There is also plenty of paid work and I did have a private student and if I had wanted I could have had a lot more. As soon as people realise that you are an English teacher they want you to teach them or their family. I have never felt so rewarded in a job before and the fact that I want to go back every year and work for nothing must say something.***

Mobile Education Partnerships (www.mobileeducationpartnerships.org) is a specialist British charity involved with teacher training along the Thai-Myanmar border, supporting education in refugee communities that have been affected by war, hardship and oppression. About 150,000 Burmese people live on Thai soil.

ON THE SPOT IN BANGKOK

Any new arrival in Bangkok would be well advised to spend a week getting his or her bearings and asking foreigners living in the city for inside information about possible employers. Many people say that the teaching scene can be somewhat exploitative and life in the city so hectic that it is better to leave Bangkok as quickly as you can. Others adore the buzz.

For those who feel strong enough to survive in Bangkok, language schools are generally easy to locate and approach on spec. As a long-term traveller, **Mark Wiens** claims not to make lots of cash, but he has discovered ways to make enough money to live overseas, partly by food blogging at http://migrationology.com, and one of the strings to his bow is English teaching. While he was in Bangkok he noticed a billboard for English courses at Wall Street English and simply went into the school and had a short friendly meeting with the HR manager, who just wanted to confirm that he would be someone that would respect and be patient with the students (though he did have a four-week TESOL certificate too):

> ***My number one task was to elicit correct English from the students. The students studied the grammar using a computer program and it was my job to confirm their comprehension of what they learned. I worked from 11am until 8pm, five days per week in a very nice air-conditioned facility located in a shopping centre. The other***

teachers were a cool group of recent university graduates who enjoyed other cultures and experiencing new things. The low point was having to teach the same material day after day. Like any job, it became too much of a routine and I did get bored.

The best place to start is around Siam Square, where numerous schools and the British Council are located. The Council has a list of private and public universities, institutes, teachers' colleges and international schools throughout the country which have English departments and therefore possible openings for a native English speaker; but most job-seekers rely on the *Yellow Pages*, which include dozens of language school addresses. Note that the Thai school year ends in mid-March and restarts the second week of May, so April is the perfect time to arrive. If you arrive after that, only the dregs are left and if you arrive in the winter, you will find very little hiring going on.

The English-language daily newspaper, the *Bangkok Post*, is a possible source of job vacancies (http://job.bangkokpost.com) though the jobs listings on ajarn.com and Craigslist (http://bangkok.craigslist.co.th/edu) are more extensive. Many ads specify 'NES' status which simply means Native English Speaker.

Travelling around Bangkok, a city of more than eight million, is so time consuming and unpleasant that it is important to plot your interview strategy on a city map before making appointments. Also be sure to pick up a map of the air-conditioned bus routes, particularly if you are contemplating a job that involves travelling to different premises.

It may not be necessary to spend too much time researching the schools with vacancies. Many of the so-called back-street language schools (more likely to be on a main street, above a shop or restaurant) look to the cheap hotels of Banglamphu, the favourite haunt of western travellers in the north-west of Bangkok. There is such a high turnover of staff at many schools that there are bound to be vacancies somewhere for a new arrival who takes the trouble to present a professional image and can show a convincing CV supported with diplomas/certificates. As usual, it may be necessary to start with part-time and occasional work with several employers, aiming to build up 20–30 hours in the same area to minimise travelling in the appalling traffic.

The teaching of children is an expanding area; if you don't want to teach the alphabet, don't accept pupils under the age of 5. On the strength of her claim that she had experience of 'working with children', **Alison Eglinton** was soon earning a reasonable wage (and she suggests that anyone teaching young children should master at least one word of Thai: *hong nam*, which means toilet).

Ajarn (teachers) are respected in Thailand and are expected to look respectable. As well as dressing smartly for an interview, try to maintain a reserve in your manner while still projecting a relaxed and easy-going image. Too many gesticulations and guffawing are considered impolite and immature and will not earn you the respect of Thai people. When visiting a school, wear your posh clothes and carry CVs and passport photos to clip onto the application forms; otherwise you'll be asked to come back with the correct documents. Don't be surprised if the application form asks some weird questions, such as asking you to give the name, age and profession of every member of your family. You won't be hired on the spot but may well be contacted by phone within a day or two. Everyone who has ever had anything to do with teaching English in Thailand emphasises the need to dress smartly, as **Bruce Lawson** describes:

The Thais like their pet farangs *(i.e. foreigners) to look as much like currency dealers as possible. I bought a suit in Bangkok for £50 especially for the job hunt. Men should take out all earrings and wear a tie (thus risking asphyxiation in the heat and humidity of the hot season). Women should wear a decent skirt, not trousers.*

Appropriate dress was also a problem for **Susannah Kerr**, who had been told by her sending agency (www.i-to-i.com) that T-shirts and flip-flops would be appropriate. But this was not the case at her school in Nakhon Nayok (population 17,000), and she was promptly taken on a compulsory shopping expedition and obliged to spend money on smarter clothes that she didn't care for.

The busiest season for tutoring is mid-March to mid-May during the school holidays, when many secondary school and university students take extra tuition in English. This coincides with the hot season. Vacancies continue to be advertised through June, July and August. The next best time to look for teaching work in private schools is October, while the quietest time is January/February.

ON THE SPOT IN CHIANG MAI

Teaching opportunities crop up in branches of the big companies such as ECC and AUA and in academic institutes. When approaching the bilingual (EP) schools, seek out the director for the 'bilingual' section of the school. Teachers are recruited for all levels from nursery school to kindergarten, primary to secondary, though in some cases a master's degree in education or a teaching degree will be required. When applying for jobs, it is best to visit the schools directly as they don't have time to answer endless emails. Most schools have websites, though they are not always easy to navigate.

There are seven international schools which may employ English teachers, though most of those hired are certified teachers recruited at international teachers' fairs such as those sponsored by the thorough and professional Search Associates (www.searchassociates.com), of which there is a long-established branch in Chiang Mai, run by Harry Deelman. Other jobs are available in the school holidays at summer and weekend camps held at resort hotels or at Chiang Mai's international schools and attended by rich children from Bangkok and other parts of Thailand. Getting into these and the summer camps run by the British Council and YMCA is by word of mouth, friends or advertisements. The advice of long-time Chiang Mai resident and owner of Eagle House guesthouse, **Annette Kunigagon,** is to be brazen, knock on doors, try hotels, shops catering to tourists, companies which export or have to deal with foreigners, pubs, restaurants, computer shops, large shops in the Night Bazaar area, etc.

Many private language schools can be found in the vicinity of Chiang Mai University and also in the area near the prestigious Thai secondary schools such as Montfort, Paruethai, Regina, Dara and Prince Royal College. The expanding expat community in Chiang Mai comprises many nationalities, most of whom use English as their second language and want to improve their skills.

ON THE SPOT IN THE PROVINCES

The number of teaching opportunities outside Bangkok has escalated; however, not many foreigners show an interest since the pay is much less than in Bangkok. The estimated four-fifths of teachers who are single males enjoying the nightlife in Bangkok are unwilling to move to a less exciting country town. Obviously few opportunities crop up on the islands since they are so constantly inundated with foreigners.

Competition for work is almost non-existent in lesser-known cities such as Nakhon Sawan, Khon Kaen, Udon Thani, Ubon Ratchathani and Pathumthani. For a job in a university you will probably have to show a higher degree or teaching certificate. The best places are Hat Yai and Songkhla. Hotels are always worth approaching, since many hotel workers are very keen to improve their English. If you find a place that suits and you decide to stay for a while, ask the family who run your guesthouse about local teaching opportunities. Sometimes the happiest and most memorable experiences take place away from the cities and the tourist resorts. **Brian Savage** returned to England after a second long stint of teaching in Thailand and describes one of the highlights for him:

My most rewarding experience was my week teaching English conversation in a rural high school in Loei province in North-East Thailand. These children had rarely seen and had certainly never spoken to a farang *(foreigner) before. My work during that week and a subsequent second visit was really appreciated by the students. The first visit came about after I was introduced to a teacher at the Chiang Mai school where I was teaching. If travellers get away from Bangkok and the resorts, they too can have experiences such as this, especially in the friendly towns of the north and north-east. A little voluntary teaching can really boost the confidence of students who are usually too poor to pay to study with native speakers.*

REGULATIONS

The goal posts keep shifting on the question of visas, and enforcement is inconsistent. The preferred alternative for people who have found a job from abroad is to apply for a non-immigrant B visa from any Thai Embassy. For this you will be asked to provide a copy of your degree certificate (essential), police clearance and various documents from your prospective employer in Thailand such as a contract of employment. With this visa, the applicant can stay in Thailand for no longer than 90 days unless his or her employer obtains a teacher's licence, for which you will need the original certificate of your bachelor's degree and transcripts or a letter/email of confirmation of graduation from your university. If your degree is in Education, that will suffice but, if in another subject, you will also need proof that you have a TESOL certificate of some kind. In addition you may need a criminal record check from your home country and from the Thai police and a medical certificate issued within the last month (obtainable from doctors in Thailand for a small fee).

To qualify for a full teaching licence, you must satisfy the requirements of the Teaching Council of Thailand, which means passing exams in Thai Language and Culture and also Professional Knowledge and Ethics. It seems that this is necessary only if teaching in a formal school that follows a Thai curriculum, so that non-formal schools, e.g. private language institutes and some employment agencies, are exempt, as are new teachers who may be granted a Provisional Teaching Permit instead of a full licence. A simpler alternative might be to qualify for the Educational (ED) visa or student visa by undertaking a course of Thai language and culture, which is valid for up to a year; renewals every three months cost 1,900 baht. Schools are being inspected and ED visa holders must show that they have attended at least 70% of the classes.

To upgrade a tourist visa to a Non-Immigrant B (Business) visa you must have a guaranteed job, the correct paperwork, patience and 2,000 baht for the fee. It is usually easier to apply for the Non-Immigrant B at a Thai embassy in another country. In this case the applicant must stay overnight and pick up the visa the next day. Most people take the overnight bus from Bangkok and arrive at whichever border town they're going to early the next morning, which makes the whole trip take at least three days. Teachers used to do a 'visa run' every 90 days, i.e. leave the country and renew their tourist status on the way back into Thailand. However the authorities have mounted a crackdown on this practice.

The paperwork forum of www.ajarn.com is a very good place to read about the evolving red tape situation and its practical (rather than theoretical) implications.

Once a work permit is granted (at a cost of 3,100 baht), tax will be withdrawn at a very modest rate of about 3%, plus up to 4% for social security contributions. However not all employers comply and some teachers take out private health insurance for instance through AIA (www.aia.co.th).

CONDITIONS OF WORK

In Thailand, the wages for *farang* teachers continue to be low. The basic hourly rate has risen only slightly over the past couple of years and is now in the 250–350 baht range (roughly £5.50–£7.50), while the monthly range is normally 27,000–35,000 baht in Bangkok, and on average 5,000 baht less in other cities. Company work can pay more depending on location, but in-company contract work is in short supply. The norm is for schools to keep their staff on as part-time freelancers while giving them full-time hours; this is primarily to avoid taxes. Most language institutes pay weekly in cash, but beware of schools that turn payday into a moveable feast.

The best remuneration is available from international schools such as the Bangkok Patana School (www.patana.ac.th). Note that the pay at international schools in Bangkok is as much as twice that paid by international schools elsewhere in the country. For a list of international schools in Thailand go to the website of the International Schools Association of Thailand (www.isat.or.th).

Few employers help with accommodation, which does not matter much since vacant apartments are not hard to locate and rental deposits not crippling as they are in Japan. Things are more relaxed in Chiang Mai, where a group of people can rent a house or live Thai-style in a studio room with attached bathroom for very affordable rents.

Remember never to touch a student on the head, which is difficult if you are teaching children. In class a show of anger will soon lose the students' respect since the Thais value a 'cool heart' (*jai yen*) and go to great lengths to avoid displays of negative emotion. They are great adherents of a 'no worries' attitude, called '*mai pen lai*' in Thai. Calm, smiling and enthusiastic personalities make all the difference. **Carlos Vega** thinks that there are two types of pupils:

> ***Primary are nice and ready to learn every day. Secondary students mostly don't care and don't want to learn anything in a system that makes it impossible for any student to fail. No one really has to do any work in order to pass the grade, so why bother? Usually if the parents are involved with the school the student tends to do well.***

LEISURE TIME

It has to be said that Bangkok may be an exciting and lively city but it is not beautiful. It has very few parks, bad traffic congestion and polluted air. Thai Labour Law stipulates that '*any employees who comport themselves in a manner which would embarrass or cause serious damage to employers' reputation may be terminated immediately, by employer, with no legal recourse available to employee*'. This applies on *and* off the clock. Many a *farang* man has been spotted in a 'night-time establishment' and been fired the next day.

With the ratio of foreign men to women teachers at least six to one, many women (although in great demand as teachers) do not enjoy the atmosphere in the city and leave as quickly as they can. Fortunately for teachers earning a low wage, the more innocent pleasures of Thailand, like street food, come cheap. Even part-time teachers should be able to afford to travel round the country, visiting jungle attractions such as Kanchanaburi, where you can ride an elephant along the banks of the River Kwai, and islands such as Koh Samet, Koh Samui and Koh Phangan where life is slow and the beaches are wonderful. Try to learn a little Thai, as **Bruce Lawson** did after getting fried battered banana when he thought he had ordered garlic chicken. He recommends organising word-swaps with students, which will also illustrate to them that they are not the only ones who have to struggle with alien sounds. Wherever you end up teaching you are sure to discover that Thailand is famously welcoming.

LIST OF EMPLOYERS

AMERICAN UNIVERSITY ALUMNI LANGUAGE CENTER
Bangkok: 21st Floor, Chamchuri Square Bldg, 319 Phyathai Road, Patumwan, Bangkok 10330
+66 2 6576 411, ext 1262
mike.white@auathailand.org
www.auathailand.org
Chiang Mai branch: AUA, 24 Rajadamnern Road, Amphur Muang, Chiang Mai 50200
+66 53 211377
chiangmai@auathailand.org

17 branches throughout Thailand (6 in Bangkok, 11 provincial).
NUMBER OF TEACHERS: About 175 in total: 40 at main branch, up to 10 at other branches.
PREFERENCE OF NATIONALITY: American, Canadian, British, Australian and New Zealander.
QUALIFICATIONS: Bachelor's degree and 120-hour certificate course taught face-to-face.
CONDITIONS OF EMPLOYMENT: 1-year commitment preferred. 4–6 hours' teaching daily (considered to be full-time). Teaching year consists of 7 6-week terms separated by 1 free week (unpaid). Courses aimed at professionals aged 18–35.
SALARY: Starting rate is 400 baht per hour on weekdays, 650 baht at weekends, depending on experience/qualifications. Annual bonus may be paid on completion of contract. Free health insurance, 1-year work permit (paid for by teacher for first 2 years), 50% discount on Thai lessons.
FACILITIES/SUPPORT: Participation in pre-service training preferred before teaching hours are assigned. Mentoring programme for new teachers and in-service professional development.
RECRUITMENT: Adverts in the *Bangkok Post*, the internet and word of mouth. Initial applications to be made online. Face-to-face interview required.
CONTACT: Mike White, Bangkok

BELL EDUCATIONAL TRUST
UK: Hillscross, Red Cross Lane, Cambridge CB2 0QU
+44 1223 275594
www.bellenglish.com/vacancies

NUMBER OF TEACHERS: Vacancies occur from time to time in partner schools in Thailand, e.g. Assumption College Rama II in Bangkok.
PREFERENCE OF NATIONALITY: For visa purposes must be from UK, USA, Canada, Australia, New Zealand or South Africa, and be a native English speaker.
QUALIFICATIONS: Bachelor's degree and CELTA (better still Young Learner speciality, PGCE and/or DELTA). Experience of and/or interest in teaching English to young learners preferred, especially experience in Thailand
CONDITIONS OF EMPLOYMENT: 1 year renewable contracts. Up to 21 contact hours per week but must be present at school Monday to Friday 9am–4pm. Much of the work is with young learners.
SALARY: 50,000–60,000 baht per month (up to 66,000 baht at Assumption College Bangrak).
FACILITIES/SUPPORT: One-way flight costs for teachers recruited outside Thailand. Hotel accommodation on arrival. Assistance in finding suitable accommodation. Visa and work permit arranged. 8 weeks' paid holiday per year plus public holidays. Health and medical insurance cover provided. Commitment to in-service training and professional development.
RECRUITMENT: Bell Recruitment, internet, telephone and face-to-face interviews.

BERLITZ BANGKOK LTD
246 Times Square Building, 2nd Floor, Sukhumvit Road 12-14, Klongtoey, Bangkok 10110
+66 2 255 6070
careers@berlitz.co.th; sunisa@berlitz.co.th
www.berlitz.co.th/en/careers-en

NUMBER OF TEACHERS: 60 for several branches.
PREFERENCE OF NATIONALITY: Must have native proficiency in the target language.
QUALIFICATIONS: University degree. Professionalism and a strong customer service orientation are essential. Both new and experienced instructors are recruited, provided they show willingness to learn and use the Berlitz Method of instruction in the classroom.
CONDITIONS OF EMPLOYMENT: 1 year. Minimum availability required is 35 hours with weekend availability required. New instructors are assigned two consecutive weekdays off.
SALARY: New instructors are paid at a rate of 220 baht per 40-minute lesson, which results in a minimum salary of 35,000 baht (net) per month, with fluctuations. Higher earnings are achievable to those willing to make themselves available for more hours. Rate of income tax is 9%–10%.
FACILITIES/SUPPORT: Berlitz works with a reliable English-speaking estate agent who doesn't charge the instructor for arranging

viewings of suitable accommodation and providing transport. HR representative assists with obtaining work permit by collecting the necessary documents from the instructor and processing the paperwork at the Ministry of Labour on the instructor's behalf. The company pays the 3,000 baht application fee.

RECRUITMENT: Websites, local recruiting classifieds (e.g. www.jobsdb.com, www.bangkokpost.com) and walk-in candidates who are welcome to leave their CV. If suitable, an interview will be scheduled.

CONTACT: Country Coordinator of Instruction.

BKS (BANGKOK SUCCESS GROUP)

184/73 Ratchadaphisek Road, Forum Tower, 16th Floor, Huay Kwang, Bangkok 10310

+66 2 645 4300

recruiting@bangkoksuccess.com

www.bangkoksuccess.com

NUMBER OF TEACHERS: 80–120, mainly teaching internships which follow on from 3-week TEFL training course on the islands.

PREFERENCE OF NATIONALITY: Native speakers only.

QUALIFICATIONS: 4-year university degree.

CONDITIONS OF EMPLOYMENT: 4.5 month stays. 25 classes of 50 minutes per week in office hours (between 7.50am and 4pm).

SALARY: 34,000–35,000 baht per month ($1,000), less 3% for income tax. TEFL training course on Koh Pha Ngan or Koh Lipe costs $1,695 including hotel accommodation.

FACILITIES/SUPPORT: Accommodation is ready and available at local prices (2,000–3,000 baht monthly). Dedicated Thai staff helps with work permits.

RECRUITMENT: Via online jobs sites, recruiting agents, and TEFL/TESOL training centres. Interviews are necessary and occasionally held in the US.

BRIGHT FUTURE INTERNATIONAL TRAINING & SERVICES (BFITS THAILAND)

SSP Tower, 11th Floor, 555/16-19 Soi 63 Sukhumvit (Ekamai), Sukhumvit Road, Klongton-Nua, Wattana, Bangkok 10110

+66 2 711 4684

hr@bfitsthailand.com

www.bfitsthailand.com

NUMBER OF TEACHERS: 120+ for about a 20 full-curriculum client schools.

PREFERENCE OF NATIONALITY: American, Canadian, British, Australian and South African. Primarily looking for native English speakers; non-native speakers must provide TOEFL/TOEIC score.

QUALIFICATIONS: Bachelor's and TEFL certification. TEFL certification is not required for licensed teachers, teachers with degrees in education or English, or for teachers teaching content subjects such as mathematics. Police clearance required.

CONDITIONS OF EMPLOYMENT: 1 year, May to February/March. 20–25 teaching hours per week for Conversational English Programme.

SALARY: 35,300 baht per month for English Conversation teachers; 35,300 baht for Intensive English, 40,300 baht for English Programme (Content) teachers. All positions come with yearly bonuses. Thai taxes are deducted at a rate of approximately 1,300 baht per month. End-of-contract bonus. Overtime paid at 500 baht per hour.

FACILITIES/SUPPORT: Assistance given in locating accommodation and translating/negotiating lease, if needed. Teachers are given necessary documents with instructions on how to obtain a non-immigrant B visa plus 2 paid working days to travel to obtain it. BFITS takes care of all costs and processing of the work permit.

RECRUITMENT: Via www.TotalESL.com, www.TESall.com, www.ESLjobfeed.com and www.TeachOverseas.ca partner sites of BFITS. Applications to HR Department with CV, photo, degrees/certificates and professional references can be emailed with contact information. Date of availability (or relocation date to Thailand) must be specified. Interviews by Skype or in person.

CONTACT: Michael Hines, Assistant Director and Owner, Icon Group of TESL websites.

ECC (THAILAND)

Teacher Service Centre (English & Computer College), ITEC House, 1st Floor, 9 Rajdamri Road, Lumpini, Patumwan, Bangkok 10330

+66 2 655 3333

garth@ecc.ac.th

www.tesol.ecc.ac.th/jobs

Teacher training centre in Bangkok and the largest private language school in Thailand with a network of many schools in Bangkok and in most major centres outside Bangkok (including Chiang Mai and Phuket).

NUMBER OF TEACHERS: Around 500 native English speakers (usually recruit 10–15 new teachers each month).

PREFERENCE OF NATIONALITY: None.

QUALIFICATIONS: Bachelor's degree plus TEFL certificate (CELTA, Trinity or equivalent).

CONDITIONS OF EMPLOYMENT: Minimum 100 hours per month (average 25–30 hours per week), 6-day week, mostly in evenings and weekends. BUPA medical insurance, end-of-contract bonus of

12,000 baht, location allowance in Bangkok (3,000–5,000 baht per month). 5 days' paid holiday in April, 13 statutory holidays.

SALARY: Depending on qualifications and experience 31,000–37,000 baht per month in Bangkok, 20,000–30,000 baht in the provinces.

FACILITIES/SUPPORT: Work permit and 1-year visa applied for after arrival. Assistance (non-financial) given with finding accommodation. Professional development with regular workshops, including a number of short courses that are free to ECC teachers: Teaching English to Young Learners and Teaching Business English. ECC offers the Cambridge CELTA course and an Introduction to TESOL course. BUPA health insurance plan.

RECRUITMENT: Adverts on the internet and qualified walk-ins.

CONTACT: Garth Marshall, Academic Director (garth@ecc.ac.th).

ECHO ENGLISH LTD

59/208 Moo 4 Tambol, Bang Kaew, Bang Phli, Samutprakarn 10540

+66 0204 71877

echoteam@echo-english.com

www.echo-english.com

Teacher recruitment and management agency.

NUMBER OF TEACHERS: 100.

PREFERENCE OF NATIONALITY: USA, Australia, United Kingdom, Ireland, Canada, New Zealand.

QUALIFICATIONS: BA is essential and a TEFL certificate is desirable. Relevant teaching experience is also taken into account as a possible alternative to qualifications.

CONDITIONS OF EMPLOYMENT: 1 school semester, i.e. about 4–5 months, with option to renew. Teachers must be at school all day Monday-Friday. No more than 24 teaching hours per week.

SALARY: 30,000 Thai baht per month.

FACILITIES/SUPPORT: Advice given on finding accommodation.

RECRUITMENT: Online advertisements, through a TEFL course partner based in the UK, and through a 3-day induction course in Bangkok which is run twice a year and costs participants 4,000 baht. Participation virtually guarantees a job. Alternatively candidates are interviewed via Skype. Work permit costs are covered by the company.

CONTACT: Jay Landles, HR & Recruitment Consultant.

GIFT SCHOOL OF ENGLISH

Nakorn Pathom, Central Thailand

+66 86 3318686

giftschoolofenglish@gmail.com

www.gift-school-of-english.com

NUMBER OF TEACHERS: 30 full-time and part-time native speaking teachers teach in small public and temple schools throughout Thailand, and at free summer camps for disadvantaged children.

PREFERENCE OF NATIONALITY: None.

QUALIFICATIONS: Only a wish to gain experience in teaching English, Thai culture and travel. Degree holder valued.

CONDITIONS OF EMPLOYMENT: One-year contracts (renewable) to start May/June and October/November. 20–25 teaching hours per week.

SALARY: 300 baht per teaching hour for graduates.

RECRUITMENT: Year round. Applicants should send CV, photo, highest certificate earned, police clearance and 2–3-minute self-introduction video.

CONTACT: Nora Ying (nora1111@gmail.com).

INLINGUA INTERNATIONAL SCHOOL OF LANGUAGES

4th Floor, Esplanade, 99 Ratchadaphisek Road, Dindaeng, Bangkok 10400

+66 2 655 3333

teach@inlinguabangkok.com

www.inlinguabangkok.com

NUMBER OF TEACHERS: 140 full-time, 100 part-time. For 19 branches.

PREFERENCE OF NATIONALITY: Native English speakers: American, Canadian, British, Irish, Australian, New Zealander and South African.

QUALIFICATIONS: Candidates must have a bachelor's degree and TESOL/TEFL/CELTA.

CONDITIONS OF EMPLOYMENT: 1 year. Children's classes are on Saturday/Sunday 9am–6pm. Teachers work a 6-day week or 5 for corporate work.

SALARY: Guaranteed minimum 35,000 baht for full-time contract teachers; possibly more, depending on workload.

FACILITIES/SUPPORT: Try to point staff in the direction of suitable accommodation. Full support given in work permit/visa applications. BUPA medical insurance.

RECRUITMENT: Internet adverts on www.ajarn.com. Applications welcomed on above email address. Mostly local hires.

CONTACT: Fraser Morrell, Director of Studies (fraserm@inlinguabangkok.com).

IST PLUS – TEACH IN THAILAND PROGRAMME
Crest House, 102-104 Church Road, Teddington, Middlesex TW11 8PY, UK
+44 20 7788 7877
info@istplus.com
www.istplus.com/teachinthailand

NUMBER OF TEACHERS: 20–30 each year for two programmes, one for paid teachers in state schools, supported by the Overseas Ed Group (www.oeg.co.th), and the other voluntary.
PREFERENCE OF NATIONALITY: None, although non-native speakers of English must have near-native proficiency in English.
QUALIFICATIONS: University degree in any field essential. TEFL training or experience is not essential but preferred. Maximum age 65.
CONDITIONS OF EMPLOYMENT: 5 or 10-month renewable contracts starting in either May or October, teaching 22 classes a week, which works out at a working week of 35–40 hours.
SALARY: Minimum 25,000 baht per month.
FACILITIES/SUPPORT: Free accommodation (usually on-campus), all-inclusive 7-day orientation in Bangkok on arrival including basic EFL training, accommodation, sight-seeing and airport transfer. IST Plus arrange school placement, visa and work permit, insurance and 24-hour emergency hotline.
RECRUITMENT: Deadlines for application are mid-March for May departure and mid-August for October departure. Teach in Thailand Programme fees from £995 for 5 months, £1,195 for 10 months. Teachers who complete 10-month contracts starting in May will receive a 20,000 baht bonus. All teachers who complete their contracts will receive a TEFL certificate.
CONTACT: Ralph Allemano, Director (rallemano@istplus.com).

KING'S COLLEGE OF ENGLISH
1093/19–21, 5th Floor, Central City Tower I, Bangna-Trad Road, Bangna, Prakanong, Bangkok 10260
+66 2 745 6001
kings.recruitment@hotmail.com
www.kingsthailand.com

A group of 4 English-language schools in Thailand.
NUMBER OF TEACHERS: 35–40.
PREFERENCE OF NATIONALITY: Native English speakers: British (majority), Canadian, American, Australian, New Zealander, South African.
QUALIFICATIONS: University degree (any subject) plus CELTA or 120-hour equivalent. Preference given to applicants with qualifications or experience teaching young learners, and/or with experience at summer camps or primary schools. Support and extensive materials are supplied.
CONDITIONS OF EMPLOYMENT: 1-year contracts mainly from August but also November/December. Contractual arrangement is 112 contact hours per month; preparation time is extra. Saturday and Sunday are working days. 2 consecutive days off a week.
SALARY: Approximately 34,000 baht per month depending on qualifications and experience. Yearly increment, paid holidays (13 days plus 13 statutory public holidays). End-of-contract bonus of 25,000 baht as contribution to flights.
FACILITIES/SUPPORT: Assistance with accommodation and non-immigrant B visa. Basic private health insurance provided by school. Free Thai language lessons plus Thai cookery and boxing programme.
RECRUITMENT: Local and web adverts and UK recruitment agency. UK applicants should send CV and photo in the first instance to John Hudson (john.hudson@firstwayforward.com or hudson.111@virgin.net). Interviews are usually by Skype and phone.

SIAM COMPUTER & LANGUAGE INSTITUTE
471/19 Ratchawithi Road, Bangkok 10400
+66 2 247 2345 ext. 364/366
hr@siamcom.co.th
www.siamcom.co.th

NUMBER OF TEACHERS: 35 for client government schools in the greater Bangkok area and 49 at 38 external locations in the greater Bangkok area.
PREFERENCE OF NATIONALITY: Native English speakers.
QUALIFICATIONS: Bachelor's degree and CELTA or equivalent required; experience preferred.
CONDITIONS OF EMPLOYMENT: 9–12 month contracts. Full-time internal teachers 6 days per week in air-conditioned facilities; 15 or fewer students per class. All ages. Full-time external teachers 5 days per week in Thai classrooms. 50 students per class from kindergarten to high school level.
SALARY: 33,000–40,000 baht per month based on experience. Bonus plans for external teachers. Hourly rates for part-time internal and external teachers.
FACILITIES/SUPPORT: Assistance with finding local accommodation. 15 paid Thai vacation days per year, assistance in obtaining a teacher's licence, work permit and 1-year visa. Complete teacher orientation and teacher training before starting in the classroom, with bimonthly teachers' meetings.
RECRUITMENT: Adverts in the *Bangkok Post* and on the worldwide web, and contacts with schools in Australia and the USA. Online application form.
CONTACT: Anthony Donnelly; Mr Bhudeb.

SIAM ENGLISH LANGUAGE SCHOOL

1199 4th Floor, Piyavan Tower, Phaholyothin Rd, Ari Samsennai, Phyathai, Bangkok 10400

+66 5234 4713

jones@siamels.org; contact@siamels.org

www.siamels.org

NUMBER OF TEACHERS: 37 at 35 school locations in the greater Bangkok area and 49 at 38 external locations in the greater Bangkok area.

PREFERENCE OF NATIONALITY: Native English speakers.

QUALIFICATIONS: College degree required; CELTA or equivalent and experience preferred. Dynamic personality, aged 25–35.

CONDITIONS OF EMPLOYMENT: 1-year contracts. Full-time internal teachers 6 days per week in air-conditioned facilities; 15 or fewer students per class. All ages. Full-time external teachers 5 days per week in Thai classrooms. 50 students per class from kindergarten to high school level.

SALARY: 30,000+ baht per month based on experience. Bonus plans for external teachers. Hourly rates for part-time internal and external teachers.

FACILITIES/SUPPORT: Assistance with finding local accommodation. 15 paid Thai vacation days per year, assistance in obtaining a teacher's licence, work permit and 1-year visa. Complete teacher orientation and teacher training before starting in the classroom, with bimonthly teachers' meetings.

RECRUITMENT: Adverts in the *Bangkok Post* and on the worldwide web, and contacts with schools in Australia and the USA. Interviews in Bangkok required.

CONTACT: Ian Jones.

SINE EDUCATION

555 SSP Tower, 11th Floor, 555/50-51 Soi Sukhumvit 63, Sukhumvit Road, Bangkok 10110

+66 2 711 4703

hr@sineeducation.com

www.sineeducation.com

NUMBER OF TEACHERS: Approximately 100 for 30 partner Matthayom level schools (for ages 13–15) in Bangkok, central Thailand and the northeast.

PREFERENCE OF NATIONALITY: UK, Canada, New Zealand, USA, Australia, South Africa and Ireland.

QUALIFICATIONS: Minimum bachelor's degree from a recognised university. Must be enthusiastic and motivated.

CONDITIONS OF EMPLOYMENT: 10 months from 1 May. Max 24 teaching hours per week between 7.30am and 4pm. Positions are in public (government) schools, with large classes and few resources. Teachers follow the SINE system which involves standardised PowerPoints so preparation time is minimal.

SALARY: 33,000 baht per month. Maximum tax deduction of 5%. Contract completion bonus.

FACILITIES/SUPPORT: Company assists teachers throughout the process and pays for permits to teach, work permits and final visas. Help given with finding accommodation. Health insurance. Training in the SINE method given.

RECRUITMENT: Internet, personal recommendation. Recruiting constantly via online form.

CONTACT: Keith James, Programme Manager.

SPENCER INTERNATIONAL

1st Fl., Muangthai Phatra Complex, 252/193 Rachadapisek Road, Bangkok 10320

+66 2 693 2901

stephen.l@spencer.co.th; recruitment2013@spencer.co.th

www.spencer.co.th

NUMBER OF TEACHERS: 60. Also for schools in Cambodia, Vietnam, Myanmar, China and Indonesia.

PREFERENCE OF NATIONALITY: None.

QUALIFICATIONS: Professional educators need an internationally accredited 120-hour training course. Degree holders are preferred, but positions for non-degree holders are also available. Inexperienced and unqualified teachers have opportunities to undergo formal or in-house training through a staff development programme.

CONDITIONS OF EMPLOYMENT: 10-month contract. Usual hours 7.30am–3.30pm Monday to Friday. Evening and weekend work is offered as overtime.

SALARY: Starting salary 32,000 baht with increments after 3 months, 6 months and 1 year. Tax is deducted at source.

FACILITIES/SUPPORT: Spencer International provides TEFL and TESOL courses in Bangkok, accredited through Chichester College, UK. Assistance given with finding accommodation in the school vicinity to suit teacher's lifestyle. School takes care of all work permit procedures for teachers holding the appropriate qualifications.

RECRUITMENT: Via TESOL training programmes or the internet. Interviews can be conducted by email, Skype or telephone.

SUPER ENGLISH

38/1–2 Bandon Road, Talad, Muang, Surat Thani 84000

+66 77 213395

teach@superenglishsurat.com

www.superenglishsurat.com

NUMBER OF TEACHERS: 14.

PREFERENCE OF NATIONALITY: American.

QUALIFICATIONS: University degree essential. Must have the right attitude: a willingness to learn, be flexible about living in an eastern culture, able to think creatively and be patient. Must enjoy working with children and have a sincere desire to teach them English and to have an impact on their lives.

CONDITIONS OF EMPLOYMENT: Standard 1-year contract from October or May. Schedules vary greatly but usually 20–25 hours per week (and hours above 25 are paid overtime rate). Some teachers work in the mornings and have their afternoons off; others prefer late mornings and continuing through the early evening. Classes finish at 6.30pm. Weekends off.

SALARY: Current flat salary is 30,000 baht or 35,000 baht per month, depending on which programme.

FACILITIES/SUPPORT: Shared, semi-furnished accommodation in Surat Thani provided free for first 2 months. Paperwork provided pre-arrival for a 3-month non-immigrant B visa. School will process that visa into a 1-year non-immigrant visa and will obtain a 1-year labour permit. 20,000 baht paid for holiday month of October.

RECRUITMENT: Adverts on www.eslcafe.com and directly via website. Interviews via Skype are essential.

CONTACT: Peter C. Meltzer, Owner and Founder.

THE AMERICAN ENGLISH LANGUAGE SCHOOL

29/492 Moo 2, Ransit Klong 3, Klong Sahm, A. Klonglu-ang, Pathumthani 12120

+66 89 922 4126

americanenglishthailand@gmail.com; teacherfinder@hotmail.com

www.americanenglishthailand.com

NUMBER OF TEACHERS: 40.

PREFERENCE OF NATIONALITY: All nationalities welcome.

QUALIFICATIONS: At least a bachelor's degree from an internationally accredited academic institution. BEd (or higher) degree holders will receive preference. At least 1 year's teaching experience required, preferably in Thailand.

CONDITIONS OF EMPLOYMENT: 1-year contract starting in early May, ending in late April. To teach Monday to Friday, 8am–4.30pm.

SALARY: Starts at 30,000 baht per month with no real ceiling. The AELS sends teachers to many levels of schools where top earnings are 50,000 baht and up. Taxes are 1,000–2,000 baht per month and 650 baht per month for health care coverage and social security (compulsory under Thai law).

FACILITIES/SUPPORT: Company helps teachers find a place that has a good location, for a good rent, with good amenities, and takes them to all the necessary offices, every step of the way, to get the necessary papers. Teachers pay for visa and work permit upfront, but will be reimbursed by AELS on completion of contract.

RECRUITMENT: By personal interviews and teaching demonstrations, followed by credential checks. Company rarely hires directly from overseas: three videoconferencing interviews have led to only one hire so far.

CONTACT: Jason Alavi, Owner & Director.

WECI TEFL (WORLD ENGLISH COMMUNICATION INSTITUTE)

70/145 Soi 112 Hua Na, Petchakasem Road, Tambon Nhong Kae, Hua Hin, Prachuap Khiri Khan 77110

+66 81 8576086 (mob)

info@wecitefl.com

www.wecitefl.com

NUMBER OF TEACHERS: 15 for 4 branches.

PREFERENCE OF NATIONALITY: Native English speakers.

QUALIFICATIONS: Minimum bachelor degree plus 120 hour TEFL training course (TESOL or CELTA).

CONDITIONS OF EMPLOYMENT: 30–25 hours per week. 1-year contracts.

SALARY: Minimum 30,000 baht (net).

FACILITIES/SUPPORT: Some schools provide housing; others help teachers to find accommodation. Full assistance given with correct visa. If applicant lacks necessary training, they can do it at WECI TEFL (as listed in Training Directory).

RECRUITMENT: Word of mouth, via universities. Interviews by Skype or email.

CONTACT: Darron Jenkins or Kannika Prakobphon, Office Manager.

LATIN AMERICA

Spanning 75 degrees of latitude, the mammoth continent of South America, together with the Caribbean islands and the eight countries of Central America, offers an eclectic range of teaching opportunities. With the important exception of Brazil, where Portuguese is spoken, South American countries have a majority of Spanish speakers and, as in Spain itself, there is a great demand for English teaching, from Mexican resorts where local people want to access jobs in the tourist industry to Punta Arenas at the southern extremity of the continent, south of the Falkland Islands.

The countries of most interest to the travelling teacher are Chile, Argentina, Colombia, Ecuador, Venezuela, Brazil and Mexico. Certain patterns emerged during the research for the various editions of this book, though sweeping generalisations are of limited value and will not apply to all countries and all situations. After problems with inflation, most countries (apart from Venezuela, where it is ballooning out of control, Argentina and Brazil which is mired in deep recession) have brought inflation rates down to reasonable levels, which means that currencies are more stable and salaries do not lose their value as they once did.

Urban life in the big cities of Brazil, Argentina and Chile is more like that of Europe than of developing countries. In such cities, the greatest demand for English comes from businesses. Because of the strong commercial links between the two American continents, the demand tends to be for American English, though an increasing number of British and Australian teachers are finding work in these countries.

Among the providers of the English language are Bi-National Centers and Cultural Centers, the American counterpart of the British Council. There are scores of these centres in Latin America, many engaged in the teaching of English, including 17 IBEUs (Instituto Brasil-Estados Unidos) in Brazil alone employing more than 200 teachers. While the English Language Fellow Program administered from Washington requires teachers with an MA in TESOL from a US university to commit to 10-month contracts, there may be more informal local opportunities for others. A good point of contact is the relevant Regional English Language Officer (http://americanenglish.state.gov/support-near-you-regional-english-language-officer-relo).

Britain also has cultural representatives in several Latin American countries; the longest-established Culturas Inglesas are in Argentina (founded 1927) plus Brazil, Chile, Mexico, Paraguay, Peru and Uruguay (Instituto Cultural Anglo Uruguayo). Among them, these *Culturas* teach English to a quarter of a million students. Usually they require their teachers to have specialised ELT training and experience. Only a few recruit abroad, so it is worth making local enquiries on arrival.

Several South American nations have a number of British or American-style bilingual schools and *colegios*. Although this book is not centrally concerned with English-medium schools, which are usually looking for teachers with a PGCE or full teacher accreditation, international schools in South America are mainly looking for local nationals (rather than expatriates) who want a bilingual Spanish-English education and have a very strong emphasis on English-language teaching. Despite the prestige of these schools, some are willing to consider EFL teachers who have not done teacher training. For example, some accept school-leavers participating in gap-year projects.

Finally, there are private and commercial language institutes, from International House, which is not particulary well represented in the continent (Argentina, Colombia, Ecuador, Mexico, Peru and Uruguay only), through to Berlitz (which is strongly represented in Latin America) to the cowboy operations where standards and wages will be extremely low. **David Hewitt**, a computer programmer from Yorkshire with no TEFL training or experience, was surprised not only to walk into a casual teaching job in Brazil but also to find himself giving lessons to the director of the school. In whatever kind of school you teach, or if you just give occasional private lessons to contacts, you will probably find the local people extremely friendly and eager to help. The ethnic diversity and Latin warmth encountered by foreign teachers and travellers throughout the continent usually more than compensate for low wages and (in the big cities) a high crime rate.

PROSPECTS FOR TEACHERS

In a land where baseball is a passion and US television enormously popular, American (and also Canadian) job-seekers have an advantage. The whole continent is culturally and economically oriented towards the USA. There is a decided preference among language learners for the American accent and for American teaching materials and course books, which explains why so many language institutes are called Lincoln and Jefferson. Business English is gaining ground throughout the region, particularly in Argentina, Chile, Colombia, Brazil and Mexico, and anyone with a business background will have an edge over the competition.

The academic year begins in February or early March and lasts until November/December. In the southernmost nations of Chile and Argentina, January and February are very slack months for language schools; while further north in Bolivia, for example, the summer holiday consists of December/January. The best time to arrive to look for work is a few weeks before the end of the summer holidays. But many institutes run 8- to 12-week courses year round and will be eager for the services of a native English speaker whatever the time of year.

FINDING A JOB

Speculative enquiries from EFL teachers are less likely to work if sent before arrival than after, although sending a 'warm-up' CV may help your job search. What the principal of a girls' school in Lima wrote is echoed by many other institutes. '*Anyone interested in a job is welcome to write to me at any time. If they happen to be in Lima they are equally welcome to come into school.*' Unless you are very well qualified or have met your prospective employer before, you are unlikely to be offered a contract while out of the country. This is unfortunate since work visas are best applied for in the country of origin of the teacher (see below). On the other hand, **Miranda Crowhurst** had a Skype interview with an institute in Bolivia, and took up a position a month or two later, where she is still teaching.

IN ADVANCE

Not many Latin American language schools advertise internationally. Even the most prestigious schools complain of the difficulties they encounter recruiting teachers abroad, mainly due to the low salaries they can offer and the bureaucratic procedures for obtaining a work permit. When 20-year-old **James Gratton** was making plans for his first trip to South America, he wrote to all the embassies in London and received quite a lot of literature, including a number of lists of language schools, for Paraguay, Uruguay, Peru, Argentina, etc. Serious candidates might ask the cultural attaché for advice.

In addition to International House and Berlitz, already mentioned, EF English First and Wall Street English have quite a few branches. Saxoncourt Recruitment is occasionally active in Peru and one or two other countries of South America and sometimes recruits on behalf of Culturas Inglesas and international schools. Denver-based Bridge TEFL (www.bridgetefl.com) offers TEFL training courses in 11 Latin American cities from Santiago to Playa del Carmen on the Caribbean coast of Mexico (costing $1,995), many of whose graduates go on to work locally. For language school listings and teaching information check http://thelajoblist.blogspot.com (which is no longer being maintained). TEFL training colleges in the US often have close ties with Latin American language schools, such as Transworld School, which sends large numbers of its graduates to posts in South America. Teaching House maintains an impressive database of teacher vacancies for CELTA holders; at the time of writing there were more than 400 listings each for Colombia, Chile and Mexico to take just three examples.

The British Council arranges for language assistants to work in five Latin American countries for an academic year: Argentina, Chile, Colombia, Ecuador and Mexico; details can be found on their website (www.britishcouncil.org/language-assistants/become/where-can-I-go). Applicants must be undergraduates studying Spanish or graduates with a Spanish A level. The level of placements and the nature of the duties are more suited to graduates than undergraduates. Deadlines for application vary among the different countries.

The Association of American Schools in South America (AASSA, www.aassa.com) coordinates teacher recruitment for its 75 full and invitational members, all American international schools in 24 Latin American and Caribbean countries. Candidates who attend a recruiting fair in December must have a degree and generally be state-certified teachers. There is a $110 registration fee and if you are hired your school pays a further placement fee to AASSA.

Volunteers are widely deployed as teachers throughout the continent. The non-profit organisation South American Explorers keeps lists of schools that employ English teachers. It has a volunteer database for members to access with information about volunteering opportunities throughout South America. Many of the organisations listed will take on English teachers without TEFL certification. Membership costs $60 per year ($90 for a couple). Contact South American Explorers for further details (www.saexplorers.org).

Patient searching of the web will unearth opportunities for volunteering, perhaps through one of the mainstream databases like www.idealist.org and http://barefootatlas.com. Specialist websites like www.volunteersouthamerica.net are always worth scouring for 'grass-roots, zero-cost volunteer work' in South and Central America. Another Latin American specialist website with a similar ambition is www.volunteerlatinamerica.com. To contact any of the organisations in their searchable directory of grassroots projects, it is necessary to join at £9 for two years' basic membership or £18 which includes personalised assistance.

Lots of commercial volunteer agencies have programmes in Latin America such as: Travellers Worldwide (www.travellersworldwide.com) with teaching programmes in Argentina, Costa Rica, Ecuador and Brazil. Knowledge of Spanish may be expected on some of these programmes and accommodation is usually with host families. The UK and Australia-based teacher recruitment agency TEFL Heaven (www.teflheaven.com) arranges jobs in Mexico, Argentina, Costa Rica, Peru and Guatemala normally involving an in-country TEFL training course.

WorldTeach at Harvard (www.worldteach.org) places paying volunteers as teachers of EFL or ESL for a year in Colombia, Ecuador, Chile and (unusually) Guyana. The Spain-based online community www.culture-gogo.com allows subscribers to arrange a live-in stay directly with a host family, many of whom are looking for English conversation practice. Listings for South and Central America include Colombia, Costa Rica, Chile, Mexico and Argentina. For a fee volunteers can join the community to post their profile and contact any registered families to teach them English in exchange for food and accommodation. Prices are $20 for one month, $30 for 3 months and $48 for a year.

ON THE SPOT

As throughout the world, local applicants often break into the world of language teaching gradually by teaching a few classes a week. Non-contractual work is almost always offered on an unofficial part-time basis. So if you are trying to earn a living you will have to patch together enough hours from various sources. Finding the work is simply a matter of asking around and knocking on enough doors. For those who speak no Spanish, the first hurdle is to communicate your request to the secretaries at language schools, since they rarely speak much English. Try to memorise a polite request in Spanish to pass your CV (*hoja de vida*) and letter (in Spanish if possible) to the school director, who will know at least some English. Check adverts in the English-language press such as the *Buenos Aires Herald* and online communities. English-language bookshops are another possible source of teaching leads.

The crucial factor in becoming accepted as an English teacher at a locally run language school may not be your qualifications or your accent as much as your appearance. You must look as neat and well dressed as teachers are expected to look, at least when you're job-hunting. Later your standards might slip a little: **Nick Wilson**, who taught for two years in Mexico, says that it is easy to spot the English teachers in banks and office buildings; they're the ones wearing jeans, T-shirts and carrying a CD player.

LIBBY GOLDSMITH

Libby Goldsmith has done a lot of travelling and lived in a number of countries, but is especially enjoying her four and a half years of teaching in South America. With a 140-hour distance learning TEFL course and a summer of teaching at a summer school completed before departure from England, she felt that she knew what she was getting into, though she wouldn't describe herself as a skilled teacher at the outset. She worked for various employers and also privately first in the capital of Chile and then in Bogotá Colombia:

I researched teaching institutes on the internet and cross-referenced these against online reviews. I then approached each institute with my CV by email or in person. I have seen two application processes in play. The first is the traditional approach where you send in your CV then await an invitation for an interview, which is usually fairly structured and standard, with questions relating to past experience, reasons for applying, etc. Upon a successful interview you are then invited back to teach a mock class on a designated topic. References are also required. The second process is based principally on a fellow teacher's recommendation, followed up with an informal interview to discuss requirements and teaching philosophies. Student feedback becomes the final character reference.

The majority of my teaching has been to business professionals, consequently the focus is on business language and business skills (e.g. emails, presentations, etc). Grammar is taught through functional language rather than directly. Peak teaching hours typically extended in bands across the week - anything between 6am and 9am were the morning slots; lunchtime slots extended from 11.30am to 2.30pm; and the evening between 4pm and 9pm. One aspect I hadn't anticipated was the highly unpredictable nature of working private or institute classes. Cancellations make scheduling and planning difficult, never mind managing finances. To date, my earliest start has been 4am and latest finish stretching to 10pm so working unsociable hours is a fact of life. Most of my classes are at business premises, either in meeting rooms or student offices. This of course means that you end up doing quite a bit of travelling between classes; though I do enjoy this as it offers variation. Few institutes arrange accommodation but Facebook groups provide a support network and there are always noticeboards.

Wages are adequate in South America. To earn more you can of course work more hours or choose the kind of company or private students that pay higher wages. Nevertheless, EFL teaching is not especially well paid here, so it can be difficult to save much. Some weeks you can find yourself with lots of spare time due to a rash of cancellations and therefore with little money. During these times it can be hard to find things to do without feeling like a pauper.

Of course all the red tape is an issue – the obligatory work visa application, immigration and/or police formalities, identity card and so on. Based on my experience you have to have a 12-month contract in order to secure a work visa. (I have started to hear of teachers with six-month contracts being turned down.) After the visa, there's tax registration, setting up a bank account, health insurance, pension; and if you were looking to stay longer, residency application. If you approach a reputable institute, they offer support (though variable) with this process which is a life-saver!

The best part of EFL teaching is seeing students achieve their dreams and knowing that in part, you helped. The business students are all well-educated, extremely motivated and enthusiastic. Teaching is fun and extremely rewarding: watching a beginner with hardly any English in the first class learn to construct sentences and give basic opinions after as little as two or three months...it is incredible. English is a valuable skill in South America which can improve job prospects and level of income, and lead to enormous opportunities and a better life. The highlight of the whole experience for me has been meeting some incredibly motivated and committed students who have such interesting stories and views of the world. The fascinating conversations you have can challenge your view of the world.

FREELANCE TEACHING

In most Latin American cities there is a thriving market in private English lessons, which usually pay at least half as much again as working for an institute. It is not uncommon for teachers to consider the language school that hires them as a stepping-stone to setting up as a private tutor. After they have familiarised themselves with some teaching materials and made enough contacts among local language learners, they strike out on their own, though this is far from easy unless you can get by in the local language and have access to suitable premises. If you are thinking of privately tutoring students you have met through a language school, check your contract carefully to make sure you are not breaking its terms. Clients can be found by advertising on online communities, by placing notices on strategic noticeboards or by handing out well-produced business cards. If the latter, use the local method of address and omit confusing initials such as BA after your name: teachers often call themselves '*Profesor*' or '*Profesora*'.

REGULATIONS

Of course requirements vary from country to country but the prospects are dismal for teachers who insist on doing everything by the book. It is standard for work visas to be available only to fully qualified and experienced teachers on long-term contracts. Often you will have to present an array of documents, from university certificates and transcripts to FBI police clearance, which have been authenticated by your consulate abroad or by the consulate of the host country. Although many schools will not offer a contract before interview and then will make it contingent on a work permit, the procedures should be started in the teacher's country of origin, which makes the whole business very difficult. All of this can take as long as six months and involve a great deal of hassle and expense, not least for the employer.

The upshot is that a high percentage of teachers work unofficially throughout Latin America. It is hardly an issue in some countries, for example virtually no one gets a work permit in Brazil, not even long-resident language school teachers. Teaching on a tourist visa or as a 'tourist' in countries where you don't need a visa is a widespread practice in Mexico and Peru. There are ways round the regulations, for example to work on a student/trainee/cultural exchange visa (as in Ecuador or Venezuela).

CONDITIONS OF WORK

Very few schools offer perks such as an extra month's salary or return flights to teachers who stay for a two-year contract. Contracts are fairly hard to come by and always require a minimum commitment of a year. The advantages are that you are guaranteed a certain income and you have a chance of applying for a work permit. Teachers without the CELTA or Trinity certificate are not greatly disadvantaged, partly because this qualification is not as widely known in Latin America as it is in Europe, although you can take the Trinity TESOL course at the Casa de Ingles in Chaco (Argentina), the British Council in Recife and São Paulo (Brazil) as well as the Cultura in Rio, the Dickens Institute in Montevideo (Uruguay) and Stael Ruffinelli de Ortiz English in Asuncion (Paraguay). Many institutes offer their own compulsory pre-job training (to be taken at the teacher's own expense), which provides a useful orientation for new arrivals.

One of the seldom-mentioned perks of teaching in Latin America is the liveliness and enthusiasm of the students. Brazilian students have been described as the 'world's most communicative students' and class-rooms around the continent often take on the atmosphere of a party. You may also be dazzled by the level of knowledge of western popular culture, and should be prepared to have your ignorance shown up. Also be prepared to lose their attention if a lesson coincides with a major sporting event.

LEISURE TIME

Whether you are a serious student of Spanish or a frivolous seeker after the excitement generated by Latin carnivals, South America is a wonderful place to live and travel. Women teachers may find the machismo a little hard to take, but will soon learn how to put it in its place. If you want to travel around, the annually revised *South American Handbook* definitely justifies the initial outlay of £23.

ARGENTINA

The teaching market in Argentina is reasonably buoyant, with hundreds of institutes operating at varying standards. However, against expectations the economy moved into a recession in 2016, with inflation climbing. So the English language market may not expand much over the next couple of years. The cost of living keeps rising, and many European visitors wonder how the local people can manage on the wages they earn, when eating out, taxis, etc are so expensive in Buenos Aires (but not basic services like public transport and haircuts). Teachers are far more likely to secure a job once they are in Argentina than by applying from their home country. Anyone with a recognised qualification like the CELTA will probably get snapped up, at least for a few hours a week initially, as Alan Chadwick did.

ALAN CHADWICK

Alan Chadwick completed the CELTA course in his home town of Cambridge, and exactly a year later set off for Argentina to work and travel.

He started in Buenos Aires and spent some time asking around and investigating teaching possibilities. But he found the city too hectic, not to mention too dangerous. Four or five mugging incidents were reported just by people in his hostel, and the final straw came when a young Finnish traveller who had set off one afternoon to catch a long-distance bus to her next destination returned within an hour having had all her bags, money and passport taken at gunpoint – possibly a toy gun but she couldn't be sure.

So Alan headed for Córdoba, second-largest city of Argentina, where he had an English friend managing a hostel. After handing round his CV to a few language schools, he was offered some hours of teaching within three days of arrival and at the first school he had approached, the British School, which has several branches around Córdoba. The wage was a decent £10 an hour. But it turned out that his teaching was to take place at a different branch, an hour and a half journey by public transport from where he was staying, which hadn't been spelt out at the interview.

His first exposure to his colleagues was a little challenging. Because he happens to be from Cambridge, home of the famous First Certificate English exam, they had lots of questions about the exam and the syllabus, with which he was almost totally unfamiliar ('To be honest, I haven't been teaching it very long ...'). On the first day the director introduced him as 'someone from Cambridge – with a DELTA', which he hastily corrected to CELTA; it seemed that she was not familiar with the substantial difference between the two qualifications disguised by one letter along in the alphabet. When introduced in the staff room, he started shaking hands, and the staff (all middle-aged Argentinian women) laughed at him, telling him that in Argentina, you kiss.

In some respects Alan loved that everyone was 'super-relaxed' about everything: students routinely arrived 20 minutes late, no one was too bothered about targets, etc. But it wasn't so great on pay day, when he had to travel to the other side of the city to collect a quarter of the wages he was owed, probably due to gross inefficiency rather than anything more sinister. With some effort, and a strategic phone call to the head of his branch to vouch for him, he eventually received all the wages he was owed.

He was teaching a total of about 10 hours a week: two-three hours on four evenings. Because he didn't speak Spanish, he was assigned high-level adults. He taught FCE prep and a conversation class, which he really enjoyed. On the assumption that everyone likes to talk about themselves, he only needed to introduce a random question such as 'What have you done that has made you proud?' to prompt a cascade of conversation. The mixed bag of students asked him all sorts of questions about British culture, life in Cambridge, etc. He corrected some of their mistakes in English but not too many because he didn't want to discourage them.

After six weeks of working for British School, he told the boss that he needed more hours to make it financially viable or he would have to leave. She could not offer him any at that time, but suggested he try to piece together work from other schools that he knew would be possible. But by then he was finding the relentless 30-degree heat and the lack of greenery rather draining, so he decided to move 1,000km west to the coast of Chile.

Language schools are linked from www.inglesnet.com/donde.htm. Courses in Argentina start in mid-March, after the school summer vacation, and finish in early December, with July off for school holidays.

Job-seekers should check community noticeboards such as Craigslist (http://buenosaires.en.craigslist.org), which includes a steady stream of teaching job ads, mostly part-time for people already living in Buenos Aires. Schools of Spanish abound and often prove good contact points for foreign residents who want to teach on the side.

Some of the 13 Bi-National Centers or Instituto de Intercambio Cultural Argentino-Americano (listed at http://ar.usembassy.gov/education-cultural/binational-centers) offer English courses, as do the two International House schools in the capital (located in Recoleta and Belgrano). To work at one of these, you usually have to have worked for IH before. A large number of full-curriculum private schools prepare students for Cambridge and other exams, such as the Belgrano Day School in Buenos Aires; www.bds.edu.ar, which has pupils from kindergarten to school-leaving age.

It is commonplace for Americans and Britons to move from learning Spanish to teaching English, as **Chris Moloney** from Queensland did (and along the way had a romance with a former Miss Argentina), and as did also **Richard Ferguson**, a New Zealander who has travelled extensively in South America:

> ***There are heaps of English schools in Buenos Aires and everyone wants to learn English. I made a few basic signs in Spanish advertising conversational classes, stuck them around Palermo (a wealthier suburb) and sometimes I'd stand on a busy corner and hand out leaflets. I charged about 30 pesos an hour per student. I think any native speaker can teach here, better with experience and better still with qualifications. Either do as I did, approach some schools or look in the papers in the jobs section. I saw at least 15 in one edition of the Buenos Aires Herald.***

The standard hourly freelance wage offered to qualified English teachers for in-company work is 90-130 pesos, while the rate at language institutes will be considerably lower.

One of the easiest routes into a job is to take a TEFL training course in situ (see Training Directory). For example US-based BridgeTEFL (www.bridgetefl.com) offers a 120-hour proprietary certificate qualification called IDELT in Buenos Aires (cost $1,995).

Luke McElderry from Texas and his girlfriend **Jenny Jacobi** spent hours researching potential teaching employers in Buenos Aires on the internet. After completing a training course locally, he sent a mass email with CV attached to at least 40 addresses and waited for responses to trickle in, and ended up hearing from about a quarter. He describes his job hunt:

> ***The first interviews were varied, some in English, one in Spanish, but all fairly casual. Most take 30 minutes and they seem to care more about your availability than your experience. I was asked a couple of times if I had any visa/permit and said no, and the employers didn't seem to care at all. I have heard the biggest institutes are the ones who care, and ironically pay the least!***

Before long, they were working for an institute, Speak Spanish, which, confusingly, also teaches English (www.speakspanish.com.ar). They were sent out to teach 90-minute classes in businesses. Sometimes they were assigned to comfortable conference rooms with whiteboards, free photocopies, faxes and coffee. Luke and Jenny found that all went smoothly, apart from finding accommodation:

> ***It is a real hassle finding an apartment as they want to charge you tourist rates and it is nearly impossible to get a lease as an expat. Accommodation prices depend on your ability to find a rental agency that doesn't require a garantiá from an Argentine property owner saying that you will pay the entire rental term in full; some places will let you pay everything up front, usually six months or more, but these places are very few and far between.***

Alicia Meta of ACM Business English, Buenos Aires (see entry), explains how the letting market works:

> ***If you are renting on a short contract the agents will ask you to pay in full. For a short-term contract you also have to pay a commission to the real estate agency of about 8% of the total amount. For a one-year contract the commission is the equivalent of one and a half months of the rent to be paid. The deposit for a long-term contract (one year) is equal to two months' rent. It is always returned once the deal is over.***
>
> ***It is difficult for tourists to rent an apartment and unfortunately I believe that there is no other way out. My advice would be to get some feedback before coming to Argentina, go to a hostel and then calmly try to look for the best option. Usually, apartments in the outskirts of Buenos Aires can be cheaper but the payment method might not differ.***

If you want to cast your net wider you can move to smaller cities where there will be fewer vacancies but also fewer applicants competing for the jobs. For example, Bariloche in Patagonia in the deep south of Argentina has an unexpectedly large market for English teachers because of its role as an international ski resort. Expect the cost of living to be much higher in Patagonia.

VOLUNTEERING AND CULTURAL EXCHANGES

Cultural exchange programmes will appeal to those willing to teach as volunteers in rural areas, normally in state rather than private schools. For example, Voluntario Global (see entry) feeds Spanish-speaking volunteers to worthy projects in schools, among others, in greater Buenos Aires, while Connecting Schools to the World (see entry) invites university graduates to live for one or two semesters in a *pueblo* or city, mainly in the Argentinian province of Córdoba. The $2,000 programme fee covers homestay accommodation with a local family and a modest monthly stipend. As with all these programmes, participants are encouraged to take up various extra-curricular activities such as tango lessons, cookery and photography.

Other possibilities, some of them more like tour operators than exchange organisations, include the following.

Connecting Worlds Argentina, Buenos Aires: see entry.

EBC TEFL Training, Buenos Aires (www.ebcteflcourse.com/tefl-courses-jobs-buenos-aires-argentina). Offers a month-long TEFL training course for €1,060 followed by a job placement programme. Accommodation can be arranged for an extra cost.

Expanish, Buenos Aires (✆ +54 11 5252 3040; www.expanish.com/spanish-courses/volunteer). Spanish language school with Volunteer English teaching programme. Volunteer placement fee of $95 plus donation of $100 following minimum 2-week language course.

Road2Argentina, Buenos Aires (www.road2argentina.com). Places English teaching assistants/interns for 4–24 weeks between mid-March and early December, as part of a cultural exchange and language-immersion programme. International interns are accepted without relevant training or experience to help in private or public school classrooms. Programme fees start at $675 for one month and include accommodation in a shared homestay. (Road2Argentina also offers its own 4-week TEFL training course for $1,250 in Buenos Aires, $1,890 with accommodation in shared flat; $2,090 in a homestay.)

RED TAPE

US nationals no longer have to buy a $160 tourist visa since in 2016 Mr Obama agreed that Argentinians will become eligible for a visa-waiver programme from 2017 for entry to the US. No visa is required for Britons either. Tourist visas can be extended beyond the initial 90 days at the Dirección Nacional de Migraciones. The tourist visa can also be renewed by crossing the border, most commonly by ferry to Uruguay for the weekend which costs about $60, which is up to ten times cheaper than an 'exchange visa'.

Working papers can be obtained from the National Direction of Migrations by employers, though a school will be willing only for long-term propositions. It will be necessary for the applicant to provide a contract of employment for a minimum of a year and birth certificate (notarised by a notary public in Argentina), as well as passport. Non-British passport holders must also provide a certificate of good conduct from the police authorities in his or her country or countries of residence in the five years prior to applying.

Irish and Antipodean young people are eligible for a six-month working holiday visa extendable by three months. Irish applicants should check out the programme options offered by USIT (www.usit.ie).

Most teachers are paid hourly by the language institutes employing them. Self-employed people are obliged to register in the *monotributo* system with AFIP (tax office) and pay approximately 15% of their full-time earnings in tax. You can become a *monotributista* only if you have a DNI (*documento nacional de identidad)* which comes with permanent residency. A detailed source of bureaucratic procedures can be found on www.urbanexpats.com.

LIST OF EMPLOYERS

ACM BUSINESS ENGLISH
Viamonte 2660, Buenos Aires
+54 911 5025 4752
info@acmbusinessenglish.com.ar
www.acmbusinessenglish.com.ar

NUMBER OF TEACHERS: 3–4.
PREFERENCE OF NATIONALITY: American, British and Canadian. Note: A strong Australian accent is usually difficult for Latin Americans to understand.
QUALIFICATIONS: TEFL, ESL or equivalent. Experience teaching ESL to adults in companies needed. Candidates with a teaching degree are the most sought after. General knowledge and high intellectual level needed for training executives who will be dealing with native English speakers at headquarters.
CONDITIONS OF EMPLOYMENT: No contracts. Part-time work so people are self-employed. Most teachers intend to stay in the country for at least 1 year, starting in March. Courses in Argentina start in March and finish in December. Usually 2–3 hours twice a week teaching in different companies. Many companies are located on the outskirts of Buenos Aires, so it can take more than an hour to reach some companies from downtown (where most candidates live) by bus. In these cases, a block of 3 hours minimum in one place is offered.
SALARY: Around 70 pesos per hour, paid at the beginning of the following month.
FACILITIES/SUPPORT: No training given. No assistance with accommodation.
RECRUITMENT: Word of mouth/posting on international websites, and in the *Buenos Aires Herald* (local English newspaper). Interviews in Buenos Aires.
CONTACT: Alicia Meta, Director.

CIL – CENTRO INTEGRAL DE LENGUAS
Leon 1753, Maipu, Córdoba
+54 351 458 1727
info@cil-method.com.ar
www.cil-method.com.ar

NUMBER OF TEACHERS: 3.
PREFERENCE OF NATIONALITY: None.
QUALIFICATIONS: Experience of teaching a second language or English.
CONDITIONS OF EMPLOYMENT: 9-month contracts. Afternoon teaching. School has developed its own methods.
SALARY: 45 pesos an hour. If the teacher can invoice school, social security contributions of about 200 pesos can be made.
FACILITIES/SUPPORT: No support with accommodation or visas.
RECRUITMENT: Via newspaper ads and local interviews.

COLONIAS DE INMERSION AL IDIOMA (CII)
Av Forest 1213, Caba, Buenos Aires 1427
+54 11 4553 8445
experienceargentina@ecolonias.com
www.ecolonias.com

Experience Argentina voluntourism programme.
NUMBER OF TEACHERS: 25–35 TEFL interns per semester who spend 20 hours per week assisting with English in a local school or camp, a few hours a week tutoring members of their host family and one weekend a month at a language camp for children and young people.
PREFERENCE OF NATIONALITY: Citizen of any English-speaking country.
QUALIFICATIONS: University students and graduates aged 20–26, no specific qualifications or experience required. Speaking knowledge of Spanish preferred and TEFL certificate (online acceptable).
CONDITIONS OF EMPLOYMENT: 3–12 months, preferably starting February or July. Most schools prefer applicants who can commit to at least a semester but shorter stays are possible. Schedules vary from school to school. Total of 25 hours a week.
SALARY: Monthly stipend from 280–350 pesos plus 200 pesos for participating in weekend language camp. Early-booking programme fees of $2,495 for up to 6 months, $2,995 for up to 12 months includes homestay accommodation throughout with full board, Spanish coaching and opportunities to travel.
FACILITIES/SUPPORT: 2-day TEFL workshop. Full support.
RECRUITMENT: Through cooperating universities and the internet. Applicants must submit a two-part 5-minute video introducing themselves and a skill they can share.
CONTACT: Joaquin Nunez, Teach Argentina Director.

CONNECTING SCHOOLS TO THE WORLD
Luis Maria Campos 545 1 D; 1426 Buenos Aires
+54 911 58899035
info@connectingschools.com.ar; connecting schools@gmail.com
www.connectingschools.com.ar

NUMBER OF TEACHERS: 20 teachers per year. All placed in rural schools in the interior of Argentina for a period of one semester.

PREFERENCE OF NATIONALITY: People from any English-speaking country.

QUALIFICATIONS: Recent college graduates.

CONDITIONS OF EMPLOYMENT: Teaching periods of 1 or 2 semesters. Up to 25 hours of work per week. First semester mid-February to 9 July and second 9 July to 5 December. Participants must wish to become part of the community and to make a contribution. They must also wish to learn the Spanish language.

SALARY: Homestay in Argentine family, private Spanish tutoring, round-trip bus ticket from Buenos Aires to location, $100 monthly stipend after fortnight of training and 1-week placement. Programme fee is $2,000.

FACILITIES/SUPPORT: Two weeks of intensive TESOL training on arrival in Buenos Aires while participants stay in a hostel (www.hostelpalermosuites.com). Supervision and help with lesson planning throughout the teaching period. 4 hours of private Spanish classes a week while teaching and homestay accommodation for 4 months arranged after initial 3 weeks. Volunteers teach on tourist visa (available at airport for $120 fee).

RECRUITMENT: Via internet. Résumé, list of references and a telephone interview with director required.

CONTACT: Cristina Rapela, Director.

CONNECTING WORLDS ARGENTINA

Marcelo T. Alvear 1459, Zip Code C1060AAA, Ciudad autónoma de Buenos Aires

+54 11 5199 5458 / +54 223 156 35 41 91

info@cwargentina.com

www.cwargentina.com

Argentine cultural exchange organisation.

NUMBER OF TEACHERS: Up to 20 per semester.

PREFERENCE OF NATIONALITY: UK, USA, Canada, New Zealand, Australia, Ireland, South Africa.

QUALIFICATIONS: TEFL/TESOL certificate preferred but not required. Bachelors degree in any subject needed. Motivated to experience new cultures and promote English language; should be flexible, open-minded and willing to learn. Medical report and police clearance needed plus international travel insurance against sickness, accidents and third party liability. Minimum age 21; average 30-35.

CONDITIONS OF EMPLOYMENT: Semesters start in March and August. 3-4 months or 9 months. 15-20 hours a week Monday to Friday.

SALARY: Small stipend for personal expenses of $1,800 pesos.

FACILITIES/SUPPORT: Homestay with local family or young Argentine professionals is included, and all meals. Programme also covers cultural and activity programme, an intensive Spanish course (4 hours a week) and airport transfer.

RECRUITMENT: Facebook page, Goabroad and strategic partnerships. Programme costs are $1,299 for 3–9 months.

CONTACT: Lic. María Cristina Acuña, Director.

FURTHER SCHOOL OF ENGLISH

Catamarca 1824, Buenos Aires 1246

+54 11 4941 0927

cv@furtherenglish.com

www.furtherenglish.com

NUMBER OF TEACHERS: 20 to teach in-company, children, teenagers and adults.

PREFERENCE OF NATIONALITY: British.

QUALIFICATIONS: University degree, TEFL/CELTA or similar, previous teaching experience. Some Spanish is a plus. Candidates should have outgoing personalities and be committed to the team.

CONDITIONS OF EMPLOYMENT: March to December. 25–30 hours per week scheduled in blocks.

SALARY: 90–100 pesos (net) per hour.

FACILITIES/SUPPORT: No assistance with accommodation or visas.

RECRUITMENT: Personal interview or via Skype.

CONTACT: Natalia A Garcia, Principal.

HOME INTERCULTURAL LEARNING

Calle 37 no. 1091 PB La Plata, CP 1900, Buenos Aires

+54 221 483 3575

info@homeenglishcourses.com.ar

www.homeintercultural.com.ar

NUMBER OF TEACHERS: Variable.

PREFERENCE OF NATIONALITY: None.

QUALIFICATIONS: Teacher training (CELTA, TEFL) or university degree needed for regular courses, other university degrees for fluency and multi-discipline consultancy work.

CONDITIONS OF EMPLOYMENT: Flexible hours and length of stay, according to teacher's wishes. School uses dynamic teaching techniques that emphasise conversation and make use of acting, singing, playing games, reading comics, listening to podcasts, etc.

SALARY: Teachers need to be enrolled in *monotributo.*

FACILITIES/SUPPORT: Spanish classes (and other languages) are offered at partner schools for special rates. Home Intercultural Learning has agreements with local hostels, but teachers must arrange accommodation on their own. Teachers are responsible for arranging their own permits.

RECRUITMENT: Skype interviews can be arranged.

CONTACT: Andrea Assenti del Rio, Director of Studies.

INTERACTION LANGUAGE STUDIO
Av. L. N. Alem 428 6 I, Buenos Aires 1003
+54 11 4311 7220
info@interactionls.com
www.interactionls.com

NUMBER OF TEACHERS: 5–8 foreign teachers and 40 local teachers.
PREFERENCE OF NATIONALITY: American and British.
QUALIFICATIONS: TEFL certificate and some teaching experience.
CONDITIONS OF EMPLOYMENT: Contracts from March to December. Usual hours from 3 to 20 a week; teaching in businesses.
FACILITIES/SUPPORT: 3-day training course for new arrivals.
RECRUITMENT: CV by mail, interview and mock lesson. Interviews essential.
CONTACT: Professor Virginia López Grisolia, Director of Studies and Owner.

LV STUDIO
Darregueyra 2394, Buenos Aires
+54 11 4637 9442
info@lvstudioweb.com, cvs@lvstudioweb.com
www.lvstudioweb.com

NUMBER OF TEACHERS: 20–30 for schools in Palermo, Abasto and Flores in Buenos Aires.
PREFERENCE OF NATIONALITY: None.
QUALIFICATIONS: TEFL/TESOL/CELTA and/or English teaching experience.
CONDITIONS OF EMPLOYMENT: 6–12 months. Variable contact hours; most teachers are part-time.
FACILITIES/SUPPORT: No support with accommodation or visas.
RECRUITMENT: Craigslist. Face-to-face interviews preferred.
CONTACT: Elvira Solis, Director.

NETWORK IDIOMAS
Entre Ríos 265, Avellaneda, Buenos Aires 1870
+54 11 4228 4900
teachers@networkinstitute.com.ar
www.networkinstitute.com.ar

NUMBER OF TEACHERS: 3–4 per year for two branches.
PREFERENCE OF NATIONALITY: None but must live locally.
QUALIFICATIONS: TEFL.
CONDITIONS OF EMPLOYMENT: Minimum 9 months (March to November); renewable for the next school year. Hours of teaching 5.30pm–8.30pm for regular courses; mornings and lunchtimes for in-company courses. Part-time openings also available.
SALARY: 85 pesos per hour for occasional teaching.
RECRUITMENT: Face-to-face interviews.
CONTACT: Cecilia Cicolini, Director.

SWITCH LANGUAGE SCHOOL
Avenida Presidente Roque Sáenz Pena 615, 7° Off. 716, Buenos Aires
+54 11 4393 4125
info@switchschool.com.ar
www.switchschool.com.ar or www.consultoraswitch.com.ar

NUMBER OF TEACHERS: 25 for in-company training.
PREFERENCE OF NATIONALITY: None.
QUALIFICATIONS: Recognised TEFL Certificate.
CONDITIONS OF EMPLOYMENT: 9-month minimum contract.
FACILITIES/SUPPORT: No help given with work permits or finding accommodation.
RECRUITMENT: Interviews with a mock class carried out at the school are essential.
CONTACT: Mara France Garcia, Director.

VOLUNTARIO GLOBAL
Avenida de Mayo 1385, Buenos Aires
+54 9 11 6206 9639
jfranco@voluntarioglobal.org
www.voluntarioglobal.org

Argentinian NGO that aims to empower people from disadvantaged backgrounds by giving them education, training and support. Cooperates with range of projects such as the Pablo Nogués English School on the outskirts of Buenos Aires.
PREFERENCE OF NATIONALITY: Half of total are English native speakers.
QUALIFICATIONS: Experience teaching English, and people skills. Minimum age of 18, average age of 22.
CONDITIONS OF EMPLOYMENT: Teaching programmes start every Monday from March to November. Minimum stay 4 weeks. Usually afternoon hours 2pm–6pm.
SALARY: Unpaid. Donation fee to be paid, from $400 for 4 weeks (2016) to $700 for 12 weeks, $850/$2,080 with accommodation. Volunteers are responsible for travel and meal costs.
FACILITIES/SUPPORT: Rooms in a volunteer house located in downtown Buenos Aires. Orientation on arrival, with weekly follow-up and joint activities for volunteers working at different projects.
RECRUITMENT: Via websites and partner organisations.
CONTACT: Jésica Franco, Director.

BOLIVIA

A little known fact in Europe is that Bolivia's economy has been doing well of late. Instead of being the basket case it was once considered to be, it has doubled the minimum wage in less than 10 years and thereby reduced poverty and inequality. The long-time socialist president, Evo Morales, had been considered a hero by the people until 2016 when his fortunes changed. He became embroiled in a bizarre paternity controversy and lost a referendum that he called in order to change the constitution so presidents would be allowed to run for a third term of office. He remains popular for having introduced a compulsory end-of-year bonus (an extra year's wages) to all workers in order to redistribute national wealth. The bad news for foreign teachers is that the benefit does not apply to those on foreign contracts though teachers on hourly contracts are eligible.

The best hourly wage you can earn in Bolivia is probably about US$11, which is still considerably less than the equivalent in Santiago or São Paulo, but allows for a comfortable lifestyle in a country where a room in a hostel costs $5 and a meal in the market $2. Bolivia is still a poor country. Outside the cities, huge swathes of the population have no interest in learning English, since learning Spanish is more of a priority for those who speak an indigenous language like Quechua. But among the growing urban middle classes, there is a huge hunger for English, often with a view to studying in North America or Europe. Therefore much of the teaching is geared to the TOEFL test and also preparing for SATs. The demand for English exceeds supply. When Language Connection (see entry) was opened in 2016 by two teachers, one American, one British, in the southern city of Santa Cruz, it was soon overwhelmed with students. Another British expat recently set up Panorama English in La Paz (www.panoramaenglish.com), demonstrating that there is plenty of scope.

According to **Elizabeth Gould**, who works at the Instituto Exclusivo in La Paz: '*Bolivia is a hidden gem and, although it is not a particularly lucrative destination, English teaching covers the living costs and a bit more. I think that La Paz has a lot to offer in terms of experiences. There is a strong indigenous culture, it is close to some amazing tourist attractions, and it is one of the safest cities in South America.*'

Many teachers touring South America prefer Bolivia to many other countries for cultural reasons. Although Bolivia is changing, it has preserved its traditional culture more successfully than other Latin American countries and retains its colourful social mix. Ten or more years ago, the class structure was often immediately apparent, with the upper class consisting of people of Spanish descent, the middle class of mixed Spanish/Bolivian ancestry and the underclass of indigenous people still wearing their traditional costume. However the rise of Evo Morales, an indigenous Bolivian, and the flourishing economy that gives the wider population a chance to prosper, have resulted in many social changes and have erased many of the class markers. Which is not to say that racism is not still a problem, with various groups openly disparaging others, but it is a complex picture.

Language schools and a couple of *colegios* (private schools) are listed in the *Yellow Pages* (www.amarillas-bolivia.com, search 'Institutos de Idiomas'). Bilingual schools are very popular among the aspiring classes, though they have become increasingly subject to unwelcome government regulations that, for example, prohibit selection. Language institutes may be worth approaching before arrival, as **Miranda Crowhurst** did, while working in Tanzania:

> ***I was lucky enough to bag myself a teaching job in Bolivia from abroad, spamming schools with my CV and picking up a couple of testing Skype interviews. My CELTA qualification and a couple of years' experience in education helped me to land a job at a reputable language school in Santa Cruz, the Cambridge College. An off-shoot of an English-medium high school, it runs English language courses for professionals and children.***

Terms normally last from early February to early September, resuming at the end of September to the beginning of December. The biggest language school in the country is the monolithic Centro Boliviano Americano or CBA (Parque Iturralde Zenón 121, La Paz; http://cba.edu.bo), with three other locations in La Paz, plus schools in other cities such as Sucre, Cochabamba (see entry below) and Santa Cruz (www.cba.com.bo). Despite its name it hires British and Irish native English speakers as well, though does little hiring outside Bolivia.

Make sure you do your research, online or on-the-spot, before pursuing a job. For example the negative feedback about one well-known centre in La Paz on the site www.eslwatch.info should serve as a warning:

> ***This place is a complete joke of a school. It is owned and run by people who don't speak a single word of English… They didn't even have a working photocopier when I was there, and nobody could be bothered to fix it. The school is closed for 3–4 hours in the middle of the day, meaning there is nowhere to plan evening lessons. The boss promised to pay the fine for overstaying the tourist visa and then on the day of leaving, tried to wriggle out of it, but I pressured her and got it.***

Various local charities and profit-making entrepreneurs arrange volunteer teaching placements for a fee, such as Bolivia Volunteers based in Cochabamba (www.boliviavolunteers.webs.com). If you hunt around you can find free or low-cost opportunities, like the teaching scheme run by the Fox Academy in Sucre (www.foxacademysucre.com).

MIRANDA CROWHURST

Miranda Crowhurst is one teacher who fell immediately under the spell of Bolivia after arriving in the southern city of Santa Cruz:

I arrived in Santa Cruz, three and a half years ago, with no Spanish, and no real idea of what to expect. It's often swelteringly hot, and always chaotic, with few traffic rules and building regulations, and although it's definitely not a tourist destination, it's a great place to live. People are friendly and relaxed here, and proud of where they come from. Plus, there are some fantastic off-the-gringo-trail places to visit nearby, like national parks and local villages. Over the past thirty years, Santa Cruz has boomed from a sleepy backwater into a boom-town, and the contradictions are evident – there are horses and carts, and it's predominantly Catholic. Old men play chess under frangipani trees in the Plaza. But there's also a famously riotous carnival, and some serious worshipping of short skirts, gyms and enormous cars. Like all large South American cities, you do have to be aware of crime, and muggings are common. You have to watch yourself in public places, as girls can receive unwanted attention, too. Having said that, nothing serious has happened to me yet!

As for the teaching, schools vary hugely in their quality. While some pay peanuts, if you're a qualified and/or experienced native teacher, you should get a very good wage here (in Bolivian, rather than international terms). There is a real need for English teachers, as the ex-pat community is pretty small, so schools are always hiring.

> Teaching here is great, mainly because of the students. They may have a typically Latino attitude towards homework ('Tomorrow, teacher!'), and to time-keeping, but they are very chatty in lessons, keen to participate, and happy to have fun and laugh. If you'd rather strike out on your own, you can charge a decent amount for private lessons, once you get your name around. Since I arrived, I've really come to enjoy the chaos, and the easygoing, friendly atmosphere, where drinking, barbecues and dancing are compulsory. I'll be here for a while!

Even if not everything in Bolivia runs with German-style efficiency, the good schools expect you to be prepared, organised and get good results. Prices have been steadily rising, so that a share of a nice flat in a trendy area will cost at least $200 a month. It is possible to live comfortably on $600 a month. Eating out is cheap – not much more than $3 for a modest restaurant meal. Miranda reports that they have the most amazing food 'all made with soul too'.

Historic Sucre is one of the most popular destinations for travellers, partly because of its fresher climate. Although known as a city of students, there are only three or four language institutes. Other teachers have recommended the city of Cochabamba, because of the perfect spring-like climate. Among them is **Jonathan Alderman**, who concluded: '*if one wants to earn a decent wage teaching English in Bolivia, one has to turn to private classes.*' When he first arrived, he advertised in the local newspaper for private classes charging 30–35 bolivianos an hour. He says you can expect to be approached in shops and restaurants as well as by your students and asked about private classes, but this will generally come from people who would find it a hardship to pay even $2 an hour. One place to advertise private English lessons is the Sunday edition of the newspaper *El Diario* (www.eldiario.net).

Most teachers arrive on a three-month tourist visa and then apply for the one-year visa once they are in Bolivia. Americans have to obtain a tourist visa before arrival and are the only nationality to be charged a fee. In theory teachers should obtain a work visa, though many continue to work on a tourist visa that has to be renewed every 90 days by leaving the country. You are allowed four 90-day stamps in a year. **Miranda Crowhurst** describes the visa process as an '*obstacle race where officials often tell you to go back five obstacles!*' She recommends using a lawyer, especially if you don't speak fluent Spanish.

LIST OF EMPLOYERS

BRITISH ENGLISH CENTRE
No. 7916, Calle 13 de Calacoto (Entre Av. Ballivian y Bustamante), La Paz
+591 2 2793320
info@britishenglishcentre.org
www.britishenglishcentre.org

NUMBER OF TEACHERS: 5 native speaker teachers and 3 non-native speaker teachers.
PREFERENCE OF NATIONALITY: Preference for British and Irish teachers, though other native speakers are also hired.
QUALIFICATIONS: Minimum TEFL/CELTA qualified with preferably at least one year of EFL teaching experience.
CONDITIONS OF EMPLOYMENT: Initial contract is for one year, with renewal available (and preferred) for subsequent years. Teachers may choose to work a selection of hours between 7.30am and 9pm. Most classes take place 7.30–9am and 4–9pm.
SALARY: Minimum salary is $5.50 per hour, increasing to take into consideration qualifications and prior teaching experience. At the end of one year, a bonus is paid which is equal to half the amount spent on the visa.
FACILITIES/SUPPORT: Red tape assistance given. All teachers must apply for a 30 day *Visa de Objeto Determinado* followed by a 1 year temporary residence visa. We help teachers with the application process. Teachers must apply for a NIT (tax) number and present *facturas* (tax receipts) every month to the tax office, in order to reduce their tax bill. One month's shared accommodation is provided for new teachers who sign a contract; teachers pay only for utilities.
RECRUITMENT: Speculative applications in person or through the website. Occasional adverts on EFL websites such as tefl.com. Interviews are essential, and are carried out in person in Bolivia or through Skype.
CONTACT: Wilson Lacio Torrez, General Director (wlacio@britishenglishcentre.org).

CAMBRIDGE ENGLISH CENTRE/CAMBRIDGE COLLEGE
Residencias del Norte, Av. Beni entre 4to y 5to Anillos, Santa Cruz de la Sierra
+591 3 341 6541
rogerc@cambridge.edu.bo; ian.cec@cambridge.edu.bo; mariarenee@cambridge.edu.bo
www.cambridgebolivia.com.bo

NUMBER OF TEACHERS: 12.
PREFERENCE OF NATIONALITY: British.
QUALIFICATIONS: CELTA required or 3 years' classroom experience. Proven success in exam preparation needed.
CONDITIONS OF EMPLOYMENT: 2-year contract with hours between 7am and 11am and/or 3pm to 9pm Monday to Friday.
SALARY: $1,000–$1,400 per month for a 25 contact hour week.
FACILITIES/SUPPORT: Assistance given finding apartments near the school and the school organises and pays for the work visa.
RECRUITMENT: Usually via adverts on TEFL websites. Candidates submit their CV and a model lesson plan, and an interview is conducted through video conferencing/Skype. Interested candidates can also send their CVs directly to esolinfo@cotas.com.bo.
CONTACT: Maria Renee Canedo Landivar, Headmistress, or Roger Castaños, Centre Manager.

CENTRO BOLIVIANO AMERICANO – COCHABAMBA
Calle 25 de Mayo N° N-0365 (PO Box 1399), Cochabamba
+591 4 422 1288
mblum@cbacoch.org; cba@cbacoch.org
www.cbacoch.org

NUMBER OF TEACHERS: 3.
PREFERENCE OF NATIONALITY: American and British.
QUALIFICATIONS: Proficiency in English. Work experience in schools/universities. International Examination Diplomas/TESOL/TEFL certificates.
CONDITIONS OF EMPLOYMENT: 2-year renewable contract. 6 hours chosen from the following teaching hours: 7am–8.30am, 8.30am–11.45am, 1.45pm–5pm, 2.30pm–3.45pm, 3.45pm–5pm, 5pm–6.30pm, 6.45pm–8.15pm, 6.35pm–9.45pm.
SALARY: Average of $4 per hour. Varies depending on academic background and teaching experience. Income tax of 13% is not deducted when the teacher submits invoices for the same amount each month. Social security deductions 12.21%.
FACILITIES/SUPPORT: Help given in finding accommodation at orientation. Health care provided. Assistance given with work permits. Teachers should come with a *visa de objeto determinado* valid for 30 days to start the paperwork for a work visa. If the teacher comes with a tourist visa, he/she has to change it to a *visa de objeto determinado* at a Bolivian consulate in a neighbouring country. After that he/she may start with the paperwork for a 1- or 2-year work visa. School also helps with

additional procedure for a work permit that incurs an extra fee.

RECRUITMENT: Via adverts in newspapers. Local interview necessary.

CONTACT: Mery Blum de Schwarz, Academic Director.

INSTITUTO EXCLUSIVO

Avenue 20 de Octubre 2315, Sopocachi, La Paz

+591 2 2421072; +591 70135112 (mob)

info@instituto-exclusivo.com; elizabeth@ie-spanishonline.com

www.instituto-exclusivo.com; www.facebook.com/institutoexclusivolapaz

School located near the city centre in the neighbourhood of Sopacachi.

NUMBER OF TEACHERS: 4–10.

PREFERENCE OF NATIONALITY: No preference because a range of native English accents is useful for catering to different customer preferences.

QUALIFICATIONS: Must have A-Levels or equivalent education, and a TEFL certificate; university education preferred. Teaching experience desirable in some cases, or experience in an education environment. In-house training provided so highly motivated teachers who lack previous teaching experience can be accepted.

CONDITIONS OF EMPLOYMENT: 6-12 months. Full-time contracts are 30 teaching hours and 10 hours of preparation per week. Part-time hourly contracts also available for hours that teachers are available.

SALARY: 3,000 bolivianos (net) per month for full-time teachers; 35 bolivianos per hour for hourly contract teachers.

FACILITIES/SUPPORT: Homestay accommodation arranged with Bolivian families for initial period while teachers adapt to the city, though it can be extended. Help and advice offered, to find a small apartment or a house share. Free in-house training lasting 5–20 hours depending on background of teacher, plus, orientation and regular feedback and class evaluations. Monthly workshops held to improve team work. Institute offers TESOL/TEFL course leading to certificate accredited by Intesol. Reimbursement given for visa costs and transport to classes. 15 days' paid holiday a year (for teachers on a salary).

RECRUITMENT: Elizabeth Gould, English Administrator (elizabeth@ie-spanishonline.com) or Academic Director (roeland@ie-spanishonline.com).

LANGUAGE CONNECTION

Avenida Barrientos, numero 10, Barrio Ubari, Santa Cruz

+591 33535097

info@languageconnection.com.bo

www.languageconnection.com.bo

NUMBER OF TEACHERS: 4.

PREFERENCE OF NATIONALITY: Any native English speaking country.

QUALIFICATIONS: CELTA or equivalent. No experience necessary.

CONDITIONS OF EMPLOYMENT: 2 year contracts. 24 hours per week.

SALARY: $10 an hour, so approx $1,000 a month (net) plus the end-of-year national bonuses.

FACILITIES/SUPPORT: Assistance given with finding an apartment. Help given with work permits: the process starts with a temporary visa obtained in the teacher's country of origin, and is completed after arrival. In-house teacher training workshops and observations. School has a swimming pool.

RECRUITMENT: Online advertising and word of mouth.

CONTACT: Miranda Crowhurst, Co-Director.

BRAZIL

Some commentators were predicting that the Rio Olympics would be a disaster because of the country's economic woes, not to mention the fear of the Zika virus. In the end, the Games went off far better than expected. However the national government is still in crisis, and the city of Rio is on the verge of bankruptcy. The deep recession into which Brazil has slumped has seen austerity measures brought to bear. The English language market is bound to suffer, though so far demand is holding up among the new middle class and business community. The school coordinator of a leading English School in São Paulo, who is responsible for recruiting, hiring and training a staff of 35 native and non-native teachers, wrote in July 2015 to say, '*It's a great time to be an English teacher in São Paulo; we are now hiring teachers every week, as we have students starting classes every week.*' Since then she has had to moderate her enthusiasm somewhat.

Dozens of Culturas Inglesas in the Associacao Brasileira de Culturas Inglesas (www.abci.com.br) and many ICBEUs (Instituto Cultural Brasil-Estados Unidos) scattered all over the fifth-most populous country in the world employ several hundred teachers to serve thousands of students. Language-teaching chains like Wizard, the largest in the country, Britannia and Brasas are worth trying once you're in Brazil.

Schools in smaller places often notify cooperating institutes in the big cities of any job vacancies for native English speakers. But speculative visits to towns of any size are likely to succeed eventually. The distinguishing feature of Brazilian EFL is the high proportion of well-qualified Brazilian English teachers. Recruiting teachers from overseas is seen to be unjustifiably costly and also very difficult from the visa point of view. Only individuals with very specialised expertise are invited to work in very senior posts.

Visas are a major headache. You are permitted to stay no more than six months on a tourist visa, after which you will have to leave the country (usually across the Paraguayan border) or get an extension from the Federal Police. Training visas are an option for some. The Administrative Director of one of Rio de Janeiro's upmarket schools describes the difficulties:

> ***Unfortunately, teaching English is not an area the government considers a priority in issuing visas. There are only two situations in which foreigners can teach in Brazil. The first is to work illegally, since there are numerous small schools that can afford to run the risk of hiring illegal foreigners. As a result, pay is usually bad and employment unstable. The alternative is available only to specialists, and is extremely rare. Because we have a web page, I get requests from foreigners all the time. I basically tell them that it is an adventure here, only for the strong of stomach, and you have to be willing to subject yourself to the unsavoury experiences that go along with working without proper papers. I have come across dozens of foreigners who have been promised work-related visas. In 27 years of living in Brazil, I have never, not once, seen this happen. The only cases I know of where a person has taught legally, it has been when they enter the country with visas issued at the Brazilian consulate in their country of residence.***

Very few language institutes in Brazil advertise on www.tefl.com, www.eslcafe.com or other international sites. However, **Alexis Heintz** did spot a vacancy online with the Speaking School (see entry):

> ***I contacted the school via email, then found them on Facebook and started chatting with the secretaries, teachers, and eventually the owner of the school, which included Q&A on both ends about the job and my experience (I had volunteered as an English teacher a few months), and then I sent them my updated CV. The students all feel that English is very important for them to know and learn. However, since the majority are Engineering students at uni, they treat their uni studies as their number one priority and English falls into second place. The business professionals also have to put their career demands above their English studies, so I feel that most students do not spend much time studying outside of class. The low point for me is when you have a 7am class scheduled and your student does not show up and does not cancel in advance. You don't get paid for the 30 minutes that you have to spend waiting around for the student before you can confirm that the class is cancelled.***

Useful information on teaching can be found on the site www.BrazilianGringo.com maintained by American Josh Plotkin who has recently set up a system by which he tries to match job-seeking teachers with teacher-seeking schools (www.braziliangringo.com/jobs-english-teachers-brazil). If you wait until after arrival to look for work, use the *Yellow Pages*, expatriate networks or informative websites such as www.gringoes.com, run by expats based in São Paulo; the latter has a classified section with jobs for native-speaker teachers. Most adverts placed by companies with names like Executive English and Talking Business specify that applicants must already be living locally. In São Paulo a good source of teaching jobs is the newspaper *Folha de São Paulo* on a Sunday. Hourly wages at institutes in Rio and São Paulo hover around R$50 (reais) but can climb to R$80 for corporate classes, whereas the average in small towns is less. When job-hunting, expect to go through quite a rigorous interview procedure, as **Jon Cotterill** discovered:

> ***When you drop your CV in, the school may ask you to take a written English test on the spot. This can consist of anything up to 100 questions plus a composition section. If you pass the test, you may get invited to a group interview, a 'dinamica de grupo'. This consists of a group of potential teachers (usually Brazilians) and you having to perform various tasks in small teams or pairs. If you are successful then you may be asked to do a two-week training course (usually unpaid). Only after all of this will you be offered work.***

Richard Ferguson, a New Zealander who has learned Portuguese, met an American who gave private English lessons in São Paulo charging more than $30 an hour. But he bemoaned the fact that the city was hard to get around (the Metro area has a population of about 20 million) and he insisted that you need to have the students pay in advance for a few lessons. This is because Brazilians are notorious for not showing up, being late or cancelling at the last minute (which they don't see as a problem), so you need to take some precautions so as not to waste your time. Demand for private tuition in Rio de Janeiro is sufficiently strong to prompt a local company On the Go Idiomas (www.onthegoidiomas.com.br) to try to match teachers to companies and to advise qualified expat teachers.

Although he is Swiss by birth, and arrived in Brazil assuming that Swiss time was a universal standard, **Hans Durrer** slowly adjusted to a different rhythm. He became familiar with the Brazilian way of life, made Brazilian friends, learned Portuguese and felt generally enriched. He attributes this to his open, curious and eager-to-learn attitude, and also to the warm hospitality of the school owners. He describes how rewarding it can be to tutor students with whom you develop a rapport, even when their attendance is sporadic, as happened when he spent two long stints working with Schutz & Kanomata (see directory entry) in Southern Brazil:

> ***Two days ago, Reinaldo attended his last conversational English class in Santa Cruz do Sul. As usual, we talked about anything and everything, from corruption to the ways of perception, from travels to how best to live your life. He enjoyed my classes a lot and thought them interesting, stimulating and helpful, he said. He wasn't, however, too sure whether his English had improved, he laughed. Well, to be honest, it hasn't, I laughed back. Reinaldo is in his fifties and works in tourism. He's been around, from Bariloche to China, and often missed his private classes with me. But whenever he managed to attend, we had a ball. Among other things, I learned what a truly special place Easter Island is and that I really need to visit a certain fabulous hotel in the jungle near Manaus.***

If you want to study Portuguese, you can apply for a student visa, which would make it easier to stay on. For example, many foreigners register at the Pontificia Universidade Católica in Rio de Janeiro. This is an excellent place to link up with students and advertise classes if you want to offer private lessons (which pay much better than working for an institute).

BARRY O'LEARY

Barry O'Leary, well-travelled TEFLer, arrived in Salvador (northern Brazil) just before Carnaval. (The best time to start work is following the Carnaval, which takes place during the week over Ash Wednesday every February.) He bought a map, borrowed a telephone directory from his hostel and walked round all the 25 language academies with his CV. His luck wasn't as quick as it had been in Ecuador (described later) because most academies couldn't tell how many students they would have until after Carnaval. But Barry managed to find an evening job at an academy outside Salvador and later found two other jobs.

I taught in three institutes: PEC (www.pec.com.br), Okey Dokey and AEC Idiomas. The business academy sent me to various offices that were all fully equipped and well organised. Generally working conditions were excellent and so was the pay; I received about $8 an hour, which was a good rate for Brazil. The students were a mixed bag, yet they all had a great sense of humour and participated in the lessons, though some students were there only because their boss wanted them to be and had little interest.

I worked at another academy one afternoon a week. The approach here was to teach English through music, followed by group conversation lessons. Each week the director would translate two or three songs for the students to sing along in English. The students enjoyed this immensely, and I thought it was a very original way to learn. Most students seemed to be more interested in asking me questions about England and my life rather than pay attention to the lessons, but it was a good way for them to improve their fluency. I found Brazilian students very happy-go-lucky people; they were always smiling and interested in learning English.

I was lucky enough to live in the old quarter of Salvador, called Pelourinho, which was the hub of the nightlife, but also the hub of any trouble. I lived in a house with 15 people including Brazilians, Nigerians, French and Irish, for which I paid a trivial amount and had a brilliant three months.

LIST OF EMPLOYERS

CalENGLISH SCHOOL
Rua Waldemar Faria Mota 85, Jardim Bongiovani, Presidente Prudente, São Paulo
+55 18 3908 6361
cris@calenglish.com.br; zac@calenglish.com.br
www.calenglish.com.br

NUMBER OF TEACHERS: 4 per semester.

PREFERENCE OF NATIONALITY: USA or Canada.

QUALIFICATIONS: TEFL certificate, any teaching experience or any experience with children.

CONDITIONS OF EMPLOYMENT: 6 months, renewable. 20 hours per week, usually in the afternoons and evenings.

FACILITIES/SUPPORT: Rooms right beside the school may be rented.

RECRUITMENT: By email and Skype.

CONTACT: Cristiane Zagol, Director/Owner.

ENGLISH CAMP
Rua Barão de Capanema 220, Cerqueira Cesar, São Paulo 01411-010
+55 11 3061 0080; +55 11 3062 6333
englishcamp@englishcamp.com.br
www.englishcamp.com.br

NUMBER OF TEACHERS: 5 international guests to act as monitors and teachers per vacation season.

PREFERENCE OF NATIONALITY: None, provided they are fluent English speakers.

QUALIFICATIONS: Must have open mind, to teach international students. Minimum age 18. Must have some experience camping or as a camp counsellor

CONDITIONS OF EMPLOYMENT: Minimum stay 15 days up to 4 weeks starting January and July. 6–8 hours a day. English language immersion camps also held throughout the year.

SALARY: None, volunteer positions only for those travelling on tourist visas. Full room and board provided free.

FACILITIES/SUPPORT: Letter of invitation sent so that volunteer teachers can arrive with tourist visa.

RECRUITMENT: Word of mouth from other teachers. Interviews can be conducted by Skype. Applications should be made at least 2 months in advance of January and July start dates to give time for a visa to be issued.

CONTACT: Sandra Goulart Urioste, Academic Director.

ENGLISH FOR BUSINESS
Rua Booker Pittman 303, Chácara Santo Antônio CEP: 04719-060, São Paulo - SP
+55 11 35717706
teacher@englishforbusiness.com.br
www.englishforbusiness.com.br

NUMBER OF TEACHERS: 20.

PREFERENCE OF NATIONALITY: UK, USA, Canada, Australia, New Zealand and Ireland.

QUALIFICATIONS: CELTA, DELTA and TESOL Certified Teacher as well as experienced professionals of other industries are welcome.

CONDITIONS OF EMPLOYMENT: 12-36 months. 3-32 hours per week.

SALARY: Ranges from R$600 to R$5,000 net per month.

FACILITIES/SUPPORT: Advice on accommodation and visas given.

RECRUITMENT: Websites and agreements with English Schools in the UK and USA. Face-to-face or Skype interviews.

CONTACT: Pricila Gaffuri, School Coordinator.

ENGLISH VOICE IDIOMAS
Edifício Barão de Monte Cedro, Rua Frei Caneca, 1407, Conj 915, Consolação, São Paulo 01307-909
+55 11 3266 6951
paul@englishvoice.com.br; comercial@englishvoice.com.br
www.englishvoice.com.br

NUMBER OF TEACHERS: 4.

PREFERENCE OF NATIONALITY: None.

QUALIFICATIONS: Teaching certificate needed, though 2 years' teaching experience would also be considered.

CONDITIONS OF EMPLOYMENT: 6-month contracts. 15–20 hours per week.

SALARY: R$40 per hour (net).

FACILITIES/SUPPORT: No assistance with accommodation. Help given with documentation.

RECRUITMENT: Via Gringoes (www.gringoes.com), a local expats community online newsletter. Most interviews take place face-to-face but in some cases can be by Skype.

CONTACT: Paul Major, Director.

IICA GLOBAL ENGLISH

Avenida 23, # 1274, Ituiutaba, Minas Gerais 38300-114

+55 34 3261 2141

jcjacy@hotmail.com; iica@netsitecom.br

www.iica.com.br

Sponsors Intercultural Exchange Programme.

NUMBER OF TEACHERS: 15 intercultural interns.

PREFERENCE OF NATIONALITY: USA, UK or Canada.

QUALIFICATIONS: Should be aged 21–32 and either a student enrolled in last year of university or within 12 months of graduation at the time of application.

CONDITIONS OF EMPLOYMENT: 12 months. 34 hours per week. Monday–Saturday.

SALARY: Allowance of about R$1,000 (US$300) per month plus free family homestay.

FACILITIES/SUPPORT: Free homestay accommodation provided. Programme eligible for special trainee visa status after participants sign a contract and provide documentation as required by Brazilian Immigration Service. Global English will assist with visa process. VITEM-IV (student) visa fees are US$195 for Britons, US$160 for Americans and cannot be refunded in the case of a visa being denied.

RECRUITMENT: Screening based on candidate's CV. Intake months are February and August, and screening, based on candidate's CV, takes place 4 months in advance.

CONTACT: Professor Jacy Pimenta, Coordinator (jcjacy@hotmail.com).

KIWI BRASIL IDIOMAS

Av Pico da Bandeira, 1542, 1º andar, Água Verde, Alto Caparaó (Minas Gerais) 36979-000

+55 32 3747 2889

jander@kiwibrasil.com

www.kiwibrasil.com

6 schools located in small towns in Minas Gerais, teaching all ages and levels.

NUMBER OF TEACHERS: 7 on contract and freelancers.

PREFERENCE OF NATIONALITY: None.

QUALIFICATIONS: TEFL, TESOL, CELTA , DELTA or equivalent. 1 year's experience is required.

CONDITIONS OF EMPLOYMENT: Contracts from 6 months to 2 years. 30 hours a week.

SALARY: $500 a month (net) plus full accommodation.

FACILITIES/SUPPORT: Seminars and ongoing teacher training.

RECRUITMENT: Via TEFL jobs websites. Skype interviews.

CONTACT: Jander Kenedy Nogueira Soares, Director/Owner.

LINGUAE – PERSONAL LANGUAGE INSTITUTE

Rua Dom José de Barros, 152, 10th Floor, Centre, São Paulo 01038-902

+55 11 3255 7975; mobile +55 11 8784 4489

plinio@linguae.com.br or contato@linguae.com.br

www.linguae.com.br

PREFERENCE OF NATIONALITY: Native speakers. For 3 branches.

CONDITIONS OF EMPLOYMENT: In-company, part-time work.

SALARY: Hourly rates from R$35 to R$45.

RECRUITMENT: Candidates should be living locally.

CONTACT: Plinio Gherardi, Commercial Director.

MAPLELEAF ENGLISH SCHOOL

Jose Rodrigues Menezes 93 Timoteo, Minas Gerais

+55 31 38491017

carl_avila@yahoo.com

NUMBER OF TEACHERS: 2 per semester.

PREFERENCE OF NATIONALITY: USA, Canada, Australia and UK.

QUALIFICATIONS: Some TEFL experience desirable, and with a university degree. Excellent communication skills, English grammar knowledge and travel experience, especially in developing countries, are a must. Must have cultural intelligence and want to learn Portuguese. Female preferred.

CONDITIONS OF EMPLOYMENT: One semester of 5 months (Aug-Dec or Feb-Jun) with option of renewing upon mutual agreement. 26 hours a week.

SALARY: $750 per month net with completion bonus of $750 at the end of the fifth month.

FACILITIES/SUPPORT: Free furnished apartment provided with all utilities and wifi included, within walking distance of the school. Regular teacher training support, including coaching, grammar and theory, and Portuguese language classes. No assistance with work permits.

CONTACT: Carlos Avila, Manager.

NEW START COMUNICACOES

Rua Uruguiana 10/1211, Centro, Rio de Janeiro 20050-090

+55 21 2508 6917

newstart@newstart.com.br

www.newstart.com.br

NUMBER OF TEACHERS: 15–20 in-company teachers.

PREFERENCE OF NATIONALITY: Must be a native English speaker.

QUALIFICATIONS: Preferably CELTA or Trinity TESOL certificate and some classroom experience.

CONDITIONS OF EMPLOYMENT: Minimum 5 months' work.

SALARY: R$34 (£8) per hour.

FACILITIES/SUPPORT: Training in Business English.

RECRUITMENT: Direct application by CV via email and telephone.

CONTACT: Stephanie Crockett (stephanie@newstart.com.br) or Adam Reid (adam@newstart.com.br).

SCHUTZ & KANOMATA ESL & PSL

Rua Galvao Costa 85, Santa Cruz do Sul 96810-012

+55 51 3715 3366

eslinbrazil@asbi.org.br

www.sk.com.br/guests/sk-lcb.html

NUMBER OF TEACHERS: 5 every semester on Brazilian Language and Culture Exchange Program located in mid-sized town in southern Brazil.

PREFERENCE OF NATIONALITY: Canadian, American and British.

QUALIFICATIONS: Main qualification is personality; must be communicative, considerate and interested in making friends. ESL-teaching experience desirable. For visa reasons must be a student or recent graduate.

CONDITIONS OF EMPLOYMENT: 10–12 month contracts; semesters run 1 March–20 July or 1 August– 20 December. Occasionally 1-semester positions are possible. Up to 24 hours per week, mostly in the evenings.

SALARY: Accommodation provided in exchange for 5 hours of teaching (one a day) per week. Above that, the rate paid is R$22 for private lessons and R$27 for groups. Bonus of US$250–$400 paid after one or $800 after two semesters.

FACILITIES/SUPPORT: Programme provides accommodation, Portuguese instruction and occasional weekend tours. Help given with obtaining study training visa valid for one year and extendable for a further year. This must be applied for in guest-teacher's own country for which enrolment on a Portuguese course is a requirement.

RECRUITMENT: Strong internet exposure. Also former teacher in Canada acts as agent. Candidates are chosen 3–4 months before semester start date, plus short-notice vacancies sometimes available.

CONTACT: Ricardo Schütz, Principal.

SPEAKING – CENTRO DE CULTURA AMERICANA

R. Cel. Francisco Bráz 969, Itajuba, Minas Gerais 37500-052

+55 35 3621 3354; +55 35 8846 1828

administracao@speaking.com.br

www.speaking.com.br

NUMBER OF TEACHERS: 7 foreign and 12 Brazilian teachers.

PREFERENCE OF NATIONALITY: American, Canadian and British. Anyone with dual Brazilian nationality especially welcome.

QUALIFICATIONS: TESL or similar. Must be young, enthusiastic and committed. Experience not needed.

CONDITIONS OF EMPLOYMENT: Standard commitment February to December. 40 hours per week, Monday to Saturday.

SALARY: Starting at R$20 (US$6) per hour net. Wage is enough for living in a small town in Brazil.

FACILITIES/SUPPORT: School provides a small, furnished house, or helps with living expenses.

RECRUITMENT: By email or via ESL websites such as www.jobstefl.com.

CONTACT: Dagmar Andrade, Director (dagmarandrade@yahoo.com.br).

CHILE

More than most other South American economies, Chile's has been flourishing, though at the time of writing the unemployment rate was rising and stood at 6.8% (2016). In terms of market competitiveness, Chile ranks most highly among South American countries. As commercial, touristic and cultural contacts with the outside world have increased, so has the demand for the English language. The most booming market is for business English, though there is also demand for teachers of children, created largely by the Chilean government lowering the age at which English is taught in state schools from 7th grade to 5th grade.

The ongoing drive to raise the level of English-language teaching throughout the country continues with the Chilean Ministry of Education's major initiative, the *Programa Inglés Abre Puertas* or 'English Opens Doors Program'. The ambitious EODP programme aims to improve English-language education in state schools in cities and small towns throughout Chile by enlisting the help of native and near-native English speakers. University graduates work alongside local teachers in classrooms to help improve listening and speaking skills among students. Participants must be university graduates (aged 21–35) and stay for one or two semesters, normally from March/April or beginning of August. Volunteers receive a small monthly volunteer allowance of 70,000 pesos (over $100) in addition to free room and board with a Chilean host family and domestic travel. Health insurance is provided. Prospective volunteers can apply directly via the Volunteer Centre in Santiago (✆ +56 2 2406 7170; voluntarios@mineduc.cl; www.centrodevoluntarios.cl).

Luke Harris was so enthusiastic about the EODP that after finishing his stint of teaching he moved into the office to help recruit further volunteer teachers:

> ***Before doing the programme I had only volunteered as a teaching assistant a few hours per week in an ESL classroom. The application process is fairly rigorous. In addition to the application form and writing two essays, you must submit various documents and photos; that is followed with a Skype interview. Since you work in a public school, teachers and students are often not very motivated, which can be frustrating. Living with a host family was awesome! It is a great way to get a feeling for the community and culture, not to mention it allows you to learn a ton of Spanish.***
>
> ***My students were extremely enthusiastic to have a native speaker for a teacher. For that reason they always received me with a great deal of warmth and appreciation. This made for a very comfortable and positive environment. However, students have a very low level of English. Despite many years of English courses most are not at a conversational level. Also, discipline can be difficult if you are used to an orderly classroom. In Chile classes are large and students have more freedom. Chileans are generally much more open and gregarious than people in the US. I was lucky to make many Chilean friends and spent a lot of time making barbecues with them, playing football and travelling on the weekends. I had not expected to receive so much attention for being a foreigner. This was great at times and difficult at times. For me, this has been a life-changing and self-defining experience. If you are a professional teacher though, and have your own ideas, styles and lesson plans, this programme could be somewhat unsatisfying in the classroom. The cultural experience is unparalleled.***

One of the advantages of the programme is that the Centro de Voluntarios will assist in the process for applying for the *residencia temporaria* before arrival, for which you will need a Criminal Background check, medical certificate and so on. As a volunteer, you're expected to teach 25 pedagogical hours (an hour is calculated as a 45-minute lesson in Chile) per week. In addition, you are required to spend 10 hours working on lesson planning with your head teacher as well as leading extracurricular activities.

Most other teaching opportunities in Chile are in the commercial sector and the majority of those are in the capital, Santiago, where there are scores of private language schools. Some relevant institutes can also be found in the Valparaiso-Viña del Mar area.

ALAN CHADWICK

Alan Chadwick spent a happy six months in Valparaiso.

October was not the best time of year to start the hunt for full-time work, but he set to work dropping off his CV in many universities and schools, sending off multiple email enquiries and putting up posters offering private tuition (which brought no response). Eventually he got a few bites from potential employers impressed with his CELTA qualification, but deterred by the fact that he didn't have a working visa or a RUT (tax/NI number). He was lucky enough to be asked by an Englishwoman he knew to take over an evening class she taught to university students which met for three hours three times a week. This was the most enjoyable as well as the most lucrative of his several jobs. The hourly rate was 15,000 pesos per hour (then worth £15, now nearly £17) less about 20% for tax. Although the students were serious about achieving good scores on a Chilean language test connected with studying abroad, the classes were friendly and informal and often involved sharing food.

Another job he did was through the International Center in Viña del Mar (www.internationalcenter.cl) which Alan reckons is a good place for newcomers to try. Among other things, it hires teachers to work on occasional all-day immersion courses constructed round a theme and an excursion, for example wine-making. A large and disparate group of learners met in the lobby of a hotel for four hours of lessons before going by bus to a vineyard for a tour, a wine-tasting and lunch. After all that red wine in 30 degree heat, Alan was not sure how useful his lessons at the end of the day could be. In any case it was well paid.

Through a recruitment agent, Alan was eventually interviewed for a full-time job at the Naval Academy in Valparaiso which he got. He appreciated the civilised hours of 8am-1pm but it took a little while to get used to the no-nonsense discipline of the place, with its regulations and dress code and hierarchy. He had to get used to seeing the students doing press-ups for the slightest misdemeanour. He was conscious of the discrepancy between his respected role as teacher of future naval officers and his bohemian life in a big shared house on the hill (cerro) where he loved the frequent barbecues, proximity to the beach and the modest rent of £65 a month for a big room shared with his girlfriend.

Alan came away with the impression that there is a huge and growing market for English in Valparaiso and Chile generally and that Britons are in very short supply in Valpo.

There will be less competition for teaching vacancies and a lower cost of living in smaller places such as the aptly named La Serena in the dry north of the country, or other towns such as Arica, Iquique, Antofagasta, Talca, Concepción, Valdivia, Osorno and Punta Arenas, all of which have possibilities for teachers, albeit on a smaller scale. Some course providers in Santiago serve clients in Valparaiso/Viña del Mar, where there are three universities.

The Instituto Chileno-Británico de Cultura in Santiago (entry below) recruits qualified teachers and has a good library that incorporates the British Council's resource library for teachers; anyone prepared to pay the membership fee can borrow materials, though many schools in Santiago have good libraries themselves. Native English-speaker teachers are also hired by the Institutos Chileno-Britanico de Cultura in Concepcion (www.ibritanico.com), Arica (www.britanicoarica.cl) and Viña del Mar (www.icbc.cl). **Libby Goldsmith** noticed that in Chile, her fellow teachers were mainly young Americans taking a break to travel and experience new things after university. Perhaps because of the scarcity of a British accent, it is at a premium and can make work easier to find.

South American language schools tend to prefer face-to-face meetings rather than emails and phone calls. **Heidi Resetarits** typed 'English schools in Santiago' into a search engine, came up with a huge list of language schools in areas she wanted to apply to and then dropped off résumés in person:

> ***I actually got an interview on the spot at the second school I applied to . . . and I happened to just walk by it – it wasn't even on my list! Santiago is a very modern city and new schools are popping up all the time. It's worth it just to walk around town and see what's there. I know that South Americans appreciate face-to-face meetings rather than emails and phone calls, so I walked in and asked to meet with a director. I decided to stay and chat a bit with the receptionist, and he made me an appointment for the next day.***
>
> ***The interview was a face-to-face with the director of the school. After we talked about my résumé and a bit about my teaching experience, we set up a teaching practice (he chose a topic and a student) for the next day. I got the job within three days.***

Doug Burgess went job-hunting in Santiago, armed with a CELTA he had acquired at home in England and some experience. He had an interview with a corporate training company and EF English First (see entry), who offered Doug a contract for 12 months with work visa and decent hourly rate, more if he had to travel more than two metro stations or worked at its other campus. In the end, Doug accepted another offer from the Instituto Chileno-Británico de Cultura. His contract was for 15 hours, which was enough to secure a work visa, although he had the option of working up to 30 hours or more. Before Doug secured a full-time teaching job, he participated in an exchange programme run by Woodward Chile. For every Spanish lesson he received, he gave an English lesson, and went from being a complete beginner in the language to fairly competent.

A further possibility is to teach at English-medium *colegios*, where a longer commitment will be necessary and a reasonable salary paid. Although they employ mainly certified teachers, often hired at recruitment fairs and through international advertising, they do need some native English speakers for their English departments. For example, **Eleanor Padfield** was determined to work abroad after finishing her A levels but did not want to go through an agency where she would be with lots of other British students. After spending the first half of her year in Salamanca, Spain, she sent emails in Spanish all over the world to find something to do, preferably in Latin America. Of the many schools and language schools she contacted, one of the few to reply was the Redland School, an upmarket private school. Although it told her that it didn't usually accept gap-year students (since so many previous gappers had left prematurely to travel), it made an exception for Eleanor when she promised to stick it out till the end of the term, beginning in March and ending in August. When June rolled round, she was tempted to leave early but her conscience (or her mother's exhortations) persuaded her to keep her promise, trying to see as much of the country as she could in her days off.

The commercial institutes in Santiago vary greatly in size, reliability in their treatment of employees and teaching methods. Newcomers to the city quickly learn which are the better schools and gradually acquire more hours with them. In-company teaching usually takes place early in the morning; middle-ranking staff tend to be taught before the official working day begins, while directors and higher-ranking executives take their classes at a more civilised mid-morning hour. In **Libby Goldsmith's** experience, business students in Santiago (unlike in Bogotá where she later worked) seemed more flexible with class hours so she was able to build up a schedule throughout the day and not just at peak times. Most teachers enjoy the variety of off-site teaching rather than classroom teaching, which tends to be more textbook based.

The academic year runs from March to December with a two-week winter holiday in July and one-week recess in mid-September, so the best time to apply for a contract is the end of February. There are 21 British curriculum schools listed on the website of the Association of British Schools in Chile (www.absch.cl).

Non-contractual work is usually paid by the hour, starting at 6,000 pesos and rising to 8,000 pesos. One business English provider in Santiago was recently offering hourly wages of up to 18,000 pesos for 90-minute lessons. Established teachers working for universities such as UNIACC in Providencia can top 15,000 pesos but this is rare. The cost of living is higher than in many other places on the continent but teachers can still support themselves. **Heidi Resetarits** says that '*you won't be able to do much saving in South America in general*', and recommends that you don't move to Chile without savings if you want to have fun and money to travel. Normally 10% of earnings must be paid in tax, which in some cases can be reclaimed the following April/May. After taking the first job she was offered, **Mandy Powell** assumed that all jobs paid roughly the same. However, later when she was working for EES (see entry) she discovered that there is a huge variation and wishes that she had looked for a better-paid teaching job sooner. It was especially tough trying to make ends meet in the quiet periods of January–February and July.

Usually the CELTA, Trinity or equivalent certificate is a minimum requirement for anyone considering working in the private sector. You can of course obtain a qualification after arrival, for example the proprietary IDELT certificate is offered for $1,995 by BridgeChile (www.bridgetefl.com/teach-english-in-chile) with the option of paying an extra $1,000 for a package that guarantees job interviews after the training. Another option for those who are not confident enough to show up and find their feet, the Teaching Chile agency (see entry) can take the stress away in exchange for a fee of $1,395.

A worthwhile volunteer teaching scheme is run by Voluntarios de Esperanza in Santiago (www.ve-global.org). VE works with partner institutions to place volunteers to work with at-risk children, including teaching English, for a minimum of four months beginning in September, January and May. The application process is competitive and no registration fee is charged.

RED TAPE

Most job-seekers arrive on a tourist visa valid for 90 days which is free for many nationalities (but not Australians, who are still liable for the reciprocity fee of US$117). Once you find a job, the most common visa to apply for is the *Visa Sujeta a Contrato* (subject to contract visa), for which you will need to take a notarised copy of a contract from an employer that shows a minimum salary of 100,000 pesos a month to the Departamento de Extrajería. If you are able to commit yourself for a year, your employer may be willing to help you obtain the more flexible temporary resident visa. The total expenses for the permits will top £1,000 for Britons, whereas Americans pay much less. After you get your work visa, you then need to register your address with the immigration police and obtain your ID card or *cedula*, which you require for joining the Chilean health care scheme, opening a bank account, etc.

Many British teachers delay applying for the expensive work permit until they are sure they are going to stay longer term. Others work for schools that are not keen to assist in the process. In this case it is necessary to leave the country before the 90-day validity of the tourist visa expires; most get a new

90-day tourist visa by crossing an international border; the most popular route is to Mendoza, Argentina. If you are from New Zealand, Australia,Canada or Ireland you may be eligible for a working holiday visa that gives complete flexibility in job-hunting in Chile for one year.

Rarely, people are offered a job before arrival. If this is the case, there are two ways to obtain the appropriate visa permit. Either your employer submits the application at the Ministry of Foreign Affairs in Chile (Direccion de Asuntos Consulares y de Imigracion, Bandera 46, Santiago) or you apply at the Chilean Consulate in your country of origin. You will need a signed and notarised work contract and a full medical report. If granted, the visa will be valid for one year. After that you may be eligible for a *visacion de residencia* that allows an unlimited stay.

Almost everything you do in Chile requires you to present a national ID number, equivalent to National Insurance, known as RUN (Rol Único Nacional) but commonly referred to as RUT (Rol Único Tributario).

ADVERTISING FOR PRIVATE CLIENTS

The average rate for private lessons is about 10,000–12,000 pesos per hour though business people will pay up to 15,000 pesos. The expatriate community – many of whom will be involved with English teaching – could open doors to more private clients; there are many ways to meet expats, from playing cricket at the Prince of Wales Country Club to frequenting the English-language bookshop Books and Bits on Av Apoquindo in Santiago (www.booksandbits.cl).

You can advertise for private clients in *El Mercurio*, the leading quality daily. Check ads on Craigslist (http://santiago.en.craigslist.org), mostly for part-time hours, or in the free ads paper *El Rastro*.

LEISURE TIME

Although Santiago is cosmopolitan and modern, there are pockets of poverty and the men can be aggressive, shouting across the street at women. However, Santiago is an interesting and on the whole safe city where young women can feel reasonably secure, even when out alone in the wee small hours. Pollution in the winter months can get a bit depressing. However, for the most part, the quality of life is enviable. **Mandy Powell** especially relished waking up after rain and seeing the fantastic mountains clearly against crystal-clear blue skies. During her two years in Santiago, **Libby Goldsmith** became part of a close circle of expats who were always meeting up for impromptu social gatherings. She noticed that with Chilean friends, scheduling became more important as their lives centred around family commitments and responsibilities.

LIST OF EMPLOYERS

ACADEMIA DE IDIOMAS DEL NORTE
Ramirez 1345, Iquique
+56 57 411 827
secretaria@languages.cl
www.languages.cl

Swiss-owned.

NUMBER OF TEACHERS: 4.

PREFERENCE OF NATIONALITY: Native English speakers.

QUALIFICATIONS: Recognised TEFL certificate.

CONDITIONS OF EMPLOYMENT: 6–9-month contracts with 6 working hours per day. School is owned by a Swiss.

FACILITIES/SUPPORT: Information on homestay families, flats, hotels, etc is given. Shared apartments with other teachers sometimes available. Work contract provided in order to get work permits.

RECRUITMENT: Interviews are essential and usually held in Chile but can be conducted by telephone or Skype.

CHILENGLISH
Ramón Carnicer 81, Of. 607, Providencia, Santiago
+56 2 665 1676
oficina@chilenglish.com
www.chilenglish.com

NUMBER OF TEACHERS: 15.
PREFERENCE OF NATIONALITY: None.
QUALIFICATIONS: TEFL-certified teachers with previous experience. Some opportunities for those who lack qualifications but have the right background and personality.
CONDITIONS OF EMPLOYMENT: Contract length is negotiable. Full-time is 25–30 hours per week with classes between 8am and 9pm, Monday to Friday. Some Saturday work available.
SALARY: Average 500,000 pesos per month.
FACILITIES/SUPPORT: Assistance given with work permits and guidance when filling in relevant paperwork.
RECRUITMENT: Interviews essential.
CONTACT: Craig Wilson, Director (cwilson@chilenglish.com).

EES EXECUTIVE ENGLISH SOLUTIONS
Coronel Pereira 62, Office 601, Las Condes, Región Metropolitana, Santiago
+56 2 335 7781 /22 232 3571
howard.spencer@ees.cl; cv_chile@yahoo.com
www.ees.cl

NUMBER OF TEACHERS: 30–40.
PREFERENCE OF NATIONALITY: None.
QUALIFICATIONS: 4+ year degree, TESOL, CELTA or TEFL and 1+ year's experience preferred.
CONDITIONS OF EMPLOYMENT: Standard contracts are 6–12 months. The usual hours are mornings, lunchtime and evenings, Monday to Friday. Normal allocation of hours is up to 18.
SALARY: 8,000–12,000 pesos per hour, 25–30 hours per week. Deductions of 10% refundable with filing of tax return.
FACILITIES/SUPPORT: Company will provide proof of employment for lease and rental agreement. All foreign employees receive a Chilean work visa.
RECRUITMENT: In-person interview.
CONTACT: Howard H. Spencer, Director of Studies.

ENGLISH FOR LIFE
Badajoz 130, Of. 1102 Las Condes, Santiago 7560908
+56 2 2760 2206
info@efl.cl; jrobertson@englishforlife.cl
www.efl.cl

Associate Member of International House.
NUMBER OF TEACHERS: Around 15.
PREFERENCE OF NATIONALITY: None.
QUALIFICATIONS: CELTA, Trinity TESOL or IH certificate are preferred and English for Life also offers its own teacher-training programme. More experienced teachers have the possibility of moving into more senior roles or teacher training.
CONDITIONS OF EMPLOYMENT: Contract is initially for one academic year (9 months). The contract specifies an agreed number of contact (teaching) hours.
SALARY: Varies with number of contracted hours. Bonus may be paid depending on location of teaching in Santiago. Teachers are guaranteed a base salary, for example, for an 18-hour contract, with extra hours and bonuses paid in addition. 7% deduction for health insurance. Overtime paid on hours worked over 24 per week.
FACILITIES/SUPPORT: Accommodation and flights are not paid for by the school, although help and advice are given in finding suitable accommodation. Teachers enter on a tourist visa and then apply for a work permit/visa when they have signed the contract. Teachers are entitled to paid holiday and sick leave on a pro-rata basis. Full academic support is given; e.g. employer pays for teachers to attend meetings and teacher-development sessions that are run once a week by in-house teacher trainer. The school is easily accessible by metro and bus. School has a garden available to staff for lesson preparation, barbecues, etc. Free wi-fi access and computers. DoS willing to supervise teachers who wish to do the online DELTA or other career-development courses.
RECRUITMENT: Through IHWO (www.ihworld.com/recruitment), www.tefl.com or direct application throughout the year. CVs should be sent to the DoS (dos@englishforlife.cl), who will contact suitable candidates for interview.
CONTACT: Justine Robertson, School Manager.

FISCHER ENGLISH INSTITUTE
Calle Cirujano Guzmán 49, Providencia, Santiago de Chile
+56 22 235 6667/9812
contacto@fischerinstitute.cl
www.fischerinstitute.cl

NUMBER OF TEACHERS: 30.

PREFERENCE OF NATIONALITY: USA.

QUALIFICATIONS: University degree and TEFL certificate or similar and 1 year's experience in teaching.

CONDITIONS OF EMPLOYMENT: Minimum 1-year contract, 20 hours a week.

SALARY: 8,000–8,500 pesos per hour.

FACILITIES/SUPPORT: None.

RECRUITMENT: References, preferably from school abroad. Interviews essential, carried out in Santiago.

GRANT'S ENGLISH
Londres 60, Oficina 4, Santiago 8330133
+56 22 638 1128
grants@grantsenglish.cl
www.grantsenglish.cl

NUMBER OF TEACHERS: 20-25.

PREFERENCE OF NATIONALITY: USA, Canada, UK, Australia.

QUALIFICATIONS: Bachelor's Degree and TEFL/CELTA certification.

CONDITIONS OF EMPLOYMENT: 6-month contracts. 20-30 hours per week minimum

SALARY: From 9,000 pesos an hour. 10% deductions for social security and tax.

FACILITIES/SUPPORT: Advice given on accommodation. Job letter given to teachers to be attached to a notarised copy of their degree, photocopy of their passport, entry stamp, photo and completed Temporary Residency form.

RECRUITMENT: Craigslist, Facebook, word of mouth. Face-to-face and Skype interviews.

CONTACT: Darshana Mahtani, Academic Director.

INSTITUTO CHILENO-BRITANICO DE CULTURA
Paseo Huerfanos 554, Santa Lucia, Santiago
+56 2 413 2350
edovas@britanico.cl
www.britanico.cl

Eight branches altogether including Las Condes, La Florida, Maipu, Providencia and Nunoa.

NUMBER OF TEACHERS: 10.

PREFERENCE OF NATIONALITY: None, but should be native English speaker.

QUALIFICATIONS: A degree in English or Modern Languages, plus a TEFL qualification. However, experience is valued more than TEFL qualification.

CONDITIONS OF EMPLOYMENT: 1 year, March to February. 30 teaching hours per week, mostly evenings.

SALARY: £700 per month.

FACILITIES/SUPPORT: Help with finding accommodation is provided. Teachers are provided with a settling-in grant towards their accommodation.

RECRUITMENT: Usually on the spot.

CONTACT: Eduardo Vasquez, General Manager.

INSTITUTO CHILENO-NORTEAMERICANO DE CULTURA
Moneda No. 1467, Santiago
+56 2 2677 7167
englishteachers@norteamericano.cl
www.norteamericano.cl

NUMBER OF TEACHERS: 15–20, also for branches in La Florida and Providencia. Norteamericano branches in the regions (Valparaiso, Curicó, etc.) recruit teachers separately.

PREFERENCE OF NATIONALITY: American and Canadian.

QUALIFICATIONS: Teaching related degree or BA in another subject plus TESL/TEFL certificate. Minimum 6 months' teaching experience requested.

CONDITIONS OF EMPLOYMENT: 1-year contracts starting in March. 30 hours per week. Peak hours of work early morning and early evening, and some Saturdays. Classes for adults, children, teens, Business and Academic English. Part-time openings for Friday evening and Saturday morning hours.

SALARY: Equivalent of US$1,100 per month in Chilean pesos.

FACILITIES/SUPPORT: Assistance given in obtaining visas. Training provided. Teachers' room with computers, email access and cafeteria privileges.

RECRUITMENT: Direct application by mail, email, phone or fax. Applicants should send cover letter, CV, recent photo, copy of diplomas/certificates and letter of reference from recent employer.

REDLAND SCHOOL
Camino el Alba 11357, Las Condes, Santiago
+56 2 959 8500
secretaria_rector@redland.cl; jobs@redland.cl
www.redland.cl

NUMBER OF TEACHERS: 72 in total.

PREFERENCE OF NATIONALITY: British or other nationalities with English as a first language.

QUALIFICATIONS: University degree and teaching qualification. Pre- and post-university students also considered for gap-year placements.

CONDITIONS OF EMPLOYMENT: 1–3-year contract, mostly starting late February for academic year March to December. Classes run from 8am to 3.30pm or 5pm. Pupils aged 4–18.

SALARY: On application. Increases are pegged to cost of living. 13th month salary given as bonus.

FACILITIES/SUPPORT: Assistance finding accommodation can be offered. Professional development opportunities and free lunches provided.

RECRUITMENT: Via email in first instance. Recruitment starts in August for following academic year.

TEACHING CHILE
Av. Vitacura 3355, Dept 113, Santiago
+1 720 221 3831 (US phone number routes calls to Santiago office); +44 20 8150 6981 (UK phone number routes calls to Santiago office)
info@teachingchile.com
www.teachingchile.com

NUMBER OF TEACHERS: Approximately 90 native English-speaking teachers per year are placed by this recruitment/placement agency.

PREFERENCE OF NATIONALITY: None. To date, TeachingChile has placed teachers from Australia, Canada, England, Ireland, New Zealand, Scotland and the USA.

QUALIFICATIONS: Varies among schools. Overall, applicants should be a graduate of a university or in their final year of undergraduate studies. ESL/TEFL/TESOL certification and teaching experience are desired but not required. Spanish language skills are not required for classroom instruction but elementary conversational language skills are recommended for the teacher's cultural enjoyment.

CONDITIONS OF EMPLOYMENT: Minimum 5–6 month contract; 10–12 months preferred. The majority of teachers choose a 1-year contract. All contracts are renewable directly with the teaching institution, assuming the school has positions available and the teacher has a good rapport with the employer and students.

SALARY: Minimum 445,000 pesos per month for a base of 18 hours of classroom time per week. For longer hours teachers earn more. Some schools deduct 13% for tax and an optional 7% for medical insurance, but salaries are adjusted accordingly and teachers make about the same net salary.

FACILITIES/SUPPORT: Guaranteed work contract, visa-processing assistance, and 3 weeks' rent-free accommodation. TeachingChile provides assistance with finding long-term accommodation and a pre-paid transfer from Santiago airport to the first night's accommodation.

RECRUITMENT: Via the internet, universities and ESL/TEFL/TESOL job placement websites. Applicants submit an application package available from TeachingChile's website prior to arrival and will be interviewed by telephone. Programme application fee is $50 plus placement fee for full service is $1,395.

CONTACT: Bruce Thompson, Managing Director (bruce@teachingchile.com) and Andrea Rodriguez, Programme Coordinator (US telephone: 1 810 415 6818).

COLOMBIA

With the welcome news in November 2016 that FARC, the dreaded guerrilla movement, had signed a peace agreement with the Colombian government, perhaps now the world will stop associating Colombia only with crime and violence. Teaching institutes may no longer have to struggle to attract qualified foreign teachers to what is (wrongly) perceived to be a dangerous corner of the world. Among those who have spent time in Colombia, memories will be of lessons with an urbane businessman or of a local carnival rather than of a neighbourhood shoot-out. **Dave Crowder** has nothing but praise for his adopted country:

> ***I have found the people of Colombia to be universally friendly and helpful to strangers. Unlike the USA, the welcome here is genuine, open and amicable, and the people are genuinely interested in the novelty of a stranger among them. There is no more drug trafficking in Medellín where I live than in any other major city anywhere in the world (I used to live in Miami, where there is much more drug gang activity). As a matter of fact, I will extend my comments about Medellín to every part of the nation that I have visited.***

With the expansion of trade, interest in English has increased especially among the business community. When in 2015/16 **Libby Goldsmith** worked for both Bogotá Business English and First Class (see entries) she found that many Colombian business students would only take classes at the peak times, usually either before or after work. This made it difficult to build a steady flow of work through the day and led to a stop-start timetable with a loss of momentum. Furthermore this made it hard to earn a decent and steady income.

A completely different teaching experience of Colombia can be found in the Ministry of Education's ambitious programme to encourage bilingualism in the state education system. To that end, SENA (the National Training Service) is recruiting a large number of English Teaching Fellows from abroad to work for at least four months alongside local teachers mainly in secondary schools throughout the country. Although TEFL experience/qualifications and a basic level of Spanish are preferred, the only absolute requirements for acceptance are being a native speaker aged 21-50 and able to pay the refundable US$400 deposit. A monthly living allowance of 1,500,000 pesos ($500) is paid in arrears to participants. SENA works with an organisation called Volunteers Colombia (www.volunteerscolombia.wordpress.com) who in turn work in partnership with various international recruiters such as Footprints in Canada (www.footprintsrecruiting.com), Greenheart in Chicago (www.greenhearttravel.org/program/adult/work/teach-in-colombia), Flying Cows in the UK (see entry) and www.ESLstarter.com. The programme attracts a lot of favourable feedback.

CHARLES BEACH

CELTA-qualified Charles Beach applied to become one of the first volunteer participants via the Nottingham-based agency Flying Cows who cooperate with Volunteers Colombia in Bogotá. After pre-screening candidates for suitability to the programme, Flying Cows handles all the lengthy pre-departure paperwork. Charles is full of praise for the programme:

The interview was conducted via Skype and was far more relaxed than other TEFL Skype interviews I had. I have two classes that total 20 hours of teaching a week.

We are expected to spend another 20 hours a week planning lessons plus 5 hours are dedicated to a special project. In practice the working week is less than 45 hours, as sometimes lessons are cancelled or lesson-planning takes less time. Accommodation was found for us and paid for during the fortnight-long orientation and the first month in our placement city.

My pupils are mostly aged 17–18 and studying a vocational course provided by the state for young adults who can't afford education otherwise. There are some expected behaviour issues and their level of English is very low, but I genuinely like spending time with them and they are a lot of fun. Having to speak in front of 30 people every day is a tremendous confidence builder.

Volunteers Colombia have been far more on the ball than I expected from a small NGO and Colombia has been far easier to settle into than I expected. My life here in Colombia is pretty busy. In my spare time I go dancing, go hiking, practise Spanish, see classical music at the local university, hang out in student bars, etc. A highlight so far is having cookery students cook us a three-course meal as a welcome to the school. Bucaramanga is a small city so you will always bump into someone you recognise who has something to do!

A newly piloted Building Opportunities Programme for older more experienced teachers is being managed by Auscom, the Australian Colombian Chamber of Commerce. TEFL-certified teachers over 25 are placed for six months (renewable) in a SENA office in one of the major cities (Bogotá, Barranquilla, Medellín, Cali or Bucaramanga) to improve the level of English among Colombian teachers. The stated wage is $800–$1,000 per month. Unfortunately this programme has not been rated as highly as the school programme. One recent participant reviewing it on www.gooverseas.com reported that promises about number of hours, availability of affordable accommodation near the work place, etc. were broken, though those may have been teething problems. One recruitment organisation that is involved with this programme is www.Teachers-latin-america.com based in Mexico.

Colombia is strongly oriented towards the USA with an extensive network of Colombian-American Cultural Centers around the country. However, **Charles Seville** from Oxford, who spent a year as an English-language assistant at the University de Los Llanos in Villavicencio, was struck by how keen Colombians were to learn British English. There is a British Council Teaching Centre in Bogotá, whose market is primarily university students and young learners (www.britishcouncil.co/en) but which also runs conversation clubs. From time to time it advertises hourly-paid teacher vacancies for people with TEFL certificates already in-country.

It is possible to access the Colombian *Yellow Pages* on the internet (www.quehubo.com) which might provide a starting place for finding school addresses; search for *Instituto Idiomas*. Some global EFL companies have a strong presence in Colombia. EF Education First in Bogotá is based at the Edificio EF (Carrera 9, No. 78-57; ✆ +57 1 616 1130; www.ef.com.co) and Berlitz (see entry) has more than a dozen centres, including five in Bogotá. The established company Inglés Bogotá offers a range of language services and is always looking for qualified teachers, and has opened offices in Medellin and Cali too. You can apply for an interview via a form on their website (www.inglesbogota.com/contactenos/apply-for-interview).

The main newspaper, *El Tiempo*, carries adverts for language schools in the capital. There are plenty of local language schools where untrained native English speakers can find work, but there are two main disadvantages.

Wages and conditions can be very poor; many schools start teachers off at 10,000 pesos an hour (about $3.50), though the schools listed below offer more attractive salaries, with an upper limit of 2,000,000 Colombian pesos per month as paid by the respected institute Bogotá Business English to qualified teachers (see entry). One tip for anyone flying into Colombia is to have an address (e.g. a hostel) where you will be staying since you can be asked for this at the airport immigration desk. The immigration restrictions have become more manageable with the passing of several recent laws. It is no longer necessary to apply for a work permit from outside the country. The application with various apostilled documents can be made in Bogotá. Good employers will assist with the process and may even underwrite the $400 fee for a one-year visa. Check the website of the Ministry of Foreign Affairs (www.cancilleria.gov.co). If a teacher intends to stay in Colombia longer than three months, he or she must register at the Foreign Registry of Migration.

LIST OF EMPLOYERS

BERLITZ COLOMBIA

Calle 125 # 21A -18, Bogotá 110111

+571 7459999

andrea.ramirez@berlitz.com.co

www.berlitz.com.co; www.berlitz.com.co/ofertas/adultos/work-abroad-program

NUMBER OF TEACHERS: 50 per year.

PREFERENCE OF NATIONALITY: None.

QUALIFICATIONS: TEFL/ TESOL/CELTA certified teachers holding a BA in any subject.

CONDITIONS OF EMPLOYMENT: 6–12 months. Working week is 40 hours Monday to Saturday. Also offer shorter placements (1 September–15 December) to teach adults; participants in this Work Abroad Program receive a 4-day initial training and free airfares.

SALARY: 2,000,000 pesos plus housing allowance of 290,000 pesos and free travel to Bogotá. Deductions of 8% for social security but no taxes are applied.

FACILITIES/SUPPORT: Free hotel accommodation for first 3 days and help with the housing search. All teachers are trained online before coming to the country. Free airfares provided, also private health care, life insurance and work visas. Berlitz provides all documents requested to obtain a work visa. Teacher pays the $300 visa fee upfront but is reimbursed at the end of the contract. Visas can be obtained in a Colombian consulate abroad or in Bogotá.

RECRUITMENT: Recruiters abroad, advertisements on TEFL sites and direct contact via web page. Applicants for the 30-month programme attend initial online training as part of the selection process.

CONTACT: Andrea Ramirez, Regional Manager of Instruction.

BOGOTA BUSINESS ENGLISH

Carrera 15 No.79-36 Oficina 402, Bogotá

+57 1 749 8148

andrew@bogotabusinessenglish.com

www.BogotaBusinessEnglish.com/jobs

NUMBER OF TEACHERS: 40.

PREFERENCE OF NATIONALITY: None.

QUALIFICATIONS: CELTA/Trinity/TESL training with observed practice element or minimum one year experience.

CONDITIONS OF EMPLOYMENT: 1 year. Split shifts between 6am and 9pm; 2-hour classes.

SALARY: 2,000,000 pesos (approximately $685) per month.

FACILITIES/SUPPORT: Deductions for compulsory medical insurance. No tax. Assistance given with finding accommodation through various rental agencies. Support for one-year foreign worker visa which costs $400.

RECRUITMENT: TESL websites, direct from CELTA recruiters in Bogotá, word of mouth. Face-to-face interviews in Bogotá only.

CONTACT: Andrew Riordan, Academic Director.

DARLINGTON ENGLISH CONSULTANTS

Carrera 16A # 80 – 06 Piso 2, Bogotá

+57 1 7557112

info@darlington.com.co

www.darlingtonenglish.com

NUMBER OF TEACHERS: 25.

PREFERENCE OF NATIONALITY: Preferably already in Colombia.

QUALIFICATIONS: ESL teaching experience.

CONDITIONS OF EMPLOYMENT: 2-year contracts. Flexible working hours.

SALARY: Hourly rates.

FACILITIES/SUPPORT: No assistance with accommodation or training. Advice given on work permits, though they are very difficult to obtain in Colombia.

RECRUITMENT: Face-to-face interviews preferred.

CONTACT: Erika Hernandez, Coordinator.

FIRST CLASS ENGLISH

Carrera 12 #93-78 Of 407, 407 Bogotá

+57 1 623 2380

info@fce.edu.co

www.fce.edu.co

NUMBER OF TEACHERS: 24+ native English speakers.

PREFERENCE OF NATIONALITY: American and British.

QUALIFICATIONS: At least 1 year's teaching experience, preferably with executives/professionals, CELTA, ICELT certification is a plus. But the bottom line is that the candidate must have 3+ years' college/university degree, hopefully in Business or related areas.

CONDITIONS OF EMPLOYMENT: Minimum 1 year, if volunteering a minimum of 4 months. Up to 8 hours of teaching within the hours of 6am to 9pm.

SALARY: Contracted hourly pay from 15,000 to 18,500 Colombian pesos per hour, disbursed every 15 days. The retention (tax) deduction, specific to this type of contract, is about 7% of income.

FACILITIES/SUPPORT: Can assist with accommodation if necessary on a case-by-case basis. School provides paperwork for working visa; however, the teacher is required to activate the visa by travelling to a neighbouring country and going to the local consulate. This process can take up to 60 days in total from the moment the visa is requested.

RECRUITMENT: Email requests and walk-ins. An interview – possible by phone – is followed by 20-hour mandatory selection process. The process includes training, simulated class, teaching crash course and administrative instruction.

CONTACT: Juan Zamora (juan.zamora@fce.edu.co).

FLYING COWS

The Hive, Nottingham Trent University, Nottingham NG1 4BU, UK

0115 824 0824

placement@flying-cows.com

www.flying-cows.com

NUMBER OF TEACHERS: Up to 50 volunteer teachers per intake, e.g. from late July, for Ministry of Education programme.

PREFERENCE OF NATIONALITY: Mostly British although can be any nationality provided they have a C1 level of English, i.e. with 'effective operational proficiency'.

QUALIFICATIONS: Having a TESOL certificate assists placement but is not essential. Experience of travelling in South America is valued.

CONDITIONS OF EMPLOYMENT: Contracts are for one or two semesters (5 or 11 months) to work in state schools.

SALARY: 1,500,000 pesos per month.

FACILITIES/SUPPORT: School arranges and pays for the accommodation for first month, but after that teachers are independent. Visas are arranged.

RECRUITMENT: Ministry asks for a $400 refundable deposit against completing the programme.

CONTACT: Amanda Middlecote, Director.

FUNDACION EDUCATIVA PERSONAL GROWTH

Transversal 25 No 53C-15 Bogotá

+57 1 300 4320

info@pgrowth.com; academicdirection@pgrowth.com

www.pgrowth.com; www.teachincolombia.wordpress.com

Private international organisation with headquarters in the Cayman Islands. Bilingual schools in Bogotá, Medellin, Cali, Barranquilla, etc.

NUMBER OF TEACHERS: 45.

PREFERENCE OF NATIONALITY: UK, USA, Australia, Canada and South Africa.

QUALIFICATIONS: Native speakers with or without experience. 120-hour TEFL course required. Teachers can take on-site TEFL course if needed.

CONDITIONS OF EMPLOYMENT: 1 year (February to November or August to June). 30–48 hours per week to teach one-to-one and in small groups (adults, teenagers and children). In bilingual schools hours are 6.30am-3.30pm Monday to Friday; 25 teaching hours a week.

SALARY: : 2 million pesos ($670) a month. Teachers are responsible for paying their own health insurance.

FACILITIES/SUPPORT: Accommodation assistance with choice of homestay for $250 per month to private furnished apartment for $700 (including furniture, bedding and internet connection). Work visa sponsorship with some jobs; visa can be arranged after arrival.

RECRUITMENT: Usually via Craigslist, www.teflgraduate.com etc. Local or preliminary Skype interviews essential.

If selected, candidates must give a demo class after arrival and have face-to-face interviews with Personal Growth and with the institution, and also a psychological test.

CONTACT: Sigfried Castell, International Academic Director.

INSTITUTO DE IDIOMAS (UNIVERSIDAD DEL NORTE)

Km 5 Via Pto Colombia, Barranquilla

+57 5 350 9736/359 8852

iidiomas@uninorte.edu.co

www.uninorte.edu.co

NUMBER OF TEACHERS: Around 5 a year.

PREFERENCE OF NATIONALITY: None.

QUALIFICATIONS: Master's degree in TESOL, Linguistics, Psychology, English, Elementary/Bilingual Education, or related areas. Must have certified experience teaching EFL, preferably outside the USA. Must be a native English speaker; be able to teach and evaluate students effectively; and have experience using language lab equipment.

CONDITIONS OF EMPLOYMENT: Minimum 1 year. 8 hours a day depending on classes assigned. Most likely 9am–5pm.

SALARY: Depends on qualifications. Other benefits include a living allowance of around US$200 for rent, ticket and visa-issuing costs. The university pays in Colombian pesos.

FACILITIES/SUPPORT: University recommends a rental agency and will serve as a guarantor. When teachers arrive, the university pays for a hotel for 1 week. The university also provides transport and documentation needed for the working visa.

RECRUITMENT: Via internet websites such as www.studyabroad.com. Interviews through Skype or videoconferencing are required. References are also checked.

CONTACT: Lourdes Rey Paba, Academic Coordinator (arey@uninorte.edu.co).

NATIVE TONGUE ENGLISH INSTITUTE

Cra. 4a Bis #35-05, B/ Cadiz, Ibagué, Tolima

+57 8 264 6595

infont@nativetongue.edu.co; ancusm@hotmail.com

www.nativetongue.edu.co

Canadian-owned and operated company in its 13th year that operates a school in Pereira as well.

NUMBER OF TEACHERS: 10+.

PREFERENCE OF NATIONALITY: Canadians preferred, Americans accepted.

QUALIFICATIONS: Native speaker with at least 1 year overseas teaching experience. Spanish is an asset but not necessary.

CONDITIONS OF EMPLOYMENT: 11 months. Teaching hours 28 per week.

SALARY: Approx 1.5 million–2 million Colombian pesos (from CAN$675) less deductions of about 40,000 Colombian pesos per month.

FACILITIES/SUPPORT: Assistance given with finding accommodation, guaranteeing contract and a stipend. Help given with obtaining work visa outside of Colombia.

RECRUITMENT: Via web postings. Phone interviews acceptable. Face-to-face interviews occasionally carried out in Canada.

CONTACT: Shawn Miranda, Owner & Canadian Operations (Grimsby, Ontario).

ECUADOR

Ecuador's economy has benefited since it was forced to adopt the US dollar as the national currency and it has been an oasis of political stability in the region for a long time. Teaching wages are still low, but obviously EFL teachers do not go to Ecuador to save money and it is still possible to live comfortably on the wages paid. For example, a night in a hostel costs from $8 and a tasty meal costs less than $5.

Demand for English continues to thrive, particularly for American English, in the capital, Quito, the second city, Guayaquil, and in the picturesque city and cultural centre of Cuenca in the Southern Sierra. The majority of teaching is of university students and the business community, whose classes are usually scheduled early in the morning (starting at 7am) to avoid the equatorial heat of the day and again in the late afternoon and evening. Many schools are owned and run by expatriates since there are few legal restrictions on foreigners running businesses.

BARRY O'LEARY

Barry O'Leary, on arriving in Quito, visited a tourist agency that had the addresses of all the possible academies and institutes. He started his first TEFL job-hunt armed only with a basic TEFL certificate and speaking very little Spanish. As luck would have it he found two jobs in 24 hours just by walking round the city with copies of his CV.

I can still remember the buzz I felt when José, my first employer, said 'Yeah we're looking for someone to start next week.' I couldn't quite believe it. With this institute there wasn't really a formal interview or application process. With another school I had a basic interview to make sure I could speak and wasn't a monster; they didn't even ask for my TEFL certificate. In Ecuador everyone I knew was working without a work visa. I remember being worried about telling them I was only staying for three months but they were just happy to have a native speaker teaching their students.

The teaching varied. In one school I was responsible for conversation classes. I had no guidance with the type of lessons they wanted so had to use resources from my course, the internet and my imagination. In every lesson a local teacher was there to help with any language barriers. The working conditions were very relaxed, no lesson plans or meetings, I was just given a timetable and left to get on with it. As long as the students were smiling I was seen to be a good teacher.

I was lucky enough to find an apartment with an Ecuadorian family through an advertisement in an internet café. I made enough money to pay for my rent, food and some social activities and even managed to travel a bit with my last pay packet – and the dollars went much further in Peru. The students were all great, the teenagers tending to be cheeky, a few times they changed the theme of the lessons to 'Make the teacher dance like a fool' before they did any work, but this was all part of the fun.

It was a very relaxed atmosphere most of the time. I really enjoyed working with local teachers and they were all very open and friendly and interested in my life in England, since many of them had never left Ecuador.

The highlight of Ecuador was helping my first students to prepare a presentation for the directors on their chosen topics of hooliganism, pollution and anorexia. The looks on their faces when they received their certificates were definitely worth all the hours of hard work we put in. The low point of my experience was unfortunately when I was held at knifepoint outside my house. Luckily I was not hurt and they did not steal anything but it should be known that certain areas of Quito are dangerous.

A qualified teacher can expect to earn from $400 to $800 a month, while the more prestigious institutes like the British School of Language (now affiliated to International House) pay $800–$1,200 net per month. Accommodation is harder to find in Quito than in Cuenca. Qualified TEFLers should not accept less than $6 an hour, though the private institutes that accept unqualified teachers pay accordingly less. All teachers (both contract and freelance) have taxes withdrawn at source of between 5% and 12%. Quito is not as large and daunting a city as some other South American capitals and it should be easy to meet longer-term expats who may be able to give advice on teaching. The helpful British Council will give you a list of ELT schools throughout the country and will (unofficially) indicate which offer the best teacher support and modern teaching methods and resources. One possible source of information is the South American Explorers clubhouse (membership costs $60). In Quito the Club is at Mariana de Jesus Oe 3-32 y Ulloa. It includes language schools in Ecuador on its database and has a useful noticeboard.

One of the most exotic locations for teaching is the Galapagos Islands. The Galapagos Language Academy which teaches Spanish to foreigners has been hiring native English teachers for the past few years. Qualified EFL teachers staying for four months are paid about $650 a month in addition to free accommodation and health insurance (www.galapagosla.com).

That salary is about twice what one recent teacher in Cuenca was paid. **Davinna Artibey** from Oregon was all set to spend two years as a TEFL volunteer in Nicaragua. However, the pre-departure experience for her Peace Corps assignment became so frustrating that she decided to pull out; they kept asking for more and more medical checks beyond the initial physical exam (which she had passed with flying colours), and these were expensive and using up all her paid leave. Instead, she went to Ecuador on her own, got a CELTA in Montañita followed by a nine-month contract position with CEDEI in Cuenca (see entry).

My employer was the largest employer of English teachers in Cuenca, a non-profit called CEDEI. There are usually about 40 English teachers on staff at any given time doing nine-month contracts that start in September, January and April. The pay was really low because all teachers are considered volunteers who receive a stipend. I earned about $350 per month, which wasn't enough to live on. In my estimate, to get by in Cuenca, around $700 to $800 per month would have been necessary; though some colleagues figured out how to make ends meet – they had multiple roommates, shopped only at outdooor markets, rarely ate out, and so on. One thing we teachers never understood was why it was that the students paid quite a bit for courses – over $300 for a ten-week course – yet somehow the institute had non-profit status and paid its teachers such a low amount. Our students were actually children of some of the wealthier families in Cuenca. One thing CEDEI was really good at was professional development of its trainers. I learned and grew professionally from the ongoing workshops provided. I absolutely loved living in Cuenca; it's a gorgeous, walkable city with a lot to do and very comfortable weather.

As throughout the continent, charitable schools for children can always use voluntary help. The department of education in the country's poorest province runs a free volunteering scheme for native speakers with a basic knowledge of Spanish to teach in primary schools. If you want to spend at least three months between September and June in the Chimborazo region in the Andes, the poorest province in the country, go to http://ecuador.teach-english-volunteer.com for details. Through the Arajuno Road Project (see entry), volunteers are given the opportunity to work and teach in schools in the Amazon jungle of Central Ecuador.

RED TAPE

Technically you shouldn't work on a tourist visa but there is little control. Britons and Americans can stay 90 days. If possible, teachers should get a 12-IX non-immigrant visa (*actos de comercio*) in their country of origin for stays of three to six months (fee $230), which can be extended by visiting a neighbouring country, usually Colombia. Most employers will help teachers who commit themselves for a reasonable stay to obtain an Intercultural visa (Category 12-VIII), valid for a year. The requirements are as follows: a notarised copy of a police report, doctor's certificate (including HIV test) and birth certificate, letter of invitation and various other documents from an Ecuadorian employer, letter of financial support from a backer/inviter and so on. The visa application fee is $50 plus the visa itself costs $400; some schools will partly reimburse this amount. The Centro de Educación Continua in Quito and CEDEI in Cuenca (see entries) both contract instructors as Cultural Exchange volunteers. For a proper teacher's work permit, a degree in English or Education plus a TEFL Certificate qualification are required.

LIST OF EMPLOYERS

ARAJUNO ROAD PROJECT
Casilla 16-01-803, El Puyo, Pastaza
 +593 99 851 1638; UK: +44 1832 275038
 info@arajunoroadproject.org
www.arajunoroadproject.org

The Arajuno Road Project supports children and their families by providing quality English instruction, improving the infrastructure and environment of their schools and working on community development and conservation programmes in the Ecuadorian Amazon. Managed by the Amazon Language & Conservation Exchange, based in El Puyo.

NUMBER OF TEACHERS: 2 Teaching Coordinator positions, 6 Teaching Volunteer positions and interns are accepted on a case-by-case basis.

PREFERENCE OF NATIONALITY: All nationalities encouraged to apply; however, all teachers must be proficient in English.

QUALIFICATIONS: Anyone over the age of 18 and in good physical/mental health is welcome to become a Teaching Volunteer. Teaching Coordinators must have a minimum of 1 year's work experience and must be bilingual in English and Spanish. It is highly preferred that applicants have previous experience working with children, working internationally, teaching and have a TESOL/TEFOL certificate. In addition, applicants should have excellent organisational skills, communication skills and people skills. Applicants should have the ability to adapt to diverse situations and be tolerant, patient and understanding.

CONDITIONS OF EMPLOYMENT: Minimum stay 4 weeks during school year (September to June), 10 weeks for coordinators. The schools run from 7.30am to 12.30pm Monday–Friday, including approximately 4 hours of English instruction. In addition, teachers travel up to 45 minutes to reach the schools. Teachers are also welcome to participate in non-formal English instruction in the afternoons and run cultural exchange activities as time and interest permit.

SALARY: None. Teaching Volunteers pay an at-cost placement fee and weekly fee covering food, housing, materials and support: $640 for first month, $135 per week thereafter.

FACILITIES/SUPPORT: All teachers stay at the project's volunteer house, unless a host family is requested. No need for work permits; volunteers enter Ecuador with an automatic 90-day tourist visa, which can be renewed if needed.

RECRUITMENT: Via personal recommendations, social media/internet (e.g. idealist.org) and partner volunteer organisations.

CONTACT: Laura Hepting, MSc, Director, Amazon Language & Conservation Exchange (laura.hepting@gmail.com).

CEDEI SCHOOL CUENCA

Gran Colombia 11-02 y General Torres Esq, Cuenca

+593 7 283 9003

jalban@cedei.org; english@cedei.org

www.cedei.org

NUMBER OF TEACHERS: 9.

PREFERENCE OF NATIONALITY: None.

QUALIFICATIONS: Degree, TEFL Certificate, teaching experience.

CONDITIONS OF EMPLOYMENT: Minimum 9 months from the last week of September, although vacancies crop up in January and April. 20–25 hours a week with opportunities for extra tutoring and conversation classes. Usual hours between 7.30am and 1.45pm, teaching children from pre-school to 9th grade.

SALARY: $6.75 per hour ($7.75 on Saturdays).

FACILITIES/SUPPORT: 3-day pre-service orientation. Teachers are responsible for their own accommodation. School assists in obtaining an intercultural visa (not a work visa); teachers pay costs for the first year. Free Spanish and salsa classes.

RECRUITMENT: Through posts on websites and links with universities. Interviews by Skype/telephone.

CONTACT: Jessica Alban, International Programmes Coordinator.

CENTRO DE EDUCACIÓN CONTINUA DE LA ESCUELA POLITECNICA NACIONAL

Edificio Araucaria, Baquedano 222 y Reina Victoria, Quito

+593 22 500068

henryguygooch@yahoo.com ;linguist@cec-epn.edu.ec

www.cec-epn.edu.ec

NUMBER OF TEACHERS: 160+.

PREFERENCE OF NATIONALITY: American, Canadian and British.

QUALIFICATIONS: BA in English, Applied Linguistics, TEFL, Drama, International Studies or a related field. TEFL certificate, 1-year experience.

CONDITIONS OF EMPLOYMENT: Minimum 1 year (40 weeks of teaching). 6 hours per day.

SALARY: Volunteers are not paid a salary, but are provided with a monthly subsistence allowance of $720–$885 net as required by law and written agreement.

FACILITIES/SUPPORT: Teachers must find their own accommodation. Instructors are contracted as Cultural Exchange Volunteers under the agreement the University maintains with the Ecuadorian Ministerio de Relaciones Exteriores.

RECRUITMENT: Word of mouth. Telephone interviews.

CONTACT: Henry Guy Gooch, Director of Linguistics and Cultural Exchanges.

CENTRO DE ESTUDIOS INTERAMERICANOS/CEDEI

Casilla 597, Cuenca

+593 7 283 9003

English@cedei.org

www.english.cedei.org

A non-profit institution dedicated to the study of American languages and cultures.

NUMBER OF TEACHERS: 50.

PREFERENCE OF NATIONALITY: Native English speakers.

QUALIFICATIONS: Minimum university degree in related field and TEFL/CELTA/TESOL certificate or university degree in TESL/TEFL. Experience in teaching EFL/ESL.

CONDITIONS OF EMPLOYMENT: Minimum 9-month stay, preference given to year-long commitments. Courses run from January to mid-March, early April to early June, end of June to early September and mid-September to the beginning of December. Teachers teach on average 20 hours per week. Most classes meet Monday to Thursday and there are also Saturday Intensives. To teach both classroom courses and individuals. In addition to classroom classes, teachers may elect to give tutorials and conversation classes to supplement their income.

SALARY: Approximately $325 per teenage/adult course, $260 per children's course, and $300 per Saturday class. Courses are 40–50 hours long and teachers are given 3–4 courses per term (10 weeks). This is a high salary by Ecuadorian standards.

FACILITIES: Apartments are very reasonably priced. Cost of living is low. Average rent for a shared apartment/house is between $90 and $140 per month. Free Spanish classes, dance classes and internet access for teachers. Beautiful school building. Very charming city in an Andean setting. Extensive help given with visas.

RECRUITMENT: Via the website www.cedei.org.

CONTACT: Elisabeth Rodas, Academic Director of English Programs (erodas@cedei.org).

EF SCHOOL OF ENGLISH – QUITO

Av. Amazonas N37-102 y Naciones Unidas, Edificio Puerta del Sol, Mezzanine, Quito

+593 2 2265 005

www.ef.com.ec

NUMBER OF TEACHERS: 20.

PREFERENCE OF NATIONALITY: None; school aims to have a mixture of nationalities and accents.

QUALIFICATIONS: CELTA or equivalent teaching qualification.

CONDITIONS OF EMPLOYMENT: 6 months to 2 years. 35 hours per week.

SALARY: Average $700+ per month after deductions of 12% for tax.

FACILITIES/SUPPORT: Accommodation arranged in local hostel, EF residence or with host family. Pre-arrival pack contains detailed information about the options. Free transfers on arrival.

RECRUITMENT: Via internet or worldwide network of EF schools. Teachers also recruited locally. For senior positions and long-term posts applicants may be asked to present themselves at a local EF centre.

FINE-TUNED ENGLISH LANGUAGE INSTITUTE
Macara entre Miguel Riofrio y Rocafuerte, Loja
+593 2578899/2563224
venalfine@finetunedenglish.edu.ec
www.finetunedenglish.edu.ec

NUMBER OF TEACHERS: 10.

PREFERENCE OF NATIONALITY: None.

QUALIFICATIONS: Minimum CELTA or equivalent.

CONDITIONS OF EMPLOYMENT: Minimum one semester. Minimum 20 hours per week, Monday-Friday.

SALARY: $6 per hour.

FACILITIES/SUPPORT: Institute finds temporary accommodation for teachers when they arrive, but does not offer financial assistance.

RECRUITMENT: Via email and Skype interviews.

IH GUAYAQUIL
Kennedy Norte, Av. Luis Orrantia Mz 110 Solar 7, Guayaquil, Ecuador
+593 4 2684404
t.bolton@ihecuador.com
www.bsl.com.ec

PREFERENCE OF NATIONALITY: None but must be native speakers or non-native speakers with a CPE certificate or valid IELTS certificate at 9.0.

QUALIFICATIONS: CELTA/TrinityCert, DELTA/TrinityDip. Minimum 1 year experience. Degree required for visa purposes.

CONDITIONS OF EMPLOYMENT: Minimum 12 months; 1 or 2 year contracts. 20 contact hours per week, 80 per calendar month. Extra hours paid (excluding prep time, admin, marking and professional development). Split shifts including Saturdays.

SALARY: Start at US$880 (net) and reach US$1,440 per month, depending on qualifications and experience.

FACILITIES/SUPPORT: Logistical support given on arrival. School obtains a non-immigrant visa before 3-month tourist stamp expires. IH Ecuador does most of the bureaucratic leg work. Professional development programme and subsidised Spanish classes.

RECRUITMENT: Via www.tefl.com and www.ihworld.com. Skype interviews. Not financially, though we do offer logistical support before and upon arrival.

CONTACT: Tom Bolton, Director of Studies, IH Guayaquil.

INLINGUA
Sebastian Quintero N37–12 y Jose Correa (behind the Atahualpa Olympic Stadium), Quito
+593 2 245 8763
inlinguaquito@inlingua.com; academic@inlingua.com
www.inlingua.com.ec

NUMBER OF TEACHERS: 25–30 mainly part-time.

PREFERENCE OF NATIONALITY: None, but native English speakers only.

QUALIFICATIONS: Recognised TEFL/CELTA and/or teaching experience (particularly Business English and/or TOEFL preparation).

CONDITIONS OF EMPLOYMENT: Minimum 6-month part-time/full-time contracts. Hours vary. Full-time position totals 20/25 hours per week.

SALARY: $6.15–$7.35 per hour depending on experience and/or qualifications.

FACILITIES/SUPPORT: Full training on Inlingua's international programme and teaching resources provided. Spanish classes and health insurance offered at discounted rates for teachers.

RECRUITMENT: Applications by email, interview and induction in Quito upon arrival.

CONTACT: David Montenegro, Academic Coordinator (academic@inlingua.com).

MEXICO

The lure of the USA and its language is very strong in Mexico. The frenzy of American investment in Mexico after the North American Free Trade Agreement (NAFTA) saw a huge upswing in both the demand for English by businesses and the resources to pay for it. That boom is now over, but the market for English is still enormous in universities, in business, almost everywhere. Proximity to the USA and a tendency towards what Australians call the cultural cringe (in Mexico called Malinchism after the lover of Cortès who betrayed her people) means that there will always be an unquenchable thirst for English taught by native English speakers in Mexico. Foreign teachers are automatically respected and are often promoted almost immediately.

Companies of all descriptions provide language classes for their employees, especially in the early mornings and evenings (but seldom on weekends or even Fridays). **Roberta Wedge** even managed to persuade a '*sleek head honcho in the state ferry service*' that he needed private tuition during his usual siesta time and that busy executives and other interested employees of a local company needed English lessons at the same time of day. (In fact, the siesta is dying out in these more striving times.)

It is not surprising that enrolment in English courses is booming, when some employees have been threatened with dismissal unless they master some English. A vet going to Dubai, a stockbroker doing deals with the New York Stock Exchange, housewives who have to go to parties with their executive husbands, teenagers with exam worries, all are keen to improve their English. After each six-year presidential term of office, the top layers of management in companies (especially oil and banking) are replaced by new staff that need new training, especially English. Elections always boost the demand for English not only in Mexico City and the border cities to which US industries looking for cheap labour have relocated, but throughout the country, including the Yucatan Peninsula and other unlikely places.

The British Council in Mexico City can provide the addresses of the 25 or so language centres attached to state universities. The British Council runs an English teaching centre in Mexico City; see www.britishcouncil.org.mx which mentions ongoing full-time and part-time teaching vacancies; applications to be sent to: HR.Mexico@britishcouncil.org. The long established Anglo-Mexican Foundation (www.tamf.org.mx) hires ESL teachers at the flagship Churchill School in Mexico City, as well as other 'Anglos' in Toluca and elsewhere. The monthly salary for working a 45-hour week at these venerable schools is 16,000 pesos, well above average for Mexico. Mexican-American Bi-National Centers (www.relacionesculturales.edu.mx) employ scores of native English speakers, mostly on a local basis. The school year starts in early August and lasts for 11 months. The Office of English Language Programs of the US State Department manages English teaching programmes in Mexico (and Central America) from its offices in Mexico City (Liverpool 31, Colonia Juarez; relomexico@state.gov).

With a TEFL qualification and a year's experience in Indonesia, Canadian **Bruce Clarke** was in a good position to make use of the Mexico's job postings on www.eslcafe.com, where he learned of the vacancy at a state university in Oaxaca that he went on to fill. He reports that his students were pleasant and fun loving, though not particularly energetic or keen to complete homework. A further possibility is to work at English-medium schools modelled either on the American or British system. Many of these advertise internationally for certified teachers or recruit through recruiting fairs but, as in Chile, Peru and elsewhere, some are willing to interview native English speakers locally to work in the EFL department. Without a TEFL background or at least a solid university education you are unlikely to break into any of these more upmarket institutes. An online recruitment agency Teachers Latin America based in Mexico City (www.teachers-latin-america.com) connects teachers with schools. Candidate teachers can upload their applications to the site, and scour the jobs posted.

CONDITIONS OF WORK

THE PRIVATE SECTOR

A host of private institutes supplies language training to business, either on their own premises or in-company. The norm is for teachers to freelance and work for a combination of companies. There are also full-time school-based jobs with teaching companies such as Harmon Hall and Interlingua, which have a national network of branches; the latter's website has an online application procedure (www.interlingua.com.mx) and seems to ask only that candidates speak English fluently, have a service-oriented personality and full-time availability; no teaching experience is required. A typical local branch of Harmon Hall might employ about 20 teachers, mainly of American English (as in Oaxaca). Hours can be unpredictable and a lot of time is taken up travelling from office to office. Getting three hours of work a day (early morning and early evening) is easy. Anything above that is much trickier. Freelance teachers must be prepared for frequent holidays cutting into earnings. Normally institutes do not pay for public holidays, sickness or annual leave. For example attendance goes into a sharp decline after Independence Day on 20 November, in the month leading up to Christmas, and there are no classes over Easter. Most courses run for three months and there may be a lapse of one or two weeks before another starts. Usually freelancers are paid cash in hand with no deductions for tax.

The spectrum of institutes varies enormously. At one extreme there is the employer who pays the equivalent of $5 an hour, but never on time, and who employs only Mexicans with poor English or native English speakers who have just arrived with their backpacks and no interest in or knowledge of teaching. The top of the range pays $15–$20 an hour, offers free training and gives contracts that aren't cancelled. These institutes are of course a lot more choosy about their teachers. Whereas a few companies want to control their teachers completely and send inspectors into classes, most leave teachers alone as long as the clients are happy. The typical institute consists only of four people: the owner who gets the contracts, a teacher coordinator, a secretary and an office boy.

While a TEFL qualification is an advantage, few employers are concerned about whether it is from a 130-hour or a 30-hour course. Business and financial experience is also beneficial, possibly more than a university degree. Patience and an ability to make a class interesting are the two key qualities that many employers are looking for. As a boss of **Nick Wilson** said: '*The most important thing is that the students enjoy their classes and think that they are learning English; don't just teach or we'll lose customers.*' Word of mouth recommendations are important in Mexican culture, and jobs are seldom filled by emailed applications.

Michael Tunison contacted half a dozen teaching organisations from the *Yellow Pages* and was interviewed by Berlitz and Harmon Hall (www.harmonhall.com/bolsa-de-trabajo). Both offered tentative positions, based more on his native English speaking than his degree and journalism background. In 2014, Harmon Hall were offering 80–90 pesos an hour, though one teacher reported recently he was paid about half that if you considered all the extra hours for planning meetings, etc. that teachers are obliged to attend. Legitimate companies will only hire teachers with working papers. Other international language companies represented in Mexico include International House, with schools in eight cities, and Wall Street English (see entry). Try also Inter-Act Speaking Centers (www.interactmexico.com) with four branches in the Distrito Federal (DF), i.e. Greater Mexico City.

Guadalajara and resorts such as Puerto Vallarta, Cancun, Acapulco and Mazatlan are places where a great many locals need to master English before they can be employed in the booming tourist industry. However, beach resorts are such popular destinations for so many foreigners and expats that it is an employers' market and much harder to find work than in the inland states where the vast majority of the population lives and receives an education.

One way around the glut in coastal areas would be to join an innovative programme run by VolunQuest in Isla Mujeres and Playa del Carmen near Cancun. It offers a TEFL training course (for $2,281 including accommodation) followed by placement in public schools and summer camps in the state of Quintana Roo.

Occasionally VolunQuest can place interns in these same positions even if they haven't done the training course locally; details are at www.volunquest.com.

American **Bradwell Jackson** had a go at funding his round-the-world travels by teaching English:

> *After reading* **Work Your Way Around the World,** *I made the decision to quit my job, leave my home, give most of my belongings to charity and sell my car, so that I could wander the earth freely. I wondered if it was really possible to get a job teaching English so easily. Well I found out that it is. I was sitting at a metro stop in Mexico City, trying to figure out what school to go to for my first planned job enquiry. After I decided that the particular school I had in mind was too far away, I looked up and saw an English school right across the street. Providence, I thought. I was right. I sauntered on upstairs, cheerfully asked if they needed an English teacher, and about an hour and a half later, I was told when to start my training. It really was that easy.*
>
> *I teach a range of students, including some teenage girls. For them I came up with the ideas of asking them to talk about a popular soap opera and to tell me about the stars in a teen magazine. I have also asked my students about popular Spanish songs and asked them to translate them into English for me.*
>
> *Mexico is the first country I have visited on my world wanderings and I can't believe how lucky I've been. The people are top-notch and I certainly must count my blessings.*

A couple of years later, Bradwell returned to Mexico after teaching elsewhere and then obtaining his CELTA in London. While in the tourist town of Oaxaca, he decided to investigate teaching possibilities. The Facultad de Idiomas of the local university Benito Juárez de Oaxaca employed 90 part-time teachers, five of whom were foreigners. All were paid less than $3 an hour.

WORKING FOR YOURSELF

Private lessons are in great demand, and may be given informally in exchange for board and lodging. But it is also possible to teach on a more business-like footing. With so many clients seeking one-to-one tuition through institutes, it is worth considering setting up as an independent tutor and offering private lessons at a rate that undercuts the institutes. In the capital, a standard rate to charge students would be 200–250 pesos an hour for a one-to-one. If you find clients who want two two-hour classes a week, you can do well. You can find students through the small ads on craigslist or segundamano. Teachers who are tempted to poach students from the organisation they work for should bear in mind that employers who find out have been known to set the immigration department on errant teachers. However, it is legitimate to advertise yourself in the press and distribute printed business cards. Teaching in companies sometimes produces lucrative spin-offs in the field of translation and editing documents in English.

REGULATIONS

The red tape situation in Mexico is difficult, although it is virtually unheard of for an English teacher working on a tourist visa to be deported. Officially, visitors are not allowed to work or engage in any remunerative activity during a temporary visit. British and American citizens can stay in Mexico for 180 days without a visa as a tourist. Some employers may be willing to help you apply for a *Residente Temporal – No Inmigrante* visa (formerly the FM3) that will be valid for one year and renewable thereafter; however, it must be applied for outside Mexico. As mentioned, established schools are not usually willing to contract people without an employment visa, unlike private institutes. Private employers do not want to become involved with the hassle and expense of applying for teachers who are unlikely to stay long-term. Some deduct a small tax (*recibos*), which makes the teacher semi-official. Among the required documents are a CV in Spanish, plus transcripts, diploma or certificate from your university, apostilled by the Mexican Consul or, in the US, by the Secretary of State in the state where you studied.

LIST OF EMPLOYERS

AHPLA INSTITUTE

Juan Escutia No. 97, Colonia Condesa, CP 06140 DF

+52 55 869016

Kallen@ahpla.com

www.ahpla.com.mx

QUALIFICATIONS: Educated, flexible, willing to work with a team and travel. People skills and personality are a must.

CONDITIONS OF EMPLOYMENT: Minimum period of work 6 months. To work 7am–9am and 5pm–7pm.

FACILITIES/SUPPORT: No help with accommodation or flights, but assistance given with working papers after teacher has shown commitment to the institute. Compulsory induction and training.

CONTACT: Karen Julie Allen, Operations Manager.

BERLITZ (CENTRO INTEGRAL DE IDIOMAS)

Av. Benito Juarez No. 2005, Local Sub Ancla M Plaza Sendero, Colonia Estrella de Oriente, San Luis Potosí CP 78396

+52 444 166 3570

salvador.estrada@berlitzmexico.com

www.berlitzslp.com.mx

NUMBER OF TEACHERS: 20; also for centres in Saltillo, Aguascalientes and Tijuana.

PREFERENCE OF NATIONALITY: None.

QUALIFICATIONS: TESOL, TEFL, CELTA certification or a university degree in Education.

CONDITIONS OF EMPLOYMENT: Standard 1-year contract. Hours mainly 7am–9am and 6pm–9pm, Monday–Friday; 8am–2pm Saturday.

SALARY: 60–80 pesos per 45–60 minutes of class.

FACILITIES/SUPPORT: School ensures the applicant has a place to stay on arrival. First month housing covered up to 1,600 pesos.

RECRUITMENT: By email and telephone interview.

CONTACT: Salvador Estrada, Regional Academic Coordinator; Lance Fajardo, SLP Academic Coordinator (lance.fajardo@berlitzmexico.com).

CARLIE ENGLISH

Plaza San Juan, Planta Alta Local 43-45, Av. Río Moctezuma #266, Col. San Cayetano, San Juan del Río, Queretaro

+52 427 264 0931

carlieenglishsjr@hotmail.com

www.facebook.com/carlieenglishsjr

NUMBER OF TEACHERS: 4–6.

PREFERENCE OF NATIONALITY: English speaking countries: UK, USA, Canada, Australia.

QUALIFICATIONS: Degree-level education is preferred; TEFL/CELTA/TESOL certificate is essential. Previous experience preferred but not required.

CONDITIONS OF EMPLOYMENT: 6 months to 1 year. 20–25 teaching hours per week.

SALARY: 105 pesos per hour. Rate of tax is 16%.

FACILITIES/SUPPORT: Assistance given with finding accommodation. Proof of employment and references for rental contracts can be given. School can provide all necessary paperwork for work permit application. Initial induction and training period of about a week. Ongoing training is provided through a peer observation programme and periodic group training sessions. Regular team excursions and social events and activities. Opportunity to help with voluntary work carried out by the school providing free courses to children from rural/marginalised areas.

RECRUITMENT: Online recruitment mainly.

CONTACT: Carlie Flack, Director.

CULTURLINGUA JALISCO

Reforma #31, Col. Centro, Tlaquepaque, Jalisco

+52 33 3344 9139

info@culturlinguagdl.com

www.culturlinguagdl.com/teaching

Franchise of the Culturlingua group of 5 schools in the states of Michoacán and Jalisco in the Highlands of Mexico; the one in Zamora was recently advertising for teachers as well.

NUMBER OF TEACHERS: 4.

PREFERENCE OF NATIONALITY: Native English speakers.

QUALIFICATIONS: TEFL/TESOL certificate is essential and one year of teaching experience.

CONDITIONS OF EMPLOYMENT: Standard length of contract is 15 weeks with 30–32 working hours per week.

SALARY: 5,500 pesos per month.

FACILITIES/SUPPORT: Fully furnished accommodation is provided for teachers and included in the salary.

RECRUITMENT: Via internet sites such as Dave's ESL Cafe. Candidates successful with their CVs and cover letters are asked to submit a sample lesson plan and then a telephone interview will be organised.

CONTACT: Greg Davies, Owner; Nancy Garcia), Teacher Coordinator at Culturlingua Los Reyes (nancygarcia@culturlingua.com.mx).

DUNHAM INSTITUTE
Avenida Coronel Urbina 30, Chiapa de Corzo, Chiapas 29160
+52 961 616 1498/0398
academic-coordinator@dunhaminstitute.com
www.dunhaminstitute.com

NUMBER OF TEACHERS: 4.
PREFERENCE OF NATIONALITY: Native English speaker.
QUALIFICATIONS: ESL certified.
CONDITIONS OF EMPLOYMENT: Minimum 5 months from end of August or February. 3.5 hours in the afternoon and study Spanish in the mornings, Monday to Friday only.
SALARY: None. Exchange of English teaching for free accommodation with a local family and 2 hours of Spanish tuition a day.
FACILITIES/SUPPORT: Work permits not required. Homestay accommodation provided. 2 hours' Spanish instruction per day.
RECRUITMENT: Interviews are necessary.
CONTACT: Joanna Robinson, Director.

GLACE LANGUAGE CENTER
Francisco I. Madero 335, Zona Centro, San Luis Potosí CP 78000
+52 444 8145526
contacto@glc.edu.mx
www.glc.edu.mx

PREFERENCE OF NATIONALITY: All native speakers from English-speaking countries welcome.
QUALIFICATIONS: BA preferred. If the degree is not related to language teaching, must have TKT (Teaching Knowledge Test) core modules and at least 3 years' experience in a regular school and/or language school.
CONDITIONS OF EMPLOYMENT: Minimum stay: 2 years. Teachers sign contracts for each class with stated number of hours. Minimum 20 hours per week for teachers with full-time availability.
SALARY: 85–100 pesos per class, so monthly income can range from 6,800 to 8,000 pesos. Taxes are 8%–12%; no social security.
FACILITIES/SUPPORT: Assistance given in finding a reasonably priced place to live within walking distance of work.
RECRUITMENT: Interviews essential, at the centre or online.
CONTACT: Elvia Rico Zermeño, Academic Director.

HELP! HESLINGTON LANGUAGE PROGRAM
2 Norte 1210 Colonia Jacarandas Tehuacan, Puebla
+52 238 384 6929
instituto_heslington@hotmail.com
www.helpenglishmexico.org

NUMBER OF TEACHERS: 20 per semester, including paid teachers, volunteers and interns.
PREFERENCE OF NATIONALITY: None.
QUALIFICATIONS: TESOL/TEFL/CELTA Certification – no experience abroad required.
CONDITIONS OF EMPLOYMENT: 4 months: August–December, January–April or May–August. 25 hours per week, Monday–Friday only.
SALARY: Monthly stipend of 4,000 pesos ($200) plus free housing (rent and utilities paid by school).
FACILITIES/SUPPORT: Free housing or host family arrangement. Spanish workshop for 3 hours a week
RECRUITMENT: Via internet adverts (e.g. www.tefl.com and www.eslteachersboard.com) and word of mouth. Interviews carried out by Skype.
CONTACT: Matthew Poy (tehuacansupervisor@gmail.com); Rachel Heslington, Director of Volunteer Services (r.heslington@helpenglish.org).

ROBINSON SCHOOL
Blvd. Everardo Marquez #200 Piso 2, Colonia Cuesco, Pachuca, Hidalgo 42060
+771 719 2247
info@therobinsonschool.com
www.therobinsonschool.com

NUMBER OF TEACHERS: 3, also for branch in Tulancingo.
PREFERENCE OF NATIONALITY: None, must be native English speaker.
QUALIFICATIONS: ESL certificate preferred. Must be enthusiastic and politically and culturally open minded.
CONDITIONS OF EMPLOYMENT: 10 weeks. Individual schedules vary. Classes begin at 7am and finish at 8.30pm.
SALARY: 2,000 pesos per week (net).
FACILITIES/SUPPORT: Housing and/or furnishings can be provided and monthly rent deducted from pay cheque. Teachers will be assisted in acquiring necessary documents.
RECRUITMENT: Internet, word of mouth, newspaper adverts. Interviews are sometimes carried out in person in the USA but mostly conducted by phone.
CONTACT: Luke Robinson, CEO and Head of Recruitment.

UNIVERSIDAD DEL MAR

Campuses in Puerto Angel, Huatulco, Oaxaca de Juárez and Juquila

www.umar.mx

NUMBER OF TEACHERS: 16.

PREFERENCE OF NATIONALITY: None but must be native English speaker.

QUALIFICATIONS: Degree-level education, TEFL teaching qualification (or an MA in TOEFL or related field) plus at least 1 year's experience working in a foreign country.

CONDITIONS OF EMPLOYMENT: 1-year commitment. Teaching hours are 8am–1pm and 4pm–7pm, Monday to Friday.

SALARY: 12,000–14,000 pesos net (more for candidates with an MA in TEFL or Education plus 2 years' experience), plus free medical service, Christmas and vacation bonuses, savings scheme and monthly shopping vouchers. Monthly deduction of about 2,000 pesos for tax and social security.

FACILITIES/SUPPORT: Teachers must arrange their own accommodation. University files paperwork for work permit on arrival; processing can take up to 3 weeks and teachers cannot start work without work visa.

RECRUITMENT: Most via internet ads and emailed CVs. Telephone interviews essential; short-listed candidates are telephoned.

CONTACT: Director of Languages.

WALL STREET ENGLISH MEXICO

Florencia 53 Col. Juárez, DF 06600

+52 55 5533 8997/8

zonarosa@wse.com.mx

www.wallstreetenglish.com.mx

NUMBER OF TEACHERS: 8 for 4 branches.

PREFERENCE OF NATIONALITY: None.

QUALIFICATIONS: CELTA or equivalent with a bachelor's degree with 1 year's experience preferably.

CONDITIONS OF EMPLOYMENT: 1 year. Full-time schedule, 35 teaching hours per week plus 5 hours every other Saturday.

SALARY: 14,000 pesos per month (gross), 12,100 pesos (net).

FACILITIES/SUPPORT: Wall Street helps teachers find an apartment near the branch where they will be working. Assistance given in obtaining a work visa. Teachers pay for the process but will be reimbursed after completing a year's contract.

RECRUITMENT: Via websites for ESL/EFL teachers. Candidates do 2 or 3 interviews with a demo lesson required in the second interview. Interviews are via Skype or Google Talk services.

PERU

Lima has in the past been considered one of the most stressful and dangerous South American cities in which to live; however, threats from guerrilla groups are a thing of the past and Peru has returned to the mainstream of destinations for English-language teachers. Modest wages and the difficulty of obtaining working papers mean that few professional teachers can be attracted to the private EFL sector. For those who are, it may be worth contacting the 11 Lima branches of the British-Peruvian Cultural Association, known familiarly as Britanico; recruitment for its 11 centres in Lima is carried out centrally (sgomez@britanico.edu.pe).

Yet the range of opportunities in Lima is enormous and the stampede to learn English is unstoppable. Many company employees have been told by their bosses to learn English or risk demotion. Some employers organise a course at their place of work, but most expect their staff to fix up private lessons, making the freelance market very promising at the moment. In-company training courses in all industries are often offered in English, so knowledge of the language is becoming essential for all ambitious Peruvians. The Peruvian economy is not in dire straits at present, as evidenced by the stability of its currency, the new sol.

A useful online resource is the LA Joblist (http://thelajoblist.blogspot.co.uk/2009/12/peru.html), although it is no longer maintained. The EL teacher who created the job list (as well as the blog http://theultimateperulist.blogspot.co.uk/2008/11/1a-finding-teaching-jobs.html) stresses how much easier it is to find teaching hours once you are in Peru than when you're trying to fix up a job from home.

Many temporary visitors to Peru who lack a TEFL background end up doing some English teaching once they have established a base in the capital, usually earning about $5 an hour, more than three times the Peruvian minimum wage which is just over 4 soles an hour or 850 soles/$250 a month. Some employers offer a free or subsidised training course to new potential recruits, at which native English speakers usually excel over the locals, whose knowledge of English is often very weak. For classified job adverts, search www.aptitus.com/buscar-trabajo-en-peru.

Ruain Burrows from Ireland turned himself from a long-term backpacker into a teacher in Lima working for Business Links (www.bl.com.pe) and English Life (see entry):

> ***I had been travelling around South America for the best part of two years and was, inevitably, running out of money. I had just enough for a flight home, yet wasn't ready to go home, so decided to invest in a 120-hour online TEFL course (with i-to-i.com) after convincing myself that it was an easy way to continue living my dream. Three hundred US dollars and five weeks later, certificate in hand, I was ready to dive into the word of TEFLing. The application process was as simple as typing up a cover email, attaching my CV along with my new qualification and sending it out in bulk to all the institutes, colleges and temping agencies with which Google provided me. The interviews were really easy, the main requisite being fluency in English (being Irish, I just squeezed into this category) and being in possession of some sort of TEFL certificate. The recurring question was concerning my availability, because apparently a lot of foreigners pass through the doors of the institutes just looking for short-term work to fund a flight home or to fill a gap between stages in their lives and they were sick of this. Fortunately they didn't expect teaching experience because, prior to the application/interview stage, my teaching experience had been restricted to teaching my dog how to play fetch. Also, the institutes in Lima generally don't insist on permits or special visas but it is required if you intend on applying to the colleges or universities.***

Ruain taught as many hours as his employers were willing to assign him, and earned decent money, up to 2,500 soles a month. He found the cost of living to be relatively low, particularly since he earned free hostel accommodation by working as a barman in the evenings.

One tip he offers is never to give out your telephone number to students. When he did this to one of his female students she used him as her personal dictionary whenever she felt like it. He really enjoyed seeing the progress his students made: '*When you take on a student who can't even count to five, then watch them progress through the levels and go on to pass an exam like the IELTS or CAE, that to me is amazing.*' It is not difficult for him to identify an even better highlight, which was when he met his wife, with whom he has settled in Peru. So his summation of the experience comes as no surprise: '*The rewards of being a TEFL teacher in Peru are that the Peruvian people are amazing, the food is next to none and it's an intriguing country.*'

Plenty of opportunities exist for volunteer teachers in remote corners of the country. For example Vive Peru (www.viveperu.org) runs an English enrichment programme at public schools in the mountain village of Otuzco and on the coast at Trujillo and Pacasmayo, all in northern Peru. Fees to join the programme are $1,800 for one month, $2,600 for three months. A small family-run charity in the Andean region of Huaraz charges volunteer teachers much less: the one-off placement is $160 plus $110 per week to cover homestay expenses (www.teachhuarazperu.org).

FREELANCING

Setting up as a freelance tutor is potentially lucrative. A standard fee is $10–$20 a lesson, though this can be reduced for clients who want to book a whole course. **James Gratton** put a cheap advertisement (written in English) in the main daily, *El Comercio*, and signed up two clients. This was straightforward in his case since he was staying at his girlfriend's house, where he had free accommodation and telephone. His new students were both employees of Petro-Peru, and soon other clients contacted James for lessons. He admits that freelancers do lose out to cancellations, though some of his students willingly paid for missed lessons. Freelancing is a continual process of advertising and getting new students to replace the ones that fall by the wayside.

REGULATIONS

Peruvian work visas are very rare and most people teach as tourists. British and Irish nationals, as well as US and EU citizens, do not require tourist visas for Peru; neither do nationals from EU countries. They are allowed to stay in Peru for up to 90 days, although they are required to possess an onward/return ticket. After that it is necessary to cross the Peruvian border. One reason which many people use to extend their stay is that they have formed a romantic attachment to a local woman/man.

In his quest for a work visa, **James Gratton** gathered together all the necessary documents, including contract, notarised certificates and documents translated into Spanish. All of this cost him a lot of money and time, and he still didn't succeed. He concluded that it would be possible only if you knew someone in the immigration department who could give your application a safe passage without having to pay fines (bribes) at every stage. Making key contacts is more important than gathering documentation. Care must be taken to keep on the right side of the tax office (SUNAT), to which about 15% of earnings are supposed to be paid. Many employers pay their staff under the table, sometimes by cash, personal cheque or via a *Recibo de Honorario* from a Peruvian friend, which uses their tax details and signature to receive your money.

LIST OF EMPLOYERS

BRITTANY ENGLISH SOLUTIONS
José Bustamente y Rivero Av, EEUU, Fl.1, Arequipa
+51 54 422964
coordinacion@brittanygroup.edu.pe
www.brittanygroup.edu.pe

NUMBER OF TEACHERS: 30 for 3 branches in Arequipa. Quite a few teachers teach remotely through 3G platforms.
PREFERENCE OF NATIONALITY: British.
QUALIFICATIONS: TESOL, TEFL, CELTA.
CONDITIONS OF EMPLOYMENT: 6–12 months. Teaching hours in afternoon.
SALARY: $600 a month.
FACILITIES/SUPPORT: Assistance given to teachers with finding suitable accommodation. School hopes to be able to offer its own accommodation to teachers in the future. Help given with permits.
RECRUITMENT: Web postings. Face-to-face interview is not necessary.
CONTACT: Christian Valdivia Chavez, Executive Manager.

ENGLISH LIFE
Av Ricardo Palma 280, Interior 402, Miraflores, Lima
+51 1 446 1968
recruitment@englishlifeperu.com
www.englishlifeperu.com

NUMBER OF TEACHERS: 20 on self-employed basis (100% of staff are native speakers).
PREFERENCE OF NATIONALITY: None. School hires native English speakers only.
QUALIFICATIONS: TEFL certificate or similar, plus some experience is desirable.
CONDITIONS OF EMPLOYMENT: 6 months. Teachers are given part-time hours, on a class-by-class basis (3–15 per week).
SALARY: $8–$10 per hour.
FACILITIES/SUPPORT: No accommodation provided but advice can be given.
RECRUITMENT: People are invited for interview after submitting their CV. Interviews are essential and so applicants must be in Peru to qualify for an interview or employment.
CONTACT: Valerie Watson, General Manager and Owner.

EXTREME LEARNING CENTERS
Av Bolognesi 118, Yanahuara, Arequipa
+51 54 250596
teflperu@gmail.com
www.extreme.edu.pe; www.vialinguaperu.com

NUMBER OF TEACHERS: 28.
PREFERENCE OF NATIONALITY: USA and Canada.
QUALIFICATIONS: TEFL, TESOL or CELTA certificate from accredited course with at least 8 hours of observed student teaching practice; bachelor's degree needed and experience of teaching preferred. Candidates without experience must have excellent natural teaching ability and 'people' skills. Those who lack a certificate can take a 4-week 120-hour Via Lingua Peru course onsite for $1,550.
CONDITIONS OF EMPLOYMENT: Minimum 6 months preferred. Normal working hours 7am–9am and 5pm–9pm. Centre operates a volunteer teacher programme.
SALARY: $4–$5 per hour. Average earnings are 1,500 soles ($435) per month based on working 6 hours a day for 18 days per month.
FACILITIES/SUPPORT: Advice and contacts for accommodation given but teachers pay for their housing. Teachers come as legal TEFL interns.
RECRUITMENT: Paid ads online and university contacts in the USA. Interviews essential.
CONTACT: J. C. Larsen, BS Ed, MA Ed/TEFL, Executive Director; Lilian Frampton, Teaching Coordinator (framptonlilian@gmail.com).

INSTITUTO CULTURAL PERUANO NORTEAMERICANO
M.M.Izaga No. 807, Chiclayo
+51 74 321241
informes@icpnachi.edu.pe
www.icpnachi.edu.pe

One of 16 Bi-national Centres in Peru.
NUMBER OF TEACHERS: Fluctuating. North American students come as unpaid interns.
PREFERENCE OF NATIONALITY: American and Canadian preferred; others considered.
QUALIFICATIONS: University degree that qualifies candidate for teaching EFL/ESL. Experience not a necessity.

FACILITIES/SUPPORT: Can find apartments for teachers or arrange homestays. Help given with work permits for long-stay teachers.

RECRUITMENT: Via TESOL conferences and the internet. Interviews not essential.

MAXIMO NIVEL INTERNATIONAL PERU

Avenida El Sol 612, Cusco

+51 84 581800; +1 800 866 6358 (Florida HQ contact number)

international@maximonivel.com

www.maximonivel.com; maximoingles.com

Primarily a TEFL training provider.

NUMBER OF TEACHERS: 10–20.

PREFERENCE OF NATIONALITY: Must be native English speaker for the Native English Program.

QUALIFICATIONS: Teachers must be TEFL, TESOL or CELTA certified from a training course of at least 100 hours with a minimum of 6 hours of practical teaching. Candidates must be dedicated, professional and passionate about teaching with a self-confident personality and a good sense of humour.

CONDITIONS OF EMPLOYMENT: 6-month contracts are the norm. Split shifts, generally with classes from 7am to 10am and 4pm to 9pm. Teachers teach 30 hours per week, Monday through Friday.

SALARY: $475 to $800 per month (net).

FACILITIES/SUPPORT: Teachers are responsible for their own accommodation, but school provides assistance in locating housing. Often the institute provides 5 days of free room and board in a family stay to a new arrival, while he or she finds more permanent housing. Work permits are available on a very limited basis, and only for long-term teachers.

RECRUITMENT: Via email and online advertising through www.goabroad.com, www.idealist.org, Dave's ESL Café and others. Many teachers are hired on graduating from Maximo Nivel's own TEFL/TESOL certification course in Cusco. In-person interviews are preferred, but interviews can be conducted via Skype or phone.

CONTACT: Ken Jones, Executive Director.

VENEZUELA

Reports of the state of the Venezuelan economy in 2016 make for sobering reading and will deter all but the foolhardy from choosing it as a destination. Government policies, together with the loss of revenue due to the fall in the price of oil, have shattered the country. Severe shortages of commonplace goods have led to massive price increases plunging a huge percentage of the population, estimated to be as high as 80%, into poverty. Inflation is completely out of control at 180%, with IMF forecasts that next year it will top 700%. Not surprisingly, this situation has led to social unrest and mass demonstrations, none of which will make the life of a foreign teacher feel safe or enjoyable.

Chris Morvan had been a professional writer in the UK for 20 years, in journalism, advertising and public relations. But when recession hit in 2008–2009, some of his freelance work dried up and he decided to move to Venezuela to marry a Venezuelan doctor he had met online. In a bid to reinvent himself he took a 100-hour online TEFL course. At first everything went (literally) swimmingly, with him '*baking in the streets of Caracas and swimming in the Caribbean even in the cooler months, rather than shivering in the UK*'. On arrival in Caracas he applied for three part-time teaching jobs with agencies, got all of them and discovered that he loved teaching. Most of his classes were one-to-one with adults in their offices. After working for agencies for a time, he found that his students preferred to deal with him direct, so he started teaching privately, mainly young adults in their offices and, in the case of oil industry personnel studying in Caracas, in their hotel rooms.

However, the idyll has ended. When the Venezuelan economy started to falter, he and his wife decided to leave, as he explained in an interview with *ExpatFocus* in 2016: '*This was just before Venezuela went into serious decline and it was still relatively prosperous and safe. I probably wouldn't walk the streets of Caracas now, because the country is in trouble – nothing in the shops, people going hungry – and it has become increasingly lawless.*' So, he and his wife left and are currently living in Suriname.

However, there are still Venezuelans studying English. According to the British Council in Caracas their teaching centre currently employs about 20 English teachers to teach 1,200 adults and 600 young learners. Lots of branches of both Berlitz and Wall Street English carry on in business. Despite a preference for American accents and teaching materials, **Nick Branch** from St Albans discovered – before the crisis – that teaching work is not exclusively for Americans, nor is it confined to the capital:

> ***Merida is very beautiful and a considerably more pleasant place to be than Caracas. The atmosphere and organisation of the institute where I worked were very good. But alas, as with all the English teaching institutes in Merida, the pay is very low. Merida is three times cheaper to live in than Caracas, but the salaries are five to six times lower.***

Nick investigated most of the schools and agencies in Venezuela and worked for several of them, including one based in the Oriente coastal resort of Puerto la Cruz. Once again the pay was less than in Caracas, but advantages such as easy access to the Mochima National Marine Park compensated. Opportunities for English teachers may even exist on the popular resort island of Margarita. At one time job-seekers consulted Craigslist Caracas; but a telling snapshot of education jobs listed at the time of writing included only one in Venezuela, and that was for a life coach; the others were for teaching jobs in Bangkok and nanny jobs abroad. Not a single job in Venezuela has been advertised on the eslcafe site in the past year.

LIST OF EMPLOYERS

CENTRO VENEZOLANO AMERICANO DEL CARACAS
Av. Principal de las Mercedes, Edif. CVA, Urbanización Las Mercedes, Caracas 1060-A
+58 212 993 7911
informacion@cva.org.ve
www.cvalasmercedes.wordpress.com
CVA also located in the state of Zulia: Calle 63, No. 3E–60, Maracaibo, Estado Zulia
+58 261 2000600
www.cevaz.org

Bi-National centre.
NUMBER OF TEACHERS: 100+.
PREFERENCE OF NATIONALITY: American, Canadian and Venezuelan.
QUALIFICATIONS: Bachelor's degree or teachers with EFL/ESL experience. A written and oral test is given to all non-native English-speaking applicants. Also placements for university students studying modern languages.
CONDITIONS OF EMPLOYMENT: Minimum 6 months with renewals up to 2 years. Choice of children's courses (for ages 9–11), teens (12–15) and regular and Saturday courses for adults. Minimum 30 academic hours per week.
SALARY: Hourly rate plus housing bonus.
FACILITIES/SUPPORT: Assistance with obtaining accommodation, health insurance and visas. 2-week pre-service training course for interns is paid. Free Spanish course. Computer lab and access to cultural centre activities.
RECRUITMENT: Send CV and recent photo.
CONTACT: Human Resources Dept (telephone extension 114).

WALL STREET INSTITUTE (WSI)
Av. Francisco de Miranda, Centro Lido, Nivel Galeria Local 6–1, El Rosal, Caracas
cv@wsi.com.ve
www.wallstreetenglish.com.ve/empleos.php

NUMBER OF TEACHERS: Variable for 17 branches throughout the country.
PREFERENCE OF NATIONALITY: None.
QUALIFICATIONS: Teaching degree not necessary but some experience teaching English as a second language is helpful. WSI trains all teachers in-house.
CONDITIONS OF EMPLOYMENT: No contract but minimum of 6 months. 8 teaching hours.
SALARY: Local average.
FACILITIES/SUPPORT: Assistance with work permits.
RECRUITMENT: Word of mouth, advertising in local papers and via AIESEC.

CENTRAL AMERICA AND THE CARIBBEAN

If you keep your ears open as you travel through this enormous isthmus squeezed between two great oceans, you may come across opportunities to teach English, especially if you are prepared to do so as a volunteer. Salaries on offer may be pitiful but if you find a congenial spot on the 'gringo trail' (for example, the old colonial towns of Antigua in Guatemala or Granada in Nicaragua), you may decide to prolong your stay by helping the people you will inevitably meet who want to learn English. You might also find openings off the gringo trail. It is always interesting to hear from a part of the world that has never been included in this book before.

COSTA RICA

As the wealthiest country in Central America, Costa Rica is a good starting (and perhaps finishing) point for many native English teachers. It is government policy to teach English in primary schools as part of its initiative to make Costa Rica a multilingual nation by 2020, which has increased the demand for English teachers both paid and voluntary. The Peace Corps deploys large numbers of TEFL teachers and trainers in the state education system. Although state schools can't afford to import expat teachers, they are often willing to accept an offer of voluntary assistance. The school year runs from 1 March to 1 December. The English language *Tico Times* publishes its classified job ads online at www.ticotimes.net, as does Craigslist for Costa Rica. If you're lucky you'll spot an ad such as: '*The Swan English Learning is looking for Native English Teachers, for Heredia, San José & Ciudad Colon. Part and full-time. Excellent pay. Training and Free Spanish Classes*'.

The majority of teaching work is available in the Central Valley, which encompasses the capital San José and the cities of Heredia and Cartago. After four years of teaching at different institutes in Costa Rica, including as a director at Intercultura in Heredia (see entry), **Lindsay Fair** is an established expat who feels frustrated with American attitudes whenever she visits her home country. She describes teaching in the corporate market:

> ***Teaching corporate in Costa Rica has advantages and disadvantages. The biggest disadvantage is having to travel by bus most of the day, especially during the rainy season, wearing business clothes. The benefits of working corporates includes nice working conditions and well-behaved students. Classes are paid for by employers and success is monitored by the bosses, so the students are for the most part very responsible. They come from the upper-middle class of Costa Rica, so are generally educated and, after having worked for North American companies, knowledgeable about North American culture. My colleagues have been almost all North Americans, and most around my age (23–28).***
>
> ***San José is not exactly what you think of when imagining Costa Rica; it's polluted, dirty and dangerous, and the closest beaches are a good two-hour bus ride away. But the company explained all that during the interview. Unfortunately, San José is where most of the work is, so the best part of living in Costa Rica is taking weekend trips to the beaches and national parks. Now that I know more about Costa Rica, I definitely recommend looking for jobs in Heredia instead of San José because it is much safer, nicer and an easier place to live for expats.***

Ex-teacher **Dev Parikh** stressed what he perceived as the dangers of travel round San José and the very high cost of living in the capital.

Bryson Patterson made use of contacts from the TEFL course he did at ALI San Diego to get his first job in San José but eventually moved away from the city:

> ***After working for a time in the capital, I moved to a town called Jaco on the Pacific Coast where I worked at a high school and then at the Marriott Hotel. I was teaching English first to high school students (that was hell) then to the hotel staff, which was cool. A lot of people will tell you that there are no ESL jobs on the coast but they are wrong.***

If you want to support the teaching of English among disadvantaged communities, English Volunteers for Change (EVOLC; see entry) places native-speaker volunteers in various English-language teaching programmes, including some in the tourism sector. Participants get a three-day weekend and plenty of cultural immersion. Programme costs including a homestay with meals are typically $750 per month for a six-month commitment.

Work visas and residency permits (temporary as well as permanent) are very difficult to get. Immigration requires that you get your birth certificate and state background check from your home region, get them notarised by a public notary and send them to the Costa Rican Consulate in your country to be authenticated. Once the documents are sent on to Costa Rica, you have to take them to the foreign ministry to be authenticated again, get a background check, get fingerprinted by the OIJ (Judicial Investigation Department) and pay a lot of money. Once all these steps are taken (and they must be taken within six months before the birth certificate and background check expire), you can bring your documents to immigration, whereupon it can take up to 18 months to get your passport stamped, and that stamp will expire.

Because the process requires so much time, energy and money, schools are not generally willing to assist teachers on standard one-year contracts, who tend to opt for taking visa runs every 90 days to Nicaragua or Panama, making sure that they stay out of the country for at least 72 hours. Not long ago, the *Tico Times* reported that 12 American students were deported in a language school dispute. This is how the article started: '*Working at a language school in Costa Rica may sound like a dream short-term job. But before signing any contract, ask first whether you'd be expected to hide in the bathroom if immigration police show up.*' Immigration police can and do raid likely premises. According to an immigration officer involved in the case, '*Even if someone is teaching English at the beach for a summer, they are legally required to have a work permit.*' Businesses that are registered with the Immigration Administration as *empresas reconocidas* (recognised companies) can reduce the time that an application to legalise a foreign worker takes.

The situation is not quite so difficult for volunteers who work for an established programme, such as EVOLC. Their volunteers enter Costa Rica on a tourist visa, and if they want to extend their stay, the parent foundation ALIARSE will ask the Immigration Center for a volunteer visa.

Allen Tracey has pursued an alternative route by becoming an 'Independent Contractor' with Pro Language (see entry). Foreign teachers can independently contract with an institute (by starting a self-employed business), which means that employers do not take on the obligations of hiring an employee. No taxes are paid, no benefits are received and there is no binding contract. However, for each class the teacher must sign an Assignment Sheet, and the services outlined become the teacher's subcontracted responsibility. The system does mean that you don't really get to know other teachers unless your institute organises group training sessions which you attend:

> ***I have been very fortunate to have been assigned a wide range of interesting and motivated students in my time teaching for Pro Language over the past three years, including top executives who are as eager to learn as tradespeople. Aside from teaching the essentials like grammar from the textbook, I do try to find ways to make each two-hour class fun and entertaining. I am always searching for viable new teaching games because students just love games. I just can't seem to find enough really good teaching games that work. Of course, you get the occasional rotten apple students, who are there only because their employer requires it. A highlight was teaching a top Walmart executive who was a very interesting and appreciative student to invest time with ... it's nice to be appreciated. A low point was having to deal with an extremely rude and controlling Venezuelan student who considered my lesson plans to be optional and negotiable.***

LIST OF EMPLOYERS

CENTRO CULTURAL COSTARRICENSE NORTEAMERICANO
San Pedro (Apartado Postal 1489–1000, San José)
+506 800 046 4537
sharon.alvarado@centrocultural.cr
www.centrocultural.cr

NUMBER OF TEACHERS: Varies. Teachers also needed for centres in Heredia, La Sabana, Alajuela and Cartago.
PREFERENCE OF NATIONALITY: None, but must be native English speaker.
QUALIFICATIONS: Experience in ESL and/or EFL is indispensable.
CONDITIONS OF EMPLOYMENT: Standard 1-year contract. Minimum 16 hours per week.
SALARY: From 4,000 colones ($7+) an hour. Deduction of about $15 a month for voluntary insurance with *Magisterio Nacional*.
FACILITIES/SUPPORT: No assistance with accommodation or work permits.
RECRUITMENT: Via newspaper adverts, work fairs and internal recommendations. Interviews carried out at CCCNCR sites in Costa Rica after applications have been processed centrally.
CONTACT: Sharon Alvarado, Human Resources Assistant.

ENGLISH TO GO – INGLES SIN FRONTERAS
Apartado Postal 271–3007, San Joaquin de Flores, Heredia
+506 2588 2204
apply@english2go.co.cr
www.english2go.co.cr/english-teaching-jobs-costa-rica

NUMBER OF TEACHERS: 15–25 sub-contracted staff mainly for business clients.
PREFERENCE OF NATIONALITY: Americans and Canadians; other native English speakers can also apply, as well as teachers of Spanish and Portuguese.
QUALIFICATIONS: Qualification like CELTA, TESOL, TEFL, etc. needed. ESL teaching experience preferred, especially if in a foreign country. Must have professional appearance.
CONDITIONS OF EMPLOYMENT: Minimum 6-month contract, 12 months preferred. Hours vary according to needs of students or companies with whom English to Go contracts. New arrivals start with 8–16 hours and work up to maximum of 20–24. Teachers should arrive with at least $2,500 start-up money.
SALARY: Sub-contracted hourly work pays $9.
FACILITIES/SUPPORT: If needed on arrival, English to Go will help with finding housing but does not pay rent.
RECRUITMENT: Ads in Craigslist, ESL sites, newspapers, and website. Applicants should submit CV, photo and copy of educational certificates. Interviews essential.

EVOLC (ENGLISH VOLUNTEERS FOR CHANGE)
Esquina SE Del Parque Francia, Barrio Escalante, 11062–1000 San José
+506 2248 0237 ext. 102
evolc@aliarse.org
www.evolc.org

Non-profit project of the Aliarse Foundation.
NUMBER OF TEACHERS: 15–20 volunteers to provide free ESL classes in a range of settings throughout Costa Rica, such as public schools, National Learning Institutes, technical education centres and community centres. Also collaborates with JumpStart (www.jumpstartcostarica.org) to put on intensive English language camps for pupils moving up from primary to secondary school.
PREFERENCE OF NATIONALITY: Any native speaker of English.
QUALIFICATIONS: University degree and TEFL certified for most positions, though for short-term community service or camps, tutoring experience is sufficient. Volunteers should be independent, outgoing, willing to adapt, be responsible and able to organise, have experience of living in another country, have commitment to service and volunteerism and have the ability to communicate well with others.
CONDITIONS OF EMPLOYMENT: 2 weeks to 1 year with monthly start dates year round. Most stay 3–6 months. 20 hours a week teaching, plus 20 hours preparing.
SALARY: Unpaid position. Volunteers pay a programme fee, e.g. $1,750 for 5 weeks, $4,500 for 6 months, $8,000 for 12 months, that covers homestay accommodation, including 3 meals per day.
FACILITIES/SUPPORT: 1–3-day intensive orientation on arrival in San José introduces TESOL methodology and cultural aspects. Assistance can be given in applying for a long term visa before tourist visa expires.
CONTACT: Mrs Chelsea Vasques, Programme Coordinator.

INTERCULTURA LANGUAGE AND CULTURAL CENTER
Apartado Postal 1952–3000, Heredia
+506 2260 8480 ext. 21
ingles@interculturacostarica.com
www.inglesintercultura.com

NUMBER OF TEACHERS: 30–36 (depending on the semester).
PREFERENCE OF NATIONALITY: Native English speakers: American, British, Canadian, Irish, New Zealander and Australian.
QUALIFICATIONS: Minimum bachelor's degree, and TEFL/CELTA certification. At least 1 year's teaching experience is preferred.
CONDITIONS OF EMPLOYMENT: 1 year starting in July or January. Average 18–24 hours teaching per week. Classes last 1.5–3 hours and are held in mornings, evenings and some afternoons. Hours of teaching mainly Monday to Thursday evenings and Saturdays. Part-time contracts are for a minimum of 6 months.
SALARY: $800–$1,000 per month net.
FACILITIES/SUPPORT: Free Spanish lessons for full-time teachers, mentor programme and ongoing training/professional development opportunities. Help setting up a bank account and support for finding housing upon arrival. Classrooms with smartboards with internet and server access with lots of shared materials. Full-time contracts require work visas; Intercultura will assist.
RECRUITMENT: Local adverts and in-person or Skype interviews. Resumés accepted in April and October in time for the start of the semester.
CONTACT: Holli Barrett, Human Resources Coordinator (holli@interculturacostarica.com); Devin Peyton (devin@interculturacostarica.com).

MAXIMO NIVEL INTERNATIONAL COSTA RICA
De La Farmacia La Bomba, 75m South (left side), San Pedro-Montes de Oca, San José
+506 2253 9220; Florida contact number +1 800 866 6358
international@maximonivel.com
www.maximonivel.com

NUMBER OF TEACHERS: 3–5 per month.
PREFERENCE OF NATIONALITY: Must be native English speaker.
QUALIFICATIONS: Teachers must be TEFL, TESOL or CELTA certified from a training course of at least 100 hours with a minimum of 6 hours of practical teaching. Candidates must be dedicated, professional and passionate about teaching, with a self-confident personality and a good sense of humour.
CONDITIONS OF EMPLOYMENT: 6-month contracts are the norm. Split shifts, generally with classes from 7am to 10am and 4pm to 9pm. Teachers teach 30 hours per week, Monday through Friday.
SALARY: $475–$800 per month (net). Some positions are unpaid internships for visa reasons.
FACILITIES/SUPPORT: Teachers are responsible for their own accommodation, but school provides assistance in locating housing. Often the institute provides 5 days of free room and board in a family stay to a new arrival, while he or she finds more permanent housing. Work permits are available on a very limited basis, and only for long-term teachers.
RECRUITMENT: Via email and online advertising through www.goabroad.com, www.idealist.org, Dave's ESL Café and others. Many teachers are hired on graduating from Maximo Nivel's own TEFL/TESOL certification course at institute on Manuel Antonio beach (costing $1,925 for 4 weeks or $2,895 for 8-week internship). In-person interviews are preferred, but interviews can be conducted via Skype or phone.
CONTACT: Tom Kearin, Chief Operating Officer; Paula Piazza, Director of Admissions (paula@maximonivel.com); Ken Jones, Executive Director.

PRO-LANGUAGE CORPORATE LANGUAGE SOLUTIONS
Edificio Langer, Of. #3, Zapote, San José
+506 2280 6053 ext. 11
info@prolanguage.org
www.prolanguage.org

NUMBER OF TEACHERS: 40 (for several branches in metropolitan San José, including in Escazu and Heredia).
PREFERENCE OF NATIONALITY: None, but native English speakers.
QUALIFICATIONS: TEFL certification or equivalent and a minimum of 6 months' experience.
CONDITIONS OF EMPLOYMENT: Minimum 4 months. Flexible part-time opportunities.
SALARY: $8 per hour.
FACILITIES/SUPPORT: Assistance with accommodation and work permits. Free Spanish lessons and free training.
RECRUITMENT: Newspaper adverts, internet and alliances with teacher training organisations. Candidates already in Costa Rica strongly preferred. Online application form.
CONTACT: Dawn Needham, Academic Co-ordinator or Mark Henker, Executive Director.

PROYECTO SAN GERARDO
600 M Norte de la Oficina de MINAE, Camino por Herradura, San Gerardo de Rivas, PZ, San José
+506 2742 5356
proyectosangerardo@gmail.com
www.proyectosangerardo.org

Proyecto San Gerardo is a Rose Charities Canada project (www.rosecanada.info) providing English classes in three locations among other skills training to improve employment prospects for rural inhabitants of the Rivas area.

NUMBER OF TEACHERS: 3 volunteer English teachers plus English conversation volunteers.

PREFERENCE OF NATIONALITY: None, provided they are native speakers.

QUALIFICATIONS: Must have TEFL qualification or teaching experience. Some knowledge of Spanish preferred. Must be patient, creative and flexible with ability to adapt to a remote rural area with few city conveniences. Minimum age 21.

CONDITIONS OF EMPLOYMENT: Minimum stay 3 months, throughout the year except December/January when schools are closed. Teachers conduct children's classes for 2–3 hours in the morning twice a week plus afternoon/evening classes for youths and adults are held on weekdays 4pm–6.30pm.

SALARY: None, but homestay is subsidised. Homestay fee is $350 per month including meals, laundry, private room and shared bathroom.

FACILITIES/SUPPORT: Orientation to the homestay and support is provided. Volunteer Resource Guide and curriculum guidance given at the outset. Follow-up meetings are held bi-weekly or as needed. Short training on a Child Protection Policy is compulsory.

RECRUITMENT: Online via idealist.org, authentic volunteer recruitment websites, and via some ESL teacher training institutions.

CONTACT: Jenny Moss, Director.

SARAPIQUÍ CONSERVATION LEARNING CENTER

Apartado Postal 9241–001, Chilamate, Puerto Viejo de Sarapiquí, Heredia

+506 2761 2082

volunteer@learningcentercostarica.org

www.learningcentercostarica.org

The SCLC takes on volunteers for a range of programmes, including environmental, community development and English teaching.

NUMBER OF TEACHERS: 3.

PREFERENCE OF NATIONALITY: English native speaking countries.

QUALIFICATIONS: TEFL, TESOL or CELTA certified, with teaching and group management experience. Intermediate level of Spanish, preferably with experience of community-driven organisations.

CONDITIONS OF EMPLOYMENT: 6 months. 18 hours of teaching, mainly 5pm–8pm. 22 hours in lesson planning and other duties at the Center.

SALARY: Unpaid positions. Room and board provided with a local family.

RECRUITMENT: Internet, volunteer websites, partnerships with language institutes in Costa Rica. Interviews can be by Skype.

THE SWAN ENGLISH LEARNING

Frente al Banco Costa Rica, Ciudad Colon Centro, San José Province

+506 2249 3598 / 4033 4910

info@theswanenglish.org

www.theswanenglish.org

NUMBER OF TEACHERS: 13.

PREFERENCE OF NATIONALITY: None.

QUALIFICATIONS: TEFL, CELTA or equivalent. Experience preferred.

CONDITIONS OF EMPLOYMENT: Minimum 4 months. 20 hours per week on average.

SALARY: 4,000–5,000 colones ($7–$9) per hour, net.

FACILITIES/SUPPORT: Advice given on finding good, cheap, local accommodation.

RECRUITMENT: Via local paper, Craigslist, website, advertising in local university and word of mouth. Interview in person or via Skype.

CONTACT: Oliver Petersen, Owner and Director.

UNIVERSAL DE IDIOMAS

Avenida 2da, calle 9, San José

+506 2257 0441; USA: +1 727 230 0563

info@universal-edu.com

www.universal-edu.com or www.ingles.cr

NUMBER OF TEACHERS: 10 English teachers. Also a large Spanish teaching operation.

PREFERENCE OF NATIONALITY: American, British.

QUALIFICATIONS: TEFL/TESOL, university diploma, a couple of years of experience.

CONDITIONS OF EMPLOYMENT: 1 year. Teaching hours mainly in evenings and on Saturdays.

SALARY: About $8 per hour. 9% deductions for social security.

FACILITIES/SUPPORT: Most teachers find their own accommodation, though homestay can be arranged at extra charge.

RECRUITMENT: Via internet ads. Local interview essential.

GUATEMALA AND HONDURAS

There are perhaps about a dozen institutes in the capital Guatemala City. But it is not nearly as appealing a destination as Antigua. Dozens of Spanish language schools in this backpacker honey pot have links with local communities that welcome volunteer teachers. To take just two examples, check out www.launion.edu.gt/volunteer-work/work-as-a-teacher and El Nahual Community Language Center in Quetzaltenango called Xela (www.languageselnahual.com). Many travellers find that Lake Atitlán is the perfect place to use as a longer-term base. The small villages around the lake are all interconnected by launch boats, and the variety in atmosphere among these villages means that you can choose one that suits. Well-known party town San Pedro attracts many foreigners who come to attend one of the many Spanish schools. Hostel beds average about 50 quetzales (£5), though cheaper places can be found, and food is also very cheap.

ANNA LING

When Anna Ling was 20 years old, she headed to Santa Cruz while pursuing her main interests, writing and performing music.

I am based at the Iguana Perdida hostel (www.laiguanaperdida.com), the first building near the launch stop. The local village is a wonderful place and home to the Amigos (www.amigosdesantacruz.org), a charity that has brought medical care and an out-reach programme to the more remote villages. They have also built a library and a school offering free education to all children under 12, and scholarship programmes for older children. They are in the process of building a large new centre for vocational education. I went up to the village to see Pam, the brains behind the operation, and within the hour I was teaching an English class. I was soon given a classroom and started an enrichment afternoon with the local kids, doing arts, craft and music projects. The organisation is so well run that anyone willing to give some time will be put to good use, whether in teaching, construction or any other interests.

Visas are not a problem at all, neither for work nor volunteering. No one even asks to see a passport. Language is no problem either. Personally I'm trying to live very much on a tight budget and paid language lessons (25-50 quetzals per hour) would push me way over my daily price watch. But volunteering at the school has been the best opportunity for learning Spanish I could imagine. I take up a dictionary and the kids speak really slowly and clearly and it has helped so very much.

Britons, Americans and other tourists are permitted to stay in Guatemala for 90 days. This can be extended by the same period at the immigration office, but when that 90-day limit expires you must leave the country and renew your visa on re-entry. Note that because Guatemala, Honduras, Nicaragua and El Salvador belong to the CA-4 border agreement pact, a harmonised visa regime, you must go outside that group to Mexico, Belize or Costa Rica.

Volunteer teachers who wish to go to Honduras can arrange a placement in La Ceiba, the third-largest city, through several fee-charging agencies, including A Broader View (www.abroaderview.org), helping local people trying to get ahead in the burgeoning tourist industry. The cost for people who know some Spanish already is from $995 for 2 weeks up to $2,240 for 12 weeks. Spanish immersion courses cost extra. It would be cheaper to work directly with the US-based charity that works in La Ceiba, Helping Honduras Kids (www.helpinghonduraskids.org), with whom you can arrange to become a volunteer teacher at a jungle school attended by marginalised children, for a one-off $100 fee plus $65 a week to cover homestay accommodation.

Another possibility is the Bilingual School in Cofradia (www.cofradiaschool.com) in northern Honduras, which relies on a team of internationally recruited volunteers to teach from August to June in exchange for free accommodation. The possibility of corporate teaching should not be discounted either. A company called Harris Communications (management@harriscom.org) employs native speakers with at least two years' experience and conducts conversation classes in the two northern cities of San Pedro Sula and La Ceiba.

LIST OF EMPLOYERS

BILINGUAL EDUCATION FOR CENTRAL AMERICA (BECA)

PO Box 7400, New York, NY 10150, USA

+1 646 820 BECA (2322) in New York; +504 9964 5352 in Cofradia, Honduras

becaschools@gmail.com

www.becaschools.org

BECA exists to promote cultural exchange and affordable bilingual education in Central America. BECA's largest school is San Jeronimo Bilingual School in Cofradia, Northern Honduras.

NUMBER OF TEACHERS: 34 volunteer teachers. Also 8–10 paying volunteers for summer camp in July.

PREFERENCE OF NATIONALITY: All nationalities welcome.

QUALIFICATIONS: BECA seeks motivated individuals who have completed a bachelor's degree. Average age is 24; most are 21–35.

CONDITIONS OF EMPLOYMENT: Minimum commitment 1 full year. Summer Institute begins mid-July and the school year finishes in mid-June of the following year. BECA schools operate from 7.15am to 2.15pm.

SALARY: All volunteers are provided with food, shared living accommodation and high speed Internet. Manager, administrators and second year teachers receive a modest monthly stipend in addition to food and lodging.

FACILITIES/SUPPORT: Accommodation provided. 5-week training course provided for incoming volunteers, which covers training on different methods of language acquisition, classroom management, curriculum planning, cultural sensitivities, social and emotional development of the child plus complimentary Spanish classes. Volunteers come with a tourist visa to Honduras.

RECRUITMENT: Via websites such as idealist.org, through BECA alumni, and through promotion by various universities and colleges.

CONTACT: Sean Bell, Executive Director (sbell@becaschools.org).

MAXIMO NIVEL INTERNATIONAL GUATEMALA

6a Avenida Norte #16–16A, La Antigua

+502 7932 1500; +1 800 866 6358 (Florida contact number)

instructors@maximonivel.com

www.maximonivel.com

NUMBER OF TEACHERS: 10–20. Also organises volunteer teaching programme for paying volunteers.

PREFERENCE OF NATIONALITY: Must be native English speaker.

QUALIFICATIONS: Teachers must be TEFL, TESOL or CELTA certified from a training course of at least 100 hours with a minimum of 6 hours of practical teaching. Candidates must be dedicated, professional and passionate about teaching, with a self-confident personality and a good sense of humour.

CONDITIONS OF EMPLOYMENT: 6-month contracts are the norm. Split shifts, generally 7am–10am and 4pm–9pm. Teachers teach 30 hours per week, Monday through Friday.

SALARY: $475 to $800 per month (net).

FACILITIES/SUPPORT: Teachers are responsible for their own accommodation, but school provides assistance in locating housing. Often the institute provides 5 days of free room and board in a family stay to a new arrival, while he or she finds more permanent housing. Work permits are available on a very limited basis, and only for long-term teachers.

RECRUITMENT: Via email and online advertising through www.goabroad.com, www.idealist.org, Dave's ESL Café and others. Many teachers are hired on graduating from Maximo Nivel's own 150-hour TEFL/TESOL certification course in Antigua (cost is $1,400). In-person interviews are preferred, but interviews can be conducted via Skype or phone.

CONTACT: Ken Jones, Executive Director.

NICARAGUA

Nicaragua is the second poorest country in the Western Hemisphere after Haiti. Yet it is blessed with a wealth of natural beauty in its volcanoes and coastlines. It is also among the safest countries in Central America and an attractive destination for travelling teachers. Unfortunately, there are few opportunities for native speaker teachers even in the two main cities of Managua and Léon. Granada is a smaller city, considered the country's tourist gem, and with a sprinkling of language schools. Granada is where the international TEFL training group, INTESOL, offers its four-week proprietary TEFL training course (www.intesolnicaragua.com). The respected cultural immersion travel company, Greenheart, offers a month-long certification course in León, followed by job placement assistance (www.greenhearttravel.org).

LIST OF EMPLOYERS

ABC SCHOOL (American British College)
519 Calle El Consulado, Granada
+505 55 2552 0812
marlonabc@hotmail.com; marlongabc@teachers.org
http://marlonabc.wix.com/school

NUMBER OF TEACHERS: 5 volunteers.
PREFERENCE OF NATIONALITY: North American.
QUALIFICATIONS: TEFL or equivalent, minimum 2 months' EFL teaching experience, some Spanish, some travel outside country of origin, interest in Nicaragua.
CONDITIONS OF EMPLOYMENT: Minimum stay of 3 months. 20 hours per week on weekdays between 3pm and 8pm and 3-hour classes taught on Saturdays and Sundays. School is open year round.
SALARY: Contribution of $160–$240 per month for housing.
FACILITIES/SUPPORT: Teachers are helped to find rooms to rent or homestays.
RECRUITMENT: Internet (including Facebook page) and word of mouth. Phone interviews.
CONTACT: Marlon Gutierrez, Owner/Director.

LA ESPERANZA GRANADA
Calle Libertad, #307, Una y media cuadras al lago, Granada
+505 8913 8946
info@la-esperanza-granada.org
www.la-esperanza-granada.org

NUMBER OF TEACHERS: 20–60 volunteers in total working in various aid projects, including some who teach English in primary schools and work in kindergartens.
PREFERENCE OF NATIONALITY: None.
QUALIFICATIONS: Knowledge of Spanish important for volunteers working with children.
CONDITIONS OF EMPLOYMENT: Minimum stay 1 month between February and November. Summer school projects run in December and January. Kindergarten hours are 7.30am–noon Monday to Friday. English team volunteers work Monday through Thursday 12.30–4pm or 1–4.30pm, and do lesson planning on Friday mornings.
SALARY: None. Volunteers pay a $20 administration fee and $5 for a project T-shirt. Volunteers are self-funding and pay $25 a week for a bed in the volunteers' dorm, plus $40–$100 in other expenses.
FACILITIES/SUPPORT: Other housing options on offer, e.g. $35–$45 per week for a single room.
CONTACT: Pauline Jackson, Operations Officer.

EL SALVADOR

After finishing high school in his hometown of Flagstaff, Arizona, **Kellen Brandel** knew that he wanted to take a year out. In his search for something affordable that would let him work on his Spanish, he settled on an NGO in the capital of El Salvador (see entry) which teaches English to local people and also supports some social justice projects around the country. Kellen spent a total of seven months in Central America and reflects on the benefits:

I mainly researched options using the internet and was most impressed with the one I chose (CIS: Center for Exchange and Solidarity) based on communication and quality of information, not to mention costs. I spent the first three months volunteer English teaching in CIS, a grassroots NGO founded by an American woman in the 1990s. I spent the next month backpacking through the countryside of El Salvador, Honduras, Guatemala and Belize before returning to San Salvador and spending an additional three months teaching again. While I volunteered abroad, I also studied the native language, Spanish, in a sister school at this particular NGO. The costs were quite reasonable. The average week consisted of spending about $80 for host family including meals and utilities, $57 for Spanish school, provided you were an English volunteer ($100 for passers-by) as well as a few additional expenses.

My volunteer position was that of an English teacher for adults, mainly in the evenings. The working conditions were great and the coordinators were very helpful in providing us with material, ideas and support. At first I was wary about teaching adults, as most of my students were in their late twenties and thirties. But I think I established respect with them and was laid back to the extent that the age difference didn't seem to matter. After that we were able to relax and eventually make jokes about my young age. It was professional, but the atmosphere at the CIS is also really laid back. Over the course of seven months I got to know my students on a much more personal level than many teachers get to, and that to me was really special. The low point would probably be the amount of English spoken. For many the balance is good, but since I already had a strong foundation in the Spanish language, I found too much English spoken at the CIS. But once I became more involved with locals outside school, that improved.

LIST OF EMPLOYERS

CIS – CENTRO DE INTERCAMBIO Y SOLIDARIDAD
Mélida Anaya Montes Language School, Avenida Aguilares y Avenida Bolivar #103, Colonia Libertad, San Salvador
US office: Los Olivos CIS, PO Box 76, Westmont, IL 60559–0076
+503 2235 1330 / +503 2226 5362
info@cis-elsalvador.org and volunteer@cis-elsalvador.org
www.cis-elsalvador.org

NUMBER OF TEACHERS: 7–10 volunteer teachers at any one time.
PREFERENCE OF NATIONALITY: None.
QUALIFICATIONS: No teaching experience or certification needed. Must be committed to social justice and reciprocal learning between students and teacher.
CONDITIONS OF EMPLOYMENT: Minimum stay of 10 weeks for complete English cycle. Time commitment includes teaching English 3 days a week (Monday, Tuesday and Thursday) 5.15pm–7pm, weekly 2-hour teachers' meeting, plus time spent on lesson planning. Please contact for more details about rural volunteer placements and longer-term placements.
SALARY: None. Volunteers must also pay a one-time programme fee of $100.
FACILITIES/SUPPORT: The CIS has a host family network with whom volunteers can live: cost of homestay with breakfast and dinner starts at $80 a week. Monthly living expenses estimated to be $400. Training for teachers provided. Tourist visa ($10 at border) is sufficient. Volunteers are eligible to receive a half-price discount on Spanish classes.
RECRUITMENT: Word of mouth, internet, travel publications.

DOMINICAN REPUBLIC

A major tourist destination, the Dominican Republic (DR) provides some opportunities for native English teachers, although these may well be low paid (or volunteer positions) because the DR is still one of the poorest countries in the Caribbean. A useful resource is the Dominican Republic One news and information service (www.dr1.com) in English, which has a classified section and a message board where you can ask the online community for information, as well as some useful tips on finding teaching work in the Dominican Republic at http://dr1.com/living/work/2.shtml. The Instituto Cultural Dominico-Americano (ICDA) carries teaching information on its website (www.icda.edu.do) and invites applicants to submit CVs (to empleos@icda.edu.do).

A small not-for-profit organisation hosts summer volunteers to run an English summer school in the area around Ramón Santana (see www.supportingguasa.com/blog). A charity called Outreach 360 based in Arizona (www.outreach360.org) sends volunteers to participate in conversational English programmes with children in the Dominican Republic (and Nicaragua). This doubles as a fundraiser for the organisation so, for example, a four-week summer stay costs $2,000. In the rural areas where the organisation works, access to native speakers of English is very limited. Volunteers are also needed to attend English-immersion summer camps. The charity Fundacion Aldeas de Paz (www.peacevillages.org) has established a base in the Dominican Republic in the seaside town of Santa Barbara de Samana, though teaching is incidental to other volunteering programmes. The participation fee for eight weeks is €1,140 which includes accommodation in the volunteer guesthouse.

LIST OF EMPLOYERS

ULAE (UNIVERSITY LANGUAGE EXTENSION) ENGLISH PROGRAM

UCNE (Universidad Cathólica Nordestana), Centro de Idiomas y Relaciones Globales (CIRG), Calle Restauracion esq. 27 de Febrero, San Francisco de Macorís, Provincia Duarte, (Apartado Postal No. 239), Dominican Republic

+1 809 588 3505 ext. 3200; +1 809 588 3151 ext. 233; +1 809 290 3355

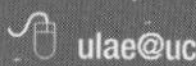

ulae@ucne.edu; darling.ulae@gmail.com

www.cirg.webs.com; www.ucne.edu

NUMBER OF TEACHERS: 30 volunteer professors of language and literature.

PREFERENCE OF NATIONALITY: English-speaking countries.

QUALIFICATIONS: Ages 21–38. Should be graduate in education-related subject or with experience working with children. Should be able to adapt to life in the Caribbean and have a love of multicultural life and tourism. Intermediate Spanish needed.

CONDITIONS OF EMPLOYMENT: 6 months or a year from beginning of terms (second Monday in September or early January). Working hours are 8am–3pm Monday to Friday with lunches provided at 1pm daily at school.

SALARY: $650 per month (paid on the 10th of the month).

FACILITIES/SUPPORT: Shared apartment next to the school with utilities, phone and internet included; teachers have their own room. Access to beaches and aquatic sports on days off. Teachers meet regularly with the coordinator to prepare tests, evaluations and lesson plans.

RECRUITMENT: CVs to be submitted. Interviews by Skype.

CONTACT: Mr Darling J. Perez, Administrative Director ULAE English Program (coordinator.cirg@ucne.edu).

NORTH AMERICA

Just about every university and college in the major cities has an ESL programme, as do a range of government and charitable organisations. Commercial schools offer a wide variety of classes but tend to focus on survival ESL and EAP (English for Academic Purposes), with writing as a major component. Berlitz and Inlingua are represented throughout the USA and are a completely different type of commercial school, concentrating on conversational skills and foreign languages for business people. Embassy English (www.embassyenglish.com) has adult English schools in Boston, New York, Fort Lauderdale, San Diego, Los Angeles and San Francisco, plus a centre in Toronto. These may be worth applying to if you are well qualified, although they normally recruit locally. Details of summer teaching jobs in New York, Massachusetts, Florida and California can be found at http://jobs.embassysummer.com/usa-application.htm, which might be of interest to non-Americans who can obtain a J-1 exchange visa by joining the BUNAC Work America programme.

Bilingual/bicultural classes are run in thousands of high schools across the country. Many require staff who are not only state-certified teachers but also bilingual in exotic languages like Hmong or Gujarati. Most larger cities have at least one free or low-cost workplace literacy/vocational ESL programme that caters for immigrants needing assistance with the basics of English. Some of these programmes operate in outposts (e.g. churches, libraries) and many depend on local volunteers as tutors. Volunteer positions can conceivably lead to better things and are sometimes a prerequisite for ESL programmes abroad (such as the Central European Teaching Program in Hungary). The largest and longest established literacy organisation is ProLiteracy (www.proliteracy.org), which offers ten hours of training. It provides volunteer tutors with the professional training and materials they need to teach basic literacy or English for Speakers of Other Languages (ESOL). Additional literacy organisations offering volunteer opportunities for prospective teachers are listed at www.LiteracyConnections.com.

While many American English teachers set off to see the world, others like **Jeffrey Machado** move back to the US (after teaching in China in his case) to teach their language to incomers, as he explains on the forum of Cambridge English Teacher (www.cambridgeenglishteacher.org):

> ***I have recently started volunteering with a literacy organisation here in my home country. I never fully understood the difference between ESL and EFL before this point. But, now, working with students who NEED English (rather than want to learn it for career purposes), the dynamic is completely different. I have found that students are less inhibited once they are here in the US.***
>
> ***There are some truly unique opportunities in the ELT field here in the United States. Just this weekend, I read an article about the state of Hawaii's difficulties retaining good teachers. Essentially, Hawaii with its English language learners, who mainly speak a combination of Hawaiian and pidgin English, represents not just a state, but an entire other country with unexplored opportunities. In addition, EAP careers are prevalent around cities and towns with large student populations. While not strictly EAP, there are also plenty of opportunities for TOEFL exam prep. The main downside is that the cost of living in the majority of these places is quite high whereas the pay for ELTs is rather paltry.***

GEMMA PIRELLI

Gemma Pirelli tried to think of ways of achieving her desire to travel after finishing a degree in psychology, and spend time with people from different cultures. She carried out lots of research on the internet and made contact with the director of www.teachingenglishinitaly.com, Sheila Corwin, a fellow American. Not only did she enrol on a distance-learning course, but took steps to get some practical experience.

In addition to putting together a portfolio of all coursework I'm doing for my distance TEFL course (the International Certificate for Applied Linguistics), I tried to find some volunteering opportunities and classroom observations here in New Jersey. Therefore, I began to research local colleges/universities in my area as well as community centres accepting volunteers. I went back to my alma mater (Seton Hall University) and arranged a couple of classroom observations with the ESL adjunct. Because I wanted more involvement in the classroom, I decided to become a volunteer at a local community centre where they have programmes for adult learners. After connecting with the director, she was able to accommodate me in a Monday evening class, and have me float around different classrooms to observe various levels. I was able to teach one class of learners at intermediate level, which went very well, and I was able to use my knowledge from the course as well as lesson planning guided by Sheila. Eventually I was put in charge of advanced learners (only one to three at a time). There are no set books and little structure so I had to arrange lessons on my own ... There is no doubt in my mind that this experience will lead me to grand frontiers.

Although the demand for ESL teachers is enormous, it is very difficult for foreigners who do not have a 'green card' to obtain the necessary working visa. The J-1 visa is available to university students participating in an approved Exchange Visitor Programme (which are mainly for the summer) and to researchers and teachers whose applications are supported by their employing institution in the USA. Similarly it is extremely difficult to obtain the H-1B 'Temporary Worker' visa, which is available for prearranged professional or highly skilled jobs for which there are no suitably qualified Americans, an increasingly unlikely circumstance as more and more Americans are becoming qualified to teach ESL/EFL. Although more US organisations now recognise the Cambridge CELTA Certificate than before, the MA in TESOL still dominates the American EFL scene. Even for qualified American teachers, part-time work is the norm, often referred to as being hired as an 'adjunct'. Many contracts are not renewed, creating a transient English-teaching population. Pay is hourly and varies according to region, for example $20–$25 in Chicago, a little more in San Francisco. Part-timers almost never get benefits, which means no health insurance or vacation pay. Even full-time teaching openings may be for just nine months, with pay as little as $20,000–$25,000 in the Midwest.

Canada has a flourishing ELT industry; however, the difficulty of getting a visa is a major stumbling block for foreign teachers. People with experience might have expected to be able to do some casual one-to-one tutoring of new immigrants, but stiff competition makes this difficult. Two sources of possible contacts are Languages Canada (www.languagescanada.ca) and TESL Canada (www.tesl.ca). Member institutes will usually consider only Canadian citizens or those with work permits or landed immigrant status. The hourly wage starts at C$20–25 per hour.

AUSTRALASIA

While Europeans tend to have a somewhat Eurocentric view of the world, the Antipodean English language industry has built itself into a giant. TEFL has a very high profile in both Australia and New Zealand. There are no fewer than 15 Cambridge CELTA training centres in Australia and nine in New Zealand, most of them attached to flourishing English language colleges. There are a further two Trinity TESOL centres in New Zealand, despite its tiny population of less than 4.5 million. **Neil Preston** of International House Brisbane has kindly contributed to this assessment of the ELT scene in Australia.

AUSTRALIA

The growth in student numbers and ELT schools has resulted in strong job prospects for TESOL qualified teachers. Approximately 80,000 students study English in Australia on student visas and the Australian immigration department estimates that another 60,000 students study on other visas, such as working holiday and tourist visas. This represents an increase of 80% over the past 10 years, although the last few years have seen shrinkage in the EFL student market, partly due to the strong Australian dollar and resultant high cost of living. Industry experts predict that the market will start to recover over the next year or two.

For obvious reasons of geography, the majority of Australia's international students are from Asia, although there are a growing number of students coming from further away, including Italy and elsewhere in Europe, plus a strong Latin America presence.

Australia has a strong market for longer-term students, e.g. Academic English students (20+ weeks) and English for high school students (20–30 weeks) who need to improve their English skills for entry into an Australian university or high school. However, the average number of weeks overseas students study is 12. This longer-term student market has resulted in relatively steady student numbers year round. Whilst Australia does experience a peak in student numbers over the warmer months (September to May), due to an influx of study tours, there is not the same dramatic seasonal fluctuation as in Europe.

There are approximately 100 English language colleges in Sydney alone, around 70% of which are accredited by the National ELT Accreditation Scheme (NEAS). The profession is strictly regulated in Australia and standards are high in both the private and public sector. The minimum acceptable qualification to teach at an Australian NEAS-accredited language school is a degree in any discipline (or 3-year full-time diploma) plus a recognised TESOL qualification and 800 hours of teaching experience. Alternatively you may be considered with a higher-than-pass grade in the TESOL qualification or if you can show references from your TESOL course director about your performance.

An acceptable TESOL qualification must have a practical component including at least six hours' supervised and assessed practice teaching in TESOL and involve no fewer than 100 contact hours in total (or the equivalent in Distance Education programmes). To check the current requirements and a list of 200+ accredited language schools see the NEAS website (www.neas.org.au). Some non-accredited schools will employ TESOL trained teachers who do not hold a degree or diploma. It is interesting to note that due to the strong demand for TEFL qualified teachers in Sydney, job-seekers with the CELTA but without a degree have still been offered positions by accredited schools.

Candidates (whether Australians or foreigners on working visas) are regularly offered employment in Sydney and in other Australian cities within a week or two of completing the Cambridge CELTA course. To find a list of English language schools throughout Australia, see the website of ELICOS (English Language Intensive Courses for Overseas Students – www.elicos.com). Job vacancies are posted at http://au.jora.com (search for ELICOS). Generally, teaching contracts are casual, as staffing is organised from one course period to the next, from week to week or month to month, depending on the college. Once a relationship has been built between school and teacher the teacher can opt to work long term with one school or short term with a number of schools. Annual salaries range from around AUS$40,000 for a newly qualified graduate teacher without experience to AUS$90,000 for a head teacher. The Fair Work Commission sets 'award rates' (agreed minimums) for different categories of TESOL teacher; these are normally reviewed in July. The median hourly wage is about $38.50.

Many foreigners teach English on a working holiday visa. British, Irish and North American travellers aged between 18 and 30 years can apply for working holiday visas for up to 12 months (renewable for a further 12 months provided visa-holders do a minimum of 88 days of fruit-picking in a designated rural area). For further information visit www.border.gov.au. One company that sometimes hires teachers with a WH visa is Lexis English (www.lexisenglish.com) with four schools in Queensland and one in Perth. When **Barry O'Leary** arrived in Sydney with a working holiday visa, he had very little money so needed a job fast. He had emailed a number of language institutes in Sydney in advance and fixed up an interview the day after he arrived. In addition to walking round all the schools he could find, he used Australian search engines such as www.seek.com.au, www.jobsearch.gov.au and www.adzuna.com.au to look for sessional positions. Soon he found a job with a college in an outer suburb of Sydney:

> ***This was my first full-time job and I was thrown in at the deep end. Initially I was doing maternity cover and working 15 hours a week, but this later increased to 45 including preparation time. The wages were fantastic, I wasn't paying any tax because I set myself up as a contractor and I was paid AUS$30 an hour (the going rate then) and AUS$300 every two weeks for the evening business course I taught. I managed to save about AUS$8,000 in three months, which paid for a brilliant trip up the east coast of Australia. There was always a laugh in the staff room and a lot of banter between England and Australia. I really enjoyed the mixed classes because there was such a range of opinions and at times they were more challenging because each nationality would have different weaknesses.***

LIST OF EMPLOYERS

ACCESS LANGUAGE CENTRE
72 Mary Street, Surry Hills, New South Wales 2010
+61 2 9281 6455
english@access.nsw.edu.au
www.access.nsw.edu.au

NUMBER OF TEACHERS: 16.

PREFERENCE OF NATIONALITY: None.

QUALIFICATIONS: Bachelor's degree plus TESOL certificate. Some experience essential.

CONDITIONS OF EMPLOYMENT: 4 weeks renewable to start.

SALARY: Depends on qualifications and experience.

FACILITIES/SUPPORT: No assistance with accommodation.

RECRUITMENT: Advertising and will respond to general enquiries about work while in Australia.

CONTACT: Tony Stock, Director of Studies.

AUSTRALIAN INTERNATIONAL COLLEGE OF ENGLISH
Level 3/303 Pitt St, Sydney, New South Wales 2000
+61 2 9299 2400
info@aice.nsw.edu.au
www.aice.nsw.edu.au

NUMBER OF TEACHERS: 15.

PREFERENCE OF NATIONALITY: Any native-speaking country.

QUALIFICATIONS: Recognised TESOL certificate/CELTA and a bachelor's or higher degree from a recognised university.

CONDITIONS OF EMPLOYMENT: 20 hours per week of teaching. Different class schedules, ie Monday–Thursday 9am–3pm or Monday–Friday 9am–1.30pm or 4.15pm–8.45pm.

SALARY: AUS$35–$45+ per hour (gross), based on state salary scale for English teachers. Deductions are made for tax and compulsory superannuation contributions.

FACILITIES/SUPPORT: Candidates with working holiday visas are welcome. No help given with visas or accommodation.
RECRUITMENT: Local advertising. Face-to-face interviews.
CONTACT: Heidi Reid, Principal.

ENGLISH LANGUAGE COMPANY
495 Kent St, Sydney, New South Wales 2000
+61 2 9267 5688
recruitment@englishlanguagecompany.com
www.englishlanguagecompany.com

NUMBER OF TEACHERS: 20.
PREFERENCE OF NATIONALITY: None but must already have right to work in Australia.
QUALIFICATIONS: University degree + CELTA or equivalent; though CELTA definitely preferred. (Under national industry regulations set down by NEAS, teaching qualifications must include 120 hours of face-to-face instruction and at least 6 hours of observed, assessed teaching.) One year's experience teaching adult learners.
CONDITIONS OF EMPLOYMENT: Most teachers start with a short contract of 10 or 12 weeks, as is common in Sydney. Teaching hours are 8.15am–4.15pm.
SALARY: Teachers are paid on a national step-based award system. Qualifications and relevant experience are factored to give a salary step. Salaries range from approximately AUS$41,500–S$60,000. Tax is deducted on a PAYE basis.
FACILITIES/SUPPORT: No help given with visas. Support to find accommodation given to teachers on working holidays.
RECRUITMENT: Applications with CV by email or post and then face-to-face interview is arranged. In certain cases the applicant is asked to do a demonstration lesson of 30–60 minutes using material given to them.
CONTACT: Lyn Scott, Academic Director; David Scott (david.scott@englishlanguagecompany.com).

ENGLISH UNLIMITED
Level 9, 138 Albert Street, Brisbane, Queensland 4000
+61 7 3003 0088
info@englishunlimited.qld.edu.au
www.englishunlimited.qld.edu.au

NUMBER OF TEACHERS: 5.
PREFERENCE OF NATIONALITY: Providing the applicant has the right to live and work in Australia and sufficient English language skills, teachers from any country of origin are encouraged to apply.
QUALIFICATIONS: Specific TESOL qualification, for example CELTA or Trinity CertTESOL are a requirement to teach within the private education industry, in colleges accredited by NEAS. TEFL training courses that are accepted must have a minimum number of hours input and a practical teaching component, which excludes online courses. University degree also required (in any discipline).
CONDITIONS OF EMPLOYMENT: Teachers are employed on ongoing sessional contracts, mostly on a casual basis. Most teachers work approximately 20 hours a week, 8.30am–2.30pm Monday to Thursday (5 contact hours per day).
SALARY: Teachers are usually paid based on a national scheme, according to qualifications and experience. Unfortunately, the majority of overseas experience is not counted, so teachers may well find themselves starting at the bottom. Salary range is from AUS$42.02 per hour at Level 1 to AUS$55 at Level 12 (less superannuation payments of 9% and income tax).
FACILITIES/SUPPORT: Teachers source their own accommodation but advice is available. No visa sponsorship is available.
RECRUITMENT: Via adverts on www.seek.com.au and www.onestopenglish.com, walk-in applications and teacher recommendations. Interview prior to appointment is essential for all positions including voluntary; paid employees must teach a demonstration lesson.
CONTACT: Ms Rufus James, Academic Manager (rufus@englishunlimited.qld.edu.au).

INTERNATIONAL HOUSE BRISBANE
126 Adelaide St, Brisbane, Queensland 4000
Postal address: PO Box 13393 George St, Brisbane 4003
+61 7 3229 3389
neil@ihbrisbane.com.au
www.ihbrisbane.com.au

NUMBER OF TEACHERS: Approximately 20.
PREFERENCE OF NATIONALITY: Native English speakers.
QUALIFICATIONS: CELTA or equivalent and minimum of 1 year's experience.
CONDITIONS OF EMPLOYMENT: Variable length contracts. Up to 25 hours per week.
SALARY: Australian award rates ($41–$54 per hour).
RECRUITMENT: CV and interview. Interviews occasionally conducted overseas.
CONTACT: Neil Preston, School Director.

MILNER INTERNATIONAL COLLEGE OF ENGLISH
379 Hay Street, Perth, Western Australia 6000
+61 8 9325 5444
dos@milner.wa.edu.au
www.milner.wa.edu.au

NUMBER OF TEACHERS: 25–35.

PREFERENCE OF NATIONALITY: None. Teachers from the UK and Canada can come on a working holiday visa if they are under 30.

QUALIFICATIONS: Degree plus CELTA (or equivalent).

CONDITIONS OF EMPLOYMENT: No contracts for casual teachers. School hours 9am–3pm.

SALARY: There is an award scale for EL teachers ranging from AUS$38.55–$50.46 per hour.

FACILITIES/SUPPORT: Teachers find their own accommodation.

RECRUITMENT: CV and interview.

CONTACT: Deborah Pinder, Director of Studies.

PHOENIX ACADEMY

223 Vincent Street, West Perth, Western Australia 6005

+61 8 9227 5538

robynne.walsh@phoenix.wa.edu.au

www.phoenix.wa.edu.au

NUMBER OF TEACHERS: 30–35 across all English programmes.

PREFERENCE OF NATIONALITY: None, but candidates must have a working holiday visa or other appropriate visa.

QUALIFICATIONS: Minimum undergraduate degree in any discipline and a CELTA.

CONDITIONS OF EMPLOYMENT: Length of stay varies according to vacancy needs, e.g. it could be a 4-week summer course contract, a 12-week Business English or Cambridge course contract or a 6-month EAP contract. Permanent contracts occasionally available. Contact hours usually 20 per week plus 3–5 hours for other duties.

SALARY: Minimum starting salary AUS$42,000–$53,000 per year. School usually pays above this award minimum according to skills and experience. Tax reduces salary by about 20%.

FACILITIES/SUPPORT: On-campus residence available for new arrivals at a cost of AUS$30 per night.

RECRUITMENT: Via teachers' websites and local advertising in newspaper media. Interviews essential and can be done by Skype for non-local applicants.

CONTACT: Robynne Walsh, Principal.

SYDNEY ENGLISH ACADEMY (SEA)

19/74 –78 The Corso, Manly, New South Wales 2095

+61 2 9976 6988

info@sea-english.com

www.sea-english.com

NUMBER OF TEACHERS: 6–12 depending on time of year.

PREFERENCE OF NATIONALITY: None, provided they already have legal right to work.

QUALIFICATIONS: An undergraduate degree plus a CELTA or equivalent certificate (as an absolute minimum).

CONDITIONS OF EMPLOYMENT: Varies according to current needs but 12 weeks is typical. Hours normally 8.15am–3.45pm.

SALARY: Based on the New Federal Award. Depending on earnings, 25%–30% is deducted for income tax and the employers adds on 9% of earnings to pay into the employee's superannuation fund.

RECRUITMENT: Face-to-face or Skype interview necessary.

CONTACT: Samantha Milton, Director of Studies.

NEW ZEALAND

The English-language teaching market in New Zealand is fairly similar to that of Australia: highly developed, although subject to demand fluctuation. Demand from Chinese, Korean and other Asian students is very high. Also there are plenty of Saudis, South Americans and many others who can see the appeal of learning a foreign language in this beautiful country. According to Marty Pilott, on the National Executive of TESOLANZ (the New Zealand Association of ESOL teachers), plenty of local teaching applicants are available, which means that language schools are unlikely to hire teachers from abroad. However, anyone with a CELTA and several years' experience who goes to New Zealand to conduct a job hunt has a reasonable chance of success. One such, a few years ago, was **Mr Roy**:

> ***When I came here, I'd never felt so popular. I was amazed how many jobs I got offered cold calling with a CV. I entered the country on a visitor visa that, as a British passport holder, gave me six months in the country. Before coming here I had looked on the internet for the addresses of English language schools and I brought a stack of CVs with me too. I just typed 'English language schools New Zealand' into the Google search engine and clicked on the second link, www.english-schools.co.nz, which gave me some useful information. I didn't jump at the first three jobs I was offered in Auckland because I wanted to check out Christchurch, the other main centre for EFL schools. There I was offered a few more jobs and decided to take up a post at Aspect [now Kaplan] at 116 Worcester Street in the city centre. The students are mainly Chinese, Korean and Japanese but there are notable groups from Taiwan, Switzerland and South America too. My school was helpfully willing to aid me with the visa bureaucracy and now I have residency. My school has a core of staff with open-ended contracts and a larger number of casual/part-time staff, including some British people with working holiday visas who work for some months and then continue travelling.***

Private language schools are regulated by the New Zealand Qualifications Authority or NZQA (www.nzqa.govt.nz/providers/index.do). Its website lists all the educational establishments in New Zealand, but is worth looking through for leads (or search for 'language' to narrow it down). The national organisation of English language teachers, TESOLANZ (www.tesolanz.org.nz), provides a free listing for job-seekers and institutions offering work, while English New Zealand is an association of accredited private and state sector English language schools which posts current vacancies (www.englishnewzealand.co.nz).

British citizens aged between 18 and 30 can work in New Zealand through the working holiday visa scheme for up to 23 months (www.immigration.govt.nz).

LIST OF EMPLOYERS

DOMINION ENGLISH SCHOOLS
8th Floor, 155 Queen St, Auckland (PO Box 4217)
+64 9 377 3280
dos@dominion.school.nz
www.dominion.school.nz

NUMBER OF TEACHERS: Up to 20.

PREFERENCE OF NATIONALITY: None, but must be native English speakers.

QUALIFICATIONS: Minimum Cambridge/RSA CELTA or Trinity CertTESOL or recognised equivalent. Preferably also university degree and experience.

CONDITIONS OF EMPLOYMENT: Flexible contracts. Part-time hours 12.5 per week from 9am to 12pm. Full-time hours 25 per week, 9am–4pm.

SALARY: Starting wage approximately NZ$30 per hour.

FACILITIES/SUPPORT: Applicants must hold a valid work visa/permit.

RECRUITMENT: Local interviews essential.

CONTACT: Julia Walton, Director of Studies.

INDEX OF ADVERTISERS

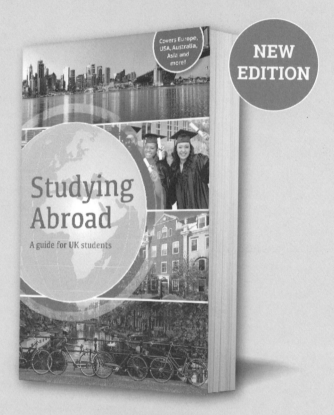